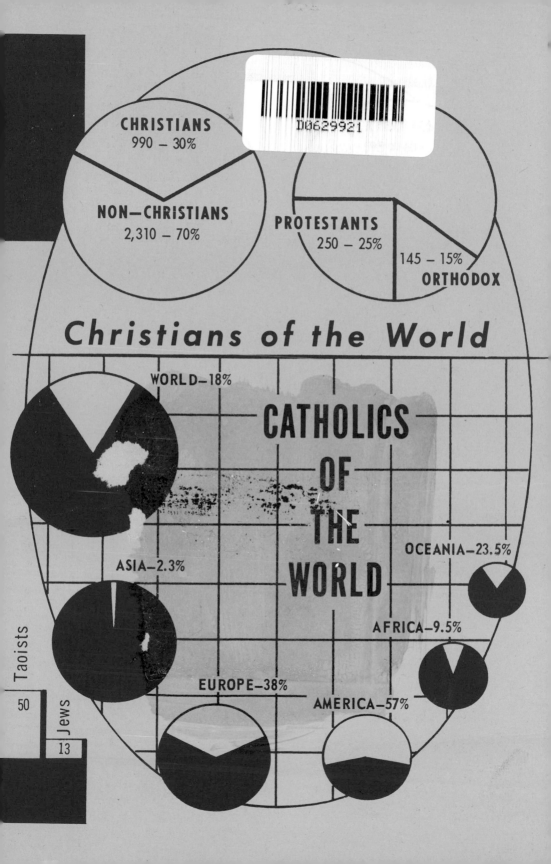

CHRISTIANS
990 – 30%

NON—CHRISTIANS
2,310 – 70%

PROTESTANTS
250 – 25%

145 – 15%
ORTHODOX

Christians of the World

WORLD–18%

CATHOLICS
OF
THE
WORLD

OCEANIA–23.5%

ASIA–2.3%

AFRICA–9.5%

Taoists

50

Jews

13

EUROPE–38%

AMERICA–57%

THE
MARYKNOLL
CATHOLIC DICTIONARY

THE
MARYKNOLL
CATHOLIC
DICTIONARY

Compiled and Edited by

ALBERT J. NEVINS, M. M.

Published by Dimension Books
Wilkes-Barre, Pa.

Library of Congress Catalog Card Number: 65:15436
First American Edition: 1965 by Dimension Books

Nihil Obstat

Rt. Rev. Msgr. James T. Clarke
Censor Librorum
November 27, 1964

Imprimatur

✠ Jerome D. Hannan
Bishop of Scranton
November 28, 1964

Contents

PREFACE

Preface

Do those of us to whom books are important ever spare a thought of thankfulness to the writers and compilers and publishers of books *of reference?* I fear that we tend to take them for granted and to use them as if they were part of the natural order of things, like water or sleep, without perhaps ever thinking of all the devoted and conscientious work that has gone into their making. Yet how often we should be at a loss without reference books, whether we use them as adjuncts to work or to recreation or to both: the dictionary or the encyclopedia which elucidates a point that crops up in conversation, the book of birds or wild flowers that enlarges the possibilities of a hobby, the learned or technical summaries which are the day-to-day companions of workers in this or that field of knowledge or activity.

Recent times have seen increasing publication in many languages of reference books of *religious* interest, from Biblical dictionaries to volumes of information concerning particular religions or Christian communities. For over half a century *The Catholic Encyclopedia* has been the principal general work of reference on its subject in the United States, Canada and all English-speaking countries, and there are various works of smaller compass much used by a wide public.

It is my happy task to write a brief foreword to the first edition of a new book of this kind, *The Maryknoll Catholic Dictionary.* Its object and scope are explained by the Editor, Father Albert J. Nevins, M.M., in his *Introduction.* It is a one-volume work giving, in alphabetical order, information about the Catholic Church in all her aspects, and it has been planned and carried out with the needs of people in the United States and Canada particularly in mind. It seeks "to offer clear and accurate explanations rather than strict definitions" and aims throughout to reflect those changes and developments of which we

are all so conscious today and with which it is our duty to become well acquainted as soon as possible.

In my considered judgment, these objects are admirably attained. Father
Nevins particularizes that his dictionary is intended "for students, for professional people . . . , for office workers, for writers and educators," and for
intelligent people in general, both Catholic and non-Catholic. I would emphasize this last, double category, and add another one, journalists, who sometimes
show an unhappy ignorance where religion in general, and the Catholic Church
in particular, are concerned. Religious and ecclesiastical matters require as
much special knowledge as any other important subject.

The trouble is that many people seem to forget the existence of reference
books: time and again I receive letters from across the Atlantic asking me
questions that the writers could answer for themselves in five minutes by
consulting a relevant reference book. It is to be hoped that *The Maryknoll
Catholic Dictionary* will circulate widely, and that teachers will persevere in
teaching their pupils what reference books are for, and how to use them. It is
true that some of these books call for a considerable degree of antecedent
knowledge in those who consult them. But *The Maryknoll Catholic Dictionary*
is not one of these: it is written for what is called the "average man" or the
"average woman," it is a "popular" work. Even so, those who consult it must
not expect to find a dead-level of "easiness" throughout. The simplest inclusive book about the Catholic Church has to deal with some very difficult and
deep ideas, some of which it is all but impossible to reduce to simple terms.

This dictionary is right up to date. It is also thoroughly practical: the value
of including articles on Moral Rearmament, Jehovah's Witnesses and similar
contemporary matters is obvious; and the accounts of the Church in each
State of the Union and in foreign lands, especially those of South America,
will be found useful far outside the places concerned.

As its name indicates, the dictionary is a product mainly of the labors of
members of the well-known Catholic Foreign Mission Society of America, the
Maryknoll Fathers. It follows that appropriate space is accorded to that most
important topic, the Church's foreign missions, whose bishops are such an
effective and enlightened force in the second Vatican Council. Another subject of special contemporary significance that receives full attention is the
Bible. In the present writer's opinion, the entries concerned with the books
of the Bible and with Biblical problems and persons are among the best in
The Maryknoll Catholic Dictionary: they will be of great value to numberless
readers. From a less serious standpoint, the writers of the 10,000 entries (I
have not counted them!) are not afraid to express themselves vigorously from
time to time, or sometimes to record small things that are curious or amusing

rather than important. For examples, it is refreshing to be reminded that the term "born Catholic" is "essentially nonsensical"; and I wonder how many altar-boys know (or care) that there is a "right" and "wrong" order for lighting the candles on the altar!

No doubt this work of Father Nevins and his collaborators will be much used by those who are not themselves Catholics, and I will end this note by a slight elaboration of something he just glances at in his *Introduction*. This book is a conveniently-arranged collection of information about the Catholic Church and associated matters; it is not a co-ordinated account, measured and proportionate, of the Catholic Christian religion, nor is it meant to be: it is a *reference* book. It is the business of a dictionary to provide pieces of information in a handy form, not to try to present a system, still less to describe a way of life. The Catholic Christian religion and Church as such can be delineated only by a different sort of book, or expounded by word of mouth. The Catholic Christian life, of the whole person, body and soul, can be learned only by observing it in action in others; eventually and fully, it can be learned only by living it oneself, with others. *The Maryknoll Catholic Dictionary* will give many people an appetite for further discovery.

DONALD ATTWATER

INTRODUCTION

Introduction

The Maryknoll Catholic Dictionary has been prepared to meet the growing demand for a Catholic dictionary intended for use in the United States and Canada—one that incorporates the many changes in liturgy, Church discipline and organization that have come about in the past few years, particularly since Vatican Council II. During this time there has been a great movement within the Church among the various Catholic Rites, between Catholics and Protestants, and in the relationship of clergy and laity. There has also been new examination of the very nature of the Christian vocation. It is the aim of this dictionary to attempt to mirror some of these movements and changes as well as to offer definitions of standard Catholic words and terms.

This dictionary has been prepared for students, for professional people who have long needed a guide to Catholic terminology, for office workers, for writers and educators, for interested non-Catholics as well as the laity. In its descriptions of frequently used words and terms, this book seeks to offer clear and accurate explanations rather than strict definitions; it does not pretend to be encyclopedic; in fact, an effort has been made to avoid being overtechnical. While the dictionary is intended to be thorough, one should not expect to find in it a logical outline of Catholic faith and doctrine.

In many cases, where they would not be readily available, the etymology and derivation of words and terms are given as an aid to better understanding. Also, for unusual and foreign words, a phonetic pronunciation is included to make the dictionary more useful to speakers, broadcasters, etc. Words and terms are arranged alphabetically, and where a term of several words appears, alphabetization is according to the most common usage. In cases where there might be confusion, or in the handling of a subject which might appear under several headings, cross reference is made. A particularly useful feature of this dictionary is the capitalization of words only in those cases when proper Catholic usage pertains. When a word or term has several meanings, these are listed in order of general acceptance or importance.

A number of supplementary features increase the value of *The Maryknoll Catholic Dictionary*. These include sections on Catholic abbreviations, Catholic forms of address, patron saints of countries and occupations, lists of Christian male and female names, the popes and anti-popes of the Church, a listing of names and addresses of Catholic international organizations (Catholic organizations in the United States are in the main section), a selective biography of deceased Catholics of the United States and Canada, and an American martyrology.

The Maryknoll Catholic Dictionary has been three years in preparation. The compiler acknowledges his indebtedness to many people. Among those who contributed definitions are the following Maryknollers: Andrew J. Balistreri, M.R.E., S.T.B., M.A.; Charles H. Cappel, B.A., M.A., Ph.D.; Donald J. Casey, B.A., M.R.E., S.T.B., M.S.; James A. Collignon, B.A., M.R.E., M.A.; Robert F. Crohan, M.A., M.R.E., S.T.B.; J. Joseph Daly, M.A., Ph.D.; Rafael R. Davila, B.A., M.R.E., M.S.; J. Leo Davis, S.T.B.; Frederick C. Dietz, B.A.; William B. Frazier, B.A., M.R.E., S.T.L., Ph.L.; Fidelis C. Goodman, B.A., M.A.; John K. Halbert, B.A., M.R.E., M.A.; Robert E. Hoffman, B.A.; Gregory J. Keegan, B.A., M.A., Ph.D.; Arthur C. Kiernan, B.A., S.T.L., Ph.L.; Thomas V. Kiernan, Ph.B., M.A.; John F. Lenahan, B.A.; Thomas J. Malone, B.A., M.A., S.T.B.; Daniel J. Maloney, B.A., M.A., M.R.E., S.T.B.; John J. McCormack, M.A.; Carroll I. Quinn, M.R.E.; George H. Ratermann, M.A.; William J. Richardson, B.A., M.R.E., S.T.B.; Edward A. Weis, B.A., M.A.; R. Felix White, A.B., M.A.; Francis J. Winslow, S.T.B., J.C.L., J.C.D. Also the following lay members of the staff of Maryknoll Publications: Neil F. Kirwan, A.B.; Peter J. Gallagher, A.B.; Raymond M. Boyle, A.B. and Daniel O'Callahan.

Acknowledgment is owed Dr. Donald Attwater who read the galleys and who offered many suggestions, particularly regarding the Eastern Rites, and helped immeasurably to improve this work. Father Paul Mailleux, S.J., Superior of the John XXIII Center for Eastern Christian Studies, was also generous in his assistance on Eastern Rite terminology.

Thanks are due to the many Maryknoll Seminarians who assisted in the project. Particular appreciation must be expressed to Father Joseph A. Grassi, M.M., S.T.L., S.S.L., and Father Vincent P. Mallon, M.M., S.T.L., S.S.L.; besides their own contributions, these two Maryknollers read and checked many other definitions, particularly in Liturgy and Scripture, for accuracy and modern approach. Two Maryknoll Sisters made invaluable contributions. Sister M. Juliana contributed many definitions, particularly the countries and states, and supervised the sections on abbreviations and forms of address. Sister Rose Benigna acted as copy editor. The essential clerical work of typing, filing, keeping records, etc., was carefully and thoroughly carried out by Mrs. Catherine Farrell and Mrs. Frances Capossela. Finally, the illustrations were all prepared by Brother Sebastian Schwartz, M.M.

ALBERT J. NEVINS, M.M., L.H.D.

Editor

THE
MARYKNOLL
CATHOLIC DICTIONARY

A

a cappella (It. in chapel style) A term applied to choral music that is not accompanied by any instrument.

A.D. (L. *anno Domini*, in the year of our Lord) Used in designating dates in the Christian era. *Charlemagne was crowned in Rome, A.D. 800.* The meaning is that the Emperor was crowned 800 years after the birth of Christ. Since, however, there is some uncertainty about the exact date of Christ's birth, the term *anno Domini* is only relative. It is estimated that our Lord must have been born before Herod the Great died, which was in April 4 B.C. If He was born shortly before the death of Herod, it would make Him "about thirty years of age" (Luke 3:23) when He began His ministry, and possibly thirty-three when He died.

ab homine (L. by man) Refers to a type of ecclesiastical censure that is inflicted by a judge because of certain conditions.

Abaddon (Heb. *abad,* perish) A late Hebrew word used to designate the place of the dead that is reserved for the wicked.

abandonment The act of completely conforming oneself to the will of God so that all one does flows from love and sacrifice. It is a high degree of sanctity and demands a special grace from God.

abba (ahb'bah) The emphatic form of the Aramaic word for father, *ab.* It is found only in the New Testament (Mk. 14:36; Mt. 23:9; Rom. 8:15; Gal. 4:6). It became a liturgical expression in the early Church.

abbé (ahb-bey', Fr.) In French-speaking countries this title may be used in addressing anyone who has the right to wear the dress of the secular clergy. *"Monsieur l'abbé"* could refer to anyone who has received tonsure, whether or not he is a priest.

abbess A feminine form derived indirectly from Aramaic *abba,* father. An abbess is the superior of an abbey or convent. Her position is similar in a general way to that of an abbot in his monastery. The title is used among the Benedictines, Cistercians, some Franciscans, and a few others. The abbess is elected by secret ballot of the professed nuns in her house. According to the Council of Trent, she must be at least forty years old and eight years professed. In case of necessity, however, a dispensation from the exact observance of this precept may be obtained from the bishop. Abbesses have authority in temporal

1

matters but exercise no jurisdiction in spiritual matters. In medieval times abbesses were often ladies of the nobility with great power and influence.

abbey A canonically erected (independent, self-governing) monastery with a community of at least twelve monks or nuns, ruled by an abbot or an abbess. Most of the great abbeys of Western Europe spring from the original foundation of the Benedictines. The monks converted and civilized the people among whom they settled. The abbeys were centers of worship, of learning, of culture, and of the arts and crafts. Before the age of printing they were the publishing houses and libraries where the great books of the past were copied by hand and kept safe for future generations. Towns and villages sprang up around the abbeys as the poor, the sick, the aged, travelers, and orphans flocked to the monks for help; and refugees from war, from famine, and from rapacious landlords came to settle on the abbey lands and to gain the abbot's protection.

abbey nullius (new-lee′us) An abbey which has as its abbot one who has the rank of abbot nullius. The abbey has territory attached to it. The abbot rules this territory, possessing ordinary power. His jurisdiction is that of a bishop. The abbey and the attached territory belongs to no diocese. Belmont Abbey in North Carolina is the only abbey nullius in the United States.

abbot (Aramaic *abba,* father) The superior of a community of monks. The title was first used in Syria and in Egypt, where it designated any monk venerated for age or sanctity. After monasticism began to flourish in the West under St. Benedict (6th century), the title was used there to

mean the father of the monastic family, the head of the monastery, the superior. In his rule, St. Benedict says, "An abbot who is worthy to be over a monastery should always remember what he is called, and live up to the name . . . for he is believed to hold the place of Christ in the monastery, being called by a name of His . . . he should show them all that is good and holy by his deeds even more than by his words." Abbots are generally elected by secret ballot of their monks. Abbots hold office for life. They administer the external affairs of the abbey, and have in general a spiritual jurisdiction over their monks —one, however, subject to the bishop of the diocese.

abbot general A monk who governs a monastery and at the same time governs the whole congregation of monasteries which follow the same rule. He may also be the one who rules the whole congregation of monasteries, without governing an individual monastery. He is sometimes called the abbot president.

abbot, titular A monk who holds the title of a monastery which has been destroyed or suppressed. He neither exercises the functions of an abbot nor does he have any monks subject to him. The office is analogous to that of a titular bishop.

abbreviations *See* Appendix.

Abdia A minor prophet, author of the book of the Old Testament bearing his name. Since the entire book contains only 21 verses, it is the shortest of the Old Testament. It denounces Edom's abuses, predicts Edom's destruction and exhorts Israel to fight against Edom. He lived about the 5th century B.C.

abdication The voluntary renunciation of a high office, princely dignity or much more rarely, the papacy.

2

Generally the abdication is irrevocable, so that once a person has renounced a high Church office, he no longer partakes of the rights of that office.

abduction The violent deprival of a person's liberty for lust or marriage. The violence can be either physical or moral. It is a violation against justice because a person has the right to personal liberty, and it is also a violation against chastity. With a view to marriage an impediment is set up between the abductor and the one abducted so that there can be no marriage as long as the abducted is deprived of freedom.

Abel (Heb. short-lived) According to the account in the Book of Genesis, chap. 4, Abel was the second son of Adam and Eve, and was slain by his older brother Cain. Both brothers offered sacrifices to God. Cain made his offering from the fruits of the field; Abel offered the first born of his herds and flocks. While Abel's sacrifice was pleasing to God, Cain's works were wicked and God was displeased with his offering. Thereupon Cain, in a fit of jealous rage, slew his brother. Abel is mentioned often in the New Testament. He is a type of Christ, by his calling as shepherd, by his offering of sacrifice, by his holiness, by his innocent and violent death resulting from the jealousy of his brother man. Christ mentions Abel (Mt. 23:34) in speaking to the scribes and Pharisees: ". . . all the just blood that has been shed on earth, from the blood of Abel the just unto the blood of Zacharia, whom you killed between the temple and the altar." It is clear that the story of Cain and Abel was intended to teach a lesson, and that the biblical writer did not intend it to be taken as literal history. The author wished to instruct his readers in the ways of God. Mankind was sinful after the fall of Adam; original sin was followed by a multiplication of crimes throughout the world; the murderer repudiates God's Fatherhood and the brotherhood of man ("Am I my brother's keeper?") ; sacrifice is shown to be useless without a heart devoted to God. The story is true—true to the purpose of its author in teaching true doctrine.

Abib (Heb. *abhibh,* kernel of grain) Nisan, the first month of the ancient Jewish calendar.

abiogenesis (Gr. *a,* not; *bio,* life; *genesis,* birth) The origin of life from a nonliving thing; spontaneous generation. This theory in its strictest sense states that life can come from nonliving matter merely by the evolution of the nonliving matter. Understood this way, abiogenesis is opposed to the principle of causality which states that a cause can only act according to its own nature. Hence a thing which is nonliving could not of and by itself produce life.

abjuration The renunciation under oath of an apostasy, heresy or schism made in the external forum according to a certain formula prescribed by Church authorities. In its strictest sense it refers to a convert's profession of faith prior to the reception of Baptism.

ablution (ab-lu'shun; L. *ablutio,* a washing away) A cleansing with water out of reverence, or as a symbol of spiritual purification. It is used for both people and things. Washing as a sign of purification has been practiced from early days, both in pagan rites and under the Law of Moses. Pontius Pilate, wishing to indicate that he was innocent of the blood of Christ, washed his hands. In the liturgy of the Church, Baptism (*q.v.,*) is the great ablution. The use of holy water on entering a church is a ritual ablution, signifying the cleansing of the heart. The Aspersion at Mass is likewise an ablution for all present. The priest celebrating Mass washes his hands at the Lavabo, cleansing the hands that will hold the Body of Christ and signifying the purity of soul necessary for the offering of the Sacrifice about to be made. The chalice too is washed after the Communion, and the priest simultaneously washes the tips of the fingers which have just held the consecrated Host. At the consecration of a church, the bishop takes possession of the new building in the name of Christ, sprinkling the outside with holy water. Then the inside is purified by sprinkling with a mixture of water, salt, wine, and ashes, called lustral or Gregorian water. An altar, when it is consecrated, is washed, in a solemn rite, with Gregorian water.

abnegation (L. *abnegare,* to deny) Self-denial. In the Christian sense it presumes dependence on God and has both a positive and a negative meaning. It presumes that one denies those inclinations, habits and conditions which would lead him from God and practices those which will lead him closer to God.

abomination of desolation This expression comes from the Book of Daniel, which makes allusion to the profanation of the Temple of Jerusalem by Antiochus Epiphanes in 168 B.C. The New Testament borrows this from Daniel 9:27 and indicates by it the invasion of the Holy Land by a pagan power, which the Romans did do at the siege of Jerusalem in A.D. 78.

abortion The expulsion from a mother's womb of a living fetus which cannot remain alive outside the womb. Abortion may be: (*a*) natural—caused by conditions beyond human control, (*b*) artificial—deliberately caused by a human agent. Direct artificial abortion is a serious sin forbidden by the law of God because it is the direct killing of an innocent person.

abortion, penalties of In addition to penalties inflicted by civil law and particular ecclesiastical law, the following penalties are inflicted on those procuring an abortion: 1. excommunication reserved to the ordinary; 2. criminal irregularity with dispensasion reserved to the Holy See; 3. deposition of clerics by explicit pronouncement.

aboulia (Gr. thoughtlessness) A form of neurotic behavior characterized by uncontrollable scruples.

Abraham The father of the Chosen People. He had an intense love of God, and for God he left his native land and was willing to sacrifice his son. He was greatly venerated by the Israelites. His story is told in the Book of Genesis.

Abraham's bosom Expression used in Lk. 16:23 to indicate the repose of the just and the joys of heaven.

abrogation (L. *abrogare,* to repeal) 1. *Of law.* Complete revocation of a law by those having the power to make the law. 2. *Of custom.* A custom with the force of law ceases the same way as law itself, namely, through revocation by lawful authority, through cessation of its purpose and through contrary custom. Generally speaking, however, a law cannot revoke customs which have existed for a hundred years, and a general law cannot destroy particular customs.

absence, ecclesiastical In its juridical meaning absence means the nonparticipation in an activity (deliberations, religious functions or juridical

4

hearings) which one must attend. It also refers to a violation of the law of residence (dwelling or remaining in a certain place) which certain individuals are bound to by virtue of their ecclesiastical positions.

absolute   1. A word referring to the conferral of a sacrament in the ordinary way without making any conditions because of a doubt that conditions for validity of the sacrament are present. 2. Also that which exists by itself independent of another being, e.g., God, the Absolute.

absolution (L. *absolvere,* to forgive) The form (words) used in the Sacrament of Penance by a duly authorized priest, while making the Sign of the Cross, by which sins are forgiven. To exercise this power legitimately, the priest must receive jurisdiction from his ordinary. However, in case of danger of death, any priest may absolve, even though jurisdiction may be lacking.

absolution, conditional   In the Sacrament of Penance, absolution from one's sins is given conditionally when the administering priest is doubtful of the disposition of the penitent or if he suspects the absence of any condition which is necessary to make the sacrament valid. Conditional absolution may be given only with serious reason.

absolution, general   Absolution given by a priest to a large group, members of which are not able to confess. Examples would be soldiers on a battlefield or passengers in an out-of-control aircraft. If the person receiving such an absolution survives, the absolved sins must be confessed in the next confession.

abstinence   1. To refrain from meat, and soups and gravies made from meat. All Catholics over seven are bound to abstinence. Abstinence is either total or partial. On days of partial abstinence, meat and soups or gravies made from meat may be taken once a day at the principal meal. On days of total abstinence no meat or soup or gravy made from meat may be taken. If a person unknowingly takes meat on a day of abstinence and then realizes the error, abstinence still obliges at the remainder of meals. Thus anyone who deliberately eats meat on forbidden days commits as many sins as the number of times meat is eaten. *See* fasting. 2. A moral virtue which inclines man to moderate use of food as required by right reason for his own moral good. Abstinence differs from temperance which regulates the sensitive appetite in the pleasures of touch, i.e., food, drink, sex.

abstinence, day of   A day on which meat and soup or gravy made from meat may not be eaten. A day of abstinence is said to be either complete or partial. A day of complete abstinence obliges at all meals; such days in the United States are all Fridays, Ash Wednesday, Dec. 7, Holy Saturday, and either Dec. 23 or 24, according to the local diocesan regulations. In many dioceses, a dispensation is given for Holy Saturday, and can be given for other days. In Canada, all Fridays, Ash Wednesday, Dec. 7 and Dec. 23 are days of abstinence. A day of partial abstinence permits meat and soup or gravy made from meat to be taken at the principal meal. Days of partial abstinence are Ember Wednesdays and Saturdays and the Vigil of Pentecost. Abstinence obliges all who are seven years of age or older.

abstract (L. *abstrahere,* to withdraw) Having no reference to a thing or things. To consider apart from any application to a particular object or instance. The opposite of concrete.

abstraction (L. *abstractio*) The act or process of leaving out of consideration one or more qualities of a complex object so as to attend to others. For instance, when one considers a tree without reference to this or that type of tree, its size or shape, etc., but merely the nature of the universal tree or "treeness."

Abuna (Arabic, Father) Former title of the Coptic metropolitan of the Ethiopian Church. The word is now used for all priests.

abuse of power The transgression of the limits or the neglect to fulfill inherent duties of a proper office.

abyss (Gr. *abyssos,* bottomless) 1. Used in Scripture to indicate a great depth. 2. The primal chaos that existed in the universe at the time of its creation. 3. In the New Testament it means the bottomless pit which is the abode of the dead (Limbo) or of evil spirits (hell).

Abyssinian Church An incorrect title for the Ethiopian Church. In the Acts of the Apostles (8:26-40), mention is made of the treasurer of Queen Candace of Ethiopia, converted by the Apostle Philip while riding in his chariot, reading the Book of Isaia. In the 4th century, Bishop Frumentius from Egypt brought the Catholic Faith to Ethiopia (Abyssinia) and the people became strongly attached to this Coptic Rite branch of the Universal Church. In the 7th century it fell into the Monophysite heresy, and from the year 675 it was isolated from the Christian world by the Muslims. Today, the inhabitants of this corner of Africa belong to three principal groups: the ancient Ethiopian Christians of the Coptic Rite, who are still out of touch with the Holy See and have fallen into many superstitions through long isolation; the Muslims who number almost as many as the Christians; and the pagan Banlus of the marginal lands. Catholics are in the minority. In the 17th century two Capuchins who penetrated the country were stoned to death. When later missionary arrivals gained a foothold, their chapels were closed and they were expelled from the country. In time, by means of works of charity and education including the care of lepers, the Church was established once more. The great Catholic missionary school at Asmara has done much to build up the Church and promote native vocations. A steadily increasing number of young men have gone to Rome to study for the Ethiopian Rite priesthood. The Pontifical Ethiopian College is situated in the Vatican Gardens. There the students are fed, housed, and educated at the expense of the Sacred Congregation for the Oriental Church. There are some 40,000 Ethiopian Rite Catholics in Ethiopia, with three dioceses of Asmara, Addis Ababa, and Adigrat.

Acacian Schism Acacius, Bishop of Caesarea in Palestine (340–366), caused St. Cyril to be deposed as Patriarch of Jerusalem in A.D. 357 and was present at the Synods of Seleucia and Constantinople (359–360) as the leader of a sect. He favored embracing a mild form of Arianism in which he and his followers denied the consubstantiality of the Second Person of the Blessed Trinity with the Father and taught that He was merely "like" the Father. From this teaching the group received the name *Omei,* Greek for "like." Acacius was deposed for heresy at the Lampsacan Synod in 365.

Academies, Pontifical (Gr. *Akadameia,* a public grove in Athens where Plato taught, hence, an institution for the pursuit of higher learning in the arts and sciences) The Roman Academies which developed at the height of the Renaissance were at first merely circles of friends gathered round a learned man or a wealthy patron. Cardinals and the clergy in general were patrons and collaborators in the movement. With the 17th century the Academy changed somewhat in character. No longer merely a group of learned men engaged in literary pursuits, it became a public body and took on a fixed, definite aim in the study of science, letters, and the fine arts. Many of these institutions remain today as Pontifical Academies. Some of these are the Academy of the Artists of the Pantheon, founded in 1542; of Sciences founded in 1603 and brought up to date by several successive popes; of Archeology, founded by Benedict XIV (1740–1758); of the Liturgy, founded also by Pope Benedict XIV and reconstituted by Pope Gregory XVI in 1840; of the Immaculate Conception, founded in 1835 by seminarians for the promotion of study among the young men of Rome and reorganized in 1921 by Pope Benedict XV; and of St. Thomas Aquinas and the Catholic Religion, founded by Pope Leo XIII in 1879, for higher ecclesiastical education.

Academy of Sciences, Pontifical In the year 1603 the Roman Prince Federigo Cesi, a distinguished scholar with an impressive library, a botanical garden, and a museum of relics of antiquity, brought together a group of scholarly men and founded the Accademia dei Lincei. The title "of the Lynx" was a symbol of keenness in the study of nature. The Academy was devoted to physical, mathematical, philosophical, and literary studies, and eventually specialized in the exact sciences. In 1651 the Academy had begun to decline, and it eventually perished. In 1847 Pope Pius revived it as the Pontificia Accademia dei Nuovo Lincei. Pope Leo XIII encouraged and developed it further, drawing up a new constitution for it in 1887. Pope Pius XI reformed the Academy on Oct. 28, 1936, under the name of the Pontifical Academy of Sciences. He chose seventy scientists of note from various countries to be life members, regardless of their religion. Its roster is a long list of some of the most distinguished names in modern scientific research.

Acadians French-speaking Catholics who lived in Nova Scotia which was ceded to England in 1713. In 1755 the forceful dispersion of the Acadians by the English took place, many being resettled in Louisiana. Longfellow's poem, *Evangeline,* commemorates the unjust incident.

acclamation 1. A way of electing a pope. According to documents of Gregory XV (1621–1623) and Urban VIII (1623–1644) there are three valid methods of papal election: the first by scrutiny, the second by compromise, the third by acclamation. This last form of election takes place when all the cardinal-electors spontaneously and unanimously proclaim one of the candidates to be pope, without casting votes. It is necessary that the acclamation take place without previous consultation or negotiation. It is then looked upon as a work of the Holy Spirit, and is sometimes called "quasi-inspiration." Clement X (1670–1676) was suddenly acclaimed pope by the people outside, whereupon the cry was echoed by the cardinals. In the case of Innocent XI (1676–1689), all the cardinals in the chapel of the conclave suddenly surrounded him and kissed his hand, thus designating him pope. 2. A greeting and solemn invocation after the Collect, at the Mass of a papal coronation.

accommodation *See* missionary accommodation.

accommodation of Scripture, biblical An adaptation or application of the words of Scripture to express ideas different from those intended by the sacred writer. While accommodation is not an inspired sense of Scripture, it is nevertheless a legitimate use of Scripture. The Church often uses accommodation in the liturgy.

acculturation The phenomena which occur when persons of varying cultures come into continuous firsthand contact with the result that each culture influences the other and cultural changes take place.

acolyte (Gr. *akolouthos,* an attendant)  A cleric in minor orders; the highest of the four minor orders recognized by the Western Church. The acolyte's duties are to offer the cruets of wine and water to the priest at Mass, to light the candles, to carry lighted candles at solemn services, and to take care of minor duties at divine worship. In practice, laymen (altar boys) usually carry out the duties of acolytes.

act of God An expression used in civil law to explain an action that arises beyond the control of man and is usually given as a reason why a contract cannot be fulfilled, e.g., a flood, an earthquake, etc.

Act of Supremacy A law passed in England in 1534 which declared the English monarch the supreme head of the Church of England and gave him the powers necessary to carry out this role.

act of worship *See* liturgy.

Acta Apostolicae Sedis (L. Acts of the Apostolic See) The official periodical of the Holy See and of Vatican City published in Latin. It was instituted in 1908 by Pope Pius X and is the vehicle of promulgation for Church laws, which become binding three months after publication in this periodical. It also contains the citations of the Roman Tribunals, appointments and papal audiences granted to foreign dignitaries (Abbreviation: A.A.S.).

Acta Sanctae Sedis (L. Acts of the Holy See) The title of the periodical which preceded the *Acta Apostolicae Sedis* (*q.v.*). It was a private publication from its founding by Father Pietro Avanzini in 1865 until May 23, 1904, when it became the official organ of the Holy See.

Acta Sanctorum (L. Acts of the Saints) A large collection of lives of the saints edited by the ecclesiastical association called the "Bollandists," who began the work in Europe during the 17th century.

active life Usually, the religious life of one engaged in the spiritual and corporal works of mercy, in contrast to the contemplative life. However, the active life may also apply to the dedicated lay person whose days are spent in works of charity for the love of God and neighbor. The active life, though full of merit when pursued from supernatural motives, is regarded as less perfect in itself than the contemplative life. However, no truly Christian life is entirely active. St. Thomas Aquinas says, "Every Christian who is in the way of salvation must partake in some way in contemplation, because it is commanded to all." When we speak of

8

active and contemplative life, we understand the terms to mean merely the element which dominates; that which is emphasized, or to which more time is given. In using the term "active" it must be understood that the activity is undertaken for the spiritual or corporal good of the neighbor.

active orders Religious orders or congregations, whether of men or women, whose field is the spiritual and corporal works of mercy. Thus members of active orders may spend their time in doing missionary work at home or in foreign fields, giving retreats and missions, administering the sacraments and doing whatever pertains to the care of souls.

actor Besides legal prescriptions to which an actor is bound by contract, the actor is also bound by strictly moral obligations flowing from the divine and ecclesiastical laws. Actors who participate in productions that offend public order and good morals are guilty of sin; if the offense is grave, the sin is grave. If the performance is indecent by reason of place, dress, action or speech, no Catholic actor can take part, for to do so would make him a material cooperator.

acts of faith Voluntary and deliberate acts, expressive of a firm belief in God and His Church, as well as acts of love, trust, contrition and resignation to God. These internal acts of faith may also be outwardly expressed either extemporaneously or by formulas such as are found in prayer books, etc.

Acts of Paul An apocryphal account of the life of St. Paul which varies greatly in detail from the account given in the Acts of the Apostles.

Acts of Pilate A spurious account of the trial and crucifixion of Jesus Christ is found in the apocryphal Gospel of Nicodemus (*q.v.*).

Acts of the Apostles The fifth book of the New Testament, written by St. Luke, the author of the third Gospel. It continues the account given in the Gospels, taking up the story after the Crucifixion, giving details of the ascension of Christ, the descent of the Holy Spirit, and the activities of the early Church including the work of St. Paul and the Church in Rome. Like the third Gospel, it is addressed to the "most excellent Theophilus," a man otherwise unknown to us. He may have been a Gentile of influence, a sponsor of the work, or some friend whom St. Luke wished to convert. The book is a remarkable historical record of the period *c*. A.D. 30–67, written by an author of distinguished literary ability.

Acts of the Martyrs The official records made at the trials of the early Christian martyrs. This name is also applied to all narratives of a martyr's trial and death.

ACTU The Association of Catholic Trade Unionists. Many of the early trade unions in Europe were founded upon Marxist principles, so that in many European countries separate Christian trade unions were formed. However, in countries where labor unions were neutral, the pope wished to have arrangements made for some form of instruction to be given to Catholic workers. A forum for the study, discussion, and adoption of Catholic social principles seemed to be called for. ACTU was therefore formed in New York in 1937, with chapters in other cities. It is an association of Catholic union members. They receive instructions such as those given in most labor schools, with added lectures on union procedures and preparation for meeting special situations. Labor and economic problems are discussed from the point of view of Christian social principles. Naturally ACTU counteracts Communist activity wherever it can, but it is not merely against Communism. It has a Christian social program that is positive, upholding and promoting social justice. It operates labor schools and forums on industrial matters. It publishes literature on labor, and gives free legal help and advice to workers who have union problems. It has centers in the main industrial states of the United States, and also in England and Scotland.

actual grace A supernatural, transient help given by God in order to enlighten the mind and strengthen the will so that we may better perform spiritual acts. Actual grace exerts its influence in a direct, moral and physical manner. This grace acts on the mind and will to set them in motion so that they seek a spiritual end. The rule is that actual grace is a necessity in order to perform any supernatural act, since there must be a proportional relationship between effect and cause.

actual sin A human act willingly done in violation of some law of God. It may consist of a thought, word, action or omission.

ad bestias (L. to the beasts) The sentence passed on Christians during the Roman persecution dooming them to be thrown to the wild animals in the amphitheater.

ad hominem, argumentum (L. argument to the man) 1. A term in Scholastic philosophy that refers to a special type of argument: arguing from principles already admitted by an opponent. 2. Arguing from some personal weakness or defect associated with an opponent.

ad libitum (L. at one's choice) The source of the expression "ad lib," to speak without written material. In the liturgical sense it is used to express a choice in the prayers (collects) at Mass.

ad limina (ad lim'ee-nah; L. *limen,* threshold) To the threshold, i.e., the tombs, of the Apostles Peter and Paul in Rome. Used in reference to a bishop's visit to Rome, obligatory every five years. Residential bishops and military vicars have to make the *ad limina* visit, presenting themselves before the pope with a written report of that section of the Church which is under their care. Bishops from dioceses outside of Europe may make the *ad limina* visit decennially, but the written report must nevertheless be sent in to the pope every five years.

ad nutum Sanctae Sedis (L. at the will of the Holy See) A person holding an office *ad nutum* can be removed any time the pope wishes.

Adam (Heb. *a-dam,* man) According to the biblical accounts (Genesis 1 and 2) the father of the human race, the first man created by God. Scientists date the arrival of man on earth from the probable age of the oldest tools and weapons which have been discovered, since the making and storing of tools for a purpose presupposes intelligence and planning, i.e., man. Most archeologists place man's first appearance at somewhere about 500,000 B.C., the earth itself being perhaps three billion years old. Regarding the possible method used by the Creator in forming man's body, the sacred author of the account in Genesis says that Adam, formed from the dust of the earth by the Creator, became a living person when God breathed into him the breath of life. The body may already have had a subhuman life when God made it a living person by giving it a soul. Some scientists think that the human body could have come into being at the end of a long series of sudden mutations, each one in turn more richly endowed, each one directed toward the end God had in mind. Unplanned mutations would never have resulted in the wonderful and complex creature that is man. But, "God incessantly mingles with His works," as St. Augustine says, and God, the Author of nature, could have directed the mutations so as to prepare for the end product, the crown, the human soul. These theories fit into the teaching of the Church. The Bible, however, does not intend to teach us how man was created, but the fact and meaning of his creation.

Adamites An obscure 2nd-century sect which claimed to have regained the innocence of Adam before the Fall. They rejected marriage and stripped naked when performing acts of common worship. These practices were revived in Holland in the 13th century and by the Beghards in Germany during the 14th century, and most recently by some in Bohemia in the 18th century.

adaptation (L. *adaptare,* to fit) In the religious sense, the word refers to the adaptation of the Church and its missioners to native cultures. It is the aim of the Church to build on what is good in native cultures and not to transplant European or Western cultures. There is discussion on how far missioners are to adapt. The Jesuit Robert di Nobili took on the dress and life of a Brahmin in order to reach that class in India. Most missioners believe in a more moderate approach.

Adeste Fidelis (L. come all you faith-ful)   A popular Christmas hymn written in the 18th century by an unknown author.

adjuration (L. *adjurare,* to swear)   A demand made in the name of God or a holy thing to induce a person to do or to omit something. Adjuration which fulfills the necessary conditions (truth, right judgment, justice) is an act of religion. Adjuration takes place in Baptism, over the salt and over the person being baptized; it is also used in the rite of exorcism.

Adjutorium nostrum in nomine Domini. Qui fecit caelum et terram (L. Our help is in the name of the Lord. Who made heaven and earth.) This verse and response, accompanied by the Sign of the Cross, is used to open blessings. It is also used near the beginning of Mass, Confirmation and Anointing of the Sick and in the Divine Office. It originates in Psalm 123.8.

administration of ecclesiastical property A charge that is primarily entrusted to the bishop of each diocese. The bishop appoints two or more persons to form a diocesan council to assist him in administration. When administration is delegated to pastors and others, each must render an annual accounting to the ordinary. Religious orders are responsible for the administration of their own property, but if engaged in parochial work, religious superiors must furnish an annual accounting to the ordinary regarding administration of parochial facilities and income.

administration of the sacraments The act of conferring the sacraments on the faithful, performed by a duly authorized minister in the name of Christ.

administrator One who administers affairs in place of another. The bishop ordinarily administers the affairs of his diocese. However, if a bishop dies, resigns, or is removed, leaving the post vacant, or if he is unable to function because of illness, an apostolic administrator may be appointed by the Holy See to administer the diocese until a permanent appointment is made. There are also administrators of parishes.

Administrator Apostolic One who receives an interim appointment from the Holy See to administer until a permanent appointment is made. Administrators Apostolic fall into two categories: 1. Appointed because a diocesan see is vacant (*sede vacante*) due to death, resignation or removal of the ordinary; or because the see is impaired (*sede impedita*) due to the inability of the ordinary to function because of illness, infirmity, suspension, etc. 2. Appointed to govern religious institutions. The obligation, rights and duties of administrators are outlined in canon law.

Adonai (*Ahd-oh-nah'eye;* Heb. *Adonay,* my Lord) One of the terms used by the Jews to substitute for Yahweh, I am, the most Holy Name of God, which might not be pronounced by man.

adoption, canonical To take the child of another as one's own. This creates a legal relationship. Canon law (canon 1059) says that where civil law recognizes a relationship, the Church also recognizes this relationship. Thus if civil law creates an impediment to marriage, ecclesiastical law recognizes this same impediment. In the United States, each state has its own laws regarding adoption, and legal relationship is difficult to establish.

adoption, supernatural The free and loving gesture by which God communicates to man a real, though limited, share in His own divine na-

ture and life, making him both son and heir. Commonly understood as the effect of sanctifying grace, divine adoption is being linked more and more closely with uncreated grace, i.e., the indwelling of the Blessed Trinity. According as the causal role of sanctifying grace is emphasized exclusively, the tendency is to regard man as son of the divine essence, lacking any particular relation to the divine persons as such. Stress on the causal influence of the divine indwelling, however, leads to the consideration of man as son of the Father, in the Son and through the Holy Spirit. The latter alternative is gaining considerable prominence.

adoptionism A heresy that developed in Spain in the 8th century which was rooted in Nestorianism. It claimed that Christ was only the adopted son of God. This heresy was condemned by the Council of Nicaea (787) and the Council of Frankfort (795).

adoration An act of honor to God. Adoration is due only to God and is distinguished from veneration which is a reverence expressed for saints, relics, etc.

adoration of the cross Strictly speaking (since adoration—latria—belongs to God alone), the solemn liturgical veneration of the cross in the cermonies of Good Friday, when clergy and faithful kneel and kiss the crucifix which has been unveiled and placed on a cushion. During the ceremony the choir sings certain hymns with the refrains "O faithful cross" and "O sweet wood" between verses.

adoration, perpetual Adoration of the Blessed Sacrament, continually exposed, as in certain convents dedicated to this end. The term is also used in connection with the Forty Hours Devotion.

adorer   A person who kneels before the Blessed Sacrament for a specified period of time (usually an hour) during Forty Hours Devotion, or at any other time the Blessed Sacrament is exposed on the altar. Some religious houses and parishes have perpetual adoration at which the watchers adore in pairs for an hour at a time.

adult (L. *adultus,* grown)   One who has reached maturity. In American civil law, 21 years. In the Church the age varies; for marriage, 16 years of age is adult for males, 14 for females. Adult baptism means when the subject has reached the age of reason.

adultery (L. *adulterare,* to pollute) The voluntary sexual intercourse between a married man and a woman who is not his wife, or between a married woman and man who is not her husband.

advena   A canonical term referring to a person living in a quasi-domicile (*q.v.*). It contrasts to *incola* (*q.v.*).

Advent (L. *advenire,* to come)   A liturgical season of the year in preparation for the solemn celebration of Christmas. In the Latin Rite, it begins on the fourth Sunday before Christmas and ends at midnight, Christmas Eve. In the Ambrosian rite it has six Sundays instead of four. Advent is a time of penance, less severe than that of Lent, and with more of a sense of expectation and desire. It celebrates the thousands of years before the coming of Christ, when the world was waiting for its Savior. The Masses and Offices of Advent are of great beauty.

Advent House   A small one-dimensional cutout house which is hung against the light of a window used in family preparation for Christmas. It has seven sealed windows containing symbols of Christ from the Old Testament. Each morning, beginning on Dec. 17, a window is opened revealing a symbol of Christ, such as the burning bush, the root of Jesse, the key of David, etc. The "O" Antiphon (*q.v.*) particular to the day is recited. On Dec. 23, the door of the house is opened, and Jesus is seen sitting on His mother's knee.

advent of Christ   Generally understood to be the Second Coming of Christ to judge the living and the dead at the end of time. The first advent of Christ took place at His incarnation and birth in Palestine over nineteen hundred years ago. This first coming of the Son of God into His world occurred in a quiet, hidden manner and was only gradually manifested. Strictly speaking, the Second Coming of Christ begins in the spirit, through His Church, in the souls of men, every day, in the sacraments and in the graces bestowed through prayer and good works; and also at the moment of each man's death, when he meets Christ, his judge. The advent of Christ will be perfected at the end of time when He returns in glory. It will be accompanied by the transformation of this world, the resurrection of the dead, and the vindication of God's sanctity. Then those who have served Christ in their neighbor will be received into glory, while those who have rejected Christ in callousness toward their brother man will depart into their own place, with the damned.

Advent wreath   A wreath of evergreen boughs or holly, hung or laid flat on a table or sideboard, with four candles fixed at even intervals around it. One candle is lighted at the evening meal on the first Sun-

13

day of Advent, two candles on the second Sunday, and so on through the fourth Sunday. A prayer is usually said during the lighting of the candle, or a brief hymn may be sung. On Christmas Eve the wreath is discarded, and may be replaced by a Crib or a statue of the Christ Child.

Adventism The doctrine that the second coming of Christ and the end of the world are near at hand. *See* Seventh Day Adventists.

advocate (L. *advocare,* to call to) One who defends a cause, a defense lawyer. There are also several specialized meanings to this word: 1. A name used for Christ. "We have an advocate with the Father, Jesus Christ the just" (1 Jn. 2:1). 2. The Holy Spirit. "And I will ask the Father and he will give you another Advocate to dwell with you forever, the Spirit of truth" (Jn. 14:16).

Advocate of God (L. *advocatus Dei)* The one assigned to promote the cause of one whose life is being scrutinized for the process of beatification or canonization.

advocates of Roman Congregations Lawyers, either cleric or lay, who plead cases before Church courts of the Holy See. These lawyers are skilled in both canon and civil law. They serve under a fixed salary, independent of the outcome of their cases.

Advocatus Diaboli (ahd-voh-cah'tus dee-ah'bo-lee, L.) The Devil's Advocate. A popular name for the Promoter of the Faith, the Consistorial official who carefully examines the life, work and miracles of a subject for beatification or canonization is more positively called the Advocate of God *(q.v).*

aequiprobabilism *See* equiprobabilism.

aer (Gr. ãr) A large veil to cover the paten or chalice used by the Eastern Church.

aesthetics (Gr. *aisthetes,* one who perceives) That branch of philosophy concerned with beauty, which seeks to determine the nature of beauty and how beauty is to be apprehended. Some philosophers make it a part of psychology which treats of sensations and emotions evoked by fine art and literature. However, since all beauty is a reflection of divine beauty, it is considered as part of ontology.

aestimative (L. *aestimare,* to esteem) One of the four internal senses which instinctively distinguishes the desirable from the noxious.

Aeterni Patris (L. Eternal Father) The title of the encyclical letter Pope Leo XIII issued in 1879 to revive Scholastic philosophy according to the mind of St. Thomas Aquinas.

affability (L. *affari,* to speak to) A moral virtue which enables its possessor to be amiable to his fellow men. It is allied to justice.

affections (L. *affectare,* to do to) Those driving and motivating forces inherent in the nature of man. The philosophers reduced these affections to four: love, joy, sorrow and hate. These affections are natural to man and cannot be denied. But they must be brought under control and so disposed that they become centered on Christ so that man may gradually become transformed into a Christlike being.

affective prayer A prayer based primarily on the emotions.

affiliation (L. *affiliare,* to adopt as a son) The union of lesser societies and confraternities to greater ones, whereby the smaller enjoy the rights and privileges of the larger. A papal indult is necessary for validity.

affinal marriage An attempted marriage with an in-law. *See* impediments.

affinity (L. *affinis,* related by marriage) A relationship which arises from a valid Christian marriage, creating an affinity between the husband and the blood relations of his wife, and between the wife and the blood relations of her husband, in the same line and degree as would be established by consanguinity. Affinity is a diriment impediment (canon 97). In the direct line (ancestors and descendants) no licit marriage can be contracted in any degree (canon 1077). In the collateral line it invalidates marriage up to the second degree, although dispensation may be given.

affusion (L. *fundere,* to pour) The method of Baptism in the Latin Rite by pouring water. Also called infusion.

Africa The continent of Africa, a mission field of gigantic proportions, was one of the very early sites of Christianity. The Acts of the Apostles relates the conversion of an official of Queen Candace of Ethiopia by the Apostle Philip (Acts 8:28-40), and the populace received the Faith later on from Egypt. St. Mark preached the Gospel in Egypt, and the Catholic Church flourished there for centuries. Closely following the apostolic age, the Faith filtered into what was called Roman Africa, in the Mediterranean coastal region as far west as Tangiers. The Church spread rapidly in these highly civilized areas, accompanied by persecutions and with many martyrs. By the third century there was a large Christian population in town and country. By the time paganism had ceased being a menace, heresies were dividing the Church. The great St. Augustine returned to his native land and built up the Church from his see of Hippo. He died in A.D. 430,

just as the Vandals were invading the country, determined to destroy the Church and establish the Arian heresy. After a hundred years marked by more martyrdoms, the Church in Africa was much weakened, but the Byzantine forces overcame the Vandals and destroyed their power. Just as the Church was recovering, though still afflicted by heresies, the Moslem Arabs came down in hordes, conquered Egypt and then swept on. By 698 the Church in Africa was practically blotted out, and Islam took over. Even today the Moslem-controlled lands remain mostly closed to Christianity. South of the Sahara lies the Africa of the Negro peoples, mostly animists for untold ages. The Muslims of North Africa made a great business of capturing the inhabitants of remote Negro villages and selling them into slavery, fostering hostility of the natives towards foreigners. The vast reaches of central Africa have been penetrated by missioners only in relatively modern times with warrior tribesmen, wild animals and tropical diseases taking a toll of many lives. Cardinal Lavigerie (1825–1892) founded two missionary societies, the White Fathers and the White Sisters, that have done much to plant and preserve the Faith in Africa. He also worked effectively to get the slave traffic abolished. Holy Ghost Missioners have also pioneered this once difficult and dangerous mission territory. Today Africa has over 25 million Catholics. There is a fine native clergy, including an African Cardinal; and counting both natives and foreign-born, there are 44 archbishops, 224 bishops, over 14 thousand priests, 35 thousand religious, more than 2,000 native seminarians, nearly 700 hospitals, and 47 thousand Catholic schools with over 4 million students.

Africa, South, the Church in The Republic of South Africa covers an area of over 472 thousand square miles, has two capitals, two flags, two official languages, two national anthems and various problems, all of which affect the Church. The Dutch settled in the area beginning in 1652, and the British gained control over Cape Colony early in the 19th century. The war between British and Boers (of Dutch ancestry) left bitter feeling which is still in evidence. When the Dutch first arrived, the only natives, Bushmen and Hottentots who were nomads and few in number, were left unmolested. However, a horde of Bantu tribesmen from Central Africa began a trek into the region between 1750 and 1850, and there were bloody battles and raids, reminiscent of those between early American settlers and the Indians. The Bantus were defeated and reduced to being servants of the white settlers, but there has never been peace between them. During all these years the Catholic Church has had a bare foothold or none at all. Early Dutch Calvinists held the Church in low regard, and both they and the British made priests and missioners unwelcome. The teaching of the Church on the equality of the races under God has been a further reason for its unpopularity in South Africa. In recent years, however, the Church has made definite progress there. The Mariannhill Missionaries at Natal train the Bantu in agriculture, in the use of cooperatives, in housing and health practices. They and others educate native teachers, and train native clergy and religious. In a population of nearly 16 million, the Bantu represent 66.9 per cent;

Africans of European ancestry nearly 21 per cent; those of mixed blood, 8.2 per cent; Asiatics, 3 per cent. Among all these people, Catholics number only 5 per cent.

African Liturgy The African Rite Liturgy as used in North Africa twelve centuries ago. It derived from the original Roman Liturgy and is supposed to have first used Latin in its services. It has long since disappeared.

African Methodist Episcopal Church A religious organization of Negroes founded in 1816 in Philadelphia which follows the doctrine and the practices of the Methodist Church.

agape (ah′gah-pay, Gr. charity) 1. A Greek word that signifies charity freely given from love. 2. The meal (love feast) that was ceremoniously taken in company with other Christians, designed to signify and cement the bonds of charity among the early Christians. It was celebrated with hymns, prayers and the reading of Scriptures. It was not the same as the Eucharistic meal, but often preceded it. St. Paul (1 Cor. 11:16-34) seems to disapprove of the custom because of abuses. 3. A friendly meal in common.

age, canonical Canon law fixes various ages for various acts, known as the canonical age. This age is reckoned from the date of birth. Thus the age of reason when a child may go to the Sacrament of Penance and incur the obligation of abstinence and Sunday Mass is set at 7 years. Fasting is of obligation for all over 21 and under 59. Marriage attempted by males under 16 and females under 14 is null and void.

age, impediment of An obstacle because of lack of sufficient chronological age, that stands in the way of a true and valid marriage. According

16

to canon law, boys cannot marry before they have completed their 16th year and girls their 14th year.

age of consent 1. The lowest age at which a person may marry. 2. The lowest age when a girl may consent to sexual relations without having her partner subject to a charge of statutory rape.

age of discretion That time in life when a person can begin to make serious and weighty decisions. In English law it is 14. It is different from the age of reason which the Church sets at the age of 7.

age of reason The age at which a child is normally able to make responsible decisions. This is said to be usually about the age of 7, but children vary greatly in this respect. Catholic children who have reached the age of reason are obliged to attend Mass on Sundays and holy days, to receive the Sacrament of Penance, and to keep the days of abstinence. (Fasting is not of obligation until the age of 21.) They receive Holy Communion when they have attained the age of reason if they have the necessary understanding of their Faith and of the nature of the Eucharist, simply expressed, and in accordance with their years. In the Latin Rite they may be confirmed at this age; in Eastern rites, infants often receive Confirmation along with Baptism.

Ages of Faith, the The Middle Ages when society in Europe was organized on Christian principles. The period culminated in the 13th century, called by many historians the greatest of centuries.

Aggai (Heb. *haggay,* born on a feast day) A minor prophet, author of the book of the Bible bearing his name. The book consists of five oracles aimed at encouraging the rebuilding of the temple. It is not cer-tain that Aggai wrote the actual book although the thoughts are his.

Aggeus Aggai (*q.v.*).

aggiornamento (It. update) A term used by Pope John XXIII when summoning Vatican Council II to seek ways of adapting the Church to the conditions of the modern world. Pope John called it "the opening of the window of the Church to let fresh air enter."

aggregation (L. *aggregare,* to collect) The right of an archconfraternity to affiliate to itself other confraternities of the same kind, and allow them to share in its rights and privileges.

aggressor, unjust It is a moral principle that one may defend himself against an unjust aggressor even to the point of killing him, provided that one does not injure him any more than necessary to ensure self-protection.

agility In the spiritual sense, agility is one of the four qualities applied to the risen body; it implies the power to pass from place to place with great speed.

Aglipayan Schism (ag-lae-pye'an, from name of founder, Gregorio Aglipay) A native Philippine "Catholic" church. Under the Spanish rule, a native priesthood in the Philippine Islands was only partly developed. There were native priests, but no native bishops. When during the 19th century the Filipinos revolted against Spain, they also turned against the Spanish-dominated Church. Most of the Spanish missioners withdrew during the revolution of 1896, and when the United States took over the islands in 1898 still more Spanish priests and friars went back to Spain. A Filipino priest named Gregorio Aglipay in 1902 proclaimed himself the pope of a Philippine Catholic Church and carried over a million believers with him. By the time of Aglipay's death in 1941, the schism had declined and its followers had diminished in number. Since that time there has been a steady return of Aglipayans to the Catholic Faith.

agnet (ahg'net; Gr. *agnus,* lamb)  The first piece of bread cut from the prosphora during the Liturgy of the Byzantine Rite. It symbolizes the action that "the Lamb of God is sacrificed, who takes away the sin of the world."

agnosticism (Gr. *agnostos,* unknowing) A philosophical system which holds that the existence and nature of God are unknowable. There have been both English and French schools of agnosticism. Agnosticism denies the possibility of knowing God through reason. Vatican Council I considered this question and reaffirmed the traditional claims of the Church as being in accord with reason.

Agnus Dei (ahyn'yus day'ee, L. Lamb of God) One of the Church's sacramentals (*q.v.*), a small wafer of wax taken from paschal candles or from those of Candlemas, solemnly blessed by the pope during the year of his coronation and every seven years afterward. The name derives from the image of a lamb, which is stamped on one side. Agnus Deis originated from the popular custom of using bits of the paschal candle as articles of devotion. The wafers of wax are usually enclosed in leather or silk and embellished with embroidery and lace.

Agony of Christ The term used to describe the particular suffering endured by Christ in the Garden of Gethsemani after the Last Supper and prior to His apprehension. The suffering endured by Christ was primarily a suffering of mental anguish, although there were physical effects. His human will wanted to flee what He knew lay ahead. His divine will compelled Him to continue His work of Redemption. This event is also called the Agony in the Garden, as in the Sorrowful Mysteries of the Rosary.

agrapha (Gr. unwritten) The sayings of Jesus which are not recorded in the canonical Gospels but which are found elsewhere in the New Testament (Acts 20:35), in the writings of the Fathers and in other documents. Many of the latter do not stand up to critical examination.

AID *See* Association for International Development.

air Symbol for giving life. The breathing of air is used in a number of Catholic ceremonies: in Baptism, exorcisms, consecrating the holy oils and blessing baptismal water. As God breathed on Adam to give him life, so the minister of Baptism breathes on the one to be baptized to symbolize the spiritual life that is being given.

aircraft blessing A formula for blessing aircraft was approved by the Congregation of Rites in 1920 and inserted in the Roman Ritual. At that time aircraft were referred to as "air machines." It follows: "O God, who has ordained all things for your own and devised all the elements of this world for the human race; bless, we beg you, this machine consigned to the air; that it may serve for the glory and praise of your name, and, free from all injury and danger, expedite human interests and foster heavenly aspirations in the minds of all who

18

use it. Through Christ Our Lord. Amen."

aisle (OF. *ele,* wing of a building) 1. A section along the side of a church, separated from the nave by pillars. An aisle may also run alongside a choir or transept. 2. The passageway between pews in a church.

akolouthia (a-ko-loo-thee′ah; Gr. a sequence) In the Byzantine Rite, any liturgical ceremony, particularly a recitation of the Divine Office in choir. The Office consists of psalms, hymns and prayers. When sung in choir it takes about eight hours.

Alabama (*Alibamu,* an Indian tribe of Muskhogean stock, possibly "thicket-clearers") The 22nd state of the Union. The first Mass was probably celebrated in Alabama in the year 1540, near the site of the city of Mobile. At that time the De Soto expedition, including twelve priests and four Dominican Friars, was exploring the area. The first European settlement was made by Tristan de Luna of Mexico in 1559–1562, at an Indian village called Nanipacna. The missioners who accompanied the party tried to make converts among the Indians, but with little success. The settlement was finally given up. In 1682 La Salle, from the mouth of the Mississippi, claimed the surrounding land for France, and in 1702 Fort Louis de la Mobile was founded by the French-Canadian explorer Iberville. The parish of Mobile was formally erected in 1703, under the jurisdiction of the Foreign Mission Seminary in Quebec. The first pastor was Father De La Vente. A church was built on Dauphin Island at the entrance to Mobile Bay in 1709, and several missions were established: Fort Toulouse, Tombigbee, and Chickasawhay. After 1721 the Discalced Carmelites, the Capuchins, and the Jesuits carried on missionary work in Mobile. France ceded the region to England in 1763, and the English lost it to Spain in 1780. From that time on, Spanish priests carried on the work of the Church in the Mobile area until 1813, when the United States took over the colony. In 1819 Alabama was admitted to the Union, and in 1825 Michael Portier was named Vicar Apostolic of Alabama and Florida. He was the only Catholic clergyman in the whole vicariate at the time. He sailed for Europe to find missionary helpers, and came back with only two priests and four men in minor orders. In 1828 he was appointed first bishop of the diocese of Mobile. He founded Spring Hill College and Seminary, later run by the Jesuits, and brought in the Visitation Nuns, the Sisters of Charity and the Brothers of the Sacred Heart, all of whom occupied themselves in works of charity and in the education of children. After the Civil War many of the churches and establishments were in ruins. The bishop repaired them, built the portico of Mobile Cathedral, and brought in Benedictines from St. Vincent's Archabbey, Pa., to do missionary work in the diocese. Later bishops introduced many other Religious Orders, paying particular attention to work among the Negroes. The Catholics of the diocese now number about 100,000, in a total population of somewhat over 3 million.

Alamo The Franciscan mission of San Antonio de Valera founded at San Pedro Springs, Tex., about 1718. It was moved to the plaza of San Antonio, Tex., in 1732, and to its present site in San Antonio fourteen years later. The buildings included a church, hospital and monastery (*convento*) surrounded by a walled enclosure. It became a symbol of resistance in the war for the independence of Texas when it was defended against a large Mexican force by a relatively small body of men.

Alaska The 49th state, entered the Union in 1959, its territory having been purchased from Russia in 1867. Its name comes from a native word meaning "Great Country." The Aleuts, the Athabaskans, the Tlingits, and the Eskimo or Innuits of Alaska practiced sorcery and had a complex moral code. They believed in a future life with rewards and punishments, and recognized the Creator of all. They practiced polygamy, and woman's life was one of considerable hardship. Abandonment of old and helpless parents to die on the frozen steppe was usual. In 1794 a band of monks under Archimandrite Ivassof arrived in Kodiak under the protection of the Russian-American Fur company and set out from there to do missionary work among the natives. They showed great zeal, led lives of hardship, set up Russian churches with parochial schools and orphanages, and trained native boys for the priesthood. Later, Protestant missionaries from the United States were very successful, establishing stations along the coast and on the shores of the great rivers. In 1878 Father John Althoff became the first resident priest. Most Rev. Charles Seghers, Archbishop of Oregon City and Apostle of Alaska, made long journeys visiting native tribes, and in 1884 was murdered by an insane companion. Mission work went on with the arrival of the Jesuits and some funds from Europe. A training school for native children was established at Holy Cross Mission. Bishop Joseph Crimont, S.J., was made Vicar-Apostolic of Alaska in 1904, and subsequent Jesuit bishops have built up the Church there. The Sisters of St. Ann, the Ursuline Nuns, the Sisters of Charity, the Daughters of Our Lady of the Snows and the Little Sisters of Jesus all have establishments in the state. It now has a growing number of parishes and missions, but it is still a field of considerable hardship and sparsely distributed personnel. In a total population of 226,000, Catholics number about 36,000.

alb (L. *alba,* white) The long white vestment used in liturgical functions, principally the Mass. It is a survival of the long inner tunic worn in Roman times. It is put on after the amice.

Albania, the Church in Albania was once a predominantly Muslim country with a minority of Christians, most of whom were members of the Albanian Orthodox Church. The Catholic Church there numbered 2 archdioceses, 3 dioceses, 1 abbacy nullius, 1 apostolic administration, 3 bishops, 48 parishes, 53 priests and a few seminarians, according to the last report from Rome before the Communists came into power. There were about 100,000 Catholics in a total population of over 1.6 million. In 1944 the Communists took over the country. Following this, the Church was destroyed, bishops and priests were murdered and many lay Catholics were imprisoned. Over 5,000 Catholic lay leaders of the professional and business community died by slow torture, starvation and other types of inhuman treatment best known to the Communists. The Church in Albania is now a Church of Silence behind the iron curtain.

Albany One of the earliest settlements in New York State and the present capital, originally settled by

Walloons and called Fort Orange. Spiritual administration was under Quebec. St. Isaac Jogues took refuge here after escaping from his Mohawk captors. The city came under Bishop John Carroll of Baltimore in 1790. It became a diocese in 1847.

Albigensianism (al'bi-jen'-see-an'ism) So called from the city of Albi in southern France. In the 12th century there had been a period of decline in the Church, resulting in the rise of various sects of heretics. The most dangerous of them were the Albigenses. They denied the sacraments and the entire ecclesiastical hierarchy, and the power of the state to punish crimes. There were two classes, the *perfect* and the *believers.* The perfect were forbidden to marry, or to eat meat or any animal products, and were obliged to observe rigorous fasts. The believers had only two duties; namely, the firm will of joining the perfect sometime before death, and the performance of certain acts of reverence when meeting one of the perfect. Whatever vices they indulged in would be forgiven upon their entering the ranks of the perfect. This transition was brought about by a ceremony called *consolamentum,* which they imagined gave them absolute certainty as to their eternal salvation, provided they fulfilled the duties of the perfect. Should they commit a grievous fault, they were irretrievably lost because the *consolamentum* could not be repeated. To prevent a relapse their friends might resort to the simple means of killing them. Such cases were not at all rare. Often, too, they would starve themselves to death.

Alcantara, Knights of A military order founded in Alcantara, Spain, in the 12th century to combat the Moors. Its powers and rights were restricted by Pope Alexander VI in 1494. It survives as a lay order of honor.

alcoholic A condition arrived at by a person when he is no longer able to control his consumption of alcoholic drink. By taking one drink, control is lost. The condition may result from psychological or physiological reasons or from both.

Aleph First letter of the Hebrew alphabet. This alphabet is used before the verses of the Lamentations of Jeremia at Tenebrae.

Alexandria, Church of Tradition says that St. Mark founded the Church in Alexandria. In its early years it made great contributions to the whole Church, producing such outstanding theologians as St. Athanasius and St. Cyril. It produced the Septuagint, the Greek translation of the Hebrew Scriptures. The rise of Arianism saw the Church of Alexandria go into decline. Today Alexandria has three patriarchates: 1. the Catholic Copts; 2. the dissident Copts; 3. the Orthodox.

Alexandria, Patriarchate of Founded (according to tradition) by St. Mark, this patriarchate was for several centuries the most important after Rome. Before the numerous schisms, the patriarchate held particularly absolute jurisdiction over all the sees of Egypt. Today this patriarchate exists under five different jurisdictions. 1. Catholic Coptic Patriarchate; title and jurisdiction restored in 1895 by Pope Leo XIII. 2. Catholic Melkite Patriarch of Antioch and Alexandria, the last title possessed as a personal concession. 3. Latin Rite Patriarchate of Alexandria, created at the time of the Crusades, but now suppressed and no longer titular. 4. Coptic Patriarchate (Dissident), in schism since the Council of

Chalcedon in 451, which condemned Monophysitism. 5. Orthodox Patriarchate, in schism since 567.

Alexandria, school of The small catechetical school of Alexandria was founded by the missionary St. Pantaenus and modeled after the school of St. Justin. The school gradually grew and produced a group of important Christian thinkers. Included among these are Clement (d. 211), Origen (d. 255), St. Athanasius (d. 373), St. Cyril (d. 444); closely associated with these were the Cappodocian Fathers, St. Basil, St. Gregory of Nyssa and St. Gregory Nazianzen. To this school the production of the Septuagint is attributed. Various members of this school are responsible for originating the great Christological heresies of Apollinarism, Monophysitism and Monothelitism.

Alexandrine Liturgy The first liturgy of Alexandria is attributed to St. Mark. This liturgy is no longer in use, except as a part of the Coptic Rite anaphora composed by St. Cyril. Today the Copts use three liturgies; namely, those of St. Cyril, St. Gregory Nazianzen and St. Basil. These differ only in their anaphoras. The Ethiopian Rite makes use of the Liturgy of the Twelve Apostles, which is the Coptic translated by St. Cyril into their own language. They also change this liturgy on various feasts by adding other anaphoras.

Alexandrine Rite One of the rites of the East, originated in Alexandria, Egypt. At the present time, represented by the Catholic Eastern Rites of the Coptic and Ethiopian (Abyssinian) Churches. *See* Alexandrine Liturgy.

Alexian Brothers A nursing congregation of men, founded in 1365 in Brabant, Belgium, by a Brother Tobias, at the height of the pestilence called the "Black Death." At first they were merely an association of pious laymen who tended the pest-stricken and buried the dead. Later they took a Syrian, Saint Alexis, as their patron, calling themselves the Alexian Brothers, and in time they became a religious order with solemn vows. They have spread throughout Germany and the Low Countries, to England and the United States. Their general motherhouse is at Aachen, Germany, and their center in the United States is at Signal Mountain, Chattanooga, Tenn. They are engaged in hospital work for the sick in general, and also for those with nervous and psychiatric disorders, inebriates as well as the aged and infirm.

Algeria Almost 1 million Catholics in a population of 11 million. There are 1 archdiocese and 3 dioceses. Formerly the Roman provinces of Numidia and Mauretania, the area was once the site of flourishing Christianity. Here St. Augustine was born, here the Council of Carthage took place. In the early 8th century, the Muslims took control and the Church disappeared. In the 19th century the Vincentians began work and Cardinal Lavigerie founded the White Fathers. Charles de Foucauld died at Tamanrasset in 1916. Obstacles to the Church are the Muslims, an underdeveloped economy, anti-French feeling, dispersion of the population, lack of priests. Positive factors are the development of a Catholic elite interested in *rapprochement* with the Muslims, the spirit and method of the missioners, the efforts of the Mission to the Sahara to find solutions to economic problems.

alienation A canonical term used in transferring the property of the Church to another. Canon law forbids alienation except for a just reason and then only in the manner prescribed by the canons.

alimentation　Provision for the necessities of life (food, clothing and shelter) for members of religious orders; the maintenance offered diocesan priests.

All Saints, feast of　Nov. 1, the feast which commemorates all the saints in heaven, whether or not they are canonized; a holyday of obligation. In the Eastern Rites it is kept at other times, but it is always a feast of highest class. In England it was formerly called All Hallows, and the eve of the feast (Oct. 31) was Hallow Even or Hallowe'en, widely known today as an evening of capers and tricks even among those who have never heard of the feast of All Saints. In the year 610 Pope Boniface IV cleansed and consecrated the Pantheon (a temple in Rome, dedicated to all the gods, known also as the Temple of Agrippa). He made of it a Christian sanctuary containing relics of many martyrs, named it St. Mary of the Martyrs, and ordered an annual commemoration of all the saints. Pope Gregory I (731–741) named Nov. 1 as the anniversary, and Gregory IV (827–844) had the feast and its vigil extended to the worldwide Church.

All Souls' Day　Nov. 2, or, if this day falls on a Sunday, Nov. 3. The commemoration of the souls of all the faithful departed. On this day special prayers are offered for the dead, priests and religious recite the Office of the Dead (*q.v.*) and each priest may say three Masses. A plenary indulgence is also granted for each visit made to a church to pray for the dead, under the usual conditions for gaining the indulgence. The practice of praying for the dead is a very ancient one. Prayers and sacrifices were offered to cleanse the souls of the dead in Old Testament times (2 Machabees 12:38–46) and the Church has prayed for the dead from the beginning. The celebration of All Souls' Day was ordered in 998 by St. Odilo, Abbot of Cluny, effective in all the monasteries under his jurisdiction. The practice spread throughout the Church. Pope Benedict XV granted to priests the privilege of offering three Requiem Masses on this day.

Allah　The Muslim name for the Supreme Being, God. Islam is a monotheistic religion, accepting Yahweh, the God of Israel.

Allatae Sunt　(ahl-lah'tay sunt, L. they were carried away)　An encyclical of Pope Benedict XIV written in 1775 and addressed to missioners in Syria and Asia Minor. It explained proper relationships of the missioner to the Eastern Churches. It laid down the important principle that converted dissidents should not be brought into the Latin Rite but into their own. "We desire most intensely," Benedict wrote, "that all should be Catholics, but not that all should be Latins."

allegorical interpretation, biblical　A method of exegesis which attempts to discover a meaning in Scripture other than the literal sense by means of a symbolic transference of the words. In the past, the term included every meaning that went beyond the meaning of the author, including the typical sense. Today the term is a narrower one and the typical sense is not included within it.

allegory　(Gr. *allegoria,* description of one thing under the guise of another) Allegory is sustained metaphor, a literary device by which the metaphor has a literal and representative meaning. It should not be confused with allegorical interpretation of Scripture which refers to the spiritual or mystical sense of Holy Scripture.

allocution (L. *allocutio,* to speak to) A formal exhortation or address, given by the pope to the cardinals assembled in a secret consistory. It may be of general interest to the world, in which case it is published later.

Alma Redemptoris Mater (ahl'mah ray-dempt-or'is mah'tare; L. loving mother of the Redeemer) The title and first line of one of the four seasonal antiphons sung in honor of the Mother of Christ at the end of Compline. It is designated for use in Advent from the Saturday before the first Sunday until Feb. 1, the eve of the Purification, inclusively. A versicle, response, and prayer proper to Advent follow the antiphon. It is said to have been composed *c.* A.D. 1050, by a Benedictine monk called Hermann the Cripple, in the monastery of Reichenau, Baden, Germany.

Almanac, National Catholic The most comprehensive handbook of Catholic information regularly published in the United States. The annual edition contains all types of facts, statistics and information on Catholic life. It is produced by the Franciscan Fathers of the Holy Name Province. For over half a century it has been a major contribution to Catholic literature in the United States.

Almighty, the Another name for God. It indicates His infinite power, His omniscience and His omnipresence.

almoner 1. An official attached to the court of a king, prince, governor, ecclesiastic, etc., who is charged with the distribution of his master's alms. 2. An almsgiver in general. 3. An Anglican dignitary bears the title of the Lord High Almoner to the king

of England. A social worker in English hospitals. 4. In France the name (*aumonier*) is used for a chaplain; e.g., to the army or a convent.

alms, giving of The giving of money or material goods to one in need is a corporal work of mercy and is one of the points on which our Last Judgment will be made. Almsgiving is commanded by the law of charity, and each one is expected to give according to his means. We are expected to give to all who are in need, enemies as well as friends. Theologians teach that we are strictly bound to give only from our surplus, after one's obligations and ordinary needs are satisfied.

alpha The first letter of the Greek alphabet. This letter is used in Christian symbolism and art, usually in connection with *omega,* the last letter in the Greek alphabet. *Alpha* and *omega* signify the beginning and end of all things, or God. St. John applies this title to Christ.

alphabet, liturgical uses of the The Hebrew, Greek and Latin alphabets have been used in various ways in the Christian liturgy. 1. During Holy Week the Hebrew alphabet is used, each of the letters preceding one of the verses of the Lamentations of Jeremia at Matins. 2. At the dedication of a church the bishop writes two alphabets on the ground, one Greek and one Latin, with the point of his pastoral staff, along two lines of ashes laid in the form of the letter X. This liturgical rite has developed from a practice borrowed from the ancient Roman land surveyors. 3. In Christian symbolism from early times the first and last letters of the Greek alphabet, *alpha* and *omega,* have signified God's absolute and eternal being. In the Apocalypse it has the additional symbolism of signifying Christ and His divinity. In early Christian ages *alpha* and *omega* were used as the monogram of Christ. The restored rite of the Paschal Vigil prescribes for the blessing of the paschal candle that the priest inscribe a cross with a stylus between the outer holes made to receive the grains of incense. At the head of this cross he then traces the Greek letter *alpha,* at the foot *omega* and between the arms, four figures for the date of the current year.

altar   The table or block upon which sacrifice is made. It is the place where the Sacrifice of the Mass is offered. In the primitive Church, the Eucharist was celebrated on a table and no particular form prevailed. Later when the Church went into the catacombs, Mass was offered on the tomb of a martyr. This custom remains in the practice today of celebrating Mass on a stone slab containing the relics of a martyr. In ancient days the altar was built so that the priest offering Mass faced the people. Later, altars were built in the apse of the Church so that the people were behind the priest. In an instruction prepared by a special liturgical commission established by Pope Paul VI for the implementation of the decrees of the Constitution on the Sacred Liturgy of Vatican Council II,

the document spoke of new churches and alterations of old ones, declaring: "It is proper that the main altar be constructed separately from the wall, so that one may go around it with ease and so that celebration may take place facing the people." The same instruction said that the Most Holy Eucharist shall be preserved in a "inviolable" tabernacle either on the main altar, or a "minor but truly outstanding altar" or with the approval of the Ordinary in some other "properly adorned part of the church." A fixed altar consists of a *mensa* (table top), *stripes* (base) and a sepulcher for the relics. A portable altar consists of an altar stone with a sepulcher for relics which is consecrated apart from its table or support. The Byzantine altar is square and has a wooden top. Vatican Council II has called for sacred furnishings that "should worthily and beautifully serve the dignity of worship." The Council stated that sacred art should "strive after noble beauty rather than sumptious display."

altar boy   One who assists a priest at a liturgical or paraliturgical function; a server. At Mass the altar boy answers the prayers, transfers the missal, brings the priest wine and water, and rings the bell. He also assists at Benediction and other ceremonies.

altar, consecration of an   A permanent altar is consecrated at the same time as a church. Rubrics set specific ceremonies. The bishop anoints the sepulcher with chrism and encloses relics. He then passes around the altar three times, incensing it each time. The altar is then anointed in the middle and at the four corners, twice with oil of catechumens and once with chrism; the five anointings are in honor of Our Lord's five wounds.

The mensa, or table, is then rubbed thoroughly with the oil and chrism, incense is burned on it, and the Sign of the Cross is made with chrism on other parts of the altar. The ritual contains the prayers and antiphons that are used.

altar, double One so constructed that Mass may be celebrated on either side, having candles and crucifix in center which serve both sides.

altar, Gregorian An altar that carries the same privilege as the altar of St. Gregory in St. Gregory's Church in Rome. This privilege is to grant a plenary indulgence for a soul in Purgatory, gained by celebration of Mass at the altar. Since 1912 this privilege is not given to new altars. *See* altar, privileged.

altar, high The main or principal altar of a church. It should be the central object in the sanctuary which in turn should be the center of interest in the church building. The Blessed Sacrament is often reserved on it.

altar linens Altar cloths (*q.v.*).

altar ornaments 1. Western Church. The high altar should have a crucifix; six candles, each in a candlestick; three white cloths of linen or hemp, the top cloth covering the entire mensa and hanging down at the sides. Over the entire altar should be a canopy (ciborium). 2. Byzantine Rite. The altar should have a crucifix placed between two or more candles in candlesticks behind which are the ripidia; the altar is covered with cloth of which the uppermost may be made of any fabric and may be colored. On this cloth is placed the antimension, a pall-like cloth corresponding to the altar stone of the West; it bears a picture of the burial of Christ and the instruments of His passion, and has relics sewn into it. The antimension is wrapped in the eileton, equivalent to a corporal. On the eileton is placed the Book of Gospels. Over the altar is a canopy (ciborium).

altar, papal An altar only used by the pope or his delegate. The major basilicas in Rome contain a papal altar.

altar, privileged An altar at which a plenary indulgence can be gained for a soul in Purgatory by the celebration and application of the Mass (canon 535). The privilege is given in different ways: *local,* belonging to the altar and the indulgence gained by any priest celebrating Mass there; *personal,* given to a priest and follows him to any altar; *mixed,* given to certain priests at certain altars. To obtain the local privilege, the altar must be permanent. Cardinals and bishops have personal privilege. On All Souls' Day every altar is privileged. During Forty Hours every altar in the church is privileged, as is that altar on which there is perpetual exposition.

altar society A group of devoted women who take it upon themselves to care for the altar and sanctuary in the parish church. Their duties may be many and varied. They see that the linens are laundered, brought back and put in place; that candlesticks and other equipment are clean and polished; flowers purchased, often with their own funds, arranged on the altar and shrines, and removed when their usefulness is over. In some churches they keep the sanctuary lamp clean, filled and lighted; do dusting and tidying up in the sanctuary; keep the vestments and linens mended and laid out ready for use, taking on themselves numerous small time-consuming duties according to the need of the church and the wish of the pastor. They sometimes have social gatherings and run bazaars or card parties to obtain money for the upkeep of the sanctuary and its furnishings.

altar stone  A solid slab of natural rock large enough for the host and chalice to be placed on it. It has a small cavity into which are sealed relics of a martyr or martyrs and if desired, of other saints. It is consecrated by a bishop or by a priest who has received the proper faculties. It is placed on the surface or mortised into the top of a table or structure on which Mass is to be celebrated, to answer the purpose of an altar when there is no consecrated altar. Missionary priests and military chaplains carry altar stones in their Mass kits. Such stones are called portable altars.

altar, stripping of The ceremony performed on Holy Thursday after the Blessed Sacrament has been transferred to the Altar of Repose. It is symbolical of Christ's being stripped of His garments before crucifixion. In the ceremony the altar is stripped of altar cloths, antependium and tabernacle veil.

alternation The response to alternate verses in singing, or alternate responses in such prayers as the litanies and the Rosary.

altruism (L. *alter,* another) Altruism is a philosophy by which the believer never acts for his own good but always for the good of another.

ambo (Gr. *ambon,* a raised place) In the early Christian churches, the ambo was a small platform in the middle of the church from which the Gospel and Epistle were read. Later a platform was placed on each side of the church, one for the Gospel and one for the Epistle. The ambo was also used for preaching and making announcements. In the Roman Church the ambo has been replaced by the pulpit or lectern. In the Greek Church the ambo is a table in front of the iconostasis, at which Baptisms, Confirmations and marriages are celebrated. In the Byzantine Church, the ambo is found on the north side of the church and is used for singing the Gospel.

Ambrosian chant The simple and beautiful plain chant used in the Ambrosian Rite. It is noticeable because only one or at the most two notes are used on each syllable. Forerunner of Gregorian chant.

Ambrosian hymnography All the hymns having the meter and strophic measure found in the hymns of St. Ambrose.

Ambrosian Rite The liturgy as used in the province of Milan, and said to have originated with St. Ambrose in the 4th century. It differs from the Roman usage in the Mass and Divine Office. The Mass makes use of Old Testament passages which like the Gospel and Epistle are sung from an ambo. The Creed is said just before the Preface. The faithful present gifts of bread and wine before the Offertory. The breaking of the bread is before the Pater Noster. The Agnus Dei is omitted except at Requiem Masses. The liturgical colors are also different; black is used in Lent when Fridays are liturgical days.

ambry (am'bree, L. *armarium,* a cupboard)  The box attached to the side of the sanctuary in which the Holy Oils are kept. The ambry should be kept locked and the door should bear the words *Olea Sacra* (Latin for "Holy Oils").

ambulatory (L. *ambulare,* to walk)

A covered walk around a cloister, open at the courtyard side; also a passage around the apse of a church which allows an uninterrupted processional path.

amen (Heb. certainly, truly) A Hebrew exclamation indicating emphatic assent or agreement. In the Hebrew synagogue the people made a prayer offered by a prayer leader their own by answering, "Amen." The use was carried over into the New Testament. Christ gave an unusual meaning to the word by beginning many of His statements with "Amen" which He sometimes even doubled. His use meant that He was giving the statement a guarantee of truth and endorsing it with His own authority. The "Amen" now said when receiving Holy Communion is a profession of faith in the Eucharist that dates back to the earliest Christianity. The word has a double pronunciation: In English it is *aye'men'*; in Latin and when being sung it is *ah'men'*.

amendment, purpose of According to the Baltimore Catechism, a firm purpose of sinning no more, including a sincere resolve not only to avoid sin but to avoid as far as possible the near occasions of sin. It does not necessarily exclude the fear that a person may repeat his sin in the future. It does mean that, at the time, a person, relying fully upon God's grace, sincerely intends never to commit this sin again. It includes the intention to remain away from persons, places or things that may easily lead to sin. The firm purpose of amendment must include all of the person's mortal sins, including those committed in the past and confessed. If a person has only venial sins to confess, he must have the purpose of avoiding at least one of them.

American Board of Catholic Missions
A committee established in 1924 for the purpose of distributing a definite share (40 per cent) of the monies collected each year on Mission Sunday by the Society for the Propagation of the Faith (*q.v.*) in the United States and its dependent territories.

American Cassinese Congregation A congregation of Benedictine Monks, erected by Pope Pius IX in 1855, headed by St. Vincent's Archabbey at Latrobe, Pa. To this congregation belong Benedictine abbeys in the archdioceses of Kansas City, Kan., of Newark and of Seattle; also in the dioceses of Bismarck, Cleveland, Greensburg, Joliet, Manchester, Mobile-Birmingham, Oklahoma City and Tulsa, Peoria, Pueblo, St. Augustine and St. Cloud; also the abbeys nullius in Belmont, N. C., and in Muenster, Sask.; and the Conventual Priory of the Pittsburgh Greek Rite.

American College (the North American College) A pontifical institution for the education of North American clergymen in Rome (address: Via del Gianicolo 14, Vatican City). In 1854 Archbishop Hughes of New York and Archbishop Kenrick of Baltimore together with other archbishops and bishops asked Pope Pius IX for permission to establish such a house of studies in Rome. The Pope was so greatly interested in the project that in 1857 he bought a convent building and presented it to the American Bishops. Archbishop Hughes took up a collection throughout his diocese to provide funds for the repairs and refurnishing of the building. On Dec. 12, the feast of Our Lady of Guadalupe, the first pontifical Mass was offered in the new college. It opened with thirteen students. After the seizure of Rome the Italian government tried to take over the property, but through the prompt action of Cardinal McCloskey and Archbishop Corrigan, President Chester A. Arthur took up the matter with the King of Italy and prevented the seizure. The American College was raised to the rank of a Pontifical College by Leo XIII in 1884. Many famous American churchmen owe part of their education to this institution.

American Protective Association A secret society known by its initials (A.P.A.) that flourished briefly in the United States during the last decade of the 19th century. Members were bound by oath to exclude Catholics from public office. It caused havoc through a number of forged documents, one being a papal bull which called for the massacre of Protestants. When the society failed to block the nomination of William McKinley (1896), it suffered a setback from which it never recovered.

Americanism Toward the end of the nineteenth century Catholics in the United States were accused of heresy because of nationalistic tendencies. The charge was precipitated in France when a biography of Father Isaac Hecker, founder of the Paulists, was translated into French by Abbe Felix Klein who also wrote a lengthy introduction. This edition, particularly the Klein introduction, was attacked as heretical, and the heresy was called Americanism. The dispute became so bitter that Pope Leo XIII wrote a letter to Cardinal Gibbons, Jan. 22, 1899, condemning Americanism. The pope pointed out that he was not condemning the American spirit and that Americanism was not necessarily a doctrine accepted by Americans, but that he condemned this term because of the way it was used in Europe.

amice (am'iss, L. *amictus*, a gar-

ment or covering) A square or oblong of white linen cloth worn by the priest when celebrating Mass. It is a sacred vestment and is blessed before it is used. Originally perhaps a kerchief or scarf to protect the throat or to prevent stains of perspiration on the richer vestments or even to cover the head, it is the first of the sacred vestments put on when the priest is vesting. He places it first on his head, then around his neck, tying it down with the long strings which are attached to it. Regular clergy, members of religious orders, still use the amice as a kind of headdress or cowl. At ordination, the amice is bestowed on the subdeacon by the bishop, who says, "Receive the amice, which signifies the discipline of the voice." This would seem to refer to it as a kind of muffler, protecting the voice of the cleric who formerly had to sing and preach in cold, drafty churches. The prayer which the priest says when putting on the amice refers to it as the "helmet of salvation," obviously a headcovering. In the Ambrosian rite the amice is worn over the alb, not under it.

Amish A strict sect that developed from the Mennonites. It takes its name from its founder, Amman. The members settled in America, particularly in Pennsylvania where they still continue primitive practices.

Amos, Book of The third of the prophetic books of the Old Testament, named after its author. Amos prophesied, during the 8th century B.C., the eventual coming of the Messianic Kingdom and the conversion of the Gentiles. His words are quoted in Acts 7:42 and in Acts 15:16 f. The

Roman Martyrology mentions him on Mar. 31. Amos was one of the minor prophets. He was a man of the soil who was a shepherd and dresser of trees. He despised pomp and the abuse of power.

amovability　A canonical term describing the rights of a bishop in removing a cleric from an office, except in cases prohibited by canon law (Canons 192, 2147-2161).

amphibology　A type of mental reservation (*q.v.*). It is a statement with several meanings. Its purpose is the concealment of truth, which in certain circumstances can be permitted and on occasion is even necessary.

amula (ahm′you-la, L. small bucket) A name given in the early Church to the cruet which contained either the water or the wine which was to be used in the Eucharistic liturgy.

amulet (L. *amuletum,* an ornament) A small object worn as a charm to ward off evil. The use of amulets is superstitious, implying belief in a power equal to or greater than God's; they are forbidden to Catholics.

Anabaptist　A member of a Protestant sect which began in Switzerland in 1524. It taught only adult Baptism, separation of church and state, and was marked by its simplicity.

analecta (Gr. collections)　A word referring to collections from the writings of the Fathers.

analogy　A comparative likeness of one thing with another, or a like condition or relation of two things to each other. Analogy is used in Christian philosophy and theology to obtain a better understanding of the existence and nature of God. Both God and created things have the same attributes or participate in the same perfections, albeit, in an unequal degree. For instance, God is good; man

is good. God is a Being (or exists); man is a being (or exists). In these examples, "good" and "being" are said to be analogous terms.

anamnesis (Gr. recollection)　That which is done in commemoration or memory of someone or something, such as the first prayer following the Consecration of the Mass.

Ananias (Heb. *hananyah,* Yahweh has been kind)　The name of a number of persons in the Old and New Testaments. The best known are: 1. a Christian of Damascus who played a role in the conversion of St. Paul by carrying God's message to Paul concerning his call to the apostolate; 2. a Christian of Jerusalem who with his wife Sapphira tried to deceive the Holy Spirit (Acts 5); 3. the Jewish high priest who persecuted St. Paul; 4. a companion of Daniel at the Babylonian court, also known as Sidrach.

anaphora (Gr. offering)　The canon of the Eucharistic liturgy in the Eastern Rite. By extension, the word also refers to the Canon of the Mass in the Latin Rite. The Malabarese and Armenian Rites have a single anaphora but the other rites have multiple anaphora with the West Syrian Rite numbering 65. The Eastern anaphora are named after saints who supposedly composed them.

Anastasis, the (Gr. resurrection) The Church of the Holy Sepulcher in Jerusalem whose proper title is the Church of the Resurrection.

anathema (an-ath′eh-mah, Gr. *anatome,* dissection)　Originally signifying an object of consecration or execration, and used as such in both the Old and New Testaments. The latter meaning gradually predominated in the sense of curse, ban or sentence of reprobation. The final biblical development is that of the severest form of excommunication (*anathema maranatha,* 1 Cor. 16:22). In canon law *anathema* is the name given to excommunication inflicted with full ceremonial of the *Pontificale Romanum* and is the word used instead of excommunication in the condemnatory doctrinal decrees of the councils. Anathema may refer to both the curse and the thing cursed.

anchor A Christian symbol of hope, particularly the hope of eternal bliss. It was used in earliest times in epitaphs inscribed in the catacomb of St. Domitilla dating from the end of the first century and in others of succeeding periods. It was usually accompanied by sentiments such as *"Pax Tecum"* (Peace be with you!) indicating the hope that the soul was safely anchored in the harbor of heavenly peace. It is sometimes found today ornamenting altars and vestments, often accompanying the symbols for faith and charity, i.e., the cross and the heart.

anchor cross A disguised symbol of  the cross of Christ and of the crucifixion, used in ancient times of persecutions to inform the Christians and mislead the persecutors. It is found many times in the early catacombs, sometimes (as in the cemetery of St. Priscilla) with two fishes hanging from the crossbar. The anchor with its crosspiece indicated the cross; the fish (in Greek, *ichthus*) spelled out the initials of the words "Jesus Christ, Son of God, Savior."

anchoret An anchorite (*q.v.*).

anchorhold The cell of an anchorite or anchoress.

anchorite (ang'ker-ite, Gr. I withdraw) A hermit, who withdraws from so-

ciety in order to devote himself to prayer and penance, to lead the contemplative life. St. Anthony (286–356) and others in the deserts of Syria and Egypt lived in solitude, some emerging to preach as did John the Baptist and Our Lord Himself after His forty days' fast. In many cases a holy man living in solitude would attract disciples who wished to imitate him, and in time a monastery would result. St. Benedict, founder of monasticism in the West, began as a hermit and founded the Benedictine Order of monks living in community. There are various degrees between the life of absolute solitude and that of the cenobite or monk living in a monastery. In many cases one who wished to become an anchorite spent a time of preparation in a monastery, then withdrew to solitude with the abbot's permission. Usually his meager wants would be provided by the monastery. The anchorites in the desert sometimes lived on fruit of the date palm, as did Father Charles de Foucauld in the Sahara in modern times. The Carthusians and the Camaldolese monks combine the life of solitude with the monastic life. Both have foundations in the United States. Women also have lived the hermit's life and are known as anchoresses. A famous English anchoress was Mother Julian of Norwich (*c.* 1343–1413) whose book, *Revelations of Divine Love* is read by succeeding generations. She lived, as some others have, in a tiny cell built into the wall of a church where she could see the altar and receive the Blessed Sacrament through a slit in the wall.

Ancient of days A term used three times in the 7th chapter of the Book of Daniel to refer to God.

ancients A term found in Matthew

31

referring to the ancestors of Israel whose traditions were the basis for the unwritten law.

Andrew, St. One of the twelve Apostles, a native of Bethsaida in Galilee, a fisherman by trade and brother of Simon Peter. He was listening to the preaching of John the Baptist on the banks of the Jordan when he met Jesus and became one of His first disciples. He introduced his brother Simon to the Lord, saying, "We have found the Messias." Later, he received his definite call to be an Apostle, and he appears throughout the Gospels as one of Christ's devoted followers. After Pentecost Andrew went out to preach Christ in foreign fields. It is said that he died a martyr at Patras in southern Greece during the reign of Nero, A.D. 60, bound to a cross made in the form of the letter X (since known as St. Andrew's cross). Both Latin and Greek Churches keep his feast on Nov. 30. St. Andrew was chosen as patron of Russia because of a legendary account of his having preached there, and as patron of Scotland because of an equally legendary tale of his relics having been transported there. St. Andrew's cross has appeared together with the cross of St. George on the Union Jack, the national flag of Great Britain, since the union of England and Scotland in 1707.

anesthetics Drugs which eliminate sensibility are permitted to allay pain and to allow greater surgical control. However, general anesthesia carries the remote possibility of danger of death from asphyxia or cardiac paralysis. Therefore it is advisable that the patient be in the state of grace before undergoing such anesthesia.

angel (Gr. *angelos,* messenger) According to the Baltimore Catechism, angels are created spirits without bodies, having understanding and free will. They are inferior to God and superior to man. Sacred Scripture frequently speaks of the angels and mentions three by name: the Archangels Michael, Gabriel and Raphael. The exact number of angels is unknown, but Sacred Scripture indicates that their number is very great. The popular method of depicting angels either as fluffy floating beings with feathered wings, or as baby Cupids, has no relation whatever to the scriptural teaching on angels. According to the Bible, they are endowed with great power and intellect and are of such majesty that those who see visions of them are usually overwhelmed with awe. When they take human form for the purpose of delivering some message to man from God, they are usually described as young men robed in dazzling white.

angel, guardian A guardian angel is one assigned by God to care for a human being; as St. Jerome says, "Great is the dignity of souls, for each one to have an angel deputed to guard it from its birth." St. Thomas Aquinas explains: "Man while in this state of life is, as it were, on a road by which he should journey towards heaven. On this road man is threatened by many dangers both from within and without . . . and therefore as guardians are appointed for men who have to pass by an unsafe road, so an angel guardian is assigned to each man as long as he is a wayfarer. When, however, he arrives at the end of life he no longer has a guardian angel; but in the kingdom he will have an angel to reign with him, in hell a demon to punish him." No man who has ever lived has been without a guardian angel.

angel-lights In architecture, small

circular windows separating subordinate arches of window tracery.

Angelic Doctor, the St. Thomas Aquinas, the "Angel of the Schools," famous doctor of the Church, author of the *Summa Theologica* and many other works. The *Summa,* a summary of sacred and secular thought, was unfinished at his death, yet it is a perfect system of philosophy and theology remarkable for harmony and intellectual depth. St. Thomas was a humble Dominican friar who refused higher office in the Church in order to continue studying, teaching and writing. He died in 1274, was canonized in 1323 and was proclaimed a doctor of the Church in 1567.

angelic hymn, the The Major Doxology, also known as the Gloria, used in the Mass except in times of penance, in ferial and nonsolemn votive Masses, and in Requiem Masses. It is a magnificent hymn, beginning with the song of the angels at the birth of Christ, "Glory to God in the highest, and peace on earth among men of good will" (Lk. 2:14). It comes down from the earliest years of the Church, mentioned by St. Ignatius about the year 107 and by others at various times up to the end of the 4th century. Known as the morning hymn, it was sung in praise of God the Father, and not until the 4th and 5th centuries, when there was much controversy on the nature of Christ, were the parts regarding Christ and the Holy Spirit added. It was at first a part of the Divine Office, but was later used in the Masses for Christmas only. In the 16th century its use in the Mass was prescribed for other days, but only by bishops. After the year 1000 priests also were allowed to recite it. *See* Gloria.

Angelic Salutation, the The best known and most widely used prayer to Mary, the mother of Christ. It is also called the Ave Maria and the Hail Mary. The first part of the prayer consists of the angel's salutation (Lk. 1:28) joined to the greeting of Elizabeth (Lk. 1:42). The second part, "Holy Mary, mother of God," etc., was not added until the 16th century. It is recited in the Angelus (*q.v.*) three times daily while the church bells ring (morning, noon and night); and it forms the main part of the Rosary. The greatest artists have illustrated different aspects of this prayer to the mother of God, and noted composers have set its words to music.

Angelicum, the The theological college of the Dominicans in Rome that was founded in the Middle Ages.

angels, fallen Those angels who rebelled against God and lost His grace, i.e., became incapable of enjoying His friendship and the place He had given them in heaven. By nature they were the same as the other angels (*q.v.*). They lost supernatural grace by their own will. St. Thomas teaches that their sin must have been one of pride, since as pure spirits they would not have been tempted by sins of the flesh or of avarice. Other theologians have surmised that God gave them a preview of the Incarnation, His Son in man's flesh, and they refused to adore Him because as man He was inferior to them. According to interpretations of various texts in Holy Scripture, the leader of the fallen angels was Lucifer, one of the brightest of archangels. When he failed his test and fell from grace, a great number of other angels followed him and were cast out of heaven after a battle with the faithful spirits under Michael's leadership. Lucifer is the chief of the fallen angels in hell. Known as Satan, the Evil One, the Devil, he tempted Christ in the desert and prowls around trying to find victims among men. The sacrifice of Christ on the cross overcame him, but he is still allowed time on earth to try men before the last day and the final accounting.

angels, names of　The only angels named in Scripture are Raphael, Gabriel and Michael. St. Jude (1:9) refers to Michael as an archangel and Church tradition gives the same rank to Raphael and Gabriel. Apocryphal Jewish books refer to angels called Uriel and Jeremiel.

angels of the churches, the　The seven angels of the Apocalypse. St. John describes a vision of Christ, the Son of Man, holding seven stars and surrounded by seven candlesticks (Apoc. 1:13–20). The candlesticks represented the seven churches in Asia at that time: Ephesus, Smyrna, Pergamum, Sardis, Philadelphia, Thyatira and Laodicea. The seven stars, said St. John, were the angels of the seven churches. He was commanded to write to the angels of the seven churches to praise or blame them according to their deserts. According to Origen, these were the guardian angels of the churches, since churches, cities and nations as well as men had guardian angels. However, St. Epiphanius and St. Augustine reject this idea, explaining that the stars, or angels, were the bishops of the individual churches. St. John accuses the angels of various faults, of having left their first charity, of being dead and so on, things which could not be said of angel guardians.

Angelus (ahn'jhe-lus; L. *Angelus Domini,* the angel of the Lord, the first words of the prayer)　A prayer said daily at morning, noon and evening as the church bell rings in a special pattern of three strokes three times and then nine strokes in succession. It is a threefold salutation to Mary, the mother of Christ, in honor of the Incarnation, the greatest event in the history of the world. Catholics, hearing the bell, stop and say the prayer, which includes the Hail Mary three times, with versicles between and a collect at the end. Many bells which survive from the 13th and 14th centuries bear the inscription AVE MARIA, indicating that they were used to ring the Angelus. In some places the evening Angelus was also the curfew bell. It was rung after Vespers were finished in the monastery. In country districts today, in some Catholic countries and in mission lands, the people regulate the hours of their days by the Angelus bell.

anger　An emotion of displeasure coupled with a desire for the punishment of an offender. To be angry for a just cause is licit and often praiseworthy. The capital sin of anger is committed: (*a*) when the anger greatly exceeds the offense; (*b*) when the punishment desired is immoderate, i.e., revenge. Anger in the Bible has two connotations: 1. the bitter, revengeful anger of men, and especially, of Christ's enemies; 2. the righteous indignation of God. This "anger (wrath) of God" in the Old Testament results both from God's holiness and righteousness, and also from the Jewish belief that a lack of anger would denote a lack of seriousness on the part of God. In the New Testament this theme is more eschatological in purpose with the theme of divine love predominating. Divine wrath, however, is still mentioned as an ethical necessity in God.

Anglican Church (L. *Ecclesia Anglicana*)　The Church of England. It is that established national church which began to take form in 1534, followed by the Act of Supremacy appointing King Henry VIII (and his successors) the only head of the church and clergy of England. This in effect declared Henry to be pope in his own realm, and aimed at giving him certain powers which he craved for personal and political reasons. At first there was no difference in dogma and practice between this new body and the Catholic Church. The Act of Uniformity in 1559 made the Prayer Book of Edward VI obligatory in all houses of worship and obliged everyone to attend the new services. In 1563 the Thirty-Nine Articles were adopted, making the Anglican Church definitely Protestant, although some Anglican theologians dispute this. The churches, monastery properties and endowments of Catholic England were confiscated by the crown or taken over for the use of the Anglican Church. The Archbishop of Canterbury now rules the See of St. Augustine of Canterbury, missionary monk sent by Pope Gregory the Great in 597. The Archbishop has a kind of primacy of honor in the Church of England, meeting with other Anglican bishops every ten years to arrive at conclusions concerning faith and order for the whole church. Their conclusions are not laws and do not bind, but they are generally observed. The bishops of the church are nominated by the Prime Minister of England, who may or may not be an Anglican or even a Christian.

Anglican orders Those orders conferred upon candidates for the priesthood or sacred ministry in the rites of ordination of the Church of England according to the Edwardian Ordinal which was issued in 1550 at the di-

rection of Edward VI. As early as 1555, Pope Paul IV declared Anglican orders to be invalid. Leo XIII in the bull, *Apostolicae Curae,* reaffirmed the invalidity of Anglican orders because of lack of due form and of intention on the part of the minister. According to Leo XIII, the intention of those following the Edwardian Ordinal did not include the essence of the Sacrament of Orders which is the power to offer the Sacrifice of the Mass. It is the teaching of theology that whoever changes a rite instituted by Christ thereby demonstrates that he does not wish to do what Christ did and which the Church repeats. It is evident from history that the Edwardian Ordinal deliberately and intentionally excluded all mention of Mass. Therefore the intention of the authors was opposed to that of Christ who instituted this sacrament so that the Eucharistic Sacrifice might be repeated over and over. The second argument was that the Anglican hierarchy descended from Matthew Parker who was consecrated a bishop according to the Edwardian Ordinal; and therefore since his orders were invalid and without power, it follows that the hierarchy descending from him has invalid orders. However, conditions have changed from the time of Leo XIII. Some Catholic theologians hold today that the validity of present Anglican orders is open to new consideration. The reason is that many Anglican bishops since the time of Leo XIII have been consecrated by Orthodox bishops and hence their consecration and the ordinations they have performed would be valid if all the other requisites for validity were present.

Anglicanism The Church of England and those bodies deriving from it and in communion with it (known collectively as the Anglican Communion), including the Protestant Episcopal Church of the United States. Also the faith and practice of the people belonging to this communion. Although Henry VIII is often credited with founding the Anglican Church, in actuality he merely broke away from the Holy See which refused to approve his attempted marriage. Henry declined to embrace Protestantism and maintained the chief tenets of the Catholic Faith except recognition of the Holy See. Henry's daughter, Elizabeth, was the real founder, kindling a bitter persecution of Catholics and adopting 39 of the 42 articles of Cranmer. The Anglican Church had troubled beginnings with groups breaking away to form the Baptists, Puritans, Presbyterians and Congregationalists. Deism and Illuminism drained a good part of the supernatural life of the church, leading to the development of various movements within it: High Church, conservative and closely allied to Catholic practice; Low Church, evangelistic and anti-Catholic with distinct Protestant ideals; Broad Church, liberal, open to the development of lay thought. The Oxford Movement developed in the High Church and led to many conversions to Catholicism, the future Cardinal Newman being chief among them. Today, the Church of England has lost considerable influence among the people and there has been a distinct drift toward secularism. Anglican clergymen are of high caliber and do magnificent missionary work in slums and foreign lands. In the ecumenical movement the Anglican Church is seen as the logical bridge between the Catholic Church and Protestantism.

Anglo-Catholics   Those members of the Church of England and the Episcopal Church who belong to the "High Church" group, following closely the Catholic Church in liturgy, ceremonies and beliefs. There is a double movement going on in the Anglican Church: one approaching union with Rome and another toward a broad mingling with Protestant groups, especially in the foreign mission field. There are numerous conversions to Rome among Anglo-Catholics, particularly among clergymen. There have been instances of monasteries of Anglican monks and nuns coming into the Church en masse.

Anima Christi (ah'ni-ma kriss'ty; L. Soul of Christ)   The name and the opening words of a prayer to Our Lord in memory of His passion; the favorite prayer of Pope Pius XII, frequently used after Holy Communion and at other times by the devout faithful. It has been attributed to St. Ignatius of Loyola, to St. Thomas Aquinas and to Pope John XXII who enriched it with indulgences in the year 1330. St. Ignatius placed it at the beginning of his book of the *Spiritual Exercises* and recommends its frequent use. It was inscribed on one of the gates of the Alcazar of Seville, dating back to 1350. Cardinal Peter de Luxembourg (d. 1387) left a prayer book now in the library of Avignon, containing the *Anima Christi*. It was evidently widely known in the 14th century, as it is today. The hymn "Soul of my Savior" is a rhymed translation of the prayer, found in most Catholic hymnals.

animals in Church art   From the earliest days animals have been used as symbols in Church art. Thus Christ has been represented by a fish, a deer, a lamb; St. John as an eagle, etc.

36

annates (L. *annus,* year) The first fruits of a benefice paid to the Papal Curia.

anniversary (L. *anniversarius,* returning yearly) The date on which some important event is commemorated each year. Also, the day of a death, on which a Requiem Mass is celebrated annually for the deceased. Christian festivals or feasts are anniversaries commemorating sacred mysteries of the Catholic Faith, such as Easter, Pentecost, the Annunciation, Christmas and other events in the life of Christ. The feast days of the saints are also commemorated yearly, and are usually the day on which the holy person died, i.e., his birthday in heaven.

anniversary Mass 1. A Requiem Mass offered for a deceased person on the 3rd, 7th and 30th day after death; or on the annual anniversary of death. 2. A Mass marking an anniversary such as the 25th anniversary of ordination, of elevation to the episcopacy, of a wedding, etc.

Annuario Pontificio (L. Pontifical Annual) Official directory of the Holy See which is published each year. It contains a list of congregations and offices of the Holy See with the major personnel, the list of cardinals, a list of all bishops and ordinaries of the world by name and see, and various other useful items.

Annunciation of the Blessed Virgin Mary, Feast of the The celebration of the greatest event in history, the beginning of our salvation, when God became man and dwelt on earth. The Angel Gabriel made the annunciation of Mary, and with her consent, the "Word was made flesh, and dwelt among us." It is celebrated on Mar. 25, nine months before Christmas. It seems to have been celebrated first at Nazareth, and in the Eastern Church there is a feast of Christ; in the Latin Church, a feast of Mary. It seems to have originated about the time of the Council of Ephesus (A.D. 431), and was celebrated on various dates in different parts of Christendom. In Rome, it was always celebrated on Mar. 25. It was a holyday of obligation in the universal Church but as such was abrogated for the United States in 1884, by the Third Council of Baltimore.

Anointing of the Sick The sacrament which through prayers and the anointing with oil is conferred on those who are seriously ill or in danger of death. Sickness and sin are the consequences of original sin and a reminder that sin defeated the original plan God had in creating man. In serious sickness there is need for strength of spirit and of body. Because the life of God is increased in the person receiving this sacrament, he becomes stronger. The sacrament destroys the remains of sin and remits all mortal sins. The Sacrament of Anointing of the Sick is for all those who are seriously ill. The purpose of the sacrament is to restore the sick to the Family of God strong and well. The form of the sacrament is the prayers and the matter is the oil of the anointing.

Anointing of the Sick, rite for A small table covered with a white cloth is placed near the bed of the sick person. On the table is placed a crucifix between two lighted candles. Also on the table should be a small bottle of holy water, a glass of drinking water (half full), a small dish of water for purifying the priest's fingers, a small napkin or towel, a small dish in which are placed six small balls of cotton for the anointing and another dish with a piece of crustless bread. The preparations should be completed before the priest arrives. The entire family should meet the priest, follow him to the sick person's room and recite the prayers with the priest. The administration of the sacrament is simple. There is an Asperges followed by three short prayers. Confession is then heard if this is necessary, at which the family withdraws. After confession, the people return. There is a short reading, some prayers and an exorcism. Then the priest touches his thumb to the oil of the sick and anoints the sick person in the form of a cross on eyes, ears, nostrils, lips, hands and feet. He says a prayer at each anointing asking forgiveness for anything done wrong by the sense involved. After the anointing, he purifies his fingers and closing prayers are said. If circumstances make it necessary, the ceremony as described can be abbreviated. In that case, a single anointing is made on the forehead, conditionally if there is doubt of life.

antediluvian (L. *ante,* before; *diluvium,* flood) One who lived before the Flood. The account in Genesis gives ten generations from Adam to Noe, naming the patriarchs and giving them fantastically long spans of life on earth. It is agreed by commentators that these figures are not historical, but symbolic, showing the great wisdom of the patriarchs, since wisdom was supposed to come with years. History, as written in ancient times, concerned itself more with the teaching of truths than with exact details and chronology. What Genesis teaches us about the antediluvian period is true; i.e., that sin begun in Adam was augmented in his children, and that civilization developed during uncounted ages of man's early life on earth.

antependium (an-te-pen'dee-um, L. *ante,* before; *pendens,* hanging) That which covers the front of an altar, from just beneath the altar table to the predella or platform on which the altar stands. It reaches from the Gospel corner to the corner on the Epistle side, completely hiding and ornamenting the front of altar. Some antependiums are highly ornamented, made of carved wood, of silver or other precious metals, embossed, set with jewels, or enriched with pearls. Cloth of gold, silks, tapestries and embroideries have been used. An antependium is prescribed by the rubrics, although its material is not designated. Wherever an altar front is richly ornamented or carved, no antependium of cloth need be used. Where an altar is set out from the wall so that its back can be seen by the people, that side too must be covered by an antependium.

anthem (Anglicized from Gr. *antiphon,* answering chant) Originally the same as antiphon, a hymn sung alternately by two sides; or as a response. Now understood of any sacred composition of choral music usually employing words from the Scriptures.

anthropomorphism (Gr. *anthropomorphos,* of human form) 1. In Biblical literature, a literary device by which the inspired author attributes human qualities to God in order that man may better understand God. Thus God is described as possessing a face, walking, being angry, etc. 2. Sometimes used as a term for religious personalism, the system of religion that places excessive emphasis on the religious experience of the individual. The accent is on how the individual can produce the presence of God in his soul. This type of religion is no longer a God-directed (theological) orientation but a man-directed perspective; it has little to do with real Christianity. It is self-centered, a "Jesus and I" type of religion, ignoring God's children.

anticamera (It. anteroom) The room next to the pope's office where cardinals and other dignitaries await papal audience.

anticipate To recite Matins of the following day in the afternoon or evening before.

anticlericalism Unjustified opposition and criticism of the clergy. Anticlericalism usually arises from secularist or prejudicial sources but it can exist among Catholics.

antidoron (Gr. a gift instead of) The particles of bread which remain after the hosts to be used for Holy Communion have been cut out. In the Eastern Church these remainders arc blessed and distributed to the faithful after Mass. The French *pain benit* is a similar custom.

Antigonish Movement An adult educational program for socio-economic action begun in 1930 at St. Francis Xavier University, Antigonish, Nova Scotia, and widely imitated in other parts of the world. During its first quarter century it organized 434 credit unions with a membership of over 100,000, 150 retail cooperative stores and 50 housing projects.

antimension (an-ti-men′shun). An antimensium (*q.v.*).

antimensium (an-ti-men′see-um; Gr. *anti,* instead of; *mensa,* table, altar) In the Greek Rite, a consecrated corporal which in general takes the place of the altar stone or portable altar in the Roman Rite. It is a strip of linen or silk, ornamented

with pictures or embroidery reminiscent of Our Lord's passion and death. It may be about ten inches by fourteen, and has relics of the saints sewn into it. It must be certified by the bishop. It must be placed on the altar before the Greek Mass is celebrated.

Antioch 1. An ancient city in Pisidia, Asia Minor, which had a large Jewish population in the first century A.D. St. Paul visited this city in the course of his missionary work twice certainly (Acts 13:14-52; 14:20) and possibly two more times (Acts 14:6; 18:23). 2. The capital of ancient Syria in the northwestern part of the country. During the persecution in Jerusalem that followed Stephen's martyrdom, Christians fled to Antioch and founded a new church. It was at Antioch that the term "Christian" was first given to members of the Church (Acts 11:26).

Antioch, Patriarchate of The office or see of the Patriarch of Antioch in Syria is said to have been founded by St. Peter. At present there are three Catholic patriarchs in Antioch, those of the Melkite, Syrian and Maronite Rites respectively. Formerly there was a Latin patriarchate here.

Antiochene Liturgy, the The earliest form of the liturgy which arose among the Greek-speaking Syrians in and around Antioch. A mid-3rd-century document, the *Didascalia Apostolorum,* gives some evidence of the form of this primitive rite. In the 4th century several usages proper to the Church in Jerusalem were introduced at Antioch, notably the Eucharistic prayer "of St. James." From then on the Antiochene Liturgy was characterized by much splendor and non-biblical hymns. The Churches of Syrian language are more or less direct successors of the old Patriarchate of

Antioch. The Eucharistic liturgies of the Eastern Churches presently traceable to the Antiochene Liturgy are: 1. West Syrian: Syrian Rite, Malankarese Rite, Maronite Rite; 2. East Syrian: Chaldean Rite, Malabarese Rite.

Antiochian Rite An Eastern Rite formed first at Jerusalem, then, and especially, at Antioch. It is the source of more derived rites than any other. The Maronites have substantially preserved the Antiochian Rite, but with Latin modifications. Originally performed in Greek and Syriac, it is today celebrated in Syriac only, with some Arabic parts. In India, the Malankarese who belong to this rite recite some formulas in the vernacular.

antiphon (an'ti-fon; Gr. sounding against, responsive singing) In reciting or singing the Divine Office, a brief section of a psalm or other part of Holy Scripture which is repeated before and after each psalm of Matins, Lauds and Vespers; before and after the three psalms of Compline and Little Hours; also before and after each of the three canticles: the Benedictus of Lauds, the Magnificat of Vespers and the Nunc Dimittis of Compline.

antiphonal chants Three chants sung at High Mass in the nature of an antiphon: the Entrance Prayer, Offertory Prayer and Communion Prayer. They are opposed to responsory chants: Gradual and Alleluia.

antiphonary The liturgical book which contains all of the sung portions of the Divine Office.

antiphons of Our Lady, the The four seasonal antiphons of the Blessed Virgin Mary: *Alma Redemptoris Mater* for Advent, *Ave Regina Coelorum* for Lent, *Regina Coeli* for the Paschal Season and *Salve Regina* for the rest of the year, which are sung or recited daily after Compline of the Divine Office. They were at first sung as antiphons connected with the psalms, but since the year 1239 have been sung as independent chants or hymns. Their melodies are exceedingly beautiful, though of simple style, as they were intended to be sung by the whole congregation present at the various feasts of Our Lady.

antipope One who claimed to be pope in opposition to the truly elected pontiff. There have been thirty or more antipopes in the history of the Church. The last of them, Amadeus of Savoy, submitted to Pope Nicholas V in 1449.

anti-Semitism (an-ti-sem'it-ism; Gr. *anti,* against Sen or Shem) Hatred for, or persecution of Jews, who are Semites, descendants, according to tradition, of Sem or Shem, one of the three sons of Noe, the ancestor of Abraham and of the Jews. However, the Arabs, Ethiopians and others, also said to be descended from Sem, and speaking a Semitic language, can be called Semites. The Jews have been a suffering and persecuted people in many places and since ancient times, even before the Christian era. Since the time of Christ, after the Church herself emerged from the catacombs, there have been unworthy Christians here and there who persecuted the Jews under the pretext that they crucified Christ. Pope Paul VI settled this in 1963 by declaring that Christ died at the hands of all the sinners in the world, and that the Jews alone were not guilty of His death. It was the Jewish high priests and leaders who had Him crucified, not the Jewish nation, and Pontius Pilate, a Roman, sent Him to His death. All persons are guilty. Jesus Himself was a Jew; so were His mother, His foster-father, the Apostles, and thousands of the early Christians and martyrs. The Church began from Judaism, which was the Church of God before Christ came. Christ offers forgiveness and full membership in His family to all peoples and nations, even to the ends of the earth.

antitrinitarian One who denies that there are three persons in the Trinity. The Unitarians in the United States are antitrinitarian in teaching.

antitype A scriptural term referring to persons, things or events in the New Testament that were prefigured in the Old Testament. It is the mystical or typological sense of Scripture. Mary is the antitype of Eve (the type).

Apocalypse (a-poc′a-lips; Gr. revelation, disclosure) The last book of the Bible, containing the revelations of St. John the Apostle. It was written on a small, rocky island called Patmos about fifteen miles west of Ephesus in the Aegean Sea. (Today it is called Patino.) It is addressed first to the seven churches of Asia to scold them for weaknesses and to encourage them during the persecutions of Domitian (d. A.D. 96). It is also addressed to the worldwide Church of all ages, for its words of warning and consolation are foreign to no age or place. It is a book full of mysteries, often misinterpreted and quoted out of context. It was written by a master of literary proficiency and a man of great mystical insight who has given us one of the most beautiful and encouraging books of all time.

Apocalyptic number A mystical number. Among the ancients, letters of the Greek, Hebrew and Roman alphabets were given numbers. Thus a person's name could be stated as the total sum of its letters. In Greek, Jesus became 888.

Apodeipnon (Gr. after-supper service) The final part of the Greek Divine Office, corresponding to the Latin Compline.

Apollinarianism A heresy taught by Apollinaris, Bishop of Alexandria, in the 4th century, which denied that Christ had human intellect and affirmed that His body was one with His divinity, brought with Him from heaven.

apolusia (Gr. washing) The washing of those to be baptized in the Eastern Rite, which takes place eight days before Baptism.

apolysis (Gr. dismissal) The concluding blessing in the Byzantine Liturgy after which the priest dismisses the people. It is given at the end of Mass, Baptism, Matrimony, etc.

apolytikon (Gr. that which delivers) The final prayer or hymn, usually sung, which is given before the apolysis.

apostasy (Gr. *apostasia,* a desertion) Abandonment of what one has totally possessed. In relation to the Church, three types of apostasy exist. 1. Apostasy from the Faith (*a fide*) is the act by which a baptized person, after possessing the true Christian Faith, totally rejects it. Such apostasy incurs an excommunication (*ipso facto*) reserved in a special manner to the Holy See. The neglect of one's Faith, even when total, is not apostasy. Abandonment of one's Christianity, even though baptized in the Catholic Church, by one who has been brought up from infancy in a non-Catholic sect is not apostasy. Apostasy differs from heresy because the latter is only partial abandonment by the denial of certain teaching of the Faith. 2. Apostasy from orders (*ab ordine*) is the act by which one who having received major orders abandons the clerical state. Excommunication is reserved to the local ordinary. 3. Apostasy from the religious life (*a religione*) is the act by which one who has perpetual vows, whether solemn or simple, illegally leaves monastery or convent with the intention of not returning, as well as one who leaves lawfully but does not return in order to withdraw perpetually from obedience. This intention must be manifested externally. It may be rightfully presumed if the individual does not return within a month or manifest an intention of returning. Such an apostate remains bound by rule and vows; and incurs excommunication (*ipso facto*), reserved to the superior.

apostate   A Catholic who, after having received the true Christian Faith in Baptism, totally rejects it. *See,* apostasy.

Apostle (Gr. *apostolos*, one sent forth)   One of the twelve friends of Christ whom He sent out to preach the Good News to the whole world. The original twelve Apostles were Jews of the working class who, after three years of training by Christ, were to set up the Church and convert the world. Their names were Simon Peter, the leader and first pope; James, John, Andrew, Philip, Bartholomew, Matthew Levi, Thomas, James of Alphaeus, Jude Thaddeus, Simon the Cananean and Judas Iscariot. After the suicide of the traitor Judas, Matthais was chosen to take his place. St. Paul, who was not one of the original Twelve, was accepted as one of them, and so was Barnabas, his companion.

apostle   1. One of those priests, bishops and missioners who followed and still follow in the apostolic succession, under the same command of Christ and performing the same duty. 2. One of those lay men and women who do a noble and essential work in bringing the Good News to friends at home and strangers abroad. Their role is becoming rapidly more important in the modern world.

Apostles' Creed, the   A brief formula made up of twelve statements covering the fundamental belief of Christians, and said to have been composed by the twelve Apostles. Rufinus (*c.* 400) describes the origin of the Creed as the work of all Twelve, who put it together on the very day of Pentecost. He states that he received the tradition from earlier ages, and mentions that the Creed was called the Symbol—a password. The term "Symbol" is used in this sense in the letters of Sts. Cyprian and Firmilian (3rd century) where it is given as part of the rite of Baptism. It is certain that some form of creed was used in Rome before the middle of the 2nd century; it may be that the present Creed is based on an outline dating from the Apostles. The New Testament mentions a "form of doctrine" (Rom. 6:17) and a "profession of faith" (Rom. 10:8-10). In many sources of the 4th and 5th centuries (Augustine, Hilary, Cyril of Jerusalem and others) it is insisted by ancient tradition that the Creed was to be learned by heart, not committed to writing. This would explain the absence of the Creed in earlier writings. Tertullian and St. Irenaeus maintain that the "rule of faith" is part of the apostolic tradition, and Tertullian shows that he means something practically the same as the Creed. He insists that it was given by the Apostles as coming from Christ. While there is no conclusive evidence that the Creed actually comes from the Apostles, it would be rash to state that it does not do so. Since it has been intimately connected with the liturgy and the teaching of the Church from very ancient times, its points of doctrine are believed to be part of the Catholic Faith, as taught by the Apostles and delivered by the living voice of the Church.

Apostles, dispersion of the　Little is known with certitude concerning the missionary endeavors of the Apostles. St. James the Elder was put to death by Herod Agrippa as early as A.D. 43. St. Peter was destined for the same fate until he escaped from prison miraculously and went probably to Antioch where he established an episcopal see. He participated in the Council of Jerusalem in A.D. 50. He first went to Rome during the reign of Claudius (41–54). It is historically certain that Peter was the first bishop of Rome and that he died there for the Faith. John, the youngest of the Apostles, probably remained in Palestine until after the death of the Blessed Mother, and then went to Ephesus where he exercised his episcopal powers. He lived to a very old age and did not, like the other Apostles, suffer a violent death. As for the other Apostles, St. Thomas preached in Parthia, St. Bartholomew journeyed to Arabia, St. Matthew worked in Palestine at first and then among the "other nations," St. Andrew traveled to Sythia. Of the missionary activities of Thaddeus, Matthias, Philip and Simon nothing is known.

Apostles, Teaching of the Twelve *See* Didache.

Apostleship of Prayer　A pious organization founded at Vals, France, in 1844, to promote devotion to the Sacred Heart of Jesus. Its world membership now numbers in the tens of millions. The League members recite the "Morning Offering" which sanctifies their prayers, works, joys, and sufferings of the day by uniting them with the Holy Sacrifice of the Mass throughout the world. The offering is made to God in reparation for sins, for the intentions of the Sacred Heart of Jesus and of all the associates, and in particular for the special monthly intentions named by the Pope. Members are also encouraged to offer Mass and Communion of reparation weekly or monthly, to say at least a decade of the Rosary daily for the League intentions, and where possible to make the Holy Hour of Reparation on the first Friday of the month. Membership in the League is highly enriched with indulgences. The society has centers all over the world, and its magazine, the *Messenger of the Sacred Heart,* is published in many different languages.

Apostleship of the Sea　A Catholic society founded in 1920, in Glasgow, Scotland, for the welfare of seamen. Its aims are religious, educational and social, and its headquarters are Piazza Pio XII, Vatican City. Its works are carried on in 14 countries under national secretariats, diocesan units being under the jurisdiction of the local bishops. Special pastoral care is provided for seamen with a social service program for sailors through Maritime Clubs in world ports. There are 70 of the Clubs, of which 7 are in the United State: in Mobile, New Orleans, Norfolk, San Francisco, San Pedro, Wilmington (Calif.) and Seattle. More than 300,-000 seamen are served in these 7 Maritime Clubs in a year. There are 74 chaplains of the Apostleship in American ports, with dockside chapels in Boston and Philadelphia. An annual event in large ports is Communion Sunday for dock workers and sailors. The Apostleship aims to unite the world of seafarers in a Christian community and to encourage sailors in the works of Catholic Action.

apostolate The ministry of the Word of God; the work or office of an apostle, which is that of preaching the Good News and setting up the Church of God, spreading the Faith and bringing souls to God. The primary work of an apostle is not only that of saving souls; it is that of setting up the Church in every place so that the Sacrifice is offered there and souls have access to the kingdom. Souls are thereby saved, that is, brought into God's family, made children of God and brothers of Christ, through Faith and the sacraments. Through the centers of Faith all over the world, where Mass is offered, and the Gospel is preached, the grace and power of Christ reach out to men of good will. The lay apostolate refers to the essential part of lay men and women in the work of telling the Good News and establishing the Church in ever widening areas of influence. Some participation in the apostolate is not merely optional; it is of obligation for the laity too.

Apostolic Canons A collection of decrees of the early Church. They mostly contain disciplinary matters but also contain a canon of Scriptures. Tradition says that they were given by the Apostles to Pope St. Clement.

apostolic delegate A representative of the Holy See who has no diplomatic accreditation since he is not appointed to deal with a civil government but the hierarchy of the country. There is an apostolic delegate in the United States with residence in Washington. His home and office are called the apostolic delegation.

Apostolic Father One of the Fathers of the Church who lived in the first or second century.

Apostolic Preacher The "pope's preacher." The priest who preaches to the Pontifical Court during Advent and Lent. He is always a Capuchin.

Apostolic Signature *See* Signatura Apostolica.

Apostolicae Curae A papal bull issued by Pope Leo XIII declaring that Anglican orders are invalid.

apparition (L. *apparitio,* appearance) The term used to refer to an appearance of someone either by vision or by bodily manifestation that is permitted by God. The appearance of Our Lady at Fatima or Lourdes would be an apparition. So would the vision that appeared to Joseph in which he was told to flee with the Child and His Mother into Egypt.

appeal An appeal from a decision of an ecclesiastical court can be made to the next highest court. However, there is no appeal from a decision of the pope.

appetite The movement or inclination of a person toward a desired object, or toward an object seen to be good for that person. Traditional Christian philosophy posits two appetites, or motions, in man: 1. sensitive appetite, a movement of the senses toward a sensible good. Some equate sensitive appetite with emotion or passion; 2. intellectual appetite, the movement of the person toward an intellectual or reasonable good, or to a good seen to be reasonable. "The will" is another name given the intellectual appetite.

appetite, irascible (L. *irasci,* to become angry) A tendency through which a person is confronted with obstacles in the pursuit of good and the avoidance of evil. Because the obstacles can arouse anger, these tendencies or passions are called irascible.

appropriation Because of the limitation of language and the finite nature of human minds, one quality is often attributed to a specific Person in God as if it did not belong equally to the other Persons. This is known as appropriation.

April Month of the Holy Eucharist.

apse (aps; Gr. *hapsis,* a loop, a bow or an arch) A vaulted recess, semicircular in shape (sometimes polygonal) at the end of the choir in a church, also at the end of the aisles or nave.

apsidiole (ap-sid′i-ol) A lesser or smaller apse, usually found in a church where there are several apses.

Ara Coeli (ahr′ah chay′lee; L. altar of heaven) St. Mary of Ara Coeli, a church in Rome, dedicated to Our Lady, once the residence of the General of the Franciscans. It is located on the Capitoline, one of the seven hills of Rome, on the site of the ancient temple and citadel of Jupiter Capitolinus. A flight of 124 steps leads up to the church. Here, says an ancient legend, the Emperor Augustus saw a vision of the Blessed Virgin standing on an altar of heaven, "ara coeli." In the sacristy of the church is kept a little figure of the Holy Child, made of olive wood from the Mount of Olives and greatly venerated by the Romans. The Christmas Crib, built in one of the chapels every year, is famous. Roman children perform playlets and make speeches before it.

Aramaic (ar-ah-may′ik) The language spoken by Jesus Christ. Aramaic is a Semitic language that was used in Babylonia and Syria. Among the Jews it supplanted Hebrew at the time of the Babylonian Captivity. It was replaced by Arabic following the Muslim Conquest. Its only existence today is in Syriac, a dialect used in the Syrian Rite Liturgy. A few words exist in the New Testament: *abba, eloi lamma sabacthani.*

arca (ahr′ka; L. *arca,* chest or box) A box in which the early Christians reserved the Blessed Sacrament in their homes.

arch 1. A structure made of separate pieces of stone or bricks, slightly wedge-shaped, built in the shape of a curve and arranged so as to stay in place by their own weight. Each stone helps to hold up the other stones and prevents the arch from falling. The arch is much used in the construction of churches, and it exists today in many forms, simple and complex. The ancient Babylonians devised it; the Egyptians and Greeks used it for underground passageways; the Romans learned it from the Etruscans. In Rome there are arches 2,000 years old still standing. The tall, pointed, vaulted arch of medieval times made the Gothic cathedral one of the triumphs of sacred architecture. 2. A prefix (Gr. *archos*, chief) meaning first, higher in rank.

archabbot An honorific title given to abbots of certain major Benedictine monasteries such as Monte Cassino. There are two archabbeys in the United States: St. Vincent in Latrobe, Pa., and St. Meinrad in St. Meinrad, Ind.

archaeology, Christian The study and evaluation of early Christian life, as revealed in the relics and monuments which remain.

Archaeology, Commission of Sacred A papal Commission set up in 1851 by Pope Pius IX to explore and study the catacombs and the Vatican excavations, and to care for the museums of Vatican State. An important discovery of this Commission was the finding of the tomb of St. Peter underneath St. Peter's Basilica.

archangel (ark'an-gel) An angel of a higher rank. Holy Scripture names three: Michael, the leader of the angels who remained faithful to God; Gabriel, the angel of the Annunciation; and Raphael, the angel of healing and the guardian of Tobias.

archbishop (Gr. *arch-*, chief; *episkopos,* bishop) In the Western Church, a bishop of an archdiocese who has a canonical role over the bishops of a province. The archbishop occupies the metropolitan see, and the bishops of the other dioceses of the province are known as suffragan bishops. An archbishop's rights in other dioceses of his province are severely limited. An archbishop can call provincial councils, and his archdiocesan courts serve as appeal courts from decisions of the suffragan courts. The archbishop takes over his archdiocese by being invested with the pallium, a circular band of white wool worn on his shoulders. He is also entitled to use a cross with a double bar. In the Eastern Church, any bishop immediately subject to his patriarch is called an archbishop.

archbishop-elect One who has been named an archbishop but who has not yet been consecrated a bishop or who has not taken possession of his archdiocese.

archbishop, titular A bishop who has been promoted to the rank and title of an archbishop but who has no ordinary episcopal jurisdiction. He may be a retired bishop or archbishop, one engaged in Church administration, a papal nuncio, etc.

archconfraternity A confraternity with the right to aggregate or affiliate to itself other confraternities of similar nature, and the power to grant them its privileges and indulgences. The archconfraternity cannot erect a confraternity, as this privilege belongs ordinarily to the bishop, or, in some cases, to the heads of certain religious orders. Some of the widely known archconfraternities are those of the Sacred Heart of Jesus, of the Precious Blood, of the Holy Rosary, of the Blessed Sacrament, of the Holy Name, and of Christian Mothers.

archdeacon In the early Church, a deacon appointed by the bishop to assist him in administration. In the Middle Ages the office grew to one of considerable power. Because of abuses, it was ended by the Council of Trent. The term is sometimes used today but only as an honorific. In the Eastern Church, archdeacons have specific duties; most of them are true deacons, not priests. In some cases, the Eastern archdeacon is the senior deacon in a monastery.

archdiocese A diocese presided over by an archbishop. It is one of several dioceses within a province. The archbishop has certain limited jurisdiction over the bishops of the other dioceses within the province, but he holds immediate and exclusive jurisdiction only over his own archdiocese.

archetype The original model from which all others are copies. Thus the attributes of God (Beauty, Truth, etc.) are archetypes for human or natural attributes.

archiepiscopal cross A cross of two bars in which the upper bar is shorter. It is part of the coat of arms of an archbishop. It is also mounted on the staff which is carried before the archbishop or patriarch in processions.

antiminsion The antimensium (*q.v.*).

46

archimandrite 1. An official of the Byzantine Church below the rank of bishop. 2. The head of an Eastern monastery, corresponding to a Western abbot.

architecture, ecclesiastical The art of building beautifully, expressively and suitably toward a primary purpose, the worship of God. A church should be a suitable place for man to pray, to take part in the Holy Sacrifice of the Mass and to receive the sacraments. It should be planned for the adequate carrying out of the liturgy. It should also be, in itself, an expression of the worship of God. In the Old Testament, God showed great concern for the details of the Ark of the Covenant and the Tabernacle. When King David determined to build a temple for God, the Lord was so greatly pleased that He told David, "I will build *you* a house," that is, the house or family of Christ to come. The great cathedrals of Europe are monuments to Faith unequaled in beauty and inspiration. The subject of ecclesiastical architecture is very complex and rich in development, and modern materials and art forms are making new approaches to the subject, many of them worthy of admiration. 1. *The Roman basilica* During the first three hundred years of Christianity the Church was outlawed, her members persecuted. Mass was offered and the sacraments administered in private homes, in the catacombs or in any shelter that could be had for the purpose. In the year 313 the Emperors Constantine and Licinius met at Milan and issued an edict granting Christians equal rights with other citizens and freeing them from persecution. The Church then began building her great houses for the worship of God, Constantine himself

giving the example with gifts of several famous Christian churches. These structures were patterned at first after the old Roman basilicas, which were assembly halls built of stone, with two or more columns of pillars inside to support the flat roof and an apse at one end for the judge or speaker. The Church put an altar in the apse where the priest and his sacred ministers officiated, and the faithful filled the aisles between the rows of pillars. "Arms" or transepts were added at the apse end of the basilica, giving the building the shape of a cross. Hence we have the general elements of a church: apse and sanctuary with altar, nave, transepts and aisles. The Church of St. Cecilia in Rome, once a patrician home, is a beautiful example of the Roman basilica. 2. *Byzantine* In the Byzantine or Eastern Roman Empire, circular or polygonal churches were crowned with domes and embellished with richly colored mosaics. The Church of Santa Sophia (Holy Wisdom) in Constantinople (Istanbul) was erected in A.D. 532–537 by ten thousand artisans and workmen under the Emperor Justinian. When the Muslim Turks captured the city in 1453, they found the church so beautiful that they spared it from destruction and turned it into a mosque. It is a magnificent example of Byzantine architecture. Its dome is nearly 100 feet in diameter and 160 feet high. Walls, floors and marble columns gleam in the richest colors. Domes and walls covered with biblical scenes and images of saints in red, blue and gold mosaics, were plastered over by the Muslims who feared idol worship. The altar and sanctuary were enriched with gold, ivory and jewels. Splendid as the Byzantine style may be, it is not suitable for present-day use, as the structures are dark, with massive walls and filled with ponderous supports to support the great domes. St. Mark's Cathedral in Venice is a blend of Byzantine, Roman and Gothic architecture. 3. *Romanesque* During the barbarian invasions of the early Middle Ages, church architecture suffered along with other arts. Then during the 11th and 12th centuries an era began with the appearance of the Romanesque style. New churches, built to take the place of those destroyed in the wars, had thick walls, heavy pillars and stone roofs in the shape of barrel vaults and domes. Windows were small and narrow to prevent weakening of the walls, making the churches dark inside. The great weight of the roofs made it necessary to keep the buildings low. Walls were thickened and buttressed, and rounded arches were built over windows and doorways and between pillars. The general effect was majestic and massive. The Romanesque style developed into something very beautiful, often used at the present day. Romanesque churches with their round arches and series of columns are found in Italy, France, Germany, England and the United States. There are many modifications and adaptations of this style. The Cathedral of St. Louis (Mo.) is one well-known example of a modern adaptation and combination of Romanesque, Byzantine and Gothic. 4. *Gothic* A term (Gothic) almost synonymous with "barbarous" was applied to a new style of architecture by those accustomed to Byzantine and Romanesque, to whom the Goths and Vandals were an unpleasant historical memory. The new trend began in the 12th and 13th centuries when the Catholic Faith was flourishing

and church building was going forward throughout Christendom. In France, and later in all of western Europe, architects tried to improve on the Romanesque style by making their arches taller and pointed. They gained stability by using rib vaulting under the roof, and flying buttresses to bolster the pillars and hold the great weight of the increasingly taller structures. In many cases stone walls were almost eliminated, and spaces between a framework of pillars were closed with great windows of stained glass. A lacework of carved stone and statuary panels together with high, vaulted interiors and colored lighting from the many windows produced an entirely new kind of sacred edifice, elaborate yet uncluttered, beautiful and inspiring. To the illiterate as well as to the scholar, the Scriptures and histories of saints were pictured in windows of rainbow hues and in the stone carvings which covered almost every surface, inside and out. The spires reaching to the sky inspired the beholder to pray. Bells called the faithful to Mass and Vespers, and rang the Angelus three times a day. Inside the cathedral, richly embroidered vestments and hangings, carved wood, and metal work in sacred vessels rounded out the picture. The great cathedrals of Chartres, Rheims, Paris, Amiens, Beauvais and of many other towns on the Continent and in England were monuments to the faith of a people, as well as examples of a great art never surpassed. In the 15th and 16th centuries Gothic architecture declined, together with the fervor of faith among many. 5. *Modern* Vitruvius, Roman architect (*c.* 10 B.C.), laid down three elements of good architecture which have never been superseded. (*a*) "commodity":

comfort, convenience, lighting, a-
coustics, ventilation, heating, acces-
sibility of one part from another—
elements that make a house suitable
for humans. A structure may be
artistically satisfying, but if it does
not have "commodity" it is not a
good building. (*b*) "firmness": good
architecture is well built. It must be
made of good materials, properly
constructed and should be more or
less permanent. If a structure does
not have "firmness" it cannot be considered architecture. (*c*) "delight":
A good building may have commodity and firmness, yet if it does not
delight the eye and the heart, it is
not architecture. In the case of a
house of worship, delight would include religious inspiration. Some of
the older churches attained a considerable degree of firmness and of
delight; but they often neglected commodity, being dank, drafty, dark,
poorly ventilated, so arranged that
many were unable to see the altar
at services, and with such poor acous-
tics that sermons, liturgical functions
and singing were heard as confusing
echoes. In the United States, much
pioneer work has been done in the
field of new styles in ecclesiastical
architecture. Even in colonial days,
the Spanish missions in the West and
Southwest originated forms of great
charm, beauty, humility and rugged
dignity. In the East, the colonial
trend provided noble unassuming
beauty in both Protestant and Catholic churches, with their white wooden
pillars and simple spires. St. Joseph's
Cathedral in Bardstown, Ky., is a
notable example. Contemporary architects are again pioneering, using
glass blocks, plate glass, copper, alu-
minum, reinforced concrete, steel
and colored ceramic tiles in new ways
for modern religious architecture;

and many of the results are remarkably good. In Chapter VII of the
Constitution on Sacred Liturgy
adopted by Vatican Council II, the
following brief extracts are apropos:
"The Church has not adopted any
particular style of art as her very
own. . . . Ordinaries . . . should strive
after noble beauty rather than mere
sumptuous display. . . . When
churches are to be built, let great
care be taken that they are suitable
for the celebration of liturgical services and for the active participation
of the faithful."

archives, diocesan A place where records are stored; also the contents of
archives. The contents would be records in spiritual matters and diocesan administration. Canon law requires a catalogue be kept of all
documents. Because much of the
records is of a secret or confidential
nature, the archives must be kept
under lock and key. Archives are also
kept by religious orders and houses.
The archives of the Holy See are
known as the papal archives.

archpresbyter An archpriest (*q.v.*).

archpriest Formerly a priest who
assisted and took the place of the
bishop in matters of public worship, paralleling the archdeacon's
assistance in matters of public worship. Today the archpriest has been
generally replaced by the dean. However, the office of archpriest has been
retained in certain Roman basilicas
and in other important churches, and
the title is used for certain parish
priests in Italy. In the Eastern
Church, the office of archpriest is
found with specific duties, such as a
dean in a city or an overseer of
churches in a particular area. It is
also applied in the Western Church
to the priest who assists a newly
ordained priest at his first Mass, or

who assists at a solemn Mass of major prelates.

arcosolium (ar-ko-sol'ee-um; L. *arcus,* arch; *solium,* seat) The recess hewn into dirt or rock which formed a burial place in the catacombs. Mass was celebrated in this recess on the grave slab.

Areopagite (ah-ree-op'ah-gite) A term applied to one who practiced law in the Areopagus, the supreme tribunal of Athens. The name derives from the hill of Ares where the court was located.

Argentina The Catholic Church was brought to modern Argentina during the period of colonization, and in 1570 the Diocese of Córdoba was founded. Today there are 11 archdioceses and 35 dioceses with over 19 million Catholics in a population of 20 million. There is a tremendous shortage of priests due to poor recruitment, lack of Catholic formation among many Argentineans, an intellectual disdain for formal religion and the fact that few priests accompanied the large number of Italian and Spanish immigrants.

Arianism One of the most important and far-reaching heresies of the early Church. The heresy takes its name from Arius (256–326), a priest of Alexandria, who taught that Christ was not the equal of the Father, nor was He true God. Christ was a creature, more perfect than other creatures, but still a part of the creation of God. Arianism was exposed by St. Athanasius, and condemned by the Council of Nicaea in 325.

aridity A spiritual dryness in the soul; the lack of consolation in prayer. It varies in degree from the lack of exultation in prayer to the dark night of the soul. In one way it has a good effect in that it makes spirituality a matter of the will and not of the emotions. In another way it can cause the undirected person to abandon spiritual practices.

Ariel (air'i-el; Heb. lion of God; also, altar, God's altar, or altar hearth of sacrifice) As used in Isaia 29: 1-8, it means the city of Jerusalem.

Aristotelianism The philosophic teachings of Aristotle, a Greek (384–322 B.C.). Aristotle was concerned with essences and first principles. He had a tendency to emphasize the empirical and the particular, to think in logical (scientific) steps and to use syllogisms. The philosophy of Aristotle was the basis for the Scholasticism (*q.v.*) of St. Thomas Aquinas.

Arizona (Indian, *arizonac,* little spring) The 48th state of the Union. In 1539 the Franciscan Father Mark of Nice made his way, unarmed and afoot, into the area, which was sparsely settled by various tribes of Indians. Next year, Coronado arrived with several priests in his company. One of them, the Franciscan Father Padilla, was killed by Indians, the first to shed his blood for the Faith on United States soil. From 1600 to 1827 the Franciscans built numerous missions and made many converts, and the Jesuit Father Kino, "Padre on Horseback," went about teaching, baptizing, setting up many missions including San Xavier del Bac. Many of the Pimas were converted, instructed in agriculture and the care of cattle and sheep, and settled in farming communities. However, it was such a dangerous mission that only men dedicated to martyrdom would undertake it. The Apaches, now peaceful citizens, were a constant menace. When King Charles III of Spain had the Jesuits arrested in 1767 and imprisoned, the missions suffered a severe blow. In 1827

Mexico expelled the Franciscan Friars too. In 1848 after the war with Mexico, Arizona was ceded to the United States, becoming a territory in 1863 and a state in 1912. Numbers of Mexicans, in the meantime, had fled political troubles and settled in Arizona. The discovery of copper and gold brought many settlers from the Eastern states. In 1850 Bishop Lamy, appointed to the Vicariate of New Mexico, Colorado and Arizona, found the missions in ruins, the only church left standing, San Xavier del Bac. He built St. Augustine's in Tucson and several other churches. In 1868 Arizona was established as a Vicariate Apostolic with Most Rev. J. B. Salpointe in charge. He built schools and hospitals and brought in several orders of religious to care for them. The first bishop was Most Rev. Peter Bourgade, who built the Cathedral of Tucson. Succeeding bishops have brought in various religious orders, taking care of the Spanish-speaking communities and building up Indian mission work once more, while at the same time caring for the English-speaking Catholics. In a total population of over 1.3 million, Catholics number about one fifth.

Ark (L. *arca,* a chest, a translation of Heb. *tēbhāh,* used of vessel built by Noe and also of the papyrus basket made for the infant Moses; also, a translation of Heb. *'ārōn,* the sacred Ark of the Covenant)

1. Noe's Ark, as described in Genesis 6:9 and 9:17, together with the history of the deluge, is believed by many biblical scholars to be based on a memory of a fact handed down by ancient tradition and embroidered by poetical license. Floods are known to have occurred in the region of Babylonia; and a holy man, warned by God, escaped death by building a structure large enough to hold his family and the domestic animals needed for farming. 2. Tightly woven baskets, such as the one described in Exodus 2:3, have been found in many tombs in Egypt. Smeared with pitch or bitumen, one could be easily made waterproof, a logical boat-cradle for a fugitive infant, like Moses. 3. The Ark of the Covenant was a sacred chest made by the children of Israel while camped in the desert, following a pattern revealed by God to Moses. It was made of precious materials and could be lifted on two poles thrust through gold rings. When the Israelites traveled, the Ark was carried forward; when they went into battle, it was with them; and when they camped, it was set up within an elaborately ornamented tent or Tabernacle. As the Sheik's tent among his people, so the Ark was the sign of God's presence and protection. The Ark contained the Tables of the Law, a golden dish of Manna and the rod of Aaron which had blossomed. It was a symbol of the Church to come which would keep the law of God, and the Eucharist where Christ would live among His people, guiding, protecting and feeding them during their journey through the desert of the world, on their way to heaven.

Arkansas (from Arkansas or Quapaw Indians) The 25th state of the Union. Early Indians lived in the areas by hunting, fishing and primitive agriculture; worshiping the forces of nature and the Great Spirit, supreme God over all. Hernando de Soto and his companions (1541) were the first Europeans in the territory; the Friars with him baptized some Indians but could not offer Mass as they had lost their supplies en route. In 1673 Marquette and Joliet visited the area on their voyage down the Mississippi. In 1682, La Salle reached the territory. After his death the two priests from his party returned to Canada. About the same time, the first European settlement was made by Henri de Tonti at a trading station named the Arkansas Post. The first priest to settle in the area was Father Nicholas Foucault of the Quebec Foreign Mission Seminary. He made his home among the Arkansas Indians in 1700 and was killed by hostile tribesmen two years later. Other missioners came in turn, resulting in the conversion of many Indians, including their chief, Sanasin, who was buried near the Church of St. Joseph, Pine Bluff. The territory passed from Spain, to France, to the United States, and was settled by English-speaking citizens. The Indians were forced out and moved to (Oklahoma) Indian Territory. Cotton plantations were run with slave labor until after the Civil War, when the "share-cropper" plan became general. Until 1843 Arkansas was part of the diocese of St. Louis; having about 2,000 Catholics but no priests. A few priests finally arrived to care for Catholic immigrants. In 1838 Father Richard Bole opened the first Catholic school in the state at St. Mary's mission with Sisters of Loretto from Kentucky. In 1843 the diocese of Little Rock was established with Rt. Rev. Andrew Byrne as bishop of all Arkansas and Indian Territory. He built churches, a cathedral, and schools. Various religious orders were brought in by him and succeeding bishops to care for scattered Catholics and to do missionary work among the Negroes. Catholics have always been a small minority in Arkansas.

Armageddon (ar'ma-ged'un; Heb. *Har-Megiddo*) The mountain of Megiddo, bordering the plain of Esdraelon in present-day Israel, the great battlefield of ancient Palestine, where the fortunes of kings and nations were decided. In the New Testament (Apoc. 16:16) it is a symbol of the struggle between good and evil that goes on in the world and in the soul of every man.

Armenian Church Founded in northern Asia Minor by St. Gregory the Illuminator. Rejecting the decisions of the Council of Chalcedon (593), the Armenian Church became a completely independent national church. Non-Catholic Armenians do not use the Sacrament of Anointing the Sick; they admit divorce, and in practice sometimes permit widowed priests to remarry. There was an attempted reunion with Rome in the 12th century. Gregorian Armenians are to be found in the United States.

Armenian Rite Several influences have combined to form the Armenian liturgy, with a few small elements from the Latin Mass. The liturgy makes use of unleavened bread, and no water is mixed with the wine. The Armenians have the four minor orders of the West. Classical Armenian is used in the liturgy.

Armenian Rite, Catholics of There are approximately 97,000 Catholics in the Armenian Rite, who are found principally in the Near East. There are some in Transylvania and the United States. Their liturgy is in classical Armenian. The head of the Armenian Catholics is the Katholikos, the Patriarch of Cilicia, who lives near Beirut in Lebanon. Those in the United States are subject to their local Latin ordinaries.

Arms of Christ, the   A term used to represent the instruments of the Passion grouped together to form a unit for a seal or an emblem.

art, Christian   That art which serves to develop Christian belief, grace, piety, modesty, worship or the holiness of the Church. Christian art existed from the earliest times. The catacombs are rich in fine Christian art, particularly in the use of symbolism. Over the centuries this art developed as a means of expressing beauty, as decoration and for teaching. Mosaics, paintings, statuary, woodcarving, gold and silver creations were made. The making of stained-glass windows, and the illumination and calligraphy of manuscripts were high forms of Christian art. Church architecture also became a high expression of Christian art. *See* art, liturgical; art, sacred.

art, liturgical   A special form of religious art pertaining to the official worship of the Church. Liturgical art involves the application of artistic craftsmanship to church architecture and decoration in order to enable a more full and meaningful worship to be practiced. In an Instruction of June 30, 1952, the Sacred Congregation of the Holy Office stated: "It is the function and duty of sacred art . . . to enhance the beauty of the house of God, and to foster the faith and piety of those who gather in the church to assist at the divine service." *See* art, Christian; art, sacred.

art, sacred   The making and expressing of what is beautiful, inspiring, noble and worthy of its purpose: the directing of the mind and heart to God. Regarding sacred art, Vatican Council II in the Constitution on the Sacred Liturgy states as follows:

"Ordinaries must be very careful to see that sacred furnishings and works of value are not disposed of or dispersed; for they are the ornaments of the house of God. Bishops should have a special concern for artists, so as to imbue them with the spirit of sacred art and of the sacred liturgy. This they may do in person or through suitable priests who are gifted with a knowledge and love of art. It is also desirable that schools or academies of sacred art should be founded in those parts of the world where they would be useful, so that artists may be trained. All artists who, prompted by their talents, desire to serve God's glory in holy Church, should ever bear in mind that they are engaged in a kind of sacred imitation of God the Creator, and are concerned with works destined to be used in Catholic worship, to edify the faithful, and to foster their piety and their religious formation."

articles of Faith   *See* dogma.

arts, the liberal   Originally, those arts which only free Romans (*liberi*) were able to pursue. In the 5th century, the term was applied to the seven subjects taught in the medieval school: grammar, rhetoric, logic, (which were called the *trivium*) and arithmetic, music, geometry and astronomy (called the *quadrivium*). Today the term applies to the subjects studied in a collegiate education, as opposed to subjects studied for a technical education.

Ascension of Christ   1. The departure of Jesus Christ from this world to take His rightful place at the right hand of the Father. The departure took place in the presence of the Blessed Mother, His Apostles and disciples forty days after His Resurrection. 2. A feast kept on the fortieth day after Easter Sunday. The paschal candle is extinguished on this day, symbolizing the departure of Our Lord and the end of the Easter season. It is a holy day of obligation throughout the world.

ascetical theology That body of principles which deals with the efforts necessary to achieve Christian perfection. It is an intermediate study between moral theology (the study of God's commandments) and mystical theology (the study of extraordinary ways to perfection).

asceticism (Gr. *askein,* to exercise) The practice of self-discipline in order to have greater union with God. This discipline can be exercised internally, such as control of the intellect, imagination and will; or externally, through fasting, bodily mortifications, etc. Asceticism is an integral part of Christian perfection.

aseity (as-aye′itee) That attribute of God by which He exists by virtue of His own nature, independently of any external cause. Aseity is of the very essence of God.

Ash Wednesday The first day of Lent, so-called because ashes, from burnt olive or palm blessed the preceding year are, on this first day of the yearly season of penance, placed on the heads of the faithful. Sackcloth and ashes were signs of penance, mourning and humiliation in Old Testament times, and were used by public penitents in the early Church. In the Ash Wednesday ceremony, the priest traces the Sign of the Cross on the forehead of the kneeling recipient, saying, "Remember, man, that you are dust, and to dust you will return."

ashes, blessed A sacramental, which obtains favors for us from God *ex opere operantis Ecclesiae,* that is, thanks to the liturgical prayers of the Church, which are always accepted by God. The ashes of burnt olive and palm branches from Palm Sunday of the preceding year are blessed solemnly before Mass by the priest, accompanied by his sacred ministers, who will celebrate the following Mass. The prayers (found in most Missals for Ash Wednesday) beg God to forgive the penitent sinner, and to bless and sanctify the ashes so that they may bring spiritual health to all those who call upon God with a contrite heart, imploring His mercy.

Asia, the Church in Asia is the world's largest land area, comprising 17,075,000 square miles, and with far the world's greatest population, approximately two billion. In Asia, conversions to Christianity began in very early days, and large areas are still unconverted or under Communist domination. Catholics in the free Asian countries number over 35 million, with 22,000 priests, of whom almost half are Asiatic. Brothers number about, 6,000, and Sisters nearly 60,000. In those parts of Asia which are under Communist tyranny, the Church is one of suffering, operating in secret, bearing martyrs whose numbers are known only to God.

Asperges, the (as-per′jes; L. *Asperges me,* Thou shalt sprinkle me) The rite of sprinkling the faithful with blessed water before the principal Mass on Sundays in churches and chapels. The name comes from the first words of the antiphon taken from Psalm 50 which follows the rite. The Asperges is sung by the choir or the congregation during the procession of priests and ministers performing the ceremony. During the Easter season the antiphon *Vidi aquam* (L. I saw water) from Ezechiel 47:1-9, and Psalm 117 are sung during the Asperges instead. The rite is meant to prepare the people for the Holy Sacrifice by penance and a reminder of their Baptism.

aspergillum (as'per-jil'um; L. *aspergere,* to sprinkle) A small brush or perforated metal ball on a handle, used by the priest for sprinkling holy water on the faithful or on articles to be blessed. Originally it was a leafy twig of some shrub such as marjoram or box, used in Jewish rites of purification and referred to as hyssop in the Bible (Psalm 50).

aspersion (L. *aspergere,* to sprinkle) 1. To baptize by sprinkling the head instead of by pouring water. This method while valid is now illicit. 2. Any sprinkling with holy water.

aspersory The holy-water sprinkler; the aspergillum.

aspidiale An apsidiole (*q.v.*).

aspirancy A period of trial given candidates for certain orders of religious women which is prior to acceptance for the postulancy. The length of time varies. The Sisters of Mercy have an aspirancy of from three and a half to four years.

aspirations Prayers said in one breath, ejaculations.

ass 1. A beast of burden mentioned in Scriptures over 130 times. Our Lord entered Jerusalem on Palm Sunday riding one. 2. A caricature used by Roman writers and artists to represent Christians. One such caricature shows Christians worshiping a crucified figure with the head of an ass.

Assemblies of God Several evangelical sects native to America which were united in 1914. They emphasize the inspiration and primacy of Scripture. In government they follow the Congregational and Presbyterian systems.

assent To give or express one's concurrence, acquiescence or compliance.

assent, external A sensible act or sign which corresponds to internal assent (*q.v.*) such as a confession of faith, preaching of the Gospel, signing a proposition as is demanded when one makes a religious profession.

assent, internal An act of the intellect whereby one accepts a proposition as true; it results with natural necessity from a free, responsible, rational, self-conscious decision to believe the truth of a proposition. Assent is the actual value one affirms and decides to accept absolutely and without conditions. Hence this act of the intellect is direct and complete in itself. Often the mind exercises it without regard for previous argument, although antecedent argument may have been a *sine qua non* for eliciting assent. In any case the truth of a proposition is so overwhelmingly evident that we assert the truth by an act of the mind.

assessor A cleric appointed as a consultor to a judge in an ecclesiastical case. He has no jurisdiction.

assist at Mass To attend Mass. The faithful attending Mass are not expected to witness the celebration as they would a drama but to participate with the celebrant in offering the sacrifice, thus to assist.

assistant at the pontifical throne Episcopal members of the papal chapel who rank after cardinals and are assigned special places on each side of the papal throne.

assistant priest 1. A curate; an assistant to a pastor. 2. A priest who assists a newly ordained priest at his first Mass. 3. An assistant to a bishop in pontificial ceremonies whose principal duties are to hold open the books for the bishop, indicate the proper place in the books, and transmit the Kiss of Peace to the choir.

Association for International Development (AID) An organization of laymen which assigns lay specialists to technical and social service with the Church in mission areas. Founded in 1957 with the approval of Bishop James A. McNulty, then of Paterson, N. J., the group is assisted by an advisory committee of missionary-priests. AID members, single persons and married couples, receive training for ten months and agree to serve in the missions for at least two years. Headquarters: 374 Grand Street, Paterson, N. J.

association, right of An association or private society is formed within the state when several persons join together to attain as a common end the private advantage of the associates. The right to form such associations follows the natural impulse that man has to join himself with others as a necessary means to attain objects which without the collaboration of others would be impossible. The state is bound to protect natural rights and unless the purposes of the associations are evidently bad, unlawful or dangerous to the state, it cannot forbid their formation by the citizens; for both they and it exist by virtue of the like principle, namely, the natural tendency of man to live in society.

associations, pious Societies such as third orders secular, confraternities and pious unions, which are formed with ecclesiastical authority for the sanctification of their members, for public worship and for the performance of works of charity. They are under direct ecclesiastical control.

Assumption of the Blessed Virgin Mary The doctrine which states that the Mother of Christ was "assumed"—taken up—into heaven bodily, by the power of God. It has always been believed in the Church, but it was defined as a dogma by Pope Pius in the year 1950. It had been celebrated as a feast for fifteen hundred years, and is kept on August 15 as a holy day of obligation.

Assumptionists 1. A shortened title for the Augustinians of the Assumption, a missionary congregation of men dating from 1845, founded by Abbe d'Alzon at Nimes, France. Its members wear a black habit and recite the Divine Office in choir, following the Rule of St. Augustine. They conduct schools, colleges, seminaries, hospices and parishes in mission countries, and publish a number of newspapers, magazines and books. 2. The title "Assumptionists" also refers to several congregations of Sisters.

Assyrian Church, the A name given to the Nestorian Church in Iraq and Iran by missionaries from the Church of England.

asterisk (Gr. *aster,* star) A device used in the Byzantine Liturgy to be placed over the *diskos* to prevent the veil from touching the particles. The device is made of two semicircular rods which cross each other at right angles. Sometimes a small star hangs from the intersection.

astrology A false science which claims to foretell the future and treats of the supposed influence of the stars, the sun and moon on human affairs. It came into influence in the Middle Ages as a development of the Arabs and Jews. Today it is having a revival among the superstitious. Astrology rejects free will. It was condemned by Pope Sixtus V in 1586, and again by Pope Urban VIII in 1631.

asylum (Gr. *asylos,* inviolable) 1. A place of sanctuary. In olden times one could take sanctuary from the law or enemies in a church and be safe as long as he remained there. 2. An institution to shelter those in need, such as orphans.

Athanasian Creed One of the three Creeds used in the Roman Liturgy. It is sometimes called *Quicumque* from its opening words: *"Whoever* wishes to be saved . . ."* It is said to have been composed by St. Athanasius, Bishop of Alexandria (A.D. 296–373), a claim that has been challenged by many ecclesiastical antiquarians. However, it seems highly probable that it was composed in the lifetime of the great bishop or shortly thereafter, and it most certainly is a reflection of his spirit. It is evidently aimed at the heresies of Arius (A.D. 256–326) and is more than a brief profession of faith. It is a detailed exposition of the mysteries of the Trinity and of the divinity and humanity of Christ.

atheism (Gr. *a,* without; *theos,* God) The denial of the existence of God. Practical atheism consists in living as if God does not exist. It may be identified with religious or moral indifference. Speculative or moral atheism consists in an attempted rational defense of the statement that God does not exist.

atomic warfare Because of the destructive powers of modern nuclear weapons and the fact that the traditional distinction of direct and indirect results of a bombing have largely disappeared, Catholic theo-

logians are more and more arriving at a position that general use of such weapons is intrinsically inhuman. Catholic thought favors an international agreement, able to be enforced, that would ban any military use of nuclear weapons for all times.

Atonement, Friars of the A congregation of men belonging to the Third Order Regular of St. Francis, whose motherhouse is at Graymoor, Garrison, N. Y. In 1898 a little band of Episcopalians formed a religious community there, keeping the rule of St. Francis, and devoting themselves especially to bringing the Anglican branch of Christianity into communion with Rome. In 1908 Father Paul Francis, an Anglican clergyman, superior of the community, inaugurated the Church Unity Octave with special prayers for the union of all Christian bodies and the conversion of non-Christians. Pope Pius X approved the Octave and indulgenced it as a form of devotion for the whole Church in December, 1909. In the meantime, Father Paul Francis and the friars of his community had been received into the Catholic Church. Their center at Graymoor has become famous for its works of charity in the Franciscan tradition, giving hospitality to vagrants with true brotherly love and offering rehabilitation to those who wish it. Their particular works as a Franciscan congregation are those of missions and the promotion of Church unity. A group of Anglican women who had been following the Franciscan Rule also came into the Church and have since persevered in their own congregation with its works of charity at Graymoor and on the missions.

Atonement, the (*lit.,* at one) The act of reconciliation between God and man, earned by the Incarnation, suffering and death of Christ. Through the Atonement, Christ earned His title and right to be Mediator of mankind. This is said to be the only theological term of English origin.

attention An act by which the mind and senses are directed to one thing to the exclusion of others. In a theological sense, it is the amount of care directed to the performance of a spiritual act. To fulfill certain obligations—such as the recitation of the Divine Office, the celebration or hearing of Mass, or the reception of sacraments—external attention is required. *External attention* requires the avoidance of all obstacles to internal attention. *Internal attention* is the exclusion of mental distraction. *Material attention* is observation of the form without paying attention to the sense. *Literal attention* implies an observation of the sense.

attributes of God The perfections of God. These perfections are one and infinite. Man, however, because of the nature of his intellect separates these perfections. Thus we refer to God as all-holy, almighty, all-good, omnipotent, omniscient, eternal, etc. In God, all these perfections are actually united.

attributes of the Church There are three. 1. *Authority:* Religious or ecclesiastical authority should be distinguished from civil. The latter's concern is to enforce obedience to the laws and regulations of the state, while the former is mainly a power to influence belief or conduct. Christianity claims to be based on revelation, i.e., it professes to know truths transcending man's natural capacities of apprehension and revealed directly or indirectly by God. These truths are not contrary to reason, but their discovery is for the most part beyond

its reach, and, as made known by God, they have the authority of God. These revelations are handed on by the Church, partly through Tradition and partly through Scripture. Catholics hold that this truth has absolute authority for the further reason that the Church is divinely guided into the whole truth of the Christian revelation by the Holy Spirit and that the organs of this authoritative teaching include general councils and the Pope in his ex cathedra pronouncements. Protestants, however, have commonly confined this authority to the Bible, guaranteed by its appeal to the individual conscience rather than by the consent of the Church. 2. *Infallibility:* The prerogative of the Church as a teacher by which, being guided by the Holy Spirit, when she actively teaches revealed truths, she is protected from error or the possibility of error. Infallibility also extends to those matters which are very closely connected with revealed truths and which the Church also as an authoritative teacher may pronounce upon. It is also a prerogative of the Pope when he speaks as head of the Church on a matter of faith or morals. 3. *Indefectibility:* The fact that the Church in its faith and morals and its infallible interpretation will remain unchangeable until the end of time. That attribute of the Church by which it will remain until the end of time essentially the same as it was established by Christ.

attrition (L. *atterere,* to rub) Imperfect sorrow for sin, which in theology is considered the lowest degree of repentence and results from fear of punishment. Perfect sorrow is when the sinner is sorry for having offended God who is all-good and loving. Imperfect sorrow is when the sinner is sorry because of some effect the sin will have on himself, e.g., the punishment of hell. Perfect contrition forgives the sin even before it is confessed. Imperfect contrition is sufficient for valid reception of the Sacrament of Penance.

audiences, papal Any reception granted by the pope to an individual or group of individuals. Audiences are public (large group) or private (an individual or small group). Those received in audience include everyone from heads of state to humble peasants. The procedure for requesting an audience varies. One way is to request an audience through the rector of the Roman college of one's country, e.g., the American College. Another way is through the Vatican master of the chamber. Other Roman officials can also make arrangements.

auditor (L. *audire,* to hear) Usually a Church official who hears and prepares a record of an ecclesiastical case which is then submitted to his superior for judgment. An auditor of the Rota is a judge of that tribunal. The Papal Auditor is in charge of the appointment of bishops.

Augsburg, Diet of Charles V summoned a diet to be held in Augsburg, Germany, in 1530 in order to plan action against the Turks and to ensure peace to Church and Empire. He ordered the Protestant states to submit a written formula of their beliefs and a statement of the abuses in the Catholic Church. Melanchthon set down the doctrinal views of his party in a document which afterward was called the Confession of Augsburg. It was approved by Luther and comprises two parts: 1. twenty-one articles of "reformed doctrines"; 2. seven articles of "abuses," which included Communion under one species, private Masses, celibacy, monastic vows, confession and the ecclesiastical hierarchy. The Confession set off a wide debate. Charles ended it when he gave the German states one year to return to the Faith of their ancestors. The Protestants reacted by forming the League of Smalkald, and Luther approved the taking up of arms against Charles.

August Month of the Immaculate Heart of Mary.

Augustine, Rule of St. A Rule used by many modern congregations, particularly of Sisters, as a basis for their constitutions and customs. It is brief, not detailed, and is easily adaptable to changing times. Its prescriptions are contained in a letter which St. Augustine wrote to a community of women in the year 423. It advises them concerning charity, holding property in common, fraternal correction, proper conduct in public places, prayer, fasting and leading the common life.

Augustinian Fathers Formally Order of Hermits of St. Augustine, established in 1256 by Pope Alexander IV when a union was made of a number of monasteries following the rule of St. Augustine. The order is dedicated to education, missionary and parochial works. There are two American provinces. The order is known in the United States for its outstanding educational achievement, Villanova University.

Augustinianism The body of teachings of St. Augustine (354–430) which expounded the necessity of grace, the divine election, and which reconciled predestination and the complete liberty of the human will. These teachings are found mainly in the *Confessions* and *The City of God*.

Augustinians A title given to several religious orders based on the Rule of St. Augustine.

aumbry *See* ambry.

aureole (awe′ree-ol, L. *aureus,* golden) In sacred art, particularly in icons, the rays of gold leaf, gilt paint or metal which surround the figures of the three Persons of the Blessed Trinity and of Our Lady. The aureole is a symbol of heavenly glory. It is not the same as the halo.

auricular confession (L. *auris,* ear; *lit.,* confession to the ear) The declaration of one's sins privately to the confessor, as opposed to public confession. In the early days of the Church, public confession was common. It is not necessary that auricular confession be spoken; sins may be written down. For valid confession, the penitent must be present; therefore, one could not make confession by telephone, radio or letter.

Auriesville Site of the Mohawk village of Ossernenon, near the present city of Amsterdam, N. Y., where St. Isaac Jogues and others were tortured. St. René Goupil was martyred here in 1642. Catherine Tekawitha was born here, later moved to nearby Fonda. It is the site of the present shrine of the North American Martyrs, and a popular place of pilgrimage.

Aurora, Mass of the (awe-ro′ra; L. dawn, daybreak, early morning light) The second of the three Masses offered at Christmas, originally celebrated in Rome at dawn in the old church of St. Anastasia. It has now become a part of the Christmas celebration in all churches of the Latin Rite throughout the world, and it is still intended to be sung at dawn.

austerity (Gr. *auein,* to parch) The rigorous practice of bodily penances and mortifications for the purpose of advancing in Christian perfection. These austerities would include such practices as flagellation, wearing chains, depriving oneself of sleep, etc. Such practices while useful, and even necessary, should be undertaken only with prudence and upon the advice of a competent spiritual director.

Australia The island continent of Australia, claimed in part for Great Britain by Captain Cook in 1770, was at that time sparsely inhabited by primitive tribesmen. At the close of the American War of Independence, Britain's prisons were full to bursting, and it was decided to send the wretched inmates to found a self-supporting prison colony in New South Wales, since they could no longer be sent to America. Although the prisoners were convicts, many of them were far from being criminals. In those days people could be hanged or imprisoned for trivial offenses, and many were political prisoners. One thousand three hundred Irish Catholic peasants, for instance, were deported during the Orange reign of terror in 1795–1796, without trial or sentence. Inmates of the penal colony were treated as beasts of burden, flogged, tortured, put to death for minor infringements. Catholics were obliged to attend Anglican services or suffer reduced rations; if the offense were repeated, imprisonment, then the stocks, then the cat-o'-nine-tails, with added strokes for each new violation. Three priests were among the prisoners, unjustly charged with taking part in the Irish insurrection of 1798. After long negotiations, one of them was permitted to say Mass once a month, and so the Holy Sacrifice was first offered in New South Wales on May 15, 1803. The chalice was of tin, the vestments were made from old curtains. Soon the permission was withdrawn, and there were 6,000 Catholics in and around Sydney without Mass or the sacraments. Father

Jeremiah Flynn, an Irish Cistercian, finally gained permission from the British Colonial Office to go to Australia and minister to the Catholics there. Upon his arrival he was informed by the governor that no popish missionary would be allowed to work in the settlement. Father Flynn, however, went "underground" and did what he could for his lonely flock; but after a few months he was seized and shipped back to London as a prisoner. He had no chance to remove the Blessed Sacrament from a cedar chest in the house where he had been offering Mass. For two years the pious Catholic who owned the house kept a vigil light burning before the chest, and sorrowing Catholics crept in to visit their Lord, and pray. The "Holy House" was later given up for religious use and the fine Church of St. Patrick now stands on the site. The harsh treatment given Father Flynn brought to light the cruel treatment of convicts in the colony and the persecution of Catholics. In May, 1821, there began a partial toleration of the Catholic Faith and some priests arrived to care for the faithful. The Church has grown since then. There are 7 archdioceses, 18 dioceses, 1 cardinal, 8 archbishops, 27 bishops, 1,241 parishes, 3,419 priests, 2,022 Catholic schools with 423,883 students, and a Catholic population of 2,137,373, comprising almost 20 per cent of the total population. Catholic missioners are also working among the aborigines, with good results.

Austria The first traces of Christianity in what is now Austria date back to 174. In 303 St. Florian and his companions were martyred. Today Austria has 2 archdioceses and 5 dioceses with a cardinal in Vienna. Catholics number almost 6.5 million in a population of over 7 million. There are many Catholic social, charitable and intellectual movements, with 4 Catholic dailies and 27 weekly newspapers. Salzburg and Innsbruck are centers of Catholic education. Austria has less than 300 priests engaged in mission work outside the country.

authentic (Gr. *authentes,* one who does a thing with his own hand) Authorized for use by the faithful. Thus, the Confraternity Edition of the New Testament is the authentic edition to use when reading the Gospel in English at Mass.

authentication of relics The act of approving a relic for veneration of the faithful. Only those relics can be venerated which have been declared authentic by one authorized to approve them. Authentication is not a guarantee of genuineness but a declaration that the relic has been investigated and no evidence found that it is spurious.

authenticity, biblical Refers to the fact that a text or edition of the Bible is substantially identical with the original text.

authority (L. *auctoritas*) 1. A person in command or who has jurisdiction. 2. A person to whom assent is given because of his knowledge. 3. The power of self-governing of the Church because it was founded by Jesus Christ. *See* authority, ecclesiastical.

authority, civil Because the state is a perfect society, having within itself the means for attaining its end, it has authority in temporal affairs. This authority derives from the authority of God, and therefore commands the respect of its members. Catholic theologians teach that this authority is conferred immediately on the state, and therefore its members are free to choose the mode by which they shall be governed. Since the basis for the authority of the state is God, the state must be careful in the use of this authority; it must not encroach on the rights of individuals, on the authority of a father over his family, or on the spiritual authority of the Church. Authority presupposes actions in conformity to divine and natural law.

authority, ecclesiastical Because the Church is a perfect society, having within itself the means for the sanctification of its members and of giving honor to God, the Church has authority in spiritual matters and in those temporal matters which affect the spiritual. The authority of the Church is the authority of Jesus Christ who delegated his authority to St. Peter, and through him to the popes and the bishops. The authority of the Church is independent of civil authority, and is actually of a higher order.

authority of papal acts Decrees and decisions promulgated by the Holy See, whether by the Pope or one of the Roman offices, are to be obeyed by those to whom they are directed; in doctrinal matters internal assent should be given, but in other matters only external assent is necessary. If no date is fixed, the decree and decision becomes binding when published in the *Acta Apostolicae Sedis*. No further promulgation is necessary unless particularly prescribed.

authority of Scripture The Bible is the written Word of God. Christ promised that the Holy Spirit would reside in the Church. Therefore, the interpretation of Sacred Scripture and the promulgation of its authority belongs to the magisterium of the Church as successor to the Apostles. The authority of Scripture is equal to the authority of Tradition, and there can be no conflict between them because they are both guarded by the Holy Spirit, and each consists of divinely revealed and guaranteed truths.

authority, parental Parents have the authority from God to command obedience from their children in order to ensure their welfare until the time they can care for themselves.

authority of the Divine Office While the Divine Office contains nothing opposed to faith and morals, its authority does not extend to its historicity. Thus one is not held to believe historical statements made in the Second Nocturns.

authority of Tradition Vatican Council I defined Tradition as a source of theological teaching distinct from Scripture, and stated that it is infallible. Tradition can exist apart from Scripture, but Scripture depends upon Tradition for interpretation. Tradition is to be looked upon equally with Scripture as the Word of God.

Authorized Version 1. Specifically, the revision of the Bible carried on by James I of England and published in 1611 with his authorization. It is also called *King James Version*. For many years it was the only standard and official Protestant Bible in English. 2. Any translation of Scripture recognized as official.

auto-da-fe (awe-toe-dah-fay′; Sp., Port., an act of faith) A ceremony held by a tribunal of the Spanish Inquisition (*q.v.*), during which an accused heretic might recant, be pardoned, given a penance to perform and be reconciled to the Church. Those who refused to abjure their errors and were judged guilty were handed over to the state for punishment according to its laws, which held heresy and treason to be practically synonymous. Although this ceremony and subsequent possible punishment are popularly attributed only to the Spanish Inquisition, civil punishment for heresy or nonconformity to the prevailing religion have existed since pre-Christian times. See Dan. 3, the three Jews in the fiery furnace; the death of St. Stephen, Acts 6:8-7:60; accounts of the martyrs of pagan Rome in the Roman martyrology; the burning of Servetus and the beheading of Gentile by Calvin; the death penalty decreed against priests in Elizabethan England and in some early Lutheran states of Europe; the hanging of Quakers in Puritan New England in 1659–1661; the harassment of Roman Catholics in most of the early American colonies; the torture and murder of Catholic churchmen and the faithful in modern Communist-dominated countries in Europe, Asia and Latin America. The Church condemns the forcing of religion on anyone.

autoeroticism Self-stimulation of the erotic areas of the body. It is sinful unless a proportionately honest cause removes guilt.

autos sacramentals (L. *lit.* self-sacramentals) A type of morality play designed to teach about the Eucharist that was produced in Spain in the 17th and 18th centuries. Because of abuses, it was suppressed.

auxiliary bishop A bishop who acts as an aid to the bishop of a diocese who may need help because of sickness, old age or great amount of work. He must be appointed by the Holy See, and is a titular bishop—that is, a bishop of an ancient see which has lapsed and no longer exists except in records.

avarice The inordinate desire for temporal goods. Covetousness is generally used as a synonym for avarice, but is more extensive in meaning,

avarice often being restricted to an inordinate desire for material wealth. The special evil of the sin is that goods and wealth become ends in themselves. The special danger arises because avarice leads to other sins usually of a more serious nature.

Ave Maria (ah'vay mah-ree'a; L. Greetings, Mary!) The first words of the Angelic Salutation, or the Hail Mary, the most ancient and popular prayer to Our Lady. *See* Hail Mary.

Ave Regina Caelorum (ah'vey ray-gee'nah chay-lo'rum; L. Hail, Queen of Heaven) An antiphon of Our Lady used in the Divine Office from Compline of the Purification (Feb. 2) to Thursday of Holy Week.

aversion (L. *avertere,* to turn away from) The state of mind which compels one to turn away from an object. Among theological writers, the term is used in a positive sense of turning away from an ordinary good or pleasurable thing in order to increase in spiritual perfection and holiness.

aviators By a decree of the Holy See in 1920, Our Lady of Loreto was proclaimed patroness of aviators. *See* aircraft blessing.

Azrael (Aramaic, *Azrail*). The angel of death in old Jewish lore. Muslims also use the name in the same context. It was believed that Azrael parted the soul from the body in death.

azyme (ah'zime; Gr. unleavened) The cake of unleavened bread used by the Jews during the Passover holy days; matzos. Hence, the unleavened bread used for consecrated hosts in the churches of the Latin Rite. (Churches of the various Eastern Rites use leavened bread.) Since the Eucharist was instituted during the celebration of the Passover meal, Christ must have used unleavened bread, hence the traditional use in the Latin Rite. However, leavened bread was originally used at Rome and has been used in emergencies, such as imprisonment, even up to the present time.

Azymites A term of reproach used in Orthodox Churches for Latin Catholics, Armenians and Maronites because of their use of unleavened bread in the celebration of the Holy Eucharist.

B

Babel, Tower of According to Genesis 11:1-9, when the human race increased after the deluge, men settled on a plain and began to build a city and a tower. But they never completed their project because God so confused their speech that they were unable to understand one another. The city was called Babel (Babylon). There are a number of interpretations of this passage. Some exegetes see that the building of a city was an evil thing to the semi-nomadic Israelite. The tower was evil further because it showed human pride which was offensive to God. Others interpret the passage as showing that man had drifted further away from his first innocence and needed more than ever the salvation of God.

Babylon, Patriarch of The Patriarch Katholikos of Babylon of the Chaldees who has jurisdiction over all Catholics of the Chaldean Rite. His seat of jurisdiction is in Al Mawsil (Mosul), Iraq. He is elected by the synod of bishops, and confirmed by the pope.

Babylonian Captivity Deportation of the Jews by their Babylonian conquerors in 598 and 587 B.C. In 538 B.C., King Cyrus gave the Jews permission to return home from Babylonia but many chose to stay in the first great Jewish diaspora.

bachelor A man who has not married. Ordinarily in the Western Church one must be a bachelor to be promoted to the subdiaconate, the diaconate or the priesthood. However, there are exceptions. A widower or a married man whose wife has entered a religious order with solemn vows may be allowed to take major orders.

bad faith Acting against the dictates of conscience; particularly applies to those who are convinced of the truth of the Church's teaching but remain outside her fold.

Bahai (Persian *baha,* glory) A modern religious movement which is derived from Islamism. It originated in Iran in the 19th century and has spread to many parts of the world. It emphasizes the spiritual unity of mankind.

baldacchino (*also* baldachin *and* baldaquin) Derived from baldacco, the Italian name for Baghdad, where the fabric was manufactured that produced the original canopy or umbrellalike covering made from rich silks and brocades that was first introduced into Europe through the Crusades and commerce with the Near East. Originally used in ceremonial occasions to hold over the heads of dignitaries. Three forms of canopies are still used in the Church. One type is projected over the altar, another over the episcopal throne and another is carried in a procession.

balm Fragrant secretion of certain trees or plants; it is mixed with olive oil to form holy chrism, which is used in the administration of Baptism and Confirmation, and for solemn consecrations or blessings.

balsam Balm (*q.v.*).

Baltimore Largest city in Maryland, named for Lord Baltimore, founder of Maryland Colony. The oldest see in the United States. Rev. John Carroll, Prefect Apostolic of the United States, established residence there in 1785, and was consecrated first bishop of Baltimore in 1790. The Sulpicians established the first seminary in the United States there in 1791. The three plenary councils held in the United States (1852, 1866, 1884) were held in Baltimore. James Cardinal Gibbons, the first American cardinal, was Archbishop of Baltimore.

Baltimore, Councils of The series of provincial and national meetings held during the 1800's in Baltimore, Md., by America's bishops. These councils laid the groundwork for Church expansion and mission work in the United States. The first of seven provincial councils met in 1829. They led to the first national council, convoked in 1852 to unify Catholics and promote Catholic education. A second followed in 1866 and a third in 1884. The latter, known as the great educational council, charged parents with the responsibility for the Christian education of their children and called for erection of parochial schools, preparation of a uniform catechism, distribution of Catholic literature and an annual collection for the home missions. These councils paved the way for establishment of the National Catholic Welfare Conference, which now functions through an Administrative Board elected by the hierarchy at their annual meeting in Washington, D.C.

bambino (It. infant) In art, a representation of the infant Christ.

bankruptcy and restitution A bankrupt person who has completed all legal requirements, and who has been legally discharged from his obligations, has no further obligation in conscience to abrogate his debts.

banner A cloth with some religious  picture or motto on it, hanging from a crossbeam above a single upright; it may be carried in processions, displayed before religious groups or used in a church.

banns of marriage To publish by proclamation an intended matrimony on three successive occasions. Banns are announced at Sunday Mass in order to learn if any impediment exists to the proposed union. The banns are announced in the parish where the wedding will take place. For proper reason, they may be dispensed with (cf. canons 1023-1030).

Baptism, conditional When there is danger of death and a person is unable to respond, or when there is doubt whether Baptism has already been given, or some doubt about the dispositions of the person, Baptism should be administered conditionally in order to safeguard the sacredness of the sacrament while ensuring the spiritual good of the person so baptized. In conditional Baptism, the words, "If you are capable of it," are prefixed to the form.

Baptism, lay Anyone, even non-Catholics, can baptize in case of emergency when a person is in danger of death and no priest is immediately available. The baptizer must have the intention of doing what the Church does, and pour water while reciting the form. If the person should recover, the full baptismal ceremonies should be supplied. It is gravely illicit for a lay person to baptize when no danger of death exists.

baptism of bells When blessed or consecrated, bells become sacramentals of the Church and are used in religious services. The rite of consecration is so elaborate that it is improperly called baptism in popular usage.

Baptism of children of non-Catholics A non-Catholic child in danger of death may be baptized without the consent of its parents when it can reasonably be foreseen that it will die before the age of reason. Otherwise the consent of one parent or guardian must be obtained and guarantees given that the child will be raised a Catholic.

Baptism of desire A perfect act of charity that includes at least implicitly the desire for Baptism by water. The implicit desire is sufficient if it is a desire to do the will of God (thus if one knew God willed Baptism by water, that person would receive this Baptism). Hence it is possible for non-Christians, even though they do not know Christ or His Church, to enjoy salvation through Baptism of desire. Baptism of desire does not imprint an indelible character on the soul, and must be followed by Baptism of water when this becomes known as God's will. Infants are not capable of Baptism of desire.

Baptism of the dead Baptism is a sacrament of the living and cannot be administered to the dead. In a case of ignorance whether a person is dead or not, it must be administered conditionally. Some heretical sects have practiced Baptism of the dead but this has been condemned by the Church as sacrilegious and superstition.

Baptism, Sacrament of The primary sacrament whereby a person is cleansed of original sin, made a member of the Mystical Body of Christ and charged with the Christian mission. This sacrament prints an indelible mark on the soul and can be received only once. It also forgives actual sins and the temporal punishment due them. The ordinary minister of the sacrament is a priest; in case of emergency, however, anyone can baptize. The matter of the sacrament is the pouring of water. The form is: "I baptize you in the name of the Father and of the Son and of the Holy Spirit." The water is poured on the forehead in the figure of the cross while the form is being recited. Natural water suffices for the sacrament but in solemn Baptism special baptismal water is used. The Church recognizes as valid Baptism by infusion (pouring of water), immersion and aspersion (sprinkling). The Church also recognizes as valid Baptisms performed in non-Catholic rites provided the proper matter and form are used. Baptism is necessary for the reception of the other sacraments. The Church requires a sponsor (godparent) at Baptism. The godparent must be a Catholic in his or her fourteenth year or older. The godparent assumes the responsibility of providing for the religious education of the child if the parents should be negligent or unable to provide such education. The Church teaches that Baptism is necessary for salvation (Mt. 28:18-20). However, if a person cannot receive Baptism of water, he may receive Baptism of blood (martyrdom for the Christian faith or a Christian virtue) or Baptism of desire (perfect contrition plus a desire to do whatever God requires for salvation).

baptismal certificate A document issued by a parochial church or other place certifying that the person named was baptized there and that the fact is recorded in the baptismal register. It is used to show membership in the Church for matrimony, entrance into a seminary, etc.

baptismal font The basin—usually  part of, or set on, a pedestal — that is used in the administration of Baptism. It is located in the baptistery, which (after the high altar) is the second most important part of the church building.

baptismal name The name given to or chosen by the person to be baptized. Usually a saint's name, but definitely a Christian name.

baptismal robe Formerly the white garment worn by the person to be baptized. Today it is symbolized in the white cloth that is placed on the head of the person receiving the sacrament.

Baptismal Water The water blessed in the font on Holy Saturday and which must be used for Baptism. However, any ordinary water suffices for the valid administration of the sacrament and can be used in emergency or conditional Baptism.

baptist One who baptizes; used as an epithet for the first St. John, the forerunner of Christ.

baptistery The room or closed-off section of a church, usually near the main entrance, which contains the baptismal font used for the administration of the Sacrament of Baptism. This is the second most important and sacred part of the church. The high altar is first.

Baptists The largest Protestant denomination in the United States. The Baptists came into being in the 17th century as a development of English Puritanism. Roger Williams founded the first Baptist church in the United States in what is now Rhode Island, although he later withdrew from the movement. The religion gained strength in New England, Philadelphia, later in the South and then moved west with the pioneers. A major schism was caused by the slavery question and resulted in the formation of the Southern Baptist Convention and the Northern Baptist Convention (now the American Baptist Convention). Negroes were drawn in large numbers to the Baptists and formed the National Baptist Convention (now the National Baptist Convention, U.S.A.), which after the Southern is the largest Baptist body. Later the National Baptist Convention of America was formed, as well as the American Baptist Convention. Northern Baptists had a great interest in education and founded many schools, the University of Chicago being among the number. A wide variety of theological opinion is found among Baptists. In general, however, practically all Baptists agree on the independence of the local church, the Bible as the sole guide to faith and practice, the priesthood of the faithful, believer's Baptism by total immersion and separation of Church and State. Doctrinally, Baptists are Calvinistic. The Baptists have a well-developed sense of mission and spend many millions of dollars each year in overseas work. Because of their beliefs in individual independence in theology, there have been numerous fractionalizations of the Baptists, many of which are numerically small. Jehovah's Witnesses, Seventh-day Adventists and Disciples of Christ are among the sects derived from the Baptists.

barangay A Christian neighborhood movement that developed in the Philippines, somewhat similar to the block Rosary. A group of people gather each evening, form a procession, recite the Rosary aloud while going to the home of one of the members. There a passage of the New Testament is read, other prayers are said and sometimes a homily is given.

Barnabas, St. (Aramaic, meaning "son of encouragement") Barnabas was a Levite from Cyprus who assisted the early Church in Jerusalem and Antioch. He was a relative, possibly the uncle, of St. Mark. He befriended the recently converted Paul and introduced him to the Apostles. Paul and Barnabas were the first missioners to Cyprus and central Asia Minor. His feast is on June 11. He is ranked as an Apostle.

baroque (Fr.) A curved and rococo style of ecclesiastical architecture found in Italy and elsewhere that was used from about 1550 to the middle of the 18th century.

Baruch (Heb. *baruk,* blessed) Re-puted author of the Book of Baruch which was composed in Babylonia after the fall of Jerusalem. The authenticity of this book is questioned, as some exegetes state it should not be dated more recently than 300 B.C. although it was formerly held that it was composed not earlier than the 1st century B.C.

Basil, Liturgy of St. The Church of Constantinople had its own liturgy derived from Antioch and said to have been edited by St. Basil the Great (330–379). It is still used both by Catholics and by dissidents of the Byzantine Rite on five Sundays in Lent and for certain feasts.

Basil, Rule of St. The method of religious life developed by St. Basil the Great, Father of Monasticism in the East and one of the four great Greek doctors of the Church. The rule was organized in the form of questions and answers aimed at inculcating a religious spirit of obedience, poverty and unworldliness. The original rule required fasting five days a week; and set hours for meditation, study, work and community prayers. It became the basis for many religious rules of a later period.

Basilian Fathers The Congregation of the Priests of St. Basil, founded in France in 1822. Members are engaged in educational and parochial work. The congregation is represented in a number of parts of Canada and the United States.

Basilians Monks of the Ukrainian order founded by St. Basil the Great. Their general motherhouse is in Rome, and members work among Byzantine Rite Catholics in the U.S.

basilica A title of honor given to various churches. There are two classes of basilicas, *major* and *minor*. Only four major basilicas exist, all in Rome, but the Pope sometimes grants the minor title to other churches, which simply gives the clergy serving there precedence of rank.

beads Popular, descriptive name for the Rosary; any form of beads connected by wire or string to aid a person in counting a repeated number of prayers.

Beatific Vision Vision is the knowledge resulting from the direct influence of the object of sight on the person seeing. There is nothing mediate, indirect, analogical, abstract or rational about vision. Today the Beatific Vision is usually described as intuitive. When used by theologians it indicates the supernatural aspect of the sight of God, as does the word "beatific." Beatific Vision then is the act of understanding by which the Blessed know God in Himself, clearly and immediately. This God in His unity and trinity and in all His attributes is the primary object of beatific vision. This knowledge is limited only by the limitations of human receptivity, for God's intelligibility is inexhaustible. Its secondary object is created things as seen in the divine essence.

beatification (be-att-i-fi-cay'shun; L. *beatus,* blessed, *facere,* to make) A process resulting in the declaration by the Pope that a person of saintly life or heroic death may be called "Blessed" and considered to be in heaven. The preliminary process is long and painstaking, with examinations into the life, reputation and works of the candidate to see whether he or she practiced heroic virtue, or died a heroic death for the Faith. Miracles must be proved to have resulted from prayers to the servant of God in the case of a confessor of the Faith, but not necessarily in case of a martyr. Miracles are needed in both cases for canonization.

beatitude 1. The eternal satisfaction that will be found in heaven according to one's merits. It consists primarily of the Beatific Vision and secondarily of enjoying the company of the Blessed. 2. In the Eastern Rite, the term is used as an honorific for patriarchs, similar to "Your Excellency" of the Western Church.

Beatitudes, the Declarations beginning "Blessed are," introducing Christ's Sermon on the Mount. The Beatitudes appear in both Mt. 5:3-12 and Lk. 6:20-23. Matthew emphasizes the moral aspect. Blessed are the poor, etc., in the sense of their deep need of God and their patience under persecution, as they await a great reward in heaven. Luke emphasizes the social aspect as well, e.g., those who are poor because they share willingly with others in the Christian community.

beatus Literally, "blessed one," the title refers to one who has been beatified; it is also applied to any canonized saint, as a soul who has reached heaven. *See* canonization.

Beauraing, Our Lady of The title given to our Blessed Mother, taken from the name of the village, Beauraing, Belgium, where she appeared thirty times to five children between November 29, 1932, and January 3, 1933.

Beautiful Gate The gate of Herod's temple mentioned in Acts 3:2 where Peter cured the lame man.

beauty That quality in an object by which it pleases a person. It consists of wholeness, proper proportion and clarity. Beauty can be spiritual as well as that perceived in material objects, and partakes of divinity and of supreme order. As St. Thomas has written, "The beauty of God is the cause of the being of all that is" (*De Div. Nom. Lect. v*).

beauty contests The body of Catholic thought toward beauty contests is that Catholics should avoid them because they are an offense to modesty and can give scandal. Beauty contests place an exaggerated importance on physical attributes; moreover, they are meaningless since they really determine nothing.

B.C. The initials for the English words *Before Christ* which are used to designate the period of years in history before Christ was born.

Beda, the The College of St. Bede in Rome which began in 1852 and is now known as the Collegio Beda. Actually a seminary, it provides special training for ex-Anglican ministers, men with late vocations and for priests doing advanced study in Rome.

Beelzebub (Heb. *b'al zebub,* lord of flies) A name in the New Testament given to Satan. The Pharisees accused Christ of working miracles through the power of Beelzebub.

behaviorism A materialistic approach to the psychological study of human behavior. It rejects consciousness and introspection, admitting only what can be studied by observation and experimentation. It attempts to forecast human reaction to any given stimuli.

being That which is. Anything that does or can exist; anything, actual or conceptual, that is identifiable with or bears a correspondence to reality. All that is known to the mind of God.

belfry An extended structure above a church, a structure housing church bells.

Belgium The Church in Belgium is organized into 1 archdiocese and 6 dioceses. The metropolitan see is Malines-Brussels under Leon Joseph Cardinal Sue-

nens. There are 8.8 million Catholics in a total population of 9.2 million. Belgium has been an important contributor to Catholic thought; in philosophy and theology through Louvain University; in catechetics and liturgy through Lumen Vitae; and considerable contributions to ecumenism, missiology and spirituality through several Benedictine abbeys. The Scheut Fathers were established in 1888 for missionary work and out of the almost 4,500 Belgian priests working in the missions over 1,000 are Belgian Scheut Fathers.

Belial A name used in 2 Cor. 6:15 to indicate Satan.

belief The assent of the mind to a truth. Belief is founded in knowledge which is either experiential (empirical) or accepted on faith.

bell, book and candle Symbolic act of medieval times; after the reading of a sentence of excommunication, a bell tolled while the ritual book was closed and a lighted candle was thrown to the ground, to indicate the person's fall from the state of grace.

bells A large bell, usually found in the church tower, is used to sound the Angelus or to call the faithful to services; small hand bells in the sanctuary are sounded during Mass to call attention to the most solemn parts of the Holy Sacrifice.

Belmont, Abbey Nullius of Founded in North Carolina in 1878, raised to an abbey in 1884, and erected into an abbey nullius in 1910. It is staffed by the American Cassinese Benedictine congregation.

bema (Gr. step) In Greek Orthodox churches the space behind the iconostasis surrounding the Holy Table, the sanctuary. It takes its name from the raised platforms in Roman basilicas containing the judges' seats.

Benedicite (bay-nay-dee'chee-tay) 1.

The Latin title of the Canticle of the Three Children (Dan. 3:51-90), a hymn of praise. 2. Literally "bless you," it is used as a greeting in monasteries.

Benedict, the holy Rule of St. The "Father of Western Monasticism," St. Benedict (d. 543), wished his monks to be self-supporting and live in community. His rule, which exacted no unusual austerities, aimed to cultivate the family spirit of the community and to establish moderation as an ideal. The Benedictines began in Monte Cassino in 529 and quickly spread to become a great force in the development of Europe.

Benedictine Sisters Founded in the 6th century by St. Benedict and his sister, St. Scholastica, there are now approximately 20,000 throughout the world, in many independent communities. The major communities in the United States and Canada will be found listed under their proper titles.

Benedictine Sisters of Perpetual Adoration Established in the United States in 1875. The Sisters lead a contemplative life within a minor papal enclosure. Simple vows are taken. There are almost 300 members.

Benedictine Sisters of the Diocesan Jurisdiction There are two independent communities. St. Scholastica Convent in Arkansas was founded in 1878 and numbers over 300 Sisters engaged in teaching, nursing and care of orphans. Holy Name Convent in Florida was founded in 1889 and numbers 58 Sisters engaged in teaching, nursing, retreats and catechetics. Simple vows are taken.

Benedictine Sisters of the Pontifical Jurisdiction Established in the United States in 1852, the original foundation has now grown to 35 motherhouses and almost 7,000 Sis-ters. The motherhouses are grouped in three confederations: 1. Congregation of St. Scholastica, 17 motherhouses, over 2,600 members; 2. Congregation of St. Gertrude the Great, 11 motherhouses, 1,800 members; 3. Congregation of St. Benedict, 7 motherhouses, approximately 2,200 members. The life of these Sisters is both active and contemplative, and simple vows are taken. The Sisters engage in teaching, catechetics, nursing and related occupations. Both home and foreign mission work is extensively developed.

Benedictines, the Monks and nuns of the order of St. Benedict of Nursia, who established a monastery at Monte Cassino about the year 525. He was the founder of monasticism in the Western Church. During his lifetime he set up twelve monasteries where he ruled as abbot. His famous rule combined prayer and manual labor. In those days of slave labor the Benedictine monastery was perhaps the only place where free men might be seen working with their hands, with honor. There a former count might not find it beneath his dignity to feed the swine, and a former slave might in time become an abbot, freely elected by his monks. The abbot was a father to his community and was to be obeyed absolutely, yet he was to consult all the monks—especially the younger ones—before any important decision was made. The praise of God—celebration of Mass with noble solemnity and the singing of the Divine Office in liturgical splendor—was the first duty of monks. Labor, ascetical practices and the keeping of the vows were glorified by charity toward one another and toward the poor who came to the monastery gate. The stranger, the guest, was to be received as Christ. The Benedictines and other congregations who followed their rule in whole or in part were the great missioners who converted the barbarians of Europe, taught them agriculture and the arts, and settled them in towns and villages near the monasteries. Forests were cleared, swamps drained, good farm land produced from wilderness where wild beasts had roamed. The example of democracy among the monks and the famous rule conditioned the peoples of Britain and continental Europe for the eventual abolition of serfdom and the democratic forms of government that were gradually to be won. Today there are Benedictine abbeys in most of the free countries of the world, many in the United States and many in mission lands still carrying on the old traditions.

benediction (L. *benedictio,* a blessing) 1. A blessing, usually accompanied by the Sign of the Cross. It is at least an implicit intention that good fortune go with a person or thing. 2. The blessing given in the Divine Office pronounced by the officiant on the reader. It is in answer to the petition: "*Jube Domine benedicere*" ("Deign, Lord, a blessing").

Benediction, Apostolic *See* Blessing, Papal.

Benediction of the Blessed Sacrament A paraliturgical Eucharistic service popular in the Latin Rite which in recent years has been adopted by some Eastern Rites, particularly the Melkites. The service began in the 14th century with the custom of exposing the Blessed Sacrament for reverence. By the 16th century, blessing with the Sacred Host was added. The service usually consists of exposing the Blessed Sacrament for reverence in a monstrance, incensing and singing the O Salutaris or other Eucharistic hymn, another incensing during the singing of the Tantum Ergo, a versicle and prayer, blessing with the Sacred Host, the recitation of the Divine Praises and the replacement of the Blessed Sacrament in the tabernacle during a recessional. For such Benediction, twelve candles should be lighted. The Second Council of Baltimore permits Benediction on Sundays, feast days, twice a week during Lent, at the Forty Hours' Devotion, every day during a mission and on other days designated by the bishop.

Benediction with the ciborium A simple form of Benediction of the Blessed Sacrament. It consists of opening the tabernacle, singing hymns and the blessing of those present with the ciborium making the Sign of the Cross. Blessing with the Blessed Sacrament also figures in Communion for the sick.

Benedictionale A nonliturgical book that contains many forms of blessings taken from the Missal, the Pontifical and other books.

Benedictus, the 1. Latin title of the canticle of Zachary as recorded in Lk. 1:68-79, which hails the Messias and prophesies about his own son, John the Baptist. 2. The short canticle that follows the Sanctus in the Mass.

benefice (L. *beneficium,* a benefit) A permanent foundation which entitles the holder to a sacred office and the revenue from it. It must be canonically erected and have a perpetual endowment; the incumbent must also have the right to the revenue. A clergyman with a benefice may use his income freely insofar as is becoming for his state of life, but he must spend whatever is over and above on the poor and good works.

benefit of clergy The right of a cleric to be tried in an ecclesiastical rather than a civil court. The right was abolished in England in 1827. It has never existed in the United States.

Benemerenti Medals (L. well-merited) Pontifical decorations started by Gregory XVI as awards to either men or women for exceptional military or civic service.

benignity (L. *bene,* well, *genus,* kind) Kindness. One of the twelve fruits of the Holy Spirit (Gal. 5:22).

Benjamin (Heb. *ben-yamin,* son of the right hand) The youngest son of Jacob and Rachel, founder of the tribe of Benjamin. He was the favorite of Jacob and was only reluctantly allowed to join his brother Joseph in Egypt.

bequest for Masses Money left in a will for Masses to be said after the decease of the donor.

berakoth (Heb. blessings) Brief prayer formulas of blessings and thanksgiving used by the ancient Jews before undertaking ordinary daily actions by which they consecrated the action to God. They began with the words: "Blessed be Thou, O Lord our God, King of the ages, Thou who hast. . . ." Then to each *berakoth* was added a citation crediting God with the initiative behind the action about to be begun. Many Catholic teachers of asceticism would restore the practice.

Bernardines Founded in 1799 by three Cistercian nuns uprooted by the French Revolution; also members of several congregations of nuns with rules modeled on those of the older order established at Citeaux, France.

berretta The biretta (*q.v.*).

bethel (Heb. *beth el,* house of God) A holy place. The word is frequently used by Protestants for a chapel.

betrothal A solemn and formal mutual agreement of intention to marry (canon 1318). A betrothal to be valid must be in writing, state the full date, have the signatures of the contracting parties, witnessed by the ordinary or pastor, or by at least two witnesses. Canon law further specifies that even then such a promise gives no legal right to demand the celebration of marriage, but only the right to damages for breach of promise. Betrothal is a prohibiting impediment to marriage with another until the betrothal is legitimately ended. This formal type of betrothal is also called espousal. A less solemn form is the engagement, which is a simple agreement to wed made between a man and woman, usually sealed by the presentation on the part of the man of an engagement ring.

Better World Movement A religious movement begun in Italy in 1952 by Father Ricardo Lombardi, S.J., which has now spread throughout the world. It is aimed principally at the unification and sanctification of the clergy and religious and through them the unification and sanctification of the laity and the world. The Movement believes that the greatest need of the Church today is to build the Christian community and, therefore, the Movement promotes the presence of Christ and the need of charity.

betting *See* gambling.

Beuron Congregation A Benedictine congregation founded in 1868 which has its archabbey in Beuron, Germany. The well-known Maria Laach Abbey belongs to this group. The Beuron Abbey is known particularly for the works of art that are produced there.

Bible reading The reading of Sacred Scripture is greatly encouraged by the Church, by the granting of indulgences to those who read it at least 15 minutes a day. It may be read privately or in company with others, always with reverence and faith. There have been times and places in history when, on account of some prevailing excess in the mistaken and arbitrary interpretation of Scripture, the Church restrained the use of certain vernacular versions. There is no restriction today upon the reading of Scripture by the laity.

Bible, the (Gr. *biblia,* books) The Holy Scriptures, the written Word of God, the collections of those writings which were inspired by God and placed in care of the Church. The Bible consists of the Old Testament, 46 volumes written before the coming of Christ, and the New Testament, 27 books written since. The Old Testament explains and leads up to the New Testament, and the New Testament crowns the Old. These, says the Council of Trent, the Church receives with piety and reverence since the one God is the Author of both Testaments. The Church has protected the Holy Scriptures, interpreted them and handed them down from ancient times. She has always taught them to her children and she reads them to the faithful at each Mass. The Scriptures are the foundation of all the liturgical worship of God which goes on in the Church day and night through the centuries. The Church invites and encourages the laity to read the Word of God with faith and reverence. She does not allow the Divine Story to be explained away in unbelief, neither does she teach that all the narratives in the Sacred Books are to be taken literally, but in the sense—sometimes, e.g., metaphorical or allegorical—that was intended by the writer. The Bible is God's letter to us, inspired but not dictated by Him, written by many authors in different times and places, telling us the Good News of our salvation. None of the sacred books of the various great religions even approaches the Bible in grandeur, in high moral teaching, in beauty, in comfort for the heart of man and in the magnificence of its promises. Its entire message is comprised in one sentence: God has visited our earth and has become one of us, has lived among His creatures, has shown us the way and given us the means to be His children sharing in His own blessed and eternal life.

Bible Vigil A service being more and more used among Catholics, consisting of readings from the Bible, usually around one theme, from both the Old and the New Testaments. After a Bible reading there is a few minutes pause to allow the community to meditate on the texts just read. This is usually followed by the singing of a psalm as the community's response to the Word of God. In conclusion a prayer is offered by the leader in the name of the whole community. There is no strict format for the Bible Vigil. It consists of the four elements: readings from the Bible, meditation, singing and prayer. The service is usually held on the vigil of first-class feasts such as the Epiphany. Texts from both the Old and the New Testaments would be chosen according as they pertain to the feast; e.g., for the Epiphany, texts depicting the Lord as King of the Universe, receiving the homage of all the nations. The Bible Vigil is also the structure for the modern Holy Hour (*q.v.*).

Biblical Commission Established by Pope Leo XIII in 1902, to the end that Holy Writ "receive more elaborate treatment which the times require and be preserved intact not only from any breath of error but also from all rash opinions."

Biblical Institute of Jerusalem School

75

for biblical studies founded by Dominicans at Jerusalem in 1889.

Biblical Institute, Pontifical Established in Rome in 1909 to promote reading and understanding of the Bible.

Biblical Introduction That discipline concerned with the origin (both divine and human) of the Sacred Scriptures, their history, authenticity, integrity and interpretation. For each book of the Bible, its interpretation depends on an attentive study of the author or authors, the time and place of writing, theme and purpose, literary forms and textual study. Basic to all Biblical Introduction, and part of it, are the principles of interpretation, the art and science of exegesis. It depends too upon many auxiliary sciences such as philology, geography, history and archaeology.

biblical revival The renewed interest among Catholics in the study of the Bible. Initiated around the turn of the century by the work of such biblical scholars as Pere Lagrange, O.P., the movement was given added impetus by the encyclical of Pope Pius XII, *Divino Afflante Spiritu,* September, 1943. This encyclical urged Catholic scholars to make use of new discoveries in archaeology; better knowledge of Hebrew, Aramaic and Greek, the languages in which the Sacred Books were written; and better understanding of the customs and rites of the ancient peoples of the Near East of whom the Hebrews, God's Chosen People, were a part. Other Christian non-Catholics had made great advances in these fields in their effort better to understand the Word of God. Now the Holy See is giving encouragement to Catholic biblical scholars to enter these fields of archaeology and linguistics, so that they will relay to the Catholic faithful the real meaning of the Sacred Books. Catholic scholars are urged to be aware of literary forms, such as sacred myth, history, poetry and proverb used by the author to convey sacred truth. Today Catholic exegetes, like Pierre Benoit, O.P. or Roland deVaux, O.P., are in the front ranks of original contributors to our knowledge of the Sacred Text. American Catholic exegetes are not to be left out either, men such as Robert North, S.J. and Barnabas Ahern, C.P. But the Catholic Scripture revival is not only taking place among the scholars. Scripture courses in the seminaries are being conducted in the light of archaeology and better understanding of the manuscripts. For the lay Catholic many parishes have started Bible study clubs.

bigamy (Gr. *bi,* double; *gamos,* marriage) The state that results when a party already married goes through a marriage ceremony with another in an attempt to contract a second valid marriage. The offender incurs infamy and is bound to separate under penalty of interdict or excommunication.

bigot A person who through ignorance or prejudice adheres unreasonably to a religious belief or practice and is intolerant of the views of others.

Bill of Rights Ten amendments to the Constitution of the United States passed by Congress on September 25, 1789, and ratified by the states on December 15, 1791. They assert individual rights which exist of themselves as inborn and inalienable, which cannot be given by the state, but are acknowledged by it. These ideas go back to the British Bill of Rights and the common-law notion of government. The British Bill of Rights (1689) confirmed freedoms which the people had gained during centuries of striving, these rights granted to its subjects generally, but not to Catholics. In England under Henry VIII, Edward VI and Elizabeth I, the establishment of a state church and the view that dissenters were traitors forbade freedom of worship. This fundamental right was confirmed in the American Bill of Rights by the provisions of the First Amendment: "Congress shall make no law respecting the establishment of religion, or prohibiting the free exercise thereof." In recent years the interpretation of this amendment has received considerable discussion. It is argued on one side that the framers of the Constitution had in mind the state church of England when the amendment was written and that its purpose was solely to prevent a national state church being erected in the United States. Its aim was to forbid preferential treatment of one denomination over another, and that it was not the intention of the framers to make the state neutral to all religions or religious values. On the other side the argument is made that the amendment prohibits state support, recognition or assistance to any religion or religions. Extremists who support this latter view claim the amendment prohibits chapels and chaplains on military installations, and forbids recognition of God in the national motto of the United States. Various cases have been brought before the Supreme Court but except in certain instances, such as school prayer, no clear adjudication has been made.

bilocation   A miraculous phenomenon in which one individual appears to be present personally in more than one place at the same time. Bilocation is contrary to reason only when

actual physical presence in several places is implied.

bination   Exercise of the faculty or permission to say two Masses. This faculty is given by the ordinary, when necessary, to accommodate all those obliged to attend Mass.

binding and loosing   The power of the keys exercised in the Sacrament of Penance. Christ gave to Peter and the Apostles (Matt. 16:18) the power to forgive sins, which in turn has been handed down to bishops and priests.

biretta   A stiff square cap, black, red or purple, used by many Western clergymen and worn at various times such as entering and leaving church and at special moments during services.

birth control   Contraception in the wide sense is any positive method used to prevent conception. Contraception is distinguished from negative birth control which consists in either continuous or periodic abstinence from sexual relations, commonly called the "rhythm" method of controlling conception. Methods of birth control vary. Permanent prevention of conception is caused by surgical operations like vasectomy and salpingectomy. Other methods of birth control are the use of condoms, diaphrams, douches, suppositories or other chemical means. All these latter means are called "artificial" means of birth control and are condemned as mortal sins by the Church, for violating the natural law and purpose of marriage.

birth control pill   A synthetic hormone that achieves an antifertility effect by suppressing ovulation, thus creating the absence of conditions necessary for pregnancy. These pills can be used for legitimate purposes (e.g., correcting a female cycle) under the supervision of a competent doctor provided that the intent is not directly contraceptive even though the infertility is foreseen.

bisexual A person who seeks sexual gratification with both men and women.

bishop (AS. *biscop,* from L. *episcopus,* bishop) One who has received the fullness of the Sacrament of Holy Orders, a successor to the Apostles. Only bishops have the power to administer Holy Orders and consecrate other bishops. Although subject to the authority of the Holy See, bishops exercise their powers by virtue of their office. Ordinarily a bishop administers the temporal and spiritual affairs of a diocese, and is responsible before God for the faithful of his diocese in the manner that a shepherd is responsible for his flock.

bishop, auxiliary A titular bishop who is appointed by the Holy See to assist a ruling bishop.

bishop, coadjutor A bishop who is appointed to administer a diocese because the residential bishop is incapable of acting. The term is also applied to a bishop who is appointed to assist a residential bishop but who is granted the right of succession.

bishop-elect One who has been named a bishop but who has not yet been consecrated.

Bishop of Rome The pope, the Supreme Pontiff of the Catholic Church.

bishop, residential The ordinary of a diocese, the bishop of a diocese.

bishop, suffragan A bishop of a diocese other than a metropolitan. For example, the Bishop of Buffalo is a suffragan bishop to the Archbishop of New York, for New York is the metropolitan see of the Archdiocese of New York.

bishop, titular Since every bishop must be consecrated with a title to a see, those bishops who are not residential bishops are consecrated to a diocese which at one time existed but because of loss of faith or population no longer exists. An ordinary who resigns his see receives a titular title. A titular bishop has no ordinary jurisdiction in the area to which he holds title.

bishopric The see or diocese of a bishop, the church district which he controls, as well as the position and authority of a bishop.

bishops, appointment of The pope reserves to himself the right to appoint all bishops in the Western Church although the mode of nomination varies. In some cases a cathedral chapter or other body may elect a nominee. In other cases the clergy hold a terna from which the three leading candidates are suggested to the Holy See. In some countries the civil authorities make the nomination; this system is permitted for specific reasons, e.g., the king of Spain was granted the *patronato real,* which included the right to name bishops; this has been carried over to some Latin American governments. In the Eastern Church the system varies greatly. In some cases the patriarch is chosen by a synod of bishops and confirmed by the Holy See. Melkite bishops are elected by the clergy from among three candidates submitted by the Patriarch of Antioch.

bishops, collegiality of The body or college of bishops, as the successors to the college of the Apostles in the office of teaching, sanctifying and ruling, which always with its head, the pope, possesses full and supreme power over the whole Church. Christian tradition has consistently regarded the college of bishops as successor to the college of the Apostles. This college of bishops is in itself a moral person. The authority of the pope is universal and sovereign. The authority of the bishops depends upon the pope, not in its origin which is divine, but in its exercise. Thus the Church is a living society with an organization and hierarchy led by the Apostles, that is the bishops; and in first place by Peter, that is, the pope.

Bishops' Committee for the Spanish Speaking An organization of the American hierarchy founded in 1945 to work for the spiritual and material welfare of the Spanish-speaking in the United States. The committee is particularly concerned with Spanish-speaking people in the Southwest, and with migrants. *See* National Catholic Council for the Spanish Speaking.

bishops, jurisdiction of Only the pope has universal jurisdiction. The bishops as successors of the Apostles govern their dioceses with ordinary jurisdiction under the authority of the pope. They cannot act against common law (the law of the Church as contained in canon law) and they have no jurisdiction over exempt religious. The bishop has supreme direction in all else.

bishops, obligations of A bishop must reside in his diocese, be present in his cathedral at certain times of the year and complete a pastoral visitation of his diocese every five years. He must make expected reports to the Holy See and perform *ad limina* visitations to the Holy See. It is also the obligation of a bishop to rule and govern his diocese, safeguarding and developing the faith of his people.

black A liturgical color used in the liturgy of the dead.

black fast A fast which excludes the use of wine, flesh meat, eggs, cheese, milk and butter. Not of obligation.

Black Friars 1. An English term applied to Dominicans because of the black mantle that is part of their habit. 2. A dramatic group organized by the Dominican Fathers in New York City, known for its experimental theater. 3. A publication of the English Dominicans carrying important articles and reviews.

Black Legend A legend perpetuated in Anglo-Saxon history that the Spanish explorers and conquerors were evil men, greedy, rapacious and cruel, who sought only their own glory and gold. On the other hand, the English explorers and conquerors were men of great sacrifice and devotion, whose only purpose in conquest was the advancement of the English crown. Henry Morgan, whose rape of Panama and Caribbean piracy made him a scourge of the Spanish colonists, was knighted for his actions. It is only later history that has shown that the Spanish conquistadors were sincere men of their times. They had a hatred and terror of heresy and saw their actions as a new crusade. They discovered a New World, conquered it, founded great cities and taught millions of natives to revere the name of Christ. It has been pointed out by some historians that in those countries settled by the Spanish, the Indians are today a major element in the population; but in those countries settled by Anglo-Saxons, the Indians have disappeared.

Black Madonna An image of the Blessed Virgin Mary which is made of black material or painted in dark shades, or which has turned black from age. One such very famous image is the jeweled icon of Our Lady of Czestochowa (chen-sto-ko′ va) in a monastery shrine on the hill of Jasna Gora in Poland, where pilgrims through the ages have come to pray. The picture has always been particularly loved by gypsies because of the dark color of its painted face and hands. The Lady of Czestochowa is the special patron of the Polish people and her basilica on Jasna Gora (Bright Mountain) is their national shrine, a solace to them in their many sorrows and persecutions. Another famous madonna is the black carved wooden statue of Our Lady of Montserrat in Spain. The statue has been venerated in her shrine on top of the "Sawtooth Mountain" (Montserrat) for over a thousand years, and millions of pilgrims including kings and saints (St. Ignatius Loyola, St. Vincent Ferrer) have worshiped there.

Black Mass 1. The Requiem Mass or Mass of the Dead, so called because black vestments are worn by the minister. 2. The name given to a mocking and sacrilegious rite performed by satanic apostates or infidels.

"Black Pope" A nickname given to the Superior General of the Jesuits who resides in Rome. The "black" comes from the black Jesuit cassock.

Blaise, Blessing of St. The blessing of throats on the Feast of St. Blaise, Feb. 3. The throat of the person to be blessed is centered between two crossed white candles while the person kneels before the altar rail and the priest says: "May God deliver you from trouble of the throat and from every other evil through the intercession of St. Blaise, bishop and martyr. In the name of the Father, and of the Son, and of the Holy Spirit. Amen."

blasphemy (Gr. *blasphemia*). Irreverent words or actions dishonoring God. Direct blasphemy is: *heretical,* which denies God's providence; and *imprecatory,* which invokes some evil against God. Indirect blasphemy is directed against the attributes of God, the Church, the saints, sacred things, etc. Unintentional blasphemies in speech are to be guarded against.

blasphemy of the Spirit, the *See* sin against the Holy Spirit.

bless oneself, to (AS. *blestian*) to make the Sign of the Cross on oneself.

Blessed The title of one who has been beatified. This is the step immediately prior to canonization. *See* canonization, beatification.

blessed earth, holy ground Ground which has been consecrated for Catholic burial. *See* cemetery.

blessed in heaven All the souls in heaven who are enjoying the Beatific Vision. After the Last Judgment, these souls will be united with their bodies in a glorified state.

Blessed Sacrament A title given to the sacrament of the Body and Blood of Jesus Christ, the Holy Eucharist, called "blessed" to indicate its preeminence among the seven sacraments.

Blessed Trinity (L. *trini,* threefold) The three Persons in one God; the Father, the Son and the Holy Spirit. The Son proceeds from the Father by generation and the Holy Spirit proceeds from the Father and Son by spiration. The term indicates the central doctrine of the Catholic Church. Each of these persons is distinct from the others, yet each is the true God with all of His infinite perfections. All life begins in the Trinity, comes from the Trinity and is destined to end in the Trinity. The Trinity is the mystery of divine mysteries. It represents a mutual giving so complete that the Divine Persons do not exist except in relation to one another. These three Persons are co-equal, co-eternal and consubstantial. The *Gloria* is the chief prayer honoring the Blessed Trinity.

blessing Placing a thing or person under the care of God. A liturgical blessing is one that uses a prescribed formula or ceremony, and is given by a priest except for those blessings reserved to pope or bishop. The simplest blessing is made with the Sign of the Cross and is sometimes accompanied by sprinkling of holy water. Official blessings of the Church are contained in the Roman Ritual. Once an object is blessed the blessing is lost only if the object is sold or totally destroyed.

blessing, apostolic A blessing or benediction given by the Pope at audiences and functions over which he presides. The power to give this blessing is delegated to bishops and others under certain circumstances, including any priest who is giving the last rites to the sick. It bestows a plenary indulgence at the moment of death, under the usual conditions.

blessing, last 1. The blessing given to a person about to die. A plenary indulgence is attached. 2. The blessing given at the end of Mass.

blessing of aircraft *See* aircraft blessing.

blessing, papal The blessing or benediction given by the pope. A plenary indulgence is attached. The blessing is given at the end of liturgical functions and sometimes at the close of papal audiences. It is also given from the window of the papal apartments to crowds in St. Peter's Square. On solemn occasions it is given *urbi et orbi* (to the city and the world) from the balcony of St. Peter's Basilica.

The blessing can be delegated; e.g., priests can give the apostolic blessing to the sick who are on the threshold of death.

bliss (AS. blithe, happy) The perfect happiness of heaven; eternal beatitude.

block Rosary A devotion in which the people of a neighborhood gather at a different home each evening to recite the Rosary.

blood, Baptism of A substitute for Baptism of water in one who, not yet baptized, suffers martyrdom for the Faith, or for a Christian virtue. Since no greater love can be shown than that of laying down one's life for God, martyrdom forgives sin and gives sanctifying grace to the soul. The martyr is "baptized in his own blood." Even infants can receive this Baptism.

blood, shedding of The reception of the Sacrament of Holy Orders is rendered unlawful, though not invalid, in the case of a candidate who has shed blood voluntarily in any of the following ways: by murder or abortion, by cooperating in these crimes or by mutilating himself or others. Clerics who have practiced medicine or surgery unlawfully and have thereby caused a death incur an impediment against the *exercise* of Holy Orders. Bloodshed in the above causes constitutes a canonical impediment or irregularity (*q.v.*). A murder or any crime of violence accompanied by the shedding of a considerable amount of blood constitutes a violation of a church if committed within its walls, but not if committed in the sacristy, the porch or the bell tower. A church which has been violated by bloodshed must have the Blessed Sacrament removed, the altars stripped and all services discontinued until it has been reconciled by a priest or (if it is a conse-crated church) by the bishop. Private chapels do not come under this rule.

blue A color much used in modern times to symbolize Our Lady. It is not a liturgical color throughout the Church at present, although it was often used in pre-Reformation times. No general rule as to color was kept throughout the Church in those days, but blue was prescribed in some places for virgins who were not mar-tyrs, and for confessors. Even to-day in Spanish and Latin American churches blue vestments are used on the feast of the Immaculate Concep-tion.

Blue Army, the (Full title: the Blue Army of Our Lady of Fatima) An institute founded in 1946 to pray for the conversion of Russia and for world peace, as urged by Our Lady of Fatima. It has world-wide mem-bership. Its headquarters are in Washington, N.J.

blue laws A term referring to laws which overregulate morality; laws which infringe on private morality; Puritanical laws. The origin of the term is contested. One reference is to the blue covers which bound the ses-sion laws of Connecticut. At various times these laws have been against gambling, Sunday travel, Sunday en-tertainment, certain wearing apparel, etc.

boat A small vessel, in the shape of an ancient boat, which holds the in-cense that is to be put into the thuri-ble or censer. When a boat is pictured as riding on waves, it is a symbol of the Church, the bark of Peter.

boat bearer The server at a Solemn Mass or other ceremony who carries the incense boat. Very often this in-dividual is omitted and the thurifer carries both thurible and boat.

bodily defect An irregularity that

prevents a person from saying Mass or fulfilling the functions of Holy Or-ders. Such irregularity might be blindness, the loss of a thumb, etc. Dispensations from such irregular-ities must be obtained from the Holy See.

body It is Catholic teaching that one's body is holy. It is the temple of the Holy Spirit and the tabernacle to which Christ physically comes in the Holy Eucharist. Therefore, one's body should be treated with respect by oneself and by others. It should be clothed in modesty and dignity, and we are obligated to keep it strong and healthy in order to serve God and mankind better. Owing to orig-inal sin, certain powers of the body tend to lead away from God. One must be alert to keep these powers under control, and to maintain them in the service of the creator and the whole man.

body and soul The whole man. Both body and soul are incomplete in themselves but when united they form man, a complete substance. Man's acts are posited by this union of body and soul.

body, glorified The body which will be assumed by the soul at the end of the world. It will be immortal and incorruptible (1 Cor. 15:53). Man is a creature of both body and soul, and to exist as a disembodied spirit would be contrary to his nature. To prove that God will reunite us with our bodies, He raised up His Son, Jesus Christ, from the grave.

body, resurrection of It is a dogma of Faith that the body will be resur-rected and reunited to the soul. There are many references in Scripture to this fact, including the words of Christ. St. Paul (1 Cor. 15:33) ex-plicitly says that we shall rise again incorruptible. This means that the body will live again after death and as such will enjoy the beatitude of heaven or the agony of hell.

Bolivia Until 1552, when the first bishop for what is now Bolivia was appointed, the area was governed from Cuzco, Peru. In 1825 the country's independence from Spain was proclaimed. Today there are 2 archdioceses, 5 dioceses and 3 prelatures nullius. In addition there are 6 vicariates apostolic which are mission territories. Although statistics claim almost the entire 4 million population to be Catholics (50,000 Protestants), this Catholicism is in name only. Bolivia is faced with grave economic and spiritual problems. The majority of the population (Indian) live in misery, lacking decent housing and food. Some 70 per cent of the population over 5 years of age is illiterate. Almost the same percentage is born illegitimate. Alcoholism, Communism, lack of communications, Indian dialects and a scarcity of priests (one priest to every 5,000 Catholics) arc some of the other problems. On the positive side is the aid being given from outside. American Maryknollers and Franciscans, priests from several United States dioceses, Canadian missioners and others are assisting to restore the Faith. A national vocational effort is being made and many parishes once closed are being reopened. The Jesuits and Maryknollers each conduct two radio stations and the Canadian Oblates have one, used for basic education and catechetics.

Bolshevism (Russ. *bolshinstvo,* majority) First applied to the political followers of Lenin in 1903 when his movement received a majority vote at the Second Congress of the Russian Social-Democratic Labor Party in London. Actually a forerunner of

the present Communist party. The movement had as part of its aim the destruction of economic capitalism. It also aimed at state ownership of goods and dictatorship of the proletariat.

Book of Common Prayer The book used in the Anglican prayer service.

Book of Hours A form of breviary used in monasteries during the Middle Ages. It contained prayers, psalms, canticles, antiphons, responses, etc.

Book of Life, the A term used in Apoc. 20:15. Those who in God's knowledge are saved or are to be saved are written in the Book of Life.

"born Catholic" A term used of one born of Catholic parents and reared in the Faith, whereas one converted and baptized later in life is said to be a convert, not a "born Catholic." The term is popularly used, but is essentially nonsensical, as there is no such thing as a "born Catholic." All Catholics enter the Church through the Sacrament of Baptism. So-called "born Catholics" are sometimes, more accurately, called "cradle Catholics."

Boston Capital of Massachusetts. The first known visit of a priest to the city was in 1646 when a ship was in port with two priests aboard who were made guests of the governor. The *Weekly Rehearsal* for March 20, 1732, carried the following announcement: "Mass has been performed in town this winter by an Irish priest among some Catholics of his own nation." During the French and Indian War, 100 French Catholics were arrested as a danger to the colony but released by the sheriff. Anti-Catholic bigotry was so strong that General Washington rebuked the soldiers who insulted the religion of those with whom he was trying to form an alliance. On All Saints' Day, 1788, the first Catholic church in New England was opened here. The first Catholic bishop, Bishop Cheverus, was appointed in 1810. By 1844 Catholics numbered one-quarter of the population but had never elected a Catholic to public office. The first Catholic member of the Common Council was elected in 1857; the first alderman in 1870. The diocese was raised to an archdiocese in 1875. Under Cardinals O'Connell and Cushing the archdiocese has made tremendous progress, and has been the home of many national movements.

bowing A lesser form of reverence than genuflecting. The latest rubrics have simplified bows of the head; a body bow may be either slight or profound. Head bows are made during ceremonies to advise the ministers when they are to perform an action.

boycott An organized severance of business relations with a firm or individual in order to punish or coerce. The word is derived from Captain Boycott, a notoriously harsh land agent in Ireland, who was first "boycotted" by the Irish patriot, Parnell. It is a common weapon in the United States, used by labor unions and minority groups. A boycott is a moral weapon, provided there is sufficient reason for its application and it is free of violence. It is generally held that a secondary boycott is an unjust infringement of one's right to free intercourse with others.

Brazil In 1500 the first priests arrived in Brazil with the early explorers, and the Jesuits arrived in 1549 for the evangelization of the Indians. Today Brazil has 29 archdioceses, 106 dioceses, 35 prelatures nullius and 1 abbey nullius. There are 3 cardinals. There are almost 70 million Catholics in a population of over 72 million (93 per cent). There are 12,000 priests, making approximately one priest for every 5,700 Catholics. There are many problems facing the Church in Brazil, not the least of which is the country itself: immense in size, great distances between cities, a scattered population, deficient communications, considerable migration and serious economic problems. On the religious side is the serious lack of priests and Sisters, religious ignorance, insufficient lay organization, weak spiritual life of most people, and superstition and spiritism. However, there are positive elements in favor of the Church. The people are basically Catholic and respond when priests are made available. Outside help is coming to Brazil: American Franciscans and Redemptorists each have sizable contingents there. The Brazilian hierarchy is socially dynamic and apostolic, with good relations between Church and State. More and more young Brazilians are entering the lay apostolate and the number of seminarians is steadily increasing. A nationwide Catholic radio apostolate is very active. Protestantism has had a phenomenal growth in Brazil, partly from immigration and partly from conversions. In 1915 there were 50,000 Protestants; today there are over 4 million, 5.7 per cent of the population.

breach of promise The refusal by one party to go through with a marriage. In the case of a canonical betrothal, breach of promise is actionable in ecclesiastical court to obtain damages. No action can be taken, however, to force the marriage.

bread One of the elements for the matter of the Mass, wine being the other. It is used as the matter for the Holy Eucharist. Bread also has some minor liturgical usages, such as cleansing the fingers after certain rites, as in the anointing of the sick.

bread, blessed　There is a form in the Roman Ritual for the blessing of bread. *See* antidoron, pain bénit.

bread, Eucharistic　The bread used in the liturgy of the Western Church is an unleavened round wafer, varying in size. Except for the Armenians, Maronites, and Catholic Malabarese, the Eastern Churches use leavened bread, usually in the form of small cakes or loaves. In some places salt and oil are added.

Bread of Life　A name Christ applied to Himself (Jn. 6:48). It refers to the Eucharistic Christ in which He appears under the species of bread.

breaking of Bread　1. The breaking of the Host into three parts in the Mass. The smallest portion is dropped into the chalice to mix with the wine (Precious Blood). 2. The act by which the disciples at Emmaus recognized Christ after His Resurrection. 3. A fresco in the catacomb of St. Priscilla that shows the Eucharistic Banquet.

breath　A biblical symbol for life itself. It is also used to express the outward form of the soul. In the latter sense it can mean a human being.

breathing　The breathing of air on a person or thing is a symbol of life and of exorcism. God breathed on Adam to give him life. Jesus breathed on His Apostles to symbolize their spiritual life. In Baptism the priest breathes on the one being baptized to symbolize the expulsion of evil spirits to make room for the spirit of spiritual life. Breathing is also used in consecrating oil of chrism and oil of catechumens, and in blessing baptismal water.

brethren of the Lord　A term used to describe cousins in New Testament times. It appears in Matt. 12:46; 13:55, and Jn. 7:3. The perpetual virginity of Mary is an article of faith which follows from Lk. 1:34. Four of these cousins are named in Matt. 13:55; they are James, Joseph, Simon and Jude. The "brethren of the Lord" were among the most important members of the early Jerusalem church (Acts 1:15).

breve　A papal brief. *See* brief, papal.

Breviarium Romanum　*See* Breviary.

Breviary (L. *breviarium,* an abridgment)　The liturgical book, divided into two volumes since Pope John XXIII's reform (1960), which contains the "Prayer of the Hours," which are set forms of prayers consisting of psalms, readings and hymns that are meant to sanctify the different hours of the natural day. All clerics in major orders are obliged to recite it daily, hence it is sometimes called "the Office." Vatican Council II approved further modifications in the structure of the various Hours. The book takes its name from that fact that it presents in a single work materials formerly to be found dispersed in the Bible, writings of the Fathers, etc. *See* Compline, Lauds, Matins, None, Prime, Sext, Terce, Vespers.

bribery　A reward, gift or favor bestowed or promised to another in order to prevent or corrupt the conduct or judgment of a person in a position of trust. It ordinarily refers to subversion of a public trust but can occur in any walk of life. Bribery in any form is immoral since it corrupts justice and duty. The guilt rests with all who participate in the bribe.

bride of Christ　A term used of women who have vowed their chastity to God, for the purpose of being more closely united to Christ. The term thus used is incorrect, since Christ has only one bride, the Church. Consecrated persons, whether men or women, who have taken vows of chastity for Christ, are merely more *deeply rooted* in the Church thereby. Like all Christians in the state of grace, though in a different degree, they partake of the nature of the Church, the virginal Spouse of Christ.

brief, papal A papal document less formal than a bull. It is signed by the secretary for briefs and stamped with the pope's ring, i.e., the Ring of the Fisherman.

Briefs to Princes, Secretariate of A papal secretariate whose task is to compose letters from the pope to heads of state and other important personages.

Brother A form of address used for novices and postulants in certain religious orders of men, and for lay brothers in orders of priests; also for men who belong to congregations whose members do not usually become priests. The term is used formally, as in documents, in referring to friars who may be priests, i.e., Franciscans or Dominicans. The collective name "Brothers" is used of those congregations and institutes of men whose members do teaching, nursing or other works of charity and do not become priests. The Alexian Brothers, the Christian Brothers and the Xaverian Brothers are some examples. The Marianist Brothers, whose work is teaching, ordain a few members to the priesthood to take care of their own religious needs. A modern foundation, the Little Brothers of Jesus, following the example of the hermit Father Charles de Foucauld, has members who make a living by manual labor and lead a life of contemplation. Another modern association, the pious union of the Little Brothers of the Poor, aims toward giving Christlike devotion and joy to the poor together with material aid.

brotherhood of man In the natural order, genetics teaches that all men are biologically the same. In the historical order, even though at present there are various races (anthropologists are not in agreement as to the criteria for distinguishing different races), there are strong indications of a common lineage of all men. In the spiritual order, our Faith teaches that all men are created equal, have a common dignity and a common destiny. In the supernatural order, all men are called to be brothers of Christ and have a potentiality for this fulfillment of their being in God's family. The Judaeo-Christian heritage teaches the brotherhood of men under the fatherhood of God; for Christians, this has a solid foundation in Faith.

brotherly love Fraternal charity. Loving everyone as a brother in the family of God, our Father. Christians are commanded by Christ to love all men in this way.

Buddhism The system of religious thought and practice taught by Siddhartha Gautama (*c.* 563 B.C.) later called the Buddha, the Enlightened One. Despite his being a prince with a young wife, a child, several palaces and great riches, he left them all when 29 and went out as a wandering monk, trying to solve the problems of human suffering, of life and of death. He came to certain conclusions which he preached for 45 years as he traveled over Northern India. The basis of his teaching is that suffering is universal, that the cause of suffering is craving, that the elimination of craving is the answer to all problems. Buddhism accepted the common Brahmanic belief in reincarnation, that after death the soul is reborn into a state higher or lower according to its merits in this life. When a man by the practice of Buddhist rules attains to sainthood, having no desires, he will escape further incarnations and at death will be absorbed in nirvana. Various groups of Buddhists differ in the exact meaning of nirvana and of the soul's state in bliss. According to some, there is a real and eternal nirvana, but the departed saint no longer exists. He has been absorbed in the eternal Entity. For him suffering is over, and so is existence. Modern versions of Buddhist teaching have modified the ancient beliefs, encourage works of charity to serve the saints (departed Buddhas) and teach that Buddha pardons sins and showers graces upon those who wish to become saints. At death they will be reborn into the Paradise of Buddha. These ideas would seem to have borrowed something from Christianity. Zen Buddhism, based on meditation and rigid discipline, is a form which was introduced into Japan about the 12th century A.D. where it has millions of adherents. Its asceticism and mysticism are attractive to some Westerners who have grown up without ever having looked seriously into the Christianity which surrounds them. Buddhism has been a great civilizing force for the Orient, where it has perhaps 500 million followers, about the same as the number of Roman Catholics in the world. Buddhism, with other great pagan religions, was founded within a century of the destruction of Jerusalem, 586 B.C., about the time the Prophet Isaia was speaking of the Christ to come.

Buddha was living in 560 B.C.; Lao Tsu in 570–490; Confucius 551–478; Zoroaster perhaps about the same time. The Holy Spirit, speaking through Isaia to the Chosen People, seemed to be making His presence felt in the pagan world as well. There, men of good will were led, according to the Natural Law, to renew their stumbling quest for their Creator and Savior. As St. Paul said to the pagans of Lystra (Acts 14: 16–17). "In the generations that are past (God) let all the nations follow their own ways, yet He did not leave Himself without testimony. . . ."

bugia A candlestick with a straight handle. It is held at the Missal in a bishop's low Mass. It takes its name from Bougie, Algeria, where candlewax was once obtained.

bull, papal (L. *bulla,* a seal) An important document issued by the pope and sealed with a disk of lead called a "bulla," whence derives the name. Each bishop is appointed by a bull. Other major papal documents are often called bulls, though they have various special names.

bullarium A collection of bulls or other papal documents.

Bureau of Information A public relations bureau established in many dioceses in the United States to represent the bishop for mass communications media. There is a national Bureau of Information set up at the National Catholic Welfare Conference.

burial, Christian Deposit of a body in a grave or tomb, usually in a cemetery or consecrated ground, preceded by Requiem Mass and/or other Christian funeral rites.

burial, ecclesiastical The interment of a deceased person in consecrated ground following the funeral rites of the Church. All baptized persons, including catechumens, are entitled to Christian burial but it is to be denied to some for grave reasons; those to whom Christian burial is denied are persons who are apostates, culpable suicides, heretics, schismatics, unrepentant public sinners, excommunicated, interdicted, and those killed in a duel. *See* cremation.

burse (L. *bursa,* a purse) 1. The  square, flat, cloth-covered case in which the corporal is carried on the chalice. It is made of the same cloth and design as the vestments. 2. The leather, silk-lined purse in which the pyx is placed when the Blessed Sacrament is carried to the sick. It usually has a string which is worn about the neck for safe carrying. 3. A fund, set up with a college or seminary, which is invested and the interest applied against the education of a student.

Burundi In 1879 the first White Fathers arrived in this nation in the very heart of Africa. Today there are 1 archdiocese and 3 dioceses; approximately 60 per cent of the population (2.3 million) is Catholic. Of the nearly 300 priests almost 25 per cent are natives of Burundi.

buskins Silken half boots reaching to  the knees and worn over the bishop's purple stockings at a pontifical Mass. They are the same color as the other vestments but are not worn with black vestments.

bussolanti Name given to the lay chamberlains who are on guard in the anterooms leading to the pope's apartment.

buying and selling The exchange be-tween persons of goods or services for an agreed price. The seller must have legitimate possession, the amount of money involved must satisfy both parties, the buyer must have true knowledge of the condition or quality of the item exchanged and it must be delivered to the buyer in the condition it was when he bought it.

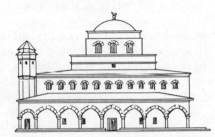

Byzantine art The art developed in Constantinople (Byzantium) after it became the capital of Constantine. It was an amalgam of Greek and early Christian art making lavish use of color and decoration, limited to painting and carving on flat surfaces, avoiding all sculpture. It has never been equaled in its miniatures and mosaic work. Byzantine architecture is noted for its vaulted roofs and its dome supported on pendentives. Decoration was rich in marbles and mosaics and high relief in sculpture was avoided. Wood was not used in construction. St. Mark's in Venice is an example of Byzantine art. The Greek Orthodox Cathedral in Los Angeles is the finest example of Byzantine art and architecture in the United States.

Byzantine Church The Patriarchate of Constantinople. The term comes from Byzantium, the old name for the city. Sometimes the term is used to include all who follow the Byzantine Liturgy.

Byzantine Empire The Roman Empire in the East founded by Constantine at his capital, Constantinople. The empire finally fell to the Turks in 1453.

Byzantine Rite The Byzantine Liturgy takes it name from Constantinople, formerly Byzantium, where it came into full flower and whence it spread across the Near East and into Europe. Popularly, it is called the "Greek Rite" because of its Greek origin. It is the second most widely used liturgy, being preceded only by the Roman Rite. It is used by many million Eastern Orthodox Christians and by several million Catholic Byzantines. Its liturgy is in many languages, vernacular and other. Two forms of Mass (Liturgy) are used in the Byzantine Rite, that of St. John Chrysostom which is the regular liturgy and that of St. Basil which is used on ten occasions during the year. The ceremonial and public prayers of both are identical but the private prayers of the priest are much longer in the Liturgy of St. Basil. In the Byzantine Mass the deacon plays an important role, acting as link between priest and people. Concelebration is frequently practiced.

Byzantine Rite, Catholics of the Those Catholics who are in union with the Pope of Rome but whose liturgy is according to the Byzantine Rite. They number nearly one million in the United States and Canada. Byzantine Catholics use leavened altar breads, give Communion under both species, baptize by immersion and permit a married clergy.

C

Caeremoniale Episcoporum Bishop's book of ceremonies, first published in 1600. Latest revision was in 1886. Some sections are out of date because of changes in the rubrics made in recent years. Vatican Council II ordered the revision of this and the other liturgical books.

caeremoniarius Master of ceremonies, a minor minister in solemn liturgical functions who directs the service, advising the others of their duties.

Caesarian operation A surgical operation designed to deliver a child through incisions made in the womb. This operation, also called Caesarian section, is performed when delivery cannot be made in the normal manner. Even in cases with some risk for the safety of child or mother, this operation is permitted when necessary.

Cain *See* Abel.

CAIP Peace Award Annual award to an American who has helped through his actions to further Christian principles of justice and charity in international affairs, made by the Catholic Association of International Peace. Among winners have been Senator Brian McMahon, Bishop Raymond A. Lane, M.M., Thomas E. Murray, Father John LaFarge, S.J.

calced (L. *calceus,* a shoe) This adjective is used to distinguish certain religious, as wearing shoes, from a branch of their order that wears sandals or goes barefoot, e.g., Discalced or Calced Carmelites.

calefactory (L. *calefacere,* to warm) 1. A heated room in a monastery where monks retire to warm themselves. 2. A kind of hot-water bottle used in medieval times by a priest to warm his fingers while distributing Holy Communion.

calendar (L. *calendarium,* an account book) 1. A system of reckoning time; an orderly arrangement of time according to days, months and years. 2. In scriptural times, the week contained seven days ending on the Sabbath (Saturday). The year consisted of twelve lunar months of twenty-nine or thirty days, for a total of 354 days. The month began with the new moon. The new year began at the new moon nearest to and preceding the vernal equinox (March 21). To make a balance between the lunar and solar calendar an extra lunar month was added every two or three years. 3. Liturgical. A cycle composed of days, weeks, months, feasts and seasons for the entire year. The liturgical calendar centers about Easter which falls on the Sunday after the full moon of the vernal equinox. From this date other movable feasts are calculated. Christmas also determines other feasts. The liturgical year begins with the first Sunday of Advent. In the Western Church many religious orders and dioceses have special calendars based on the Roman calendar. At Vatican Council II the Fathers stated that they were not opposed to the establishment of a universal calendar.

calendar, Armenian Has seven feasts on fixed dates; Christmas–Epiphany, Circumcision, Entry into the Temple (Candlemas), Annunciation, Our Lady's Birthday, Presentation of Our Lady, Immaculate Conception. The Sundays are reckoned as occurring after Easter. Only about 130 saints' feasts are observed in a year. Many saints' feast days commemorate groups of saints; e.g., the Martyrs of Persia, the Hermits of Egypt. Armenians in communion with Rome have taken over various Western practices. The dissidents of this rite are the only non-Protestant Christians to celebrate Christmas and the Epiphany as one feast, on January 6.

calendar, Byzantine The Church year begins Sept. 1. Of special importance is the period running from the Sunday falling ten Sundays before Easter to the Saturday after Pentecost. Feasts are divided into those of Our Lord, of Our Lady and of the Saints. Each day one or more feasts are commemorated; there is much variety from country to country in these celebrations. Sundays are named after the subject of the Gospel of the Sunday in question; cf., "Good Shepherd Sunday" in the Roman Rite. The calendar devotes days to Old Testament saints: Dec. 11, The Ancestors of the Messias; Sunday before Christmas, All the Fathers,

from Adam to St. Joseph, who were pleasing to God.

calendar, Chaldean Divides the Church year into ten unequal periods from Advent to the general feast of the Dedication of the Church. The customs and discipline of Chaldeans in communion with Rome have drawn steadily closer to the customs and discipline of the Latin Rite. They follow the Gregorian Calendar. There are about sixty saints' days and feasts; and many of these are movable, occurring very often on Fridays before or after some given point in the Church year; thus, the Four Evangelists are commemorated on the first Friday after Epiphany. Some special Chaldean feasts are the feasts of St. Addai the Apostle, St. Mari, St. James of Nisibis.

calendar, Coptic The Copts reckon their ecclesiastical years from the Era of the Martyrs; that is, from the year A.D. 284, which is the first year of the reign of the Roman Emperor Diocletian. They have seven great feasts of Our Lord and seven lesser feasts of Our Lord. These feasts are celebrated on days differing from the day of celebration elsewhere. About one hundred feasts and saints' days are common to the Coptic and Roman calendars. The Birthday of Our Lord, the Birthday of Our Lady and the Feast of St. Michael are supposed to be celebrated at least once a month.

calendar, ecclesiastical A list of the days of the year with feasts, saints' days, vigils, fasts, liturgical season and the like, noted therein. A very ancient extant calendar is that of Philocalus for Rome (4th century), noting the anniversaries of over thirty martyrs. Ecclesiastical calendars today usually list many more than thirty feasts; and in the general list will be inserted the arrangement of the special feasts of a diocese or a religious community. The liturgical seasons depend on the date of Easter so the ecclesiastical calendar differs from year to year. Harmonization, according to liturgical rules, of feasts having movable dates and feasts having fixed dates is the basis for the annual arrangement of the ecclesiastical calendar.

calendar, Gregorian A reform of the Julian calendar introduced by Pope Gregory XIII in 1582. Under the Julian calendar, fixed days such as the vernal equinox were occurring earlier and earlier. The change was made when Oct. 5, 1582, was called Oct. 15, 1582; thus ten days were dropped from reckoning. To prevent errors in the future, it was decided that only those hundredth years (1600, 1700, 1800, etc.) exactly divisible by 400 should be leap years. This calendar was adopted in England and in British North America in 1752. The Julian calendar is still used by some Eastern Churches. Today, the difference between the two calendars is thirteen days. Since 1900, July 4 by the Julian calendar would be July 17 by the Gregorian calendar. Christmas, according to some Eastern Christian calendars, occurs on Jan. 6 according to Gregorian reckoning.

calendar, Islamic A lunar calendar whose year is made up of twelve months. Its reckoning begins with the year A.D. 622, the year of the Hegira, Muhammad's flight from Mecca to Medina. A Christian year is dated, for example, A.D. 1964 (Anno Domini: in the year of the Lord); so an Islamic year is dated, for example, 1384 A.H. (Anno Hegirae: in the year of the Hegira). Thirty years make up a cycle. The ordinary year has 354

days. Every eleventh year in the cycle is a leap year, counting 355 days. The extra day in a leap year is added at the end of the 12th and last month of the year. The year 1384 A.H. will begin May 13, 1964 A.D. A strict fast is practiced each year in the ninth month, the month of *Ramadhan*.

calendar, Jewish A lunisolar calendar in use among Hebraic peoples, reckoning from the year 3761 B.C., the date traditionally given for the Creation. The Jewish year is made up of twelve months; the week, of seven days. The seventh day is the Sabbath or day of rest. Feasts of the Jewish year are: Rosh Hashanah, New Year, occurring usually in September; Yom Kippur, Day of Atonement, at the end of September or the beginning of October; Hanukkah, Feast of the Dedication, occurring usually in December; Pesach, the Passover, in March or April; Shabuoth, Feast of Weeks, or Pentecost, occurring fifty days after Passover. There is a relation between the Jewish and the Christian year. The day of rest was changed from the seventh to the first day of the week: Sabbath, Sunday. Easter is the fulfillment of the Passover. The coming of the Holy Spirit occurred on Pentecost, the Jewish Feast of Weeks.

calendar, Julian Introduced by Julius Caesar, the hero of the Gallic Wars, in 46 B.C. According to this calendar the year was made up of 365 days. The months had the same names, length and order that they now have in the Gregorian reform of the Julian calendar. But, since every fourth year was a leap year, the year was too long; and fixed days—the vernal equinox, for example—began occurring earlier and earlier. The Julian calendar was in force in the West until A.D. 1582, and is used

92

today by many Christians of Eastern Rites.

calendar of the Roman Church, the general The latest general calendar of the Roman Church was issued in a *Motu Proprio* of Pope John XXIII, dated July 25, 1960. This calendar notes by month and by day, the feasts and observances generally celebrated in the Western Church among those who follow the Roman Rite. Only feasts with fixed dates are noted; the date of Easter, of course, changes from year to year. This calendar is in general use throughout the Western Church; but provinces or divisions of the Church may depart from the general calendar for some peculiar or local observance. For example, December 12 is a day not marked by any saint's feast in the general calendar. In North and South America, though, December 12 is celebrated as the feast of Our Lady of Guadalupe in many regions. Other regions with feasts peculiar to themselves would differ from the general Roman calendar's usage on the days of these feasts and observances. Vatican Council II went on record as not being opposed to additional calendar reform.

calendar, Syrian The feast days in this calendar often occur on unusual dates. Our Lady's Visitation, for instance, comes on the sixth Sunday before Christmas. Catholics of this rite have added Western feasts to their calendar. The Maronite calendar was worked out from this calendar.

California The 31st state of the Union. Named for a mythical island, said to be "next door to Paradise" in the old Spanish romance. Nicknamed "El Dorado" (Sp. gilded). Early Indian inhabitants were Stone Age culture, many of them desert diggers and gatherers. Hernando de Alarcon in 1540 sailed from Aca-pulco into the Colorado River, sighting the lay of the land. In June, 1542, Juan Cabrillo sailed up the coast as far as Drake's Bay and took possession of the land for the King of Spain. In 1579, Francis Drake, after pirating Spanish ships, and before continuing on his voyage around the globe, put in at Drake's Bay near San Francisco. He left there a brass plate claiming the land for England—a relic discovered by picnickers in 1936. In 1602 Sebastian Vizcaino landed on the shore at Monterey. Carmelite Friars who came with him and who may have celebrated the first Mass in Upper California, named the beautiful neighboring valley for our Lady of Mount Carmel. Vizcaino planted a cross, mapped the coast and wrote glowing descriptions of the place. In 1763 France ceded the Louisiana Territory to Spain—including all the land west of the Mississippi, though Spain had always considered both Upper and Lower California part of Mexico. Under Catherine the Great (1762–1796) Russia was extending its fur trade down the west coast of North America. The Spanish grew alarmed and decided to make settlements in Upper California. In 1769 they sent several parties, consisting of troops, artisans and Franciscan Friars, to make settlements and establish missions under the leadership of Don Gaspar de Portola, first governor of California. California was claimed by the United States in 1845 and ceded to it at the end of the war with Mexico. Gold was discovered in 1848, and thousands of "forty-niners" arrived by land and sea from all over the continent and from Europe and Asia. On September 9, 1850, California was admitted as the 31st state of the union. Even after the gold rush subsided the population continued to grow, rich soil and a fine climate contributing. In 1840, while still under the Mexican government, the Franciscan Garcia Diego y Moreno had been appointed Bishop of both Californias. After the United States took over, California was made into two dioceses, with the Vincentian Thaddeus Amat as Bishop of Monterey–Los Angeles, and the Dominican Joseph Alemany as Archbishop of San Francisco. Many Catholics were among the new settlers and the Church was thriving. In 1868 the diocese known later as Sacramento was established, followed in 1922 by the diocese of Monterey–Fresno. In 1936 Los Angeles was raised to archdiocesan rank and the diocese of San Diego established. In 1962 the dioceses of Oakland, Santa Rosa and Stockton were erected. The Jesuits had come to California in 1851, and had begun their work of higher education with Santa Clara University and St. Ignatius College, University of San Francisco. Dominicans, Sulpicians and many other orders of priests and Brothers, as well as numerous groups of Sisters, have established charitable institutions, hospitals, schools, colleges, and centers of social work in the state. California received its first cardinal in 1953, Most Rev. James Francis McIntyre, Archbishop of Los Angeles. There are about three and one-half million Catholics in the state, in a total population of almost 16 million.

California missions, the　A religious, social and economic project of tremendous import, perhaps surpassed only by the Jesuit Reductions of Paraguay and by the conversion and civilization of Europe by the Benedictines and allied orders of monks. In 1769 Don Gaspar de Portola, accompanied by Father Junipero Serra and his band of Franciscan Friars, led an expedition from Mexico into Upper California. Included were a small number of troops (to impress possible hostile Indians), bakers, cooks, blacksmiths, a surgeon and also a few Mexican Indians who could learn the local Indian dialects easily. The Friars brought along cattle, sheep and other livestock, camping outfits, farm implements, church ornaments and vestments. They either brought with them (or procured from home, later) seeds for major field crops and for vegetables, as well as young nursery stock of the olive, orange, fig, lemon, lime and grape. Father Serra founded San Diego (St. James) in the same year (1769), the first of 21 missions built along the Royal Highway (El Camino Real) ending with St. Francis Solano, north of San Francisco. The procedure was the same in all. A cross was set up, a booth of boughs was built, booth and ground were blessed and named for a saint. A bell hung from a tree branch was rung, and any Indians in the neighborhood were invited to attend, were given trinkets, treated kindly and invited to come again. Two Friars were left in each station to build the mission and to instruct and convert the Indians. A few soldiers, artisans and Indian interpreters remained as long as necessary. Father Serra, suffering from a leg ailment, limped from one mission to another as the work grew, overseeing, directing, spending himself for the Indians, his dear children. These usually came in large numbers, many of them half starved, primitive men, Stone Age diggers of desert roots, eaters of ants, grasshoppers, snakes and lizards. Naked savages were clothed, taught agriculture and irrigation, animal husbandry and nearly fifty useful trades. They were instructed in Christian doctrine, taught to speak Spanish, to sing hymns and to play simple musical instruments. In a period of 65 years the Friars built 21 missions, converted over 80,000 Indians, tamed thousands of acres of land, developed grazing lands, pastures, fruitful irrigated fields and orchards. The missions and the mission Indians prospered. As one instance: in less than 50 years from its foundation, Mission Dolores at San Francisco (in 1825) had 76,000 head of cattle, 950 riding horses, 2,000 breeding mares, 820 mules, 79,000 sheep, 2,000 yoke of oxen, 18,000 bushels of wheat and barley and quantities of other products. The missions were the only inns for travelers, who could always find bountiful hospitality there. The Indians attached to the mission shared in the goods they helped to produce, having the use of implements and work animals without owning them. Adult children as they were, it was necessary to protect them until such time as they would be able to protect themselves. The padres had stringent rules against the fraternizing of the Spanish with their Indians, especially with Indian women, and they tried to keep peace between the races and prevent the exploitation of their charges. The Indian families lived in or near the mission, a regular, settled life with daily Mass, prayer, work, with good food and security, with Sunday rest and plenty of fun and dancing on fiestas. Between 1826 and 1845 the Mexican government, having declared its independence from Spain, seized the missions, took over their property, plundered the buildings and gave small fields to individual Indian families, who were supposed to become independent thereby. Within one year the Indians were cheated and despoiled by white settlers and traders of everything they had. Left destitute, they died by thousands, leaving a remnant who fled to a bare existence in the hills. After California became a part of the United States, the authorities in Washington gave the mission buildings, now ruined, back to the Church. A great experiment in Christianity and civilization had failed through man's inhumanity and greed. Some of the old mission buildings remain, in partial use and visited by tourists, humble yet magnificent examples of religious architecture, lonely relics of a lost vision. Compared with the treatment of the Indians by English colonists on the Atlantic coast, the results were in the end the same—total or partial genocide. But in California, at least, there had been the vision.

calumny (L. *calvi,* to deceive) To impute to a person something derogatory of which he is not guilty. It is a sin against the Eighth Commandment, and the gravity of the sin is in proportion to the seriousness of the charge and the damage done.

Calvary (L. *calvaria,* skull) The hill near Jerusalem where criminals were executed and where Jesus was put to death. The hill took its name from its resemblance to a head or skull.

Calvinism A system of religion propounded by the French theologian John Calvin (1509–1564) from which Unitarianism, Puritanism and Presbyterianism developed. Calvin taught absolute predestination, that some are destined to hell, and others to heaven, independently of one's own efforts. He retained two sacraments, Baptism and the Lord's Supper.

camauro A close-fitting, brimless,

red velvet hat, trimmed with white fur, that comes down over the ears. It is worn by the pope on extra liturgical occasions. Its use had disappeared until John XXIII adopted it for frequent wear.

Camera, Apostolic (L. *camera,* vault) An office of the Roman Curia that dates back to the 11th century. It supervises and administers the temporal goods and affairs of the Holy See.

camerieri segreti (It.) Privy chamberlains attached to the Roman court.

camerlengo (It. chamberlain) In its Italian form this title is applied to two high-ranking Roman prelates, both Cardinals: 1. The "Camerlengo of Holy Roman Church" is the head of the Apostolic Camera or Chamber, which is charged with responsibility for the temporal goods and the vindication of the rights of the Holy See. When a pope dies, it is this Camerlengo who takes over the administration of the affairs of the Church, makes the arrangements for the conclave and remains in charge until a new pope has been elected. 2. The "Camerlengo of the Sacred College" is the Cardinal charged with the administration of the properties and revenues of the College of Cardinals and with the official registry of all business conducted in the consistories.

camisia (L. shirt) A name given to the alb. *See* alb.

campanile (L. *campana,* bell) The name given to the bell tower of a church. It is usually a tall, slender structure, semidetached from the church. The campanile of the National Shrine at the Catholic University is a good example.

Campion Award Annual award of the Catholic Book Club for distinguished service to the cause of Catholic letters. Among winners have been Jacques Maritain, Paul Horgan, Helen C. White and Sister M. Madeleva.

Cana Conference A movement organized at diocesan level that aims to strengthen married and family life. It takes its name from the marriage feast which Jesus attended at Cana in Galilee. The movement is coordinated by the Family Life Bureau of NCWC. Conferences are held at regular intervals, centering about relationships between husband and wife, parents and children, God and the family, and society and the family. Marriage experts, experienced priests and doctors give the conferences. There have been two outgrowths from the movement. The first is the Cana Club organized by a half dozen couples who meet in each other's homes at regular intervals to discuss matters of mutual concern. The second comprises Pre-Cana Conferences for engaged couples, which prepare them for matrimony.

Canaanite (Hurrian, *kinahuhu,* crimson wool) A person inhabiting Canaan (Chanaan) which became ancient Palestine and Phonecia. It came into being about 3000 B.C.

Canada, Catholic Church in Catholicism came to Canada with the French explorers. The first Mass celebrated in Canada was offered in Gaspe in 1534 by a priest accompanying the explorer Jacques Cartier. In 1615 French Recollects arrived to begin mission work among the Indian tribes. Jesuits were invited to assist. In 1628 Acadia fell to the English and the following year Quebec was conquered; all missioners were compelled to return to France. The treaty of 1632 restored Canada to France and mission work resumed. Jesuits, Sulpicians and Ursulines planted deeply the roots of the Church. In 1659 François de Montmorency Laval was appointed the Vicar Apostolic of New France, and in 1674 Quebec was made a diocese with Laval the first bishop. Dark days came to the Church with the fall of Quebec in 1759 to the British General Wolfe. Great Britain attempted to anglicize her new subjects. Various restrictions were put upon the Church. Bishops were not allowed any title, religious orders were not permitted to accept new novices, and the Anglican Church was the only recognized Church. However, the French support for Great Britain in the War of 1812 under the leadership of Quebec's Bishop Plciss won recognition. In 1819 the government assented to the elevation of Bishop Pleiss to archbishop. Immigration to Canada by European Catholics spread the Church across the continent. An apostolic delegation was established in 1899. Today there are 15 ecclesiastical provinces of the Western Rite in Canada with 63 archdioceses, dioceses, vicariates and one abbey ordinary. There is also one Byzantine Province with a metropolitan sec in Winnipeg and three eparchates. There are over 7,500 secular priests caring for over 6.5 million Catholics and 200,000 Byzantine Catholics. There are 16 diocesan seminaries for the secular clergy. In addition religious orders have great strength in Canada and have contributed many personnel to the overseas mission of the Church. The Quebec Foreign Mission Society and the Scarboro Fathers are nationally organized foreign mission sending societies. The Oblates of Mary Immaculate have considerable strength in Canada and have long been noted for their labors in Canada's arctic regions. The hierarchy of Canada is organized into the Canadian Catholic Conference, similar to the United States National Catholic Welfare Conference; there are commissions for Latin America, Liturgy, Education, Communications Media, Catholic Action, Social Action, Home Missions, Hospitals and Welfare.

Canadian Catholic Conference An association of Canadian bishops similar to the National Catholic Welfare Conference in the United States. It was founded in 1943 in order to advance the Church and to coordinate activities of the hierarchy. It has its headquarters in Ottawa.

cancellus The altar railing separating the sanctuary from the rest of the church.

Candelmas A name given to the Feast of the Purification of the Blessed Virgin Mary, celebrated on Feb. 2. It is so-called because on this day candles are solemnly blessed and distributed before the Mass.

candles (L. *candere,* to shine) From Baptism to the Requiem Mass, candles are used in many of the ceremonies and rites of the Church. They are required on the altar for the solemn recitation of the Divine Office, for the celebration of Mass and other services. Twelve candles are required for Benediction. During the ordination to acolyte, a candle is presented the candidate. During the ordination to the priesthood, the candidate presents a candle to the ordaining bishop. They are used at the dedication of a church, at the blessing of the baptismal font, at the churching of a new mother, at the singing of the Gospel, during liturgical processions and even at excommunications. The blessing of the paschal candle is one of the most solemn ceremonies of the Church. Candles are blessed solemnly on the Feast of the Purification. Liturgically, candles are not used for the purpose of giving light, but as a symbol of joy and to show honor to God, to holy persons or holy things. Definite records exist to show that candles were in use in the Church in the 4th century. They probably developed from the catacombs where they were used to illuminate the darkness. It is required that all candles used for liturgical purposes contain a proportion of pure beeswax, and that they be white, except for Requiem Masses, when they should be unbleached. Blessed candles are also used in private devotions by members of the Church in times of trouble or temptation, during thunderstorms, when receiving Communion of the sick, at the hour of death.

candles at Mass Placed beside or on the altar to signify the place of importance. Formerly, Roman officials were flanked by candles on important occasions; this custom was adapted by the Church. Two are used for Low Mass, six for a High Mass. Normally, Mass may not be said without lighted candles.

candles, blessing of Performed before Mass on Feb. 2, even if there is a transferal of the Feast of the Purification to the following day. After the celebrant has put on a purple stole, he blesses the candles with five prayers. Following this, he sprinkles them with holy water and incenses them. He then distributes them to the clergy and people while the Nunc Dimittis is being sung. Next a procession is formed in which lighted candles are carried and three antiphons sung. The whole ceremony has been borrowed from the East and the chant used is of an unusual type. On the day of the blessing of the candles, the candles are lighted again at the Gospel and from the Consecration to the Communion, unless the Mass be that of a Sunday and not of the Purification.

candles, lighting altar The candles are lit beginning with the candles nearest the crucifix on the Epistle side of the altar and working out, i.e. from left to right; next on the Gospel side, but the process is from right to left. The candles are extinguished in reverse order; i.e., starting with the furthest one on the Gospel side. The reason for this procedure is reverence for the crucifix or tabernacle.

candles, votive Burning tapers in receptacles of glass placed before an altar, shrine or statue. Originally used to beautify these places. Now the most important function they serve is as a source of revenue.

candlesticks The furnishings of any altar which are mounts for holding candles in place.

canon (Gr. *kanon*, rule) A rule, decree or principle by which other things are measured or judged. The word has a number of specific meanings. 1. *Law*. One of the 2,414 decrees of the *Code of Canon Law*. 2. *Liturgy*. That part of the Mass which begins immediately after the Sanctus–Benedictus and ends with the "Amen" just before the Pater Noster. 3. *Scripture*. A list of the inspired books of the Bible confirming their true inspiration. 4. *Persons*. A priest who is a member of a cathedral chapter, appointed by the bishop after consulting the other canons. He has a stall in the sanctuary choir of the cathedral, a voice in the cathedral chapter, which is the "senate" of the diocese, and may receive revenues if there are any belonging to the chapter. He resides in the cathedral city, helps the bishop in administering the diocese and sings the Divine Office in the cathedral in choir with the other canons. At the death of a bishop the chapter of canons takes over the ordinary duties of the bishop, elects a vicar to administer the diocese during the vacancy and sometimes nominates a new bishop. Cathedral canons are found in Catholic dioceses in European countries but not in the United States.

canon coadjutor　A canon appointed to carry out the choir duties of another canon who is busy with some other official work. A canon coadjutor has the right of succession.

canon, honorary　A canon who has the title as an honor, but without the duties and privileges of a canon.

canon law　The body of laws by which the Church is governed. The present *Code of Canon Law* (*Codex Juris Canonici*) with its 2,414 canons (laws) became effective in 1918. This Code has been supplemented by numerous decrees, interpretations and replies to questions submitted to a permanent committee.

canon, lay　An honorary appointment of a layman to a canonry by a chapter.

canon of honor　A French custom whereby a bishop names another prelate to this honorary office. It has no canonical standing.

Canon of the Mass (Gr. *kanon,* rule) The solemn consecratory prayer of the Mass which begins with the versicles and responses before the Preface and ends with the "Amen" of the people before the Pater Noster. It is fixed and has minor variations only at Christmas, Epiphany, Easter, Ascension and Pentecost.

canon penitentiary　A member of a chapter of a cathedral who is appointed a general confessor for the diocese. His power includes sins and censures reserved to the bishop.

canon, pontifical　A liturgical book containing the Ordinary and Canon of the Mass used for a Pontifical Mass.

canon, privilege of the　It is a sacrilege to violate the person and dignity of a religious or cleric. Canon law specifies that a person doing so incurs excommunication reserved to the bishop or the Holy See according to the dignity of the person violated.

canon, titular　A titular dignitary. He varies from an honorary canon in that he is a member of the chapter and has a vote in its deliberations.

canon theologian　An official of a diocesan chapter who acts as the authority on dogmatic and moral theological problems.

canoness　A name given to several orders of nuns such as the Canonesses Regular of St. Augustine and the Canonesses Regular of the Lateran. The title was formerly applied to a woman holding a canonry.

Canonesses Hospitallers of St. Augustine　Founded in France in the 12th century, established in Canada in 1639 where they bulit the first Canadian hospital, the Hotel Dieu in Quebec. Members are engaged in hospital and medical work. A mission is staffed in Paraguay. Over 800 members. The life is both active and contemplative. Simple vows are taken.

canonical hours　Seven divisions of the day on each of which a part of the Divine Office is recited, according to Psalm 18:164, "Seven times a day I praise you." Matins is the night office, Lauds at dawn; Prime at 6 A.M.; Terce at 9 A.M. Sext at noon; None at 3 P.M.; Vespers at 6 P.M.; and Compline at the end of the day. They all are centered around the Mass of the day, receiving their direction and tone from the Holy Sacrifice, and in turn contributing their worship to it. The rules permit numerous variations in the exact hour of recitation, whether alone or in choir.

canonical marriage A marriage performed according to the laws and regulations of the Church.

canonicals 1. The vestments prescribed by law for Mass and other ceremonies. 2. The examinations taken by numbers of the junior clergy (three years after ordination) as required by canon law.

canonicity Belonging to the canon of Sacred Scripture.

canonist An authority on canon law.

canonization (Gr. *kanon,* rule or list) A solemn declaration by the Pope that a person is now in heaven and entitled to the full honors of the Church. There are two steps to canonization. The person's cause must be introduced which, if the Congregation of Rites decides that it shows virtue to a heroic degree, allows that person to be referred to as Venerable. The cause is then considered by a detailed examination of the person's life, writings, reputation and miracles. Martyrs do not need miracles in this process. If the Congregation of Rites finds in favor of the person, a declaration is issued by the Pope naming him Blessed (beatification). A Blessed is honored locally or in a religious community. The process is then carried forward. Re-examination is made of the person's life and two new miracles must be proved. If this part of the process is

successful the canonization declaration is made to the universal Church.

canons, chapters of Those groups of men who hold the Church office of canons. These clergymen on the staff of a cathedral or other large church have the basic office of possessing a stall or place in the choir and of voting in the chapter. The chapter is considered a moral person just as a corporation is a moral person.

canons, ecclesiastical The rules, laws and decrees of the Church. The major body of Church law is to be found in the 2,414 canons which have been gathered into a book, *Codex Juris Canonici* (*Code of Canon Law*).

Canons of the Apostles See Apostolic Canons.

canons regular Ecclesiastical persons bound by vows and living in community under a common rule. They are different from secular canons who take no vows. Their origin is unknown.

canopy (Gr. *konopos,* gnat) Originally a bed with a  mosquito curtain. In the liturgical sense the word has a number of meanings. 1. The structure covering the altar in both the Western and Eastern liturgies. 2. The four-staffed white canopy used to shelter the Blessed Sacrament when carried in procession. 3. The covering over the throne used by bishops or other dignitaries. 4. The small single-staff canopy used when moving the Blessed Sacrament from one altar to another or in taking the Blessed Sacrament to the sick.

Canterbury The mother church and primatial see of England. The first bishop was St. Augustine (597) and the last, Cardinal Pole (d. 1558). Among the prelates who ruled this see were St. Theodore (668–690), St. Dunstan (960–988), St. Thomas of Canterbury (1162–1170) and St. Edmund Rich (1234–1240).

canticle A sacred hymn whose words are taken directly from the Bible. The Benedictus and Magnificat are among the best known canticles.

Canticle of Canticles, The That book of the Old Testament whose Hebrew title means "song of songs," i.e., song without equal. Protestant versions refer to it as "The Song of Solomon." Scripture scholars are not agreed on its interpretation; some see it merely as a collection of love songs, others as contrived drama, others as an allegory of the relationship of Yahweh to Israel. While authorship has been popularly attributed to Solomon, evidence indicates otherwise.

cantor The leader or leaders of the choir who intone the antiphons, begin psalms, etc.

cantoral staff The large staff sometimes carried by the cantor of an ecclesiastical choir to show his dignity and that he is exercising his duties.

cantoris (L. *canere,* to sing) The side of the choir occupied by the cantor. It is the right of the choir, the north side.

capital punishment The death penalty. It is Catholic teaching that society has the clear right to take life in order to repel unjust aggression against itself or its members. From this it follows that the state has the right to inflict the death penalty for serious crimes. There is much debate, however, on the value of the death penalty. Those in favor argue that it is necessary for the protection of society, to satisfy justice, as a deterrent to crime and as an act of kind-

ness to the criminal. The opponents of capital punishment argue that society can be protected without killing, by substituting life imprisonment; that eye-for-an-eye justice is not Christian, and can be invalid because of many extenuating circumstances; that capital punishment does not deter crime, as proved by statistical studies; and that instead of being a kindness, it is a cruel type of mental torture which causes an apprehension of death that is unjustifiable. In the United States, 41 states and the District of Columbia have the death penalty. In most non-Communist countries of Europe capital punishment has been abolished (exceptions being England, France and Spain). In most Latin American countries, executions for crime no longer take place.

capital sins (L. *caput,* head) The seven principal tendencies of fallen nature viewed as the fountainheads or prime sources of all sin. These inordinate inclinations are: pride, covetousness, lust, anger, gluttony, envy, sloth. They are sometimes less appropriately called "The Seven Deadly Sins."

capitalism An economic system to produce and distribute wealth based on private ownership by an individual or group of individuals of the means of production, and for which ownership and risk the individual or group of individuals receive profit. Capitalism is recognized as a legitimate economic form by the Church. However, the Church has condemned unbridled capitalism and has pointed out the responsibilities of capitalism and of private ownership in many social encyclicals beginning with the famous one of Leo XIII, *Rerum Novarum.*

capitalism, absentee The investment

of capital in a business by stockholders who will have no contact with the business or workers. In *Mater et Magistra* (n. 104) Pope John XXIII warned of the dangers to the common good of a country under a system of absentee capitalism.

capitular Mass   When a chapter is held, the canons attending celebrate a principal Mass called a capitular Mass. In cathedral churches where the Divine Office is said the capitular Mass would be sung daily.

capitulary   The name given to the canons or laws passed by provincial councils. It can mean a set of chapters, each of which is a law. Historically, it refers to the laws, each of which was called a "chapter," that were promulgated by the Frankish kings of the first and second dynasties.

capitulum (L. a little chapter)   1. A collegiate or cathedral chapter (*q.v.*). 2. A brief reading from Sacred Scripture, usually connected with a liturgical or prayer service. The capitulum is usually a brief summary of the theme of the service or other Scripture reading. The Divine Office has many capitula, found in the hours of Vespers, Compline, Lauds, Terce, Sext and None.

cappa (L. cape)   The word usually refers to the cape worn by a religious; a choir cape.

cappa magna (L. the great cape)   It is the robe or cope worn by Cardinals or bishops on ceremonial occasions. It has a long train, requiring a trainbearer, and a large hood. Canons and certain prelates wear a cappa magna but the train is considerably shortened.

capsula (L.)   The small metal-frame container holding the large Sacred Host in the tabernacle. The capsula with the Host is placed in the monstrance for Exposition of Benediction of the Blessed Sacrament. *See* lunette.

Captivity Epistles   The four Epistles (Ephesians, Philippians, Colossians and Philemon) which were written by St. Paul while in captivity. Except for Philemon, which is a short personal letter, the Epistles are remarkably alike in style and content. They stress the role of Christ in the plan of Redemption and for this reason are sometimes called the Christological Epistles. The traditional opinion is that they were written by St. Paul during his first imprisonment in Rome. There are some who hold that they were written at Ephesus.

capuche   The cowl on the habit of a Capuchin.

Capuchins (kap′hew-chins; It. *scappucini,* hermits)   Popular name of the Order of Friars Minor Capuchins, a branch which broke away from the Franciscans in 1525 in order to restore the literal observance of the Rule of St. Francis. The Capuchins wear the brown Franciscan habit. Their general motherhouse is in Rome but Capuchins are found throughout the world and represent one of the Church's largest missionary societies. There are several provinces in the United States. The Apostolic Preacher is always a Capuchin.

cardinal (L. *cardinalis* fr. *cardo,* hinge)   An ecclesiastical prince of the Church who is a member of the pope's supreme council, the Sacred College of Cardinals. He is an adviser and assistant to the pope. The *Code of Canon Law* promulgated in 1918 states that a cardinal must be at least a priest; previous to that time cardinals could be drawn from the laity. Cardinals elect a pope when the Holy See becomes vacant. They act as protectors for religious orders and institutes and serve on the Sacred

Congregations. The College of Cardinals goes back to 1150, although before that time, the pope had a body of advisers. In 1179 the right of appointing cardinals was reserved exclusively to the pope. *See* consistory.

cardinal bishop A cardinal who is the bishop of one of the cardinalatial (suburbicarian) dioceses, which are those dioceses that surround Rome: Ostia, Palestrina, Velletri, Frascati, Sabina and Poggio Mirteto, Albano, and Porto and Santa Rufina.

cardinal canons The holders of seven canonries at the Shrine of St. James at Compostela, Spain. They are the only priests allowed to celebrate Mass there. They have the privilege of wearing a mitre and a cassock of cardinal red.

cardinal deacon Cardinal deacons are priests assigned to the service of the Holy See.

Cardinal Dean The dean of the Sacred College of Cardinals. He is the president of the College. He presides at the coronation of a new pope and has the right to wear the pallium at all functions. He is traditionally appointed Bishop of Ostia.

Cardinal Gibbons Medal An annual award made by the Catholic University of America to a person who has rendered outstanding service to the Church, the United States or the Catholic University. Winners have included Carlton J. Hayes, General Carlos Romulo, Fulton Oursler, John F. Kennedy.

cardinal in curia (L. at the court) A cardinal who resides in Rome. All cardinals who are not ordinaries are bound to live in Rome.

cardinal in petto (L. in the bosom) A cardinal who has been chosen by the pope but who is not named. Such a cardinal has no rights, privileges or duties until he is named. When his name is published, his seniority ranks from the time he was chosen.

cardinal priest A cardinal priest formerly represented one of the titular churches of Rome. Today he is usually a bishop whose diocese is outside Rome.

cardinal protector A cardinal who was formerly assigned the care of a particular religious community. The appointment gave no jurisdiction over the community but the cardinal represented the community's interest before the Holy See. Pope Paul VI announced his intention of not appointing new cardinal protectors. Protectorates presently assigned will continue to exist as simple titles but without duties; they will expire on the death of the holder.

cardinal see A see occupied by a cardinal bishop. These sees are referred to as cardinalatial or suburbicarian dioceses. They surround Rome and are: Ostia, Palestrina, Velletri, Frascati, Sabina and Poggio Mirteto, Albano, and Porto and Santa Rufina.

cardinal vicar The cardinal who is the vicar-general of the See of Rome.

cardinal virtues (L. *cardo,* a hinge) The four basic natural virtues: viz., prudence, justice, fortitude, temperance; so named because all other virtues are regarded as "hinging" or centering upon them. Also known as the "moral" virtues in contradistinction to the supernatural "theological" virtues of faith, hope and charity.

Cardinals, College of *See* College of Cardinals.

cardinals, creation of The naming of cardinals is reserved exclusively to the pope. Cardinals are appointed during a private consistory. The creation is formalized by the delivery of the cardinal's scarlet skull cap. The red hat is presented in a public consistory, usually by the pope. A private consistory follows during which takes place the ceremony of opening and closing the mouth, signifying that it is the cardinal's duty to give counsel and to keep counsel on private matters of the Holy See.

care of souls   *See* cure of souls.

Caritas Christi   A secular institute founded in France in 1938 and established in the United States and Canada in 1954. Membership is limited to single or widowed women. Members remain at home in ordinary occupations. Vows are taken.

Carmel, Mount   A mountain in northwest Palestine associated with the Prophet Elias (3 Kings 18:20), where he sacrificed and brought down fire from heaven. It is where the Carmelite Order was founded.

Carmelite Rite   The liturgy used by the Calced Carmelites. It is derived from the liturgy of the Holy Sepulcher as used in Palestine in the 12th century, and closely resembles the Dominican Rite in that the bread and wine is prepared at the beginning of Mass. There are also differences in the Divine Office, the burial service and the administration of the sacraments.

Carmelites   An order of monks formally titled "Brothers of the Order of the Most Blessed Mother of God and Ever Virgin Mary of Mount Carmel." They trace their origin back to Elias and hermits who lived on Mount Carmel with him. Generally, however, 1155 is considered the date of their foundation, when St. Berthold established a hermitage on Mount Carmel. A century later, under St. Simon Stock, they modified their religious life and became mendicant friars. A community of Carmelite nuns was founded in 1452. The reforming activities of St. John of the Cross and St. Teresa in the 16th cen-

tury resulted in two independent branches of the order. Those of the Old Observance, also known as Calced or Shod Carmelites, have modified their original rule in regard to fasting, abstinence and night Office, but retain their ancient liturgy derived from the rite of the Holy Sepulcher. The Discalced, Barefooted or Teresian Carmelites use the Roman Rite, say Divine Office daily in choir, rise from bed for night Office and meet in common for mental prayer twice daily.

carnal knowledge   A legal term for sex relations.

carnival   (L. *carnem,* meat, *levare,* to take away)   A period of feasting and revelry immediately preceding Lent, practiced mainly in Latin countries. The Mardi Gras celebration in New Orleans is a carnival.

carol   A vernacular semisacred and popular hymn used by the faithful at festivals. At the present time the carol is associated with Christmas.

Cartesianism   The system of philosophy of René Descartes (1596–1650) that has been described as being "intuitive in intellect, angelic in mode." Descartes set out by doubting all truth. But there was one truth he could not doubt: "I think. Therefore I am." The deduction or self-evidence of this principle becomes the criterion for all further judgments. On this basis Descartes went on to develop a new philosophy.

Carthage, Councils of   Four councils of bishops held in Carthage, North Africa. The first was in 220. The second, in 397, published a canonical list of Sacred Scriptures. The third, in 404, condemned the heresy of Donatus which held that sacraments administered by an unworthy minister were invalid and that sinners were not members of the Church.

The last was held in 411, at which St. Augustine refuted the Pelagians.

Carthusian Rite That variation of the Latin liturgy used by the Order of Carthusians. The rite extends back to the 11th century and the chant used has been preserved note for note from that time. In the Mass, hands are extended in the form of a cross; there are no complete genuflections; the bread and wine are prepared before Mass and offered together at the Offertory. There is no Last Gospel. The Carthusians were founded in 1084 at Grand Chartreuse in France by St. Bruno. There is an American foundation in the Diocese of Burlington, Vt.

Carthusians An order of contemplative monks founded by St. Bruno in France in 1084. Members live in individual cells or cottages and follow a schedule of prayer, reading, manual work, gardening, eating and sleeping. They meet in church on Sundays and feast days for the Divine Office, in the refectory for two meals, at scheduled times for recreation and once a week for a long walk. On other days they sing Mass, Vespers, Matins and Lauds in church.

case of conscience *See* casus.

cask The small barrel which holds the wine a new bishop presents to his consecrator after the Offertory of the Mass. Two small casks are presented, along with two loaves of bread and two candles. The same presentation is made by an abbot at his solemn benediction.

cassock (It. *casacca,* great coat) A soutane. The long outer gown worn by priests and clerics. It is usually black, although in tropical countries white cassocks are worn. It is also worn by altar boys when they assist at ceremonies. A prelate's ceremonial cassock is purple, and his house cassock is black with red or purple trimming. A cardinal wears a scarlet-red cassock. The pope's cassock is white.

Castel Gandolfo Summer residence of the popes dating from the time of Pope Urban VIII in the 17th century. It is situated in the town of the same name about 15 miles southeast of Rome in the Alban Hills.

Casti Connubii An encyclical of Pope Pius XI, issued in 1930, which proclaimed the fundamental law governing Christian marriage.

Castrensis, Episcopus (L. bishop of the camp) Latin title for a bishop who is in charge of military chaplains.

casuist One who uses casuistry to demonstrate the presence or lack of conformity of our actions to divine law manifested by conscience or based on the authority of Holy Scripture and Catholic Tradition.

casuistry A method of studying cases of conscience or solving questions of obligation by application of general principles in ethics or moral theology in regard to concrete problems of human conduct. The word often takes on a debased meaning, e.g., quibbling, moral laxity, confusing the issue.

casus (kah'sus, L. case) A real or fictional problem for discussion and solution arising in theology, canon law or liturgy.

catacombs (L. *ad catacumbas,* used to designate the church built over the Catacombs of St. Sebastian in Rome) Catacombs are intricate mazes of subterranean galleries used by early Christians as cemeteries and places of refuge. Graves were recessed in tiers along the walls and faced with slabs of marble or terra-cotta which carried Greek and Latin inscriptions. Occasionally the more open spaces where galleries converged served as halls or gathering places for the celebration of the divine mysteries. Under Roman law cemeteries were immune from disturbance. After the 4th century the catacombs were gradually abandoned and forgotten until rediscovered in the 15th century; later they were systematically explored and publicized by the noted archaeologists J. B. Rossi and Joseph Wilpert. It is estimated that the various catacombs in the Roman area alone contain over 500 miles of galleries, many of which have not yet been explored in detail. Similar catacombs were brought to light in Naples, Sicily, Sardinia, Malta and North Africa. The inscriptions and paintings found throughout the catacombs are valuable sources of information concerning the early Christian centuries. Besides many allusions to Old Testament stories about Noe, Abraham, Moses, Daniel, Jonas, etc., there are historical and symbolical references to Christ's Baptism, the resurrection of Lazarus, the Good Shepherd, the Last Supper, the fish symbol for Christ, the sacraments, the nature of the Christian life and other matters.

catafalque (It. *catafalco,* a scaffold) The platform used before the sanctuary to receive the coffin of a deceased person, or the simulated coffin used when the body is not present. It is covered with a long black pall. It is usually flanked by three candles on each side. With or without the body, it is treated with the same respect.

cataphatic theology A theology in which is applied to God images and thoughts drawn from natural experience.

catechesis Instruction given to Christian catechumens preparing for Baptism, especially those in the primitive Church. The word was also used of the books containing such instruction, of which the most celebrated is that of St. Cyril of Jerusalem.

catechetical revival The bringing together of 2,000 years of teaching experience in the Church. From contemporary times the revival has borrowed a theology of salvation, and the progress in educational methods and child psychology; from the beginning of this century, a concern generally for methodology; from the mid-1500's, the religious instruction of all children and the catechism; from the Middle Ages, a recognition of the milieux and catechetical formulas; from the early Church, the spirit of the catechumenate and a live liturgy. Finally, there is a re-emphasis of the kerygma, i.e., the original nucleus of the Christian message preached to non-Christians with the person of Christ at its center.

catechetics The science of teaching catechism; the study of the catechism and catechetical methods. Today much study is being done regarding the methods and pedagogy of catechetics. The catechism has become Christ-centered and the old system of rote and memory has yielded to understanding and explanation.

catechism (Gr. *katechein,* to instruct verbally) A manual for moral and religious instruction which is a summary of Catholic doctrine. The basic catechism in the United States is the so-called Baltimore Catechism which takes its name from the compilation of instructions authorized by the Third Baltimore Council. It is traditionally issued in question-and-answer form. Today the catechism has undergone considerable streamlining and updating, not because of doctrinal change, but because methods of teaching and catechetical approach have been improved.

catechist Originally, one who prepared catechumens for Baptism; today, an instructor in Christian doctrine. In mission territories, catechists play major roles because they extend the work of the missioner. In many areas, these lay catechists are full-time workers. Catechists are used widely in Latin America because of the shortage of priests, and in many areas have restored an otherwise lost Faith.

catechumen A nonbaptized person who is taking instruction to enter the Catholic Church. In some areas, particularly Africa and parts of the Orient, catechumens are brought into a central place, called a catechumenate, where they undergo long and intensive instruction. In the early Church, catechumens were only allowed to attend the first part of the Mass, and had to leave when the Mass of the Faithful began.

categories (Gr. *kata,* down, *agoreuein,* to assert) A set of ultimate and primary mental conceptions to which all knowledge can be reduced. These were explored and listed by Aristotle.

cathedra (kath'ay-dra; Gr. chair) 1. The throne of a bishop in his cathedral church. It is located in the sanctuary against the wall of the cathedral on the Gospel side. 2. The seat of authority, as in "ex cathedra." 3. The seat used by the celebrant at a Carthusian sung Mass.

cathedral (Gr. *cathedra,* seat) The official church of the bishop of a diocese. It is usually in the see city from which the diocese takes its name. The United States has many beautiful cathedrals; particularly those of St. Louis, Mo., Hartford, Conn., Baltimore, Md., and New York, N.Y., to mention a few. St. Louis Cathedral in New Orleans, La., is the oldest in the United States.

cathedral priory A monastery attached to a cathedral. This is the common practice in England and many places in Europe. A priory is a religious house, governed by a prior and ranks next to an abbey.

cathedraticum (kath-ayd-ra'tee-kum; Gr. *kathedra,* episcopal chair) A moderate contribution payable annually to a diocesan bishop for his support and in recognition of his authority by the various churches subject to his jurisdiction.

catholic (Gr. *katholokis,* universal) A term first applied to the Church by St. Ignatius of Antioch (d. 107). As the word was further used, it came to mean not only the Church but also a member of that Church. Its use today refers to the Church, teachings and hierarchy which has descended from the Apostles. It is also one of the marks of the true Church as listed in the Nicene and Apostles' Creeds: "One, holy, catholic and apostolic Church."

Catholic Action The apostolate of the laity. Strictly speaking, Catholic Action is "the participation of the Catholic laity in the apostolate of the hierarchy" (Pius XI); in this sense it included only those organizations or activities commissioned by a bishop and under his control. However, the term is commonly used in a broader sense to include the organized activities of Catholics to witness to Christ in their everyday lives and to apply Christian principles to the social structures in which they are involved. For, strictly speaking, every Christian, by reason of his incorporation into Christ through Baptism, is required to act as a leaven in society. To be a Christian means to build up the Kingdom of God on earth and to restore all things in Christ.

Catholic Action Inquiry Composed of three steps: to observe, to judge, to act on the part of those engaged in Catholic Action.

Catholic Almanac, National A very valuable and complete reference book edited in the United States by the Franciscan Fathers of the Holy Name Province. It contains Catholic information of every sort on the history and organization of the Church, the hierarchy, Catholic doctrine, liturgy, the Catholic Church in the United States, etc. It is the most valuable Catholic reference book published in English. A revised edition is produced each year.

Catholic Charities An agency of each diocese which plans, coordinates, supervises and finances social work within the diocese. The main fields of aid are child care, family welfare, health, care of the aged and recreation. The various diocesan directors have organized into the National Association of Directors of Catholic Charities.

Catholic Charities, International Conference of A federation of some forty nationwide organizations of Catholic charities existing throughout the world with its headquarters in Rome. It was organized on the initiative of the Holy See in 1951 and has nongovernmental status at the United Nations. The American member is the National Conference of Catholic Charities with headquarters in Washington, D.C.

Catholic Church Popular and short form for the one, holy, catholic and apostolic Church. The Church founded by Jesus Christ, which was first governed by the Apostles under Peter, and continuously over the centuries by his and their legitimate successors. The Catholic Church is a world-wide Church whose members are united in the same Faith, participate in the same sacraments and recognize the same universal spiritual leadership of the pope.

Catholic Directory, Official An annual publication of P. J. Kenedy, New York, N.Y., which contains personnel listings and ecclesiastical statistics on the United States and its possessions, Canada, Ireland, Great Britain, Australia, New Zealand, Oceania, parts of the Caribbean, Mexico and the Philippines. It also lists foreign missioners, military chaplains, officials of the Roman Curia, personnel of National Catholic Welfare Conference, statistics of religious orders, an American clerical necrology, etc. With the *Catholic Almanac* (*q.v.*), it is one of the two standard reference books published annually in the United States on the Catholic Church.

Catholic Epistles A name given to seven epistles of the New Testament: St. James; 1 and 2 Peter; 1, 2 and 3 John; St. Jude. The term originates in the fact that they were addressed to the universal Church, whereas those of St. Paul were addressed to individual churches.

Catholic Foreign Mission Society of America Legal title for the Maryknoll Fathers. *See* Maryknoll Fathers.

Catholic Hospital Association The national organization of the Catholic hospitals in the United States. The official publication is a monthly magazine, *Hospital Progress*. Headquar-

108

ters for the Association is in St. Louis, Mo.

Catholic Literary Foundation An organization established in Milwaukee in 1943 by the Bruce Publishing Company which has the aim of promoting worthwhile Catholic literature and of making it easily available to the Catholic public. The Foundation operates a book club.

Catholic Medical Mission Board An organization to assist the staffs of Catholic medical institutions in all parts of the world with material supplies and lay personnel, and to improve the care given charitably to the destitute sick of all religions. CMMB maintains a placement service to supply doctors, nurses and technicians to medical institutions overseas. The headquarters for the organization is at 10 W. 17th Street, New York, N.Y., 10011.

Catholic Order of Foresters Fraternal orders of men and women that carry on charitable, social and mutual beneficial activities. The order is organized into courts and has its main strength in the midwest. Headquarters: Chicago, Ill.

Catholic–Orthodox A term used to describe Russian Catholics of the Byzantine Rite.

Catholic Press Association A trade association composed of Catholic newspapers, magazines and Catholic book publishers in the United States and Canada. There are 150 newspapers and over 400 magazines with a total circulation of approximately 30 million. The Catholic Press Association publishes the *Catholic Journalist,* the *Catholic Press Annual* and the *Catholic Press Directory*. A national office is maintained at 432 Park Avenue South, New York City. The Association makes an annual award for the most distinguished contribution to journalism in the preceding calendar year.

Catholic Press Association Award Annual award of bronze statue of St. Francis de Sales for the most outstanding example of Catholic journalism in the preceding calendar year.

Catholic Students' Mission Crusade A national federation of student mission societies established in high schools and colleges with the aim of making the students more conscious of the needs, opportunities and problems of the so-called mission countries in order that the students will become personally involved in the fulfillment of their Christian vocation. Several editions of the magazine *The Shield* are published in the school year. Headquarters: Cincinnati, Ohio.

Catholic truth Truth is one and absolute. The Catholic Church has all the truths of religion (not necessarily all explicit and declared). All religions whatsoever have varying amounts of the truth in them, which they share with the Church, but the Church alone has all. It is impossible to qualify truth except by way of classification of truths, so the expression "Catholic truth" must be understood in the sense of "the truth about the Catholic Church, her life and teaching."

Catholic Truth Society A name for a number of organizations in English-speaking countries that have the purpose of publishing Catholic literature both for the education of Catholics and as an apologetic to non-Catholics.

Catholic University of America Founded in Washington, D.C. in 1889 by the archbishops of the United States, the official Catholic University is empowered to grant both civil and canonical degrees. The trustees and administration of the University are appointed by the bishops of the United States and are directly responsible to them. The chancellor is the Archbishop of Washington *ex officio.*

Catholic Youth Organization Organized originally by Bishop Bernard Sheil of Chicago in 1930, CYO is the name of the official, parish-centered diocesan Catholic youth programs throughout the country. CYO has a program of spiritual, cultural, social and physical activities. National CYO is the constituent member of the National Council of Catholic Youth, Diocesan Section.

catholicate The area of jurisdiction of a catholicos (*q.v.*).

Catholicism A term used to include all those different rites of the true religion that are dependent on the pope in Rome. This includes both the Roman Rite and the numerous Eastern Rites (*q.v.*).

catholicity (Gr. *catholicos,* universal) A term that designates the universality of the true religion which is found among all the peoples of the world and is not limited to a certain linguistic or ethnic group.

catholicos A title given to certain patriarchs of the Eastern Church.

Catholics in National Statuary Hall In 1864 Congress established National Statuary Hall and invited the states to nominate two distinguished persons whose representation would be placed therein. The following states have nominated Catholics: Arizona, Father Eusebio Kino; California, Father Junipero Serra; Illinois, James Shields; Louisiana, Edward Douglass White; Maryland, Charles Carroll; New Mexico, Archbishop Jean Baptiste Lamy; Nevada, Patrick A. McCarran; Oregon, Dr.

John McLoughlin; West Virginia, John E. Kenna; and Wisconsin, Father Jacques Marquette.

Caughnawaga A Catholic Iroquois reservation situated on the St. Lawrence River near Montreal. Originally founded at Lapraire opposite Montreal in 1667, it was moved several times before being established at its present site in 1716. It is under the care of the Jesuits. Catherine Tekakwitha died and was buried there.

causae majores (L. major cases) Important cases which are reserved to the pope for decision. An example would be a canonization.

causality That relationship between events or things, so that one (the cause) has the power to produce the other (the effect). Philosophy relates each effect back to the First and Supreme Cause: God.

cause A word used theologically and philosophically in a number of senses. The word refers to God as the First or Supreme Cause. In a restricted sense, it refers to the process of beatification and canonization.

CCD The Confraternity of Christian Doctrine (*q.v.*). The abbreviation is commonly used in place of the long title.

CELAM (Sp. Consejo Episcopal Latino Americano) Latin American Bishops Council: an ecclesiastical organization which represents the hierarchies of the twenty Latin American countries. From the Bishops' Conference following the International Eucharistic Congress of Rio de Janeiro in 1955 came the foundation of the hierarchies of the twenty republics with a central office in Bogota. Its pattern is somewhat similar to the National Catholic Welfare Conference in the United States.

celebrant The presiding officer at a liturgical ceremony. He may be a bishop, a priest or, for certain ceremonies such as Baptism and Holy Communion, a deacon.

Celebration of the Word of God, the Sacred   In places where no priest is available for Sunday or a feast of precept, the ordinary may permit a special ceremony presided over by a deacon or layman. The ceremony follows the Service of the Word of the Mass. The Epistle and Gospel of the day are read in the Vernacular with chants, especially from the Psalms. A deacon shall give a homily; a layman shall read a homily indicated by the bishop or pastor. The service shall close with the prayer of the faithful and the Lord's Prayer.

celebret (L. he may celebrate)   The name for a commendatory letter which is given to a priest who is traveling out of his home diocese. It affirms that the priest is in good standing, free from censure, and therefore permitted to celebrate Mass.

celestial hierarchy   While there is no degree of authority in heaven except that of God, this term is applied to the three categories of angels according to rank. Theologians, basing their reasoning upon an enumeration given in Scripture by Isaia, Ezechiel, St. Paul (Col. 1:16, Eph. 1:21), list three hierarchies, in each of which there are three orders, making nine types of classifications. The first threesome is: Seraphim, Cherubim, Thrones; the second: Dominations, Principalities and Powers; the third: Virtues, Archangels and Angels. The classes or choirs of angels differ in the degree of perfection of their nature and grace, and they do so in a descending order in the listing above.

celibacy (L. *caelebs,* unmarried) The state of being unmarried; especially in Church parlance, the state of persons obligated by vow to remain single. The celibate life, advocated and practiced by St. Paul (1 Cor. 7:8), gained gradual acceptance as being more fitting for ministers of the Gospel. It became established as the regular discipline in the Western Church toward the end of the 6th century when Pope Gregory the Great imposed it on all clerics in major orders. In present practice, all clergy of the Latin Rite implicitly accept the obligation of celibacy from the day of their ordination to subdeaconate, the first of the three major orders. As a result, clerics in sacred orders who presume to contract a marriage, even only civilly, incur by the very fact an excommunication specially reserved to the Holy See. The requirement of celibacy is a matter of Church discipline established by positive ecclesiastical law. As such it is not immutable. Among the Catholics of most Eastern Rites many of the clergy are married in accordance with the common tradition in the East but there is a notable movement toward the adoption of celibacy. At all events marriage must precede ordination to the diaconate or priesthood; and bishops are chosen from among the single or widowers.

cell   1. A small monastery or convent dependent upon a larger religious house to which support must be given. 2. The small room of a monk, nun or hermit, used mainly for sleeping but also for study and prayer. 3. The group of individuals who form the nucleus of various efforts generally described by the term Catholic Action (*q. v.*).

cellarer   An officer of a monastery concerned with the ordinary temporalities such as the buying of food, the physical operation of the monastery, etc. Also called an econome, procurator, purchasing agent, etc.

Celtic cross  An ancient type of cross that originated in Ireland. It is distinguished by having a circle about the juncture of the cross arms.

cemetery (Gr. *koimeterion,* a sleeping place) A place set apart for the burial or entombment of the dead; a graveyard. The first Christian burial places were the catacombs. After the peace of Constantine, it became common practice to bury the dead in church graveyards or beneath the church; later, graveyards apart from the church developed. Canon law requires the faithful to be buried in blessed ground and whenever possible a section should be set aside for clerics and priests. Canon law also requires that neither cemeteries nor individual tombs contain inscriptions or ornaments contrary to a spirit of religion. Burial can be by inhumation (*q.v.*), burial in the ground; or by tumulation (*q.v.*), burial in a tomb above ground. *See* cremation.

Cenacle (L. *caenaculum,* dining room) 1. The upper room in Jerusalem where Christ and His Apostles celebrated the Last Supper and where He appeared to them after His Resurrection. It was here also on Pentecost that the Holy Spirit appeared as tongues of fire. 2. A name given to a convent of Cenacle Nuns.

Cenacle Nuns Popular name for the religious community formally known as the Congregation of Our Lady of the Retreat in the Cenacle. Although enclosed and devoted to daily exposition, these nuns lead a very active life giving retreats to women. The group

was founded in France in 1826 and was established in the United States in 1892. There are two American provinces.

cenobite (Gr. *koinos,* common; *bios,* life) An obsolete word for a monk. The term is opposed to *anchorite,* one who lives alone.

cenobium (sen-oh'-bee-um; Gr. *koinos,* common; *bios,* life) A community of monks, a monastery. Sometimes the word is used to designate the church of the monastery. The word is used in contrast to anchorite or hermit who dwells alone.

censer  A vessel in which incense is burned at liturgical functions. It has a perforated cover and is suspended on chains by which it is swung. It is also called a thurible.

censor librorum (L. censor of books) A diocesan official appointed to examine certain books before publication to assure that they contain nothing against faith and morals. The Church requires that all writings pertaining to Scripture, theology, Church history, canon law, ethics, prayer and religion be submitted for examination in order to protect the faithful against false or misleading doctrines. In addition all printed sacred pictures must likewise be examined. After the book is approved for publication, the censor gives the *Nihil obstat* (Nothing is prejudicial) which is printed in the book over his name. The bishop of the diocese adds his *Imprimatur* (It may be printed) which is also printed in the book over his name and the date it was given. The imprimatur can be given in the diocese where the author resides, where the book is published, or where the book is printed. The imprimatur does not imply agreement with the contents, but merely that there is nothing in the contents that would be harmful to faith or morals of the reader.

censorship of books The examination and judgment of writings before their publication by an ecclesiastical authority especially appointed for the task. All books and printed matter dealing with religious or moral subjects require this censorship. This is a purely preventive measure against the spreading of doctrine harmful to faith and morals. If approval of the Church authorities is given, it is merely negative; i.e., the book contains nothing harmful, and so may be read by the faithful. This negative approval or permission to publish (*Imprimatur*) is printed at the beginning or at the end of the book. In order to protect the faith and morals of her children, the Church strongly forbids Catholics to read, to keep, to sell, to translate or to give away without proper permission any book which is dangerous to faith or morals, which defends heresy or schism, or is published without the required imprimatur.

censure Ecclesiastical censure is a penalty by which a baptized person, who has committed a crime and is contumacious or obstinate, is deprived of certain spiritual goods, or goods connected with the spiritual, until he has given up such contumacy. Censures are imposed only for crimes that are external, grave and consummated. A necessary condition for a valid infliction of censure is contumacy on the part of the delinquent, that is, contempt or disregard of the threatened penalty or formal warning. Upon repentance and the removal of contumacy, absolution from the censure is given. Three types of censure exist in canon law: excommunication, interdict and suspension.

centurion The Roman military commander of a century (100 soldiers). The word occurs several times in the New Testament.

cerecloth A linen cloth, waxed on one side, that is placed on the mensa (*q.v.*) of an altar after its consecration, over which the altar cloths are placed. It is retained on the altar as long as any remains of the holy oils are on the mensa.

Ceremonial of Bishops A liturgical book containing the procedures to be followed in such ceremonies as the Pontifical Mass, the death and election of a bishop, the singing of the Divine Office in cathedral chapters, etc. It also contains directions for extra-liturgical functions.

Ceremonial, Roman A book containing the ritual for papal ceremonials, such as the election and coronation of a pope, canonization, creation of cardinals, etc.

Ceremonies, Master of That person who guides and directs ceremonial ministers in the performance of the ritual.

Ceremonies, Sacred Congregation of That congregation of the Roman Curia that regulates ceremonial protocol of the papal court. It decides precedence of cardinals and ambassadors to the Holy See.

cessatio a divinis (L. suspension of divine services) A type of interdict imposed by an ordinary suspending religious services in a particular church as an act of reparation and horror for some violation to which the church has been subjected.

Ceylon The first Mass was offered in Ceylon in 1505 and St. Francis Xavier visited the country in 1548. In 1656 under the Dutch conquerors there was a violent persecution and a period of decadence set in for the Church until the middle of the 19th century. Today there are 1 archdiocese and 5 dioceses with a Catholic population of 750,000 in a total population of over 10 million. Although the constitution guarantees religious freedom, the Buddhist majority have caused the government to bring strong pressures on the Church with the result that Catholic institutions have had to close and some foreign missioners had to leave the country while others were denied entry. Catholic schools have been nationalized and ecclesiastical goods are taxed.

CFM *See* Christian Family Movement.

chains of St. Peter The two chains with which St. Peter was bound (Acts 12:6) when he was imprisoned by Herod and from which he was miraculously released. There was formerly a feast of this title but it is now suppressed.

chair A word that in its religious sense refers to a seat of authority, such as the Chair of Peter. It also refers to an episcopal throne.

chair of St. Peter A portable chair in the Vatican Basilica said to have been used by St. Peter in Rome. There were formerly two feasts by this name, one for St. Peter's Chair in Rome and the other for a chair in Antioch. Today they have been combined into a single feast on February 22.

Chair of Unity Octave The Unity Octave founded by Father Paul Watson of Graymoor for the reunion of all Christians begins on January 18, formerly the Feast of the Chair of St. Peter in Rome. This feast has now been suppressed and a new one instituted on another date; however,

it helped to give its name to the Unity Octave. *See* chair of St. Peter.

Chalcedon, Council of The fourth ecumenical council that was held in Chalcedon, a city in present-day Turkey, near Constantinople, in 451. The council defined Christ's nature and person, and condemned Monophysitism.

Chaldean A member of an Aramaic tribe that became prominent in Babylonia during the first millenium B.C. Also the language of the Chaldeans.

Chaldean Catholics Descendants of converts from Nestorianism. They use an adaptation of the Antiochian Rite. They live chiefly in Iran and Iraq and are governed by the Patriarch of Babylon who makes his residence at Mosul, Iraq. Historically the Malabar Catholics belong to the Chaldeans but in fact are organized separately.

Chaldean Rite Used by the Chaldeans and Malabarese. It is derived from the Antiochian Rite and uses the Syriac language.

chalice (L. *calix,* cup) 1. The sacred  vessel used in the sacrifice of the Mass to hold the wine to be consecrated into the blood of Christ. It is usually in the form of a cup with a stem and base, made of metal of any type with stipulation that the inside of the cup be gold. Chalices are consecrated with chrism by a bishop or his delegate and should not be touched directly by anyone not in Holy Orders unless permission is given them. 2. The "chalice" spoken of by Christ in the Agony of the Garden (Mt. 26:42 and Jn. 18:11) signifies the "portion or lot" of suffering accepted voluntarily.

chalice veil The square piece of cloth made of the same material and color as the other vestments of the Mass which is used to enclose the chalice until its unveiling after the Creed, and again covers the chalice after the final ablutions. It is not used by the Carthusians.

Challoner's Bible The 18th-century revision and translation of the Douay-Rheims Bible by Bishop Richard Challoner which became the standard Catholic English text throughout the world. It has been replaced in modern times by the Confraternity Version.

chamberlain Title of several classes of officials serving at the papal court. It includes members of the Roman Curia and those who serve in the apartments of the Pope; it is usually an honorary title.

chamberlain, privy A title bestowed on certain Vatican functionaries whose duty it is to render personal assistance to the pope in his immediate entourage. The *Pontifical Yearbook* lists five classes: three for clerics, two for laymen. The vast majority of privy chamberlains are either "supernumerary" or merely "honorary." The best known class are the Supernumerary Privy Chamberlains of His Holiness, numbering nearly 3,000 clerics scattered throughout the world. Their distinctive garb is a purple cassock and, for ceremonial occasions, a *mantellone* or Roman cloak. Their title of address is "Very Rev. Monsignor." Their appointment lapses on the death of the Pope who named them but is customarily renewed by his successor. The corresponding distinc-

tion of honor for laymen is that of Supernumerary Privy Chamberlain of Sword and Cape. Chamberlains of this class, when visiting Rome, may take a turn of active duty at the Vatican; when doing so, they wear their medieval court costume featuring sword and cape.

chancel (L. *cancelli,* railings) The area of the sanctuary of a church between the altar and the nave, or body of the church. The name comes from the railings which formerly separated this area from the rest of the church. Today the altar rail serves this function.

chancellor (L. *cancellarius,* a legal Roman official) The official priest appointed by the bishop of a diocese with the charge of the chancery. His duties include the drawing up of official reports on the government of the diocese, the authentication of documents and supervision of the diocesan archives.

chancery office That department of the diocesan curia, headed by the chancellor of the diocese, which conducts the affairs of the diocese as delegated by the bishop, handles correspondence, and which cares for official documents.

Chancery, the Apostolic The Roman office or bureau which, on instructions from the various Congregations or by order of the Sovereign Pontiff personally, prepares and dispatches Decretal Letters of Canonization and papal bulls concerned with appointments to Consistorial benefices and offices, the erection of new dioceses and chapters, and certain other affairs of major importance. Its origins go back to the 4th-century Notaries of Holy Roman Church who were charged with drafting pontifical documents and supervising the archives.

change The passage from one form of perfection to another. Change is either substantial or accidental, according as a being passes from one substance to another, or from one accident to another. An example of a substantial change is the change which takes place at Mass when the bread and wine are changed into the Body and Blood of Christ. This change is known as the Transubstantiation (*q.v.*). Change can be accidental; e.g., when a thing changes from cold to hot. To Aristotle is due credit for the philosophical classification of the types of change.

chant (L. *cantare,* to sing) 1. A type of music, largely monodic, characterized by singing an indefinite number of syllables on one tone and used in liturgical worship. There are a number of versions of plain chant (*q.v.*) but the type used in the Western Church is some form of Gregorian Chant (*q.v.*). There is also a chant in use in the Eastern Churches which sounds strange and monotonous to most Westerners. Several of the churches, such as the Slavonic Byzantines, have music of rich harmony and beauty. 2. A monotonous incantation used in primitive cultures, largely by chemans and witch doctors, to cure disease, cause rain, drive away an evil, etc.

chapel (L. *capella,* a small cloak) 1. From the sanctuary where the cloak of St. Martin of Tours was enshrined. Today it is applied to a building, or part of a building, or room set apart for public worship for the use of a community, religious group, a family or individual, and not for the faithful at large. It may be designated as a public or semipublic oratory by the bishop. 2. A partially enclosed portion of a larger church containing an altar where Mass may be celebrated or the Blessed Sacrament reserved or the relics of a particular saint may be enshrined.

chaplain One who serves a chapel. 1. A priest appointed to exercise the sacred ministry for a religious institution, lay group or organization; or for a public institution such as a hospital or prison; or for an orphanage. He has no parochial rights over the community unless by special privilege or faculties accorded him by the bishop. 2. Military chaplain. A priest member of the Army, Navy, or Air Force assigned by his military superiors to units or areas of military personnel to exercise the sacred ministry in the place of assignment. He is under the jurisdiction of the Military Vicar or Bishop Ordinary of the armed forces.

chaplet (Fr. *chapel,* a hat) Originally, a wreath or garland worn on the head; now, a circular string of beads for counting prayers. The size of a chaplet varies according to the devotion.

chapter (L. *capitulum,* a chapter in a book) 1. A canonical meeting of superiors and delegates of a religious order or institute. 2. A daily meeting of religious at which their rule is read. 3. A group of secular canons attached to a cathedral or a church. 4. A division of the Old or New Testament.

chapter, cathedral A group of clergy that constitutes the council of the bishop at his episcopal seat, upon which devolves the care of souls exercised through a vicar chosen either from its own number or outside. The body is responsible for the temporal as well as the spiritual concerns of the cathedral church.

chapter, collegiate A group of clergy upon which devolves the care of souls exercised through a vicar (chosen either from its own number or outside) who are attached to a collegiate church, i.e., a church which is endowed for a body of canons, but is not, like a cathedral, the see of a bishop.

chapter, general A canonical meeting of the heads and representatives of a religious order, congregation or society especially for the purpose of electing new superiors and dealing with business concerning the whole order. They are regularly held every three, four, six or ten years, and apart from the pope they constitute the highest authority for their respective religious.

chapter house A meeting place of the canons of the cathedral. Also the meeting place of monks or religious within their monastery.

chapter of faults An exercise carried out in monasteries and convents at regular intervals through which the religious confesses known faults and transgressions of the rule (not sins) publicly and receives suitable penance. In some religious houses one member may accuse another of faults, but generally counteraccusations are not allowed. The exercise is conducted in the spirit of charity and is one of its finest manifestations.

chapter, provincial The assembly of delegated members of a religious community for the discussion, improvement or change of the rules of their order or society. It is provincial in that it pertains only to the members of a certain territory, termed a province. In this province are included all the members of all the religious houses of that order; the religious superior of a province is termed the provincial.

character 1. *Theological:* a spiritual mark imprinted upon the soul by the reception of the sacraments of Bap-

tism, Confirmation and Holy Orders. It is indelible even after serious sins, including apostasy. 2. *Psychological:* internal dispositions coming from heredity, environment, education, or deliberately formed habits which preside over one's habitual conduct.

charism (Gr. *charismata,* gifts) Extraordinary gifts of the Holy Spirit, granted to an individual for the sanctification of others. The term is sometimes limited to the personal gifts referred to by St. Paul in 1 Cor. 12 and Rom. 12:6 ff.

charismata *See* charism.

charismatic gifts Supernatural gifts, e.g., ability to heal the sick, prophecy, etc.

charity Christian charity is the love of God and the love of all men for the sake of God. This love compels one to set aside his own selfish desires in order to do that which is desired by God and others.

charity, act of Any act of the will which expresses a supernatural love for God. It is most commonly used as a form of words, such as, "O God, I love Thee above all things and my neighbor as myself for your sake"; but these words are not necessary for the act.

charity, heroic act of An act by which an individual offers to God on behalf of the souls in purgatory all the indulgences, merits gained by good works and suffrages which may be due him after death. It is called "heroic" because the maker is willing to accept the pains of purgatory without any merits of his own in order to benefit others. Priests who make this act may gain a plenary indulgence for a soul in purgatory of their choice each time they offer Mass; laymen, when they receive Holy Communion. The act is revocable when that is desired.

Charity, Sisters of   A title given to numerous congregations of religious women who are often distinguished by a secondary title. They are in general devoted to the works of mercy. The original foundation was a daring venture on the part of St. Vincent de Paul in Paris in 1633. St. Vincent, learning from the failure of St. Francis de Sales, took great care in trying to found an unenclosed order, to avoid any resemblance to cloistered nuns in the congregation which Francis had founded. He called them "Daughters of Charity," avoiding the title of Sisters or of nuns; had them wear the ordinary peasant dress of the time; gave their superiors the title of Sister Servant instead of Abbess; and carefully arranged for them never to be bound by final vows, but to renew their vows annually. All these precautions were taken to prevent their being enclosed inside cloister walls, according to the laws governing religious women of that time. He wanted them to serve the poor in their homes and in the streets. Numerous modern orders have now adopted a similar life, and though the Daughters of Charity were a great innovation in their time, today such active congregations abound throughout the world. It is no longer necessary to observe all the precautions taken by St. Vincent regarding dress, vows, etc.

charity, works of   Primarily, the corporal and spiritual works of mercy stressed unceasingly by Christ. They are key concepts of Christianity upon which our judgment will rest. In general they are actions of a social nature which are resultant from the love of God, actions primarily directed toward our neighbors. We are enjoined to practice works of charity in Eph. 2:10 and Tit. 2:14. Sometimes works of charity are an obligation.

charm.   A word, text or object supposed to have occult power to avert evil or to bring something desired to pass. Use of such articles is a superstition (*q.v.*) and as such is forbidden to Catholics. As a religious belief it is thought to be irrational, an excess in religion.

Chartres, Our Lady of   One of the most historic, famous and beautiful cathedrals in Christendom, located at Chartres, France. The first church was built on the site *c.* A.D. 67. A rebuilding of the present cathedral was begun in 1020 and completed in 1220. It is one of the world's most magnificent examples of Christian art and architecture. The cathedral was the site of many pilgrimages to the Blessed Virgin and a threefold devotion was paid there: 1. to venerate the statue of Notre-Dame-sous-terre, a reproduction of a Druid figure; 2. to venerate the Black Virgin of Notre Dame; 3. to honor the Veil of the Blessed Virgin, a relic obtained by Charlemagne, which was transferred to Chartres about 876.

Chartreuse, the Grand   The motherhouse of the Carthusians, founded in 1084 by St. Bruno. It is located in the Alps, near Grenoble, France. It gave its name to a liqueur that was made there, the sale of which helped to support the monks. It was the center of many charities. The monks were expelled from the monastery in 1903 by the French Republic. In 1941 the monastery was returned to the Carthusians.

chasse (Fr. reliquary)   A box built in the form of an ark, used to contain major relics of a saint. Other meanings of the term relate to a certain form of dance and to a light liqueur.

chastity (L. *castigare,* to chastise)   1. As a *virtue,* chastity applies to all

Christians, married as well as single. It denotes deliberate abstention from all unlawful sexual pleasure of mind or body by way of conscious control. As applied to persons lawfully married it implies a *relative* restraint in keeping with the observance of the marriage vows and right reason; with respect to the unmarried, *absolute* subjection of the flesh to the spirit is called for. Chastity is a special gift of God, one of the fruits of the Holy Spirit; while difficult, it is always obtainable through prayer and mortification. 2. The *vow* of chastity involves a deliberate promise to God to observe chastity as an *evangelical counsel*. The obligation undertaken under pain of sin binds for a time or in perpetuity according to the intention of the vower; and every infraction will be a twofold sin, against the virtue as such and against religion because of the vow. Clergy of the Latin Rite are bound by a solemn obligation to observe perpetual chastity from the time they receive the subdiaconate, the first of the three major orders. Members of religious congregations of men and women take a vow of absolute chastity according to the terms of their particular profession. A "solemn" vow made publicly for life in certain religious communities constitutes a diriment impediment to matrimony; a "simple" vow, unless dispensed from, acts as a prohibitive impediment to the same.

chasuble (L. *casubula*, a hooded garment) The outer garment worn by the priest at Mass. Its color is according to the feast of the day. It is a sleeveless vestment. Former spellings are *chasible* and *chesible*.

chasuble, folded At one time, the chasuble was folded when worn during penitential seasons. Now, however, the only time it is worn folded is during the ceremonies for the ordination to the priesthood. This signifies the gradual conferral of the spiritual powers of the priesthood. It is unfolded to its full length at the Postcommunion prayer of this Mass.

Cherubikon The "Cherubic Hymn" of the Byzantine liturgies sung by the priest in a low voice and set to very elaborate music which is continued by the choir.

cherubim (Heb. plural of cherub) One of the classes of angels, usually ranked below the seraphim. The name appears in the prefaces of the Latin Rite Mass.

chi rho The first two letters in the Greek name for Christ (X P).  These two letters are most often written one imposed upon the other to make the Christogram, or symbol, for Christ.

Chicago In December, 1674, Father James Marquette and two companions reached the mouth of the Chicago River. They wintered at the site and in Father Marquette's cabin the first Mass was offered. In 1696, Father Pinet established a mission among the Miami Indians. In 1846 the first Catholic school opened under the direction of the Sisters of Mercy. In 1860 the parochial school system was begun. Successive waves of immigration saw both city and diocese grow with large groups of Irish, Poles, Germans and Lithuanians settling there. Today the archdiocese is a leader in apostolic movements.

Childermas Day Another name for the Feast of the Holy Innocents, December 28. Many parents use the day to bless their children solemnly.

children, duties of The duties of children to their parents can be obliga-

119

tions of charity or piety. In charity, children owe their parents a special love. Children sin gravely by hating their parents, by wishing them serious evil, by treating them with great unkindness or neglect, or by causing them great sorrow or worry. As duties in piety children must respect and assist their parents. They show serious disrespect when they express contempt, or seriously dishonor a parent in words (e.g., by injurious or mocking names), in deeds (e.g., by speaking against them), in omission (e.g., by refusing to acknowledge or to show the usual marks of courtesy). A child is not disrespectful, however, in disliking or protesting against evils done by parents. Children are bound to assist parents spiritually by prayers and by obtaining the sacraments, and by giving them bodily help if they are poor, persecuted or suffering. Children living at home should contribute a fair share to the upkeep of the home, if their parents need it and wish it.

Children of Mary Members of one of the various sodalities which have for its purpose the promotion of devotion to the Blessed Mother among youth. Since the 12th century there have been a number of such confraternities established by individuals or religious organizations; e.g., Bl. Peter de Honestis; St. Peter Fourier, 1600; Canons Regular of the Lateran, 1864; Sisters of Charity, 1876.

Children's Crusade, the In 1212, some 50 thousand children, mostly French and German, under the leadership of the shepherd boys Stephen and Nicholas, set out for Palestine on a tragic and unfortunate crusade. A monk had persuaded them that the Holy Land could be reconquered only by innocence, not by military valor and strategy. Those children who did not perish of hunger and fatigue were betrayed into the hands of the Saracens and sold as slaves.

Chile In 1541 the first priest arrived in Chile and in 1561 the Diocese of Santiago was erected. Today there are 4 archdioceses, 15 dioceses, 2 vicariates and 2 prelatures nullius. Out of a total population of over 7.5 million, 6.7 million are said to be Catholics; Protestants claim 850,000 followers, a phenomenal growth from the 6,293 Protestants in 1915. While the Church in Chile has many problems, few Latin American countries have made the progress in solving internal difficulties as has Chile. Led by several of the most progressive of Latin American bishops, the Church through its Rural Education Movement, its *Centro Bellarmino* in Santiago and through other social movements has brought the doctrine of Catholicism to the masses. The Church pioneered in land reform, has an organized program of catechetics, conducts a national vocational effort. Unofficially, members of the hierarchy have encouraged the Christian Democratic Movement both among workers and university students. In the so-called mushroom villages, shanty towns which have sprung up around the larger cities, the Church has organized a movement of *pobladores,* the people who live in these hovels. The Episcopal Conference of Chile with 7 departments represents the hierarchy in its effort to reform Catholic life. There is a Catholic university in Santiago, another in Valparaiso with a branch in Antofagasta. Priests and Sisters from the United States are assisting the Chilean hierarchy; Maryknoll, the Holy Cross Fathers and the Precious Blood Fathers have been active for some years.

China The Nestorian Church first brought Christianity to China, probably in the 7th century. In the 13th century Dominican and Franciscan friars visited the country. When the Franciscan, John of Monte Corvino, the first papal legate, reached Peking in 1292 or 1293, he found Nestorians in the city and suffered from their opposition. After the fall of the Mongols, however, all Christian missions disappeared. Christianity was reintroduced by the Jesuits in the 16th century, the most famous of whom was the mathematician and astronomer, Matteo Ricci. In the years that followed there were misunderstandings and controversy that hindered the development of the Church. It was not until the imperial dynasty crumbled in 1911 that the Church was able to function freely. Following World War I, Popes Benedict XV and Pius XI launched a vigorous program for the Sinification of the Church. Following the Synod of Shanghai, the first National Synod ever held in China, Pope Pius XI in 1926 consecrated six Chinese bishops. In 1939 Pope Pius XII promulgated the decree which ended the quarrel over Chinese rites (*q.v.*). In 1946 Archbishop Thomas Tien, S.V.D., was appointed Cardinal, the hierarchy established, an internuncio appointed to the Republic of China and a solemnization of the beatification of the Boxer martyrs took place. The Church seemed at last ready to blossom after all the centuries of spade work. Then in 1949 after a military drive, the Communist Party drove the Nationalist government into exile and took over control. The Reds immediately began to remove foreign influences using arrests, false accusations, imprisonment and public trials to discredit foreign missioners. Bishop Francis X. Ford, a Maryknoll bishop from Brooklyn, N.Y., died in a Chinese prison in Canton. Bishop James E. Walsh, another Maryknoll bishop and former Superior General, was tried and sentenced to twenty years for "espionage." The Chinese Communists attempted to set up a patriotic church, divorced from the Holy See, with which they have had some success; by the end of 1962, they had consecrated 42 "patriotic" bishops.

China, People's Republic In 1949 when the Communists overran China there were almost 4 million Catholics, with a conversion rate of about 50,000 Chinese a year. Today very little is known of the Catholic Church in China. The only American missioner left in the country is Bishop James Edward Walsh of Maryknoll who is in a prison in Shanghai. All other foreign missioners have been forced out of the country, many Chinese bishops and priests are in jail, others sent to work camps. Churches, convents, schools and seminaries have been closed. The Communist government made considerable effort to set up a national church with some success but evidence reaching the outside world tells of priests and faithful who have chosen death rather than cooperation with the atheistic government.

China, Republic of When the Communists overran the mainland in 1949, the Chinese government withdrew to the Province of Taiwan (Formosa) until the day it could return to China proper. For some years the Dominicans had been working on the island and at the time of the arrival of the Chinese government there were about 9,000 Catholics. Today out of the 11 million people of Taiwan, there are a quarter of a million Catholics. A Catholic university is being organized in Taipei, the capital. There is a Catholic radio station in Taichung. From the United States, Jesuits and Maryknollers are represented in the largest numbers.

Chinese Rites From time immemorial, Chinese have had a great respect for their ancestors. To honor them, a small wooden tablet containing the name of the ancestor and the date of death, was placed in the ancestral hall of each clan and in the residence of the family. On the anniversary of death and at other special times, elaborate ceremonies took place in the ancestral hall. In the home, offerings of tea and rice were placed before the tablets. Accompanying these rites were solemn ceremonies performed in honor of Confucius, the great sage who left his teachings of wisdom and virtue to the Chinese. When Mateo Ricci, the founder of the 16th century Jesuit mission to China, came into contact with these rites, he studied them carefully and concluded that they could be tolerated and gradually purified and brought into harmony with Christian principles. However, Franciscans and other missioners attacked the rites as superstitious and intolerable. A great controversy arose that did much to hinder the spread of Christianity. In 1715 Pope Clement XI issued a bull declaring that the rites were superstitious and prohibited. Pope Benedict XIV ended all further discussion in 1742 by requiring every missioner to China to take an oath that he would not enter into discussion or argumentation about the rites. The first move to upset these decisions came in the 20th century when the Japanese government ruled that bowing at the shrines was not a religious act. The Japanese ordered all students in the empire to pay homage to Confucius, declaring that such honor was a mark of respect and not religious worship. The Bishops of Manchuria (Manchukuo) requested permission of the Holy See to perform these ceremonies and in 1935 Pope Pius XI chaired the meeting that approved the request. In 1939 Pope Pius XII promulgated an instruction that accepted the prevalent interpretation that the rites were nonreligious and which left particular cases to the consciences of Christians, thus ending a controversy of many centuries.

chivalry (Fr. *chevalier* from L. *caballarius,* horseman) The religio-social moral code of medieval knighthood. It was an order entered into through a vow-rite in which the knight pledged himself to the service of God and the Church in behalf of the weak and oppressed. *See* knight.

choice The act of using one's rational nature to select from among two or more possibilities. Man has the power to choose because of his free will.

choir (L. *chorus,* singers) 1. That part of a church or chapel where the Divine Office is sung. 2. That part of a church used by singers; sometimes called a choir loft. 3. Those men and boys who sing the proper parts of the Mass, the Divine Office, etc. 4. By extension, men and women singers who for certain reasons take the place of a liturgical choir.

choir dress The costume worn by the clerics present in choir at a sacred function. Secular priests wear a surplice over their cassock; bishops and other prelates entitled to them, wear the *mozzetta* or *mantelletta* over the rochet and cassock; all wear the biretta. Monks wear a large cowl over their habit, and some friars have a cloak or *cappa* for choir use.

choir monk One professed "for the

choir," i.e., with the obligation of saying the Divine Office daily in choir, as opposed to a lay Brother. In the Western Church all choir monks must proceed to Holy Orders. Only two European monasteries now have the privilege of professing men for the choir who may not intend to be ordained (Prinknash and Amay). Earlier monasticism was essentially a lay life; it is still so to a great extent in the Eastern Churches, Catholic and dissident.

choir screen A construction separat-

ing the choir from the nave found in many medieval churches.

choirs of angels, the nine The whole company of angels arranged in hierarchic (graded) order. The nine choirs, from the lowest hierarchy to the highest, are: Angels, Archangels, Principalities, Powers, Virtues, Dominations, Thrones, Cherubim and Seraphim. These nine choirs are divided into three orders. The last three are spoken of as being closest to God and are sometimes called counselors. The middle three are sometimes called rulers because their names seem to indicate a certain governing power. The first three are spoken of as workers. They are God's messengers, and among them are the guardian angels.

choral vicar The choir director of a group of canons of a cathedral chapter.

chorale A religious hymn or psalm whose music is arranged for many voices.

Chosen People, the 1. The Jews of the Old Testament who were chosen from among all peoples in virtue of a promise made by God to Abraham (Gen. 17), becoming a privileged society. Their election did not necessarily imply worldly success, but supernatural privileges, especially the fact that the Redeemer was to come from among them. 2. In a narrower sense the term is applied to such of them as were faithful to their calling, and who persevered in justice in the time of trial (cf. Is. 14:9 ff; Wis. 3:9).

chrism (Gr. *chrisma,* an anointing) A mixture of olive oil and balm consecrated by a bishop on Holy Thursday and used in administering Baptism, Confirmation and Holy Orders; and in the consecration of a bishop. This oil is also used in the consecration of churches, the blessing of baptismal fonts, the consecration of chalices, patens, altar stones and church bells.

chrism, consecration of Takes place after the Communion of the Mass on Holy Thursday. In the East the consecration of chrism is a sign of patriarchical authority. The Catholic patriarchs consecrate it for the bishops and clergy under their jurisdiction.

chrismal 1. A baptismal robe (*q.v.*). 2. An oilstock or small metal vessel in which the holy oils are kept.

chrismale A cerecloth (*q.v.*).

chrismarium 1. The area in a church formerly set aside for the administration of Confirmation. 2. The vessel in which chrism is kept.

chrismation (Gr. *chrisma,* an anointing) The act of anointing persons or things.

chrismatory A chrismal (*q.v.*) for storing the holy oils.

chrisom child A name given to a child that dies during the first month after birth.

Christ (Gr. *Christos*) A name translated from the Hebrew *messia* (masiah) meaning "the anointed one." It was a title added to the name "Jesus."

Christ-Candle A large white candle used on the family table during the Christmas season. It is lighted during the family meals. The candle signifies that Christ is the Light from the Root of Jesse.

Christ of the Andes A large statue of  Christ erected on the Andean border of Argentina and Chile. Cast from melted-down guns, it commemorates a peaceful settlement of a border dispute between those two nations. It stands on a mountain pass 14,000 feet above sea level.

Christ the King A feast established by Pope Pius XI in 1925, celebrated on the last Sunday in October by the Western Church. Its object is to reassert the authority of Our Lord to rule over men's hearts and wills, as well as over whole nations; and of His Church to teach the human race and bring mankind to salvation in the Kingdom of Christ. Christ is King by reason of His Sonship of God; and by right, as mankind's Redeemer.

Christendom The Kingdom of God on earth to which modern thought gives a personal rather than a territorial connotation. It refers to the religious, ethical, legal and social life of Christians united in the common life of the Mystical Body which transcends merely state or national boundaries. In the Middle Ages the term referred to countries which were wholly or predominantly Christian, though there is a tendency to confine the word still to Europe.

christening The traditional English word for the conferral of the Sacrament of Baptism and the act of baptizing: i.e., making one Christlike or Christian. A Christian name is so called because it is the name given when one is christened.

Christian 1. One who believes that Jesus Christ is the Risen Lord and Savior of the world. 2. One who has been initiated into a personal relationship with Jesus Christ through the rite of Christian Baptism. 3. One who lives in accord with the teachings of Jesus Christ. The term is also applied to all churches, denominations and sects professing belief in Christ.

Christian Brothers Catholic laymen devoted to teaching youth. There are two separate but similar congregations: 1. The Brothers of the Christian Schools (F.S.C.) founded by St. John Baptist de la Salle in 1680 at Reims, France. They take the three religious vows, and are found throughout the world. The motherhouse is in Rome. There are six provinces in the United States. 2. The Christian Brothers of Ireland, founded in 1802 in Waterford, Ireland, by Brother Edmund Rice. Motherhouse is in Dublin, and the American provincial headquarters is at Iona College, New Rochelle, N.Y.

Christian Democrats Those engaged in the political, economic and social movement known as Christian Democracy; it is a movement in which lay men and women, under the inspiration of their Christian Faith, take up their responsibility in the area of directing or becoming involved in political parties, trade unions, unions of farmers, etc. Leo XIII said of Christian Democracy (in *Graves de Communi,* 1901), "It is concerned primarily, though not exclusively, with the problems of the working class. It is aimed at so improving the conditions of life as to allow people to feel themselves to be men, not animals; Christian men and not pagans . . . enabling people to strive with more facility and earnestness to attain that one thing needful, that final good for which we came into the world." Today, however, the movement is no longer confined to the working class, but consists of laymen of whatever class who are working out the solution of political, social and economic problems in the light of Christian principles; they are convinced that in the modern world democracy is the best form of government, and that all government should be of, for, and by the people, not only in the state but also in the firm, in the local community or in the family. The Christian Democrats have produced practical Christian principles for the solving of the social, political and economic problems of our times. These principles are built upon the foundations laid by the Church of the Apostles and the great Christian Doctors, St. Augustine, St. Thomas Aquinas and others, who proved that Christian thought could be applied to every detail of life. The doctrine of the "just price" in the Middle Ages, for instance so long disregarded in our secular, *laissez-faire* environment, is coming to light again as an ideal and a way of solving problems in the modern, disorganized world. The Church with her Christian approach to everyday life has made a slow recovery in the 400 years since the Protestant revolt destroyed the integrity of Christendom. However, in the 19th and 20th centuries the tide has begun to turn. Catholic social science has flourishing schools in European universities. Institutes of social action have sprung up everywhere. The last century has seen a

Christian revival, both Catholic and ecumenical; and Christian Democracy is an integral part of the pattern. Its Catholic, Orthodox and Protestant movements today combine to look at the problems of life on earth as Christians, and to exert a Christian influence on them.

Christian doctrine 1. The body of Catholic doctrines and teaching. 2. The matter of the catechism which summarizes the truths of the Catholic faith.

Christian Doctrine, Confraternity of A national organization reaching down to the parish level that has for its purpose the religious education of Catholic youth. It is responsible to the Bishops' Committee on the Confraternity of Christian Doctrine. The national organization is geared to service the diocesan organization which in turn services the parish units. These latter are the basic and essential units which fulfill the purpose of the organization wherein the laity, under the guidance of the hierarchy and clergy, play leading roles in learning, living and teaching Christian doctrine. The CCD carries on programs on all levels from preschool to adult. The CCD uses the laity in many capacities as members of the organization: teachers; discussion club leaders; fishers, who promote attendance at catechism classes; helpers, who provide transportation and give other assistance; apostles of good will, who work in the program for non-Catholics; and parent-educators, who promote religious education in the home. The national organization has a broad publications program which includes translations of the Old and the New Testaments. It has headquarters in the NCWC building in Washington, D.C.

Christian era 1. That time since the

birth of Christ. 2. The period in a Christian country following its evangelization.

Christian Family Movement (CFM) Aims to restore family life to Christ and to create a community which is conducive to Christian living. The program, which first took form in Chicago in 1947, combines religious elements, informal and practical discussions, and action by members to influence their parishes and communities. Headquarters: Room 2233, 111 West Monroe Street, Chicago 3, Ill.

Christian name Strictly speaking, it is the name conferred at Baptism, i.e., christening name. In general usage, it is any name of a saint prefixed to the family name whether given in Baptism, at Confirmation or otherwise chosen.

Christian Science A religion known as the Church of Christ, Scientist. It is a sect founded by Mary Baker Eddy (1821–1910) in 1879 in Boston. The sect claims to be Christian but in reality denies most of the truths of Christianity. It professes to be scientific but bases its belief in faith-healing while it denies the existence of sickness and evil as errors of the mind. The followers of the sect are relatively few and found predominantly in the United States. The foundations for the religion are in Mrs. Eddy's book, *Science and Health, with Key to the Scriptures,* a volume that borrows extensively from the writings of P. P. Quimby, founder of the "New Thought" movement. The sect is exceedingly well-organized and wealthy.

Christian Socialism A political and economic system which seeks to accomplish the social reorganization of socialism but on the basis of Christian principles. It advocates protec-

tion of small property owners and aims to make man economically, politically and socially free.

Christianity The religion founded by Jesus Christ; the teachings and moral practices given by Jesus Christ. The word includes not only the Catholic Church but also members of the Eastern Churches not in union with the Holy See and many Protestant churches. The doctrine of Christianity was a revolutionary doctrine that completely remade the Western world. There are two keys to Christianity: the first is a world consciousness and concern for all humanity; the second, flowing from the first, is the Christian doctrine of love. A personalistic religion or individualistic Christianity is a type of personal egotism and is a false Christianity.

Christianity, world See world Christianity.

Christlike An adjective describing a person who deliberately tries to resemble Christ in his actions, spirit and thought.

Christmas (O.E. *Cristes Maesse,* Christ's Mass) The Feast of the Nativity, Dec. 25, the anniversary of Christ's birth. The day commemorates a threefold birth that is meant for all members of the human race: 1. the birth of God into the world— the uniting of the Second Person of the Blessed Trinity, the Word, in the Person of Christ; 2. the birth of Jesus, the true Son of Mary, weak nature assumed by God in order that mankind might not be blinded by His splendor; 3. the day of potential spiritual birth for all men. In the early Church there was no such feast, the commemoration of birth being observed on the Feast of the Epiphany. St. Clement of Alexandia, *c.* 200, first mentions the feast and the Latin Church began celebrating it on Dec. 25 about 300, although there is no evidence that this date is the actual birthdate of Our Lord. Christmas is a holyday of obligation, and should it fall on a Friday there is no abstinence. Priests are permitted to celebrate three Masses on this day.

Christmas crib A representation of the manger in Bethlehem where Christ was born. The representation usually contains the Holy Family, the Wise Men, the shepherds and various animals. The devotion was popularized by the Franciscans beginning in the middle of the 13th century.

Christmas cycle The liturgical period beginning with the First Sunday of Advent and extending through the Saturday after the last Sunday of Epiphany. The Christmas cycle has four minor or subcycles: 1. Advent, a time of preparation. The liturgical color is purple. It begins with the First Sunday of Advent and ends with December 23. 2. Christmas, a time of celebration. The liturgical color is white. It begins with the Vigil of Christmas and extends through January 5. It includes Christmas and New Year's Day and the Feast of the Holy Name of Jesus. 3. Epiphany, a time for thanksgiving. The liturgical color is white. It begins January 6 and extends through the Saturday after the Feast of the Holy Family. 4. Time after Epiphany. The liturgical color is green. It extends from the second Sunday after Epiphany through the Saturday after the last Sunday after Epiphany. There may be as many as six Sundays after Epiphany, depending on the date of Easter.

Christmas Eve The day, and particularly the night, before Christmas; the Vigil of the Nativity.

Christmas tree A tree, usually an evergreen, which is decorated and used as part of the Christmas celebration. Its origin is uncertain although it developed in Germany. It was popularized in England by Prince Albert, consort of Queen Victoria, about 1840. Since then its use has spread to other parts of the world.

Christology 1. The study of Jesus Christ, His sayings, His nature, His times, etc. 2. The body of knowledge scientifically collected concerning Jesus Christ.

Christo-paganism The theologically untenable amalgam that results from the fusion of Christian and pagan beliefs. Some Guatemalan Indians are a prime example of this fusion.

Christopher, medal of St. There is an ancient legend of a saintly ferryman who once carried a child across a stream; the child turned out to be the Child Jesus. The ferryman was called Christopher, Greek for Christbearer. He has been celebrated as the patron of travelers and it has long been a custom to wear or carry a medal of St. Christopher to seek his protection while traveling. In recent years, he has become the patron of motorists, and plaques made in the fashion of a St. Christopher medal are carried in automobiles to ask his protection from accident.

Christophers, The A movement without memberships, meetings or dues founded in 1945 by Father James Keller, M.M., for the purpose of encouraging each individual to show a personal and practical responsibility in restoring the love and truth of Christ to the market place, especially in government, education, labor-management, literature and entertainment. The Christopher movement reaches millions of individuals through 3,000 radio and television stations every week and through its publications. The philosophy is expressed by the motto: "Be not overcome by evil, but overcome evil with good."

Chronicler 1. That section of the solemn singing of the Passion in Holy Week that narrates the events that happened in Christ's Passion. This does not include spoken words which are taken by the ministers who represent Christ and the Synagoga. 2. The person who sings this section of the Passion. 3. The author of the Book of Chronicles (Paralipomenon) whose real name is unknown.

Chronicles, Book of An old Testament work also known as Paralipomenon ("the book of what was omitted"). It is divided into two sections which are mainly concerned with history from the time of Adam to the edict of Cyrus at the end of the Babylonian captivity. It was written about the 4th century B.C. The theme is that God is the omnipresent ruler of creation; it emphasizes the holiness of God's people, centered in worship around the Temple.

chronology, biblical The record by years of the history of the Old Testament. These dates can only be reached by exhaustive research. The problem is made more difficult because of the different methods of keeping dates that existed in Egypt, Assyria and Babylonia.

church (building) Any physical structure designed or adapted primarily for the Christian community's worship of God in the Eucharist (the Mass), and the other sacraments, the Divine Office but also for private prayer.

Church The Catholic Church is the family of God on earth. It is a true family into which a person is born by Baptism. The Church unites its members in a strong mutual love and gives a common life. The purpose of the Church is to build up the Kingdom of God on earth, and in doing such becomes the visible representation of the Mystical Body of Christ.

Church and State The medieval state was a unity with two poles of authority—the Church and the State. In many cases the authority was one and the same. The Founding Fathers of the United States conceived a new type of society, one in which there would be no state religion and in which state every man would have the freedom and choice of any or no religion. This conception made the Church and the State two distinct powers, each autonomous in its own sphere. It is the task of the government to create an atmosphere wherein its citizens can choose their own religion to work out their eternal welfare.

church history The account of the rise and continuance of the Catholic Church from its founding to the present time; the written account which gives the history of the Catholic religion. Eusebius of Caesarea in the 4th century is said to be the father of church history.

Church Militant All members of the Mystical Body of Christ now living on earth. They are termed "militant" in light of the conception of this life as a warfare in which the soldiers (all the members of the Mystical Body) are fighting Satan and their own dispositions to sin in order to attain salvation.

church, national 1. Commonly applied in the United States to those parishes established to care for Catholics of a common language and cul-

128

ture such as the Italians or Chinese who have not as yet been assimilated into American life. 2. Also used to refer to the one church which has or had the official backing of the government of a country and which may or may not not be subject to anyone outside of that country, as the Church of England or the Catholic Church in Spain, or the Greek Orthodox Church.

Church of Christ The human means set up by Christ for the continuance of His presence among men, as manifested most typically in the community life of Christians with their bishop.

Church of Rome 1. A popular term among non-Catholics, particularly Protestants, for the Catholic Church, so used because the center of this Church is at Rome. 2. The gathering of Christ's faithful at Rome where Peter was the first bishop. Since then the pope, bishop of the diocese of Rome and successor to Peter's office of chief of the Apostles, has primacy among the bishops, and is patriarch of the West.

Church of Silence The term refers to the Churches in those nations which are persecuted and cut off from the outside world, particularly those in Communist countries.

church property Anything that is possessed by the Church as a corporation or as a moral person. Any property, movable or immovable, owned by a moral personality created by the Church, such as a parish, religious house and the like.

Church Suffering A designation for the souls in purgatory who comprise a part of the Mystical Body of Christ.

Church Triumphant Comprises all the blessed in heaven, forming part of the Mystical Body of Christ. The Church Militant, Suffering and Triumphant form the Communion of Saints.

Church Unity Octave Eight days of prayer in Catholic, Protestant and Orthodox churches throughout the world for the religious unity of Christians and all men. It is held from Jan. 18, the commemoration of St. Peter's Chair, to Jan. 25, the Feast of the Conversion of St. Paul. The exercise was begun at Graymoor, N.Y., by Father Paul Watson before his conversion from Anglicanism to Catholicism. Piux X and succeeding popes have blessed and encouraged this observance. Promotion of the octave is in the care of the Friars of the Atonement.

churches, classification of Places (other than oratories) designated for worship are distinguished according to their use and fame. Churches are named "metropolitan," "cathedral," "collegiate" and "parochial" through function. "Basilica" is exclusively a title of honor. Oratories are classified as: public, semipublic and private.

Churches of Christ Founded in Western Pennsylvania in 1832 by Thomas and Alexander Campbell, its members are sometimes called the Conservative Campellites. Members believe that Scripture is the sole rule of faith, rejecting all creeds. Baptism is by immersion. The Lord's Supper is commemorated every Sunday. Each church is independent. There are over 1.5 million members. *See* Disciples of Christ.

churching of women A blessing given to women after childbirth; it is recommended as an act of thanksgiving. The custom of receiving such a blessing according to the ritual is symbolic of the re-entrance of the mother into the Church.

ciborium (L. a cup) A vessel usu-

 ally made of gold, goblet-shaped with a cover, in which the communion hosts are contained for distribution and reservation in the tabernacle.

CICOP, The Catholic Inter-American Cooperation Program A program launched in 1963 by the United States Bishops' Committee for Inter-American Cooperation in order to create programs specifically designed to promote understanding and friendship and accelerate mutual concern between Catholics of the United States and those of Latin America.

cilicum (L. a hairshirt) Used as a penitential garment or for mortification.

Cincinnati A city in Ohio. Catholics in the area made an unsuccessful attempt to establish a parish in 1811. When Bishop Flaget visited Cincinnati in 1814 he said the first Mass there in the house of a Catholic layman. He encouraged the Catholics to renew their attempt of 1811. Because of anti-Catholicism within the city and an ordinance forbidding a Catholic church within corporate limits, the first church, a log cabin, was built just outside the city limits. The first bishop of Cincinnati (1821), Bishop Edward Fenwick, used the structure as his cathedral. Bishop Fenwick was responsible for having the discriminatory ordinance removed and St. Peter's Cathedral was completed in 1826. On a visit to France Bishop Fenwick was given a printing press, which printed the first edition of the *Catholic Telegraph* in 1831. The Sisters of Charity arrived in Cincinnati in 1829. The city was a center for strong elements of the Know-Nothing Movement. In 1850 the diocese was raised to the rank of an archdiocese.

circumcision (L. *circumcidere,* to cut around) The Hebraic rite which consists in cutting the membrane of the foreskin of the penis. God in the Old Testament prescribed this practice to Abraham and his descendants and made it a sign of the religious pact with Abraham and all his heirs. Circumcision in the Old Testament had an effect analogous to Baptism in the New. It was performed on boys on the eighth day after birth with a ritual flint knife, bestowal of name, godparents, formulae and prayers. Many of the ancient pagan peoples also practiced this rite.

Circumcision, Feast of The feast which commemorates the subjection of the Child Jesus to the Jewish rite of circumcision. The rite signified the admission of the Child to the Covenant which God established with Abraham and through him with the Jewish people. The feast is celebrated on Jan. 1 and is a holyday of obligation. It is the octave of Christmas day and is observed in Anglican and Orthodox Eastern Churches as well as Roman Catholic.

circuminsession 1. The attribute of the Blessed Trinity that the Three Persons exist totally within each other. The mutual indwelling or inexistence of the three distinct Persons means that the Father is wholly and entirely in the Son, wholly and entirely in the Holy Spirit; the Son is wholly and entirely in the Father and Holy Spirit; and that the Holy Spirit is wholly and entirely in the Father, and wholly and entirely in the Son (Council of Florence). 2. The expression denotes the mutual inexistence of the human and divine natures in Christ.

circumstances The conditions or facts that prompt one's action or prevail during the action, and which must be taken into account when judging the action. Cimcumstances are: 1. *aggravating,* when they increase culpability; 2. *extenuating,* when they lessen culpability. Circumstances can often mean the difference between a venial and mortal sin (and vice versa), and therefore must be confessed when they alter a sin.

Cistercian Rite Following the reform of the missal in the 17th century, the Cistercian Rite closely follows the Roman Rite. The Rite has its own "Ritual" and a breviary developed from the Monastic Breviary.

Cistercians Monks of the Order of Citeaux founded by St. Robert in 1098 to follow a more strict observance of the rule of St. Benedict. They in turn divided into two Observances, the Common and the Strict. Those of the latter, often called Trappists, practice perpetual silence except in times of necessity, and abstinence from flesh, fish and eggs unless sick. Their primary daily work is farming, and they rise for night Office at 2 A.M. Those of the Common Observance, who are fewer in number, follow a modified version of the original rule. There also are Cistercian nuns who live cloistered, contemplative lives.

citation A canonical term referring to a summons to appear before an ecclesiastical court.

City of God 1. One of the most celebrated Christian apologetic works. It was written by St. Augustine to defend the Church against the attacks of paganism. 2. Jerusalem, so called because it was the center of religious life for the people of Israel. This term is reflected in many of the psalms and has a close association with the worship of Israel before the exile.

civil allegiance Each citizen owes loyalty and obedience to the state. Allegiance is a religious duty since the authority of the state shares in the authority of God.

civil law That law which is directed toward the private rights of individuals in a community and to legal proceedings in connection with them. It is distinct from criminal, political or ecclesiastical law. Civil law is binding in conscience but whether it binds under pain of sin depends on the intention of the legislator. Civil law that touches on spiritual matters only binds when sanctioned or tolerated by ecclesiastical authority.

civil marriage Marriage performed before a civil official as opposed to an official representative of the Church. A merely civil marriage is not recognized by the Catholic Church when one of the parties is a Catholic.

civil rights The rights which belong to a citizen by law. In the United States these would be the rights that belong equally to all citizens as guaranteed by the Constitution, various laws and decisions of the courts. These include the rights of thinking, writing, or acting without interference, except in the interest of public order.

clandestinity A lack of the proper matter and form prescribed by canon law for the valid contracting of a marriage. The matter and form prescribed consists in the exchange of vows in the presence of a priest and at least two witnesses.

clapper (L. *crotalus*) A wooden device used in the place of bells from Holy Thursday to the Easter Vigil. It is variously made. Some have a swinging hammer which hits a piece of wood. Others have a piece of wood which when swung over a gear makes a clicking noise.

Claretian Fathers   Popular name for Missionary Sons of the Immaculate Heart of Mary and taken from the name of its founder, St. Anthony Mary Claret. Founded in Spain in 1849. There are two provinces in the United States. The society is devoted to missionary work, preaching and parochial work.

clausura (L. enclosure)   1. A cloister (*q.v.*). 2. The closing ceremony of a cursillo. The clausura is usually attended by veteran cursillistas who come great distances to welcome the new cursillistas to their ranks.

Clementine Epistle   A letter written by Pope St. Clement about A.D. 95 to the Church at Corinth. It gives a valuable insight into the early Church and the position of the papacy.

Clementine Instruction   The regulations issued by Pope Clement XII in 1736 governing the Forty Hours' Devotion (*q.v.*).

Clementine popes   Clement VII (1378–1394) and Benedict XIII (1394–1423) who claimed the papal throne and who resided at Avignon during the Schism of the West (*q.v.*).

clergy (Gr. *kleros,* an allotment) Generally those who are by state of life consecrated to the divine service. Specifically those persons in the Church legitimately deputed to exercise the power of Holy Orders and jurisdiction. A person becomes a member of the clergy by receiving the ecclesiastical tonsure.

clergy, married   Those members of the Eastern Catholic Rites who are legitimately deputed to exercise the power of Holy Orders and jurisdiction and who are not bound by the oath of celibacy (bound by vows to an unmarried life). In the Eastern

Catholic Rites a man may be ordained to the diaconate and priesthood although he is married. He may not be married after receiving the diaconate; or if his wife dies, marry again. Bishops, however, must be single men or widowers.

cleric (Gr. *kleros,* a lot)   Anyone who has received the ecclesiastical tonsure is strictly speaking a cleric. This includes not only members of the clergy but also students preparing for the priesthood who have been tonsured. The English word "clerk" is derived from the same root.

clerical privilege   The special fourfold favors granted to clerics because of their office. 1. Privilege of Forum —exempts the cleric from subjection to the lay courts and puts him under the ecclesiastical court. 2. Privilege of Canon—prohibits violence against the cleric and punishes with excommunication anyone who dares to strike him unjustly or with malice. 3. Privilege of Personal Immunity— frees the cleric from the burden of secular duties or obligations. 4. Privilege of Competency—gives the cleric the right to proper sustenance. These privileges are usually only by a concordat. They do not apply in the United States.

clericalism   Usually refers to an attempt on the part of the clergy to extend ecclesiastical authority and influence beyond its proper sphere. It may also refer to a tendency to become involved in areas which are the proper responsibility of civil authority. It is often, however, a derogative term for any attempt by the clergy to apply religious principles to questions of social, moral, economic or political life, no matter how legitimate.

clerics, obligations of   Rules set forth in canon law (can. 108–144) providing for the conduct of the clergy:

1. Positive. The leading of exemplary lives, obedience to their ordinary, study of sacred sciences, recitation of the Breviary, practice of celibacy, wearing of ecclesiastical dress. 2. Negative. Abstention from everything unbecoming their dignity and from the practice of certain professions which would interfere with their priestly duties.

Clerks Regular   Groups of men in the Church professing solemn vows and living a community life according to a rule solemnly approved by the sovereign pontiff. They are distinct from monks in that they: 1. are primarily devoted to the sacred ministry; 2. are obliged to cultivate the sacred sciences; 3. must retain some appearance of clerical dress distinct from the habit and cowl of a monk; 4. are less given to the practice of austerity.

client (L. *cliens*)   A person who has a devotion to a particular saint and who puts himself or herself under that saint's care and protection.

cloister (L. *claudere,* to close)   1. A canonically enclosed place reserved for religious. The laws governing such enclosures are found in canons 597–606; 2342. An enclosure is established by the Holy See or the bishop of the diocese in which it is located. Papal cloisters for men hold a penalty of excommunication for any woman who enters and for anyone who permits her to enter. This excommunication is reserved to the Holy See. 2. The covered passageway around the inner square or garden often found in monasteries.

closed time   *See* forbidden time.

cloth of gold   A color for liturgical vestments. It may be used to replace other colors except purple and black.

clothing   The name given to a ceremony in which an aspirant is clothed in the habit of his or her religious community.

coadjutor   Auxiliary or assistant. 1. One appointed to assist a bishop or priest. A bishop may be appointed to aid a bishop in his duties and become an administrator bishop. He may or may not have jurisdictional capacity with the right of succession. If he is a coadjutor bishop to an incapacitated bishop, he usually has all the rights and duties of a residential bishop. 2. In the Society of Jesus, the Brothers are called coadjutors.

coat of arms   A heraldry device of a bishop, diocese, school, religious corporation, saint, etc. *See* hat; heraldry, ecclesiastical.

co-consecrators   The two bishops who assist the consecrating bishop in the creation of a new bishop. They join with the consecrator in imposing hands and calling down the Holy Spirit on the new bishop.

Code of Canon Law (L. *Codex Juris Canonici*)   The whole body of rules which forms the legal system by which the Church governs her life and that of her members. The canon is the standard unit of subdivision within the code and each is numbered for convenience.

codex (koe′decks; L. *caudex,* tree trunk, book)   An ancient book or manuscript in leaf form which distinguishes it from a roll. Great manuscripts of the Bible are in codex form and are named accordingly, Codex Vaticanus, Codex Alexandrinus, etc. The word when used alone refers to the *Code of Canon Law.*

Codex Vaticanus   The name of a Greek manuscript of the Bible that dates back to the early 4th century.

It is one of the most important biblical manuscripts extant. It is preserved in the Vatican Library.

coeducational The educational practice of teaching both sexes the same subject matter together. In the Catholic school system, coeducation is practiced at all levels; but for the secondary schools, separate or co-institutional schools are preferred.

cohabitation Living together under one roof in a familial way. It is the principal obligation of married couples. Cohabitation creates the presumption that a marriage has been consummated, and positive and conclusive proof must be given by parties claiming otherwise.

cohort One-sixth of a Roman legion, consisting of 1,000 infantrymen and 120 horsemen. The term is mentioned in John and Acts.

coinstitutional Educational practice of teaching differentiated subjects to the sexes in separated classes. Usually only the major facilities of the school are shared by the two separated divisions.

coition (L. *coire,* to come together) The loving embrace of man and wife in the fulfillment of sexual union. The act is unlawful if the persons concerned are not husband and wife.

collateral relationship That relationship of persons descended from a common ancestor but not from one another. Thus brother and sister are collaterally related. It is taken into account in determining impediments to marriage.

collation (L. *collatio,* a bringing together) 1. A light meal which was taken on fast days in addition to the full meal. The word came from *Collationes,* the spiritual writings which were read in monasteries during this meal. 2. A light repast taken outside of time of regular meals. In the United States, the repast taken after Midnight Mass is called a collation. 3. The presentation of a vacant benefice to an incumbent.

collect (L. *colligere,* to collect) A brief prayer of the priest recited before the Epistle at Mass. It is the "gathering together" or collection of prayers and consists of three elements: 1. the invocation to God; 2. a petition that usually contains some spiritual objective; 3. The ending, which calls upon the name of Jesus Christ. Collects vary according to the feast of the day or season of the year. Also, they may be prayers or orations for a special intention. The sources for most collects are from the Latin *Sacramentaries* of Leo I (5th century), Gelasius (492), and Gregory (590).

collection 1. In general, contributions of money given for the support of the church, clergy, religious institution or religious project. 2. Offertory collection. A collection taken up following the Creed (at the Offertory) to meet church expenses. Formerly, this collection represented Offertory gifts to be used in the Eucharistic Liturgy; later, gifts of food and money were given to support the priest and purchase the necessities for Mass. 3. Seat collection. A practice of collecting "seat money" at the door of the church. The practice began as a substitute for pew rent. However, because of the many misunderstandings that arose from it, particularly because many interpreted it as a "charge" for admission, the practice has been banned and voluntarily halted in many places.

collection, offertory The voluntary giving by the faithful during the Offertory part of the Mass. Its purpose is to symbolize the faithful giving themselves to God and to support their church and priest. In former times the giving consisted of food, clothing, alms for the poor, money, etc. and this was the income for the church and priest. Today, money is the common form of contribution for the collection.

collects, solemn   The nine collects or prayers which form the second part of the Good Friday Liturgy. They are for the Church, the pope, the clergy and faithful, rulers, catechumens, the needs of the faithful, the unity of the Church, conversion of the Jews, conversion of the heathen.

college (L. *collegium*)   The most familiar application is to a society of persons engaged in the pursuits of literature or science, including both professors and students. The college is subordinate to the university in the degrees it can grant, being limited mainly to bachelor degrees. In American usage, college commonly indicates the stage of instruction between high school and graduate studies.

College of Cardinals, Sacred   A corporation or college of cardinals, after the manner of the cathedral chapters. The nomination to the college is by the pope alone. According to the decrees of the Council of Trent, the college should contain doctors of theology and at least four theologians from the mendicant orders. The cardinal must swear that he will defend conscientiously the papal bulls concerning nonalienation of the possessions of the Roman Church, nepotism, papal elections and his own cardinalitial dignity. As a legal corporation the cardinals have their own revenues, which are administered by a camerlengo chosen from their own body. It is the duty of the cardinals to assist the pope at the chief liturgical services; also to

counsel him and aid in the government of the Church. They are obliged to reside at Rome, and cannot leave without the permission of the pope. The share of the cardinals in the government of the Church is exercised partly in the consistories, partly in curial offices in the Roman Congregations and in various ecclesiastical commissions. The dean or head of the college is the Bishop of Ostia, the first of the cardinal priests. The subdean is the Bishop of Porto, and is the supervisor of discipline of the Roman clergy and administrator of the possessions of the Roman Church. The dean, as president of the College, has first place in general councils after the pope, and has the duty to convoke the council, to conduct its deliberations and to represent it abroad.

colleges, national   Institutions for the education of ecclesiastics established and maintained in Rome, which have been founded under the auspices of the pope and of the bishops of the country to which they belong.

colleges, Roman   Institutions established and maintained in Rome for the education of ecclesiastics which have been founded under ecclesiastical auspices and are under ecclesiastical direction. These colleges are equivalent to a seminary, having in addition the advantages for study which Rome offers, and serve in a certain measure to maintain in the various countries of the world that spirit of loyal attachment to the Holy See which is the basis of unity. With this end in mind the popes have encouraged the founding of colleges in which young men of the same nationality might reside and at the same time profit by the opportunities which the city affords. The Roman colleges are grouped in several clusters. Each college has at its head a rector designated by the episcopate of the country to which the college belongs and appointed by the pope. The schedule of the colleges is that of a seminary.

collegiality *See* bishops, collegiality of.

collegiate (L. *collegium,* a society) A term used for a moral body of persons and their acts. A collegiate church is one served by a group of secular clerics, called canons; they form a chapter. Canon law distinguishes between collegiate and non-collegiate personalities. The former are chapters, boards, councils, etc., that consist of more than three persons. Non collegiate would include hospitals and other institutions.

collusion Conspiracy between two or more persons for a deceitful purpose. It is an agreement formed in secret for a fraudulent or illegal purpose—a secret understanding by two parties to defraud a third. The moral guilt lies in the deceit.

Colombia The first episcopal see created in South America was set up in Colombia in 1513. Today there are 6 archdioceses, 26 dioceses, 11 vicariates, 7 prefectures and 1 prelature. Of the more than 15 million people in the country, 90 percent are Catholic. In the large centers such as Bogotá, Medellin and Cali, Catholic life is active and vigorous. A substantial number of vocations come from these areas. In the matter of native vocations and organized Catholic life, Colombia is probably the leader in South America. Bogotá, the capital, is the headquarters for the Episcopal Conference of Latin American Bishops. It is also the center for *Popular Accion Cultural,* the pioneering effort of education by radio which has had considerable success and imitation.

Colorado (Sp. colored, from red silt-laden waters of the Colorado River) The 38th state of the Union, 8th in area, 33rd in population, a Rocky Mountain state. It is the highest state in the Union, with an average altitude of 6,800 feet with 1,500 peaks over 10,000 feet high. One of its famous sights is the Mount of the Holy Cross (13,986 feet) whose peak shows a cross outlined in snow. Colorado was part of the Louisiana Purchase and of areas ceded by Mexico and Texas. The early Indian tribes, Utes, Arapahoes and Cheyennes, were nomads and big-game hunters. They were animists, believing also in the Great Spirit, the Supreme Being. Many Spanish explorers traversed parts of the area, the first being, perhaps, Coronado, in 1540. The Franciscan Fathers Dominguez and Escalante passed through the territory in 1776, looking for a route to California. In the meantime French fur traders had made their way into the Colorado Rockies, followed in later years by American traders and explorers. The first white settlers were Spanish-speaking families from New Mexico, who brought the Catholic Faith with them to the San Luis Valley in the 1850's. In 1858 gold was discovered, and in the gold rush which ensued, numerous immigrants arrived from all over the Union and from Europe. Among the Germans and Irish there were many Catholics, who settled in the northern parts of the state, the date of the gold rush marking also the first parish in Colorado. Sisters of Loretto at the Foot of the Cross established Loretto Heights Academy for girls in Denver, and the Sisters of Charity of Leavenworth branched out into numerous schools and hospitals in the state. Sisters of various other religious orders also set up educational and charitable institutions. Colorado was combined with Utah as a vicariate apostolic, headed by Most Rev. Joseph Machebeuf, who invited the Jesuits, Benedictines, Carmelites and many others to work in the state. In 1887 Msgr. Machebeuf was appointed first bishop of the new diocese of Denver. In 1941 Denver was raised to the rank of an archdiocese, and the diocese of Pueblo was established. Colorado has a little over three hundred thousand Catholics, in a total population of 1,700,-000.

colors, liturgical A sequence of colors at different seasons of the ecclesiastical year for vestments and other liturgical objects was first used by the Augustinian Canons at Jerusalem at the beginning of the 12th century. The colors prescribed by the modern Roman service books are five: white (*albus*), red (*rubeus*), green (*viridus*), purple (*violaceus*), and black (*niger*). White is used on feasts of Christ (so far as they are not memorials of His Passion) and of the B.V.M.; red, on the feasts of the Apostles and of martyrs; green, on Sundays and ferial days between the octave of the Epiphany and Septuagesima, and between Trinity Sunday and Advent; purple, in Lent and Advent; and black on Good Friday, and in Masses and offices of the dead. In the Eastern Church there are no definite rules about colors, though there is a natural tendency to use more somber colors at penitential seasons, while white is used at all services, including funerals from Easter to Ascensiontide.

Colossians An Epistle written by St. Paul to the Christians of Colossae, a city in Phrygia, in the Roman province of Asia, an important trade and wool center. The Epistle was written to correct certain doctrinal errors. Paul develops the supremacy of Christ over the spiritual world and the mystical union of the faithful with Christ, who is our Mediator and Head of the Church, His Body. The letter was written during Paul's imprisonment in Rome. The subject is the same as that of the Epistle to the Ephesians.

Columban Fathers, the St. Columban's Foreign Mission Society, founded in 1918 in Ireland by the Most Reverend Edward J. Galvin; an organization of secular priests devoted to the foreign missions. It was approved by Pope Benedict XV soon after its foundation. The general motherhouse is in Navan, Ireland; headquarters in the United States is at St. Columbans, Nebraska. They have houses in the archdioceses of Boston, Chicago, Los Angeles, Philadelphia, St. Paul and San Francisco, and in the dioceses of Brooklyn, Buffalo, Galveston, Providence and San Diego. They publish a magazine, *The Far East,* which promotes their mission work among English-speaking readers. They carry on foreign mission work in Korea, Japan, the Philippine Islands, Burma, the Fiji Islands, Peru, Chile and Argentina. They number nearly 700 priests and over 400 students.

Columban Sisters, the The Missionary Sisters of St. Columban were founded in Ireland in 1922, by Father (later Bishop) Edward Galvin, founder of the Columban Fathers. After Father Galvin had spent some time as a missionary in China, he saw the great need for Sisters to instruct the women and children and carry on works of mercy. Upon a return to Ireland, he sent out a call for young women to volunteer for foreign missions. A group of twelve became the first candidates for the Columban sisterhood, at their motherhouse in County Clare. They were trained in the religious life by the Irish Sisters of Charity whose rule they adopted—that of St. Ignatius. The congregation took its name from St. Columban (545–615) the great Irish missionary who converted much of Europe. The Sisters conduct schools, orphanages, dispensaries and hospitals in the foreign mission field. Their motherhouse in Ireland is at Wicklow. They came to the United States in 1930, where they founded a center house at Hyde Park, Mass. They also have houses in Boston, Chicago, Los Angeles and Buffalo. Their mission works are mainly in Burma, Hong Kong, Korea and the Philippine Islands.

comb, liturgical Used in the liturgy of the consecration of a bishop to comb the hair of the newly consecrated bishop after the chrism has been wiped off his head. Combs were used extensively in the liturgy during the Middle Ages.

Comma Johanneum The word "comma" used in the phrase is from the Greek, meaning "to cut off." The phrase refers to the following italicized clause in 1 Jn. 5:7–8: "For there are three that bear witness *in heaven: the Father, the Word, and the Holy Spirit; and these three are one. And there are three that bear witness on earth:* the Spirit, and the water, and the blood; and these three are one." The italicized words appear in no important Greek manuscript and most exegetes believe that they are a later insertion by some copyist.

Command, Great See Great Command.

commandery 1. The houses in charge of a commander knight of a military order. 2. The area or territory under a commander knight of a military order. 3. An assembly or lodge of a secret order. *See* preceptory.

Commandments, Great *See* Great Commandments of the New Law.

Commandments of the Church Practical laws of a moral and ecclesiastical nature for the spiritual good of the Catholic faithful. They are: 1. Assistance at Mass on Sundays and holydays of obligation and rest from servile labor on Sunday and the holydays. 2. Fasting and abstinence on the days appointed by the Church. 3. Confession at least once a year. 4. Reception of the Eucharist at least once a year during the Easter season. 5. Support of the pastor and the Church according to one's means. 6. Refraining from marriage within certain degrees of kinship and refraining from marriage with solemnity at forbidden times.

commandments, root Those commandments (love of God, love of neighbor) given by Christ out of which all other commandments flow. *See* Great Commandments of the New Law.

Commandments, the Ten The moral commands or laws given by God to Moses (Ex. 20:1–21) on Mount Sinai. It is certain that the Decalogue was made up of the distinct commandments (Deut. 5:2–23) no matter how they may be grouped. These commands are interpreted by Christ in the New Testament (Mt. 5:17–47). The first three are concerned with the love and true worship of God, and the other seven are directed to the love and justice due our neighbor. The order traditional in the Church is *First table, or group*: 1. I am the Lord, your God, you shall not have false gods before Me. 2. You shall not take the Lord's name in vain. 3. You shall keep holy the Sabbath day. *Second table*: 4. Honor your parents. 5. Do not murder. 6. Do not commit adultery. 7. Do not steal. 8. Do not lie. 9. Do not have adulterous desires. 10. Do not covet your neighbor's goods.

commemoration (L. *commemorare,* to mention)   On days when two feasts coincide due to the coincidence of the temporal and sanctoral cycles of the Church's liturgical year, the greater feast is celebrated and the lesser feast is generally kept by adding commemoratory prayers of the lesser feast in the Mass and Office of the greater feast.

commemoration of the living and dead in the Mass   Two prayers of the canon of the Mass, both beginning with the word *Memento* (Remember). The Commemoration of the Living is the second prayer of the Canon of the Mass, and is before the Consecration. The Commemoration of the Dead comes four prayers after the Consecration.

commendation of a soul, the (L. *dare in commendam,* to give into the care of someone)   The prayer for the dying said by a priest or another beside a dying person in which the dying person's soul is sent forth in the name of God, pardon is asked for the person's sin and the soul is commended to God.

commendatory letter   *See* celebret.

commentaries, biblical   A work attempting to give the meaning and purpose of a text or texts of Sacred Scripture for the purpose of study and understanding.

Commissary Apostolic   A person delegated by the pope to take evidence, make judgment or act as an administrator.

Commissary of the Holy Land   A Friar Minor (Franciscan) whose duty

it is to collect alms within a defined area for the maintenance of the Holy Places of Palestine. The Holy See has given these friars a special commission to care for these places.

Commissary, Provincial   A superior of the Friars Minor or Conventuals who is put in charge of a group of friars whose number is not sufficient to form a province, and who are dependent on an established province.

commission, ecclesiastical   1. A body appointed by the pope or other authority to perform some specific duty. There are many papal commissions: for Biblical Studies, of Sacred Archeology, for the Protection of the Historical and Artistic Monuments of the Holy See, for Latin America, etc. 2. A document conferring rank or power on an individual. 3. The duty or rank to which one is commissioned.

Commission for Catholic Missions among the Colored People and the Indians   An organization established in 1886 to support and maintain mission work among Negroes and Indians in the United States. Funds for disbursement are received from an annual national collection. The headquarters is in Washington, D.C.

commixture   A term which refers to the dropping by the celebrant of the sacred particle broken from the large Host into the chalice. The action takes place after the Pater Noster. It symbolizes the union of the Body and Blood of Christ and His union with His Church in the Mystical Body.

common good   The sum total of those conditions of social living whereby men are enabled more fully and more readily to achieve their own perfection. The general welfare. The well-being of all or almost all of the people of a community or a state.

common life Religious communities in which the members submit to a rule of life and to a common superior. They hold their goods and property in common, recite the Divine Office in choir and eat together at the same table. The degree of material communalism varies in different institutes: i.e., the Carthusaian daily life is almost solitary whereas the Cistercians even sleep in a common dormitory.

Common of the Mass The ordinary of the Mass; or those parts of the Mass which never or hardly ever change: in contrast to the Proper of the Mass.

Common of the Saints A division of the Missal used in the Mass and a division of the Divine Office. Here are found Masses and Offices for all those saints who do not have any or only some parts special to the Mass and Office prayers assigned to them. Those special Mass and Office prayers which are lacking are supplied from the Common Mass and Office prayers.

common prayer, the *See* prayer of the faithful.

common teaching of theologians A doctrine held by the theologians of all schools which they declare binding on the Catholic conscience. As such, it is to be held as infallibly true as it partakes of the ordinary magisterium of the Church. The unanimity required is a moral unanimity. Disagreement by a body of important theologians would invalidate the infallibility of the doctrine.

Communicantes (L. in the unity of holy fellowship) The third prayer of the Canon of the Mass, which takes its name from the first word. It is also called the Remembrance of the Saints because it calls to mind a list of saints including the Blessed Virgin, St. Joseph, the Apostles and others and asks that "we may ever be strengthened by the help of your protection." There are special Communicantes for Christmas, Epiphany, Easter, Ascension and Pentecost. There is a special Canon on Holy Thursday.

communicatio in sacris (L. joining in sacred actions) The act by which a Catholic actively and publicly joins in divine worship with non-Catholics. The Church tolerates mere passive presence for a grave reason; e.g., weddings and funerals of close non-Catholic relatives and friends. Active participation is forbidden.

Communion 1. The reception of the Eucharist, the Sacrament of the Body and Blood of Christ. Catholics speak of receiving, rather than taking, Communion. 2. The antiphon which is sung during the distribution of Communion.

Communion, frequent The reception of Holy Communion several times during the week or even daily. A decree of the Congregation of the Council, Dec. 16, 1905, stated that frequent and daily Communion is most earnestly desired by Christ and the Catholic Church, and that all that is necessary is the state of grace and the right intention. The decree also forbids any further controversy over dispositions required for frequent Communion. Since that time the Church has made many reforms to make frequent Communion more easy.

Communion, manner of receiving 1. *Latin Rite*. The priest or deacon approaches the communicant, takes a sacred particle from the ciborium, making the Sign of the Cross with the particle over the ciborium, saying,

140

"Body of Christ." The communicant replies, "Amen." The celebrant then places the Host on the extended tongue of the communicant. 2. Byzantine Rite. The communicant stands before the celebrant holding the veil of the chalice under the chin. The celebrant then administers with a spoon the Holy Body after it has been immersed in the Precious Blood. He says in the liturgical language, "The servant of God, (*name*), receives the Precious and All-Holy Body and Blood of our Lord, God, and Savior Jesus Christ for the forgiveness of his sins and life everlasting. Amen."

Communion of children In 1910 the Congregation of the Sacraments issued the decree *Quam Singulari* which restored the practice of reception of Communion by children when they reach the age of reason (about seven years of age). The children must know the difference between right and wrong, have an elementary idea of the main mysteries of Faith, and be able to distinguish between the Sacred Host and ordinary bread.

communion of saints The sharing of spiritual goods between the faithful on earth, the Church Triumphant in heaven and the Church Suffering in purgatory. It is shared in by the angels and by those non-Catholics in good faith who belong to the Church invisibly.

Communion of the sick The rite when administered apart from anointing begins with the priest's greeting, "Peace be to this house," sprinkling with holy water and the recitation of the Confiteor. After giving Communion the priest recites a special prayer and gives the blessing either with the pyx, if any Hosts remain in it, or with his hand.

Communion outside of Mass Although normally Communion should be received at Mass, the Church allows for its reception at other times, not only for the sick who cannot assist at Mass but also for those who are impeded by legitimate cause from receiving at the proper time. The rite includes the Confiteor before and an antiphon and prayer of the Blessed Sacrament afterward, and concludes with the priest's blessing.

communion plate A round or oblong concave metal dish placed under the chin of a person about to receive Holy Communion. Its upper surface should be at least gilt. Some communion plates have small metal handles on each side, others a long wooden handle. It is to protect the Blessed Sacrament and to catch any particles which may come off as Communion is being given. Also called a paten.

Communion, refusal of Holy Persons who are excommunicated, under interdict, or infamous are to be refused Holy Communion. If a priest knows (apart from the seal of the confessional) another to be in the state of unrepented mortal sin, he must refuse to give Holy Communion privately but not publicly unless there be danger of scandal.

communion, spiritual The desire to receive Holy Communion when one is not able to do so. In place of actual reception, an individual through acts of adoration, faith and thanksgiving creates a spiritual union between self and God.

Communion under both kinds The reception of the Eucharist under the species of bread and of wine, practiced in the Western Church until the 13th century and in the Eastern Churches until the present time. Vatican Council II permits bishops to allow it in cases to be determined by the Apostolic See, e.g., to newly or-

dained priests, newly professed religious and newly baptized adults.

Communion under one kind The reception of the Eucharist under only
one species, usually that of bread,
which has been the prevalent custom
in the Western Church since the 13th
century. The Council of Trent justified the practice from the doctrinal
point of view, since those who thus
receive are deprived of no grace
necessary for salvation, but the way
was left open for a return to the ancient practice when the Church
should judge it useful.

Communion Verse An antiphon, usually from the psalms, that is recited
in the Mass following the Communion and ablutions. It is sung during
the distribution of Communion at
sung Masses.

communion with, to be in To be
united and associated in matters of
religion, creed, worship or spiritual
intercourse. All Catholics are in communion with the pope, the faithful on
earth and the saints in heaven. This
communion is destroyed only by heresy or schism.

communion with Rome Applied to a
group of baptized Christians who
share in the sacramental life common
to all peoples and Churches recognized by the Church of Rome, the See
of St. Peter and the Vicar of Christ,
as living in the same confession of
Faith and in the one bond of unity.
This can be said of a particular congregation, diocese, or of a whole hierarchical organization. It is manifested by the common peace under
the successor of St. Peter as head of
the Church on earth, and as common
father and teacher of the faithful of
Christ, and by the mutual recognition
of priests and liturgies. The special
sign of the communion is the common sharing of the Body of the Lord

as the cause and the sign of that unity.
Communion with Rome implies a
common life of faith and love and
sacraments, but not necessarily of
practices, laws, or customs, of
which a great variety are possible,
and are indeed found among the various Churches which enjoy this communion.

Communism The most logical and
extreme form of socialism following
the theory of Karl Marx. It is materialistic and deterministic; the social
order evolves through economic
struggles between the classes in the
direction of a violent revolution followed by the substitution of a society
where ownership of all things is in
common. Communism per se is not
in conflict with Catholic doctrine,
since many religious orders lead a
communal life. The Church's opposition is to Marxian or atheistic Communism because of its denial of God,
materialism and betrayal of human
rights. For statement of the Church's
position consult *Divini Redemptoris*
by Pope Pius XI (1937). In 1949
the Sacred Congregation of the Holy
Office decreed that the penalty of excommunication is automatically incurred by any Catholic who voluntarily professes, defends or spreads
Communism. Communism puts the
state above the individual and family, and whenever the rights of the
latter come into conflict with the
state, the state prevails. Communism
is materialistic and besides denying
God, teaches that there is no life after
death. Under Communism there is no
moral law, no personal liberty. No
man has rights over material goods
or the means of production. All forms
of private property are to be eradi-
cated. Marriage and the family are
artificial institutions. The primary
responsibility for the education of

children belongs to the state. The idealism of Communism does not work out in practice. New classes arise and inequities continue.

community The assembly of God's people, the Church. In a more particular sense, the assembly of God's people celebrating the liturgy.

community development "A process of social action in which the people of a community: 1. organize themselves for planning and action; 2. define their common and individual needs and problems; 3. make group and individual plans to meet their needs and solve their problems; 4. execute these plans with a maximum reliance on community resources; 5. supplement these resources when necessary with services and materials from governmental and non-governmental agencies outside the community."

commutation (L. *commutare,* to change) To change a greater thing for something less. In canon law, the term refers to the substitution of a lesser penalty for a greater one.

Company of Mary, the A congregation of women founded in France in 1607 by St. Jeanne de Lestonnac, a niece of the famous Michel de Montaigne. She was married at 17 to Gaston de Montferrant (related to the royal houses of France) but was left a widow in middle age. She entered the Cistercian novitiate, but was forced to leave on account of ill health. Two Jesuit priests at Bordeaux suggested that she devote herself to the Catholic education of girls, a work greatly needed where the Calvinist influence was strong. A number of companions joined Mme. de Lestonnac, and the Archbishop of Bordeaux gave them the religious habit in 1608. Their schools prospered greatly and spread to many towns. However, one of the nuns spread calumnies about the foundress and had her deposed. She was later vindicated, but she refused the office of superior and retired to a life of prayer and penance. Her holy life and the miracles worked after her death gave evidence of sanctity. During the Revolution the schools were destroyed, the nuns scattered and St. Jeanne's body lost. She was canonized in 1949. Her order came to Mexico, and from there to the United States in 1926. The Sisters conduct schools, kindergartens and catechetical centers in the archdioceses of Los Angeles and Santa Fe and in the dioceses of Monterey–Fresno and Tucson. Their American motherhouse is in Sun Valley, Calif.

comparative religion The study of various religions of the world as to their similarities and dissimilarities. While the study of comparative religion does produce information of value, care must be taken lest the study make religion a purely human phenomenon or equate all religions.

competence In the canonical sense, it means the authority or faculty pertaining to an office; the ability to carry out some function. The word indicates a power but only when jurisdiction is added to it.

Compline (L. *completorium,* the completion) The final hour of the Divine Office. Considered to be the night prayer of the Latin Rite, it is said shortly before retiring. It corresponds to Apodeipnon in the Byzantine Rite.

compunction (Gr. *penthos,* godly sadness) A Christian attitude of sorrow for sin coupled with the hope of pardon. It leads the sinner to comprehend his offense and the need of begging pardon. As the attitude develops, the sorrow is based more on love than fear. The Christian loves

God to such an extent that he becomes sorrowful when he realizes how many things still separate him from God.

concelebration The simultaneous celebration of Mass by two or more priests who consecrate the same bread and wine. It was common in the Western Church until the Middle Ages and then gradually disappeared; however, the Eastern Rites preserved the practice. The Constitution on Sacred Liturgy adopted by Vatican Council II praised the practice as manifesting the unity of the priesthood and restored its use at the Masses of Holy Thursday; at Masses during councils, bishops' conferences and synods; and at the Mass for the blessing of an abbot. It also empowered bishops (ordinaries) to permit concelebration at the principal Mass and at a conventual Mass where the needs of the Church do not require all priests present to celebrate individually and at Masses celebrated at any kind of meeting of priests.

conception 1. In biology, the process in the reproduction of man involving the union of two unlike sexual cells, the sperm and the ovum or egg. Theologians refer to this as active conception. 2. Passive conception is the infusion by God of the soul in the human embryo. It is in this sense that the Church speaks of the Immaculate Conception.

Conception, Immaculate The privilege of the Mother of Jesus Christ by which she was conceived without any trace of original sin in view of the work of her Son. Under this title the Blessed Virgin is patroness of the United States. *See,* Shrine of the Immaculate Conception.

conciliar theory A theory, condemned by Vatican Council I in 1870, that maintained that an ecumenical council has greater authority than the pope. The theory was one of the decrees approved by the Council of Constance (1414–1418) but was not approved by Pope Martin V. It later appeared among the teachings of Gallicanism.

conclave (L. *cum clave,* with a key) The closely regulated assembly of the College of Cardinals to elect a new pope. Also, the place of the assembly. *See* election of a pope. The word is also sometimes used of any private meeting or close assembly.

concomitance The Body and Blood of the glorified Christ cannot be separated and so, in the Eucharist, both are present under the species of bread and also under the species of wine.

concordance, biblical A reference work on the Bible, containing an index of all the principal words used in the Bible. The concordance gives a listing of all the texts in which a particular word will be found. One of the most famous concordances is Alexander Cruden's *Concordance,* first published in 1736, and reprinted to the present day.

concordat A pact or treaty drawn up between the Vatican and the civil government of a country regarding the spiritual welfare of its Catholic citizens and regulating the part of the state in the religious affairs of these nationals. Two of the most famous concordats were: 1. the concordat between Napoleon and Pope Pius VII in 1801 which re-established the Church in France, and later was repudiated by the French Government in 1905 with its Law of Separation of Church and State; 2. the concordat resulting from the Lateran Treaty in 1929, ensuring the independence of the Holy See, its *de jure* and *de facto* international sovereignty with its absolute jurisdiction of a state called

Vatican City, and providing for the religious welfare of the citizens of the Kingdom of Italy.

concubinage The cohabiting of a man with a woman outside of wedlock or any enduring liaison whether the parties are free to marry or not. Also, the state of two persons living together maritally more or less permanently without being married.

concupiscence (L. *concupiscere,* to desire) Morally, the word "concupiscence" is a disordered inclination to sense pleasures against the direction of reason, and a general propensity of human nature to sin as a consequence of the sin of Adam. Like all passions, concupiscence is a natural property good in itself, but which may be used for good or for bad.

concurrence of liturgical days The coming together at Vespers of two offices, one of which will usually be commemorated in the other. The rules have been much simplified in nos. 103-105 of the latest rubrics.

concursus (L. *concurrere,* to bring together) 1. That act by which divine energy is transmitted to the operations of creatures. 2. An examination held to select appointees to parishes and benefices.

conditional administration of the sacraments When there is a reasonable doubt as to the fact or validity of the sacraments of Baptism, Penance or Holy Orders, they should be administered conditionally, i.e. the form is stated as a condition. Thus an unconscious person in danger of death would be baptized with the form beginning, "If you are not baptized, I baptize you, etc." While absolution must be given absolutely, the conditional form is used when the sacrament might be invalid when given absolutely or some notable spiritual harm might result to the penitent if

absolution is refused. The main reasons for conditional absolution are: doubt whether the penitent is alive or dead, doubt whether an absolution was given correctly, doubt whether a penitent has use of reason or is morally present, doubt concerning the jurisdiction of the confessor, doubt whether the penitent has sufficient sorrow or purpose of amendment and there is danger of a greater harm resulting from any postponement of absolution. The conditional absolution must be in regard to a present event and not the future. Thus if absolution was given on the condition that restitution be made, it would be invalid.

confect To administer a sacrament. The term has a sense beyond the actual act of administration. It has the idea of an effect caused by the action of both God and man as initiated by the person administering the sacrament. These theological meanings of the word derive from the root sense of putting together.

conference, clergy A meeting of parish priests and all those engaged in pastoral activity. These meetings are usually held monthly in each diocese or deanery to discuss problems of dogmatic, moral and pastoral theology.

Conference of Major Superiors of Men's Institutes in the United States An organization founded in 1956 to promote the general welfare of the religious societies and congregations in the United States. The major superiors meet annually and have a national office at the NCWC building in Washington, D.C. The conference is subject to the Sacred Congregation of Religious.

Conference of Major Superiors of Women Religious An organization founded in 1956 to promote the professional welfare and efficiency of women religious and to coordinate activity. The conference is responsible to the Congregation of Religious of the Holy See. It has an office in Washington, D.C.

Conference, Sister Formation Founded in 1954, it is now a body of the Conference of Major Superiors of Women Religious and of the National Catholic Educational Association. The purpose of the Conference is to advance the spiritual and professional training of Sisters, and to assist in intercommunity cooperation. It has an office in Washington, D.C.

confessio (L. confession) 1. The tomb of a martyr. 2. The crypt beneath the high altar where relics are enshrined. The crypt of St. Peter's Basilica where the relics of the first pope are kept is known simply as The Confessio.

confession 1. *Sacramental*. The auricular confession of sins committed after Baptism made to a priest who has jurisdiction in order to obtain absolution. 2. *Annual*. The obligation imposed on all who have reached the use of reason to confess at least once a year. 3. *Sacrilegious*. A confession in which the penitent willfully conceals the mortal sin or sins of which he is conscious, or has no contrition or purpose of amendment or intention of making satisfaction. 4. *Legal*. A statement made freely and deliberately in a lawsuit against oneself and in favor of one's adversary, relieving the other party of the obligation of proving the matter confessed.

confession, lay 1. The practice of telling one's sins to a lay person as an exercise of humility and in order to receive direction. In general, this is not recommended. 2. A practice prevalent in the Middle Ages of confessing one's sins to a lay person when in imminent danger of death and no priest was available.

confession of a martyr See confessio.

confession, seal of A most grave obligation of keeping secret all knowledge the confessor has obtained in the Sacrament of Penance, under the pain of mortal sin; no exception is made, not even to save one's life. Direct revelation of such matter places the confessor under excommunication by the very action itself, pardon of which is reserved to the pope himself. The obligation is based upon the natural law, positive divine law and Church law. Superiors may never use confessional information outside the confessional. Courts of law respect the seal of confession and make information so obtained inadmissible in court cases.

confessional An enclosed area constructed within the church itself usually consisting of three sections: two side parts with gratings so the priests may easily hear the penitents' confessions, with kneeling benches for the penitents; and a center section with a chair for the priest to sit upon. In the Latin Rite, it is obligatory to use the confessional for women's confessions, except in the case of emergency.

Confessions of Faith Formulae of doctrine drawn up and promulgated by the various Protestant bodies from time to time. In the early days of Protestantism it was not the reading of the Bible which held the various Protestant bodies together but their respective Confessions of Faith, inculcated by preachers and enforced by the civil power. The "Word of God" was interpreted in accordance with formulae devised by men. The most famous were the Anglican

Thirty-Nine Articles, the Lutheran Augsburg Confession, the Heidelberg Catechism of the Reformed Churches, the Confession of Dort (Calvinist), and the Scottish and Westminster Confessions of the Presbyterians.

confessor (L. *confiteri,* to confess) 1. One whose life gave testimony to the faith and who is a canonized male saint, not a martyr. 2. A priest with required faculties from the bishop of the diocese who hears confessions of penitents and administers the Sacrament of Penance. 3. An extraordinary confessor, one appointed to hear the confessions of men or women religious over and above their regular confessor.

Confirmation Name A saint's name chosen by the recipient and imposed by the bishop in the conferring of the Sacrament of Confirmation, recommending that the person confirmed imitate the virtues of the saint he has chosen. It is not a legal name.

Confirmation, Sacrament of A Sacrament of the New Law by which the recipient receives the Holy Spirit through the anointing with chrism by the bishop in the form of a cross on the forehead, the imposition of hands and saying the words, "I sign you with the Sign of the Cross and confirm you with the chrism of salvation in the name of the Father and of the Son and of the Holy Spirit." Only a baptized person may be confirmed. The sacrament imparts a seal or character on the soul (and may not be repeated), strengthens actual grace so that the person may fearlessly profess his Faith and fight against temptation should the need arise. A bishop is the ordinary minister of confirmation, and the extraordinary minister is a priest who has been granted the power by office (as

a cardinal, prelate nullius, prefect apostolic) or by apostolic indult. It is customary to have a sponsor and to choose a saint's name for the sacrament. We learn of the sacrament in the Acts of the Apostles (1:5; 2:38; 11:16).

confiteor (L. I confess) The name given that prayer in the Prayers at the Foot of the Altar at the beginning of Mass where the Christian, in the honest admission of his being a creature or of his being in sin, praises God and asks His forgiveness through the intercession of His saints.

conflict of laws In the presence of conflicting obligations or duties, preference must be given to the stricter and more urgent one.

confraternity An association under religious authority of the faithful who come together to perform some work of piety, charity or instruction that redounds to the glory of God or the Church.

Confraternity Edition of the Bible A translation of the Old and New Testament by outstanding American biblical scholars under the sponsorship of the Confraternity of Christian Doctrine. The Gospels and Epistles read at Mass are from the Confraternity Edition.

Confraternity of Christian Doctrine, the A society for the religious education of Catholics not in Catholic schools, originating in 1905 (in its modern form) when Pope St. Pius X directed that it be set up in every parish in the world. The laity are to be trained, guided and encouraged for this work by the clergy and hierarchy. The confraternity plans religious instruction in the home by parents, providing materials and guidance. It furthers instruction classes in released time and in vacation schools for elementary school pupils and discussion clubs for high school and college students. Catholic adults and non-Catholic enquirers are also provided for in special ways. The confraternity includes teachers, discussion leaders, fishers (who seek out possible members of classes), helpers to drive buses or cars bringing children to class and various other assistants. The local parish priest is the director of each C.C.D. parish unit. In 1934 the American hierarchy appointed an episcopal committee on the C.C.D., and a publications department was organized at the center in Washington, D.C., to service programs throughout the nation. National and regional congresses are held, special institutes and leadership courses are sponsored. Trained leaders may be procured through the center for help in local C.C.D. development.

Congo (Leopoldville) One of the major Catholic nations in Africa. In 1865 the Holy Ghost Fathers took charge of a mission in the Congo. They were followed by the White Fathers and Scheut Fathers who with great sacrifice and devotion gave themselves to the development of the Congolese. Unfortunately, the Belgian rulers made a policy of nonprofessional training for the Congolese, except for native clergy, and it was not until 1957 that the Church was able to open the first university. In 1960 when the Belgians suddenly withdrew, the nation was left a legacy of chaos which has affected the work of the Church and brought death to some missioners. There are 41 ecclesiastical divisions in the Congo, and of the total population of over 14 million, 35 per cent are Catholic. Tribal jealousies, disorganization of government, anticlericalism, the revival of pagan practices

are all hindrances to the growth of the Church.

congregation 1. *Religious*: a group of men or women who have given themselves to the service of the Church, sealing it with promises of poverty, chastity and obedience for a time or for life. 2. *Hierarchical:* a permanent committee of cardinals, bishops, etc., to whom some aspect of the Church's life is committed for its organization, government, and stimulus; e.g., the Congregation of Propaganda Fide is in charge of the missions. 3. *Liturgical*: a gathering of the people of God to worship as a family with one another and with Christ at their head.

Congregation of Antonian Sisters of Mary, Queen of the Clergy Founded in Canada in 1904, established in the United States in 1932. Primary purpose is domestic work in seminaries, colleges and rectories; also teaching, care of orphans, home missions. Simple vows are taken. About 300 members.

Congregation of Our Lady of the Sacred Heart Founded in Michigan in 1871 by Mother Mary Aquinata Fiegler as an offshoot from the Congregation of the Most Holy Rosary in Newburgh, N.Y. Teaching and nursing are the main works. There is a mission in Guatemala. There are approximately 850 Sisters. Vows are simple.

Congregation of the Blessed Sacrament Founded in Paris in 1856 by Blessed Pierre Julien Eymard, the society is devoted to devotion to and promotion of the Blessed Sacrament. The society maintains a number of parishes and has missions in England, the Philippines and Uganda.

Congregation of the Holy Cross A community for women founded in Brooklyn, N.Y., in 1853. It is a diocesan institute with simple vows. Teaching is the primary work. There are approximately 1,600 Sisters.

Congregation of the Most Holy Rosary Founded in Michigan in 1877. There are 5 provinces in the United States with close to 2,500 Sisters. Teaching is the primary work of the community. Missions are staffed in the West Indies and Peru. The congregation is pontifical with simple vows.

Congregation of the Sisters of Charity of the Incarnate Word Founded in San Antonio, Texas, by Bishop C.M. Dubuis in 1870. The community is engaged in teaching, nursing, social work. There is a province in Mexico. Simple vows are taken. There are well over 1,000 Sisters.

Congregation of the Sisters of the Third Order of St. Francis Founded in Indiana in 1851 by Mother Theresa Hackelmaier, the congregation is engaged in teaching, nursing and social work. Missions exist among the Negroes and Indians and in New Guinea. There are approximately 850 Sisters. Simple vows are taken.

Congregation of the Third Order of St. Francis of Mary Immaculate Founded in Illinois in 1865, the congregation now has close to 800 Sisters who are engaged in teaching, social work and the care of the youth and aged. Simple vows are taken.

congregational singing Both Pope St. Pius X and Pope Pius XII encouraged the participation of the laity in liturgical singing. The Constitution of the Sacred Liturgy of Vatican Council II says that pastors of souls have the responsibility to see that "the whole body of faithful may be able to contribute that active participation which is rightly theirs." Article 118 of the Constitution states: "Religious singing by the people is to be skillfully fostered, so that in devotions and sacred exercises, as also during liturgical services, the voices of the faithful may ring out according to the norms and requirements of the rubrics."

Congregationalism One of the three major forms of Protestantism, the others being Episcopal and Presbyterian. The Congregationalists developed from the Anglican Church. The Pilgrims and the Puritans brought the religion to the United States and it found great strength in New England. Congregationalists hold the Bible as the sole rule of faith. They are strong believers in individual freedom and in the autonomy of the local congregation. Harvard, Yale, Williams and Bowdoin are Congregationalist foundations. Congregationalists believe that their churches are patterned on the early Christian communities, both in organization and in government. The Unitarians are derived from Congregationalism. In 1957 the Congregationalists joined with the Evangelical and Reformed Churches to make the United Church of Christ.

Congregations, Sacred Permanent commissions of cardinals for handling the business of the Church. The title of Prefect of the Congregations of the Holy Office, Consistory, and the Oriental Church is reserved to the pope. The other Congregations are Sacramental Discipline, Council, Religious, Propagation of the Faith, Rites, Ceremonies, Extraordinary Ecclesiastical Affairs, Seminaries and Universities and Basilica of St. Peter.

conjugal rights See marriage rights.

Connecticut (Mohegan Algonquian, place of the long river) The fifth of the original 13 states, 48th in area, 25th in population. It was explored by the Dutch in 1614; and settled by the English in the 1630's, first by traders from Plymouth, and then by Puritans from Massachusetts, who founded New Haven. In 1638 they drew up the "Plantation Covenant" making the law of Moses the final rule in all matters, both religious and civil. In 1639 the colonists adopted a basic law for the colony, called the "Fundamental Orders," which carried no religious test for citizenship. The frame of government made no provision for trial by jury; and the Congregational church was the "established" church, supported by a general tax. In 1636–1637 there was war with the Pequot Indians, who were in the end slaughtered and their stronghold destroyed by troops under Captain John Mason. The people of Connecticut have always had a great regard for education. In 1650 a law obliged all parents to educate their children, and every township of fifty householders or over was obliged to provide a school. However, this was only for boys. Girls were educated at home, or placed in "dame schools" where a few girls were taught ladylike accomplishments by a woman in her own house. There were free public schools for boys in some places as early as the 1640's, and Yale University (1701) is only one of many institutions of higher learning in the state. The principle of interchangeable parts developed by Eli Whitney was first applied in Connecticut. It was used in the manufacture of firearms in 1799—a giant step in the direction of the assembly line and later automation. The first Catholic priest in Connecticut was Father Gabriel Druillettes, S.J., sent to New Haven as an envoy of the governor of New France. In 1755 there were about 400 Catholic Acadians among the settlers, immigrants expelled from Nova Scotia, but no

priest is known to have been with them. During the American Revolution some priests, chaplains to the French forces, were in the state. In 1808 Connecticut was made part of the diocese of Boston, from where Bishop Cheverus and later Bishop Fenwick made occasional missionary trips into the state. The first resident priest was the Rev. Bernard O'Cavanaugh, who arrived in 1828 and built the first Catholic church in Hartford a year later. The diocese of Hartford was established in 1843, the first bishop being Rt. Rev. William Tyler (1844–1849) who had both Connecticut and Rhode Island in his charge. The Society for the Propagation of the Faith in Lyons, France, and the Leopold Society of Vienna helped out with funds. In the middle 1800's, thousands of Irish and French-Canadian immigrants came into the state, to work in factories and mills. During the Civil War Connecticut's factories prospered in the manufacture of munitions and other necessities of war. Italian immigrants flooded in during the early 1900's, working in the numerous industries of the state. The Sisters of Mercy from Ireland started parochial schools in 1852; and Sisters of Charity, Franciscans, Sisters of Notre Dame and many others staffed institutions of learning and charity. Jesuits, Dominicans, the Fathers of La Salette and others built churches, schools or colleges and cared for parishes. Connecticut has a Catholic population of 1,168,000, in a total population of 2,500,000.

conopaeum The Latin name for the tabernacle veil. It should be the color of the day; however, purple (not black) is used for a Requiem Mass.

consanguinity The blood relationship which is reckoned in canon law by lines and degrees. In the direct line there are as many degrees as there are generations; in the collateral line there are as many degrees as there are generations in the longer line. Marriage is never permitted if there is any doubt of the parties being related in the direct line or in the first degree of the collateral line.

conscience A judgment of the intellect, dictating what is to be done as morally good, or what is to be avoided as morally wrong, in the particular circumstances in which one is now placed. Conscience is said to be certain when it dictates something as right or wrong, without experiencing any reasonable fear that the opposite is true. It is doubtful when it is undecided which of two contradictory views is true. One is bound to follow a certain conscience; one may never act while in a state of positive practical doubt. Conscience is true when it correctly dictates what is right or wrong; it is erroneous when it falsely judges right as wrong or wrong as right. An erroneous conscience must be followed if the false judgment is not culpable; that is, when one judges in good faith that he is allowed to do something that is in truth forbidden. A lax conscience is a habitual condition that lightly judges wrong as right, sin as no sin, mortal sin as venial sin. Conscience, as the norm of action here and now, must be followed when it is certain and true, or certain and invincibly erroneous.

conscience, cases of Problems in the application of moral or canon law to the conduct of men and women in various circumstances. Often these laws are quite clear and evident, but their application in a given set of circumstances is not evident. In other circumstances there seems to be a conflict of laws or moral principles;

e.g., whether to go to Mass on Sunday or to miss Mass in order to nurse a sick person. Over the years many cases have been resolved and settled by expert theologians and canonists; some have not, because there has been no authoritative decision of any kind. New cases are coming up; e.g., the atom bomb, flouridation of water, the morality of prize-fighting, the morality of inhaling cigarettes, etc. When a case of conscience is submitted to a priest by anyone, the priest's solution may be safely followed in practice.

conscience, examination of That act in which one reflects on his moral state and its conformity to the will of God. An examination of conscience is a preliminary to confession. The penitent should determine the sins of which he must accuse himself since his last confession. He should also determine the approximate number of times the sin was committed. Sins which are not recalled are included in the absolution but if remembered afterward, should be included in the next confession. Spiritual writers recommend a daily examination of conscience, preferably at time of retirement. In many seminaries and religious houses it is the custom to make an examination of conscience (particular examen) at noon, usually in relation to one particular fault.

conscientious objector A name given to a person who is opposed to war on grounds of conscience. The Church holds armed conflict between nations is morally permissible under certain conditions, one of which is that there be an adequate proportion between the seriousness of the cause and the evils resulting from the war. A growing number of Christians maintain that because of the consequences of nuclear weapons this condition cannot be met and that therefore no modern war is justified. In the United States, civil law recognizes the right to objection to war on the grounds of conscience but maintains its right to assign the objector to some noncombatant status. The Church recognizes the right of conscience and teaches that for anyone to violate his conscientious beliefs is to commit sin.

consciousness (L. *conscire* to know) A realization of one's own mind toward internal and/or external matter. In case of an accident or illness where consciousness cannot be ascertained, the sacraments of Baptism and Penance should be administered conditionally.

conscription (L. *conscribere,* to enroll) The compulsory enrollment of an individual, especially for governmental use. Today, the word applies primarily to enrollment for military service. The Church holds that the state has the right of self-protection and therefore is entitled to use this drastic measure in self-defense. However, provision must be made for respecting the right of individual conscience, and those whose consciences are opposed to war or to justified killing should not be forced. Exemption should also be made for clerics and ministers of religion whose vocation is opposed to violence.

consecrate (L. *consecrare*) 1. To make or declare sacred or holy; setting apart for service or worship of God. 2. Mass: that integral part of the canon when the priest by divine right changes gifts of man, bread and wine, into the Body and Blood of Christ.

consecration That act whereby a person, place or object is made holy, sacred and set aside for the service of God.

Consecration at Mass The short, but very important, part of the Mass in which the bread and wine are changed into the Body and Blood of Christ by the power of God acting through the priest. The words of the Consecration are those of Christ Himself as taken from Scripture.

consecration crosses These are the twelve small crosses carved or painted on the inside walls of a church which serve as permanent signs that the church is a holy place, consecrated exclusively for the worship of God. They are anointed by the bishop in the consecration ceremony with the holy oil (chrism).

consecration of a church Each permanent church should be consecrated, an act which dedicates it to sacred use. The consecrator is a bishop, usually the bishop of the diocese where the church is located. The highlights of the consecration are the triple sprinkling of the exterior walls, the tracing of the alphabet on the floor, the anointing of the door posts with chrism, the consecration of at least the main altar, the anointing of the walls at twelve consecration crosses, the celebration of Mass.

consent An act of the will, a voluntary compliance or approval of something presented to it as good. 1. *Consent to sin.* Consent is full if given with that ordinary degree of liberty that we have when we are still exercising control over our decisions, though we may be under the impulse of some passion. 2. *Consent for a contract.* To have a contract it is necessary that two or more wills agree and consent to the same thing. Contractual consent must have the following: (*a*) it must be internal, true and deliberate. Hence if a person feigns external consent without the intention of binding himself, the contract is void, but leaves him liable to a claim for damages. If, however, the intention is actually to contract, but not to fulfill the obligations implied, the contract is valid; (*b*) it must be external, i.e., the consent must be externally manifested, either expressly or tacitly; (*c*) it must be mutual, i.e., the two wills of the contracting parties must be morally united in agreement. Consent in marriage is the very essence of the contract. It can only be given by a person who is not legally hindered from giving it; it must be voluntary, without a degree of compulsion that would prevent the exercise of free will; it must be mutual, given not by one but by two; and it must signify that the parties take each other then and there (not conditionally, not at some future time), with the intention of living together as husband and wife until death will part them. The essential object of matrimonial consent is the right to the body (*jus in corpus*) for the purpose of conjugal intercourse, not the exercise of this right. The transfer of the right to each other's body is perpetual and exclusive.

consent, defect of An impediment that can invalidate marriage. The consent may be defective because of lack of reason, or of certain kinds of ignorance or error, or by any fact that hinders the full consent of the will such as force, grave fear or a condition that makes sufficient consent impossible.

consent of the Fathers, unanimous When the Fathers of the Church are morally unanimous in their teaching that a certain doctrine is a part of revelation, or is received by the universal Church, or that the opposite of a doctrine is heretical, then their united testimony is a certain criterion of divine tradition. As the Fathers are not personally infallible, the counter-testimony of one or two would not be destructive of the value of the collective testimony; so a moral unanimity only is required.

conservatism That philosophy which wishes to preserve the existing order or to retain certain elements considered of value as contrasted to those movements which seek to change existing order or values. The order and values can be religious, social, political, economic, educational, etc., or a combination of any or all of these.

Consistorial Congregation, Sacred Although of ancient institution, this Congregation was organized in stable form by Pope Sixtus V in 1587. At the present time, in addition to its ancient task of providing for the erection of dioceses and preparing business for the Consistory, it is in charge of government of dioceses, except those dependent on Propaganda and the Oriental Church. It belongs to this Congregation to erect and divide dioceses and ecclesiastical provinces, nominate bishops, coadjutors, auxiliaries and Apostolic Administrators. It is also in charge of spiritual assistance of emigrants belonging to the Latin Rite, the selection and appointment of their missioners and ship chaplains, the discipline of European priests going overseas, and the direction of the Apostolate of the Sea.

consistory (L. *consistorium,* a place of assembly) A meeting of the cardinals presided over by the pope. Consistories are of three kinds. 1. *Secret.* Only the pope and the cardinals are present. The pope delivers an allocution on some subject and then directs the cardinals in any pertinent business. At this consistory the pope appoints bishops, creates new dioceses, presents the cardinal's ring, and takes a vote on proposed canonizations. 2. *Public.* Prelates and lay spectators are permitted to attend. At a public consistory, the pope bestows the red hat on new cardinals, and hears status reports on beatifications and canonizations. 3. *Semipublic.* Bishops and patriarchs may attend on invitation. At this consistory, the advisability of proposed canonizations is discussed.

constancy   Refers to steadfastness or firmness of mind. It is fidelity to a certain way of acting, such as a firmness in one's faith.

Constantinople, Patriarchate of   Soon after Constantine moved the capital of the Roman Empire to Constantinople (formerly Byzantium) in 330, the city became an ecclesiastical center as well as a political and cultural one. Its ecclesiastical influence increased until it became a patriarchate along with that of Antioch, Jerusalem, Alexandria and Rome. After the final split of the Orthodox in 1054 Constantinople became the principal patriarchate of the Orthodox Church.

Constantinople, Patriarchs of   The Patriarch of Constantinople is considered by the Orthodox as the leader of the Orthodox Church. But his primacy is not like that of the pope in the Catholic Church; rather he is considered "first among equals." Yet to some degree he represents the whole Orthodox Church, as when he and the pope had their historic meeting in 1964.

Constantinople, Rite of   The Rite of Constantinople is one of the many rites in the Catholic Church other than the Latin Rite. These various rites are chiefly concerned with the manner of liturgical worship. The presence of them in the one Catholic Church is a sign of its universality

and richness.

Constantinople, the Liturgy of   formerly the Antiochene Liturgy as used at Caesarea in the 4th century, edited by St. Basil and perhaps again by St. John Chrysostom. With the further modifications of centuries it is still in use and usually referred to as the Byzantine Rite. By the end of the 13th century it had been adopted by the other Orthodox partriarchates of Alexandria, Antioch and Jerusalem.

Constitutional Clergy   Those clerics who took the oath to the constitution drawn up for the Church by the French National Assembly in 1790 despite the fact that Pope Pius VI condemned the constitution and forbade clerics to swear obedience to it. Those priests who did not take the oath were persecuted and many had to flee to England and the United States. Those who came to the New World did much for the development of the Church in the United States. The schism ended with the Concordat of 1801.

constitutions   1. *Papal:* the communications of general authority which the Pope issues in his own name. 2. *Religious:* the regulations governing religious institutes in all the phases of their daily life. They are the principles on which the particular society is based.

consubstantial   The three Persons of the Trinity are of one and the same substance and essence. This was defined by the Council of Nicaea in 325. The word is also used by philosophers to designate "of the same kind or nature."

consubstantiation   A Eucharistic heresy put forward by Lutherans and condemned by the Fourth Lateran Council and the Council of Trent. According to this heresy, the substances of bread and wine remain together with the substance of Christ's Body and Blood after consecration.

consuetudinary According to religious custom.

consultors Men of highly specialized knowledge who advise the various Sacred Congregations in Rome. In English-speaking countries the term is applied to advisers of a bishop.

consummation The actualization of marriage fulfilled by the marital act of sexual intercourse. The consummation of a ratified marriage is a condition which makes that marriage indissoluble by any human power or any other cause except death.

contact 1. *Physical*: the union of two bodies in a purely corporeal way. 2. *Virtual*: the union of two bodies in an intellectual way.

contemplation A high and absorbing interest on some perception of God accomplished by the mind and will engrossed in Him.

contemplative life An austere vocation adapted to foster union with God through a continuous life of prayer and love for Him. By seclusion and freedom from the world the contemplative chooses a life of mortification and atonement for sin as a further means to this union.

contemplative orders A member of a religious order whose rule and activity are adapted to induce contemplation. These orders are of both men and women. Among the men's orders are the Carthusians, Trappists and Camaldolese. Among the women's orders are the Poor Clares, Trappistines and Carmelites.

continence That virtue which in practice preserves the mind from impure thoughts and desires, and restrains the will from actions following aroused sexual desire. In the context of marriage, abstinence from marital intercourse for any period of time by mutual consent of husband and wife.

contingent The possibility of an occurrence not predictable by any rule. The Scholastic philosophers used this term to distinguish what is accidental from what is logically necessary. The word is also used to designate that which is, but might not have been.

contrition The sorrow which arises in the soul, making one's mind repent for past sins and resolve not to sin again.

contrition, act of A formal prayer said by Catholics to express their sorrow for their sins and to resolve amendment. This prayer is said by the penitent following confession to the priest in the Sacrament of Penance. The words of the prayer: "O my God, I am heartily sorry for having offended Thee, and I detest all my sins, because of Thy just punishments, but most of all because they have offended Thee, my God, who art all good and deserving of all my love. I firmly resolve with the help of Thy grace, to sin no more and to avoid the near occasions of sin. Amen."

contrition, imperfect That sorrow for sin aroused when the motive is other than God but is supernatural in that it refers to God; e.g., through fear of God's punishment.

contrition, perfect That sorrow for sin which arises when the motive is the love of God, the highest Good, and for God as God. With this are all the elements of contrition including the desire to confess.

contumacy (L. *contumax,* insolent) Defiance of religious authority. A person who fails to appear in ecclesiastical court without a just reason after he has been summoned can be declared contumacious. Censures may be inflicted only on those who are contumacious.

contumely (L. *contumelia*) Contemptuous treatment of a person in order to bring him into disrepute, or refusing to extend a person due honor. It is a sin against charity and justice and demands reparation.

convent Building in which men or women live in a religious community; it is also used to refer to the community itself. It is most often used today in reference to where women live, and "monastery" is used more when referring to the living place of men.

Conventual A member of the Friars Minor Conventual, sometimes called a "Black Franciscan." The Conventuals broke away from the regular Franciscans and received the approbation of John XXII in 1322. The first foundation in the United States was in 1852; they now have four provinces.

conventual Mass The daily community Mass offered in a conventual church of regulars who have the obligation of public recitation of the Divine Office.

conversion (L. *convertere,* to turn) 1. A changing of religion, e.g., conversion to Catholicism. 2. A changing of one's way of life, e.g., a sinner's conversion to Christ. 3. A technical term used in theology to express the complete changing of bread and wine, both matter and form, into the Body and Blood of Christ in the Holy Eucharist. *See* change; transubstantiation.

conversus (L. *convertere,* to turn around) A term for a lay brother as one who has "turned around," i.e., converted. It comes from the fact that he has renounced the world and adopted a new way of religious life.

convert 1. One who has changed

from one religion to another. 2. To change from one religion to another.

converts, reconciliation of Before an adult can be received into the Church, he must renounce his errors (even though he may not be guilty before God for having held them) and be absolved from excommunication by the ordinary or his delegate in the presence of two witnesses. Conditional Baptism is usually administered unless there is certain evidence of valid Baptism.

cooperation in another's sin In general, any and every physical or moral assistance in the commission of a sinful action in union with others. Cooperation is formal by concurrence in which one takes part in the external sinful deed of another and at the same time consents to his evil intention. This is always sinful. Merely material cooperation is concerned with a good or at least with an indifferent act which is misused by another in his sinful activity. The cooperator has no evil intention but foresees with certainty or probability that his act will be misused. There can be sufficient reason for this merely material cooperation and that without sin. Many knotty problems arise under this head of merely material cooperation, and each case must be solved on its own merits; the great difficulty lies in judging whether or not there is sufficient reason in each case for cooperating materially in the sin of another. Formal cooperation or complicity in the sin of another is as follows: by command; by counsel—advising or urging another to commit an injustice; by consent or approval; by flattery or challenge or praise or ridicule; by sheltering; by furnishing aid, shelter, protection; by concealing weapons or stolen goods; by buying and selling stolen property, etc.; by participation —by helping another commit a crime or by sharing in the loot; by silence on the part of one bound to protect life and property—e.g., the police, a watchman; by not restraining the criminal when one is bound to keep order; by not denouncing the criminal when one is bound to do so.

cooperative The joint effort of a people of a community to improve their socioeconomic life by capital improvements, increase of production and income, more efficient marketing or to furnish the means to meet the crises of family life. Cooperative activities which are encouraged by the social philosophy of the Church fall into five general classes: 1. credit unions; 2. processing and market cooperatives; 3. service cooperatives; 4. consumer cooperatives; 5. multipurpose cooperatives, i.e., containing functions from the first four. St. Francis Xavier University in Antigonish, Nova Scotia, noted for its work in cooperatives, has a six-point philosophy for successful structure: 1. the primacy of the individual; 2. social reform through education; 3. education must begin with the economic; 4. education must be through group action; 5. effective social reform involves fundamental changes in social and economic institutions; 6. the ultimate objective is full and abundant life for everyone in the community.

cope (L. *cappa,* cape) A mantle-like vestment which reaches from the shoulders to the ankles. It is open in front and clasped at the neck. It has a flat hood that covers both shoulders. It is worn by the celebrant at nearly all solemn functions

except the Mass. It is white or gold for Eucharistic functions; otherwise its color follows the liturgical color.

Coptic Church The native Egyptian Church supposedly founded by St. Mark at Alexandria. Its adherents are Christian Egyptians and are distinguished from the Greeks and other churches of Egypt. After the Council of Chalecdon (491), they professed Monophysism and today they are in union with the Syrian Jacobites. They are governed by the Patriarch of Alexandria. They allow certain causes for divorce and remarriage, e.g., adultery; but their orders and sacraments are valid. Copts deny the supremacy of the pope. They number under a million members and Arabic is the main liturgical tongue. The Catholic Coptic Church united with the Roman Catholic Church in the 18th century; Pope Leo XIII appointed for them a Patriarch of Alexandria.

coram (L. before) A Mass *coram episcopo* is one said in the presence of a bishop who assists from his throne or faldstool. *Coram cardinale* is a Mass said in the presence of a cardinal. *Coram Sanctissimo* is a Mass celebrated with the Blessed Sacrament exposed.

Corinthians, Epistles to the Two Epistles of St. Paul addressed to the Christians of Corinth which were written during the course of his third missionary journey (*c.* 53–57). The first calls on the Corinthians to end their quarrels and vices, and then goes on to develop various points of Catholic doctrine. The second is more personal; Paul speaks of his own actions and teachings, closing with an appeal for the Corinthians to support a collection being taken up for the poor Christians of Jerusalem.

cornerstone A stone placed in the

corner of a foundation of a building, usually with a blessing ceremony. It is inscribed with the date and is hollowed out at the top to receive mementos related to the period or the builders. The cornerstone symbolizes Christ who is the Foundation of the Church.

cornerstone, blessing of There is a specific ritual prescribed for the blessing of the cornerstone of a church. Following the blessing of the spot where the main altar is to stand, the bishop blesses the cornerstone, engraving crosses on each side with a knife, after which it is set in position.

cornette (Fr.) The large, starched white headdress worn by Sisters of Charity of St. Vincent de Paul.

corona (L. a crown) 1. The narrow strip of hair left on a cleric's head when he receives a large tonsure. 2. Five mysteries of the Rosary. 3. A circlet of lights or candles found in some churches.

coronation (L. *corona,* a crown) It has special reference to the coronation of the pope, which takes place after a Mass that the pope celebrates shortly after his election and during which he is solemnly blessed by three cardinal-bishops. The tiara (triple crown) is placed on his head by the senior cardinal-deacon. His reign dates officially from this day, although he has full jurisdiction from the moment he accepts election.

Coronation of Our Lady The fifteenth mystery or fifth Glorious Mystery of the Rosary. The term symbolizes the reception of Our Lady into heaven following her Assumption.

coronet A narrow strip of cloth worn about the temples as part of a nun's headdress.

corporal (L. *corpus,* body) The white linen napkin on which are placed the host and chalice during the Mass. It is also used whenever the Blessed Sacrament is placed on the altar, such as at Benediction or when filling the pyx for Communion of the sick. When it is not in use it is kept in a burse. It receives special washing, and is usually starched for the easy gathering of particles.

corporal works of mercy Seven works of mercy affecting the physical man. They are: to feed the hungry, to give drink to the thirsty, to clothe the naked, to visit the imprisoned, to shelter the homeless, to visit the sick, to bury the dead.

corpus (L. body) The name given the representation of the body of Christ as found on a crucifix.

Corpus Christi (L. Body of Christ) A feast in the Catholic Church commemorating the institution and gift of the Holy Eucharist, observed in the Western Church on the Thursday after Trinity Sunday.

correction, fraternal Any direct influence on our neighbor guided or directed by love, which has as its object to confirm him in the way of virtue and to turn him from evil. It may consist of instruction, advice, encouragement, rebuke, warning. The strict obligation to correct others in individual instances exists only when the following conditions are all present: 1. when the salvation of another's soul is in serious peril; 2. when there is a reasonable hope that the instruction or correction will prove fruitful; 3. when the admonition is the sole means of averting the evil according to one's prudent judgment. The term is derived from 2 Thes. 3:15.

158

corruption of minors Any action aimed to promote moral perversion in a minor, generally considered such under age 16. Persons guilty of this crime may incur the following penalties: 1. a lay person is automatically infamous and made subject to appropriate penalties imposed by the ordinary; 2. a cleric in minor orders is discharged from the clerical state; 3. a cleric in major orders is suspended, declared infamous, deprived of office or benefit, or deposed. However, for these penalties to be inflicted there must be evidence that an impure act has been committed.

costs The expenses of a trial in an ecclesiastical court are usually paid by the loser. However, in certain cases the costs are divided between the parties engaged in the case.

cotta (It.) A surplice.

council, diocesan A meeting of the bishop and chief members of the clergy. It must be summoned at least every ten years by the bishop in order to discuss the condition of the Faith and other diocesan matters. As a body it is only advisory; the bishop alone makes any final decisions.

council, ecumenical (Gr. *ecumenos,* of the whole world) A meeting of all the bishops and Church authorities of the whole world. The bishops and others who have the right to vote are called the Council Fathers. A general council must be summoned by the Holy Father and continue under his direction. The decisions of the council must be approved and promulgated by the Holy Father. The Catholic Church to date recognizes twenty-one councils as being ecumenical and therefore binding in conscience upon all Christians.

council or synod, national A meeting of the bishops and other ecclesiastical authorities representing an entire nation or state. It can be either plenary or provincial. A delegate of the Holy See presides over a plenary council; the Holy See must approve its decisions before they take effect. A provincial council is one summoned by the metropolitan bishop at least every twenty years. Its decisions must be approved by the Holy See.

council, plenary The meeting of all archbishops, bishops, apostolic administrators, abbots nullius, vicars apostolic, prefects apostolic and vicars capitular of a given area. The area always exceeds the confines of a province and generally includes an entire nation. The Holy See must authorize a plenary council, appoint a delegate to preside over it and approve the acts of the council before they are promulgated. In the United States there have been three plenary councils (Baltimore, 1852, 1855, 1884). A plenary council for Latin America was held in 1899.

council, provincial (L. *concilium,* a coming together, an assembly) A meeting of the bishops and other local ordinaries of a province, convened at least once every twenty years by the metropolitan with the permission of the Holy See. The provincial council deals chiefly with matters of a disciplinary nature.

Council, Sacred Congregation of the Founded by Pope Pius IV in 1564. Today it has competence over the discipline of the clergy and faithful, directs catechetical instruction and sees to the observance of the precepts of Christian life. It exercises authority over pastors, canons, confraternities, pious associations, Catholic Action, pious legacies, benefices, offices, ecclesiastical property, taxes and tributes; and it still retains the right to revise the acts of councils and episcopal conferences.

counsel (L. *consulere,* to consult) An exhortation or an invitation to do more for God than is strictly commanded.

counsels and precepts The precepts are strictly required for perfection or salvation. Disregard of the precepts (or the commandments) involves sin. The counsels, while not so strictly required, are necessary for perfection; i.e., necessary for perseverance in living a life pleasing to God.

counsels of perfection Traditionally there are three ultimate or apostolic counsels of perfection: 1. poverty, complete renunciation of personal property; 2. chastity, complete abstention from sexual relations; 3. obedience, complete submission of the will in all things, sin excepted, to a superior. Those who are not bound by vows are expected to live in the spirit of the counsels. The counsels of perfection are contrasted to the commandments of perfection: love of God and love of neighbor.

Counter-Reformation, the The religious upheaval which gave birth to Lutheranism, Calvinism, Anglicanism and to the radical Christian sects in the 16th century, was matched by a veritable revolution in the Catholic Church, called the Catholic- or Counter-Reformation. Following the example of Cardinal Ximines who renewed the Church in Spain, and in response to urgent demands by Catholics everywhere, Pope Paul III (1534–1549) began the work of reform by appointing virtuous and learned men to high Church offices; by naming a zealous reform commission whose report on abuses in the Church (1537) was a turning point; by summoning the Council of Trent. Pope Paul's policies were continued: Paul IV (1559–1565) brought the Council of Trent to a successful conclusion in 1563 with the help of Cardinals Borromeo and Morone; St. Pius V (1566–1572) put into force the decrees of the Council of Trent by a thorough reorganization of the Church and began a movement which led to the re-establishment of the Faith in many parts of Europe; Gregory XIII (1572–1585) reformed the Julian calendar; Sixtus V (1585–1590) carried on a campaign of reform in Germany, Switzerland, Poland and the Low Countries. During its trials in the 16th century, the Church was strengthened by a number of new religious orders. The Society of Jesus, founded by Ignatius Loyola in 1534, did the greatest work in preserving the Faith in southern Europe, and in checking the spread of Protestantism in the north. The Theatines, founded by St. Cajetan and Giovanni Caraffa in 1524, did noble work in fighting heresy by preaching and teaching. In 1535, St. Angela Merici founded the Ursulines, the first modern order of teaching nuns, to provide young ladies with a Catholic education. The Capuchins, the Congregation of the Oratory of St. Philip Neri, the Oblates of St. Charles Borromeo and other new orders all contributed special kinds of services to the reform of the Church. While these new orders of religious contributed the major effort to the Catholic revival, the older orders, the Benedictines, Franciscans, Dominicans, etc., with renewed zeal and devotion preached by word and example the Christian way of life not only to their fellow Europeans, but also to people in all parts of the world as the revival led to a tremendous outburst of Catholic missionary activity.

court An ecclesiastical tribunal for trying cases pertaining to persons or things of the Church. Each diocese has its own court; and in Rome, there is the tribunal known as the Roman Rota. The most common case heard by these courts is a marriage case involving Catholics. The courts hand down decisions regarding the validity or nullity of marriages. Cases involving clerics should be presented before the ecclesiastical court unless the bishop gives permission for the case to be tried before the civil court.

cousins, marriage of   Canon law prohibits two Catholics from marrying if they are related to each other as first or second cousins. Although a dispensation from this restriction is commonly granted, to attempt such a marriage without the dispensation would result in an invalid marriage.

covetousness   Any inordinate or unreasonable desire for what one does not possess. It is listed as one of the seven capital tendencies in our nature which inclines us to evil.

cowl   The hood of the habit of a monk or friar. The word originally referred to the great cloak or mantle worn by members of monastic orders. Today it generally refers only to the hood.

craniotomy   The operation of crushing the head of an infant still in the womb. This operation is immoral when performed on a living fetus. It is performed most commonly by some doctors instead of a Caesarean section when the pregnant woman is weakened, or when the head of the fetus is larger than the opening between the pelvic bones.

creation   The story of creation is contained in the first chapter of the Book of Genesis. The author is showing that one God created the entire universe. To provide a model for man's work and rest he divides the period of creation into six sec-

tions (days). The author had no scientific intention, and he was using terms understood by the people of his times. The Genesis account does not rule out the evolution of man, but it may be that in some point in history God created life, and at another point He infused a human soul to create man. From Genesis, Catholics are bound to believe that the universe and everything in it were created by God, that the universe was created in time, and that all created things were good. True creation is to bring something out of nothing and this is an activity that is proper only to God.

creationism   The doctrine that each human soul is created directly by God so that the soul derives neither from the body nor from any physical seed. This doctrine is opposed to traducianism which claims that the human soul is handed on by the simple act of propagation. It is opposed also to an extreme form of transformism which holds that the human race, body and soul, is solely the product of evolution. The doctrine of creationism leaves the door open for any theories of the evolution of the human race which protect the direct creation of the soul by God. As to when the soul is infused into the body, theologians hold two different theories: either at the moment of conception or at a time in the fetus' development when it begins to take a shape recognizably human.

creator   One who makes a thing from nothing; one who causes to exist. A title proper to God alone, who creates, sustains and commands the universe by His laws.

creature   In general, anything that has been created. In particular, it refers to animal life. In specific, it is restricted to human beings who have been created by God in His likeness.

credence (L. *credentia,* side table)   A table placed on the Epistle side of the sanctuary to hold the articles that will be used at Mass, such as the cruets, Lavabo dish and towel.

credit union, parish   A small, cooperative, banking and loan association made up of the members of a parish who wish to belong. Members purchase shares of stock or place their savings in the credit union, and may then apply for small loans at low rates of interest when desired for reasonable and productive purposes. The cooperative movement has been praised by Pope John XXIII in *Mater et Magistra* and enjoys the backing of many social-minded Catholics. The credit union is a recognized means of raising the standard of living, rescuing the poor from the hands of loan sharks, bringing about a degree of financial security and uniting the members of a parish in mutual help and Christian fellowship. In 1962 there were 1,383 Catholic parish credit unions in the United States, with nearly 500,000 members. Missioners among people of substandard living conditions find that the parish credit union can literally change the face of the earth. Improved housing, water supply, good roads, sanitation, health, education, follow in the wake of the increase in human dignity and decent living standards brought about by the credit union. As one instance, a Maryknoll Missioner started a credit union in Peru among the laborers of a depressed area, and within a few years it had 4,000 members and $300,000 in capital.

Credo (L. I believe)   First word of the Nicene Creed recited after the Gospel at certain Masses. It is used in both East and West.

creed   A form of belief. In the Latin Church it may refer to the Nicene, Athanasian or Apostles' Creed, each of which is a summary statement of the beliefs of Christian Faith.

Creed in the liturgy   The great profession of Faith which the baptized recite after the celebration of the Word, as their "Amen" to their reception of the Word.

cremation (L. *cremare,* to burn up)   The destruction of a human corpse by means of fire or intense heat. Cremation may be an ordinary or common practice, i.e., cremation properly so called; or it may be an exceptional action caused by war, epidemic or natural catastrophe in order to prevent the spreading of contagion. While cremation is not wrong in itself, the Church is opposed to ordinary cremation as being against the most ancient Christian tradition. The Church teaches that it is not proper that the human body, once the living temple of the Holy Spirit, should at death be destroyed; and that respect should be paid the human corpse which will one day rise in glory. Another reason for the Church's prohibition is the anti-Christian tendency shown by some of the advocates of cremation who use it as a manifestation of their disbelief in immortality. In Japan where cremation is the universal practice, except for some rural areas, the Church does not legislate against the practice. Many parishes have made it part of the funeral rite. After the funeral Mass, the final absolution is given at the city crematory. The urn containing the ashes is returned to the church where it is placed on a special shelf while the priest recites prayers. It is kept in the church for an indefinite period after which it is buried in a Catholic cemetery.

crib The manger in which Jesus Christ was laid after His birth. In Christian homes and places of worship the manger with the figure of the Infant is a symbol of the Incarnation. Used especially during the Christmas season.

crime In canon law, an external and culpable violation of a law to which a penalty is attached. Malicious intent or serious negligence is necessary for a crime to be committed. Mental defect, ignorance, violence and fear can lessen or remove the culpability of the crime. The positive motive of a return of love to God the Father must be the foundation of observing Divine and Church law. The avoidance of crime is not to be motivated by the degrees of culpability, but in the Christian living of sharing the divine life with God.

crosier A staff conferred upon bishops and mitred abbots at the time of their consecration and investiture. It is a symbol of authority and jurisdiction.

cross (L. *crux*) The vertical trunk and transverse beam on which Christ was crucified. It is today the most common symbol of Christianity. In art the cross takes many forms.

cross, altar The crucifix which is placed behind or above the tabernacle on the altar. It is usually visible to all in the body of the church and, with the tabernacle, is in the center of the altar.

cross, archiepiscopal Also called a patriarchal cross. It is a cross with two crossbars, instead of the single crossbar, of which the upper is shorter than the lower. This cross is usually carried before an archbishop in processions in his own province.

cross bearer One who carries a processional cross. In less solemn processions the cross bearer is usually a cleric in a surplice. In lay processions worthy laymen are selected for this function. In solemn processions the subdeacon, vested in an amice, alb and tunic, bears the processional cross.

cross, feasts of the According to the Roman calendar, there are two feasts of the cross: the "Finding of the Cross" on May 3 and the "Exaltation of the Cross" on Sept. 14. The Eastern Church observes these two feasts as well as additional ones.

Cross, Finding of the True The cross on which Chirst died is said to have been found by the Empress Helena about 326, after it had been hidden and buried for 180 years. A feast commemorating the event was formerly celebrated on May 3. Later the cross fell into the hands of the Persians. It was recovered by King Heraclius of Judea in 629. Relics of the cross made their way to many parts of the world, and many relics still exist. A relic of the true cross is the only relic that can be carried under a canopy in procession, and it is the only relic which receives a genuflection when exposed. The charge is sometimes made that if all the relics of the cross were put together they would be enough to make several crosses. Actually all the known relics that exist or are known to have existed would make up only a small portion of the original cross.

cross, Greek An equilateral cross.

cross, hand A small cross held in the hand. It is most frequently used in giving blessings, both liturgical and nonliturgical; commonly employed by priests of the Armenian, Maronite and Syrian Rites, and by bishops of all Eastern Rites.

cross, Latin The cross in which the transverse beam is shorter than the upright, and the headpiece projects above the transverse bar.

cross on vestments Speaking generally, this is a comparatively modern development. The cross on most modern chasubles does not seem to have been originally adopted with any symbolic purpose. Probably the cross concealed the seams. The Roman-type vestment has a cross in front; the French type, in back.

cross, papal The cross carried before a pope. A cross with three transverse bars of varying length, the smallest at the top.

cross, pectoral (L. *pectus,* breast) A cross worn on the breast by a bishop. It is suspended from a cord or chain, and worn outside the clothing. It is usually of gold, ornamented with precious stones, and contains relics. It can be worn by others, not bishops, such as a prefect apostolic, when they have the privilege of pontificating.

cross, processional A crucifix mounted on a long shaft of metal or wood. It is carried aloft at the head of processions with the figure turned forward, and is accompanied on either side by an acolyte with candle.

cross, Russian A three-barred cross used by the Russian Church. The upper bar represents the title of the cross, the second the arms, and the lowest, which is always inclined at an angle, the foot rest. The last is angled because Christ is said to have pushed it down in a moment of extreme pain.

cross, St. Andrew's A cross shaped like the Greek letter *chi* (X). Also known as *crux decussata,* so called from its resemblance to the Greek symbol for the numeral 10. St. Andrew is said to have suffered martyrdom on such a cross, his hands and feet bound to its four arms.

cross, veneration of the The honor and esteem which Christians render to relics of the real cross or images of it because upon this tree of sorrow Jesus Christ Our Savior was crucified for the sake of our salvation. Veneration of the cross is worship given to Christ indirectly through the relic or image and it differs from divine worship which is given to God alone. *See* Adoration.

crown, baptismal The crown is a wreath of plaited red-and-white ribbons with a small cross attached, symbolizing the grace of the Holy Spirit. It is put on after Confirmation which follows Baptism and is worn for eight days. It is then taken off while the priest says a prayer. It is a peculiarity of the Armenian rite.

crown, episcopal A headdress similar to the Latin mitre which is worn by Byzantine bishops when celebrating the liturgy. It is a tall, bulb-shaped, highly ornamented crown fashioned after the imperial crown of Constantinople.

crown, Franciscan A Rosary of seven decades in honor of the seven joys of our Lady. It is also called a Seraphic Rosary.

crown, marriage A metal crown or wreath which is placed upon the heads of the bride and groom during the marriage ceremony in the Eastern Rites. The wreath of flowers familiar in the West may be a survival of the same custom, symbolizing virginity.

crown of thorns ". . . And plaiting a crown of thorns, they put it upon his head, and a reed into his right hand, and bending the knee before him, they mocked him, saying, 'Hail, King of the Jews'" (Matt. 27:29–30). Christ's Resurrection and Ascension to the right hand of the Father, from which He rules the world, as King of the universe, heightens in retrospect His suffering and death for us. Our final possession of the Kingdom of heaven is our inheritance because Our Lord suffered and died and rose again to restore all creatures and creation to right order with the Father. Our Lord's crown of thorns is reputed to be in the Notre Dame Cathedral of Paris. St. Peter's in Rome and the Passionists celebrate a feast in honor of the crown of thorns on the Friday after Ash Wednesday; the Dominicans, on April 24.

crown, papal *See* tiara.

crown, virgin's Among the Greek and Romans a crown made of branches was presented to one who had won a victory. Today the symbolism is preserved in the reception of a virgin into one of the Sisterhoods. One of the articles presented to her during the ceremony of her consecration to a life of virginity is a crown which symbolizes the unperishable crown that is laid up for her in heaven.

crucifix (L. *crux,* cross, *figere,* to fix) A cross on which is represented the figure of Our Lord. The usual crucifix today represents Our Lord suffering, but traditional crucifixes, particularly those of Spanish influence, depicted Christ as crowned, robed and reigning from the cross. The crucifix is placed on or above all altars where Mass is offered except in the Nestorian and Coptic churches. In the Eastern Churches because of the prohibition against rounded representations, the crucifix is usually painted, or a cross with a painted figure is used. In Catholic terminology the word "cross" usually refers to a crucifix. The Protestant preference is for a figureless cross.

crucifixion (L. *crucifixio*) 1. The

infliction of the death penalty by means of nailing or binding the victim to or impaling him on a cross. A mode of capital punishment employed in the Roman Empire. 2. The death of Jesus Christ on the cross at Calvary.

cruelty (L. *crudelitas*) The quality or state of mind of being cruel. The disposition to inflict pain or suffering or to enjoy the infliction. Cruelty is a sin against charity and justice.

cruets (OF. *crue,* a small bottle) Two small containers, glass or metal, used to contain the water and wine used during the sacrifice of the Mass. Sometimes considered as part of the cruets is the small dish or bowl used to receive the water poured over the celebrant's fingers at the Lavabo.

Crusade, the Fourth The one thought that was always uppermost in the mind of Innocent III was to launch a universal crusade for the complete recovery of Palestine and all the Christian lands of the East. It proved to be the only purpose of his life that was not attained. The Fourth Crusade was diverted from its purpose and, instead of driving the Turks from the Holy Land, the so-called crusaders, mostly French and Venetians, captured and sacked Constantinople (1204) and converted the Greek Empire into a Latin one. Innocent condemned in the strongest terms this war of Christians upon Christians and excommunicated the leaders. In spite of this dismal failure, he spared no efforts to unite Christendom against Islam. He kept calling for a crusade to the day of his death, but people were unwilling to listen to him, for they had no leader. The tales of the brutality of Christian to Christian do not make for pleasant listening.

crypt (Gr. *krypte,* hidden) A vault

or tomb beneath a church or chapel. Originally such a place was a catacomb but after the freedom of the Church the custom of burying inside the church was adopted. Later the crypt became a large area under a church used not only for burial but also for worship.

Cuba The Catholic Church arrived in Cuba with the Spanish conquerors and until the overthrow of Spain in 1898 was completely under Spanish domination. Even at the beginning of 1962 (the last statistics available), 83 of the 187 priests in Cuba were Spanish, 68 were Cuban, 19 were Canadian and 10 were nationalized Cubans. Early in 1961 Fidel Castro expelled 135 priests, of whom 46 were Cubans and most of the others were Spanish. In November, 1961, 598 priests, 970 Brothers and 2,401 Sisters were forced to leave the country. While churches are open in Cuba, the 187 priests left in Cuba in 1962 (7 of whom were in prison) are hardly sufficient to give adequate spiritual care to the population which is subject to continual Marxist propaganda. A few Spanish priests were admitted in 1964. The national Catholic movements have been suppressed.

cubiculum (L. *cubicle*) A tomb hewn out of the wall of a catacomb.

culpa (L. fault) A fault or infraction of discipline. The sin of Adam and Eve is referred to as *"felix culpa"* (happy fault) because it was the cause of Christ's Incarnation and the Redemption.

cult (L. *cultus*) A great or excessive devotion or dedication to some person, idea or thing. Strictly speaking, it is either a religious practice or worship, embracing all the acts of adoration, direct or indirect, by which honor is given to God.

cult of saints Reverence and ceremonial veneration paid to the saints or to objects that symbolize or otherwise represent them.

culture shock An extreme psychological reaction to an alien culture resulting from improper adjustments to cultural frustrations and misunderstandings. A person suffering from culture shock reacts in one of two ways. Either he becomes antagonistic to the misunderstood culture, depreciating its members and becoming more and more American, or else the sufferer goes to the opposite extreme by "going native" which is an exaggerated desire of belonging. It is for this reason that missionary formation and orientation are so necessary.

cultus (L) A body of religious beliefs.

cultus disparitus (L. *cultus,* adornment, reverence, *disparitus,* divide, separate) Because of the new relation that the Christian has with God his Father, the Church, realizing the difficulty of married life between two persons not sharing the same outlook in religious practice, has placed an impediment restricting or forbidding marriage between the Christian and one who is not officially a member of the Church.

cura animarum (L. the care of souls) The obligation entrusted to an ordained priest involving instruction, the administration of the sacraments and in general all pastoral duties.

curate (L. *curatus*) An ordained priest who has the care of souls. The title of those priests who are assistants to the pastor of a parish.

cure of souls (L. *cura,* charge) The pastoral care of the faithful carried out by Mass, the sacraments, preaching and catechizing, and empathy for all. This obligation of service belongs to the pope, bishops and pastors.

curia, diocesan The assistants of a diocesan bishop who assist him in the administration of his diocese, acting under his authority.

Curial office One of the three departments of the *Curia Romana,* namely, the Chancery, *Dataria* and *Camera Apostolica.*

cursillista A man or woman who has made or is making a Cursillo.

Cursillo (kur-seal'yo; Sp. little course) One of the most vigorous movements of grace in Christianity today. Bishop Juan Hervas of Spain founded the *Cursillos de Cristiandad* (short courses in Christianity) in 1949. The movement spread throughout Spain, soon caught on in Austria, Germany, Belgium, France and Italy. In 1952, the Cardinal Archbishop of Bogotá brought it to Colombia, and it spread rapidly to other Latin American countries. Two Spanish air cadets brought the movement to the United States in 1957. Three full days (Thursday evening to Sunday evening) are spent in an atmosphere quite different from the familiar retreat. Except for the first evening, there is no rule of silence. Discussion, singing, jokes, even skits are encouraged. In this informal community atmosphere, participants hear 5 meditations and 15 lessons on Christian doctrine. Five of the instructions are given by priests, the others by lay persons. Each talk is followed by small-group discussions. Dialogue Mass, prayer and visits to the Blessed Sacrament are integral parts of Cursillo activities.

cursing and swearing Cursing is calling upon God to inflict a harm on the object cursed. Swearing is calling upon God to witness the truth of a statement. Without proper reason, cursing is a sin of irreverence, akin to blasphemy, and can also be a sin against charity. In Scripture there are justified curses: God cursed the serpent (Gen. 3), Noe cursed Chanaan (Gen. 9), and Our Lord cursed the barren fig tree, the Pharisees and the scribes. Swearing is sinful whenever it is false or unnecessary. The gravity of the sin is judged by the degree of irreverence, perjury or scandal involved.

cursus (kur'-sus; L. a course) A word having a variety of meanings. It refers to a Mass in which certain parts follow a prescribed rhythm; or to the order in which the psalms are arranged; or a prescribed order of study; or the order of the Divine Office.

curtain 1. A term used to denote the tabernacle veil. 2. In the Armenian liturgy this term denotes a large curtain which is drawn to hide the sanctuary during the Prothesis, before the Great Entrance, and from the people's Communion to the final prayer before the Last Gospel.

custodia (kus-toe'dee-ah; L. guard) Any temporary receptacle wherein the Blessed Sacrament is kept.

Custodian of the Holy Land The Franciscan who is the superior of the Friar Minors in the Near East. The Custodian is always the Guardian of Mount Sion. Until 1847, when the Latin Patriarchate was re-established, the Custodian in addition to his duties as provincial of the Franciscans had jurisdiction over the clergy and faithful of the Patriarchate of Jerusalem and still has the use of pontificals. Since 1558 the Custodian has resided in the Convent of the Most Holy Savior in Jerusalem.

custom An unwritten law introduced by the continuous acts of people. It is the frequent and free repetition of acts concerning the same thing. In Church law, established usage gives custom the force of law only with the consent of competent ecclesiastical authority.

custos kus'tos; L. custodian) An official of the Franciscans, having various responsibilities according to the branch of the order.

cycle A period of time marked by the beginning and completion of one round or course of events, recurring in the same order in a series; as, the cycle of the Church year or, of the saints.

cycle, liturgical *See* liturgical year.

C.Y.O. Abbreviation for Catholic Youth Organization (*q.v.*).

Czechoslovakia This Iron Curtain country has a population of 14 million of which 77 per cent is Catholic. There are 2 archdioceses and 10 dioceses. The Church is subject to continual harassment by the Communist government. Bishops have been imprisoned and driven from their sees. In 1957 alone, some 500 priests were sent to prisons and concentration camps. In 1960 Bishop Hlad was condemned to 9 years in prison for exercising episcopal functions without the authority of the state. Only 3 Czech bishops were allowed to leave the country for Vatican Council II.

D

dalmatic (L. *dalmatica)* A liturgical vestment worn by the deacon at Mass and other solemn ceremonies and by the bishop (under the chasuble) at Solemn Pontifical Mass. A loose - fitting robe with open sides and wide sleeves, it is of proper liturgical color (of the feast), decorated with two vertical stripes, running from shoulder to bottom, which are joined with two horizontal stripes. It receives its name from Dalmatia, possibly because the garment was first made from Dalmatian wool or because it was introduced to Rome from that region during the reign of Diocletian (284–305).

damage, unjust Any action which inflicts harm on another without material benefit to the person doing the harm. It is a grave sin that admits of slight matter and which imposes the obligation of restitution provided the damage was unjust in the strict sense, formally sinful, and the effective cause of the damage. No obligation of restitution arises from damage which is materially unjust unless a judge orders restitution to be made or it is voluntarily agreed that restitution be made.

damnation (L. *damnare,* to condemn) The state of everlasting separation from God and punishment in hell which is the result of mortal sin.

damned, the Those souls condemned to eternal punishment in hell, the lost souls (*q.v.*). The Church has no teaching on the relative number of people in hell and forbids Catholics to maintain that any particular person has been condemned.

damnification Damage, unjust (*q.v.*).

Daniel (Heb. God is my judge) A book of the Old Testament, certain parts being deuter-canonical, named from its chief character and traditional author. The first part of the book is historical; the second part records Daniel's visions which look forward to Christ and Antichrist; the third part is the appended stories of Susanna and elders, and of Bel and the dragon. Either of two viewpoints on the question of authorship may be held: 1. Daniel was the original author; the book was added to and translated into various languages; finally a compilation occurred with a final translation into Greek. 2. The book first appeared about 164 B.C., adapting older stories to Daniel, whom the author invented. Daniel is named in the Roman Martyrology on July 31.

Dark Ages A misnomer applied to the period following the fall of the Roman empire to the 13th century, sometimes with the implication that enlightenment did not come until the Protestant Reformation. Actually, this period was an Age of Faith. It saw the founding of Monasticism and the spread of the Benedictine movement. Great missioners such as Columban, Patrick, Augustine, Boniface, Willibord and others advanced the frontiers of the Church. In this period Byzantine culture reached its apogee. It is true that the Roman empire decayed and collapsed and that there were wars and invasions by the Huns, Visigoths, Vandals, Mongols, and Saracens. But that period was not one of retrogression but one of realignment and Christian advance.

Dark Night of the Senses A name given by St. John of the Cross to trials sent by God which are designed to detach a person from things of sense. It is an arid quietude of the prayer of quiet (*q.v.*). "God establishes the soul in the dark night of the senses," says St. John of the Cross, "that He may purify, prepare and subdue its lower nature, and unite it to the Spirit, by depriving it of light and causing it to cease from meditation."

Dark Night of the Soul A name given by St. John of the Cross to trials sent by God which detach a person from spiritual consolations and all self-love. The light of contemplation that the soul receives is so faint and so crucifying that the soul feels plunged in darkness and abandoned by God. The person sees himself as so loathsome that he cannot understand why God does not loathe him. These aridities make the soul advance in the pure love of God and finally bring a great spiritual peace.

Dataria, Apostolic An office of the Roman Curia from which certain types of dispensations and appointments to ecclesiastical benefices are issued. The name is derived from the formula used to date the documents, *Datae Kalendiis Martiis,* "given (sent) on the first of March."

Daughters of Charity of St. Vincent de Paul Founded in France in 1633 by St. Vincent de Paul and St. Louise de Marillac. Established in the United States by Mother Elizabeth Seton in 1809. The Sisters are primarily engaged in teaching and hospital work. There are 45,000 members in the world. There are two provinces in the United States with approximately 3,000 members, and one province in Canada. The Sisters staff missions in Formosa, Bolivia and Japan. Simple vows are taken.

Day of Atonement (Heb. Yom Kippur) The day of penance and atonement of ancient Israel which became the most solemn day of the Hebrew year. It falls on the tenth day of the seventh month. Sacrifice was offered by the high priest both as atonement for himself and the people. The feast is still observed in the Jewish religion.

day of recollection A religious practice of setting aside a special day of the month or year for developing an increased awareness of the presence of God in the soul.

de condigno (day-con-dig'nyo; (L. from worthiness) A type of merit that is due a person from justice or a promise. Thus the good works of a just man merit grace and eternal life *de condigno*.

de congruo (day-con'grew-oh; L. from fitness) A term applied to merit that is not due in justice and for which a person has no claim of reward although such a reward is fitting.

De Profundis (day pro-fun'dis, L. from the depths) The name given to Ps. 129, one of the penitential psalms, derived from the first two Latin words. It is a frequently used prayer for the dead.

deacon (Gr. *diakonos,* servant) A man who has received the second of the major orders in the sacrament of Holy Orders. Deaconate is received prior to ordination to the priesthood with the conferring of the stole and dalmatic by the bishop and the words, "Receive the power of reading the gospel in the church of God both for the living and the dead, in the name of the Lord." The main functions of the deacon are ministration at High Mass, exposing the Blessed Sacrament at Benediction, distributing Communion in case of need and administering solemn Baptism with permission. Although celibacy is normally required for Holy Orders, Vatican II ruled that married laymen of mature age could be ordained deacons when there is need of their services.

deaconess In the modern Church there is no order of deaconess, but prior to the 4th century women who received a special consecration were permitted to exercise certain definite functions in the Church. Among the duties were guarding the doors, maintaining order among members of their own sex in church and acting as intermediaries between the clergy and the women of the congregation. They were also used in the adult Baptism of women since Baptism at this time was by immersion and was preceded by the anointing of the whole body. The order of deaconess was discontinued after the Council of Nicaea.

Deacons, the Seven The seven men of Greek origin who were ordained by the Apostles (Acts 6:1-6). They had at least the powers of preaching and baptizing.

Dead, Mass for the A Mass offered for the repose of the soul of a person, or persons, who have passed away. The intention of such a Mass is that the deceased person arrive as quickly as possible into God's presence. There are different Masses for the dead. There is the Mass on the day of the funeral and burial; the Mass for the third, seventh, and thirtieth (Month's Mind Mass) days after death or burial; and the daily Mass for the Dead. In addition there is the Mass for All Souls' Day (Nov. 2), which remembers all deceased souls. The color of the vestments in the Mass for the Dead is black. *See* Requiem.

Dead, Office of the Those psalms, readings and prayers to be said before the burial Mass. The Office consists of First Vespers, Matins and Lauds; thus it differs from other Offices in the Breviary in that it does not have Little Hours, Second Vespers or Compline. The custom of singing psalms while carrying the corpse to the grave seems to date from the 3rd century. It was not until the 8th century that an Office for the Vigil of the Dead was established. Essentially the Office was always much as it is today. Today this Office has been reduced to a devotional status.

dead, prayers for the A religious service of psalms and lessons modeled on the Divine Office used in commemoration of the dead or as part of the funeral service.

Dead Sea Scrolls Scroll manuscripts or fragments of such manuscripts found following World War II in caves in the cliffs along the Dead Sea in the vicinity of Jericho. The manuscripts contain portions of most of the books of the Old Testament. They also contain the valuable documents and writing of an Essene community living in Palestine in New Testament times. Some of the manuscripts date to the 2nd century B.C. The scrolls are very important for the textual study of the Old Testament. They also provide valuable information for a better understanding of the New Testament.

deadly sins, the seven Sinful propensities which reveal themselves in particular sinful acts. An attempt to enumerate the primary instincts which are most likely to give rise to sin; e.g., pride, covetousness, lust, envy, gluttony, anger and sloth. *See* Capital Sins.

dean (L. *decanus,* head of a group of ten) 1. A priest, usually appointed by the bishop, having general supervision over a group of parishes constituting a deanery. 2. The head of a cathedral or collegiate chapter. 3. An ecclesiastical official, such as the Dean of the College of Cardinals, or a dean in a college.

deanery A territory consisting of several parishes presided over by a dean.

death The end of life. It is usually used in connection with physical life. The Church teaches that physical death is the penalty for original sin (Gen. 2:17); and that spiritual death, the loss of the state of grace, is the punishment for personal sin.

Debora A Hebrew prophetess who helped free the Israelites from the Chanaanites. Because of her deeds, she was afterwards called the "mother of Israel."

debt Something owed someone. It also has the meaning of sin or trespass. The Church teaches that Christ paid for the debt, or sin, incurred by the evil acts of man.

decade The fifteenth part of a rosary consisting of an Our Father, ten Hail Marys, and one Glory be to the Father; one meditates on the inner meaning of a mystery while saying the above prayers or at least puts oneself in the presence of God.

Decalogue (Gr. *deka,* ten; *logos,* word) The Ten Commandments (*q.v.*) or moral precepts given to Moses on Mt. Sinai. They are found in Ex. 20:1-17 and Deut. 5:6-21. They were the basis of the Old Law.

deceit A form of lying; the deceit of the liar who tries to mislead others by concealing or twisting the truth or by giving false alibis.

December Month of the Holy Infancy.

Decency, National Legion of An organization founded in 1934 to evaluate moral standards for the judgment and patronage of motion pictures. For many years the Legion operated on standards that were largely negative but in recent years has worked from positive principles of encouraging attendance at good motion pictures.

declaration of nullity The decree of nullity is a judgment by a competent court that a certain marriage was and is invalid, i.e., never a marriage. A marriage may be null because of defective consent, a diriment impediment or a substantial defect of form. The ordinary can declare the following null: marriages invalid because of defect of form: e.g., a Catholic who went before a civil authority or a Protestant minister; cases in which the invalidity of a previous marriage is based on one of these diriment impediments, namely, disparity of worship, Holy Orders, solemn vows, previous bond of marriage, consanguinity, affinity, or spiritual relationship. If the impediment can be proved by a certain and authentic document, and if there had been no dispensation, no trial is required. But if the invalidity of a previous marriage arises from some other causes such as impotence, defective consent, etc., a formal judicial trial is necessary and two concordant sentences to the effect that the invalidity of the former marriage has been proved.

decollation   Beheading; used in connection with John the Baptist.

decorations, pontifical   1. The ornaments used by a bishop. The *pectoral cross* (L. *pectus,* breast), suspended from the neck, by a chain or cord, to the chest; made of gold and decorated with gems, it usually contains the relics of a martyr. The *ring* with a precious stone, worn on the third finger of the right hand, signifying the seal of faith and the wedding of the bishop to his diocese. (The ring is kissed by the bishop's subjects as a sign of respect; an indulgence of fifty days can be gained.) The *mitre* (G. *mitra,* turban), a headdress made of two stiff parts (front and back) joined by cloth which allows the two parts to fold together; two lappets hang down from behind. There are three types or grades of the mitre: *precious,* adorned with gold and precious stones, used on major feast days when standing or in procession; *golden,* made of cloth-of-gold, worn when sitting during a sacred ceremony and during penitential times; *simple,* made of plain white silk or linen, used at funerals, on Good Friday, when blessing candles on Candlemas and when in solemn attendance on the pope. The *crosier* (L. *crocia,* crook), the "pastoral staff," an ornate metal tubing taller than the bishop, symbolizing (by its crook)

the bishop's office of tending the members of his flock and (by its pointed end) the spiritual "prodding" some may need. At Solemn Pontifical Mass, in addition to these and the ordinary vestments, the bishop wears *buskins,* knee-length embroidered silk stockings of the proper liturgical color; *sandals,* or slippers, of embroidered silk the same color as the buskins and worn over the buskins. Decorated silk *gloves* are worn up to the Offertory; a *tunic* and a *dalmatic* of proper liturgical color are worn under the chasuble. The *gremial veil* (L. *gremium,* lap), an oblong cloth of the same material and liturgical color as the vestments, placed over the knees of the bishop when sitting at Solemn Mass or during the distribution of ashes, candles or palms, and during anointing. The *mozzetta,* a short cape reaching to the elbows and is fastened only at the neck although it has buttons all the way down. The *cappa magna,* a long cape with a train and the *throne* are also considered as pontifical decorations (*pontificalia*). 2. Honors conferred by the Holy See on lay people such as knighthood, titles to nobility, and medals and crosses.

decree (L. *decretum*)   1. An order issued by a person or body in authority. 2. The decision or the judgment of a court.

decree of nullity   A decree from a competent court which declares a marriage null and void; invalid, as if it had never taken place; annulled. For a list of some types, *See* declaration of nullity.

decretals (dee-kray't'ls; L. *decretalis*) Decisions given by the popes in reply to questions on matters of discipline are called decretals. These replies had the force of law, so that as a result, before the promulgation of the new *Code of Canon Law* in 1918, all bishops had to possess collections of them. Each bishop's collection included decretals addressed to him personally as well as copies of decretals addressed to other bishops which would be of help to him in judging similar cases in his own diocese. In the 12th century, Gratian, a Camaldolese monk, made a collection of these decretals. When the phrase "the Decretals" is used, reference is being made to the collection of laws made by St. Raymond of Penafort at the command of Pope Gregory IX. In 1918, by the promulgation of the new *Code of Canon Law,* the use of the decretals and the commentaries on them as directives was abolished.

Decretals, False A collection of letters and decrees ascribed to the popes and councils of the first six centuries. After several centuries these documents became suspect and in the 17th century were proved to have been forgeries. The purpose of the collection was to increase the powers of the bishops against the civil rulers.

decretist One who is a student of law or is expert in canon law. *See* decree, decretals.

Dedication, Feast of the 1. The anniversary of the dedication of a cathedral or church. The anniversay of a cathedral is celebrated in all the churches of the diocese. 2. A Jewish feast instituted by Judas Machabee (64 B.C.) to celebrate the purification of the Temple which had been defiled three years earlier by Antiochus Epiphanes. The feast is mentioned in the New Testament as the day on which the Jews attempted to stone Our Lord (Jn. 10:22).

dedication of a church The setting apart of it for divine worship. This may be done by a simple bless-ing or by solemen consecration. All churches, public and semipublic oratories, must be at least blessed, with the rite of prayers, aspersions and Mass provided in the *Rituale,* by a bishop or a delegated priest. In case of pollution it may be reconciled by a priest. A church so blessed has no right to the liturgical feast of the dedication (*q.v.*) until consecration (*q.v.*) has been performed by a bishop.

defamation Unjust defamation, either calumny or detraction, is a grave sin against charity and justice.

defect, irregularity from A canonical impediment which prohibits the reception of Tonsure and Holy Orders, or prevents the exercise of orders already received. The irregularities, intended to safeguard the dignity of the Church's ministry, may be divided into those of: 1. *Crime* (*ex delicto*), which includes apostasy, heresy, schism, marriage of those in major orders or in vows, attempted suicides, voluntary murders (abortions); and 2. *Defect* (*ex defecto*) which abides in the subject, such as defects of health, whether mental or physical. Other defects are bigamy, a bad reputaion, a lack of liberty. Some irregularities cease when their cause is removed, e.g., age or freedom. Others need formal dispensation, either from the local bishop or directly from the pope.

defendant The party against whom a claim or charge is brought in a law proceeding. When a trial or hearing is in process, the defendant must be present throughout, either in person or by proxy, and, if accused of a crime, must be represented by counsel.

defender of the bond (L. *defensor vinculi*) That priest who is appointed to the diocesan court to defend the marriage bond in all cases where it is challenged or where a dispensation is sought. If the court passes down a ruling of nullity, he is required to appeal to a higher court.

definition, papal (L. *definire,* to determine) A solemn and irrevocable decision rendered by the pope as pastor, teacher and supreme head of the Church. When it pertains to faith and morals and is made by the pope as universal teacher of the Church (ex cathedra) or by an ecumenical council acting with the pope's consent and sanction, it binds the universal Church. This is not a decision as a sentence of law, but a statement of truth which always existed in the deposit of faith.

definitively (L. *definire,* to limit) 1. This adverb, which modifies verbs of definition and decision, conveys the notion of preciseness, conclusiveness and finality. 2. To speak infallibly and irrevocably as does the pope when he speaks ex cathedra on matters of faith and morals; thus the pope is said to define a doctrine that has always existed in the deposit of faith.

definitor 1. A person given charge, under canon law, over ecclesiastical property in one of the districts into which a deanery is divided. Such a person is also designated as an adviser to the dean. 2. The name also applies to a member of a general chapter in some religious orders. 3. A member of a governing council in a religious order, assisting the superior.

definitors Officials who are appointed as counsellors of a provincial or general superior with certain determinate powers. In religious orders definitors are those who form the governing council.

defrauding spouse One who without sufficient cause denies his wife (her husband) the due conjugal rights.

Such a denial is an offense against justice.

defrauding the state (L. *defraudare,* to cheat) To take or withhold from the state by fraud what is its right. The state has the right to collect from individuals and corporations revenue for the support and the maintenance of certain public services. Individuals of a state have an obligation to support the state. A state has a right to levy a fair tax, and individuals have an obligation to pay such a tax.

defrauding workers of their wages To take or withhold from a worker by fraud what is his by right. Employees have a right in justice to receive a living wage, and employers are bound to honor this right. This is a sin crying to heaven for vengeance.

degradation Deposition of a cleric from clerical orders or from the performing of the functions of his office, together with the deprivation of his benefice; the act reducing a cleric to the state of a layman. It is the most serious canonically vindictive penalty which the Church can inflict upon a cleric.

degrees, academic Title of scholarship conferred by universities as a mark of having completed certain prescribed studies, such as the degrees of bachelor, master and doctor; e.g., A.B., A.M. and Ph.D.

deism A philosophical system which admits an intelligent First Cause but denies any Providential God.

Deity In ordinary language, the same as God, but in theology there is a distinction between God and Deity. Although they are in reality one and the same, yet their signification is different. God is concrete and signifies the divine essence in the possessor, and, as such, can stand for a divine person. Deity is abstract and signifies the divine essence as an abstract, i.e., as for but apart from, the possessor, and as such cannot stand for a divine person.

delate To denounce to authority, such as reporting a book dangerous to faith and morals. Solicitation in confession must be delated under penalty of excommunication.

Delaware (Named for Lord De La Warre, first governor of Virginia company) One of the 13 original states, and first to ratify the Constitution. It is 49th in area, 46th in population, and has the highest per capita income in the United States except Washington, D.C. It was originally the home of the Lenni-Lenape Indians (later called Delawares). The first permanent settlement, at Wilmington in 1638, was named New Sweden, and was seized by Peter Stuyvesant, then by England, later governed by William Penn. There was religious freedom from the first. Settlers from Sweden, Holland, Finland, Scotland, Ireland and England swarmed into the colony. Catholics, few in number, were visited by Jesuits from Maryland. After the Revolution, the population increased, farming and industry flourished. The first Catholic church was built in 1772 at Coffee Run by Father Sittensperger, and in 1816 Father Patrick Kenny built St. Peter's in Wilmington. This later became the cathedral, with Thomas Becker as first bishop of the diocese (1868). Daughters of Charity from Emmitsburg, Md., opened the first school and orphanage, and other religious orders followed, establishing numerous educational and charitable institutions. Delaware has a Catholic population of about 106,-400, out of a total population of 446,292.

delegate, apostolic *See* apostolic delegate.

delegation The act of turning over authority to another by one who has ordinary power by reason of his office, done totally, or in part, unless restricted by law. Also, the commission given to the delegate.

Deluge, the The Flood of the Old Testament as narrated in Genesis 6:9; 8:14. The main figure of the Flood is the ark which is a figure of the Church (1 Peter 3:20). Noe and his family were saved by God by means of the ark, so the Church is God's means of mankind's salvation.

demiurge A word used by Plato to indicate the supreme architect or maker of the universe. The Gnostics used the word to mean a world-maker, distinct from the Supreme God. By some it was interpreted as the force of evil responsible for matter and the imperfect God of the Old Testament.

democracy Government by the people, either directly or through elected representatives. In this state, citizens have rights which authority must respect: the right to a personal opinion on the rights and duties imposed on them, the right to be consulted and to have their opinion put into effect, in a manner consistent with the common good. "The state should be the organic and organizing unity of the true people" (Pope Pius XII).

demon A person or thing regarded as evil or cruel. Usually applied to a messenger or minister of the Devil.

demoniac (Gr. *daimon,* a demon) A person possessed by a devil; a person whose actions are controlled by an evil spirit.

denomination A category or class of the Christian religion to which a given person belongs, such as Methodist, Baptist, Episcopal, etc.

denunciation The revealing to a superior of the crimes of one of his subordinates. In canon law, the act of reporting the major crimes of churchmen, or their suspected heresy, to the proper authority.

Deo gratias (day'oh grah'tse-ahs, L. thanks be to God) This is an old Latin formula used as a grateful response in the Mass.

Deo volente A pious Latin expression meaning "God willing." It is appended to statements of determination, thus: "I shall go to New York tomorrow, Deo volente."

deposit of faith The sum total of truths revealed by Christ, taught infallibly by the Church, and witnessed by Scripture and Tradition.

deposition (L. *deponere,* to remove) An ecclesiastical penalty where one who is a cleric is forever deprived of his office and of the right of exercising the functions of his orders.

deposition, day of The day of death of a saint or martyr. The term is used in the *Roman Martyrology* (*q.v.*).

descent from the Cross A phrase used for the act of removing the body of Christ from the Cross following His crucifixion. After the death of Christ, Joseph of Arimathea went to Pilate and asked for the body of Christ. He was given permission and with the assistance of some followers of Christ removed the body from the Cross, wrapped it in clean linen and placed it in his own new tomb.

descent into hell The fifth article of the Apostles' Creed which states that at the death of Christ, His soul "descended into hell." The word "hell" is used to represent Limbo where Christ went to the souls of the just who were held captive there awaiting the Redemption and who were brought by Christ into everlasting life with Him.

desecrate 1. To profane or misuse a sacred object or thing; to treat a holy object in an unholy manner. 2. To treat in a sacrilegious and unholy manner any object or place, such as a church, altar, chalice, etc., which has been either blessed or consecrated for a religious purpose.

design, argument from The fifth argument of St. Thomas in his *Summa Theologiae,* I: q.2, a.3, for the existence of God. It is variously known as the argument from the governance of the world, from order, from ordered multiplicity, from providence, and from final causality. The argument states: "We see that things which lack knowledge, for example, natural bodies, act for an end, and this is evident from their acting always, or nearly always, in the same manner, so as to obtain the best result. Thus it is clear that they obtain their end, not by chance, but by design. Now that which lacks knowledge cannot move toward an end, unless it is directed by some being endowed with both intelligence and knowledge. Therefore some intelligent being exists by whom all natural objects are directed to their end. This being is God."

desolation A condition of shocking abandonment to confusion and dejection in which a person finds himself when he feels that God has withdrawn His love and concern for him.

despair A willful and complete abandonment of hope and assurance that God will bring man to life everlasting.

destiny A man's destiny is understood differently, according to the philosophy by which a person is influenced. To Catholics it means the ordering of secondary causes, such as a man's own acts cooperating with grace, in order that they produce their effects in accordance with Divine Providence. Fatalists regard destiny as something over which they have no control.

detachment In the ascetical sense, the result of the ability to have control over the use of material things and over one's own will. It is usually spoken of as a state of preference for the things which pertain to the spirit over the things which pertain to the flesh. The thought of man's eternal union with God motivates man to strive to subordinate all lesser things to this ultimate end, not rejecting things that are good, but not being dominated by anything that might interfere with man's union with God ultimately.

determinism A philosophic doctrine which teaches that every event results from a preceding event, that the progress of events is determined by what has occurred, and that everything comes to be of necessity. The doctrine denies free will and holds that actions are determined, mechanistically, by the most powerful motive. The result of the doctrine is that it dispenses with morality, responsibility, and right and wrong.

detraction The injuring of another's reputation by the unjust telling of the true but hidden faults of another. It is a violation of the command to love one's neighbor (charity) and of the seventh commandment (justice). Guilt varies with the damage done. Since it is a sin against justice, restitution must be made as far as possible. For a just reason and only to the proper persons, the faults of another may be revealed to prevent evil.

Detroit An archdiocese in Michigan. La Salle and his companions visited the site in 1679, and named the Detroit River. Fort St. Joseph was established within the present city limits and by 1701 a few French families had settled around the fort.

On July 26th of that year, the first pastor, Father Constantine Delhalle, began the still existing records of the parish of St. Anne. In 1796 Detroit was drawn from the jurisdiction of Quebec and placed under Baltimore. During the first third of the 19th century, Father Gabriel Richard, a Sulpician, was pastor. He published the first Catholic paper (1809) in the United States, was the founder of the University of Michigan and was elected to the House of Representatives, the only Catholic priest ever elected to Congress. The diocese was established in 1833 under Bishop Frederick Rese.

Deus in Adjutorium meum intende (L. O God, come to my assistance.) To which is replied: *Domine, ad adjuvandum me festina* (O Lord, make haste to help me.) This invocation is the first line of Psalm 69 (70), used at, or near, the beginning of all Hours of the Divine Office.

deuterocanonical books Those books of Sacred Scripture about whose inspiration there was doubt on the part of some of the Fathers or some local churches although the Church as a whole received them as inspired. The Greek Fathers called them "disputed" books. Protestants refer to them as "apocryphal" because they are not listed in the Jewish canon of the Bible.

Deuteronomy (Gr. *deuter*, second; *nomos,* Law) Book of the Old Testament cast in the form of discourses delivered by Moses shortly before his death. Although it is thought to have been originally composed around 700 B.C., it contains the essence of the Mosaic tradition, commended by Our Lord as the "first and greatest commandment" (Mt. 22:37, quoting Deut. 6:5).

devil (L. *diabolus*) 1. A fallen angel.

A purely spiritual being cut off from God because of the sin of rebellion. 2. An evil spirit, such as those driven out by Christ. 3. Lucifer, the chief of the rebellious angels who goes through the world like "a roaring lion seeking whom he may devour" (1 Pt. 5:8). He is a rational spirit, embittered over his loss of the Beatific Vision, who has turned to an unending hatred of God and things holy.

Devil's Advocate *See* Advocatus Diaboli.

devolution (L. *devolvere,* to roll down) 1. Transference of a power or right from one person to another. In Church law this is an appeal to a higher authority when a previous appeal did not change the effect of a decision of a superior. 2. It also refers to the filling of a vacant benefice on the part of the Holy See when the ordinary had not acted to fill it by appointment after six months. Or, if an election is not completed within a prescribed period, the right of appointment devolves on that superior who has the right to confirm the election.

devotions (L. *devovere,* to vow) Public or private prayer and/or worship regularly performed such as the Holy Hour, Bible Vigils, Stations of the Cross, various novenas in honor of the Blessed Virgin or some saint, or for some special intention. These devotions would include any regular church service or private worship that is not part of the Church's liturgy; i.e., part of the official public worship of the Church such as the Mass, the sacraments, the Breviary (the Divine Office), or Benediction of the Blessed Sacrament. Such devotions receive a certain amount of ecclesiastical recognition.

devotions, popular Extraliturgical devotions such as the Rosary, Little

Office of the Blessed Virgin, Stations of the Cross, etc. They are personal and private devotions. The Church has always encouraged private prayer; however, care must be taken against individualism, subjectivism and sentimentality. Liturgical prayer always takes precedence as it is Christocentric, rich in the entirety of Christian doctrine and full of the spirit of Christian community.

diabolism (L. *diabolus,* devil) Any attempt to deal with or have intercourse with an evil spirit whether it is successful or not. It is a very serious sin because the evil spirits are the unalterable enemies of God who by their perversity seek to turn men away from God. *See* possession; spiritism.

dialectics The science which treats of the rules by which the mind in its search for the truth may judge rightly and proceed correctly. It proceeds by weighing and reconciling juxtaposed or contradictory arguments for the purpose of arriving at truth, usually through discussion or debate. It is the method of many Western philosophers, especially Socrates and Hegel. Marx applied the method to matter. He taught that matter and history unfolded and developed in a dialectical way. Dialectics is also important to the modern philosophies, existentialism and phenomenology.

dialogue (Gr. *dialogos,* a conversation) A theological conversation between members of separated Christian churches which seeks for mutual doctrinal understanding in the light of the ecumenical movement.

Dialogue Mass While the Solemn High Mass (*q.v.*) is the complete and perfect liturgy of the Mass, expediency and custom have made the Low Mass the more common ceremonial form. Expediency and custom also lessened the role of the faithful in the Mass, delegating to one or two servers what was once a personal and communal role of all. The Constitution on the Sacred Liturgy of Vatican Council II (nos. 48, 50) declares that the faithful should not be present at the liturgy "as strangers or silent spectators" but that they "should take part in the sacred action." The Constitution ordered revisions so that "the devout and active participation by the faithful may be more easily achieved." An instruction from the Congregation of Rites calls for the faithful to make liturgical responses to the celebrant. This type of Mass is known as a Dialogue Mass.

diaspora (Gr. a scattering) 1. The countries outside Israel (Palestine) to which the Jews were dispersed. 2. The Jews living in these countries. The Jews were dispersed from their homeland by various conquerors, culminating in the capture of Jerusalem by Emperor Titus in A.D. 70. 3. By extension to other groups that have spread beyond their homelands and the areas to which they have dispersed, e.g., the overseas Chinese.

Didache (did'a-kee; Gr. teaching) A book written in the 1st or 2nd century called "The Teaching of the Twelve Apostles." It was known to the Fathers of the Church, who put great value upon it. It is divided into two parts, the first being moral and the second concerned with liturgy and discipline. It speaks of a hierarchy of Apostles, bishops and deacons. It speaks of Baptism, confession and Communion.

Dies Irae (L. day of wrath) A sequence or hymn which is part of the Requiem Mass, attributed to St. Thomas of Celano who lived in the 12th century. It is a highly poetical description of the last judgment, neither joyful nor triumphant in tone, but is filled with concern over the suffering souls. It paints death and judgment in dark and fearsome colors.

Diet of Augsburg *See* Augsburg, Diet of.

difference of worship, religion This is a dire impediment to marriage, which arises when one of the parties has been baptized in the Catholic Church or is a convert to the Church and the second party is an unbaptized person. This impediment however can be dispensed when a grave reason is present.

dignitary (L. *dignus,* worthy) A person holding a position of exalted rank, honor or dignity. An example of an ecclesiastical dignitary would be a cardinal or a bishop.

dimissorials, letters dimissorial (L. *litterae dimissoriales,* dismissal letters) Letters given by a bishop or a regular prelate to his subjects, thus allowing them to be ordained outside their territory by another bishop. In general, they can also refer to letters given by an ecclesiastical superior to his subjects, which are to have effect outside the superior's jurisdiction.

diocesan clergy The secular clergy as distinguished from the regular or religious clergy. This clergy comes under the jurisdiction of the ordinary of a diocese and it is its duty to administer the spiritual and temporal affairs of the diocese and its parishes.

diocese (Gr. *dioikesis,* a province) A territory under the jurisdiction of an ordinary (*q.v.*) which has been canonically erected by the Holy See. It embraces all those parishes and people within the given area. The pope alone can create or divide or suppress dioceses. All secular priests are attached to some diocese (incardinated).

diplomatic corps Personnel who are involved in the diplomatic relations of one country with other countries. As a sovereign state the Vatican has its own diplomatic corps of ambassadors, envoys, ministers as well as attaches and secretaries who help carry on diplomatic relations with many countries.

diptych (Gr. *diptychon; dis,* twice; *ptyssein,* to fold) A diptych is made from two tablets hinged together and folded over. The tablets have been used variously for writing, painting, carving and sculpturing. In the early centuries of the Church, they were used for liturgical texts, or for listing the names of living and deceased members of the Church to be read out at some point in the Mass. Traces of this practice are seen in the Roman Liturgy in the remembrance of pope and bishop, the lists of several saints, the commemoration of the living and the remembrance of the dead. Later they became sculptured or painted as devotional panels. It also became the custom to add extra leaves, thus obtaining a triptych or polyptych, etc.

direct line A term used in matrimonial legislation to denote consanguinity (blood relationship). It includes all ancestors and descendants, legitimate and natural. Marriage between any two of these parties is invalid.

direction, spiritual In every work which implies a special competence and a long-term effort there is need of guidance from one who has already demonstrated skill in this competency and who has acquired through experience and study the necessary knowledge to instruct others. In striving to reach a higher degree in spiritual, religious matters a guide is needed who furnishes direction. Spiritual direction both for those who dedicate themselves totally to the service of God and for lay people who endeavor to attain a closer union with God while continuing their secular occupations has been part of Christianity from the beginning. Direction ordinarily means telling people what to do and how to do it, as in a factory where orders and commands are issued. In spiritual matters it would mean rather enlightening, encouraging, counseling and guiding in matters that pertain to Christian life. The spiritual content of direction would include the actual prayer life, communal worship and individual conversation with Christ; it would also include discussion of the way to live the Christian life existentially, in the environment in which one is placed. This would include assistance in the cultivation of virtue, especially that of Christian prudence, which, as it grows, will make the need of direction less and less until the mature Christian has reached full manhood in Christ. Spiritual direction may be given by parents, especially in the early stages of religious training, by teachers, student counselors and advisers in the field of guidance. Cardinal Suenens recommends that nuns enter more vigorously into the field of spiritual direction of women. In a more restricted sense, spiritual direction is given by priests, especially by those who have done studies in ascetical and mystical theology as a preparation for work in this important field of Christian holiness.

director, spiritual 1. The person, usually a priest, who gives spiritual direction. He should have certain qualities. The most important is *competence,* i.e., knowledge of theology adequate to fulfill the position. This has always been a prime necessity, as St. Teresa of Avila and St. John of the Cross point out. 2. In these modern times, he should also have an

adequate *knowledge of psychology*
so as to supplement his theological
knowledge. Often the basic needs of
nature are overlooked as the spiritual
director recommends spiritual poul-
tices for wounds that need natural
remedies. 3. He should have *good
judgment,* a kind of practical wisdom
or common sense that concerns both
the natural and supernatural and enables him to distinguish between
both. In many cases, this seems to be
a gift. The spiritual director who
lacks it is greatly handicapped. 4. *Experience and spiritual maturity,* i..e,
a man who has striven to live the
spiritual life himself. The spiritual
director ought to have a vital superiority in this matter over the one who
seeks his direction. 5. *Empathic understanding,* i.e., the readiness to try
to see through the eyes of the person,
the difficulties the person is facing
and the opportunities he enjoys. This
calls for much *patience* in listening,
silence to allow the Spirit to work,
and *understanding* through the generosity and zeal that he brings to direction. 6. *Paternal firmness.* Father
Thils says: "A director who is not
firm would do well not to occupy
himself with direction. By firmness
we understand the quality of one who
knows what must be enacted and
holds to it, recalls it and aids in its
realization." He adds that it should
be fatherly, possessing a fundamental
and natural kindness, that never looks
down from above, never judges,
never condemns but like the Prodigal
Father is always ready to pardon. 7.
Discretion hardly needs to be mentioned. As in the case of doctors,
psychiatrists and psychologists, spiritual directors are bound to protect
the confidence placed in them.
Church law requires that every seminary have a priest who is available

for spiritual direction of the students.

Directorium An obsolete term for
the ordo (*q.v.*).

dirge This word is taken from the
first word (*dirige*) of the Antiphon
of Psalm 5 which begins the first nocturn of Matins of the Office of the
Dead. It was originally used to refer
to the public recitation of this Office.
It is now applied to any psalm or
hymn sung for a deceased Christian.

diriment impediment (L. *dirimere,* to
take apart; *impedire,* to hold back)
An obstacle from natural or Church
law which renders an attempted marriage invalid. In some cases the
Church can give dispensation from
the impediment, after which a valid
marriage can take place. Among
these impediments are disparity of
worship, impotence, insufficient age,
spiritual relationship, consanguinity,
Holy Orders, solemn vows, crime,
violence and fear, previous marriage
existing, etc. An impediment created
by the natural law can never be dispensed.

disabilities of Catholics A term used
in Great Britain to describe legal restrictions placed against Catholics because of their religion. Many of these
were removed by the Emancipation
(Relief) Act in 1829 and more by
the Act of 1926. Some disabilities
still remain: A Catholic or a person
married to a Catholic cannot be king
or queen; no Catholic may be regent;
no Catholic may hold divinity posts
at Oxford, Cambridge or Durham.
Catholic priests are also barred from
sitting in the House of Commons (as
are Anglican priests).

disarmament The reduction of military force. Pope John XXIII, in his
encyclical *Pacem in Terris,* gave the
Catholic doctrine on disarmament.
He pointed out that economically active countries are storing huge stocks

of arms and as a result other countries are deprived of the collaboration they need to progress economically and socially. People live in constant fear of war and there is a danger that a conflagration might be set off by some obscure event. Therefore, justice, right reason and humanity demand an end to an arms race. Military stocks should be equally reduced. Nuclear weapons should be banned. Agreement should be reached on disarmament and control. The Holy Father further pointed out that peace will come only through mutual trust.

discalced (L. *dis,* without; *calceus,* shoe) A term applied to religious orders and congregations whose members go barefoot or wear sandals, such as the Discalced Carmelites. At one time Capuchins, Franciscans and all Carmelites followed this practice, but over the years they have taken to wearing sandals and shoes.

Discalced Carmelite Nuns The Second Order of Our Lady of Mt. Carmel, called "Discalced" because sandals are worn instead of shoes. It is not certain when the order was founded but its modern history begins with St. Teresa of Avila and St. John of the Cross who restored the original rule. It is a contemplative, enclosed order. There are more than 15,000 Carmelite Nuns in the world with some 60 convents and monasteries in the United States and 3 in Canada.

discernment of spirits The act of determining whether a person is acting genuinely from a virtue and grace of God or only simulating the virtue or is influenced by the Devil. This may be an acquired gift or an infused gift by God as mentioned by St. Paul, (1 Cor. 12:10; Gal. 5:19-23) and St. John (1 Jn. 4:1-6).

disciple (L. *discipulus,* a pupil) Title or name applied to the twelve Apostles and the seventy-two sent out, two by two, by Christ (Luke 10:1). The name was extended later to cover others appointed by the Apostles (Acts 1:15).

Disciples of Christ Founded by Thomas and Alexander Campbell in Lexington, Ky., about 1827, its members are sometimes called the Progressive Campbellites. Members believe that Scripture is the rule of faith and life and no other guide is necessary. Baptism and the Lord's Supper are practiced. Each church is independent. There are approximately 2 million members. *See* Churches of Christ.

discipline A name given a small scourge or whip used for self-inflicted mortification and penance. It should not be used except on the advice of a spiritual director.

discipline, ecclesiastical The instruction and laws which the Church legislates for the governing of the actions of the faithful.

Discipline of the Sacraments, Sacred Congregation of the A congregation of the Roman Curia which was established by Pope St. Pius X in 1908. To it is entrusted all legislation on the discipline of the seven sacraments. For such matters the entire territory of the Latin Church, including that under Propaganda, depends on this Congregation. It handles dispensations to matrimony and Holy Orders and rules on the validity of marriages and ordinations.

discipline of the secret (L. *disciplina arcani*) In the first five centuries of the Church, the unbelievers were not permitted to witness the Christian worship or told certain doctrines, in order that blasphemy, persecution or interruption of the worship would not occur. Catechumens were slowly instructed and their faithfulness tested in order to avoid false instruction. They were fully instructed by the time they received Baptism. Symbols kept secret were: the fish, the lamb and the shepherd. In the liturgy only "the Mass of the Catechumens" was attended by those being instructed. This system is being used today in some missionary areas.

discursive prayer Another name for meditation. It is praying silently to God without using the words of formal prayers, such as the Our Father or the Hail Mary. A person practices discursive prayer when he uses his intellect and imagination to recall and think about a doctrine of the Faith or an incident in the life of Our Lord. From thinking about the mystery, the person is led to make acts of love, adoration, thanksgiving or sorrow to God.

Dismas, St. Also called the Good Thief. Nothing is known for certain about the man who confessed Christ on the cross other than the simple event narrated in the Gospels. His feast is celebrated on Mar. 25. The name Dismas was first given in the fanciful Gospel of Nicodemus, an apocryphal work that appeared about the 5th century.

dismissal 1. A custom at the end of the Mass where the minister dismisses the congregation with the words, *"Ite Missa est"* (Go, you are dismissed). It is a custom adapted from the ancient Roman public courts and imperial palace to announce the end of a session or audience. 2. It also is an act where one is dismissed from a religious institution, after being found guilty of a

law requiring this sentence. A public apostasy from the Faith, flight with a person of the opposite sex, or an attempt of marriage are acts requiring dismissal from a religious institution.

disparity of cult A difference of worship (*q.v.*).

disparity of worship A canonical term which strictly speaking refers to the marriage impediment between a baptized Catholic and a nonbaptized person. If a marriage is contracted without a dispensation from this impediment, the marriage is null and void. The strictness of this legislation is based on the sacramental nature of marriage and the desire of the Church to protect and nourish the Faith of parents and children.

dispensation (L. *dispensatio*) 1. An act whereby the lawful superior grants relaxation from an existing law. It is only the lawgiver, his delegate or his successor who can dispense a person from observing a law. The law itself is not changed or altered but the operation of the law is suspended in a given case. 2. A system of revealed truths and sacred rites. For example, the Christian religion is called the New Dispensation in contrast to the older Mosaic system.

disposition (L. *disponere,* to arrange, set in order) The state or quality of being disposed *to* or *to do* something; inclination. 1. Of the body: nature or constitution, tendency, aptitude. 2. Of the mind: temperament of mind; or natural or prevailing spirit. 3. Psychological: relatively permanent tendency to act in any certain way. To receive the sacraments properly, one should have the proper dispositions; i.e., have the right relationship to God (loving submission).

dissident (L. *dissidere,* to sit apart, to

disagree) 1. That which is dissenting, discordant, or not agreeing. A dissident note in music is one that is out of harmony with the others. 2. A church that disagrees with, and teaches contrary to, the Catholic Church is called a dissident church.

dissolution of a marriage No *human* power can dissolve a valid marriage. For a very grave reason, the Pope, using *divine* authority, can dissolve a ratified but not consummated marriage between Catholics. If a marriage between Catholics has been consummated, it cannot be dissolved. By ecclesiastical law, solemn profession in a religious order with solemn vows annuls a previously existing ratified (but not consummated) marriage. The consummated marriage of two pagans may be dissolved if one of them is converted to the Faith and the other will neither be converted nor live in peace without trying to draw the convert to sin. *See* Pauline Privilege.

distraction The voluntary or involuntary taking of the mind away from a particular train of thought, usually in regard to prayer. If it is involuntary, the distraction can be a means of merit because the person has to make much more deliberate and sustained efforts to keep united with God than when the prayer goes easily. Voluntary distraction is a sign of disrespect for God.

Dives (L. rich man) The name given to the rich man who is described in the parable of Christ in Lk. 16:19-31.

divination The foretelling of contingent future events or the discovery of what is hidden or obscure by supernatural or magical means. The word has a sinister signification. As prophecy is the lawful knowledge of the future, divination, its superstitious counterpart, is the unlawful. As magic aims *to do,* divination aims *to know*.

divine 1. In its infrequent use as a noun it designates a priest, a clergyman and a theologian. 2. As an adjective, it usually refers to anything partaking of the nature of God, or to something "Godlike" whether given by or proceeding from God, or addressed or devoted to God, such as divine worship.

Divine Comedy (It. *La Divina Commedia*) Dante Alighieri's epic masterpiece, written in 1321. The poem consists of three canticles, "Inferno," "Purgatorio" and "Paradiso." Dante's experiences in the three realms of the Beyond were symbolical of mankind's quest of God and achievement of salvation. To himself, as well as to his fellow men beset by sin and ignorant striving, Dante wanted to show that there was a way out. Illuminated by divine inspiration, helped by heavenly grace and by a severe spiritual discipline, man could achieve salvation from the maze of life. Of Dante's three guides, Virgil, Statius and Beatrice, the first two—symbols of reason—can guide him through "Inferno" and up "Mount Purgatorio," but in "Paridiso" it is Beatrice—the symbol of faith—who alone can assist him. The work shows Dante's great insight into the theology of the Fathers of the Church and the philosophy of the 13th century.

Divine Office The term is used in the sense of a work done for God. It is the public liturgical prayer of the Church distinct from the Eucharistic and sacramental liturgies, through which the Church praises God and intercedes for the salvation of the world. Its purpose is the sanctification of the day through formal prayer at stated hours. Hence the term *Canonical Hours*. The history of the Divine Office is co-extensive with that of the Church. Its roots lie in the practice of the early Jewish Christians who patterned their formal prayer life on the Jewish Temple customs of the time. Further development came with the appearance of *vigils* or night prayer services preparatory to the celebration of Mass on Sundays and major feast days. The present format of the Divine Office was completed with the additions traceable to the prayer habits of early Christian monastic life. The Office consists chiefly of the recitation of psalms and readings from Sacred Scripture, the Fathers, Doctors and ecclesiastical writers, plus accounts of martyrdom and the lives of the saints. Through the centuries there has been a gradual evolution in the Canonical Hours of the Office. Present liturgical law decreed by Paul VI, Dec. 4, 1963, proposes the following canonical distribution of the hours: Lauds as morning prayer; Vespers as evening prayer; Compline as a prayer suitable for the end of the day; Matins, while containing the character of nocturnal praise when celebrated in choir, at any hour of the day; the daylight hours of Terce, Sext and None, all three of which are to be recited in choir, but only one of which need be prayed outside choir. The Divine Office is celebrated in choir by ecclesiastical communities so obliged as well as by the chapters of Canons, and in private by all other individuals who are obliged to its recitation. The first of the Little Hours, Prime, is now said only in choir.

Divine Office, obligation of the In the Latin Church the obligation of saying the Divine Office, at least privately, unless dispensed or legitimately prevented, is a grave one for all clerics in sacred orders; i.e., those who have been ordained to the subdeaconate, for all those who have benefices, and for religious, both men and women, who have solemn vows in communities that have the choir obligation. The time within which one must recite the Divine Office is a natural day; i.e., from midnight to midnight. Private recitation of the Office does not require movement of the lips, but does include a thoughtful and devout completion of the prayer.

Divine Praises A series of brief ejaculations praising God, Christ, the Holy Spirit, Mary and the angels and saints. They originated at the end of the 18th century as an act of reparation for blasphemy and profanity, and their number has been increased periodically up to the present. Although not strictly prescribed by liturgical law, they may be recited, and almost universally are, by priest and people in the vernacular after the blessing with the Host during Benediction of the Blessed Sacrament. In several dioceses in the United States, diocesan regulations require that they be added after the Leonine prayers at the end of Low Mass as a petition for peace. At present they are: Blessed be God; Blessed be His holy Name; Blessed be Jesus Christ, true God and true man; Blessed be the name of Jesus; Blessed be His most Sacred Heart; Blessed be His most Precious Blood; Blessed be Jesus in the most holy Sacrament of the Altar; Blessed be the Holy Spirit, the Paraclete; Blessed be the great Mother of God, Mary most Holy; Blessed be her holy and immaculate Conception; Blessed be her glorious Assumption; Blessed be the name of Mary, virgin and mother; Blessed be St. Joseph, her most chaste spouse; Blessed be God in His angels and in His saints.

divine right of kings   A claim on the part of sovereigns that their kingship is divinely instituted and that they can therefore exercise absolute power without any responsibility for the use of such power to those whom they govern. The doctrine was used by kings to defend their actions against the papacy and came to fruition with such leaders as Henry VIII, the Russian czars and the German Hohenzollerns. Authority comes from God but is entrusted to the people who transfer it as a channel to those who will exercise it for the good of the people; therefore, rulers have responsibility to the people they govern.

Divine Service   1. The term used to denote the Eucharistic Liturgy in the Ruthenian Rite. 2. A general term for acts of liturgical worship.

Divine Word, Society of the   A missionary society of men, founded in Holland by Father Arnold Janssen in 1875, established in the United States in 1879. Father Janssen (1835–1909) was born in northern Germany. As he grew up and went on to seminary studies and ordination to the priesthood, he became more and more concerned because Germany had no foreign mission seminary, as France, Italy and England had. His friends discouraged him from trying to found such an enterprise, as he had no influential connections and lacked the appearance and personality thought to be necessary in a leader. He tried to spread the idea in Germany through the press, hoping to get someone interested in foreign missions. In 1875, as the German government was persecuting the Church, Father Janssen went to Holland and started a mission seminary in the village of Steyl. The students who came to his small institution were few and diffident at first, but Father Janssen made up in courage and devotion for any and all shortcomings. He called his group the "Society of the Holy Ghost" and he attributed its eventual rapid growth to his trust in the Holy Spirit. Before he died, he saw his missioners working in China, West Africa, New Guinea, Japan, the Philippine Islands, Argentina, Paraguay, Brazil, Chile and among the Negroes in the United States. They now have three provinces in the United States. Their motherhouse is in Rome.

Divini Redemptoris   An encyclical letter of Pope Pius XI issued in 1937 which considers the nature, errors and evils of atheistic Communism.

divinity of Christ   Jesus Christ, in virtue of the hypostatic union is a divine person, the Second Person of the Holy Trinity. "For God so loved the world that he gave his only-begotten Son" (Jn. 3:16). This communion of essence of Son and Father is the revelation made in majestic simplicity which John reports that Jesus makes of himself: "I am the Father, and the Father in me" (14: 10 f.); "Philip, he who sees me sees the Father" (14:9); "I know mine and mine know me, even as the Father knows me and I know the Father" (10:14). These passages mean that no one has such a close communion of life with the Father as the Son; nor has anyone such a close communion of life with the Son as the Father. They are both one single life. His communion of life with the Father is unique and exclusive. No created being has part in it. It is a unique, eternal relationship, necessary to divine being, far transcending all created relationships, this relationship that makes God the

Father of Jesus Christ; and Jesus Christ the Son of the Father. Their existence is rooted in their reciprocal exchange of life and love.

divorce A legal separation of married persons. 1. *In canon law: (a)* from the bond of matrimony, which is an absolute divorce, which is given only for a marriage that has not been consummated or through the Pauline Privilege; (*b*) from the bed, which makes lawful the denial of the marriage debt; (*c*) from bed and board, which denies the rights of cohabitation. In the latter two cases there is a separation of the parties with the marriage bond remaining. 2. *In civil law:* As divorce implies the right to marry again, it is contrary to divine law which has established the indissolubility of marriage, a law which binds both the baptized and unbaptized. Protestants base their doctrine of divorce on Matt. 19:9 where Christ, speaking on the indissolubility of marriage, makes the exception "except it be for fornication." However, Christ was addressing this text to the Pharisees, therefore he parenthetically included the privilege of Moses which was meant only for Jews. In parallel texts (Mk. 10; Lk. 16, 1 Cor. 7), the clause does not appear. The teaching of the Church is that in such an important matter, it would not have been omitted by inspired writers if it were meant to regulate the relationship between man and wife.

divorce a toro et mensa Separation from bed and board; cessation of married life in common.

divorce, civil Result of court proceedings where a civil magistrate declares a marriage null and void. A civil divorce is permissible for a Catholic under certain circumstances: 1. breaking of legal or civil

bond when ecclesiastical authority has declared a marriage null and void previously; 2. divorce *a toro et mensa* (from bed and board), without intention or freedom to remarry, when the union has become "unbearable." In the first case, there was no valid, sacramental marriage bond; in the second, the valid, sacramental marriage bond remains. *See* Pauline Privilege; Petrine Privilege.

Docetism A heresy of early Christianity which taught that Christ only seemed to have a human body but really did not. It also averred that Christ did not really die on the Cross.

doctor (L. *docere,* to teach) Refers generally to a teacher or learned man; technically, it is an advanced academic title. *See* doctor of the Church.

Doctor Angelicus (L. Angelic Doctor) St. Thomas Aquinas, 1225–1274. A Dominican, author of the *Summa Theologica.*

Doctor Communis (L. Common Doctor) Another title for St. Thomas Aquinas. He was the teacher for all people for all time.

Doctor Ecstaticus (L. Exalted Doctor) Denis the Carthusian, 1402–1471.

Doctor Eximus (L. Excellent Doctor) Francis Suarez, 1548–1617, a Jesuit theologian.

Doctor Gratiae (L. Doctor of Grace) St. Augustine of Hippo, 354–430.

Doctor Mellifluus (L. Mellifluous Doctor) St. Bernard of Clairvaux, 1090–1153, a Cistercian.

Doctor Mirabilis (L. Wonderful Doctor) Roger Bacon, 1214–1295, a Franciscan who taught at Oxford.

doctor of the Church A title officially conferred by the Church on ecclesiastical writers of eminent learning and a high degree of sanctity who have distinguished themselves by their defense, exposition and preservation of the doctrine of the Church.

Pope Boniface VIII was the first to confer the title in 1205. At present there are 29 doctors officially acknowledged by the Church.

Doctor Seraphicus (L. Seraphic Doctor) St. Bonaventure, 1231–1274, a Franciscan theologian.

Doctor Subtilis (L. Subtle Doctor) John Duns Scotus, 1270–1308, a Franciscan theologian.

Doctor Universalis (L. The Universal Doctor) St. Albert the Great, 1206–1280, a Dominican theologian who taught St. Thomas Aquinas.

doctrine (L. *doctrina,* teaching) 1. The teaching of the Church. It does not consist in definitive ecclesiastical pronouncements, as does dogma, but rather refers to the truths of the Word of God, as found specifically in Scripture. 2. The body of principles on which Faith is based.

dogma A truth of faith or morals authoritatively proposed by the Church as revealed by God and requiring the belief of the faithful. The proposition may be in the form of a solemn judgment or through the ordinary and universal magisterium.

dogmatic fact A truth, not itself revealed, but so closely connected with some dogmatic truth as to be necessary for its preservation and integrity. Such a truth falls within the competence of the magisterium (*q.v.*) and can thus be proclaimed infallibly.

Dogmatic Theology A speculative science which implies the highest principles of natural reason to the data of revelation in order to derive further insight into the revealed deposit. Distinct from Moral Theology (*q.v.*) which deals with the actions of man, Dogmatic Theology confines itself to the consideration of God Himself and His activity.

Dolors of Our Lady *See* Seven Sorrows of Our Lady.

Dom (L. *dominus,* master) 1. Title placed before the name of professed Benedictines, Carthusians, Cistercians and Canons Regular. In Italy, Don is used for most clerics. 2. The German word for cathedral. 3. Used as the abbreviation for L. *Dominica,* Sunday.

domestic prelate An honorary title granted by the Holy See to certain priests because of their service to the Church. As such they are counted as members of the papal household even though they do not reside in Rome. They dress similarly to a bishop, omitting the pontifical insignia; the biretta is black with a red pompon. In speech a domestic prelate is addressed as "Monsignor"; in writing the proper form is "Right Reverend Monsignor."

domicile Place where one has a fixed abode, where he intends to stay.

Dominations One of the choirs of angels; usually called Dominations but also referred to as Dominions.

Dominic, Rule of St. Not an original rule but an adaptation of the Rule of St. Augustine. It was approved in 1216. The rule has been considerably modified over the years.

Dominica (L. Sunday) Frequently used in the liturgical writings.

Dominica in Albis In the Western Church, the name given to Low Sunday as that on which those newly baptized at Easter put aside their white robes. The previous Saturday is correspondingly known as "Sabbato in Albis."

dominical letters A system devised by early Church chronologers to indicate the days of the week. The first seven letters of the alphabet were used and applied to each day of the week beginning with Sunday. These letters were called dominicals because their purpose was to show the dates of the year on which Sundays would fall.

Dominican Congregation of St. Catherine of Siena Founded in Kentucky in 1822 by Father Samuel Wilson as the first American community of Dominican Sisters. The primary work is teaching. The Sisters take simple vows and there are over 800 members.

Dominican Congregation of the Most Holy Rosary Founded in Wisconsin in 1847 by Father S. C. Mazzuchelli. The congregation is both active and contemplative and is engaged in contemplation, teaching and nursing. There is a mission in Bolivia. Approximately 2,000 members.

Dominican Republic The first bishop in the New World arrived in the Dominican Republic in 1512 and from this country the Faith began its spread to the rest of the Americas. Today there are 1 archdiocese, 3 dioceses and 1 prelature nullius, staffed by almost 300 priests (half of whom are foreigners) to care for 3 million Dominicans. American Redemptorists and Canadian Scarboro Fathers are among the island's clergy. Many more priests are needed, as each priest has 10,000 people to serve. Also hindrances to the Church are social inequalities which leave the masses desperately poor, and a lack of Catholic schools except for the upper class.

Dominican Rite The liturgy proper to the Dominicans, essentially the same as the Roman Rite. The chalice is prepared before a Low Mass begins, the chalice and host are offered together, and there are certain differences in the wording and order of prayers.

Dominicans Popular name for the Order of Preachers, taken from St. Dominic, the founder of the order.

His real name was Domingo de Guzmán (1170-1221) and he was of Spanish origin. Foundation was at Prouille, France, in 1215. The salvation of souls, particularly through preaching, is the aim of the order. The Dominicans have made important contributions to scholarship, particularly in the fields of philosophy and theology; SS. Albertus Magnus and Thomas Aquinas hold a distinct place in Catholic scholarship and the work of St. Thomas has never been equaled for clarity and synthesis. Dominicans have also contributed greatly to the mission of the Church and were among the main mission societies that evangelized the New World.

dominion (L. *dominium,* ownership) 1. John Wycliffe used dominion as that spiritual authority and material ownership which should be denied to sinful clerics. Both support and obedience should not be given to such clerics, and civil powers should deprive such of their property. 2. In the plural (Dominions), it refers to one of the choirs of angels.

Dominus vobiscum. *Et cum spiritu tuo.* A Latin liturgical salutation and response, meaning "The Lord be with you. And with your spirit." These words of greeting are probably as old as Latin Christianity. It is used frequently in the Mass and in the Divine Office.

doom A common Anglo-Saxon word for the condemnation of the body and soul at the Last Judgment.

doorkeeper The doorkeepers constitute the lowest of the minor orders of the Church. The order was probably established in Rome during the first half of the 3rd century. At that time, doorkeepers were responsible for excluding unauthorized persons from receiving the Eucharist. The order is now largely symbolic. In the United States "porter" is generally used.

Doors, Holy The door in the facade of St. Peter's which is nearest the Vatican Palace. The Holy Door is normally sealed with brickwork, except during the Holy Year when it is opened for those who wish to gain the Holy Year indulgence by entering. The opening and closing, by the pope, are at the beginning and end of the Holy Year.

Dorcas Another name for Tabitha (*q.v.*).

Dormition of the Blessed Virgin Another name for the Feast of the Assumption (Aug. 15). It refers to the passage of the soul and body of the Blessed Virgin into heaven. Because Mary was born without original sin, she was freed from the debt of that sin. Her death was a death without corruption, an ineffable passing. That is why it is often referred to as dormition (a sleeping). It is also a title of a church on Mount Zion.

dorsal (L. *dorsum,* back) A curtain hung behind an altar.

dossal A dorsal (*q.v.*).

Douay A city in northern France which shares with the city of Rheims the honor of being the site of the first complete translation and publication of the Catholic Bible into English, 1582–1609. It was in the English Seminary, founded there in exile by William Allen (later cardinal), that the Douay Bible was translated and hundreds of seminarians educated for the apostolate in Britain, over 160 of whom were martyred in the persecutions of loyal Catholics during the reigns of Queen Elizabeth I and her successors.

Douay Bible Also called the Rheims-Douay or Douay-Rheims Bible, it was the first complete Catholic Bible in English to be translated from the Latin Vulgate Bible. The translation was made by English scholars in exile from the English persecution of the Church who conducted the English College at Douay and, for a time, at Rheims. The New Testament appeared in 1582; the Old Testament in 1609. Bishop Challoner of London published a new version of the Douay Bible in 1750, and Bishop F. P. Kenrick of Baltimore edited another in 1859 for use in the United States. It is now being replaced by the Confraternity Version.

doubt The suspension of judgment concerning the right or wrongness of an action to be done or avoided. If the judgment is formed there yet remains a reasonable chance of erring. It is never lawful to act with a doubtful conscience. If a person acts with such a doubt he is taking the chance of committing an evil act. However, according to one opinion, that of probabilism (*q.v.*), it is safe to follow a solidly probable opinion permitting a certain course of action. In the realm of law, a doubtful law does not bind. This rule refers to a doubt of the law's existence or obligation. In the case of doubt as to the justice, or penalty, of a known law, the law must be observed until the doubt is dispelled. Otherwise there is some danger of reckless behavior, or of depriving others of their just rights.

double effect, principle of This principle is applied to an action which will have a good and a bad effect. Such an action is lawful if the following conditions are fulfilled: 1. the performer of the act must intend the good action; 2. that the evil effect be tolerated and not desired; 3. that the good effect precede the evil (evil means can never be employed to produce a good end); 4. there must be sufficient reason for performing this act which allows the bad effect.

douillette (Fr. a padded greatcoat) A long black coat reaching to the ankles worn over the cassock by priests.

Doukhobor (Russ. *dukh,* spirit; *borets,* wrestler) A sect originating in Russia in the 18th century which believes in inner lights and which rejects both ecclesiastical and religious authority. Members of the sect settled in Western Canada and have been repeatedly embroiled in disagreements with the Canadian government against which they practice disobedience both actively and passively.

dove The symbol of innocence and simplicity (Canticle of Canticles); of the creative spirit of God (Gen. 1:2); and of the new creation, the rebirth at the Baptism of Jesus (Mt. 3:13-17).

downtown church A Catholic Church in a metropolitan business area that does not have regular parishioners but depends on transients and people working in the area for its support. It provides extra services on holydays of obligation and usually offers noon Masses which can be attended by workers during their lunch hour.

Dowry of Mary A title, sometimes given as Our Lady's Dowry, which was applied to England in the 14th century. It included the islands of the realm.

dowry of religious A gift of money given to a religious community or order by a girl about to become a postulant in that order. The dowry is returned to the girl if she leaves the order for whatever reason.

dowse The act of using a divining rod to discover water or minerals below the surface of the earth. At times this practice can involve superstition, but usually its effect is attributed to some natural power of the individual or the instrument.

doxology (Gr. *doxa,* glory, praise) This term is usually used to refer to the "Glory be to the Father." Strictly speaking, this is the lesser "doxology"; the "Glory to God in the highest," the Gloria of the Mass, is the "greater doxology."

Draft Riots A draft act was put into law by the Union in order to raise troops for the Civil War. The act permitted exemption for those who could provide a substitute, usually obtainable for about $300. Since the poor could not raise this sum, they felt they were discriminated against. The result was riots throughout the larger cities of the North. Since a good portion of the poor were Catholics, bishops in various parts of the North used their influence to end the riots.

dreams, interpretation of God may speak to us through dreams, as the Sacred Scriptures frequently testify. If the dream comes from God, the meaning and fulfillment is apparent to the one concerned. Some dreams arise from sane premonitions of the subconscious and point to the immediate future somewhat after the manner of so-called "second-sight" or clairvoyance. Particularly for people with sound and healthy natural instincts, the dream may be the expression of many true premonitions of this kind of well-founded fear or hope. Perhaps this is the normal function of the subconscious. In the Middle Ages it was not uncommon for sincere Christians, even for saints, to search for norms in the discernment of dreams with distinctions between the futile and meaningful, and to interpret the latter. In fact, the interpretations of dreams in present-day depth psychology (especially the work of Carl Jung) is an earnest scientific effort as long as it does not presume to forecast the future by means of dreams, but investigates psychic traumas and depressions and their remedies. Prudence dictates that we place little or no trust in dreams as signs of what is to come.

dress, clerical 1. In the Western Church clerical dress consists of the black cassock, with or without a cincture, and the Roman collar. A long black coat and a black hat are worn outdoors. This dress is common street garb in many parts of the world. In the United States, Canada, Great Britain and in growing areas of Latin America, this dress is confined to rectory and church; a black suit with rabat and Roman collar is worn outdoors. 2. In the Eastern Church a black gown is worn. Some of the Eastern Churches add the *rason,* a long, loose black gown with wide sleeves, open down the front. Caps and turbans vary according to the Church. The Malabarese follow the Western garb.

droit du seigneur (Fr. right of the lord) A reputed medieval custom by which the lord had the right to his vassal's bride on her wedding night. There is no positive evidence that such a custom ever existed.

drugs *See* narcotics.

drum While ordinarily the drum would not be considered an instrument for liturgical use, it has been employed in liturgical music composed for use in Africa. Several Masses composed in the Congo make extensive use of the instrument.

drunkenness This term means that the individual is deprived of the use of reason and moral freedom through the use of alcoholic beverages. It is

a grave sin if there is culpability; this would not be true in a case where a person was overcome once or twice because he did not realize the potency of the drink served him, or overrated his own capacity to resist its effects. In such cases there are usually the lack of premeditation and full deliberation which are necessary for mortal sin. Direct and premeditated drunkenness is an even graver sin where the individual knew of his weakness but went ahead regardless. The drunkenness is then directly willed and intended, with the accompanying loss of reason and moral freedom.

dry Mass (L. Missa sicca) 1. A term derived from the rite of Communion for the sick which included all the elements of the Mass except the Canon along with the giving of Communion under the form of bread only (hence the term dry). The classical example of this type was the Blessing of the Palms used on Palm Sunday until 1955. The Carthusians say daily this type of dry Mass of our Lady in their cells. This rite is not truly a Mass but merely a recitation of the nonessential prayers. 2. This term has been extended to apply to the practice Masses which students for the priesthood say as part of their preparation for ordination.

duel (L. *duellum,* war) A combat between two persons with the deadly purpose of killing or seriously injuring one's opponent. It is a gravely immoral act both for challenger and challenged and is a form of private vengeance. The malice follows from the elements of intent to kill or seriously injure and the exposure of oneself to possible serious injury or death. A person's honor can be only defended by moral means. Those who engage in a duel, even to the witnessing of the contest, are *ipso facto* excommunicated with sanation reserved to the Holy See. A person who dies unrepentant from wounds received in a duel is forbidden ecclesiastical burial.

Dukhobors   A Russian sect that emigrated to Canada in 1898, settling in the western part of the country. Members deny the Holy Spirit and place little importance on Scripture. They reject civil authority and have come into many conflicts with the Canadian government. *Also* Doukhobor (*q.v.*).

dulia (Gr. *douleia,* service)   Veneration and homage paid to saints and angels. It is to be distinguished from latria (*q.v.*) which is given to God, and hyperdulia (*q.v.*) which is paid to Mary, Mother of Jesus.

Dunker   A member of a sect deriving from German Baptists. The sect baptizes by immersion, practices the agape and avoids taking oaths.

duplication   *See* bination.

duration   A limited extent of existence in time, from a fraction of a second to countless ages. In general it is the condition of continued existence.

duty   Obligation imposed upon a free person to use his freedom in a given manner.

dying, prayers for the   The prayers for the dying said by a priest or another person as contained in the Roman Ritual.

dynamism   The philosophic attempt to account for cosmic phenomena by reference to force or energy.

E

Earthly Paradise, the The Garden of Eden (*q.v.*) original home created for Adam and Eve, lost by original sin.

Easter (ÓÈ eastre) The English term for the Sunday on which is celebrated the Resurrection of Christ from the dead. It is the most important liturgical feast in the calendar year. It commemorates Christ's triumph over death and the proof of His divinity, as St. Paul said in his Epistles.

Easter cycle The liturgical period of time beginning with Easter and ending with the Friday after the Sunday after the Ascension. This is a time of celebration. The liturgical color is white. It includes Easter, Low Sunday, the Sundays after Easter, Ascension Thursday and the Sunday after the Ascension.

Easter, date of The Council of Nicaea in 325 set the date of Easter on the first Sunday of the first full moon which occurs after Mar. 21. Easter therefore falls from Mar. 22 to Apr. 25 inclusive. Vatican Council II has gone on record as having no objection to assigning the Feast of Easter to a fixed Sunday of the Gregorian calendar, provided that those whom it may concern, particularly the Eastern Rite Churches not in communion with the Apostolic See, give their consent.

Easter duty The obligation of receiving Holy Communion during the Easter period. In the United States this is between the first Sunday in Lent and Trinity Sunday inclusive. The period varies elsewhere.

Easter eggs In many places it is the practice to color eggs at Eastertime and to bring them to church for a blessing.

Easter Vigil The solemn celebration of Christ's Resurrection, which begins on Holy Saturday night and includes the blessing of the paschal candle, symbol of Christ, the Light of the world; readings from the Old Testament which prefigure the mysteries of the New Testament; the blessing of the baptismal water; the Baptism of candidates and the renewal of the baptismal promises by all present. Mass follows, normally after midnight, in which the Easter Alleluia is solemnly intoned. In 1951 Pius XII restored this Vigil and revised the ceremonies.

Easter water This is water blessed at the Easter Vigil service, along with the water to be consecrated for Baptisms, but separated from the baptismal water before the holy oils are poured into it. It is used to sprinkle the congregation at the ceremony of renewal of the baptismal vows during the Vigil service and also for sprink-

195

ling during Easter week. Its use is a good reminder of the connection between the sacramental of holy water and the Sacrament of Baptism.

Eastern Church, the The term used by the Holy See to mean the totality of churches of Catholics of the Eastern Rites. Another meaning is to use the term for the Eastern Orthodox Church.

Eastern Congregation, the Sacred *See* Oriental Church, Sacred Congregation for the.

Eastern controversy This controversy was based on the proper time for observing Easter. There were three different stages of the conflict over the centuries, ending only after the Synod of Whitby in England (664) when the Celtic practice gave way to the Roman tradition. *1st stage:* The discussion arose late in the 2nd century of the Christian era and concerned the way in which the date of Easter should be determined. Despite the apostolic tradition of celebrating the memory of the Resurrection of Christ on the "first day of the week," the Sunday following the Jewish Passover, Churches in the East often celebrated it on the day of the Passover itself, i.e., on the 14th day of Nisan, regardless of the day of the week on which it might occur. Pope Victor (189–199) took strong measures to secure conformity with the apostolic and Roman practice. Even Origen considered the Eastern practice as wrong. *2nd stage:* About the time of the Council of Nicaea (325) a new controversy arose as to how Easter Sunday itself, celebrating the Resurrection, should be determined. The Council of Nicaea approved a decree ordering all to follow the Roman practice of celebrating Easter on the Sunday following the spring equinox. Great confusion existed in

various areas in the astronomical calculation of the lunar calendar and coordinating it with the solar calendar, which led to different practices in such remote regions as Ireland and Britain. *3rd stage:* The final stage was centered in England after the arrival of Augustine (of Canterbury) who brought with him the Roman practice regarding the dating of Easter which differed somewhat from that used by the early Irish missioners who had spread the Faith in so much of England earlier. The Easter dispute caused friction between the English Catholics of the Celtic tradition and those stemming from the labors of Augustine and his followers. The question was finally settled at the Synod of Whitby when the Roman practice was accepted for all of England (664).

Eastern Rites, Catholics of Those Catholics of Oriental Churches which hold the same essential beliefs, morality and purpose as the Catholics of the Western or Latin Church. They are in communion with the Holy See. They retain their own canon law and customs not by concession but by right. They include Catholic Copts, Ethiopian Catholics, Syrians, Chaldeans, Catholic Armenians, Malabar Catholics, Maronites, and the Catholics of the Byzantine Rite such as Melkites, Ruthenians, Greek Catholics, Bulgarian Catholics, Russian Catholics, etc.

Eastern Rites in the United States There are five eparchies of the Byzantine Rite in the United States. 1. *Archeparchy of Philadelphia.* This has jurisdiction over all Byzantine Catholics of Ukrainian origin, except those in New York and New England and west of Ohio, Kentucky, Tennessee and Mississippi. This archeparchy counts as subjects those Catholics of the Byzantine Rite who emigrated to the United States from Galicia, Bucovina and other Ukrainian provinces, their descendants and other persons as provided in canon law. 2. *Ukrainian Catholic Eparchy of Stamford.* This Connecticut see has jurisdiction over all Byzantine Catholics of Ukrainian origin in New England and New York. 3. *Ukrainian Eparchy of St. Nicholas of Chicago.* This has jurisdiction over all Byzantine Catholics of Ukrainian origin who live west of the Archeparchy of Philadelphia. 4. *Byzantine Rite Eparchy of Pittsburgh.* This eparchy is immediately subject to the Holy See whereas Stamford and Chicago are suffragan sees of the Archeparchy of Philadelphia. It has jurisdiction over all Byzantine Catholics of Russian, Magyar and Croatian nationality or descent in the United States, except those in the Eparchy of Passaic. 5. *Byzantine Rite Eparchy of Passaic.* Immediately subject to the Holy See, this New Jersey eparchy has jurisdiction over all Byzantine Rite Catholics of Russian, Magyar and Croatian nationality or descent in New England, New Jersey, New York, part of Pennsylvania, Delaware, Maryland, District of Columbia, Virginia, North Carolina, South Carolina, Georgia and Florida. 6. In addition there are other Eastern Rite Catholics represented in the United States who, because they have no ordinary, come under the jurisdiction of the Latin Rite ordinary. These include Armenians, Byelorussians, Chaldeans, Melkites, Russians, Romanians, Maronites and Syrians.

ecce homo (ech'che hoe'moe; L. Behold the man) 1. The words used by Pilate (John 19:5) when he showed Christ to the Jews after his scourging and crowning with thorns.

2. An image of Christ, crowned with thorns and wearing a purple cloak.

ecclesia (ek-leh'see-ah; L. church) The term can mean a church building, e.g., St. Mary's Church; or a body of believers, e.g., the church of Antioch.

ecclesia discens (dis'chens; L. the learning Church) Used to describe that portion of the Church which is subject to the authority of the magisterium (*q.v.*), the universal college of bishops under the headship of the pope (*ecclesia docens, q.v.*).

ecclesia docens (doe'chens; L. the teaching Church) Designates the teaching office or magisterium (*q.v.*) of the Church. Applied strictly only to the papacy and the episcopate, the expression can be extended to others insofar as they function as channels of this teaching power, e.g., priests, catechists, teachers of religion.

Ecclesiastes (Gr. preacher) A book of the Old Testament that was supposedly written by Solomon but the internal evidence of which shows that it came long after Solomon's time. The purpose of the author was to exhort his readers not to seek transitory goals but to perform the duties imposed by God and thus enjoy the pleasures of life.

ecclesiastic A cleric. One in major orders. A Church dignitary.

Ecclesiasticus One of the more important deutero-canonical books of the Old Testament, sometimes called the Book of Sirach after its author, "Jesus, son of Eleazer, son of Sirach." From internal evidence we know that the author was well-to-do, a traveler, a friend of important people, a literary man and one who was well respected. The author wrote this book in his declining years to set down his teachings on wisdom, which is not only a God-given gift to man but also an attribute of God Himself.

ecclesiology The science or study of the Church in any or all of its aspects.

ecology The study of the influence of physical environment on culture. The missioner cannot be indifferent to the difficult physical environment of the people among whom he works but through education and socio-economic programs must labor to aid man to cope with the problems of climate, food and health.

economy A theological term used to refer to God's mysterious plan for the salvation of mankind. St. Paul (Eph. 3:9) calls it the "dispensation of the mystery which has been hidden for eternity in God." The Greeks have a special branch of Economic Theology which is concerned with the restoration of communication between God and man in Jesus Christ.

economy, divine A term popular in Roman Catholicism which refers to the inimitable way in which God sees to it that His work is done with or without the help of man. More formally it can be considered the providential and orderly plan employed by God in the exercise of His divine will, which is the best possible plan as it comes from the all-knowing and perfect God.

ecstasy (Gr. *existanai,* to put out of place) That state in which the soul is absorbed in God and the activity of the senses is suspended. It is the highest form of spiritual and mystical union with God.

Ecuador Quito, the capital of Ecuador, was founded in 1534 and 10 years later was erected as a diocese. Today there are 3 archdioceses, 6 dioceses, 2 prelatures nullius, 4 vicariates and 4 prefectures; the vicariates and prefectures are mission territories under the Congregation of the Propa-

gation of the Faith. Ecuador has 4.5 million people with 1 priest for every 2,300 people, a relatively good figure for Latin America but very poor by North American standards. There are many obstacles to the development of the Church: great masses of Indians and Negroes who are poor and illiterate, poor national economy, great distances between parishes in the rural areas, the absence of modern apostolic movements. Working in favor of the Church are the devotion of the dedicated clergy, the desire of the people for Catholicism, the extensive charitable works of the Church, the decline of laicism and anticlericalism.

ecumenical (Gr. *oikoumene,* the inhabited world) Universal, general, world-wide in extent. An ecumenical council is one in which the entire Church takes part. The word has also come into use to describe the movement toward greater understanding between Catholics and Protestants, between Catholics and Orthodox, between Orthodox and Protestants and between Protestants themselves.

Ecumenical Councils (Gr. *oikoumene,* the inhabited world) Assemblies of the bishops of the whole world, presided over by the pope or his legate. The pope alone can summon a general council, and he must approve of its decrees or they are valueless. The bishops in general council do not define new doctrines; they define or give witness to the teachings received from Christ and handed down in the Church from the beginning. In addition to bishops, it has been customary to invite abbots, superiors of religious orders, lesser prelates, canonists and theologians and others to participate in the deliberations of the councils. After the first council at Jerusalem in A.D. 51, there had been 20 ecumenical councils before Pope John XXIII summoned the 21st Council (Vatican II), in September, 1962; his successor, Paul VI, continued the work of this council. Of the 20 councils preceding Vatican II, the first 8 were held in the eastern Mediterranean area, the remainder in Italy, France or the Holy Roman Empire.

1. The *First Ecumenical Council* was convoked by the Emperor Constantine at Nicaea in Asia Minor in A.D. 325. It was attended by 300 bishops; the pope was represented by two Roman priests (some historians hold that Bishop Hosius of Cordova was Pope Sylvester I's legate). The council condemned the teaching of Arius, a priest of Alexandria, who taught that Christ was not equal to God the Father. The Nicene Creed was formulated, which declared the Son to be "consubstantial with the Father," thus affirming that Jesus Christ, Second Person of the Blessed Trinity, is divine.

2. The *Council of Constantinople* called by Emperor Theodosius in 381, proclaimed again the doctrine of the divinity of Christ as enunciated at the Council of Nicaea, and showed that that Eastern Church was opposed to Arianism. Only bishops of the East attended this council; the pope was not represented. The council became an ecumenical council when it was acknowledged by the Council of Chalcedon and by the actions of Pope Hilarius (461–468) and other popes.

3. The *Council of Ephesus* (431) was called by the Emperor Theodosius II to settle a dispute concerning the teachings of the Patriarch of Constantinople, Nestorius, who held that Mary was the Mother of Christ but not the Mother of God. Over

200 bishops attended this council; Pope Celestine sent three legates from Rome. The pope wrote a letter to the fathers of the Council in which he referred to Nestorius' doctrine as "treason to the Faith," and he urged them to unite against the heresy and to condemn it courageously. The fathers declared that Tradition had always used the term *"theotokos"* —i.e., Mother of God—of the Blessed Virgin.

4. The *Council of Chalcedon,* (451) was sponsored by the Emperor Marcian to resolve the question of the human and divine nature in the one Person of Christ. The Monophysite Heresy, which had a large following at the time, taught that there was only one nature in Christ—the divine. This council clearly enunciated the true doctrine that the two natures in Christ were united in the one Person without confusion, change, division, separation or suppression. The sessions were attended by 500 bishops, including 5 papal legates. The fathers enacted 28 canons on church discipline. Of these, the last one gave Constantinople ecclesiastical jurisdiction over a large territory including the ancient and apostolic secs of Antioch and Alexandria, and also claimed equality with Rome. Pope Leo I (440–461) refused to endorse this canon, declaring that the See of Constantinople had not been founded by an Apostle and therefore could not be superior to sees of apostolic origin, such as Antioch and Alexandria. The Patriach of Constantinople, however, ignored Leo and continued to claim jurisdiction over the ancient sees, thereby doing untold harm to the Church in Syria, Palestine and Egypt.

5. The *Second Council of Constantinople* (553) was called by the

Emperor Justinian in order to condemn Nestorianism. No Western bishops attended. Pope Vigilius, although he was in Constantinople at the time, refused to participate. He was compelled, however, to grant recognition to the council before the emperor would permit him to return to Rome. This council approved of Justinian's condemnation of the Three Chapters—three treatises by three Eastern bishops denouncing the Monophysite Heresy— and thereby seemed to repudiate the Council of Chalcedon. The validity of this council was questioned for a long time, but eventually it came to be accepted.

6. The *Third Council of Constantinople* (680–681) reiterated the teaching of the Council of Chalcedon that Jesus Christ possesses both a divine and a human will. This was, in effect, a repudiation of a heresy that was prevalent at the time—Monothelism—a heresy that taught that Christ did not possess a human will. This council reconciled the Eastern Church, separated temporarily by a schism, with the Roman See.

7. The *Second Council of Nicaea* (787) was convened in order to settle a savage controversy concerning the right or wrong of veneration of holy images and relics. The council was a source of much controversy in Western Europe due to a mistranslation of the canons. The erroneous document had the fathers of Nicaea asserting that statues and relics should be "worshiped." After the correct documents were received in Rome, Pope Adrian I accepted this council.

8. The *Fourth Council of Constantinople* (869–870) was convoked by the Emperor Basil and was presided over by three representatives of the pope. It repudiated Photius, who had replaced the Patriarch of Constantinople, Ignatius, upon the latter's ouster by the regent Bardas. In addition to approving Ignatius, the council condemned iconoclasm.

9. The *First Council of the Lateran* (1139) was attended by 300 bishops and 600 abbots. Pope Calistus II presided, guiding the fathers in the enactment of 22 disciplinary decrees concerning clerical marriage, episcopal jurisdiction, appropriation of Church property, etc. The main work of the fathers was to confirm the Concordat of Worms, which had put an end to the lay-investiture controversy. The temporal lord retained the right to invest bishops with their secular powers, the Church recovered the right of investing bishops with their spiritual powers and jurisdiction.

10. The *Second Lateran Council* (1139) was called by Pope Innocent II (1130–1143) to put an end to a schism caused by an antipope, Anacletus.

11. The *Third Lateran Council* (1179) was summoned by Pope Alexander III to restore order after the defeat of Emperor Frederick I Barbarossa by the Lombard League. This defeat put an effective end to the schism that sent Alexander into exile and placed in Peter's chair a series of antipopes between 1159 and 1180. The schism resulted from the actions of Alexander in excommunicating Frederick when the latter ordered Alexander and a rival pope, Victor IV, to appear before him for judgment. Alexander had to flee, and Frederick supported Victor IV as pope. During the sessions of the council the sacred orders conferred by Frederick's antipopes were annulled; the Albigensian and Walden-

sian heresies were condemned. It was at this council that a canon was adopted requiring a two-thirds vote of the cardinals present at a conclave for the election of a pope.

12. The *Fourth Lateran Council* (1215) was one of the greatest of the councils. It was not surpassed in importance until the Council of Trent. Called by the pre-eminent medieval pope, Innocent III, it was attended by more than 400 bishops, 800 abbots and priors of monastic orders, and most of the royalty of Christendom. The council ratified Innocent's candidate for Holy Roman Emperor, Frederick II (Hohenstauffen), and supported the pope in suspending Langton, Archbishop of Canterbury, for failure to publish Innocent's bull denouncing the barons of England for forcing King John (present in person at the Council) to sign the Magna Carta. This, the Great Council, issued 70 canons on government of the Church, discipline, free school for clerics, etc. Here the word "transubstantiation" (*q.v.*) was used for the first time. Many canons concerned the weaknesses of the clergy and prescribed punishment and corrective measures for reform; new orders of religious were henceforth banned; confession at least once a year and reception of Holy Communion at Easter time were decreed for the laity; heretics were to be punished. The 6th canon provided the means of enforcing the reforms of the council, calling for provincial meetings of bishops annually for the purpose of maintaining discipline.

13. The *First Council of Lyons* (1245) was called by Pope Innocent IV to try the Holy Roman Emperor, Frederick II. Innocent, forced into exile in France by Frederick, deposed him. The decree of deposition was signed by 150 bishops. Frederick's envoy then appealed to a future pope and to a more general council. Frederick, however, died in 1250, and so did not live long enough to appeal to a future pope.

14. The *Second Council of Lyons* (1274). St. Thomas Aquinas died on the way to this council; St. Bonaventure died during it. The Dominicans and Franciscans were formally approved. Pope Gregory X presided over the council, which succeeded in uniting, however briefly, the Orthodox Greek and the Roman Churches, a matter dear to the heart of Gregory.

15. The *Council of Vienne* (1311–1312). The history of this council is obscure. It was called by Clement V under pressure from King Philip IV of France, to suppress the Order of the Knights Templar. It was held in Vienne, now Grenoble, France. Philip was present with his army at the council. Despite the threat from Philip, the fathers recommended that the Knights be allowed to defend themselves, but Clement decided to abolish the order for the welfare of the Church. Philip also wanted the council to condemn the actions of Pope Boniface, who died in 1303, the former enemy of Philip. The council compromised; the pope was acquitted of all charges brought by Philip, and the king was exonerated of all blame for the injuries suffered by Boniface at the hands of his agents.

16. The *Council of Constance* (1414–1418) was summoned to settle the scandalous condition of Christendom brought on by the election of Urban VI (1378–1389) to the papacy. For seventy years prior to that time the popes had been French, living at Avignon, an enclave within the Kingdom of France. Urban was

an Italian. His tactless, high-handed methods of reform antagonized the French cardinals, who fled Rome and elected a rival pope, Clement VII (1378–1394). Clement went back to the papal court at Avignon. The condition of two popes reigning, one from Rome and one from Avignon, lasted until 1409, to the great confusion of Christians everywhere. In 1409 cardinals from both papal courts met at Pisa to put an end to the schism. After excommunicating both popes, they elected a third pope, Alexander V (1409–1410). Instead of healing the schism, these actions only broadened it. Now there were three popes. Alexander's successor, the antipope John XXIII (1410–1415), at the urging of Emperor Sigismund, called a council to meet at Constance in Switzerland in 1414. The council met on Nov. 4 of that year with John XXIII presiding. Six months later, fearful of his life because of charges of crime brought against him, John fled Constance in disguise, deserting the council. Without a head, the council proceeded to pass the Five Articles, the first two of which declared the supremacy of a general council over the Pope, in accordance with the conciliar theory. Earlier, Pope Gregory XII (1406–1415) had sent a message from Rome to the council offering to resign if the two other popes would do likewise. Now the fathers of the council requested Gregory to *convoke* the council. By gaining the right to call the council, Gregory not only saved the supremacy of the pope, but he also obtained acknowledgment of himself and his predecessors as the true popes. It also followed that the canons concerning the council's superiority in spiritual power over the pope, which had been voted on be-fore Pope Gregory convoked the council, had no validity. Later, in 1417, the cardinals at Constance met and elected Martin V (1417–1431) as sole pope. The council had settled the Great Western Schism. Aside from this one great accomplishment, little else was achieved. John Hus and Jerome of Prague were burned at the stake for heresy, thus providing two martyrs for the Hussite heresy in Bohemia. A program was drawn up for future councils to act upon, which, it was decreed (by the decree *Frequens*), must be held at regular intervals. Very little was done for the reformation of the Church, despite much talk concerning "reform of the Church in head and members."

17. The *Council of Basle-Ferrara, Florence* (1431–1445). In accordance with the provision of Constance, Pope Martin V summoned a council to meet at Pavia in 1423, but when a few bishops had gathered there, an epidemic drove them to Sienna. Very little had been accomplished by the fathers when the council was suspended eleven months after it started. The decree *Frequens* of Constance, calling for frequent councils, was exercised, and another council was scheduled for Basle, Switzerland, in 1431. Eugene IV was pope when a handful of bishops met at Basle, where Guilano Cesarini eventually took over the presidency as representative of the pope. The council had hardly opened, however, when Pope Eugene tried to dissolve it. When the bishops refused to go home, a veritable rebellion against the pope ensued, during which the papacy struck bottom in power and prestige. These defiant fathers at Basle not only compelled Pope Eugene to withdraw the bull issued to

dissolve the council, but also forced him to admit that he was wrong in issuing the bull. The council then assumed the general administration of the Church. It seemed that the conciliar theory (namely, that a council superseded the pope), after its defeat at the Council of Constance, had been revived and was about to triumph over the papacy. A general council was superior over the pope for the moment. At this point, the Greek emperor, in fear of the destruction of his empire by the Ottoman Turks, appealed to Pope Eugene, rather than to the council at Basle, for reunion with Rome. Taking heart at this unexpected support, the pope denounced Basle, and ordered the council transferred to Ferrara (1438). A remnant of the bishops at Basle refused to go to Ferrara and stirred up a storm in Basle for two years or so. After much discussion of the question of reunion between the Eastern and Western Churches at Ferrara, the council was transferred to Florence (1438) due to a plague. It was at the latter city that the Act of Reunion between the Churches was signed on July 6, 1439. It was one thing to reunite in Florence, quite another to persuade the Greek Christians at home to accept reunion with the hated Latin Church. Upon their return home, the Greek bishops who had signed the Act of Reunion at Florence, met with bitter opposition. The reunion was never accepted in the East. Behind the theological questions at Florence was the grim fact of the Muslim threat to Constantinople. In vain did Emperor John VI appeal to the Christians of the West to come to the aid and defense of his besieged city. He returned home emptyhanded. In that age Western Christians were indifferent to the fate of the Byzantine Empire.

18. The *Fifth Lateran Council* (1512–1517) was summoned by Pope Julius II to counteract a schismatical council assembled at Pisa in 1511. Eventually Pisa was repudiated. This council held twelve sessions, during which it ratified the Concordat of Bologna between Julius II and Francis I of France. The council voted for a tax to support a war against the Ottoman Turks, but nothing came of it.

19. The *Council of Trent* was summoned by Pope Paul III to meet in 1543, but the opening session had to be postponed because of the Hapsburg-Valois war. The council finally opened in December, 1545, and sat until 1547, when a plague forced the fathers to flee to Bologna. All attempts at reopening the council failed. The second period of the council, convened by Pope Julius III in 1551, was attended only by bishops in the territories of the Holy Roman Emperor, the French bishops being forbidden to attend by Henry II. Very little was accomplished during this period, but an attempt to negotiate with the Lutherans was made. Nothing came of the efforts at reconciliation, however, because this part of the council came to an abrupt end when Maurice of Saxony, betraying Emperor Charles V, invaded the Tyrol in 1552, forcing the emperor and the fathers to flee for their lives. The third period of Trent began in January, 1562, when Pope Pius IV reconvened the council. Despite the conflicting demands of the various rulers of Europe upon the council, Cardinals Borromeo and Morone guided the fathers to a successful conclusion in December, 1563. The decrees of Trent were

signed by more than 200 fathers and approved by Pope Pius IV in the bull *Benedictus Deus*. The work of the Council of Trent was both dogmatic and disciplinary. A clear statement of Catholic doctrine was made to refute the errors of the new religions in Europe. The main teachings of the Catholic Church were confirmed. Historic tradition as well as the Bible was to be the basis of Christian Faith. The teachings of the new religions concerning grace, justification by faith alone, the effect of original sin on the human will, were rejected. The seven sacraments were declared necessary. The sacrificial nature of the Mass was reaffirmed. Faith was sustained in the intercession of the saints in heaven, in the belief of purgatory, the veneration of images and indulgences. The evils of the times connected with these practices were banned. The spiritual jurisdiction of the papacy over all Christians was reasserted, and the Holy Father was admitted to be the head of the bishops and the chief authority in matters of faith and morals. The second great accomplishment of the council was a volume of discipline. The sale of benefices was forbidden; bishops and other Church authorities were ordered to live in their dioceses, thus putting an end to the evil of absenteeism. Seminaries were to be established for the proper training of young men to the priesthood. Indulgences were not to be dispensed for money. The government of the Church was thoroughly reorganized; a catechism for the instruction of the faithful was composed; the Breviary and Missal were published; a new edition of the Latin Bible, the Vulgate, was issued. The Council of Trent, in spite of the almost insurmountable difficulties of the age, achieved a great reformation and made an enormous contribution to the preservation of the Catholic Church.

20. *Vatican Council I* (1869–1870), was called by Pius IX, who in 1865 named a commission of cardinals to make preparations for this first council since that of Trent three centuries earlier. The council formally opened on Dec. 8, 1869, in St. Peter's, attended by 774 of the 1,500 eligible prelates. Invitations to bishops of the Eastern Churches not in union with Rome, and to Protestant leaders brought no response. The first schemata "On Catholic doctrine against the errors stemming from rationalism" resulted in the unanimously accepted decree *Dei Filius*. The decree declares that God, the Creator of all things, can be known by natural reason; it also treats of the necessity of divine revelation and faith, stating that there can never be any real discrepancy between faith and reason. The most important and most debated work of the council dealt with papal infallibility. The decree *Pastor Aeternus* (July 18, 1870), passed with only two dissenting votes, teaches that St. Peter and his successors, the bishops of Rome, enjoy full and supreme power of jurisdiction over the whole Church and the capacity for teaching infallibly on matters of faith and morals. The following day the Franco-Prussian War began. In the same year the Italian government occupied Rome and the council was unable to proceed even though it had not completed more than a fraction of the work planned. Pius IX suspended the council indefinitely and thus it technically continued until officially closed by John XXIII.

21. *Vatican Council II*. Pope John

XXIII presided at the opening session of Vatican II which met on Oct. 11, 1962. There were 2,540 council fathers, mostly bishops, present. This session began with a declaration of independence by the fathers who then proceeded to show the Church to the world in a new garb; they opened the way for ecumenism; they reorganized the work of the council. The fathers concluded the work of the first session with the formulation of the basic standards for the liturgical reform, to be implemented in the second session of the Council. The session ended on Dec. 8, 1962. By the time the council reconvened in September, 1963, Pope John had died, and so his successor Pope Paul VI addressed the opening meeting. The Constitution on the Sacred Liturgy was the chief accomplishment of the second session of the council. The Constitution placed the main emphasis in liturgical worship on the Old and New Testaments. A decree on communications dealing with the duties of the press, the radio, television and motion pictures was the only other document formally promulgated at this session. The third session in 1964 considered the nature of the Church and the ecumenical movement.

Ecumenical Patriarch A title used by the Patriarch of Constantinople. The Holy See has never formally recognized this title.

ecumenism (eh-kue′men-ism, Gr. *oikoumene,* the inhabited world) The principles and practices promoting or tending toward world-wide Christian unity. According to Father Schillebeeckx, O.P.: "An attitude of mind attuned in faith to a visible unity, not only of love and hope, but also of faith, among people who confess Christ the Lord, and, in fact,

more generally among all people who acknowledge the value of the religious in human life."

Eden, Garden of (Sumerian, *edin,* prairie) This term is used in the Book of Genesis as the name of the place where God planted a garden that was to be the home of Adam and Eve. They lived here until their fall from God's pleasure. The word is also used to refer to an Aramaic state along the Euphrates.

Edict of Nantes A decree signed by King Henry IV of France at Nantes on Apr. 13, 1598, terminating the religious wars of the 16th century between the Catholics and Huguenots and granting the Huguenots full civil liberty and freedom of private worship. In addition they were given complete control of 200 towns with the right of public worship in them, as well as in 3,000 domains of the nobility, although Paris and episcopal see cities were excluded. In 1685 King Louis XIV, in order to suppress what amounted to a state within a state, revoked the edict following many years of strife during which the Huguenots tried to preserve and extend its advantages. The revocation sparked an intense persecution of the Protestants; thousands of refugees fled to England, Holland and America. While Pope Innocent XI had approved the general plan for the conversion of the dissidents, he did not countenance the bloody atrocities perpetrated in the pretended interest of the Catholic religion by the French court and the partisans, nor was he able to influence the king and the Gallican clergy to stop the persecution.

edification (L. *aedificare,* to build up) A term used by St. Paul (Eph. 4:12) to express the building up of the Mystical Body of Christ. Today the word is used to denote a state of emotional approval for some religious act.

edify (L. *aedificare,* to build up) To spiritually enlighten and strengthen an individual or the Church by instruction, example or exhortation. St. Paul tells the members of the Church to help and to strengthen one another as members of the same Body of Christ.

Editio Typica (L. typical edition) The original Vatican edition of a book to which other editions printed elsewhere should conform.

education The law of the Catholic Church is that parents have a grave obligation to provide for the religious, moral, civil and physical education of their children (canon 1113). Canon 1374 forbids Catholic children to attend non-Catholic, neutral or mixed schools, unless the ordinary decides otherwise. Canon law also affirms the right of the Church (canon 1375) to establish schools at every grade level. The Third Plenary Council of Baltimore (1884) urged the establishment of parochial schools and bound Catholic parents to send their children to these parochial schools unless the ordinary allows them to do otherwise for a sufficient cause. The American bishops in a joint statement in 1919 affirmed that "An education that united intellectual, moral and religious elements is the best training for citizenship." They declared that Catholic schools have not been created as a divisive element but are "simply the concrete form in which we exercise our rights as free citizens, in conformity with the dictates of conscience." In a decision made in 1928, the Supreme Court affirmed the right of private and parochial schools to exist; and it has always

been the position of the Church that Catholic schools are subject to some regulation by civil authority, particularly the subject matter required under state educational law. The Supreme Court has ruled that it is a violation of the First Amendment of the Constitution to use federal funds to aid religious schools, although bus transportation of pupils is constitutional. A growing body of Catholics hold that the interpretation of the First Amendment is incorrect, that the amendment was designed to prohibit the establishment of a national religion and to avoid preferential treatment of any one religion. The Supreme Court in the Zorach case ruled that the State can cooperate with the Church as long as basic liberties of the community are respected. The Court has also ruled that Bible reading and the saying of prayers in public schools are unconstitutional.

effect That which results from a cause.

ejaculation (L. *ejaculare,* to throw out) A short prayer that can be said quickly and many times (e.g., "My Lord and My God"). A list of indulgenced ejaculations can be found in the Raccolta. These short prayers are also called aspirations and invocations.

ekphonesis (eck-phone′ess-iss, Gr. lifting the voice) The final words of a prayer said or sung aloud after the previous part has been said in silence. The purpose of the ekphonesis is to allow the faithful to know what part of the Mass the celebrant has reached. It is used in all liturgies.

elect, the A term used to mean: 1. those who have been chosen by God for the gift of faith, namely, the members of the Christian Church; 2. the saved in heaven.

election 1. A theological term that refers to the divine decree by which God intends to give to the predestined eternal happiness with Him, together with the necessary graces for gaining this eternal happiness. St. Thomas Aquinas teaches that the predestined are the object of a true election on the part of God. 2. A canonical term referring to the selection of a person for an ecclesiastical office (canons 160 ff.). 3. Papal election. The usual method of selecting the pope. *See* election of a pope.

election of a pope Under the revised system as decreed by Pope John XXIII, the Roman Pontiff is to be chosen through *election* by a two-thirds majority, provided the number voting is divisible by three; or by a two-thirds plus one majority (if the number is not divisible by three). A pope can also be elected by *acclamation* (when the electing cardinals unanimously choose a pope without previous consultation) or by *compromise* (when the cardinals agree to accept the choice of a committee of not less than three or more than seven cardinals). The pope is elected in a conclave (*q.v.*), which is held behind locked doors. The conclave must begin by the 18th day following the death of a pope but may open as early as the 15th day. Balloting takes place in the Sistine Chapel, at the rate of two secret votes in the morning and two in the afternoon until the required majority is reached. The Dean of the Sacred College then asks the elected if he accepts the office of pope. As soon as the pope accepts, the conclave comes to an end. The cardinals then declare their obedience to the new pope, after which his name is announced to the world.

eleemosynary (L. *elemosyna,* alms) Connected with or related to charity or alms. The word can refer to one who is collecting alms, dispensing alms or receiving alms.

Elesha Eliseus (*q.v.*).

Elevation, the At the Consecration of the Mass, the priest identifying himself with Christ pronounces slowly over the bread the words of Christ at the Last Supper. At this instant transubstantiation takes place. The celebrant genuflects, rises, lifts the Host so that the faithful can see it, lowers the Host and places it on the corporal, then genuflects again. This action is repeated with the chalice. Both Host and chalice are raised for the silent adoration of the faithful. As members of the Mystical Body the faithful should unite in the sacrifice. The Elevation was added to the Mass at the end of the 12th century in Paris by Bishop Eudes de Sully to correct an erroneous teaching that Christ's body was not present until the wine was consecrated. There is no comparable action in the Eastern liturgy.

Elevation, Little The doxology at the end of the Canon of the Mass beginning with the words *"Per ipsum, et cum ipso . . ."* (Through Him and with Him) and concluding with the *"Per omnia saecula saeculorum."* Throughout the entire doxology, the celebrant lifts the Host and chalice a few inches above the altar, genuflecting only after the response "Amen" is given by the people. The prayer is chanted or recited in a loud voice. Formerly three signs of the Cross were made over the chalice but these are now omitted.

Elia (Heb., my God is Yahweh) A

prophet of the Old Testament who lived in the first part of the 9th century B.C. He defended the religion of Yahweh against Queen Jezebel who tried to make the worship of Baal the official religion. Elia appeared with Moses to witness the transfiguration of Jesus.

Elijah   Elia (*q.v.*).

Eliseus (L. form for Heb. *Elishah,* God saves)   A prophet who lived in the latter half of the 9th century B.C. He was the disciple of Elia. He was reputed to be a worker of miracles.

Elohim (Heb. unknown derivation)   A term used in the Old Testament for "gods," "god" and "God." It is used more than two thousand times to refer to Yahweh, the God of Israel.

ELV   *See* Extension Lay Volunteers.

Elvira, Council of   Held early in the 4th century at Elliberis, or Illiberis, in Spain, a city now in ruins, not far from Granada. First council held in Spain, attended by 19 bishops and 26 priests. There is a dispute as to the exact year, but A.D. 324 is assigned to it. Its 81 canons on disciplinary matters give a good insight into the conditions in Spain at that time. Of the first three centuries of the history of the Church in Spain, we know almost nothing. It was important because it was the first to impose celibacy on bishops, priests and deacons. There is also interesting legislation on the use of images.

emanation   Radiating or proceeding from another. Pantheism teaches that the universe is an emanation of God, which makes it a part of God.

emancipation, Catholic   The removal of the disabilities (*q.v.*) affecting Catholics in England. This took place over a long period beginning in 1778 and culminating in the Act of 1926 which has left only a few existing disabilities.

embassy chapel   A chapel attached to a foreign embassy. Since such a chapel enjoys diplomatic privilege and extraterritoriality, it becomes a device to bring religious services to a country where religion may be otherwise banned. In the 17th and 18th centuries, embassy chapels were popular in London in order that the Mass might be said for Catholics. The French established an embassy chapel in Moscow.

Ember days (AS. *ymbren,* running around)   Three days each quarter which are set aside as days for special penance and prayer. They are the Wednesday, Friday and Saturday following Dec. 13, the first Sunday in Lent, Pentecost, and Sept. 14. Ember days are days of fasting and partial abstinence (meat may be taken only at the principal meal), except Friday which is a day of fast and total abstinence.

embolism (Gr. *embolismo,* interpolation)   An addition to the petition made in the Pater Noster of the Mass which amplifies and extends this petition. The embolism begins with the words, "Deliver us, we beseech you, O Lord."

embryotomy (Gr. *embryon,* fetus; *tome,* excision)   Any surgical intervention on the human fetus. It is direct homicide and a grave sin.

emeritus (L. honorably retired)   A word appended to such titles as rector, professor, doctor, etc., to indicate that the person has retired with honor from such a position.

Eminence   A term of address used for cardinals, as in "Your Eminence." The only other person to whom this term applies is the Grand Master of the Knights of St. John of Jerusalem.

Emmanuel (Heb. With us is God) A term used by Isaia and St. Matthew to refer to the Messias. In recent years, some biblical scholars hold that the Old Testament passage does not necessarily refer exclusively to Christ, and that it must be interpreted in a typical sense.

empathy A sympathetic understanding of a people's customs and psychology. It is a type of apostolic identification, which does not necessarily signify approval. It implies that the missioner understands the reasons behind the actions of people. Thus, in a polygamous area, the missioner does not approve polygamy but understands why the people are polygamous.

empiricism (Gr. *empeiros,* experience) A system of philosophy that attributes all knowledge to sensual experience.

employers, duties of Employers, as "custodians" of God's world in a highly industrialized socioeconomic order, have duties in social justice and charity toward the common good. Toward their workers the following are due: 1. To provide a living family wage. 2. To respect the rights of their employees to form a union for mutual cooperation. 3. To provide a safe and healthy environment for their workers. 4. To cooperate in promoting the well-being of the whole community.

Encaenia (en-kay-nee′ah) A feast kept in the Byzantine Rite to commemorate the dedication in 335 of Constantine's Basilica of the Resurrection which was built between Calvary and the Holy Sepulchre.

Enchiridion (Gr. en′ki-rid′ee-on) Title of a frequently quoted source book which lists council decrees along with condemned propositions.

enclosure *See* cloister.

Encratites Followers of encratism. Early Christians, chiefly Gnostics, who abstained from use of wine, meat and marriage because of heretical views regarding the origin of matter.

enculturation The process of learning a culture, a *sine qua non* for the religious worker.

encyclical (L. *encyclicus,* circular letter) A letter written by the pope and usually addressed to ordinaries of the whole Church or to the hierarchy of a particular country or region. Some encyclicals are addressed also to the clergy and the faithful. Pope John XXIII addressed his encyclical *Pacem in Terris* to "all men of good will." The encyclical is written in Latin and usually takes its name from its first words. The popes use encyclicals to express their minds on doctrinal subjects and as a method of teaching. An encyclical is not necessarily an infallible document, although the pope could speak ex cathedra by this method. Catholics are expected to give both external and internal assent to doctrinal encyclicals. *See* epistle, papal.

encyclical epistle A written message from a pope which concerns less important subjects than those of an encyclical letter, or which concerns a particular event, such as a Holy Year.

end That for which something is done. It is a supposed good. There are different types of ends according to scholastic philosophy. *Finis operis* (end of the work) is the good to which a work is directed by its agent. *Finis operantis* (end of the one working) is the good which the agent intends. *Finis proximus* (proximate end) is the good which the work or agent immediately intends. There are also intermediate and ultimate ends. Other ends are: *finis qui* (the end which), the good intended; *finis cui* (the end of whom), that in whose favor the good is intended; *finis quo* (the end by which), the actual attainment of the thing intended. An end is natural or supernatural. Any end is primary or secondary, if it is sufficient in prompting to action or auxiliary in prompting to action.

end justifies the means A condemned principle that evil or sinful means may be used to arrive at a good effect. This principle has been wrongly attributed to Jesuit philosophers. It is Catholic teaching that no sinful act may be committed to accomplish a good.

end of man The end of man is God, the Beatific Vision. All actions of man should be directed to this end.

end of the world The Old Testament books speak often of the last days (Gen. 49:1; Num. 24:14; Deut. 4:30; 32:29; Osee 3:5; Mich. 4:1; Is. 2:2; Jer. 30:24; Ezech. 38:16) without actually defining the limits of such times. These times did, however, include the messianic times. These expressions of the last days indicate at the very least that Israel will not continue forever and that some day it will come to an end. In the New Testament, Christ speaks of the passing of this world (Mt. 4:18; Lk. 16:17). Christ speaks of it in terms of fulfillment when He shall return as the Kyrios, the King of Glory. It is spoken of in the New Testament as a time of judgment and retribution when the just shall rise to glory and the wicked to punishment. It is considered a time when all things will be brought to fruition and completion.

endowment 1. A talent considered to be a gift from God or nature. 2. A gift of property or money to be used in the maintenance of an institution such as a college or hospital.

The regular offerings of the faithful may be considered as endowment.

ends of sacrifice There is a fourfold reason for sacrifice: adoration of God, reparation for offenses committed against God, thanksgiving for God's many blessings and petition for needs.

energumen (eh-ner'goo-men, Gr. worked up) A person possessed by the devil, a demoniac.

engagement *See* betrothal.

engagement, Christian All Catholics by Baptism have a role in the mission of the Church. The Laity's basic role is to bring Christian influence to bear on secular life and society, the *consecratio mundi*. This fundamental duty is keeping the Word and bearing witness to it by applying it in all phases in the life of men and of society. The engaged Christian accepts this responsibility and duty. Involvement is not a matter of choice but a sought opportunity to fulfill one's Christian mission.

England *See* Great Britain.

English Martyrs The English men and women who suffered and died for their Catholic Faith in the 16th century. The earliest and best known of these martyrs are St. John Fisher and St. Thomas More, who suffered the ultimate penalty for refusing to take the Oath of Supremacy by which they would have acknowledged Henry VIII (1509–1547), instead of the pope, as supreme head of the Church in England. Under Henry VIII, both Catholics and followers of the new doctrines were executed for their beliefs, the former for refusing to admit Henry was head of the Church, the latter for denying the Six Articles, basic tenets of the Catholic Church. On July 30, 1540, three Catholics were hanged for denying the supremacy of Henry; three dissidents were burned at the stake for holding heretical doctrines. Under the penal laws of the reign of Elizabeth I (1558–1603), Catholics were fined, imprisoned and put to death. One of the most famous of these was Father Edmund Campion, who (with two other priests) was executed for "treason" in 1581. He died bravely, professing his loyalty and devotion to the Queen. During Elizabeth's reign 124 priests were put to death for the sole exercise of their ministry, and 32 laymen and women were executed for sheltering or helping priests. Most violators of the penal laws, after their possessions were seized by the government, were hanged, drawn and quartered on the trumped-up charge of treason. Of those who died for the Faith in England, there are 2 saints, 200 Blessed and many other cases awaiting the decision of the Holy See.

enkolpion (en-kol′pea-on, Gr. that which is worn on the breast) The large medallion worn by bishops of the Byzantine Rite. It hangs from a chain worn about the neck. It bears a representation of Christ or the Blessed Mother, and sometimes contains relics.

ens The participle of the Latin verb "esse" ("to be"), and usually rendered "being." The term "being" refers to any person or thing existing in the world. There are grades of being. God is the Highest, or Supreme Being. Angels, men, animals, vegetables and inanimate objects are lesser beings.

Enthronement of the Sacred Heart The act of acknowledging the kingship of Jesus Christ by placing an image of His Sacred Heart in the home. The Enthronement of the image is usually accompanied by the prescribed prayer of consecration, entrusting the family and the home to the Sacred Heart.

Entrance, Great That part of the Byzantine Liturgy in which the bread and wine are carried from the *prothesis* out of the sanctuary, by the north door of the screen, into the nave and to the altar through the holy door.

Entrance Hymn The first prayer of the variable part of the Mass. It consists of an antiphon, a psalm verse, the Gloria Patri and the antiphon repeated. This prayer sets the mood for the day's Mass, and suggests the main thought to be found in the Reading and Gospel. It is a hymn to the dignity of Christ, who comes to sacrifice Himself through the ministry of the celebrant and of the worshiping community.

Entrance, Little That part of the Byzantine Liturgy in which the Book of Gospels is carried out of the sanctuary through the north door to the middle of the church. After some prayers the celebrant and those accompanying him return to the altar through the holy doors.

Entrance Rite That part of the Mass up through the Collect or Prayer. The Entrance Hymn (Introit), the Litany (Kyrie) and the Glory to God (Gloria) are permitted in the vernacular in public Masses. Many liturgists include this as part of the Liturgy of the Word of God (*q.v.*).

envy (L. *invidus,* envious) That capital sin which creates sadness at the good of another.

epact (Gr. *epactos,* added) The period added to equalize the lunar and solar calendars. It is used to determine the time of the ecclesiastical new moon.

eparch The name formerly used for an exarch (*q.v.*) in the United States.

eparchy   The name used for a diocese of the Byzantine Rite.

Ephesians, Epistle to the   One of the Captivity Epistles of the New Testament, possibly a circular letter, written by St. Paul. However, some biblical scholars challenge the Pauline authorship, holding that the Epistle was probably written by a disciple of Paul who used the Epistle to the Colossians as his model. The central theme of the Epistle is the mystery of Christ; God's plan to unite all men, both Jew and Gentile, in communion with Christ.

Ephesus, Council of   Third ecumenical council, held in 431. It defined that the Blessed Virgin was the Mother of God, and it condemned Nestorianism and Pelagianism. *See* ecumenical councils.

Ephphetha, ceremony of (ef'fay-tah; Aramaic, to open)   During the ceremony of Baptism according to the Catholic ritual, the priest touches the ears and nostrils of the person to be baptized with saliva. This rite is reminiscent of Jn. 7:6-12, when Jesus healed the man blind from birth by mixing clay with His spittle and rubbing it on his eyes, then sending him off to wash in the Pool of Siloam. It symbolizes the opening of the soul to the light of heavenly truth and wisdom. According to the new *Collectio Rituum* for use in the United States the use of saliva in touching the ears and nose may be omitted for a reasonable cause, to safeguard cleanliness or to avoid the danger of spreading or contracting disease.

Ephraim (Heb. *efrayim,* fruitful land)   Son of Joseph, founder of the tribe of Israel that bore his name.

epigonation (Gr. thigh)   A diamond-shaped vestment, 12 in. by 10 in., suspended over the right thigh to symbolize the spiritual sword of justice. It is worn in the West only by the Holy Father, but in the East all the bishops wear it as a Eucharistic vestment.

epikeia (eh-pea-kai'ah, Gr. reasonableness)   Equity. The interpretation of a law not from the words of the law but from the mind of the lawmaker, since there are situations in which the lawmaker would not intend the law to apply. Epikeia must be used prudently and with discretion. It may not be used for acts which are intrinsically evil or for acts already invalidated by law.

epiklesis (ep-ee-klay'sis; Gr. invocation)   A prayer found in all the Eastern liturgies which is said following the consecration, calling on God to send down the Holy Spirit upon the sacred species so that the recipients will be filled with Grace. The non-Catholic Eastern Churches hold that the consecration is not completed until this prayer has been said.

Epiphany (Gr. *ephihainein,* to show oneself)   A feast celebrated on Jan. 6 which is a holyday of obligation in the universal Church, although the United States is exempt. Traditionally, it was one of the important feasts of the Church ranking only after Easter and Pentecost, and in the Eastern Church still maintains that importance. The Feast of Epiphany is believed originally to have commemorated the date of the Baptism of Christ, as attested to in the 2nd century. The feast of Christmas was not added until the 4th century, to supplant a pagan festival. Even in the Western Liturgy, the Epiphany was of higher rank than Christmas until 1955 when its octave was abolished and thus its rank reduced. In the Eastern Church the feast has a broad concept commemorating the Birth, the Baptism of Christ (His manifestation to the world) and also the beginning of His public life. In the Western Church, emphasis was on Christ's revelation to the Gentiles, symbolized by the story of the Magi (*q.v.*).

episcopacy (Gr. *episkopos,* overseer) 1. The bishops of the Church as a group. 2. The state of being a bishop. The Council of Trent defined the episcopacy as being the fullness of the sacrament of Holy Orders.

Episcopal (Episcopalian) Church A term which refers to the American and Scottish branches of the Anglican Church, so-called because the church is ruled hierarchically on the belief that the bishops have been given authority by God. The Episcopal Church in the United States has a spiritual but not a juridical affinity with the Church of England. The Episcopal Church is divided into High Church, which is generally conservative but which preserves many Roman Catholic practices, such as the Mass, Penance, etc.; and the Low Church, which is radical and evangelical, rejecting many Roman Catholic practices as "pomp."

episcopate 1. The office of a bishop. 2. The period of rule by a bishop. 3. The body of bishops of the universal Church or of a specific area.

episcopus castrensis (L. bishop of the camp) The Latin term for the military ordinary, the bishop who has charge of all military chaplains. The Archbishop of New York is the military ordinary for the United States. He is in charge of the military ordinariate which is set up in the manner of a special diocese with its own rules and regulations.

epistle, papal A formal letter from the Holy Father addressed to the entire Church and commonly called an "encyclical" (world letter). The idea comes from the letters of instruction circulated in the early Church by the Apostles—what we call today "the Epistles." Though not necessarily infallible documents, the encyclicals could become such if the Holy Father so wished and if certain conditions are met. If the contents treat of doctrinal matters Catholics are bound to give internal as well as external assent. *See* encyclical.

Epistles of the Captivity, The *See* Captivity Epistles.

Epistles, Pastoral The three Pauline Epistles, 1 Tim., 2 Tim., Tit., which are concerned with the pastoral duties of the men to whom they are addressed. They give instructions on the care of souls and the organization of the Church.

epistolae ecclesiasticae (L. ecclesiastical letters) There are specific types of letters written by the pope and other Church dignitaries which fall into specific categories. Some of these are: 1. encyclical letters; 2. apostolic letters, written on the authority of the pope; 3. dimissorial letters, excardinating a priest from a diocese to take on another title; 4. pastoral letters of a bishop; 5. decretals; etc.

epistolary, epistolarium The book containing the Epistles used by the subdeacon at High Mass.

equality A term referring to the fundamental natural and spiritual rights enjoyed by every man because he is made in the image and likeness of God. But in the natural order we uphold a certain inequality between man and man: one possesses natural abilities, characteristics and gifts that the other will not have. When justice is at work, equality is the result.

equiprobabilism (L. *aequus,* equal; *probabilis,* worthy of belief) A teaching which solves the problem of probability by holding that a law must be obeyed unless the opinion favoring freedom is equally probable as that favoring the law.

equivocation The use of phrases or words having more than one meaning in order to hide information to which the questioner has no right.

era, the Christian The time since the birth of Christ. It was calculated by a monk in Rome about 527 who estimated that Christ was born in 753 A.U.C. (*ab urbe condita,* from the foundation of the city). He set this year as A.D. 1. The estimate was probably off by several years but it makes no difference for chronological purposes.

Erastian One who advocates state supremacy in religious affairs. Named after Thomas Erastus, d. 1583, a Zwingalian theologian who taught this doctrine.

erection, canonical When a religious organization or body is raised up and given canonical status by qualified ecclesiastical authority, that organization or body is canonically erected. Only the Holy See, for example, is qualified to erect religious orders or societies, dioceses, cathedral-churches, abbeys of monks or nuns or archconfraternities. A bishop or religious order may erect a confraternity, a seminary or a convent.

eremite Another term for a hermit (*q.v.*).

ermine A name sometimes given to the office of a cardinal whose ceremonial robes are bordered with ermine.

error (L. a wandering about) In one way or another the result of ignorance is error. Due to a lack of knowledge or an improperly formed conscience a man is prone to make an error in judgment or in conscience where faith and morals are concerned. Once he is aware of his ignorance in the matter in question he has a Christian obligation to fill the lack with the truth. Salvation is not endangered by error for which one is not responsible. But a personal lack of moral diligence or a personal, conscious hardness against the truth as the Church presents it, can make a person responsible for the moral evil of sin.

error, invincible A type of error that arises out of a person's ignorance of a fact or a condition through no fault of his own. It means the person has taken reasonable means to dispel this lack of knowledge, but due to conditions beyond his control or a lack of ability to understand on his part he cannot come to a definite knowledge of something. Such a type of ignorance presupposes good will on the part of the person so that if he could dispel his ignorance he would. It also excuses him from the responsibility that a definite knowledge of a fact or condition would impose upon him.

error, toleration of The Church tolerates error in persons but not in her doctrine. She loves the one who errs but hates the error itself, and by her living magisterium is a guide to the true road to follow in matters of faith and morals. She welcomes all to follow this road but respects the conscience of all who in good faith follow other paths.

erroneous (L. *erronea*) The Church condemns as untrue or erroneous any proposition which contradicts a truth that is certain from the cooperation of faith and reason. If, for instance, it were to be said that a Negro does not have an immortal

214

soul, this statement would rightly be condemned as erroneous. For our faith tells us that God has created every man with an immortal soul; and our reason tells us that the Negro is a man.

Esau (Heb. *esaw,* hairy) Son of Isaac and Rebecca, twin brother of Jacob. He sold his birthright for a meal.

eschatology (Gr. *eschatos,* the furthest, the last) Study of the doctrine about the "last things," such as death, resurrection, immortality and judgment. It is concerned with the final destiny of man, both as an individual and as a species. It is also concerned with the present order on the earth and the establishment of that of eternity.

Esdra (Heb. *ezra,* help) An Old Testament author of priestly descent who was one of the leaders in the Jewish restoration at the end of the 5th century B.C. In the Septuagint the book known as Esdra (1 Esd.) and Nehemia (2 Esd.) are joined simply into the Book of Esdra. Because of the similarities in style and language between the Books of Esdra and Paralipomenon, some exegetes hold that Esdra is also the Chronicler (*q.v.*).

esotericism (Gr. *esoteros,* inner) The holding of secret doctrines known only to a few initiates.

espousal (L. *spondere,* to promise) Originally a solemn betrothal. Today the word is synonymous with wedding or marriage ceremony.

esse (ess'say, L. to be) A Scholastic term for being, the state of existence.

essence (L. *esse,* to be) That which makes a thing what it is. It is that in being which underlies all outward manifestations. It is permanent and unchangeable. It is the real character or nature of a thing within which its attributes inhere. Often essence is said to be the same as being, substance, nature or even form.

Essene A member of a monastic brotherhood which existed in Palestine in the time of Christ. Little was known of this ascetical group until the discovery of the Dead Sea Scrolls (*q.v.*).

establishment, church 1. Specifically, recognition by the state of a particular religion as the official state religion. The Catholic Church is the established church in Italy and Spain. In England, the Anglican Church is the established church. In Norway, it is the Lutheran Church. 2. Generically, to establish the Church means to raise up a native hierarchy, the ultimate purpose of missionary labor. 3. The Church is a fact established by God for our salvation. Christ first appointed Apostles who were witnesses to His Resurrection. They and their successors proclaimed the reign of Christ to others. Pius XI in *Rerum Ecclesiae* (1926) said: "The Church was established precisely for this task, to spread the Kingdom of Christ throughout the world and to afford all men a share in His Salutary Redemption."

Esther, Book of Old Testament book recounting the story of the heroine of the same name who averted a threatened pogrom of the Jews by their enemies at the Persian court and the institution of the Feast of Purim (Lots) to commemorate their deliverance. The events supposedly took place in the 5th century B.C. The Catholic Bible after 10:3 contains enlargements not found in the Hebrew text but accepted by the Church as inspired Scripture. Recent Catholic commentators have inclined to believe that an original historical nucleus has

been freely treated for purposes of
edification, to teach that one should
not despair in adversity.

eternal life 1. The perfect possession
of life without beginning or end. In
this sense the term applies only to
God. 2. In a broad sense the term
is used to refer to man's life after
death which has a beginning but no
end (immortality). 3. In an ontological sense, St. Thomas Aquinas
says that man shares in the divine
eternity which transcends all time.
Because the blessed have full happiness, there is no sense of past,
present or future (*Summa Theologica* II-II. 18:2:2).

eternity 1. *Absolute eternity.* That
endless state which has no beginning
or end or succession. This state is
proper to God alone. 2. *Relative
eternity.* That state in which a being
brought into existence will always
continue to exist. *See* eternal life.

ethics (Gr. *ethos*) The study of
moral conduct. By moral conduct
is meant conduct regarded as right
or wrong or as involving deliberation and choice among ends viewed as
good. Ethics directs a man how to
act if he wishes to be morally good
and sets before him the absolute obligation he is under of doing good
and avoiding evil.

Ethiopian Church 1. The Ethiopian
(Abyssinian) National Church that
fell into the Monophysite Schism. It
is now independent of the Coptic
Patriarch of Alexandria. The liturgical language of the Church is Geez
and its services are of Alexandrian
type. 2. Ethiopian Catholics who are
converts or descendants of converts
from the Ethiopian National Church.
They follow similar liturgical rites to
the non-Catholics, and in Geez.

Eucharist (Gr. *eucharistia,* thanksgiving) 1. The sacrament of the New

Law in which, under the species of
consecrated bread and wine, the body
and blood of Christ is truly, really
and substantially contained for the
purpose of giving spiritual nourish-
ment to the soul. It is the teaching
defined by the Council of Trent that
Christ is present in the Eucharist
through transubstantiation, i.e.,
through the transformation of the entire bread and wine into the body and
blood of Christ although the original
appearances remain. It is also the
definition of the Council of Trent
that Christ is complete and entire
under both or either species, and
should that which appears as bread or
wine be divided Christ is wholly
present in each and every part. Once
the bread and wine have been consecrated, Christ permanently remains
as long as the bread and wine remain incorrupt. Therefore, the Eucharist is properly the subject of
adoration (latria). The matter of the
sacrament is bread and wine; the
bread must be made from wheat
and the wine from grapes. The water
that is mixed with the wine is not
matter for the Sacrament but its use
obliges gravely. The form of the
Sacrament is double, one set of words
pronounced over the bread (*Hoc est
Corpus Meum*) and another pronounced over the wine (*Hic est
Calix Sanguinis Mei*). Reception
of the Eucharist confers *ex opere
operato* (*q.v.*) the actual grace of devotion and fervor and a spirit of delight and excitement to charity;
venial sin is also blotted out. The
Eucharist can only be consecrated
by a priest although a deacon may
distribute Holy Communion. For the
reception of the Sacrament a state of
grace is necessary, and the recipient is
expected to fast before reception.
The Sacrament of the Eucharist is

the highest of all sacraments because of its intimate connection with Christ. The name comes from the prayer of thanksgiving made by Christ at the Last Supper, during which He founded the Sacrament and commanded His followers to continue the Unbloody Sacrifice in commemoration of Him. 2. The Sacred Species, i.e., the consecrated Host or wine.

Eucharistic adoration　Worship given to Jesus Christ under the Eucharistic species of bread outside of Mass and Holy Communion. While the Blessed Sacrament was always worshiped, this adoration did not become formalized until the Middle Ages. The creation of the Feast of Corpus Christi (1264), the Forty Hours Devotion (1527), and such devotions as Benediction and Perpetual Adoration formalized this adoration. Religious orders such as the Fathers of the Blessed Sacrament were founded to advance this devotion. Some religious orders such as the Blessed Sacrament Sisters practice perpetual exposition and adoration. Private devotions are expressed by the faithful in frequent visits to the Blessed Sacrament. It is customary for Catholic men to tip their hats when passing a Catholic Church as a gesture of honor and respect to the Blessed Sacrament.

Eucharistic Congress　1. Strictly, an international assembly of Catholics to honor the Blessed Sacrament, approved by the Holy See, and presided over by a papal legate. It consists of a series of Masses, processions, Benedictions, sermons, etc., aimed at giving honor to the Blessed Sacrament and increasing devotion of the faithful. The first such congress was organized in Lille, France, in 1881 as a means of answering growing secularism. Originally confined largely to France and Belgium they are now held at regular intervals in such diverse parts of the world as the United States, the Philippine Islands, India and Brazil. 2. A similar gathering on a regional or national level.

Eucharistic elements　The bread and wine used at Mass. The bread must be made of wheat. In the Roman Rite, the bread must be unleavened; leavened bread is valid but illicit. In the Eastern Rite, for the most part, the beard is leavened. The wine must be made of grapes, and it should not have less than 5 per cent alcohol, nor more than 18 per cent.

Eucharistic fast　The fast from food and drink which must be observed before the reception of Holy Communion. The faithful must fast from food and alcoholic beverages for one hour before receiving Holy Communion, and from other liquids for one hour. The same rules apply to a priest who is offering Mass but in the case of bination (*q.v.*) or trination (*q.v.*) nonalcoholic liquids may be taken between Masses. For both celebrant and laity the time is to be figured from the actual time of reception of Holy Communion.

Eucharistic Liturgy　The Mass, the central and most solemn act of Christian worship. On the night of His betrayal, Jesus instituted the Mass and Sacrament of the Eucharist, commanding His disciples that they should celebrate and use the Eucharist in His memory. It was not to be an act of personal religion, something isolated from the act of Christ, but it was to be offered for the glory of God in memory of the redemptive sacrifice of His Son. While the Eucharist adds nothing to the Sacrifice of the Cross, it does prolong it and extend it until the end of the world. In the early Church the Eucharist became the reason of religious assembly, forming the community of the faithful and giving bond to their unity. The Eucharist was not something solely for adoration but it was a means for the Christians to share the lives of one another in Christ's Mystical Body. In the Constitution on the Sacred Liturgy issued by Vatican Council II emphasis is placed on the restoration of liturgy as the center of Christian life, declaring: "The renewal in the Eucharist of the covenant between the Lord and man draws the faithful into the compelling love of Christ and sets them on fire. From the liturgy, therefore, and especially from the Eucharist, as from a fount, grace is poured forth upon us; and the sanctification of men in Christ and the glorification of God . . . is achieved in the most efficacious possible way." In the Eucharist, contact with Christ is very personal and real, and by reception of Holy Communion this contact even becomes physical, not only between Christ and the person receiving Holy Communion but with all the faithful who receive Holy Communion.

Eucharistic Service   *See* Liturgy of the Eucharist.

eugenics (u-jen'iks; Gr. *eugenes,* wellborn) Science which aims to improve the human race by genetic means. Stress is laid on the genetic misfits whose heritable defects ("bad genes") would be passed on to their descendants. *Negative eugenics* advocates preventing these people from reproducing. *Positive eugenics* aims to encourage reproduction of those having more desirable traits ("good genes"). There is no objection to positive eugenics. But with negative eugenics, laudable as are its aims, and lamentable as are some of the cases of heritable defects, there is

also a question of ethics. Some of the means proposed to bring about the desired effect, such as sterilization and contraception, are morally unacceptable. In addition, the principles of justice and individual rights must be considered. "Public magistrates have no direct power over the bodies of their subjects; therefore, where no crime has taken place and there is no cause present for grave punishment, they can never directly harm, or tamper with the integrity of the body, either for the reasons of eugenics or for any other reason" (Pius XI, *Casti Connubii*). Even biologists are not agreed on the effectiveness of eugenics programs, especially in the case of recessive genes. Where legalized, eugenics programs are open to possible abuse and in some places have been used as a justification for racist policies. In the present state of our knowledge of human genetics, it would be rash to embark on an uncertain program of negative eugenics; and some geneticists even hold the hope that some day, with the discovery of the genetic code of DNA, controlled mutations may be possible to correct genetic defects. *See* spontaneous generation.

eulogia (Gr. a blessing) A name given to a blessed object but particularly to blessed bread which is distributed after Mass.

euthanasia (Gr. *eu,* well; *thantos,* death) The act or practice of painlessly putting to death persons suffering from incurable conditions or diseases. It is gravely immoral when direct means of killing the person are used; however, there is no obligation to use extraordinary means to keep the person alive.

evangel (Gr. *euangelion,* glad tidings) The good news of man's redemption by Christ, thus one of the four Gospels. The use of the word is archaic.

Evangeliarium The book of Gospels used by the deacon at High Mass.

Evangelical A name applied to some Protestant churches which place great emphasis on the authority of Scripture and the importance of preaching over liturgy. Salvation is by faith in Jesus Christ, apart from good works.

Evangelical Counsels This term refers to voluntary poverty, chastity and obedience, used to arrive at perfection in the service of God and neighbor.

Evangelist (Gr. *euangelistes,* a bearer of glad tidings) A term applied to the authors of the four Gospels. In apostolic times the word was used of those who preached the good news of Christ, such as Philip (Acts 21:8) and Timothy (2 Ti. 4:5). Some Protestants use the word today for a preacher, usually one who moves from pulpit to pulpit.

evangelize To preach the Gospel to a people, to Christianize. It is the mission of every Christian to carry his faith to others. Christ's command to teach all nations was meant for all of His followers.

eve (AS. *aefen,* evening) The evening or day before a religious feast.

Eve (Heb. *hawwah*) The name which according to Genesis 3:20 the first man gave to the first woman. The Blessed Virgin is sometimes referred to as the new Eve.

evening Mass A Mass offered in the late afternoon or evening. A decree of Pope Pius XII in 1953 gave every ordinary power to permit evening Mass. This decree was strengthened in 1957 by allowing daily Mass after midday for the spiritual welfare of the faithful.

evensong The name for the evening service of the Anglican Church. It

was formerly used for Vespers in Catholic England but is now archaic.

evil (AS. *yfel*) Evil is the impairing of a perfection or good that should be present in a person, action or thing as part of its reality. Evil is of two types: 1. *physical,* when a physical good is missing or deprived, as the loss of sight in a blind man; 2. *moral,* the deprivation of a moral good, such as the loss of truth by a lie.

evil eye A look by a person that is said to inflict blight or injury. The belief is widespread in backward cultures and people often wear some charm or amulet to ward off the evil eye.

evil, material The limitation by one another of the various component parts of the natural world. Through this mutual limitation natural objects are prevented from attaining to their full or ideal perfection whether by physical conditions or by sudden catastrophes. It does not necessarily connote suffering.

evil, moral The turning of the human will from the prescriptions of the moral order to that which is opposed to it; the evil action which results from that deviation.

evil, problem of The philosophical and theological problem confronting all men which revolves around the question: "If there is a good God, how can He permit moral and physical evil to exist in the world?" Philosophically, the Church teaches that God does not cause evil, but merely permits its presence in the world. Theologically, the Church teaches that suffering and hardship are part of each man's limited life in this world.

evil spirits The fallen angels and other condemned spirits associated with Satan. It has been a historical and universal belief that there are bad spirits, or evil life forces, that roam the world. Primitive and ancient cultures attempted to deal with these spirits through sacrifices and prayers. It is Catholic teaching that evil spirits have no authority over human beings against their will, nor can evil spirits read one's secret thoughts.

evolution (L. *evolvere,* to unroll) Developmental change or unfolding of any kind. Biological theory that all species of living things have arisen by gradual transformation from other species—also called theory of common descent. The theory has given rise to wider extensions of its meaning to include evolution of living from nonliving (*see* spontaneous generation), chemical evolution, evolution of matter, evolution of mind, evolution of society and others. Most biologists hold that biological evolution took place from the most primitive form of life to the most complex through mutations, genetic isolation, natural selection and other factors. Historically, Darwin gave the greatest impetus to the theory by presenting a mass of evidence in its favor. Subsequent research of a hundred years has supported the main outline of biological evolution. Darwin's publication generated much opposition from theologians accustomed to look upon the first chapter of Genesis as a scientific account of creation. Further study, however, has made it clear that this chapter means to teach religious rather than scientific truth. Catholics are now free to envisage any evolutionary hypothesis which leaves room for the Creator, that is, for God as the ultimate cause of all things that exist. On the evolution of man, Catholics must hold some reservations. 1. The soul itself does not evolve, but is created immediately by God. The intellect and will are spiritual faculties of the soul; therefore any theory of the evolution of the mind which denies this qualitative difference would be untenable. 2. "The faithful cannot embrace that opinion which maintains either that after Adam there existed on this earth true men who did not take their origin through natural generation from him as from the first parent of all or that Adam represents a certain number of first parents" (Pius XII, *Humani Generis*), for this theory of polygenism seems to be incompatible with the doctrine of original sin. 3. Even if God used an animal's body to make man, man could not be called (for philosophical reasons) the "son" of a brute animal (Pius XII, Allocution 1941). 4. A decree of the Biblical Commission requires Catholics to hold that the first woman was formed from the first man; many Catholic scholars now interpret this to mean that the first woman was formed on the model of the first man, taken from him as a copy from an original. Within these guide lines one may hold for evolution of species and evolution of man's body from other primates.

ex cathedra (L. from the chair) By virtue of, or in the exercise of, one's office; with authority; as when the pope speaks ex cathedra in matters of faith and morals, he is infallible.

ex opere operato, operantis (L. on the part of the work, on the part of the worker) Theological terms which distinguish between an act and the one performing the act. The grace of the sacraments does not depend on the doer but on the deed itself, i.e., by the reception of the sacrament. The term *ex opere operantis* refers to the priest's right in conferring the sacrament, *ex opere operato* refers to validity. Thus regardless of whether or not the one administering the sacrament is in the state of grace, the sacrament itself is always valid as far as the one receiving is concerned, its fruitfulness depends on the worthiness of the reception.

ex voto (L. *votum,* vow, solemn promise to God) 1. That which has been vowed, a votive offering. 2. In general, a prayer, a wish, desire, as in something we do *ex voto.*

Exaltation of the Cross A second-class feast celebrated on Sept. 14.

examen (L. *exigere,* to weigh accurately) That examination of conscience usually made daily, which is not necessarily connected with confession. It is called *particular* when directed against a particular fault, and *general* when directed to all faults or sins.

examination of a bishop The series of questions put to a bishop-elect before his consecration, concerning rejection of false doctrine, obedience to the authority of the Church and the episcopal life.

examination of conscience *See* conscience, examination of.

examiners, synodal An office established by the Council of Trent to provide members of the clergy to conduct competitive examinations or a *concursus* (*q.v.*) and in some cases, other types of examinations. The minimum number required for each diocese is six; they are elected at a diocesan synod. They are sometimes called examiners of the clergy.

exarch (Gr. *exarchos,* a commander) Formerly, the ruler of a Roman province. Now used in the Eastern Church as the title of one who is the deputy of a patriarch. *Also* eparch.

exarchate That territory or group of churches ruled by an exarch. *Also* eparchy.

excardination The legal and canonical release of a cleric from one jurisdiction in order that he may be incardinated under another jurisdiction.

Excellency A term of address (Your Excellency) and reference (His Excellency) used for archbishops, bishops and certain other prelates.

exceptional children Those children who need special care and training because of some physical or mental difference which sets them apart from ordinary children. The term does not refer only to mentally retarded children or to physically handicapped children but includes also gifted and intelligent children who are exceptional for their age or educational level and thus need special attention.

exclaustration (L. *extra,* outside; *claustrum,* cloister) An indult granted by ecclesiastical authority allowing a religious to live outside his or her religious house but retaining the obligations of vows and affiliation with the religious community.

excommunication A censure by which a person is deprived of communion with the faithful of the Church. Excommunications are of two types: 1. *shunned* (*vitundi*), if he is completely excluded from communion with the faithful; 2. *tolerated* (*tolerati*). Only the Holy See has the power under present discipline to declare a person shunned. A person who is tolerated may assist passively at divine liturgical rites.

exeat (L. he may leave) A letter of excardination necessary for a priest to leave one diocese and become incardinated in another.

execution *See* capital punishment.

exegesis (Gr. *exegeisthai,* to interpret) The critical interpretation of the Bible (*q.v.*). The scholar who practices this interpretation is called an "exegete."

exegete A scriptural scholar who deals in exegesis, i.e., interpretation of the Bible.

exempt 1. For an ecclesiastical person, corporation or institution to be released from the authority of his immediate superior and placed under the authority of a higher superior. 2. To be free from the obligation to obey a particular law or regulation.

exequatur (L. he may perform) A right claimed by civil rulers to examine papal commissions and to decide whether they would take effect in their territories. This claim was condemned by Pius IX in his *Syllabus of Errors.*

exequial (L. *exsequi,* to follow) The requiem Mass said at a funeral. It is followed by the absolutions and burial.

exercise, spiritual Prayer or any other religious act required by a systematic approach to Christian perfection. *The Spiritual Exercises* is the title of a work on the spiritual life by St. Ignatius Loyola.

existence Being, either actual or potential. The act of being in the real order. That quality of a being which is the first object of the judgment.

Existence of God, Arguments for Arguments for the existence of God depend upon our accepting two truths that are self-evident: (*a*) Our reason and senses can generally be trusted; (*b*) All effects have causes. Granted that these axioms are true, the following statements can be made. 1. Motion exists in the universe, therefore there must be a Prime Mover. 2. Order exists in the universe, so there must be a Planner. 3. Certain natural laws exist, so there must be a Lawgiver. 4. From the effects which exist, we reason that there must be a

First Cause. 5. Dependent, contingent, unnecessary beings exist, so there must be an Independent, Necessary Being. Of all these, perhaps the second, the one on Order, appeals most to the modern mind. Science gives us continual evidence of greater mysteries, greater planning, more marvelous order in the universe. Could blind chance have invented the human eye or ear, the evolutionary growth of life on earth, the development of a human embryo from single cells to an unbelievably complex, purposeful, structure containing human life, an individual person, a world in itself, with the power to think and choose and love? How did the electrons get into the atom? Who planned the transformations of matter and energy? From these first proofs of the existence of God, one can go on to others proving that God is a Person, that He is good and that He has certain attributes such as omnipotence and omniscience.

existentialism A term used to designate a certain philosophical attitude or school that has come into prominence since the end of World War I. This is not a single philosophical school, but refers rather to a trend in philosophical thought which had its beginnings in Germany and France. The philosophers who call themselves existentialists, as well as those who are named such by others, profess a variety of thoughts. Central to existentialist thought is the contingency of man's existence. The stress is on the concrete particular existence of each man. The existentialist is not worried about what man is, so much as he is concerned with what man becomes; what man makes of himself becomes his essence. Man's existence comes first and man's nature comes only later from his use of human freedom. Thus Sören Kierkegaard sees man as a synthesis of infinite and finite, of temporal and eternal, of freedom and necessity. Martin Heidegger says that man is a shepherd of being, and that the substance of man is existence. Jean-Paul Sartre writes that man is nothing else than his plan; he exists only to the extent that he fulfills himself and is nothing else than the totality of his acts. Existentialists vary widely in fundamental beliefs, some professing atheism while others are believers in God. Other existentialist thinkers are Karl Jaspers, Gabriel Marcel and Albert Camus.

Exodus (Gr. *exodos,* going out) The second book of the Pentateuch, a continuation of Genesis. It has a varied content, containing historical narrative, poems, songs, folk tales, laws, genealogical lists, etc. The book is divided roughly into four parts: 1. Israel's attempt to escape Egypt; 2. the exodus from Egypt to Sinai; 3. the covenant of Sinai; 4. the erection of Yahweh's dwelling.

exorcism (Gr. *exorkizein,* bind with an oath) 1. The expelling of evil spirits in cases of possession and obsession according to the rite prescribed in the Roman Ritual, and presently performed by a priest with the permission of his bishop. 2. Lesser exorcisms are used in the ceremony of Baptism and in blessing water and salt. This exorcism does not imply possession.

exorcist The second of the minor orders which in the past gave the recipient power to expel the Devil in the ceremony of exorcism and to take charge of the water needed for divine service. Exorcisms today are reserved to priests. In the Eastern Orthodox Church, exorcists are not ordained.

expiation (L. *expiare,* to appease) 1. That act whereby Christ made complete satisfaction for the sins of men. 2. In general, to atone for sin.

explicit Clear, definite, not hidden; usually referring to faith or truth. The ability to give a reasonable explanation, including knowledge of the details.

exposition A ceremony, either private or solemn, whereby the Blessed Sacrament is removed from the altar tabernacle for the adoration of the faithful.

exposition of relics The display of relics of a saint (and in certain cases of the beatified) for veneration by the faithful. The relic is kept in its reliquary and is flanked on both sides by lighted candles. Relics cannot be exposed for veneration on the same altar where the Blessed Sacrament is exposed.

Exsultet The great Easter hymn of praise sung by the deacon in which he invites all heaven and earth to join with him in the song of joy. He asks the grace of Easter for the Church and her children. He prays for the pope, the bishop and all the people of God. The hymn is sung during the Easter Vigil service, following the entrance of the lighted Easter candle.

Extension Lay Volunteers A lay apostolate organization dedicated to service in the American home missions. Founded in 1960 under the patronage of Albert Cardinal Meyer of Chicago, the ELV is a department of the Catholic Church Extension Society of the United States of America. Single laymen as well as married couples aged 21 to 45 are accepted for service in the United States or her territories. One may serve as a teacher, parish worker, nurse, campus or Newman Club volunteer, promotional worker or secretary. Headquarters: 1307 South Wabash Avenue, Chicago 5, Ill.

Extension Society, Catholic Church An organization established in 1905 to assist the extension of the Church in the United States, principally through the collection and disbursement of alms. The organization is under the direction of the American hierarchy which operates through a board composed of resident archbishops and elected members. The official publication is *Extension. See* Extension Lay Volunteers.

extern A member of a cloistered order who lives outside the cloister but within the convent. An extern is the contact with the outside world. She answers the door, does the shopping and handles any business that must be done outside the convent. Such a Sister wears a different habit than the cloistered Sister.

extra Ecclesiam nulla salus (L. outside the Church there is no salvation). *See* salvation and unbelievers.

extra-liturgical worship *See* paraliturgical.

Extraordinary Ecclesiastical Affairs, Sacred Congregation of Established by Pope Pius VII in 1814. Its task is to erect and divide dioceses and to appoint bishops in those cases in which it is necessary to take these matters up with civil governments, and to discuss those matters referred to it by the pope, especially those dealing with civil laws, concordats, or other agreements entered into between the Holy See and different countries.

Extreme Unction *See* Anointing of the Sick.

Ezechiel An Old Testament prophet, son of Buzi, the priest. He was one of the captives taken from Jerusalem to Babylonia in 597 B.C. Five years later in Babylonia he had a vision of a heavenly chariot and received his commission from God. In his teaching, he announced the punishment of Jerusalem for her sins and prophesied the restoration of Israel.

Ezechiel, Book of An Old Testament book that relates the vision of Ezechiel and his prophecies. The book has been considerably re-edited and additions have been made. However, the contents are essentially the work of the prophet. The book is especially important for its teaching on the new covenant and the new temple, which was fulfilled by Christ Himself.

Ezra Esdra (*q.v.*).

F

fabric (L. fabrica)   1. Church building and its furnishings. 2. Funds for repair, reconstruction, maintenance as distinct from the funds for the living of the priest and curates. 3. One who has charge of maintenance.

faculties *See* faculties, canonical; faculty.

faculties, canonical   The permissions or commissions given to a deacon, priest or bishop by a legitimate superior to use the sacred powers he possesses by reason of his ordination or consecration, e.g., the faculties to hear confessions and to preach.

faculties of the soul   Powers by means of which the soul operates. St. Thomas lists: 1. the sensory faculties, which act through a bodily organ, (*a*) external senses, (*b*) internal senses, (*c*) sensory appetites; 2. the vegetative faculties, comprising the achievements of nutrition, growth and procreation; 3. locomotive faculty; 4. the rational faculties, intellect and will found only in man.

faculty   A faculty is a power, authority or permission to act. 1. In scholastic philosophy, a power of the soul that enables it to act. Each faculty is an ability or active potency to perform a certain act or actions. The nature of each faculty determines the actions that it enables the soul to per-form. The faculties are accidents inhering in the soul, which is a substance. Examples of the faculties of man's soul are: intellect and will. 2. In canon law, authority, privilege or permission to perform an act or function. In a restricted sense, it means the conferring on a subordinate, by a superior, of certain ecclesiastical rights, denied to him by the common law.

faith   A gift of God, a share in his Divine vision by which the person exercising it has the virtue or strength to believe what God reveals because of God's authority in revealing truth.

faith, act of   Generally, this act is a person's response to the grace of faith. In it a person strives to understand, believe and live the truths God reveals. More specifically, this act is a man's firm assent to any formal, authoritative teaching of Church doctrine because of the Church's power to interpret revelation.

faith and morals   There is an essential connection between faith and morals. "The just man lives by faith." Although man's morality is rooted in the natural law, revelation was necessary in order to bring to his attention the important moral obligations. These revealed truths are believed by faith. In addition, faith spurs and mo-

225

tivates the believer to a moral life pleasing to God, to a strong trust in God and His infinite Mercy, and to that greatest essential of all, the love for God.

faith and reason (*See* science and religion) Faith and reason are two sharply distinct modes of attaining to knowledge of truth. The first of these, faith, begins and ends with the action of God. Reason begins and ends in our own action. In the words of Vatican Council I: "Faith is a supernatural virtue, by which, guided and aided by divine grace, we hold as true what God has revealed, not because we have perceived its intrinsic truth by our reason but because of the authority of God who can neither deceive nor be deceived." Reason, on the other hand, is a natural power by which, guided by the rules of logic or intellection, we arrive at new truths because they are perceived to be intrinsically contained in or follow from some original truth already known. Faith and reason insofar as they both attain to truth can never be at odds with one another. It is only when error creeps in that a conflict appears.

faith and works Faith without works is a dead faith (James 2:26). The existence of faith is a purely internal act; the existence of works proves the existence of faith which produces them.

faithful, the Those members of the Church who have been baptized in contrast to those members who have not been baptized, such as catechumens. In other words, those people who have been accepted into the Community of the Church through the rite of Baptism are called the faithful. The faithful are united to Christ and to each other in the Mystical Body (*q.v.*).

falda A papal garment made of white silk with a long train that is worn over the cassock on solemn occasions.

faldstool Portable folding chair of wood or metal without a back, used at pontifical functions by a bishop in the sanctuary when he is not at his throne, also called a genuflexorium. It is also used as a kneeling bench for liturgical functions.

Fall of man The account in Genesis of how the first woman was induced by a serpent to eat of forbidden fruit and how she persuaded her husband to do the same. As a result God drove them from the Garden of Eden, and sin entered the world. The Genesis account can be interpreted in three ways: literally, symbolically and a mixture of the literal and symbolic. Few scriptural scholars accept the Genesis account as a literal, detailed, historical account. By the Fall man was cut off from supernatural grace so that neither he nor his descendants could enjoy the vision of God except for the Redemption by Jesus Christ. Catholics may not hold that the Fall was a gradual evolution away from God but must believe that our first parents committed serious sin that led to disinheritance of themselves and their progeny.

fall of the angels Neither the Old nor New Testament is clear on the cause of the fall of the angels. The most that can be said is that they were punished for some sin, possibly a revolt against God. Since God does not force the love of his creatures, it is logical that He put free will to some test. How the angels were tested is unknown. Those who failed the test were driven from heaven. These fallen angels have Satan (Lucifer) as their leader.

fallen nature The state in which every man exists prior to God's infusion of sanctifying grace into his soul. It is the inheritance of all men since Adam's fall from grace, from which Christ redeemed mankind.

false witness Perjury is the crime of taking a false oath, or making a false statement supported by an oath. A false oath in addition to the evil of a lie contains the evil of a sin against the virtue of religion, which of itself is always a grievous sin.

false worship The practice of superstition by worshiping the true God either in an unfit or false way; the worshiping of a false god; or rendering worship, in whatever way, to a creature rather than to the true God.

fame (L. *fama,* report) Fame is a lofty reputation or name. It carries the notion of a person's being renowned or well-known. Fame does not have to connote a good reputation.

familiar An old term for a domestic employed by and living in a religious household, e.g., a seminary, a monastery, a bishop's household, etc.

family Bible A Bible which has a special section in which can be recorded family history such as births, baptisms, marriages, deaths, etc.

Family Rosary The recitation of the Rosary in common as a family prayer. The devotion is promoted by the Family Rosary Crusade under the motto, "The family that prays together, stays together."

family, the The first of all societies, prior to the state (like the family, a natural society) and having as its example and guide the Church (a supernatural society). Christian marriage, the foundation of the Christian

family, is holy, a great sacrament, conferring three blessings: 1. the blessing of children; 2. the blessing of mutual faithfulness between husband and wife; and 3. the blessing of the sacrament, which gives grace. The family was founded by God at the beginning of the world, and it was blessed by Christ as a sacrament— Christ who declared plainly that marriage was indissoluble, thus giving stability to the family and security to wife and children. The family in a larger sense includes not only parents and children, but grandparents and other relatives who may or may not live in the same house or in the neighborhood. Clean moral living as well as financial security and care of children are more likely found in a closely knit clan, with relatives ready to give a helping hand in sickness or need, and ready also to censure a member who begins to deviate from rules of decent living. The education of children is the right of the family, and no state can abrogate this right. It is the parents' sacred duty and absolute obligation under God to see to the education of their children and their training as Christians on their way to heaven. Children are talents, entrusted to the parents by God who will demand a return of the loan with interest on the day of reckoning. Many modern conditions hinder holy family life: apartments or houses too small and too expensive; mothers who go to work outside the home from choice, not need, who neglect their children during the day, and are too exhausted at night to mother them; inducements to adultery and divorce on every side; drinking, gambling and dissipation; teenage "going steady" with subsequent ill-prepared and unsuitable marriage; birth control (*q.v.*) and refusal to have children; unemployment of the father; inadequate wages, particularly when wife and children have extravagant tastes; "keeping up with the Joneses" and so on. A living wage is necessary for the family, and it means not only enough for the support of the man himself, but enough to keep his wife and children, enough to pay for education and modest recreation; enough to put by something for sickness, unemployment, old age and death. A family home can be a happy place reflecting heaven, or a hell on earth, depending upon the good will and grace of those who live in it. Membership in a family apostolic movement is a great help in initiating and preserving good Christian life. *See* Cana Conference; Christian Family Movement.

fan In the early Church, a liturgical instrument used to keep insects away from the sacred vessels. Now, a large flat spread of feathers, serving only an ornamental purpose, mounted on a long staff and carried in papal processions by an attendant. It is also called a flabellum.

fanon Capelike vestment made of two pieces of white silk with narrow red and gold stripes, placed over the alb on the shoulders. It is worn by the pope when celebrating Pontifical High Mass.

farcing (L. *farcire,* to fill up) The medieval practice of inserting or repeating texts or words between verses of a psalm or canticle. It became an abuse and is no longer practiced.

fast (OE. *fasten,* observance) 1. The act or period of fasting. 2. An ancient practice of asceticism by which the use of food and drink are limited. It is done as a penance, a mortification, a means of gaining control of sensuous appetites. *See* abstinence; fast, Eucharistic; fasting.

fast, Eucharistic According to the revised regulations established in 1964 the following rules pertain to the Eucharistic fast. 1. *Water.* May be taken anytime before Communion since it does not break the fast. 2. *Food.* May be eaten one hour before the time when Communion will be received. 3. *Alcoholic beverages.* May be taken up to 3 hours before the time when Communion will be received. 4. *Nonalcoholic beverages.* May be taken up to one hour before the time Communion will be received. 5. *The sick.* Even for those not confined to bed, nonalcoholic beverage and true medicine—whether liquid or solid, even if the medicine contains alcohol—may be taken up to the time for Communion. 6. *Viaticum.* No fast is required. 7. These rules oblige all whenever they receive the Holy Eucharist, even at Midnight Mass. 8. Priests who binate or trinate may take nonalcoholic beverages between Masses.

fasting To refrain from food. Fasting must be distinguished from abstinence (*q.v.*). All over 21 years and under 59 are obliged to fast unless exempt or dispensed. Days of fast only are all weekdays of Lent including Holy Saturday, excepting Ash Wednesday, Fridays; Ember Wednesday and Saturday. Days of fast and partial abstinence are Ember Wednesday and Saturday, the Vigil of Pentecost. Days of fast and total abstinence are Fridays of Lent, Ember Fridays, Ash Wednesday, Dec. 7, Dec. 24 (unless transferred by the bishop). On days of fast only one full meal is allowed. Two other meatless meals may be taken according to one's needs; but together they should not equal a full meal. Persons not obliged to fast may eat meat several times on days of fast which are not also days of abstinence. It is the teaching of theologians that the law of fasting is a positive precept. Therefore a man who has broken his fast, whether through his own fault or not, does not commit a new sin by taking a third or fourth meal; thus a fast once broken does not have to be resumed that day. *See* abstinence.

Father   1. The First Person of the Trinity, the Creator of heaven and earth. He who begets a coeternal and coequal Son, the Word. By Divine adoption God is our Father and we are His children. 2. A title originally reserved for members of a mendicant or religious order but which now is used for all Catholic priests in English-speaking countries. The name originates from the function of the minister, that of begetting the faithful, as the bestowal of the sacraments creates a type of paternal relationship. Thus the name helps to signify what a priest is really doing as he performs his ministry.

Father of Lies   The Devil (Jn. 8:44). This is a very common figure of speech in the East, where a man is often thus addressed from a notable characteristic or the goods he deals in. The Devil tempted the first man with a lie and in doing so helped him to sin.

Fathers of the Church   1. The Apostolic Fathers of the Church. Those Christian writers of the first and second centuries who had some connections with the Apostles and whose writings reflect apostolic teachings. Among these Fathers are SS. Ignatius, Clement and Polycarp, disciple of St. John. 2. Those theologians of the first eight centuries who are celebrated for both sanctity and scholarship. St. Gregory the Great (d. 604) is the last Father of the West, while St. John Damascene (d. 749) is the last Father in the East. The acceptance by the Fathers of a doctrine indicates that it belongs to the deposit of faith (*q.v.*) left by the Apostles. To be a Father of the Church the person must have lived in the early centuries of the Church, have led a holy life, have taught and written with wisdom and truth, and have at least the consensus of approval of the Church.

Fathers of the Desert   Hermits (also called ascetics or monks) who renounced the world to lead a more perfect Christian life in the Egyptian deserts beginning in the 3rd century. Most of these hermits were not priests. They chose the desert as a dwelling place because they believed it to be the only environment in which they could fulfill their ascetical ideals. The names most prominently connected with this early form of monasticism are St. Paul of Thebes (d. 347) and St. Anthony (251–356). St. Paul, the earliest leader of the monks in the desert, is said to have lived in a cave for ninety years. St. Anthony lived alone for years on the banks of the Nile River; eventually, however, so many disciples gathered around him that he agreed to organize them into a community life. To each monk he gave a solitary cell, the whole group was called together at stated times for spiritual exercises in common. St. Athanasius wrote the life of St. Anthony, a volume that exerted tremendous influence on the development of monasticism.

Fatima   Shrine of Our Lady in Portugal which commemorates her apparitions there to three children. These apparitions took place in 1917 and are said to have been verified by many miracles.

fear   An agitation of the mind, often with physical effects, produced by a present or threatened evil to oneself or another. Grave fear does not remove responsibility for an act unless it is so grave that it destroys reason; however, it may lessen responsibility. A grave fear can invalidate contracts, thus agreement to marriage given under conditions of grave fear would be invalid.

fear of God "The fear of the Lord is the lesson of wisdom" (Prov. 15:33). There are two kinds of fear of God. 1. *Servile fear* is the agitation of mind that results from knowledge of the punishment due because of sin. 2. *Reverential fear* is the agitation of mind that results from the dread of losing or offending God because of sin. Although the Bible makes frequent mention of fear of God, our motives in serving God should not be based on fear but on love.

feast, cardinal A feast that is followed by a series of Sundays with the name of the feast; i.e., Easter, Pentecost, Epiphany.

feast of nine lessons For certain more solemn feasts of the Church, the Divine Office has nine lessons to be read at Matins. On days of lesser feasts there are three lessons.

feast of Our Lady A day set aside for special commemoration of Our Lady or some event connected with her. On such a day the liturgy makes special mention of her and gives particular veneration (dulia). Feasts of Our Lady are Purification (Feb. 2), Apparition at Lourdes (Feb. 11), Annunciation (Mar. 25), Visitation (July 2), Our Lady of Mount Carmel (July 16), Our Lady of the Snow (Aug. 5), Assumption (Aug. 15), Immaculate Heart (Aug. 22), Nativity (Sept. 8), Name of Mary (Sept. 12), Seven Sorrows (Sept. 15), Our Lady of Ransom (Sept. 24), Our Lady of the Rosary (Oct.

7), Maternity (Oct. 11), Presentation (Nov. 21) and Immaculate Conception (Dec. 8). In addition there are other feasts that are particular to certain dioceses and religious orders.

feast of Our Lord A day set aside for special commemoration and worship of Our Lord because of some event or mystery connected with Him. Feasts of Our Lord are Circumcision (Jan. 1), Holy Name (Sunday between Jan. 1-6, otherwise Jan. 2), Epiphany (Jan. 6), Holy Family (Sunday after Epiphany), Easter, Finding of the Holy Cross (May 3), Ascension (forty days after Easter), Corpus Christi (Thursday after Trinity Sunday), Sacred Heart (second Friday after Corpus Christi), the Precious Blood (July 1), Transfiguration (Aug. 6), Exaltation of the Holy Cross (Sept. 14), Christ the King (last Sunday of Oct.), Christmas (Dec. 25).

feast of precept Holyday of obligation.

feast, proper A feast is said to be proper to a certain place if it celebrates the titular saint of the place, the patron of the place, a saint whose body or major relic is preserved there, or a saint who has some particular or important relationship to the place. Feasts proper to the United States are St. Peter Claver (Sept. 9), St. Isaac Jogues and Companions (Sept. 26), St. Isidore the Farmer (Oct. 25), St. Frances Xavier Cabrini (Nov. 13), and Our Lady of Guadalupe (Dec. 12). In addition there are many feasts proper to particular dioceses in the United States and to some religious orders and congregations.

feast, suppressed Feasts that were formerly holy days of obligation. They are: Easter Monday and Tuesday, Pentecost Monday and Tuesday, Finding of the Cross (May 3), Purifi-

cation (Feb. 2), Annunciation (Mar.
25), Nativity of the Blessed Virgin
(Sept. 8), St. Michael (Sept. 29), St.
John the Baptist (June 24), St. Stephen (Dec. 26), Holy Innocents (Dec.
28), St. Anne (July 26), the principal
feast of each Apostle, the patron of
the country, the patron of the locality, the titular feast of the parish.

feasts, rank of The revision of rubrics for Mass issued by the Sacred
Congregation of Rites in 1960 sys-
tematizes and clarifies all prior legislation. 1. Sunday Masses. These are
of two ranks, first class (during Advent and Lent) and second class (all
others). 2. Feasts of Our Lord, the
Blessed Virgin, the Apostles, some
Evangelists and a few other saints
are ranked as first and second class.
3. Feasts of the saints, generally
speaking, are ranked as third class.
A less solemn way of giving a saint
honor is as a commemoration (by
adding a Prayer, Secret Prayer and
Postcommunon Prayer in their honor
to those of another Mass). 4. Ferial
Masses have four classes: 1st class,
Ash Wednesday and all weekdays
of Holy Week; 2nd class, Ember days
and the last eight days of Advent;
3rd class, days in Lent and Advent
except for the last eight days; 4th
class, other days of the year that do
not have a proper feast of their own.
5. Octaves. The eight days after
Christmas, Easter and Pentecost. 6.
Vigils. The day preceding certain
feasts (Christmas, Pentecost, Ascension, Assumption, St. John the Baptist, SS. Peter and Paul, St. Lawrence) may be of first, second or third
class. *See* commemorations; Masses
for the Dead.

February Month of the Passion

federal aid to education Basically a
dispute over the interpretation of the
First Amendment to the United

States Constitution: "Congress shall
make no law respecting an establishment of religion." It is argued on historical evidence by Catholics and
others that the amendment was enacted to prevent the establishment of
a national religion but that it does not
mean, as argued by secularists, that
any cooperation with religion is opposed to the intention of the amendment. This latter interpretation is put
forth as an argument that no federal
assistance should be given to parochial schools but only to public
schools. Catholics and others who
favor aid to private schools argue
that the federal government, without
constitutional hindrance, has given
aid to church-related schools under
the GI Bill of Rights, the National
Defense Education Act, the College
Housing Program, the Federal School
Lunch Act and the Hill-Burton Act.
It is pointed out that it is an inconsistency to allow aid in higher education but not in the elementary level.
It is further argued that aid can be
given to students, if not to schools,
without any violation of constitutional conditions. Another argument
is that the denial of federal aid to
church-related schools constitutes an
abridgment, because of economic
hardship, of the freedom of parents
to provide for the education of their
children in the schools of their choice
as guaranteed by the Constitution and
stated in 1925 by the United States
Supreme Court.

Felician Sisters Founded in Poland
in 1885 by Venerable Mary Angela
Truszkowska, established in the
United States in 1874 where there
are now seven provinces, plus one in
Canada. The primary work is teaching but social work and catechetics
are also part of the apostolate. The
congregation has missions in Brazil

and staffs home missions. Simple vows are taken. There are over 4,100 Sisters in the United States.

felix culpa (L. happy fault) A term used for original sin. While the sin of our first parents was a great tragedy, it is sometimes referred to as "felix culpa" because as a result of it Christ came to earth, worked the Redemption and established His Church.

felo-de-se (L. a felon concerning oneself) A person who commits suicide while of a sound mind, i.e., the act is done deliberately as contrasted to a suicide while of unsound mind; a self-murder. *See* suicide.

ferendae sententiae (L. bearing the sentence) A censure imposed by the sentence of a judge in contrast to one imposed by the very fact of committing the act (*latae sententiae*).

feretory (feh'ray-taw'ree, L. *feretrum,* a bier) 1. A large reliquary able to be carried in procession. 2. That part of a church or chapel reserved for a shrine of a saint or where the saint's relics are kept.

feria (fe'ree-ah, L. holiday) The word as used liturgically today has lost its original meaning. It means a day of the week other than Saturday (*Sabbatum*) or Sunday (*Dominica*) when there is no feast or vigil. It is used for the days of the liturgical week thus: Monday, *Feria Secunda;* Tuesday, *Feria Tertia;* Wednesday, *Feria Quarta;* Thursday, *Feria Quinta;* Friday, *Feria Sexta.*

ferial Pertaining to a feria, as a ferial office, etc.

fermentum (L. leaven) A particle of the Host broken off during the Mass of a bishop and carried by the deacon to other churches where it was placed in the chalice at the *fractio panis*. It showed the identity of the bishop with his flock and the unity of the

Eucharistic Sacrifice. The custom was in use in the early Church but has now disappeared.

ferraiola (fair-rey-oh'lah, It.) A short cape worn over the cassock and reaching half-way down the upper arm.

ferraiolone (fer-ray-oh-lo'nah, It.) A large full-length cloak having a large flat collar, varying in color according to the wearer's rank, and forming the necessary complement of full ecclesiastical dress among Latin Catholic clergy on nonliturgical occasions.

ferule (L. *ferula,* a rod) 1. The rod formerly used to discipline penitents. 2. A discipline or punishment. 3. The imperial scepter of the Byzantine empire. 4. A staff surmounted by a cross used as a support in religious ceremonies in those days before sitting was allowed. It is still in use in choir by Maronites, and by Ethiopians and Copts.

Festival of Lights Hanukka (*q.v.*).

fetus (L. offspring) The child in the womb, a human being from the first moment of conception. To kill it, by abortion or any other way, is murder. The fetus should be baptized whenever it is expelled from the womb; although in case of doubt of life, Baptism shall be given conditionally. In case of the death of the mother, the fetus should be removed from the womb, even surgically, and be baptized.

feudalism (L. *feodum,* a fief) A system of vassalage which prevailed in Europe in the Middle Ages and which was concerned with the relationship of lord and vassal; it still prevails in modified form in some areas of Latin America. Although feudalism had a proper role at one time, it is now outmoded and unjust. The Church also at one time was part of the feudal system but because of the encroachment of secular power into spiritual matters and many other abuses, reform gradually came about and the Church became free.

fideism A philosophical system which relies on faith in opposition to reason.

Fides News Service A news-gathering and distributing agency of the Sacred Congregation for the Propagation of the Faith. Through correspondents in all parts of the mission world, Fides gathers religious news of major importance and issues it to the world press in English, Italian, Spanish, French and German editions.

Field Mass A Mass service for the faithful at a place in the country or outdoors. It is particularly applied to Mass offered outdoors by a military chaplain.

fighting Fighting (or quarreling) is wrong because it is a sin against the Fifth Commandment unless it is done in self-defense or to protect someone else. Wrestling and boxing are not wrong in themselves; however, when anger or hatred develops as a result, they do become sinful and should be stopped; they are also sinful if a deliberate attempt is made to inflict physical injury.

filiation The relationship between Jesus Christ as Son and Second Person of the Blessed Trinity and God the Father, First Person of the Trinity.

Filioque (L. and from the son) A term inserted in the Nicene Creed to describe the procession of the Holy Spirit from God the Father and from the Son. The Greeks objected to its being inserted into the Creed and to the doctrine implied. The term has long been a principal point of division between Catholics and Eastern Orthodox.

final absolution The short-form ab-

solution given as part of the Sacrament of Penance to one who is in proximate danger of death. It should be given conditionally if the person is unconscious or unable to communicate.

final perseverance The gift from God whereby one possesses the state of sanctifying grace and friendship with God at the time of death, which alone assures sufficient grace for one's salvation. God offers this gift to those frequently receiving the sacraments, offering sincere prayers daily and working actively in the service and care of others.

finding of the True Cross In 326 the Empress Helena is said to have discovered the True Cross buried in a cistern near Calvary. Her son, Emperor Constantine, built a basilica over the spot. Tradition says that the basilica was dedicated on the anniversary (Sept. 14) of the finding of the Cross. On this date the Church celebrates the Feast of the Exaltation of the Cross. There was formerly a Feast of the Finding of the Cross on May 3 but this has now been suppressed.

finite That which has a nature, character or existence subject to limitations or marked by imperfections. Man is a finite being in contrast to God who is infinite.

fire Long a symbol of purification and total oblation, fire has played an important role in many religions. In the Christian religion fire is used in three ways: 1. The blessing of the New Fire as the first ceremony of the Holy Saturday Liturgy. Adapted from the Celtic usage, this is a symbol of the life and death of Jesus Christ. All candles and lamps are extinguished on Good Friday and then relighted from the New Fire. 2. The use of candles as a mark of respect and honor. This would include the sanctuary lamp, candles used at liturgical functions, etc. This practice comes from Roman law where certain officials were preceded by lighted torches. 3. The burning of charcoal to consume incense, used during High Mass, Benediction, certain blessings, Lauds and Vespers, absolutions of the dead, etc. This symbolizes the consuming zeal of the Christian and the rising of prayers to heaven.

fire, hell In the New Testament, the principal description of hell is a place of everlasting and unquenchable fire. In the Jewish tradition fire was looked upon as a purifying agent, and something that could destroy the unclean. The term is used to describe the secondary punishment which is real and exterior to those in hell. It cannot be the same as earthly fire which consumes, because the punishment of hell is eternal.

fire, holy Fire is one of the most expressive and most ancient of liturgical symbols. Man, at an early time, saw in its mysterious nature and irresistible power a principle of heat and light for the earth. Christianity adapted this belief, seeing here the symbols of the divinity that enlightens and warms humanity. The symbolism led quite naturally to the liturgical rite by which the Church on the Eve of Easter celebrates the mystery of the Death and Resurrection of Christ, of which the extinguished and rekindled fire furnishes the expressive image.

First Blessing The blessing of a newly ordained priest, to which an indulgence is attached.

first cause A philosophical term applying to the first in any series of causes. A first principle from which things originate with dependence. A

"first being" which in some way influences "all other beings," as the reason for the existence of "all other beings." A traditional argument (taken from St. Thomas' *Summa Theologica*) demonstrates the existence of God as the First Cause of all things, and as immediately operating in all finite causality.

First Communion A term designating the reception of the Eucharist for the first time. This event usually takes place after the child has reached the age of reason (or as an adult, as is the case with converts) and after sufficient instruction on the doctrine of the Eucharist. The day on which one receives the Eucharist for the first time is called "First Communion Day," a very solemn occasion in the life of a Christian.

First Friday A devotion in which the first Friday of each month is set aside in honor of the Sacred Heart and in reparation for sin. Among the promises said to have been made to St. Margaret Mary Alacoque was that the reception of Holy Communion on nine consecutive First Fridays would gain the grace of final repentance.

first fruits A biblical term describing the fruits, vegetables and grains which ripen first and are a token of the coming harvest. The first ripe fruits, like the firstborn (usually of men, though sometimes of animals) and the firstlings (always of animals) were to be offered to God, the Creator of all life. The offering of the first ripe fruits figured prominently in the corporate worship of Israel (Lev. 23:9-21) and in individual worship (Exod. 23:19; Deut. 26:1-11). The term "first ripe" or "first fruit" was used metaphorically by several New Testament writers and came to have popular theological connotations.

fiscal procurator A diocesean official whose appointed task is to start proceedings against offenders of the law of the Church and bring them to trial in Church courts.

fish A symbol for Our Lord found  in the catacombs. The Greek word for fish is *ichthus,* and each Greek letter in this word begins a word in the phrase *Iesous Christos, Theou Uios, Soter* (Jesus Christ, Son of God, Savior).

Fisherman, Ring of the The official papal ring. It is engraved with a picture of St. Peter fishing from a boat. Around the edge of the ring is engraved the pope's name. It is used to seal briefs, and is destroyed on the death of the pope.

fistula (L. tube) A type of tube or straw once used by the faithful to sip the sacred species from the chalice. Today it is the golden tube used at solemn papal Masses by means of which the pope receives the Precious Blood while standing at his throne.

Five Wounds, the There were five prominent wounds in Our Lord's body at His crucifixion: in His feet, hands and side. They are an object of special veneration and in some places are venerated on the fourth Friday of Lent.

flabella (L. fans) Fans made of ostrich feathers and set 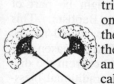 on long poles. When the pope is carried on the *sedia gestatoria* and wearing pontifical vestments, a flabellum is to be seen on either side of the papal chair. No longer used as fans, the flabella are hardly more than decorations.

flagellants Any group which fanatically or excessively inflicts, on itself or others, scourging by rod or whip as penance. Mostly found among primitive peoples. Self-flagellation traces back to the 13th century as a common penitential practice among religious orders. The practice was prohibited by papal order in 1261. Popularized again after the Black Death plague, the flagellants were condemned by Pope Clement VI in 1349.

flectamus genua (fleck-tah′mus ge′ new-ah, L. let us bend the knee) A versicle used during Masses on Ember Days and in Holy Week as a prefactory bidding for certain prayers. The response is, *"Levate"* (arise).

Flood, the The Deluge. The rain of waters upon earth for forty days by an Act of God as narrated in Genesis 6:9; 8:14. It signifies: 1. punishment for the unrepenting sinners; 2. the ark of Noe was a means of freeing and protecting those who had remained faithful to God from the prevailing corruption. God set these people apart as ancestors of the Chosen People. The ark is a type or symbol of the Church, which is divinely appointed by God as the means of mankind's salvation. The Flood, while described in cosmic terms, was local in nature. Parallel ancient records attest to the biblical account of a great flood.

Florida The 27th State to be admitted to the Union (1845). It is 22nd in area and 10th in population. It was discovered by Ponce de Leon during the Easter season in 1513, and was named for *Pascua Florida,* "flowery Easter." St. Augustine, the oldest city in the U.S., was founded in 1565. The earliest Spanish settlers were killed by Indians, and several Dominican missioners were martyred. Jesuits and Franciscans later did missionary work there, and the leading tribe, the Apalachee, were entirely converted, but they were all slaughtered by the English and their Indian allies, and a number of the missioners were killed, so the missions were abandoned. The Seminoles arrived in 1750 and fought the whites who tried to drive them out during the next century. A small band, never conquered, still live in the Everglades. Florida was ruled in turn by Spanish, French and English, and it sided with England during the Revolution. After the war, the Church was again introduced, as Irish priests from their college in Salamanca came in 1783 to care for Spanish and Irish Catholics. In 1821 Florida was acquired by the United States; Andrew Jackson was then governor. In 1825 Father Michael Portier was made Vicar Apostolic of Alabama and Florida. At the time of the Civil War, Florida seceded with the Southern States. After the war, as immigrants from Europe poured in, the diocese of St. Augustine was established with Most Rev. Augustin Verot as first bishop (1870–1876). Religious communities set up schools and charitable institutions, and carried on missionary work. Florida has 2 dioceses, 176 parishes and 77 missions. Catholics number over one-tenth of a total population of 5 million. Special attention is given to numbers of elderly people who retire there, to the young through Newman Clubs at Colleges, and to the Apostolate of the Word through such groups as the Daughters of St. Paul.

flowers, altar Natural or artificial flowers may be used for decoration of the altar, especially during festival days. They must be removed when Mass or Office of the season is said in Advent, Lent and other penitential times, and at Requiem Masses. They may not be put upon the altar table itself.

flowers, blessing of In the *Rituale Romanum* is a form for blessing flowers and fruit on the Feast of the Assumption.

flowers, funeral The use of flowers at the funeral of an adult is discouraged though not forbidden.

folk religion The religious beliefs and practices of an ethnic group or a small, isolated section of society as distinguished from that theological religion practiced by a more sophisticated people.

font A permanent receptacle for baptismal water, generally placed near the entrance of a church, symbolizing the entrance of the new Christian into the Church, the Mystical Body of Christ.

font, blessing of the The solemn blessing of baptismal water takes place at the Easter Vigil on Holy Saturday night. The liturgy recalls the wonders done by God through the use of water, and candidates for Baptism may be baptized at that time. Vatican Council II decreed that a somewhat shorter form of blessing should be drawn up for use during the conferring of Baptism, so that the blessing of the water with its rich doctrinal content might be part of the ceremony of Baptism. This shorter rite, however, would not be used during the Easter season, for nothing should detract from the dignity of the ancient traditional blessing of water at the Easter Vigil.

forbidden books *See* Index of Forbidden Books.

forbidden degrees Those degrees of relationship whether by blood (consanguinity) or marriage (affinity) within which it is forbidden to contract matrimony. In the case of blood no dispensation can be given in the direct line. In the collateral line, no dispensation can be given in the first degree (brother and sister). In the case of affinity, no dispensation is given in the direct line (i.e., for an ancestor or descendant of a deceased partner); in the collateral line the impediment extends to the second degree but a dispensation may be given for the first or second degrees.

force   *See* violence.

foreign missions   Those areas outside the United States, as contrasted to the "home missions," where missioners work to bring Christianity to the people. The term generally refers to Africa, Asia, Oceania and Latin America; more accurately, it includes those areas under the Congregation of the Propagation of the Faith. Actually, the distinction is artificial since the mission of the Church is one and indivisible. Every Catholic by Baptism has a role in the mission of the Church, namely, in making Christ known, in establishing His Church and in giving the opportunity of living a complete and full life of Faith to those people who have never heard the Good News of salvation. However, because of His needs, God gives some people the vocation to work as a foreign missioner—to leave home, country and family in order to preach the Gospel and build up the native Church. The role of the foreign missioner is achieved in the establishment and flowering of this native Church.

forgiveness   The taking back into favor of one by whom another has been injured in some way. In the spiritual sense this refers to God's restored friendship for a person who

has lost it because of serious sin. Forgiveness does not necessarily involve the remission of punishment.

forgiveness of sin   The guilt and stain of sin can be removed by the absolution given in the Sacrament of Penance. Sorrow for sin and purpose of amendment are necessary conditions. A perfect act of contrition can also bring about the forgiveness of sin. Finally, sin is forgiven when the Sacrament of Baptism is received. It is Catholic teaching that although the sins have been forgiven, the temporal punishment due these sins may remain.

forgotten sins   Those not recalled during one's confession. They are forgiven by the absolution of that confession but in the case of mortal sins there still exists the obligation to confess them in the first confession after they have been remembered.

form   (L. *formis*)   1. In philosophy and theology, the formal, intrinsic cause which constitutes the nature of things, e.g., the soul is the form of the body. 2. In sacramental theology, one of the two elements of any sacrament. The form of a sacrament is the words of the minister of a sacrament which determines the sacramental sign; e.g., in Baptism the form is: "I baptize you in the Name of the Father, and of the Son, and of the Holy Spirit." *See* matter.

formale   A morse (*q.v.*).

formalism   A religious overconcern with the external aspects of worship or devotion or with the mere speculative content of religion; an incongruity between the externals of religion and the internal, motivating spirit.

fortitude   (L. *fortis,* strength)   A gift of the Holy Spirit and a cardinal virtue. As a gift of the Holy Spirit it endows its possessor with strength to pursue spiritual good in the face of difficulties. As a virtue it is strength of soul, firmness in the practice of virtue in the pursuit of good. It is that strength which overcomes fear of not doing right. It prompts us to be brave in the face of obstacles to the performance of duty.

fortune-telling The pretense to know and foretell the future, or the destiny of individuals. Some means used include astrology, crystal-gazing, reading palms, numerology, and the inspection of cards, tea leaves, etc. It can be a grave sin of either divination or superstition, against the virtue of religion. There is no divination if the religious element is wanting. The moral malice or moral defect in any case may lie in the irrationality and folly of the practices which are a clear indication of the weakness of the religious penetration of thought and life. Instead of turning wholeheartedly to God in loving trust of His providence, one attempts, even though it may be only half-heartedly, to seek His good fortune in stupid practices.

Forty Hours A devotion that arose in Renaissance Italy as a means of promoting reparation and atonement through the cult of the Blessed Sacrament. The Sacred Host is solemnly exposed for a period of forty hours in parish churches and in other churches and chapels where the Blessed Sacrament is usually reserved. This devotion, to which various ceremonies and prayers are attached, takes place once a year in each church, at a time designated by the local ordinary. It is customary that the days set aside for this devotion be so established that the Blessed Sacrament is exposed in at least one church or chapel in the diocese each day of the year.

forum In canon law, the exercise of jurisdiction over the faithful. The internal forum (also called the forum of conscience) refers to the private good of the faithful, governing their private actions as individuals in their relationship to God. The external forum refers to the public good of the faithful and governs their social actions as members of the Church.

forum competens (L. proper court) An ecclesiastical judge is a *forum competens* when he has the authority to hear a particular case. The local bishop is the *forum competens* in causes of first instance; the metropolitan, in causes of appeal.

forum, external The Church acts in the external forum when she exercises her juridical authority over temporal and spiritual affairs of groups or individuals as members of society. In this tribunal the accused is absolved or condemned exclusively on the basis of the evidence.

forum, internal That which is concerned directly with the sanctification of souls and deals with matters of conscience of the individual. In the internal forum the judge relies on the penitent who accuses or excuses himself, unless the contrary is evident. Generally, the Church acts in the internal forum in the Sacrament of Penance. This is the sacramental forum. There is also the extrasacramental forum or forum of conscience which is outside the Sacrament of Penance. The forum of conscience is that in which everything dealt with outside the Sacrament of Penance and related to the spiritual welfare of the individual is exercised. Absolution from censures (ecclesiastical penalties) and certain dispensations are given in this forum.

forum, privilege of the The exemption of clerics from secular courts in all cases. Only the pope can remove the exemption for cardinals, legates, bishops and certain other clerics. Unless the local bishop has a grave reason, he should allow an ecclesiastic to be cited in civil court, especially if the plaintiff is a lay person.

fossor (fos'ser; L. digger) A representation in relief of a gravedigger found in the crypts of the catacombs.

foundation Masses The stipends for these Masses are received from canonically established endowments. The bishop or provincial council decides the sum for the Masses and how it is to be invested and administered.

Four Horsemen, the Refers to Apoc. 6:1-8. The first horseman is usually interpreted as being War; the others are Civil Strife, Famine and Plague. Some of the Fathers considered the first (white) horse to be the conquering Christ.

four last things Death, Judgment, Heaven, Hell. That branch of theology which deals with them is called eschatology (*q.v.*).

Fourth Gospel, the Another name for the Gospel of St. John.

fraction, the (L. *fractio,* breaking) The breaking of the Host, the sacred bread, takes place in the Latin Mass between the Lord's Prayer and the Agnus Dei. The Host is broken in half, with a third piece, quite small, broken from the piece in the left hand and mixed with the Precious Blood.

France It is uncertain when Christianity first reached Roman Gaul, but in 177 there was a Christian community at Lyons which was persecuted. The country was evangelized by missioners from Rome and religious community life was introduced by St. Martin of Tours (315–397). As the nation was united, the French royal house remained ardently loyal to the Holy See through the Middle Ages, earning for the French king the title of "Most Christian Majesty" and for the French nation the name "Eldest Daughter of the Church." In the 16th century, Lutheranism, Calvanism, Jansenism and Gallicanism weakened the Church. There was a revival in the 17th century led by Jean Olier and his Sulpicians, and by St. Vincent de Paul and St. Francis de Sales with the missionary spirit revealed in America and the Far East. The 18th century was a period of great trouble for the Church with the Constituent Assembly confiscating Church property and dissolving religious orders and with the establishment of the "Civil Constitution of the Clergy" which allowed the people themselves to nominate priests and bishops without contact with Rome. Relief came under the Concordat of Napoleon in 1799. In 1905 the government abrogated the Concordat, and Church and State were separated. Diplomatic relations with the Holy See were resumed in 1920. The position of the Church gradually strengthened and there has been a revival of Catholic intellectual life. French theologians and apostolic movements have been in the forefront of the modern Church. In the nation as a whole secularism has great influence and there has been widespread apostasy from religion.

Francis, Rule of St. There are three Franciscan Rules, for the Friars, the nuns and the Lay Tertiaries respectively. The definitive Rule for the Friars is that of 1223. Franciscan life is summed up in these words: "To observe the Holy Gospel of Our Lord Jesus Christ by living in obedience, without goods and in chastity."

Various interpretations and constitutions in regard to the Rule have been made from time to time by the Holy See.

Franciscan Sisters of Christian Charity Founded in Wisconsin in 1867, the community is engaged in teaching, nursing and caring for the aged. There are approximately 1,100 Sisters. Simple vows are taken.

Franciscan Sisters of Glen Riddle Founded in Philadelphia in 1855 by Blessed John Neumann as the first American Franciscan sisterhood. The Sisters are engaged in teaching, hospital work, nursing, caring for the aged, catechetics. Missions are maintained among the Negroes, Indians and in Puerto Rico. Simple vows are taken. There are approximately 1,800 Sisters.

Franciscan Sisters of St. Bernardine of Siena Founded in Pennsylvania in 1894, the community is primarily engaged in teaching and nursing. There are three provinces in the United States with approximately 1,100 Sisters. Foreign missions are staffed in Brazil and Liberia. Simple vows are taken. Also known as the Bernardine Sisters.

Franciscans Popular name for members of the Order of Friars Minor, the Order of Friars Minor Conventual, the Poor Clare nuns and other societies of women following the Franciscan Rule, and more rarely to the Capuchins. The Order of Friars Minor was founded by St. Francis of Assisi and legally approved in 1209. The Conventuals broke away from the parent body in 1415; members do not wear the regular Franciscan habit but one of black and hence are sometimes called the Black Franciscans. The Capuchins began in 1525 in a desire to return to the more primitive rule of St. Francis. The

Franciscans are one of the major orders in the Church and their contribution to the Church in the United States is incalculable.

frankincense (OF. *franc encens,* incense of high quality) A fragrant resin which exudes when the bark of a particular Arabian tree is burned. It was one of the gifts offered Christ by the Magi (Mt. 2:12).

Frater (frah'tare, L. brother) A title given to a religious brother or to a student preparing for the religious priesthood.

fraternal correction Aid given to another to help him to avoid sin or to overcome a fault or imperfection. It must be done from the motive of Christian love and given privately. It arises from positive divine law (Ec. 19:13) and from natural law since fraternal correction is a form of spiritual almsgiving. There is no grave obligation to give fraternal correction unless one is certain that the other is in grave spiritual need from which he cannot be saved without correction, and that the correction can be given without serious consequences to the corrector.

fraud As a kind of trickery, it is the execution of clever plans by means of dishonest actions, as when a person cheats by not observing the rules of the game, or defrauds by selling inferior goods, or imposes on others by passing himself off as their friend, etc. In contracts, fraud is any unlawful conduct on the part of one party to a contract that puts the other party under a disadvantage in agreeing to the contract, or that takes away the equality that should exist between the parties. Fraud may be a grave or light sin; if an injustice is involved, restitution must be made to the person defrauded.

free love The state of a man and

woman who have entered into an open agreement to live together without the benefit of marriage on the understanding that the relationship may be dissolved by either party at any time. Such an arrangement is opposed to the Sixth and Ninth Commandments and is gravely sinful.

free will That responsible choice every man possesses, by which he responds to the Creator or turns away from Him.

freedom of man Every man is endowed with a free will which has for its object any good. To the extent that an object lacks some perfection of goodness the will is necessarily indifferent to it. Hence, given all the prerequisites for acting, it is able to choose or not to choose it.

freedom of the will The power of free choice. When a person's will is free one is free from all internal determinism, in virtue of which he would of necessity wish whatever he wishes. This internal freedom is the essence of free will.

freedom of worship The inalienable right of every man to worship God according to the dictates of his conscience.

Freemasonry An international secret society, ostensibly set up for mutual assistance and social association but in actuality promoting a religion diametrically opposed to Christianity. It has been condemned by the Church and membership to Catholics is forbidden under pain of excommunication. Most Protestant Americans who join a Masonic Lodge do so sincerely and not from any hatred of the Catholic Church or religion; the usual reasons are social and business. They do not progress far enough into Masonry (beyond the third degree of Blue Lodge Masonry) to realize its inconsistency,

nor do they know the anti-Catholic activities that in the past have been directed against the Church, which in Europe and Latin America undermines basic Christian doctrine by the Lodge's teaching of a religion of reason and naturalism. One of every twelve American men belongs to the Masons, attached to one of the 16,-000 Blue Lodges. Although Masons deny that they practice a religion, they follow a ritual that mixes rites of sun cults to the attainment of "light" through the death and resurrection of Hiram Abiff, a minor biblical character. They have temples with altars, sacred books, candles, plus a system of dogma and natural morality, all of which are used to deify reason. Membership in the Masons is condemned by others than Catholics. The Missouri and Wisconsin Synods of the Lutheran Church refuse communion to anyone belonging to a Lodge. The American Lutheran Church has called Masonry "anti-Christian." The Assemblies of God, Church of the Nazarene, Christian Reformed Church, Seventh-day Adventists and Jehovah's Witnesses all condemn membership in the Masons. The *Lutheran Cyclopedia* states: "Freemasonry in England and the United States has always called itself a supporter of morality and doctrine of the Protestant Church. Very few candidates realize that they are joining an organization that is essentially antagonistic to the Christian belief in the inspiration of the Bible and the divinity of Jesus Christ."

fresco (Fr. *fresco,* fresh) The art of painting on freshly spread plaster before it dries. It is commonly used in church decoration. Many masterpieces exist in this form such as Michelangelo's paintings in the Sistine Chapel and Da Vinci's Last Supper.

friar Term applied to members of mendicant orders (such as Dominicans, Franciscans, Carmelites, Augustinians) whose physical and spiritual duties represent a mixture of the active and contemplative life, to distinguish them from religious who devote their lives almost exclusively to solitude and contemplation in monastic institutions.

Friars Minor *See* Franciscans.

friary 1. A monastery or residence of a group of friars. 2. The community that occupies such an establishment.

Friday abstinence (L. *abstinentia,* abstain) From the beginning of Christianity, Friday has been the day on which no flesh meat is taken in order to honor the memory of Christ's suffering and dying on that day of the week.

frontal (L. *frontale,* an ornament for the forehead) An appendage which covers the entire front of the altar from the lower part of the table (mensa) to the predella, and from the Gospel corner to that of the Epistle side; an antependium (*q.v.*).

fruits of the Holy Spirit Name that collectively refers to types of acts that result from the working of the Holy Spirit in the Christian. The Christian responds to God's graces and inspirations within him and his acts are accordingly "godly," hence are fruits or products of the Holy Spirit. St. Paul in his counsels to the Galatians on Christian living contrasts the fruits of evil such as contention, murder, jealousy and the like with fruits or actions of people who are led by the Spirit: "But the fruit of the Spirit is charity, joy, peace, patience, kindness, goodness, faith, modesty, continency" (Gal. 5:22). The Church adds benignity, longanimity and chastity.

fruits of the Mass The effects of the Mass that benefit men by obtaining new graces for them and moving the divine mercy to the pardoning of sins. They can be distinguished: 1. the general fruit, in favor of the whole Church; 2. the special fruit, in favor of the person for whom the Mass is celebrated; 3. the most special fruit, in favor of the celebrant.

full of grace From the angel's greeting to Mary in the Gospel of St. Luke (1:28). "Hail, full of grace" means "Rejoice, most favored one." It has been the firm traditional teaching of the Church from earliest days that Mary, the "Lord's servant girl," never displeased God in the slightest; she never sinned and therefore was "full of grace." Also she was preserved at the moment of her coming into being from original sin by a special gift of God due to the anticipated merits of Jesus, later to become her son. This privilege is formally known as her Immaculate Conception.

Fundamentalism A strict Protestant profession of literal biblical interpretation in which the Bible is the sufficient and final authority for faith. Although rooted in 16th-century Protestantism, Fundamentalism came to fruition in the United States, drawing widespread attention in the Scopes trial of 1925 in which William Jennings Bryan defended the Fundamentalist teachings against biological evolution.

funeral rites Various customs arose through the centuries by which men were able to humanize the yielding of the bodies of their dead to the earth. These customs originated in and were shaped by the religious convictions of people. Ancient peoples are known to have employed cremation as well as interment. That the belief in some kind of life after death often determined the nature of these rites even in ancient times is evident from the discoveries of Paleolithic burial sites in which stone implements were placed for the future use of the dead person. Among other funeral methods used through the centuries are: embalming, exposure to birds of prey, river or sea committal, disposal in two stages when the soft tissue is first allowed to decay after which the bones are gathered up. The Church has generally rejected the practice of cremation (*q.v.*). The center of the Church's funeral rites is the Requiem (Rest) Mass. *See* wake.

G

Gabbatha Paved space occupying the highest point of the court at the eastern side of Jerusalem, the place where Pilate tried and condemned Christ.

Gabriel (Heb. *gabar-el,* God prevails) An angel mentioned in Jn. and Lk. In the New Testament Gabriel appears to Zachary to announce the birth of John the Baptist. He also appears to the Blessed Virgin to announce that she has been chosen by God to be the mother of the Messiah.

Galatians, the Epistle to the An Epistle of St. Paul written to correct the teachings of Judaizing Christians who wished to restore certain Jewish practices (e.g., circumcision) and who questioned Paul's authority. The Epistle is addressed "to the churches of Galatia." However, it is not certain where these churches were. The similarities between Galatians and Romans suggest that it was written slightly before Romans, around 56–57.

Galilean A term applied to Jesus Christ because Galilee was the country of His origin.

Galilee (Heb. *galil,* a district) The northernmost area of Palestine, home of Christ. Southern Galilee, a country of rolling hills, was the main area of the ministry of Christ. The New Testament mentions the following towns of Galilee in connection with Jesus: Nazareth, Cana, Capharnaum, Naim, Bethsaida and Tiberias.

Galileo case In the year 1616 and again in the year 1633 the Holy Office of the Roman Inquisition condemned as formal heresy the new scientific proposals of Galileo. This condemnation resulted from misunderstanding of Scripture and excessive caution in doctrinal matters, or at least in matters at that time thought to be doctrinal. Galileo's theory placed the sun as the center of the universe and made it immovable. He claimed that the earth moved with both an annual and diurnal motion. In the minds of some, both of these theories contradicted happenings recorded in Scripture. When Pope Paul V and Pope Urban VIII sanctioned the condemnation, they did so without involving the doctrine of papal infallibility, since they did not claim to be speaking ex cathedra.

Gallery of Living Catholic Authors Founded in 1932 at Webster College, Webster Groves, Mo., for the purpose of promoting Catholic literature. The Gallery gives recognition to Catholic authors of the United States and foreign countries.

244

Gallican Liturgies That group of early Western liturgies with Eastern influences, broadly divided into the Mozarabic and Celtic branches. They were used with many local variations in Gaul, Germany, Ireland, England and northern Italy. All, with the exception of the Mozarabic privilege in the Toledo cathedral chapel, were superseded by the Roman Rite between the 9th and 10th centuries. However, in the process, the Roman Liturgy itself assimilated many elements of the Gallican Liturgy and was enriched thereby.

Gallican Psalter St. Jerome made a translation of the psalms from the Greek Septuagint some time after he had edited and corrected the *Vetus Latina* or *Itala* version, known as the Roman Psalter. This translation from the Septuagint is the one contained in the Vulgate and became known as the Gallican Psalter because it was used in Frankish territories. Pope Pius V imposed the Gallican Psalter on all those subject to the Roman Rite when he had the Divine Office revised in the 16th century. In recent years Pope Pius XII authorized the use of a new version of the psalms made from the original Hebrew.

Gallicanism Essentially, Gallicanism is a theory or policy regarding the relation of the French Church and the papacy, equivalent to a demand for an independent national church. In 1628 the French clergy adopted a program called "The Gallican Liberties" with four propositions: 1. denying any divine authority of the papacy in temporal matters; 2. affirming the force and validity of the laws and customs of national and local churches; 3. proclaiming the supremacy of ecumenical councils over the pope; 4. denying the infallibility of the pope apart from an ecumenical council. Successive popes denounced it and Vatican Council I condemned many of its concepts as heretical. It is a term commonly used to designate any opinion which exalts the rights of national churches to the derogation of the rights of the Holy See.

gambling To play or game for some stake. It is a more generic form than betting which is an act of wagering between two parties on the result of some contest or issue. Gambling and betting are permissible if they do not lead to waste of money needed to pay a debt or support one's family, and provided cheating and fraud are absent. Betting is wrong if one of the parties has certainty of the outcome, while gambling may be undertaken even though the person wagering knows that he cannot win.

garth (Old Ger. *gart,* enclosure) An open courtyard surrounded by cloisters (covered walkways) especially in a group of buildings of a monastary or college.

gate of heaven 1. A metaphor standing for heaven itself. It is Catholic belief that the "gate of heaven" was closed until the Son of God obtained redemption for all men. This means, according to the theologians, that those holy people who died before the coming of Christ, e.g., the Old Testament saints, and who deserved to be with God, did not come into God's presence until the Redemptive Act of Christ. This opened "the gate of heaven" to all men, and the holy people before Christ entered into the presence of God. 2. A title of Our Lady found in the Litany of Loreto.

gates of hell A metaphor standing for hell itself. The phrase occurs in the Gospel of Matthew in the passage where Christ gave St. Peter the power to rule and govern His Church. Our

Lord promised St. Peter that the forces of hell would have no power over the Church. "Thou art Peter, and upon this rock I will build my Church, and the gates of hell shall not prevail against it" (Mt. 16:18).

Gaudete Sunday The third Sunday of Advent which takes its name from the first word of the Introit. The word *gaudete* is a Latin imperative meaning "rejoice." The day is a minor pause in the liturgical season of Advent. Rose-colored vestments may be worn, flowers can decorate the altar and use of the organ is permissible.

Gedeon (Heb. *gidon,* the hewer) One of the principal "Judges" who was an opponent of Baal-worship, who defeated the Madianites with only 300 men, and who ruled for 40 years over Israel.

Gehenna (Heb. *ge-bene-hinnom,* valley of the sons of Hennom) The name used in the New Testament to denote hell. The valley of Hennom, south of Jerusalem, was notorious for its terrible worship of the god, Moloch. The Jews detested it and used its name to designate the place of the damned. An alternate interpretation: Hinnon was a refuse dump where fires continually burned, hence a place of torment and burning.

genealogies of Jesus, the There are two genealogies for Jesus given in the Synoptic Gospels, one by Matthew and the other by Luke. Matthew derives his genealogy from Abraham to show Christ's right to the throne of David. Luke goes as far back as Adam to show that Jesus, son of Adam, was born for all men. No clear explanation for the different names in the two genealogies has been found. It is possible that Matthew's genealogy gives the royal line while Luke's gives the genealogy according to blood.

general 1. Refers to a whole class, not particular, usual, not special. 2. The head of a religious order.

general chapter A meeting, at regular intervals, of the members of a religious community, either personally present or through delegates, wherein community affairs are discussed and regulated.

general confession A pious practice of confessing all the sins of one's past life or at least some definite segment of life already sacramentally forgiven.

General Judgment The event at which God will pronounce final judgment on mankind (Jn. 5:22, Matt. 25:31-46, Apoc. 6:14-17; 7:8-9). *See* Judgment.

general welfare *See* common good.

generationism A doctrine, opposed to the teaching of the Church, which states in general that the soul of a child is transmitted to it by its parents. More particuarly it asserts that this soul derives from the souls of its parent in a mysterious way similar to the way he derives his organism from his parents.

Genesis, Book of (Gr. *genesis,* beginning) The first book of the Old Testament which sets forth the origins of mankind and Israel. This book is heavily dependent on oral tradition. Genesis outlines God's plan for salvation which is constantly being thwarted by man's inclination to sin. The author made use of revelation and the limited scientific information possessed by the Israelites of his time. The Biblical Commission ruled in 1903 that the first three chapters of Genesis relate real facts corresponding to objective reality and cannot be considered allegorical or fictional. However, it is not necessary to take the literal sense of every word or phrase where terms are anthropomorphic. The author wrote to be understood by the men of his time in the language they spoke and was not attempting a scientific thesis.

Gentiles, the (L. *gentes,* people) A New Testament term used to designate those who were neither Christians nor Jews. In the Old Testament the corresponding word was *goyim,* "the other nations." The Jews were taught that everything Gentile was to be avoided. After His rejection by the Jews, Christ instructed His Apostles to take His teachings to all nations. Attempts were made to Judaize the Gentiles; but after the Council of Jerusalem, the Gentiles were exempt from Jewish law. St. Paul received a special commission from God to carry the Faith to the Gentiles and, as a result, is known as "the Apostle of the Gentiles."

Georgia One of the 13 original States, it is 21st in area and 16th in population. De Soto traversed it in 1540, and a Spanish fort was built on St. Catherine's Island in 1562. Dominicans, Jesuits and Franciscans in turn did missionary work, suffering numerous martyrdoms, but by 1634 Indian converts in Florida and Georgia numbered 30,000. The English colonists of South Carolina (who had introduced African slaves in 1610) attacked and devastated the Spanish missions, slaughtered their personnel, and took over the colony beginning in 1701. England's penal laws against Catholics were enforced. Catholics served with distinction in the War for Independence. Georgia became part of Bishop Carroll's diocese of Baltimore, and the first parish church was built in Savannah in 1799. In 1820 John England was made the first bishop of the Carolinas including Georgia. In 1850 the diocese of Savannah was established and succeeding bishops continued to carry on missionary work among the poor and the Negro slaves, and brought in religious orders to staff schools and orphanages. After the Civil War Georgia was left devastated. A community of Negro Sisters was founded by Mother Matilda Beasley in the late 19th century. In 1956 the diocese of Atlanta-Savannah was divided in two, and in 1962 Atlanta was raised to an archdiocese and metropolitan see. Catholics in Georgia have been a small minority since its beginning as an English colony. Today there are approximately 70,000 Catholics, in a total population of 4 million.

Germany The history of the Catholic Church in Germany goes back to the time of Constantine. In the 5th century St. Columban and other Irish missioners worked along the Rhine but it was St. Boniface in the 8th century who gave solid organization to the Church and who became the Apostle of Germany. Today there are 5 archdioceses (two cardinals) and 18 dioceses. There are 25 million Catholics in a population of over 55 million in West Germany and 1.5 million Catholics in a population of 15 million in East Germany. The Church in West Germany (the Federal Republic) is exceptionally strong and vigorous. There are numerous works of Catholic Action and charity. Many millions of dollars are collected annually and distributed overseas by the Adveniat and Misereor collections. West Germany has a strong Catholic press, many centers of Catholic thought and a vigorous social-action movement. More than 2,600 German priests, 1,100 Brothers and 7,000 Sisters are working in the missions. Germany has 1,480 priests at work in Latin America alone.

gesta (L. deeds) A word sometimes used after the 5th century for accounts of the life and death of martyrs (instead of *acta, passio,* etc.).

Gethsemani (Aramaic, *gat semani,* olive presses) A garden on the Mount of Olives where Jesus often went to pray. It was here that the agony in the garden took place and where He was taken prisoner.

Ghana A country in Africa. In 1503, the chief of Efutu was baptized along with 1,300 of his subjects and the Catholic Church took roots in what is today modern Ghana. Today there are 600,000 Catholics in a population of 7 million. One handicap the Church encounters in Ghana is a movement of nativism (*q.v.*) which developed following independence.

ghost Catholic theology has nothing to say against the possibility of a ghost in the sense of one dead. It is within the providence of God to permit departed souls to appear for some good purpose, e.g., to give help or warning or to obtain prayers. The Church also fully recognizes the possibility of apparitions or illusions caused by diabolical agency. Because of this common meaning of the word "ghost" the expression "Holy Ghost" for the third Person of the Trinity is now objected to because it is archaic. The term "Holy Spirit" is preferred.

Gideon Gedeon (*q.v.*).

gift of tongues The gift, first bestowed by the Holy Spirit at Pentecost on those present in the Upper Room, of singing the praises of God in divers tongues, most of which must not have been known to the speakers. The gift was not used for the purpose of preaching, but of praising God. If the Apostles later possessed the gift of speaking the languages of the foreign nations they evangelized, the Scripture texts themselves never make reference to it. From the words of St. Paul (1 Cor. 12:7-10) we conclude that speaking with tongues was a gift given both to laity and to religious leaders and consisted, not in addressing the faithful, but in praising God in an unknown tongue understood only by a person of that speech who happened to be present. The gift was common in the Church for over one hundred years, for St. Irenaeus had known people who possessed it. Christ promised the continuance in the Church of this gift of "new tongues" (Mk. 16:17). Some later saints are said to have had the gift of preaching "with tongues."

gifts of the Holy Spirit Wisdom, understanding, knowledge, counsel, piety, fortitude and fear of the Lord. These seven gifts dispose us to the inspirations of the Holy Spirit and aid us in the practice of virtue.

gifts, supernatural The gifts which are above and beyond the nature of man and which cannot be achieved by man for himself. They are completely free gifts of God. An example would be the share we have in God's life through Baptism.

girdle The cincture. A cord, approximately 12 to 14 feet in length, used to bind the alb at the waist.

glebe (L. *gleba,* land) A parcel of revenue producing land belonging to a parish or ecclesiastical benefice.

Glenmary Home Missioners Legal title: The Home Missioners of America. Founded in 1939 by Father William Bishop to train missioners for the priestless sections of the United States. The society includes priests and Brothers. The Glenmary

Sisters work in close cooperation with the priests.

Gloria (L. Glory to God on high) The opening word of the Greater Doxology. It is also called the Angelic Hymn because these words were sung by the angels at the time of the birth of Christ. It was originally part of the Proper of the Christmas Mass but has now become part of the Ordinary of the Mass, following the *Kyrie.* It is omitted from Mass during Advent and Lent or whenever the priest wears purple vestments. It is always omitted from Requiem Mass. *See* angelic hymn.

Gloria Patri (L. Glory to the Father) The first words of the Lesser Doxology from which the Doxology takes its title. It is used as a prayer of praise. It is recited after the psalms of the Mass and the Breviary, except in the last three days of Holy Week and in the Liturgy of the Dead.

Glorious Mysteries Those five decades (of the fifteen) in the Rosary which are concerned about the Resurrection of Christ, his Ascension, the descent of the Holy Spirit on the Apostles, the Assumption of Mary and her coronation as Queen of heaven. While reciting each decade, the mystery commemorating the event in the life of Jesus and Mary should be meditated upon.

glory The old Hebrews used this term in the sense of weight. It was a real value measurable in money, flocks, herds, lands, etc., and it was not taken in the abstract sense of fame. The glory of God was seen in the infinite weight of His power in behalf of Israel. This sense is carried over into the New Testament when the glory of Christ includes His life, His miracles and wonders.

glory, formal This phrase describes the praise, honor or worship given to God by his intelligent creatures. It is distinguished from material glory, which is the unconscious testimony of the universe to its Creator.

gloss (Gr. *glossa,* tongue) An entire commentary on scriptural passages. Today the term "glosses" would be likened to "footnotes."

glosses, scriptural Words used in the Bible which do not belong to the original text. It is not the intention of the glosser to insert new material in the text (interpolation) but to explain something already there.

gloves, episcopal A bishop at his consecration is invested with gloves which are strictly of a ceremonial use. They are worn by the bishop while he is celebrating a Pontifical High Mass. They are worn only until the washing of the hands at the Lavabo. The liturgical color of the day determines their color.

gluttony One of the capital sins, of a twofold nature. It is the inordinate longing for indulgence in food or drink; the taking of food or drink in excess or in such a manner that is harmful to the body.

Gnosticism (nas'ta-siz-m; Gr. *gnosis,* knowledge) A doctrine originated in the philosophic schools of the pre-Christian age and influenced by doctrines of the religions of Egypt, India and Judaism. In its primeval state its central form was characterized by the belief that human perfection came through knowledge which freed the human spirit from the slavery of material things, all of which were deemed evil. With the advent of Christianity, Gnosticism acquired a certain corrupt Christian ideology. It was a heresy of the first centuries of Christian times causing great harm to souls in various areas of the Roman Empire. It taught that all matter was evil; that Christ was an aeon, and an intermediary of God with the material universe; that only knowledge could save men from an existence which they held as essentially evil. In the Middle Ages, the Catharists and Albigensians professed doctrines which were basically Gnostic. Some have argued that modern idealism is a variant of this ancient teaching, thus emphasizing the persistence of this ancient teaching.

God St. John says that God is love. God is the one supreme and infinite personal Being, the Creator and Ruler of the universe, to whom man owes obedience and worship. In the Old Testament, God describes Himself to Moses as "I am who am."

God the Father The First Person of the Blessed Trinity, omnipotent, eternal with the Son and the Holy Spirit, equal to and one with the Son and the Holy Spirit. The Father is of no one, but of whom the Son is begotten and from whom with the Son, as one principle, proceeds the Holy Spirit (Rom. 8:15; Gal. 4:6; Mk. 14:36; Mt. 26:39).

God the Holy Spirit The Paraclete, Holy Spirit, the Spirit, the Third Person of the Blessed Trinity, consubstantial with the Father and the Son, proceeding from both the Father and the Son by an eternal procession, a person distinct from both, uncreated, omnipotent, equal to, eternal and one with the Father and the Son. The Holy Spirit proceeds as from a co-principle. He dwells in us at Baptism making us sons of the Father and brothers in Christ. Thus, through the Holy Spirit, Christian life flows to men from the Trinity and moves men toward the Father (Rom. 8:15).

God the Son Second Person of the Blessed Trinity, the Word, the only-begotten, Jesus Christ, also called the Son of Man. He is the only-begotten of the Father by eternal generation, a person distinct from the Father and the Holy Spirit, uncreated, omnipotent, eternal, equal to the Father and one with the Father and the Holy Spirit (Lk. 10:22; Mt. 11:27; Mk. 13:32).

godchild A name given to a baptized person to indicate his or her spiritual relationship to godparents, i.e., sponsors at the Baptism. There is a spiritual relationship between a godparent and godchild which is an impediment to marriage. Furthermore, any carnal sin committed between them takes on the character of incest.

Godhead (L. *Trinitas,* Trinity) The truth or dogma professing the existence of Three Persons in One God, the Father, the Son, and the Holy Spirit, these three being truly distinct one from another. Christ revealed the doctrine in explicit terms when He bade His Apostles to go and teach all nations, "Baptizing them in the name of the Father, and of the Son, and of the Holy Spirit" (Mt. 28:19).

godparents The godfather and godmother who are sponsors at Baptism. Canon law requires the presence of a sponsor at solemn Baptism whose duty it is to make the profession of faith for the one to be baptized and thereafter to assume responsibility for the spiritual education of the child. However, this obligation binds only when parents neglect their duty or die. Sponsorship creates a spiritual relationship which creates an impediment to marriage between sponsor and one sponsored. For valid sponsorship, a godparent must be baptized; have attained the use of reason; have the intention of sponsorship; must not belong to a heretical or schismatic sect; must not be under a sentence of excommunication; must not be father, mother or spouse of the person baptized; must be designated as sponsor; and must physically touch or hold the person being baptized.

God's Acre A name given to a burial plot of a religious order or society.

God's Kingdom (Gr. *basileia,* assembly) In the New Testament the term refers to life eternal for individuals (Mt. 25:46) and communion with the saints for the collectivity of people (Mt. 26:29). It is the realm in which God's will is fulfilled.

golden bull 1. Metal sculpture representing a cow, calf or bull, which becomes an object of idolatry. In biblical literature, the Hebrews fabricated a golden bull when Moses, who had led them out of Egypt, went on Mount Sinai for forty days. They became discouraged at the thought that Moses would not come back and therefore begged Aaron to make a god who would lead them in the fashion of Egyptian divinities personified as bulls (Ex. 24:18; Deut. 9:11). 2. A name given to a number of papal bulls either because they were sealed in gold or because of their exceptional content.

Golden Legend A collection of biographies of saints compiled *c.* 1260 by Blessed James de Voragine, a Dominican friar. The work was very popular and was translated into many European languages. Today it is read for devotion but not for historical accuracy.

Golden Rose An ornament of gold and gems in the form of a rose. It is customarily blessed by the pope on the Fourth (*Laetare*) Sunday of Lent when rose-colored vestments are used. It is then presented to a distinguished Church or community as a mark of special honor. This custom dates back to the 11th century.

golden rule The name given to the rule that one should do unto others as he would have others do unto him. It was stated by Christ (Mt. 7:12). It also appears in negative form in Tb. 4:16.

Golgotha (Aramaic *gulgulta,* skull) A dialectical pronunciation of the Aramaic word for skull, the name of the place known as Mount Calvary where Christ was crucified.

gong A musical instrument made from a slightly convex metallic disc, which is sounded by hitting with a hammer. This is quite popular in the East where it is used in pagan religious celebrations. Christianity has been slow to adopt it.

good and evil 1. The two opposing ways of human moral choices, according to Gen. 3:22. "Then God said, 'Behold man has become like one of us knowing good and evil.' " The choice is often difficult, because of contrasting desires and because the full understanding of the good quality of a deed comes easily only by the grace of Faith and a life of virtue. 2. In events not under the moral choice of man, evil is a present lack of a perfection or removal of a good which a nature is owed; good is the possession of due perfection or the increase in this valued quality.

good faith One who conscientiously believes that his statements or beliefs are true and his actions honest is said to be in good faith. Guilt is not imputed to one in good faith even if he is not acting rightly. Many outside the true Church are in this state of good faith.

Good Friday The Friday before Easter commemorating the day on which Christ died. The vestments worn are black because the Church is in mourning. At the beginning of the Good Friday service, the priest lies prostrate before the altar as a sign of man's desperate and desolate condition before being redeemed. The Veneration of the Cross is one of the high points of the day's service. First, Christ on His cross is dramatically unveiled and adored. In worship, we thank God for the salvation He has given us at so great a cost. The climax of the ceremony is the Communion service. The primary purpose in receiving the Body of Christ is to obtain "more abundantly the fruits of redemption." On Good Friday the attention of the faithful is not directed to the unbloody sacrifice of the Mass but to the bloody sacrifice of Calvary itself.

Good Friday Liturgy The solemn Liturgy of Good Friday is celebrated in the afternoon about 3 P.M. For sufficient reason, however, it may be celebrated from noon on but not after 9 P.M. The liturgy has four parts: 1. the lessons which consist of sacred readings and responses, and concluding with the Passion of St. John; 2. the solemn collects or prayer of the faithful; 3. the adoration of the cross and the Reproaches; 4. the Communion service.

Good News A paraphrase of the term "Gospel." Christianity must be the presentation and proclamation of something desirable and valuable, as something to be received with joy and to be experienced as joyful. In its essence, catechesis cannot be restricted only to religious instruction, to something that need only be "known." The power of faith and knowledge must be channeled into action; it must be fostered into a believing acceptance of the divine message of "good news." *See* kerygma.

Good Shepherd A term used in the

Gospel of St. John (10:11) to describe Christ. The symbol of a young man with a lamb over his shoulders was used in the catacombs to indicate Christ. The Second Sunday after Easter is known in many places as Good Shepherd Sunday because of the Gospel of the Mass.

Good Shepherd Sisters Founded in France in 1641 by St. John Eudes and reorganized in 1835 by St. Mary Euphrasia Pelletier, the community was established in the United States in 1843. Its apostolate is to help girls who have problems of social or emotional adjustment. In addition to the customary three vows of religion, the Sisters take a fourth vow of zeal for souls. Americans staff missions in the Philippines and Hong Kong. There are over 1,200 Sisters in 48 cities of the United States, professionally treating and rehabilitating over 8,000 teenage girls each year.

good, the That which is of the highest ethical worth and value; that which a man consciously and unconsciously strives for all his life.

Good, the Supreme Every real thing has some good, some have more than others, but there is only one Being who possesses the highest possible degree of good, because He is the maker of all good things. He is God. This is a title of God.

Good Thief, the The name given to one of the two thieves crucified with Christ. This thief, who confessed his belief in Christ (Lk. 23:39-43), is traditionally given the name of Dismas (*q.v.*).

good works 1. Generally, moral actions of kindness and generosity toward others that are performed from a spiritual motive, and are rewarded by God. 2. Specifically, those works resulting from following the precepts and counsels and those which fall under the headings of prayer, fasting and almsgiving. Good works in themselves are not the cause of justification. The Council of Trent requires for justification primarily Faith, but also acts of fear, hope, love and sorrow. Thus in this latter sense good works are necessary for salvation.

Gospel (AS. goodspell, good tale) The glad tidings or teachings of Christ which must be preached to all men. In a restricted sense, it refers to each of the scriptural accounts written by Matthew, Mark, Luke and John.

gospel, apocryphal Matters relating to the teaching and life of Christ that were written from the 1st to the 5th centuries to fill gaps in the canonical Gospels. They are, for the most part, made up of legendary and often fantastic stories.

Gospel, liturgical That portion of the Scripture read or sung following the Gradual of the Mass. The selection is always from the work of one of the Evangelists.

Gospel of Nicodemus An apocryphal Gospel which was written in the 4th century and which purports to have been composed by Nicodemus, the Pharisee, who had a nocturnal conversation with Christ and who later assisted in His burial. It is a very fanciful account of the trial and death of Jesus. Many of its legends persist as facts to today. It is also called the *Acts of Pilate.*

Gospel of Peter An apocryphal passion gospel that appeared toward the end of the 2nd century. Only a fragment copy exists today.

Gospel of Thomas An imaginative

apocryphal gospel that supplies information about the youth of Christ. It was the product of Gnostics.

gospel side Gospel side is that side of the sanctuary or altar from which the priest or the deacon reads or sings the Gospel of the Mass being said. Today, it is usually sung either from the pulpit or from an ambo nearby facing the people.

Gospel, the Last The Scriptural reading, usually the introduction to the Gospel of St. John, which formerly ended the Mass. The Mass now ends with the blessing and the Last Gospel is entirely omitted.

Gospels, dates of the According to the *Catholic Commentary,* the following dates are offered, such a matter being disputed and open to many opinions: Matthew, 40–50; Mark, 53–63; Luke, 60–62; John, 100.

Gothic architecture A method of  construction, Franco-Norman in origin and developed during the 13th and 14th centuries. The distinguishing characteristic of this type of building is the pointed arch and the system of stone vaulting thereby made possible. Ornament is but a minor detail of Gothic, especially in the early periods, but in the later periods it became the custom to fill the large windows with carved stone tracery of rich and intricate design. As a system of construction, pure Gothic had been out of use for 300 years. There has been a revival using it in a modified form.

Gothic Rite Another title used for the Mozarabic Rite. It was derived from the Gallican Rite and used in Spain and what we now call Portugal until the 11th century. It is preserved in only one church in Toledo, Spain, at the present time.

Gothic vestments The name given to a style of vestments that is less formalized and looser than the Roman style. Whereas the chasuble in the Roman style covers only the shoulders, leaving the sides open, the Gothic chasuble is full, flowing all around. Very often Roman-style fabrics are stiff and heavily ornamented while Gothic fabrics are softer and more simple. In the Roman-style maniple and stole, the ends are splayed while in the Gothic both vestments are designed with straight lines, equally parallel throughout. The name was adapted from Gothic architecture which has a free style and uses straight lines.

government The exercise of administrative powers by those in authority; the office and function of governing. 1. Of God. The execution of God's plan or providence. It is a teaching of Vatican Council I that God guards and governs by His providence all that He has created. 2. Ecclesiastical. Because the Church is a perfect society it has supreme authority over its members. The pope governs the universal Church assisted by the Roman Curia. A bishop governs in his diocese assisted by his chancery. The government of the Church embraces the legislative, judicial and executive. 3. Civil. Society is a grouping of men for the common good, but very often the common good clashes with individual preferences. Therefore some authority is needed. This authority is demanded by man's nature, therefore it is not conferred on society by man any more than man can confer nature on himself. This authority comes from God. It is man, however, who decides how this authority is to be exercised. The Church is not as interested in who exercises authority as in how that authority is exercised and how much power the authority has. Between forms of government (democracy, monarchy, dictatorship) the Church is neutral because under any one, God can be obeyed and man can fulfill his destiny. But in the question of extent of power the Church cannot be neutral. The state cannot act against natural law because then it would be acting against the source of its authority.

grace 1. *Biblical.* (*a*) God's favorable disposition toward man. (*b*) The result of divine favor; the state and condition of spiritual life into which the recipients of this favor come. 2. *Theological.* (*a*) The supernatural gift freely given by God to a rational creature for his eternal salvation. (*b*) Uncreated Grace: God Himself, communicating Himself to man. Created grace: The supernatural reality produced in man by this communication of God.

grace, actual An internal grace which enlightens the intellect and strengthens the will. It is "internal" in that it influences the will and intellect directly. It differs from habitual grace, which is permanent in that actual grace perdures only for the duration of the act itself.

grace, baptismal The grace of Baptism takes away sin and intrinsically sanctifies man.

grace, efficacious The characteristic note of this function of grace is the infallibility of the effect. This divine influence infallibly, but freely as befits men, brings us to act with respect to eternal life.

grace, elevating Grace is by itself above the natural; and thus when it is united to the natural, grace lifts the natural to its order, the supernatural. The function of elevating grace is being a principle of activity which surpasses absolutely human nature, and thus elevates the human operation to a new order, the supernatural order.

grace, external Any happening, fact or event which by its moral influence helps man attain his final end. Such a grace would be Sacred Scripture, the preaching of the Gospel, the example of the life of Christ or a saint, etc.

grace, habitual The created supernatural gift of God which places a person in a state of permanent friendship with God. It is not something merely extrinsic or imputed to the person "as if" he were pleasing to God, but rather it is a real and intrinsic change by which the person is now an adopted child of God. Through habitual grace the person is united to God Himself, Uncreated Grace or Gift. Habitual grace is lost by any mortal sin, and may be regained through sacramental confession or, if this is impossible, through an act of perfect contrition.

grace, illuminating An actual grace which enlightens the intellect in order that the person receiving the grace may perform some action which will contribute to his eternal salvation. This illumination is usually thought of as something given directly and internally. But at other times the grace may be in the form of some natural mental experience such as a sermon, a book or the sight of a crucifix. Most frequently however, illuminating grace refers to a direct or immediate enlightening of the intellect.

grace, imputed Heretical teaching of some of the Protestant reformers on the nature of the habitual grace which man receives when he is justified. They taught that justification was simply a judicial declaration of the nonimputability of sin. Then they proceeded to say that the merits of Christ were positively imputed, so that the sinner was cloaked in the grace of Christ.

grace, interior A help or gift from God which directly influences the soul. All grace, in the strict sense, is interior, e.g., habitual grace. Interior graces are distinguished from exterior graces (not graces strictly speaking) which operate through some sensible medium like a prayer, a sermon, or a reading, and from other natural gifts of God.

grace, irresistible A type of interior help of God which the receiver supposedly cannot oppose. According to Jansen and Calvin man is forced to doing good by irresistible grace. Their stand on irresistible grace was condemned at the Council of Trent. Catholic teaching does not hold that grace, even so-called efficacious grace, is irresistible, because this would destroy man's free will.

grace, natural Any good (thing, event, person) enjoyed by someone, inasmuch as all goods and gifts are ultimately from God; any natural good used by God for the supernatural good of man.

grace, prevenient (L. *praevenire,* to come before) The supernatural power (actual grace) given by God which enlightens the mind and stirs up the will. It is given to lead one to perform a good work (action, thought, prayer, omission of something evil) that directs a man to eternal salvation. Because of man's radical dependence on God, he stands in need of divine impulse and power for each work that aids his salvation and glory.

grace, sacramental This grace both

sanctifies man intrinsically and helps him to attain the end of the sacrament.

grace, sanctifying A constant supernatural quality of the soul which sanctifies man intrinsically and makes him just and pleasing to God.

grace, substantial Also called uncreated grace because it is God as He gives Himself to man. It is the divine indwelling whereby God has established a special relationship of presence with His people as a whole or individually. It is the Shekina (*q.v.*) that we read of in the Old Testament whereby God is present in a cloud, in a pillar of fire, in the Temple. It is the presence of the spirit of God in the Christian as in 1 Cor. 3:16, Rom. 8:9-11.

grace, sufficient A supernatural gift which gives a man the power to act in the supernatural order and thereby in a way affecting salvation. This grace does not determine an act to be supernatural but it enables a man to act. It requires the cooperation of man to be effective.

Grace, Your Mode of address to an archbishop in England and elsewhere. It compares with the American use of "Your Excellency."

gradine (Fr.) The ledge above and behind the altar upon which the cross, candlesticks and other ornaments are placed.

gradual (L. *gradus,* a step) A short text usually taken from Holy Scripture, which the priest says (and which is sung by the choir at High Mass) immediately after the Epistle reading. In most Masses it represents a pithy summary of the Epistle lesson.

Gradual Psalms Psalms 119 to 133 as numbered in the Vulgate which have a somewhat similar theme, namely joy and trust in the providence of God. Their name has been variously explained; some scholars attribute it to their being sung on steps of the Temple; others, to their use on pilgrimages to Jerusalem.

Graduale Romanum A liturgical book used during the worship of the Church. It contains the chants that are incorporated into the Mass.

graffiti (It. *graffito,* scribbling) Drawings or scribblings on early Christian monuments. Valuable to historians and archeologists, they are chiefly found in the catacombs and on relics from the Crusades.

Grail, the A movement established in Holland in 1921 which aims to train women as leaders in the lay apostolate to work in Christian and non-Christian lands. The Grail movement was established in the United States in 1940 and has its headquarters at Loveland, Ohio. It is active in mission work, work among foreign students, etc.

Grail, the Holy The platter or cup used by Christ at the Last Supper. According to legend it was brought to England but disappeared when its guardians became impure. Many legends exist of how medieval knights sought the Holy Grail.

gratitude A moral virtue which enables a person to be grateful and thankful for a kindness received, returning such kindness according to opportunity and means.

grave An excavation in the earth used for burial. A Catholic should be buried in consecrated ground. If burial takes place in nonconsecrated ground, the grave should be blessed before the coffin is lowered. Canon law prescribes that whoever desecrates a corpse or grave from an evil motive shall be punished with personal interdict, *ipso facto* infamous; if the person is a cleric, he shall be deposed.

Great Britain Although there were already many Christians long established in Celtic Wales and southwest England, the conversion of the Anglo-Saxons was begun as the result of a decision by Pope Gregory the Great in 596 to send the Benedictine monk Augustine to that island. The following year, Ethelbert, one of the English kings, was baptized and Augustine was consecrated a bishop with his see at Canterbury. The relationship between the Church and the English crown varied over the centuries, although the long list of English saints testifies to the fervor of the English people. In 1170 Archbishop Thomas Becket was murdered following a quarrel with Henry II. The divorce of Henry VIII began a schism with Rome in 1534 and brought death to St. John Fisher and St. Thomas More. Under Elizabeth I, Protestantism was promoted and Catholic clergy were hunted and put to death. In Scotland Catholicism was proscribed in 1560. The political emancipation of Catholics did not come until 1829. Today Catholics compose 15 per cent in Scotland and slightly better than 8 per cent in England and Wales. Scotland has 2 archdioceses and 6 dioceses; Wales, 1 archdiocese and 1 diocese; England, 3 archdioceses and 13 dioceses. Catholic life is well organized.

Great Command This is the command given by Christ immediately before His Ascension. This command closes the Gospel of St. Matthew. "Going therefore, teach ye all nations: baptizing them in the name of the Father, and of the Son, and of the Holy Spirit" (Matt. 28:19).

Great Commandments of the New Law Christ came upon earth to amplify the Mosaic commandments and the Old Law. In the New Law which He established He gave two great commandments, love of God and love of neighbor (Matt. 22:36-40). These two commandments are root commandments out of which all other commandments flow.

great silence, the The silence observed in religious houses and seminaries after Compline or night prayers and kept until after Mass the next morning. In most cases it is prescribed by religious rule. The purpose is to give time to prepare for meditation and Mass the next morning.

Greater Antiphons The "O" Antiphons to the Magnificat recited on the seven days preceding the vigil of Christmas. The opening words are *O Sapientia* (O Wisdom), *O Adonai, O Radix Jesse* (O Root of Jesse), *O Clavis David* (O Key of David), *O Oriens* (O Orient), *O Rex Gentium* (O King of the Nations), *O Emmanuel. See* "O" Antiphons, O Sapientia.

Greater Litanies (L. *Litaniae Majores)* A procession, in which the Litany of the Saints is sung, followed by a Mass of rogation. It is observed on Apr. 25, the feast of St. Mark.

greca (It. Greek) The long black clerical overcoat worn in Rome. The name probably derives from its resemblance to the long black outer garment worn by the Eastern Rite clergy.

Greek This has always been considered the second language of the Church. Up to the middle of the 3rd century, the services of the Church were in colloquial Greek, the same language found in the New Testament. A relic remains in the modern Mass in the Kyrie and in Good Friday's *Agios o Theos.* Among Catholics, only Italo-Greeks, a few Greek nationals and occasionally Melkites use Greek in the liturgy; but the whole Orthodox Church of Greece uses it.

Greek Catholics Those few Greek Christians who recognize the Bishop of Rome as the visible head of the Catholic Church; but the term is often applied, misleadingly to other Eastern Catholics, e.g. Melkites.

Greek Church One of the four leading churches of the Eastern Orthodox Church. It separated itself from the patriarchal jurisdiction of Constantinople in 1833 and is now independent, but it recognizes the patriarch of Constantinople's primacy of honor among Orthodox bishops. The Archbishop of Athens is its head, ruling with a holy synod.

Greek Church, Uniate A loose and incorrect name for Catholics of the Byzantine Rite (*q.v.*). Very few of them are Greeks.

Greek Fathers The Fathers of the Church are those men from primitive stages of the Church who witness the tradition handed on to the Church from the Apostles. Their orthodox teaching and their holiness of life are the means through which they bring this witness to the Church. These writings of the Fathers are very important; in fact, when there is universal consent of the Fathers on an interpretation of Scripture, the Church regards this opinion of the Fathers as an infallible position for the whole Church. The Greek Fathers are the Fathers of the Eastern Church whose literary production was in Greek. This Church received the Faith from the Jewish Christians first and was converted to the Faith earlier than the western part of the Roman Empire. Therefore, the Greek writers are of special importance because they witness the earliest tradition of the Church's history. The greatest of the Greek Fathers were Athanasius, Basil, Cyril of Alexandria, Cyril of Jerusalem, Gregory Nazianzen, Gregory of Nyssa, John Chrysostom, John Damascene, Origen and Clement of Alexandria.

Greek Rite A term often used incorrectly to designate the Byzantine Rite. Although it was originally celebrated in Greek, as was also the Roman Rite, the Byzantine Rite is properly celebrated in many languages.

green Color for hope, prescribed for Mass vestments used on Sundays after the feasts of the Epiphany and Pentecost.

Gregorian Armenian Church The Christian Church in Armenia in northern Asia Minor which grew up around the figure of Gregory the Illuminator. After a few centuries of growth, nationalistic tendencies greatly influenced the adoption of Monophysitism by the majority and eventually the Church was split. Efforts at reconciliation have failed.

Gregorian chant. A term for plain chant that is no longer used by competent musicologists. The term "Gregorian chant" did not stem from any of the "Gregory" popes or from Italy but developed in France and Germany. *See* chant; plain chant.

Gregorian Mass One celebrated at a Gregorian altar.

Gregorian University, Pontifical Founded by St. Ignatius Loyola and erected by Pope Julius III in 1552, the Gregorian is an autonomous part of the central pontifical university. It is sometimes called the Roman College. It has faculties of theology, canon law, ecclesiastical history, philosophy and missiology. The Pontifical Biblical Institute and the Pontifical Institute for Oriental Studies are connected with the Gregorian. The university is directed by the Jesuit Fathers.

Gregorian water A special purificatory water blessed by a bishop which is made by mixing water, wine, salt and ashes. It is sprinkled on various parts of a church during its consecration, and is also used in the reconciliation of a defiled church. It is called after Pope St. Gregory I who is said to have prescribed its contents.

gremial (L. *gremium,* lap) The rectangular veil or silk apron which is laid across the lap of a bishop when he sits at some pontifical ceremony. The object is to protect the vestments from drops of oil, wax, etc. At ordinations a white linen gremial is used.

Grey Nuns of Montreal Founded in Montreal in 1738 by Bl. Marguerite d'Youville and established in the United States in 1855, the community today numbers over 8,000 Sisters who are engaged in medical work, nursing and care of children. Simple vows are taken.

Grey Nuns of Quebec Founded in Quebec, Canada, in 1849, the community was an offshoot from the Grey Nuns of Montreal. An establishment in the United States was made in 1890. The community is primarily engaged in nursing and medi-

cal work. There is a mission in Japan. There are 2,000 members.

Grey Nuns of St. Hyacinthe A community founded in St. Hyacinthe, Canada, in 1840 as an offshoot from the Grey Nuns of Montreal. The Sisters began an American establishment in 1878. The work is primarily medical and nursing and there are missions in Haiti and Brazil. There are over 800 Sisters. Simple vows are taken.

grille In the confessional, the screen or lattice work partition separating priest and penitent. In a cloister, the wooden or metal grating which separates the enclosure of cloistered nuns from the visiting room used by the public, also the opening in the chapel wall through which the nuns receive Holy Communion.

Grotto of the Nativity The cave in Bethlehem where Our Lord was born. It is now covered by a basilica built by Justinian. It was the special object of pilgrimage on the part of Pope Paul VI in 1964 following the closing of the second session of Vatican Council II.

group dynamics Systematized interworking influences within a small group of people. The term is also used to describe the critical examination of these influences as a sociological study. The system is being used to make the work of Catholic apostolic groups more effective.

Guadalupe, Our Lady of The title of the Blessed Virgin Mary as the special patroness of Mexico, also the basilica dedicated to her near Mexico City. In 1531, during the episcopate of Juan de Zumarraga, first bishop of Mexico, a poor Indian catechumen named Juan Diego beheld a vision of a radiant lady on Tepeyac hill, a place formerly dedicated to pagan deities. She told him she was the mother of

Christ, and that she wanted a church built on the hill. To impress the bishop with the authenticity of Juan's message, she worked a miracle, causing her image to appear as if painted on the rough sackcloth of Juan's cloak. The basilica of Our Lady of Guadalupe was built, and devotion to her did much toward bringing the Indians into the Church. This devotion has remained fervent, even during later periods of religious persecution. The cloak of Juan Diego hangs over the altar in the basilica, with the image clearly visible on it. Many miracles have been reported as having taken place there. Pilgrims from all parts of Mexico walk, some barefoot, in processions as much as five miles long, singing hymns and praying aloud, coming to visit the shrine. Our Lady of Guadalupe is the patroness, not only of Mexico, but of all the Americas. Her feast day is Dec. 12 and is celebrated in the liturgical calendar of the United States.

guardian　1. The superior of a Capuchin or Franciscan monastery. In those monasteries which are also parishes, the guardian is usually different from the pastor. 2. One who has the legal custody of another person and/or property.

guardian angel　A proximate teaching of faith (not defined) that an angel is assigned to each person to watch over and protect him and to act as an intermediary between that person and God. (Mt. 18:10; Acts 12:15). The Church encourages prayer to one's guardian angel. Pope Clement X approved a feast for the guardian angels for the Western Church to be celebrated on Oct. 2.

Guatemala　Colonized from Mexico, Guatemala became the center for mission work in Central America, as the magnificent ruins of Antigua still

testify The revolution of 1871 separated Church and State, took away juridical personality from the Church, dissolved religious orders and left a religious poverty that still exists. Today there are 1 archdiocese, 6 dioceses and 1 prelature serving a population of 4 million with 1 priest for every 10,555 inhabitants. The United States is represented by Franciscans, Maryknollers and Christian Brothers. In recent years tremendous progress has been made in restoring Catholic life: parishes have increased 50 per cent since 1949; diocesan priests 100 per cent, order and society priests, 200 per cent; Sisters, almost 200 per cent. During the same period the population increased only 24 per cent.

guest master　1. A Brother or priest who has been appointed to care for guests in a monastery or religious house. The Christian is expected to see Christ in every guest. "I was a stranger and you entertained me" (Matt. 25:35). 2. The term is also applied to the guest master of one about to be ordained or professed, caring for the individual's relatives and friends.

guilds, the　Associations of people who have interests or employment in common. Workingmen's guilds have been known since ancient times, and certain modifications of guilds are still in existence. The guild which flourished in Christendom in the Middle Ages, is a notable example of a whole society guided and transformed by Christian principles applied to labor and craftsmanship. Workingmen banded together according to the craft in which they made their living. Each guild might put up its (sometimes magnificent) guild hall where business and social meetings connected with the guild were held. Guilds were not organized with workers and employers in opposition as happens today in a different system of labor and capital. All those who were engaged in a craft —masters, journeymen, apprentices —belonged to the same guild. They settled by democratic methods matters of employment, wages, hours, types of products made and prices to be charged. They took care of workers when ill; when one died they attended his funeral, had Masses said for his soul, and helped support his widow and orphans. They supervised the training of apprentices and saw to it that the boys were educated in their craft and in their Catholic Faith. If apprentices were abused by a master, the matter might be taken up at the guild meeting and justice administered. Journeymen who had served their apprenticeship and were not yet masters were accustomed to travel through various cities and countries in Christendom, where they stayed with members of their guild, worked a while, learned new ways and broadened their education in general. The decay of the guilds came about through the Protestant revolt, the Industrial Revolution with the invention of power-driven machinery, the necessity for immense amounts of capital to set up a factory under the new conditions, and various other causes. The guilds were not pious confraternities; they were primarily associations of craftsmen, yet they were definitely Catholic in character and received their inspiration from the Church. They were a bright light in a time of turbulence and warfare, and they showed the way for modern adaptations that would solve many problems in our time.

guilt   The responsibility for one's sinful acts.

H

Habacuc, Book of A book of the Old Testament, written somewhere between 605 B.C. and 597 B.C., containing the message of the prophet Habacuc. No information is had from the book itself on the person of the prophet, who is identified in the Jewish Canon as one of the twelve minor prophets among the latter prophets. In the three chapters of the prophecy, Habacuc questions God's severe punishment of Juda at the hands of the pagan Chaldeans and answers with the message that this punishment is preparing the final triumph of all just men who live by faith.

Habakkuk Habacuc (*q.v.*).

habit In general, the disposition to do certain things with ease, or to act the same way in given circumstances: with ease because the disposition proceeds into action without much thought or deliberation, and at times nearly involuntarily, as in the use of profanity. It is acquired by repeated acts. The more frequent the repetition, the stronger the acquired tendency; often the forming of acquired habits is favored and facilitated by natural and congenital dispositions. A habit makes the doing of the respective act prompt, easy and pleasurable, and conse-

quently makes resistance to such an act increasingly difficult. Habit, therefore, is one of the elements to be taken into consideration in evaluating the morality of an act.

habit, religious The special attire or dress proper to members of a religious organization or group. The law of the Church at the present time requires every religious organization to have its own particular habit. The external form of the habit should differ from that of secular priests and lay persons. Pope Pius XII on several occasions strongly recommended that the habits worn by female religious be simplified and more adapted to modern conditions. Once the religious habit has been approved by the Holy See, it may not be changed without permission of the same Holy See.

habitual grace Supernatural gift of God infused into the very essence of the soul as a habit. Also called sanctifying grace or justifying grace, "God abiding in the soul" (Jn. 14: 23). Habitual grace also includes the virtues and gifts of the Holy Spirit. It enables man always to act in a supernatural way and ultimately to enjoy the vision of God supernaturally. It is lost by mortal sin; increased through good acts done for and through God and particularly through the reception of the sacraments.

Haceldama (Aramaic, field of blood) The New Testament gives two accounts of this field where the destitute were buried. Acts 1:18 refers to it as the place where Judas killed himself. Matt. 27:6 calls it the field purchased by the thirty pieces of silver returned to the priests by Judas.

Haggai (*also* Aggai, Hagai, Aggeus; Heb. born on the feastday) One of the minor prophets who encouraged the rebuilding of the Temple at Jerusalem. Author of the Book of Aggeus. He was called to be a prophet in 520 B.C.

hagiography (Gr. *agios,* holy; *graphos,* writing) 1. Writings concerned with the lives of saints. Such writings are more than historical biography; they are interpretative, requiring a knowledge of theology, particularly ascetical theology. 2. A scriptural term referring to Old Testament writings which are concerned with neither the law nor the prophets.

hagiology Writings concerned with the lives of holy people. Since the term includes legends of saints, many of which are a strain to credulity, the word is sometimes used disdainfully.

hagiosope An architectural term referring to an opening in the wall of a church which allows those in the transept to view the altar.

Hail Mary, the A favorite prayer also known as the Ave Maria and the Angelic Salutation. It takes its name from the first two words of the prayer. It is composed from the words addressed to Mary by the Angel Gabriel at the time of the Annunciation (Lk. 1:28) and those spoken to Mary by her cousin Elizabeth (Lk. 1:42). The Church then adds its own supplication. The prayer is used in the Divine Office and in the Rosary. The prayer is as follows: "Hail Mary, full of grace, the Lord is with thee. Blessed art thou among women, and blessed is the fruit of thy womb, Jesus. Holy Mary, Mother of God, pray for us sinners now and at the hour of our death. Amen."

hair In the Western Church clerics are distinguished by the tonsure. In the Eastern Church, hair is worn long and the face is unshaven. However, in recent years, the tonsure is less frequently worn and is the rare exception in the United States, Canada and the British Isles. In the Eastern Church, particularly in America and Europe, many clerics cut their hair and are clean shaven.

hair shirt A penitential garment made of hair and worn next to the skin. It varies in length.

Haiti One year after the discovery of the New World by Columbus, Mercedarian, Franciscan and Jeronymite missioners were at work in Haiti, but the island's turbulent history has always been a handicap to the sound building of the Church which claims 3.4 million of the total 3.5 million (1960) population. Actually the majority of the population is Catholic only in name. There are many obstacles to the Church, one of the greatest being the present government which heads a nativist movement closely allied with voodoo. The Archbishop of Port-au-Prince, his auxiliary and the Bishop of Les Gonaives have been expelled along with numerous priests. Other obstacles are the lack of parishes, the difficulty of communications with the interior, the lack of priests and native vocations; 85 per cent of couples never marry in the Church; 90 per cent of the people are said to have some attachment to voodoo and to be subject to religious ignorance and Communist propaganda.

halfway house A place to which a person goes after being discharged from a sanatorium or hospital in order gradually to readjust to the world. Such a place could exist for a person discharged from a mental hospital, after a narcotics or alcoholism cure, etc.

hallucination An imaginary sense experience, usually visual or auditory, which is misinterpreted as real. It can be distinguished from an illusion (an erroneous perception), in that an external stimulus is either lacking or not at all relevant to the imagined experience. Hallucinations can be experienced by normal persons, but they are more usually found in the mentally ill and those under the influence of certain drugs. Some common types of hallucinations are voices or visions of a religious nature, divine commands, supernatural visions. Caution should be exercised in judging claims of this sort, and consultation with professional persons in theology and psychology is advisable.

halo (Gr. *halos,* disk of the sun) A circle or solid disk about the head as used in representations of blessed, saints or God. It is of pre-Christian origin and was used to denote power and majesty. The halo used for Christ or other persons of the Blessed Trinity usually contains a cross. *See* nimbus.

Ham One of the three sons of Noe. He is mentioned as the ancestor of the Egyptians. The term Hamitic derives from his name and is used for certain languages of North Africa.

Hanc Igitur A prayer of the Mass leading up to the Consecration; it takes its name from the first two words. It begs God to accept the offering that is about to be made and to grant salvation to all of the members of the community at Mass. As the priest begins this prayer, he extends his hands over the bread and wine and the server rings the bell to alert the congregation to the coming Consecration.

Hanukka The Jewish Festival of Lights which commemorates the dedication of Solomon's temple. While over the centuries it was a minor feast, modern Jews have given it more importance since it falls near Christmas.

happiness The possession of a good which satisfies a person's desires. Man's happiness is in the attainment of his ultimate end, which is God Himself; the attainment of this end is perfect happiness.

happiness, celestial Celestial happiness is the ultimate goal of man. This happiness consists in and is a result of man's possession and sight of God in the Beatific Vision. God's being is one with our intelligence in the order of knowledge.

harmony, biblical The essential agreement among various texts of the Bible which deal with the same subject. There have been many apparent contradictions found in the Bible, but as biblical studies advance, the original meaning of the various texts is more clearly understood and as this happens, very often, one by one, the apparent contradictions are resolved, or the particular theological import of the variations is recognized. A Harmony of the Gospels, or Gospel Harmony, is: 1. a combination of the four Gospels into one continuous narrative;

2. an arrangement of the Synoptic Gospels (Matthew, Mark and Luke) into three parallel columns, so that similarities and differences in them can be readily compared; 3. an arrangement of the four Gospels into parallel columns. Synoptic harmonies usually take Mark or Luke as the basic text, and rearrange the order of the verses in the other Gospels to parallel the basic text.

hat 1. Ecclesiastical. A flat, wide-brimmed black hat worn by clerics in Rome. A red broad-brimmed hat presented to a cardinal following his appointment; after the death of the cardinal it is hung from the ceiling of his cathedral. The hat used by priests for liturgical services is called a biretta (*q.v.*) and that of a bishop a mitre. The insignia for priest and bishop is a black-and-green flat hat with tassels, but it does not exist as an article of apparel. Various types of caps, turbans, etc., are worn in the Eastern Rites. 2. It is the Christian custom for men to be bare-headed in church and for women to wear a hat or veil but in some Eastern countries men wear a tarboosh in church.

hatred The sharpest conflict against the law of love of others is in attitudes and acts of hostility against one's neighbor and in any conduct which hurts the welfare of another in a positive way. The principal sins are hatred toward the person of another shown by strong dislike or ill-will: diabolical hatred which is deliberately against the spiritual good or salvation of a neighbor. Such hatred and any hatred of God are mortal sins.

Hawaiian Islands, the The 50th state of the Union. A group of volcanic islands in the Pacific, discovered by the Englishman Captain Cook in 1778. The inhabitants, a branch of the Polynesian family, were living in an island "paradise" where nature was usually kind and man's needs were simple. They worshiped the deified forces of nature, comprising some 400,000 gods, though there seem to be traces of the knowledge of a Supreme Being, Lord of all the gods. The islander's life was made complex and fearful by multitudes of taboos, and cannibalism was practiced. A cultured upper class lived at ease upon the labors of a numerous underprivileged lower class. The first Catholic priests, three members of the Picpus Society (Sacred Hearts of Jesus and Mary), were sent by Pope Leo XII and arrived in 1827. The Protestant missionaries who had arrived from the United States in 1820 had gained great favor with the king and the chiefs, and they influenced the authorities to oppose the Catholic missioners. A fierce persecution broke out. The Catholic native converts were ill-treated, imprisoned and tortured. They were also forced to attend Protestant services. The priests were expelled from the islands. Ten years later an Irish Picpus priest who was a British subject arrived in Honolulu but was forbidden to make converts. Later the French government forced the Hawaiian ruler to allow freedom of religion to all, and to give the same privileges to Catholics as to Protestants. Father Maigret, one of the three pioneers who had been expelled, returned and later became the first bishop. The Vicariate of the Sandwich Islands was erected in 1844, and later (1941) became the Diocese of Honolulu. The Protestants had translated the Bible into Hawaiian, had taught the people to read and write and to wear clothes. In 1873 Father Damien de Veuster began his work at Molokai among a numerous and neglected leper population. Franciscan Sisters aided in the work, and they still maintain a hospital there for the treatment of Hansen's disease. Catholics had early begun serious education work in Hawaii, and today there are well over 200 thousand Catholics, with numerous schools, organized social services and a general hospital in Honolulu. Members of various religious orders are working in the state.

hear Mass, to This is a popular expression meaning to assist at, or be present at, Mass for the purpose of worship, and especially, to fulfill the Sunday obligation. "To assist at Mass" is a better expression since the laity does have a role in the Sacrifice of the Mass. Bodily presence is necessary in the place where Mass is celebrated, or in the immediate precincts, to hear Mass. Mass must be heard with devotion and attention, although any form of prayer at Mass fulfills the obligation.

hearse (Fr. *herce,* a harrow) 1. A framework with spikes for candles which is placed over a coffin in church and which holds the pall or hearsecloth. 2. An elaborate framework built over a coffin or the tomb of an illustrious person to which memorial verses or epitaphs were affixed. 3. The vehicle which carries the coffin to the church and grave.

Heart of Jesus The physical heart of Jesus Christ which is an object of adoration and devotion as a symbol of His love and mercy.

Heart of Mary Immaculate The physical heart of the Blessed Virgin Mary which is venerated as a symbol of the great love and purity of Mary.

heathen Those who practice a religion other than Christianity, Islam or Judaism, as these religions believe in the One, True God. The word is the English equivalent of pagan (country dweller) and meant "one who dwelled on the heath."

heaven (AS. *heofen*) The place or state of perfect happiness and bliss where God will show His glory to the blessed and where the blessed will see God.

hebdomadarian (Gr. *hebdomas,* a week) In monasteries and churches where the Divine Office is sung in choir, the priest who is appointed for a week to make the intonations at the beginning of the canonical hours, to sing the prayers and give the blessings. His duties usually include singing the daily conventual Mass.

hebdomadary The choir official appointed to act for a week at a time as the officiant at choral recitation of the Divine Office and the celebration of conventual or capitular Mass.

Hebrew (Aram. *Ebrai*) 1. That variation of the Chanaanite language as used by the Israelites. The Bible refers to it as the "language of Chanaan" (Is. 19:18). Rabbinical texts call it "the sacred language." Biblical Hebrew varies widely from modern Hebrew. 2. A person who speaks Hebrew. In the New Testament the word refers to one who spoke Aramaic in contrast to the Hellenists or Greek-speaking Jews.

Hebrew Bible, the The Christian Old Testament made up of the Torah (Pentateuch), Neviim (Prophets), Ketuvim (Writings). The *Torah* includes the five books of Moses: Genesis, Exodus, Leviticus, Numbers, Deuteronomy. *Neviim:* Josue, Judges, Samuel, Kings, Isaia, Jeremia, Ezechiel, Minor Prophets. *Ketuvim:* Psalms, Proverbs, Job, Five Scrolls (Song of Songs, Ruth, Lamentations, Ecclesiastes, Esther), Daniel, Ezra, Nehemia, Chronicles Paralipomenon).

Hebrews, Epistle to the A letter under the name of St. Paul addressed to Christian Jews. The precise community to which the Epistle was sent is unknown but it was probably meant for the Jews of Palestine. It is an important part of the scriptural canon because it demonstrates the superiority of the New Testament over the Old, and it deals with the mediating priesthood and sacrifice of Christ. In language and style it differs much from other Pauline Epistles. Its contents are also unusual when compared with other Pauline Espistles. Hebrews' central theme of Christ's High Priesthood is not found in any other Epistle. The view of some Catholic scholars is that it was written by an unknown author from an outline provided by St. Paul who approved the finished work and allowed his name to be signed to the letter.

hedonism (Gr. *hedomai*, take pleasure) The teaching that pleasure is the end of human conduct with the result that actions which give pleasure are good in themselves and that those which give displeasure or pain are thereby wrong.

hell The place and state of eternal punishment for all who die in mortal sin; the place of the Devil and evil spirits.

heortology (Gr. *heorte*, feast; *logos*, knowledge) The science and study of the feasts of the Church: their origin, history and meaning.

Help of Christians A title in the Litany of Loreto that was inserted by Pope St. Pius V following the battle of Lepanto.

heraldry, ecclesiastical The science of devising distinguishing marks or emblems such as the arms of a religious corporation, the arms of a bishop, the insignia of ecclesiastical rank or office; the emblems or devices of saints and popes. The devices used by a bishop are a mitre, crosier, a flat, wide-brimmed green hat with tassels, and a shield. The pope has the tiara and the crossed keys of St. Peter, one gold, the other silver. *See* coat of arms; hat.

heresiarch A Greek derivative that refers to a person who originates or leads a heresy.

heresy (Gr. *hairein*, to choose) Originally a division among Christians; the false doctrine or false interpretation of true doctrine. Formal heresy is a grievous sin; it is rebellion against God.

heresy, material The error of a Christian who rejects some truth of the Catholic faith without knowing that it is the truth. It is opposed to formal heresy in which there is pertinacity in the will. Material heresy is not sinful since it is not voluntary. Thus a Protestant incurs no guilt from material heresy.

heretic A baptized person, who while retaining the name of Christian, obstinately denies or doubts a truth of the Catholic Faith. Such persons choose on their own authority what beliefs to accept or reject contrary to the truths revealed by God and taught infallibly by His Church.

hermeneutics (Gr. *hermeneuein*, to interpret) The science that treats of the principles upon which the correct interpretation of the Bible is based.

hermit (Gr. *eremos*, solitary) One who lives alone in order to devote himself exclusively to God. Hermits were the forerunners of modern monks. In the early Church hermits lived entirely solitary, subject only to whatever rule they adopted for themselves. Later they grouped together under a common rule and these groupings evolved into the monastic orders. Today the solitary hermit is a rarity but some communities of hermits still exist, such as the Carthusians and Camaldolese.

Herodians A group mentioned in Mk. 3:6 and 12:13. Although it is not clear to whom the term refers, it is generally held that they were Jewish partisans and courtiers of the Herod dynasty who supported the Romans. They conspired with the Pharisees against Christ.

heroic virtue (L. *virtus,* manliness) Manifestation of a particular moral excellence, doing more than one is required to do. The practice of virtue to a degree worthy of salvation.

Hesychasts (Gr. quietist) Followers of a system of mysticism defended by monks of Athos in the 14th century. They believed that by a rigorous system of asceticism they would be able to see a mystic light, the uncreated light of God which was present at the Transfiguration.

hesychia (Gr.) The perfect tranqility of flesh and spirit; interior peace. In the Eastern Church monks who achieve this peace are called hesychasts.

heterodoxy (Gr. *heterodoxos,* of another opinion) The quality of holding different opinions from accepted doctrine; erroneous; not orthodox.

hexateuch (Gr. *hexateuchos,* six scrolls) The six books which are made up of the Pentateuch and the Book of Josue. Some scriptural scholars hold these books as a unit taken from the same literary sources.

hierarch (Gr. *hierarchia,* sacred rule) In general, any member of the hierarchy but especially an archbishop or patriarch.

hierarchical orders The episcopate, priesthood and diaconate; the three

main grades of the Sacrament of Holy Orders.

hierarchy, celestial Angelic orders collectively. Theologians and early writers, basing their reasoning upon an enumeration given in Scripture by Isaia, Ezechiel, St. Paul (Col. 1:16, Eph. 1:21), list three hierarchies in each of which there are three orders, making nine types of classifications. The first three: Seraphim, Cherubim, Thrones; the second: Dominations, Principalities, Powers; the third: Virtues, Archangels, Angels. The classes or choirs of angels differ in the degree of perfection of their nature and of grace, and this in a descending order in the listing above.

hierarchy, ecclesiastical A body of Church rulers, disposed organically in ranks and orders each subordinate to the one above it. A system of Church government or its authority. The hierarchy of the Church has two distinctions: 1. by reason of Holy Orders, the hierarchy is composed of bishops, priests and deacons; 2. by reason of jurisdiction, the hierarchy is made up of the pope and the bishops under his authority. The jurisdiction of the second group may, by delegation, be shared in part by clerics of the first group. Thus the hierarchy of the Church includes all grades of the clergy.

Hieronymites Members of any religious order of hermits named after St. Jerome. Refers specificially to an order founded in the 14th century in Spain and Italy by an amalgamation of groups of hermits which became very influential in Spain in the 15th and 16th centuries. There is no historical link between St. Jerome and this order, although he is their model and patron. This order rose to great influence in Spain and Portugal at the time of the discovery of the New

World, and participated in the conquest of the island of Santo Domingo, which was under the government of the order for a time.

hierugia (Gr. *hieros,* sacred) A sacred action, the Eucharistic Liturgy, the Mass.

High Church That movement in the Anglican or Episcopal Church which follows Catholic practices in liturgy, doctrine or other usages.

High Holyday A name given to two important Jewish feasts: Rosh Hashanah and Yom Kippur.

High Mass The Solemn Mass. The celebrant is assisted by a deacon and subdeacon plus other servers. This is the complete ritual of the Mass in which parts of it are sung; the ministers, people and altar are incensed; the Kiss of Peace (Pax) is given.

high places 1. Altars of the Old Testament set up on hills or elevations. 2. The upper places of space as referred to by St. Paul (Eph. 6:12). 3. Exalted positions in State or Church.

hindering impediment A condition which renders a marriage illicit but not invalid. *See* impediments.

Hispano-Gallican Rite Commonly known as the Mozarabic or Toledo Rite. It is a Latin liturgy of the Gallican group—the ancient Spanish Rite, basically Roman with overtones of Milan and southwest France. Its origin can be traced to the 3rd or 4th century. From the 11th century on, the Holy See gradually succeeded in replacing it with the authentic Roman Rite. Its continuation is provided for in a chapel of the cathedral of Toledo, Spain.

history, Church The history of the Kingdom of God on earth. The statement of the foundation and development of the Catholic Church, its personages, its spread from age to age, its adversities and persecutions. The subject matter of Church history is all those events which have touched the life of the Catholic Church since its foundation. Church history considers the relations of the Church with various nations among which it is established, explains the developments of dogmas and the conflicts with schism and heresy, and shows how the Church adapts to every people in all times. Church history can be broken down into four periods: 1. from the birth of Christ to A.D. 680, the period of Christian Antiquity; 2. from A.D. 680 to A.D. 1500, the Middle Ages when all Western Christendom was under one head, the Pope; 3. from 1500 to 1870, the Reformation and Post-Reformation periods when much of Western Christendom was lost to the Church but when the Church made new advances in America, Asia and Africa; 4. from 1870 to the present, the modern period. Church history should be presented with secular history since the Church cannot exist out of the context of its times.

Hoey Award A medal conferred annually by the Catholic Interracial Council on the two Catholic laymen, white and Negro, who have done the most during the year to promote racial equality.

holiness (AS. *halignes,* perfect) 1. Divine: the infinite perfection and wholeness of God. 2. Human: an inherent quality by which man is united to God. It is the possession of sanctifying grace and separation from sin. 3. Objective: the dedication of a person or object to the service of God. In this sense, a church, a nun, a priest, a chalice, etc., are said to possess holiness. 4. Mark of the Church: one of the signs by which the true Church of Christ can be recognized and distinguished from false churches. It is found in the Church because its faith and discipline are for the purpose of sanctifying its members. Its holiness is revealed in its worship, doctrine and laws, in its miracles, and in its many saints. 5. A title reserved in the West for the pope (His Holiness, Your Holiness). In the East it is used for metropolitans and bishops.

holocaust (Gr. *holos,* whole; *kaustos,* burned) A sacrifice wholly consumed in fire. The Jews burned animals as their expression of reverence and dependence on God, and as a means of atonement. These sacrifices foreshadowed the perfect sacrifice of Christ.

Holy Alliance A treaty signed between Austria, Prussia and Russia in 1815 and later subscribed to by France and England. It took its name from the fact that it pledged the subscribing governments to base their rule on Christian morality and not to make war on one another. It finally degenerated into a mere political alliance.

Holy Child Jesus, Religious of the A religious society of women founded in Derby, England, by Cornelia Connelly, under the direction of Bishop (later Cardinal) Wiseman in 1846. Mrs. Connelly, a native of Philadelphia and a convert, had agreed to separate from her husband Pierce, a convert from Anglicanism, to allow him to fulfill his wish to become a Catholic priest. She lived in Rome for a while near the Convent of the Sacred Heart, and was persuaded by Pope Gregory XVI to found a much needed order for the education of girls in England. She, with a few companions, began living the religious life at Derby, following a rule inspired by that of the Religious of the Sacred Heart. The order grew

and was soon established in many countries, due to its reputation for imparting a sound education and a thorough grounding in religion. The widowed Duchess of Leeds donated two thousand acres of land in Pennsylvania, making it possible for Mother Connelly to begin work in her native America. A school was opened at Sharon Hill, Pa., in 1864, and soon a chain of educational institutions sprang up in the United States—notable among these, Rosemont College near Philadelphia. The motherhouse of the order is in Rome.

Holy Childhood Association A children's association founded in 1863 by Bishop Charles de Forbin-Janson of Nancy, France, for the purpose of cooperating with missioners in saving children of non-Christian lands from sin and death. Members cooperate by the practice of Christian charity, mortification and small monetary offerings.

Holy Coat, the Several garments that purport to be the seamless garment taken from Christ at His Crucifixion. One, located at the cathedral in Treves, Germany, tradition says goes back to St. Helen; another at Argenteuil, France, reportedly came from Charlemagne.

Holy Communion The body, blood, soul and divinity of Christ whole and entire which is received under the form of bread and wine alone or together and consumed by the recipient. All baptized persons, in the state of grace, having the right intention and observing the proper fast may receive the Sacrament of the Eucharist. Moreover, all Catholics are bound to do so at least once a year.

Holy Cross, Congregation of the A religious congregation of men who take the simple vows of poverty, chastity and obedience, and devote themselves to missionary work and to the education of youth. It was founded in France in 1837, in reaction to the inroads in Catholic education due to persecutions during the French Revolution. It resulted from the official union of two previously constituted societies—the Brothers of St. Joseph (educational) and the Auxiliary Priests of Le Mans (missions and retreats). Father Basile-Antoine Moreau was the first superior. The congregation spread rapidly through France and its North African colonies until by the Law of Associations of 1901 the French government closed all their schools and colleges and confiscated their property. Only a few old, feeble Brothers and one priest remained in France, at Angers. The members of the congregation, forbidden in France, set out for Bengal, India, and for Canada and the United States. Father Edward Sorin, at the invitation of the Bishop of Vincennes, had founded the humble beginnings of Notre Dame University in 1842. As the institution grew, missionary work and educational institutions were carried on in other parts of the United States. The Congregation of the Holy Cross now has two provinces in the United States. The generalate is in Rome.

Holy Face, the   The suffering face of Christ in His Passion. The devotion is rooted in the representation of the face of Christ said to have been left on the towel or veil used by Veronica to wipe the face of Jesus. An Archconfraternity of the Holy Face was established in Tours, France, in 1884, whose members make reparation for the blasphemies hurled at Christ. The great devotion of St. Thérèse to the Holy Face has brought it to the attention of many of the faithful.

Holy Family   The family which consisted of the Child Jesus, Mary and Joseph. The Holy Family has long been a subject of devotion and inspiration, and has given its name to a number of pious associations and religious institutes. A feast honoring the Holy Family, instituted in 1893 by Pope Leo XIII, in 1921 became universal. It falls on the Sunday after Epiphany.

Holy Father   The pope (*q.v.*).

Holy Ghost   *See* Holy Spirit.

Holy Ghost Fathers   Congregation of the Holy Ghost and of the Immaculate Heart of Mary. A religious congregation of men founded in France in 1703, by Claude Poullart des Places, a young Breton nobleman. The young congregation prospered and sent missioners to the French colonies, India and China. However, after the French Revolution only one member was left alive. A young Alsatian Jew, Francis Libermann, was converted in 1826, became a priest, and set out to found a society for work among the Negroes of Africa. The pope suggested that he unite his new Society of the Immaculate Heart of Mary with the older one of the Holy Ghost, an amalgamation which took place in 1848 with Father Libermann as Superior General. Over the years the society has prospered. The Holy Ghost Fathers arrived in the United States in 1872. Although the organization conducts missions in many parts of the world, it is best known in the United States for Duquesne University and its African missions.

Holy Hour   An hour set aside to honor the Blessed Sacrament exposed. In many places it is a monthly devotion, often on the First Friday of the month. In some places it consists of recitation of the Rosary, hymns, litanies and other prayers, closing with Benediction. A recent trend is to a more biblical approach with passages being read from Sacred Scripture, meditation on the Scripture and the singing of psalms.

Holy Innocents A feast celebrated in the Western Church on Dec. 28 to commemorate the children murdered by King Herod (Matt. 2:16-18). The Eastern Church venerates them under the title "the Holy Children" on various dates. Although they are venerated as martyrs, when their feast falls on a week day, purple vestments are worn. This indicates the mixed joy and sorrow for the innocent victims of the first persecution.

Holy Land The land in which Christ lived, Palestine. There is a Commissariat of the Holy Land in the care of the Order of Friars Minor which is charged with collecting alms for the support of the holy places and shrines which are now found in Israel and Jordan.

Holy Name Together with the names of God and the Holy Spirit, the name of Jesus is the most revered in the language of Christians. It was a name given under instructions from God Himself (Lk. 1:31). The name comes from the Greek *Iesous,* derived from the Aramaic *Yeshu.* It means "Jahweh is salvation." The name has been treated with the greatest respect from the earliest days of the Church, and the custom is to bow one's head whenever it is spoken. In the 13th century the Dominicans preached devotion to the Holy Name, and in the 15th century SS. Bernadine of Siena and John Capistran, Franciscans, promoted devotion to the Holy Name with the result that the Franciscan Order was given a feast in honor of the Holy Name. This feast became universal in 1721. When possible, it is observed on the Sunday after Jan.

1, For many years the Holy Name Society has promoted reverence and respect for the Holy Name.

Holy Name Society, the An indulgenced confraternity of men whose purpose is: 1. to promote love and reverence for the Holy Name of God and of Jesus; 2. to discourage profanity, blasphemy, perjury, unlawful oaths and improper language. It originated at the Council of Lyons in 1274 and spread rapidly through the preaching of the Dominicans after Pope Gregory X asked the Master General, Blessed John of Vercelli, to have the Friars Preachers promote it. Devotion to the Holy Name has always been a particularly Dominican trait. It was the Spanish Friar Didacus of Victoria (d. 1450) who founded a confraternity of the Holy Name and drew up a rule and constitution for it, which was approved by Pope Pius IV in 1564 and richly indulgenced. The Pope commanded all priests and bishops to favor it. This confraternity merged with the Society of the Holy Name and was promoted by later popes, continuing under the direction of the Dominicans. Branches of the society are found all over the Christian world and have flourished in the United States since 1882. There are about 5 million members. Group reception of Holy Communion in the parish church or cathedral at stated intervals, together with reverence for the Holy Name, and hatred of all blasphemy and foul language, are the main characteristics of the Holy Name Society. It has an official organ, the *Holy Name Journal.*

Holy of Holies The innermost room of the Jewish Temple. In Solomon's Temple it was where the Ark of the Covenant was kept. It was entered once a year by the high priest on the

Day of Atonement to offer sacrifice for the people.

Holy Office, Congregation of the Founded by Paul III in 1542 to combat heresy. Since that time the Congregation has gone through various reforms. Since this Congregation is also a Tribunal, there are, in addition to an Assessor, a Commissary and two Companions of the Order of Preachers who prepare investigations. For the study of doctrinal questions, the Congregation is assisted by scholars known as Qualificatores. Its competence extends to all questions dealing with faith and morals, the Pauline Privilege and mixed marriages. It watches over publications and the reading of books contrary to Faith. In criminal cases, it has jurisdiction over offenses against faith and the unity of the Church (such as apostasy, heresy, schism, profanation of the Eucharist, etc.). All matters are handled under strictest secrecy.

holy oils Oils of catechumens, oil of the sick, chrism consecrated by the bishop on Holy Thursday and given to the priests of the parishes.

Holy Orders, Sacrament of (L. *ordo*, rank) A sacrament of the New Law instituted by Christ by which spiritual power is handed on and grace is conferred for the confection (*q.v.*) of the sacraments, especially of the Eucharist, and, therefore, for offering sacrifice, and for the proper carrying out of other ecclesiastical duties. Subdiaconate, diaconate and priesthood are called major, sacred or holy because of their dignity, powers and obligations. Of these orders two are sacramental, namely, the diaconate and the priesthood which confer upon the recipient an indelible character and the power to administer divine grace to the faithful both by the sacraments and by the Word. The conse-

cration of a bishop is not a special order because the episcopal order is that of the priesthood in its highest perfection. In the bishop are vested the full powers of the priesthood; but not all these powers are conferred upon the ordinary priest, who is therefore a priest of lower rank. Major orders must be conferred during Mass, and, as a rule, on the Ember Saturdays, the Saturday before Passion Sunday and Holy Saturday. For a good reason, however, the bishop may also confer them on any Sunday or feast of obligation. The rite of conferring major orders is more solemn than that of minor orders. The features of the preceding ordinations remain: the call, the instruction, the bestowal of the office and prayer. More prayers and other ceremonies are added, however, in accordance with the nature of the respective order. Despite the various grades in the ministry, only one Sacrament of Holy Orders exists.

holy places Those places in Israel and Jordan which were connected with Jesus Christ. It was to visit these sacred shrines that Pope Paul VI made his historic trip to the Holy Land. Some are in the custody of the Western Church, some in the custody of the Orthodox and some in the custody of Muslims. The chief holy places are Calvary, the Via Dolorosa (Way of the Cross), the Cenacle, the Holy Sepulcher, Gethsemani, the grotto of the Nativity at Bethlehem, the Church of the Annunciation at Nazareth, the River Jordan where Christ was baptized, the Sea of Galilee and Mount Tabor where Christ was transfigured. Many of the sites are fixed only by tradition, others by archeology.

Holy Roman Empire An imperial domain of west central Europe, consisting of numerous states and countries (Austria, Bavaria, Bohemia, Brandenburg, Franconia, Lorraine, Saxony, Swabia, to name but a few), whose people were principally German-speaking. Besides being governed by their own rulers, these states were theoretically under the authority of the Holy Roman Emperor. Moreover, for centuries the Empire had interests in Italy and at various times it claimed sovereignty over territories outside Germany proper. Historians date the origin of the Empire either from the reign of Charlemagne (who was crowned by Pope Leo III in A.D. 800) or from that of Otto the Great when a permanent union of the German states with the Empire had its beginnings (A.D. 962). The history of the Empire is bound up with the papacy and Germany. The Empire was dissolved in 1806 after Napoleon, victorious over the Austrians and Russians at Austerlitz in December, 1805, formed the Confederation of the Rhine out of much of the territory of the Empire. The emperors were elected to office. The number of electors, who chose the emperor upon the death of an incumbent, was fixed at seven by the Golden Bull, promulgated by Emperor Charles IV in 1356. The seven electors were divided; there were three ecclesiastical (the Archbishops of Mainz, Trier and Cologne) and four lay electors.

Holy Saturday The day before Easter, Easter eve. It is a day of mourning for Christ in the tomb. The bare altar reminds Catholics to think of the suffering their sins have caused. In the evening the Easter Vigil service takes place. The purpose of this beautiful liturgy is to live, in a great act of worship, the mystery of how the Christ-life within us springs from the death of Christ on the cross. The Easter Vigil service consists of two parts. 1. *Service of Light.* A fire is kindled as a symbol of Christ newly present and active in this Easter mystery. The Easter candle symbolically represents Christ. Just as all the candles in the church are relighted from the Easter candle, so all spiritual life and light come from Christ alone. There is a solemn procession of the Easter candle. 2. *Service of Baptism.* The light and life of Christ come to men through Baptism when the infusion of grace cleanses them from sin. Baptismal water is blessed. Baptismal promises are renewed. The Easter Vigil Mass concludes the service.

Holy See The episcopal see of Rome, the Apostolic See. The term includes the pope and the various congregations, offices and tribunals which aid him in governing the Church.

Holy Sepulcher, Church of the Officially, the Church of the Resurrection. It was built over the remains of the sepulcher in which Christ was buried. It is situated a short distance northwest of Calvary. The original church was built by Constantine. The church which now shelters the sepulcher and Calvary was built by the Crusaders. The Orthodox, Copts, Syrians and Armenians share the building with the Catholics. The Catholic guardians are the Friars Minor. The authenticity of the site has been attacked but today its location is accepted as genuine.

Holy Sepulcher, Knights of the A papal order of knighthood whose origin is uncertain. It is known that the order appeared in the Holy Land and was in existence in 1113 when it was approved by Pope Paschal I. The prestige of the order decreased with the overthrow of the Latin Kingdom of Jerusalem, and the withdrawal of its members to Perugia. Over the years, the Order has undergone many revisions. Today the Order of the Holy Sepulcher has five classes: Grand Cross, Commanders with Plaque, Commanders, Knights and 12 Knights of the Collar with four degrees. Women are accepted for membership.

holy souls   The souls of the dead who died in the grace of God but are detained in purgatory to make satisfaction for temporal punishment due to sins. Their release into heaven may be obtained by prayer and works of suffrage on the part of the living faithful; such works and prayers are a work of charity. The commemoration is kept on Nov. 2.

Holy Spirit   The third Person of the Blessed Trinity. The spirit of the Father and Son, moving in a common spiration. He is also known as the Sanctifier because He sanctifies us by the graces and virtues He infuses; the Creator Spirit; the Spirit of Truth; the Comforter because He continually comforts and nourishes the Church. The Holy Spirit is symbolized by the dove (under which form He appeared at the Baptism of Christ) and by tongues of fire (as He appeared above the heads of the Apostles on the first Pentecost).

Holy Spirit, indwelling of the   The presence of the Holy Spirit in the soul of a person in the state of sanctifying grace.

Holy Thursday   The Thursday before Easter. On this day in the cathedral of the diocese the bishop consecrates the holy oils. To encourage confession on this day, the Church grants a plenary indulgence to anyone who visits the altar of repose after having confessed and received Holy Communion. The liturgy of Holy Thursday centers about the Eucharist. Holy Thursday celebrates the institution of the Mass at the Last Supper as the sacrifice and sacrament of Christian unity. On this day Jesus first shared His priesthood with men by ordaining the Apostles. Then He uttered the command that is the reason for every Mass: "Do this in remembrance of Me." This is the day to think of the great love Jesus showed in instituting the Eucharist through which we are united to Christ and one another. Everyone should spend some time on Holy Thursday adoring Jesus at the altar of repose. The stripping of the altars after Mass is a sign that Mass will not be offered again until the evening of Holy Saturday.

holy water   A sacramental. Water blessed by a priest to impart God's blessing on those who use it. The use of holy water goes back to the earliest days in the Church and today it is blessed according to a formula in the Roman Ritual. There are many kinds of holy water; the principal kinds are: 1. ordinary, used for the Asperges, at the door of the church, for blessings and in the home; 2. baptismal water, which contains oil of catechumens and holy chrism, used only for Baptism; 3. water of consecration or Gregorian water, with wine, salt and ashes, used in the consecration of a church.

holy water font   A vessel for holding  holy water found at the doors of a church, also called a stoup. The vessels are sometimes fixed to the wall and at other times set on a pedestal. There are also private fonts usually affixed alongside the door of a private room.

Holy Week The week preceding Easter, the most solemn week of the liturgical year. It begins with second Passion Sunday (Palm Sunday) and concludes with Holy Saturday. During the week Christians worship Christ as the King who went to His death voluntarily, with a royal freedom, because it was His Father's will. Catholics are urged to put themselves in a proper disposition for taking part devoutly and fruitfully in the Holy Week services by going to confession early in the week. A living, active participation by word, song and deed brings a greater spiritual profit to each worshiper.

holy women 1. Those women associated with Christ, particularly with His Passion and Death. These include Mary, His Mother; Mary Magdalene; Joanna; Mary, the mother of James; Mary of Cleophas; and others who prepared His body for burial. 2. Those female saints for whom there are common Masses, e.g., widows, virgins, married, penitents, martyr virgins, martyr married.

Holy Year A year set aside by the pope as one of special grace and prayer during which the Jubilee Indulgence can be gained under prescribed conditions. Since the middle of the 15th century a Holy Year has been proclaimed every 25 years. The year begins with the opening of the holy doors in the major basilicas on Christmas Eve and ends on the following Christmas Eve when the doors are resealed.

holyday of obligation Days other than Sunday on which the faithful are bound to attend Mass. In the United States these are New Year's Day (Jan. 1), Ascension (forty days after Easter), Assumption (Aug. 15), All Saints' Day (Nov. 1), Immaculate Conception (Dec. 8), Christmas (Dec. 25). In Canada, the Assumption is dropped from the list but Epiphany (Jan. 6) is a holyday. All of the days already mentioned are holydays of the universal Church, plus Feasts of St. Joseph (Mar. 19), Corpus Christi (Thursday following first Sunday after Pentecost), SS. Peter and Paul (June 29). In Ireland, the Feast of St. Patrick (Mar. 17) is a holyday.

homicide The killing of one human being by another. If the killing is direct and unlawful it is murder. Homicide may be justified in self-defense or war to protect one's own life. It is direct killing but not unlawful to kill in self-defense against an unjust aggressor, whether as a private citizen or a soldier. Killing another through culpable carelessness or negligence is culpable homicide, although not directly intended.

homiletics (Gr. *homilein,* to have communication with) The art or study whereby one learns the composition of sermons and homilies and the effective means of preaching them. Especially concerned with Biblical themes.

homily A short sermon expounding the mysteries of faith and the guiding principles of the Christian life as found in the Gospel or Epistle of the Mass. According to the Constitution on the Liturgy promulgated by Pope Paul VI in 1963, the homily is to be highly esteemed as part of the liturgy itself. The Constitution further provides that at those Masses which are celebrated with the assistance of the people on Sundays and holydays of obligation, the homily must be given.

homoiousion (hoe-moy-oo'see-on Gr. like in substance) A word used by Semi-Arians to indicate that Christ was like the Father in substance but not identical with the Father in substance and nature. This word is the key to Semi-Arian doctrine.

homoousian (Gr. of the same substance) This is the key word used by the Council of Nicaea (325) in condemnation of the doctrine of Semi-Arianism which affirmed that Christ was only like His Father. The Council in using this word declared that Christ was consubstantial with the Father, and therefore coequal and coeternal with the Father. *See* homoiousion.

homosexual A person who is sexually orientated toward persons of the same sex, i.e., the attraction of one man for another, or one woman for another. A male homosexual does not necessarily appear effeminate; nor a female homosexual, masculine. Although the term may be used for male or female, it is usually reserved for the male while the word "lesbian" is used for the female. In some instances, homosexuality seems almost innate, while in others it is definitely acquired. Homosexuality does not diminish responsibility for one's acts, and the person so afflicted has the same responsibility to avoid venereal pleasure as does an unmarried normal person.

Honduras Evangelized by Franciscans about 1550. Honduras today has 1 archdiocese, 2 dioceses, 1 vicariate and 1 prelature. There are 154 priests to serve a population of almost 2 million, or approximately 1 priest for every 13,000 people. This lack of priests is the chief handicap of the Church as the rural people have a natural religious sentiment.

honest day's work 1. The amount of work an employer can expect for the wages or salary paid a worker. 2. An unwritten agreement among workmen as to the amount of work that should be done despite what can ac-

tually be done. To do more is "rate busting" and to do less is "chiseling."

honor The external recognition of a person's excellence. This recognition can be conveyed by words (praise), by actions (a bow) or by external objects (a medal). Honor is violated by contumely which is the unjust dishonoring of another in his presence. Honor is a person's prime external good, and all are bound to give honor when it is due (Rom. 13:7).

hood That part of a monk's habit that serves as a covering for the head. It is commonly called a cowl.

hope One of the three theological virtues infused into the soul at Baptism which makes us desire the possession of God and which gives us the confidence that we will receive the necessary grace to accomplish this end. Hope is necessary for salvation. The sins against hope are despair and presumption.

hope, act of A prayer expressing our confidence in God's promises of eternal happiness and in obtaining the means to accomplish this end.

Horae Diurnae (L. day hours) A book containing the Day Hours of the Divine Office.

Hosanna (Heb. "Do save!") A Hebrew exclamation used both as a cry for help and as a joyous shout of homage. In Catholic worship the term occurs in the *Sanctus,* following the *Preface.*

Hosea Osee (*q.v.*).

hospital (L. *hospes,* guest) Hospitals have long been a means of expressing Catholic charity. The earliest known Catholic hospitals were founded in the 4th century by Fabiola, St. Pammachus and St. Basil. The latter's foundation in Caesarea had a special section for lepers, and as far as is known was the first such asylum. The oldest hospital in existence is the Hotel Dieu which was founded under religious auspices in Paris about A.D. 660. Many religious orders have been established to assist the sick, and to staff hospitals. The members of the latter are known as hospitallers.

Hospital Sisters of St. Francis Founded in Germany in 1844 and established in the United States in 1875. The Sisters are engaged primarily in hospital work and nursing. There are home missions among Indians and in the Ozarks and a foreign mission in Japan. Simple vows are taken. There are approximately 800 Sisters in the United States.

hospitality, Christian An extension of Christian charity. The term is most often applied to the opening of one's home to a stranger or visitor. Christian hospitality was practiced by the early monks, who had the motto: *Hospes venit, Christus venit* ("A guest comes, Christ comes"). A traveler or stranger was always welcome at a monastery. Catholics in America have the opportunity to practice Christian hospitality among the foreign students and visitors who come to our country each year. There are approximately 65,000 men and women from other countries studying at American colleges and universities. Most of them have no friends or acquaintances when they arrive on America's shores. It is a great opportunity for American Catholics to practice Christian hospitality by opening their homes to these foreign students and visitors. Hospitality can be practiced by an invitation to dinner or by an invitation to spend the weekend or Christmas holidays with an American family. Such a visit would do much to dispel the loneliness of the foreign student, and it would also give the American family a better understanding of another country and culture. Such hospitality will not go unrewarded, for Our Lord will one day say: "Come you blessed of my Father, take possession of the kingdom prepared for you from the foundation of the world, . . . for I was a stranger, and you entertained me" (Mt. 25:34-35).

host (L. *hostia,* hostage) The consecrated bread used in the Eucharistic Liturgy. 2. The unconsecrated wafer. 3. A title applied to Jesus Christ as victim for our sins.

This is the meaning of the word in the Benediction hymn "O Salutaris Hostia" and as found in the Mass.

hot cross buns Small buns decorated with a glazed sugar cross and eaten on Ash Wednesday and Good Friday. It is not known how the custom arose although it is of fairly recent origin.

Hotel Dieu (Fr. house of God) A name applied to a large Catholic hospital. The most famous in North America are in Quebec City and Montreal in Canada, and in New Orleans, La.

hour 1. Canonical. One of the divisions of the Divine Office, called a canonical hour because it is prescribed to be said at or near a particular time. 2. Scriptural. In the time of Our Lord the civil day was reckoned from sunset to sunset. There were twelve hours in the day beginning approximately at 6 A.M. and ending at 6 P.M. The third, sixth, ninth and twelfth hours were particularly sacred to prayer. The night was divided into four watches: 6 P.M., the "midnight watch" at 9

P.M., cockcrow at 12, and the morning watch at 3 A.M.

house, blessing of a There are a number of blessings for a house in the Roman Ritual. One is for the blessing of houses at Easter and another for the Feast of the Epiphany. The most commonly used blessing is the one for a new house. The priest vested in surplice and stole (the color of the day) says two versicles and their responses, then comes the blessing proper during which the priest makes the Sign of the Cross six times. The blessing ends with the priest sprinkling the house with holy water.

household of the pope The pontifical family. All those in the immediate service of the pope. These include the *major domo,* the *maestro di camera,* the auditor, the master of sacred palace, the sacristan, the apostolic preacher and many others.

humanitarianism The devotion to the cause of humanity as a substitute for religion. *See* secular humanism.

humanity of Christ Jesus Christ was true man, like all men except for sin. He was a perfect man with a complete human nature, with body, soul, intellect, will, human affection and human passions. The Gospels tell of Christ's love, sorrow, anger, hunger, weariness. In the tortures of the Passion He suffered in all of His senses, and finally He encountered death as all men must.

humeral veil (L. *humerus,* shoulder)
 A long oblong of white or gold worn over the shoulders by a priest when he carries the Blessed Sacrament in procession. It is so arranged that it covers the hands, thus preventing them from touching the monstrance. A humeral veil is used by the subdeacon to transfer the chalice. In this case the veil is the same color as the vestments. It is also used for the blessing at Benediction.

humerale (L. *humerus,* shoulder) The name given to shoulder coverings that preceded the amice.

humility (L. *humilitas*) A supernatural virtue which, through the self-revelation it imparts, inclines us to know our true worth and to seek self-effacement. Its foundation is our knowledge of self and a realization of our relationship to God. Its basis, therefore, is in truth and justice. Truth makes us realize that what is good in us comes from God and what is evil comes from self. Justice compels us to render to God alone all honor and all glory.

humility, degrees of The twelve degrees of humility as set down in the Rule of St. Benedict. They are: 1. fear of God; 2. preference for will of God to one's own; 3. obedience; 4. embracing patiently hard and contrary things; 5. openness to one's superior; 6. contentedness with the lowest position; 7. believing oneself lower than his companions; 8. following the rule completely; 9. observing silence; 10. restraint in laughter; 11. speaking gently, gravely and sparingly; 12. showing humility to all.

Hungary Catholicism was introduced into Hungary in the 8th century. Today of the 10 million people in Hungary, 70 per cent are Catholic. Nevertheless since 1946 the Church has been under constant pressure and subjected to both direct and subtle persecution by the Communist government. There are 3 archdioceses, 7 dioceses and 1 abbey nullius. Two archbishops, including Cardinal Mindszenty, and 3 bishops are not allowed to function. Many priests have been arrested and some have been executed. Catholic organizations have been taken over and Catholic institutions closed. Virtually all Church administration is under state-appointed commissars.

husband The correlative to wife; the head of a family to whom is due respect and obedience (Eph. 5:22-24). In return, the husband must love his wife, treating her with the respect given to a partner (Eph. 5:25-33). The husband has the obligation to consent to reasonable desire for marital intercourse. He is bound to support his wife and children. According to Church law, children follow the rite of the father, provided he is a Catholic.

hylomorphism (Gr. *hyle,* matter; *morphe,* form) The name given in Scholastic philosophy to the theory of matter and form.

hymn (Gr. *hymnos*) A song of praise. In the religious sense, a hymn is a poetic composition set to music in praise of God or His saints.

hymnal A hymn book. A collection of hymns to be used by the faithful.

hymnody All hymns and religious lyric poetry; hymns taken collectively.

hymnology The science and study of hymns.

hymns, liturgical Hymns appointed for use in the liturgy, i.e., in public official worship. They are divided into hymns used in the Mass and those found in the Divine Office. They may also be sung apart from the liturgical service, at Benediction or in processions.

hymns, nonliturgical Hymns used for private devotion or used as private prayer. These can be either in Latin or in the vernacular. They consist of religious verse, carols, folk-hymns, etc. There is a movement away from sentimental, pietistic verse to a form with more substantial meaning.

hyperdulia (Gr. *hyper,* above; *douleia,* servitude) The veneration given the Blessed Virgin as the mother of God. It is a higher homage than that (*dulia*) given to saints and angels. It contrasts with *latria,* the worship given to God alone.

hypnosis (Gr. *hypnos,* sleep) The process of inducing a sleeplike state which renders the person extremely responsive to any suggestion made by the hypnotist. This state is usually attained by bodily relaxation accompanied by attention, at the suggestion of the hypnotist, to a narrow range of objects or ideas. Because of the state of heightened suggestibility which this process can induce, it should be practiced only by those who are professionally competent and morally reputable. The practice is useful as a technique for bringing unconscious attitudes and feelings into awareness and for relieving disturbing anxieties and fears. It also has reputable uses for anesthetic purposes. The use of hypnosis by the unskilled can result in harm to the person hypnotized.

hypocrisy That attitude by which one pretends to be holy or virtuous. It is a species of lying. Christ made bitter condemnation of hypocrites.

hypostasis (Gr. *hypo,* under; *histemi,* stand) Literally, that which lies beneath something. The term is used to indicate a complete and individual substance that is not communicable. Thus when this substance is endowed with intelligence, a personality (hypostasis) develops. The word was

280

used by the Council of Chalcedon to indicate that the two natures in Christ are combined in the one person of the Son of God.

hypostatic union   A theological term to indicate that the two natures of Christ (God and man) are united to form the one person Jesus Christ. These natures do not lose their dis-tinction and as a result there are two wills.

hyssop (Gr. *hyssopos,* an aromatic plant)   A plant mentioned in Scripture and used by the Jews in sprinkling the blood of the paschal lamb or in sprinkling water for purification. It is thought to have been the thorny caper (*Capparis spinosa*).

I

ICA *See* International Catholic Auxiliaries.

icon (Gr. *eikon,* image) Representa-

tions on wood or metal, or Byzantine-style paintings of Our Lord, the Blessed Virgin and other saints, which take the place of statues in Eastern Churches.

iconoclasts (Gr. *eikonoklasmos,* image smashing) Followers of a heretical doctrine of the 8th and 9th centuries that taught that the use and veneration of sacred images was unlawful. It began with an edict of Emperor Leo in 726 which supported the heresy and ordered images destroyed. It was condemned by the Seventh Ecumenical Council in 787. It had its greatest effect in the Eastern Church but also had echoes in Europe.

iconostasis The image screen used in the Byzantine Lit-

urgy. It is a partition that separates the nave from the sanctuary with two small side doors and a large double door in the center. The screen is decorated with many icons.

id (L. that) A term coined by Freud to describe the sum of the unconscious biological urges of a person which drive him to seek pleasurable satisfaction.

Idaho One of the Rocky Mountain states, bordered on the east by the Continental Divide. It is 13th in area and 42nd in population. Early tribes of Indians were animists, and lived by hunting and fishing. The name "Idaho" in Shoshone tribal tongue means Salmon Tribe. Lewis and Clark, sent by President Jefferson, explored the area in 1805. Spain, Russia, England and the United States all claimed Idaho as part of Oregon Territory. By treaty with Britain in 1846, United States territory begins at the 49th parallel. Gold was discovered in 1860, railway construction began and towns sprang up. The Indians, their way of life disturbed, took to the warpath, but were subdued. The first priest to say Mass in Idaho (1840) was the Jesuit, Father De Smet, Apostle to the Indians. Jesuits also began work at Sacred Heart Mission among the Coeur d'Alenes, and built the first Catholic Church in Idaho in 1848. Father De Smet in particular made great progress among the Indians of the Northwest Territory, but most of the missions were later lost to the Church when the U.S. Commission

282

on Indian Affairs arranged for Protestant missionaries to take charge of them. The territory was under the jurisdiction of Archbishop Blanchet of Oregon City, who sent two priests in 1863 to care for the placer miners of Boise Basin. In 1867 Sisters of the Holy Names opened the first Catholic school at Idaho City. In 1868 Bishop Lootens was placed in charge of the Vicariate Apostolic of Idaho, and in 1893 the diocese of Boise was erected with Most Rev. Alphonse Glorieus as first bishop. In the meantime, Idaho had been admitted to the Union in 1890. Various religious orders were brought in and many Catholic schools built. Children out of reach of parochial schools were given correspondence courses in Catholic doctrine. Today there are over 45,-000 Catholics in Idaho, in a total population of 667,000.

idealism A philosophical system that denies the reality of matter, affirming that it exists solely in the spirit (the mind). Also an attitude toward things as one would wish them to be.

idleness In the spiritual sense, a vice which inclines a person not to work. It is different from sloth.

idol (Gr. *eidolon,* an image) Any person or thing which receives the worship properly due only to the true God. The images used in the Catholic Church do not receive worship.

idolatry (Gr. *eidololatreia,* image worship) The worship given to a person or thing which properly belongs solely to God. It is a sin against the virtue of religion. Idolatry is material (external) if the worship given is only external and fictional. It is formal (internal) when the worship is meant. Idolatry is against the First Commandment, and is not sinful only when it arises from invincible ignorance.

Ignatian Method *See* meditation.

ignorance (L. *ignorare,* to be ignorant) A lack of due knowledge, i.e., the absence of knowledge in a person capable of possessing this knowledge. Ignorance in relation to its object is either ignorance of fact or ignorance of law. In relation to its object, it is either vincible or invincible. In relation to the will, ignorance is either antecedent, if it exists prior to the act of the will, or consequent if it is the result of an act of the will which desires it. Ignorance is different from nescience (knowledge which the subject has no obligation to possess) and error.

ignorance, invincible A lack of knowledge which persists despite ordinary efforts to dispel it. Actions which proceed from invincible ignorance are neither voluntary nor imputable since nothing can be willed unless it is previously known. Thus a bad action done out of invincible ignorance cannot be a formal sin.

ignorance, vincible Ignorance that is due to a lack of reasonable effort to remove it. Although vincible ignorance may diminish the voluntariness of an act, it does not completely remove it. This is because vincible ignorance is of itself voluntary. Thus, if a confessor gives a penitent wrong advice from vincible ignorance, he is less sinful than if he gives wrong advice with full knowledge.

IHS A monogram formed from the first three Greek letters which spell the name of Jesus. As a monogram, it does not take a period after each letter. Various fanciful interpretations (I Have

Suffered; *Jesus Hominem Salvator;* etc.) have been given for the letters but they are erroneous.

illegitimacy Not according to law; the condition of one who is born out of wedlock. Illegitimates are children not conceived or born of a valid or putative marriage. (A putative marriage is an invalid marriage that was celebrated in good faith by at least one of the parties and contracted with the form to which the parties were bound.) An illegitimate child can be legitimated and thus acquire a juridical status similar but not always equal in canon law to the status of legitimate children. Legitimation in canon law can be granted: 1. By the subsequent valid or putative marriage of the parents, whether the marriage is only now contracted, or was contracted before (invalidly) and is now convalidated, the children are made legitimate provided the parents were legally capable of contracting marriage with each other at the time of the child's conception, or of the pregnancy, or of the child's birth. 2. By a dispensation granted from a diriment impediment in virtue of ordinary power or of power delegated by a general indult, there is automatically granted the legitimation of offspring already born or conceived by the persons receiving the dispensation; 3. If the Holy See grants legitimation as a favor. Effects of illegitimacy: illegitimates may not be admitted to the seminary; they are irregular; they cannot obtain ecclesiastical offices and benefices. Foundlings are presumed to be legitimate. For details in the matter of illegitimacy in civil law, the reader must consult the particular civil legislations.

illicit Acts are licit or illicit, depending on whether they are permitted by law (sometimes even commanded) or forbidden by law. Some acts require certain essential requisites or conditions in order to produce a legal or juridical effect: they are valid if they have these requisites, and invalid if they lack an essential condition necessary to produce their proper effect. An act can be valid but illicit; it can be invalid, but licit. This distinction is important in the sacraments and in contracts, including the contract of marriage. Thus, if a Catholic layman baptizes anyone, except in an emergency, using natural water and the proper words (which are necessary for validity) the baptism is valid, but illicit, because forbidden. If anyone having a prohibiting impediment (not, however, invalidating) marries knowing he has the impediment and receives no dispensation, the marriage is valid, but illicit.

Illinois A north central state in a prosperous farming and industrial area. It was the 21st to be admitted to the Union, is 24th in area and 4th in population. Jesuit Father Marquette and Louis Joliet explored the country in 1673 and Mission Immaculate Conception was founded near Utica. The first martyr was Father Ribourde, O.F.M., whom the Kickapoos killed at Seneca. The first permanent settlement was made by La Forrest and Tonti in 1692 at Lake Peoria. A chapel was built there and blessed by Father Gravier, S.J., who wrote the first grammar and dictionary of the Illinois Indians. Various forts and missions were established by the French, who were defeated in the Seven Years' War, the territory being then held by the British until the Treaty of Peace in 1783. Illinois Territory (1809) was admitted as a State in 1818. In 1833 the Catholics of Chicago received their first resident pastor, Father St. Cyr, sent by Bishop Rosati of St. Louis, and the first Mass was offered in a log cabin. In 1844 the diocese of Chicago was established. Numerous congregations of religious men and women arrived and built up works of education and charity. St. Frances Cabrini worked in Chicago and died there in 1917. Today there is 1 archdiocese (Chicago) and 5 dioceses in Illinois. The Eparchy of St. Nicholas (Ukrainian Catholic) is also established at Chicago. There are about three and one-half million Catholics in a total population of over ten million.

illuminative way, the   The second stage of the spiritual life which takes its name because the desire of the soul is the following of Christ by the positive exercise of Christian virtue. Jesus said: "I am the light of the world. He who follows Me does not walk in the darkness, but will have the light of life" (Jn. 8-12).

Illuminism   A teaching affirming the autonomy of reason independent of all authority, hostile to tradition. One of the leaders was the Englishman, Herbert of Cherbury (d. 1648), who professed a naturalistic religion that consisted of a few noncontroversial fundamental truths.

image (L. *imago,* an imitation)   A representation of Our Lord, Our Lady or of a saint. It may be a sculpture, a painting or some other form of representation. The Constitution on the Liturgy of Vatican Council II called for such images to be of high artistic value and to avoid sentimentality. Images are not the object of worship but are only venerated because of the person they represent.

image not made with hands   A term used to refer to an image not made by man but which is reputedly mirac-ulous. The best known of such images are Veronica's Veil and the portrait of Our Lady of Guadalupe. There are also several such icons in the Eastern Rite. The term would probably include the Holy Shroud although it is not claimed that this image is miraculous but the result of natural forces.

image of God   According to Gen. 1:26, man is made in the image of God. St. Thomas Aquinas says that this likeness to God is chiefly in man's intellect and reason which distinguish him from the brute animals. To this, theologians add free will as another point of likeness. The likeness also is found in man's dominion over all other living things (Gen. 1:26).

images, veiling of   Covering of a statue or representation of a saint or of some holy object. This is done during the last week of Lent so that we may think solely of the Passion and Death of Christ.

images, veneration of   When sacred relics and images are honored, the honor is called relative because it is referred to God or the saints. Thus we regard with respect, awe and admiration God or the saint represented by the image.

imagination (L. *imago,* image)   An internal sense which reproduces absent objects, persons and actions. It may take these from memory or completely create them. The imagination plays an important role in the movement of the intellect and will and as such may be a force for good or evil. It can excite passion, blur the intellect and weaken the will; or, as in meditation, it can be a means of drawing closer to God. The imagination should be kept under the control of the intellect and not allowed vain meanderings and daydreaming.

Imitation of Christ A devotional book of practical spirituality based on the life of Christ that has become a Christian classic. It is sometimes called *The Following of Christ*. The book was written in the Netherlands and its authorship is attributed to either Thomas à Kempis or Gerard Groote. It was first published in 1418.

Immaculate Conception, the 1. The doctrine that Mary, the mother of Jesus, "in the first instant of her conception was, by a singular grace and privilege of Almighty God and because of the merits of Jesus Christ the Saviour of the human race, free from all stain of original sin" (Pius IX, Dec. 8, 1854, defining the doctrine of the Immaculate Conception). From all eternity Mary was chosen to be the Mother of the Word Incarnate. It is unthinkable that such a mother should have been defiled by sin for even a moment. Therefore, in the instant of her conception she was made immaculate. She was truly saved, redeemed, not from an evil already present, but from an evil that threatened. 2. The term is sometimes used as a personification of the Blessed Virgin. Under this title Mary is the patroness of the United States.

immanence (L. *in manere,* to remain in) 1. Philosophically, a term which refers to a cause which begins in an agent and remains there. Immanent action is the Scholastic definition for life. Immanence is the property of organic beings. Transience, or transient action, is the property of inorganic objects. 2. Theologically, immanence means that we are "in God and God is in us. It is the understanding of St. Paul that in God we live and move and have our being." We are in God because we are His creatures and God is in us through the Eucharist and the presence of sanctifying grace. A pantheistic heresy has resulted from a misunderstanding of this notion which avers that man is an emanation from God.

immediately subject to the Holy See A term referring to an exempt diocese which is not subject to any metropolitan but is directly subject to the Holy See.

immensity (L. *immensus,* boundless) That attribute of God by which we understand Him to be without limits. By His very nature God is everywhere on earth, in the universe, in heaven, every place. This is essentially a negative turn by which we affirm that God is absolute.

immersion (L. *immergere,* to immerse) A type of Baptism in which the subject is immersed in water. Most Eastern rites practice immersion or semi-immersion. It was the method generally employed in the early Church but because of difficulties and inconvenience it has become almost obsolete in the Western Church. It is practiced by some Protestant sects.

immortality That quality of the soul by which it consciously exists in perpetuity after separation from the body. It is a fundamental Christian doctrine because on one's attitude toward it depends one's actions in the present life. The doctrine can be demonstrated logically without appeal to revelation. The arguments are the spirituality and substantiality of the human soul, man's innate desire for perfect happiness and the need for an adequate sanction for the moral law which is not found in this life. St. Thomas Aquinas has given a complete philosophical development to these arguments.

immortality of Adam Adam and Eve

286

were conditionally promised immortality but because of their failure to meet the condition they then became subject to death. The Council of Trent condemned those who denied that death did not result from the sin of Adam and Eve.

immovable feast A feast assigned to a particular date. Many such feasts can be supplanted by a movable feast or transferred to another date.

immutability (L. *immutabilis,* unchangeable) An attribute of God; His unchangeableness. Change implies the addition of something new or the subtraction of something present, and therefore something imperfect. But God is infinitely perfect and therefore cannot change. He is immutable in His very essence for one simple eternal act is His essence.

impanation (L. *in panis,* in bread) A heretical teaching which affirms that the bread and wine are not changed into the body and blood of Christ following the consecration but that He enters the bread and wine in a sort of hypostatic union. It is opposed to the Church's teaching of transubstantiation (*q.v.*).

impassible (L. *impassibilis*) Incapable of suffering. A quality attributed by the common teaching of theologians to Adam and Eve before the fall. It means that they were free from those evils due to a fallen state of human nature. The risen and glorified bodies of the saved will enjoy this quality in its completeness.

impeccability (L. *im,* not; *peccare,* to sin) Unable to sin. Christ was impeccable. Theologians hold that Mary was impeccable, not by nature, but by divine privilege.

impediments of marriage Any circumstance which prevents the marriage contract between two persons from being valid or at least lawful. Al-though the impediment may exist in only one party, the marriage is illicit or invalid for both. Impediments are of many kinds but in general fall into the following categories: 1. By reasons of their effects, annulling or prohibitive. 2. By reason of their origin, from natural law, ecclesiastical law, divine law. 3. By reason of their scope, absolute or relative. 4. By reason of the way they are known, public or occult. 5. By reason of their liability to dispensation.

impediments to ordination Temporary obstacles or hindrances (contrasted with irregularities) because of which a candidate to the priesthood cannot be ordained. These impediments can cease or be dispensed. Among these impediments are: being a soldier in the army, illegitimacy of birth, being the child of non-Catholics while the parents remain in error, the condition of slavery, a person guilty of a public crime (infamy in fact), and other matters specified by Canon Law.

impenitence, final A sin against the Holy Spirit which is unpardonable because it is not repented. It is the denial of repentance in a sinner that is willful at the moment of death.

imperata (L. commanded) Prayers or orations added on to those assigned to the Mass at the order of the Holy Father, the bishop of a diocese or another having such authority. *Imperata* are not said on major feasts. In many dioceses, it is the custom to say the *imperata* "For Peace."

imperfection Something that causes a lack of perfection in one's spiritual life. Imperfection is said to be positive or negative. It is positive when a violation of God's known will is a matter that does not oblige. It is negative when the failure is in a desire to do a good action to which one is not bound though one is moved toward that action. It is the teaching of theologians that imperfections are not sins and therefore are not sufficient matter for absolution.

impetration (L. *impetrare,* to obtain a request) A word synonymous with petition, supplication. It is asking God for a favor. It is one of the four ends of the Mass and the result of good works. It is theological teaching that God hears every prayer made with the right disposition and that He answers every such prayer.

implicit In a theological sense, the word is used to refer to a truth that is contained, though not necessarily expressed, in another truth. Thus an explicit belief in the second truth presupposes an implicit belief in the first.

impotency The inability of a husband or wife to complete sexual intercourse arising either from some natural or physical cause or from some psychic cause. It is an impediment to marriage. It is to be differentiated from sterility which is not an impediment since it does not prevent conjugal intercourse in the natural way but only the procreation of children. Antecedent and permanent impotency whether known or not annuls marriage by the very law of nature.

imprimatur (L. it may be printed) Permission from a competent ecclesiastical authority to publish a book that may be safely read without damage to faith or morals. Ecclesiastical approval is required for the publication of all books and pamphlets pertaining to Sacred Scripture, theology (sacred and natural), Church history, canon law, ethics, prayer, devotions, catechism, asceticism, mysticism, religion and morals. Printed sacred images must also receive an imprimatur before publication. The imprimatur may be obtained where the work is written, printed or published.

imprimi potest (L. it may be printed) Many religious orders require approval of a manuscript by the superior general, a provincial, or a delegated authority before printing. When such approval is given, the name of the approving authority appears under the words "Imprimi potest" in the front of the book together with the Imprimatur and Nihil obstat.

impurity (L. *impuritas*) Any unlawful indulgence of sexual pleasure. It is one of the capital sins and can be committed either by act or in the mind.

imputability (L. *imputare,* to impute) The quality by which sin or virtue can be ascribed to a person, however, it is usually applied in a derogatory sense. The degree of imputability depends upon advertence, and the full imputability of an act is known only to God.

in articulo mortis (L. in the presence of death) A theological term to refer to the immediate danger or moment of death. Thus a person in *articulo mortis* should be given final absolution and the Last Sacraments. A pagan child in *articulo mortis* should be baptized.

in cena Domini (L. at the Lord's banquet) Pertaining to the Last Supper of Christ with His disiciples; the Holy Eucharist; the feast celebrating the institution of the Blessed Sacrament.

in fieri (L. in becoming) A term in scholastic philosophy referring to the transference from potency to act. *In fieri* is opposed to *in facto esse* which expresses the existence of being.

in globo (L. ball, globe, sphere) A group of people; e.g., to baptize *in globo* rather than individually.

in nomine Patris (L. in the name of the Father)   First words of the Sign of the Cross said in blessings and to begin prayers.

in paradisum (L. into paradise)   First words of an antiphon of the Catholic burial services, "May the angels lead thee into paradise." It is supposed to be sung while the body is being carried from the church to the grave. In the United States it is usually sung by the choir following the sprinkling and incensing of the coffin, and before the priest reads the burial prayers in English, after which the body is carried out of the church.

in partibus infidelium (L. in the regions of unbelievers)   A term formerly used in referring to honorary or titular sees which were located in areas lost to the Faith. Today the term refers to mission territories where the majority of the people have not been converted to Christianity.

in petto (L. in the breast)   A secret. It refers to the creation of a cardinal whose name the pope keeps secret and does not disclose. If the name is not revealed before the death of the pope, the appointment ceases upon the pope's death. There are many reasons for such an appointment. For example, the cardinal so named might be in a Communist prison or behind the Iron Curtain where such an appointment might bring him further persecution.

in plano (L. on the level)   Technical term in the rubrics for the liturgy, meaning the floor of the sanctuary, as distinct from the altar steps; e.g., at Forty Hours when Mass before the Blessed Sacrament is said, the celebrant descends to the floor to wash his hands.

in principio (L. in the beginning) The opening words of St. John's Gospel.

in se (L. in itself)   Philosophical expression; e.g., a tax cut *in se* is very desirable, but not without decreased government expenditures.

in sin   A popular and loose expression to indicate that a person is in the state of mortal sin.

incardination (L. *incardinare*)   The canonical act whereby a man is attached to a diocese and made subject to its bishop. By reception of tonsure, a man enters the clerical state and is incardinated into the diocese which he is to serve. It also refers to the formal reception of a subject of another diocese into a new diocese. However, for the religious, his vows bind him to his religious order, congregation or society.

Incarnation, the (L. *in; caro,* flesh) The assumption of human nature by the second person of the Blessed Trinity. The Incarnate God accepted all human characteristics, except sin, "so that He, as a new Adam, might be the source whence the grace of the Holy Spirit should flow unto all the children of the first parent." The Incarnation means a threefold birth that reaches into the soul of every member of the human race. 1. The birth of God into the world. 2. The birth of Jesus, the true Son of Mary. Weak nature assumed by God so that mankind will not be blinded by His splendor. The day of potential spiritual birth for all men. "It is not for His own sake," says St. Thomas Aquinas *(Summa Theologica* III, 37), "that the Son of God became man, but in order to make us, as it were, gods by His grace." Thus through the Incarnation, God descended to the manger that all men may rise toward divinity.

incensation   The act of incensing. In the Western Church, it is done by swinging the thurible by the middle of the chain so that the smoke of the incense arises. In the Eastern Church, the thurible is held by the upper extremity of the chain.

incense (L. *incensum,* a burnt thing) Powder or small crystals made from resins which when burned give off an aromatic smoke. Also the smoke itself. Incense is burned over charcoal in a thurible, and is used at High Mass, Benediction and other ceremonies. It symbolizes sacrifice for God, and prayer and good works ascending to God. Unburned incense is put into the sepulcher of an altar along with the relics. Five large grains are set in the paschal candle in the form of a cross.

incest Impurity committed with a person related to one within the degrees in which marriage is forbidden. Internal desires are mental incest; sexual intercourse is actual incest. It is committed with one related by blood, with one related by marriage (affinity), with one related in spiritual relationship (between the baptizer and the baptized, and godchild with godparents), and with one related by adoption. Incest with a blood relation also violates piety. Incest with a spiritual relation violates piety also and is against religion. Incest can be committed only within forbidden degrees. If a dispensation from an impediment of relationship had been granted to parties about to marry, a sexual sin between them would not be incestuous.

inclusus (L. *inclusus,* an enclosed person) A custom of the Middle Ages whereby a religious was walled into his or her cell. A small opening was left for reception of Holy Communion, the passage of food and other necessary articles. The act was a voluntary penance and required ecclesiastical permission.

incola A canonical term referring to a person who is living in his domicile. It contrasts to an *advena,* a person living in a quasi-domicile.

incorruptibility A quality of the soul whereby the soul being simple, spiritual and indivisible is not subject to dissolution after death.

incumbent (L. *incumbere,* to devote oneself to) The holder of a benefice. In a wide sense, any holder of an ecclesiastical office.

indefectibility A quality possessed by the Church which makes it not liable to failure. It was assured the Church by Christ when He promised to be with the Church until the end of time (Matt. 28:20).

Index of Forbidden Books The official list of condemned books and writings issued by the Holy Office which are held to be against faith and morals or inimical to the Church. A Catholic may not read a work included in this list without permission of his bishop. The Index was first published in 1559, and for a time was the work of a special congregation. In 1917, the Index was put in the care of the Holy Office. Canon 2318 prescribes the penalties for violation of the law regarding forbidden books. Canons 1384-1405 record the Church's legislation regarding forbidden books.

India One of the historic mission fields of the Catholic Church, India claims to have been first evangelized by St. Thomas the Apostle. In 1349 the first diocese was erected for the St. Thomas Christians. In 1534 the Diocese of Goa was created. In 1542 St. Francis Xavier arrived in India. By the end of the 16th century there were 600,000 Latin Christians and

75,000 belonging to Oriental Rites. Today there are well over 4 million Latin Rite Christians, 1.5 million of the Malabar Rite, and 124,000 of the Syro-Malankar Rite. The total Catholic population is 6 million served by 6,850 priests. There are 16 archdioceses, 50 dioceses and 7 prefectures.

Indian missions Those missions established to work among the American Indians, and which are found almost entirely on or immediately proximate to Indian reservations. There are 129,070 Catholic Indians on reservations and about 25,000 more living among the general population; this total represents 38 per cent of the Indian population. Franciscan and Jesuit priests have long pioneered in Indian work. There are 240 priests and 650 Sisters, Brothers and lay people staffing Catholic Indian missions, and particularly 54 schools. In proportion to size, no other racial group has the services of so many clerics and religious as do the Indians.

Indiana The 19th State of the Union, 38th in area and 11th in population, a prosperous farming and industrial region. The aborigines were warlike hunters of various tribes who traded with both the French and the English. La Salle and Father Hennepin traversed the area en route to the Mississippi in 1679. Father Allouez built Mission St. Joseph near the present site of Notre Dame University, where he and succeeding missioners worked among the Indians until General Harrison defeated them at Tippecanoe in 1811. Forts Wayne and Lafayette were built by the French during the early 18th century, a post was also built at Vincennes. After the Seven Years' War, in 1763, the territory was ceded to England. Dur-ing the Revolution Vincennes was captured by George Rogers Clark and became American property in 1779, the priest, Father Gibault, having persuaded the French to fight on the side of the Americans. Indiana became part of Indiana Territory in 1800 and was admitted to the Union in 1816. Immigrants were pouring in from New England, Germany and Ireland. After the Civil War there was great development in railroad construction, industry and agriculture. Vincennes became a diocese in 1834 with Simon Brute as first bishop. He had 3 priests in his diocese, which comprised all of Indiana and one-third of Illinois. He brought in the Sisters of Providence and Congregation of the Holy Cross, who began work at Notre Dame. Benedictines, Franciscans and many others followed. There are 4 dioceses in Indiana today—Evansville, Fort Wayne-South Bend, Gary and Lafayette. Indianapolis was raised to the rank of archdiocese in 1944. Catholics number about 660,600 in a total population of 4,662,498.

indifferent act A theological expression to indicate a human act which in the concrete is neither good nor bad. An act derives its moral character from its object which in many cases is indifferent, such as sleeping, walking, etc. However, in the concrete, human acts are never indifferent because every act is done for a motive and the morality of the act depends on whether the motive is good or bad.

indifferentism A rationalist doctrine that professes absolute indifferentism when it affirms that man need not be concerned with any religion; or relative indifferentism, when it affirms that one religion is as good as another.

individual (L. *individuus,* indivisible)

That indivisible being distinct from all other entities. Two qualities are necessary to have an individual: 1. that it be incommunicable, not able to be in any other; 2. that it be distinct, divided from all others.

individualism 1. That doctrine which makes the individual and not society the primary end. It exaggerates individual liberty and individual action. 2. Religious individualism. *See* personalism.

Indonesia The first evangelization of the islands now belonging to Indonesia began in 1522. In 1546 St. Francis Xavier founded the mission of Amboina. Today there are 1.2 million Catholics in a population of almost 100 million. There are 6 archdioceses, 19 dioceses and 2 prefectures. There are slightly less than 1,000 priests of whom one-third are native. Obstacles to the Church are Islam, reaction to Dutch occupation, excessive nationalism, Communism and restrictions on foreign missioners. Favorable factors are constitutional freedom, an increasing number of Indonesian bishops, the high percentage of Catholic intellectuals and the influence of Catholic schools.

induction A term in canon law that means a personal introduction of one assigned to a benefice at the time of his taking possession of that benefice.

indulgence (L. *indulgere,* to be kind to) The remission in whole or part of temporal punishment due to sin, provided the sin has already been forgiven. To gain an indulgence one must be in the state of grace, have the intention of gaining the indulgence and perform the required work. No one can gain an indulgence for another living person but most indulgences can be applied to the deceased. The power of granting indulgences is founded in the "Power of the Keys" which was given to St. Peter and his successors (Matt. 16:19). Indulgences are drawn from the treasury of the Church, particularly from the infinite merits gained by Jesus Christ.

indulgence, apostolic The indulgence which is attached to religious objects such as crucifixes, rosaries, medals, etc., which have been blessed by the pope or an authorized priest. The indulgence is gained only by the first person to whom the object is given.

indulgence, jubilee A plenary indulgence granted by the Holy See for a special occasion, e.g., a Holy Year, an anniversary of a pope, etc.

indulgence, partial The remission of part of the punishment due to sin. It is granted in terms of time: days, quarantines, years. (A quarantine is a period of forty days.) The indulgence equals the merit that would be gained by doing penance for the prescribed period.

indulgence, plenary The remission of all temporal punishment due to sin. However, due to imperfections of our own disposition, one can never be sure that the full plenary indulgence can be gained. Besides the regular requirements to gain a plenary indulgence, one must detest sin and be free from all attachments even to venial sin. In applying the indulgence to a soul in purgatory, its acceptance depends upon the will of God.

indult (L. *indultum,* a concession) A faculty granted by the Holy See to ordinaries and other authorities to do something that is not permitted by the general law of the Church. It is not the same as a dispensation.

Ineffabilis Deus (L. Ineffable God) The title of the bull issued by Pope Pius IX on Dec. 8, 1854, defining the dogma of the Immaculate Conception.

inerrancy (L. *inerrans,* not wandering) The quality of being free from error and exempt from mistake. The pope is inerrant when making an infallible pronouncement.

inerrancy of the Scriptures The immunity and freedom from all error which belongs to Holy Scripture because of its divine inspiration, as St. John testifies when he writes, "The Scripture cannot be broken" (Jn. 10:35). Inerrancy of Scripture is an article of faith because God, the author of Scripture, is incapable of error.

infallibility (L. *in,* not; *fallere,* to deceive) That quality in the Church by which it is preserved from error in matters of faith and morals. This incapability to err is a special gift of the Holy Spirit who resides in the Church. Infallibility does not mean that the Church defines new revelations but that it interprets the deposit of faith. Infallibility is necessary so that the faithful may be assured of the validity of their beliefs. The doctrine of infallibility was defined by Vatican Council I and promulgated on July 18, 1870. The decree defined infallibility in three areas: 1. In the pope. When the pope speaks ex cathedra, i.e., in virtue of his office and apostolic authority, on a matter of faith and morals. Papal infallibility does not extend to Church policy, discipline or the pope's private opinions. 2. In the ecumenical council. The pronouncements of this council on faith and morals when issued with the approval and by the authority of the pope are infallible. 3. In the body of bishops. The ordinary teaching of the bishops when in union with the pope is infallible.

infallibility of the pope The doctrine that the pope is free from error insofar as he is head of the Church on earth and when he speaks in that capacity to define a doctrine of faith or morals. Such statements are irreformable by nature, not by reason of the Church's consent. Infallibility of the pope is neither impeccability nor inspiration. Infallibility refers only to the pope's ex cathedra statements, not to his every doctrinal act. Infallibility resides primarily in the Church. The pope is one of the three organs of this infallibility of the Church, the other organs being the bishops spread throughout the world in union with the Holy See and the bishops gathered together with the pope in an ecumenical council. Even when the pope proclaims that a doctrine must be believed, he can do so only after first examining the belief of the Church in the particular matter.

infamy (L. *infamia*) A canonical penalty whereby is suffered the loss or diminution of a person's good name. There are two kinds of infamy. 1. Infamy of fact. This vindictive penalty is incurred for some evil conduct or the commission of some crime. A person declared infamous of fact is excluded from receiving orders, dignities, benefices and ecclesiastical acts. Clerics are excluded from exercising their sacred ministry. Infamy of facts ends when the ordinary judges that the person has recovered his good reputation with practicing Catholics. 2. Infamy of law. This is a vindictive penalty imposed for certain crimes. Incurring this infamy *ipso facto* are: those who join or publicly adhere to a non-Catholic sect; those who desecrate the consecrated species; those who violate the bodies or graves of the dead; those who lay violent hands on the pope, cardinals or legates; those who fight a duel, including the seconds; those who commit bigamy; lay people convicted of crimes of impurity with minors under 16 years of age, or for rape, incest or sodomy. This infamy is to be declared on apostates, heretics, schismatics, unless they return to the Faith after they have been admonished; clerics who commit sins of impurity mentioned above for lay people, also those who commit adultery, bestiality or incest in the first degree. The effects of infamy of law are irregularity; inability to obtain benefices, pensions, offices or ecclesiastical dignities; inability to exercise legal ecclesiastical actions.

infant A person is considered a canonical infant until the seventh year is completed. Adults without the use of reason are considered as infants.

infants, anointing of Infants who have not reached the age of reason cannot receive the Sacrament of the Anointing of the Sick. This is because the sacrament is administered only to a baptized person capable of sin. Since a person cannot sin before the use of reason, such a person is not subject to this sacrament. If the infant has reached the use of reason even though the age of seven has not been reached, the sacrament may be administered. In case of doubt, administration should be made conditionally.

infants, Baptism of Infants are to be baptized as soon as possible after birth. The Constitution on the Sacred Liturgy of Vatican Council II ordered a revision of the rite for Baptism of infants that adapts itself to the circumstance that those being baptized are indeed infants. The revision enlarges and clarifies the roles and duties of parents and godparents.

In place of the rite called the "Order of supplying what was omitted in the baptism of an infant," the Council Fathers ordered a rite that would clearly manifest that the infant, baptized by the short rite, has already been received into the Church. The short rite is used in danger of death. Foundlings are to be baptized conditionally.

infants, burial of The Constitution of the Sacred Liturgy of Vatican Council II ordered a revision in the rite for the burial of infants and the replacement of the Mass of the Angels with a Mass special to the occasion.

infants, communion of It is the custom not to give Holy Communion to infants except when the age of reason (*q.v.*) has been reached and there is some knowledge of Catholic doctrine. In danger of death, Holy Communion should be given provided they can distinguish the Body of Christ from ordinary bread and are able to adore It reverently. The insane are considered as infants and are given Holy Communion only as Viaticum when there is no danger of irreverence.

infants, confession of The Church's law of annual confession does not apply to infants. However, an infant may be admitted to the sacrament if it has sufficient use of reason to understand the nature and meaning of confession.

infants, unbaptized It is the teaching of the Church that unbaptized children do not go to heaven, but nothing has been defined as to the fate of such children. It is the common opinion of theologians that unbaptized children go to Limbo (*q.v.*) where they enjoy a natural happiness and adore God through their natural faculties.

infidel (L. *in,* not; *fides,* faith) One

who does not accept Christianity as a divinely revealed religion. Particularly, a Muslim.

infidel, marriage with an   In the law of the Church an infidel is an unbaptized person. A Catholic who marries an infidel must have a dispensation from difference of worship; otherwise the marriage is invalid.

infidelity   A sin of detect against faith. It is positive (formal) when it is a culpable lack of faith in a person who refused to believe. It is negative (material) when it exists in a person to whom faith has not been revealed. It is privative when it is culpable because of negligence in examining the credentials of the Church on the part of one who realizes the necessity of examining them. Negative infidelity is involuntary while positive infidelity is voluntary. Heresy and apostasy are types of positive infidelity. Positive infidelity is a grave sin, negative infidelity is not a sin, privative infidelity must be judged on the degree of negligence.

infinite (L. *infinitum,* boundless)   Infinity is an attribute properly predicated of God alone because God alone is infinite in duration (without beginning or end) and in perfection (without admixture of limitation or restriction of any kind).

infinity of God   The infinite is that which is without limits. When referred to God, who is omnipotent, perfect and transcendent, infinity is the attribute declaring that there is no limit to God's perfection and that He has complete fullness of every perfection in Himself, above all things existing or possible of existing by His creation.

inform (L. *informare,* to give form to)   Give being to; to permeate with an animating quality. A philosophical term describing the manner in which a form gives being to that which receives it. Thus the soul informs the body, or gives being to it.

infra actionem (L. within the action)   A rubrical direction to the celebrant of a Mass at the Communicantes (*q.v.*) to remind him that a proper Communicantes should be substituted at that point when it is necessary.

infulae (L. fillets)   1. The two lappets which hang down from the back of the mitre. 2. Sometimes used in the singular (infula) to mean the mitre itself.

infused virtues   *See* virtues, infused.

infusion (L. *fundere,* to pour)   The method of Baptism by pouring water, as used in the Latin Rite. Also called affusion.

ingressa (L. *ingressus,* entrance)   The entering act of the Mass in the Ambrosian Rite corresponding to the Latin Entrance Hymn (Introit). It consists of an antiphon and psalm verse.

inherence (L. *inhaerere,* to stick)   The relation of an accident to a substance. An accident must have something in which to inhere, it cannot exist apart by itself.

inhumation (L. *inhumare,* to cover with dirt)   Burial in the ground, i.e., in a grave. The mode of such burial follows local custom and law. In some states, bodies must be exhumed after a period of time and the bones placed in a common ossary. *See* cemetery.

innocence, baptismal   The state of one after receiving Baptism when there is no attachment to sin and the soul enjoys sanctifying grace. It is used to refer to one who has never actually sinned and has thus preserved baptismal innocence.

innocence, original   The name given the original state of Adam and Eve which was lost by original sin, The greatest gift lost by this sin was sanctifying grace.

inordinate affections Those affections (*q.v.*) which lead man away from God. Hate directed against an individual is destructive of charity. A fear of pain or sacrifice leads to tepidity in the spiritual life. The affection must be reorientated toward its proper end, e.g., fear of loss of God, hatred of sin, etc.

inordinate attachment To prefer a creature before God.

I.N.R.I. Letters often found on the sign board at the top of many crucifixes which are the Latin initials of the inscription Pilate ordered put there: *Iesus Nazarenus, Rex Iudaeorum* (Jesus of Nazareth, King of the Jews).

Inquisition (in′kwa-zish′on; L. *inquirere,* to look into) An ecclesiastical tribunal first instituted by Pope Gregory IX in 1229 to deal with heretics. Although very extensive, the Inquisition did not comprise the whole of Christendom, nor even all the Latin countries. The Scandinavian kingdoms escaped it almost entirely. England experienced it only once in the case of the Templars. Castile and Portugal knew nothing of it before the reign of Ferdinand and Isabella. It was almost unknown in France—at least as an established institution—except in the south in what was called the country of Toulouse, and later on in Languedoc. It was in full operation in Aragon. The Cathari were wont to travel frequently from Languedoc to Lombardy, hence upper Italy had, from an early period, its contingent of Inquisitors. Frederick II had it established in the two Sicilies and in many cities of Italy and Germany. Its activities in Flanders and Bohemia in the 15th century were very considerable. These were the chief centers of its operation. The condemnation of heresy was not something peculiar to the Middle Ages. From the beginning of the Christian Era we find both the Church and the populace expressing definite views on this matter. The death penalty by stoning, which apostates merited under the old dispensation, was changed to a purely spiritual penalty—excommunication. When emperors became Christians, they considered themselves as rulers not only in civil matters, but also in the religious. We find them severely punishing all those who denied the orthodox Faith, or rather their own faith which they considered, rightly or wrongly, the Faith of the Church. The penalties differed in severity: exile, confiscation, the inability to transmit property. The severer penalties, which included the death penalty, were reserved for those heretics who were disturbers of the public peace. The practice was for the Church, after passing judgment, to pass over the heretic to the civil law for punishment. The inquisition was generally administered by the Dominicans. Although the numbers are greatly exaggerated of those who were burned at the stake, some of its procedure and punishments must be set down as utterly unreasonable and cruel.

inquisition, canonical The secret judicial investigation made before anyone is summoned to appear in an ecclesiastical court in a criminal action. The inquisitor makes his report to the ordinary.

Inquisition, the Spanish Queen Isabella of Castile obtained the formal foundation of the Inquisition from Pope Sixtus IV. It began operations in 1480. Her husband Ferdinand joined her wholeheartedly; and gradually the institution struck root throughout the peninsula. The Inquisition in Spain was severe, and Pope Sixtus strongly criticized its methods; but his objections were ignored. To find an explanation of this cruel repression we must try to imagine what that still inadequately unified Spain of the 15th and 16th centuries was like. It was a country in which the very numerous Moriscos constituted a people apart, especially in certain regions such as Andalusia and the Kingdom of Valencia. The coast populations lived in perpetual dread of raids by Barbaresque or Ottoman pirates. A Mussulman invasion or a disembarkation of Turks or Africans was a constant obsession and often a very real danger. There was even reason to believe that the Moriscos would turn traitors. The men responsible for the government of Spain were afraid of these people who waited in silence for the hour of deliverance foretold by their prophecies. Unity of Faith was taken as a necessity and as a security. That subjects should follow the religion of their sovereigns was then an accepted proposition in practically the whole of Europe, Protestant as well as Catholic.

insanity (L. *insanus,* unhealthy) Any mental disorder or defect of sufficient severity to bring a person under special legal custody and immunities. It is a vague term but still used in the legal sphere. Canon law declares an insane person irregular for the reception or exercise of Holy Orders. A person so afflicted can be impeded by his illness from exchanging valid matrimonial consent. The term no longer has acceptable usage in psychiatric and clinical practice.

insemination, artificial The implanting of human semen by some means other than the natural marriage act. The use of donor semen is illicit and never permitted; a child born after such use is considered illegitimate. The use of any act to obtain semen that is contrary to nature is immoral. In the view of the Church there is no substitute for intercourse because it is the will of God that children be the fruit of a personal union. However, artificial means are permitted in order to help natural conjugal relations to be fruitful.

insignia (L. *signum,* sign) Distinguishing marks of authority of office such as badges, ornaments, dress, etc. Examples would be the tiara of the pope, the pectoral cross and ring of a bishop, the cassock of a priest, etc.

inspiration of Holy Scripture "A supernatural impulse by means of which the Holy Spirit excited and moved the sacred writers to write and helped them while they wrote in such a way that they could conceive exactly, wished to report faithfully and expressed with infallible accuracy, all that God commanded them to write and nothing else" (Leo XIII, *Providentissimus Deus*). God and the human writers are both true authors of the Scriptures; God is the principal Author who communicates His message to us by means of the human writer. God did not destroy or interfere with the freedom or personality of the human author but rather so worked in conformity with the human nature that often the human author was unaware of any special working of the Holy Spirit. It is God who initiates the process, but He carries it out by causing the human author to will himself to write and effectively accomplish what God wills. God is thus involved from the first impulse to write to the final verbal formation of the Scriptures. Since God is the Author, Scripture contains no formal error. But because God concurs with men, only that which the human author intended to affirm, and only to the degree to which he wished to affirm, is necessarily true, except in the case where, unknown to the author, God intends a fuller sense of the Scripture (*q.v.*) over and above the one intended by the sacred writer. (*See* inerrancy.) Thus the human writer was subject to the same limitations as his contemporaries in those things that were not directly judged and affirmed to be true by him. Furthermore, the individual writer's unique personality and style necessarily shine through in his writings. Inspiration applies equally to all books of the Bible and to every word of the Bible, whether new revelation is involved or only things naturally known by the writer. However, inspiration is guaranteed only for the original text; not for the various translations of the original book. The sole judge of which text is inspiried is the Church. Apart from the common tradition of the Church, the fact of inspiration is attested to by Scripture itself (2 Tim. 3:16; 2 Pt. 1:21).

installation (L. *installare,* to put in a stall) The act of investing a person with an office. The ceremony by which a cleric takes possession of his office. Originally it was the leading of a new canon to his stall in the cathedral or collegiate church. By extension it refers to the installation in any office, e.g., a bishop, new pastor, etc.

institute, religious *See* religious institute.

institutes, pontifical Attached to the Pontifical Gregorian University are the Pontifical Biblical Institute (1909) and the Pontifical Institute for Oriental Studies (1917). In addition there are the Pontifical Institute of Sacred Music (1911), the Pontifical Institute of Christian Archeology (1925) and the Pontifical "Regina Mundi" Institute.

institution 1. The act of founding or establishing; a long-standing custom, practice, system, etc.; an organization having a social, educational, or religious purpose, as well as the building housing such an organization. 2. In sacramental theology, the establishment of a sacrament by Christ. 3. In canon law, the appointment of a legitimately presented candidate by a legitimate authority to an ecclesiastical position or benefice.

instruction 1. Doctrinal explanations, admonitions, rules, directions and recommendations issued by the Holy See. In themselves they do not have the force of law unless they recall former law. 2. Every Catholic child has the right to be instructed in the Catholic faith and the obligation of seeing that this is done rests on both parents and pastor. Pope St. Pius X directed that the Confraternity of Christian Doctrine be established in every parish and this directive was later made part of canon law. Converts are to be instructed in accordance with their age, education and intelligence.

Instruction Clementina (L. Clementine Instruction) The instructions given by Pope Clement XII in 1736 governing the celebration of the Forty Hours Devotion (*q.v.*).

instruments of the Passion The cross, nails, hammer, lance, etc., that were used in the Passion of Our Lord.

integralism (L. *integer,* untouched, whole) Also known as Christian humanism, refers to the philosophy of many Christian philosophers today. It advocates the development of the whole man. Applied to the makeup of a person, it means that a person's emotions or passions, for instance, are under the control of reason. A person is said to be integral or whole when his intellectual powers are developed to their capacity and are in coordination with his physical and emotional powers. A person receives help from God's grace through the sacraments to attain to this wholeness, or integrity of being.

integration (L. *integratio,* a renewal) A mixture of people, ideas, institutions or anything else. As regards interracial justice, the situation in which barriers (in housing, schools, employment, etc.) between people based on race have been removed. The opposite of segregation to which the doctrine of the Church is opposed.

integrity (L. *integer,* whole) 1. Theologically, freedom from concupiscence, a gift given to our first parents by which impulses to sensuality were kept completely under control. 2. Generally, a moral wholesomeness of unusual honesty and uprightness.

intellect That power of the human soul which enables its possessor to think, the faculty of cognition.

intelligible Those things than can be apprehended by the intellect, capable of being understood. The intelligible world is the object of philosophy; the sensible world is the object of the physical sciences.

intention 1. The efficacious tendency of the will toward some good that has been proposed by the intellect as desirable. An intention is actual when it exists here and now; virtual when a residual force of a once actual intention still exerts its influence; habitual when it has never been retracted but no longer exerts a positive force; interpretative when a person does not will a particular end but it is assumed he would have if he had adverted to it. 2. In conferring the sacraments the minister must have at least a virtual intention. This is the intention of administering the sacrament, of doing what the Church does. An adult who receives a sacrament should have a positive intention except for Penance and Matrimony for which a habitual intention suffices. 3. The person or object for which a Mass or prayer is offered. It may be spiritual or temporal, for oneself or another, for the living or the dead.

intercession (L. *intercessio,* an intervention) A prayer said on behalf of another. Thus Catholics ask saints to intercede with God for them. There are two intercessions made in the Mass, one for the living and the other for the dead. Christ is the great Mediator who intercedes with the Father of all mankind.

intercommunion 1. An agreement between two religious bodies whereby each extends membership to the other members without consideration of dogma. Such an arrangement exists between the Anglicans in England and the Lutherans in Sweden. 2. The administration of a sacrament by the minister of one religious body to a member of another religious body even though the minister knows that the person is not of his communion. Vatican Council II ruled that under certain circumstances Catholics may receive certain sacraments from an Orthodox priest and members of an Orthodox religion may receive certain sacraments from Catholics. This is possible because the Church recognizes the legitimacy of Orthodox baptism and orders.

interdict (L. *interdicere,* to prohibit)

A censure, vindictive penalty or prohibition whereby a person while remaining in communion with the Church is forbidden the use of certain sacraments or other sacred things. It is a less severe form of punishment than excommunication. An interdict may be local, personal, general or particular. A general interdict affecting a diocese or region can be inflicted only by the Holy See. A general interdict affecting a parish and some particular interdicts can be inflicted by the ordinary. An interdict ceases as do other vindictive penalties, namely, by dispensation or lapse of the stated time.

interest   The profit lawfully acquired from a loan for consumption. It differs from usury which is an excessive return. Interest is permissible because of the risk involved, loss of profitable investment the money could be put to and the legal reward to encourage trade. *See* loan for consumption.

internal acts and law   Those acts which are completely internal, existing in the will and accompanied by external acts only accidentally, such as meditation; or partly internal, when they proceed from the intellect and will but are directed to the production of an external act, such as attention in mental prayer. There is agreement that acts that are partly internal can be commanded by both civil and ecclesiastical law; it is also agreed that acts that are completely internal cannot be the subject of civil legislation but there is a dispute on the degree to which the Church can command internal acts. There is wide agreement among theologians that the Church can command internal acts in the following cases; by a confessor in the internal forum; when the Church determines divine law,

such as the reception of Easter Communion; when a religious superior commands something legitimate under the vow of obedience, e.g., an intention for a Mass.

International Catholic Auxiliaries (ICA)   Official title of the Lay Auxiliaries of the Missions founded in Europe in 1937 under the inspiration of Father Vincent Lebbe, a famous missionary to China. Auxiliaries are women who dedicate their lives to the formation of a native Catholic laity in mission countries. They pledge themselves by oath to live in the spirit of poverty, in chastity and in obedience to the society and the local bishop. They wear no distinctive dress or habit. National Headquarters: 1734 Asbury Avenue, Evanston, Ill. (International Headquarters are at Brussels, Belgium.)

internuncio   An ambassador of the pope of a lower rank than a nuncio. He fulfills the same duties as a diplomatic ambassador assigned to a particular country.

interpellations (L. *interpellare,* to interrupt)   The questions put to a person before granting the Pauline privilege. They are usually made by the ordinary of the converted party; however, they can be made in other ways, even privately, provided there is written proof or the testimony of two witnesses. Two questions are asked the unbaptized party: 1. whether he or she wishes to be converted to the Faith; 2. whether he or she is willing to live in marriage peacefully without offense to God.

interpretation   1. Of Scripture. The science of hermeneutics by which the rules are formulated for determining and explaining the true sense of Scripture. Study is made of the history and culture of the people of the time, the sacred writer, the literary character of the writing, the vocabulary, the translation against original texts, etc. It is a highly specialized science, and the laity and even clerics are not competent to determine the true sense. 2. Of canon law. No one is authorized to determine the interpretation of canon law except the legislator, his successor or persons delegated by these. One of the pontifical commissions of the Holy See concerns itself with the interpretation of canon law.

interpretation, private One of the distinguishing marks of Protestantism is the use of private judgment in interpreting Sacred Scripture so that each man bases his religious practice on the meaning he personally draws from Scripture. One of the results of this teaching is the fractionalization of Protestant religious bodies. Basically it is a form of religious pride since a person places his own judgment foremost, while faith in the interpretation of the Church is an act of humility by submission to the teaching of the Church.

interpreter in confession If a priest and penitent are unable to converse because they lack a common language, the penitent may give permission for the use of an interpreter. In such a case, the interpreter is strictly bound by the seal of the confessional (*q.v.*). However, since confession must be secret, no one is obliged to make use of an interpreter.

Interracial Council, Catholic An integrated organization with the following goals: 1. to spread the doctrine of the spiritual dignity of the human person and the universality of the Church and apply this to race relations in the United States; 2. to combat racial prejudice; 3. to strive for equal justice for all. The first council was established in New York City in 1934. Over 45 similar councils have been established throughout the United States.

interregnum The period between the death of a pope and the election of his successor.

interstices (L. *interstitium,* interval) The space between one thing and another. The term is used canonically to mean the intervals between the reception of the various minor and major orders. The ordinary may determine the time between minor orders. Between acolyte and subdeaconate there should be one year, and between each major order, three months.

intervenient (L. *interveniens,* coming between) A term used in the Constitution on the Sacred Liturgy to refer to the prayers or chants of the Mass that come between the Epistle and Gospel, such as the Tract, Gradual, Sequence or Allelulia.

intinction (L. *intingere,* to dip into) The practice of dipping the consecrated bread into the consecrated wine so that the communicant receives under both species.

intolerance (L. *in,* not; *tolere,* to bear) A refusal to tolerate other people, other opinions, other religious beliefs. It is the want of a reasoned patience toward others. In the sense that it means a complete avoidance of compromise on religious principles, intolerance is not wrong. Nor is intolerance wrong in other cases, such as a doctor who is intolerant of disease. However, it is important in the matter of religion that intolerance does not extend to the person. Because a man hates a sin is no reason for him to hate the sinner. The Church preaches freedom of conscience and therefore we must respect persons honestly holding opinions other than our own.

intoxication The state of drunkenness. It is a sin of gluttony when done deliberately; venially sinful when it results in a partial loss of reason, mortally sinful when it results in a complete loss of reason.

intransigence (L. *in,* not; *transigere, transact*) The refusal to compromise in principle; it must be differentiated from intractability. It is used of the Church in its resistance to political pressures.

Introit *See,* Entrance Hymn.

investiture (L. *investire,* to clothe) 1. In the Middle Ages, the act by which a lord or prince granted title and possession to bishops, abbots, priests. It led to many abuses since it put a laymen in charge of spiritual benefices. It led to the appointment of ambitious and unworthy men and to long vacancies in offices. 2. Today the word is used in its etymological sense: to invest a postulant with cassock or habit, to present a monsignor with his robes of office, etc.

invocation of saints It is the teaching of the Church that saints can hear the prayers of men and that they can intercede to God for us.

Iowa The 29th state to enter the Union, 25th in area and 24th in population, is said to have taken its name from the Iowa Indians. A prairie state, it has one-fourth of all the Grade A soil in the United States, is 97 per cent under cultivation, has a record of prosperity in both agriculture and industry and a literacy rate 99.2 per cent. The Illini Indians who lived there were destroyed by the Sacs and Foxes, nations from New York, who were dominating the area when Julien Dubuque settled and began mining lead at the site of the modern city named for him. La Salle took possession of the area for France in 1682, and the United States acquired it with the Louisiana

Purchase in 1803. White settlers began moving in at a rate that alarmed the Sacs, who fought the Black Hawk War in 1832. After the war the Indians signed away 6 million acres to the settlers. Missioners were sent in by Bishop Rosati of St. Louis; the first Mass was offered in 1833 by a Father Fitzmorris in the home of Patrick Quigley of Dubuque. Father De Smet and other Jesuits opened a mission (St. Joseph's) for the Potawatomis in 1838; Father Mazzuchelli, a saintly Dominican, built the first Catholic church in Dubuque. Dubuque became a diocese in 1837, with Mathias Loras as bishop. Religious congregations arrived and opened schools and works of charity. During the Civil War over 75,000 Iowans served in the Union army. After the war, immigration began again; and schools, academies, colleges and works of charity were multiplied. In 1861 the Diocese of Davenport was established, and in 1898 Dubuque was made an archdiocese. The Diocese of Sioux City was established in 1902, and the Diocese of Des Moines in 1911. Today Iowa has a Catholic population of almost a half million in a total population of almost 3 million.

ipso facto (L. by that very fact) Philosophical term, as in one who is excommunicated *ipso facto:* i.e., without due process of adjudication, directly he posits an act that breaks the law forbidding such an act. It is sometimes called "automatic excommunication."

ipsum esse (L. by its very being) A philosophical term that refers to something that exists of itself compared to nonexistence, namely, God, who alone is true Being. God is Being, who exists in Himself and of Himself, who by His very nature is.

Ireland (Eire)　St. Patrick brought the Faith to Ireland in 432 and shortly thereafter the Irish began carrying their new religion to other parts of Europe. Today the tradition is maintained with 7,000 Irish missioners scattered over the world, or 1 missioner for every 457 Irish Catholics, a record difficult to match. Ireland has almost 3 million people of whom 93 per cent are Catholic. There are 4 archdioceses and 22 dioceses. The leading missionary societies of the country are, in order of size: the Holy Ghost Fathers, Missioners of St. Columban, Missioners of St. Patrick, and the Redemptorists. One important lay movement, the Legion of Mary, began in Ireland in 1925.

Iron Virgin　A spurious torture device falsely imputed to the Inquisition but now attributed to the 19th century. It was a hollow, larger than life-sized figure of a woman, which opened in half. Inside it was lined with spikes. The person to be tortured was put inside and the figure was closed.

irreformable　An act of the Church which is unchangeable, such as the definition of a doctrine.

irregularity　An irregularity is a canonical impediment which permanently bars a man from receiving Holy Orders. Generally it also forbids the exercise of orders already received. Irregularities are based on defects or crimes.

irregularity from crime　An irregularity from crime is a canonical impediment arising from mortal sin which is external; i.e., public or occult. Designated to protect the dignity of the Sacrament of the Eucharist and withhold the reception to worthy individuals, it makes it unlawful for a person to receive ordination, and in-

directly forbids the exercise of orders already received. Irregularities arise from the following crimes: 1. Apostasy, heresy, and schism. 2. Voluntary acceptance of a non-Catholic baptism. 3. Civil marriage while bound by a prior marriage, Holy Orders, or a religious vow. 4. Voluntary homicide, procured abortion or cooperation in an abortion or homicide. 5. Self-mutilation or attempted suicide. 6. The practice of surgery or medicine, without permission, by a cleric, with the consequent death of the patient after this practice. 7. The performance of acts reserved to clerics in major orders by persons not in these orders.

irremovable offices　Certain offices in the Church are granted by canon law the right of stability. Thus a pastor, once appointed, may not be removed without due process. However, one in such an office could retire and vacate the office at his own request.

Isaia (also Isaias, Isaiah; Heb. Yahweh is salvation)　The name of the first of the major prophets. He was called to the office of prophet about 742 B.C. He is the author of the Book of Isaia.

Isaia, Book of　This is the first and greatest prophetic book of the Old Testament. The first part (chaps. 1-39) reflects the situation of Israel in the 8th century B.C. God promises to save those who trust in His promises made to the Davidic Dynasty. The Emmanuel Prophecies (6:1-12:6) promise deliverance through a future descendant of David. The second part (chaps. 40-60) is often called the "book of consolation." God promises liberation, especially spiritual, to His people in exile or recently returned.

Islam (Arabic *aslama,* to surrender) The religion taught by Muhammad which has the Koran (Qu'ran) for its sacred book. It takes its name from the surrender by its followers of their wills to God. It is monotheistic and counts Christ as one of the Jewish prophets. The religion has its center in Mecca, its sacred city, now in Saudi Arabia. It spread across North Africa and into the Middle East through the jihad or holy war. The teachings of Muhammad were set down in the book called the Koran which has a close resemblance to the Bible. The Koran teaches one God who punishes evil and rewards good. Life on earth is a period of testing after which man will go either to hell or to paradise, the latter being a place of sensuous delights. The Koran denounces idolatry, gambling, alcoholic beverages, the eating of pork, and the representation of human and animal figures; it permits slavery and polygamy. The follower of Islam is expected to pray five times daily, and on Friday (the Muslim holy day) to attend noon prayers at a mosque. During *Ramadham,* the ninth month of the Muslim year, Muslims may not eat or drink from sunrise to sunset. Every Muslim is expected to make at least one pilgrimage to Mecca. Islam has split into several sects, the Sunnites and Shiites being the largest. In recent years a missionary movement has grown up in Islam, and missionary work is carried on in Europe, Asia, Africa and America.

Israel 1. The name given to Jacob when he wrestled with an angel. 2. The immediate family of Jacob. 3. The descendants of Jacob. 4. The people of the Northern Kingdom in contrast to the Kingdom of Juda. 5. Used by St. Paul to denote Christians.

Israel, modern A republic established in 1948 by the United Nations as a homeland for Jews, many of whom were refugees from Nazi Germany. It was the result of the partition of Palestine, which had once been the Jewish homeland. Following World War I Great Britain took over the mandates of Palestine and Transjordan. Britain gave its support to the Balfour Declaration which agreed with the Zionist aspirations but nothing was done because of the opposition of the Arabs. In 1948 the United Nations General Assembly voted the partition of Palestine, and the Republic of Israel was proclaimed in May, 1948. From the start Israel was engaged in disputes with the Arab world and even today peace is uneasy. Almost 900,000 Arab refugees fled Israel to Jordan and remain today as innocent victims of political struggle. Despite many problems Israel has made tremendous progress in building up its agriculture and economy and creating a modern state. All religions are constitutionally free but there have been individual instances of discrimination against Christians. Israel has 1 Catholic diocese, 1 bishop and 43 parishes, with about 42,000 Eastern Rite Catholics (Melkite, Maronite). Catholics of the Latin Rite are not numbered among these since they come under the jurisdiction of the Patriarch of Jerusalem and are counted as belonging to Jordan. Nazareth, Cana, the Mount of the Beatitudes, the Sea of Galilee, Mount Sion, Mount Carmel and Mount Tabor are all in Israel.

Itala Vetus The ancient Latin version of the Bible which was supplanted in the 4th century by the Vulgate of St. Jerome. Sections of it are still in use.

Italy The country of Italy is a product of the 19th century but Catholic contacts with the Italian peninsula go

304

back almost to the very foundation of the Church. It was to Rome that St. Peter came and it was Rome that became the primatial see of the Catholic Church. There are over 50 million Italians, and while Catholic statistics claim 99.5 per cent of the population, it is evident that a substantial percentage are nominal Catholics. Italy is reputed to have the strongest Communist party in Europe outside of Russia. In the 1963 election the Communists won 166 seats in the Chamber of Deputies to 273 by the Church-supported Christian Democrats. There are 284 archdioceses, dioceses and abbeys nullius in Italy. They are staffed by approximately 44,000 secular priests and 19,000 religious priests. Among the gifts of Italy to the Church were St. Francis of Assisi and the Franciscans, St. Thomas Aquinas, St. Bonaventure, St. Bernadine of Siena, St. John Capistran, St. Charles Borromeo, St. Philip Neri and his Oratorians, St. Paul of the Cross and the Passionists, St. Alphonsus Liguori and the Redemptorists. Today Rome is the center for many Catholic movements. Except for the Franciscans, Italy's mission effort is fairly modern. The main societies of men with more than 200 Italian members in the missions are in order of size: Salesians, Scalabrini Fathers, Verona Fathers, Franciscans, Foreign Missioners of Milan, Consolata Fathers, Capuchins, Conventuals and Jesuits. Women's societies with more than 200 members in the field are the Verona Sisters, Consolata Sisters, Canossians and Franciscan Missionaries of Mary.

Ite, Missa Est (L. Go now, Mass is finished)   Words of dismissal immediately before the final blessing at Mass. *See* dismissal.

Itinerarium (L. *itinerari,* to travel) The prayer of the Church for those about to set out on a journey. It is found at the end of the Breviary. It consists of the Benedictus, an antiphon, some prayers and four collects. Some mission-sending societies have enlarged the formula into a departure ceremony.

J

Jacobites Those Syrian Christians who clung to the Monophysite heresy after its condemnation by the Council of Chalcedon in 451. They became united under Jacob Baradai in 543. In the 7th century many embraced Islam. From the 17th century many were reunited to Rome. Indian Jacobites are Christians of East Syrian ecclesiastical origin, who broke away from the Catholic Church in 1653 due to local misunderstanding and lack of communication with Rome. They resemble the Syrian Jacobites in liturgy, customs and doctrine but they do not come under the actual jurisdiction of the Jacobite Patriarch of Antioch.

Jahveh Another spelling for Yahweh (*q.v.*).

James, Epistle of St. The first of the Catholic Epistles which has been traditionally credited to the Apostle James the Less. It is largely a collection of moral sayings treating on temptation, the uselessness of faith without good works, the care of the sick, confession, abuse of wealth, etc.

James, Liturgy of St. A refinement of the Antiochene Rite. It is used once a year in Greek by the Orthodox at Jerusalem, and in Syria by the Jacobites and Syrian Uniates.

James, St. 1. The Greater. An Apostle who was elder brother of St. John. Tradition says that he preached in Spain, and Compostela claims his relics. The Spaniards knew him under the name of Santiago, a patron of Spanish soldiers. His feast day in the Western Church is on July 25, and on Apr. 30 in the Byzantine Rite. 2. The Less. An Apostle who was the son of Alpheus. He was probably one of the "brethren of Christ." He was the first bishop of Jerusalem, and author of the New Testament Epistle that bears his name. Tradition says he was martyred by being thrown from the wall of the temple. He has a joint feast with St. Philip on May 11 in the West, and on Oct. 9 in the Byzantine Church.

Jansenism Heretical doctrines of Cornelis Jansen (1585–1638), bishop of Ypres, Belgium, who taught predestination, loss of free will, the irresistibility of grace, that human nature was completely corrupted by original sin and that Christ did not die for all men. This false system gave birth to a heated controversy in theological circles and spawned a rigoristic and severe type of morality and asceticism which afflicted the Church for nearly a hundred years despite the condemnation of its errors by Urban VIII, Innocent X and Clement XI.

Januarius, miracle of St. The relics of St. Januarius are kept in the Cathedral of Naples. Many miracles are attributed to them including the halting of eruptions of Mt. Vesuvius. The dried blood of St. Januarius is kept in a glass phial. It is said to liquefy when the phial is placed near the saint's head; this ceremony takes place eighteen times a year in public. It has been studied and investigated and no natural explanation has been found. St. Januarius was a bishop during the persecution of Diocletian. For visiting some imprisoned Christians, he was arrested, tortured and beheaded.

January Month of the Holy Name of Jesus.

Japan (Nihon, Nippon; Land of the Rising Sun) The legendary founder of Japan was Emperor Jimmu, 660 B.C., supposedly descended from the sun goddess. The national religion, Shinto, a mingling of nature worship and patriotism, centered upon the emperors, descended from the original Jimmu and therefore divine. However, following World War II, this claim to divinity was repudiated by the emperor. Buddhism, introduced from China, existed alongside Shinto without rivalry. Today, many people are both Buddhists and Shintoists. In 1549 St. Francis Xavier introduced Christianity. Within a generation or so there were an estimated 600,000 Catholics in a population of 30 million. A period of persecution began which decimated the Church. When French missioners entered Japan at the end of the 19th century only a small number of Christians were discovered in the Nagasaki area. These people had kept their faith over 200 years without priests or churches. The Church suffered a severe blow when an atom bomb was dropped on the Christian section of Nagasaki. Today out of a population of over 95 million there are more than 300,000 Catholics and some 400,000 Protestants. There are 2 archdioceses and 13 dioceses.

Japanese Christians, finding of the Japanese Christians (crypto-Christians) whose ancestors had preserved and handed down the Faith in secret and without priests for more than two centuries, were discovered by Father Bernard Petitjean, a Paris Foreign Missioner, on St. Patrick's Day, 1865. Commodore Perry had succeeded in opening Japan to foreigners only ten years before this discovery. In the meantime, Catholic priests and Protestant ministers had been permitted to enter Japan to care for the souls of foreigners only. The laws banning foreign religions were still in force. It might be more accurate to say that the Japanese Christians discovered Father Petitjean. On that fateful March 17, a group of Japanese visited Father Petitjean's newly built church near Nagasaki and inquired about *Santa Maria.* Father led them to the altar of the Blessed Virgin where they knelt and wept for joy. Their next query to Father was: "Have you no children?" Father replied that his Christians were his only children since, as a priest, he observed the vow of celibacy. This information pleased the Japanese very much, since it was believed by them that the priests who had converted their ancestors did not marry. They were convinced that they had discovered a priest and a church of their own religion. Thereafter, about 6,000 crypto-Christians were discovered in all of Japan. Because of the laws against foreign religions, these Christians still had to maintain the utmost secrecy. Even so their activities became known to the authorities and they were warned to cease going to the foreign church. Then, almost miraculously, on Apr. 10, 1867, the Governor of Nagasaki granted toleration to the Christians. March 17 is celebrated in Japan as the Feast of the Finding of the Christians.

Japanese Martyrs   After the death of St. Francis Xavier, Christianity made rapid progress in Japan. The number of Christians soon rose to 200,000. In 1587, during the reign of the Emperor Taikosama, a persecution against the Church broke out which continued, with slight interruptions for fifty years. In order to prevent Christian merchants from entering the country, every visitor had to trample a crucifix under his feet. Likewise soldiers were sent into every town and city with a replica of a crucifix and the people there summoned to step on it. Those who did not do so were considered Christian and were subject to torture and death. In 1596 a Spanish ship en route to Mexico from the Philippines was driven off course in a storm and thrown against the Japanese seacoast. When cannon and ammunition were discovered aboard the ship the ruler, the viciously anti-Christian Hideyoshi, accused the Spanish of a plot to conquer Japan. The enraged ruler ordered the arrest of a group of Franciscans in Kyoto. In the days that followed, more Catholics were arrested. The prisoners had their ears cropped and were paraded through Osaka and Kyoto. On Feb. 5, 1597, after a long march and much suffering they arrived at Nagasaki. The group included 6 Franciscan missioners (among them the Mexican, Philip of Jesus), 3 Japanese Jesuits and 17 lay Japanese Christians. Among the latter was thirteen-year-old Thomas Kosaki. On the last night in prison the Japanese boy wrote to his mother: "Oh, mother, our life in this world is but a fleeting dream, and as the cherry blossoms in springtime are scattered before the wind, so do our days on earth disappear. Farewell, my dearest mother, I thank you for all the goodness you have shown me from the time that God gave me to you as a tiny baby. Father and I are going to heaven, hand in hand, and there we shall wait for you." The next morning the 26 martyrs were hung from crosses where they sang hymns until soldiers pierced their hearts with spears. They were canonized in 1862. Their feast is on Feb. 5.

Japeth (Heb. *yafet*)   One of Noe's three sons.

jealousy An unpleasant emotion arising from suspicion, resentment or mistrust of another; apprehension that a rival is supplanting one in some cherished relationship. In Scripture, jealousy is attributed to God, arising from the infringement or denial of His right of exclusive possession of the Chosen People.

Jehovah   A hybrid form of Yahweh (*q.v.*).

Jehovah's Witnesses   A sect founded in the United States in 1872 by Charles Taze Russell, following a visit to a Seventh-day Adventist meeting where he heard a sermon on impending doomsday. Following Russell's death in 1916, Judge Joseph Rutherford became head of the sect until his demise in 1942. He was succeeded by Nathan Knorr who has done a remarkable organizational job which has seen a phenomenal growth in membership. The sect owns the magazine, *The Watchtower,* and the publishing house, the Bible and Tract Society, which prints an abundance of literature that the Witnesses sell, often from door to door. The sect has a peculiar appeal to people of the lower middle class and to Christians who have little knowledge of their faith. The Witnesses believe that the Bible is a more reliable source of faith than tradition is. They believe in Christ as God's Son but hold Him inferior to the Father. They claim to belong to Jehovah's New World State, all other governments being of Satan. They therefore refuse to serve in the armed forces, to salute the flag, to vote or hold political office. Though they have often been brought into court for refusing to be drafted or to salute the flag, they are generally supported by law. They also forbid blood transfusions. Each Witness is considered an ordained minister responsible for spreading the message of Jehovah.

Jeremia A Hebrew name used by many in the Old Testament of whom the best known is Jeremia the prophet. He was born about 650 B.C. of a priestly family. He was called to be a prophet about 627 B.C., and exercised the prophetic function for forty years, during the reigns of the last kings of Juda. Jeremia warned these kings of the disaster that was approaching because of the sins of Jerusalem and Juda. He had to flee to Egypt during the Babylonian rule of Jerusalem.

Jeronymites *See* Hieronymites.

Jerusalem (Heb. city of peace) The ancient Chanaanite and Israelite city that became spiritual and political capital of the Jews. It was first mentioned during the 12th Egyptian dynasty (*c*. 1700 B.C.) in the "excreation" texts. However from the Amarna Letters, it is known that there was a Semitic-Hurrian settlement there as early as the 14th century B.C. Jerusalem was in the

possession of the Chanaanites until it was captured by David. Both he and Solomon extended and enlarged it. For Christians, the city has important significance because of its connections with Christ who died there. In an allegorical sense, the word is used to mean the Church militant, heaven and just souls.

Jerusalem, Council of The assembly of Apostles, presbyters and early Christians held in Jerusalem to decide matters proposed by Barnabas and Paul, questioning the necessity of obliging Gentile converts to observe such prescriptions of the Mosaic Law as circumcision, etc. (Cf. Acts 15:4-29). St. Peter settled the dispute by declaring the Gentiles had no such obligation. St. James's proposal for a practical *modus vivendi* to avoid unnecessary injury to Jewish scruples in regard to food offered to idols, dietary regulations and immorality was incorporated in a letter of instruction to the converts in Antioch, Syria and Cilicia. While not listed as an ecumenical council, theologians maintain that its doctrinal regulations are infallible. The force and application of its disciplinary norms was gradually dissipated by the elapse of time and the altered circumstances of new peoples who became Christians.

Jerusalem, Liturgy of The Liturgy of St. James (*q.v.*). A form of the ancient liturgy developed in Antioch. This form was used in Jerusalem, and remnants of it appear today in the liturgies of some of the Eastern Churches. The Orthodox of Zakynthos and Jerusalem use the ancient Greek Liturgy of St. James on the saint's feast even today. The Syriac and Maronite Liturgies are derived from this primitive form.

Jerusalem, patriarchate of The see

of Jerusalem became a patriarchate under the Council of Chalcedon. Cut off by Muslim conquest, it had very little contact with the Western Church, and as a part of the Eastern Orthodox Church gradually became separated from Rome.

Jerusalem, Patriarchs of There are three Patriarchs of Jerusalem: Latin, Armenian, Orthodox. The see of the Latin Patriarch was established during the Crusades but was only titular until 1847 when it was made residential. The Latin Patriarch is the equivalent of an archbishop without suffragan sees.

Jesse (Heb. *yisai*) The father of David and the ancestor of Jesus Christ.

Jesse-Window 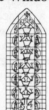 A stained glass window depicting the characters in the genealogy of Jesus Christ. It takes the form of a multi-branched tree with Christ at the summit. Jesse, the father of King David, is the root of the line of descent to Christ. From him it derives its name.

Jesu's Psalter A form of devotion popular in the 16th century and after, made up of petitions for graces necessary to the spiritual life. It contains 15 principal petitions, each of which is repeated 10 times. Every 5 petitions have an antiphon or short verse and are followed by Our Father, Hail Mary and I Believe in God. Often other prayers and verses were included within it. When found in modern prayerbooks it is often shortened or outlined. It is incorrectly called "The Jesus Psalter."

Jesuit Estates The Quebec Act, 1774, recognized the status of the Roman Catholic Church in Canada but did not consider the consequences of the suppression of the Jesuits the previous year. The Jesuits held 891,-845 acres in Canada. The British Government vested the Jesuit properties in the crown with the revenue to be used for education. After the restoration of the Society by Pope Pius VI, a number of Jesuits returned to Canada and for many years there was a dispute over the expropriated lands. Finally in 1888 the Jesuits were given $400,000 in compensation, an act vigorously opposed by anti-Catholic groups.

Jesuit Reductions *See* Reductions.

Jesuit Relations Letters, diaries and official reports of Jesuit missioners which may be classified under three headings: 1. intimate and personal letters to relatives, friends and superiors which may or may not have been intended for publication; 2. excerpts from annual reports to superiors which were circulated only among members of the Society; 3. excerpts from diaries, reports and letters for general publication. These have been collected, translated into many languages and published in forty-one volumes with the title *Jesuit Relations,* mostly covering the apostolic activities of the *Jesuits* in the North American missions among the Indians. They contain probably the most authentic and detailed description of the Indians, explorations, and colonial life of that period. They are a veritable gold mine of historical information, inspired by missionary zeal. Due to the controversy about Chinese Rites the continuation of this form of publication was halted by a decree of Pope Clement X which forbade the dissemination of such missionary literature without the antecedent approval of the Holy See.

Jesuits A popular title for members

of the Society of Jesus. A religious order of men founded by St. Ignatius Loyola at Montmarte, Paris, in 1534 and approved by Pope Paul III in 1540. Ignatius, a Basque and a captain in the Spanish army, was wounded in battle. While convalescing he read a volume of the lives of the saints and resolved to devote his life to God. After a period of prayer and penance, Ignatius decided that a solid education was necessary for his plans. He entered the University of Paris, gathering a few men around him with the idea of doing apostolic work. They called themselves the Company of Jesus. Among the early followers was Francis Xavier who was to become the great Apostle of the Indies. The Jesuits dedicated themselves immediately to the service of the papacy in whatever capacity the Holy Father chose to use them. The growth of the Society was rapid and the work broadly expanded. Almost from the beginning, the Jesuits engaged in foreign mission work and their progressive methods are models to this day. Those early missioners included such outstanding figures as St. Francis Xavier; Robert de Nobili, the Christian Brahmin; the Jesuit martyrs of North America; the Jesuits who smuggled themselves into England in order to keep the Faith alive during days of persecution; Mateo Ricci, teacher of astronomy and Chrisian doctrine at the Chinese royal court; the founders of the Reductions of Paraguay; Eusebius Kino, builder of missions in Mexico and the American Southwest. In early Maryland, Father Andrew White and fellow Jesuits ministered to Catholics and worked among the Indians. However, it was not until 1833 that the Jesuits were established in this country. Since then, they have been leaders in American Catholic thought and progress. Organized into 12 American provinces under the general motherhouse in Rome, American Jesuits today number approximately 6,000 priests and 700 Brothers. They operate such outstanding universities as Fordham, Holy Cross, Georgetown, Detroit, St. Louis, Marquette, Santa Clara, Boston College, Creighton, Gonzaga, Seattle University, Loyola of Chicago, Loyola of New Orleans and the University of San Francisco. Their publications such as *Catholic Mind, Thought* and *America* have contributed greatly to the formation of Catholic intellectuals. Jesuit scientists, sociologists, and labor and welfare experts have national reputations. The Jesuits have always met with extraordinary opposition from powerful individuals, from governments and from areas within the Church itself. One of the main reasons is that the Jesuits are devoted to the universal Church, rather than to any sectional or particularized area. Thus in seeking the broader interests of the Church, the Jesuits often conflict with particularized interests. No matter what the struggle —be it against poverty, ignorance, race prejudice, Communism or unbelief—Jesuits will be found deeply engaged. *See* Society of Jesus.

Jesuits, suppression of the Before the mid-18th century the political powers were bent on the ruin of the Jesuits. In 1759 the Society was expelled from Portugal and her possessions. In 1764 France suppressed them. A few years later the Spanish dominions were closed to them. Finally in 1773 Pope Clement XIV, under the coercion of the Bourbon monarchs, issued a brief suppressing the Society of Jesus. The Society was restored by

Pope Pius VII in 1814. Many charges were made against the Society and its individual members. The real reason for the antagonism against them was that they did their work well and successfully, thus making enemies of those who would oppress the Church, her members and their rights.

Jesus The Latin form of the Greek *Iesous* which in turn is derived from the Aramaic *Yeshu* which means "Jahweh is salvation." The name was announced to Mary by the Angel Gabriel (Lk. 1:31). It is a common name in the Near East and in Spain and Latin America.

Jesus Christ The second person of the Blessed Trinity made man. The name Jesus (Heb. *Yeshu,* Savior) was His personal name. The name Christ (Gr. *Khristos,* anointed or chosen) refers to his office as the Anointed One, chosen by God for a mission.

Jews, the A term that can refer to race or religion. More properly it refers to religion. As a race it refers to the Hebrew people. As a religion it refers to those people who follow the Law of Moses, and the revelation of the true God of the Old Covenant. However, they do not accept the divinity of Christ in the New Covenant.

Job, Book of A book of the Old Testament whose central figure is a man named Job, a religious man who having been formerly blessed by God is suddenly afflicted with great sufferings in both spirit and body. However, he bears his sufferings and refuses the temptation to blame God, giving us the key to understanding the problem of suffering.

Jocist movement The Young Christian Workers. The name comes from its French title, *Jeunesse Ouvrière Chrétienne.* The movement was founded in Belgium by Canon Cardijn shortly after World War I with the aim of making work and all activities a Christian apostolate. It follows the methods of Catholic Action (*q.v.*). It spread through Europe, then moved to Canada and the United States. Branches of the movement are now gaining strength in Latin America.

Joel, Book of (Heb. Yahweh is God) A prophetic book of the Old Testament dealing with the approaching day of the Lord. Joel wrote this book for Juda and Jerusalem. The book is placed second among the minor prophets.

John Chrysostom, Liturgy of St. The usual form of the liturgy (Mass) in the Byzantine Rite currently used in the Eastern Orthodox Church and by Byzantine Catholics.

John, St. One of the twelve Apostles and an Evangelist. He and his brother James are spoken of as the sons of Zebedee. He is also called the "Beloved Disciple" because of the special favor he had with Jesus. He was present at the Transfiguration, was with Jesus in the place of the agony in the garden and is said to have rested on the bosom of the Lord at the Last Supper. Jesus, on the cross, committed Mary to his care. He wrote his Gospel in Greek between A.D. 90–100. He also wrote three Epistles, most likely from Ephesus, continuing the message of his Gospel. He is often symbolized by an eagle because his Gospel soars beyond the other Gospels. He is the only Apostle, as far as we know, not called to martyrdom. He is believed to have lived at Ephesus until an old age. There is a tradition that he was cast into a vat of boiling oil at the command of Emperor Domitian and was delivered unharmed.

Jona, Book of (Heb. dove) This Old Testament book gets its name from the hero of its story, Jona, a prophet who lived about 750 B.C. Jona is commissioned by God to go to Ninive, the Assyrian capital, to preach repentance. On the way, he is thrown into the sea, swallowed by a large fish and cast up unharmed three days later. He reaches Ninive where the people repent as the result of his preaching. The Book of Jona was written after the Babylonian Captivity, about 400 B.C. Most modern exegetes do not consider the story of Jona a historical account but rather a parable that in part prefigures Christ. The whole theme of the book is the universality of salvation.

Jonathan (Heb. *yonatan,* Yahweh has given) The son of Saul and close friend of David. He was a brave fighter against the Philistines but finally with his father and two brothers was killed by them in the battle of Mount Gelboe. When news of the tragedy reached David, he composed the moving dirge found in 2 Kings 1:17-27.

Jordan, the Hashemite Kingdom of An Arab kingdom in S.W. Asia, containing parts of the ancient Holy Land, Palestine. Its capital is at Amman; it has an estimated area of 37,500 square miles, and a population of less than two million. It is roughly coterminous with biblical Moab, Gilead and Edom, with parts of ancient Juda and Israel. It takes its name from the Jordan River which rises in the Anti-Lebanon Range and flows 200 miles south, mostly through the Kingdom of Jordan to the Dead Sea. The partition of the ancient land was made in modern times by a combination of forces during two world wars, the action of Great Britain and the United Nations, the creation of the state of Israel out of its territory, and the conquest of added areas by Israel's armed forces. Jordan is mostly desert, though productive and well cultivated wherever water can be obtained. Its distress at losing much of its arable land to Israel is aggravated by the presence of thousands of Arab refugees from Israel. Most of the people are Muslims (Muslim Arabs conquered the country in the 7th century) though there are about 180,000 Arab Christians, 47,000 of whom are Catholics. The Catholic Church in Jordan is free, conducting many institutions for the poor, schools and hospices for pilgrims. Nearly all of the Catholic children are in Catholic schools. The Franciscan Order (Friars Minor) have been caretakers of many of the holy places of pilgrimage since the Middle Ages, and they do archaeological exploration, research and publishing as well. The Church was established in this ancient land about A.D. 33 by Christ and His Apostles. Today there are three patriarchates with numerous churches and institutions. There are various religious orders as well as the Franciscans who keep up widespread works of charity caring for refugees and the poor in general. The Catholic Near East Welfare Association (U.S.A.) supports missions in Jordan and aids refugees. Jordan contains most of the holy places of pilgrimage: Calvary and the Holy Sepulchre, besides other places in Jerusalem; Gethsemani; the Mount of Olives; the place of the Ascension; Bethany; the tomb of Lazarus; Jericho; the Jordan where John the Baptist preached and Christ was baptized; the Mount of Temptation in the desert; the Dead Sea; the caves of the Dead Sea scrolls; Bethlehem; Sa-maria and the Well of Jacob; and Hebron, city of Abraham, beloved ancestor of both Arabs and Jews and spiritual father of Christians.

Joseph (Heb. *josef,* may he add) 1. Saint. Husband of Mary and legal guardian of Jesus. By trade he was a wood-worker and traditionally has been held to have been a carpenter. Very little is said about him in the Gospels other than in the account of the infancy of Jesus; the last mention being in the finding of the twelve-year-old Jesus in the temple. Although it is generally held that he died before Jesus began His public life, Jn. 6:42 would seem to indicate otherwise. Joseph has been named patron of the universal Church, and his feast day is celebrated on March 19. 2. An Old Testament patriarch, the son of Jacob and Rachel. He was sold as a slave into Egypt by his brothers where he rose to great power, becoming governor of Egypt. When his brothers came to Egypt seeking grain, Joseph revealed himself to them. He persuaded his family to settle in Egypt. He died there at the age of 110. At the Exodus, his mummy was taken by the Israelites and buried at Sichem. 3. A native of Arimathea who probably had a residence in Jerusalem since he had pre-prepared his tomb there. He was a rich man who had a reputation for goodness and was a member of the Jewish Sanhedrin but who disapproved that body's acts against Jesus. With Nicodemus, he took care of the burial details of Christ following His crucifixion.

Joshua Josue (*q.v.*).

Josue Son of Nun, assistant to Moses and his successor as leader of the Israelites. Also known as Osee. Josue led the tribes across the Jordan where he captured Jericho and Hai, and was responsible for the conquest of Chanaan. The Book of Josue is attributed to his authorship but is probably the work of the Deuteronomy.

joy A feeling experienced by a person either in his will or in his sense appetite that results from the possession of a desired god.

Joyful Mysteries Those five decades (of the fifteen) in the Rosary which are concerned about the Annunciation, Mary's visit to Elizabeth, the Nativity, the presentation of the child Jesus in the temple and the finding of Jesus in the temple. While reciting each decade, the mystery commemorating the event in the life of Jesus and Mary should be meditated upon.

Joys of the Blessed Virgin Mary, Seven There are two enumerations for the seven joys of Mary. 1. Mary nursing her Son, Jesus curing the lame, Jesus giving sight to the blind, Jesus reading the Bible, Jesus raising the dead, Jesus' Resurrection and Jesus going into heaven. This enumeration is taken from an old English carol and is the enumeration given by common people, who made the song. 2. The Annunciation, the Visitation, the Birth of Jesus, the visit of the Wise Men, the finding of Jesus in the temple, Jesus' rising from the dead and the Assumption of Our Lady. This is the list given by the theologians and is the accepted list today.

jubilee A season of great public joy and festivity. A time when a plenary indulgence is granted by the Holy See with special solemnity together with special faculties to confessors. *See* Jubilee Year.

Jubilee Sunday The third Sunday after Easter, so named from the first word of the Introit of the Mass for that day.

Jubilee Year In Jewish history, this was a year-long celebration held every 50 years according to the Levitical Law at which time slaves were to go free, lands and houses in the open country were to be restored to their original owners and the land was to be left unworked. In the Church, the year of Jubilee has been adopted as a year of remission from the penal consequences of sin, providing the faithful perform certain pious works to gain a plenary indulgence and fulfill the conditions for repentance. Confessors receive special faculties during this time for absolution of reserved cases. Ordinary Jubilees occur every 25 years but they may be proclaimed at other times also.

jubilus (L. joyous)   A long melodious group of notes of a joyous nature to which is sung the final "a" of the second and third "alleluias," after the Gradual in the Roman Mass.

Juda (Heb. *yehudah*)   The son of Jacob and Lia, founder of the tribe of Juda. He is named among the ancestors of Jesus.

Juda, the kingdom of   Juda was a kingdom in southern Palestine in ancient times. It existed from *c.* 922 to 587 B.C. It was the southern kingdom of the divided monarchy which was formed after the schism of Jeroboam in 62 B.C. More powerful and populated than Israel, it was composed of the tribes of Juda and Benjamin, with Juda predominating. It remained loyal to the house of David when the other tribes broke away. Its capital was Jerusalem, and the Jews of today are descendants of these people.

Judah   Juda (*q.v.*).

Judaism   The distinctive form of religion revealed by God to Israel and developed over the years among the Jews. Since the destruction of the temple in Jerusalem, A.D. 70, the Jews have had no altar or sacrifice. Worship is conducted in synagogues by a rabbi, and consists of prayers and readings. Modern Judaism is divided into many factions with varying beliefs, extending from the strict orthodox to the very liberal.

Jude, Epistle of St.   A short letter written probably to a particular Christian community to warn the Christians about certain men who have entered the community to spread false teaching about Christ and whose bad example is a serious danger to the faith of the Christians. It was written by St. Jude the Apostle, probably between A.D. 66–80.

Jude, St.   Brother of James the Less and a kinsman of Christ. He wrote the Epistle which bears his name. He preached in Mesopotamia and later teamed with St. Simon to go to Persia where tradition says he was martyred. In the Western Rite, Jude shares a feast with Simon on Oct. 28. In the Byzantine Rite he has a feast alone on June 19. He is also known as St. Jude Thaddeus and St. Thaddeus.

judge, ecclesiastical   According to canon law one who has the authority to preside over an ecclesiastical court of justice. He is a person who possesses ecclesiastical jurisdiction.

Judges, Book of   A book of the Old Testament that takes its name from the charismatic leaders whose deeds are recounted within its pages. It is the story of the struggle to liberate Israel from its enemies during the period between the death of Josue and the beginning of the monarchy with Saul and David.

judgment   The act wherein God, after a person's death, determines whether or not the soul has in it His life, namely, sanctifying grace. On the basis of this judgment, the soul is admitted to heaven and the Beatific

315

Vision (following purification in purgatory, if necessary), or condemned to eternal separation from God. Judgment takes place twice for every person: at the moment of death, in a particular judgment; and at the end of the world when all persons will be judged in the company of all who have ever lived, in the general judgment.

judgment, general   At the end of the world as we now know it, Christ will come again to earth; this will be the Parousia *(q.v.)* and the general judgment, or the last judgment, will then take place. Christ will assemble before Him all men who have lived and will gather the good for Himself into heaven, while driving the evil into hell. The judgment depends on whether people have accepted or rejected God's grace.

judgment, intellectual (L. *judicare,* to speak right)   An act of intellect whereby two concepts are compared by way of affirmation or negation.

judgment, moral   A judgment is an act of the intellect which compares two ideas or realities and decides whether they agree or not. 1. A *moral judgment* is a decision as to whether an action is good or bad, whether it is in conformity with God's will, or not. 2. A *speculative moral judgment* is abstract and theoretical and its decision is a principle of action in general terms. 3. A *particular moral judgment* deals with a particular action and all the circumstances surrounding it. 4. If a particular judgment is made by an individual regarding an action he is about to perform or omit, it is called the *judgment of conscience.*

judgment of God   The judgment of every man, according to his merits, by God. 1. The *particular judgment* is the judgment of each individual

immediately after his death, after which he will be sent to heaven, hell or purgatory. 2. The *general judgment* will come at the end of the world when Jesus Christ will triumphantly come in all His glory and power to judge the living and the dead.

judgment of the soul   The judgment in which is fixed personal reward or punishment according to the merits and moral state of the person as these result from the individual's response to the graces of God.

judgment, particular   The judgment by God of the individual which takes place immediately after death.

judgment, private   Luther rejected the teaching authority of the Church, maintaining that private individuals were competent to get all the guidance they needed from their own reading of the Scriptures, and that the claim of the Church to teach was an intrusion on the liberty of the individual. This is called the right of private judgment.

Judica Psalm   Psalm 42 in the Catholic version, Psalm 43 in the Protestant. This psalm was formerly recited by the celebrant at the foot of the altar at the beginning of Mass. In the liturgical changes of Vatican Council II it was omitted from the Mass.

Judica Sunday   Another name for Passion Sunday, taken from the first word of the Introit.

Judith, Book of   A book of the Old Testament. It is not in the Hebrew Bible and therefore is ranked as apocryphal by Protestants. The Catholic Church has always ranked the book as part of the Old Testament canon. The book has two parts. The first deals with events leading up to the Assyrian invasion and the siege of Bethulia. The second part recounts

Judith's successful raising of the siege.

July　Month of the Precious Blood.

June　Month of the Sacred Heart.

juniorate　1. A two-year course of instruction for Jesuit students preparatory to the course in philosophy. 2. A junior (minor) seminary. 3. A training period in some religious orders for women.

juramentado (hoor-a-men-tah'doe, Sp. *juramento,* an oath) The name given to a Moro oath ceremony in the Philippines by which the oathtaker swears to kill as many Christians as possible in an act that will probably cost his own life.

jurisdiction　Jurisdiction is the power or authority belonging to the Church of ruling her members. This power was given to the Church by Christ in order that the Church may achieve her spiritual end. It includes all types of authority: legislative, judicial and executive. The pope has jurisdiction over the whole Church. It extends to all baptized persons everywhere, independently of any civil authority, in all that concerns the salvation of souls. Bishops have this power over those in their dioceses, and pastors have jurisdiction in certain things over the members of their parish. The jurisdiction of the bishop and pastor is limited by law. Jurisdiction is either *ordinary* if attached to the office which the cleric holds, or is *delegated,* if committed to the person apart from any office. Jurisdiction is needed in order for an ordained priest to hear confessions. It is given to him by the bishop if he is not a pastor.

jurisdiction, delegated　Delegated power of jurisdiction is that which is not attached to an office but is committed to a person. It is exercised in the name of and in virtue of the principal right vested in another.

jurisdiction, ordinary　Ordinary power of jurisdiction is that which the law itself attaches to an office. Two important elements must be present: 1. an office in the strict sense of the word, e.g., the episcopate; 2. the union of the jurisdiction with the office by either divine or ecclesiastical law.

jus primae noctis (L. right of the first night)　*See* droit du seigneur.

just price　*See* price, just.

just wage　That which is sufficient to lead a life worthy of man and to fulfill family responsibilities. In determining what constitutes a just wage the following must be considered: the contribution of an individiual to the economic effort; the economic state of the enterprise within which he works; the requirements of each community, particularly regarding overall employment; and what concerns the common good of all peoples, namely, of thc various states associated among themselves, but differing in character and extent.

justice　The rendering to a person of that which is his due. The virtue of justice is the constant and permanent determination to give everyone his duc. The subject of justice is the will, and the object is the good or right due to another.

justification　The act by which a person is accepted by God or made worthy of salvation. One receives the grace of justification (Sanctifying Grace) at Baptism, which must be preceded by an act of faith. The Council of Trent teaches that faith is "the foundation and root of all justification."

justification by faith　A religious system that attributes a person's redemption not to any good work that the individual might do but solely to his faith in Jesus Christ who has redeemed him. Luther proposed this principle which was condemned by the Council of Trent.

justification by works A religious system that would hold that man can earn the right to eternal happiness solely by the merit of his own effort. Justification comes from both faith and works (Js. 2:24, 26).

K

K. of C. *See* Knights of Columbus.

kanon A type of canticle found in the Byzantine Divine Office. Each Sunday and feast has its own kanon, many of which are acrostic.

Kansas Sioux for "South Wind." The 34th state admitted to the Union, it is 14th in area and 28th in population. Located on the Great Plains, it is an important farming and stockraising area, with growing oil production and industries. In former times numerous tribes of Indians, nomadic hunters and village dwellers lived there with huge herds of bison as their source of supply. In 1541 Coronado touched Kansas soil, accompanied by Franciscan padres who probably offered Mass. French explorers and traders came later. The United States gained the region with the Louisiana Purchase in 1803, and shortly afterwards it was explored by Lewis and Clark, Z. M. Pike, and S. H. Long in turn. In 1822 Bishop Dubourg of Louisiana sent Father La Croix on a mission to the Osage, and Father Van Quickenborn, S.J., followed. In 1836 St. Francis Xavier's mission to the Kickapoo was established by the Jesuits and the first Catholic church in the state was built. Jesuits, Religious of the Sacred Heart and Sisters of Loretto pioneered with schools for Indians and white settlers. Fort Leavenworth was built by the government in 1827, one of a series to protect traffic on the Santa Fe Trail, as covered wagons carried a constant stream of settlers to the west. The California gold rush (1848) and the Homestead Act (1862) further increased the multitudes en route. After the Civil War (1865) Texas cattle men began driving their herds through Kansas, wild cow-towns sprang up and men of the law like Wild Bill Hickock and Buffalo Bill (Cody) discouraged cattle thieves and robbers. Kansas became a state in 1861. Catholic schools, colleges and hospitals were founded by Sisters of Charity, Benedictines and others. Leavenworth became a diocese in 1877 with the Benedictine Louis Fink as first bishop. (In 1947 it was changed to the Diocese of Kansas City.) In 1887 Salina and Wichita were established as dioceses, followed by the Diocese of Dodge City in 1951. In 1952 Kansas City was promoted to the rank of archdiocese. Today there are well over 300,000 Catholics in Kansas, among a total population of over 2 million.

katholicos *See* catholicos.

kenosis (Gr. an emptying) St. Paul in Philip. 2:7 says of Christ that He

319

"emptied Himself," i.e., made Himself as of no account. For the Second Person of the Trinity to become man by assuming a lower nature was an abasement. It does not mean Christ gave up any of His divine attributes.

Kentucky Named for the Wyandot word for "plain," it is the 15th state admitted to the Union, is 37th in area and 22nd in population. In 1669 La Salle arrived, the first white man in the region. In 1749 Bienville took possession of it for France. The English explorers Finley and Boone arrived about the same time. James Harrod set up the first permanent white settlement, Harrodsville, in 1774. In 1775 the first two Catholic settlers arrived from Maryland, a Mrs. Coomes starting a school in Harrodsburg, and a Dr. Hart setting up a medical practice. The first priest, Capuchin Father Whelan, was sent by Bishop Carroll in 1787. Early priests traversed the mountains and plains on horseback, offering Mass at mission stations in settlers' homes. There were 300 Catholics in the state in 1796, the first Catholic church having been built at Holy Cross by Father De Rohan in 1792, the year the state was admitted to the Union. Sisters of Loretto, Sisters of Charity, Jesuits, Dominicans, Trappists, Ursulines, Sisters of Notre Dame and others established themselves and the works of education and mercy flourished. Bardstown was the first diocese (1808) and Bishop Flaget, S.S., built there the first cathedral in the west—St. Joseph's. The see was later transferred to Louisville. Covington became a diocese in 1853, and in 1937 Louisville was raised to the rank of archdiocese and Owensboro became a diocese. Catholics number somewhat over 300,000 today, in a total population of over 3 million.

kerygma (Gr. *keryssein,* to proclaim) The heralding or announcing of the king's coming. In the primitive Church it meant the proclamation of the Gospel as the good news of salvation. Today this term refers to the emphasis to be given to preaching, catechesis and theology, as a proclamation of God's word among men, centered in Christ.

keys A symbol of the power and authority of the pope (Mt. 6:19). Also a symbol of St. Peter, many of whose representations contain a key.

Keys, Power of *See* binding and loosing.

kindness A form of charity that leads a person to assist others by word and deed. It is a gift of the Holy Spirit.

King James Version of the Bible King James VI of Scotland succeeded Queen Elizabeth I in 1603 (becoming James I of England) and his own consuming interest in biblical studies induced him to appoint a committee of some 54 scholars to undertake a new official translation. The best original Hebrew and Greek texts were to be used as well as the existing translations. Some 15 rules to guide the translators were set up, exhibiting a remarkably prudent and even conservative spirit. The first edition of the King James Version (known officially as the Authorized Version) appeared in 1611. Despite the occasionally violent opposition to this new translation, the King James Bible in its various revisions became the official Bible for the vast majority of English-speaking Protestants for over three hundred years.

King of Kings Title given to our Lord by St. Paul (1 Tim. 6:16).

King of the Jews 1. A name applied to Christ by the Magi (Mt. 2:2). 2. The name tauntingly given Christ by his military torturers (Mt. 27:30). 3. The name given by Pilate and placed on the sign at the top of the cross (Mt. 27:11, 37).

Kings, Books of Two books of the Old Testament that relate the history of the kings of Israel and Juda from David's reign to the destruction of Jerusalem in 587 B.C. There is a short final part on the Babylonian exile. In its present form Kings dates from about 560 B.C., although there was an earlier version.

Kingship of Christ *See* Christ the King.

kiss, liturgical 1. *See* Kiss of Peace. 2. The celebrant kisses the altar during Mass. At the end of the Gospel, the missal is kissed. In a High Mass, the deacon kisses the celebrant's hand when he asks for the blessing before the Gospel. 3. A bishop kisses those whom he has just ordained.

Kiss of Peace A special kiss that is given at a Solemn High Mass. After the Agnus Dei and the following prayer for peace, the celebrant kisses the altar, turns to the deacon and places his hands on the deacon's shoulders while the deacon supports his forearms lightly. They then bow to each other, left cheek to left cheek. The celebrant says, *"Pax tecum"* (Peace be with you) and the reacon replies, *"Et cum spiritu tuo"* (And with your spirit). The deacon then gives the kiss to the subdeacon who passes it on to the clerics present. The Kiss of Peace is no longer given in the West to the laity. In the Eastern Church usage varies.

kissing cousins Cousins of opposite sex who are so closely related that marriage is forbidden; therefore, in kissing each other they can be presumed to have no romantic intentions.

kneeling While in most Eastern liturgies kneeling is unknown, it is part of the worship of the Latin Liturgy. In the Low Mass, the faithful kneel after the Sanctus and remain kneeling through the Eucharistic Prayer (Canon) up through the great "Amen" concluding the Canon. They stand for the Lord's Prayer and kneel again after the Agnus Dei up to the Postcommunion, stand for this prayer, and then kneel for the final blessing. A genuflection is made at the *Incarnatus* of the Creed. In extraliturgical functions, such as Benediction, kneeling is the ordinary posture.

knight (AS. nit) 1. A mounted warrior of the Middle Ages who was pledged under oath to fight for just causes only, to be subject to the Church and her priests, and to be a vassal of the Blessed Virgin and thus to protect all women by acts of chivalry. 2. One raised to the dignity of one of the six pontifical orders of knighthood.

knight, papal A member of one of the pontifical orders of knighthood. The *Pontifical Yearbook* lists the following five: 1. Supreme Order of Christ, founded by Pope John XXII in 1319; 2. Order of the Golden Spur, restored by Pope St. Pius X in 1905; 3. Order of Pius, founded by Pius IX in 1847 and reformed by Pius XII in 1957; 4. Order of St. Gregory the Great, founded in 1831 and reformed by Pope St. Pius X in 1905; 5. Order of Pope St. Silvester, reconstituted in 1841 and reformed by Pope St. Pius X in 1905. These orders are all honorary; the second and third are occasionally conferred on non-Catholics as well as Catholics.

Knights of Columbus A fraternal ben  efit society of Catholic men founded in Connecticut by Father Michael J. McGivney in 1882. In line with the general purpose of the K. of C. to be of service to the Church, the society has been active in promoting the Legion of Decency, the Organization for Decent Literature, laymen's retreats and days of recollection, the Catholic Press, discussion groups, public lectures, radio and television work, Catholic Evidence Guilds, public Good Friday observances, welfare drives and other projects. Since 1947 the Supreme Council has sponsored a program of Catholic advertising in secular publications with national circulation. Headquarters: New Haven, Conn.

Knights of Columbus "Oath" A bogus "oath" reputedly taken by the Knights of Columbus and used by anti-Catholic bigots to prove that the organization is un-American and anti-Protestant. Proof for the existence of the oath has been the *Congressional Record* of Feb. 15, 1913. However, the oath was printed in the *Record* as an exhibit in a contested Congressional election and to prove its falsity. The Knights of Columbus have had a long standing offer of $25,000 for anyone who can prove that such an oath was ever taken or subscribed to by the Knights of Columbus. Moreover, many persons who have circulated the oath have been prosecuted and convicted of criminal libel.

Knights of Malta A military order, originating as the Knights Hospitallers of St. John of Jerusalem toward the end of the 11th century, in hos-pital service for sick pilgrims in the Holy City. In time the order grew wealthy and acquired great influence. While its grand masters ruled as temporal sovereigns in Rhodes from 1309 to 1523, the members became known as Knights of Rhodes. Shortly afterward they established themselves in Malta and ruled there till defeated by Napoleon in 1798, whence the name Knights of Malta. Because of abuses the order was suppressed in many countries. It survives as the Sovereign, Sacred and Military Order of St. John of Jerusalem, in common parlance, Knights of St. John. Because of its sovereign character, the order enjoys diplomatic representation at the Vatican.

knights, orders of Certain brotherhoods of knights which arose during the Middle Ages. Chivalry had become a well-established institution in feudal Europe by the end of the 10th century. It represented a fusion of Christian and military ideals; the rough warrior of the earlier centuries had been tamed and transformed into the knight: the embodiment of honor, valor and other noble virtues; the protector of the innocent, weak and defenseless. When, in the centuries that followed, the Christians of Europe were called on to join forces for the sacred purpose of liberating the Holy Places, the Crusader became the pattern of the perfect knight. From then on a variety of brotherhoods or orders of knights appeared, each designed to meet a particular need or espouse a special cause. The earliest orders of knighthood were of a *religious* character, i.e., they combined with the insignia of knighthood certain features of the monastic life. One type of these, like the Knights Templar, was purely military; another type, e.g., the Teutonic Knights, was partly military and partly "hospitaller," i.e., engaged in service of the sick; still a third class devoted itself wholly to the care of the sick and needy, e.g., the Order of St. Lazarus of Jerusalem. Later, beginning with the 14th century, there arose a variety of *secular* orders of knighthood. Such are, e.g., the Order of the Garter and the Order of St. George in England, the Order of the Annunziata in Italy, of the Golden Fleece in Spain, etc. Now many fraternal organizations of recent origin with no historical connection with chivalry have appropriated the title of "knight," e.g., Knights of Columbus, Knights of the Blessed Sacrament, etc.

Know Nothings Members of a lawless and violent movement in American politics, 1852–1858, which aimed to deprive all foreigners, particularly Irish Catholics, of civil rights. The movement took its name from the answer given by members when questioned about their activities: "I know nothing." Members swore an oath of secrecy and had great political power. At one time the Know Nothings had 75 members in Congress and controlled 9 states. They practiced violence against the foreign-born and Catholics, burning schools and convents, and inflicting personal injury. Members of the movement threw a stone, donated by the pope for the Washington Monument, into the Potomac River from which it was never recovered. In 1856 they were defeated in elections by the Democratic Party and began to decline quickly.

knowability of God This term refers to having knowledge of God apart from faith, i.e., from natural reason. Vatican Council I declared: "If anyone say that God, one and true, our Creator and Lord, cannot be known by the natural light of human reason from the things that are made, let him be anathema." By philosophic deduction we can learn of the existence of God and some of His attributes. 1. Principle of causality. Every effect must have a cause, up to the First Cause. 2. The contingency of the universe. A contingent universe cannot produce itself and must be dependent on another being, and the ultimately independent Being is God. 3. Design in the universe which presupposes a Supreme Intelligence, or God. 4. Perfections in the universe, none of which can produce themselves, so the Ultimate Perfection is God. 5. Conscience. Man knows moral obligations which are impossible without law. The Supreme Lawgiver is God. This limited type of knowledge of God is confirmed by revelation.

knowledge An act of understanding; information gained through learning or actual experience. An intellectual virtue. A gift of the Holy Spirit.

knowledge, infused That knowledge which exceeds the nature of someone and which can only be obtained by divine communication. Ordinary knowledge comes through the senses to the intellect but infused knowledge is given directly by God, independent of the senses. The blessed in heaven have infused knowledge in the Beatific Vision. Christ had infused knowledge, as did the prophets.

knowledge of God In God, knowledge is perfected. God knows Himself intuitively and completely. Related to external things, God knows all things existing (past, present and future), whether possible or conditionally future. This means that God knows infallibly the future decisions of free will.

knowledge of Jesus Christ As God, Christ had the knowledge of God. As man, Christ had intuitive vision of God from the moment of conception; He had, according to St. Thomas, infused knowledge; He also had experiential knowledge, namely, that knowledge acquired through senses and intellect.

Koran Qu'ran (*q.v.*).

Korea One of the few countries of the world where the Catholic Church was established by laymen. Members of an embassy to China brought back Catholic books to Korea in 1777. On another embassy Peter Ni Scunghoun was baptized and with some friends began making converts. When a Chinese priest reached the country in 1794, he found 4,000 Catholics; a persecution broke out and he was put to death. Later the first Korean priest, Blessed Andrew Kim, was put to death for his religion. In the persecution 2 bishops, 7 missioners and a large number of the faithful were killed. Today Korea has 3 archdioceses and 8 dioceses. In North Korea the clergy has been eliminated and Catholic life suppressed by the Communist government. In the south where the Church is free there are 600,000 Catholics. Half the priests in Korea are Koreans. There are 3 American bishops heading dioceses in the south—Archbishop Harold Henry, a Columban, and Bishops William McNaughton and James Pardy, both of Maryknoll. American Jesuits founded a university in Seoul in 1960. Maryknoll Sisters conduct a large hospital in Pusan. The Protestants have had considerable success in Korea. Presbyterians claim more than 700,000 members and the Methodists have 250,000 followers.

kosher (Heb. *kasher,* proper) 1. That which is sanctioned by Jewish law.

2. Food that is prepared according to the ritual of the Jewish law.

Ku Klux Klan A term to refer to various secret organizations at different periods of American history. 1. Order of the Ku Klux Klan (1866–1869) was organized to oppose the abuses of Reconstruction with the purposes of protecting the weak, safeguarding the Constitution and preventing lawlessness. The organization, however, soon became lawless and violent with the result that President U. S. Grant suppressed it in the South. It continued in a semiorganized state for many years. 2. Knights of the Ku Klux Klan, "reborn" in 1915 to uphold Americanism, which was interpreted as attacks on Catholics, Negroes, Jews and the foreign-born. Because of its violence and terror it fell into disrepute and declined after 1926. There was an unsuccessful attempt to resurrect the organization to meet the presidential campaign of 1928. 3. In the late 1950's, there was a new attempt to revive the organization to oppose Negro integration movements. It has never gathered much strength or force.

Kulturkampf (kool-toor'kampf) A German term referring to the struggle between the German Empire and the Catholics. Following the foundation of the German Empire in 1871 the emphasis was put on unity. The conservative Protestants wanted an essentially Protestant state in which the members of the official Protestant Church were to possess weight and influence. The liberals wanted a nation disassociated from any positive religious teaching; and the state, with the help of the state schools and the Legislature, was to secure absolute control over the intellectual life of the nation. Since the Catholics opposed irreligious education, the liberals naturally regarded them as their principal enemies. During the last years of the confederation the Catholic body had grown in numbers and unity of purpose. They banded together in the Center Party to win constitutional guarantees for the freedom of the Church. Bismarck inaugurated a persecution of the Catholics. A series of laws were passed designed to separate the Catholics from the influence of the Holy See. The preaching of the clergy was put under the surveillance of the police; the Jesuits, the Redemptorists and other religious orders were expelled from the country; the clergy was deprived of all influence over the schools. Finally the "May Laws," so-called because they were passed in the month of May of three successive years (1873–1875), were enacted. Among other things they suppressed the free exercise of papal jurisdiction in German and interfered with the proper education of the clergy. All this force and persecution seemed to unite the Catholics more firmly, and finally they all rose to the defense of their Faith. Gradually Bismarck realized that he had undertaken a hopeless task. With the election of Leo XIII to the papal throne in 1878, negotiations for peace began. By 1887 when the pope declared the conflict officially closed, most of the laws had been revoked. Obligatory civil marriage was the most lasting achievement of the Kulturkampf.

Kyriale A choir book containing the music and words for the Ordinary of the Mass, plus the Asperges and Vidi Aquam. The book takes its name from its first music, the Kyrie.

Kyrie eleison (Gr. Lord, have mercy) An ancient Greek ejaculation used in Catholic liturgies. In the Roman Rite it appears six times before the Gloria of the Mass; the Kyrie is said three times, "Christe eleison" (Christ have mercy) is said three times, and the Kyrie is repeated three more times. It is also used in the Breviary and in the Litany of the Saints. In Masses attended by the faithful it is said in the vernacular.

L

La Salette 1. A village in the diocese of Grenoble in southeast France, where, it is said, the Blessed Virgin appeared to two little shepherds, Melanie Calvot and Maximin Giraud, on Sept. 19, 1846. A shrine in honor of Our Lady of La Salette was built on this spot and has been visited each year by a large number of pilgrims. 2. Missionaries of La Salette. An order formed to care for the pilgrims by a band of priests, later expanded into a missionary society and approved by Rome for work in French parishes in Canada, United States, Brazil, Belgium, Poland and Malagasy Republic.

labor 1. Any skilled or unskilled work done for another person for wages. 2. Any human effort to create an economic good or to provide a service in order to make money. 3. The body of laboring men as a collective unit. 4. The act of bringing forth a child.

labor, dignity of In a strict economic sense labor is defined as the activity of man on external objects in order to obtain an economic gain. In a broader sense, it is that work done by a man in order to obtain a livelihood for himself and his family. The laboring man is more than a machine or piece of merchandise because in leasing his physical and intellectual energies his work is a human act. As a human being his labor involves the dignity of the human person. Therefore labor is not a negotiable item in the same sense as is capital. Man's labor involves decent working hours and conditions, proper protection against injury, and social legislation to protect his rights. The efforts of recent popes, together with Catholic social philosophers, have sought to vindicate these rights.

Ladies of Charity An association of Catholic women founded by St. Vincent de Paul in 1617, organized internationally and in many dioceses in the United States. The organization claims a half million members in 47 countries. Members are dedicated to works of charity. The national headquarters is in St. Louis, Mo.

Lady Day A term used for a feast of the Blessed Virgin. In Ireland the feast of the Assumption, Aug. 15. In England the feast of the Annunciation, Mar. 25.

Lady, Our A familiar form of address Catholics often use in referring to the Virgin Mary, Mother of God.

Laetare Medal, the An award bestowed yearly since 1883 by the University of Notre Dame upon some Catholic layman or woman of exemplary conduct and citizenship, as a recognition of extraordinary accomplishment in literature, the arts, science, social activity or some other field of endeavor.

laicism (L. *laicus,* layman) The secularization of areas once belonging to the sphere of religion; exclusive administration of the affairs of the Church by laymen. There are many functions that once belonged exclusively to the Church such as marriage, hospitals, charity organizations, education, etc. Laicism is the movement by which the state moves in and takes over these functions. It has historically appeared under many names: Gallicanism, Josephinism, Febronianism, etc. At the present time it appears in the form of secularization that seeks complete separation between Church and State, with the Church confined within the walls of her buildings of worship.

laity, the The Church is a community established by God in and through his divine action on men, which is grace. As a living human community it has an organic unity which proceeds from its divine origin, which manifests itself in this Church in the form of people and their leaders, i.e., a hierarchical authority. In Christian semantics the term laity has both a juridical and a theological connotation, which derives very clearly from Scripture. Canon law uses it in the sense of *Christifideles,* i.e., those who believe in Christ as God's Revelation to mankind and have been baptized in His name. The laity, therefore, are the people of God; that is, the Church of Christ, subject to the leadership and control of the Church's hierarchy. Early Christian writings make the distinction between the clery and the laity within the community of the Church. The laity consequently are the people of God assembled in the Church, but within that community are set apart from the hierarchy, the separation implying a reference to what is not directly connected with the mystery of Christian worship. The laity is characterized by its membership in the Church and its relation to secular affairs. The distinction between clergy and laity in the Church is not merely the result of historical or sociological development; it originates in the will of Christ Himself. The laity has its part to play in the apostolate of the Church, the clergy in the apostolate of the hierarchy. There is no essential difference between those who hold ecclesiastical office and the laity, even though by the very nature of the Church the priest has functions which the laity cannot fulfill. The clergy are the shepherds who are to guide the laity, who are called to the common task of the Church: the work of salvation, the building up of the Body of Christ. Therefore, while not forgetting the differentiation resulting from ordination and ministry, the laity does share in the priestly, prophetic and regal office of Christ. As the people of God the laity has a right to instruction and the sacramental ministrations necessary to spiritual growth, as well as a right to pursue its proper task in the work of salvation.

lamb 1. A symbol of Jesus Christ. In the old Jewish traditions a lamb was used for sacrifice and thus prefigured Christ. A lamb is sometimes pictured with a halo and a cross or banner, or lying as if dead on a book with seven seals, as described by St. John in the Apocalypse; in these instances it symbolizes Our Lord. 2. A symbol of the faithful. A common Christian portrayal of the Good Shepherd (Christ) is a man carrying a lamb on his shoulders. 3. A sym bol for modesty and innocence, hence a lamb is generally portrayed with St. Agnes.

Lamb of God   1. A title applied to Christ by John the Baptist. 2. The name for Christ under the Eucharistic species. In the Mass a prayer beginning with the words "Agnus Dei" is said immediately after the mingling of the Sacred Species. The term is also used when the priest holds the Host for the adoration of the faithful immediately before Communion: "Behold the Lamb of God, behold Him who takes away the sins of the world."

Lamentations   Four elegiac poems and one prayer attributed to Jeremia, which were written to mourn the fall of Jerusalem. They make up a short book of the Old Testament.

land, private ownership of   The Church has always recognized the right to private property, which includes the ownership of land. However the right to private property is not an end in itself but a means. God created the wealth of the world for the use of all His children. This is the real end, and the right to private property merely guarantees that use. When a people fail to use natural wealth for the good of all, they relinquish the right of property. This is the reasoning of St. Thomas Aquinas when he says that the use of natural wealth is a common use. There is a great need for land reform in many parts of the world. The cry of "Land to him who tills it" has a validity, but justice requires that fair compensation be given to the absentee owners so far as possible.

language of the Church   *See* Latin.

Laodicean   A person who is lukewarm in faith or the practice of religion. The term comes from Apoc.

3·14-16 where St. John speaks of the Laodiceans who are neither hot nor cold in their witness to religion.

lapsed Catholic   1. A term (*lapsi*) which was applied in the 3rd century to Catholics who relapsed into heathenism and sacrificed to the pagan gods. They were divided into three classes: *sacrificati,* those who had actually offered sacrifice; *thurificati,* those who burned incense at a pagan shrine; *libellatici,* those who made a sworn statement they had sacrificed without actually having done so. Later another class was added, called *traditores,* mostly clerics who gave sacred books to the persecuting authorities. 2. A general term today for one who has fallen away from belief in or practice of the Catholic religion.

lapsi (L. backsliders)   The term originally referred to those Catholics who during the Roman persecution acquired a certificate of conformity and thus in effect gave up the Faith. Today it means fallen-away Catholics.

last blessing   1. The blessing given at the end of Mass. 2. A special blessing given following the sacrament of Anointing of the Sick to which is attached a plenary indulgence at the moment of death.

last sacraments   *See* sacraments, last.

Last Supper, the   The traditional name given to the Passover meal which Jesus shared with His disciples before He took leave of them. It was at this meal that Jesus instituted the Holy Eucharist and delivered His farewell discourse. The traditional site in Jerusalem of the meal is known as the Cenacle.

last things, the   Man is exhorted to keep in mind the four things which will face him at the end of life: death, judgment, heaven, hell.

latae sententiae, censure   A censure

that is automatically imposed by the very fact of committing a crime.

Lateran, the   The church and palace at Rome. The name is derived from Plautius Lateranus whose estates were confiscated by Nero. 1. The Lateran Palace. Presented to Pope Melchiades in 312 by the Emperor Constantine. It was the residence of the popes from the 4th to the 14th centuries. It is now the Pontifical Museum of Christian Antiquities. 2. The Lateran Basilica. The Church of the Holy Savior, popularly known as the Lateran, or St. John Lateran. It is the cathedral church of the Bishop of Rome, the pope, and the highest-ranking church in Christendom. Above the high altar are enshrined the supposed heads of SS. Peter and Paul.

Lateran Treaty   The treaty made between the Holy See (Pope Pius XI) and the Kingdom of Italy (King Victor Emmanuel III), signed Feb. 11, 1929, and later made part of the constitution of the Italian Republic. By this treaty, Vatican City became an independent state, Catholicism became the official religion of Italy and the Holy See gave up all claims to the former Papal States and declared the "Roman Question" closed.

Latin   The official language of the Roman Empire, was originally the speech of Latium, a little district on the Tiber. It became the predominant tongue of the western portion of the Empire only after a long history of the usual cultural, military and social struggles. 1. *Christian Latin*. In origin this was the special language of small, closely organized and secluded groups. It came into being through the gradual increase in Latin-speaking converts among what was in the beginning a community of Greek and bilingual Christians. It bore the heavy imprint of its Greek matrix. 2. *Ecclesiastical Latin*. This was the form which the Latin language assumed in the hands of the Fathers of the Western Church and of their successors up to the time of the Renaissance. A fundamental uniformity of culture and language existed throughout the Latin-speaking part of the Roman Empire. The Christian group absorbed the whole community; and its special language, now influenced by the speech of the middle classes as it grew out of Classic Latin, became the common tongue of the Western world. Three stages are apparent in the gradual adoption of Latin as the language of the Church: the emergence of a Christian spoken idiom; the latinization of the Roman Church, the use of Latin in the official correspondence of the Church, which dates from the middle of the 3rd century; the latinization of the Eucharistic liturgy during the pontificate of Damascus 360–382. As a living language it developed for many centuries, conditioned by the practical requirements of daily life. At the Renaissance attempts were made to purify the language along the lines of classical usage. Reforms in terminology and a new standard of correctness were the result. These are the standards maintained to this day in the so-called "curial style" Latin of the official correspondence and documentation of the Holy See. By decree of the Apostolic Constitution *Veterum Sapientia* of Pope John XXIII, issued Feb. 22, 1962, Latin remains the official language of instruction in the sacred sciences taught in seminaries. 3. *Liturgical Use*. Clearly the use of Latin in liturgical worship in the Western Church arose through a gradual and natural historical development. The early translation of the Scriptures into the vernacular Latin of the day, crystallized in Jerome's Vulgate, offered a framework of sacral language ideally suited to the liturgical expression of Christian Faith. In similar fashion the developing sacral language for the several vernaculars extant found its way into the liturgical expression of the Eastern Church. While Latin has remained the predominant language of the Latin Liturgy, it has not been the exclusive one. The Church has never demanded uniformity of liturgical language, nor does she forbid vernacular liturgies. The Constitution on Sacred Liturgy, issued by Vatican Council II on Dec. 4, 1963, while stating that the Latin language is to be preserved in the Latin Rites, actually encourages extensive use of the vernaculars in the Mass, the administration of the sacraments and other parts of the liturgy, as of great advantage to the people.

Latin America Bureau NCWC *See* Latin America, religious revival in.

Latin America, religious revival in Following World War II, there developed a growing consciousness of the religious ills of Latin America. The root of the trouble was traced back to colonial days and the expulsion of the Spanish clergy. Great masses of people were left without priests or instruction with the result that there were large numbers of baptized Catholics but only a minority of practicing Catholics. Following the Eucharistic Congress of Rio de Janeiro in 1955, there began a great struggle to rebuild the vitality of the Church. One of the most important steps was the foundation of the Pontifical Commission for Latin America, a section of the Vatican State Department, that was given exclusive responsibility for developing the Church in Latin America. The Pontifical Commission sparked many programs. One of the chief was the creation of CELAM (*q.v.*), the Latin American equivalent of NCWC, which for the first time brought the hemisphere's Latin American bishops together as a unit. CELAM set up headquarters in Bogotá and appointed a number of commissions in vital areas. Emphasis was placed on catechetics and seminary training. Meanwhile in the United States, the bishops formed the Latin America Bureau NCWC which was to coordinate that country's effort in behalf of the Latin American nations. Out of the Latin America Bureau came PAVLA (*q.v.*) and coordinated programs such as CICOP (*q.v.*) and other movements. Large numbers of clergy and lay apostles were recruited for Latin America in both the United States and Canada. The bishops of Latin America meantime were issuing social directives, stepping up Catholic education, reorganizing Catholic life, emphasizing Church use of mass communications, developing a new clergy and religious spirit, and prosecuting vigorous action to reawaken the Catholic spirit. The result has been the development of new and young leaders, the growth of Christian democracy, the spread of the Christian trade union movement, and a complete reversal of the drift away from the Church. Many problems remain in Latin America but religious leadership is aware of them and has plans for overcoming them.

Latin American College The pontifical seminary founded in 1858 in Rome to train students from Latin American countries for the priesthood. The Brazilians have their own seminary in Rome (Pontifical Brazilian College) founded in 1934.

Latin, ecclesiastical, pronunciation of
There are no native speakers of
Latin. There is, however, sufficient
evidence available to establish rather
accurately the significant sounds or
phonemes of Latin as spoken in the
time of Caesar. About sentence intonation there is no evidence. Latin
continues today in the Romance languages, including French, Spanish,
Portuguese, Italian and Romanian.
As Latin was gradually supplanted
by the vernacular languages, it continued to be used in the universities,
the liturgical and administrative life
of the Church, and the political chan-
ceries of Europe. Slowly there arose
the French, Spanish, Italian, etc.,
"ways" of pronouncing Latin. Pope
St. Pius X strongly urged ecclesiastics
to follow as closely as possible the
Latin pronunciation used at Rome
by native speakers of Italian. The
description of this pronunciation is
based upon the writing system, rather
than upon a scientific study of the
sound system or set of phonemes. 1.
In the period of the Roman Republic
the Latin alphabet consisted of 21 letters: *a b c d e f g h i k l m n o p q r s
t u x.* At the end of that period *up-
silon,* written as *y* and representing
i, and *zeta,* written as *Z* and representing *z* were added. The Romans
wrote *V* and *I, u* and *i;* the letters *j*
and *v* date from the Renaissance. 2.
Accent and syllabification. Words of
two syllables are accented on the
first syllable. Words of more than two
syllables are accented on the penult,
if that is long; otherwise on the ante-
penult. Every Latin word has as many
syllables as it has vowels or diph-
thongs. In dividing syllables in Latin
one should pronounce and write with
the following syllable any consonant,
including *i* and *v,* and any group of
consonants which can begin a Latin
word. 3. Vowel Sounds. In Latin
there are five basic phonemes: *a, e, i,
o, u.* The closest English equivalents
would be *ah, eh, ee, oh, oo.* Latin
phonemes have a uniform sound
throughout, keep their same quality
to the end of a word, do not have
glides.

Latin Letters, Secretariate of One
of the offices of the Roman Curia,
closely connected with the Secretariate of State, which handles briefs of
princes and has the general duty of
the Latin editing of all documents
committed to it by the Supreme
Pontiff.

Latin Rite The form of liturgical
worship used in the Western, or Roman, Church which centers around
the Eucharistic liturgy, the Mass. The
canonical prayer of the Latin Rite is
the Divine Office. The rite has its
own rituals for administering the
sacraments.

latinization A term referring to the
influence which causes change in
Eastern Rite customs and the adoption of practices of the Western
Church. This can be in liturgical
usages, i.e., the adoption of Roman
vestments or devotions, and in the
transfer of a person from the Orthodox Church to the Latin Rite.

latria (Gr. service) The worship that
is given only to God. Because God
is infinite perfection and our Creator, He is entitled to homage and
reverence given to no creature. *See*
dulia, hyperdulia.

Lauda Sion (L. Praise, O Sion) A
hymn written by St. Thomas Aquinas
which is the Sequence in the Mass of
Corpus Christi. It is considered one
of the best examples of theological
poetry.

laura (Gr. a passageway) 1. The
name for a monastery where the
monks live in separate hermitages

around the church. It is a quasi eremetical system in which the monks come together for certain liturgical functions and live as hermits the rest of the time. The particular type of monasticism to which the word refers no longer exists although the Carthusians are close to it. 2. The name for any big monastery of the Byzantine Rite.

laus perennis (L. endless praise) A defunct monastic custom of singing the Divine Office in relays so that it never ceases.

Laval University Founded at Quebec City, Canada, in 1852. It grants civil and canonical degrees. The Archbishop of Quebec is ex officio chancellor of the university.

law A rule of reason for the common good promulgated by the proper authority. For law to be effective there must be a reason for the law. Arbitrary laws or laws that are not needed interfere with the rights of others and are an abuse of power. It is a necessary purpose of any law that it exist for the common good. A law which is not directed to the welfare of society is not a genuine law; a law which benefits one small segment of society to the unfair detriment of the remainder of society is not a genuine law. An unjust law is a species of violence. The author of the law must have the authority to make the law. While the most probable opinion is that promulgation is not part of the essence of law, it is required for its integrity. No ordinance can actually oblige unless it is made known to the people subject to it.

law, canon The law of the Catholic Church, consisting of rules, regulations and laws that affect faith, morals, discipline and ecclesiastical affairs, and contained in a book, *Codex*

Juris Canonici These laws bind all over the age of seven, unless dispensed or exempted. These laws carry penalties. The present *Code of Canon Law* was put into effect in 1918. It has 2,414 canons divided into five books: General Norms, Concerning Persons, Concerning Sacred Things, Concerning Trials and Concerning Crimes and Punishments. As a result of Vatican Council II extensive revisions are now being made in sections of the *Code*.

law, civil The state as a perfect society has the power to legislate in all material and temporal matters as long as it does not infringe on natural, divine or ecclesiastical law. It is the teaching of the Church that civil law must be obeyed because all authority comes from God. The modern opinion that all civil laws are purely penal laws must be rejected. Civil laws which determine rights or transfer ownership normally oblige in conscience. It is the more probable opinion that civil laws which render acts invalid oblige in conscience after judicial sentence. When in doubt about the binding quality of civil law, a person acting contrary does not commit sin. As long as a civil law does not violate natural, divine or ecclesiastical law, a citizen can follow the law in conscience. Civil law that attempts to bind in spiritual matters has no binding force unless it has been sanctioned or is tolerated by the religious authorities.

law, common Another name for the law of the Church which is contained in the *Code of Canon Law*.

law, divine positive The supernatural laws made known to man through revelation. They are found in both the Old and New Laws. Those precepts of the Old Law are moral, judicial and ceremonial; those of the

New Law concern morals, the offering of sacrifice and the reception of the sacraments. The Old Law bound only the Jews but the New Law binds all men.

law, eternal The law of God which directs the universe. It existed from eternity. St. Thomas calls it "the plan flowing from God's wisdom directing all acts and movements." The eternal law includes both the moral and physical orders. It is the authority for all laws, which cease to be laws when they contravene eternal law.

law, human The law which has been instituted by man. It is either ecclesiastical or civil, depending upon the instituting authority. St. Thomas assigns three qualities to human law: it must be consistent with religion, i.e., it cannon contradict divine law; it must be consistent with discipline, i.e., it must conform to natural law; it must promote human welfare, i.e., the good of society. Every just human law, either ecclesiastical or civil, binds in conscience; St. Paul declared: "He who resists authority resists the command of God." He adds that we should be obedient for the sake of conscience (Rom. 13:1-5).

law, international The law between nations arrived at through agreements. It is rooted in natural and divine law and is based on civil law common in most states. At the present time it depends for its power on voluntary adhesion. There is nothing in Catholic doctrine that is opposed to international law with sanctions as long as it does not contravene divine or natural law or offend the common good.

Law, Mosaic That body of civil, ceremonial, moral and religious law and regulation found in the Pentateuch and attributed to Moses by Jewish and Christian tradition. The Mosaic Law is divided into the following classifications: the Decalogue, the Book of the Covenant, the Priestly Code, the Law of Holiness, and the Deuteronic Code.

law, municipal A canonical term differentiating laws of a country from Roman civil law upon which is based most of the law of the West.

law, natural According to St. Thomas, "Natural law is nothing else than the rational creature's participation in the eternal law." This law is called "natural" because a man is subject to it from birth, it is made of precepts which derive from the very nature of man, it can be understood by man's reason without the aid of divine or human authority. All men are subject to the natural law and since it is based upon the essential character of man's nature, it cannot be changed or dispensed from.

law of illegitimate births The rate of illegitimacy in society varies inversely with the amount of family solidarity, and is correlated to the extent of poverty.

law of religious conservatism A sociological declaration which states that religious society is the last institution of society to adopt innovations in ideas and practices.

law, penal That law which immediately binds under pain of punishment and not under pain of moral guilt. However, some penal laws are mixed, i.e., not entirely penal. Such a law can bind in conscience and create moral guilt. Moreover, the transgression of a penal law can be the indirect cause of a moral fault if due to culpable neglect, inordinate passion, formal contempt; or if the transgressor refuses to accept a justly imposed punishment. Thus, a driver who goes through a red light deliberately and causes an accident has a moral responsibility for the contemptuousness of his act and its consequences.

law, positive That law which is promulgated by an act of the lawgiver and which is contrasted to natural law. It is either divine or human.

Laxism A theological system condemned by Pope Innocent XI in 1679. It held that a doubtfully probable opinion favoring liberty dispenses a person from fulfilling an obligation.

lay apostolate The mission of the Church (the salvation of mankind) entrusted by Christ to the Apostles is to be accomplished by the "People of God," living as a witness in the world. The laity share in the Church's apostolate, directly in the temporal order, and indirectly in the pastoral order under the direction of and in cooperation with the hierarchy.

lay Baptism Administration of the sacrament of Baptism by a lay person in case of necessity, i.e., danger of death. See Baptism, lay.

lay Brother (Gr. laikos, of the people) A Brother who is concerned with secular affairs as distinct from a choir Brother. They devote themselves to the service of the community of which they are real members. Some teach and others nurse while others perform mechanical tasks, skilled and unskilled. They contribute greatly to the welfare of their community. The vocation to be a Brother is a special vocation given by God and is distinct from the vocation of a priest, being neither greater nor less, but of another order.

lay communion 1. The state of a layman in communion with the Church, i.e., not excommunicated. 2. The state of a priest who is forbidden to say Mass but who may receive Holy Communion. See degradation.

lay confession See confession, lay.

lay institute A society of men or women living in the world who dedicate themselves by vow or promise to observe the evangelical counsels and to carry on apostolic works suitable to their talents and opportunities in the areas of their everyday life. Members oblige themselves by vow to observe perfect chastity, and by vow or promise to be obedient to superiors of the institute, and to practice poverty to the extent that it can be practiced in their position in the world. They do not wear a distinctive religious habit, nor are they bound to live in community like the members of religious orders. They remain in the world, pursue their professions and earn their own livelihood, and perform their apostolic tasks in the environments in which they live and work.

lay missioner A lay person working in the direct apostolate of the Church either here at home or abroad. In recent years the lay mission movement has taken on organization, and various lay mission groups have been formed. Some specialize in serving particular areas, others in providing special types of vocational skills. One of the most significant developments is the evolution of specific training programs, such as that offered at the Catholic University of Puerto Rico. Some of the lay mission groups are Grail, International Catholic Auxiliaries, Extension Lay Volunteers, Association for International Development, Lay Mission-Helpers, Catholic Medical Mission Board and Papal Volunteers for Latin America (qq.v.).

lay organization An organization of lay people formed for a religious purpose. In order to encourage and assist such organizations, the American hierarchy has created a special department to assist these organizations, particularly the National Council of Catholic Men, the National Council of Catholic Women and the National Council of Catholic Nurses. The department is called the Department of Lay Organizations and it promotes and assists the participation of the laity in the apostolate of the hierarchy.

lay Sister   A Sister who serves in a religious order but who is not a choir nun. Their duties correspond somewhat to those of the lay Brother, and their prayers of obligation are simpler and shorter than those of choir nuns. In some cloistered communities they are the extern Sisters.

lay state, the   The people of God are considered under various aspects according to their function in the Mystical Body. The lay state would be those living and working in the temporal order, as distinguished from the clerical state referring to those involved directly in the pastoral or hierarchical order of the Church in the service of God's people.

laying on of hands   The imposition of hands to convey or symbolize spiritual power. In the rite of ordination of both deacons and priests there is an imposition of hands on the head of the one being ordained; it is also done in the consecration of a bishop. In the sacrament of Confirmation hands are imposed.

layman (L. *laicus*)   Strictly, one who is not a cleric. Thus a Brother or Sister would be considered a member of the lay state and for this reason is correctly called Lay Brother or Lay Sister. However, the use of the term today means those who are neither clerics nor in religious life, and thus

Brothers and Sisters are not considered part of the laity. Also the term has come to include both men and women. Today the laity have awakened to their role in the Church and in the Church's mission which is the Christianization of the world and the salvation of mankind. Many of the laity are taking an active role in the missionary work of the Church and many more have accepted their obligation to bring Christian influences to bear on secular life and society. It is an organic cooperation with the ecclesiastical part of the Church. In Baptism Faith is committed to the laity as a "deposit" sealed by the Holy Spirit and they are committed to the Church's mission. That which is given in Baptism is completed in Confirmation, where one of the essential effects is to make the confirmed person a witness to Christ in the temporal order.

laziness   *See* sloth.

leaven   A type of yeast used in making bread. Christ used the term as a metaphor to portray the hypocrisy of the Pharisees.

lectern (L. *lector,* a reader)   A high bookstand or reading desk used to support sacred books. They are used for the solemn singing of the Passion, in chanting the Divine Office, or even sometimes for preaching. The most commonly seen lectern is the folding missal stand used at Mass.

lectio brevis (L. brief reading)   The Short Lesson which consists of a variable verse of Scripture that is said at the end of Prime and the beginning of Compline.

lection   Another word for lesson (*q.v.*).

lectionary   A book containing passages that are to be changed or read aloud in some Church service. This would include the book which contains the Gospels and Epistles used in the Mass, or the book which contains the lessons that are read at Matins.

lector 1. The second minor order of the Roman Rite. The duties are now obsolete. 2. An office in the Eastern Church not necessarily conferred by ordination to which is assigned the duty of singing the Epistle and other passages. 3. A name applied to the person who reads during meals or leads in prayer in a religious house. 4. The first of the Dominican theological degrees and one which permits the holder to teach as a professor.

legate (L. *legatus*) A representative of the Holy See, either diplomatic or ecclesiastical. The principal kinds are nuncio, internuncio, apostolic delegate and *legatus a latere* (*qq.v.*).

legatus a latere (L. legate from the side) A cardinal sent by (from the side of) the Holy Father on a particular mission.

legatus missus (L. a sent legate) A papal ambassador with the title of nuncio or internuncio.

legatus natus (L. born legate) A person who is a legate by his very office. This right is attached to certain German sees and formerly was held by the Archbishop of Canterbury. However, since the Middle Ages the title gives only honorary privileges.

legend 1. A book containing popular biographies of saints. 2. An individual story coming from tradition. The word does not mean a wholly false story but one which, while basically true, is considerably embellished. While such legends may be used for the purpose of instruction, it is the task of good scholarship and pedagogy to discard that which is fictitious.

Legend, Golden *See* Golden Legend.

Legion of Decency, National An organization established in 1934 to encourage motion pictures of moral quality. The organization has a review and rating service for motion pictures, basing its judgments on moral standards. The Catholic people are asked to make an annual pledge to support the findings of the Legion of Decency by abstaining from immoral pictures and avoiding places that habitually show them. In recent years a new pledge has been issued that is more positive and which pledges the viewer to support wholesome motion pictures.

Legion of Mary An association of lay men and women founded in Ireland in 1921 for the spiritual growth of its members and for the apostolate, including home mission work among fallen-away Catholics and non-Catholics, and a widespread activity on the foreign mission field. The Legion was set up in the United States in 1931. It is found throughout the world, with centers in a thousand or more dioceses. It did heroic service in China after the Communist takeover, and was the organization most hated and feared by the Commissars. It was established widely in Africa by the outstanding young Irish woman, Edel Quinn, who died there a martyr to her dedicated work. The Legion of Mary is a form of Catholic Action which seems to be most uniformly successful under varying conditions.

legitimacy The condition of the offspring of a valid marriage. Canon law presumes the legitimacy of all children born of a valid marriage unless the contrary is positively proved. A child born illegitimate is legitimatized by the subsequent marriage of its parents. However, a child begotten while its parents were under an impediment of age or cult is not legitimatized by a subsequent marriage. Legitimacy is required for the reception of Holy Orders.

legitimate marriage A valid marriage between two unbaptized persons. Children born of such a marriage are legitimate.

legitimation The act of removing the irregularity caused by birth out of wedlock.

Lent (OE. *lencten,* spring) A penitential season preceding Easter that begins on Ash Wednesday and ends with Easter. It contains 40 days for fasting in remembrance of the 40-day fast of Jesus Christ and is a time of mortification and penance. Although Sundays are a part of Lent, they are not fast days. In the Byzantine Rite the strict fast lasts 48 days. During this period the solemnization of marriage is prohibited, purple vestments are worn, the Gloria and Alleluia are not said at Mass, each day has its own Mass and there is a special Lenten Preface. In this period, the Church prepares for the central act of history, the Redemption of the human race by Jesus Christ. The liturgy beginning on Septuagesima (the three weeks before Lent are a pre-Lenten preparation) tells of creation, the Fall of man, the promise of a Redeemer and finally leads up to the act of salvation on Calvary. Although the Redemption is an objective achievement that has attained its goal, each human being must subjectively apply it to himself.

Lenten cycle The liturgical period of time from Septuagesima Sunday through Holy Saturday (until the Easter Vigil). The liturgical color is purple. There are three subcycles. 1. Pre-Lenten. A time for preparation. Begins on Septuagesima Sunday and extends to Ash Wednesday. 2. Lent, a time for atonement. From Ash Wednesday to Passion Sunday. 3.

Passiontime, a time for reparation. From Passion Sunday through Holy Saturday. This period includes the two Sundays of the Passion, Maundy Thursday, Good Friday and Holy Saturday.

Lepanto, Battle of The celebrated victory of 1571 in the Straits of Lepanto by Don Juan of Austria over the Turks. The combined Christian fleet completely destroyed the invading armada, liberated Christians and is credited with saving Europe from being overrun by Muslims.

leper window A low window in the chancel of a church used in medieval times to permit lepers to attend Mass from the churchyard.

Lesser Litanies The Litany of the Saints used on Rogation Days.

lesson (L. *lectio,* a reading) 1. A portion of Scripture or other ecclesiastical writing designated to be read. 2. *Mass.* The Epistle and Gospel. Today the name "Reading" is often substituted for "Epistle." On certain Ember Days, there are lessons other than the Epistle before the Gospel. 3. *In the Divine Office.* Those scriptural, historical and patristic readings found in Matins; the short lessons found in the Short Lesson and the Capitulum of other Breviary hours.

lesson, historical The historical readings of the Divine Office as found in Matins. They relate the life of the saint whose feast is being celebrated or other historical narration. Originally given to legend and historical inaccuracy, the Constitution on the Sacred Liturgy of Vatican Council II has ruled that the "accounts of martyrdom or the lives of saints are to accord with the facts of history."

levitation (L. *levis,* light of weight) 1. A spiritual phenomenon attributed to certain saints and ecstatics by which the body rises and hangs suspended in air. Many cases of the phenomenon have been recorded but the best known are the experiences attributed to St. Joseph Cupertino. 2. A spiritualistic term by which a medium causes objects to rise and float through the air. It has been demonstrated that the condition results from the use of hidden gadgets but it is possible for diabolical powers to intercede. Catholics are strictly forbidden to participate in seances.

Levite 1. Descendants of Levi, third son of Jacob and Leah, founder of the tribe of Levi. Members of this tribe were set aside for the service of God. 2. By extension, a levite is a Christian priest or cleric.

Leviticus, Book of The third book of the Pentateuch. It takes its name from the fact that it is about the worship of the Israelites led by the tribe of Levi. Authorship is not certain but if not wholly from Moses, the spirit is Mosaic.

lex orandi, lex credendi (L. the law of prayer is the law of belief) An axiom attributed to a saying of Pope St. Celestine I. It means that the liturgy of the Church is a main source of the Tradition of true doctrine. However, everything in the liturgy does not have to be accepted as dogma.

libellus martyrum (L. certificate of a martyr) A letter given by one in prison for his religion or otherwise suffering for the Faith to a repentant *lapsus* asking the bishop to use the merits being gained by the martyr for forgiveness of the temporal punishment due the *lapsus*.

Liber Pontificalis (L. pontifical book) A collection of biographies of popes. Several such collections have been made.

Liber Usualis A liturgical book containing the Gregorian chant for all the Proper of the Masses and the feasts that might replace these Masses as well as some of the hours of the Divine Office. The unsung parts are also included.

Libera Nos (L. Deliver us) The embolism which follows directly after the Lord's Prayer in the Mass. It is a paraphrase of the last petition of the Our Father. It is now chanted or recited in a loud voice.

Libera, the (L. deliver) The first word of a prayer sung as part of the Absolutions of a funeral Mass.

liberalism 1. That philosophical doctrine which would make man independent of all restraints. 2. A historical movement among some Catholics which sought to limit or reject the authority of the Holy See. 3. Today, a forward movement among progressive Catholics desirous of bringing the Church to bear on modern conditions. The modern Catholic liberal is very sensitive to opportunities to bring them into the life of the Church. He is quick to distinguish between the essential and accidental, and he resists all attempts to absolutize that which is relative.

liberality A spirit of generosity in the use of temporal goods. It is illustrated in the Old Testament by the contributions of Chosen People for the construction of the temple and tabernacle. Since everyone has an obligation of liberality in some measure, one who squanders his goods sins with avarice, and one who gives excessively is guilty of extravagance.

Liberals, Catholic Those Catholics who sought to reject or limit the authority of the Holy See and as such are heretics. Not to be confused with liberal Catholics who are individuals trying to inject Catholic social teachings, as outlined in papal encyclicals, into social and economic life in order to spread the Spirit of Christ throughout all phases of man's existence.

liberty 1. Liberty can be attributed only to a person. In its essence, liberty is power to do good. Its presence is manifested also in the ability to overcome evil. Freedom is better understood as *freedom for* morally good action and not *freedom from* law or force. Freedom, thus understood, is the very foundation for morality. For unless a man is free to act for or against God, he is not responsible for his actions and cannot merit the salvation promised to him. 2. *Human freedom:* Man can act in a manner conformable to his spiritual and material existence. In the individual man, the two orders are inseparable because man is one. As a man, he has the *psychological freedom* to do all that he sees to be conformable with the demands of the natural law, and with its expression in positive civil law. He exercises his psychological freedom when he acts according to the judgment of his conscience with regard to any action. This may also be called *moral freedom.* When civil authority legislates for the common good, a man then has an external criterion by which he may judge certain actions. In performing these actions, he is exercising his *juridical freedom.* In the realm of his relations with other people, a man may or may not have the *social freedom* to do what he judges to be morally good or to avoid what he judges to be morally evil. 3. *Freedom in God:* God's freedom knows no limits because it is governed by the unlimited holiness of the divine essence. Therefore God's will is infallibly effective. Man's freedom, a participation in the divine freedom, is manifested in an eminent way when

he freely surrenders to the guidance of grace. In submitting to the power of the Holy Spirit, he makes use of the very power of God to render Him loving obedience.

liberty, defect of A man who is unfit to be ordained is said to have an impediment as a result of the Church's disciplinary regulations. He is therefore said to have the defect of liberty.

licentiate A Catholic academic degree awarded in theology, philosophy, canon law or other sacred subject, roughly equivalent to that of Bachelor.

lie A statement, sign or action by which one expresses the opposite of what he thinks or wills. This is often done to deceive others. Lying is of itself essentially wrong because one deliberately expresses something at variance with what he really thinks. Hence it is not a lie to express something false if one thinks it is true. According to the purpose for which they are spoken, lies may be: 1. *jocose,* told merely for the sake of amusement (no sin if the untruth is quite evident, otherwise a venial sin); 2. *officious lies* (white and courtesy lies), told as an excuse to prevent an injury, inconvenience or embarrassment (this is a venial sin); 3. *malicious lies,* harmful and injurious to another (venial or mortal sins in accordance with the harm intended).

life Many definitions of life have been attempted but none have been found wholly satisfactory. The word is negatively defined as "those forces that resist death" and scientifically defined as "metabolism in action." For the Christian, the best definition is the possession of those forces which make the owner capable of immanent action (self-movement). A living being is not only the source of this self-movement but also the term; the efficient cause immediately causing the action is a power within the being, and the immediate term of the action remains as a perfection of the being. There are three types of life: vegetable, sensitive and intellectual. The most perfect life is God who moves all other beings but is Himself unmoved by anything outside Himself.

ligamen (L. a tie)   The effect or bond of an existing marriage which prevents the contracting of another marriage.

light   The Church uses candles and lamps as ceremonial lights. They symbolize the burning ardor of faith and Christ, the Light of the World.

Lights, Feast of   Another name for the Feast of the Dedication which was instituted by Judas Machabee in 164 B.C. to commemorate the purification of the Temple which had been defiled by Antiochus Epiphanes IV.

lily   Often used in Christian art as a symbol of chastity.

Limbo (L. *limbus,* the edge)   1. The place where the souls of the just who died before the Redemption went to await entrance into heaven. It takes its name from an old belief that it was situated near hell. St. Luke referred to it as "Abraham's bosom." 2. It is Catholic teaching that only the baptized can enter heaven and see God. Therefore, those children and adults who leave this world in the state of original sin without Baptism of water, desire or blood but who are free of actual grievous sin go to Limbo where they will enjoy a natural happiness.

liquefaction   The act of liquefying. It is reputed that the dried blood of St.

Januarius, which is kept in a glass phial, liquefies when it is exposed and placed near his head. The same thing is said to happen to blood-relics of other saints.

litany   Prayer in the form of alternate statements or petitions and responses, such as, "St. Joseph, pray for us." In shortened form, the Kyrie of the Mass is an example. Six litanies are approved for public devotions: of the Blessed Mother, of the Holy Name, of the Saints, of the Sacred Heart, of St. Joseph and for the Dying. Others may be said privately.

Litany of Loreto   The Litany of the Blessed Virgin, so-called because it originated in Loreto, Italy.

Litany of the Saints   A solemn series of invocations calling on certain saints. Beginning with the Blessed Trinity, it proceeds down through the Blessed Virgin, angels, Apostles, patriarchs, martyrs, pontiffs, confessors and virgins; petitions are made for preservation from the evils of the world and the preservation of the Faith and the Church. There are three forms to this litany. The longest form is used during the Greater Litanies, on Rogation Days, when major orders are being conferred, when a bishop is consecrated, during Forty Hours, etc. The shortest form, the Litany of the Departing, is used at approaching death.

literal sense of Scripture   The actual meaning intended by the sacred writer.

Little Chapter (L. capitulum) A verse used in the Divine Hours. It follows the psalms in Lauds, Terce, Sext, None and Vespers and the hymn at Compline. It is taken from Scripture and is responded to with, *"Deo gratias."* In fact it is a very short lesson.

Little Flower   St. Thérèse of the

340

Child Jesus (1873–1897), who entered the Carmelite convent in Lisieux, France, at the age of 15. Her simple but heroic religious life of nine years was dedicated to saving souls and praying for priests. She wished to lead her hidden life of prayer in a mission land, but illness kept her in France. In 1927, two years after her canonization, Pope Pius XI declared her the patron of all missions, together with St. Francis Xavier, Apostle of the Orient.

Little Hours, the   The shorter hours of the Divine Office: Terce, Sext, None. The form is the same for all: hymn, antiphon and three psalms, short Scripture reading, versicle and response, and final prayer.

Little Office   The Office of the Blessed Virgin Mary. The structure resembles the Divine Office. It is recited by some religious communities of Sisters and Brothers and as a private devotional practice. However, the trend is for these users to adopt the Divine Office.

Little Sisters of the Assumption Founded in France in 1865, established in the United States in 1891. Purpose is to nurse the sick poor regardless of race or religion and take care of sick person's household. Members staff missions in Africa, South America and New Zealand. Simple vows are taken. More than 2,600 members.

Little Sisters of the Poor   A religious community of women founded in France in 1839 and established in the United States in 1868. In addition to the usual three simple vows, members take a fourth vow of hospitality. The work is the care of the aged poor. There are 3 provinces in the United States (one of them with a house in Canada) with approximately 850 Sisters.

liturgical assembly   The gathering of the Christian faithful for participation in some liturgical action, such as the celebration of the Eucharistic Liturgy or the recitation of the Divine Office.

liturgical books   All those books connected with the liturgy. They contain rubrics, formulas and prayers. The chief liturgical books in the Latin Rite are the Missal, the Roman Ritual, the Pontificale Romanum, Ceremonial of Bishops, the Breviary, the Liber Usualis and the Memoriale Rituum.

liturgical language   The Church has no single liturgical language, and the vernacular is being used more and more in liturgical services. However, there are a number of languages favored in the Church for use in the liturgy. These include Latin, Slavonic, Romanian, Syriac, Arabic, Armenian, Greek, Coptic, Magyar, Geez, Georgian and Malayalam.

liturgical movement   Any effort by a church to make its worship meaningful. As applied to the liturgy of the Catholic Church it is that form of renewal in the Church that concerns itself with the worship of the Church and its expressions. There have been many renewals in the Church's worship in her history. The present liturgical movement goes back to the 19th-century movement of Dom Gueranger in the monastery of Solesmes in France. His efforts brought new attention to the central place of worship in the Christian life. This start was continued by a Benedictine monk, Dom Lambert Beauduin of Belgium, who saw the need to take worship from the monastery setting to the peoples of the parishes. He together with St. Pius X who restored the practice of frequent reception of Holy Communion, is largely responsible for the impetus given to the liturgy in this century. The Abbey of Maria Laach in Germany, the liturgical writings of Pius Parsch in Austria and developments in France before and after World War II—all furthered the desire for liturgical renewal.

liturgical rites, origin of Liturgical rites center about the prescribed forms for celebrating the Eucharistic sacrifice instituted by Christ who commanded that His followers do likewise in commemoration of Him. This liturgical rite was carried out by the Church founded by Jesus Christ, united under the Bishop of Rome, the representative of Jesus Christ on earth. In the course of time some people broke away from the unity of the Church as it exists under the Bishop of Rome. Since the Middle Ages, however, many have reunited to the visible, incarnate Church of Jesus Christ and they have brought with them their liturgical languages (often vernacular) and the liturgical rites of their own long standing traditions. The Holy Fathers, welcoming the return of these separated brethren, have assured them that their own legitimate rites and ancient institutions are to be regarded with equal esteem and reverence as the Latin Rite and will never have to be exchanged for the Latin Rite. Varied as these Christian rites may be in language, chant and rubric, the basic pattern of the Sacrifice of the Mass is the same in all liturgies: 1. The Eucharistic prayers and readings (homiletic liturgy); 2. the Eucharistic Sacrifice (the Consecration); 3. the Eucharistic sacrificial banquet (the Communion). Holy Mass is celebrated daily in many different languages: Latin, Greek, Syriac, Armenian, Coptic, Geez (Ethiopian),

Gregorian, Old Slavonic, and such modern languages as Romanian, Hungarian, Arabic and Malayalam Indian. With the permission for vernacular use granted by Vatican Council II many other languages have become part of the Mass.

liturgical worship Public worship of God by the Church, the Church being the Christian community with Christ as its Head. Normally it is conducted by a designated official, a bishop, priest, etc.

liturgical year The liturgical year is made up of four major cycles: Christmas, Lent, Easter and Pentecost (*qq.v.*). These cycles in turn are broken down into minor cycles. The Church year begins with the first Sunday in Advent and ends with the Saturday following the last Sunday in Pentecost. Each minor cycle has its own liturgical color.

liturgy (Gr. *leitourgia,* a public service) The official worship of God by the Church through the celebration of the Eucharistic Sacrifice, the recitation of the Divine Office, and the administration of the sacraments with the annexed use of the sacramentals. The liturgy is the life of the soul because in liturgical action the divine and human meet and pass into one another. The culmination of the liturgy is the Eucharist because here the encounter with Christ is personal and very real, the closest contact that can be obtained with Christ and salvation. Through the sacraments we are joined in the actions of Christ, with salvation being offered us in many forms. While the liturgy helps us to partake of the love of Christ for the Father, it also enables us to share His love for mankind. Through it we are led to love of neighbor as well as of God. Thus through the liturgy besides worshiping God we build up the Christian community and through this same liturgy the faithful become the people of God.

Liturgy, Constitution on the Sacred The decree issued by Vatican Council II on Dec. 4, 1963, which sets down the principles concerning the reformation and promotion of the liturgy. The decree considers the Eucharistic Liturgy, sacraments and sacramentals, the Divine Office, the liturgical year, sacred music, sacred art and sacred furnishings. Among the highlights of the Constitution were the reordering of the Mass and sacraments with permission for greater use of the vernacular, and the reordering of the Divine Office with permission for the vernacular.

Liturgy of the Eucharist The name given to the solemn part of the Mass which is made up of the Preparation of the Gifts (*q.v.*), the Eucharistic Prayer, the Eucharistic Banquet and continuing to the end of the service. The vernacular may be used in public Mass in the Offering Antiphon (Offertory), the Sanctus, the Lord's Prayer, the Libera Nos and the following Pax, the Agnus Dei, the Communion of the Faithful, the Communion Prayer, and the Dismissal and Blessing.

Liturgy of the Word of God That preliminary part of the Mass consisting of the Entrance Rite (*q.v.*) and the Word of God (*q.v.*).

liturgy, study of The decree on the liturgy issued by Vatican Council II ranks the study of liturgy among the compulsory and major courses to be taken in the seminary. The decree states that it is to be taught under its theological, historical, spiritual, pastoral and juridical aspects. It is to be made relevant to other theological subjects. Seminarians are to be given a liturgical formation in their spirit-

ual lives. Priests who teach liturgy should be trained at institutes that specialize in liturgical training.

living wage The remuneration for labor which enables the workingman to support his family decently, provide for education and reasonable security. All of the social encyclicals of modern popes, beginning with *Rerum novarum* of Pope Leo XIII, stress the right of a workingman to a living wage arising out of natural justice. This wage should enable a man to raise a family; provide shelter, clothing and food for that family; to educate his children according to their station in life; take care of medical expenses; to provide some recreation; and to provide for old age. Defrauding a laboring man of his wages is one of the sins which cry to heaven for vengeance.

loan for consumption A contract whereby a fungible good is given by its owner to another who undertakes the obligation of returning its equivalent at a future date. A fungible good is that good which may be used in place of another to satisfy an obligation; today it is usually money. *See* interest, usury.

loci theologici (L. theological places) Sources where theologians obtain their arguments. Scripture and Tradition are the main sources of theological proof, but other sources such as history or philosophy or even the natural sciences can be used for theological proofs.

locutions, supernatural 1. Words produced supernaturally which are audible. 2. Words supernaturally created in the imagination. 3. Thoughts of supernatural origin transmitted directly to the intellect. Supernatural locutions are an experience parallel to visions. There are many examples in Scripture of supernatural locutions, such as God speaking to Moses, the warning of Joseph received to flee to Egypt with Mary and the Child, and the voice from the heavens at the Baptism of Jesus. However, care must be taken in the discernment of such supernatural experiences since they can arise from the Devil or from some psychogenic state.

logia Jesu (Gr. words of Jesus) 1. The words of Christ as they appear in the four Gospels. 2. An alleged collection of the sayings of Jesus which antedated the Gospels. The conclusion that such a text existed is based on a mention by Papias of the *logia* of Christ. It is the opinion of scriptural authorities that Papias was referring to the Gospels and not to any separate collection of sayings. 3. A name given to some sayings of Christ discovered in Egypt by B. P. Grenfell and A. S. Hunt. They were on a papyrus that dated back to the 2nd or 3rd century, and each begins "Jesus says."

Logos *See* Word.

Lollards (Dutch, *lollaerd,* a mumbler) A popular name given to the followers of John Wycliffe who flourished in England in the 14th and 15th centuries. The term was used earlier in Flanders to apply to heretics and for this reason may have been given to the followers of Wycliffe.

longanimity (L. *longanimis,* patient) Long-suffering, a disposition to bear trials and wrongs patiently. It is a fruit of the Holy Spirit. It differs from patience in that it contains the notion of patience over a long period of time.

Longinus Traditionally accepted as the soldier who pierced the side of Christ. He was subsequently converted by the Apostles. The name "Longinus" is found also in the Acts of Linus as that of a prefect who was

charged by Nero with the execution of St. Paul.

Lord 1 A title for God in the Old Testament. 2. A title used by the Apostles and disciples for Christ, and one of the proofs that they considered Jesus to be God. The Church continues to use this title. 3. An English title used for a bishop. It has never gained acceptance in the United States.

Lord's Prayer, the This is the prayer composed and taught by Christ (Lk. 11:2-4; Mt. 6:9-15). It is probably the most loved and used of all Christian prayers.

Lord's Supper, the 1. The Last Supper at which Christ established the Eucharist. It is a literal translation of the Latin, *Coena Domini.* 2. A Protestant name for their Communion Service.

Loreto, Litany of The Litany of the Blessed Virgin. The litany takes its name from Loreto, Italy, where it was first recited.

lost souls The damned. There is no Catholic teaching on the number of the damned. Likewise the Church has never asserted that any particular person has been condemned to hell.

Louisiana The 18th state admitted to the Union, it is 31st in area and 20th in population, and was named for King Louis XIV of France. Father Zenobius Membre was with La Salle in 1682 when he arrived at the mouth of the Mississippi and claimed the region for France. The Spanish had made some brief explorations there the previous century and De Soto died in the region. Father Du Rhu, S.J., came with the Canadian Iberville to do missionary work among the Indians when the colony of Louisiana was founded in 1698. Father St. Cosme from the

Quebec seminary was the first American-born priest killed by the Indians (1706). Sugar cane was brought in by the Jesuits in 1751. The first Catholic nuns in the United States were the Ursulines who came to New Orleans in 1727, set up hospitals and a school and did charitable work. In 1755 numbers of destitute French arrived, expelled from Acadia by the British. During the Revolution Louisiana, then under Spanish leaders, helped the United States in the war against England. During the Spanish period, Bishop Penalver, a native of Havana, was placed in charge of the Church in Louisiana and the Floridas. He found religion at a very low ebb and tried to reform the nominal Catholics with little success. When Spanish rule gave way to United States territorial government after the Louisiana Purchase, the whole area was part of Bishop Carroll's vast see until Bishop Dubourg, and later Bishop Rosati, arrived. During the Civil War the state was reduced to ruins, and Sisters of different orders distinguished themselves nursing the sick and wounded. Numbers of religious congregations were brought in to educate the youth and direct the adult Catholics. New Orleans became an archdiocese in 1850. Later the dioceses of Alexandria (1853), of Lafayette (1918) and of Baton Rouge (1961) were established. Today there are over 1,150,500 Catholics in Louisiana, in a total population of 3,257,022.

Lourdes A town in southern France, famous as a place of pilgrimage since 1858, when 14-year-old Bernadette Soubirous was granted 18 visions of the Blessed Virgin Mary at the nearby grotto of Massabielle. While a crowd of people watched, Bernadette, at the bidding of the vision, dug into the floor of the cave with her fingers, whereupon a trickle of water started, grew to a torrent, and now pours out 27 thousand gallons a day. The Lady bade the girl have a chapel built near the grotto. When Bernadette asked her name, she said, "I am the Immaculate Conception." She gave the girl a message for all: "Pray and do penance for the conversion of the world." Miracles of healing began at the grotto, resulting in a constant stream of pilgrims in search of health of body and peace of soul. A medical bureau was established in 1882 to test the authenticity of the cures. The doctors include unbelievers as well as believers, and any doctor is welcome to take part in the examination of the alleged cures. As many as 500 medical men, of all faiths or none, have taken advantage of the invitation each year. Though many cures are claimed by pilgrims, no cure is regarded as miraculous if science can show any natural explanation of it. The bureau is most exacting. Only 57 of the many cures have been admitted as miraculous by the medical bureau, placed on record and recognized by the Church. Several churches have been built at Lourdes to accommodate the immense crowds. The underground church of St. Pius X, consecrated in 1958, holds 20 thousand persons. As many as 3 million pilgrims visit Lourdes every year. Bernadette entered the convent of the Sisters of Charity of Nevers, where she died in 1879. She was canonized in 1933. The feast of Our Lady of Lourdes is on Feb. 11.

love In general, a tendency of the soul toward good. Christian love is a supernaturalized tendency of the soul toward good. St. Thomas Aquinas points out that true love has certain characteristics. We desire the loved one to be and to exist. We desire good for the person loved. We do good for the one loved. We desire to be with and share with the person loved. The person who truly loves, therefore, cannot escape involvement. The supreme type of love is charity, and though all charity is love, not all love is charity. Charity is a theological virtue that causes us to love God above all things for Himself and to love our neighbor for the sake of God.

love feast *See* agape.

love of enemies It is a mark of Christian love that it is universal. Christ specifically said: "Love your enemies: do good to them that hate you: and pray for them that persecute and calumniate you" (Matt. 5:44). This love that is commanded is a love of respect and regard, not necessarily a love of affection. To all people we are obliged to give the common marks of Christian charity.

love of God 1. *On the part of God.* God is love and because of this creation exists. The Scriptures continually reveal this love of God for mankind. Out of a love that wishes to share itself God created the world and peopled it. Even when man sinned against God His love was not withdrawn, but Scripture reminds us that God so loved the world that He sent His only-begotten Son for man's redemption. This love will never desert man even though he turns away from God. 2. *On the part of man.* Although man is commanded to love God in Scripture, both charity and justice also demand it. God is to be loved for His own sake and we are to love our fellow man for God's sake. While God can be loved because He is our Creator and all that we have comes from His beneficence,

the higher love is to love God for Himself because He is perfect and is to be preferred before all things.

love of neighbor Christ gave two great commandments: love of God and love of neighbor (Matt. 22:36-39). Pope Paul VI has said, "If anyone wants to convert the world, he must first love it." We love because every man's soul is created by God to His own image and likeness, and this makes us one spiritually. We love because we have descended from common ancestors, and this makes us one physically. We love because every man is the object of redemption by the blood of Christ. We love so that we can become one with Christ. This love is the desiring of good (including the supreme good of salvation) for every man in the world. This love does not have to be a love of affection, an emotional involvement, but a love of respect.

Low Mass A simplified form of the Mass as said by one priest in contrast to High Mass which is sung and has three ministers. An intermediate form is the *Missa Cantata* or Sung Mass which uses one minister, but in which the parts sung at the High Mass are also sung. The Low Mass is the usual form. There are generally only one or two servers; only two candles are lighted; there is no incensing and the entire action takes place at the altar.

Low Sunday The first Sunday after Easter. It is also called Sunday *in albis* (in white) because of its ancient relationship to the new Christians who had been baptized on Easter Eve. As such it should not be confused with Whitsunday, the British name for Pentecost.

Lucifer (L. light-bearer) The leader of the fallen angels, Satan, the prince of darkness. The term occurs in Is.

14:12 where it refers to the King of Babylon. The Fathers, however, applied this in a spiritual sense to the Devil, indicating the high and bright position to which he had been destined but which, because of rebellion, he lost when he was condemned to the eternal night.

Luke, Gospel of St. Except for a particular development of the Infancy Gospel, the Gospel according to St. Luke follows the general pattern of the Synoptic Gospels. The Gospel does have information not common to Mark and Matthew. The Gospel is noted for its excellent Greek literary style. Most Catholic scholars believe the Gospel was written in Rome shortly before A.D. 62.

Luke, St. (Gr. for L. *Lucius*) Author of third Gospel and the Acts of the Apostles; physician; companion of St. Paul. Luke met Paul about A.D. 50 at Troas and then accompanied him on his missionary travels. When Paul was arrested, Luke went with him to Rome. It is believed that Luke was a Gentile Christian, not a Judeo-Christian.

lukewarmness To be tepid in one's spiritual life and practices. Christ condemned those who are neither hot nor cold in the practice of religion.

Lumen Christi (L. the light of Christ) Our Lord said, "I am the light of the world. He who follows me does not walk in darkness, but will have the light of life" (Jn. 8:12). At the beginning of the solemn procession of the Easter Vigil service, after the new fire has been made, the deacon enters the church carrying the lighted paschal candle. As he enters, he sings, *"Lumen Christi."* The congregation replies, *"Deo gratias"* ("Thanks be to God"). This is repeated twice more in slightly higher tones as the deacon makes his way to the sanctuary.

lunette (L. *luna,* moon) A thin circular receptacle, having a glass face which holds the consecrated Host used at Benediction. It slides into the monstrance on a track.

lust (AS. *lut*) 1. inordinate appetite for sexual pleasure. It is a capital vice and one of the seven deadly sins because it leads to other sins. In the Sermon on the Mount, Christ said that to lust with the eyes or heart is already a sin. 2. By extension the word is used to express any passionate appetite or desire, such as a lust for money.

lustral water (L. *lustrum,* purified) Holy water.

Lutheranism The religious beliefs of the oldest Protestant religion as founded by Martin Luther (1483–1546). Originally it was a term of derision and Luther himself preferred the word "Evangelical," which even today is often used in the term "Evangelical Lutheran Church." The religion may be said to date from Oct. 31, 1517, when Luther, an Augustinian friar, posted his 95 theses on the church door in Wittenberg, Germany. Lutherans accept the Nicene, Athanasian and Apostles' Creeds; they make Scripture the sole authority for faith; they believe in justification by faith alone; they hold the doctrine of consubstantiation in connection with the Eucharist. Because of Luther's teaching on private judgment, there are many divergent doctrines. In the United States there are a number of synods or groups with over 7 million members.

luxury (L. *luxuria,* excess) 1. To live

sumptuously with a multitude of fine possessions. While in itself it is not sinful, it can lead to sins of gluttony or drunkenness, or sins against charity and justice. Luxury has the tendency to blind one to the needs of others and to the excessive waste of goods which others may desperately need. 2. A sinful indulgence in sexual pleasures. While its use in this sense is archaic in English, theological texts in Latin frequently use the Latin form in this sense.

M

mace (L. *mateola,* mallet) An ornamental staff carried at the head of a procession as a symbol of authority. It is used by individuals and moral bodies, such as a bishop or a chapter.

Machabees, the Books of Two Old Testament books which give an account of the wars waged for religious liberty in the 2nd century B.C. under the leadership of the priest Mathathias and his five sons, including Judas Machabeus. The books were written in Greek.

Machabees, the Holy Jewish martyrs whose feast is celebrated throughout the Church; on Aug. 1 in the Western Church. They were seven brothers who with their mother and their teacher, Eleazar, suffered heroic martyrdom rather than conform to anti-Jewish rites. They lived in the 2nd century B.C. There is no scriptural evidence that they were all Machabees but the word was used to include all the Jews who opposed the paganizing efforts of the Seleucid kings.

Madonna (L. *mea domina,* my lady) 1. A title used for a representation of the Blessed Virgin in art. In painting and sculpture Mary is traditionally shown with the Christ Child. Madonnas were favorite subjects for artists of the Renaissance. 2. A title given to Our Lady.

Madonna House Apostolate A secular institute founded in Canada by Baroness Catherine de Hueck, now Catherine Doherty. The purpose of the institute is to promote social justice in neglected areas, particularly among minority peoples. Both men and women are accepted in membership. Members live at one of the houses of the Apostolate for training and then are sent to home or overseas missions.

maestro di camera (It.) A Roman official who is in charge of the anticamera of the pope and the personnel attached to it. He regulates papal audiences and assists the pope wherever he goes, taking his place at the left. He loses his office on the death of the pope. He resides in the Vatican.

magdalen 1. An obsolete term which formerly referred to a woman of loose morals who had reformed and withdrawn to a religious institution to lead a life of reparation. The term derived from Lk. 7:36 ff. 2. Sometimes, the institution itself where such women went to reside.

Magen David Star of David (*q.v.*).

Magi (Gr. *magos*) The title of a priestly caste of Medes and Persians which has been applied to the wise men from the East who followed a star to Bethlehem where they gave gifts to the Christ Child. The Western Church holds them to be three Persians, although the actual number is not known. A 7th-century tradition gives their names as Gaspar, Melchior and Balthasar, the first named being a Negro.

magic The art of producing surprising results by occult means. Magic is distinguished into white magic (use of natural means) and black magic (with the aid of evil spirits). Magic intended to harm someone is called sorcery. White magic is perfectly lawful in itself and can be used for entertainment. Black magic is a grave sin of superstition against the virtue of religion. Sorcery is a sin of superstition and also offends charity and justice. *See* witchcraft.

magisterium (L. *magister,* teacher) The teaching authority of the Church entrusted originally to the Apostles with Peter at their head, and residing now in the bishops under the headship of the Pope. The magisterium is: 1. *solemn or extraordinary* when exercised in the form of doctrinal definitions whether of a Pope or of a General Council; 2. *ordinary,* continual, everyday exercise of this authority.

magnanimity (L. *magnus,* great; *animus,* spirit) A moral virtue, closely allied to fortitude, that reveals a greatness of soul. It enables one to bear honors without pride, to suffer trouble without rebellion and to make sacrifices without expecting reward. It inclines to deeds recognized by faith as great before God.

Magnificat (L. it magnifies) The title of a canticle spoken by Our Lady on the occasion of her visit to her cousin Elizabeth. The name comes from the first word of the Latin version. It is found in Lk. 1:46-56. The Magnificat appears in Vespers of the Divine Office in the Latin Rite; at Lauds in the Byzantine.

Maine A New England state, the 23rd admitted to the Union, it is 39th in area and 36th in population. It was named for an ancient French province. The Norsemen came to Maine in the 11th century; the Cabots in the 15th century and a succession of explorers arrived during succeeding years. French and English colonies were founded at about the same time. The first Mass was offered in the New England area when Father Nicholas Aubry arrived with de Monts and Champlain in 1604. French Jesuit Father Pierre Biard set up an Indian mission in 1609 on an island in the Penobscot River. Catholic Indians, descendants of his converts, still live there on Indian Island near Oldtown, Me. Mission St. Sauveur was founded four years later on Mt. Desert Island but it was destroyed by gunfire from a British ship which attacked the unarmed mission. A Jesuit lay brother was killed and two priests taken away as prisoners to Virginia. In 1694 Jesuit Father Rasle made converts among the Indians and wrote an Abnaki dictionary (still preserved at Harvard). He was killed by the British in 1724. French and British continued in conflict over settlements in Maine and Nova Scotia until 1763 when the French gave up their claims and the Acadian settlers were evicted and dispersed. New France became British property by treaty, and English laws against Catholics greatly reduced missionary effort among the Indians. After the Revolution Maine was part of the state of Massachusetts, but was admitted to the

Union as a separate state in 1820. Numbers of Irish Catholic immigrants now arrived, and Bishop Fenwick of Boston sent Jesuits and Picpus Fathers to care for them. By 1859 there were 33 missions in the state. However, the "Know-Nothing" brand of bigotry had sprung up, and at Ellsworth in 1856, Jesuit Father Bapst was tarred and feathered, his church burned. Portland became a diocese in 1853, the first bishop, Most Rcv. David Bacon. At his invitation various religious communities established institutons for education and charity in the state. The second bishop, Most Rev. James Healy (1875–1900), was the first bishop of Negro blood to be consecrated in the United States. He and succeeding bishops continued building up the Church and bringing in religious congregations of men and women to work among the people. Maine today has almost 300,000 Catholics in a total population of a million.

major orders In the Western Church, the orders of priesthood, diaconate and subdiaconate. In the Eastern Church, the orders vary. Some rites include the episcopacy along with the priesthood and diaconate. Only the Gregorian Armenians include the subdiaconate as a major order.

majordomo (L. *major,* elder; *domus,* house) 1. The title of an official who was the chief governor of the papal household. The position was abolished in 1929. 2. The name is now applied to a chief steward or a person who is in charge of a great household.

Malabar Rite The liturgy used by the Eastern Catholics of Malabar in India. They are among the so-called St. Thomas Christians. The liturgy follows closely that of the Chaldean Rite with Latin modifications. The Maylayam and Syriac languages are used. The calendar is that of the Roman Rite.

Malabar Rite Catholics These are the original Christians of southwest India who claim to have been evangelized by St. Thomas the Apostle. They accepted the authority of the Latin Archbishop of Goa in 1599 and thus the jurisdiction of the pope. When the Portuguese attempted to Latinize the Malabar Catholics in the 17th century, large numbers of them went into a schism which still endures.

Malabar Rites controversy A controversy that took place in India in the 17th and 18th centuries similar to the controversy over the Chinese Rites. The Jesuit missioners allowed converts to retain some Hindu and Brahmin customs, including caste, which they believed had no religious significance. Other missioners accused the Jesuits of permitting idolatry. The controversy continued spasmodically until the suppression of the Jesuits in 1773.

Malachia, Book of The last prophetic book of the Old Testament, written about the middle of the 5th century B.C. by an anonymous writer who used the name Malachia (Heb. My Messenger) to shield his identity. The author tells of God's love for the Israelites. He reproves the priests for poor sacrifices and the people for their divorces and mixed marriages. Yahweh will purify the temple and the priesthood. His justice will be seen on Judgment Day when the wicked will be punished. The conclusion is an exhortation to observe the Law of Moses and a prediction that Elia will return before Judgment Day.

Malagasy Republic (Madagascar) In

1648 the Vincentians began the first mission but were forced to withdraw. Modern missions began in 1845. Today there are well over a million Catholics in a total population of 5.5 million. The population breaks down to 20 per cent Catholic, 13 per cent Protestant, 4 per cent Muslim and 63 per cent animist. Obstacles to the Church are long association of the Church with the former French colonial power, rural poverty, difficulty of communication, superstitions and lack of native vocations. There are 3 archdioceses and 12 dioceses.

malice (L. *malum,* evil) The evil quality of an act that is freely and deliberately committed against the law of God. Malice may be in the act itself, in the purpose of the act or in the conditions surrounding the act.

malum in se (L. evil in itself) An act morally reprehensible. It is an indecent or inhuman act that is obviously evil.

mammon (Aramaic *mamona,* wealth) A term that occurs in certain sayings of Jesus as recorded in the New Testament. It is used in the sense of wealth as being a force hostile to God and a source of evil.

man (AS. a person) A creature composed of body and soul; a rational animal. The soul is produced by a creative act of God; and since the rational quality is spiritual, it is also immortal. Man's purpose in life is the service of God and his fellow men. His ultimate end is happiness with God for eternity but because man has free will, he can reject this end.

Manicheism A heresy of the third century which takes its name from its founder, Mani (216-276). It teaches that from the beginning there existed two opposed principles, good and evil, out of which the world developed. Christ came on earth as a visible spirit to teach men the difference between the kingdom of light and the kingdom of darkness. Initiates abstained from meat, wine and marriage in order to more closely approximate the ethereal. The heresy was refuted by St. Augustine of Hippo, himself a convert from Manicheism. A distinction was made between the perfect Manichaeans (the elect) and the secular Manichaeans (the auditors).

manifestation of conscience A custom in some religious houses whereby a member reveals his entire conscience to a religious superior, a spiritual director or a confessor. Affections, inclinations, temptations, trials and difficulties are all made known so that the subject can be guided to improvement in the spiritual life. Canon law forbids a religious superior to induce a subject to reveal his conscience to him, although it may be done voluntarily by the subject.

maniple (L. *manus,* hand) Originally a handkerchief carried by a Roman official, today it is a vestment worn only at Mass. It is the sign of a subdeacon and should not be worn by those in lower orders. It is worn over the alb across the left forearm, half on either side.

manitou An Algonquin word meaning "Great Spirit," "God." It has the idea of the supernatural essence.

manna (mahn'nah) The food that was miraculously given to the children of Israel in the wilderness. The word is used as a type for the Holy Eucharist, the spiritual Bread of Life.

manslaughter A legal term which refers to criminal homicide that lacks the premeditation (intention) necessary to commit murder. It is not imputable as a mortal sin if the person committing it did not advert to the danger of his action.

mantelletta (It. small cloak) A sleeveless cloak, open at the front and reaching to the knees, fastening at the neck. It is worn by cardinals, bishops, abbots and certain other prelates.

mantellone A purple cloak worn by certain prelates of the papal court. It is similar to the mantelletta except that it reaches to the ankles.

mantum A special cope (*q.v.*) worn by the pope. It is white or red in color, and is longer than the ordinary cope.

Manual of Prayers A book of prayers authorized in 1886 by the English hierarchy. Formerly common in the United States, it is now seldom seen.

manuterge (L. *manus,* hand; *tergere,* to wipe) The small towel used in the Lavabo of the Mass and on other occasions. It is sometimes called by its Latin name, *manutergium.*

March Month of St. Joseph.

Marian priests A term referring to priests in England who had been ordained before or during the reign of Queen Mary (1553–1558) and who lived under Queen Elizabeth I. The term was in contradistinction to seminary priests, i.e., those ordained abroad in Douai and elsewhere.

Mariolatry A contemptuous term used by some non-Catholics who charge Catholics with adoring (*latria*) the Blessed Virgin, i.e., giving her the honor only due God. The charge is false because adoration is reserved solely for God while veneration (*hyperdulia*) is given by Catholics to the Virgin as mother of Christ. *See* dulia, hyperdulia, latria.

Mariology 1. The study of the Blessed Virgin. 2. That branch of theology which treats of the Blessed Virgin, particularly in her relationship to the Incarnation and Redemption.

Marists A society which originated in Lyons, France, in 1816, with a group of seminarians. One of their members, Father Jean Colin, later, when he was pastor at Cerdon, founded the Sisters of the Holy Name of Mary. Another member, Father Marcellin Champagnat, established at Lavalla the Little Brothers of Mary. In 1823 Father Colin and a few companions under Bishop Devie of Belley resigned their parochial assignments and formed themselves into a band of priests for missions in the rural districts of France. Pope Gregory XVI approved the Marist Fathers in 1836 and asked them to take Oceania as a foreign mission field. They made their first foundation in the United States in 1863, where they now have two provinces and a vice-province, and engage in secondary and college education. They staff overseas missions in Hawaii, New Hebrides, Samoa, the Solomon Islands, Tonga Island and do medical, educational, charitable and social work. The Marist Brothers and the Marist Sisters have remained as separate institutes.

marital infidelity The act of being unfaithful to one's spouse by being romantically involved with another; adultery, sexual intercourse between a man and woman, one or both of whom is married to another.

Mark, Gospel of St. Mark wrote his Gospel to give the good news about Jesus Christ, the Son of God. Earliest tradition assigned this Gospel to Mark, Peter's interpreter, who recorded Peter's teaching. The Gospel was written in simple Greek for Gentile Christians. The exact date of its composition is unknown, but from intrinsic evidence it would seem to have been written before either of the other two Synoptic Gospels.

Mark, St. (Gr. *Markos*) Also known as John Mark. Author of the second Gospel. Mark was the son of Mary, in whose house in Jerusalem the early Christians met for prayer. He was related to Barnabas. Acts 12:12 indicates that Mark was a friend of St. Peter. According to common patristic opinion and according to indications of Scripture (Mk. 1:14 ff. and 1 Pt. 5:13), Mark became Peter's companion, disciple and interpreter; he recorded Peter's preaching and wrote his Gospel under this influence. Some scriptural authorities equate Mark with the young man who ran naked from Gethsemani on the night Jesus was arrested. When Paul and Barnabas returned to Antioch from Jerusalem, they brought Mark with them. Later he accompanied them to Cyprus and to Pamphilia in Asia Minor. There some disagreement arose and Mark returned to Jerusalem. Paul later refused to take Mark on his second missionary journey. However, the matter was eventually patched up because Mark was with Paul when the latter wrote his Captivity Epistles. Again in Paul's Epistle to Timothy, the Apostle of the Gentiles asks Timothy to bring Mark with him because Paul needs him. Peter in his First Epistle sends his greetings to Mark. Tradition says that he was martyred at Alexandria in A.D. 74, but there is no evidence to confirm this fact. Tradition also says his relics were transferred to Venice and are in St. Mark's Cathedral. His feast is celebrated on Apr. 25. Mark is represented in Christian art as a lion because he begins his Gospel as "one crying in the desert."

marks of the Church The four essential characteristics by which the true Church of Jesus Christ can be recognized and which are possessed by the Catholic Church alone. These marks are: 1. *oneness,* or unity; 2. *holy,* in itself and capable of sanctifying its members; 3. *catholic,* or universal, embracing men of all ages and nations; 4. *apostolic,* tracing its succession to Peter, first pope and prince of the Apostles.

Maronite Rite The liturgical worship used by the Maronites which is a modified Antiochian Liturgy in the Syriac language, with some Arabic.

Maronites Arabic-speaking Syrians who belong to the Maronite Rite. The name is derived from Bait-Marun, the shrine of St. Maro (d. 433). The Maronites (all Catholics) are found principally in Lebanon, Syria, Egypt, Cyprus, United States and Australia. Those in the Near East are under the Patriarch of Antioch who resides at Bekerke. They have a college in Rome. Those in the United States and Australia come under the ordinaries of the Latin Rite dioceses in which they live.

marriage A mutually concluded contract between a qualified man and woman by which they freely give themselves to each other in order to live together for the purpose of having and rearing children, and of cherishing each other in a common life. The marriage of baptized persons has a spiritual and sacramental nature. The marriage between unbaptized persons, or between persons only one of whom is baptized, is a natural contract only. The essential properties of any marriage are unity and indissolubility. For Christian marriage, *see* Matrimony, Sacrament of.

marriage by proxy A marriage when

354

one of the parties is absent but is represented by an agent. Canon law must be followed. The agent must have written authority from the absent person, signed by the one who is absent and witnessed by the pastor or ordinary or their delegate, or by two witnesses. In case the absent party cannot write, the fact must be noted on the document of authorization and there must be an additional witness (canon 1088).

marriage ceremonies The rituals observed at the celebration of a marriage. The marriage is ordinarily to be celebrated within a Mass after the reading of the Epistle and Gospel. Other rituals included in the ceremonies are the witnessing of the mutual declaration of consent, blessing of ring and final blessing of the Church. The schema on the liturgy of Vatican Council II orders a revision of the present marriage rite, and encourages the use of local rites when permitted by the local Church. The prayer for the bride is to be amended to remind both spouses of their equal obligation to remain faithful to one another and may be said in the mother tongue.

marriage, civil In those countries which do not recognize the validity of a religious wedding, the civil ceremony must be observed to give civil sanction to the marriage. In such a case, a religious ceremony must also take place so that the marriage will be a sacrament as well as a civil contract. The religious ceremony should take place before if the law permits or otherwise immediately afterward.

marriage, conditional A marriage can be contracted with a lawful condition regarding the future, and in this case its validity is suspended until the condition is fulfilled (canon 1092). If the condition is unlawful and contrary to the substance of the marriage, the marriage is invalid; if the condition is unlawful but not contrary to the substance of the marriage, or if impossible, the marriage is valid and the condition is to be ignored. A marriage is valid or invalid in the case of a past or present condition depending upon whether the condition has been met or not.

marriage debt The right of both husband and wife to sexual relations. For one party to withhold himself or herself from the other without the other's consent requires a serious reason.

marriage impediments An impediment is a circumstance arising from some human or divine law which prohibits the contracting of marriage either lawfully or validly. *Impeding impediments* make a marriage valid but unlawful (illicit). They are: 1. the impediment of simple vows; 2. the impediment of different religions; 3. the impediment of legal relationship (does not exist in the United States). *Diriment or nullifying impediments* render a marriage null and void. They are: 1. impediment of age; 2. impediment of impotency; 3. impediment of an existing bond; 4. impediment of a disparity of worship; 5. impediment of sacred orders; 6. impediment of religious profession; 7. impediment of abduction; 8. impediment of crime; 9. impediment of relationship; 10. impediment of public honesty. Where an impediment exists, dispensation must be sought and granted before the marriage can take place.

marriage, indissolubility of Catholic teaching is that every valid marriage that has been consummated is absolutely permanent and indissoluble. This means simply that no human power can break the bond of a valid marriage. The indissolubility of marriage is founded in the natural law (*Syllabus* of Pius IX, n. 67). In certain cases, the Church allows married persons to separate but without the right of marrying again. Christians who seek civil divorce fall into grave error because they are denying the doctrinal teaching of the indissolubility of marriage. A legitimate marriage, even consummated, between nonbaptized persons can be dissolved in favor of the converted party. *See* Pauline Privilege.

marriage, morganatic (OG. *morgengeba,* morning gift)　A marriage between a man of high station and a woman of low station in which the woman agrees to remain in her low station and forfeit for her offspring any right to title or possessions of her husband. In the eyes of the Church if properly performed this marriage is as valid as any other. It takes its name from the gift which was formerly given by a husband to his wife on the morning after the marriage day because this was the only right such a wife had to any of her husband's property; some authorities state that in such a marriage it was customary for the husband to give his wife a large dowry on the morning after marriage to care for any offspring of the union, hence the name.

marriage of clergy　The marriage of a priest is an invalid marriage in the Western Church and in most instances in the Eastern Church. It is an ecclesiastical ruling that the clergy cannot marry, therefore the rule can be changed or altered in particular cases (the conversion to Catholicism of an Anglican priest who wished to become a Roman Catholic priest).

marriage of conscience　One that has been celebrated secretly in the presence of a priest and two witnesses, and without the proclamation of banns. It is allowed only for an urgent reason and with the permission of the local ordinary (cf. canons 1104-1107).

marriage of the unbaptized　A true marriage when mutual consent is given. This is a nonsacramental marriage but the essential rights and duties are the same. The marriage becomes sacramental upon the Baptism of both parties without the renewal of consent.

marriage, putative　A marriage that is invalid because of an annulling impediment and yet was contracted in good faith by at least one of the parties. The marriage ceases to be putative when both parties become aware of its nullity. The marriage is recognized by the Church provided it was contracted publicly and without the Church forbidding it. Children born of such a marriage are legitimate.

marriage rights　The rights common to both husband and wife unless they are withheld by mutual consent or grave reason. Grave reason may be: 1. danger of death or serious illness; 2. an inordinate request (a number of times in immediate succession); 3. an unreasonable request (drunkenness or insanity on the part of the partner constitutes in the eyes of moralists a sufficient reason for withholding the marriage right).

marriage, spiritual　The union between God and a person, referred to by spiritual writers as a mystical marriage. St. John of the Cross and St. Teresa of Avila have written a great deal on this subject. It is a complete surrender into the hands of God in a union that is so close that there is a type of spiritual oneness. God and the person do not really become one, however, because God and His creatures are always separate and distinct.

marriage, unity of The natural law requires that marriage be between one man and one woman only. Polyandry (a wife with several husbands) disrupts the peace of the home and handicaps the offspring since it cannot be said for certain who is father and head of the home. Polygamy (one husband with several wives) was permitted by God for a time among the Israelites but it has been abrogated under the New Law.

martyr (Gr. a witness) 1. One who has suffered death rather than give up his religion; one who by death has witnessed for Christ. 2. In the early Church the name was applied to those who witnessed for Christ in a notable way. Since many of these met death, the word gradually came to be restricted to those who gave their lives for the Faith. There is a difference between a martyr *coram Deo* (before God) and a martyr *coram ecclesia* (before the Church).

martyrdom 1. The act of being put to death for one's religious beliefs. 2. The state of being a martyr. To be a martyr one must be put to death or die because of suffering endured for the Faith. An unbaptized person who dies for the Christian Faith receives Baptism of blood. Since God has given man liberty (freedom of conscience), it is possible for a person to be a martyr even though he may not belong to the Catholic Church and even may die in defense of an objectively erroneous doctrine. Such a person is said to be a martyr *coram Deo* (before God) but not *coram Ecclesia* (before the Church).

martyrion 1. The burial place of a martyr. 2. A church built over a martyr's tomb. 3. The name given

to a basilica built by Constantine over the spot where his mother found the True Cross.

martyrology A catalogue of martyrs and saints arranged chronologically, either according to feast day or day of death. Such a list may be local, national, regional or universal. The best known martyrology is the *Roman Martyrology* (*q.v.*) which first appeared in 1584 and which has undergone many revisions. In many religious houses it is customary to read the daily list from this book. Another famous martyrology is the *Hieronymian* which dates back to the 5th century and which was probably compiled from local martyrologies. *See* American Martyrology in *Appendix.*

Martyrs of Japan *See* Japanese Martyrs.

Martyrs of Uganda *See* Uganda Martyrs.

Mary (Aramaic, *Maryam* from Heb. *Miryam,* L. Maria) A name in common use in Palestine at the time of Our Lord. It has been given a number of meanings, none of which is certain. It is today the most common female name. The first Mary mentioned in the Old Testament is the sister of Moses. A number of women named Mary were connected with Our Lord besides His mother; e.g., Mary the sister of Martha, Mary Magdalene, etc. The New Testament also mentions Mary, the mother of John Mark, at whose home the Christians were gathered in prayer when Peter escaped from prison.

Mary, Blessed Virgin The mother of Jesus Christ, daughter of Joachim and Anne, a native of Nazareth. Mary was of the tribe of Juda and could trace her lineage to the royal house of David. She was born free of original sin (Immaculate Conception). She was betrothed to Joseph, a carpenter of Nazareth, who had been chosen by God to be her protector. Shortly after her betrothal, the Angel Gabriel announced to her that she was to be the mother of the Messias, the Son of God. She carried the good news to her cousin, Elizabeth, and chanted the beautiful Magnificat as a hymn of praise. With Joseph, Mary went to Bethlehem in obedience to a decree of the Emperor Caesar Augustus concerning a census of all Jews. Here Jesus was born. Mary presented her Child in the Temple according to custom. Afterward she, Joseph and the Child fled to Egypt to escape the wrath of Herod. When Jesus was twelve years of age, the Holy Family again went to Jerusalem, where Jesus became separated from His parents. Finding Him three days later in the Temple, Mary and Joseph took Him home to Nazareth. The next eighteen years are unknown. At Cana, Jesus began His public life, working the miracle of changing water into wine at the request of His mother. Mary accompanied Christ during His public life and was with Him when He died on Calvary. She received His body from the cross, helped in His burial and rejoiced in His Resurrection. She was present with the Apostles on Pentecost Sunday. It is thought she died in Jerusalem *c*. A.D. 48. She was assumed bodily into heaven. She is the patroness of the United States under her title of the Immaculate Conception. It is the teaching of the Church that Mary was born without sin and remained sinless for life, that she was always a virgin and that she is truly the mother of God.

Mary-Candle A candle decorated with white or blue ribbon which is placed before a small statue or picture of the Blessed Virgin on the Feast of the Immaculate Conception. The candle is lighted during family meals and evening prayers. It serves as a reminder of Mary's expectation of the "Light of the World," and helps members of the family to keep their own light of grace burning brightly in preparation for the coming of Christ.

Mary, Feast of A day set aside to commemorate some title or event in the life of the Blessed Virgin. Some of these feasts are of regional nature, others are universal. Those observed in the United States are Our Lady of Prompt Succor, Jan. 15; Purification of Mary, Feb. 2; Our Lady of Lourdes, Feb. 11; Annunciation, Mar. 25; Queenship, May 31; Visitation, July 2; Our Lady of Mt. Carmel, July 16; Our Lady of the Snows, Aug. 5; Assumption, Aug. 15; Immaculate Heart, Aug. 22; Nativity of Mary, Sept. 8; Holy Name of Mary, Sept. 12; Seven Sorrows, Sept. 15; Our Lady of Ransom, Sept. 24; Holy Rosary, Oct. 7; Motherhood of Mary, Oct. 11; Presentation of Mary, Nov. 21; Immaculate Conception, Dec. 8; Our Lady of Guadalupe, Dec. 12.

Mary, Feast of the Holy Name of A feast celebrated in the Latin Rite on Sept. 12. First fostered in Spain, then invoked against the Turks at Vienna in 1683, this devotion to Mary inspired King John of Poland to save Christendom from the devastation of the Turks. Pope Innocent XI (1683) extended the feast to the universal Church.

Mary, Immaculate Heart of A feast of the Blessed Virgin celebrated on Aug. 22. It is an ineffable mystery that it was possible for God to form a human soul so beautiful, so pure, so immaculate, so full of grace, that it actually became quite fitting for this soul to give the Eternal Word the flesh and blood with which He saved the world.

Mary, month of The month of May which is dedicated to the Blessed Virgin. Processions and special devotions take place in this period.

Maryknoll Fathers (The Catholic Foreign Mission Society of America) A society of secular priests and auxiliary Brothers founded by Fathers James Anthony Walsh and Thomas Frederick Price. It was established by the archbishops of the United States at their annual meeting in 1911 as a national organization to train young Americans and send them to foreign mission fields. It was authorized by Pope St. Pius X in 1911, and its first four priests left for China in 1918. Father (later Bishop) Walsh was Boston director of the Society for the Propagation of the Faith and publisher of a small missionary magazine, *The Field Afar,* later called *Maryknoll.* In 1910 he met Father Price, a veteran home mission priest from North Carolina. They agreed on the need for an American Catholic foreign mission society, and began to interest others in their project. The seminary was eventually built near Ossining, N. Y., on a hilltop christened Maryknoll. After the departure of the first small mission band in 1918, the work grew rapidly. The Communist take-over in China merely released workers for other fields. The Maryknoll Fathers now staff missions in Africa, Mexico, Guatemala, El Salvador, Peru, Bolivia, Chile, Hawaii, Japan, Korea, Formosa, Hong Kong and the Philippines. Their chief work is directly apostolic, the conversion and care of souls, but they also go out well prepared for the

works of mercy, knowing that it is hard to preach to starving people. In different localities, according to need, they conduct or supervise social service work, educational institutions, medical work, student hostels and native seminaries; and they have done well with credit unions and cooperatives, housing projects, better-farming movements, cooperative factories and the establishment or maintenance of leprosariums. In cases of extreme need they simply feed the poor until more permanent solutions can be found—for instance, in cases of disaster and refugees from Communist oppression. The Maryknoll Fathers have a house in Rome. Besides their center at Maryknoll, N. Y., they staff 22 houses in different parts of the United States.

Maryknoll Sisters, the (Legal title, the Maryknoll Sisters of St. Dominic) A congregation of Dominican Sisters, devoted to foreign mission work, whose motherhouse is at Maryknoll, N. Y. Their founder, Mary Josephine Rogers (later, Mother Mary Joseph) began donating her spare time to mission work in 1906, doing editorial work on *The Field Afar* mission magazine for Father James Anthony Walsh, Boston director of the Society for the Propagation of the Faith. Miss Rogers was then an instructor at Smith College. In 1912, when Father Walsh was training a small group of young men for foreign mission work at the newly founded seminary of the Catholic Foreign Mission Society of America, Mother Mary Joseph and several other young women were active helpers in editorial, secretarial and domestic work, having given up their positions to devote all their time to the new venture. They were trained in the religious life by Dominican novice mistresses from

Sincinawa, Wis , and in 1920 Cardinal Hayes formally erected the group (then numbering 39) into a religious congregation. In 1954 the congregation was made directly subject to Rome, with the title of the Maryknoll Sisters of St. Dominic. The Maryknoll Sisters—now over 1,600—do various types of mission work, including educational, medical, catechetical, social welfare, etc. Their houses number 130 in the United States, Asia, Africa, Latin America and the Pacific Islands. They also have a cloister for those called to the contemplative life.

Maryland One of the 13 original states, it is 42d in area and 21st in population. It was named by Charles I of England for his Catholic queen, Henrietta Maria, but since it was a colony for the oppressed English Catholics, to them the name indicated a more illustrious Queen. George Calvert, first Lord Baltimore and a convert to the Church, planned the colony and his son Cecil founded it under a charter granted by King Charles. The *Ark* and the *Dove* anchored at St. Clement's Isle on Annunciation Day, Mar. 25, 1634, with about 200 immigrants aboard, including Jesuit Fathers Andrew White and John Altham who celebrated Mass in the new land. Religious toleration was allowed for the first time in British colonial America and the Jesuits, working among the Indians, made friends with them and there were no Indian difficulties. The colony was well managed and began to prosper, but soon Protestants and especially Puritans from England and neighboring Virginia poured in, became a majority and seized the government, establishing the Anglican Church and putting into practice the English laws against Catholics. In the Revolution Maryland's Catholics fought bravely against England, led by Charles Carroll, who signed the Declaration of Independence. In 1789 Baltimore was made a diocese with John Carroll as first bishop. He founded Georgetown College in 1789 and placed the Jesuits in charge of it. He also built the first seminary for priests in English-speaking America, Sulpician St. Mary's at Emmitsburg. Religious Orders began their work of consolidating the Faith in the new diocese; schools, convents, monasteries, churches were built. The Cathedral of Baltimore was erected between 1806 and 1821. Under succeeding bishops the Church in Maryland continued to prosper. Mother Seton founded the Sisters of Charity in 1808 and parochial schools sprang up. The Oblate Sisters of Providence (a Negro congregation) began work for the Colored in 1828. In 1808 Baltimore was raised to the rank of an archdiocese, and in 1858 the Holy See gave its archbishops precedence over all other bishops and archbishops in the United States. James Archbishop Gibbons, a religious leader with great foresight particularly in the Labor Movement, held the Third Plenary Council of Baltimore in 1884. He was made a cardinal by Pope Leo XIII in 1886, and laid the cornerstone of the Catholic University of America at Washington, D.C., in 1889. Today there are about 459,000 Catholics in Maryland, in a total population of 3,100,-689.

masochism The act of deriving pleasure from being hurt or humiliated by another. Masochism has the idea of abnormality and in the minds of most psychologists is connected with sexual pleasure.

Masonry *See* Freemasonry.

Masoretic The name given to the original Hebrew text of the Old Testament, dating back to the 4th and 5th centuries B.C., it was codified by Hebrew scholars between the 6th and 10th centuries A.D.

Mass (L. *missa,* from the Mass dismissal, "Ite missa est"; Go, it is ended) The common word used to designate the official worship of the Church. The gathering together of God's family around the altar through Christ's love to hear the Word of God and to become one in the Eucharistic Meal. "We though many are one, all who partake of this one Bread."

Mass, application of At Mass the Christian community, gathered together through Christ's love around the altar to offer Christ to the Father, can pray for a particular intention or person as determined by the celebrant. This is called application of the Mass and refers to the special or ministerial benefit of the Mass, which is for the person or object, for which it is expressly applied, as distinguished from the general benefits which accrue to all mankind and especially to those participating; and the personal benefits which belong to the celebrant himself.

Mass at Dawn The second of the three Christmas Masses. This Mass originated in the 6th century. There were originally two Christmas Masses; one was celebrated at night (Midnight Mass) at St. Mary Major and one on Christmas day at St. Peter's. The Byzantine governor of Rome requested the Pope to celebrate a Mass at dawn for himself and his court in honor of St. Anastasia at the nearby church dedicated to her. Later the text of the Mass was changed to Christmas but the station remained as well as a commemoration of St. Anastasia. The third

Christmas Mass was changed from St. Peter's to St. Mary Major.

Mass card A card which states that a Mass will be offered for a particular person or intention, giving the name of the donor of the Mass, and sometimes the time and place of the Mass and the celebrant.

Mass, evening The first Mass at the Last Supper was celebrated as was customary for the eating of a paschal meal in the evening. With the liturgical movement, the celebration of evening Masses has become customary in many places.

Mass, ferial The Mass of the Day. To each day of Lent a proper Mass is assigned in the liturgy. The weekdays of Advent have no proper Mass but the Mass of the Day is the same as the preceding Sunday. During Lent the Mass of the Day takes precedence over feasts of third class rank. In Advent only Masses of the Day from Dec. 17 to Christmas outrank third class feasts. Outside of Lent the ferial Mass is of the preceding Sunday and is ranked as ferial of the fourth class. When the Mass of a preceding Sunday is repeated during the week, the Preface is of weekdays and the Profession of Faith is omitted.

Mass for the people A pastor of a canonically constituted parish must offer Mass for the spiritual and temporal welfare of his people (canons 339 and 466) on the following days: all Sundays, the ten holydays of obligation in the universal Church, all the feasts that were formerly days of obligation (see suppressed feasts), the Feast of St. Sylvester (Dec. 31), the Feast of the Sacred Heart and the Solemnity of St. Joseph. A pastor in the missions has the same obligation (canons 306, 466) on eleven days of the year: Easter, Pentecost and all the holydays of obligation of the uni-verbal Church, except Circumcision. No stipend may be accepted for the Mass for the people.

Mass, Low (L. *Missa privata*) The ordinary manner of celebrating Mass as contrasted to the Solemn Mass or Sung Mass (*qq.v.*). The Mass is spoken, not sung; there is no deacon or subdeacon but only an acolyte, no incense, and only two candles are lighted. All essential elements of the Mass remain the same, and it is a sacrifice in the fullest sense.

Mass, Midnight The term given to the first of the three Masses of Christmas Day, which begins at midnight. Except by apostolic indult, only a conventual or parochial celebration is allowed at this hour. Its liturgy has particular reference to the birth of Jesus.

Mass, obligation of Every Catholic who has reached the age of reason is obliged to attend Mass on Sundays and holydays of obligation. The obligation may be fulfilled at any place where the Mass is legitimately offered, and does not have to be of one's own rite. The minimum requirement is that one must be present from the Offertory until after the Communion and external attention at least is required. One is excused from Mass because of sickness, distance, the requirements of charity or for some urgent reason.

Mass of a Saint Although Mass is addressed and offered solely to God, it may be said in honor of a saint, usually on the day assigned in the Church calendar. The prayers of the Mass usually make direct or indirect reference to the saint and call upon the faithful to imitate the virtues of the saint.

Mass of Exposition Strictly, the Mass celebrated to open the Forty Hours' Devotion when the Blessed Sacrament is exposed. Loosely, any Mass celebrated when the Blessed Sacrament is exposed.

Mass of the Catechumens The beginning of the Mass from the entrance of the priest to the Offertory. In olden days it was customary for catechumens to be present only for this early part of the Mass after which they were dismissed from the solemn (secret) parts, known as the Mass of the Faithful.

Mass of the Dead *See* Requiem Mass.

Mass of the Faithful That part of the Mass which follows the Gospel and Profession of Faith until the end. It takes its name from ancient times when only the baptized were permitted to attend and from which catechumens were excluded.

Mass offering A stipend given to the celebrant by a person who has Mass offered for his or her intention. The offering is set by the ordinary or local custom. A priest who accepts a stipend has a grave obligation to offer the Mass and should keep careful records of Masses said and not said in case he should be incapacitated. Except for Christmas, only one stipend Mass may be offered a day.

Mass, Ordinary of the That part of the Mass which is relatively unchangeable in contrast to the Proper of the feast or season. It is the regular or standard part of the Mass into which is fitted the changeable prayers of the Proper.

Mass, parochial A mass celebrated at a fixed hour in a church for the people.

Mass, private A Mass that is not a sung or conventual Mass, nor a Mass celebrated at an assigned hour in a church for the faithful.

Mass, Solemn (L. *Missa solemnis*) Sometimes referred to as a Solemn

High Mass. It is a sung Mass with a deacon and subdeacon assisting the celebrant in which the complete ritual is observed. When celebrated by a bishop it is called a Solemn Pontifical Mass; and by the pope, a Solemn Papal Mass.

Mass, sung (L. *Missa cantata*) A Mass celebrated by a priest in which parts of it are sung but which has no deacon or subdeacon. It is a Mass between Low and Solemn.

Mass, the four ends of the Adoration, reparation, thanksgiving and supplication. Can be remembered easily by the word ARTS. Sometimes reparation is called contrition, in which case the ends of the Mass are remembered by the word ACTS.

Mass, the liturgy of The external manifestation of the "mystery of faith," the worship of God's people gathered around the altar. This external form takes on different aspects according to the different languages, customs and cultures of the worshipers. Thus we have various rites in the Church throughout the world. In our own day we see the changing of the Roman Rite to become more meaningful to the people gathered together to hear God's Word and partake of the Communion meal. In mission countries the adaptation of the liturgy to the people is of great importance, as expressed by the missionary bishops at Vatican Council II.

Massachusetts The 6th of the 13 original states, it is 45th in area and 9th in population. It is named for an Indian tribe meaning "Big Hill Place." It was explored by the English navigator Bartholomew Gosnold in 1602, and it became known as New England after John Smith made a map of the coast in 1616. In 1620 the Pilgrims made the first permanent settlement at Plymouth. They were seeking religious freedom for themselves but refused it to others, as did the Puritans who arrived to settle other parts of Massachusetts during the next few decades. In 1755 more than 1,000 Acadian deportees landed in Boston but the Puritans would not allow a priest to serve them. George Washington was incensed at the ridicule given the pope on Guy Fawkes Day, and reprimanded his soldiers for their discourtesy toward the Faith of the French people of Canada. In the Revolution great numbers of Catholics fought bravely, yet the Puritans still refused to allow Catholics to hold government office. The constitution of Massachusetts made Calvinism an established religion, providing government funds for the support of their religious instructors. Though Mass was probably said under cover at times for the Irish and French Catholics scattered among the population, the first public Mass was offered on Nov. 2, 1788, in Boston by Abbé de la Poterie, the first resident priest. In 1803 the Church of the Holy Cross was built in Boston with aid from Protestants led by John Adams, but Catholics were forbidden to hold office until 1821. In 1810 Bishop Cheverus was placed in charge of the new diocese of Boston, which included all of New England. Catholic immigrants—Irish, French, Canadians, Italians, Portuguese from the Azores—settled in the state and worked in the newly developed textile mills. Working conditions were little better than slavery, yet the immigrants increased, prospered, educated their children and helped develop the state and establish the Catholic Faith. The Jesuit Bishop Fenwick (1825–1846) began the training of young men for the priesthood in his own house. During his episcopacy and succeeding ones, the Church flourished, works of education and charity multiplied, and numerous religious congregations were established. In 1870 Springfield became a diocese; in 1875 Boston was promoted to the rank of archdiocese; in 1904 the Diocese of Fall River was established; in 1911 Pope Pius X made Archbishop O'Connell of Boston a cardinal, and the Diocese of Worcester was instituted in 1950. Today the severely pious followers of Calvin would hardly recognize their descendants, and Massachusetts is one of the most Catholic of states. It approaches 3 million Catholics in a total population of over 5 million.

Massacre of the Innocents *See* Holy Innocents, the.

Masses for the dead Masses offered for a deceased person are divided into four classes. 1. *First class*. The Mass of All Souls (Nov. 2) and a funeral Mass. 2. *Second class*. A Mass said on the day of death, the day the news is received or on the day of final interment. 3. *Third class*. The 3rd, 7th or 30th day after death, the annual anniversary of death or burial, Masses said for deceased in a church or chapel of a cemetery, Masses for the dead said during the eight days following Nov. 2. 4. *Fourth class*. The daily Mass for the dead. This Mass may be celebrated only on ferial days of fourth class outside of the Christmas-Epiphany season.

Masses of Christmas Each priest is allowed to offer three Masses on Christmas Day. The Missal contains the three Propers which are to be used, one for each Mass.

Masses, Votive Any Mass other than that designated for the day of the year, either by the season or by the cycle of saints in the calendar, is called a Votive Mass. It is a Mass offered for a special intention or out of special devotion. Votive Masses are graded into four classes which indicate the feasts over which they may take precedence. (*See* feasts, rank of.) On a liturgical day of fourth-class rank, any Votive Mass may be said. The missal contains a special section of Votive Masses and the celebrant may choose any of these Masses. A few Votive Masses are assigned to particular days of the week but the celebrant is not bound to follow these designations. On the First Thursday of each month, a Mass may be offered to Jesus Christ, the High Priest; on the first Friday, to the Sacred Heart; on the first Saturday of the month to the Immaculate Heart of Mary. These days have special privileges for a Votive Mass; and the Mass of Jesus Christ, the High Priest, of the Sacred Heart or of the Immaculate Heart of Mary may be said on liturgical days of third-class rank.

Master 1. A title of address to Christ used by His disciples. 2. An academic degree higher than that of Bachelor but below that of Doctor. It is given upon fulfillment of certain agreed academic standards.

master general The head of the Dominicans or Mercedarians.

master of ceremonies A layman or cleric who directs and assists at religious ceremonies. He guides the celebrant and directs other observers. He wears cassock and surplice.

master of novices An experienced religious who is in charge of the training of novices and the administration of the novitiate. Canon law lays down qualifications which he must meet. The female title is mistress of novices.

Master of the Chamber *See* Maestro di Camera.

Master of the Sacred Palace The origin of this office apparently goes back to St. Dominic and Pope Honorius III. The Master of the Sacred Palace is the confidential theologian of the Holy Father, Consultor of the Supreme Sacred Congregation of the Holy Office, Prelate Official of the Sacred Congregation of Rites and Consultor to the Congregation of the Holy Office. The Master is a member of the papal household and resides in the Vatican.

masturbation That sin against the Sixth Commandment known as self-abuse.

Mater et Magistra (Mother and Teacher) Pope John XXIII's first encyclical letter, issued on May 15, 1961, the seventieth anniversary of Pope Leo XIII's social encyclical, *Rerum Novarum*. In *Mater et Magistra* Pope John restates the Church's stand behind the natural-law principles of the dignity of man and the primacy of the common good in the socioeconomic order as originally set forth in *Rerum Novarum* and later in Pius XI's *Quadragesimo Anno*. The contents of the encyclical are as follows: 1. Teachings of the encyclical *Rerum Novarum* and timely doctrinal developments during the pontificates of Pius XI and Pius XII. 2. Explanation and development of the teachings of *Rerum Novarum*. 3. New aspects of the social question. 4. Reconstruction of social relationships in truth, justice and love.

materia prima (L. prime matter) A philosophical term for that of which a thing is made. It is essential and substantial rather than accidental.

Thus the prime matter of man is his material reality which allows him to share in the species of humanity and to be individuated.

material elements Those things used in the worship and ritual of the Church. They are to be pure and natural. Thus it would be wrong to use an electric light in place of a sanctuary lamp. Wine must be made from grapes. Candles are made from beeswax and not petroleum products. The principal elements used are water, air, wine, bread, fire, incense, oil, ashes and palms.

materialism Materialism is a philosophical theory that explains the origin and nature of the world solely by the existence and nature of physical, material things. Accordingly, spiritual, nonmaterial beings cannot explain the phenomena of experience. This is because their very existence is denied. The best known modern theory of materialism is Marxism. It attempts to explain all of human existence in terms of a determined process of history, which is economical in its basic structure.

Matins (L. *matutinum,* morning) The first of the canonical hours of the Divine Office. It is composed of psalms, scriptural readings, lessons, homilies, antiphons and responses. It is sometimes called the night office and dates back to the vigils which preceded the Eucharistic Assembly.

matrimonial court A diocesan tribunal which handles cases pertaining to marriage. Decrees to be effective must be approved by the ordinary, and appeal can be had to the Holy See.

Matrimony, Sacrament of The sacrament which sanctifies the contract freely made between a man and woman, each of whom is baptized, to live together for the purpose of having and rearing children, and of cherishing each other in a common life. Through the sacrament grace is conferred to enable them to meet the responsibilities of the married state. The bride and groom are the ministers of the sacrament. The matter and form are the consents mutually given and received to the contract. *See* marriage.

matter and form An Aristotelian theory developed by Scholastic philosophers which attributes to all corporal beings two principles: one, active and determining; the other, passive and indeterminate.

matter of the sacraments Each sacrament possesses matter and form. The matter is the indeterminate substance or act which receives its meaning from the accompanying form (words). The matter of Baptism is the pouring of water; of the Eucharist, bread and wine; of Penance, the acts of the penitent (contrition, confession, purpose of amendment and reparation); of Confirmation, anointing the forehead with chrism; of Matrimony, the mutually given consent; of Holy Orders, the imposition of hands and the presentation of the instruments of sacrifice; of the Anointing of the Sick, the anointing of the eyes, ears, nose, mouth, hands and feet.

Matthew (Aramaic, *mattat,* gift) One of the original apostles, author of the first Gospel, a former tax collector. He is also known as Levi. After his calling, he gave a banquet for Christ which was attended by other tax collectors. Since his revenue position was in Capharnaum, he was probably in the employ of Herod Antipas rather than the Romans.

Matthew, Gospel of St. This Gospel was written originally in Aramaic and later translated into Greek, but of the Aramaic original there is no trace. Matthew's purpose was to show that Jesus was the promised Messias, and that rejection of Him means the loss of salvation. While a considerable time passed between the death of Christ and the composition of the Gospel, its exact date of completion is unknown. Irenaeus said it was composed while Peter and Paul were preaching in Rome (A.D. 61–67), but some scholars hold that the final Greek version was written after the Gospel of St. Mark, possibly close to the year 70, the date of the destruction of Jerusalem.

Matthias, St. (short for Mathathias; Heb. gift from Yahweh) Matthias was the disciple chosen to take the place of Judas Iscariot, and was elected, according to Acts, between the Ascension and Pentecost. He and Joseph Barsabbas were proposed as the most suitable candidates with the final selection left to the Holy Spirit through the drawing of lots. Nothing more is known of him. His feast day is kept in the Western Church on Feb. 24, and in the Eastern on Aug. 9.

Maundy Thursday *See* Holy Thursday.

May Month of Mary.

May devotions Those devotions in honor of the Blessed Virgin practiced during the month of May, which is a month dedicated to the Blessed Virgin. They include such devotions as processions, crowning the statue of Our Lady, setting up a special shrine, a daily hymn before a statue of Our Lady, special prayers in church, etc.

measure, biblical The reference in Jn. 2:6 refers to the Hebrew *bath,* a liquid measure (44.6 quarts). Lk. 16:7 refers to the *kor,* a dry measure equal to one tenth of an *epha* (about one bushel).

meat When meat is forbidden on days of abstinence soups and gravies made from meat are also forbidden. Fridays are days of total abstinence from meat. On most other days of abstinence meat is permitted at the main meal only. Meat refers to the flesh of birds and animals born upon the land.

medal, religious A flat metal disk bearing an image of Our Lord or a holy person or some mystery of religion, etc. It is blessed by the Church and often carries an indulgence. Wearers of medals are to guard against superstition but are to use the medal as a reminder of honor to be given to the image thereon and of the need for advancing in Christian perfection. There are many types of medals but among the most popular are the Miraculous Medal, the Scapular Medal, the St. Christopher Medal, Medal of Our Lady of Guadalupe, Medal of the Sacred Heart, etc. Their use is ancient since medals have been found in the catacombs.

Mediator (L. *mediare,* to be in the middle) 1. A title given to Christ because of His reconciliation of God and man. St. Paul uses this title in 1 Tim. 2:5. 2. (not cap.) A saint who intercedes for a person or group as the result of prayer.

Mediatrix of All Graces A title given to the Blessed Virgin because of her role of dispensing grace on mankind through the Holy Spirit because of the infinite merits of her son, Jesus Christ. Theologians hold that because of her role in the Incarnation and Redemption and her own sorrows and sufferings, Mary becomes a channel of grace flowing from these same acts.

Medical Missionaries, the Society of Catholic A religious society of women founded in the United States in 1925, under the auspices of Archbishop Curley of Baltimore, by Dr. Anna Dengel. Dr. Agnes McLaren, a convert Scotchwoman familiar with Protestant medical mission work had tried to interest Catholic religious orders in training Sisters as doctors for countries where the inmates of harems often died without medical help, owing to the prohibition against the entry of males into the women's quarters. Canon law did not then allow nuns to practice surgery or obstetrics, so Dr. McLaren took up her cause among young Catholic lay women. Anna Dengel, an Austrian girl, decided to study medicine and go to India. After four years in Dr. McLaren's hospital in the Punjab, she came to the United States to find helpers in the work. Father Mathis of the Holy Cross Fathers encouraged and guided her, and the first house of the Society was founded in Brookland, Washington, D.C., with Dr. Dengel as superior. In 1926 they made their first promises, to keep the evangelical counsels. They built their first hospital in Rawalpindi, India, in 1928. The Medical Mission Sisters are doctors, nurses, social service workers, housekeepers, secretaries and general helpers—all real missioners who influence many to turn to the Church. Their Generalate is in Rome, their United States provincial house in Philadelphia. They have houses in various parts of the United States, in England, in Pakistan and many parts of India, in Venezuela and in West Africa.

meditation (L. *meditari,* to ponder) A type of mental prayer consisting of reflection on some spiritual theme with the aim of stirring the will to make practical resolutions. It is an important means for advancement in the spiritual life. There are two main

367

forms of systematized meditation. 1.
The Ignatian Method, based on the
Spiritual Exercises of St. Ignatius
Loyola. There is a remote preparation (usually the night before) of the
subject. In the meditation proper
there is a re-creation of some incident
to which all the senses are applied.
Thus in a meditation on hell one
imagines the sights, sounds, feelings,
etc., and from this, proceeds to
speculative considerations and finally
to practical resolutions. 2. *The Sulpician Method* also begins with a remote preparation the evening before.
There is an immediate preparation
in which the subject acknowledges
his unworthiness to appear before
God; there are acts of adoration and
a petition to the Holy Spirit. The
body of prayer follows with adoration and communion during which
consideration of motives leading to
virtue and withdrawing from vice are
made. The conclusion centers about
definite resolutions and the adoption
of a "spiritual nosegay" which is to
recall the meditation from time to
time.

meekness A virtue derived from
temperance which makes one quietly
obedient in heart and actions, patient
under offense and rebuke, moderat-
ing anger and irritation, and controlling disorderly affections.

Melchisedec (Heb. the king is the Just
One) The priest-king who brought
bread and wine to Abraham; a prefigure of Christ. While the bread and
wine offered to Abraham was not a
sacrifice, the passage is applied in an
accommodated sense as an image of
the Eucharistic Sacrifice.

Melkite Rite The Byzantine Rite as
used by the Melkites. It uses both
Arabic and Greek.

Melkites Byzantine Rite Catholics
found mainly in Egypt, Syria and Is-

rael. They are subject to the Patriarch of Antioch. There are about
25,000 Melkites in the United States
who are subject to the Roman Rite
bishop of the diocese in which they
reside.

memento (L. a remembrance) 1. *In
general,* a remembrance in prayer of
a person or an intention. 2. *Memento
of the Living.* The commemoration
made at Mass at the beginning of the
Canon in which the celebrant prays
for the Holy Father, the bishop and
"all faithful guardians of the Catholic and Apostolic faith," all present
at the Mass and any others whose
name he wishes to insert. 3. *Memento
of the Dead.* The fourth prayer after
the Consecration of the Mass in
which the celebrant prays God to
"Remember also, O Lord, your servants [here the names are inserted]
who have gone before us with the
sign of faith, and rest in the sleep of
peace. To them, O Lord, and to all
who rest in Christ, we entreat you to
grant a place of comfort, of light and
peace."

Memorare, the A popular prayer to
the Blessed Virgin which takes its
name from the first word in the Latin
version. It is said to have been written by St. Bernard of Clairvaux. In
English it begins: "Remember, O
most gracious Virgin Mary, that
never was it known. . . ."

memoria 1. A shrine or reliquary
containing the remains of one or
more martyrs. 2. A church or chapel
dedicated to a martyr, built over his
tomb or containing his relics. 3. A
commemoration. The lowest ranking
feast in the Dominican and Benedictine calendars.

mendicant friars (L. *mendicare,* to
beg) Members of those religious
orders who through a vow of poverty
renounce all personal and com-

munity property and who depend upon work and charity to subsist. The principal mendicant orders are the Augustinians, Capuchins, Carmelites, Dominicans, Franciscans, Mercedarians and Servites. Formerly most of these communities depended on begging but the Council of Trent modified this prescription.

Mennonites A sect derived from the Anabaptists which takes its name from Menno Simons (1492–1559), an ex-priest. Simons did not found the sect but became its leader. The sect has strong belief in the separation of church and state and rejects oaths and public office. Mennonites came under heavy persecution in Europe, many of them being put to death. Seeking religious freedom, Mennonites fled Holland to the American colonies and Russia. A large settlement was made in Germantown, Pa., in 1683, and from there the group spread to other states and Canada. There are a number of Mennonite bodies, including the Amish (*q.v.*).

mensa (L. table) The flat, stone top of a consecrated altar on which the Holy Sacrifice is celebrated. In an unconsecrated altar, the mensa properly is the altar stone, although the term is used loosely to mean the whole top of the altar.

mental reservation An act of the mind whereby a speaker restricts the meaning of words to what is not their obvious meaning. Mental reservations are strict and broad: strict when it is impossible for the hearer to perceive the truth; broad when a prudent man could gather the intended meaning. A strict mental reservation is never permitted because it is an odious lie (*cf.* Prümmer); the broad mental reservation is permitted in certain cases because its purpose is

not to deceive but to withhold a truth or part of a truth which for some reason should not be disclosed.

mercy 1. An attribute of God which causes Him to shower benefits on His creatures, despite the fact that they may have offended Him. God is willing to forgive out of love and goodness. 2. A moral virtue which is shown by compassion for those in need; a tempering of the strict demands of justice. It is a function of the virtue of charity.

mercy, corporal works of Seven external acts of charity toward one's neighbor. They are: to feed the hungry, to give drink to the thirsty, to clothe the naked, to shelter the homeless, to visit the sick, to visit the imprisoned, to bury the dead.

mercy killing *See* euthanasia.

mercy, spiritual works of Acts of charity done for the souls of persons in spiritual need. They are seven: instruct the ignorant, counsel the doubtful, admonish sinners, be patient with wrongdoers, forgive offenses, comfort the afflicted, pray for the living and the dead.

mercy, works of These are works done to alleviate the bodily or spiritual distress of another, founded on compassion with a ready desire for assistance. They are of two kinds: corporal and spiritual (*qq.v.*).

meridian (L. *meridies,* midday) An hour's rest taken in many monasteries shortly after noon, especially in hot countries, or when the night is broken by recitation of the Divine Office; a siesta.

merit (L. *merere,* to earn) The right to a reward ordained by God for a good and supernatural work done for God. Because in merit there is a relationship between the good done and the return due, merit is considered under a twofold aspect. Merit *de* *condigno,* or strict merit, is had when the relation between the act performed and the return due is one of equality, thus a laborer strictly merits his wages. To gain spiritual merit *de condigno* a person must be alive and in the state of sanctifying grace. His act must be supernaturally good, freely done as a service to God in order to gain a supernatural reward. Merit *de congruo,* or lesser merit, is had when the relation between the act performed and the return due is not equal and the return comes not from justice but from the liberality of the one served, thus a bonus given over and above wages would be merit *de congruo.* To gain this merit a man must be alive but need not be in the state of sanctifying grace.

messianism A type of nativism (*q.v.*) which has for its leader a magico-religious personality or messias (*q.v.*).

messias One who believes he has a divine ordinance to lead his people and that he has been appointed to save them from something. He also believes that he and he alone knows the will of God in this regard.

Messias, Messiah (Aramaic *mesiha,* anointed one) Translated into Greek the word became *Christos.* The word has its origin in the Hebrew custom of anointing men set apart for high offices, especially kings or priests. It was thus applied to the Hebrew king, who was the "anointed one" of the Lord. A foundation for the messianic hope is God's promise always to protect the Davidic dynasty. The prophets pointed out that God's promises would be fulfilled in a future ideal king, a "Messiah." The late Jewish apocalyptic writings after the time of Daniel spoke of a heavenly figure who would be associated with the "day of the Lord," the restoration of Israel and the resurrection of the

dead. These last writings were extant and had a great influence on the people of Jesus' time.

metempsychosis (Gr. *meta,* between; *psyche,* soul) The transfer of the human soul from one body to another; reincarnation. The theory is held in India where through a progression of such purifications one enters the final purified state of Nirvana. Modern spiritism also advocates this teaching. The teaching is both philosophically and theologically ridiculous.

Methodism A denomination which had its remote beginnings in a pious club at Oxford University, led by Charles (1707–1788) and John Wesley (1703–1791), sons of an Anglican minister in Lincolnshire, England, who were both later ordained ministers. They had begun their movement as a *methodical* way of holiness and devotion within the Anglican church, but when they found no ecclesiastical support but rather resistance to their work they broke away and John Wesley began to ordain his own ministers. The members followed a strict monastic type of schedule: weekly communion, daily attendance at church services, Scripture study, meditation and examen of conscience, prayer aloud in common three times daily, and a stop for silent prayer every hour. They combined these spiritual exercises with the teaching of poor children and regular visiting of prisoners and the sick. John Wesley's inspiration, outside of Scripture, came largely from the study of the *Imitation of Christ.* Charles Wesley became famous for his devotional hymns; among them: "Jesus, Lover of My Soul" and "Hark! the Herald Angels Sing." The Wesleys were later influenced by the Moravians, absorbed some of their spirit and set out doing street preaching with great success. They gained a numerous following not only in England but in the United States even during their lifetime. Methodists today place great emphasis on good works and fellowship. They are usually in the forefront of movements such as temperance, labor reform and peace; and they are leaders among Protestants in the number of missions, colleges and hospitals. They emphasize the inner experience of conversion, revivals and the giving of testimony, although individual Methodist churches differ greatly in some details. They observe democratic practices in church organization and government, and give a prominent place to lay leadership. The Methodist founders were undoubtedly devout and sincere persons, earnestly seeking God. In the Catholic Church they might have become canonized saints, founders of religious orders in the footsteps of St. Francis of Assisi or St. Vincent de Paul. As it was, their revivalist movement brought about an awakening of piety among Protestants and led many to an appreciation of a more spiritual life. There are about 19 million Methodists in the world, with nearly 13 million in the United States—of these, over ten million are in "the Methodist Church, formed in 1939 by union of the three main Methodist branches; the remaining 2 million are in 21 groups, some obviously quite small.

metropolitan (Gr. *metropolis,* a city) 1. An archbishop in the Western Church who is placed over a number of suffragan dioceses. Every metropolitan is an archbishop but not vice versa since there are titular archbishops. The metropolitan may call a provincial council and preside over it, and appeals from suffragan courts are made to his. He takes precedence over suffragan bishops and may use the pallium in his province. (*See* archbishop.) 2. In the Eastern Churches the title tends to supplant that of archbishop, even though most archbishops have no suffragan sees. 3. The word is also used to refer to the see (metropolitan see), cathedral (metropolitan church), etc., of such an archbishop.

Mexico The conquest of Mexico under Cortes (1519–1520) is one of the great military feats of the history of the New World. Once the Aztec Empire was overthrown, missioners began replacing its cruel paganism with Christianity. The appearance of the Virgin of Guadalupe to Juan Diego (1531) was an important factor in the conversion of the Indians and in keeping Mexico Christian in the vicissitudes that lay ahead. Following the overthrow of the Spanish in a revolution that was led by two priests (Father Miguel Hidalgo and Father José Morelos), the new governments were anticlerical. The Constitution of 1857 separated Church and State and put severe restrictions on the Church. Religious orders were suppressed, property confiscated and religious demonstration forbidden. Persecution continued against the Church in varying intensity until the violent and full-scale persecution begun under President Plutarco Calles in 1924. With the consent of the Holy See all public worship came to an end in Mexico. Priests were hunted down and executed; there were popular boycotts and religious revolts. In 1937 President Cardenas ordered state governors to relax their persecution of the Church and declared the Mexican Catholics had complete liberty to worship. The restrictive laws against the Church are still carried in the Mexican Constitution but today are not generally enforced. In 1964 for the first time in many years a president was elected who admitted to being a practicing Catholic. Despite successive waves of persecution, the Church in Mexico revived each time, and today has the strongest Christianity in Latin America. One unique development is that Mexico has its own national foreign mission society and today is sending missioners to the Orient.

Michaelmas A term used in England for the feast of St. Michael the Archangel (Sept. 29). There is an old tradition of eating roast goose on this day.

Michea (Heb. *Mikayah,* who is like Yahweh?) A minor prophet, a contemporary of Isaia, author of the book of the Old Testament that bears his name. He was a passionate defender of the little man against the rich and his work strikes out sharply at injustice. He predicted the conversion of the Gentiles and his prophecy concerning Bethlehem as the place of Christ's birth is the most definite of any prophecies in the Old Testament.

Michigan The 26th state admitted to the Union, 23rd in area, 7th in population, its name derives from Chippewa *michigama,* "big water." Champlain's emissary Brule is said to have explored the region of Lake Superior in 1621, where the Hurons were mining copper. Several Jesuits including Saint Isaac Jogues came to the site of Sault Ste. Marie in 1641 to work among the Chippewas. Father Marquette, S.J., founded the first permanent settlement there and built a mission among the Hurons at St. Ignace in 1671. Cadillac established the

settlement of Detroit in 1701 where, five years later, the Ottawas killed Father Constantin Delhalle, O.F.M. Michigan was ceded to England by France in 1763, to the United States in 1783 and became a state in 1837. In the meantime immigrants from the east and from Europe were swarming in. In Detroit Father Gabriel Richard, famous for zeal and charity, published the first Catholic newspaper in the United States, the *Western Catholic Register.* He died of cholera while nursing the stricken, 1832. Detroit became a diocese in 1833, Most Rev. Frederic Rese being the first bishop. Succeeding bishops brought in religious congregations to aid in education and works of charity. In 1857 Sault Ste. Marie (later changed to Marquette) became a diocese, followed by Grand Rapids in 1882. In 1937 Detroit was raised to the rank of archdiocese, and the Diocese of Lansing was created. Saginaw became a diocese in 1938, and in 1946 Archbishop Mooney of Detroit was made a Cardinal by Pope Pius XII. There are well over 2 million Catholics in Michigan, in a total population of 8 million.

Middle Ages That period of European history beginning with the coronation of Charlemagne (A.D. 800) and ending with the invasion of Italy by the French in 1494.

Milan, Edict of The proclamation of Constantine in 313 which gave freedom of religion to Christians and all others.

Milanese Rite *See* Ambrosian Rite.

mildness A gentleness and temperateness that is a fruit of the Holy Spirit. It is not to be taken in the etymological sense of "softness."

mildness, defect of An irregularity (*q.v.*) to Holy Orders incurred by a judge who has sentenced someone to death, by one who has held the office of executioner, by one who voluntarily acts as immediate assistant at an execution, by one who knowingly takes part in an unjust war, and probably by the members of a sworn jury who return a verdict of death. The Latin term is *defectus lenitatis*.

militarism A predominance of the ideals of the military class which glorifies war for its own sake. The Church condemns such aggressiveness as being against justice and Christian charity.

military orders Associations developed during the Crusades which attempted to combine religious and military status. Members of these associations fought in defense of the holy places of Palestine, staffed some of the holy places, protected pilgrims, etc. The members were called knights and they took religious vows. They had the rights and duties of monks and monasteries. The members tried to belong to two different worlds and for this reason the orders were not successful. The principal orders were the Knights Templar, the Knights of Alcantara, the Mercedarians, the Hospitallers of St. John and the Teutonic Knights.

military service Canon law forbids all clerics from bearing arms unless compelled to do so. In the United States clerics are exempt from military service; this is also the condition in most Christian nations. In those countries where civil law compels military service, reception of tonsure is usually postponed until the service is completed.

millenium, the Literally, a thousand years. It refers to the thousand-year reign on earth of Jesus Christ as mentioned in Apoc. 20:5. Catholic scholars interpret the number 1,000 to indicate an indefinite period of time, and the reign of Christ on earth as a spiritual reign in His Church. In the early Church many held a literal interpretation and are known as millenarians. Among these were Papias, Tertullian and Justin. The doctrine is still held by some extreme fundamentalist sects.

mind of the Church 1. The general belief of the Church in matters not defined as dogma but declared in serious pronouncements and in the teaching of theologians. Lack of respect for the mind of the Church is imprudent and can lead to sin and loss of faith. 2. To think or to act with the Church so that a person can be said to have the same mind as the Church.

minister (L. servant) 1. One authorized to administer a sacrament. 2. The deacon and subdeacon at High Mass are ministers to the celebrant. They are usually referred to as sacred ministers. 3. The minister general and minister provincial of the Franciscans and Trinitarians. The second in authority in Jesuit communities. The prior of La Grande Chartreuse is ex officio minister general of the Carthusians. 4. There is no Catholic usage of the word to mean an ordained cleric as is the fashion in Protestantism.

ministerium A term that embraces all the ordained members of the Church who are charged with preaching, teaching, sanctifying and administrating; the ministry.

Ministers of the Sick Another name for the Camillians, an order founded in 1582 by St. Camillus of Lellis to serve the sick in hospitals.

ministry *See* ministerium.

minitanti Minor officials in the Roman Curia. They work in the Sacred Congregation for the Propagation of the Faith, the Sacred Congregation for Extraordinary Ecclesiastical Affairs and the Secretariate of State.

Minnesota The 32nd state admitted to the Union, 12th in area and 18th in population, its name comes from a Dakota Sioux word meaning "clouded" or "milky water." Chippewas and Sioux fought for the hunting grounds of Minnesota for 200 years until the 1860's when the white warriors overcame both and settled them on reservations. The French explorers Radisson, Groseilliers and Du Luth took possession of the area for Louis XIV in the mid-17th century. Franciscan Father Hennepin discovered the falls which he named for St. Anthony in 1680. Jesuits started a mission on Lake Pepin in 1727. Father Jean-Pierre Alneau, first to shed his blood for Christ on Minnesota soil, was killed by the Sioux in 1732 near Fort St. Charles. Part of Minnesota became United States property in 1783, and the rest was acquired in the Louisiana Purchase in 1803. The United States government made treaties with the Indians, had the territory explored and opened it up to settlers, who came in large numbers from the East and from Europe. Minnesota became a state in 1858. After the Civil War, the Homestead Act (offering free land to settlers), increasing industrialization and road-building brought rapid growth in population; and Catholics grew more numerous. It was Father Galtier from Dubuque whose log chapel, built in 1841, gave its name to the future great city and archdiocese. St. Paul became a diocese in 1850, with Most Rev. Joseph Cretin as bishop. He started a seminary with two students for the priesthood in his own house. He brought in several religious congregations, notably the Benedictines who arrived in 1856 and began the work which developed into St. John's Abbey and University, Collegeville. Succeeding bishops continued building up the Church. In 1888 St. Paul became an archdiocese; a year later, Duluth, St. Cloud and Winona were made dioceses. In 1909 Crookston was established as a diocese, followed by New Ulm in 1958. Minnesota has about 1 million Catholics, in a total population of 3½ million.

minor orders The first four orders following tonsure through which all aspirants to major orders must pass. They are not part of the Sacrament of Holy Orders but requisites. Those in these orders are clerics with clerical privileges but are free to withdraw at any time. In the Western Church these orders are four: porter, lector, exorcist and acolyte. The duties connected with these orders are now performed by others. In the Eastern Church only the Armenians and Malabarese follow the Western custom.

miracle (L. *mirari,* to wonder at) An observable effect in the moral or physical order which is in contravention to natural laws and which cannot be explained by any natural power but only by the power of God. It is opposed to the law of nature for one dead to be restored to life or to walk upon water. It is independent of the law of nature to make a sudden and immediate cure without medical care or treatment. Since God is the author of the laws of nature, He alone has the power to act independently of this law or to set it aside. Christ promised to continue the power of miracles in His Church. The Catholic Church has displayed miracles throughout its history and will continue to do so. Every Catholic must believe this truth. However, belief in individual miracles depends upon evidence and investigation. The Church admits a miracle only when every possible natural explanation has been exhausted. Evidence of miracles of the present time can be found at Lourdes, Fatima, St. Anne de Beaupré in Canada and elsewhere. Ordinarily at least two miracles must be proved for canonization.

miracle of grace   A spiritual conversion. This is not a miracle in the literal sense but is due to the operation of God's grace in an unusual way which has the result of working a remarkable change in a soul. Such changes would be from ignorance to faith, from doubt to certainty, from attachment to sin to holiness.

miracle play   Also called a mystery play, a popular type of religious drama of the Middle Ages. Miracle plays dealt with events from the Old and New Testaments, the lives of saints and with mysteries of faith. They originated within the Church, having a connection with the liturgy. They were originally in Latin. As they appeared in the vernacular, they moved outside the Church as the liturgical connection ceased, but they retained their religious motivation.

miracles of Christ   The miracles performed by Jesus Christ are given as proof of His divinity. God alone can work a miracle and as St. Thomas Aquinas points out, "any single miracle done by Christ by his own power is sufficient proof that he is God" (*Summa Theologica* III, xliii, 4 ad 3). The miracles of Christ are traditionally divided into five classes. 1. *Nature miracles*. Nine of these are listed: water into wine at Cana (Jn. 2), first draught of fishes (Lk. 5), calming of the tempest (Matt. 8), first multiplication of loaves (Matt. 14), walking on the water (Matt. 14), second multiplication of loaves (Matt. 15), stater in mouth of fish (Matt. 17), cursing the fig tree (Matt. 21), second draught of fishes (Jn. 21.) 2. *Healing miracles*. There are many references in the Gospels to cures worked by Jesus that are not recorded in detail. However, twenty such cures are given fully: the nobleman's son (Jn. 4), the mother-in-law of Peter (Matt. 8), the leper (Matt. 8), the paralytic (Matt. 9), the impotent man at Bethesda (Jn. 5), the man with the withered hand (Matt. 12), the centurion's servant (Matt. 8), the one blind and dumb (Matt. 12), woman with an issue of blood (Matt. 9), the two blind men (Matt. 9), the dumb man (Matt. 9), the deaf and dumb man (Mk. 7), the blind man at Bethsaida (Mk. 8), the lunatic child (Matt. 17), the one born blind (Jn. 9), the woman with the infirmity caused by a spirit (Lk. 13), the man with dropsy (Lk. 14), the ten lepers (Lk. 17), the blind man near Jericho (Matt. 20), the servant of the high priest (Lk. 22). 3. *Miracles of raising the dead*. To prove His Messiahship to John the Baptist, Christ gave as one sign the fact that "the dead rise again." This statement has made some scriptural scholars think that there were more cases of resurrection than those recorded in the Gospels. This is quite possible. Those cases listed are: the daughter of Jairus (Matt. 9), the son of the widow of Naim (Lk. 7), Lazarus (Jn. 11). 4. *Miracles of the possessed*. Scriptural scholars on the basis of Mk. 1:39 believe that there are many more cures of demoniacs than mentioned in the Gospels. Those related are: the demoniac at

Capharnaum (Mk. 1), the blind and dumb demoniac (Matt. 12), the Gerasene demoniacs (Matt. 8), the dumb demoniac (Matt. 9), daughter of the Syro-Phoenician woman (Matt. 15), lunatic child (Matt. 17), woman with the spirit of infirmity (Lk. 13). 5. *Victories over hostile wills.* It is not clear whether those cases in which Christ wielded extraordinary power over His enemies were miraculous or not. He may have succeeded simply by the superiority of His will to their wills. Typical of these cases is Jn. 7:30 in which no man dared to lay hands on Him because His hour was not yet come. However, a substantial number of commentators hold that two incidents involve a supernatural display of power: the casting out of vendors (Jn. 2) and the escape from the hostile crowd at Nazareth (Lk. 4).

Miraculous Medal An oval medal of  the Blessed Virgin that originated with St. Catherine Labouré, a Sister of Charity of St. Vincent de Paul, who had three visions in 1830 during the course of which the medal was revealed to her. It bears on one side the image of the Blessed Virgin with the words: "O Mary, Conceived without Sin, Pray for Us Who Have Recourse to Thee." On the reverse side is the letter M with a cross and twelve stars, and beneath are the hearts of Jesus and Mary. It is highly indulgenced. The medal takes its name not from any miracles it works but from its origin. In the United States the Vincentian Fathers are responsible for its promotion.

Miserere (me-say-ray'ray; L. have mercy) The name for Psalm 50 which begins with this word. This is the fourth penitential psalm; the Church has always considered it the chief psalm of penance. It is traditionally the repentance and confession of David after his sin with Bethsabee. It is used in the Divine Office, in the consecration of a church and altar, at burials, in reconciling a profaned church and on many other occasions. In those monasteries and convents where the discipline is taken, it is recited during the exercise.

misericord (me-say'ree-cord; L. *misericordia,* pity) A narrow ledge on the underside of a choir stall. When the seat is raised, a standing person can lean against it and support some of his weight.

Missa (mees'sah) The Latin term for Mass.

Missa Cantata The Latin name for a sung Mass. In common use it means a sung Mass with one priest as distinguished from a Solemn High Mass.

Missa de Angelis 1. The Latin name for the votive Mass of the Holy Angels which is assigned to Tuesday. 2. The name of the Eighth Mass of Gregorian plain chant as found in the *Liber Usualis.* The name was used because of its beautiful melodies.

Missa pro Populo (L. Mass of the People) Canon law requires pastors and bishops to offer Mass for their people on Sundays, holydays of obligation and certain other days. It must be offered by the pastor or bishop himself unless he is legitimately impeded. No stipend can be taken for this Mass.

Missa Recitata (L. Recited Mass) *See* Dialogue Mass.

Missa Solemnis The Latin term for High Mass (*q.v.*).

missal (L. *missa,* Mass) The liturgical

book of the Roman Rite containing the formulas and prayers used in the celebration of the Mass. It contains the Ordinary and Proper. It contains special Masses, plus prayers to be said before and after Mass. The official text is the *Missale Romanum* from which translations are made. More and more of the laity are using missals at Mass; these missals take many forms, such as the "Dialogue Missal," used at Dialogue Masses; "Sunday Missal," containing only Sunday and Holy Day Masses; "Continuous Missal," which prints the Ordinary and Proper of the Mass together so that there is no turning to other sections.

missal stand The wooden or metal stand which supports the missal when it is placed on the altar at Mass. In some places a cushion is used as the support. It is also becoming more common to place the missal flat on the altar, particularly when Mass is said facing the congregation.

Missale Romanum (The Roman Missal) The official liturgical book used in the celebration of Mass. It is in Latin. The missal began to take form in the 9th century. The present Roman Missal appeared in 1570 under Pope Pius V and has gone through revisions under various popes. It is the source for various translations into the vernacular.

missiology A specialized branch of scientific theology which concerns itself with the theological and pastoral postulates governing the establishment of the Church in those geographical areas where it has not as yet taken root as a visible, hierarchical, social entity capable of independent growth. As is evident in its New Testament origins, the Church is essentially missionary, founded by Christ to actualize among men the universal redemption which He accomplished. The history of the last nineteen centuries gives proof of the Church's consciousness of her essential nature. Christian missionaries have roamed over the world endeavoring to build up the Body of Christ. What is recent in this consciousness of the Church is an awareness of the need to clarify the principles and techniques which energize this missionary activity. As a scientific study missiology has its roots in the work of the German Protestant theologians of the late nineteenth century, chiefly in the work of Gustave Warneck, 1834–1910. Catholic interest in missiology may be traced to the work of two German-speaking priests, Father Robert Streit, O.M.I., 1875–1930, and Father Joseph Schmidlin, 1876–1944. The early years of Catholic missiology were characterized by the strong emphasis placed by Schmidlin, following in the footsteps of Warneck, on the conversion of individual pagans. A new current in Catholic mission thought is evident with the appearance of the writings of the Belgian Jesuit, Pierre Charles, which insist that the only adequate object of missionary endeavor is the establishment of the visible Church in any region where it does not exist. It is this latter teaching which was appropriated in the missionary encyclicals of Pius XII, *Evangelii Praecones,* and of John XXIII, *Princeps Pastorum.* Current missiology is engaged in clarifying the theological basis for mission work in biblical, dogmatic, patristic, ethical and apologetic sources. Missiologists have isolated and developed canon law in its specific reference to missionary endeavor, and are responsible for the growth of a detailed and analytical history of the missions. To missiology is to be credited also the enlightened interest in the assistance for missionary methodology and technique which is to be found in a study of the social sciences such as ethnology, cultural anthropology, sociology, linguistics and the history of religions.

mission country Strictly speaking, those nations whose religious jurisdiction in the Western Church falls under the Sacred Congregation of Propaganda. Formerly the ecclesiastical territories were divided into vicariates and prefectures but in recent years it has been the growing custom to make established missions into ordinary dioceses. However, many other parts of the world are, loosely speaking, mission territories. This is particularly true of Latin America in which many areas have long been without priests with the result that the people are Catholic in name but not in practice.

Mission Indians A term applied to members of those California Indian tribes who had been evangelized by the California missions. When the missioners came they found these Indians living in great squalor and poverty with little organization and no agriculture. The missioners domesticated the Indians, taught them trades and the practice of farming. However with the suppression of the missions, the Indians rapidly disappeared and are now practically extinct.

mission of Christ The salvation of the world was the mission given Christ by the Father. Christ declared this Himself when He said: "I have not come to judge the world, but to save the world" (Jn. 12:47). Christ

founded His Church to continue this mission, to reveal Him to the world that through Him all mankind might find salvation. Through the Church every member is to partake in this mission. Therefore, the mission of every Catholic is the same mission as that of Christ, namely, the salvation of the world. God and the Gospels are world-conscious. "God so loved the world that He gave His only-begotten Son." The last instruction given by Christ before He departed this earth carried the same concern for humanity: "Go, therefore, and make disciples of all the nations." The Church exists to carry on this work of salvation; this is its reason for being, its essential apostolate.

mission of the Christian Every Catholic through Baptism has the same mission as Christ, namely, the salvation of all men. This salvation must affect man in all his human aspirations and spiritual complexities.

mission of the Church A notion derived from Christ's mission into the world. The second Person of the Trinity was sent (mission) into the world by the Father for the redemption of mankind by gathering together in His love the human race that had been divided and dispersed by sin. This "gathering together" was to be brought about through His threefold office of Prophet (preaching), King (jurisdiction) and Priest (sacrifice). Christ extended through space and time is the Church continuing His mission in history throughout the world.

mission, popular Another name for a parish mission. These missions are preached in parishes at regular intervals, usually separately for men and women. They last up to a week and have the purpose of restoring the spiritual fervor of the parishioners. Special mission bands go from parish to parish in this work. At one time the preaching of these missions was confined to members of religious orders but in recent years it has not been uncommon for a diocese to organize its own mission band of secular priests.

Mission Secretariat An organization founded in 1950 and composed of United States societies that send missioners to foreign lands. The aim of the organization is to provide a means for mutual cooperation and the interchange of information. Additional objectives are: to provide a convenient means of contact among missionary communities and with governmental and nongovernmental agencies touching on mission work; to serve as an inquiry center for community headquarters and American missioners in the field; to assist United States Catholic mission-aid societies in their relationships with governmental and nongovernmental agencies; to compile statistics and other information on mission work.

missionary accommodation The adaption of the Church to the living culture in which it is placed. Father Louis Luzbetak, S.V.D., calls it "the respectful, prudent, scientifically and theologically sound adjustment of the Church to the native culture in attitude, outward behavior, and practical apostolic approach." The modern popes have insisted that the missioner goes to another land not to take Western culture but to take Christ, and that Christ belongs to all men and, therefore, is adaptable to all cultures. The Catholic nature of the Church is also able to embrace all cultures so that the Church is nowhere a stranger.

Missionary Benedictine Sisters Founded in Germany in 1885, established in the United States in 1923. The Sisters lead an active life and take simple vows. Sisters are engaged in teaching, catechetics, nursing and filling posts as hospital technicians. There are 1,200 members.

Missionary Franciscan Sisters of the Immaculate Conception Founded in Minnesota in 1873 by Mother Mary Ignatius Hayes, the community is primarily engaged in teaching and social service. There is a Negro mission in the south and missions in Egypt, Australia and New Guinea. The community numbers over 850 Sisters. Simple vows are taken.

Missionary Sisters of St. Augustine Founded in India in 1897, established in the United States in 1919. Members are engaged in teaching, nursing, social work and training native Sisters. Missions are staffed in India, Hong Kong, Taiwan, Philippines, Congo, West Indies. Simple vows are taken. There are approximately 1,300 members.

Missionary Sisters of the Immaculate Conception The first Canadian missionary foundation for women (1902) and established in the United States in 1946. Missions are staffed in Bolivia, Chile, Peru, Guatemala, Haiti, Japan, Taiwan, the Philippines, Africa and the Malagasy Republic. There are approximately 1,000 members.

missions, foreign Mission in its broadest sense refers to any commission or power for carrying out an assignment. In theology "mission" or "sending forth" has its principle in the Trinity, the Father sending forth the Son into the world. Christ in turn sent forth the Apostles to "preach the gospel to every creature." In this sense of "preaching the gospel," mission may be described as a preaching to Christians to stir up the grace that is in them, or as a preaching to pagans to announce the good news of salvation *(see* kerygma). The latter is usually termed "foreign" missions, since historically Christianity developed in Western civilization, and countries not in the geographical sphere of this civilization were considered "foreign." The missionary, however, is an emissary of Christ not of a continent, a country, a culture or of commerce.

missions, home   Those areas of the United States where the Church is not now established or which lack sufficient priests or means to maintain and extend the Church. It is estimated that over 700 counties in the United States do not have a resident priest. In order to counteract these conditions, many religious congregations have been taking up work in these priestless areas. Several societies in particular are devoted exclusively to this work, the chief of which are the Glenmary Fathers and Sisters, and the Trinitarians. Financial assistance is given by the Extension Society and 40 per cent of the Mission Sunday collection is assigned to the home missions.

missions, various   *See* Indian missions; Negro missions, etc.

Mississippi   (Chippewa, Big River) The 20th state admitted to the Union, it is 32nd in area and 29th in population. Before the coming of the white man, tribes of hunting and fishing Indians had developed the culture of corn in the rich Mississippi basin. De Soto explored the area in 1539, Father Marquette and Joliet came in 1673, and La Salle claimed the entire basin for France in 1682, naming it Louisiana for the king. Spain, France and Great Britain at times held parts of the area. The first Mass was offered near Fort Adams by Franciscan Father Membre, who came with La Salle in 1682. Between 1716 and 1730 the Natchez Indians were given genocidal treatment by white planters, and by 1832 the Choctaws and Chickasaws were deported to Indian Territory. Between 1729 and 1736 three missioners, Fathers du Poisson, Souel and Senat, were martyred by the Arkansas Indians. The United States having gained possession of the area in piecemeal fashion, Mississippi was admitted to the Union in 1817. The few Catholics had been served by Spanish priests or transients until Natchez was made a diocese in 1837, with Most Rev. John J. Chance as first bishop. He arrived in 1841, having no church, priests, schools, or funds. During his 11-year episcopate he built a cathedral, founded an orphanage and a school with Sisters of Charity from Maryland in charge, and managed to get 11 priests established in 11 churches. Succeeding bishops brought in more religious congregations and established the Church more firmly. Catholics in Mississippi number less than 70 thousand in a total population of over 2 million.

Missouri   The 24th state admitted to the Union, it is 19th in area and 13th in population. Its name, from the Missouri Indians and the Missouri River, means "has canoe." The first white men in the area came down the Mississippi: Father Marquette and Louis Joliet in 1673; La Salle in 1682. French traders were doing business with the Osage and Missouri Indians on the Missouri River in the late 17th century. Priests from the Quebec Seminary set up St. Francis Xavier Mission in 1700–1703, near present day St. Louis. Frenchmen from New Orleans founded St. Louis in 1764. After the American Revolution and the Louisiana Purchase immigration increased and Missouri was admitted to the Union in 1821. Louis Du Bourg, Bishop of Louisiana Territory made St. Louis his headquarters (1818–1826). He established Kenrick Seminary and brought in religious orders of men and women who staffed educational and charitable institutions. In 1824 Louisiana was divided into different dioceses and Bishop Rosati was placed in charge of St. Louis. St. Louis College, a Jesuit institution, received its charter as St. Louis University in 1832, the oldest university west of the Mississippi. Many Catholic immigrants came from Germany and Ireland during the 19th century, building up a strong Catholicity. In 1847 St. Louis became an archdiocese; in 1868 the Diocese of St. Joseph was established; Kansas City in 1880. In 1956 Kansas City and St. Joseph were combined into one diocese. In the same year Jefferson City and Springfield-Cape Girardeau were erected as dioceses. In the meantime, in 1946, Archbishop John Glennon was made a Cardinal by Pope Pius XII; in 1961 Pope John XXIII gave the red hat to Archbishop Joseph Ritter. Catholics today number three quarter of a million in a total population of 4½ million.

mitre (Gr. *mitra,* a turban)   The liturgical headdress of bishops and abbots of the Latin Rite. It is made of linen, cloth of gold or silk and is often ornamented. The front and back of it are stiffened and each part comes to a peak. It has two lappets hanging down the back. The golden mitre of plain cloth of gold

is worn during Advent and Lent and at other penitential times. The ornamented mitre which is adorned with gems is worn on feasts; in paschal time; and on Sundays outside of Septuagesima, Lent and Advent. The simple mitre which is of plain white material is worn at funerals, on Good Friday, when blessing candles on Candlemas and when attending the pope. Minor prelates are usually restricted to the simple mitre.

mixed marriage   The marriage of a Catholic and non-Catholic, also called mixed religion. While the Church disapproves of mixed marriage because of the danger to the Faith of the Catholic partner and the offspring, dispensation can be granted. The Church requires that the marriage be performed only before a priest, and that the non-Catholic party sign an agreement that he or she will not interfere with the practice of religion of the Catholic party and that any offspring of the union will be baptized and brought up in the Catholic religion.

Modernism   A term used by those who followed a doctrine condemned by Pope St. Pius X in his encyclical *Pascendi Gregis* (Sept. 7, 1907) which called it a "synthesis of all heresies." The movement began with the Reformation and developed to the point under Pius X that it was an aggression against true religion. It taught that the Christ of faith was not the Christ of history, that He did not personally found the Church or sacraments but that these were historical developments. Its advocates sought freedom from religious authority and the emancipation of conscience; they assumed that everything modern was more perfect that what had gone before. Modernism denied dogma, the true efficacy of the sacraments and the authority of Scripture. The doctrine was penetrating the clergy when Pius X exposed its falsity and sounded its death knell.

modesty (L. *modestus,* modest) The virtue of moderation in one's personal life, in habits, attitudes, speech, dress, etc. The virtue has a certain relativity depending on place, time and circumstance. Thus what is permissible for a lay person is not necessarily permissible for a cleric, or what is allowed a husband and wife is not necessarily allowed an engaged couple. Dress suitable for swimming or for a beach would not be suitable in church. Also standards change with time; the dress of a modern woman would have been considered immodest in Victorian days. The virtue is closely allied to temperance.

Mohammedanism *See* Islam. The followers of Muhammad object to this term because they hold that their religion preceded Muhammad and that the use of this name gives the false impression that they worship Muhammad.

monachism (Gr. monos, alone) Another term for monasticism (*q.v.*).

monastery (Gr. *monasterion,* a hermit's cell) Strictly, the home of a community of monks or nuns devoted to the contemplative life and who usually recite the Divine Office in common. It is canonically erected and ordinarily has an enclosure. Today the term is also applied to the dwelling places of clerics such as the Capuchins or Passionists and nuns who lead a cloistered life. Franciscan custom speaks of their dwelling place as a friary, while Dominicans call their home a priory.

Monastic Breviary (L. *Breviarium Monasticum*) The Office used by Benedictines and others, differing in many respects from the Roman Breviary. The Psalms are assigned differently, lessons differ, and so on.

monasticism That manner of life practiced by monks who live together under a common rule, who are secluded from the world in order to devote themselves fully to the service of God. Monasticism is either eremetical (solitary) or cenobitical (community). It is found both in Western and Eastern Christianity but is not exclusive to Christianity since Buddhists, Shintoists, Confucianists and Muslims also practice monasticism. In monasticism the life is lived primarily for its own sake and therefore such religious orders as Capuchins, Dominicans, Franciscans, etc., are not strictly monastic but follow particular works such as preaching, teaching, etc.

monasticism, Eastern 1. *Monasticism* is said to have begun in Egypt when St. Anthony gathered various hermits about him (305) in northern Egypt. No rule governed the monks who led individualistic lives, following their own preferences in religious practices. St. Pachomius (*c.* 318) developed the monastic system where the monks led a common life. St. Basil (*c.* 360) developed Greek monasticism, placing a higher value on work than austerities. He founded a monastery at Pontus in Neo-Caesarea in which prayer, work and scriptural readings were balanced. 2. *Catholic monasticism.* This would include such groups as the Basilians, Antonians, Mekhitarists, etc. 3. *Orthodox monasticism.* These monks follow what they call the "Angelic Life." It is little changed since the 4th century. Each monastery is independent and under its own rule. In place of the work advocated by St. Basil, these monasteries have returned to austerities and are contemplative, given to much prayer and fasting. They practice great austerities and fasts, abstain from meat, engage in much prayer and the singing of the Divine Office. Mount Athos is the center for Orthodox monasticism.

monasticism, Western St. Benedict of Nursia (*c.* 480–547) and his rule are largely responsible for the development of Western monasticism. St. Benedict adapted the monastic ideas of St. Pachomius and St. Basil to European conditions: many of the austere practices were dropped, monks were bound by a vow of stability to their monasteries, the singing of the Divine Office in common and daily work were the principal features. "To work is to pray" became one of the guiding rules of the new communities. At first only those needed to serve the community were ordained but by the year 1000 it had become the ordinary practice to ordain members. Today the Cistercians live close to the original Benedictine Rule while other branches of the family are engaged in teaching, writing, liturgical promotion and mission activities.

money, biblical At the time of Jesus the main coins used in Palestine were the standard Roman coins and a variety of coins of local mintage. The most important Roman coin was the silver *denarius,* which represented a day's wage for an ordinary laborer. It was approximately equal to the Greek *drachma,* another coin commonly used. An important coin also was the silver *shekel,* a Jewish coin worth four drachmas, which is the coin mentioned in the "thirty pieces" paid to Judas. The *didrachma* or half *shekel* was the coin used in the yearly temple tribute. A *talent* equaled 3,000 *shekels.* The "widow's mite" was a *lepton,* the smallest Greek

copper coin, or the *kodrantes,* the Greek name for the *quadrans,* the smallest Roman copper coin.

Monism (Gr. *monos,* single) A philosophical system which makes reality the ground of all existence. It is materialistic in mode, basing its teaching on the doctrine that all things proceed from matter which is in evolution. It denies all duality of matter and spirit.

Monita Secreta (L. secret instructions) A forged document attributed to the Jesuits which outlined methods for the Jesuits to increase their power and influence. It gave instructions for the cultivation of rich widows, the enticement of rich young men into the Society, the belittling of other orders and how Jesuits were to become bishops. The document first appeared in Cracow, Poland, in 1612 and was written by Jerome Zahorowski, who had been expelled from the Jesuits the previous year. Historians have long discounted the authenticity of the document.

monk (Gr. *monos,* alone) A member of a religious community of men, living a life of prayer and penance apart from the world, under the vows of poverty, chastity and obedience. The name is sometimes extended to Capuchins, Franciscans, Dominicans and like groups, but it is not accurate since members of these communities move about in the world teaching and preaching. Members of the Benedictines, Carthusians, Trappists, Premonstratensians, Camaldolese and Cluniacs are monks in the strict sense.

monogenesis (Gr. *mono,* one; *gignesthai,* be born) The teaching of the Church that the human race has descended from a single pair of parents. It is opposed to polygenesis which gives multiple origins for the human race.

monograms, sacred The combining of two or more letters to form one character is often used in Christian art. Two of the most popular are IHS to represent the Greek name of Jesus and the chi rho to represent the Greek name of Christ.

Monophysism (Gr. one nature) A heresy of early Christan times claiming that there is only one nature in Jesus Christ, His humanity being entirely absorbed in His divinity, and His body not of the same substance as ours. In reacting against the Nestorian heresy of two persons in Christ, the Monophysites erred in denying the hypostatic union of the divine and human natures in the one divine person. The Greek Archimandrite Eutyches and the Patriarch of Alexandria were among the chief original proponents of this heresy about 448. It was condemned in the Council of Chalcedon in 451.

Monophysitism Monophysism (*q.v.*).

Monotheism (Gr. one God) The doctrine of belief in the existence of only one God.

Monothelism (Gr. one will) In an effort to reconcile the Monophysites to the Church certain Eastern zealots fell into error concerning the human will of Jesus Christ, teaching that He had only one will. This was condemned by the Third Council of Constantinople in 680, which stated the Catholic doctrine that Christ has two wills, divine and human, not contrary to each other but that the human will follows and is subject to the divine will, hence, operating together in perfect harmony.

Mons Pietatis (L. mountain of piety) The name given to pawnshops begun in the 16th century with the object of making small loans to the poor at low rates of interest. They were en-couraged by the Fifth Lateran Council (1511) which cleared them of charges of usury. They began in Italy and spread to France, Spain and the Low Countries. Today they are no longer operated by the Church but have become municipal institutions. In Mexico City there is a *Monte de Piedad* operated by the national government; it was founded in 1775.

monsignor (It. my lord) 1. A title of distinction given to minor prelates of the Roman court. In the United States the title is bestowed on members of the clergy for their services to the Church. Monsignors are entitled to wear violet vestments. In the United States the following classes of monsignori (pl.) are to be found: Protonary Apostolic, Domestic Prelate and Papal Chamberlain. The formal title for the first two is Right Reverend, and the latter is Very Reverend. There are other grades in Rome: Auditor of the Rota, Privy Chamberlain, Honorary Chamberlain. 2. In certain countries a bishop is addressed as monsignor.

monstrance (L. *monstrare,* to show) A tall vessel, generally silver- or gold-plated, used to expose the Blessed Sacrament. The top is usually circular with simulated sun rays coming from the center where the lunette (*q.v.*) is inserted so that the Host can be seen by the people. Below the circular part is a handle for carrying and lifting the monstrance, and at the bottom is a base on which it stands. It is used at Benediction and for Exposition of the Blessed Sacrament. It is also called an ostensorium.

monstrosities A monstrous form of the fetus must be baptized absolutely if living or conditionally if there is any doubt of life. If there is doubt whether there is one or more persons, one should be baptized absolutely (if alive) and the other conditionally.

Montana The 41st state admitted to the Union, it is 4th in area, 41st in population. Its name is Latin for "mountainous." Indians of various tribes hunted buffalo, elk and deer, and fought a losing battle against the white man's advance. Montana was partly explored in 1743 by Canadians, Sieur de la Verendrye and his sons, accompanied by Jesuit Father Cloquart. The United States acquired the territory by the Louisiana Purchase in 1803, and Lewis and Clark traversed it the following year. Fur-trading companies did a thriving business; cattle ranches prospered; gold, silver and copper were discovered; the Northern Pacific Railway was finished in 1883—all combining to bring in settlers. The Jesuits cared for Indian missions in the area from 1833, the Flatheads having sent 4 delegations to St. Louis asking for Blackrobes to teach them to pray like the Iroquois of Canada, with the "great prayer" (the Mass). Father de Smet made seven trips to Europe gaining funds and more than 100 priests for the Indians; missions were established in Bitter Root Valley, at St. Ignatius and at Alder Gulch. Sisters of Providence and of Charity were brought in to care for Indians and whites. In 1866 eastern Montana was placed under the bishop of St. Louis, the western section under Oregon. In 1877 the sections were united under Most Rev. J. Brondel as bishop of Helena. Succeeding bishops continued to build up the Church, establishing a seminary, numerous churches and works of education and charity staffed by men and women religious.

The Diocese of Great Falls was established in 1904. Today there are about 158,000 Catholics, in a total population of 674,767.

Monte Cassino Monastery founded by St. Benedict in 529 on a hill in central Italy near a place called Cassino, hence the name Monte Cassino. It is considered to be the mother-monastery of all the Benedictine foundations in the world. It was here that St. Benedict wrote his famous rule which became a model for Western monasticism. St. Benedict died here Mar. 31, 547. When the original structure was destroyed by the Lombards in 577, the monks fled to Rome. The monastery was not rebuilt until 717. During the long course of its history Monte Cassino has been destroyed many times: by the Saracens in the 9th century; by an earthquake in the 14th; the latest destruction was by Allied bombers during World War II (Feb.-May, 1944). The monks began rebuilding the monastery after the war and by 1954 the structure had been nearly completed. American soldiers contributed generously to the cost of reconstruction. In May of 1963 the new church was dedicated. Pope John XXIII was scheduled to perform this ceremony (the churches of Monte Cassino had all been dedicated by popes) but he was struck down by his final illness and the task was finally performed by Paul VI in 1965. The monastery, which, in addition to the cloister, houses a minor seminary and a major seminary for the training of secular priests, has been an abbey nullius (*q.v.*) since John XXII erected it to that rank in 1322. John XXIII named the present abbot as bishop of Monte Cassino, a large diocese of 70 parishes with a population of more than 100,000 people.

Montessori Method A system of child pedagogy developed by Dr. Maria Montessori (d. 1952) which is based on a principle of freedom in a prepared environment. It creates a natural atmosphere for the child and provides education through the senses, sense training and self-activity. It aims to develop the child's capabilities and creativeness, using the child's own psychological growth. The first schools were started in Europe before World War I but were slow to gain hold in the United States due to the resistance of the disciples of John Dewey. In recent years, largely through the efforts of Nancy Rambusch, Catholic-orientated Montessori schools have been opening in various parts of the United States.

Month's Mind Mass A name given to a Requiem Mass offered for a deceased person a month following death.

Montreal The second oldest diocese in Canada; established in 1836. It takes its name from the city founded by the Company of Our Lady of Montreal which had been formed by the Sulpician, Father Olier, and a M. de la Duaversiere. Father Olier persuaded Philip Maisonneuve to purchase the island for the purpose of colonization. Maisonneuve arrived at the foot of Mount Royal in 1642. The colony ran into many difficulties and growth was slow. In 1663 the company ceded its rights to the Society of St. Sulpice and within five years eleven Sulpicians were working in Montreal. Growth from that time on was slow but steady. Montreal became a refuge for priests driven from France during the Revolution. Today, the city is one of the more important cities in the Western hemisphere.

moral conduct That conduct which conforms to the norms of Christian morality.

moral person A canonical term that refers to a juridical person other than a human being. Thus a parish, a collegiate chapter, certain pious associations, religious orders, benefices and seminaries are constituted as moral persons. A moral person by its very nature is perpetual; it can be legitimately suppressed; it also ceases when *de facto* it has not existed for a hundred years.

moral philosophy A system of thought which derives guiding principles for moral action from philosophical reflection on man and on his environment.

Moral Rearmament A movement whose adherents deny that they constitute a church or a distinct religion. They have no church buildings, no ministers, no sacraments, no rites and may attend various churches according to their choice. The aim of MRA is to change the hearts of men and so to change the world, overcoming Communism, bringing social order, peace and prosperity. It uses all means of communication: teaching, preaching, the press, the theater. It follows Protestant revivalism in many ways, with orthodox Christian teaching in regard to Christ, prayer and the work of the Holy Spirit in souls. MRA was founded by Dr. Frank Buchman, a Lutheran minister, born in Pennsylvania and converted to a new type of thought while in England. There his following was called the Oxford Group; later in Germany in 1938 Moral Rearmament was adopted as the official title. One of Buchman's means is the "spiritual house party," which in Catholic circles would be called a weekend retreat, held in some wealthy person's home or in a hotel. There are spiritual talks, games, recreation, hours of silence, meals in common, confessions and testimonials. The house parties drew hundreds, then thousands. The Hollywood Bowl was filled for a MRA rally in 1939. They have two training centers, one at Mackinac Island, Mich., and the other in Switzerland. Full-time workers, some thousands in number, give all their property to MRA and receive room, board and minimum expense money. Sympathizers and informal members number hundreds of thousands. Like the Catholic Christophers and Better World Movement, they have no formal initiation; they simply begin living according to Buchman's ideas. These include public confession of all personal sins, a practice which has caused considerable trouble. After confession, the neophyte accepts Jesus Christ as his personal Savior, then spends 15 or more minutes a day in silent meditation, seeking guidance from the Holy Spirit and jotting down the thoughts which come to him as being inspirations from God. He then sets out to share his faith, trying to change the lives of others. MRA is considered to be more a spiritual discipline than a church.

moral sense An ethical theory that the basis for a moral judgment resides in an independent intuitive power, apart from the intellect. One thereby makes a moral judgment on the basis of one's feeling of the rightness or wrongness of an action. This is opposed by Catholic moral teaching. The basis for a correct moral judgment is objective knowledge acquired through the power of the intellect.

morality A term applied to human conduct. It is a norm which determines whether human actions are right and fitting, or bad and unbefitting. It is intimately bound up with religion. The act must be considered, its circumstances, and the ends.

morality play A type of religious drama that was popular in the 15th and 16th centuries. *Everyman* is the best known example of this type of play. These dramas were concerned with the struggle between vice and virtue. They were often performed outdoors on the steps of a cathedral, and were very popular with strolling players.

Moravian Brethren A Christian evangelical sect that developed from the teachings of John Huss. It takes its name from the fact that it first flourished in Bohemia and Moravia. Members of the group came to the American colonies settling first in Georgia and then in Pennsylvania where they founded Bethlehem and Nazareth.

morganatic marriage *See* marriage, morganatic.

Moriscos The Moors, especially of Spain; originally the natives of Morocco or Muslims of North Africa, especially the Saracenic invaders of Spain and their descendants.

Mormons Popular name for members of the Church of Jesus Christ of the Latter-day Saints. A religious sect founded in America in 1830 at Fayette, N.Y., by Joseph Smith, a farm laborer. Smith claimed he received a revelation, through the Angel Moroni, from a prophet named Mormon who told him to establish a church, since all existing churches were unworthy. Smith gained followers, led them west and set up headquarters at Nauvoo, Ill. Here Smith added polygamy to his teachings, which stirred up neighbors who rioted, during which Smith was shot (1844). A remarkable man named Brigham Young then took over leadership and organized a heroic trek westward. In Salt Lake Valley they set up their theocracy, and through good planning and industry were soon thriving. The church ordered the discontinuance of polygamy in 1896 so that Utah might be admitted to the Union and the practice is now believed by all to be at an end. The Mormon doctrine is a confusion of spiritualism, materialism, Freemasonry, Judaism, Swedenborgianism, Campbellism, several pagan philosophies and Protestantism. Mormons believe that God the Father is a material being, a perfect man and a polygamist. God did not create matter; He organized it. Christ after His Resurrection set up His church in North America among the Indians, remnants of the lost tribes of Israel. God the Father procreated many souls destined to be gods after being born on earth if they receive Mormon baptism and keep the law of the church. "What man is now, God once was; what God is now, many may become." The Mormons have one doctrine which they preach, and another which is explained to initiates. Thousands of young Mormons, at their own expense, are serving as missionaries in many parts of the world. Brigham Young University has a $60 million campus with over 12,000 students. Every Mormon settlement has its meeting house, its social hall, a "seminary" close to a public school for released time instruction. The Mormons are distinguished by large families; high esteem for education; love of culture, music, the theater. Smoking and drinking alcoholic beverages are prohibited, also the use of tea and coffee. Mormons pay tithes to their church, which also engages in profitable business enterprises. Their self-supporting missionaries are in many parts of the world.

Morning Star 1. A title given to Christ in the Apocalypse (2:28). 2. A title given to Our Lady in the Litany of Loreto (Litany to the Blessed Virgin).

morse A metal clasp ornamented with jewels on a cope. It is worn only by a bishop or higher prelate when in his place of jurisdiction. Also called a *formale*.

mortal sin A grievous offense against God which destroys sanctifying grace and brings death to the soul. Three conditions are necessary for mortal sin: 1. grave matter determined by the object and circumstances of the act which is made known by the teaching authority of the Church, by theologians and the universal belief of the faithful; 2. full advertence to the moral nature of the act; 3. full consent. The latter is presumed to be present when there is full advertence. Advertence and consent are said to be imperfect when an act is committed when one is half-asleep or half-drunk; when the penitent is suffering from some psychosis such as hysteria, insanity, phobia, etc.; when the penitent is not in complete possession of himself because of blinding anger, vehement passion, etc.; when the penitent can positively and truthfully state that he would never have acted in the manner he did if he had thought about it seriously beforehand.

mortification (L. *mortificare,* to cause death) The struggle against one's evil inclinations in order to make them subject to the will, and the will, in turn, subject to the will of God.

It can also be practiced as a penance for past sins. Ascetical writers affirm that mortification is necessary for union with God, conformity to Christ and individual sanctification.

mortuary chapel   1. A chapel built as a burial place or shelter for the dead. 2. A chapel built in a cemetery and used for funeral purposes.

Mosaic Law   *See* Law, Mosaic.

Moses   The messenger and servant of God who was selected to lead the Israelites from Egypt and who was Israel's lawgiver. His burial place is unknown.

Most Reverend   The style of address in the United States used for bishops. Thus: "Most Reverend John Jones, Bishop of Peoria."

motet (Fr. *mot,* word)   A polyphonic choral composition, usually from Sacred Scripture. It is generally sung *a cappella* (*q.v.*).

mother church (L. *ecclesia matrix*) 1. The cathedral of a diocese. 2. In canon law a church (*ecclesia matrix*) with several chapels or outstations (*filiales*).

Mother of God   From earliest times the Church has held that Mary is the Mother of Jesus Christ who is both God and man and for this reason has paid her unusual honors. Early titles used for Mary were *Theotokos* (God-bearer), *Dei Genitrix* (Mother of God) and *Deipara* (God-bearing). Christ is the Incarnate Word, a divine Person who subsists in both divine and assumed human nature. Mary gave birth to Christ. Therefore Mary is the Mother of God. This does not mean that Mary generated the Godhead. Christ as God is immutable, not subject to change. The Word was eternally generated by the Father, and temporally generated by Mary. St. Cyril explained this by saying that our human soul is infused by God and does not derive from our parents, yet none of us would hesitate to call himself the son of his mother.

Mother Seton Sisters of Charity Founded in 1870 at Altoona, Pa., as an off-shoot of the Cincinnati foundation. Main work is teaching and hospitals; has missions in Korea. Takes simple vows. Approximately 750 Sisters in the United States.

motherhouse   1. The first religious house of an order or society from which other foundations developed. 2. The convent where a mother general resides.

motive   The cause that moves to action. The quality of an act depends upon the motive of the person performing the act. The motive of the person performing the act may turn an indifferent act into a good or evil act, increase or diminish the goodness of an act, increase or diminish the evil of an act; however, even a good motive cannot make an evil act good. The end does not justify the means and a good motive cannot justify the use of immoral means (Rom. 3:8). The motive for Christian action should be to do the will of God.

motu proprio (L. on one's own accord)   A papal doument that begins with the words *"motu proprio."* It is drawn up at the pope's own accord, bears no seal and lacks other formalities, and is signed by the pope. These documents can be instructive, administrative or confer special favor. The instruction of Pope St. Pius X on the use of plain chant was a *motu proprio.* Pope Paul VI has issued a number of such documents one of which was the *motu proprio* "In fructibus multas" which established the Pontifical Commission for Social Communications (*q.v.*).

Motu Proprio of Pius X   The instruction on sacred music issued in 1903 by Pope St. Pius X. It restored the primacy of plain chant in the liturgy of the Church and condemned many musical abuses that had crept into services.

Mount Carmel, Our Lady of Title and feast of Our Lady, originally proper to Carmelites, commemorating the reported vision, in July, 1251, of the giving of the brown scapular to St. Simon Stock. The feast is commemorated on July 16.

movable feast A feast which does not fall on a set calendar day. The Church calendar is based on the lunar-solar cycle. The key to setting feasts from this cycle is Easter, which falls on the first Sunday following the first full moon after the vernal equinox (which may be as early as Mar. 22 or as late as Apr. 25). From the date of Easter other movable feasts are determined. Besides Easter, movable feasts are Septuagesima, Sexagesima, Quinquagesima, Ash Wednesday, Ascension, Pentecost, Corpus Christi.

Mozarabic Rite *See* Toledo Rite.

mozzetta (It. *mozzo,* shortened) A short cape of silk or wool reaching to the elbows and with a modified hood in back. It buttons down the front. It is worn over the rochet (*q.v.*). It is worn by cardinals, archbishops and bishops in their own dioceses, and by an abbot in his abbey as a sign of jurisdiction. It is not a liturgical vestment.

Muratorian Canon, Muratorian Fragment The oldest and most important list of the books of the New Testament. It was discovered by L. A. Muratori in the Ambrosian Library of Milan, and published in 1740. The list on which it was based was written *c.* 185 in or near Rome.

murder (AS. *morthor*) The direct

and unlawful killing of another person. Direct killing is unlawful and never permitted except in the case of self-defense against an unjust aggressor, and then may not be used if a lesser degree of resistance will deter the aggression; it is also permitted in carrying out a death penalty which is justly and lawfully inflicted. Murder is a sin against justice since it deprives a person of life and God is deprived of His right to dispose of human life. *See* capital punishment; self-defense.

music, Church That music which is sung or played in the celebration of the Church's liturgy. It includes in the traditional order of importance and preference, 1. plain chant, 2. sacred polyphony, 3. modern sacred music, 4. popular religious song, and 5. religious music. The quality of this music must express holiness, beauty and form and universality. In mission lands where the people have their own musical traditions, these too are given a suitable place in native liturgical participation.

musical instruments In the Latin Church the pipe organ is held in high esteem as the traditional musical instrument in the Church's ceremonies. Other instruments may also be admitted for use in divine worship, with the consent of the territorial authority. The instruments must be suitable for sacred use, in keeping with the dignity of the place and the occasion and should contribute to the edification of the people.

Muslim A follower of the teaching of Islam, a religion founded by Muhammad. Its main strength is in Arabic countries, although it is the religion of Pakistan, and is making large gains in sub-Sahara Africa. It once flourished in North Africa and parts of Europe. Also Moslem.

mutilation of self An action by which one deprives himself of a bodily organ or its use. Mutilation belongs to the category of murder: the difference is that mutilation is partial destruction of the individual. One could, in an emergency when no one is present to help, remove a badly diseased or infected part of his body in order to save his life. In itself, mutilation of self is a grave sin, although it may be venial if the mutilation is slight. The gravity of the sin is measured by the importance of the organ involved.

mystery (Gr. *mysterion,* something closed) Theologically, a hidden or secret thing of a sacred character. Vatican Council I defined: "The divine mysteries by their very nature so transcend the created intellect that, even when revealed and believed, they still remain veiled and obscure during this mortal life." Thus a mystery can only be known by revelation while its essence cannot be fully understood or explained even after revelation. God is omniscient and infinite and it is a logical conclusion that the finite mind of man cannot fully understand or comprehend infinite truth. However if a mystery cannot be demonstrated by reason, it can be explained and defended.

mystery of faith 1. The Eucharist, so called because the words occur in the form of consecration. 2. A mystery (*q.v.*) such as the Blessed Trinity or the Incarnation. Such mysteries can be defended, but not comprehended by reason.

Mystical Body The Church of which Christ is the head; the Holy Spirit is the soul; and the faithful, living and dead, the members. The word "mystical" is not opposed to "real" but rather denotes a supernatural reality that is not physical. The doctrine derives from the teaching of Christ wherein He likens Himself to a vine of which all men are branches. St. Paul elucidated this teaching by showing that Christ is the new Adam who is the Head of humanity which has been redeemed in Him. Christ constitutes with humanity a body which is the mystical Christ. The body in a wide sense embraces all mankind, the object of salvation. But in a strict sense it is the Church which man enters through Baptism to participate in a supernatural life which flows from the Head into the members by the action of the Holy Spirit. Pope Pius XII develops this doctrine in his encyclical *Mystici Corporis.* Pope Pius declared that in defining the Church "we shall find nothing more noble, more sublime, or more divine than the expression 'the mystical body of Jesus Christ.' " There are many consequences flowing out of this doctrine, not the least of which is the identification of all members of the Mystical Body with one another and with Christ and the Holy Spirit. The Christian by his very nature becomes involved in the affairs of others, and this involvement is personal and proximate. Care must be taken however against a false mysticism which would absorb man and his personality in Christ to the point of fusing them in one physical person. At the same time there is a type of physical identification of one Christian with another and with Christ through the reception of the Holy Eucharist.

mystical interpretation of Scripture That interpretation of Scripture whereby a person, a thing or an event is used to typify something in the future. Thus Melchisedech typified the High Priesthood of Christ, and manna prefigured the Eucharist.

Mystical Rose A title of the Blessed

Virgin in the Litany of Loreto.

mystical theology The science that studies mysticism from a theological viewpoint. It is the highest development of ascetical theology since it considers the extraordinary ways of perfection, such as infused contemplation and mystical union.

mystical union The union of the soul with God in contemplation in order that the ascetic will come to know and love God in Christ as He knows and loves Himself, insofar as this is possible. There are specific grades of mystical union: the prayer of quiet, full union, ecstatic union and spiritual marriage.

Mystici Corporis Christi (L. Mystical Body of Christ) In modern usage it usually refers to Pope Pius XII's encyclical on the Mystical Body of Christ.

mysticism (Gr. *mistikos,* secret things) A superior, experimental knowledge of God's presence in the soul which results from a special movement of God, who allows the soul to feel His presence. Definite physiological or psychological phenomena are not essential to mysticism, but accompanying mysticism are often such phenomena as the stigmata, ecstasies, visions, levitations, supernatural caresses, fragrant odors, etc. However, St. Teresa of Avila and St. John of the Cross state that such experiences indicate an embryonic state in the mystical life. The mystics who have been canonized have gone beyond such experiences, and many never had them. The end of mysticism is the full realization that: "It is no longer I who live, it is Christ who lives in me."

N

Nahum A minor prophet, a patriot, author of the short Old Testament book bearing his name. It was written sometime about the fall of Ninive (612 B.C.).

Nails, the Holy The nails with which Our Lord was crucified are reputed to have been discovered with the True Cross by St. Helena. According to tradition Helena used one to make a crown for Constantine; and another, a bridle for his horse. The Iron Crown of Lombardy at Monza is said to be this crown. There are numerous claimed relics of the Holy Nails, some supposedly containing filings of the original nails, but none have been authenticated.

name, Christian 1. The name of a saint given to an individual at Baptism. 2. A name taken by a person at Confirmation, usually a saint's name, although in some areas the name of a feast is adopted. 3. The religious name given to a novice when the habit is received. Usually the person is addressed by this name and not by the family name. *See* religious name; *see* Appendix IX.

name day The feast of the saint after whom a religious or member of a religious institute has been named. In the religious life it is usually of more importance than one's birthday. In many areas of the world lay Catholics also pay particular celebration to the feasts of the saints after whom they have been named.

names of Our Lord Various names have been given to Christ in Sacred Scripture and in the liturgy. The liturgy (Mass and the Divine Office) gives Our Lord 64 different names, the Apostles and Evangelists give 62, the Old Testament gives 26, and Our Lord Himself gives 12. Terms used by Christ to describe Himself are: Bread of Life; Door; Good Shepherd; Life; Light of the World; Lord; Master; Resurrection and Life; Son; Son of Man; Vine; Way, Truth and Life.

narcotics It is not permissible to use narcotics—morphine, opium, barbituates, etc.—unless there is sufficient reason conducive to bodily health; e.g., by prescription of a doctor. Such remedies must be used with great care as they can cause grave harm to health and lead to addiction and its consequent moral breakdown. The taking of drugs without proper reason is mortally sinful when loss of reason occurs, although the act can be also mortally sinful if there is danger of addiction.

narthex (nar'theks, Gr.) Porch, vestibule or division of a church or basilica before the entrance proper. It was the part of a primitive Christian church near the entrance separated from the rest of the church by a screen of some type and used for catechumens and penitents; sometimes it is set aside for women.

Nathanael, St. First-century apostle mentioned in John (1:43-51) as a friend of Philip, who brought him to Christ; generally considered the personal name of Bartholomew.

National Catholic Community Service Established in 1940 by the United States hierarchy to serve members of the armed forces, and defense production workers and their families. It has been continued since World War II to serve the peacetime soldiers and patients in hospitals attached to the Veteran's Administration. It is the Catholic participating agent in the United Service Organizations (USO).

National Catholic Council for the Spanish Speaking An organization formed in 1960 under the auspices of the Bishops' Committee for the Spanish Speaking which has the purpose of furthering pastoral work among Spanish-speaking migrants and permanent residents of the United States.

National Catholic Educational Association An organization formed in 1904 to unite Catholic educational institutions, to create mutual understanding and to promote Catholic educational interests in the United States. The organization holds an annual national convention and regional meetings throughout the year. It has a national office in Washington, D.C.

National Catholic Welfare Conference Voluntary association of the hierarchy of the United States, established in 1919 to serve as a central agency for organizing and coordinating the efforts of American Catholics to carry out the social teachings of the Church. It is a clearing house of information and a national service center for Catholic efforts in broad fields of social significance—education, the press, immigration, social action, legislation, youth and lay organizations. Leadership is vested in an administrative board of ten members elected at the annual meeting of the United States hierarchy. It functions through this board, its Executive Department, and comprises seven departments with various offices and bureaus for specific fields of service and seventeen special episcopal committees.

National Council of Catholic Men, Women Federations of Catholic groups; NCCM is composed of representatives of nearly 8,000 affiliated lay organizations of men with approximately 9 million members; NCCW is a federation of 14,000 women's organizations with approximately 10 million members. Each serves as a central clearinghouse for information on Catholic lay activities and carries out its program through national committees in specialized areas, with counterparts on diocesan and parish levels. NCCM is best known perhaps for its work in the fields of radio and television. It produces and sponsors "The Catholic Hour" and "Christian in Action" for radio; "The Catholic Hour," "Look Up and Live," "Lamp Unto My Feet" and special films for television. NCCW provides representation for American Catholics at national and international meetings concerned with the welfare of women, and has international affiliation with the World Union of Catholic Women's Organizations. The NCCM has committees on Legislation, Youth, Family Life, Public Relations, Religious Activities, Communications, Civic and Social Action, International Affairs, Organization and Development. One of its principal activities is its television and radio apostolate which produces programs for all the major networks. The NCCW has committees on Catholic Charities, Christian Doctrine, Civil Defense, Family and Parent Education, Foreign Relief, Immigration and Americanization, International Relations, Inter-American Relations, Legislation, Libraries and Literature, Organization and Development, Public Relations, Rural Life, Social Action, and Spiritual Development and Youth.

National Council of Catholic Nurses Organized in 1940 under the Episcopal Chairman for Lay Organization of NCWC, it functions through diocesan councils and is affiliated to NCWC through the National Council of Catholic Women. Its aim is the strengthening of Christian principles in the field of nursing. Its headquarters are at the NCWC building in Washington, D.C.

National Federation of Catholic College Students A division of the Youth Department, NCWC. NFCCS aims to broaden the apostolic outlook of students in Catholic universities and colleges, to involve them in apostolic activity, so that they will become better Catholics and citizens. Headquarters, Washington, D.C.

nationalism An inordinate affection for one's own country to the detriment of justice toward other countries. It is distinguished from patriotism, which is a legitimate and necessary virtue. Nationalism takes on the aspects of a false religion and as such is condemned by the Church. Nationalism is also opposed to the Church's teaching on the unity of the human race and the brotherhood of man under the Fatherhood

of God. The logical development of the doctrine of nationalism is the omnipotent state in which the people exist for the state and not vice versa. Nazism, Fascism and Communism are results of this false doctrine. *See* patriotism.

Native American Party A political organization founded in 1841 aimed at keeping Catholics and all foreign born out of political and governmental office. It later merged with the Know-Nothing Party.

native clergy An unpopular term to describe indigenous clergy, or clergy born in a particular country. The term is used to apply to clergy of the so-called mission country to distinguish them from foreign missioners. The aim of the foreign missioner is to have the Church take local roots and develop with its own clergy. When that work is solidly done, the foreign missioner is able to withdraw. For many years little effort was made to develop an indigenous clergy—a fact that was to give rise to centuries of trouble in Latin America for example. Pope Benedict XV in *Maximum Illud* gave impetus in modern times to the development of local clergy. Pope Pius XI and his successors consecrated indigenous bishops. At Vatican Council II their policies were vindicated, for some of the most advanced thinkers were from the so-called mission countries.

nativism 1. A movement of reaction, usually associated with underdeveloped peoples or those who have been discriminated against, which seeks to restore ancient or traditional ways in opposition to new cultural forces. An example is the Black Muslim movement in the United States. The nativistic movement seeks to restore group integrity and solidarity, usually from negative principles. The movement begins with a "prophet" or "messias" who preaches racial or national purification and the restoration of the "good days." It develops its philosophy by teaching hatred and contempt for the dominant society or culture. It is for this reason that many nativistic movements today are anti-Christian and antiwhite: anti-Christian because Christianity replaced the old pagan or animistic religion, antiwhite because of former colonial or discriminatory status. 2. The ideology that would favor a native-born people in political opportunity, economic status and social acceptance over those who may be citizens but who are not native born.

nativity (L. *nativitas,* a birthday) Only three birthdays are celebrated in the Church. They are the births of Our Lord (Dec. 25), the birthday of Our Lady (Sept. 8) and that of St. John the Baptist (June 24).

Nativity, Feast of the Christmas Day, Dec. 25, celebration of the birth of Our Lord Jesus Christ in a cave in Bethlehem. The exact day of the birth of Christ is unknown. In the earliest days of the Church, the birth of Christ was commemorated with the Epiphany (*q.v.*). The Latin Church began to observe the feast on Dec. 25, about 300. The feast is a holyday of obligation. Priests are allowed to celebrate three Masses on this day. *See* Christmas.

Nativity of Our Lady A feast observed in both the Latin and Byzantine Rites commemorating the birthday of the Virgin Mary on Sept. 8; observed on other dates elsewhere.

Nativity, Vigil of the Vigil of Christmas. All Advent seems focused on the Vigil Mass. All the desires and hopes of mankind point to this night of the miraculous birth.

natural law That ordinance or rule that is rooted in the nature of things. In nonrational creatures the operation of this law is uniform and predictable because freedom is lacking to violate or change it. In rational creatures, natural law is operative as the sum total of the ethical precepts implanted by God in the rational nature of man. The fact that man has freedom of will to violate these precepts does nothing to lessen their validity. Natural law is indelibly written into the hearts of rational creatures by their Creator, urging them to do good and avoid evil. St. Thomas Aquinas says: "Just as grace presupposes nature, the Divine Law presupposes the natural law."

natural religion That religion which flourishes in the soul from the thought of a God and Creator. It is based on or influenced by natural phenomena in contrast to supernatural religion which is based on revelation.

natural theology That branch of philosophy which concerns itself with knowledge of God derived from human reason, apart from revelation. This branch of knowledge attempts to demonstrate the existence of God from natural reasons and causes, and to ascertain the attributes of God as well as God's actions from these same reasons and causes. Thus man shows the existence of God through the principles of finality and causality. Also, since effects resemble causes, we can learn something concerning the Truth and Beauty of God.

naturalism A philosophical and theological system which denies the existence of anything supernatural, with the consequent rejection of revelation, and centers its foundation on nature alone, thus raising nature itself to the level of deity.

nature (L. *nasci,* to be born) 1. The substance or essence which is the complete ultimate principle of a natural unit. There is a basic opposition between nature and grace, nature and art, natural and artificial. 2. The broad application of the term to a whole collection of single substances, the universe as a whole. Thus we speak of the laws of nature, the natural order, etc.

nave (L. *navis,* a ship) The central  or open space in a church reserved for people. In the broad sense this includes the central and side aisles, and crossing transepts. Architecturally, it is that area west of the choir and sanctuary reserved for the people. If it is flanked by aisles, these are not architecturally considered part of the nave. In most Western churches, seats for the faithful are located in the nave. In Eastern Rite churches, the nave is usually devoid of seats.

Nazarene 1. A name applied to Christ because he was a native of Nazareth. 2. A contemptuous name applied to a follower of Christ. 3. A Judaizing sect of early Christians. 4. A 19th-century school of German painters who attempted to restore spirituality to Christian art.

NCWC News Service The press department of the National Catholic Welfare Conference which has a world-wide coverage of Catholic news, a Catholic radio and TV news script, a feature service, a picture service and special syndications by noted authors. NCWC News Service syndicates its material to the Catholic press both in the United States and abroad. The news is gathered by professional journalists, all over the world. It is the largest religious news service in the world, and its releases can be recognized by the abbreviation NC. Its main office is located at NCWC headquarters in Washington, D.C.

Ne temere (nay tay-mare′ey, lest rashly) The opening words of the celebrated matrimonial decree issued by Pope Pius X on Easter, 1908. This decree extended to the whole world the provisions of the decree *Temetsi* of the Council of Trent. It provided that no pastor or bishop can perform a marriage outside of his own jurisdiction without permission of the new jurisdiction, that the impediment of clandestinity be extended to the whole Church, that a marriage is invalid unless performed with proper jurisdiction before two witnesses, that under certain circumstances a valid and licit marriage may take place without a priest. Exceptions to the decree were subsequently made only for local reasons. *See* clandestinity.

Nebraska The 37th state admitted to the Union, it is 15th in area and 34th in population. Name from Omaha Indian, "flat." Early Indians hunted the buffalo and raised a few crops near their earthen dwellings. Coronado, searching for the fabled city of Quivera, passed through the area in 1541. Father Padilla, O.F.M., who accompanied him, remained there to do missionary work and was killed by Indian arrows in 1544—the first martyr in the United States—in what is now Hall County, Neb. More than a hundred years later French Jesuit Father Marquette again offered the Faith to the Nebraska Indians. In 1720 another Spanish priest, Father Minguez, was martyred near present-day Columbus. Nebraska became part of the

United States with the Louisiana Purchase in 1803. The first white settlement was made at Fort Atkinson north of Omaha in 1820, but as late as mid-19th century the population was still mostly Omahas, Pawnees, Sioux and other Indians. A few white settlers came in with the Forty-niners in the California gold rush. After the Civil War Nebraska became a state (1867). Immigrants from Europe arrived in the following century. After the railroads were built settlement proceeded more rapidly from the eastern states. Father De Smet and other Jesuits had made many missionary expeditions and had baptized numbers of Indians after the 1830s. In 1857 the Vicariate of Nebraska was carved out of a previous Rocky Mountain vicariate with Bishop John Miege in charge. Omaha was made a diocese in 1885 under Bishop O'Connor. The wealthy pioneer telegraph builder and banker, Edward Creighton, and his family underwrote the Bishop's building of a Catholic college which later became Creighton University. Many religious congregations and orders were brought into Nebraska by Bishop O'Connor and succeeding bishops. Lincoln was made a diocese in 1887, Grand Island in 1912; and Omaha was raised to the rank of archdiocese in 1945. In 1917 Father Flanagan began his famous experiment in boy-care, founding Boys' Town just outside Omaha. Catholics number about 300,000, in a total population of 1½ million.

Necessarianism Another name for the doctrine of Fatalism which affirms that all things happen of necessity.

necessary to salvation Some theologians hold that the minimum of truths a person must hold in order to enter Heaven are these two: 1. that there is a God; 2. that He is the rewarder of good and the punisher of evil. Other theologians hold that in addition to those two truths, a person must believe in the Trinity, i.e., that there are Three Persons in One God, and believe in the Incarnation, i.e., that the second Person of the Trinity became Man and redeemed all men.

necromancy (Gr. *necros,* corpse; *manteia,* divination) An attempt to summon forth the spirit of the dead in order to discover hidden or future things. It has been common to all primitive civilization, and has been generally prevalent among higher pagan civilizations. In recent times it has reappeared under the name of spiritism (*q.v.*), in which through seances the spirit of one dead is "contacted." It is a grave superstition, sometimes associated with evil spirits, and as such is a grave sin.

negligence The responsible omission of a duty. It is a failing of the intellect to arouse and direct the will. The degree of culpability is in proportion to the bad results that are foreseen. It can include negative cooperation in the wrongdoing of another.

Negro missions Catholic missions among the American Negroes, largely in the South. In 1963 out of 19 million Negroes, 703,443 were Catholics. Of this number 270,000 were in the South, the remainder in big cities of the North. Annual conversions average almost 13,000, and the proportion to white converts is 10 per cent, or approximately equal to the Negro proportion to the general population. There are 775 priests working among the Negroes, and some societies such as the Josephite Fathers have been organized specifically for this work. There is a growing body of Negro priests and Sisters.

Nehemia (Heb. Yahweh consoles) The man who worked diligently for the restoration of Jerusalem. Born in exile, he rose to become cupbearer to the Persian king. In 440 B.C. he was appointed royal commissioner in Jerusalem. He immediately began the repairs of the walls of the Holy City. His activities are recorded in Chronicles (*q.v.*), the Hebrew name for 1 and 2 Paralipomenon.

Nemours, Edict of The results of the Treaty of Nemours (1585) which the Catholic League, under the leadership of Henri de Guise, forced upon King Henry III of France, forbidding Protestant worship in France and denying Henri de Navarre the right to succession of the French crown. It opened the 8th and longest (15 years) of the wars of religion between the Huguenots and the Catholics.

neophyte (Gr. *neophytos,* newly planted) 1. A newly baptized convert. 2. One who has entered upon a new state in life, such as a seminarian or postulant.

nepotism (Gr. *nepos,* nephew) Preference shown by one in authority by granting positions, benefices and emoluments to relatives on grounds of relationship and not merits. Although many popes legislated against nepotism, there were others who practiced it. The system was given its death knell in the bull, *Romanum decet Pontificum,* issued by Innocent XII in 1692.

Nestorianism 1. A heresy advocated by Nestorius, Patriarch of Constantinople, d. *c.* 451. It held that Christ had two separate personalities and natures, also that Mary was the mother of the human nature but not of the divine nature. The heresy was condemned by the Councils of Ephesus and Chalcedon. 2. The movement of the Nestorian Christians. They were probably the first Christian missioners to India and China. 3. The body of doctrine of the Nestorian Christians. They have declined today to about 35,000 in number and are usually referred to as Syrians or Assyrians.

Netherlands One of the best organized and active Catholic bodies in Europe is found in the Netherlands where Catholics number 4.7 million in a population of 11.5 million. There are 1 archdiocese and 6 dioceses, staffed by nearly 6,000 priests. In addition the Netherlands has over 4,000 priests working outside their country, almost 75 per cent of them in territories under the Congregation for the Propagation of the Faith. More than 1 million children are in Catholic schools. Particularly well organized is the Catholic press. There are 20 Catholic dailies, 2 of which circulate nationally.

neum (newm, Gr. a sign) A term in Gregorian chant referring to a group of notes that are sung on one syllable. It derives from the medieval use of the term referring to a series of notes sung without words, generally on the final vowel of the text.

Nevada The 36th state admitted to the Union, it is 7th in area and 49th in population. In early days Shoshones, Paiutes and other Indians sparsely inhabited the region which is largely arid. In the late 18th century Franciscan priests traversed the area en route to the California missions. Trappers and explorers came and went before Nevada was taken by the United States after the Mexican War (1848), being at that time part of California. White settlements really began after one of the world's richest gold and silver mines was discovered on the claim of Henry Comstock, the Comstock Lode. President Lincoln proclaimed Nevada a state in 1864. In the meantime, in 1858, the Archbishop of San Francisco had sent Father Gallagher to serve the miners and others in the boom towns. He built the first Catholic Church in the state at Genoa in 1861. A miner named Patrick Manogue became a priest and came to work in 1862 in the area of the Comstock Lode. He built up a parish in Virginia City, with schools, an orphanage, a hospital and also did excellent missionary work among the Indians. Other priests followed, including members of several religious orders. In 1931 Reno was made a diocese, covering the whole state, with Most Rev. Thomas Gorman as first bishop. He founded a newspaper, built up schools, catechetical works and welfare services. Today Catholics number some 60,000 in a total population of almost 300,000.

New Fire, Blessing of the A ceremony of the Easter Vigil of Holy Saturday which takes place at the entrance of the church; a new fire is kindled from which are lit the paschal candle and other candles.

New Guinea (Papua) The world's largest island after Greenland lies in the South Pacific near Australia. The western section, now governed by Indonesia and known as West Irian, was a Dutch colony until 1963. The eastern area is an Australian mandate. There are several smaller islands included in the territory. All are mostly covered with tropical jungle, swamplands and precipitous mountains. The natives are Mela-

nesians, Negritos and Papuans. There are still areas unexplored and great potential wealth unexploited. The first European to land on the island was the Spaniard Ortiz de Retes, who reached the north coast in 1545 and named it for the African coast of Guinea which it resembled. More than 300 years later the Missionaries of the Sacred Heart, starting from Australia, settled in New Guinea and began missionary work in the British section. Father Verjus was so popular with the mountain tribes that they elected him a tribal chief. The Fathers of the Divine Word set up schools and started economic enterprises with excellent results in the islands of New Britain and New Ireland (under Australian mandate). A mass conversion movement began here toward the end of the 19th century. By the end of World War II, 95 per cent of the mission property had been destroyed and 53 per cent of the personnel, priests, Brothers and Sisters had perished. However, Divine Word Fathers, Holy Ghost Sisters, Sisters of Mercy, Australian Franciscans and lay missioners returned to work there. In Australian New Guinea there are 11 vicariates and 2 prefectures apostolic. In West Irian, under Indonesia, there are 2 vicariates apostolic and 1 prefecture.

New Hampshire The 9th of the 13 original states, it is 44th in area and 45th in population. It was named for the English Hampshire County. Early Indians of various tribes lived by hunting and farming before the coming of the white man. Martin Pring, British naval commander, discovered the mouth of the Piscataqua River in 1603. Champlain sailed along the coast two years later, and Captain John Smith wrote accounts of the region. The first settlement was led by a Scotsman, David Thomson, in 1623, and established at Little Harbor (now Rye) where fishing and trading were carried on. Settlement and development were accelerated; Dover was founded in 1623, and soon afterward Puritans driven out of Massachusetts made other settlements. In 1629 London merchant John Mason, having received a grant of land, named it New Hampshire. After 1760, the Indians having been conquered, immigrants poured in from Massachusetts and Connecticut. During the Revolution the fine tideless inland harbors made possible the building of many navy vessels, including Captain Paul Jones' ship *Ranger*. In the 19th century thousands of Irish immigrants poured in. New Hampshire was under the care of the Bishop of Boston until 1853. The first Catholic Church was built at Claremont in 1823 by a convert from the Episcopal clergy, Father Barber. Many French-Canadian immigrants added to the Catholic population. In 1853 New Hampshire was placed under Bishop Healy of Portland, Me. In the meantime the state constitution barred Catholics from public office, but this law was abolished in 1877. Manchester was made a diocese in 1884, with Bishop Denis Bradley in charge. He set up more than 30 new parishes and founded St. Anselm's College in charge of Benedictines from New Jersey. Successive bishops continued to develop the Church, adding schools, parishes, hospitals and works of charity. Catholics number about one-quarter of a million in a total population well over one-half million.

New Jersey The third of the 13 original states, it is 46th in area and 8th in population. It was named by the Duke of York in 1664 for the Isle of Jersey. The Delaware Indians inhabited the area in early days. Verrazano was the first white man in New Jersey (1524); Henry Hudson explored the country in 1609 and a Dutch trading post was built at Bergen in 1617. Fort Nassau, the first permanent settlement, was built by the Dutch in 1625. The Swedes built a trading post but the Dutch had ousted them by 1655. The British took over the colony in 1664. During the late 17th century Fathers Harvey, Gage and Schneider, under constant danger of arrest, visited the few scattered Catholics in New Jersey. Father Farmer, S.J., worked among the Catholics all over the state from 1758 to 1786. Since Catholics had no civil rights or religious freedom in the English colonies, these priests worked under great difficulties. After the Revolution, in 1799, the first parish church in the state was built in Trenton—St. John's, now Sacred Heart. Parishes were established in many cities during the following century and schools were founded. The Diocese of Newark was created in 1853, with James Roosevelt Bayley as first bishop. During his episcopate the Benedictines started a priory, later to become an abbey providing far reaching spiritual and educational services, and the Vincentians founded a seminary at Princeton (1867). Numerous religious congregations were brought in by Bishop Bayley and succeeding bishops. Seton Hall University was founded in 1856; the Diocese of Trenton was established in 1881, and Newark was raised to the rank of archdiocese in 1937. In 1963 the Byzantine Eparchy of Passaic was established. Catholics today number about one-third of the population.

New Law (*also* New Covenant, New Dispensation) The covenant between God and man established by Jesus Christ, fulfilling and infinitely surpassing the covenant established between God and Moses. The Mosaic Covenant was based on the Decalogue but in the New Law Christ added the great commandments on love of God and love of neighbor. The New Covenant, therefore, is one of love.

New Mexico The 47th state admitted to the Union, it is 5th in area and 37th in population. Its name was given by the Spanish in Mexico to the territory north and west of the Rio Grande. The original inhabitants were Pueblo Indians, village dwellers, agricultural people, worshipers of the Sun-Father and Earth-Mother. The warlike nomad Apaches, Comanches and Navajos made war on the Pueblos. Friar Marcos de Niza was at Zuni in 1538; and Coronado and his party, exploring the region, brought along several Friars, who with their followers remained to Christianize the Indians. Up until 1731 there were 34 martyrs in New Mexico. Juan de Onate brought 400 colonists in 1598, made a settlement at San Juan de los Caballeros and built a chapel. This became the headquarters for missioners and explorers, and by 1680 there were 28 established missions and 16 mission stations. That year Indian rebellions against Spanish rule destroyed the property and caused many deaths, but by 1710 the missions were rebuilt. After the war with Mexico the United States annexed New Mexico and it was made a vicariate apostolic, with Most Rev. John B. Lamy as bishop (1850–1885). He brought in religious congregations of men and women to open schools and care for orphans. He was made Archbishop of Santa Fe in 1875, and he built there the Cathedral of St. Francis. With the development of the country and the pacification of the Indians numbers of immigrants came in. New Mexico was admitted to the Union in 1912. The Diocese of Gallup was established in 1939. Today Catholics number better than one-third of the total population of one million.

New Orleans Archdiocese in Louisiana. Catholic missioners were with the explorers de Soto, La Salle, Iberville and Bienville in their explorations of the territory. The French discovers placed the region under the jurisdiction of the bishop of Quebec. New Orleans was founded in 1718 when Bienville selected the site and picked the spot where old St. Louis Cathedral was built. By 1725 New Orleans had 600 Catholic families. In 1727 the Ursulines arrived to found the first convent in the present United States. Following the sale of Louisiana to the United States the diocese, which had been created in 1793, saw a rapid growth.

New Testament One of the two general divisions of the Bible. The other is the Old Testament. The words "New Testament" mean a new contract or covenant between God and mankind. Christ came on earth to make this new covenant with man. The 27 books of the Bible that explain this new covenant are called the New Testament; these include the four Gospels, the Epistles, the Acts of the Apostles, and the Apocalypse. The inspired writers of the New Testament are SS. Matthew, Mark, Luke, John, Paul, Peter, James and Jude.

New York The 11th of the 13 original states, it is 30th in area and first in population. It was named for the Duke of York and Albany. Verrazano, Champlain and Hudson all had a part in exploring New York.

The Dutch soon began trading in "New Netherlands" and Peter Minuit bought Manhattan Island from the Indians for about $24 worth of trinkets. The Dutch began to develop the new colony in 1647. French Jesuits in the meantime had begun to work among the Indians and established successful missions among the people of the Five Nations. St. René Goupil was martyred in 1642 and St. Isaac Jogues, in 1646 near Auriesville; St. John Lalande was killed by Mohawks in the same year. The chapel of St. John Baptist was built near Syracuse in 1655. Under the Dutch there was little religious freedom, but after the British captured the colony (naming it New York) a Catholic governor, Thomas Dongan in 1683 gave a charter of liberties granting freedom of religion to all Christians. When the Stuarts lost the throne bigotry broke out again and the Jesuits had to close their missions in 1709. Many battles of the Revolution were fought in the area, and George Washington was inaugurated in the city of New York in 1789. St. Peter's Church on Barclay Street was built in 1785. Commerce and industry flourished in the state; and immigration from Ireland, Germany and Italy brought in thousands of Catholics. New York became a diocese in 1808, with Dominican Luke Concanen as first bishop. The Jesuits were brought back, and various congregations of men and women established schools and institutions. Fordham University and Manhattanville College were founded. In 1850 New York was raised to the rank of archdiocese. St. Patrick's Cathedral was begun in 1858. The first American cardinal was the Most Rev. John McCloskey, Archbishop of New York, given the Red Hat by Pope Pius IX in 1875.

In 1911 the Catholic Foreign Mission Society of America (Maryknoll) a missionary-sending society for the whole nation—the first in the United States—was founded near Ossining. In 1930 the Jesuit Martyrs of New York were canonized. Catholics today number over 6 million, in a total population of 17 million.

Newman Club An organization formed by Catholic students attending a non-Catholic institution of higher learning. These student-formed and student-operated clubs provide the opportunity for individual persons to reach out, to strive after the fulfillment of their own capacities and to spark others through leadership, initiative and in general through creative Christian activity. Each province or individual club cooperates with the local ordinary and the Newman Club chaplain to deepen the spiritual and enrich the temporal lives of its members through a balanced program of religious, intellectual and social activities. Newman Clubs are federated nationally and are an integral part of the Youth Department of the National Catholic Welfare Conference (NCWC) with headquarters in the NCWC building in Washington, D.C.

Nicaragua The first missioners arrived in 1526 and the following year the first diocese was erected. Today Nicaragua has 1.5 million people, almost all of whom are baptized. There are 1 archdiocese, 4 dioceses, 1 prelature and 1 vicariate. The latter is staffed by American Capuchins and Christian Brothers. There are 213 priests (1964) and 126 parishes. Nicaragua is gravely handicapped by a lack of priests and a lack of priestly vocations.

Nicene Creed Profession of Faith

which states the major truths of the Catholic Church, composed at the Council of Nicaea in 325. It was the answer to the Arian teaching that Christ was not divine but simply a more perfect creature. This Creed is recited or sung at all Sunday Masses and at Masses of principal feasts. It is as follows: "I believe in one God. The Father almighty, maker of heaven and earth, and of all things visible and invisible. I believe in one Lord, Jesus Christ, the only-begotten Son of God. Born of the Father before all ages. God of God, Light of Light, true God of true God. Begotten, not made, of one substance with the Father. By whom all things were made. Who for us men and for our salvation came down from heaven. And he became flesh by the Holy Spirit of the Virgin Mary: and was made man. He was also crucified for us, suffered under Pontius Pilate and was buried. And on the third day he rose again, according to the Scriptures. He ascended into heaven and sits at the right hand of the Father. He will come again in glory to judge the living and the dead. And of his kingdom there will be no end. And I believe in the Holy Spirit, the Lord and Giver of life, who proceeds from the Father and the Son. Who together with the Father and the Son is adored and glorified and who spoke through the prophets. And one holy, Catholic and Apostolic Church. I confess one baptism for the forgiveness of sins. And I await the resurrection of the dead. And the life of the world to come. Amen."

Nigeria The modern mission effort in Nigeria began in 1861 with the entrance of priests from the African Mission Society of Lyons. Today there are almost 2 million Catholics in a total population of over 30 million. There are 3 archdioceses, 14 dioceses and 4 prefectures, staffed by 818 priests. Some of the problems facing the Church in Nigeria are lack of native clergy, the spread of Islam, the lack of Catholic secondary schools and the lack of Catholic leaders in political and social movements.

night Office In the early Church the night was divided into four parts during which public or official prayers were offered. The custom remains in some monasteries of singing Matins and Lauds sometimes between midnight and 4 A.M.

nihil obstat (L. nothing hinders it) The phrase used by the censor of books to indicate that he has examined the book and found nothing that would prevent its publication (i.e., nothing against faith and morals). *See* imprimatur.

nimbus (L. cloud) A circle of light (halo) or a cloud-like light surrounding the head in representations of God or the saints. It was a pagan custom to use the nimbus to indicate the power and majesty of the gods and goddesses. The nimbus should not be used in the representation of one who has not been beatified or canonized. A nimbus with a cross is used for Our Lord and sometimes for God the Father and God the Holy Spirit.

Nine Choirs Also known as the Celestial Hierarchy. Three hierarchies of angels, each of three choirs: 1. Seraphim, Cherubim, Thrones; 2. Dominations, Principalities, Powers; 3. Virtues, Archangels, Angels. The choirs differ in the degree of perfection of their nature.

Nine Fridays A popular name given to the devotion of devout Catholics in attending Mass and receiving Holy Communion on nine successive First Fridays of the month in honor of the Sacred Heart. In one of the promises purportedly made to St. Margaret Mary, Our Lord said that no one would die unrepentant nor would a person die in His displeasure or without receiving the Last Sacraments if this devotion was practiced. Catholics must guard against superstition and presumption in making the Nine First Fridays.

Noah Noe (*q.v.*).

nobis quoque peccatoribus (L. and to us sinners also) Words beginning a prayer of the Canon of the Mass immediately after the Memento for the Dead, begging God to grant us fellowship with the holy Apostles and martyrs. These three words are said by the celebrant in an audible voice.

Noble Guard Personal bodyguard of the Holy Father, highest rank in the corps of papal military service. Its 77 members are chosen with great care from Roman nobility. They wear a blue uniform with gold trimmings, and also red tunics and white breeches on major feasts.

nocturn (L. *nocturnus,* at night) 1. Formerly the night office. 2. Presently one of the three divisions of Matins of first- and second-class feasts consisting of three psalms, antiphons, readings, versicles and responses. The nocturns of Matins are referred to as first nocturn, second nocturn and third nocturn. In some offices, Matins consists of only a single nocturn.

Noe Hebrew patriarch associated with the great Deluge as told in Gen. 6:9 ff. In tradition Noe is the first winegrower. He is the father of Sem, Japeth and Ham. St. Luke names Noe as one of the ancestors of Jesus.

non expedit (L. it is not expedient, useful, advantageous) Not clear from entanglements, not free or ready for action or unimpeded.

non-Catholic A person who is baptized but is not a member of the Catholic Church; a Protestant. The term is used incorrectly to refer to Jews, Muslims and heathens, who are non-Christians.

None (L. *nona,* nine) The last of the lesser hours of the Divine Office to be said at the ninth hour (3 P.M.), which commemorates the death of Our Lord which took place at this time of day.

nones The ninth day before the ides of the month, according to the old Roman system of calculating dates. It is occasionally used in ecclesiastical documents.

North America Today the term is generally used to refer to Canada and the United States with Mexico and Central America being considered as a unit called Middle America. *Canada,* a member of the British Commonwealth, was pioneered by the French. Jesuits and Franciscans were the early missioners, many of whom gave their lives in martyrdom. Today half the country is Catholic, with the preponderance of Catholics being in the French (eastern) half. There is a movement by a French-speaking radical group for French-speaking independence. *Alaska,* now a state of the United States, was originally a Russian possession. Although Russian Orthodox priests established churches there, they were to serve the Russians and were not missionary. American Jesuits were the real missioners, and today continue this work. Except for the Southwest where early Spanish missioners colonized and converted, the Catholic history of the United States is largely the result of migrations of European Catholics. Missioners, largely French, did work among the Indian tribes. Today the United States is about one-fifth Catholic. *See* Central America; Mexico.

North American College A seminary founded in Rome in 1859 by Pope Pius IX to train North Americans for the priesthood.

North Carolina The 12th of the original 13 states, 28th in area and 12th in population, it was named Carolina for Charles I of England. It was divided into North and South Carolina in 1729. Iroquois, Cherokees and Catawbas were living in the area, hunting, fishing and raising some crops including tobacco and potatoes when the explorers Verrazano (1524), Ayllon (1526) and a British expedition sent by Sir Walter Raleigh arrived in 1585. Though the colony failed, the Indians' tobacco was brought back to Sir Walter Raleigh and smoking was introduced to the world of palefaces. Albermarle, the first successful colony, was settled about 1660. Catholics were few in the colony; the English laws against the Faith were in force. Even as late as 1776 the state constitution made ineligible for office anyone who denied the "truths of the Protestant religion." Father Thomas Murphy was for a while the one priest in the state. In 1835 the article denying the right of Catholics to hold office was repealed, and the first church was built in Charlotte. By 1863 Catholics gained full civil liberty. In 1868 James (later Cardinal) Gibbons was made Vicar Apostolic of North Carolina. At his invitation Belmont Abbey was founded, and in 1924 Raleigh was made a diocese with Most Rev. Wm. Hafey as

first bishop. However the Benedictine Abbot of Belmont has the jurisdiction as a bishop over Gaston County, Belmont being an Abbey Nullius. Various other religious congregations have become established in the state and the work of the Church goes on. Catholics are still a small minority, numbering 1 per cent in a total population over 4½ million.

North Dakota The 39th or 40th state (with South Dakota) admitted to the Union. It is 17th in area and 44th in population. The name Dakota means "friend" or "ally" in Sioux. The Sioux made war against the advancing white man until after General Custer's defeat on the Little Big Horn River in 1876. LaSalle had claimed the region for France in 1682, and in the following century Canadian explorers and fur traders frequented the area. Part of North Dakota came to the United States in the Louisiana Purchase (1803) and American fur traders began operations in the area soon after the expedition of Lewis and Clark (1804–1805). Bishop Plessis of Quebec sent in some priests in 1818, and they built the first church and school at Pembina. In 1823 Canada withdrew its personnel as the area was settled as part of the United States. Father Peter De Smet made five of his long journeys into the region of the Dakotas from 1839 to 1861, doing missionary work and trying to make peace with the Indians. Father George Belcourt arrived from Minnesota in 1848 and reopened the mission church at Pembina. The Grey Nuns came to teach at the Indian agency in 1874. In 1873 Dakota territory was opened to homesteaders, forts were erected to give protection from hostile Indians, and the railroads came—all combining to bring in swarms of immigrants. North Dakota became a state in 1889. The entire state was included in the Diocese of Fargo in the same year, with Most Rev. John Shanley as first bishop. At his invitation the Benedictines came from St. Gall, Switzerland, founded a monastery and college at Richardton, and did mission work among the Indians. The monastery was raised to the rank of abbey in 1903 and the Abbot, Father Vincent Wehrle, was made the first bishop of the new Diocese of Bismarck in 1910. Succeeding bishops of Fargo and Bismarck have brought in other religious congregations and continued to build up the Church. Catholics today number about 166,600, in a total population of 632,446.

notary (L. *notarius,* a secretary) An official who draws up documents for Roman Congregations and diocesan offices. He also records the proceedings of ecclesiastical tribunals.

notes of the Church *See* marks of the Church.

notorious Generally said of a fact or an act which is unquestionably public, manifest and evident. Notoriety of law and notoriety of fact are referred to in canon law. Notoriety of law is had after a sentence of a competent judge which cannot be revoked, or after the confession of a criminal has been accepted by the court; notoriety of fact arises when a fact is so widely known that it cannot be denied, concealed or condoned by any excuse admitted by canon law. Ecclesiastical courts accept the principle "notorious things need no proof," but generally civil law does not accept it.

Notre Dame (Fr. Our Lady) 1. A name used for the Blessed Virgin. 2. The University of Notre Dame in South Bend, Ind., operated by the

Fathers of the Holy Cross. 3. The popular name of a celebrated church in Paris, the Cathedral of Notre Dame.

November Month of the Holy Souls.

novena (L. *novenus,* a set of nine) A prayer extended over a period of nine days and said for some special petition or occasion. Originally the novena was made for repose of a deceased person. This meaning is still used for the novena of Masses said after the death of the pope.

Novena, Pope's The nine days of Masses and prayers which are offered by the court of a deceased pope.

Novena of Grace The name given to a novena to St. Francis Xavier made March 4-12, asking his intercession for the favor of living and dying in the state of grace.

novice (L. *novus,* new) One who undergoes a period of probation and religious training in preparation for the taking of religious vows as a member of a religious community. *See* novitiate.

novitiate 1. A place for the training of novices. 2. That period of religious training following postulancy in which the novice is prepared for assuming temporary vows in a religious community. To be canonical the novitiate must last at least one year.

nullity of marriage The fact that a marriage is null and void because of some diriment or annulling impediment. The result of one of these impediments is to invalidate a marriage even though it has been entered into with good faith by both parties. The purpose of these impediments is threefold: 1. for the public good; 2. for the good of the contracting parties; 3. for the good of religion. Theologians have various methods for reckoning the number of such impediments but generally they are the following fourteen: 1. error and servile condition; 2. duress and fear; 3. abduction; 4. impotency; 5. existing marriage bond; 6. insufficient age; 7. disparity of worship; 8. Major Orders and religious profession; 9. crime; 10. consanguinity; 11. affinity; 12. public property; 13. spiritual relationship; 14. legal relationship.

number of the beast The number 666 found in Apoc. 13:18. The cryptographic value is still an unsolved problem. Its solution has been worked in Hebrew, Greek and Roman values. It is generally agreed that the number is a cryptogram standing for some great power, probably personal, such as an emperor, rather than impersonal such as an empire. It was used because prudence judged that the actual name should not be mentioned. The prevailing opinion today is that it probably refers to *neron qesar* (Emperor Nero). Irenaeus interpreted the number to mean the Roman Empire; Grotius interpreted it as Trajan; others as Caligula, etc.

Numbers, Book of The fourth book of the Pentateuch, so called because of the many numbers in the double census it contains. It relates events concerned with the Israelites over a period of 38 years. This book has been attributed to Moses but may have been from material left behind by Moses.

nun (L. *nonna,* a child's nurse) A member of a religious order or congregation of women. The word has a very specific meaning and should not be used interchangeably with "Sister," although the latter word is prefixed to the religious name of a nun when addressing her. Canon law distinguishes between *moniales* (nuns) and *sorores* (Sisters). Nuns belong to institutes having solemn vows while Sisters belong to institutes having simple vows.

Nunc Dimittis (L. Now thou dost dismiss) A short canticle named after its first Latin words. It was spoken by Simeon in the Temple at Jerusalem on the occasion of the presentation of Jesus. Simeon thanks God that he has been allowed to live long enough to see the Messias. The canticle is daily in Compline, the liturgical night prayer of the Church. In the Byzantine Rite, it is said at Vespers.

nunc pro tunc (L. now for then) Something done or given with a future result in view; e.g., a plenary indulgence for the moment of death; to make restitution now rather than in the next life; observe God's commandments for your own sake hereafter.

nunciature The home and office of a papal nuncio. It is the equivalent of an embassy.

nuncio apostolic (L. *nuntius,* messenger) An ambassador of the Holy See to a foreign power; a permanent diplomatic representative of the pope accredited to a foreign civil government.

nunnery An archaic word referring to a community of nuns and the building in which they live. The word in common use today is "convent," or in some cases "monastery."

Nuns of the Battlefield More than 600 Catholic Sisters volunteered their services as nurses immediately behind the battle lines and in military hospitals during the Civil War. The country's gratitude was expressed by the erection of the monument, *Nuns of the Battlefield,* in the nation's capital, close to St. Matthew's Cathedral.

408

Nuptial Blessing The solemn blessing said over the bride and groom immediately after the Pater Noster of the Mass at which the couple are wed. It is forbidden during Lent and Advent, on Easter Sunday and Christmas.

Nuptial Mass The special Mass to be said at a wedding. It is forbidden at certain liturgical times of the year.

O

O Antiphons On the seven days preceding Christmas Eve, Dec. 17 through Dec. 23, the antiphons to the Magnificat at Vespers are called the "O Antiphons" or the "Greater Antiphons": "O Antiphons" because the first word of each antiphon is the vocative "O"; "Greater Antiphons" because the whole substance of the Advent liturgy is contained therein through an impassioned appeal to the Messias under the form of His titles and prerogatives. Although these antiphons were in use in the eighth century, their authorship and date of composition are unknown. *See* Greater Antiphons; O Sapientia.

O Salutaris Latin hymn taken from the last two verses of the hymn *Verbum Supernum* which was written by St. Thomas Aquinas for Lauds of Corpus Christi. Ordinarily it is sung when the Host is exposed at Benediction.

O Sapientia (L. O Wisdom) The opening words of the first of the greater antiphons preparatory for Christmas. The day on which the antiphon is solemnly sung is Dec. 17. The antiphon is from Sir. 24:5 and Wis. 8:1. "O Wisdom, who proceed from the mouth of the Most High, reaching from end to end and disposing all things with mightiness and sweetness; come to teach us the way of prudence."

oath (AS. *ath*) The calling upon God to witness the truth of something. Since an oath is an act of religion it should not be taken lightly. Two conditions are necessary for validity: the intention of taking the oath and a specific formula. Three conditions are necessary for an oath to be licit: truth, justice and right judgment. An oath is either promissory or assertory, depending upon whether God is called upon to witness something promised or vowed for the future, or whether God is called upon to witness the assertion of a fact that is past or present. The violation of an oath is perjury.

oath against modernism Pope Pius X called "modernism" the synthesis of all heresies. The term "modernism" in this connection must not be confused with our present-day usage. Modernism, as condemned, is a system of theology which would destroy historical and scriptural Christianity, reducing it to a mere cultural fantasy. It applies to those heretical doctrines current at the start of the 20th century, with roots going back to the "Enlightenment," which were condemned in the papal encyclicals, the *Syllabus* of Pius IX in 1864 and the

Pascendi of Pius X in 1907. As a result of these errors, the Holy See has required all clerics before ordination and prior to their assumption of important ecclesiastical offices to swear a solemn oath that they neither hold nor will teach any of the condemned propositions.

Obadiah Abdia (*q.v.*).

obedience A supernatural moral virtue which inclines a person to submit his will to that of a lawful superior. The authority of the superior shares in the authority of God. Obedience, therefore, rests on the submission each person owes to God. Obedience is not due any command which is opposed to divine or ecclesiastical law, nor is one obliged to the impossible; however, in case of doubt the presumption is in favor of the superior. A superior cannot exceed the limits of his authority and a command beyond those limits does not have to be obeyed.

oblate (L. *oblatus,* one offered up) 1. A lay person who unites with a religious order or institute in order to live by its rule and assist in its work and thus share in its merits and spiritual rewards. 2. A child vowed and given by its parents to the monastic life according to the Rule of St. Benedict. The Council of Toledo (656) forbids the acceptance of such boys before the age of ten. 3. In the United States the word, capitalized, usually means a member of the Oblates of Mary Immaculate or the Oblates of St. Francis de Sales. The word is also used in the plural to mean either institute.

Oblate Missionaries of Mary Immaculate A secular institute established in Canada in 1952 and in the United States in 1956. The purpose is to re-Christianize society. There are two types of memberships: In-

terns who live in groups and perform the work of the Institute; Externs who remain at home, perform regular jobs and do not disclose membership. Membership is confined to single persons and vows are taken.

oblation (L. *oblatur,* pp. of *offerre,* to offer) 1. The action of a religious or ritualistic offering which carries the connotation of an inanimate offering; e.g., the Offertory of the Mass with the oblation or act of offering bread and wine. 2. The object or thing which is offered in a religious or ritualistic ceremony; e.g., the bread and wine at the Offertory of the Mass. Most probably the essence of sacrifice lies in oblation, because man thus refers himself and all creation to God as his final end.

obligation (L. *obligare,* to oblige) The moral necessity of doing or avoiding something. It is of the very essence of all law. Every right imposes a corresponding obligation. The ultimate basis of moral obligation is the will of our Creator who imposed upon man certain duties under the penalty of eternal loss of heaven.

obreption (L. *obrepere,* to deceive) A canonical term which refers to a false statement made in order to obtain a papal rescript or dispensation. A favorable answer is valid despite the obreption provided that the one motive cause for granting the favor is truth, or where a number of causes are given, one of them is true.

obsecration (L. *obsecrare,* to beg) An appeal to God for assistance on the basis of some sacred thing; e.g., "By your agony and death, O Jesus, deliver us from our enemies."

observance The rule of a religious order. The word is usually modified by a word which gives the strictness of the rule: e.g., strict observance, regular observance, primitive observance, etc.

obstinancy in sin Clinging to the intention of offending God in spite of opportunities for amendment; refusing the forgiveness of God and the help of the Holy Spirit.

occasion The immediate effective circumstance as distinct from the primary cause. Thus a boy steals candy. The cause is the boy's desire for the candy, the occasion is that the candy was at hand.

occasion of sin Any person, place or thing that is a temptation to commit sin. Catholics are bound in conscience to avoid all occasions of sin.

occasion of sin, proximate A grave external danger of sinning either for all men or for those of a particular type. When placed in certain circumstances a person nearly always falls into sin. The gravity of the danger depends on general experience, the frequency of relapse and the character of the penitent. Absolution must be denied to any penitent who refuses to give up a free proximate occasion of sin.

occult (L. *occulere,* to cover up, hide) 1. Having to do with the pseudosupernatural; e.g., fortune telling. 2. Having to do with the mysterious or hidden; e.g., occult crimes. 3. Having to do with evidence not able to be used in the external forum; e.g., occult impediments to marriage.

occult compensation The act by which a creditor pays himself from the goods of the debtor without the latter's knowledge. Such compensation is permissible only when the debt is just and certain, when no other means of redress is possible and when harm to others is avoided.

occurrence Two feasts falling on the same day. When this happens the major feast takes precedence and the minor feast is transferred, commemorated or omitted.

Oceania A collective name for thousands of small islands and a few big ones scattered over a million square miles of the central and south Pacific Ocean, including groups designated as Micronesia, Melanesia and Polynesia, sometimes also including the Malay Peninsula, but not including the Philippines. The inhabitants, originally Polynesians, Melanesians and others, are today mostly mixed races. They were animists, living in fear of ghosts and taboos, practicing cannibalism. With a few exceptions the Protestant missionaries arrived in the regions years before the Catholics came, but both were too late. Traders, whalers, pirates, sailors, adventurers, colonists already had exploited whole populations, introduced the slave trade, rum, measles (often fatal in the islands), smallpox, cholera, tuberculosis, the white man's vices and their accompanying diseases. Trade in dried coconut meat (copra) being profitable, the natives were often forced to labor on the white man's plantations, sometimes whole populations being removed to perish as slaves. Native races rapidly declined in numbers and were largely replaced by immigrants from Asian and Western countries. Pope Gregory XVI (1831-1846) divided the islands for missionary purposes into Eastern, Central and Western Oceania, and established ecclesiastical jurisdiction in the Pacific. Mass had been celebrated in the Marquesas Islands as early as 1595 when Mandana landed there on a voyage from Peru. Four Franciscans started a mission in the Solomon Islands in 1568 but had to give it up because of ferocious cannibals. Serious missionary work did not begin in the island regions until the 19th century, and although the story varies somewhat from group to group, it is generally one of martyrdom; of heroic labors trying to civilize and Christianize primitive savages; of death-dealing climates, hurricanes, shipwrecks, arduous journeys on foot through tropical forests; of constant struggle against antagonistic colonial governments; of the animosity of Protestant missionaries already entrenched, who went so far as to have Catholic missioners deported, their converts punished; of seeing mission institutions, fruits of a century or more of labor, in ruins after two world wars. In spite of all the difficulties, many of the islands today are largely or partly Catholic, a few entirely so. The native people, once headhunters and cannibals, have made excellent Catholics, furnishing many vocations to native Sisterhoods and recently, some to the priesthood. The leading pioneer missioners of East Oceania were the Picpus Fathers (Missionaries of the Sacred Hearts of Jesus and Mary) arriving in 1827. Central Oceania, since 1836, has belonged particularly to the Marists. West Oceania, since the 1880's, is a mission field shared by the Missionaries of the Sacred Heart (of Issoudun), the Missionaries of Steyl, the Franciscans, the Jesuits and the Capuchins. Maryknoll Sisters operate a few schools in this area. The total Catholic population of East, Central and West Oceania is about 700,000. This sum represents 140 years of heroic labor.

octave (L. *octo,* eight) The commemoration of a feast over a period of eight days, counting the feast itself; the final day of the commemoration. Only the octaves of Christmas, Easter and Pentecost are now cele-

brated. Easter and Pentecost have first-class octaves, whose days are all feasts of the first class. Christmas has a second-class octave, whose days are all feasts of the second class. Historically, octaves seem to have sprung up in the 4th century, and to have their origin in devotion rather than in the Jewish religion.

October Month of the Holy Rosary.

Odd Fellows, International Order of An international, fraternal society with headquarters in the United States. It grew as a rival to the Masons. It is noted for its fraternal care of sick and distressed members and their families. Because of its secret character, it is forbidden to Catholics.

odium theologicum (L. theological hate) The bitterness that arises because of difference of religious belief. It may arise between persons of different religions or between persons of the same religion holding differing theological opinions. It is wrong because, while a belief may be disliked, this distaste should not be carried over to the person.

oecumenical *See* ecumenical.

of Faith A teaching is said to be "of Faith" when it is an article of belief which a Catholic must hold as a doctrine of Faith.

offensive to pious ears An expression referring to a teaching or statement that is opposed to Catholic belief, piety or reverence, or to a true statement that is expressed crudely or unbecomingly.

offering 1. The Offertory of the Mass. 2. The bread and wine used in the Mass. 3. A voluntary gift for a religious purpose, such as a donation in the Offertory collection, a gift to the missions or a stole fee.

Offertory The offering of the bread and wine by the celebrant, and the prayers surrounding the act, at Mass after the Gospel or Credo and before the Canon. At High Mass the celebrant is assisted at the Offertory by deacon and subdeacon, and the offerings are incensed. The Carthusians, Carmelites and Dominicans offer chalice and host together, as was done in pre-Reformation England. The Offertory prayers were not finally established until the Middle Ages. Originally the Offertory was the beginning of the Mass of the Faithful. In the Eastern Rite, the Offertory takes place at the outset of the whole service, the Prothesis.

Offertory Hymn A varying verse taken from a psalm which is recited by the priest and sung by the choir at a High Mass immediately after the Profession of Faith (Creed). It is both a reflection upon the Gospel in relation to the feast of the day, and a prayer or song of immediate preparation for the Holy Sacrifice. It is a relic of what was once a whole psalm and antiphon, sung while the faithful made their offerings. The offertory Hymn for Requiem Masses, ordination Mass, the Mass of episcopal consecration, and Masses at Milan Cathedral are preserved more in their original state.

office (L. *officium,* duty) 1. A position in the Church to which one is lawfully entitled; e.g., the office of a priest or bishop. 2. The Divine Office (*q.v.*). 3. The prescribed prayers and ceremonies for some particular purpose; e.g., the Office of Holy Week, the Office of the Dead, etc. 4. A term for the Introit or Entrance Hymn.

Office, Monastic (L. *Breviarium Monasticum*) A variation of the Roman Breviary used by certain religious communities. The Benedictines follow an outline contained in the Rule of St. Benedict. The Cistercians and Carthusians use a variant of the Benedictine Office. Other groups follow slightly varying formulas depending on historical factors.

Office of the Dead *See* Dead, Office of the.

officialis (off-fi'see-al'-is; L. official) A name given to certain diocesan officials: a judge, a vicar general, one who has charge of marriage and criminal cases.

Ohio The 17th state admitted to the Union, it is 35th in area and 5th in population. Its name comes from an Indian word meaning "great" (applied to the river). Pre-Columbian Mound Builders left evidences of a village-and-farming culture. Iroquois and Algonquins later inhabited the area, but with the coming of the white man they lost their land and migrated west of the Mississippi. La Salle, in 1669, explored the region, and Bienville claimed it for France in 1749. Two Jesuits, Fathers Portier and Bonneville, came with him. Father De la Richardie, S.J. established a Catholic settlement among the Hurons at Sandusky. English traders and colonizers were at work in the region, and it was ceded to England after the Seven Years' War. During the American Revolution George Rogers Clark won it for the United States. The Northwest Ordinance provided for religious freedom and encouraged colonization. Statehood came in 1803, and the population increased greatly. The bishop of Bardstown, Ky., sent Dominican Father Fenwick to the new state in 1818, and in 1822 he became the first bishop of the new diocese of Cincinnati. He built St. Peter's Cathedral, founded a seminary, started the *Catholic Telegraph* and brought in Sisters for teaching and charitable works. Catholic immigrants flocked in from Germany and Ireland, and succeeding bishops continued to build up the Church. Cleveland was made a diocese in 1847, and in 1859 Cincinnati became an archdiocese. During the Civil War, Sisters of Charity and of Mercy did nursing service for the wounded. The Church increased greatly after the war. In 1935 Archbishop McNicholas founded the Institutum Divi Thomae for scientific research. Catholics number well over 2 million in a total population of 10 million.

oil The use of oil for anointing antedates Christianity. Historically it has symbolized strength and spiritual perfection. The use of oil in the Anointing of the Sick is based on the injunction of St. James in his Epistle (5:14). Rubrics prescribe the use of pure olive oil for the oil of catechumens, the oil of the sick and as an ingredient in chrism.

oil of catechumens Olive oil blessed by the bishops on Holy Thursday. This oil is used in Baptism when the anointings are made on chest and shoulders. It is used in the Sacrament of Holy Orders when the palms of the hands are anointed for the priesthood. It is also used in the consecration of altars, and in the blessing of the baptismal font on Holy Saturday and the vigil of Pentecost.

oil of chrism *See* chrism.

oil of saints Liquids which exude from the tombs or shrines of saints and which are collected and used by the faithful for anointing the body, in order to keep or restore health, while asking the intercession of the particular saint.

oil of the sick One of the three sacramental oils blessed by the bishop on Holy Thursday. It is pure olive oil. It is used in the sacramental anointings of the sick.

oil stock A cylindrical metal container usually made in  three parts, each to contain one of the holy oils. Each stock is packed with cotton and then saturated with the proper oil. The oil is removed by pressing the right thumb on the cotton. The stock is kept in a safe place in the church, usually in the ambry.

Oklahoma The 46th state admitted to the Union, it is 18th in area and 27th in population. Its name is Choctaw for "Red Man." Original tribes inhabiting the area hunted the buffalo which supplied most of their needs. Later (1819) the United States government made of the region a home for more than 30 tribes of Indians who were dispossessed in other states and forced to migrate to Indian Territory. The earliest explorers were Coronado, in 1541, with Father Juan de Padilla in his company, and De Soto in the same year with two priests in his party. In the following century Father de Sales and other Spanish priests crossed the Rio Grande to minister to Indians and traders. La Salle claimed the region for France in 1682. The first settlement was made by the Chouteau Brothers at their fur trading post in 1796. The region came to the United States with the Louisiana Purchase in 1803, and Fort Smith was built to protect white settlers from the Indians. After 1822 the Jesuit Fathers de la Croix, Van Quickenbourne and others began regular missionary work among the Indians. In 1826 the territory was entrusted to the Diocese of St. Louis and more priests were sent from there. In 1844 it was made part of the Diocese of Little Rock.

During the Civil War many Indians joined the Confederate forces, subsequently suffering the loss of their lands. However, "Indian Territory" was still a reservation for the Indians, part of it, the territory of Oklahoma being still "unassigned." Texas cattlemen began driving their vast herds through on their way north; white settlers in nearby states wanted more land. So, beginning in 1889, Oklahoma was opened up to homesteaders—free land for farms and ranches. In 1906 Congress passed an act joining Oklahoma and Indian Territory together in one state, and the Indian lands were opened to white settlers. The first Catholic Church was built at Atika in Indian Territory in 1874, Father Robot, O.S.B., the first resident priest. He was made Prefect Apostolic of Indian Territory in 1876, built a monastery at Sacred Heart, and in 1878 was made Titular Abbot. Various congregations of Sisters opened schools for Indians and whites. Oklahoma was made a diocese in 1905 with Most Rev. Theophile Meerschaert as first bishop. He established numerous churches and schools, aided by religious congregations, particularly the Sisters of the Blessed Sacrament for Indians and Colored People. In 1930 the Diocese of Oklahoma was changed to Oklahoma City and Tulsa. Catholics number about 5 per cent in a total population of two and one half million.

Old Catholics A group of small national churches, formed by and consisting of Christians who have at various times separated from Rome.

Old Testament Those books of the Bible pertaining to the Old Law which were written before the birth of Christ, and which for the most part are accepted as official texts by the Jews. They are divided into 45 books or sections. Historical books (21): Genesis; Exodus; Leviticus; Numbers; Deuteronomy; Josue; Judges; Ruth; 1, 2, 3, and 4 Kings; 1 and 2 Paralipomenon; 1 and 2 Esdras; Tobias; Judith; Esther; 1 and 2 Machabees. Doctrinal books (prayers and holy maxims, 7): Job, Psalms, Proverbs, Ecclesiastes, Canticle of Canticles, Wisdom and Sirach (Ecclesiasticus). Prophetic books (17): Isaia, Jeremia, Baruch, Ezechiel, Daniel, Osee, Joel, Amos, Abdia, Jona, Michea, Nahum, Habacuc, Sophonia, Aggeus, Zacharia and Malachia.

Old Testament saints 1. Men not necessarily of Jewish origin, some of whom were not even acquainted with the revealed Word of God which we generally consider to begin with Abraham. Noe, Lot, Abel, Henoch and Melchisedec would be examples of this type. 2. Men who worshiped God by responding to His grace to the extent that they saw Him reflected in the world around them and in their own mind. Those who came after the time of Abraham were considered Old Testament saints of Jewish origin. Any man who shared in the Covenant of Israel with God and who was faithful to such a commitment can be considered an Old Testament saint. There were some outstanding men, such as the prophets, who by their mission stood out above the rest of Israel and are the more renowned among the Old Testament saints, but even these men were considered saints only in relation to their devotion to the Covenant with Yahweh.

olive branch A symbol for peace.

ombrellino (It. umbrella) The small canopy set on a single pole which is carried over the Blessed Sacrament when it is taken from one altar to another. It is sometimes used when the Blessed Sacrament is carried to the sick. It is also used on Good Friday in place of a canopy.

omen A chance occurrence or phenomenon believed to foretell a future event or direct a course of action. To believe in omens is a form of superstition.

omnipotence of God (L. *omnis,* all; *potentia,* power) God is all-powerful and able to do anything but contradict Himself. He acts wholly from within Himself without change or diminution of capacity. God's power is not distinct from His knowledge and will, except conceptually.

omniscience of God (L. *omnis,* all; *praesens,* present) A word used to indicate that God is everywhere present at all times.

omnis utriusque sexus (L. everyone of either sex) A term used to indicate that each sex is bound to observe a certain law or commandment.

omniscience of God (L. *amnis,* all; *scientia,* knowledge) God knows all things, even our most secret thoughts. He alone comprehends His infinity and essence. He knows all things outside Himself that concerns His creation; He alone knows the entire past, present and future. In God there is no time or succession, but all things of the past, present and future are present to Him immediately.

onanism A word which refers to the act committed by Onan as described in Genesis 38:8-10. Withdrawal in coitus so that the semen is deposited outside the usual receptacle. The word does not properly apply to masturbation.

opinion An attitude of the intellect which inclines toward one of two or more differing propositions without definitely excluding any that are left. It is distinct from certainty and doubt. Adherence to a probable opinion should be given only after proper deliberation.

oppression of the poor One of the sins which cry to heaven for vengeance.

Opus Dei (L. work of God) The Sacerdotal Society of the Holy Cross and Opus Dei. A secular institute, the first to receive full approval from Rome, originating in Spain in 1928. It has a men's section, for laymen and priests, which was given final approval in 1950. It was established in the United States in 1949. The women's section was founded in Italy in 1930. Opus Dei consists of members of 50 nationalities, deployed over most of Europe and the Americas, and in parts of Asia, Africa and Australia. Members of lay institutes do not wear religious garb and may be employed in ordinary professions or jobs. They do not take religious vows but do make promises that approximate them. They are distinguished by complete self-dedication, and dedication to employment in the apostolate and the Christian ministry.

opus operatum, opus operantis (L. the work worked, the work of the worker) *See* ex opere operantis.

oral tradition The oral handing down from generation to generation of doctrine, practices and other information. In the Christian sense, it is handing down doctrine and teachings which are not contained in Sacred Scripture. The Holy Spirit assists the Church in keeping pure the deposit of Faith.

orans (L. *orare,* to pray) As in the expression, the *praying* Church, or a person in the act of praying; figures with outstretched arms, as frequently depicted in the catacombs.

Orate Fratres (L. pray now, brethren) First words of the priest's exhortation at Mass after the Offertory, that their offering and his be acceptable to the Lord.

oratio (L. *orare,* to pray) 1. A prayer, the Collect of the Mass. 2. A sermon or discourse (oration).

oratio imperata (L. commanded prayer) Mass prayers (Collect, Secret and Post Communion) ordered to be added as commemorations to the Mass by the pope or bishop on the occasion of some great public need or calamity. Rubrics govern when such prayers should or should not be said.

oratio super oblata (L. prayer over the offerings) The Secret. It is the prayer "over the offerings set apart for sacrifice." This prayer completes the Offertory and introduces the actual oblation of the sacrifice in the great prayer of the Canon which follows the Preface.

oratio super populum (L. prayer over the people) A special Lenten prayer said after the Postcommunion for and on behalf of the people of the Church.

orationes diversae (L. various prayers) Prayers (collects) for different occasions, formerly inserted after the one proper to the day out of special devotion or at the order of the Bishop. These *Imperata* are for unusual intentions; e.g., for peace in time of war, or danger of war; for the guidance of the Holy Spirit during the time of the Council; for the pope; against persecutors of the Church.

oratorio 1. A musical composition on a religious theme, usually adapted from a biblical story, involving recitation, dialogue, aria, chorus, and orchestral interlude and accompaniment. 2. The performance of the composition, also called an oratorio, is without action, scenery or costume. St. Philip Neri (1515–1595) was responsible for the development of the form in his popular evening services held at his Oratory in Rome.

oratory (L. *oratorium,* a place of prayer) 1. Technically, in canon law, it is a distinct class of buildings intended primarily for divine worship by a special group or by an individual. 2. A church or house of the Congregation of the Oratory. 3. A small chapel or place of prayer.

oratory, private or domestic Erected solely for the benefit of one family or private person and regulated by strict Church laws.

oratory, public Erected for some group in such a manner that all the faithful may legitimately have access to it at the time of the divine services.

oratory, semipublic Erected for some group but in such a way that others do not have free access to it.

Order of Preachers Known as the Dominicans and the Friars Preachers. This order founded by St. Dominic in the early part of the 13th century is devoted to preaching, teaching and study. *See* Dominicans.

Order of the Holy Sepulcher Although its origins are unclear, this papal order of knights first appeared in the Holy Land at the end of the 11th century. Claimed as founders in various quarters are St. James the Apostle, first bishop of Jerusalem; St. Helena, builder of the Basilica of the Holy Sepulcher; and Godfrey of Bouillon, French crusader. The religious superior of the Franciscan Friars, who had been appointed guardians of the Holy Land in 1342, had the faculty of conferring the order of knighthood until 1847, when it was given to the Latin Patriarch of Jerusalem. The Order of the Holy Sepulcher has five classes, headed by Knights of the Collar and followed by the Grand Cross, Commanders with Plaque, Commanders and Knights, with separate divisions of each for men and women. Three honorary decorations are awarded: Palm of the Order, Cross of Merit and the Pilgrim's Shell.

order, religious An institute fully approved by the Holy See and having the solemn vows of poverty, chastity and obedience. There are two classes: 1. each monastery is independent with a perpetual abbot; 2. each house is dependent on a province with superiors being elected for terms of office. *First order* refers to men with solemn vows; *second order,* to women with solemn vows; *third order,* to others without solemn vows. The name arose in the 10th century to designate certain communities of religious or certain communities following one religious rule; now widely accepted as the term for a group or groups of persons living a religious life according to a rule and professing solemn vows; groups of religious.

orders, minor The inferior degrees of the ministry, below the major orders of priests and deacons to which, in the West, have been added subdeacons. The last order was formally placed among the major orders by Innocent III in 1207. Until then the subdiaconate was commonly reckoned a minor order, as it is still in the East. In the Western Church the four minor orders—porters, lectors, exorcists and acolytes—were first mentioned in a letter of Pope Cornelius to Fabius of Antioch in

252. In the East, since the Trullan Council of 692, lectors have survived, whereas the other three—porters, exorcists and acolytes—have been merged in the subdiaconate. Since minor orders are not sacraments, the rite by which minor orders is conferred differs essentially from that of major orders. The external features of the rites for both major and minor orders are much the same, however: 1. the Call; 2. the Instruction; 3. the Bestowal of the Order; 4. the Prayer. The essence of each order consists in the bestowal of the order: chiefly a benediction and a handing-over of the instruments required for the office. The main points of the rites were laid down in the *Statuta Ecclesiae Antiqua* (*c*. 500). Since the liturgical functions of the minor orders have been taken over either by the priesthood, as in the case of exorcism, or by the laity, as in the case of serving Mass, they are now no more than transitory steps to the priesthood and are usually conferred on students during their time in the seminary. One who has received minor orders is not thereby bound to any obligations with regard to the pursuit of the priesthood. Minor orders are conferred on Sundays and double feasts, outside of Mass, but always in the morning. Not more than two minor orders may be received on the same day; nor is it allowed that tonsure and a minor order be received by the same candidate on the same day. Vicars, prefects apostolic, abbots and prelates nullius, even though not bishops, can confer minor orders on those subject to them or on those having dimissorial letters. *See* Holy Orders, the Sacrament of; major orders.

orders, number of There are seven separate degrees of Holy Orders in the Western church *minor:* door keeper or porter, lector or reader, exorcist and acolyte; *major:* subdeacon, deacon, priest. Tonsure is not an order. Bishops have the plenitude of the priestly power; archbishop, patriarch and pope are degrees within the episcopate. The cardinalate is an office, not an order, as are abbacy, canonry and other prelatures. In the East the number and reckoning of both major and minor orders varies in the different Churches.

ordinal A book containing the prayers, forms and ceremonies for conferring Holy Orders.

ordinariate 1. A chancery office, such as the military ordinariate. 2. A nonterritorial grouping of clerics and faithful presided over by an ordinary whose jurisdiction is personal rather than geographical.

ordinary The title of one who exercises ordinary jurisdiction in the external forum over a specified territory; one who directs a diocese or what is tantamount to a diocese, such as a vicariate, prefecture, prelature, etc.

Ordinary of the Mass *See* Mass, Ordinary of the.

ordination That ceremony of the Church during which men who have been called by God and judged worthy by their superiors receive one of the minor or major orders, culminating in ordination to the priesthood. The making of a bishop is called consecration.

ordination, conditional When there is grave or positive doubt that the conferring or reception of any of the Holy Orders was not truly given or actually received, the ordination ceremony may be repeated conditionally as a precautionary measure.

ordo (L. order) The annual liturgical calendar of the Catholic Church, listing feasts and ferial days with the prayers to be said in the Mass and Divine Office. The ordo varies as to diocese and religious orders.

Ordo Missae That part of the Missal that contains the Ordinary and Canon of the Mass.

Ordo Romanus A collection of rubrics and liturgical directions in use in the Roman Liturgy between the 7th and 15th centuries.

Oregon The 33rd state admitted to the Union, it is 10th in area and 32nd in population. It was named for what is now the Columbia River, which the Algonquins called Wauregan— "beautiful water." Various hunting and fishing tribes of Indians inhabited the area in early days. The coasts were explored by Spain, by England, and by Russia. English and American merchant vessels carried on a trade in furs, and trading posts were built in many places. French Canadian missioner Father Blanchet built the first church, at St. Paul, and was made Vicar Apostolic in 1838. In 1842 Dr. John McLoughlin, in charge of the Hudson Bay Company, and called the "Father of Oregon," was received back into the Church of his youth. Father De Smet, S.J., arrived in the same year, and brought in some Sisters to open a school. He founded the mission of St. Francis Xavier, near St. Paul. In 1846 the Vicariate was made an ecclesiastical province, with Bishop Blanchet as Archbishop of Portland. Oregon became a state in 1859; and settlers swarmed in after the discovery of gold in 1861 and the building of railways in 1884. In the meantime anti-Catholic bigotry had sprung up, until in 1922 the Scottish Rite Masons pushed the passage of a bill forbidding private schools, directed mainly at destroying Catholic education. However, in 1925 the United States Supreme Court declared the bill unconstitutional. A Trappist Monastery was founded in the Willamette Valley in 1953. Catholics today number almost 15 per cent in a total population of near 2 million.

oremus (L. Let us pray) Invitation given frequently before liturgical prayers of the Latin Rite. It invites all to join with the celebrant in praying for the same object.

organ The Constitution on the Sacred Liturgy issued by Vatican Council II declares that in the Latin Church the organ is to be held in high esteem, for it is the traditional musical instrument which adds a wonderful splendor to the Church's ceremonies and powerfully lifts up man's mind to God. The use of the organ is prohibited at certain penitential times; e.g., after the Gloria on Holy Thursday through Holy Saturday. The rubrics also command its use at certain times; e.g., to the end of the Gloria on Holy Thursday.

Oriental Church, Sacred Congregation of the Created by Pius IX in 1862 and united with the Congregation for the Propagation of the Faith. In 1917 Benedict XV made it autonomous. It exercises over the dioceses, bishops, clergy, religious and faithful of the Oriental Rites, all the powers which the Consistorial Congregation and the Sacred Congregations of the Council, Religious and Seminaries have in the Latin Rite. In addition it has exclusive jurisdiction over Egypt, the Sinai Peninsula, Eritrea, Northern Ethiopia, Southern Albania, Bulgaria, Cyprus, Greece, the Dodecanese, Iran, Iraq, Lebanon, Syria, Palestine, Turkey, Afghanistan, the Vicariate of Addis Ababa and the Prefecture of Endebar.

Oriental Rite *See* Eastern Rites.

Oriental Studies, Pontifical Institute for An institute for Eastern studies founded by Benedict XV in 1917 and affiliated with the Gregorian University in Rome.

Orientalium Dignitas (L. the dignity of those of the East) A constitution of Pope Leo XIII which asserted the dignity and rights of the Eastern Rite Catholic Churches and which defined the relations between East and West. The constitution ruled that any Latin Rite priest who tried to persuade an Eastern Rite Catholic to become a Latin Rite Catholic would be *ipso facto* suspended.

Origenism An early Christian system of theology attributed to Origen (*c.* 185–254) mixed with Greek ideologies, many doctrines of which are clearly heretical. It denied the equality of the three divine Persons; the Christian concept of the Incarnation; eternal punishment; the general resurrection; the factual sense of the Sacred Scriptures. It was suspected of Gnostic influences. Whether or not Origen held and taught such doctrines is a matter of dispute. It may be significant that despite the fact that he died as a result of severe torture suffered for the Faith, the early Church did not classify him, as it did others who suffered less intensely, among its martyrs.

Origin of Species Complete title: *On the Origin of Species by Means of Natural Selection,* by Charles Darwin. A book written in 1859, which popularized the theory of evolution known as Darwinism, and greatly influenced the thought of modern man. Its argument is that every species is developed from previous species and that both plant and animal life are part of a pattern which varies from one generation to the next. All life, according to Darwin, survives and bears offspring only if it has inherited characteristics which make it better able to survive in the fierce "struggle for existence." This struggle and survival, according to him, bring about that "natural selection" which influences future generations in an evolution toward an ever higher development. This was further described in a later book (*The Descent of Man,* 1871). Darwin was not the sole originator of the theory of evolution (*q.v.*). Even as early as the 4th century St. Augustine (Lib. vi, 16-17) speaks of the first creations of the world, wherein man was made so that he should exist afterwards; of created things in the elements of the world carrying invisibly within themselves a hidden power of generating; that they were incorporated with the world created before they rose up in the visible appearance of their kind. The Catholic Church has no quarrel with evolution as a method by which God may have peopled His increasingly amazing universe. However, the *Origin of Species* brought about a storm of criticism, particularly from Protestant fundamentalists. On the other hand, many readers of Darwin's books found more in them than the author himself dreamed. In the first place, the time was ripe. Malthus in his *Essay on the Principle of Population* (1798) had shown that the increase of population would lead to a grim struggle against starvation among earth's peoples. "Natural selection" became, in the words of Herbert Spencer, the "survival of the fittest." Atheists seized eagerly upon Darwin's theories as proof that God did not exist. Karl Marx emphasized the struggle for existence as a class struggle and demanded the removal of religion as a mirage. Since men were considered hardly more than animals by the followers of Marx, in setting up Communism they slaughtered and enslaved millions without a qualm. Spengler declared that man is a beast of prey; that there is no absolute right or wrong; that the German race was destined to be supreme. Nietzsche arrived at the doctrine of Superman, the Great Blonde Beast, who is beyond good and evil, and who needs no morals. Hitler and the Nazis claimed the Germans to be the Master Race, destined to enslave inferior peoples, and privileged to destroy whom they pleased. Mass murders and slaughter of millions followed there as well as in Communist countries. Darwin's books have had a great indirect influence upon our generation. Many, who have never read Darwin or any of the distorted thinkers who followed him, feel vaguely that "science" proves the Bible a fable, and religion mere superstition. People with a smattering of science think it smart to scoff at Faith. The greater scientists, however, think differently. "The probability of life originating from accident is comparable to the probability of the unabridged dictionary resulting from an explosion in a printing shop" (E. Conklin, biologist).

original justice All those supernatural and preternatural perfections which were given our first parents and which were lost by original sin. The supernatural gift was sanctifying grace; the preternatural gifts included freedom from concupiscence, bodily immortality, the absence of suffering and habitual infused knowledge. These gifts were to be passed on to the descendants of Adam and Eve. Theologians describe in detail the exact meaning of these perfections.

original sin One of the consequences

of the sin of our first parents which is passed on to their descendants. As a result of their sin man was denied original justice and instead was made subject to death and concupiscence. Original sin also meant the deprivation of sanctifying grace. This teaching of the Church is based on St. Paul (Rom. 5:12-14).

ornaments of the altar *See* altar ornaments.

Orthodox Church, Eastern The collective name for those self-governing churches of eastern Europe' and western Asia deriving from the ancient churches of Jerusalem, Antioch, Alexandria and, later, Constantinople; principally the Orthodox churches of the Near East, Greece, Russia, Rumania, Serbia, Bulgaria and their later worldwide extensions. The separation of the Eastern Orthodox from the Catholic Church came about gradually between 1054 and 1472. Their chief bishop is the Patriarch of Constantinople (the Ecumenical Patriarch), but he is not a sort of pope. Orthodox orders and sacraments are valid and under certain circumstances (according to Vatican Council II) certain sacraments can be received by Catholics and vice versa. Except for the supremacy of the pope, the Orthodox hold the Catholic Faith, without those developments and clarifications which have come to it since the 11th century. Their liturgy of worship is that of the Byzantine Rite, in many languages. The Orthodox Church is so called to distinguish it from the small Nestorian and Monophysite churches of the East.

orthodoxy (Gr. *orthodoxia,* purity of faith) Belief in the true Faith founded by Jesus Christ.

Orthodoxy A feast of the Byzantine Rite celebrated on the first Sunday of Lent to commemorate the restoration of icons to the churches in 842 and the triumph of the true Faith over Iconoclasm (*q.v.*).

oscula solita (L. the usual kisses) Those kisses formerly given to the hand of the celebrant and to the instruments of the Mass during a Solemn High Mass. In a Low Mass, the celebrant kisses the altar a number of times, and kisses the Missal after the Gospel.

osculatorium Another name for the peace plate, a plaque of metal or wood decorated with some religious carving and having a handle. It was formerly used to convey the kiss of peace to the congregation. It would be brought to the altar at the Pax and be kissed by the celebrant and then carried to each member of the congregation to kiss.

Osee, Book of (Heb. Yahweh is salvation) Old Testament book written by Osec (*also* Hosea) son of Beeri, the first of the Twelve Minor Prophets. The Book of Osee deals with God's love of men and their lack of appreciation for God.

Osservatore Romano (It. Roman Observer) A Vatican City daily newspaper, founded in 1860 under lay auspices. Later Pope Leo XIII turned it into a semiofficial organ of the papacy. It contains current events and comments on Vatican news, and often reflects the views of the Holy See.

ostensorium (L. *ostendere;* to show) Another name for the monstrance.

Ostiarius (L. doorkeeper) Latin title for porter or doorkeeper, the first of the minor orders on the way to the office of priesthood.

Our Father, the A title given to the Lord's Prayer, based on the first two words. *See* Lord's Prayer, the.

Our Lady An English title of respect  for the Blessed Virgin. It is often combined with some attribute or connection of Mary, such as Our Lady of Ransom, Our Lady of Victory, Our Lady of Mount Carmel, Our Lady of the Snows, Our Lady of Perpetual Help, etc.

Our Lord A short form for Our Lord Jesus Christ. "The Lord" usually refers to God.

Oxford Movement A movement within the Church of England, promoted by University of Oxford professors in an attempt to restore their communion to what they considered uncorrupted Catholicism. It was begun in 1833 by Keble and promoted by Newman, Hurrell, Froude, Pusey, Williams, Faber, Marriott, Dalgairns and Ward, mainly by the publication of "Tracts for the Times," which spotlighted Anglican departures from Christian doctrine and ritual that had been continuously held by the Christian Church up to the Middle Ages, thereby implying not only schism but heresy in their own ranks and urging a return to a more truly Catholic belief and practice. Many of its advocates later became Catholics, in particular Newman who eventually became a cardinal. The movement had a deep influence on Anglicanism although it was strenuously opposed by the advocates of the status quo. It opened the minds of countless Englishmen to a knowledge of the Catholic faith and Church not available to them since the reign of Henry VIII. Thousands of English converts entered the Catholic Church as a result during the succeeding generations. Its effects are still discernible in the "Anglo-Catholic" and "High Church" Anglicans and Episcopalians of our day. The movement also deeply affected the Catholic Church in England by providing a new impetus to its enlightening of fellow citizens with the assistance of important and influential converts, especially in the field of apologetics.

P

Pacem in Terris (Peace on Earth)
Pope John XXIII's last encyclical
letter, issued on April 11th, 1963,
just eight weeks before he died. This
encyclical can be described as a document of Christian political philosophy. In *Pacem in Terris* Pope John
presents and interprets the natural-
law principles which govern the political order. The encyclical is divided
into five sections as follows: 1. Order
between men. 2. Relations between
individuals and the public authorities within a single state. 3. Relations
between states. 4. Relationship of
men and of political communities
with the world community. 5. Pastoral exhortations.

pacifism (L. *pacis,* peace) Philosophical or religious attitude with regard to war or violence. 1. *Absolute,*
denying all use of force even in self-
defense, is foreign to authentic Christian tradition. However, absolute
pacifism as a personal way of life is
a possible Christian attitude. It is to
be compared to the counsels of poverty and chastity. Such counsels are
not demanded of all Christians but
are freely followed by some out of a
desire to provide a particular witness to the world. 2. *Relative or nuclear,* a conviction that while self-
defense and force can always be just

and often obligatory, modern ther-
monuclear weapons are of themselves
immoral and therefore no war today
can be moral.

padre A word used in Spanish, Italian and Portuguese for a priest,
meaning "father." It is sometimes
used in English by those who do not
wish to use the more formal term of
address. The British tradition also
uses the word for a military chaplain.

padroado (Port. patronage) The privilege of patronage granted to the king
of Portugal, similar to the Patronato
Real (*q.v.*).

paenula (L. traveling cloak) A long,
woolen outer cloak worn in Roman
times from which the chasuble (*q.v.*)
is derived. Another name for chasuble.

pagan (L. *paganus,* a country person)
One who does not believe in the true
God. Christianity spread rapidly in
the cities but for many years idolatry
lingered in the country districts. The
country people (*pagani*) thus lent
their name to all unbelievers. Jews
and Muslims are not considered pagans since they believe in the one
true God even though they do not
admit the divinity of Christ.

pain of loss One of the pains of hell
and purgatory. It is the realization
that one is deprived of the Beatific

425

Vision and life with God either permanently or temporarily, and as a result there is suffering and pain.

pain of sense The second type of pain that a condemned person will experience in hell. It will be a torment of both body and soul. Traditionally it is called a torment of fire although its exact nature is unknown.

palanca (Sp. a lever, an influence) Specifically, a written promise of prayers or acts of sacrifice for the success of a Cursillo (*q.v.*) by a person or persons not making the Cursillo.

Palatine (L. *palatium,* palace) 1. The most central hill in Rome and the first settled. It was the site of *Roma Quadrata,* the village attributed to Romulus. The Caesars had an imperial palace there, and so the term took on the meaning of a person or thing connected with a palace. The word was transferred to the pope's court. 2. A person or thing connected with the Vatican Palace. 3. Two states of the German Republic which until 1620 were united and were known as Upper Palatinate and Lower Palatinate. 4. An area ruled over by a count or lord in England in which the lord palatine exacted feudal rights and was an indepedent prince simply swearing fealty to the king. Maryland was granted to Lord Baltimore as a county palatine.

palatine cardinals Two cardinals closely connected to the pope because of their duties. They are the Cardinal Secretary of State and the Cardinal Datary.

Palatine Guard of Honor Instituted by Pius IX in 1850. It is a force of volunteers making up two batallions for a total of 500 men. The guards live in the Vatican or in Rome and come directly under the authority of the Secretary of State.

palatine prelates Prelates personally attached to the pope and who live in the Vatican. They are the major domo, the master of the chamber, the auditor to the Holy Father and the master of the apostolic palace.

palatine secretariates Three offices closely associated with the pope: the Secretariate of State and its two offices, the Secretariate of Briefs to Princes and the Secretariate of Latin Letters.

pall (L. *pallium,* a cover) 1. A heavy piece of starched linen, folded several times, and about six inches square; it can also be made of hemp. The pall is placed over the paten when that is on the chalice; and after the chalice is uncovered, it is placed directly on the chalice to protect the contents. Most palls in use today are sewn on three sides to make a pocket into which is slipped a piece of stiff cardboard that can be removed when the pall is washed. Because the pall can come into contact with the Sacred Species, it should receive its first washing from one in major orders. 2. A large black mantle draped over a coffin or catafalque at a Requiem Mass. 3. The veil held over the bride and groom in the Mozarabic (Toledo) rite which is still used in many parts of Spain and Latin America.

pallium (L. a covering) A white woolen circular band two inches wide, ornamented with six small black crosses, having a weighted pendant in the front and in the back. It is worn during ceremonies by the pope, archbishops and patriarchs. Until an archbishop receives a pallium, he may not exercise metropolitan jurisdiction and if he should be transferred to a new archdiocese, he must ask for a new pallium. It is a symbol of the fullness of the priesthood and of union with the Holy See. Pallia are woven from the wool of two lambs blessed in the Church of St. Agnes on her feast day. When they are made they are blessed by the pope on the Feast of SS. Peter and Paul, June 29.

palm 1. Branches of a tree of the palm family, blessed and used on Palm Sunday. Most palm in the United States comes from the Florida Everglades. In some areas the custom perdures of using a local evergreen. 2. Symbol for victory by martyrdom.

Palm Sunday The great memorial of Our Lord's entrance into Jerusalem where He was about to suffer and to die. This Sunday is the gateway to Holy Week. Palms are blessed on this day and distributed to the faithful. The liturgical name of the day is Second Sunday of the Passion.

palms, blessing of Palms are blessed and distributed to the faithful on the Second Sunday of Passiontide, formerly called Palm Sunday, the feast celebrated one week before Easter. The Mass is devoted to the Passion. The palms are blessed before Mass and distributed to the faithful. There is a procession, if possible outside the church. The Mass follows. The Passion according to St. Matthew is sung, during which the palms are held, in memory of Christ's triumphant entry into Jerusalem. On that occasion the people welcomed Christ by placing palms on the ground and waving them before Him. In many places, local evergreens are used in place of palms.

Panchristianity A movement to bring Christian faiths together in mutual cooperation by good will and doctrinal compromise. Pius XI in 1928 warned against participation in the Panchristian movement and stated that there can be no compromise of dogma.

Pange Lingua (L. Sing, tongue) A hymn to the Blessed Sacrament written by St. Thomas Aquinas. It is used during processions of the Blessed Sacrament, Forty Hours, etc. The last two verses form the *Tantum Ergo* which is sung at Benediction.

pantheism (Gr. *pan,* all; *theos,* god) A false teaching that identifies God and the world, that says everything is part of the divine or the divine is part of the world, that makes the world an emanation from the essence of God. Spinoza, Goethe and Hegel are some of the better known pantheists.

papabile (pa-pa-bee′lay, It.) A term applied to a cardinal going into a conclave who has a good chance of being elected the new pope; sometimes the good chance is only in the popular mind.

papacy (Gr. *pappas,* father) 1. The office of the pope as spiritual or civil ruler. 2. The period of papal office, such as the papacy of John XXIII. 3. The entire body of popes extending back to St. Peter.

papal Of or pertaining to the papacy or the pope.

papal blessing 1. The blessing given by the pope. 2. After High Mass (offered by the bishop or presided over by him) on Easter Sunday and two other solemn feasts chosen by him, a bishop of a diocese may give the papal blessing to which is attached a plenary indulgence.

papal chapel 1. Those ecclesiastics who take part in the sacred ceremonies of the papal palace in liturgical vestments or in those proper to their rank or office. Formerly, a sung divine service was held at the papal palace daily. Present at these sacred functions were the palace attendants, cardinals and prelates, ambassadors, etc. These solemn and public functions were held in the Sistine Chapel or the Vatican Basilica. Presently, services are limited to certain special and extraordinary circumstances and solemnities. 2. The Sistine Chapel.

papal choir The Sistine Choir (q.v.).

papal flag The standard of the Supreme Pontiff as the highest official of Vatican City. It is the emblem of the pope as a temporal ruler. It is also accepted by Catholics as a symbol of the supreme authority of the pope, and as such is given a place of honor inside a church and in parades and processions. The flag has two equal vertical stripes of yellow and white. The yellow one hangs closest to the flag staff. On the white half appears the insignia of the papacy. A triple crown (or tiara) is above two crossed keys, one of gold and the other of silver. The crown represents the teaching, sanctifying and ruling offices of the Holy Father. The keys symbolize the power of the keys given to Peter.

papal flag, display of While the papal flag is the national flag of the sovereign State of Vatican City, Catholics all over the world have accepted it as a symbol of the spiritual authority of the pope, and as such it is displayed in churches, parades and processions. Flag etiquette gives precedence on all occasions to the American flag. In parades the American flag is carried on the marchers' right. In church, the American flag is displayed on the Gospel side and the papal flag on the Epistle side.

papal legate An official representative or ambassador of the pope. *See* apostolic delegate; nuncio.

papal letter A publication or announcement made by the pope or in his name by a delegated papal official. It can be a constitution, encyclical, rescript, bull, brief or apostolic letter.

papal Mass A Pontifical High Mass sung by the pope. It has a number of differences from an ordinary Pontifical High Mass. The Epistle and Gospel are sung in both Latin and Greek. At the Elevation both Host and Chalice are moved in a half-circle. The pope receives Holy Communion standing at his throne and the Precious Blood is received through a golden tube. Both deacon and sub-deacon receive under both species.

Papal States Those states under the civil authority of the papacy from 754 to 1870. At their height they included the duchies of Castro, Modena, Parma, Piacenza, Romagna, Spoleto and Urbino; the Marches of Ancona; the provinces of Bologna, Orvieto and Perugia. The possession of these states made the pope a sovereign and enabled him to exercise freely his spiritual authority. But they were also the source of much strife and political maneuvering. In the 19th century a movement swept the Italian peninsula to unite Italy in one nation. By 1870 all of the papal territory was lost. The pope did not regain temporal authority until the Lateran Treaty of 1929.

papal teachings, modern The modern period of the papacy can be said to begin with the reign of Leo XIII who gave new meaning to social teachings in harmony with reality and the Gospels. Pius X laid the basis for revitalization of the community on the foundation of the Eucharist and encouraged personal prayer life. Pius XI exposed the fallacies of Communism and determined an implacable hostility to the conspiracies of the totalitarian state. Pius XII called the whole of humanity to join with the Church in freeing the human person. John XXIII summoned all Christians to seek a basis of unity among themselves. Paul VI developed the themes of his predecessor.

Papal Volunteers for Latin America (PAVLA) A lay apostolate organization of men and women who work in co-operation with the priests and lay people of Latin American countries as members of a worldwide organization which is directed by the Pontifical Commission for Latin America of the Roman Catholic Church. In the United States the program is under the direction of the United States Bishops' Committee for Latin America. PAVLA teams are composed of single men, of single women or of married couples between the ages of 21 and 45 who volunteer to serve full time in Latin America for three years. Headquarters: 1330 South Wabash Avenue, Chicago 5, Ill.

papist An opprobrious term used in English-speaking countries for a Catholic. It originated in England to distinguish a person who supported the supremacy of the pope from an Anglican who believed in the supremacy of the British crown. It has various forms in literature and history.

parable (Gr. *parabole,* a comparison) A story or narration used to illustrate a supernatural truth of the moral or religious order. Christ made frequent use of the parable in His teaching. It must be distinguished from allegory. A parable is to be understood literally, the words being used in their ordinary sense; an allegory is

figurative, its words having metaphorical sense.

Paraclete (Gr. advocate) A name applied by Christ to the Holy Spirit (Jn. 14:16). John also used the term to describe Christ, but in modern usage it refers only to the Holy Spirit.

paradise (Gr. *paradeisos,* an enclosed park) 1. The name given to the Garden of Eden, home of Adam and Eve which was lost by their sin. 2. A synonym for heaven. 3. A place of happiness. Used in this sense by St. Paul as referring to the third heaven to which he was lifted in ecstasy.

Paralipomenon *See* Chronicles, Book of.

paraliturgy (Gr. *para,* besides; *leitourgia,* public service) Any public act of worship or religion that is not part of the liturgy; an extraliturgical function. The paraliturgy takes many forms such as a Bible Vigil, Holy Hour, Rosary, novena, Advent Wreath ceremonies (*qq.v.*), etc.

parallelism The balancing of one line of verse against another. It is used frequently in the psalms and was a distinctive feature of Hebrew poetry.

paraments (L. *paramenta*) Ornamental vestments or ornamental sacred hangings.

paratus (pah-rah'tuss; L. ready) A liturgical term meaning that one is dressed in proper vestments for a ceremony. To wear surplice and stole, as when distributing Holy Communion, is also considered to be *paratus.*

parclose (L. *claudere,* to shut) A screen, usually of metal or wood, which divides a chapel from the main body of a church.

parents, duties of Parents are expected to educate their children in the things of God in order that these children may work out their salvation. Implicit in this is the Baptism of the offspring. Parents are obliged to the material and temporal welfare of their children, to educate them and to develop their talents so that they will be able to provide for themselves in later life.

parish 1. A group of people within a community, organized on the basis of their common Christian belief. It is the heart of the Church in which the people of God lead a sacramental life. It is a territorial division of a diocese. A parish becomes canonical when its boundaries are defined by the ordinary, when it has sufficient means of support and when it has a parish priest with the ordinary power of that office. 2. A national parish is one based on language and embraces speakers of that language even though they may reside in another parish. 3. A religious parish is one entrusted to a religious order, taking its pastor from that order.

parish church The official church of a parish where the people of God gather to form a Eucharistic assembly. It is the place where the sacramental life of the people is carried out. The parish church should be consecrated as soon as the proper conditions are met.

parish priest 1. Loosely, any priest assigned to a parish. 2. Strictly, a pastor, in contrast to a curate, has ordinary power in the parish, governing under the authority of his bishop. *See* pastor.

parish worker A lay person, employed by the Church, who helps to develop the life of a parish so that it becomes a living vital organization which will effect the common good of the community. A parish worker acts under the direction of the pastor to develop a program to strengthen parish life through parish organiza-

tions, the liturgy and educational programs. The parish worker brings the parish to participation in community activities.

parishioner A resident of a parish; one who has a domicile or quasi-domicile within the territorial limits of a parish. Thus if one attends a church outside the territorial limits of the parish where he resides he does not become a parishioner of that second parish. The only exception is a member of a national parish.

parochial Pertaining to a parish. The term is frequently applied to the Catholic school attached to the Church.

parochial Mass 1. That Mass which a pastor is obliged to celebrate for the people of his parish. 2. The main Mass of a parish offered on Sunday or a holy day. It is usually a Sung or High Mass.

parochial school (L. *parochia,* parish) A school established by the Catholic people of a parish for the Christian education of their children. The school is usually attached to the parish church and has the same name as the church. In most cases, Sisters staff these schools as teachers, although in recent years many lay teachers have entered the parochial school system. The parochial school came into national prominence in the United States during the first years of the Kennedy administration. A debate arose concerning federal aid to church-related schools. The proponents of such federal aid feel that the parents' right to educate their children in a religious manner is hampered by denial of federal aid. The parents are taxed to support the public schools. Yet, Catholic parents likewise must pay the tuition of any children they send to parochial schools. This is a double burden for many. The Catholic parent would wish some tax credit for the money he pays voluntarily for the support of the parochial schools. Another reason for support of parochial schools is the national interest. Nearly 13 per cent of the students attend private and church-related schools. In the school year 1960–1961, there were 5.3 million children attending Catholic schools, while there were 36.3 million students enrolled in public schools. With such a large number of the nation's students attending private schools, it is in the nation's interest, proponents argue, to support these students. Opponents of federal aid to private and church-related schools say that such aid is unconstitutional because it supports an established religion.

parochialism That narrow point of of view which is concerned primarily with family or community good and only secondarily with conditions in the greater community.

Parousia (Gr. presence, arrival) It denotes the second coming of Christ at the end of time when He shall judge the living and the dead.

partakers of the divine nature A phrase found in 2 Pt. 1:4. It does not mean that man becomes one in nature with God but that through Christ man becomes like Christ and through Him enters into communion with God. If we fashion ourselves after Christ we have the promise of victory over the world.

particle 1. The small host used for the communion of the faithful. 2. The small piece of consecrated Host which is dropped into the chalice to mingle with the Precious Blood.

parvis A porch at the entrance to a church. Sometimes it is enclosed.

Pascendi An encyclical letter written by Pope St. Pius X in 1907 which condemned Modernism.

Pasch (Heb. *pesah,* passover) 1. A Jewish feast, commemorating the deliverance of the Israelites from the Egyptians. It was celebrated by slaying a lamb, whose blood was sprinkled on the doorposts of the houses. All Jews took part in this feast, and the head of the household explained its significance to all of the circumcision. *See* Passover. 2. Because the Christian Feast of Easter and the Passover coincide, the word has been extended to mean the Christian Feast of the Resurrection and the days that follow. Christ is likened to the paschal lamb.

paschal candle The large candle which is lighted from the new fire at the Easter Vigil during the Exsultet (*q.v.*). It stands in a high candleholder on the Gospel side of the sanctuary. Five grains of incense are inserted in the candle in the form of a cross as symbols of the five wounds of Christ. The candle itself symbolizes Christ, the Light of the World. It is lighted at various services until the Feast of the Ascension when it is extinguished after the Gospel.

paschal lamb 1. Originally, the lamb that was sacrificed by the Jews and whose blood was sprinkled on the doorpost of each Jewish house on the night before the Jews were delivered from Egyptian bondage. 2. The lamb eaten by the Jews during the festival of Passover.

Paschal Lamb Jesus Christ, the spotless Lamb of God, through whose sacrifice mankind was set free from the bondage of sin, and restored to the friendship of God and the life of grace.

Paschal Praise, the The solemn Praise of Easter, also known as the Exsultet, which takes place in the Easter Vigil Liturgy following the Blessing and Procession of the paschal candle. It is a song of great joy.

paschal precept The obligation of receiving Holy Communion during the Easter season. This obligation can be fulfilled up to and including Trinity Sunday.

paschal time The liturgical period between Easter and Trinity Sunday. It is a period of happiness and rejoicing because Christ is risen; it corresponds to the time Jesus spent with His Apostles after the Resurrection.

passion (L. *passio*) 1. A desire or emotion which builds up to an intense pitch. Passions are movements of the sensitive appetite toward a believed good. The passion, however, can be directed by and made subject to the will. Eleven passions are generally enumerated: love, hatred, desire, aversion, joy, sadness, courage, fear, hope, despair and anger. The first six arise in the concupiscible appetite (pleasure passions) and the latter five in the irascible appetite (aggressive passions). 2. The suffering and death of a martyr. 3. A written account of such suffering and death. 4. Passion (cap.). The suffering and death of Jesus Christ. 5. Passion (cap.). One of the four Gospel accounts of Our Lord's suffering and death.

Passion, instruments of the The articles associated with the suffering and death of Christ. They are sometimes included in a single picture, showing the cross, hammer, nails, crown of thorns, lance and scourge.

passion of a martyr 1.The suffering and death of the martyr. 2. The written account of the suffering and death of a martyr.

Passion of Christ 1. The sufferings, torture and death of Jesus Christ. 2. The Gospel account of the events leading up to the death of Jesus as read or sung at Masses during Holy

Week. Each of these is more simply called "the Passion."

passion play Religious drama centering about the Passion of Christ. One of the most famous is at Oberammergau in Bavaria.

Passion, relics of the A number of relics connected with the suffering and death of Our Lord are said to exist. St. Helena is reputed to have discovered the True Cross, various relics of which exist in many parts of the world. The shroud in which the body of Christ was wrapped in the tomb is at the Cathedral of Turin, Italy. The Holy Lance and Veronica's Veil are preserved in St. Peter's. Holy Cross in Rome claims the Title of the cross, one of the Sacred Nails and two of the Thorns. Near the Lateran Archbasilica are the Holy Stairs. A portion of the Pillar of scourging is claimed by the Church of St. Prassede while another part is in Constantinople.

Passion Sunday The fifth Sunday of Lent, two weeks before Easter. It begins the liturgical season of Passiontide. Jesus became mortal man to mediate our redemption, to form a new people who would be His Mystical Self. Since Christians share Christ's priesthood through Baptism and Confirmation, His Passion becomes their passion for an "eternal inheritance."

Passion Week 1. In the West, the second week prior to Easter; the week following the first Sunday of the Passion. 2. In the East, the week prior to Easter, Holy Week.

Passionists Officially, Congregation of the Holy Cross and Passion of Our Lord Jesus Christ; known in the United States as Congregation of the Passion (C.P.). Founded by St. Paul of the Cross who wrote his rule in 1721, which is taken as the year of foundation. The purpose of the congregation is to keep men mindful of the Passion and death of Our Lord. The priests conduct missions, retreats, staff parishes and do foreign mission work. The Divine Office is recited in choir, and once a week Matins and Lauds are cited at 2 A.M. There are three fast days a week and members practice other penances. The motherhouse is in Rome. There are two provinces in the United States, eastern and western. The eastern province publishes *The Sign* magazine.

Passiontide   The period from Passion Sunday to the Easter Vigil. During this time the Church is in mourning, all images are covered and the liturgical color is violet.

passive resistance   Non violent refusal of a minority or dominated group to cooperate with the majority or dominant group.

Passover   A solemn Jewish feast commemorating the events of Ex. 12 which describes how God passed over Egypt and struck dead the first born of every family whose doorpost had not been sprinkled with the blood of a sacrificial lamb. As a result of the tragedy which befell the Egyptians, Moses was permitted to lead the Jewish people out of Egypt. It is kept on the 14th of the lunar month Nisan and approximates the Christian Easter. It foreshadowed the Christian Passover when through the sacrifice of the immaculate Lamb of God, mankind was freed from the bondage of sin and restored to life with God.

pastor (L. shepherd)   A priest who is appointed in charge of a parish. He is assisted by one or more curates when the congregation is large enough. He has certain rights, privileges and obligations as defined in canon law.

Pastor Aeternus (L. Eternal Shepherd)   The name of the constitution of Vatican Council I which defined the primacy and infallibility of the pope.

Pastoral Epistles   The three Epistles, 1 Timothy, 2 Timothy and Titus, are known as the Pastoral Epistles because they are principally concerned with the pastoral duties of the men to whom they are addressed. Timothy and Titus were two of Paul's closest workers. The Epistles were not merely personal letters but were also meant for the communities over which these men presided.

pastoral letter   A written communication addressed by an ordinary to the faithful and/or clergy of his diocese. A pastoral letter directed to the faithful is read at the Masses on Sunday and is usually published in the diocesan newspaper. The pastoral letter can touch on anything affecting the spiritual life of the people of the diocese.

pastoral offices   Those offices which are directed toward the care of souls; these would be offices of the pope, bishop and pastor of a parish.

pastoral staff   Another name for a crosier (*q.v.*).

paten (L. *patena,* a dish)   1. A saucerlike disc of the same material as the chalice, which is used to hold the host to be consecrated; and after the Pater Noster it holds the Consecrated Bread. It, with the chalice, is consecrated by a bishop. 2. The communion plate (*q.v.*).

Pater Noster (L. Our Father)   The first two words in the Latin form of the Lord's Prayer. *See* Lord's Prayer, the.

paternalism An attitude of pity which causes a person to do everything for others rather than teaching them to do for themselves. It is opposed to charity and is allied to pride and racism. Endless hours of passing out food to a hungry people ceases to be charity if no effort is made to teach the people how to improve or vary their crops.

patience (L. *patientia*) A virtue which enables its possessor to endure with equanimity all physical and moral sufferings for the love of God. There are three degrees of patience which correspond to the three stages of spiritual development: 1. suffering is accepted as coming from God; 2. suffering is embraced that we might be more like Christ; 3. suffering is loved and sought for the sake of God.

patriarch (Gr. *pater,* father; *archos,* chief) 1. *Biblical.* The father or founder of a tribe. 2. *Ecclesiastical.* In the Latin Rite, the Patriarch of the West (*q.v.*) or one of the titular patriarchs (*q.v.*). In the Oriental Church the patriarch exercises actual jurisdiction over one of the rites of churches. *See* patriarchate.

Patriarch of the West The Patriarch of Rome, the pope. It is one of the titles given the pope and distinguishes him from Vicar of Christ, or head of the entire Church, and from his lesser titles as Primate of Italy and Bishop of Rome.

patriarch, titular A Latin Rite bishop who has the title of patriarch without duties of the office. There have been eight such patriarchs: Constantinople, Alexandria, Antioch, Jerusalem, Venice, West Indies (Madrid), East Indies (Goa) and Lisbon. The first three are no longer listed in the *Annuario Pontificio.* The first four patriarchates were set up in the Crusades but, except for Alexandria, which was always merely a title, the other three had jurisdiction. After the Crusades, these Latin patriarchs resided in Rome and were titular only.

patriarchal cross The archiepiscopal cross (*q.v.*).

patriarchate 1. The territory over which a patriarch has jurisdiction and of which he is the chief bishop. Following the Council of Chalcedon (451) the title of patriarch was reserved to the titulars of the great sees of Rome, Constantinople, Alexandria, Antioch and Jerusalem. Some of the dissident Oriental patriarchs, on returning to Catholic unity, preserved their title and privileges, as well as jurisdiction. In this way there exists today a Patriarchate of Alexandria for the Copts; three of Antioch, for the Melkites, Syrians and Maronites; one for the Armenians; one for the Chaldees. (*See* patriarch, titular.) 2. The office of patriarch. Patriarchs in union with the Holy See have the following patriarchates: Rome and all the West, the pope; Alexandria, Egypt (Coptic); Antioch, Syria (Syrian, Melkite and Maronite); Jerusalem (Latin, Melkite); Babylon of the Chaldeans, in Baghdad, Iraq (Chaldean); Cilicia, in Beirut, Lebanon (Armenian); Western Indies, in Madrid, Spain (Latin); Eastern Indies, in Goa, India (Latin); Lisbon, Portugal (Latin); Venice, Italy (Latin).

Patriarchate of the West The territory governed by the Pope as Patriarch of the West. It includes all that territory where Latin is the classical liturgical language, where the Roman Rite is followed and where Roman canon law obliges.

patriarchs, scriptural (Gr. *patriarches,* chief father) A patriarch in the Old Testament was the founder of a family. The Old Testament labels many as patriarchs: the early heads of families before the Flood (1 Par. 24:31); the heads of the 12 tribes of Israel (1 Par. 27:22). This title is especially applied to the three great ancestors of the Jewish people before Moses–Abraham, Isaac and Jacob.

patrimony One of the necessary canonical titles under which a cleric is ordained, the others being "benefice" and "pension." It means that the cleric has sufficient means of support so that he does not have to be dependent on others. This patrimony should be secure and sufficient.

patriotism Love of one's country. St. Paul (Ti. 3:1) defined the Christian attitude toward the state: "Admonish them to be subject to princes and authorities, obeying commands, ready for every good work." Thus Catholic teaching has always required patriotism. It is a virtue akin to justice to pay one's debts to one's country, and charity demands that we love those neighbors who are our fellow countrymen. Therefore, we are not only allowed to love our own country but are expected to do so. Patriotism must be distinguished from nationalism which is an excessive patriotism.

Patrology (L. *pater,* father; *logos,* science) A study of the writings, sermons and teachings of the Fathers of the Church. Also called Patristics.

patron saint 1. Saints chosen to intercede with God for a region, country, city or other locality and approved by the Holy See. The Immaculate Conception is the patron saint of the United States; St. Francis of Assisi of San Francisco, etc. 2. A saint chosen to represent a diocese before the throne of God or one after whom a church, altar or other religious institution is named. 3. A saint after whom a person is named

in Baptism or Confirmation. *See* Appendix: Christian Names. 4. A saint who is connected in a particular way with a profession, occupation or state in life. *See* Appendix: Patron Saints.

patronage (L. *jus patronatus,* patronage right) The total of privileges and duties which are granted to founders of churches, chapels and benefices. Patronage according to the Code is real or personal; ecclesiastical, lay or mixed; hereditary or pertaining to a family or group of families. The Code does not permit new patronages to be established. The principal rights of patrons are to present a cleric for the vacant church or benefice, an allowance of support over and above that needed for the benefice and a precedence of honor.

Patronato Real (Sp. royal patronage) Concessions granted to monarchs by the Church for service to the Catholic religion. The term is usually used in reference to the New World (*Real Patronato de Indias*). There had been precedents for royal patronage before the discovery of the New World. A quarrel in 1482 over the appointment of the Bishop of Cuenca, Spain, was settled when Sixtus IV allowed the Spanish monarchs to propose candidates they would favor in filling vacancies. The same pope at the time of the Granada Crusade allowed the Spanish monarchs the right of patronage over all benefices to be reconquered, plus a third part of all tithes collected. The bull *Inter Caetera,* issued in 1493 by Alexander VI, empowered Ferdinand and Isabella to send missioners to the New World and to be responsible for the Christianization of the Indies. Because of the expense involved, Alexander issued *Eximiae Devotionis* in 1501 which allowed the monarchs to collect the tithes due to the Church in the colonies and to use this money to defray the expense of Christianization. In 1508 Julius II in his bull *Universalis Ecclesiae* allowed the Spanish crown to name the candidates for all ecclesiastical offices (from archbishops to curates) in the Indies, plus the right to define the territory of bishops and the right to sanction the extension of mission activity. Over the years there were some abuses but the Spanish crown on the whole used the *Patronato* loyally. When the revolutionary movement began in the New World and Spain was driven from her colonies, the new governments claimed the right of *Patronato*. It still exists in some Latin American countries in one form or another. In Spain, the Head of State still proposes candidates for all bishoprics.

patroness of the United States In 1846 the 23 bishops of the United States, assembled at the Sixth Provincial Council of Baltimore, petitioned the Holy See that Mary under the title "Our Lady of the Immmaculate Conception" be made patroness of the United States. Pope Pius IX approved the request in 1847.

Paul, St. Author of many New Testament Epistles, Apostle of the Gentiles. Born *c.* A.D. 5-10 in a Jewish ghetto at Tarsus in Cilicia, a Roman colony in Asia Minor in which the Greek language was spoken. Taking as his trade that of making tents and cloaks, he studied in Jerusalem at the rabbinical school of the famous teacher Hillel. St. Paul first enters New Testament history when he is present around the year 36 at the stoning of the deacon, Stephen. Saul, as he was then called, held the cloaks of some of those who martyred Stephen. It was after this that Paul was converted when, on the road to Damascus, a sudden dazzling light shone about him and the voice of Jesus asked the question, "Saul, Saul, why dost thou persecute Me?" (Acts 9:3-9). After his conversion Paul set out on a missionary life that took him all over Asia Minor and to Rome. He went on three great missionary journeys, from A.D. 45-49, A.D. 50-52 and A.D. 53-58. While on these journeys he helped establish and strengthen local churches both by his presence and words, and by his Epistles to these churches. Fourteen Epistles are attributed to Paul. In A.D. 67 Paul was beheaded in Rome.

Pauline Privilege This privilege of dissolution of a marriage is based upon the dispensation of the Apostle St. Paul (1 Cor. 7:12-15). It may be used under the following conditions: after two unbaptized persons have contracted marriage (even though it may be consummated), one of them receives Christian Baptism. The unbaptized party departs either physically (by desertion), or morally (by refusing to live with the Christian in such a way that his or her Christianity can be practiced). Upon questioning, the unbaptized party refuses to live in peace with the Christian. A marriage in which all these conditions are fulfilled can be dissolved by the Church.

Paulists, the The Society of Missionary Priests of St. Paul. A society of priests, generally called the Paulist Fathers, founded in 1858 by Father Isaac Thomas Hecker (1819–1888), a convert to the Catholic Faith in 1844, who first joined the Redemptorists in Belgium, returning to work with them in their missions in the United States. Owing to a misunderstanding, he and several other American priests were expelled from the

Redemptorists. In Rome they obtained the approval of Pope Pius IX and recommendations from Propaganda to the American hierarchy for the founding of a new society. Father Hecker, with Fathers Hewitt, Deshon, Baker and Walworth, all converts and all Americans, began work in New York with the hearty approval of Archbishop Hughes. Their special work was the conversion .of America. They were devoted and dedicated; they knew how to approach the people; and they were well received everywhere. Paulists observe the evangelical counsels without making the vows, aspire after Christian perfection and dedicate themselves to the apostolic life. Their work among non-Catholics is carried on by prayer; by good example; by their devotion to their people; by using the press, missions, retreats, Information Centers, Inquiry Classes. They publish numerous pamphlets and books. Their magazine, *Catholic World*, founded by Father Hecker in 1865, has a wide reputation for literary excellence. Their headquarters is in New York City.

PAVLA *See* Papal Volunteers for Latin America.

Pax Romana A union of national Catholic university student federations. With the main objective of promoting international peace, it formulates Catholic student opinion on leading questions of the day. General Secretariate is in Fribourg, Switzerland. United States headquarters is in the Youth Department of NCWC, Washington, D.C.

Pax, the *See* Kiss of Peace.

Pax vobis (L. Peace to you) The greeting given by the bishop instead of the *Dominus vobiscum* following the Gloria. If the Gloria is omitted, the *Pax vobis* is also omitted.

peace The tranquillity of order. Man's inner world has been disordered by sin as well as his relation to others and to the world around him. Peace is the establishment of order within man (in his psychological, imaginative, mental, emotional and spiritual life) and in society (community, state, national and international).

peace of Christ One of the results of sin, as a separation from God, was confusion and division both in man's inner world and in his outer world. One of the results of Christ's redemptive mission was to bring peace into man's life. The Church, in her preaching and teaching of an order founded on Christ, and through the sacraments, seeks to instill peace in men's hearts and in society.

peace of the Church *See* peace of Christ.

pectoral cross *See* cross, pectoral.

peculiar (L. *peculiaris,* of private property) A parish or church exempt from the jurisdiction of the ordinary of the diocese where it is located.

peculium (L. property) An allowance made by a superior to one who has the vow of poverty in order that certain necessary expenses be met. Thus a religious who is a military chaplain and receives a salary would turn that salary over to his superior. In return the superior would give the chaplain an allowance for his ordinary living expenses and needs.

Pelagianism A heresy taught by Pelagius in Rome (*c.* 405) and condemned by the Councils of Carthage and Orange. Pelagius denied original sin and the necessity of grace. Pelagius admitted the existence of grace;

however, its function was not to initiate an act but only to perfect a good work. St. Augustine refuted the Pelagian doctrines.

penalty, ecclesiastical The deprivation of a spiritual or temporal good inflicted by legitimate authority for the punishment of a crime or the correction of a delinquent. There are three types of penalties: 1. medicinal, or censures (*q.v.*); 2. vindictive, or punitive, directly intended to punish the guilty person, e.g., degradation or deposition; 3. penal remedies and penances, for lesser guilt or lesser crimes, e.g., a canonical admonition.

penance (L. *poenitentia,* repentance) 1. A detestation of sins one has committed with the intention of refraining from them in the future; repentance. 2. Canonical: prayers, acts of self-denial and good works imposed by religious authority for offenses against canon law. 3. Sacramental: the satisfaction, imposed by the confessor and accepted by the penitent, in the Sacrament of Penance (*q.v.*). It is commonly a specified number of prayers, although a confessor may impose an alms or specific work. If the penitent forgets the penance, he is not obliged to it. 4. Spiritual: any work of reparation imposed by oneself or a superior as satisfaction for wrongdoing or sin.

Penance, Sacrament of Sins committed after Baptism are forgiven by the absolution of a priest who represents Christ. Christ told his Apostles, "Whose sins you shall forgive they are forgiven and whose sins you shall retain they are retained" (Jn. 20:23). This sacrament is popularly called confession. In order that the penitent's sins be forgiven he must be sorry for them and resolve to avoid sin or the occasion of sin in the future. Penance not only forgives

the sins committed and confessed but gives abundant graces which will help the Christian lead a better life.

penitence The virtue of being sorry for one's sins or faults; the state of being penitent.

Penitentes Officially, *Los Hermanos Penitentes* (the Penitent Brothers) A group of flagellants found in New Mexico. Because of the severity of their practices, they have been condemned by ecclesiastical authority.

Penitential Psalms, the seven Especially designated because in a very powerful way they awaken sorrow for sin in those who pray them. They are Ps. 6, "O Lord, rebuke me not in thy anger"; Ps. 31, "Blessed is he whose iniquity is forgiven"; Ps. 37, "O Lord, rebuke me not in thy anger"; Ps. 101, "O Lord, hear my prayer"; Ps. 129, "Out of the depths, I cry to Thee, O Lord"; and Ps. 142, "O Lord, hear my prayer." Cassiodorus, who died in 583, referred to these psalms as "Penitentials," but they were probably known as such before his time.

Penitentiary, Chief The director of the Sacred Apostolic Penitentiaria, one of the three tribunals of the Roman Curia. He is a cardinal who generally exercises complete jurisdiction of the court.

Penitentiary, Sacred Apostolic The first of the Roman tribunals which deals with cases in the internal forum, granting absolution from censures, dispensations reserved to the Holy See, deciding cases of conscience, and handling secret cases such as private vows and secret matrimonial impediments. The Office of Indulgences was removed from the Holy Office and placed under this tribunal in 1917 by Benedict XV. It is of ancient origin and has undergone many revisions over the centuries.

438

Pennsylvania The second of the 13 original states, 33rd in area and third in population. Hudson explored part of the area in 1609; Argall, Brule and Hendrickson followed soon after. LaSalle traversed the area in 1670; and soon afterwards, Jesuits, Recollects and Sulpicians began successful missions among the Indians. In 1681 Charles II granted to William Penn the area which he named "Penn's Woods"—Pennsylvania. Penn, a Quaker of high moral principle, paid the Indians for all land acquired and made a treaty which was never broken. In 1683 he drew up a Charter of Liberties which guaranteed religious freedom to all, a most unusual idea in those days. Penn and his followers established the City of Brotherly Love, Philadelphia. There, in 1733, Father Greaton built the first Catholic chapel, St. Joseph's. In 1796 two Augustinians built a church. In the meantime, the first priest to receive all his Orders in the United States was ordained by Bishop Carroll. He was the Russian prince, Demetrius Gallitzin, who spent his priesthood as a missioner in western Pennsylvania, covering the area that now includes the present dioceses of Pittsburgh, Altoona, Erie and part of Harrisburg. The diocese of Philadelphia was established in 1808 with Michael Egan as first bishop. Pittsburgh became a diocese in 1843. In 1844 the Know-Nothings caused the death of 13 people and burned a school and two churches in Philadelphia. In 1846 the Benedictines made their first foundation in America, near Latrobe. The fourth bishop of Philadelphia was the Redemptorist, Blessed John Neumann, beatified by Pope Paul VI in 1963. Philadelphia was raised to an archdiocese in 1875.

In 1913 the Byzantine Rite Exarchate of Philadelphia was established and in 1924 the Byzantine Exarchate of Pittsburgh was established. Catholics today number about a third of a total population of 12 millions.

pension Canon law specifies that the ordinary may levy a pension on a parish for the support of a pastor or priest of that parish who has been disabled or who has resigned. The pension cannot exceed a third part of the revenue of the parish and ceases on the death of the holder.

Pentateuch (Gr. the seven-scroll book) The name given to the first five books of the Bible. Also called the Book of Moses. These books are: Genesis, Exodus, Leviticus, Numbers and Deuteronomy.

Pentecost (Gr. *pentekoste,* the fiftieth day) A major Christian feast celebrated fifty days after Easter to commemorate the descent of the Holy Spirit on the Apostles (Acts 2:2-4) and the beginning of the mission of the Church to reach out and offer salvation to all mankind. It is one of the truly great feasts of the year, honoring the third Person of the Trinity, and thanking Him for His grace, which remits sin, makes efficacious the sacraments, bestows supernatural life upon all the children of the human race who answer the promptings of the Holy Spirit in their hearts.

Pentecost cycle The liturgical period of time from the Vigil of Pentecost through the Saturday before the First Sunday of Advent. It is a time of application to Christian duty. There are three subcycles. 1. *Pentecost.* The liturgical color is red. It begins with the Vigil of Pentecost and extends through Ember Saturday. 2. *Trinity Sunday.* The liturgical color is white. It includes the week after

Trinity Sunday with the Feast of Corpus Christi on Thursday. 3. *Sundays after Pentecost*. The liturgical color is green. It begins with the Second Sunday after Pentecost and extends through the Saturday before the First Sunday of Advent. The number of Sundays varies from 24 to 28 according to the date of Easter.

Pentecost, Vigil of Pentecost, or Whitsun, eve. The Vigil of Pentecost, like Holy Saturday, is a great baptismal day. It is a day of fast and partial abstinence.

Pentecostal Assemblies A number of bodies which developed from the revival movement and founded in Kansas in 1901. They are fundamentalist and evangelical, accepting Scripture as the sole rule of faith. They await the Second Coming. They meet annually in a general assembly.

Pentecostal Churches A group of Protestant sects, offshoots from Methodism. The Pilgrim Holiness Church was founded in Ohio in 1897. The Holiness Church began in California in 1896. The Pentecostal Holiness Church was organized in 1898 in South Carolina. They are Wesleyan in spirit and practice, use Baptism and the Lord's Supper.

per accidens That which is not of the nature (essence) of a being but which is accidental to it. Thus the color of skin is *per accidens* to man since it does not pertain to his essence which is animal and rational.

per breviorem (L. in a brief way) A liturgical direction indicating that one may ascend or descend the altar by the shortest route instead of going around the steps.

per modum suffragii (L. in the manner of suffrage) *See* suffrage.

per se A term from Scholastic philosophy meaning in, or through, itself. It is that which rises from the very nature of the thing. Thus man *per se* is capable of laughter.

peregrinus (L. stranger) A canonical term for a person who is temporarily living outside his domicile or quasi-domicile. As such he is subject to the ecclesiastical laws of the place where he actually is.

perfection 1. An attribute of God. Only God has complete and full perfection; any perfections attributed to humans are only relative. 2. That state of the Christian which according to St. Thomas consists "in charity, first and foremost in the love of God, then in the love of neighbor."

perfection, divine In created things we find perfection in varying degrees. Some creatures are more perfect than others. Of created things we often hear it said, "Nothing is perfect." Yet God, an uncreated Being, is perfect. Because God is the first cause of everything that comes into existence, we can say that He contains all the perfections found in His creatures but in a perfect way. As an example, an artist can make a copy of a famous masterpiece. The original is perfect. The copy achieves perfection inasmuch as it measures up to the original from which it is copied. Yet, since it is a copy, it will never achieve the absolute perfection of the original. God is a masterpiece, the masterpiece. His creatures achieve perfection inasmuch as they reflect His perfection, yet they can only reflect.

perfection, state of God has given us not only a natural life but also a share in His spiritual life. All life must be perfected. Perfection is of two kinds: 1. *absolute,* in which the end of perfection is attained only in heaven; 2. *relative,* which is the perfection we can reach here on earth, namely union with God. This perfection is reached by three stages:

the purgative way, the illuminative way and the unitive way.

pericope (Gr. *perikope,* a section) A selection from Sacred Scripture that is used as a lection. Mass pericopes would include Epistles and Gospels. The Divine Office also has selected pericopes.

perjury Deliberately lying under oath. It is a mortal sin because it calls on God to witness an untruth. A cleric who gives perjured evidence before an ecclesiastical court incurs suspension; a layman, personal interdict.

perpetual adoration The worship of God in the exposition of the Blessed Sacrament. This worship is continuously carried on by one or more persons day and night. The Forty Hours (*q.v.*) is a type of perpetual adoration. The worship is carried on more formally in certain communities, such as the Sacramentine Nuns, whose purpose is continual adoration of the Blessed Sacrament.

Perpetual Help, Our Lady of A title given to a picture of Our Lady which was painted in Byzantine style about the 13th century. Tradition says that it was stolen from a church on the island of Crete and for many years was hidden by the family of the thief. In 1488 it was enshrined in the Church of St. Matthew in Rome. During the Napoleonic Wars it was hidden. It was finally publicly enshrined in the Redemptorist Church of St. Alphonsus in Rome. Many miracles have been attributed to the picture and the Redemptorists promote devotion to Mary under this title.

persecution Attempts by the state to suppress or harass religion by physical or moral means. There have been many persecutions against the Catholic Church. The major ones are: the Roman persecutions, ten in number and culminating in the persecution of Diocletian in which 20,000 died; the English persecution which began with the Act of Supremacy in 1534 and which in a single year (1587) saw more than a hundred die for their beliefs; the Irish persecution under Queen Elizabeth and Cromwell; the German persecution between 1830 and 1886 which resulted in confiscation of property, imprisonment of bishops, laicization of education and expulsion of religious; the French persecution which began with the anticlerical spirit of the French Revolution; the Mexican persecution which began with antireligious laws in 1822 and continued over the decades and finally broke into full violence in 1926 through pillage, robbery, torture, murder and deportation, resulting in the torture and murder of over a hundred priests; the persecution of religion by the Nazis; the Communist persecutions which have taken place in every land where the Communists have taken control and in which priests and bishops are imprisoned and put to death, religious property is confiscated, and Catholic educational institutions are closed.

perseverance A moral virtue by which one continues in performing a good action despite difficulties.

person (L. *persona*) The complete individual substance of a rational or intelligent nature which subsists of itself and is incommunicable to every other being. The human person is neither body nor soul but the rational totality arising out of both. In individuals, person and nature are so irretrievably united that the multiplication of the person causes the multiplication of the nature; this is not the case with God. God has but one nature, although there are three Persons with essential but subsistent relations.

personalism 1. A form of existentialist thought developed in France which aims at discovering how man ennobles himself through action. 2. An informal religious philosophy of particularism which makes religion solely a matter between an individual and God without any social or community aspects. Since the mission of the Christian is to work for the salvation of all men, a religion of personalism prevents the Christian from partaking in the universal mission of the Church. 3. A philosophy that places stress on regard for the individual person in trying to preserve human values in a mechanized society.

personality The changing mental organization within an individual of all the thinking, emotional and physical characteristics which have enough consistency to establish him as a unique person. The term is the abstract of person. It is what enables a rational substance to become incommunicable.

Peru Once the center of Spanish colonial power, Peru has given 4 saints to the Church: St. Rose of Lima, St. Martin de Porres, St. Francis Solano and St. Turibio. Today Peru is 95 per cent Catholic (population, 11 million) but for the majority this is a nominal Catholicism. In the altiplano, the high Andean plateau, many of the Indians practice a mixture of Christianity and paganism; in the urban areas Catholicism is traditional and cultural. This weakness of the Church has resulted from a lack of clergy. In recent years, however, a new vitality has come into the Church, largely the result of a social-minded and apostolic hierar-

chy. Peru today is one of the Latin American leaders in Catholic social progress. Over 300 credit unions have been founded, a building and loan association is responsible for much new housing, religion and basic education are taught by radio, and there are training centers for Indian teachers. The Pontifical University in Lima is educating many leaders. A center of information in Lima is giving the proper image of the Church to the nation's communications media. *Noticias Aliadas,* a Catholic news agency, gathers and disseminates Catholic news to Catholic publications all over Latin America. A strong Catholic parochial life is being established and a new emphasis has been placed on Catholic elementary schools. A great deal of the activity is possible because of the influx of priests, Brothers and Sisters from outside the country. Among the major groups from the United States are, in order of numbers: Maryknoll Fathers, Immaculate Heart of Mary Sisters, St. James the Apostle Missioners, Marianists and Maryknoll Sisters.

Peter, primacy of Peter was the first to publicly profess his faith in Jesus and as a reward is promised primacy in the Church (Mt. 16:16-19). This promise was fulfilled after the Resurrection when Peter made a threefold statement of his love for Christ (Jn. 21:15 ff.). After the Ascension, Peter acted as leader of the Christian community, presiding at the election of Matthias. He gave the first sermon on Pentecost, was the first Apostle to perform a miracle. He pronounced the sentence on Anania and Sapphira, and on Simon Magus. Peter and Paul had their differences over missionary methods but not on doctrine. Paul referred to Peter as Kephas, a Rock, which indicated his acceptance of Peter as foundation stone of the Church.

Peter, St. A fisherman from Bethsaida who was chosen by Christ to become His vicar on earth. Peter was a disciple of John the Baptist, at whose bidding Peter followed Christ. It was Jesus who gave him the name Peter and appointed him head of the apostolic band. Jesus showed many favors to Peter. He cured Peter's mother-in-law, chose him to witness the Transfiguration. It was Peter who drew a sword to defend Christ in the Garden but who a few hours later denied knowing the Master. After the Resurrection, Christ renewed Peter's commission as chief pastor. After the Ascension, Peter acted as spokesman and head of the Church. Delivered from prison by an angel, Peter left Jerusalem and began his apostolic journeys which finally took him to Rome. He suffered a martyr's death during the persecution of Nero, dying, according to tradition, on a cross, head downward. He was buried at the foot of the Vatican Hill. Constantine built a basilica over the site, which was replaced by the present St. Peter's. He wrote two Epistles in Rome, addressing them to new converts in Asia Minor. They are included in the canon of Sacred Scripture. The aim of the Epistles was to strengthen the faith of the Christians and to encourage them in virtue.

Peter's Chair, St. In the apse of St. Peter's Basilica in Rome there is enshrined in bronze a chair said to have been used by the first Pope when a bishop in Rome. There formerly was a feast under this title on Jan. 18, and this is still the date when the Church Unity Octave begins. There was also a Feast of St. Peter's Chair in Antioch, celebrated on Feb. 22. These feasts have now been combined to a single Feast of St. Peter's Chair which is celebrated on Feb. 22.

Peter's Pence An annual collection taken up among all the faithful of the world for the support of the Holy See. The funds are transmitted through the local bishop. The collection takes its name from the fact that in the Middle Ages each English householder was expected to give a penny. The collection is said to have begun during the reign of King Offa in 787 and spread from England to other countries of Europe. It ceased at the time of the Reformation but was reinstituted by Pope Pius IX.

petition to the pope Any Catholic is free to address a petition to the pope either for a favor or an appeal, and during a trial may have recourse to the Holy See at any time. However the jurisdiction of the ordinary or lower tribunal is not suspended unless the Holy See decides to reserve decision to itself. The petition should be addressed to the pope and begin "Beatissime Pater" (Most Holy Father). It should be sent in care of the sacred congregation within whose scope the matter falls.

Petrine privilege The pontifical power to dissolve a marriage between a baptized person and an unbaptized person that may be consummated but is not *ratum*.

Pharisees One of the three main political parties in Palestine at the time of Christ. They were laymen who devoted themselves to special study and strict observance of the law. They were "progressives" insofar as they held for development and progress in interpreting the Law over the centuries, in contrast to the Sadducees. Politically, they advocated freedom from the Romans. They were the real religious leaders of the people. Their insistence on very literal interpretation of the Law made it difficult for common people to follow them. Many of them were sincere and zealous men who were responsible for the preservation of the Jewish faith. Some of them became bitter opponents of Jesus because of their failure to be open to His teaching.

Philemon, Epistle to　A revealing letter from St. Paul to his convert, Philemon, a rich man of Colossae. It is one of the Captivity Epistles. In the letter Paul tells Philemon that he is sending back Onesimus, Philemon's runaway slave, who (once worthless) will now, because of his conversion, be very useful. Paul asks that the man be treated kindly; and adds that if Philemon lost any money because of his slave's flight, Paul himself will pay it. He suggests indirectly that Onesimus be given his freedom. It is believed that the Onesimus who later became Bishop of Ephesus was the former slave.

Philip and James, SS　Philip was a Greek-speaking Apostle, to whom tradition imputes the preaching of the Gospel in Asia Minor. James, the son of Alphaios, also was an Apostle. He must be distinguished from James the son of Klopas, the brother of the Lord and the Bishop of Jerusalem, who wrote the so-called Epistle of James. This latter James was probably not an Apostle. The Feast of SS. Philip and James is celebrated by the Roman Church on May 1, and in the East the Feast of Philip is celebrated on Nov. 14, while that of James the son of Alphaios is celebrated on Oct. 9. The East also celebrates the feast of James the Less, Bishop of Jerusalem, on Oct. 23.

Philippians, Epistle to the　A warm, friendly letter written by Paul to the Christians at Philippi either at

Ephesus (54–58) or during his imprisonment at Rome (61–63) The Epistle has a twotold theme. Christian love and the false teachings of the Judaizers.

Philippines, Republic of the　A group of some 7,000 islands off the coast of Southeast Asia. The only predominantly Catholic nation in Asia. There is a complete freedom of religion for all citizens, including numbers of Muslims, members of various Christian sects and tribes practicing animism. The first European to visit the islands was Magellan who was killed there by natives in 1521. Villalobos arrived from New Spain (Mexico) in 1542 and named the islands "Las Felipinas" in honor of the Spanish prince, later Philip II. Spanish expeditions gradually conquered the native islanders and set up a government under a viceroy. Several Augustinian monks arrived from Mexico in 1564; the Franciscans came in 1577; the Dominicans, Jesuits and Recollect Fathers not long after. Missionary work was rapid and fruitful, missions and schools were founded even in the interior. The University of Santo Tomas in Manila, at present granting degrees in theology, canon law, philosophy, secular law, letters, engineering, architecture, medicine and pharmacy, was founded in 1645. Literature and science flourished from the beginning. Converts were made by the thousands, especially since the missioners upheld the rights of the native people against oppressive civil governors. According to the practices of the 16th and 17th centuries, religious houses acquired large tracts of land which they improved and turned into farmlands and villages. The people often preferred to live on Church property, where their lot was easier than under a secular landlord. The Jesuits, who had done a tremendous work Christianizing the natives, were banished from all Spanish possessions in 1767, but their places were taken by other religious orders and the work went on. Freemasonry entered the Philippines in 1860, became a powerful and disastrous influence and led to a persecution of the Church. Toward the close of the 19th century, uprisings took place in which Spanish priests were killed and churches destroyed. Some of the native clergy were hostile also to the Spanish friars. An insurrection in Cuba encouraged another in the Philippines, and led to the Spanish-American War. Admiral George Dewey was victorious over the Spanish in Manila Bay in 1898, but war continued in the islands until 1901. In the course of the Spanish-American War, most of the Spanish priests and religious were expelled, and far too few clergy were left for the needs of the Catholic Filipinos. Funds were lacking for the maintenance of Catholic schools, and many former tenants on the estates of the churches became the poverty-stricken victims of exploiting politicians. Churches and institutions were left largely unstaffed until Jesuits, Franciscans, Maryknollers and others began to arrive from the United States. The United States governed the Philippines until 1935 when a commonwealth was established. The people were given their independence and elected their own president in 1946. American armed forces defended the Philippine Commonwealth during the war with Japan, paying with many lives. At present there are American members of almost 20 different religious orders of men and of 10 different orders of women at work in the islands. There are 7 archdioceses, 18 dioceses, with 1 cardinal, 8 archbishops, 36 bishops, 1,516 parishes, over 3,000 priests, more than 800 schools and numerous other Catholic institutions. Catholics number nearly 22 million, 75.7 per cent of the population.

philosopher 1. One skilled in the science of philosophy. 2. A seminarian who is engaged in the study of philosophy as his major. This usually takes place in the seminary curriculum in what would correspond to the last two years in regular college.

philosophy (Gr. *philosophia,* lover of wisdom) The science of natural reason which consists of the criticism and organization of all knowledge, be it drawn from empirical science, rational learning or other sources.

phobia (Gr. *phobos,* fear) A fixed or compulsory idea. Phobias greatly diminish the voluntariness of an act, and hence reduce the gravity of a sin.

phoenix A mythological bird that is a symbol of immortality. According to legend it came out of Arabia every five hundred years and appeared at Heliopolis, where it burned itself on the altar and then arose, young and beautiful, from the ashes. Sometimes used as a symbol of the Resurrection of Christ.

phylacteries (fie-lack'ter-ees, Gr. *phylakterion,* charm) Two small leather cases containing verses from Exodus and Deuteronomy, worn by Jews during prayer. One is worn on the forehead and the other on the left arm. They are a literal answer to Moses' admonition in Deut. 6:8. The Hebrew name is *tephillim.*

piano The everyday house dress of prelates consisting of a black cassock with red buttons and piping, and a purple cincture. It originated among the prelates of a particular Italian dis-

445

trict and its use was extended by Pius IX to the Western Church, hence its name (*abito Pian,* Pius' dress).

picketing Picketing by strikers in a just cause in order to induce others to strike or to refuse work is lawful but only so long as it is peaceful. Moral pressure, however, may be used to prevent someone from crossing a picket line, such as the fact that he may lose business with other firms. It is a sin against justice to use threats, violence or other coercion, and those so doing are bound to restitution for damage caused to another thereby.

pieta (pee'ay-tah, It. pity) 1. Any representation of the Blessed Mother mourning over the dead body of Christ. 2. The name of the famous Michelangelo sculpture in St. Peter's Basilica, life-sized figures, of Mary receiving the Body of Jesus at the foot of the cross.

piety A gift of the Holy Spirit that perfects the virtue of religion. It is a gift which develops a filial affection for God in order that we might fulfill our religious obligations with happiness, and which also develops a respect and regard for all things pertaining to God. The words "pious" or "piousness" are sometimes used in a pejorative sense to indicate a false piety that is external, affected and hypocritical.

pilgrimage A journey to a shrine for a religious purpose; i.e., for worship, to fulfill a promise, to seek spiritual aid. From the earliest days of the Church pilgrimages to the Holy Land have been made by Christians. The most popular places of pilgrimage in North America are the Shrine of Our Lady of Guadalupe in Mexico; the Shrine of the North American Martyrs, Auriesville, N.Y.; and the Shrine of St. Anne de Beaupré in Canada. The Shrine of the Immacu-

late Conception in Washington, D.C., attracts several million visitors each year, but in most instances these would not be strictly pilgrims.

pillar of scourging The pillar to which Christ was tied when He was scourged during His Passion. A number of relics of this pillar are said to exist, one at St. Praxedes in Rome, another in the Church of the Holy Sepulchre. However, it must be remembered that these relics are not the whole pillar but only sections of it.

pillar saint *See* stylite.

pious belief A belief which while not defined is held by competent theologians, contravenes no doctrine of the Church and is not offensive to common sense.

Pisan Popes Two claimants to the papacy elected because of the Council of Pisa in an attempt to settle the Schism of the West. They were Alexander V in 1409 and John XXIII in 1410. They are generally considered antipopes, a fact testified to by the late Pope John who used the same number as his supposed predecessor of 1410.

piscina (L. fish pond) A basin with a drain leading directly into the ground which is used to receive sacred water that remains after a ceremony. This may be baptismal water, the water blessed at Mass, water from the first purification washing. Formerly it was the custom to build the piscina in the wall at the Epistle side. Today the general custom is to have the basin built in the sacristy. It is also called a *sacrarium* (*q.v.*).

Placeat (plah'chee-aht, L. may it be pleasing) The prayer the celebrant says while bowed at the center of the altar immediately before the Final Blessing. It is addressed to the Holy Trinity, asking the Divine Persons to accept the Sacrifice just offered.

plain chant Often miscalled Gregorian chant. It is the traditional music of the Latin Rite of the Church. This music had its origins in the pre-Christian temple and synagogue worship music of the Jews. This Jewish influence was transmitted to the West via the Syrian and Byzantine Liturgies. The music seems to have flourished in Western Europe, particularly in present-day Germany and France from the 7th to 11th centuries. Its form and use then deteriorated until the late 19th century when efforts to restore it to its original form were initiated by the monks of Solesmes. This ancient music is unisonous and free-rhythmed and is written on a scale of four lines. The scale is diatonic, although *ti* of the scale is sometimes flatted. *See* chant; Gregorian chant.

Plain People A term used for the Amish and Mennonites because of their simple and formal dress.

planeta (L. *planare,* to wander) Another term for the chasuble (*q.v.*) probably taken from the fact that it developed from an outer garment for street wear.

pleasure A feeling of gratification and enjoyment. Each faculty has an appropriate pleasure put there by God. As a result pleasure in itself is good and rewarding. However, morose pleasure (deliberate pleasure in something sinful) is a sin in itself even if only internal and not even accompanied by a desire for the object. The amount of guilt is determined by the object and the circumstances.

plenary indulgence One that remits all temporal punishment due for forgiven sin. To gain it one must be in the state of grace, perform the good works required, have the intention of gaining it and the intention to avoid all sin.

pleroma A Greek term to indicate the completion of Christ which is the Church; the fullness of Christ.

plumbator An official of the Holy See whose duty is to affix the papal seal to documents.

pluralism 1. The illegal holding by one man of several benefices. 2. In the United States the term is used to refer to the American society in which a number of beliefs validly exist. In the religious sense it is the existence of numerous religious systems all of which are equal before the law and which should have each other's respect.

pluviale (ploo-vee-ahl'ey, L. raincoat) Another term for the cope (*q.v.*).

pneuma (Gr. spirit) 1. Man's spirit as rising above the body and matter. 2. The Spirit of God, the Holy Spirit. 3. God's gift of grace to man which comes through the Holy Spirit.

Pneumatomachi (new-mah-toe-mah' chee, Gr. *pneuma,* spirit; *machomai,* fight) Members of a heretical 4th-century sect who denied the divinity of the Holy Spirit.

podium (L. platform) The large portable platform on which the pope kneels, which is carried in processions of the Blessed Sacrament.

Poland Of Poland's 30 million people, 25 million are Catholics. Nevertheless the Communist government continues to treat the Catholic Church with disfavor. Diocesan administrators have been deposed, seminaries closed, priests arrested and jailed, and Catholic newspapers and magazines forced to suspend publication. Cardinal Wyzynski was arrested and interned in a monastery in 1953 and kept there until the abortive uprising in 1956 when students and workers released him. Since then the Cardinal and other bishops have worked out an uneasy truce.

polemics (Gr. *polemos,* war) The act of theological disputation and controversy.

politics and religion Politics and religion are both concerned with human actions. Therefore, the Church, in its concern for all things human, must necessarily become involved to some degree in the political order. While the Church does not, except in rare cases, interfere in the private political views of its members, she must occasionally interfere in political matters, especially when moral issues are at stake. The arranging of concordats, the receiving of diplomats, the sending of legates and nuncios are a few examples of the Church's political activity.

polyandry (Gr. *polys,* many; *andros,* man) The state of a woman having more than one husband at the same time. This state is much less common than its opposite, polygamy, and occurs where men greatly outnumber women. It is found today in certain Himalayan regions and in very primitive society.

polygamy (Gr. *polys,* many; *gamos,* marriage) The state of having more than one wife at the same time. This type of marriage was permitted to the Jews under the Old Law in order to populate the world. Under the New Law and the sacramental marriage of the Church, marriage is a contract between one man and one woman. Polygamy is prevalent in many parts of the world, particularly in Africa, the Far East, and among Muslims. It found strength in the United States among the Mormons; it is now outlawed in civil law.

polygenesis (Gr. *polys,* many; *gignesthai,* be born) The theory that the human race descended from more than one pair of parents.

The Church teaches monogenesis, namely, that all humans have descended from one pair of parents.

polygenism (pol-i'gen-ism, Gr. *polys, genos;* multiple origin) Theory that many men evolved independently (*see* evolution) is contrary to Catholic teaching.

polyglot Bibles (Gr. *poly,* many; *glotta,* tongues) Those editions of the Bible whose text is given in many languages. The purpose of scholarly polyglot editions is to help establish the original text of the Scriptures. In such Bibles the present form of the biblical text is compared with the original language version to see how the text has been preserved. Origen, an early Church Father, composed a famous polyglot Bible, the Hexapla, to establish the correct form of the Septuagint text. There are several other scholarly polyglots and many others in a popular vein that bring together different versions of the Scriptures.

polyphony (Gr. *polyphonia,* many sounds) Music made up of several contrasting melodies. It is contrapuntal. It is a type of harmony in which the melodic parts are independent. It had its highest development in the fugue.

polytheism (Gr. *poly,* many; *theos,* god) The belief in and worship of many gods. It is common in pagan religions.

Ponce Institute for Inter-cultural Communication Founded in 1957 to prepare priests, religious and laity for apostolic work in Latin America. The Institute provides intensive courses in conversational Spanish, apostolic methods, theology of the apostolate, cultural orientation and area studies. It is located at the Catholic University of Puerto Rico in Ponce.

ponente (It. one who proposes) The official who submits and reports on a case for a Roman Congregation.

Pontifex Maximus (L. greatest high priest) A name applied to the pope. It is translated into English as Supreme Pontiff. It affirms the pope's supremacy over the Church.

pontiff (L. *pontifex*, high priest) A term used for the pope but also applied to all bishops. Its origin is not certain but it is commonly assumed to come from: *pons,* bridge; *facere,* to make (a bridge builder). In this sense it refers to the pope as Vicar of Christ, the bridge between God and man, or to one who develops the Church as such a bridge.

pontifical 1. In a restricted sense, pertaining to the Pope. Thus a pontifical university, a pontifical society, the pontifical family. 2. In a general sense, pertaining to a bishop. Thus, a Pontifical Mass, pontifical vestments, etc.

Pontifical Annual *See* Annuario Pontifico.

pontifical chapel *See* papal chapel.

Pontifical Commission for Latin America A commission authorized by Pope Pius XII in 1958 to study problems of the Catholic Church there, to coordinate collaboration of the Congregations and other offices of the Roman Curia in their solution, and to cooperate with the Latin American Bishops Council (CELAM).

Pontifical Commission on Social Communications A commission established in 1964 by Pope Paul VI to implement the decree on communications of Vatican Council II. The competence of the Commission includes press, radio, television and motion pictures, insofar as they concern the Church.

pontifical family All those who are members of the pontifical household and in the service of the pope. The *Annuario Pontificio* (*q.v.*) lists the following: the Majordomo, the Master of the Camera, Auditor, Master of the Sacred Palace, Master of the Sacred Hospice, sacristan, apostolic preacher, Cardinal Palatine, Pro-Secretary of State, privy chamberlains participating, Privy Chamberlains of the Sword and Cape, domestic prelates, Pontifical Noble Guard, supernumerary privy chamberlains, honorary chamberlains, Swiss Guard, Palatine Guards, Pontifical Gendarmes, privy chaplains, the Apostolic Almonry and others.

Pontifical Gendarmes Pius VII in 1816 organized a unit of Pontifical Carbineers. These were replaced in 1849 by Pius IX with a unit called the Pontifical Gendarmerie. At the present time the Gendarmes are under the Cardinal President of the Pontifical Commission for the State of Vatican City. The duties of the Pontifical Gendarmes, in addition to guarding the pope, are defending Vatican City, providing police protection, maintaining internal security and assuring the observance of the laws of the state; they provide services of honor, services at papal audiences, etc. They also guard Castelgandolfo and other papal properties in Rome.

Pontifical Mass 1. A solemn Mass celebrated by one of pontifical rank. It is celebrated either at the throne or at the faldstool. It is properly sung at the throne by cardinals, by a bishop in his own diocese or an abbot in his own abbey. There are more ministers than at a Mass sung at the faldstool. This latter Mass is celebrated by bishops not in their own dioceses, titular bishops and certain other prelates. 2. Any Mass celehrated by the pope.

pontifical services Religious services in which the celebrant has the right to wear the pontificals.

Pontificale Romanum A liturgical book used by bishops for rites and ceremonies other than the Mass. It consists of three parts. 1. *Persons:* rites for Confirmation, Holy Orders, consecration of a bishop, bestowal of the pallium, consecration of a virgin, blessing of an abbot, etc. 2. *Things:* consecration of a church, consecration of an altar, consecration of a chalice, blessing of bells, consecration of a cemetery, laying the foundation stone of a church, etc. 3. *Miscellaneous:* blessing of the holy oils, order of a synod, absolutions of the dead, solemn degradation of a cleric, etc.

pontificals (L. *pontificalia*) The ornaments and paraphernalia exclusive to one in pontifical rank (cardinal, bishop, abbot, etc.). There are eight pontificals common to all: sandals, buskins, gloves, dalmatic, tunicle, ring, mitre, pectoral cross. Among the pontificals not common to all are the crosier, gremial, pallium, archepiscopal cross, throne.

pontificate 1. To preside or officiate solemnly by one who has the right to wear the pontificals. 2. The reign of a pope.

poor box A receptacle for alms to 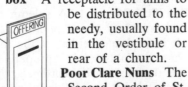 be distributed to the needy, usually found in the vestibule or rear of a church.

Poor Clare Nuns The Second Order of St. Francis founded by St. Francis and St. Clare at Assisi, Italy, in 1212. The first Poor Clare Nuns came to the United States from Italy in 1875. Solemn vows are taken and there is a major papal enclosure. The life of the Poor Clare is austere, given to prayer, mortification and contemplation. There are 24 monasteries in the United States and 7 in Canada. World membership is 13,000 nuns.

Poor Sisters of St. Francis Seraph of the Perpetual Adoration A German foundation that came to the United States in 1875 and which now has two provinces in this country with 950 Sisters. Missions are staffed here at home and in the Philippines. The work consists of teaching, staffing hospitals and caring for youth and aged. Vows are simple.

pope (Gr. *pappas,* father) 1. The visible head of the Church founded by Jesus Christ; successor to St. Peter. The pope rules the entire Church and is infallible when he speaks ex cathedra on faith and morals. The title was used for the Bishop of Rome as far back as 521 and came into general use in the 11th century. The pope exercises supreme jurisdiction in the Church but for smooth operation delegates many of his powers. His full title is Bishop of Rome, Vicar of Jesus Christ, Sucessor of the Prince of Apostles, Supreme Pontiff of the Universal Church, Patriarch of the West, Primate of Italy; Archbishop and Metropolitan of the Roman Province, Sovereign of the State of the City of the Vatican. 2. For the list of popes, *see* Appendix. For a study of papal privileges, functions, other special matters, consult the proper entry.

pope, abdication of the A pope may validly abdicate his office without the consent of any other person or persons in the Church. Papal abdication should be made to the College of Cardinals which will elect his successor. The popes who abdicated were: Marcellinus, Liberius, Benedict IX, Gregory VI, St. Celestine V, Gregory XII. A conditional abdication was signed by Pius VII in case he should be imprisoned when he went to France to crown Napoleon.

pope, authority of the The authority of the pope is derived directly from Jesus Christ and is not dependent on the cardinals or any ecclesiastical body. He has supreme jurisdiction over the whole Church and his authority extends to every Catholic. This authority is exercised by divine right as successor of St. Peter, who was chosen by Christ to be the first head of the Church.

pope, deposition of a As long as the pope remains the head of the Church no power or ecclesiastical body can depose him. However, if he should cease to be the head of the Church through heresy, a general council can declare this fact. No pope has ever been deposed. Antipopes have been deposed but their assumption of the papacy was not valid and they never were popes.

pope, election of The ordinary method of selecting a pope is by voting. The constitution *Vacantis Apostolicae Sedis* issued by Pope Pius XII in 1945 defines the method. Two-thirds plus one of the votes of the cardinals electing are necessary for a valid election. *See* conclave.

pope, primacy of the The pope has supreme episcopal jurisdiction over the entire Church. To establish this two proofs are necessary: the establishment of the primacy of Peter and the establishment that the pope shares in this primacy. It is readily obvious in a study of New Testament texts that Our Lord singled Peter out for a special place. He was the rock on which the Church was to be founded, the keeper of the keys, the one commanded, "Feed my sheep." Christ established Peter as supreme legislator, judge, ruler and teacher, and Peter exercised this power in the early Church and was so recognized. Since Christ meant His Church to continue to the end of time, He had to will the means for this, one of which is someone to head the Church, to have primacy of jurisdiction. The only logical person was the successor of Peter who had this power originally. Distinction must be made between primacy of jurisdiction and primacy of honor (first among equals). The successor of Peter has primacy of jurisdiction, for this power is necessary if the unity of the Church is to be preserved and the Church is to be governed.

population control *See* birth control.

portable altar *See* altar stone.

porter (L. *porta,* gate) 1. A doorkeeper. 2. One of the minor orders in the Church. This order was given to those who would have charge of the physical maintenance of the church building. Today it is the first of the minor orders given to an aspirant to the priesthood.

Portiuncula Indulgence A *toties quoties* indulgence (*q.v.*) originally attached to the chapel of Portiuncula, rebuilt by St. Francis near Assisi, which became the birthplace of the Franciscan Order. As often as one visited the chapel between noon of Aug. 1 and midnight of Aug. 2 a plenary indulgence could be gained under the usual conditions including six Our Fathers, six Hail Marys and six Glorias for the intention of the pope. The indulgence was extended to all Fanciscan and Capuchin churches and is still in effect.

Portugal At the Council of Illiberis held in the 4th century, historical mention is first made of Portuguese bishops; how long the Church was established in Portugal before that is unknown. During the age of exploration Portuguese navigators and colonizers took the Church to many parts of the world—Brazil, Asia and Africa. Following the proclamation of the Republic in 1910, there was suppression of religious orders and a break in relations with the Holy See. Religious fervor was renewed among the Portuguese people following the apparition of the Blessed Virgin at Fatima. Of the 9 million inhabitants of the country today 8.3 million are baptized. There are 3 archdioceses and 14 dioceses, staffed by almost 6,000 priests. Portugal also must supply priests to her colonies. There is a concordat with the Holy See.

posadas (poe-sah'dahs; Sp. lodgings) A religious ceremony carried out by lay people that takes place on the nine nights before Dec. 25, the birth of the Christ Child. A procession is formed each evening in which are carried small statues of Mary and Joseph. The procession goes to a predetermined house at which lodging is sought in the name of Mary and Joseph. Various prayers and hymns are sung during the procession and at the designated house after entry is permitted.

Positivism A system of philosophy developed by Auguste Comte (1798–1857) which denies the ability to know a personal God. It accepts only sense experience and positive knowledge, and it affirms that a person is able to know only relations and not causes. It is a rejection of metaphysics.

possession A word used in a very limited sense to indicate the possession or control of a person by a demon or demons. There are many instances in the Gospel narrative of demoniacal possession. The Church recognizes its existence in its ritual of exorcism. Only a priest can exorcise a possessed person and then only with the permission of his ordinary. Possession is not necessarily the result of sin or a pact with the Devil, for God permits it to occur in an innocent party. There are numerous cases of possession on record but the Church makes no official judgment on whether they are real instances or not.

Postcommunion The final prayer of the Proper of the Mass. It follows the Communion Hymn, and often refers to the feast while expressing thanks and petition for the graces of the mystery. It is said (sung at a High Mass) by the celebrant standing before the Missal on the Epistle side of the altar. There are the same number of Postcommunion Prayers as there are Collects or Opening Prayers.

postulant (L. *postulare,* to request) One requesting admission to the religious life. A person in the first period of religious life. The candidate for admission to a religious order usually spends a year or less in this stage before entering the novitiate.

postulate the pallium Within three months after the appointment of a metropolitan (archbishop), he must petition the Holy See for the pallium (*q.v.*). He must request it three times: "earnestly," "more earnestly," "most earnestly." Until the pallium is received, he may not exercise metropolitan rights, although he has full power and rights within his own archdiocese.

postulator The priest who is appointed to prepare and submit to the Congregation of Rites a cause for beatification or canonization. His assistants are known as vice-postulators.

Poverello, Il (po-ver-el'lo, It. *povero, poor*) "The little poor man." A name given to St. Francis of Assisi, beloved for his holy poverty.

poverty 1. The voluntary renunciation of possessions in whole or in part either by an individual or by a religious community. 2. A vow by which an individual religious possesses nothing in his or her own name. In such a case property may be held in common, in the name of the order or under some other title. 3. One of the three evangelical counsels recommended by Christ as a means of spiritual perfection.

poverty, Christian There is no possibility of salvation unless the Christian senses his radical poverty and dependence on God. The poor in spirit are those who are given the Kingdom of God (Mt. 5:3). The man who is self-sufficient proclaims his independence of God. We are always poor because we are constantly searching for truth, the will of God. Material poverty is a powerful aid in acquiring poverty of spirit.

poverty, vow of Poverty, in Catholic belief and ascetical practice, is one of the three evangelical counsels. A vow of poverty may be taken by a lay person or by a member of a religious order, or by an entire order or religious community such as the Franciscans and other mendicant orders. The vow obliges either an individual or a community to the renunciation of the rights of ownership, in part or in toto, and it also indicates the moral obligation to use material goods in the same way as do the ordinary poor —i.e., frugally, but not in destitution.

Powers The angels who compose the lowest choir of the second order of the celestial hierarchy.

practicing Catholic A popular term for a member of the Catholic Church who faithfully carries out the precepts of his religion, frequents the sacraments and is faithful in general to his religion.

praegustatio (L. pretaste) At a Pontifical High Mass when the offerings are prepared, two large Hosts are on the paten. The deacon takes one of the two breads and gives it to the sacristan or acolyte, who eats it. He does the same with the wine, pouring it into the chalice and giving it to the sacristan or acolyte to drink. This ceremony is a relic of ancient times and is obviously a precaution against poison. It is often omitted today. It does not break the Eucharistic fast.

pragmatic sanction 1. An edict given by the Roman emperor. 2. The name is applied to some of the edicts of the Kings of France and Spain. An example is the Pragmatic Sanction of Bourges, issued in 1438 by Charles VII of France which accepted the reforms of the pseudocouncil of Basle.

Pragmatism A philosophical system which makes the truth of something dependent on its practical result. It affirms the superiority of the practical over the speculative, the will over the mind. It is basically anti-intellectual. It was advocated by William James.

prayer An elevation of the soul to God to offer Him adoration and thanksgiving and to beg His favors in order that the petitioner may grow in holiness and thus give glory to God. In regard to its end, prayer is either prayer of worship or prayer of petition. In these two notions are concerned the ends of prayer: adoration which is due God as our Creator and Sovereign, thanksgiving because all we have or shall have is God's gift, reparation because we have offended God and must ask His forgiveness, supplication because we have need of His help. Prayer is also distinguished by its method, mental or vocal; mental prayer takes place wholly within the soul while vocal prayer is given outward expression. Finally, prayer is distinguished according to the offerer, i.e., public or private; public in the name of the community or private in the name of an individual. Christians are urged to unite in prayer, particularly in the offering of the Mass which is basically a community act. Prayer produces three main effects: 1. it detaches us from creatures; 2. it unites us to God; 3. it enables us to mirror God in our souls. The Our Father has been called the most sublime of all prayers because it was composed by Christ Himself.

Prayer, Apostleship of　*See* Apostleship of Prayer.

prayer book　A book containing non-liturgical devotions and prayers for private Catholic use that was formerly in common use by the faithful; such a book was published in many different versions and was not official. These books have been replaced by the missal, many editions of which contain prayers and other devotions in addition to the Mass.

prayer, attitude of　Prayer is communication or conversation with God. One can pray in the midst of work or recreation by simply recalling God's presence and offering the activity to Him. One does not have to be in a church to pray. This ability to pray to God at anytime and in any place is known as the attitude of prayer.

prayer, mental　Prayer which is interior, proceeding from the mind and will. This is in contrast to vocal prayer which requires the use of the organs of speech. Meditation, affective prayer and contemplation are forms of mental prayer. It is an es-

sential part of the daily life of priests and religious. The practice of mental prayer is recommended for all individuals who wish to grow in the Christian life.

prayer of Christ　1. The prayer Christ offered to the Father in the Garden of Gethsemani on the night of His arrest. 2. A former feast commemorating the prayer in the garden which was celebrated on the Tuesday after Septuagesima Sunday.

prayer of full union　The final prayer of the contemplative way which is marked by the suspension of all faculties and the complete and absolute certitude that God is present in the soul. It differs from quietude in that in quietude only the will is captured by God and the intellect questions at times whether the soul is really united to God. In the prayer of full union there is absolute certitude that this union has taken place.

prayer of quiet　A name given by St. Teresa of Avila to a type of prayer which other writers call a prayer of silence. It has three distinct phases: 1. first is passive recollection, an action of grace upon the faculties which creates a gentle and affectionate absorption of the mind and heart in God; 2. then the soul passes into quietude, a supernatural state which causes the soul to feel and relish God present within it; 3. and finally, the soul reaches what spiritual writers call "the sleep of the faculties," which is marked by a complete abandonment into the hands of God.

prayer of simplicity　That prayer of the unitive way (*q.v.*) which gives to life a unity of purpose and makes it more and more like the life of God. It is a work of simplification of the spiritual life which consists in the diminution of reasoning and a growing trust in God, the simplification of affections into one motivation and eventually the simplification of one's whole life. It is not a prayer in the strict sense but a method of contemplation and love with a purpose of making them habitual.

Prayer of the Faithful The common prayer which Vatican Council II ordered to be restored to the Mass. The prayer is to be said after the Gospel and homily. It is to be said in the vernacular. By this prayer, in which the people are to take part, intercession is made for the Church, for civil authorities, for those oppressed by various needs, for all mankind and for the salvation of the entire world.

prayer of union That prayer which has as its end the habitual and intimate union with God through Jesus Christ. It is the prayer of contemplation and is the prayer which marks the soul's development in the unitive way (*q.v.*).

prayer over the people The *oratio super populum* (*q.v.*).

prayer, vocal Prayer in which the organs of speech are used. Ordinarily such prayer is audible, although this is not essential (e.g., the silent recitation of the Rosary by an individual). Vocal prayer often consists in the repetition or reading of set formulas. All public or common prayer is necessarily vocal. The highest form of vocal prayers is the liturgy —the official, public worship of the Church.

prayers after Mass Prayers ordered by the Holy Father or the ordinary or both for some specific purpose. From 1884 to 1964, prayers ordered by Leo XIII were said at the end of Mass. Under the liturgical reform of Vatican Council II these are now entirely omitted.

praying to saints *See* invocation of saints.

preacher (L. *praedicare,* to proclaim) 1. One who through the commission of his bishop proclaims or expounds the Christian message of salvation. A priest or deacon by this act exercises the ministry or service of the Word, received in the Sacrament of Holy Orders. 2. (*cap.*) The English title for Ecclesiastes, one of the books of the Old Testament. The Hebrew root-word bears the meaning of a solemn announcement of sublime truths.

prebend (L. *praebenda,* a subsistence allowance from the state) 1. Specifically, an endowment held by a cathedral or collegiate church by which the occupant of a prebendary (canonry) is supported. There can be as many canons as the prebends will support. 2. Loosely, any revenues set aside for the support of the clergy.

precedence The right to a specified place of honor at church ceremonies or in processions. The pope enjoys the primacy of precedence over the rest of the faithful in the Church, an archbishop over his suffragan bishops, a bishop over the clergy and faithful of his diocese. Among persons of the same rank, precedence is given to the person who first attained that rank.

precentor (L. *prae,* before; *canere,* to sing) A choirmaster in a cathedral or collegiate church who presides over the chanting of the Divine Office and over other liturgical functions. Today the name is often extended to the cleric who is in charge of the arrangements for liturgical worship.

precept (L. *praecipere,* to command) A command given to an individual. The word is often used loosely, but properly it must be distinguished from counsel and law. A counsel is something good but optional, while a **precept** must be obeyed from necessity. Law is enacted by one who has public and official power, while a precept can be given by a private person, such as a father of a family. Law obliges everyone, while a precept obliges only the individual on whom it has been placed. Law endures after the passing of the lawgiver, while a precept ends with the death of its maker. The end of law is the common good, while the end of a precept is an individual good. A precept follows an individual and is in force everywhere, while law is in force only in the territory of the lawgiver.

preceptive 1. The quality of imposing an obligation of compliance. 2. A precept. Used in this form to distinguish from directive which differentiates something that must be done (preceptive) from that which is only advised or recommended (directive).

preceptory A house or community of the Knights Templar which was dependent on a commandery (*q.v.*) or another house or community. The knight in charge was known as a preceptor.

precepts of charity A term used to refer to the two great commandments of the New Law which were given by Christ; namely, love of God and love of neighbor. *See* Great Commandments.

precepts of natural law Those things which are commanded to be done or to be avoided according to natural law. Distinction is made between primary and secondary, between affirmative and negative precepts of the natural law. Primary and negative precepts are those which are unchangeable and oblige always in every instance. This is so because transgression against such precepts

frustrates the law itself and posits an act which is intrinsically wrong, e.g., the use of artificial contraceptives to frustrate the law of creation. Secondary and affirmative precepts oblige but not in every instance, yielding to an excusing cause, e.g., the fear of death; through this distinction God permitted the Israelites to practice polygamy.

precepts of the Church *See* Commandments of the Church.

preces feriales (pray'ches fay-ree-al'es; L. ferial prayers) Special prayers which according to the new code of rubrics (260) for the Missal and the Roman Breviary are said only in Offices of the Season and then only: 1. at Lauds and Vespers of Wednesdays and Fridays of Advent, Lent and Passiontide; 2. at Lauds and Vespers of Ember Wednesday and Friday in September; 3. at Lauds of Ember Saturday except the Saturday within the octave of Pentecost. The preces are introduced by a threefold invocation, followed by the Our Father and a short responsory prayer, and are concluded with the proper oration of the day.

Precious Blood, Sisters of the A congregation of women, founded in Switzerland in 1857 by a little group of pious women who belonged to the Archconfraternity of the Precious Blood. They looked upon the founder of that society, St. Caspar del Bufalo, as their original founder. The congregation took form under the direction of Father Karl Rolfus and their first superior, Mother Theresa Weber. They established two convents in Switzerland, and intending to be contemplatives they carried on perpetual adoration of the Blessed Sacrament. When discouraged by a hostile goverment they moved to Germany, where one community conducted a boarding school and the other carried on the contemplative life. In 1867 the active branch was asked to open schools in the United States. As the German Bismarck government was very hostile to the Church in 1870 the Sisters happily established themselves in Belle Prairie diocese of Springfield, Ill., and later in St. Louis (Mo.) archdiocese. They built their motherhouse and novitiate at O'Fallon, Mo., near St. Louis. They also carry on educational work in the dioceses of Lincoln, Neb., Omaha, Neb., and St. Joseph, Mo. They do overseas missionary work in Finland.

Precious Blood, the   1. The blood of Jesus Christ which was shed for mankind's redemption; a symbol of the sacrifice and suffering of Jesus. The early Fathers say that the Church was born from the pierced side of Christ, and that the sacraments were brought forth through His blood. 2. The wine which through the Consecration has been transformed into the blood of Christ. It is the teaching of the Church that the Precious Blood is received equally with the Body under the appearance of bread. 3. A feast celebrated on July 1. Devotion to the Precious Blood is as old as Christianity but it was not until the early 19th century that a feast was instituted for and celebrated by the Society of the Precious Blood, an Italian missionary society. In 1849 Pope Pius IX extended the feast to the entire Church.

preconization (L. *praeconizare,* to publish)   The solemn proclamation of a new bishop made in Consistory. Formerly, all bishops were appointed by preconization; however, today many bishops are appointed outside of a Consistory but solemn proclamation must later be made in Consistory and it is this preconization that deter-

mines the bishop's seniority.

Precursor, the (L. *praecursor,* forerunner)   A name given to St. John the Baptist, who *went before* Our Lord to prepare the way for His coming (cf. Lk. 1:17, 76).

predella (It. little stool)   1. The floor of the platform on which an altar is set. 2. The shelf behind an altar; the gradine (*q.v.*). This shelf is not liturgical since the altar is supposed to be a table.

predestinarianism   A heresy that came to full bloom in the Reformation which says that man cannot be saved by his own free will but only by the elect choice of God. The heresy denies that God wills the salvation of all mankind.

predestination (L. *praedestinare,* to determine beforehand)   A word that is given a number of meanings, and unless distinguished carefully, can lead to confusion and error. 1. In a heretical sense, it is a belief that one's actions are not only preknown by God but predetermined. It teaches that God from all eternity has decreed what He shall do in time and therefore whatever a person does for good or evil has already been decreed by God. It implies that God can will sin and eternal damnation, and thus denies man's free will. It fails to make a distinction between God's omniscience by which He knows what a man will do, and man's own free will which determines his acts. Thus while God may know a man will be lost, it is still God's will that that man be saved. 2. In a theological sense, it is that Divine Providence by which God rules the world, immutably decreeing the salvation of all rational creatures. In God's knowledge human beings are predestined for salvation and others to be lost, yet it is God's desire that all men be saved and to this end He gives graces and aids which man is free to accept or reject. Thus while in God's knowledge certain individuals are to be lost, this is not by the choice of God but by the choice of the individuals.

predetermination The doctrine of the Thomist theologians which states that God moves all creatures to activity. God's influence on the creature is physical, real and efficient. The doctrine of predetermination is based on the Aristotelian distinction between potency and act: it takes a being already "in act" to move another being to act. In the case of God and His creatures, God who is Uncreated Act moves His creatures to act. A problem arises concerning God's predetermination of man to act and man's free will. However, God moves each being according to its nature; i.e., necessary beings necessarily, and free beings freely.

pre-evangelization The remote preparation of a people in order to remove those obstacles which would prevent effective preaching of the Gospel to them. This preparation might be psychological, spiritual, socioeconomic, etc., depending on particular conditions. Thus a people in great poverty whose daily concern is merely to exist would have to be helped to improve their lot before effective evangelization could begin. Also a people whose lives are centered about personal pleasures and material comforts would have to be psychologically reoriented in order to receive effectively the Gospel message.

Preface (L. *praefatio*) The beautiful prayer of praise that precedes the Canon of the Mass (in the Western Rite) and is part of the anaphora (in the Eastern Rite). It concludes with the Sanctus. In the Eastern Rite it does not vary but in the Western Rite there is a Preface for Sunday (that of the Holy Trinity), weekdays, Christmas, Epiphany, Lent, the Holy Cross, Easter, Ascension, Pentecost, the Blessed Virgin, St. Joseph, Sacred Heart, Christ the King, the Apostles and the Dead. There are also special prefaces particular to certain feasts of religious orders.

prefect 1. The head of a Roman Congregation. 2. Prefect of the Apostolic Palaces. The majordomo of the pope. 3. The Master of Pontifical Ceremonies, 4. Apostolic. A priest who has jurisdiction over a district, known as a prefecture apostolic (*q.v.*), where the hierarchy has not been established. He has the ordinary powers of a bishop except that of bestowing Holy Orders. 5. A term used for a secondary official in a seminary or college, such as a prefect of discipline or of studies, or the priest who supervises a study hall, etc.

prefecture apostolic An ecclesiastical territory not yet organized on hierarchial (episcopal) lines, usually in a mission area, ordinarily dependent on the Congregation of the Propagation of the Faith. It is headed by a prefect apostolic who is rarely a bishop but who has wide episcopal powers, excluding the power of Holy Orders.

prelate (L. *praelatus,* one set aside)
1. An ecclesiastical authority who
exercises jurisdiction by his office.
This would include bishops, vicars,
prefects apostolic, heads of prelatures, abbots and major superiors in
exempt religious orders. 2. Those
honorary prelates who because of
service to the Church are granted
the title "Monsignor" and the right to
the special dress of their office. They
do not have jurisdiction as prelates
or any special duties.

prelate, domestic *See* domestic prelate.

prelate nullius (L. prelate of no diocese) One who rules a territory
that belongs to no diocese but is subject directly to the Holy See. Such a
prelate has ordinary jurisdiction over
the area, and is usually a titular
bishop. In recent years there has been
a growing move on the part of the
Holy See to set up this type of prelature rather than a prefecture apostolic. Such prelatures are particularly
common in Latin America.

prelates di fiochetti (It. of the tassels)
Three prelates of the Pontifical
Chapel, so called because they wear
ten purple tassels instead of the usual
six. They are the Vice-Chamberlain
of the Roman Church, the Majordomo of His Holiness, the Auditor
and Treasurer General of the Apostolic Camera.

prelatical dress That worn by prelates on ceremonial occasions, color
and garments varying with the rank
of the prelate. In general it consists
of a cassock, cincture, rochet, mantelletta and biretta (*qq.v.*).

prelature nullius A territory under
the jurisdiction of a prelate nullius
(*q.v.*).

presbyter (Gr. *presbyteros,* elder) 1.
A Christian priest as distinguished
from a bishop. 2. In the early Church,

one who advised a bishop. He could
be deputized by the bishop to perform
certain priestly duties such as baptizing, preaching, celebrating Mass,
etc. He ranked above deacon but below the bishop. Irenaeus gives the
word as a title of honor for prominent
and worthy members of the Christian community. Ordinarily, the
presbyters were chosen by the congregation as were bishop and deacons.

Presbyterian (Gr. *prebysteros,* elder)
One of the larger church bodies that
has a system of government based on
equal representation between clergy
and laity. The local congregation
possesses the right to select its own
pastor and its church officers, which
includes the Session, composed of the
installed minister and elected lay representatives (elders), the Board of
Trustees and the Board of Deacons.
The Presbytery, a district grouping,
is made up of installed pastors, ordained ministers and elected representatives (elders) from each church
in the area. Groups of Presbyteries
constitute a Synod. The highest court
of the church which meets annually
is the General Assembly; it is composed of ordained pastors and
elected elders. Presbyterianism began
at the time of the Protestant Reformation. The central figure was John
Calvin (1509–1564) who was trained
for a career in the law but abandoned
this vocation for one in theology.
Most of his reforming work took place
in Switzerland where his capacity for
organization and administration was
evidenced. One of his followers,
John Knox (1513–1572), established the Presbyterian Church of
Scotland which became the dominant
faith of that country. Northern Ireland and England also have strong
Presbyterian bodies. The first

Presbytery in the United States was founded in 1706 in Philadelphia. John Witherspoon (1723–1794), the only cleric to sign the Declaration of Independence, was closely associated with the Presbytery of Philadelphia. Today there are 47 million confirmed members of the Presbyterian Church throughout 52 lands. Nearly 4½ million Presbyterians, divided into 11 branches, are in the United States. Modern Presbyterianism is less legalistic than that advocated by its founder. The Westminister Confession of Faith, adopted by the Church of Scotland in 1698, is the statement of belief to which all Presbyterian ministers subscribe. Two sacraments, Baptism and the Eucharist, are practiced. Due to a renewed interest in liturgy, Presbyterians today are making an effort to adopt an official liturgy. In Europe the term "Reformed" is generally used instead of "Presbyterianism" to designate churches of the Calvinist tradition.

presbytery In the early Church, a term applied to the gathering of clergy within a diocese; later, a name for that part of the church in which the clergy assisted at divine services. Today it sometimes is used as a name for the residence of a parish priest.

prescription (L. *praescriptio,* limitation of subject matter) A legal method of acquiring ownership, right to or title of something, or of relieving oneself from a limitation or burden. Certain conditions are necessary for prescription: the person must be capable of having dominion over the object or thing, possession or use must be uninterrupted, the possession must be public, the possessor must be in good faith and the possession must be for a period of time fixed by law. Canon law holds that certain rights are not prescriptible; e.g., benefices, clerical privileges, Mass stipends.

presence of God, practice of the The prayerful act of recalling God's presence to this place at this moment. The practice is based on the belief in in the omnipresence of God, which holds that God is everywhere, conserving man in being and moving him to operation. God is believed to be physically present to each man. God is also present in a special way to a person in the state of grace. In Baptism a person becomes a temple of God, and the three Persons of the Trinity are related to him in a special way. This is known as the indwelling of the Trinity in the soul. In practicing the presence of God, a person recalls these two ways that God is present to him.

Presentation of Mary The liturgical feast of Nov. 21 that celebrates the presentation of the Blessed Virgin in the Temple. The feast goes back to a very early date, being celebrated in Jerusalem by the 6th century. The feast arose from the piety of the people toward the Mother of God and is based solely on an apocryphal legend of Mary's being brought to the Temple and presented to God at an early age. In the West this feast was not adopted until the 14th century when Gregory XI authorized it in 1372. Later Pius V suppressed it, Sixtus V re-established it and it was extended to the whole Church in 1585. The feast has become a part of liturgical piety not so much for the legendary Presentation, but for the honor it gives to Mary, the Mother of God, the "true temple of the Lord and sanctuary of the Holy Spirit," as the Magnificat antiphon for that feast says.

presentation, right of The right held by a person or corporate body to present the name of a cleric for a vacant benefice; the right of patronage held by a person or corporation endowing a church or benefice. The person so nominated must be accepted by the ordinary or religious superior unless he can be shown to be canonically unfit.

press, Catholic The first Catholic paper to appear in the United States was the *United States Catholic Miscellany* founded by Bishop John England in 1822. In 1829 Bishop Joseph Fenwick founded the *Catholic Sentinel* in Boston, known later as the *Boston Pilot* and still published. In Cincinnati, Bishop Edward Fenwick founded the *Telegraph,* and it too survives. Today the Catholic Press in the United States numbers some 131 weekly newspapers and 375 magazines which have come together to form the Catholic Press Association.

presumption A capital sin contrary to the virtue of hope which it offends by excess. It is a rash confidence of obtaining eternal happiness by other means than those ordained by God. Associated with presumption are the sins of tempting God and formal heresy.

preternatural gift That gift from God which is above and beyond the nature that enjoys it but which is not beyond the capacities of that nature. Thus it differs from a supernatural gift, e.g., habitual grace, which is above created nature and which belongs properly to God. An example of a preternatural gift would be the immortality granted to Adam and Eve.

previous marriage When a previous marriage exists, an impediment remains by which another marriage cannot be contracted; such a marriage creates a diriment impediment

(*q.v.*). *See* ligamen; Pauline Privilege.

price, just Value expressed in money. It is difficult to determine how this value is to be measured. St. Thomas Aquinas bases a just price on: 1. the intrinsic value of the article; 2. the resultant loss and loss of profitable investment which the seller suffers by reason of his sale.

pride The inordinate love of one's own excellence. It is a capital sin which leads to such other sins as presumption, ambition, disobedience, hypocrisy. It leads to contempt for authority and for one's equals and inferiors. Pride is complete when a man holds himself in such regard that he refuses to submit to God; such pride is always mortally sinful. Imperfect pride is when a man holds himself in too high esteem but still submits to God and his superiors. Pride destroys the merit of good deeds, is insidious in the way it grows, and is often difficult to recognize and admit.

prie-dieu (pree'dew; Fr. pray God) An individual kneeling bench with a raised desklike front on which the arms can be rested and which usually contains a shelf to hold books. In the United States they are set up in the sanctuary for a wedding, and are used by priests when kneeling in the sanctuary and participating in services.

priest (Gr. *presbyteros,* elder) A deputy of Jesus Christ who is charged directly and primarily with the extension of the Mystical Body of Christ, and who through the reception of Holy Orders is enabled to offer the Eucharistic sacrifice of the New Law. It is Catholic teaching that the priesthood was instituted by Christ as a sacrament, imparting a sacred and unending character on the soul. A

461

priest has the power of administering all the other sacraments, except Holy Orders, but for the valid administration of Penance and Matrimony he must be given jurisdiction by his ordinary or superior, and for Confirmation he must have an indult. A bishop is said to have the "fullness of the priesthood" because he has the additional power of bestowing Holy Orders and consecrating other bishops. A priest is often called *alter Christus* (another Christ) because the faithful should be able to see Christ reflected in his life.

priesthood 1. The office of a priest. 2. The character imprinted on the soul of one who has received Holy Orders. 3. The total body of priests and bishops. 4. Levitical. The institution founded by God when He chose Aaron and his descendants to act as mediators between Himself and Israel. The Levitical priesthood was charged with offering sacrifice, and the Book of Leviticus lists many additional duties. This was the priesthood of the Old Law. 5. Of Christ. Jesus Christ was the supreme mediator between God and man, and by His sacrifice of becoming incarnate and the sacrifice of His life on the cross became the High Priest of the New Law, in whose priesthood all those ordained in Holy Orders were to participate. 6. Of the laity. The Church is Jesus Christ spread abroad and communicated, the continuation of Christ in the world, the Mystical Body of Christ. The people of God who make up the Church are united to Christ in a very real and efficacious way. Through the liturgy all participants, lay and clerical, receive a real and direct participation in the Passion and death of Christ. Thus in a very real sense the identification of the laity with Christ in the Mystical

Body gives them a share in His priesthood, the laity enter this priesthood through Baptism, are strengthened in it through Confirmation and are vitalized in it through the Eucharist.

primacy 1. The office, rank or character of one who is an ecclesiastical primate, held by a bishop who exercises jurisdiction over all the metropolitans and bishops of a country. Today a primate does not have such power under canon law but in many places the title has been retained, e.g., the Archbishop of Lima is also the Primate of Peru. 2. Papal primacy. The office, rank or character of the pope who has supreme and universal jurisdiction. The pope as the successor of St. Peter is the supreme legislator, ruler, judge and teacher.

primacy of honor First among equals. It is a type of primacy held by the Orthodox Patriarch of Constantinople. Some of the dissident Eastern churches assign this type of primacy to the pope but do not recognize any primacy of jurisdiction.

primate (L. *primus,* first) A title formerly assigned to a bishop who exercised jurisdiction over all the metropolitans and bishops of a country or region. Present canon law does not recognize this power of jurisdiction for anyone but the pope. However in many countries the title has been retained and gives a rank of seniority. *See* primacy.

Prime The first of the Little Hours of the Divine Office. It takes its name because its choral recitation was at the first hour (6 A.M.) It is no longer said in private recitation of the Breviary but only in choir.

primicer The name given to certain superiors of chapters of canons.

prince 1. The chief ruler of civil society. He is expected to rule for the common good and general welfare with impartiality and justice. 2. The title is sometimes used for a cardinal who is called a "prince of the Church."

prince assistant at the throne The highest lay dignity of the papal court. Formerly held by such dignitaries as the prefect of the city and the senate. Pope William II designated that the post should be filled only from the Orsini or Colonna families, an act that was confirmed by Sixtus V and Clement XI. In order to end a controversy over precedence, Benedict XIII decreed that the duty would alternate between the two heads of the families. The office is ceremonial. The prince assists the cardinal-deacon at the throne, and ministers to the pope at the Lavabo.

prince-bishop One who formerly held both civil and spiritual jurisdiction over a territory. The title remains as one of honor in certain areas, e.g., the Archbishop of Vienna, Austria.

prince of darkness A title for Satan. The New Testament likens the struggle between good and evil as one between light and darkness.

Prince of the Apostles A title given to St. Peter and derived from the Latin, *princeps,* leader.

Principalities The highest choir in the lowest order of angels. They are God's ordinary and immediate servants to the world.

principle of subsidiarity *See* subsidiarity, principle of.

prior (L. superior) The superior of a house or several houses of a religious community. There are various kinds of priors but the most important are three. 1. Prior conventual. The independent superior of a monastery. The term of office differs among various communities, from life to a year. Some are elected, others appointed. 2. Prior provincial. The head of a province or national group of religious houses. They are elected and their term varies according to the constitution of the religious order. 3. Prior general. The head of certain religious orders (Augustinians, Servites, etc.). They are elected for terms according to their constitutions.

prior, cathedral Formerly, the office of superior of a cathedral-priory. It corresponded to the office of abbot. It existed only in England.

prior, claustral The coadjutor of an abbot. He is appointed by the abbot.

prior, titular Honorary title with no corresponding duties.

prioress The superior of a female monastic community. Her duties correspond to those of a prior. Some convents are directed by a mother superior and not by a prioress.

priory A religious house of men or women ruled by a prior or prioress. Some are independent (conventual), others are dependent on another house (obedientiary).

privation A type of vindicative penalty by which a cleric for serious crime is deprived of the fruits of a benefice or other ecclesiastical right.

privilegium canonis (L. privilege of the canon) Canon law states that anyone who lays violent hands on a cleric or religious (male or female) or who gravely attacks their liberty or dignity incurs excommunication by the very fact.

privilegium fori (pre-vee-lay'gee-um, L. privilege of the court) A cleric is exempt from trial in a civil court unless permission is given by the competent religious authority. Permission of the pope is required for cardinals, bishops, legates and others of superior rank. Otherwise jusisdiction belongs to the local ordinary. This privilege is not everywhere recognized.

pro aliquibus locis (L. for some places) Those sections of the Missal and Breviary containing Masses and Offices which are special to certain countries, dioceses and religious communities.

Pro Ecclesia et Pontifice (L. For Church and Pope) A papal decoration instituted by Pope Leo XIII for services to the Church, awarded to both men and women.

pro re gravi (pro ray grav'ee, L. for a grave matter) An oratio imperata which is ordered said for some serious reason. *See* imperata.

probable A theological term meaning "possible." It is used of theological opinions which may or may not be correct but which are possibly correct because of the weight of argument and the authority of the theologians holding them. Such an opinion can also be qualified as "more probable" or "less probable," again dependent on the weight of authority and argument.

Probatica (Gr. *probaton,* sheep) A pond mentioned in Jn. 5:2 where Jesus cured an infirm man. In Hebrew it was called Bethsaida. It took its name either because sheep were washed in it before being offered for sacrifice in the Temple or because it was near the sheep market and the sheep were brought there to drink. Some writers prefer the former explanation because they see therein a prefiguration of Christ in the sheep for sacrifice and the fact that cures were wrought there.

procathedral A church which is used as a temporary cathedral. They are common in mission dioceses where the building of a permanent cathedral is postponed because of lack of development.

process A term referring to the events, testimony, etc., leading up to a beatification or canonization. The preliminary process takes place in a diocese where the candidate for public honor lived, worked, died. If the findings are approved by the ordinary, they are then submitted to the Holy See and the final apostolic process is begun.

procession 1. A religious function by which people and clergy go from one place to another. They may be conducted within or without the church. They are prescribed either by the liturgy (Palm Sunday or Corpus Christi processions), by a superior for an extraordinary reason (rain, peace, etc.), or from devotion (May procession to Our Lady). A procession should be preceded by a processional cross followed by the laity and then the clergy in order of dignity and seniority. 2. A term used to describe the spiration of the Holy Spirit as proceeding from the Father and Son.

procurator (L. *procurare,* to look after) 1. The representative of a religious community who resides in Rome. 2. The econome of a religious house who is in charge of such temporal affairs as the upkeep of the house, purchasing food and other supplies, etc. 3. An agent who has been delegated by another to handle his affairs. What the procurator does in accordance with his delegation is regarded as done by the principal.

profanation A canonical term referring to the secularization of a church, i.e., turning it over to nonreligious use.

profane (L. *profanus,* outside the temple) 1. (*v.t.*) To make irreverent or blasphemous use of something holy. 2. (*adj.*) Secular as opposed to sacred; nonreligious use.

profanity The quality of being irreverent by the use of such expressions as "damn" or "God" in an unbecoming way. Unless the expression is directed deliberately against God it is at the most venially sinful.

professed Those persons who have been received into a religious community by the taking of vows. The term is opposed to postulant or novice. It can be used as singular or plural.

profession (L. *profiteri,* to confess) 1. The act of entering a religious community by taking solemn or simple vows of poverty, chastity and obedience. In addition the candidate pledges observance of the constitution of the community. Before profession the candidate must pass through a postulancy and at least one year of novitiate. Perpetual, or solemn, profession is not allowed except after a period of simple (temporary) profession in which the vows are renewed each year, usually for a period of three years. Vows taken in simple and solemn profession can be dispensed but in the latter case it is more difficult. 2. Of Faith. The public declaration accepting the teachings of the Church. This is usually done according to the formula of Pius IV which was drawn up after the Council of Trent, with later additions. This profession must be made by bishops and priests on certain occasions, e.g., when taking part in councils and synods, when appointed bishops, etc. In the United States, converts must make a profession of Faith before Baptism, except where Baptism is given without condition.

profit-sharing It is the teaching of the Church that workers should be given some share in an enterprise in those cases where the economic system is such that large and medium-sized productive enterprises achieve rapid growth precisely because they finance replacement and plant expansion from their own revenues. Pope John XXIII in *Mater et Magistra* declared that only an equitable share of the fruits of production should accumulate in the hands of the wealthy, and a sufficient and ample portion should go to the workingmen.

prohibited occupations Clerics are forbidden to engage in certain occupations. Among these are medicine and surgery, military service, legal practice in civil courts, trading and business, etc.

prohibiting impediments The prohibition by which the Church forbids a particular marriage for a just cause. The *Code of Canon Law* gives three prohibiting impediments: a simple vow, legal relationship, difference of religion. Dispensation must be obtained for the marriage to be licit.

promise A free and spontaneous contract whereby a person obliges himself to give something to another or to admit something. It is a unilateral action. If the person takes the promise in a grave way (e.g., by oath or swearing before a notary) or if its breaking would result in grave damage, then it binds gravely. St. Thomas says that a promise ceases when the matter promised is unlawful, and when the object promised or circumstances surrounding it undergo a notable change. To these must be added cessation, when the person who promised is voluntarily released from the promise or if one of the parties does not stand by his part of a mutual promise.

Promised Land Chanaan, the land promised by God to Abraham. The Jews returned to it following the flight from Egypt under Moses.

promoter of justice An ecclesiastic appointed by an ordinary to act as a judge in the diocesan tribunal. He represents the bishop and there is no appeal from him to the bishop.

promoter of the Faith An ecclesiastic appointed to represent the Church in various cases, particularly in the process (*q.v.*) of canonization and beatification. In the latter, he is known as the Advocate of God, but is popularly referred to as the Devil's Advocate, since it is his duty to question all evidence for error or flaws so that the person proposed for the honors of the Church may be proved worthy.

promulgation (L. *promulgare,* to publish) An official announcement or an authentic publication of the law in order that it may be known by the community. The ecclesiastical laws of the universal Church are officially published in the Vatican publication, *Acta Apostolicae Sedis.* Peculiar ecclesiastical laws for any given diocese are published in the official diocesan newspaper.

proof (L. *probare,* to prove) The compelling force of evidence which leads the mind to give assent to an argument or fact.

Propaganda 1. The popular title for the Pontifical Urban Athenaeum De Propaganda Fide which was founded by Urban VIII in 1627 to train students for the priesthood from mission territories and those from nonmission territories in missiological subjects. 2. The Congregation for the Propagation of the Faith.

Propagation of the Faith, the Society for the A world-wide society founded by Pauline Jaricot at Lyons, France, in 1822, in order to gather alms for foreign mission work. In 1923 the Society ceased to be a private organization and was taken over by the Holy See as a pontifical-aid Society and placed under the jurisdiction of the Congregation for

the Propagation of the Faith. The Society gathers funds which are distributed each year under the direction of the Congregations of the Propagation of the Faith, the Oriental Church and the Consistory. These funds are assigned to three general categories: 1. to all ordinaries in territories under jurisdiction of the Congregation of the Propagation of the Faith, to many ordinaries under the Oriental Church, to a few ordinaries under the Consistory for partial support of missions; 2. to certain institutions in mission lands (e.g., Catholic universities), judged by the Holy See to deserve special consideration; 3. for certain promotional efforts that will advance interest in the missions (e.g., Fides News Service). The Pontifical Society for the Propagation of the Faith takes no responsibility for other mission expenses; these are expected to be raised by the mission-sending societies themselves. In the United States, the Society is organized nationally and on the diocesan level.

propassions A name given to the sensitive passions which were part of the human nature of Christ, such as sadness, anger, etc. These passions were completely under the control of Christ's reason and were in no way disordered; moreover, Christ was impeccable (*q.v.*). Therefore these passions of Christ are called "propassions" to differentiate them from the ordinary human passions which can incite to sin or cloud the intellect or will.

Proper of the Mass Those parts of the Mass which change everyday. Such parts are the prayers assigned for a particular Mass; e.g., the Collects, Secret, Communion and Postcommunion, and the Readings from Scripture: the Epistle and Gospel, which vary according to the feast or season celebrated. The unchanged parts of the Mass are known as the Common or the Ordinary of the Mass; e.g., the Kyrie, the Gloria, etc.

Proper of the Saints The collection of Masses peculiar to each saint. The Masses in the Proper of the Saints have their own special prayers and readings for the feast day of each saint.

proper of the season The annual cycle by which the Church in her liturgy re-enacts the mystery of Christ's birth, life, death, Resurrection and Ascension. This cycle is composed of four periods beginning four weeks before Christmas: Advent, the Christmas season, Lent and the Pentecostal season.

property (L. *proprius,* one's own) That which a person owns or which may be owned. In the usual sense, it refers to the material world and its things as they are or as they may be subjected to ownership. There are many opinions on the origin of property rights; some say that the ownership of property comes from civil law, others from social agreement, and still others from occupation by force. There are also those who would limit or deny private ownership, such as the socialists and Communists. It is Catholic teaching that private ownership is a right flowing from natural law since it is useful both for peace and for orderly administration. In *Mater et Magistra,* Pope John XXIII states: "Private property, including that of productive goods, is a natural right possessed by all, which the state may by no means suppress." Pope John then adds that the right to private property implies a social responsibility. The right to property is not an end in itself but a means. God created the wealth of the world for the use of all men. This is the end, and the right of private property merely guarantees that use. When a people fail to use natural wealth for the good of all, they relinquish the right to property. This is the reasoning of St. Thomas Aquinas when he says that the use of natural wealth is a common use. Pope Pius XII elaborated this point when he declared: "Undoubtedly, the natural order, deriving from God, demands also private property and the free reciprocal commerce of goods by interchange and gift, as well as a functioning of the State as a control over both these institutions. But all this remains subordinated to the natural scope of material goods and cannot emancipate itself from the first and fundamental right which concedes their use to all men; but it should rather serve to make possible the actuation of this right in conformity with its scope." Thus the right to property is not absolute, neither is it unlimited. The right to one's property may be defended even by violence if that is necessary for repelling an unjust aggressor; however, the resistance must be proportionate to the attempted damage.

property, ecclesiastical The Church and any moral bodies or persons of the Church have the right to own and administer property. Christ instituted the Church as a perfect society. As such it has the right to support its ministers, build churches, maintain and establish religious institutions, and work for the conversion of mankind. It follows, therefore, that the Church has the right to the means to attain these ends and thus the right to property. It follows, then, that the Church has the right to exact from its members the material means necessary to carry out its mission.

Prophecies, the The four lessons chanted in the Easter Vigil following the Blessing of the New Fire and the Solemn Procession. Each is followed by a versicle, response and a prayer. The first from Gen. 1:1-31; 2:1-2 tells of the creation of man to share God's life; the second from Ex. 14:24-31; 15:1 reminds us that as God delivered His people from Egyptian slavery, so now He redeems from sin; the third from Is. 4:2-6 foreshadows the new Jerusalem, the Church, that is born out of the death of Christ; the fourth from Deut. 31:22-30 warns that even though we have a new life in Christ many selfish instincts will remain.

prophecy (Gr. *prophetes,* speaker for) 1. The foretelling of certain events which cannot be known from natural knowledge. The gift of prophecy comes from God. The only prophecies which the Church teaches as divinely inspired are those found in the Old and New Testaments. 2. In the Old Testament sense, a making known of the will of God, not only by foretelling the future, but by rebuking sin and evil, and by preaching the law.

prophetic literature of the Bible In this classification belong those books of the Bible whose literary form is that called prophecy, which contain the messages of the prophets. These are: Isaia, Jeremia, Ezechiel, Baruch, Daniel, Osee, Joel, Amos, Abdia, Jona, Michea, Nahum, Habacuc, Sophonia, Aggai, Zacharia, Malachia. These books are all found in the Old Testament.

prophetism Another name for messianism (*q.v.*). *See* nativism.

prophets, the 1. Collectively, refers to all who spoke for God or interpreted His message. (In the case of pagan or polytheistic nations, they spoke for the various gods.) 2. In the Old Testament, prophets were men under divine inspiration who, for a time, were to make known God's will: to lead the Jews back to Him by encouraging the more perfect practice of the Mosaic Law; to defend the oppressed; to offer advice to the rulers of Israel; and, occasionally, to make statements about the future. Those prophets who offered a written message were called the "literary prophets," while those who restricted themselves to the oral transmission of their message were termed "non-literary prophets."

propitiation (L. *propitiare,* to appease) 1. Reparation in order to appease God for offenses against Him. 2. One of the four ends of the Mass. 3. One of the three fruits of every good act, the others being merit and impetration.

Propositions, the Condemned Specifically, the 80 propositions condemned by Pius IX in his bull *Quanta Cura* which was issued in 1864. Also called the *Syllabus,* the *Syllabus of Errors.*

proprium de tempore Latin, the proper of the season (*q.v.*).

proprium sanctorum Latin,, the Proper of the Saints (*q.v.*).

proselyte (Gr. *proselytos,* one who has come) A person who has converted from one religion to another. It is used in a depreciating sense, since proselytizing has come to imply the making of converts by unfair methods.

prosphora (Gr. oblation) The rounded loaf of leavened bread that is consecrated in the Byzantine Liturgy. It is stamped with religious symbols.

prostration (L. *prosternere,* to prostrate) The act of lying face downward on the floor, or kneeling so that the head touches the floor. The act symbolizes submission, sorrow, petition or adoration. The act is used on a number of occasions in Catholic ceremonies. At the beginning of the Good Friday Liturgy, the celebrant and ministers enter the sanctuary and prostate themselves before the stripped altar. During ordination, the ordinandi prostrate themselves before the bishop.

Protestant One who professes Protestantism. The term originated when the Elector Frederick of Saxony made a solmen "protest" against a decree of the Diet of Speyer, 1529, which affirmed the right of Catholics to attend Mass, A "Protestant" became one who opposed Catholicity and the pope.

Protestantism A generic title applied to all Christian denominations outside the Catholic or Eastern Orthodox Churches. The term came into use in Germany in 1529 when the Diet of Speyer decreed that Mass should be restored in those German states where it had been discontinued. A formal protest was made against the decree, and those who made the objection became known as Protestants. The name soon came to mean all those who separated from the Catholic Church. There are hundreds of Protestant denominations, and Protestant doctrine is widely divergent. In general, Protestants accept three basic principles: 1. the Bible as the final source of information about God and salvation; 2. justification by faith alone; 3. the priesthood of all believers. Many Protestants believe that all men are lost through original sin but that some persons, through no merit of their own, are saved by God's grace. Protestantism minimizes the liturgical and sacramental aspects of Christianity. There are two main branches of Protestantism. One is classical or traditional Protestantism which includes the original groups that broke away from the Catholic Church: Lutherans, Calvinists and Anglicans. The second group is known as radical Protestantism: Baptists, Congregationalists, Methodists, the evangelical sects and the fundamentalists. Despite doctrinal differences Protestant denominations are actively ecumenical. In 1948 the World Council of Churches was founded, bringing together many Protestant and Eastern Orthodox groups.

proto- A Greek prefix used in English to mean "first." Thus Father Juan de Padilla is called the protomartyr of the United States.

protocanonical books Those books of the Old Testament the canonicity of which was never challenged. These books are in the Hebrew canon approved by the Jewish Council of Jamnia (*c.* A.D. 90). They contrast with the deuterocanonical books which are mostly found in the Greek translation of the Old Testament called the Septuagint.

Protoevangelium of James, the An apocryphal gospel attributed to St. James the Less, dating from the 2nd century. Although regarded as heretical from early times, it has had wide influence.

protomartyr The first martyr of the Church or in a country or territory. Thus St. Stephen is called the protomartyr of the Church. Father Juan de Padilla, O.F.M., is the protomartyr of the United States.

protonotary apostolic One of the chief colleges of prelates of the Roman Curia. They trace back to the 3rd or 4th century, and in the 5th century formed a college. They had various functions: legations and visits, investigation of processes, the drawing up of Council acts and of letters in the Apostolic Chancery, reports to the Pope and preparation of decisions. In the 13th century, they lived in common. In the 14th century there appears a distinction between the protonotaries (the seven ancient regional notaries) and the apostolic notaries, who could be also outside of Rome. From the time of Martin V a distinction was made between protonotaries *officio fugentes* and honorary protonotaries. The number of the former, which had been elevated to twelve by Sixtus V was later reduced to seven by Gregory XVI (1838). The office, the faculties and the privileges of the protonotaries were newly determined by Pius IX in 1853, by St. Pius X in 1905, and by Pius XI in 1934, through the Constitution *Ad incrementum,* which distinguishes: protonotaries apostolic in actual service, supernumerary protonotaries, protonotaries *ad instar* and titular protonotaries. Sometimes spelled "prothonotary."

prototype Theologically, the image of each created thing as conceived in the mind of God.

Proverbs, Book of This book of the Old Testament is really a collection of groups of wise sayings and terse statements about life that were written over a span of five centuries. The earliest group of these sayings dates back to 800 B.C. and comes up to the 4th century before Christ. Their purpose was to teach people, especially the young, to live correctly and to follow the word of God. This book belongs to a group of Old Testament writings called "Wisdom Literature." The Wisdom Books not only contained fundamental moral teachings, but also presented the reader with a correct human way of doing things, not excluding any part of life. Hence there is a great variety in the type of sayings contained in the book. There are proverbs that make no judgment, merely commenting on the world as it is; some judge the right or wrong of things; others give reasons why the good succeed and the evil fail. Throughout the book there are many proverbs that are arranged in artificial orderings, e.g., in one group each proverb begins with the Hebrew letter *beth* (11:9-12).

providence, divine (L. *providere,* to provide) That act by which God ordains all things to an intended end so that His purpose of creation may be accomplished. God's providence in relation to man is that ordering of events so that man can accomplish the purpose for which he was put on earth. St. John Damascene describes it as: "The will of God by which all things are ruled by right reason."

Providentissimus Deus A historic encyclical on the Bible, issued by Leo XIII in 1893, which contained an important exposition of the Church's teaching on inspiration.

province An ecclesiastical territory of the Church. 1. The territory of a metropolitan (*q.v.*) which consists of an archdiocese and one or more suffragan sees (*q.v.*). Thus the Province of Chicago embraces all the sees of Illinois. 2. A division of a religious order, embracing all the houses belonging to that order and located in a specified territorial area.

provincial The superior who is the head of a province of a religious order. He administers the province as the delegate of the superior general. In most cases the office is elective, but in some, as with the Jesuits, it is appointive.

provision, canonical A concession

to an ecclesiastical office made by competent ecclesiastical authority according to the norms of canon law. It is the right to a benefice for support. No appointment to canonical office can be validly given without canonical provision.

provost (L. *praepositus,* one placed before) 1. The head of a cathedral or collegiate chapter. 2. An administrative officer in a university, usually in charge of educational activities. 3. The second dignitary under a dean (*q.v.*). 4. Provost general. The superior of certain religious orders and congregations such as the Passionists.

proximate occasion *See* occasion of sin, proximate.

prudence A supernatural and moral virtue which inclines the intellect to choose the best means for attaining its aims by subordinating them to man's ultimate end. To act prudently three qualities are necessary: mature deliberation, a wise choice and right execution. The use of prudence is necessary for the practice of virtue and for self-control.

psalm (Gr. *psalmos,* song for a stringed instrument) One of the 150 religious poems found in the Old Testament Book of Psalms. They are the accepted prayer of both the Old and New Law. Many verses of the psalms are found in the Mass, and psalms form the principal part of the Breviary. Other religious poems are found in the Old Testament that can fit into the category of psalms, such as Ex. 15:1-19.

psalm tone One of the nine chants used when singing the Psalms. They are numbered one through eight, with the ninth tone called *tonus peregrinus* (wandering tone). The latter tone is used only for the psalms *In exitu Israel* and *Laudate pueri.* Each chant consists of two parts. The first is the monotonic with an inflected intonation and mediation; the second is monotonic with an inflected conclusion.

psalmody The singing of psalms.

psalms, alphabetic Alphabetic or acrostic psalms are those which follow the Hebrew order of letters in the Hebrew alphabet; that is, each verse or group of verses begins with consecutive letters of the Hebrew alphabet.

Psalms, Book of (Gr. *psalterion,* a stringed instrument) The Psalter, as the Book of Psalms is called, is a collection of 150 Psalms. It takes its name from the stringed instrument that accompanied the psalms as they were sung. In general the psalms are songs that were sung in worship by the Jewish people. There are three types of psalms: hymns praising God, prayers begging help, and songs of thanksgiving to God for saving His people. The psalms were written over a long period of time. More than half the psalms are attributed to David; the others to the sons of Asaph, the sons of Core, Moses, Solomon and others. Attributing the psalms to these men was the Old Testament way of showing that these psalms had some relationship to the men named as authors. The themes that these 150 songs touch are varied. There are psalms about the king, many of which look to a future messianic king and redeemer. Many psalms narrate the beauties that God has placed in nature. But most of the Psalter is devoted to psalms that are either individual supplications for God's mercy or group pleas for God's aid. The Church uses the psalms frequently in the liturgy: i.e., the Mass contains parts of many psalms and the prayer book of the priest, the Breviary, has all 150 psalms in it.

psalter 1. That part of the Breviary which contains the psalms. 2. A book containing the psalms in numerical order. 3. (Also "psaltery"). A harp-like stringed instrument on which music is produced by strumming the strings.

Psalter, Gallican A second translation of the Book of Psalms made by St. Jerome. It found greater popularity than the first (also by Jerome) and was immediately accepted in France from which it took its name. It was in use in the universal Church (except St. Peter's) until the issuance of the Vatican Psalter. *See* Psalter, Vatican.

Psalter, Roman The first translation of the Book of Psalms made by St. Jerome (*c.* 393).

Psalter, Vatican A new translation of the Book of Psalms made in Rome and issued in 1945. It was based largely on the Masoretic Hebrew text and differs considerably from the Gallican and Roman Psalters. It may be used in the Divine Office.

psychiatry A medical specialty dealing with the prevention, diagnosis and treatment of mental illness. The practice of psychiatry is often very similar to that of nonmedical specialties that deal wth problems of personal adjustment. Psychiatric training is not exclusively medical, but it usually does not include as much background in normal psychological functioning as is studied in fields of applied psychology. Many Catholics still maintain a certain reserve about the benefits which psychiatry can render. Pope Pius XII, however, has encouraged research and therapeutic practice in the field of psychiatry. There is a greater recognition of the ways in which priest and psychiatrist, each within the sphere of his competence, can collaborate in helping their penitents and patients to achieve a more adequate mental balance and growth.

psychoanalysis Properly, a specialty within psychiatry, which attempts a deep penetration into the patient's psyche in order to deal with unconscious influences on his feelings, thoughts and behavior. It uses the techniques of free association, dream analysis and sometimes hypnosis. The method was originated by Freud for the treatment of certain kinds of psychoneurotic reactions; it has been modified and extended by his followers and other psychiatrists. The term is also used loosely in reference to the system of psychological theory which has grown out of the clinical experiences of Freud and others. This "analytic theory" has been considerably modified in some respects, so that currently there is much more recognition of rational processes of control in personality-functioning than was proposed in Freud's original propositions. Initial Catholic reaction to psychoanalytic technique and analytic theory of personality was at best suspicious. There was an understandable defensive reaction to Freud's hostility to religion and the mechanistic and materialistic assumptions on which many of his theoretical statements were based. There has been, however, an increasing willingness to accept the usefulness of many of his insights for understanding human psychology. Further, the testimony of Catholic doctors, priests and patients indicate that analytic treatment does not, if competently employed, violate in any way the tenets of traditional morality. The statements of Pope Pius XII point out the limits which moral considerations place on the practice of psychoanalysis but offer no over-all moral objection to it.

psychologism The reduction of the spiritual life to certain states of consciousness and the production of these states by certain psychological means. However, the successive states of consciousness in Christian spiritual life cannot be understood by immanent analysis alone. Moreover, psychologism tends to underplay or deny the workings of grace.

puberty (L. *puber,* adult) That state in which a person first becomes able to beget or bear children. According to canon law legal puberty is reached by boys at the age of 14, by girls at 12.

public decency A diriment impediment, also known as quasi-affinity, public honesty, public propriety, which is the relationship between two persons arising from an invalid marriage or from public and notorious concubinage. By this impediment a civil marriage contracted by a Catholic is regarded as public or notorious concubinage. The impediment annuls marriage to the first and second degree of the direct line between a man and the blood relations of the woman and vice versa. It may be dispensed.

public worship The official worship of the Church as distinguished from private devotions. It is the liturgy of the Church.

publican (L. *publicanus,* taxgatherer) It was the custom of the Romans and their vassal kings not to collect taxes directly but to give the tax concessions to private individuals who were known as publicans because they gathered the public revenue. Each publican was assessed a fixed sum and it was up to him to collect this amount plus whatever was to give him a profit. This system encouraged the tax collector to become greedy and unjust. For this reason publicans were disliked, and also because they were working for foreign overlords and their native collaborators.

pulpit (L. *pulpitum,* scaffold, stage) An elevated platform or enclosed stage in a church from which the ministers of the Mass proclaim the Gospel and Epistle, and preach.

punishment 1. Suffering inflicted for wrongdoing. 2. The divine punishment inflicted by God for offenses against Him. In some instances this may take place in this life. After death, mortal sin is punished eternally in hell while venial sin is atoned in purgatory. 3. Canon law defines particular ecclesiastical punishments. An ecclesiastical penalty, according to the Code, is the privation of some good, inflicted by legitimate authority on the delinquent for his correction and the punishment of the offense. These punishments are for the good of the individual and the good of society. There are a number of types of penalties according to their purpose. A penalty is *vindictive* when its purpose is the expiation of delinquency and the reparation of damage caused the social order, such as the deprivation of a benefice. A penalty is *medicinal* when its purpose is the correction of the delinquent, such as a censure. Penal remedies (admonition, reproof, precept, vigilance) are preventive medicinal penalties since they are intended to prevent delinquency. By reason of their object penalties are either *spiritual* (deprivation of a spiritual benefit) or *temporal* when they subject one to a temporal evil such as a fine.

punishment, capital *See* capital punishment.

pure act (L. *actus purus*) That which in no way is mixed with potency. God alone is pure act since He has no potency.

purgatory (OF *purgatoire*) The state in which souls exist for a time after death to work out the temporal punishment due to venial sins or forgiven mortal sins. The soul is purified in this state to prepare it for its entrance into the delights of heaven and the Beatific Vision. "It is therefore a holy and wholesome thought to pray for the dead, that they may be loosed from their sins" (2 Mac. 12:46).

purgative way, the The first or beginning stage in the spiritual life. The aim of this stage is to purify the soul in order to attain union with God.

Purification of the Blessed Virgin Mary The feast that is celebrated on Feb. 2. This feast commemorates the day that the Blessed Virgin Mary presented the Christ Child in the Temple. At that time Simeon welcomed the Child, accepted Him into his arms and sang the hymn praising God, the Nunc Dimittis. A more correct title for this feast would be the "Presentation of Our Lord in the Temple." Naming the feast the "Purification of the Blessed Virgin Mary" goes back to the Gelasian Sacramentary. But the real object of the feast is not the traditional legal purification to which Mary submitted herself forty days after the birth of Christ. In the Gospel for the feast, St. Luke emphasizes that Mary and Joseph came to the Temple to offer the newborn Child to God His Father. The feast originated in Jerusalem, being a customary feast there in the 4th century. The feast has another popular name, Candlemas Day. It is so called because of the blessing of candles and the procession that usually takes place before the Mass on that day.

purificator A triple-folded band of white linen cloth, 18 inches long and generally 3 to 5 inches wide when folded, which is used by the celebrant at Mass to cleanse the chalice both before and after the Holy Sacrifice, and to dry the thumbs and forefingers after the last ablution. In setting up the chalice preparatory to Mass the purificator is placed over the mouth of the chalice, and the paten with the Host is placed on top of it. Since the purificator can come in contact with the Sacred Species, it should not be handled by a layman until it has received one washing by a cleric in major orders. In the Byzantine Rite a small sponge is used in its place.

Purim A Jewish feast celebrated on the 14th of Adar (February or March) to commemorate the deliverance of the Jews from dangers which threatened them in the Persian empire. The ones who played important roles in the deliverance were Esther and Mardochai. The feast is also known as the Feast of Lots.

purity (L. *puritas*) 1. Detachment from whatever may lead to sin, avoidance of all deliberate venial sin and even of any willful resistance to grace. In this sense, one speaks of purity of heart or purity of intention. 2. Specifically, the observance of chastity according to one's state in life. It moderates the desire for venereal pleasure according to right reason. Modesty is an important element in purity for it concerns itself with external as well as internal behavior.

purple 1. A liturgical color which is a symbol of sorrow and penance. Purple vestments are used during the seasons of Advent and Lent, on the three Sundays preceding Lent, on Ember Days and most Vigils. 2. The color used in the ceremonial dress of prelates in the Western Church. Cardinals, however, wear scarlet.

pusillanimity (L. *pusillus*, petty;

anima soul) A smallness of soul, opposed to the virtues of magnanimity and fortitude. It is an exaggerated humility, often resulting from the vice of sloth. A person having this vice has contempt both for himself and for God.

putative marriage *See* marriage, putative.

pyx (Gr. *pyxis,* box) A small vessel in which the Blessed Sacrament is kept. This may be either the vessel in which the Host in its lunette is reserved for exposition, or the watch-shaped case in which the Blessed Sacrament is brought to the sick.

Q

Quadragesima (L. *quadraginta,* forty) The fortieth day before Easter; a term which has become the liturgical name for both the First Sunday of Lent and the forty days of Lent.

Quadragesimo Anno (L. fortieth year) An encyclical issued May 15, 1931, by Pope Pius XI to commemorate the fortieth anniversary of Pope Leo XIII's great encyclical on labor, *Rerum Novarum* (*Of New Things*). After praising Leo's letter as the source of a true Catholic social science and the font of teachings that have bettered the conditions of the workers everywhere, Pope Pius condemned the economic dictatorship of big business as responsible for social injustices. He called for the practice of Christian social principles as a counterbalance to the evils of the then present economic system. Only a renewal of the Christian spirit could provide a remedy for those evils. Pope Pius warned that unless a social order is founded which is based on justice and charity no real cure of the injustices of contemporary economic life can be realized.

Quadragesimo Anno Medal Annual award by the Association of Catholic Trade Unionists to an individual who makes an outstanding contribution to the solution of industrial problems.

Among the winners have been Joseph Bierne, Philip Murray, George Meany and Robert F. Kennedy.

Quaestor (L. one who seeks) A cleric appointed to collect alms for some worthy project. Usually indulgences were granted to contributors. The famous Dominican Johann Tetzel was sent to Germany as a Quaestor to collect alms for the construction of St. Peter's in Rome. Martin Luther took the occasion to break with Rome and publish his "Ninety-five Theses." Because of abuses, the system was terminated by the Council of Trent.

Quakers (The Religious Society of Friends) A religious sect founded in England by George Fox (1624–1691), the son of a Leicestershire weaver. At the age of 19 he "forsook all things" and wandered through the countryside, carrying his Bible, preaching contempt for the decadence affecting the Anglican and Protestant clergy and for "steeple houses" (church buildings). He condemned lawyers and soldiers, refused to bear arms or take an oath or to doff his hat to anyone, reasoning that all men were equal before God and were forbidden by Scripture to swear or to kill. He and his followers called themselves "Friends," trying sin-

476

cerely to be friends of God and all men. The term "Quaker" was applied when the court trying Fox "trembled at the Word of the Lord" at his command. The Friends believe that they are led by the Holy Spirit, the Inner Light, which is that of God in every man. They have no priesthood, no ministers, believing that Christ speaks to the soul directly. There are no creeds, no sacraments. Weddings are celebrated in the meetinghouse with the Friends present, the bride and groom simply making their vows to each other in the presence of all. The Society of Friends has a history of social service and works of charity out of proportion to their small numbers. Though often persecuted (banished or put to death indeed in Puritan New England in colonial times) they have persisted and are highly respected. Pennsylvania and Philadelphia owe their origin to the good and kindly Quaker William Penn, and in this colony founded in 1681, brotherly love, toleration and peaceful negotiations with the Indians set it apart from many of the other colonies. In 1780 the Friends declared that not one of their members owned a single slave. Today the Friends have divisions and modificacations of practice among them, but with no enmity over the different viewpoints. They have small groups practically all over the world, especially in depressed regions where they engage in social and charitable works.

Quam Oblationem (L. this offering) A prayer of the Canon of the Mass said directly before the Consecration. The celebrant, while reciting the prayer, makes the Sign of the Cross five times over the offerings of bread and wine. The prayer asks God to make the offering acceptable so that it may become the Body and Blood of His Son.

Quam singulari The first words of the decree issued at the direction of Pope St. Pius X in 1910 which restored the right of children who have reached the age of reason to receive Holy Communion and which advocated the frequent reception of the sacrament. It was the final blow against the heresy of Jansenism *(q.v.)*.

quarantine (L. *quadraginta,* forty) A period of forty days. In the ancient Church it was a rigorous fast of forty days during which water, bread and salt were allowed once a day. Later it became a term used with indulgence meaning that the indulgence remitted that amount of temporal punishment due to sin as would be remitted by such a fast.

quarter tense An old term used mainly in Ireland for the Ember Days.

quasi-domicile A place where a person dwells with the intention of remaining there a greater part of the year or where he has actually dwelt for a greater part of the year. A person living in a quasi-domicile is called an *advena.*

Quasimodo Sunday Another term for Low Sunday, taken from the first words of the Entrance Prayer.

quasi-parish Another name for a mission, a division of a vicariate or prefecture that is the equivalent of a diocesan parish.

quest The begging of alms by one from a mendicant order.

quiet, prayer of A term used by St. Teresa of Avila referring to that state of the soul in which for the first time the presence of God is felt by a kind of spiritual delight; it is the beginning of mystical union. It is the first step in the prayer of infused contemplation.

Quietism A false mysticism that arose in the 17th century which held that man in relation to God must be wholly passive and self-repressive, allowing God only to act on the soul. It was characteristic of some of the religions of the Orient. It taught that once man had made the act of submission to God, he should make no further attempt to acquire virtue or even resist temptation. The doctrine was condemned in 1675.

Quinquagesima (L. fiftieth day before Easter) The Sunday before the beginning of Lent. Excitement and tension are in the prayers and lessons of the day's Mass.

quire An old variant for choir. It is sometimes used to distinguish the quire area of the church from the choir singers.

Quirinal, the A papal palace built by Gregory XIII in 1574 on the Quirinal Hill in Rome. In 1870 it was taken over as the residence for the Italian royal family. It is now used for the residence of the president of Italy and for the entertainment of state guests.

Qu'ran (Arabic, a recitation) A compilation of the revelations Muhammad claimed were given him by God. It is the Muslim Scripture, and the final authority in all things pertaining to Muslim religious practices. It drew heavily on the Old and New Testaments. Also known as the Koran.

R

rabat (Fr. it is turned down)   A stiff piece of cloth, divided in the middle, attached to the collar and coming down over the chest. It is perhaps the origin of the necktie. It is seen today as part of the habit of the Brothers of the Christian Schools and in the court dress of lawyers in Great Britain and some of the Commonwealth countries.

rabbi (Heb., master)   1. A term in general use in the time of Christ as an honorific title, especially for an outstanding teacher. Literally it meant "my great one." 2. It is used today as a title for the Jewish clergy, the spiritual heads of the Jewish communities who lead in prayer, give rulings on law and customs, attend to the ritual purity of food and vessels, etc. 3. A corruption of rabat (*q.v.*) and used for the clerical shirt front worn as part of street dress. It is of black and can be attached to or hold the Roman collar.

Raccolta (It. a collection)   A book containing all the indulgenced prayers, aspirations and devotions which have been approved by the Church. The book also contains the indulgence for each item, necessary conditions and the date the indulgence was granted. The official version issued by the Holy See is called *Enchiridion Indulgentiarum,* for which the Holy See authorizes vernacular translations.

race prejudice   Because of the dignity of each individual, both in being created in the image of God and in being in fact either a brother of Christ through Baptism or at least having a possibility of becoming a member of God's family, any division because of different race, color or belief is a sin against the belief of God and our Father, and against the very nature of the Church as the unity of all men in Christ.

racial discrimination   Treatment of an entire race in a discriminatory and prejudicial manner as compared to treatment of another race. It has been condemned by the Church.

racial integration   A situation in which members of different races live and work together in equality. Integration describes the efforts of citizens who through the courts of law and other lawful methods seek to bring equal rights to all citizens. The term is especially used to describe the attempt to bring to Negroes in America equal opportunities for housing, education, social and economic life in areas where they are discriminated against. Since segregation is against the teachings of Christ which the Church has constantly proclaimed, the Church favors movements that seek to bring equality to all men. The Church is the Mystical Body of Christ, seeking to integrate all men into its fold, and is an active force to integrate all men equally into society.

rank of feasts   *See* feasts, rank of.

Ransom, Our Lady of   Title and feast of Our Lady, originally proper to Mercedarians, commemorating her reported vision in 1218 to St. Peter Nolasco, St. Raymond of Penafort and King James of Aragon requesting the foundation of an order for ransoming captives. This feast is commemorated on Sept. 24.

rape   The sex act committed by force without the consent of the other person. In addition to the sin of fornication and/or adultery there is a sin of injustice since it is an act of unjust violence.

rapture (L. *raptus,* seized)   A synonym for ecstasy. However on the basis of St. Paul's use of the term (2 Cor. 12:2), spiritual writers use the word for a more intense type of ecstasy.

raptus (L. seizure)   1. Latin term for rapture (*q.v.*). 2. The deriment impediment to matrimony of abduction.

rash   An adjective applied to a teaching or proposition that goes considerably beyond the common teaching of the Church.

rash judgment   The first assent of the mind to the existence of sin in another without sufficient reason. It is a sin of injustice and can become grave if it is deliberate, completely rash, concerns another's grave sin. These conditions are not often met.

rashness   The state of one who makes a judgment without sufficient reason. It is a vice opposed to prudence and the gift of counsel.

ratified marriage   A valid marriage between two Christians in which conjugal intercourse has not yet taken place.

ratio studiorum (L. method of studies)   The educational system of the Jesuits, established in 1599, and still followed in somewhat revised form. In its broad scope and method, it sets up the orderly system and subjects which serve to train the minds of students while at the same time giving basic knowledge in the arts, particularly in grammar and rhetoric. The aim of the system is not only to train students to think, but to prepare them for passing oral public examinations. Today the system has been greatly modified to meet the demands of modern scientific education. The term is an abbreviation of *Ratio atque Institutio Studiorum Societas Jesu* (The Method and System of Studies of the Society of Jesus).

rational soul   A philosophical term which indicates the substantial form of the human body.

rationale   A clasp of precious metal worn on the breast and over the chasuble by a bishop. It is no longer in use.

rationalism   The theory which places human reason above revelation, applying it preferentially to the solution of life's problems, including religion. Its ultimate development is the denial of the supernatural.

rationalism, theological   A tendency to overrate the dominion of reason, subjecting to its control every aspect of the supernatural. Its most explicit exponent in modern times was Christian Wulff (d. 1754) who denied revelation and made observance of the moral law the equivalent of religion.

Ratisbon chant   A type of Gregorian

chant that was popularized by the Ratisbon school of music in Bavaria. It is no longer in use.

ratum non consummatum, marriage (L. ratified, but not consummated) A marriage which is ratified by a valid contract and ceremony but is not yet consummated by subsequent physical union (sexual intercourse suitable of itself for generation) of husband and wife. If the partners have lived together after the wedding, the marriage is presumed consummated until the contrary is proved. But if it can be proved that the marriage has not been consummated (even though ratified), the Church can annul the nonconsummated marriage for a grave reason.

reader Another name for a lector (*q.v.*).

real presence The teaching of the Catholic Church that Jesus Christ is truly, really, substantially and completely present in the Holy Eucharist under the appearance of bread and wine. The presence takes place following the Consecration by the act of transubstantiation (*q.v.*). This doctrine opposes Protestant teaching that Christ is only representatively or figuratively present, or that Christ is virtually present by the effects of the sacrament.

reason (L. *ratio,* a reckoning) The ability to distinguish between right and wrong. The age at which children are presumed to attain the use of reason is seven, although in individual cases it can vary. Most Church laws bind only when one has reached the use of reason (e.g., Easter duty, annual confession, etc.).

reason, principle of sufficient Whatever begins to be cannot itself be the reason of its beginning. Everything that begins to be, has not only an efficient cause but also a final and formal, and in certain cases, a material cause.

reasoning The logical process whereby the intellect proceeds from the known to the knowledge of the unknown.

rebaptism The Council of Trent affirmed that Baptism imprints a spiritual and indelible character on the soul. Therefore once validly administered any attempt to rebaptize is a grave sin. However, where there is a doubt concerning previous Baptism the sacrament can be administered conditionally. This is not rebaptism, since if the sacrament was administered validly the first time, there is no effect from the second. If a person who has received Baptism by the short form in danger of death later recovers, the missing ceremonies are supplied but there is no rebaptism.

received teaching *See* accepted teaching.

recidivism (L. *recidere,* to fall back) Lapsing into the same sin after many confessions of it, showing little or no amendment.

recollection (L. *recolligere,* to come together) 1. The attempt to keep the presence of God in the soul by attention to and concentration on spiritual matters. It is necessary for the development of the spiritual life. 2. A day of retreat, usually monthly, made by clerics and religious.

reconciliation 1. The coming to agreement of two or more persons after a misunderstanding or an estrangement. The great act of reconciliation was that one by which man and God were brought back together —namely, the redemptive act of Christ. 2. In canonical language: the act of reblessing or reinstating. When a church is violated, it must be reconciled by the bishop before it can be used for sacred services.

reconventio A Latin term for the counterclaim made by a defendant in an ecclesiastical court.

recto tono (L. *rectus,* straight; *tonus,* tone) The simplest form of Church music in which one note is held without variation for the length of the phrase or paragraph sung. Also called "reciting tone."

rector (L. *regere,* to rule) A priest put in charge of a church, college or other institution (seminary, etc.). He has charge of both spiritual and temporal matters. In the United States the term is now not ordinarily applied to the pastor of a parish but vestiges of the old practice are found in the name for the priest's house: rectory. The head of the Redemptorists is called the Rector Major.

rector magnificus A title given to rectors of certain universities, such as Louvain.

rectory Residence of the rector of a church or other institution. It is the residence for the parish priests.

recusant (L. *recusare,* to reject) One who despite the law refused to attend Church of England services. Although the term included others than Catholics, the greater majority of recusants were Catholics. Laws existed to punish recusants from the time of Queen Elizabeth I up until George III, although enforcement varied. Recusants could be fined, debarred from holding office, not allowed to move more than five miles from home, etc. Convicted recusants had to renounce their belief in papal supremacy within three months of conviction or, if required, abjure the realm. If they did not deny the pope or leave the realm, they were guilty of a capital offense.

red The liturgical color used in Masses of the Holy Spirit, the Cross, the Precious Blood and martyrs. It is used on the Feast of the Holy Innocents when it falls on a Sunday. The pope wears red vestments when he celebrates a Requiem Mass. Red is also the color for cardinals.

red hat The wide-brimmed, flat scarlet hat with tassels presented by the pope to a new cardinal at a public consistory after his appointment. The hat is not used again until after the cardinal's death when it is hung from the ceiling of the church.

Red Mass A Mass to the Holy Ghost celebrated for lawyers and jurists that they may exercise prudence and equity in their duties. It is celebrated in both England and the United States.

Red Pope A nickname for the Cardinal Prefect of the Sacred Congregation of the Propagation of the Faith. It was given him because of his widespread power and jurisdiction in so much of the world.

Redemption, the Through original sin man forfeited the friendship of God and a life of sanctifying grace. However, God's love would not allow Him to abandon man. He promised a Redeemer who was Christ. By the infinite merits of His life and death on the cross, Jesus restored man to friendship with God. By His sacrifice, Christ restored a life of sanctifying grace to those who unite with Him in His Mystical Body. In this union, man is joined with Christ and is able to expiate his sins and satisfy divine justice and thus regain the kingdom of heaven.

Redemptorists, the Congregation of the Most Holy Redeemer. A religious congregation of men, founded in Italy in 1732 by St. Alphonsus Liguori. Alphonsus, an intellectual genius, was born near Naples in 1696 of distinguished parents and was given a good education under tutors. He began the study of law at 13 and received his doctor's degree in both civil and canon law, with acclamation, at 16 from the University of Naples. He abandoned his career after practicing law for 8 years, refused the marriage his father had arranged for him and studied for the priesthood. As a priest he began missionary work among the poor of Naples, preached simply and earnestly, treated sinners with love and understanding, and organized Christian Doctrine classes among outcasts. He developed clubs of thousands of working men who met daily for prayer and instruction, and directed a convent of nuns, the Redemptoristines, to pray and do penance for his missionary work. In 1732 he went to Scala where he founded his Congregation of the Most Holy Redeemer to do missionary work among poor peasants in remote districts. Numbers of followers joined him, but the political power of those days over Church affairs brought about a schism in his community, and Alphonsus was deposed from his own congregation. Then Bishop of St. Agatha of the Goths, he spent his remaining years writing numerous books of guidance and devotion still widely used in the Church. He was active in converting innumerable sinners until his death at 91, in 1787. St. Clement Hofbauer, the second general of the Congregation, managed to heal the schism and extend the Redemptorists into other parts of Europe. Today they are widespread through the Christian world. Their general motherhouse is in Rome.

reduction The name given to the ceremony which takes place at an altar in a church that is being turned over for profane use. It includes the taking away of the mensa if it is a fixed altar or the small altar stone if the altar is unconsecrated.

Reductions of Paraguay One of the most important and characteristic works of the missions in South America carried out by the Jesuits. The Reductions were so called because they were groups formed by Indians who had been "reduced" from their forests, and formed a kind of state governed by the Jesuit missionaries. The Jesuits, authorized by the Kings of Spain, held almost absolute authority over the Indians not only in things spiritual but also in material things. They administered justice and observed a patriarchal vigilance in which there was also a certain community of goods. The Jesuits were encouraged by their General, Father Claudio Aquaviva, and the competent authorities granted them land in Parana, along the Parana and Uruguay Rivers. The Jesuits began their famous work in 1610. At the same time the Jesuit Father Lorenzana acting with permission of his Provincial Father Diego Torres Bollo founded the Reduction of St. Ignatius and Father Catoldino that of Loreto among the Guaranies of Guayra. Nevertheless the Jesuits had to contend with unheard of difficulties in order to defend their work. The first enemies were the Spanish merchants, who saw in the Reductions an impediment to their abusive trade with the Indians. The second, the civil authorities who did not want the independence of the Indians. The third, unfortunately, were some bishops, as in the case of the celebrated and unfortunate Bernardino de Cardenas, Bishop of Asuncion. Together with these, the Jesuits had to contend with the indolent character of the

Indians, and the invasions of the half-castes from São Paulo in Brazil, who between 1628 and 1641 invaded with fire and blood the Reductions and hunted the Indians. They destroyed a great number and took many prisoners. The missioners began again and were able to arm the Indians for their own defense; so from 1641 onward they were able to repel such invasions. From this date forward they increased in numbers. There were from 30 to 33 Reductions with 150,000 Indians. They continued on in a state of prosperity to the middle of the 17th century. After the suppression of the Jesuits and the independence of the South American republics they gradually disappeared.

refectory (L. *reficere,* to refresh) The dining hall of a monastery, convent, seminary, etc. Meals are usually taken in silence, accompanied by a lector reading aloud from some spiritual work.

reform (L. *reformare,* to form again) To improve by changing and removing faults and abuses. There are many types of reform in the Catholic Church: reform of a religious order, by bringing it nearer its primitive observance; reform of liturgy; reform of Church music; reform of canon law; etc. Reformation is necessary at intervals to bring the Church current with the times. Pope John XXIII began the major reform of modern times by summoning Vatican Council II.

Reformation, the Protestant The revolt in religious life in Western Europe in the 16th century which resulted in the formation of Protestant Churches. The premise was taken that Christ left no authoritatively teaching Church but only the Bible, which each individual may read and interpret on the principle of "private judgment." Faith was sufficient for salvation. The door was thus left open for every conceivable type of prophet. The spark that kindled the flames of religious revolt was struck when Martin Luther, an Augustinian monk, nailed his Ninety-Five Theses to the doors of the church at Wittenberg, Oct. 31, 1517. The occasion of Luther's posting his theses was the preaching of indulgences by a Dominican monk, Tetzel. Pope Leo X was raising funds for the building of the new St. Peter's Basilica and had renewed a Bull of Indulgences designed to stimulate donations for this work. *Causes.* 1. Growth of nationalism. In the 14th and 15th centuries there gradually developed the modern concept of the state. The passions of nationalism and pride of race began to assert themselves in the jealousy of kings and princes concerning the rights and prerogatives of sovereignty. Collisions between the officials of the state and those of the Church became the order of the day. The situation was further complicated by the fact that many bishops were also civil lords and exercised a feudal sway. 2. Weakening of the authority of the Holy See due to the sojourn of the papacy at Avignon, France, and the Western Schism. It seemed incongruous to have the center and head of the universal Church in a provincial center, outside the influence of the Holy Roman Empire which still conveyed to men's minds the sense of general authority in temporal affairs, paralleling the authority of the pope in spiritual matters. Scarcely had the papacy been re-established at Rome when there arose two and even three claimants to the papal throne. The exile at Avignon lasted from 1307 to 1377.

The Western Schism from 1377 to 1418. 3. Moral laxness. A widespread spirit of worldliness which prevailed among the clergy and the laxity of morals which obtained among the laity, the clergy and the papal curia were an underlying cause. In many places bishops and abbots were likewise territorial rulers and all too frequently they bore themselves as secular princes rather than as servants of the Church. 4. Neopaganism. The revival of the art and literature of the Greco-Roman paganism brought with it a tendency to copy the pagan ideals of morality and to set aside the Christian code as old-fashioned. Higher intellectual culture which had been largely fashioned by the clergy and bore a monastic mark now began to assume a secular character that veered more and more to pagan practices. Among the upper classes a crude materialism and a voluptuousness of life dimmed the values of the supernatural. *Results*. The principal results of the Reformation were: 1. the true reform of the Church and the revivification of Catholicism effected by the Council of Trent; 2. the separation of countless souls from the means Christ gave to attain their salvation.

regent (L. *regere,* to rule) One who exercises vicarious authority; a member of a governing board, as of a university. The term is used in many Catholic universities.

Regina Coeli (L. Queen of Heaven) The opening words of an antiphon to Our Lady which is said during Eastertide in place of the Angelus. It is also used in the Divine Office during this period. It is said standing.

register, parochial Canon law requires that every pastor keep five distinct books in which are recorded respectively: Baptisms, Confirma-

tions, marriages, deaths and the spiritual state of his parish. Marriages of conscience and other secret matters are recorded elsewhere. Subsequent Confirmation, marriage, ordination to the subdiaconate and religious profession are to be recorded alongside the baptismal name. These books are to be kept in a protected place, in a safe if possible.

regium placet (L. it pleases the ruling authority) At the pleasure of the king or his government. A thing is satisfactory to the powers that be.

regnans in excelsis (L. reigning on high) Said of Christ who now sits at the right hand of the Father, or of the Church triumphant in general.

Regular clergy Also Regulars. Canonically, religious men in solemn vows.

relationship There are three types of relationship: 1. natural—by blood, consanguinity; or by marriage—affinity; 2. legal—by adoption; 3. spiritual—by Baptism between the baptized and the baptizer, and the baptized and the godparents; in Confirmation between the confirmed and the sponsor. The relationship through Baptism creates a diriment impediment to marriage.

relativism Any doctrine which denies the existence of absolute values. It is more commonly applied to theories which treat of the nature of knowledge and reality.

released time A program of religious education for public school children in some states of the United States, in which a period of time in the weekly school schedule is allotted for religious instruction. Only those children who have their parents' permission are permitted to leave the school buildings, for instruction by their priest, minister, rabbi or others chosen by them. This instruction is not conducted in publicly owned buildings, nor at any expense to the state. Released time is made available so that the public-school children may receive some organized religious instruction without any violation of the First Amendment of the Constitution.

relic (L. *reliquiae,* remains) First class, the corpse of a saint or any part of it. Second class, any object intimately connected with the saint. Third class, anything touched to the body of a saint. Veneration (dulia *q.v.*) is paid these relics by the Church and the faithful. An excommunication reserved to the ordinary is incurred by anyone who manufactures, knowingly sells or distributes false relics or exposes them for public veneration. It is also forbidden to buy and sell relics. No relic may be publicly honored unless it has proper authentication. Relics of a martyr are placed in the sepulcher of every altar, and thus the ancient tradition of saying Mass on the tomb of a martyr is continued.

relics, duplication of There are many cases where a relic is said to exist in more than one place. This does not necessarily mean that there is fraud or manufacture. A number of relics can be the result of division. Thus, the many relics of the True Cross (*q.v.*). There are, for example, three pillars of the Scourging, one each at Rome, Constantinople and Jerusalem, but when examined it is readily seen that each is only a piece of a pillar. A major portion of the neck bone of Blessed Theophane Venard is preserved at the Maryknoll Preparatory Seminary in Clarks Summit, Pa., while a piece taken from the whole is at Maryknoll Seminary, Maryknoll, N.Y. Also, the body of the Maryknoll co-founder, Father

Thomas Frederick Price, is in a crypt at Maryknoll while his heart is buried near the body of St. Bernadette of Lourdes in Nevers, France.

religion (L. *religio,* reverence) The moral virtue which inclines man to give due reverence and worship to God. Objectively, religion is an established body of beliefs and manner of worshiping God. The necessity of religion is founded in the natural law which commands the worship of God; in the divine positive law, revealed in both the Old and New Testaments which commands the worship of God; and in human law, which commands the worship of God and punishes the absence of religion. The chief acts of religion are sacrifice, adoration, prayer, devotion, the use of the sacraments, vows and the sanctification of certain days. Religion dictated by right reason is called natural religion and that revealed by God is called supernatural religion. The chief sins against the virtue of religion are blasphemy, sacrilege, idolatry, tempting God, superstition and simony.

religion, natural Man can give homage to God even though he does not have the help of divine revelation. The knowledge he has comes from his natural insights and experiences, and so his religion is a natural rather than a supernatural one.

religiosity Religiousness that is affected or sentimental; false piety. It lacks intellectual or true spiritual foundation.

religious A member of a religious institute who is devoted to the service of God.

religious house The dwelling place of religious; a monastery, priory, abbey, convent, etc.

religious institute Canon law defines a religious institute as a religious society of men or women living in common, under a common rule, observing the vows of poverty, chastity and obedience, and approved by legitimate ecclesiastical authority (canons 487-488).

religious liberty To force religious belief on anyone is opposed to the teaching of the Catholic Church. Faith is a supernatural gift that the Holy Spirit gives freely. To believe, man must accept God freely. A religion that teaches the free gift of faith and then forces man to receive it, contradicts itself. Man's greatest gift and treasured possession is his God-given freedom. It would be a strange God that gave man freedom and then instituted a Church that forced man to accept God. Bishop de Smedt of Belgium synthetized this doctrine for Vatican Council II: "Catholics must respect and esteem the right and duty of non-Catholics to follow the dictates of their own conscience even when, after sincere and sufficient study, it errs in good faith." Such a respect forbids any direct or indirect coercion of non-Catholics by Catholics or vice versa.

religious life The mode of life of a religious. It is a quest for perfection under a common rule and by practicing vowed poverty, chastity and obedience. The work and duties of the religious vary from active apostolate to the strict contemplative life.

religious name In the religious orders and most religious institutes the custom is followed of giving the novice a new religious name, usually at the time the religious habit (clothing) is given. Sometimes a feast or the name, Mary, is added to this religious name. It is a common practice among women to adopt Mary as a first name and then add the name of a saint, male or female. It is the usual custom that the person is addressed by the religious name and that the family name is dropped; i.e., Sister Mary Robert, Brother Jude, Father John. The Jesuits do not follow this practice but retain the family name, as do the Religious of the Sacred Heart.

Religious of the Assumption Founded in France in 1839, established in the United States in 1919. Members are engaged in teaching, retreats, social work. Missions are staffed in Africa and the Far East. The life is both active and contemplative. Simple vows are taken. There are 1,500 members.

Religious of the Sacred Heart A religious order for the education of girls, founded in 1800 in France by St. Madeleine Sophie Barat. Mother Barat was born in Burgundy in 1779 and lived through the Reign of Terror, contriving through a keen intellect and hard study to obtain an excellent education. She developed a religious vocation, and was tending toward the contemplative life of Carmel when Father Varin, her director, turned her attention to the idea of founding a society for the education of girls. Soon several young ladies including Mother Barat began living a community life in a home in Paris. They made their vows in 1800, and in 1801 the first convent was founded, with Mother Barat as superior. First, a free school was opened for the children of the poor. There followed a long succession of notable schools, academies and colleges, which offered the highest type of training, both religious and secular, for the daughters of the wealthy and highly placed. In connection with each of these institutions, wherever possible, a free school for the poor has always been provided. As the Society of the Sacred Heart flourished and developed, foundations were made all over Europe and in mission countries. In 1818 Mother Philippine Duchesne brought the Society to the United States.

Religious of the Sacred Heart of Mary Sometimes referred to as the Marymount Sisters, the community was founded in France in 1848, established in the United States in 1877 and in Canada in 1943. There are missions in Latin America and Africa. There are two provinces in the United States, Eastern and Western. Members are engaged in teaching. There are approximately 850 members in the United States.

Religious, Sacred Congregation of Founded in 1586 by Sixtus V, this Congregation has gone through a number of revisions. It handles everything pertaining to religious orders or congregations, whether of men or women, and also societies living in common without vows, in everything touching upon their government, studies, discipline, temporal goods, rights, privileges. Its competence includes all aspects of the life of religious: Christian life, religious life, clerical life. The jurisdiction of the Congregation is personal and has no territorial limits. Lastly, it has competence over Third Orders Secular and over Secular Institutes.

reliquary A vessel, usually of metal, 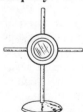 used to contain and expose one or more relics. It often resembles a miniature monstrance or tiny pyx but varies according to the size and nature of the relic.

remarriage A party to a valid marriage (*ratum et consummatum*) can-

not remarry as long as the other party is alive. Upon the death of one of the marriage partners, the surviving party is free to remarry. The partners to a marriage that has been ruled null because of invalidity are free to marry. In a *ratum non consummatum (q.v.)* marriage that is dissolved by the Church, the parties are free to marry. However, except for death or a case of Pauline privilege, the use of the word "remarriage" is not accurate since there was no first marriage.

remission An act of pardon and forgiveness. 1. Of sin. The removal of the guilt and stain of sin and the restoration of sanctifying grace in the soul. Sin is remitted in three ways: (*a*) by Baptism; (*b*) through the sacrament of Penance, of all postbaptismal sins: (*c*) through an act of perfect contrition (*qq.v.*). 2. Of temporal punishment due sin. By the gaining of an indulgence (*q.v.*)

removal from office The proper procedure to be followed in removing any person who holds an ecclesiastical office. The ordinary of a place may remove anyone who holds an ecclesiastical office within his territory. If the office-holder is termed "irremovable," he may still be removed but the ordinary must follow the proper procedure in an ecclesiastical court.

Renaissance, the The period in Italy beginning in the 14th century and reaching its height in the early 16th century. 2. A term used to designate the movement that had a profound effect on the moral, spiritual and artistic life of Western Europe. It had its roots in a revival of Greek culture and scholarship. It was directed by a series of profound social changes that were taking place: invention of the printing press, the compass and gunpowder; the circumnavigation of

Africa; the discovery of America; and the astronomical theories of Copernicus. It resulted in a humanistic approach to the arts. Among the outstanding men of the period were St. John Capistran. St. Bernadine of Siena, Machiavelli, Donatello, della Robbia, Michelangelo, Raphael, da Vinci, Botticelli, Fra Angelico, Titian and Correggio. In England St. Thomas More and others initiated a Renaissance that resulted in the Elizabethan era. In the Low Countries, Erasmus, Melanchthon and others began a movement that ended in a rationalistic approach to the Bible. In France Rabelais, Villon and scholars of the University of Paris headed a reaction to Scholasticism. 3. A style of architecture and ornament, also known as Classical, which borrowed from the ancient Greeks and Romans. St. Peter's Basilica is a good example.

renewal of consent   Canon law requires that when there is a defect of form or public impediment of a marriage, the consent of the parties is to be renewed publicly or privately according as the defect was of a public or private nature.

renunciation   The act of repudiating some attachment, right or privilege. In Baptism the godparent in the name of the child promises to renounce Satan and all his works. Certain rights can be suspended but not renounced, e.g., the marriage rights which can never be ceded to a third party.

renunciation, Christian   Putting aside all that is not of God and putting God above all other things.

reordination   Formerly when a priest who had received Holy Orders from a schismatic heretical bishop was converted to the Church of Rome, he partook of another ordination ceremony thus ensuring the validity of his priesthood. In the 12th century, however, the practice was discontinued because the indelible mark of Holy Orders is present despite the erring bishops, as long as it has been performed witih the right intention and in the prescribed manner.

reparation   The act of making amends for the wrongs and injustices done to others. When God is the object of reparation, it is termed *satisfaction*; when man, *restitution*.

repentance   Contrition or sorrow of sin, including a purpose of amendment. Also an act whereby the effects of sin are removed because of God's promise.

Reproaches, the   Those sung verses of the third part of the solemn afternoon Liturgy on Good Friday. They immediately follow the unveiling of the crucifix. They are addressed to the Jewish people for the ingratitude with which they received the gift of Christ's redemption. The verse, "O, my people, what is it I have done unto you? How have I grieved you? Answer me," is repeated after each Reproach. In content, the Reproaches dwell upon the favors that God had done for His people, and that they in turn rejected His Son by crucifying Him. While the Reproaches are being sung, the faithful present at the ceremony go up and kiss the crucifix that has been unveiled.

reprobation   A Calvinistic term referring to the act by which God rejects an individual, deeming him beyond pardon or redemption. Caution must be taken in using the word in a Catholic sense. Only a person who dies in final impenitence can be called a reprobate, and that state is known only to God.

reputation   The esteem which men express regarding the character and excellence of another. This esteem is violated by defamation either through detraction or calumny. Unjust defamation is a grave sin against both charity and justice that admits of slight matter. A person who unjustly defames another is bound to make restitution of the loss of good esteem and all the material losses which are foreseen as resulting from the defamation.

Requiescant in pace (L., May they rest in peace) The dismissal words in the Requiem Mass substituted for the regular "*Ite, missa est.*" No blessing follows as is customary at other Masses.

reredos (OF. *rere-*, rear; *dos,* back) An ornamented screen or partition wall behind an altar, a painting behind the altar or a combination of both. The side facing the altar is called a retable and the rear a counterretable.

Rerum Novarum (Reh'rum no-vah' rum; L. of new things) The revolutionary encyclical letter of Pope Leo XIII on the condition of labor and the need of social reform, addressed to the world on May 15, 1891. Laissez-faire capitalism was widespread through Europe and America, and as the pope wrote, "Working men have been given over, isolated and defenseless, to the callousness of employers and the greed of unrestrained competition. . . . The evil has been increased by rapacious usury . . . so that a small number of very rich men have been able to lay upon the masses of the poor a yoke little better than slavery itself." Pope Leo declared (contrary to the socialist teachings), "Every man has by nature the right to possess property as his own." "Man," he said, "has a natural and primitive right to marry and raise a family, to provide for their necessities, and to accumulate property which he can transmit to his children by inheritance." Though man has a right to private property which the state may not suppress, yet he who uses this right must consider the welfare of others as well. The state should see to it that labor agreements are entered into with justice and equity, and the environment of work should be such that human dignity is not violated in body or spirit. Workers have the right to enter into associations, and to act freely within them. Workers and employers should regulate their mutual relations in accordance with Christian brotherhood. Unregulated competition on the one hand, and the class struggle of Marxism on the other hand, are both contrary to Christian teaching and to the very nature of man. The pope wrote of the guilds (*q.v.*) of a former day, and of their excellent results. He urged that new associations along the same lines be formed, adapted to the present times. He ended by stating that "happy results would be brought about chiefly by charity . . . ready to sacrifice itself for others' sake, man's surest antidote against worldly pride and immoderate love of self . . . charity."

rescript, papal A response of the pope or a sacred congregation, in writing, to a question or petition of an individual. A rescript usually affects only the person to whom it is addressed although at times it can have the force of a general law.

reservation of the Blessed Sacrament The practice of preserving, after the celebration of the Mass, a portion of the consecrated Species for the communion of the sick or for other good purposes.

reserved case A term used for sins and censures whose absolution is not within the power of every confessor. By reservation an ecclesiastical superior, usually a bishop, reserves absolution to himself or to those confessors delegated by him. Some sins are reserved directly. One sin, the false accusation of a priest for solicitation in confession, is reserved directly to the Holy See. In danger of death, any confessor can absolve from all censures and sins under specified conditions.

residence 1. *Clerical.* Canon law has a number of laws regarding the residence of clerics. A parish priest may not be absent from his parish for an extended period without the permission of his ordinary. Clerics must live in their own diocese. Cardinals in curia, bishops and canons must reside in the place of their office and length of absence is specificed in law. 2. *Lay.* Canon law rules that a lay person acquires a domicile or quasi-domicile (*qq.v.*), and one without either is a person of no fixed abode (*vagus*).

resignation 1. Canonical. One of the ways an ecclesiastical office can be lost. Canon law legislates modes and types of resignations. 2. To the will of God. An active cooperation with the divine intention in order to advance in the spiritual life. It must be distinguished from Fatalism, which is passive submission to the inevitable.

resisting evil In Matt. 5:39 and elsewhere in Scripture the admonition is given "not to resist the evildoer." Quakers and others have used this and similar texts to justify their pacifism and nonresistance to oppression. The Church's interpretation is that these texts teach a higher and voluntary good to which not all men are called. Moreover, these admonitions do not apply to the state, which has the obligation of protecting the public welfare. St. Thomas Aquinas makes the distinction of not resisting evil in two ways: 1. the forgiveness of a wrong done to oneself, which may pertain to perfection; 2. the tolerating of wrongs done to another without protest, which pertains to imperfection and may even be a vice.

resisting known truth A sin against the Holy Spirit. It is stubborn resistance to a truth known to come from God. Because it is a sin from contempt it reveals a state of mind which makes repentance difficult and is therefore called one of the sins for which there is no forgiveness, although if the sinner does repent, forgiveness will be given.

response (L. *respondere*, to reply) A reply to a versicle, prayer, etc., spoken or sung by the server, ministers, choir or people.

responsibility The moral accountability of a person for his voluntary act. This responsibility is measured by the attention which is given to the act, the presence of violence or fear, the influence of passion and other circumstances.

responsorial chants *See* antiphonal chants.

responsory A series of versicles and responses recited or chanted in the Divine Office. They follow each lesson of Matins, and the Little Chapter in the other hours.

restitution Restoration of any article whatsoever to its rightful owner. In moral theology; an act of commutative justice by which one repairs the unjust damage done to another or to another's possessions.

restriction, mental   *See* mental reservation.

Resurrection of Christ   The physical rising from death by Jesus Christ on the first Easter as related in the four Gospels. By His own power, Christ reunited His soul with His body and rose in triumph from the dead. It was the greatest and final proof of His teachings, for as St. Paul tells us, "If Christ has not risen, vain then is our preaching, vain too is your faith" (1 Cor. 15:14).

resurrection of the body   It is Catholic dogma that the body will be resurrected and reunited with the soul; the dogma is affirmed in the Creed. This resurrection and reunion will take place immediately before the Last Judgment. St. Paul gives proofs for the dogma in 1 Cor. 15:1-58. There is no teaching on what matter will form the resurrected body, whether it will be the same matter as at death or new matter.

retable   The front of the reredos. Also a name used for a low panel erected behind an altar, often richly ornamented, to support candles, etc.; properly called "gradine" (*q.v.*).

retreat   (L. *retrahere,* to withdraw) 1. A spiritual exercise varying from a few days to a month or more during which the retreatant, either religious or lay, withdraws from his usual activities to meditate, pray and carry out other devotions aimed at advancing in the spiritual life. The retreat is conducted under a retreat master who gives spiritual conferences. Silence is generally observed, though sometimes there is a recreation period. There are a number of systems for such a retreat, the Spiritual Ex-

ercises of St. Ignatius being the best known. Growing in popularity is a new kind of a retreat called "cursillo" (*q.v.*). 2. The place set apart for retreats, a retreat house.

retribution   1. That punishment afflicted as a recompense for sin. 2. A recompense for good. This positive use of the word is now rare.

reunion, corporate   The reconciliation of a church or large body of Christians with the Holy See.

Reunion Councils   The three ecumenical councils whose main purpose was the healing of the differences between East and West. They were the Councils of Bari, Florence and Lyons II.

reunion of the Churches   The rejoining of the different Christian sects into one communion under the leadership of the sovereign pontiff.

revalidation   The manner in which a putative marriage is validated or rectified, either by dispensation or by retrospection (*sanatio in radice, q.v.*).

revelation   Making known to others something previously unknown to them. Divine revelation makes known to us things about God which otherwise we would not know, or would know only imperfectly. Revelation forms the basis of supernatural religion and of knowledge of God, His Nature and His saving deeds, which is beyond ordinary human reason, or if knowable by human reason, it becomes known in a manner outside the usual human processes of gaining knowledge. God tells of His wisdom, His goodness and His wishes for man in and through a living assembly, His Church, in both the Old and New Testaments, and calls for their grateful response. Discussions about whether written and unwritten revelation are to be regarded as one or two sources occupied many sessions at Vatican Council II and showed the need for further study on their complementary and interpenetrating nature. It seems likely that further study will follow the lead of Hebrews 1:1-2 and start from its view of Christ as being "the" revelation of God.

Revelation, Book of *See* Apocalypse.

revelation, private A revelation given by God to an individual for his own use or the use of others. It is contrasted to the revelation given to Israel and the Apostles which was universal revelation for all men. Examples of this type of revelation are the revelations given to St. Joan of Arc and the children at Fatima.

revenge (L. *vindicare,* to avenge) The punishment inflicted on a person for a wrong he has done voluntarily so that reparation is made for the injury and satisfaction is had by the injured party. Revenge in this sense is not wrong but is lawful. Thus punishment inflicted by authority for the good of society is an act of legal justice. In this positive sense, revenge is a virtue allied to justice. Vices opposed to revenge are: 1. by excess, cruelty and savagery; and 2. by defect, excessive laxity in giving punishment.

reverence (L. *reverentia*) A virtue which enables a person to show worship and honor for persons of dignity. Reverence is of four kinds: 1. *civil,* given to civil authorities; 2. *religious,* given to ecclesiastical dignitaries, from pope to parish priest; 3. *supernatural,* given to the saints (dulia). Reverence to God is inaccurate, for to Him man owes worship. Sins opposed to reverence are disobedience and failure to give reverence to those to whom it is due; 4. *natural,* given to those persons who because of legitimate authority have it as their due,

such as parents, teachers, etc.

reverences, ceremonial Bowing, genuflection and the greater *metany* of the Byzantines (a prostration).

Reverend A title given to clerics and extended to choir nuns and all who have the title of "Mother." Most priests prefer to be addressed on mail as Reverend Father or simply Father rather than as Reverend. In vocal address to a priest it is incorrect to say "Reverend Jones." In this case, "Father" is always used. *See* address, modes of.

Revised Version An English translation of the Bible published between 1881 and 1895, which was a revision of the Protestant Authorized Version popularly known as the King James Version, published in 1611.

revolution Active opposition to civil power. Citizens are bound to obey civil rulers in all lawful matters in which they have a right to command. Ordinarily, it is forbidden to rebel against a lawful ruler, even if he is a tryant. However, passive resistance is permitted when his demands are unjust. It is lawful to rise against a gravely unjust tyrant who is working for his private good, rather than the common good. Peaceful means must be used first. There must be a reasonable hope of success, and the need for revolution must be the opinion of a substantial part of the populace.

Rhode Island The 13th of the 13 original states, it is 50th in size, 39th in population. It was first named "Red Island" by Dutch explorer Adriaen Block (1616) because of the red clay soil. Roger Williams changed it to the Island of Rhodes. In the 11th-century Norsemen, sailing down the coast of Vinland, are thought to have frequented the coast, and to have erected a fortified church about 1355. The remains, at Newport, would be, if authentic, the oldest building of the white man in America, and the oldest Catholic church. The first white settlers known today were refugees from Puritan harassment in Massachusetts. Roger Williams, the leader, treated the Indians fairly, bought land from them for his settlement of "Providence Plantations," and granted religious liberty, but after his time Catholics were denied the right to hold office by the laws of 1719. Though continually plagued by attacks from Massachusetts, Williams was made president of the colony. The first known Mass was offered in the state during the Revolution by chaplains with the French forces commanded by Rochambeau. Catholic immigrants increased the population particularly when Rhode Island became an industrial region, the Church in the area being under the care of Bishop Fenwick of Boston. French-Canadians, Irish and others worked in the spinning and weaving mills. Schools, parishes, institutions increased, staffed by an ever increasing number of religious orders of men and women. In 1872 the Diocese of Providence was established with Rt. Rev. Thomas Hendricken as first bishop. Succeeding bishops continued to bring in religious congregations, and to build up a strong Catholicity in the state. Rhode Island today has the highest percentage of Catholics of any state —61.11 per cent.

rhythm method About 1930, two doctors, Knaus and Ogino, working independently announced the discovery of definite fertile and sterile periods in the menstrual cycles. The principle of the discovery was that all women have periods of fertility and sterility which succeed each other in an orderly pattern, and that given certain known facts, these periods can be accurately predicted. Dr. Ogino discovered that ovulation took place between the 12th and 16th days before the first day of the next menstruation. After exhaustive tests Dr. Knaus concluded human ovulation takes place between the 14th and 16th days before the next cycle begins. Since pregnancy can only develop during the period of ovulation, the rhythm method allows a married couple to know fertile and infertile periods and thus naturally space births. However, the rhythm method can be successful only on the basis of careful records, and the menstrual cycle can change due to illness, overwork, drugs, change of life or other cause.

rhythmical signs Those directions used in plain chant to facilitate singing. They consist of two signs of length and five of rhythmical division.

riddel (Fr. *rideau,* a curtain) The name given to the curtain that hangs at the side of some altars. It is often used to divide one altar from another or to separate an altar from a passageway.

right A moral power by which a person may claim something as due to him or as belonging to him. That which is just, lawful and opposed to wrong.

right intention In all actions, internal and external, man is moved to action by that which he considers simply a good, which he loves and seeks simply for what it is; i.e., he intends something as an end. This intention is right if it conforms to the requirements of the moral law.

right of goods of nature, the The right to property is not an end in itself but a means to an end. God created the wealth of the world for the use of all men, and for this reason

St. Thomas Aquinas says that the use of natural wealth is a common use.

right of succession, with A phrase sometimes used in the appointment of a coadjutor or auxiliary bishop which means that his appointment includes the right to succeed to the office of the ordinary upon the death, resignation or removal of the incumbent ordinary.

Right Reverend A title given to abbots, protonotaries apostolic and domestic prelates. In the latter two cases it is followed by the title "Monsignor." In Great Britain the term is used for bishops.

right-to-work laws State laws which, in effect, prohibit any type of compulsory union membership. They are aimed against three principal forms of union security requiring membership in a union as a condition of employment: the closed shop, which allows the employer to hire only workers who already are union members; the union shop, which provides that a new employee must join the union or at least pay dues within a specified time, usually from 30 to 90 days; and the maintenance-of-membership clause, an agreement whereby no employee is compelled to join the union but no one who becomes a member may drop out for the duration of the contract. While there is no official Catholic position on right-to-work laws, a majority of the American bishops and priests who have taken a stand on them have registered opposition. Some hold that, in practice, the laws are inconsistent with firm Catholic social principles; others, accepting the same principles, conclude that, in concrete circumstances, the laws do not violate basic human rights or the rights of labor. Those in favor maintain that the laws are directed against compulsory unionism, not against unions themselves, and guarantee the right to join as well as the right not to join. Opponents argue that a worker has the obligation to join in organizations to protect the common rights of all and to seek the common good. To supporters who argue that the laws are directed against corruption in some areas of organized labor, opponents maintain that such laws are not an effective way or the proper means to eliminate such abuses.

righteousness The quality or state of doing what is right, upright, honest, virtuous, good and without sin. It is a perfection of God in which man can share.

rights, fundamental human It is Catholic teaching that every man is born with certain basic rights. These include: the right to life and a decent standard of living; the right to security in case of sickness, old age, inability to work, widowhood; the right to security when a man is deprived of his means of subsistence through no fault of his own; the right to respect for one's person; the right to one's good reputation; the right to share in benefits of culture; the right to education according to merits; the right to worship God according to conscience; the right to free initiative; the right to work; the right to own property; the right of meeting and association; the right to emigrate and immigrate; the right to take part in public affairs.

rights of animals Although animals have no rights, strictly speaking, they are creatures of God and as such deserve respect. Animals cannot suffer injury in the strict sense of the word; nevertheless cruelty to animals (without grave cause) is sinful insofar as it is contrary to right reason.

rights of women A woman has a double life-task: as an individual, her own moral perfection; as a member of society, in union with man, to develop humanity in all its aspects. As individuals, man and woman are morally equals. Each requires the other for its social complement. All activities impairing woman's chief social duty, maternal influence, whether in the spiritual or material sphere, are to be avoided. The Christian's view of woman's sphere is that her proper influence should extend to Church and State, provided her double life-task is not thereby impeded.

rigorism (L. *rigere,* to be stiff) A moral teaching that when there is a doubt between law and liberty, the doubt must be resolved in favor of the law, even if the opinion in favor of liberty is very probable or more probable. It gave rise to the heresy of Jansenism which did great harm to the Church.

ring (AS. *hring*) A circular band of metal, often ornamented with precious stones, to be worn on the finger. 1. Wedding. A simple circular band of gold or silver used in the marriage ceremony. Formerly, it was only given to the bride but the custom is growing of an exchange of rings between bride and groom. 2. Clerics. Ordinarily, clerics are not permitted to wear rings. However, some clerics like the Marianists have permission to wear a special ring. Doctors of canon law and theology have the right to wear a ring but not during the celebration of Mass. 3. Virgins. At the consecration of a virgin a plain ring is placed on the ring finger as is also done at the solemn profession of many nuns. 4. Pontifical. A ring usually with a stone, presented to a bishop at his consecration or to an abbot at his blessing. It is a symbol of authority. It is customary for the faithful to kiss a pontifical ring.

ring, bishop's In pagan Rome, priests consecrated to the service of Jupiter wore rings, as did Roman senators. Therefore, rings took on the notion of consecration and authority. St. Augustine mentions sealing a letter with a ring. By the 6th century they were used by higher prelates. The conferral of the ring then became a part of the episcopal consecration. Cardinals receive special rings bearing the arms of the pope who names them. However, this ring is not worn.

Ring of the Fisherman A gold seal ring presented to the pope at his election. It represents St. Peter fishing. The pope uses it only to seal briefs and it is broken up by the Chamberlain on the pope's death.

risen body *See* body, glorified.

risorgimento (It. resurrection) The popular name given the movement for the unification of the Italian states in the 19th century. Out of it came the House of Savoy and the seizure of the papal states from the Holy See. As the result of it, the pope became the "Prisoner of the Vatican." The injustice was not righted until the signing of the Lateran Treaty in 1929.

rite (L. *ritus*) 1. A distinction within the Church as determined by the liturgy practiced. There are nine such rites: Latin (Roman), Byzantine, Coptic, Ethiopian, Chaldean, Armenian, Maronite, Syrian and Malabar. 2. Special variations in the Latin ritual which are permitted to certain groups, such as in the Toledo Rite or the Dominican Rite. 3. The prescribed form for conducting a religious ceremony, such as the rite of Baptism or the rite of Good Friday. 4. A ceremonial act that follows a prescribed form, such as the Last Rites.

rite, change of Under canon law (canon 98), it is forbidden for a Catholic in one rite to pass over to another without permission of the Holy See. But one is free to attend the services of another Rite. Schismatic Catholics who return to the Catholic Church belong to the same rite as that which was schismatic, thus a convert from the Armenian National Church would become a Catholic Armenian. A Western priest who persuades an Eastern Catholic to join the Latin Rite incurs suspension.

rite, determination of A person belongs to the rite of his father, even though that person may have accidentally been baptized in another rite. If the father is not a Catholic, the child follows the rite of its mother. A non-Catholic who is converted belongs to the rite of his conversion.

Rites, Congregation of Sacred A Congregation of the Roman Curia established by Sixtus V in 1587 to direct the carrying out of divine worship and to handle the causes of saints. Pius XI added a Historical Section to handle the historical causes of Servants of God and the correction of liturgical books. It also handles the causes of saints and everything pertaining to sacred relics. It has competence over all the rites and ceremonies of the Latin Church (canon 253) insofar as they refer to the Sacrifice of the Mass, the administration of the sacraments, sacred ceremonies and divine worship in general (canon 253).

Rites of the Eastern Church There are five principal rites in the Eastern Church: Byzantine, Alexandrian (Coptic and Ethiopic), Antiochian (Maronite and Syrian), Armenian, Chaldean (Chaldean and Mala-barese).

Ritual 1. A liturgical book containing the prayers and ceremonies for the sacraments, blessings, etc. 2. The ceremony that follows the prescribed order (ritual).

Rituale Romanum *See* Roman Ritual.

Ritus Servandus The name given to that section of the Roman Missal which contains the rubrics for celebrating the Mass.

Robber Synod of Ephesus A meeting held in 449 under the leadership of Dioscorus of Alexandria, a heretic. The synod condemned St. Flavian, Patriarch of Constantinople, and Theodoret, Bishop of Cyprus; it also advanced Nestorian doctrines. Pope St. Leo excommunicated all who had taken part in the assembly and nullified all of its acts.

robbery Distinguished from theft (*q.v.*) because robbery is accomplished by violence or putting the victim in fear.

rochet (OF. *roc,* coat) A garment that is like a shortened alb or an elongated surplice. It is made of linen or cotton, reaching to the knees with tight-fitting sleeves, the cuffs and hem of which are adorned with lace, the length of lace depending on the dignity of the wearer. It is worn by the Pope, cardinals, bishops, abbots, prelates and canons. It is worn under the mozzetta.

rock A play on words made by Christ (Matt. 16:18) to indicate both Peter and the foundation of His Church. The play is lost in English but in the original Aramaic Peter's name was Kepha and *kepha* also meant a rock. Thus the passage could be rendered: "Thou art Kepha, and upon this *kepha* I will build my Church."

rococo (Fr. *rocaille,* shellwork) A name given to a style of decoration and architecture that was popular in France and Germany in the 18th and early 19th centuries. It was used for the decoration of churches although its frivolity and ornateness make it unsuitable. It was exaggerated baroque with the heavy lines of the baroque broken by shell-like curves and curlicues.

Rogation Days The Monday, Tuesday and Wednesday before Ascension Thursday. They are the Christion substitute for the ancient feast called *Robilgalia,* celebrated for the purpose of obtaining a good harvest.

rollista A layman who addresses a cursillo (*q.v.*).

rollo A cursillo (*q.v.*) talk.

Roman Catholic A term that originally arose among Protestants to derogate the Catholic Church and distinguish it from the One, True, Holy and Apostolic Church. Today the term is not controversial and has legal standing even though incorrect. It is true that Catholics look to Rome for the seat of their Church, but because of the connotation of the term to Protestants it is better to avoid it.

Roman Church, Holy 1. Specifically, the Diocese of Rome. 2. By extension, the Western or Latin Rite Church. Technically, its use is incorrect. 3. By further extension, the whole Catholic Church both Latin and Eastern Rites. Again, the use is incorrect.

Roman collar The stiff linen collar which fastens at the back of the neck. It is worn under the cassock and with street dress. Formerly, it distinguished Catholic priests from Protestant ministers but is now being adopted by many of the latter.

Roman Congregations Departments organized by the Holy See to assist in transactions which canonical discipline and the individual interests of the faithful bring or send to Rome. *See* Congregations, Roman.

Roman Curia All of the departments set up to assist the pope in the government and administration of the Church. These bodies consist of the Congregations, Tribunals and Curial Offices. Canon law specifies the organization, functions and powers of the various divisions of the Curia. In general, the Congregations have executive and administrative power; the Tribunals, judicial; and the Offices, ministerial.

Roman Martyrology A book that lists martyrs and saints together with observations on their lives. The book does not have historical authority.

Roman Patriarch The pope, by title Patriarch of the West, with actual jurisdiction over all the Catholic Eastern Churches and the Church of the Roman Rite.

Roman Rite The Latin Rite. The manner of celebrating Mass, administering the sacraments, praying the Breviary and performing other ecclesiastical acts in the manner prescribed by the Roman Ritual. It is opposed to such variants as the Carthusian, Dominican, Ambrosian and Mozarabic Rites. It is the most widely used rite, being found in almost every part of the world.

Roman Ritual The official and authorized publication of the Holy See which contains the prayers, ceremonies and rubrics for the administration of the sacraments, blessings, special prayers, devotions and so on. In addition to the Missal and Breviary it is an essential book for a priest.

Romanesque A style of art and architecture common in Europe from the time of Constantine to the 11th century. It was distinguished by the cruciform church with aisles and transepts. From it developed the

Gothic style.

Romania Christianity entered Romania in the 3rd century and for many centuries the country was under the influence of Constantinople. The annexation of Transylvania by Austria in 1688 gave the opportunity for organizing the Catholic Church. Following World War I, relations between Romania and the Holy See were excellent, culminating in the concordat of 1927. However, Soviet troops entered Romania in 1944 and a Communist government was organized. Violent attacks were made in the press against the Church and the Vatican. In 1948 the Catholic press was interdicted and the concordat with the Holy See was broken. Since then the Church has existed precariously with frequent arrests, closed seminaries and suppression of religious orders. The Latin and Byzantine Rites each have 1 archdiocese and 4 dioceses in Romania. Latin Rite Catholics number 11.25 million and Byzantine Catholics number 1.5 million in a total population of 16 million. Since 1948 the Byzantine Catholics have been driven "Underground."

Romanism A derogatory name given to the Catholic faith. A person who believed in the Catholic faith was called a Romanist.

Romans, Epistle to the About the year 58, probably from Corinth, Paul wrote his Epistle to the Church at Rome to introduce himself and to state some of the doctrinal problems which concerned him in those years.

Rome 1. The city and diocese of the pope, also known as the See of Peter, the Holy See, the Apostolic See. It was inhabited as early as the 8th century B.C. Under the Caesars it came to the zenith of its glory and power, and became the center of the world. Because of this St. Peter set up his episcopal seat in Rome and there was put to death and buried. All of the popes, except the Avignon popes, resided in the city. From 800 to 1870 the popes were the sovereigns of the city. Garibaldi invaded the Papal States and in 1870 Rome was taken from the popes and made the capital of the Kingdom of Italy. In 1929 the Holy See recognized this fact and under the Lateran Treaty of that year the Vatican was restored to the sovereignty of the Holy See. 2. Figuratively, the word is used to mean the Holy See, the Catholic Church.

rood (OE. *rod,* a cross) A large crucifix.

rood beam A beam across the chancel arch supporting a large crucifix.

rood loft A choir loft above the rood screen found in medieval churches.

rood screen An ornate screen of stone or wood placed between the chancel and the nave, usually surmounted by a crucifix either directly on the screen or hanging from a proximate beam, whence its name.

Rorate (roe-rah'tey; L. *rorare,* to drop dew) 1. An Advent hymn based on Is. 45:8. 2. The Fourth Sunday of Advent, which takes its name from the first word of the Introit.

Rosary, the A series of prayers, counted as they are repeated, on a string of beads or a knotted cord. Also, the string of beads on which the prayers are counted. The word "bead" came originally from Middle English *bede,* a prayer. There are various forms of the Rosary. In the Latin Rite, the best known form consists of five decades (five series of ten beads each) divided with a larger bead between the decades. The two ends of the chaplet are joined by a single string consisting of one large

bead, three small beads, and another
large bead, ending with a crucifix.
The Lord's Prayer or "Our Father"
(Pater Noster) is repeated on each
large bead, and the Angelical Salutation or "Hail Mary" (Ave Maria)
on each of the small beads. The Glory
be to the Father (Gloria Patri) is repeated after each decade. Scenes representing the mysteries or episodes
in the life, death and glorious triumph
of Christ and His mother are meditated upon during the recitation of
the successive decades. The vocal
prayers, themselves holy and inducing to piety, are an accompaniment
to the meditations on the joyful, sorrowful and glorious mysteries (*q.v.*).
The history of the Rosary goes back
to the days of early Christianity and
the monks in the desert. A devout
ascetic, wishing to say a certain number of prayers (Pater Nosters usually), would gather a hundred or
more pebbles or seeds into a basket
and place them one by one in another container as he said his prayers.
It was often customary to make a
low salaam or genuflexion with each
prayer. In some of the Eastern Rites
these customs have been retained,
the prayers being recited upon
knotted cords or strings of beads. In
the Western Church, the Hail Mary
came into general use in the middle
of the 12th century. Hail Marys and
Our Fathers were then used when
reciting the Rosary, especially in
monasteries by lay Brothers and
Sisters who could not read the psalms
of the Divine Office. Instead of the
fifty psalms which were sung daily
by choir monks and nuns, the fifty
Hail Marys with the accompanying
Pater Nosters and Glorias were substituted. The laity in general took up
the recitation of the Rosary, which
is a source of deep devotion for both
learned and illiterate, combining as it
does both mental and vocal prayer.
There seems to be no proof that St.
Dominic originated the Rosary, or
even preached it in his missionary
work. However it is known that
Dominican Friars later spread the devotion far and wide. The practice of
meditating during the recitation of
the vocal prayers is said to have been
introduced by Dominic the Prussian,
a Carthusian monk, after St. Dominic's death. The beads of the Rosary
are made of all materials—olive
stones, wood, Job's tears, pearls both
imitation and real or precious stones
strung on gold chains, as used by
many a great lady both past and present. The Rosary is a beloved and universal devotion in honor of Christ,
son of Mary, leading the worshiper
gently along through their joys, sorrows, and on into glory. Said in common with others it is a communion
of prayer with fellow Christians on
earth and the blessed in heaven. To
one who loves God, the repeated
prayers are neither tiresome nor rep-
etitious.

rose window A circular stained-glass

window with mul-
lions and tracery gen-
erally radiating from
the center. The rose
window is a develop-
ment of Gothic archi-
tecture and is usually
found in the façade of
the nave or at the ends of the transepts.

Rosh Hashanah (Heb. beginning of
the year) The Jewish New Year
which falls on the 1st of Tishri, the
month of the autumn equinox. According to tradition, this was the time
the world was created. On this day
the *shofar* (Ram's horn) is blown as
a summons to repentance. With Yom

Kippur (*q.v.*) it is a Jewish High Holyday.

Rosicrucians Members of a secret brotherhood who claim to have occult and mystical knowledge. The organization grew out of literary satire written by John Andrea (1586–1654) which he attributed to a mythical Christian Rosenkreutz. Andrea ridiculed and condemned Rosicrucianism as nonsense. The group spread to the United States and has headquarters in California.

Rota, Sacred Roman A historic tribunal of the Holy See. It took its name from the circular hall where the auditors sat to hear a cause. It originally began as an extension of the Apostolic Chancery in the 13th century, and has slowly developed over the centuries. Essentially it is a tribunal of appeal (*c.* 1599) for all ecclesiastical cases in which the Roman Curia is competent. It is also the tribunal of appeal for the Vatican State. Finally, it is the Tribunal of the First Instance in those cases reserved to the pope or Holy See.

rubrics (L. *ruber,* red) Directions in liturgical books for carrying out ceremonies, so called because usually printed in red.

rule of Faith The Word of God as contained in Sacred Scripture and Tradition, and the teaching of the Church. Theologians refer to the former as the remote or indirect rule of Faith and the latter as proximate and direct. The characteristic of Protestantism is to make the Bible the proximate rule of Faith. Vatican Council I affirmed that Tradition which the Church "by a solemn judgment or by her ordinary and universal teaching, proposes for belief as having been divinely revealed" is a matter of Faith.

rule, religious The regulations which direct the life and discipline of a religious. The rule varies according to the purpose of the order or congregation. There are four great rules on which most of the others depend: St. Basil, which directs all monks of the East; St. Augustine, all canons regular and many orders; St. Benedict, all Benedictines, Cistercians, etc.; St. Francis, all Franciscan orders. Other rules are the Jesuits, Carthusians, Carmelites, etc. The rule binds under the virtue of obedience but generally not under grave sin.

rural dean (L. *decanus,* one set over ten) A priest of experience who is given charge of a section of a diocese (a deanery). It is his duty to bring together the clergy of the area for theological conferences, days of recollection; to care for the spiritual welfare of the priests of the area; to make certain that ill priests are cared for; and to report annually to the bishop on the condition of the deanery. *See* vicar forane.

Rural Life Conference, National Catholic Founded in 1923 to promote rural welfare through extension services, publications and other activities.

Russicum, the Popular name for the Russian Pontifical College of St. Teresa of the Child Jesus which was founded in Rome by Pius XI in 1929 to train priests in the Byzantine Rite to work in Russia. It is entrusted to the Jesuits.

Ruth, Book of An Old Testament Book of edifying history extolling Divine Providence and familial piety. It records the story of Ruth, a Moabitess, who through her loyalty to her mother-in-law, Noemi, became the wife of the Jew, Booz, and consequently the great-grandmother of David, and an ancestress of Jesus as listed in Matthew's genealogy of Christ.

Ruthenian Catholics A name sometimes applied in the United States to
those Catholics of the Byzantine Rite
who originate from the Podkarpatska
Rus ("Rusins"), Slovakia, Yugoslavia and Hungary. In Roman documents the name is sometimes extended to include the Catholic
Ukrainians. All of these people
shared the Orthodox separation from
Rome, but were reunited in 1595
and at other dates. In Europe, the
Rusins share the sufferings of their
Ukrainian brothers under Soviet rule.
See Ukrainians.

Ruthenian Rite The Ruthenians have
no distinct liturgy although the rite
used by them is often called by that
name. They use the Byzantine Rite
with some modifications based on
Latin Rite practices. The language
is Old Slavonic.

S

sabaoth (Heb. armies)   A term used to refer to God in the Sanctus and Te Deum (L. *Dominus Deus sabaoth*, Lord God of hosts). It is also found in the Old Testament.

Sabbatarians   1. A puritanical sect which tries to restore the rigors of the Jewish Sabbath on Sunday. Although the Jewish law forbids all secular activity on the Sabbath, this sect is mainly concerned with forbidding recreation and entertainment. 2. Certain Christian sects which advocate keeping the seventh day of the week (Saturday) as the Sabbath, such as the Seventh-day Adventists.

Sabbath (Heb. *sabbat*)   The seventh day of the week which was set aside by the Israelites. In Judaism, the day was excessively strict with many legalistic ramifications. This led to several conflicts between Christ and the Scribes and Pharisees. In the early Church the Christian community probably observed the Sabbath as they did other Jewish customs. It was St. Paul who made the first day of the week the special day for Christians.

Sabbatine privilege   The belief that those who wear the scapular of Our Lady of Mt. Carmel, who observe chastity according to their state, abstain from meat on Wednesdays and Saturdays or daily recite the Little Office of the Blessed Virgin, and who otherwise lead a virtuous life, will upon death be a special object of the intercession of the Blessed Virgin.

sacral   Sacred, holy.

sacrament (L. *sacrare,* to make sacred)   An exterior act of worship established by Christ by which, through the Church and her ministers, He signifies and effects the sanctification of the person properly disposed to receiving it. A visible sign instituted by Christ to give grace and which requires the proper disposition on the part of the receiver to be effective.

Sacrament of the altar   The Blessed Sacrament; the Holy Eucharist which is reserved in the tabernacle.

sacrament, root   A term that refers to the Church, which is a visible sign instituted by Christ to confer grace. It is from this root sacrament that the seven sacraments flow.

sacramental character   A spiritual sign or formation conferred by the sacraments of Baptism, Confirmation and Holy Orders, which shapes the soul in the image of Christ.

sacramentals   Canon law defines sacramentals as "those rites, actions and things which the Church uses in imitation of the Sacraments in order to obtain through her intercession certain effects, particularly of a spiritual nature." A sacramental produces grace indirectly not *ex opere operato* (*q.v.*) but *ex opere operantis*. The Church, because of her holiness, dignity and intercessory power, obtains from God, though not infallibly, the spiritual effect for which the sacramental was instituted. Among the sacramentals are prayers, holy water, blessings, ashes, medals, the Rosary, candles, vestments, etc.

Sacramentine Nuns Popular name of the Order of the Blessed Sacrament and of Our Lady. The order was the first one established for perpetual adoration of the Blessed Sacrament. Founded in 1639 in Marseilles, France, thirteen Sacramentine-Adorers were martyred by the guillotine during the French Revolution. They were beatified in 1925. When the anticlerical laws of 1901 closed the Sacramentine Convent at Bernay, France, the exiled religious founded monasteries in Belgium and at Yonkers, N.Y. The Yonkers foundation has since given birth to a foundation at Conway, Mich. The Holy Eucharist is the center of Sacramentine life, that through prayer and adoration all members of the Mystical Body will be helped. The Sacramentines make particular remembrance in their prayers and sacrifices for those actively engaged in spreading the Good News of Christ.

sacraments, last Anointing of the Sick and Viaticum (giving of Holy Communion). Sometimes, but incorrectly, conditional absolution to a dying person is called by this name.

sacraments, non-Catholic In those Eastern and other dissident churches which have valid episcopal orders, the sacraments that require only valid orders are in themselves valid. In practice, the Church also recognizes the validity of Penance and Confirmation when administered by an Orthodox priest. In those churches which do not have valid orders, the sacraments other than Baptism and Matrimony have no validity. They may be a means of grace but do not produce grace of themselves.

sacraments, the seven As defined by the Council of Trent, these are the sacraments of the New Law, instituted by Christ. They are Baptism, Confirmation, Holy Eucharist, Penance, Matrimony, Holy Orders and the Anointing of the Sick. Christ is present in all the sacraments either with His whole personality (the Eucharist) or through the effects of grace. A sacrament is used by Christ in the way a tool or instrument is used by whoever gives it power; grace passes through it.

sacrarium (sak-rah'ree-um, L. depository for holy things)
A basin in a sacristy draining into the ground. Water used for a sacred purpose is emptied here. Also the first washing of the sacred linens takes place here.

Sacred College of Cardinals The collective body of cardinals, who ordinarily elect the pope from among themselves, and who hold prominent places of authority and responsibility in Church government. They are chosen by the pope ordinarily from the rank of bishops and usually preside over important archdioceses or direct some administrative body within the Vatican.

Sacred Heart, League of *See* Apostleship of Prayer.

Sacred Heart of Jesus A devotion whereby the heart of Jesus is honored as a symbol of Christ's love for men, a logical consequence of the Incarnation, since Jesus Christ is perfect God and perfect Man in one divine Personality. By showing us His heart, wounded by sin, Our Lord calls men to the duties of love and expiation.

Sacred Orders Another name for the three Latin Rite major orders: subdiaconate, diaconate and priesthood.

Sacred Roman Congregations *See* Congregations, Sacred.

sacred vessels Vessels which touch the Blessed Sacrament: chalice, paten, ciborium, pyx and luna. Less sacred are the monstrance and paten. Other vessels used at Mass but not sacred are the cruets, thurible, incense boat and aspergillium. Except for grave emergency, only a priest or deacon should handle a vessel containing the Blessed Sacrament.

sacrifice The highest public and external act of divine worship by which a material offering of a victim is made to God by a legitimately appointed priest in recognition of His supreme dominion over all creation. In the supposition of sin, it expresses consciousness of guilt and hope of pardon. "Every visible sacrifice which is offered to God by exterior acts is a sign of that invisible sacrifice whereby a man offers himself and all he has to the service of God" (St. Augustine). The Sacrifice of Calvary was the one universal and absolute sacrifice. Consequently, to have any efficacy, the sacrifices offered at the Last Supper and in the Mass must bear some essential relation to that of Calvary; and actually in all three sacrifices the Victim and the principal Offerer are the same, namely Christ; the difference is in the manner of offering—in a bloody manner on the cross, in a bloodless manner at the Supper and in the Mass.

sacrifice of expiation The Mass, from the point of view of its value as an act of propitiation and of impetration (*qq.v.*) respectively.

sacrifice of praise All acts of religion may be described as sacrifices, inasmuch as the purpose of sacrifice is to manifest the interior worship of God externally; a sacrifice, however, strictly requires the offering of a victim by a priest for its external sign. The Mass is a sacrifice of praise, but it must be noted that the Council of Trent condemned the Reformers' opinion that "the Mass is only a sacrifice of praise and thanksgiving"; i.e., effectively imploring pardon and offering satisfaction for our sins.

Sacrifice of the Cross The free offering made by Christ of His Life for the salvation of men by gathering them together in Him. "And I, if I be lifted up, will draw all things to Myself." The one universal and absolute sacrifice by which the world was redeemed, so that every means of grace before or since Calvary derives its efficacy from the Sacrifice of the Cross.

Sacrifice of the Mass The true sacrifice of the Body and Blood of Christ made present on the altar by the words of consecration. A representation and renewal of the offering made on Calvary, inasmuch as all the separate Masses throughout time are included in that one and only Sacrifice of the Cross. "In this divine sacrifice the same Christ is present and immolated in a bloodless manner who once for all offered himself in a bloody manner on the altar of the cross; . . . only the manner of offering is different." The sacrificial action is held by the majority of theologians to be contained in the separate consecration of the bread and wine.

Sacrifice of the New Law Since the Sacrifice of the cross was the one universal and absolute sacrifice, every other sacrifice must derive from whatever efficacy it has. Those of the Old Law were types of the supreme Sacrifice of Calvary. Similarly, the Sacrifice of the New Law is the Mass, one and the same sacrifice with that of the cross, instituted by Christ to satisfy the needs of mankind for sacrifice and as the means whereby the fruits of the Redemption might be applied to men for the remission of their daily sins.

sacrilege (L. *sacer,* sacred; *legere,* to carry off) The violation of sacred persons, places or things; thus sacrilege is personal, local or real and should be so distinguished in confession. Sacrilege is a grievous sin against religion which admits of slight matter. Personal sacrilege can be committed in four ways: violation of the *privilegium canonis* (*q.v.*), violation of the *privilegium fori* (*q.v.*), violation of personal immunity, violation of a public vow of chastity. Local sacrilege may be committed in three ways: defilement of a sacred place, grave theft in a sacred place, violating the immunity of a place. Real sacrilege is reduced to three categories: the Sacraments and sacramentals, sacred vessels and church decorations, ecclesiastical property.

sacristan One charged with the care of the sacristy, the altar, the sacred vessels, etc. The sacristan prepares the vestments and articles needed for a Church ceremony. Although the Council of Trent ruled that all sacristans should be clerics, this is not possible today in most parishes and the function is carried out by laymen. *See* sexton.

sacristy (L. *sacer,* sacred) A room usually adjoining the sanctuary in which the ministers vest for Mass and in which the sacred vessels and vest-

ments are stored.

Sadducees One of the three main religious parties in Palestine at the time of Christ. They were a priestly group who were the "ultra conservatives" in religious matters. They accepted only the older views on the future life in the Bible and refused to acknowledge later developments such as belief in the angels and the resurrection. They rejected the centuries of oral interpretation and development of the law that was championed by the Pharisees. In political matters, the Sadducees tended to favor the Romans.

saint 1. A member of the Church Triumphant who by an exemplary life of holiness and virtue has been officially listed in the roll of saints by the Church following the processes of beatification and canonization, and to whom the Church Militant may render veneration (dulia) and request his intercession before the throne of God. 2. Each member of the Church Triumphant who has been admitted to the Beatific Vision.

St. Elmo's fire A visible discharge of static electricity sometimes seen at the top of a mast of a ship or on the wing of an airplane during a storm. It takes its name from St. Elmo (Erasmus), patron of sailors.

St. James the Apostle, Society of An organization founded in 1958 to accept secular diocesan priests for work in Latin America. Richard Cardinal Cushing, Archbishop of Boston, was the founder. The Society has priests in Peru and Bolivia.

Saint Mary Major One of the main patriarchal basilicas in Rome. It was founded by Pope Liberius in 366. It is the major church in Rome dedicated to Our Lady and is sometimes called Our Lady of the Snow.

Saint Peter's Basilica The patriarchal church adjoining the Vatican palace and the largest church in the world. It is built on the site of the Circus of Nero where St. Peter was crucified. It is not the first church of Christendom as so many believe, that honor belongs to St. John Lateran which is the papal cathedral and formerly the residence of the popes. Constantine replaced the original church on the site with a magnificent basilica. This was partly demolished during the early Renaissance and the present basilica begun. Successive popes and architects changed and re-changed the plans. Michelangelo succeeded in restoring most of Bramante's design. The tremendous dome was designed by Michelangelo but the effect was spoiled by later architects who extended the nave and thus cut off the view of the dome at close range. The basilica is a church of treasures. The tomb of St. Peter was recently located. The chambers beneath the pavement contain the bodies of many popes and emperors. The present building was completed in 1626. It holds 50,000 people. The covered colonnades leading to the front of the building with the huge Doric columns are an integral part of the design.

Saint Sophia A popular name for the Basilica of the Holy Wisdom (Gr. *Hagia Sophia*) in Constantinople. It ranks first among the churches of the East. It was dedicated to Christ, the Word of God.

Saint Thomas Christians A name given to the Christians of the Malabar Rite in southwest India who claim that they are descendants of converts made by St. Thomas the Apostle who was supposedly martyred at Mylapore. Their liturgy is taken from that of the East Syrian Church.

Saint Vincent de Paul Society An association of Catholic laymen devoted to personal service of the poor through the spiritual and corporal works of mercy. The first conference was formed at Paris in 1833 by Frederic Ozanam and his associates. The first conference in the United States was organized in 1845 at St. Louis. Headquarters: Railway Exchange Building, St. Louis 1, Mo.

saints (L. *sanctus,* holy) 1. In strict modern usage, those men and women who by exemplary holiness and after scrutiny by the Church are declared saints by the pope. They are martyrs or confessors if men; virgin-martyrs, virgins or widows if women. They are entitled to veneration (dulia) and intercessory prayer. 2. Any person who dies and goes to heaven is a saint. However, the only certain saints are those officially canonized by the Church. 3. In the early Church, men and women of eminent holiness. 4. In the apostolic Church, all Christians. Thus St. Paul began his Epistle to the Colossians: "To the saints and faithful brethren in Christ Jesus, who are at Colossae."

saints, intercession of the From the earliest days the Church has recognized the power of saints to intercede before the throne of God. It encourages the faithful to pray to saints.

saints, veneration of While saints cannot be worshiped since this act of religion belongs solely to God, the Church does encourage veneration (dulia) of the saints. This is a type of honor paid them because of their model lives. By veneration we adore God through the saints.

sale of indulgences Until the Council of Trent in 1545, there were many abuses in granting indulgences. The most publicized was connected with the indulgence preached by Johann Tetzel to which Martin Luther responded with his ninety-five theses in 1517. Although Tetzel never said it was possible to "buy" salvation, there was still a mercenary character to the whole controversy. The true Catholic teaching is that it is lawful to make an offering on the occasion of receiving an indulgence provided there is no danger of simony. Anyone granting an indulgence for money is guilty of simony and liable to excommunication reserved to the Holy See. If the object to which an indulgence is attached is sold, the indulgence is lost.

sale of Masses This practice is an evil arising out of the centuries-old custom of offering Mass stipends. A stipend helps in the support of the priest who offers Mass and thus takes the place of the bread, wine, vegetables and other gifts which were, in former times, given the priest for his own upkeep and to help the poor. No Mass can be bought or sold, for the fruits of the Mass are a free gift of God. The sale of Masses, i.e., "the commercial traffic in stipends," was formally denounced by Pius IX in 1869; anyone guilty of this practice is guilty of simony and incurs the penalty of excommunication.

Salesians, the Society of St. Francis de Sales; Salesian Society of St. John Bosco. A religious society of men, founded in 1846 by St. John Bosco in Turin, Italy. John Melchior Bosco was born of a poor family near Castelnuovo, Italy, in 1815. As his mother was left a widow with three small boys, John spent his early years herding sheep and had his first schooling from the parish priest, keeping up his studies between his duties in the fields. In 1835 he entered the seminary at Chieri and was

ordained a priest six years later. Doing pastoral work in Turin, he was shocked at the numbers of boys in prison under evil influences. He began to instruct homeless boys, showing kindness and friendship. His little group of 20 increased to 400, and he obtained an old shed for them. He began night schools for child factory workers, organized a band, led them on picnics. Neighbors complained, criticized, even tried to have him confined to a mental hospital. Mamma Margaret, his mother, joined them, selling her small property and mothering the waifs. Funds began to come in, and Don Bosco erected technical schools and workshops. As priests and lay teachers joined him, he formed a society with a rule which was approved by the pope in 1874. He led the boys to a Christian life, teaching them, hearing their confessions with love and understanding. "Instruction alone," he said, "is not enough, but frequent confession, Communion, and daily Mass are the real foundation." He liked his boys to play and be active. He never found it necessary to punish, but won everything by kindness, love and patience. He named his Society after St. Francis de Sales, the special apostle of gentleness and love. Don Bosco died in 1888, and was canonized in 1934. At the time of his death the Salesians had 250 houses widely dispersed over the world, with an enrollment of 130,000 children, graduating 18,000 apprentices each year. Today the Society has houses with trade schools for boys all over Europe and in most mission countries, with 12,000 priests and 10,000 Brothers. Their first house in the United States was founded in 1898 in San Francisco, and there are now two provinces in the country.

salt, liturgical use of Baptismal salt is given to the catechumen during the ceremony of Baptism. Blessed salt is used in the preparation of holy water before High Mass on Sunday. Salt symbolizes wisdom, though perhaps it originally had an exorcistic signification.

Salvador, El Evangelized with and from Guatemala. A diocese was not erected in El Salvador until 1842, more than 20 years after independence. Today that diocese has grown to 1 archdiocese and 4 dioceses. The country has long been beset by a lack of priests, and its present 2.5 million people make a ratio between priest and people of 1 priest for 15,619 people. There has been some improvement in recent years due to outside aid. From the United States have come Franciscans, Benedictines and Maryknollers. The Diocese of Helena, Mont., operates a parish in Salvador.

salvation (L. *salvatio,* act of saving, state of being saved) A state of freedom and its consequences; living temporarily or permanently in favor in God's eyes. It is a result of man's free will cooperating with God's grace.

Salvation Army A Protestant sect founded in England in the latter half of the 19th century by William Booth. It was established in the United States in 1880 and today has approximately 2,000 centers of operation with over 5,000 officers and a quarter of a million members. Although the major portion of its work is evangelical, it is best known to the American public for its social and welfare activities.

salvation of unbelievers It is generally agreed that the grace of Christ is of universal application and that no souls of good will lack the concrete means of salvation in the full sense. There is no man, no unbeliever, whose supernatural conversion to God is not possible. The method of salvation will differ according to whether the unbeliever has or has not encountered the Church. If he does not know the Church, the only condition of salvation is that he wants to do what God wills and would belong to the Church outwardly if he came to know it.

Salvatorian Fathers Popular name for the Society of the Divine Savior, founded in 1881 in Rome for the evangelization of the world. The American province has a mission in Africa, conducts missions among the Negroes and a number of high schools.

Salve Regina (saal'vey ray-jee'nah; L. Hail, queen) An antiphon to Our Lady and the most widely used prayer after the Hail Mary. It takes its name from the first two words and is known in English as the Hail Holy Queen. It is used in the Divine Office, has been set to music as a hymn and is one of the prayers said after a Low Mass when the prayers are mandatory.

Samaritans A mixed people descending from the Israelites and various groups of immigrants who lived in central Palestine near the city of Sichem. The Samaritans and the Israelites broke their ties with one another and became rivals in the 5th century B.C. The Samaritans considered themselves as the authentic Israelites, whereas the Israelites considered them heretics. The Samaritans revered Moses and the Pentateuch (but no other book of the Bible) and were awaiting a Messiah. They set up on Mount Garizim a temple to rival the Temple in Jerusalem. At the time of Christ there was great mutual contempt between the Samaritans and the Judaeans. Orthodox Jews carefully avoided any contact with the Samaritans. A tiny colony of about two hundred Samaritans still lives in the same area of Palestine which their ancestors inhabited in the time of Christ.

sampietrini (It. St. Peter's men)   The body of skilled craftsmen and artisans who maintain St. Peter's Basilica.

Samuel, Books of   Two Old Testament books also commonly referred to as 1 Kings and 2 Kings, after the titles given them by St. Jerome. These two books originally formed a single work which was divided for greater convenience. The books were called "Samuel" probably because the birth and life of Samuel were the subjects treated in the beginning of the work. The two books are concerned with the history of three persons whose destinies are closely connected with one another: Samuel, Saul and David. The narrative contains a marked unity in that it progresses toward, and converges on, the Kingship of David. These books seem not to have originated at one period of time. It is more reasonable to believe that accounts were written both in the Northern Kingdom and in the Southern Kingdom, and were then edited some time before the Babylonian exile.

San Francisco, Archdiocese of   In 1776 Father Junipero Serra, Father of the California Missions, ordered the founding of a mission to be called after St. Francis of Assisi. The mission prospered until 1834 when it was confiscated by Mexican authorities and renamed the village of Yerba Buena. In 1847 the city was seized by a United States gunboat and renamed San Francisco. It was part of the territory ceded to the United States

in 1848. In 1853 it was created an archdiocese with Monterey named as a suffragan see.

sanatio in radice (L. a healing at the root)   A secret validation of a previously invalid marriage without securing a renewal of consent. This *sanatio* can be granted by the Church only for a marriage which was invalid because of some ecclesiastical obstacle; not, however, for a marriage which was invalid because of an obstacle of natural or divine law. The *sanatio,* by a legal fiction, considers the marriage valid retroactive to the beginning of the union, thus legitimating any children already born of the couple.

sancta sanctis (L. holy things to the holy)   An ancient formula used in all rites but the Latin to remind the faithful that one must be in the state of grace to partake of the Eucharist.

sanctify (L. *sanctus,* holy)   To make holy, to fill with holiness (*q.v.*).

sanctifying grace   A divinely produced quality or perfection of the human soul whereby it participates in, is drawn into, the nature and life of God and is made to resemble Him as He is; it elevates man's nature to the level of the divine, giving man both divine life and a spiritual end. It is "God abiding in the soul" (Jn. 14:23). Sanctifying grace is lost through mortal sin and is increased by reception of the sacraments and the performance of good acts.

sanction (L. *sanctio*)   That system of rewards and punishments attached by a legislator to induce observance of a law. A moral sanction has a twofold object: the first, deterrent, influencing through the hope of reward or promise of punishment; the second, retributive, rewarding the observance and punishing the violation. The final sanction due man for his acts is found not in this world but in the next where man will enjoy life with God or suffer eternal separation from Him.

Sanctissimum Procession (L. most holy) The procession with the Blessed Sacrament to the altar of repose on Holy Thursday and the procession from the altar of repose to the high altar on Good Friday.

Sanctissimum, the (L. most holy) The Blessed Sacrament.

sanctity of the Church Holiness, one of the marks by which the Church can be identified. The Church is holy because it is the Mystical Body of Christ, because it preaches holiness to its followers so that they can merit eternal life with God, and because many of its followers have attained eminent holiness as revealed by the lives of its saints.

Sanctorale That section of the Missal or Breviary that contains the proper offices of the saints.

sanctuary (L. *sanctuarium,* holy place, shrine) 1. That area of a church immediately surrounding the altar, usually marked off by altar rails, but not necessarily so. 2. A name given to a holy place or a shrine. 3. Because of its sacred nature it is held that worldly affairs should not be conducted in a sanctuary or in its immediate vicinity. Thus results what is known as the "privilege of sanctuary." This privilege though not recognized today is still provided for in canon law. It considers the sanctuary and its vicinity a place of refuge from which a person cannot be taken in order to administer public justice to him. If a person were to commit a serious crime, civil authorities could not apprehend or try him while he remained in a sanctuary or its immediate boundaries.

Sanctus The prayer of praise that introduces the Canon of the Mass: "Holy, holy, holy Lord God of Hosts! Heaven and earth are full of Your glory." This prayer is based on Isaiah 6:3.

sanctus-bell The bell rung at the Sanctus to signal the beginning of the Canon of the Mass. The bell is also rung at other parts of the Mass; e.g., the Elevation, the prayer *Hanc igitur,* the priest's *Domine non sum dignus.*

sandals A shoe made of a sole strapped simply to the foot. This type of footwear has come to be a symbol of poverty, and as such is worn today by several religious orders in the Church.

Sanhedrin, the (Gr. *synedrian,* seat) The supreme council and court of justice among the Jews. Consisting of 71 members, including the High Priest who presided over it, the Sanhedrin combined the functions of a council of state, a supreme court and a theological conclave. The practical power of the Sanhedrin varied from time to time. When Judea was independent, the Sanhedrin held unlimited power even in civil matters. When Judea was made a Roman province ruled by procurators, the Sanhedrin had the authority to arrest an alleged criminal and to gather evidence for the case, but the Roman procurator alone had authority to hear the case and pronounce sentence.

santos (Sp. saints) A Latin American word for a religious representation such as a statue, holy picture, etc.

Sapienti Consilio The constitution of St. Pius X published in 1908 which removed the United States, Canada and other countries from the jurisdiction of the Congregation for the Propagation of the Faith and placed them under the Consistorial Congregation. The effect of this action was to declare that these countries were no longer missionary countries but had come of ecclesiastical age and were responsible for spreading the Word of God to other lands.

Sapiential Books, the The name given to a group of books of the Old Testament largely dedicated to the praise and inculcation of divine and human wisdom. These books are: Job, Proverbs, Ecclesiastes, Ecclesiasticus (Sirach) and Wisdom. To this group are added the Canticle of Canticles and the Book of Psalms.

Satan (Heb. adversary) A proper name given to the Devil, who is the cause of all evil. This name is used frequently in the New Testament.

Satanism The worship of the Devil, mainly by persons who profess a hatred for Catholicism. Statanists are a fanatical group who show this hatred for the Church by worshiping the Devil through profaning a validly consecrated Host in what is known as the "Black Mass."

satisfaction (L. *satis,* enough; *facere,* to make) 1. To make amends for sins committed against God by undertaking some form of reparation. 2. Sacramental satisfaction, the performing of the penance assigned by a confessor in the Sacrament of Penance. 3. An act of penance performed in a monastery for a violation of the rule. It usually consists of kneeling in one's place until the superior gives a signal to arise.

satisfaction, vicarious Because the offense of man against an infinite God took on infinite aspects, no reparation on the part of man could satisfy for it. Christ took man's place and by His passion and death atoned for the sins of mankind; He thus made vicarious satisfaction for man.

Saturday The seventh day of the week, the Jewish Sabbath. It is a day specially dedicated to the Blessed Virgin, having no other meaning to the Catholic Church. A few Protestant sects, e.g., the Seventh-Day Adventists, make Saturday their weekly holy day.

Saturday abstinence The penance of abstinence from meat on Saturday as well as Friday. The Church at one time required that the faithful abstain from meat on both Saturday and Friday, probably to honor the time in which our Lord was in the tomb.

Scala Sancta (L. the holy stairs) The flight of 28 steps that go up to the chapel in the Lateran Palace which, for protection, are now covered with wood. The faithful customarily ascend the stairs on their knees as an act of penance. Although never authenticated, tradition holds that these stairs originally led to the praetorium where Pilate condemned Christ, and that they were brought to Rome by St. Helen.

scamnum The Latin word for the long bench that has no back or arms, which is found on the Epistle side of the sanctuary. It is used by the celebrant, deacon and subdeacon at a High Mass.

scandal (Gr. *skandalon,* a snare) Bad example in thought, word or deed which causes another's Faith to be weakened, or causes him to sin. Some persons may take scandal if a good action is performed which to them appears to be evil. In this case a sufficiently good reason is needed to per-

512

form the action. If a person, however, customarily sees evil in good actions he need not be considered.

scandalous A proposition is said to be scandalous when it can be the cause of wrong thinking or acting by another.

scapular (L. *scapula,* shoulder) 1.  A long narrow piece of cloth about the width of the shoulders with an opening in the center so that it can be slipped on over the head and hang in equal lengths in front and back. It is worn over the tunic, sometimes under a belt. In some cases it has a hood attached as with the Benedictines. It began as a working garment to protect the tunic but has now become part of the habit. 2. Two pieces of cloth about three inches long and two inches wide attached by two strings so that the scapulars can be worn front and back with the cloth strings going over the shoulders. The scapulars have embroidered or stamped representations. There are almost a score of such scapulars, each attached to a particular third order or confraternity. The scapular gives the wearer a share in the merits and good works of the particular group of which it is a badge. The wearer should be invested in the scapular by religious authority. It must be worn as described. If set aside for any period, the spiritual benefits cease during that time. Care must be taken in the use of scapulars to guard against superstition. *See* scapular medal.

scapular medal A blessed medal which may be worn in place of one of the small scapulars. It was authorized as a substitute by St. Pius X in 1910. The priest who blesses it must have the faculties to invest in the scapular it represents. On one side of the medal is a representation of the Sacred Heart and on the other the Blessed Virgin. Investing in any scapular cannot be done with the medal; the actual scapular must be used. Afterward the medal may be substituted.

scapular promise *See* Sabbatine privilege.

Scarlet Woman, the The woman mentioned in the Apocalypse (17:3-6) who was clothed in purple and scarlet and rode a scarlet-colored beast. She has the symbolic name of Babylon. She represents the immorality and decadence of imperial Rome.

schism (Gr. *schisma,* to split) The separation from the unity of the Church, from communion with the Church, from the head of the Church or from the jurisdiction of the Supreme Pontiff.

Schism of the East A series of disagreements, quarrels and breaks which led up to the severance of the Eastern Church from the Western Church. The assumption of power by Photius in the 9th century caused one break. The schism of Cerularius in the 11th century was another. The disagreements came to a head with the fall of Constantinople in 1453. The Council of Florence (1439) had affected a brief reconciliation but political pressures on the Eastern Church by the Turks led to a final and complete break in 1472 when Constantinople withdrew from the Church. The break has hardened over the years and it was not until Vatican Council II that a serious attempt was begun to explore differences.

Schism of the West Also called the Great Schism. It was not really a schism but a dispute rooted in politics. The background was the residence of the popes in Avignon, France. Upon the death of Gregory IX in 1378, the residence of the pope was a major issue at the conclave to elect his successor. The conclave elected Urban VI, an Italian. However, some of the electors, largely the French, complained of Italian pressures on the election and asserted that the election was invalid because it was made under threats of violence from the Roman mob. They reassembled and elected Clement VII, a Frenchman, who took up residence at Avignon. The various princes divided their loyalty between the two claimants of the papacy. The Latin and French monarchs supported Clement, and the German and English supported Urban. The quarrel ended with the election of Martin V in 1417. Historians are generally agreed that the Urbanist popes were the valid successors to the chair of St. Peter.

schismatic One who knowingly and deliberately separates himself from the Catholic Church and voluntarily embraces schism. Thus anyone born in a schismatic church and not knowing that the Catholic Church is the one, true Church cannot properly be called a schismatic.

schola cantorum (L. a body of singers) 1. A choir specially trained for the singing of liturgical chant. 2. In general, a place for the training of singers in ecclesiastical music. Pope Hilary (d. 468) founded the first such school but it was St. Gregory the Great who put it on a firm footing. The Roman school was imitated in other parts of the world.

scholastic 1. A follower of Scholastic philosophy, a Schoolman. 2. A Jesuit seminarian who has completed his novitiate and taken simple perpetual vows.

Scholasticism The systematic philosophy developed in the Middle Ages from Aristotelian and Augustinian roots, highly developed by St. Thomas Aquinas, marked by the tendencies to metaphysical, theistic and humanistic interests, and by conformity to Catholic orthodoxy. The word is used for methods in which the doctrines of revealed truths are explained and systematized with the help of philosophical concepts.

school *See* parochial school.

school, apostolic A minor seminary for the training of candidates for the foreign missions. The term is not as common as formerly. In the United States the Maryknoll preparatory seminary at Clarks Summit, Pa., was originally known as the Venard Apostolic College.

School Sisters of Notre Dame A community of women that was re-established in 1833 after having been suppressed by Napoleon. The American foundation was made in 1847. Today there are 6 American provinces with 6,500 Sisters; and one Canadian province. Missions have been begun in Bolivia, Brazil, Guam, Guatemala, Honduras, Japan, Puerto Rico and the Ryukyu Islands. Teaching, nursing and catechetics are the primary work. Simple vows are taken.

School Sisters of St. Francis Founded in Wisconsin in 1874, the community is engaged in teaching, hospital work and catechetics. Foreign missions are staffed in Costa Rica and Honduras. Simple vows are taken. There are almost 3,000 members.

Schoolmen An English word to designate the medieval leaders in Scholasticism. The Schoolmen effected a synthesis with ancient philosophy, particularly that of Aristotle, and Christian revelation. The greatest of the Schoolmen was St. Thomas Aquinas; others were St. Albert the Great, St. Bonaventure, St. Anselm, Peter Abelard, Alexander of Hales, Duns Scotus, etc.

science and religion, conflict between Throughout the history of the Church, much has been made of the conflict often raised between science and theology. Invariably it has resulted from one or the other going beyond the legitimate range of its own discipline. Physical science deals with the nature and properties of things and the laws by which they are governed; religion deals with the truths, both of the physical and of the moral order, which lead men to God. The two ought to work hand in hand. Physical science gives a detailed knowledge of this universe, which is God's handiwork, and religion seeks to have man use this knowledge as a means toward attainment of full happiness with God. At times the conflict has been the result of confusing the era of an idea or concept with its truth. At other times it has come from excessive attachment to mere opinion. Thus many battles have been waged from misguided zeal in defense of notions mistakenly thought to be doctrine or necessary concomitants to dogma; e.g., the Galileo Case. Scientists on the other hand have been overeager at times to castigate all religions as superstition and sheer nonsense. Thus science and religion have appeared utterly opposed. When attention is given to the methods and ends of science and religion, the two are seen to be incapable of opposition. Since they concern themselves with types of knowledge and truth that are only indirectly related, and since they use different starting points, neither can be said to conflict or oppose the other. Ultimately insofar as all truth can be said to have its beginnings and end in the Godhead, there can never arise a fundamental disagreement between the findings of science and the teachings of the Church.

Scourge of God The name given Attila, king of the Huns, who advanced in 441 with little opposition through eastern Europe and into Italy. He was persuaded from sacking Rome by Pope Leo the Great. He died in 453.

screen *See* choir screen; iconostasis; parclose; rood screen.

Scribes The learned class among the Jews. They were authorities on the Law and on tradition. They were the editors, teachers, notaries and copyists, especially of the Bible; they generally favored the Pharisees.

scriptorium (L. a writing place) A large room in a monastery used by scribes, copyists, illuminators, artists, etc. The room was under the care of a precentor who provided all the supplies needed. Silence was maintained and artificial light was forbidden lest the manuscripts be damaged.

Scriptures A term used from the earliest times to denote the Bible—both the Old Testament and the New Testament and any part thereof. (*See* Bible). Also, the term describes one of the three divisions of the Hebrew Bible, "The Law, the Prophets, and the Writings."

Scriptures, sense of the In general there are three kinds of "senses" found in Scripture: 1. *Literal,* the meaning that the author intended by his *words*. This is an inspired sense of Scripture. The fuller sense (*sensus plenior*) is a term frequently used. Its meaning is that a text which completely conveys the meaning intended by its original inspired author is now given an additional meaning by another inspired author. Since the second meaning is beyond that intended by the first author this sense of Scripture cannot strictly be termed inspired. Nor would it be fair to classify it as merely accommodative. Since it has to do with the *words* of a sacred author, it is placed under the literal sense. There is much discussion of this term. 2. *Typical,* the meaning that arises by considering the *reality* expressed by the words of a text of the Old Testament as prefiguring certain later realities of the New Testament. This is an inspired sense of Scripture. 3. *Accommodative,* an adaptation of the words of Scripture to express ideas different from those intended by the sacred author. This is not an inspired sense of Scripture. It is a legitimate use of Scripture, however.

Scriptures, the Church and the The Catholic idea of the relationship between the Church and the Scriptures is fundamentally that the Scriptures come to us from within the Church and in this vivifying atmosphere of Christ's Mystical Body, they are explained to us. The Christian Church already existed and was an active and expanding organization before even the first sentence of the New Testament was written. These Scriptures were written in the Church, for the Church and by members of the Church. The Holy Spirit not only impelled the human authors of that first century to write as members of the Church, but also gives the Church the power to determine what books are to be considered as having divine authority. The unique supernatural quality of the Scriptures can be perceived and made known only by a supernatural authority. Natural criteria are not enough to establish or disprove this quality in the Church's writings. Ultimately, apostolic tradition, transmitted through the centuries within the Church, is the one means by which the divine authorship of the Scriptures can be made known to us and thus we accept this divine authorship by means of our faith in the Church's authority. It would be wrong to conclude from this that the Scriptures are simply subordinated to the Church. The Church sees them for what they are. She did not make them the Word of God; she received them as such, as gifts bestowed upon her by her divine Spouse. She has both the privilege and the responsibility of preserving them and of using them in whatever way she can for the salvation of men. She uses them as she sees fit; she understands them and claims the power to declare authoritatively, if necessary, their meaning. But she is aware that the divine origin of these Scriptures is parallel to her own; both are the work of God. The Scriptures, a work of the Holy Spirit within her, she humbly receives but does not control. Even though individuals in the Church are fallible, and even though they must be guided by the judgment of the Word of God, nevertheless, the Church, as the people of God and the Spouse of Christ, is the mother and teacher who speaks of the authority of Christ and therefore has the right to preach and interpret the Scriptures infallibly.

scruples (L. *scrupulus,* a small sharp stone) The source of difficulty in determining what is right or fitting. An excessive severe judgment on one's own conduct based on an erroneous conscience.

scrutiny (L. *scrutari,* to examine) 1. The method of election to ecclesiastical office by secret ballot. It is the way a conclave elects a pope. 2. The examination of a candidate for Holy Orders to determine his spiritual fitness.

seal of an altar The sepulcher (*q.v.*) of an altar and the relics therein.

seal of confession The obligation which binds a priest in administering the Sacrament of Penance to maintain absolute secrecy concerning facts learned through sacramental confession. This obligation also binds all who have knowledge of matter confessed in this sacrament.

séance (Fr. sitting) A meeting of followers of Spiritism under the direction of a medium which attempts to make contact with the dead. Catholics are strictly forbidden to attend such a séance even out of curiosity or as a spectator. *See* spiritism.

seat money Although it is specifically forbidden by canon law to charge money for attendance at Church services, many churches collect small voluntary contributions from those entering for the upkeep of the church. The custom is open to many misunderstandings and is a source of scandal to non-Catholics, and as such is being discontinued in many parishes. In some places it is called "door money."

Seat of Wisdom A name given the Blessed Virgin in the Litany of Loreto.

Second Coming, Christ's Christians adopted the Greek word *parousia* (presence) as a technical term to signify the time of Christ's return at the end of time, a time when the power and glory, which are now His by virtue of His exaltation and heavenly session at the Father's right hand, will be disclosed to the world. This coming will see the time of full and final triumph of Christ over evil and the full manifestation of our new

life in Christ. It will be a time of joy for those who truly believe, and a time of sorrow for those who have hardened their hearts to His love (cf. Matt. 24:3; 1 Cor. 15:23; 1 Thess. 5:1; Apoc. 22:17).

second order A noncanonical term applied to orders of women that have a founder in common with and a rule similar to an order of men (first order). The term is applied to such communities as the Dominican and Franciscan Sisters.

secrecy The act of remaining silent about things which a person is bound not to reveal. The obligation binds gravely in matters of professional secrets and where revelation would gravely offend justice or charity.

secrecy of confession *See* seal of confession.

secret (L. *secretum*) 1. Secret of the *Mass* (*q.v.*). 2. The keeping of silence about matters which should not be revealed. Moral law condemns the unwarranted revelation of a secret as well as the effort to steal the secret of another, particularly through dishonest means such as stealing documents, opening letters, wire tapping, etc. It is permissible for parents to read letters of their children and for religious superiors to read letters of their subjects, provided there is a good reason, i.e., for the protection of the children or subjects. Religious superiors may not open letters sent by a subject to the Holy See, the apostolic delegate, major or local superiors. The obtaining of secrets from a suspected criminal through the so-called "third degree" narcoanalysis (truth serum) or lie detector is held as morally wrong by most theologians since it violates a basic right of a person not to accuse himself and to protect his reputation; it is also held to be a violation of the common good. In the clinical and medical field the use of narcoanalysis is licit for a serious reason, provided consent is obtained.

secret, discipline of the *See* discipline of the secret.

Secret of the Mass A variable part of the Mass in the form of a prayer, said over the offerings and completing the preparation of bread and wine. It immediately precedes the Preface. When there is a commemoration (*q.v.*), it is an additional prayer. The prayer takes its name because it was formerly said *sotto voce* but from the liturgical changes of Vatican Council II it is now said aloud or chanted so that the people can respond.

secret societies Groups which are founded with the purpose of plotting against the Church or the State, whose members are bound by oath not to reveal the proceedings to lawful authorities and who give obedience to the head of the group. Catholics are forbidden to join such groups.

Secretariate of State This office of the Roman Curia dates back to the 15th century, and has slowly evolved to its present functions. This office handles affairs between the Holy See and civil powers, and other special matters.

secretarium (L. a place set apart) The chapel where a cardinal, bishop or abbot vests for pontifical ceremonies.

secreto (L. privately) A rubrical direction to say a liturgical prayer secretly, i.e., inaudible to servers and others around.

sect A religious group dissenting from the parent body. The term has a note of disapproval. The old and main Protestant bodies prefer to be called churches.

secular (L. *saeculum*, the world) 1. Pertaining to the world, temporal; opposed to the spiritual, eternal. 2. Pertaining to the secular clergy. 3. A secular priest. 4. A lay person as opposed to a cleric.

secular arm, the The civil authority. In other times it was the custom in the case of certain serious crimes, or where a severe penalty was to be meted out, to turn a prisoner over to the civil authority for trial. This happened in the cases of Savanarola and St. Joan of Arc. The practice is no longer followed because of the many abuses it created.

secular clergy A term applied to the clergy who are not religious and who come under the jurisdiction of the bishop of a diocese; the usual parish priests. The secular priest lives in the world, not under the rules of the monastery. He is permitted to hold property. He takes no vows, other than the implicit vow of chastity.

secular humanism A type of humanitarianism which is a devotion to the cause of humanity as a substitute for religion. It is a natural philanthropy coupled with a desire to bring the greatest good to the greatest number. It operates from no spiritual or supernatural motives.

secular institutes Organizations of men and women living in the world who dedicate themselves by vow or promise to observe the evangelical counsels and to perform apostolic works. They wear no distinctive habits. Secular institutes were given recognition and approval in 1947 by the Apostolic Constitution, *Provida Mater Ecclesia,* of Pius XII. Secular institutes are subject to the Sacred Congregation for the Affairs of Religious.

secularism A rejection of every form of religious faith and worship so that a person tries to live in a world separate from God and all religious realities. In education and civil matters, it is a rejection of any religious element; in world affairs, it is a rejection of any need for supernatural help in making a better world. Theologically it is a rejection of the immanent presence of God in the world and in history, and a rejection of the Incarnation as God entering into human affairs.

secularization 1. Permission given to a professed religious to leave his institute permanently, with a corresponding dispensation from the religious vows. 2. The abolishment of the Church's title to property by the giving of that title to the secular authorities, or a forcible taking of that title by secular authorities.

secundum quid (L. according to the thing) A philosophical expression meaning less than "complete" or "absolute," or completely; a qualifier. Thus the statement, "It is a good newspaper *secundum quid,*" could mean that the newspaper is relatively good when compared to other small newspapers but that it is not good when compared to superior newspapers.

sede impedita (say'day im-ped-ee'ta; L. the obstructed see) A term used when a bishop for any reason is not able to administer his diocese.

sede vacante (say'day vah-cahn'tey; L. the see is vacant) A term used when a see is empty because of the death, removal or transfer of its ordinary. The term is best known for its use when a pope dies and the Chair of Peter is vacant. Special stamps are issued by the Vatican in place of ordinary stamps, bearing the words "SEDE VACANTE" and the crossed keys of Peter under an umbrella.

sedia gestatoria (It. portable chair)

The portable throne set on a platform on which the pope is borne in procession. The platform is carried by six men wearing red damask who are known as *sediarii.*

sedilia (say-dill'ya; L. *sedile,* a seat) Seats formed from a recess in the wall on the Epistle side of the sanctuary, usually three in number. They have been replaced by the scamnum (*q.v.*).

see (L. *sedes,* a seat) The area in the care of an ordinary, a diocese or archdiocese. The creation of sees is reserved to the Holy See. An ordinary is known by the name of his see, e.g., Archbishop of New York, Archbishop of Toronto, etc.

seed-Christ The philosopher Justin, 2nd century, said that since Christ is God, everything created is an image of Christ. Christ is already present in "seed form" among non-Christians. The work of the Church is to look for the seed-Christ and bring Him to fullness of growth in the Church.

segregation (L. *segrego,* to separate from the flock) Keeping a group of people apart from normal contact with the whole community. As regards interracial justice, the situation in which members of a particular race are artificially and unjustly separated from the members of another race. The opposite of integration. In February, 1956, Archbishop Rummell of New Orleans enunciated the Church's position when he said: "Racial segregation as such is morally wrong and sinful."

self-defense One is able to resist an unjust aggression by whatever means is necessary even to the point of killing, provided that no greater force is brought against the unjust aggressor than is deemed necessary for self-protection.

Sem The oldest of the three sons of Noe, mentioned in the genealogy of Luke as an ancestor of Jesus. He was the founder of the Semites, the *bene sem* or famous people. In Sir. 49:16 together with Enos and Seth he ranks only next to Adam as an ancestor of the human race.

semi-Arianism (Ar'i-an-iz'm) The doctrine that the Son was not *identical in essence,* but of *similar essence.* In the year 313 Constantine published his famous Edict of Milan, by which full liberty was granted to the Christians. Soon after the Edict had been proclaimed, Arius, a priest of Alexandria in Egypt, began to preach the doctrine that Jesus Christ is not God but only God's noblest creature. In 325 Constantine, with the approval of the Pope, caused a council to assemble at Nicaea in Asia Minor where a creed was adopted stating that the Son is identical in essence with the Father. The semi-Arians were constrained to sign the document. After the closing of the council they began to assail the Nicene Creed (*q.v.*). The sons of Constantine continued to favor the semi-Arian party, which included a large number of Eastern bishops. With the death of Constantius II in 361 the Arian party was left without imperial support and lost some of its influence. With the accession of Valens in 363 it flared up again. External and internal conditions caused it again to lose ground. A second ecumenical council held at Constantinople in 381 reaffirmed the Nicene Creed. Arianism was soon suppressed within the empire, although it continued to flourish for a long time among the barbarians.

semi-Pelagianism (Pe-lay-jee'an-izm) After Pelagianism was condemned by the Council of Ephesus in 431, a modified form, called semi-Pelagianism became somewhat popular. It held that God's grace is given to all men, but the individual must take the first step toward salvation. This doctrine was condemned by the Synod of Orange in 529.

seminarian A student for the priesthood who attends a seminary.

seminarian, major A seminarian who is in the major seminary, i.e., the institution where the last six years (two years devoted to the study of philosophy and related subjects and four years to theology, Scripture, etc.) of the preparation for the priesthood are conducted. There is a growing tendency in the United States to depart from the 6-6 formula of Europe and to institute a 4-4-4 arrangement; four years of high school, four years of college and four years of postgraduate theological training.

seminarian, minor A seminarian who attends a minor seminary where the first six years (the four years of high school and the first two years of college) are conducted. *See* seminarian, major.

Seminaries and Universities, Sacred Congregation of One of the curial congregations. This congregation was established as the Congregation of Studies by Pope Sixtus V in 1587. In 1915 Pope Benedict XV added to this congregation a section dealing with seminaries and its name was changed to its present form. All seminaries depend on this congregation except those under the jurisdiction of the Congregations for the Oriental Church and the Propagation of the Faith. It likewise has jurisdiction over all Catholic universities and faculties and over all educational institutions dependent on ecclesiastical authority. This congregation also has charge of the Pontifical Work for

Priestly Vocations.

seminary (L. *seminarium,* a seed plot) An institution for the training of candidates for the priesthood. There are two levels: the minor or junior seminary which provides the high school and first two years of college training; and the major seminary where the last two years of college and the four years of theology are provided. This division is carried over from Europe. The present trend, however, more in conformity with the American system of education, is to divide the seminary training into three levels instead of two, i.e., to provide separate institutions for the high school, college and theology and consequently operate on the 4-4-4 division instead of the 6-6. The purpose of the seminary is to provide the special training in the spiritual life that is required for the priesthood, as well as the usual academic preparation received in other schools. A young man who desires to offer himself to Christ to continue His work on earth in the capacity of a secular priest may apply to the diocesan authorities. Usually there are yearly examinations for the candidates. When accepted, they enter on the year of education for which they are qualified. Expenses are borne by the individual if his family can afford them or they are taken care of by the diocese. After ordination a priest pays back the cost of his seminary education to his bishop. Seminaries were a late establishment in the history of the Church. Some kind of training has always been provided by the bishops. It was on an individual basis up to the time of St. Augustine. This great educator established a school near his residence where candidates for the priesthood lived in community, observed rules and carried out certain studies, especially theology and Scripture. This became the model for the Cathedral Schools established in other dioceses from the time of St. Augustine up to the Middle Ages. Out of these schools grew the universities where theology, philosophy and Church law held first rank; but the Cathedral School itself declined because the universities drew the best professors and most promising students, which led to serious defects in the holiness and preparation of priests. The Council of Trent saw in the reformation of the clergy one of the most important means of reviving the holiness of the Church. In 1556 the Fathers decreed that separate institutions should be established for the exclusive training of candidates for the priesthood.

senicide 1. The practice of killing the aged. 2. One who puts an aged person to death.

sense, accommodated The application of a passage of Scripture to a person or event for which the passage was not originally intended by the author. An example of accommodation is the application of the Wisdom passage in Ecclesiasticus, chap. 24, to Our Blessed Mother used in the Epistle of the Mass of the Common of the Blessed Virgin Mary. The accommodated sense of a passage of Scripture is not the genuine sense. Therefore, it should not be used as a proof for a doctrine. The sense intended by the author is known as the literal sense.

senses, dark night of *See* soul, dark night of the.

sensible That which is capable of being perceived by the senses. Something that is felt, thus sensible prayer involves the emotions.

sensualism An inordinate attachment to the pleasures of the senses

521

Sentences, Book of The popular theological textbook of the Middle Ages. It was compiled by Peter Lombard.

separated brethren A term coming into use among Catholics for all Christians outside the Catholic Church. Thus it includes Protestants and Orthodox. It is a development of ecumenism (*q.v.*), recognizing the common Fatherhood of God and the universal Brotherhood of Jesus Christ.

separation 1. Marriage. Marriage partners are obliged to live together by the very nature of their bond which is an undivided partnership. However, for a just cause a separation (imperfect divorce) may be had although the bond remains. Causes which permit a separation are: (*a*) adultery; (*b*) danger to the Faith, by heresy or apostasy of the other partner; (*c*) grave danger to body or soul; (*d*) mutual consent, when there is sufficient reason and no danger of scandal, harm to offspring, etc. Children are to remain with the innocent party or with the Catholic party unless the ordinary decides otherwise. 2. Of Church and State. *See* Church and State.

September Month of the Queen of Martyrs.

Septuagesima (L. seventieth) The third Sunday before Ash Wednesday. It begins the preparatory penitential period before Lent. Purple vestments are worn. The Gloria, Allelulia and Te Deum are omitted in the ferial liturgy.

Septuagint (L. *septuaginta,* seventy) That translation into Greek of the Hebrew and Aramaic Old Testament which was made in Egypt by various authors during the period of time between 250 B.C. and 100 B.C. The Septuagint is by far the most im-portant ancient version of the Old Testament. Its name comes from the fact that legend ascribes the work of translation to a group of seventy-two scholars. The Septuagint Version contains not only translations of the protocanonical books of the Old Testament, but also contains the deuterocanonical books. Still in general use in the Eastern Church, the Septuagint Version is of great importance, since, until recently, it has been our sole witness for the state of the original text of the Hebrew Old Testament before the Christian era. The Septuagint was the Bible of the primitive Church.

sepulcher (L. *sepulchrum,* a burial place) 1. Of an altar. The cavity in an altar stone to hold the relics of a martyr. After the relics are placed in the cavity, the hole is sealed. It is the spot on the altar which the priest kisses during Mass. The stone is a reminder that in the early Church it was customary to offer Mass in the catacombs on the tomb of a martyr. 2. Holy Sepulcher. The tomb northwest of Calvary where the body of Christ was laid after being taken from the cross. It was a new monument hewn out of rock, belonging to Joseph of Arimathea. Tradition passed down its location and in 326, Constantine erected a basilica over the spot where now stands the Church of the Holy Sepulchre, officially named Church of the Holy Redeemer. *See* Holy Sepulchre, Church of the.

Sequence (L. *sequentia*) A hymn inserted in the Mass of certain feasts after the Gradual. The use of such hymns was once very great but now is quite limited. There are also certain Sequences proper to some religious orders. An example of a Sequence, the *Victimae Paschali Laudis*

(Praise of the Paschal Victim) of the Easter Mass.

seraphic (Heb. *seraphim,* members of the angelic choir) A term used in the sense of angelic and applied originally to St. Francis of Assisi. Later it was extended to his Order and some of its illustrious members. Thus the Franciscans are called the Seraphic Order, St. Bonaventure is referred to as the Seraphic Doctor, etc.

seraphim (Heb. members of the angelic choir) The name given to the highest of the nine choirs of angels. Is. 6:2-3 describes them as attendants at the throne of God where they sing His praise.

sermon (L. *sermo,* speech) A formal religious discourse, as opposed to a homily which is an informal explanation of Sacred Scripture. The Constitution on the Sacred Liturgy of Vatican Council II has restored the place of the homily in the Mass ruling that at those Masses celebrated on Sunday and feasts of obligation with the assistance of the faithful, a homily should not be omitted except for a serious reason. "The homily," declared the Council Fathers "is to be esteemed as part of the liturgy itself."

Sermon on the Mount The discourse of Christ to the multitude. Matt. 5:1 says that Christ went up the mountain to preach the Sermon while Lk. 6:17 says the Sermon was given after Christ came down from the mountain. Although the Sermon as recorded by Matthew and Luke is the same in essence, Luke includes many parts of the Sermon elsewhere. Scriptural authorities explain this discrepancy by saying that Matthew was including many of the sayings of Christ which were spoken on other occasions. Luke also dropped parts which he did not think would apply to the non-Jewish audience to whom he was writing. The Sermon proclaims the teachings of the New Law. It is strikingly original in its content, teaching detachment from the goods of the world, the love of one man for another, and proclaiming the brotherhood of man under the Fatherhood of God.

Serra International Founded in 1938, this organization fosters vocations to the priesthood and assists in the education of young men with religious vocations. Headquarters: 38 South Dearborn Street, Chicago 3, Ill.

Servants of the Blessed Sacrament Founded in France in 1858, established in the United States in 1947. The Sisters lead a cloistered and contemplative life, take simple vows. There are choir nuns and lay Sisters. Perpetual adoration of the Blessed Sacrament is practiced. There are 500 members.

server One who serves the priest at liturgical functions, also called an altar boy or acolyte (in a broad sense). The server at Mass moves the Missal and brings the wine and water when required. He may also at a Sung Mass (*Missa cantata*) sing the Epistle (Rubrics of Pope John XXIII, 1960). Along with the congregation (or in place of them when they do not answer) he makes the responses to the prayers of the celebrant. Women may not enter the sanctuary to serve, but like the rest of the congregation they may and should respond from their place in church.

Service of the Word *See* Liturgy of the Word.

servile work Any occupation or labor performed by bodily action. It is forbidden on Sunday and holydays of obligation. However the law is to be interpreted on the basis of charity and grave inconvenience to oneself or others, not in the tyranny of mere legalism divorced from meaning and reality.

Servite Sisters There are a number of independent communities in the United States of religious women who derive their foundation from the Third Order of Servites which was founded in Italy in the early 14th century by St. Juliana Falconieri. Most of them are engaged in teaching. The largest community consists of several hundred members.

Servus Servorum Dei (L. the servant of the servants of God) A title the pope applies to himself. It was first used by Pope St. Gregory the Great in 591.

Seth (Heb. set) Son of Adam and Eve, father of Enoch.

Seven Churches, the The seven churches of Asia which St. John mentions in the Apocalypse as being the ones to whom he was directed to write concerning his vision (Apoc. 1-3): Ephesus, Smyrna, Pergamum, Thyatira, Sardis, Philadelphia and Laodicea. Only Smyrna remains as a residential see.

Seven Councils The first seven ecumenical councils of the Church which are accepted by the Eastern Orthodox Church. They are the Councils of Nicaea I, Constantinople I, Ephesus, Chalcedon, Constantinople II, Constantinople III and Nicaea II.

Seven Holy Founders Seven men of Florence, Italy, who lived in the 13th century. In response to a vision of the Blessed Virgin, they withdrew from the world to Mount Senario where they founded the Servite order. They have all been canonized.

Seven Last Words The seven utterances of Christ as He hung on the cross. They are recorded in the Gospels and are a frequent subject for Lenten preaching. They are: 1.

"Father, forgive them for they know not what they do." 2. "Amen, amen, I say to you, this day you shall be with me in Paradise." 3. "Woman, behold your son. Son, behold your mother." 4. "My God, My God, why have you forsaken me?" 5. "I thirst." 6. "It is finished." 7. "Father, into your hands I commend my spirit."

Seven Sorrows of Our Lady A feast granted to the Servite Fathers in 1668 and later made universal; it is celebrated on Sept. 15. The Sorrows as popularized by the Servites are: the prophecy of Simeon, flight into Egypt, the loss of Jesus in Jerusalem, meeting Jesus on the way to Calvary, standing at the foot of the cross, the removal of Jesus from the cross, His burial. They are also called the Seven Dolors.

Seventh-day Adventists A sect with more than a million members, spread over the world, who preach the near approach of doomsday and keep certain Orthodox Jewish observances such as abstention from pork and the observance of Saturday as the weekly day of rest. They believe that there is no hell; that at death the soul falls into a sleep from which the just will be raised at the Last Day to live with Christ forever, while the souls of the wicked will be destroyed. They claim that God wishes Saturday to be observed as the Sabbath; that the pope, who was the anti-Christ, changed the observance to Sunday. The Seventh-day Adventists contribute double tithing or 20 per cent of their income to their good works; have a high moral sense; believe in plain, healthful living and hard work; forbid liquor, tobacco, coffee, tea, cosmetics, the theater, movies, dances, playing cards and joining lodges. Their institutions for medical care and the training of doctors have top rating.

They provide for the religious education of their children from kindergarten through college, having three times as many college graduates as the general population. They are conscientious objectors in military matters but train their young men for medical and noncombat duty. They run 44 publishing houses, putting out books and tracts in 200 languages, operate a radio program over 860 stations and a TV program on 153 stations. They are a fine people, with many good ideas and great generosity, understandably misled, once the "reformers" had rejected tradition and authority, from their only source, Christ's own Catholic Church.

sex education A duty of parents which should never be omitted and should always be combined with education to purity. Instructions should begin very early, fitted to the occasion that arises and to the growth and maturity of the child. Parents must prepare themselves for the proper imparting of sex education. There are excellent Catholic books and pamphlets which give detailed instructions and diagrams for the use of parents and teachers in giving these lessons. Instruction should be kept up over the years, linked with the child's interests and needs at the time. Explanations should be given frankly, questions answered truthfully, but only as fully as the child can grasp at the time, calmly, in a matter-of-fact manner, showing the dignity and holiness of sex. Sex should be accepted as a normal part of life, treated in a wholesome, realistic manner. Prepare children beforehand for the birth of a new baby. They should love it and welcome it. When a baby is bathed, let them watch it and be instructed in the differences of the sexes "because God planned it so." As children grow into their teens, instructions should be full and complete, and the right kind of reading material on sex matters should be given them to supplement the instructions of parents. Here, too, instructions should be linked with the choice of a vocation in life. There are parents unfortunately who have shirked their responsibility in the matter of sex education, and in such cases the duty falls upon the teacher in the Catholic school, the C.C.D. catechist or the parish priest. Sisters in the lower grades can give the teaching necessary for that level, and here too, the many excellent books and pamphlets can be of great value. For higher grades, the parish priest might take the boys, and one of the Sisters might teach the girls if she is mature, poised and knows how to teach the subject. Questions should be settled individually by private interviews afterward. However, if necessary, a priest may take the group of older girls separately and instruct them himself. In any case, it is necessary to use the proper terms, to use them with dignity and authority, and to explain clearly. Finally, every teacher, parent, Sister-teacher or priest, should make clear the rules of Christian courtship, preparation for marriage, conjugal chastity, the Church's attitude on the raising of a family, on birth control, on divorce, on prayer and the sacraments as aids to holy family life, and to many Catholic family practices which are helpful. Particularly good is the consecration of one's purity to Jesus through Mary, for any state of life. This might be done at the conclusion of the course of instruction.

Sexagesima (L., sixtieth) The name given to the second of the three Sundays preceding Ash Wednesday. It is in the period of Lenten preparation.

Sext (L. *sextus, sixth*)   The third of the lesser canonical Hours; so called because belonging originally to the sixth hour of the day.

sexton (L. *sacristanus,* sacristan)   One having care of the fabric of a Church and its contents, opening and closing the Church, and the care of the altar.

shaman (Russian *saman*)   A witch doctor. One who uses magic to cure illness, to determine future events and to control happenings. In some areas of Latin America the word "chemane" is used for a shaman.

shared time   The division of school time between public and parochial schools, in which the student attends public school to study neutral subjects, such as mathematics, languages, physical sciences and vocational crafts, while subjects bound up with value judgment, such as history, literature, social sciences, the arts and religion are taught in the parochial schools. In shared time, the student divides his time between both schools. The system has many advantages. It allows children to receive a religious education which today is a serious concern to many parents because of the legally enforced secularism of the public school. At the same time it saves private groups the added expense of building science and language laboratories, and of training and hiring teachers for the subjects that are taught in public school.

Shekinah (Heb. *shakan,* dwell)   A term indicating God's presence among His people. The Jews thought of the Shekinah as an enveloping cloud or indwelling presence. The Incarnation is a new Shekinah; thus the angel told Mary that the power of the Most High would overshadow her, and St. John speaks of the Word dwelling among us. The term is also

used of the Father who spoke from a cloud of glory at the Transfiguration, and the Holy Spirit who clothed the Apostles with power at Pentecost.

Shem   Sem (*q.v.*).

Shepherd, Good   A figure Christ used to describe Himself in a parable recorded in John 10:11. There Christ says, "I am the good shepherd. The good shepherd lays down his life for his sheep." Here Christ emphasizes the love He has for all men, using the figure of a shepherd keeping guard over his sheep. In this parable we also find a scriptural definition of the Church, the flock over which the true Shepherd, Christ, presides. The figure of the shepherd has a strong biblical background: Ps. 22,77; Is. 40; Jer. 23; Ez. 34; Zach. 13, all refer to the Shepherd of Israel who takes care of His people. In saying that He is the "Good Shepherd" Christ points out the mutual knowledge and love that exist between Him and all the members of His Body. Just as sheep know the shepherd and follow him, and the shepherd knows all the traits of his flock and care for them, so Christ as the Good Shepherd knows all men for whom He gave His life.

shofar (show'far, H.)   The ram's horn used in Jewish synagogue services on Rosh Hashanah and Yom Kippur (*qq.v.*). The use of the horn is traditional and it was formerly blown to summon the Israelites to assemble. It was the horn which Josue used to "blow down" the walls of Jericho.

short lesson (L. *lectio brevis*)   A verse of Scripture said near the end of Prime and at the beginning of Compline. They are shortened forms of Bible reading that were once inserted in these parts of the Divine Office.

short responsories   A series of versicles and responses said after the

Capitulum of the Little Hours and Compline. In the Monastic Office it is found only in Lauds and Vespers.

shrine (L. *scrinium,* a case for paper or books) 1. A case, box, niche or reliquary where a saint's relics are kept. 2. A holy place where the faithful gather for some particular devotion. This may be the tomb of a saint, a place of apparition such as Lourdes, Fatima or Guadalupe, etc. 3. It can also be a shrine in the home or in a church set aside out of particular devotion.

Shrine of the Immaculate Conception, National In 1846 the American hierarchy placed the United States under the protection of the Blessed Virgin Mary, under her title of the Immaculate Conception. In 1914, on the ground of the Catholic University in Washington, D.C., a national shrine was begun to the Immaculate Conception. The foundation stone was laid in 1920, and the crypt church was completed in 1926. The upper church and shrine were dedicated on Nov. 20, 1959. The shrine is complete except for the addition of one chapel and the finishing of the interior of the upper church, now being carried out. Since its dedication, the National Shrine has drawn pilgrims from all parts of the United States. The Shrine is the largest Catholic church in the United States and the seventh largest in the world. The Byzantine roof of the main church and the towering campanile are outstanding additions to the Washington skyline.

Shroud, Holy The winding sheet which covered the body of Christ while in the tomb. It is claimed that the original shroud is in the cathedral of Turin, Italy. In 1898 in celebration of the 400th anniversary of the cathedral, the Holy Shroud was ex-

hibited and photographed for the first time. As the photographer developed his plates he saw a positive image form. It was the face and body of a man. The stains on the original shroud were like a negative photograph, made by vapors rising from the body in the tomb. In 1931 the Holy Shroud was again exhibited and photographed under controlled conditions. Scientists have deduced the following information from study of the Shroud and photographs. The man who had been covered by the burial cloth was 5'11". He had been scourged, crowned with thorns, forced to carry a large heavy object, and was crucified. He had been nailed to the cross through his wrists. There was a wound in his side, which had been made when the body was erect. The Church has not spoken on the authenticity of the relic, but there is great private devotion to the Holy Shroud.

Shroud of Christ *See* Shroud, Holy.

Shroud of Turin *See* Shroud, Holy.

sign (L. *signum*) Something which indicates the existence of something else. In this sense a sacrament is described as an outward sign of interior grace.

Sign of the Cross A sacramental made by the right hand which describes a cross on the body. In the Byzantine Rite it is made with the thumb and first two fingers joined, touching the forehead, breast, right shoulder and left shoulder. All other Catholics make it with all fingers joined touching the forehead, the breast, the left shoulder and right shoulder. It is usually accompanied by the words: "In the name of the Father, and of the Son, and of the Holy Spirit." It is the most frequently used sacramental, summing up Christian doctrine, particularly the Redemption. It is also made with the hand or with a crucifix as a blessing.

Signatura Apostolica (L. Apostolic Signature) The supreme tribunal of the Catholic Church. It judges with ordinary power: 1. in appeals based on a violation of secrecy by the Auditors of the Rota and on damages caused by the same through unjust or invalid acts; 2. in objections of suspicion against the Auditors of the Rota; 3. in claims of nullity against decisions of the Rota; 4. in requests for restitution against Rotal decisions which have become final; 5. in appeals against Rotal decisions in matrimonial cases which the Rota has refused to admit for further investigation; 6. in conflicts of competence between ecclesiastical tribunals which are not apostolic. Also, in virtue of delegated jurisdiction, it deals with petitions of commission to refer a judgment to the Sacred Rota. Lastly, through decisions to be submitted for the approval of the Holy Father, it passes judgment on any question connected with the administration of justice. It has other duties deriving from the juridical organization of the State of Vatican City and from certain concordats.

Signature *See* Signatura Apostolica.

silence (L. *silere,* to be still) The absence of occupation, particularly conversation. Silence can be either interior or exterior. Interior silence is the abstention from willful distraction so that the inspirations of the Holy Spirit may be more easily recognized. Exterior silence is the absence of exterior occupation so that a spirit of recollection may be induced. Silence is necessary for effective prayer.

Simon and Jude, SS. Two Apostles who are usually linked together. In the Gospels Simon is called "the zeal-ous one." Jude, also called Thaddeus, was the brother of James the Less, and therefore related to Christ. He is the author of one of the seven Catholic Epistles in the New Testament. Tradition says that SS. Simon and Jude went to Persia to preach the Gospel and were martyred there. They are mentioned together in the Canon of the Mass. Their feast is celebrated on Oct. 28 unless the Feast of Christ the King should fall on that day, in which case it is omitted and not commemorated.

simony A word taken from the name of Simon Magus who offered SS. Peter and John money for the power of bestowing the Holy Spirit and was rebuked by St. Peter (Acts 9). It is the expressed will of buying or selling something spiritual or related to something spiritual. Simony can be against divine law when an attempt is made or accomplished in buying or selling something which by its very nature or the law of the Church is set aside for the supernatural welfare of the soul, such as the sacraments, grace, the power of Holy Orders, etc. Simony can also be against ecclesiastical law by exchanging ecclesiastical goods in a way contrary to the prohibitions of the Church. Simony against divine law is always a grave sin against religion. Simony against ecclesiastical law is ordinarily a grave sin but may be venial.

simpliciter (L. simply) 1. The opposite of *secundum quid* (*q.v.*); that which is absolute and without limitation. 2. A term meaning "simply" or without complications. Thus a case can be reserved *simpliciter* to the Holy See.

simplicity of God An attribute of God who is the most simple of beings. God has no physical composition; He has no body, He has no matter or form, nor does He have quantitative parts. In God there is no metaphysical composition; in God real composition is not given to essence and existence, to substance and accidents. In God there is no logical composition because this would suppose act and potency while God is pure act.

simulation   A lie told by means of an action, or performing an act to give a false impression. It is permissible to simulate one's Faith provided there is sufficient reason and it does not entail either a direct or indirect denial of Faith. Thus a priest passing through dangerous territory of unbelievers could wear lay attire. The simulation of a sacrament consists in the minister changing secretly and unlawfully either the matter, form or necessary intention so that the sacrament is invalid and the recipient is led into error. Simulation of a sacrament is never permitted because it is a dangerous lie and a sacrilege. However, distinction should be made between simulation and pretense. For instance, a confessor who has to deny absolution to a penitent and tells him so and then gives him a blessing so that onlookers will not know absolution has been refused, is not simulating the sacrament but making a pretense.

sin   A deliberate transgression against the law of God. It is a willful act of disobedience whereby the sinner prefers his will to that of God and for this reason violates the right of God to the submission of His creatures. It has many divisions but the main ones are mortal and venial.

sin, actual   A transitory act or omission against the law of God. It arises from the free will of the sinner. It is committed by thought, word or deed, or a combination of these. It can be a sin of commission or omission, of weakness or malice, or a sin of ignorance. There are sins that cry to heaven for vengeance: sins against the Holy Spirit and the capital sins.

Sin against the Holy Spirit   The unforgivable sin (Matt. 12:31-32). St. Augustine explains this sin as final impenitence, or the rejection of God at the moment of death. There are other sins against the Holy Spirit which can be forgiven when repented: despair, presumption, resistance to truth.

sin by silence   A person shares in the sin of another when by his silence he does not warn of the injury to be done or by failure to denounce the guilty party to the legitimate authority after the injury is done. This is particularly true in damage to property.

sin, formal   A voluntary and free transgression of divine or ecclesiastical law. It presupposes knowledge that the act is sinful and then a deliberate placing of the sinful act.

sin, habitual   A permanent habit of sin resulting from repeated actual sins.

sin, material   A transgression which is in itself sinful but which is unknown as sinful or is involuntary. An example would be taking another's hat from a rack, thinking it was one's own.

sin, mortal   The transgression in a grave matter of law which is made with full advertance and full consent. It is called mortal (bringing death) because it cuts the sinner off from sanctifying grace and in a sense brings death to the soul. Since it is a grave rebellion against God, a person who dies in mortal sin dies cut off from God. Full advertance or full consent is absent when there is external violence, when an act is committed while half asleep or drunk,

When a person is not in complete possession of himself (e.g., temporary insanity through anger), when a person is afflicted with a pathological state, when a person can truthfully state that he would not have acted in such a manner if he had thought about it seriously beforehand.

sin, occasion of Any extrinsic circumstance (person or thing) which creates a strong urge to sin and a suitable opportunity. An occasion of sin is remote when it offers slight danger to sin under circumstances where a person rarely commits sin and proximate when it offers a grave danger of sin. Absolution must be denied to a penitent who refuses to leave a free proximate occasion of sin.

sin of another It is possible to share in the sin of another without actually committing the sin. He shares in another's guilt by commanding the sin, advising the sin, acting as partner with the sinner, by silence, by cooperation, by aiding the guilty person to escape, by receiving stolen goods, etc.

sin of commission An act which transgresses a negative precept of the divine or ecclesiastical law, such as stealing. It is a willful choice not to observe the precept.

sin of omission An act which transgresses a positive precept of the divine or ecclesiastical law, such as failure to attend Mass on Sunday.

sin, original 1. The sin committed by Adam and Eve through disobedience. 2. The effects of the original sin of Adam which is shared by all his descendants, the chief of which is the loss of sanctifying grace. Original sin does not so corrupt human nature that it is incapable of natural virtue, but it does deprive of grace which leads to the practice of virtue beyond the natural powers of man. Thus original sin as it affects mankind today is not sin in itself but a deprivation of life with God which was intended for all men but lost through sin. This life is restored through Baptism.

sin, venial (L. *venia,* pardon) An offense against God not serious enough to cause the loss of sanctifying grace. Venial sin is likened to an illness of the soul, and not its death. A sin is venial when its matter is not grave (e.g., stealing a nickel, a jocose lie), or when there is wanting full advertence or full consent to grave matter. Venial sins can become mortal sins through an erroneous conscience, through malicious intent and through the accumulation of matter, as in theft.

sindon (Gr. cloth) The Holy Shroud. The cloth on which Christ's body was placed and which was then used to cover His corpse. *See* Shroud, Holy.

sinlessness of Christ It is the teaching of the Church that in Christ there was never any actual or original sin. Since He was God, He was incapable of sin. Likewise, He was free from all concupiscence since this is a result of original sin.

sinlessness of the Blessed Virgin It is the teaching of the Church that the Blessed Virgin was kept free of original sin (the Immaculate Conception, *q.v.*) and from all actual sin either mortal or venial. This is proper as befits the one who was to be the mother of God.

sins against the Holy Spirit The six sins that lead one to resist grace: presumption, despair, resisting known truth, envy, obstinancy, final impenitence.

sins, capital Those seven sins which are the roots from which other sins arise: pride, envy, covetousness, anger, lust, gluttony, sloth.

sins crying to heaven In Scripture the following sins are described as crying to heaven for vengeance: willful murder (Cain kills Abel, Gen. 4:10); perversion (Sodom and Gomorra, Gen. 18:20); oppression of foreigners, widows or orphans, the poor (Ex 22:20, Sir. 35:14-17); and defrauding laborers of their wages (Js. 5:4). All these sins in some way are sins against our neighbor, especially those in need.

Sion A Chanaanite word used as a synonym for Jerusalem. It also was used to indicate the nation of Israel. In Christian times its usage was broadened to mean the household of God.

Sister Adorers of the Most Precious Blood A community of women founded in Italy in 1834 by Bl. Maria de Mattias and established in the United States in 1870. There are three provinces in the United States with approximately 1,100 Sisters. The principal works are teaching, nursing and care of the aged. There are missions in Brazil and Puerto Rico. Simple vows are taken.

Sister Adorers of the Precious Blood A contemplative community of women with a minor papal enclosure that was founded in St. Hyacinthe, Canada, in 1861 and established in the United States in 1890. There is a mission in Japan. There are 25 monasteries in Canada and 6 in the United States with approximately 900 members.

Sisters Members of various sisterhoods of women, bound by the simple religious vows of poverty, chastity and obedience, usually living together in communities and devoting themselves to the spiritual and corporal works of mercy. The terms "Sisters" and "nuns" are often used interchangeably, but "nun" is more properly used of members of contemplative orders, bound by solemn vows, and "Sister" of women bound by simple vows and practicing a mixed life of contemplation and active service as teachers, nurses, social workers, catechists, etc.

Sisters of Charity of Cincinnati Originally part of the Maryland community, this branch of the Sisters of Charity became independent in 1852. The Sisters are engaged in teaching, nursing and social work. There is a mission in Peru. The Sisters take simple vows. There are approximately 1,500 Sisters.

Sisters of Charity of Leavenworth, Kansas Founded in Kansas in 1858 by Mother Xavier Ross. The Sisters are engaged in teaching, nursing and Negro missions. Simple vows are taken. There are approximately 1,000 members.

Sisters of Charity of Nazareth Founded in Kentucky in 1812 by Bishop John David and Mother Catherine Spalding. Teaching and hospital work are the principal works. There is a medical mission in India. Simple vows are taken. There are over 1,600 members.

Sisters of Charity of Providence Founded in Montreal in 1843 by Mother Emelie Gamelin and established in the United States in 1854. Engaged in teaching and hospital work with a mission in Argentina. There are 3,500 Sisters with over 750 in the United States.

Sisters of Charity of St. Elizabeth Founded in New Jersey in 1859 by Mother Mary Xavier Mehegan. The order is engaged in teaching and nursing. The community staffs a mission in the Virgin Islands. Simple vows are taken. There are approximately 1,800 members.

Sisters of Charity of St. Vincent de Paul, Halifax Founded in Halifax, Nova Scotia, in 1856, The Sisters are engaged in teaching and nursing. Simple vows are taken. This is a provincialate in the United States. There are over 1,600 members.

Sisters of Charity of the Blessed Virgin Mary Founded in 1833 in Philadelphia by Mother Frances Clarke. Primary work is teaching, has missions in Colombia. There are approximately 2,500 Sisters.

Sisters of Christian Charity A German foundation that was established in the United States in 1873. Teaching, nursing, child care and catechetics are the principal works. There are approximately 1,150 Sisters in the United States.

Sisters of Divine Providence A German foundation that was established in Pennsylvania in 1876. The Sisters are engaged primarily in teaching. There are two provincialates in the United States with approximately 850 Sisters. Simple vows are taken.

Sisters of Divine Providence of San Antonio, Texas A French foundation that was established in the United States in 1866. Teaching, nursing and catechetics are the primary works. Simple vows are taken. There is a mission in Mexico. There are approximately 750 Sisters.

Sisters of Loretto at the Foot of the Cross A community of women founded in Kentucky in 1812 by the veteran and pioneer missioner, Father Charles Nerinckx. It is the oldest community completely native to the United States. The Sisters are engaged in teaching and nursing. There is a mission in Bolivia. There are approximately 1,200 members; simple vows are taken.

Sisters of Mercy A community of women founded in Ireland in 1831 by Mother Mary Catherine McAuley and first established in the United States at Pittsburgh, Pa., in 1843. The community has had remarkable growth and today numbers some 30,000 Sisters throughout the world, almost half in the United States. They operate through independent motherhouses except for the Sisters of Mercy of the Union in the United States (*q.v.*) who joined together in 1929 to form one community. Apart from this group there are still 17 independent motherhouses with close to 6,500 Sisters. The largest independent motherhouse is in Hartford, Conn., with approximately 750 Sisters. Work varies according to the motherhouse but teaching, nursing and assisting handicapped children are the primary occupations.

Sisters of Mercy of the Union in the United States A congregation formed in 1929 by the voluntary union of formerly independent motherhouses of the Sisters of Mercy (*q.v.*) in the United States. There are provinces in Illinois, Maryland, Michigan, Missouri, Nebraska, New York, Ohio, Pennsylvania and Rhode Island. Missions have been established in British Guiana, British Honduras, Honduras and Peru. The motherhouse is in Washington, D.C. The almost 7,000 Sisters of the congregation are engaged primarily in teaching, nursing and caring for orphans, underprivileged children and the aged. Simple vows are taken.

Sisters of Notre Dame A community that began in Germany in 1850 and then moved to the United States in 1874 because of religious persecution. There are five provinces in the United States with more than 1,500 Sisters. Teaching, nursing and social service are the primary works. Simple vows are taken.

Sisters of Notre Dame de Namur A community of women founded in France in 1803 by Bl. Julie Billiart and established in the United States in 1840. There are five provinces in the United States with some 3,000 Sisters. Missions have been established in Brazil and Japan. Most of the community's personnel are engaged in education. Simple vows are taken.

Sisters of Our Lady of Perpetual Help A community of women founded in Canada in 1892. Teaching and care of foundlings and orphans are among the main works of the community. There are missions in the West Indies and Africa. Members number 825; simple vows are taken.

Sisters of Our Lady of the Holy Rosary Founded in Canada in 1874 and established in the United States in 1899. Teaching is the principal work. There are approximately 900 members. Simple vows are taken.

Sisters of Providence A religious congregation of women founded in the diocese of Le Mans, France, in 1806, by Abbe Francois Dujarie, to help repair the ravages of the Revolution by teaching children and nursing the sick. A small band of devout women were joined by Madamoiselle Josephine du Roscoat of a noble Breton family, who was elected superior, and is called the foundress. The new congregation grew rapidly, and its schools were well known for their efficiency. In 1840 they came to work in the foreign missions of North America by invitation of the Bishop of Vincennes, Ind. They began their religious life in America in a small farmhouse near Terre Haute, and so established St. Mary-of-the-Woods, the motherhouse of the Sisters of Providence in the United States. The congregation prospered; schools, academies and high schools sprang up; St. Mary-of-the-Woods had its college. Work began in the archdioceses of Boston, Chicago, Indianapolis, Los Angeles, St. Louis, Washington, and in the dioceses of Corpus Christi, Evansville, Fort Wayne, Gary, Lafayette, (Ind.), Manchester, Oklahoma City and Tulsa, Peoria, Raleigh and Rockford. In the spirit of the Apostles, the Sisters also set out from the United States and founded a group of Chinese catechists who are still doing work in the mainland, and they are engaged in educational work and the training of native novices on Formosa.

Sisters of Providence of St. Mary-of-the-Woods Founded in France in 1806, the community was established in Indiana in 1840 by the pioneer missioner, Mother Theodore Guerin. There are missions in Taiwan and Peru. Primary works are teaching and nursing. There are approximately 1,500 Sisters. Simple vows are taken.

Sisters of St. Anne Founded in Canada in 1848, established in the United States in 1867. The purpose of the foundation is to teach poor children in rural areas. Missions are staffed in the Yukon and Haiti. Simple vows are taken. More than 2,200 Sisters.

Sisters of St. Casimir An American community founded in 1907 in Pennsylvania by Mother Maria Kaupas for teaching and social work. It is a diocesan institute with simple vows and has approximately 500 members.

Sisters of St. Francis of Assisi of Penance and Charity Founded in 1849 in Wisconsin by Mother Aemiliana Duerr, the community today is approaching a membership of 1,000. The Sisters are engaged in teaching, social work and care of the deaf, retarded, underprivileged, orphans and aged. Simple vows are taken.

Sisters of St. Francis of the Holy Family Founded in Germany in 1864, the community moved to the United States in 1875 to escape religious persecution. The nearly 1,000 members are engaged in teaching, nursing and caring for youth and aged. Simple vows are taken.

Sisters of St. Francis of Penance and Christian Charity The community was established in the United States from the Netherlands in 1874. There are now over 800 Sisters in the United States. Teaching, nursing and social works are the main activities. There are three provinces in the United States, and missions among Indians and Negroes and in Java, Bali, Indonesia, Tanzania. Simple vows are taken.

Sisters of St. Joseph A name given to a group of independent communities of Sisters which trace their foundation back to the original foundation of 1836 at Carondelet, Mo. With the original Carondelet community, they total 17,500 Sisters, almost a tenth of all the Sisters in the United States. The primary work is teaching. Motherhouses are found in Orange, Calif.; La Grange, Ill.; Tipton, Ind.; Concordia, Kans.; Wichita, Kans.; Boston, Mass.; Springfield, Mass. Nazareth, Mich.; Brentwood, N. Y.; Buffalo, N. Y.; Rochester, N. Y.; Watertown, N. Y.; Cleveland, O.; Erie, Pa.; Philadelphia, Pa.; Pittsburgh, Pa.; Rutland, Vt.; Wheeling, W. Va.; Superior, Wisc. The largest communities are Philadelphia, 2,400; Brentwood, 1,900; Boston, 1,800; and Rochester, 860.

Sisters of St. Joseph of Carondelet A community of Sisters established in Carondelet, Mo., from France in 1836. There are 4 provinces and 1 vice-province in the United States with missions in Japan and Peru. Teaching and medical works are the primary concerns of the community. There are approximately 4,700 members. Simple vows are taken.

Sisters of St. Joseph of Newark A community women founded in England in 1888 and established in New Jersey the same year. Two provinces exist today. The Sisters are engaged in teaching, catechetics and care of blind, retarded and disturbed children. Missions have been established in the Philippines. There are approximately 750 Sisters. Simple vows are taken.

Sisters of St. Joseph of the Third Order of St. Francis In 1901 the community was founded in Wisconsin and today has grown to 1,300 Sisters in three provinces and a mission in Puerto Rico. Teaching and nursing are the principal occupations. Simple vows are taken.

Sisters of the Assumption of the Blessed Virgin Mary Founded in Canada in 1853, established in the United States in 1891. Members are engaged in teaching and catechetics. Missions are staffed in Japan and Brazil. Simple vows are taken. Approximately 2,700 members.

Sisters of the Blessed Sacrament Founded in 1891 by Mother Katherine Drexel to aid Indians and Negroes in the United States. The Sisters lead an active life of staffing missions in rural areas, large cities and Indian reservations. There are over 500 members.

Sisters of the Congregation of St. Agnes Founded in Wisconsin in 1858. Members teach, staff hospitals, care for aged and orphans, staff missions in Nicaragua. Simple vows are taken. Over 800 Sisters.

Sisters of the Holy Cross A French foundation that was established in the United States in 1843. Teaching and nursing are the principal activities. Missions are conducted in Brazil and Pakistan. There are approximately 1,600 Sisters in the United States. Simple vows are taken.

Sisters of the Holy Cross of the Seven Dolors A French foundation that was established in Canada in 1847 and in the United States in 1881. Missions have been established in Haiti and Pakistan. Teaching is the primary work. There are two provinces in Canada and one in the United States with a membership of 2,300 Sisters. Simple vows are taken.

Sisters of the Holy Family A society founded in 1872 in San Francisco by Miss Elizabeth Armer under the direction of the Very Rev. J. J. Prendergast. Miss Armer (later, Sister Mary Dolores) had been doing catechetical work, organizing sewing clubs and sodalities and had pioneered in caring for children of working mothers. This last she particularly loved as it gave her a chance to be of aid to the weary and underpaid mothers, particularly in counseling and religious instruction. As the foundress of a religious order, Sister Mary Dolores simply continued and extended the same catechetical and social service work. They have houses in the Archdioceses of Los Angeles, San Francisco and San Antonio; and in the Dioceses of Honolulu, Monterey-Fresno, Reno, Sacramento, Salt Lake City and San Diego.

Sisters of the Holy Family, Congregation of the Founded in 1842 by four pious Negro women in New Orleans, to provide catechetical and educational advantages for children and adults of their own race. Harriet Delisle of New Orleans was the first superior, and Archbishop Blanc encouraged and watched over the young community. The demands for the Sisters' services were many. Soon after their foundation an epidemic of yellow fever broke out in the city, leaving many orphans whom the members of the new order cared for. Parochial schools, academies for girls and homes for the aged are among the many works of education and charity under their charge, not only in New Orleans, but in many other cities, mainly in the South. They are also in the foreign missions.

Sisters of the Holy Family of Nazareth An Italian foundation that was established in the United States in 1885, the community now has 4 provinces in the United States and missions in Australia and Puerto Rico. Teaching, nursing and catechetics are the main works. There are approximately 1,600 Sisters in the United States. Simple vows are taken.

Sisters of the Holy Names of Jesus and Mary Founded in Canada in 1843 by Mother Marie Rose Durocher, the community was established in the United States in 1859. Missions are staffed in Basutoland, South Africa and Latin America. Work is primarily teaching. There are approximately 1,700 Sisters in the United States, 900 in Canada. There are choir and lay Sisters and simple vows are taken.

Sisters of the Order of St. Basil the Great Founded in Capadocia in the 4th century by St. Basil and his sister St. Macrina. There are two branches in the United States. One attached to the Byzantine Rite Diocese of Pittsburgh was established in the United States in 1921, and is engaged in teaching, catechetics, nursing and retreats; it has 142 Sisters. The other is attached to the Ukrainian

Catholic Archeparchy of Philadelphia; it was established in the United States in 1911 and its 160 members are engaged in teaching, catechetics, nursing and retreats.

Sisters of the Presentation of Mary A religious community of women founded in France in 1796, established in Canada in 1858 and in the United States in 1873. There is a mission on Mindanao in the Philippines. The primary work is teaching and catechetics. There are approximately 900 Sisters in the United States. Simple vows are taken.

Sisters of the Presentation of the Blessed Virgin Mary A religious community of women founded in Ireland in 1776, established in Canada in 1833 and in the United States in 1854. There are 14 foundations in the United States and 1 in Newfoundland, Canada. Some of these foundations are independent motherhouses, others are attached to motherhouses in Ireland; some are pontifical and others are diocesan institutes. Simple vows are taken. Work consists of teaching, catechetics, social work and some nursing. There are 1,850 Sisters in the United States and 400 in Canada.

Sisters of the Third Order of St. Francis Founded in New York in 1859 by Mother M. Teresa O'Neill, the community is engaged in teaching, nursing and social work. There are missions in Brazil and Jamaica. The community was the first United States foundation to send missioners overseas. Simple vows are taken. There are approximately 950 Sisters.

Sisters of the Third Order of St. Francis of the Congregation of Our Lady of Lourdes Founded in Minnesota in 1877, today there are approximately 900 Sisters. Teaching and nursing are the primary object of the group. There is also a mission in Colombia. Simple vows are taken.

Sisters of the Third Order of St. Francis of Perpetual Adoration The community was founded in Wisconsin in 1849. Teaching, nursing and social work are the main activities. There are Indian and Negro missions, and also missions in El Salvador and Guam. The community is composed of approximately 1,200 Sisters who take simple vows. The Sisters have perpetual adoration of the Blessed Sacrament.

Sisters, Servants of the Immaculate Heart of Mary A community for women founded in Michigan in 1845 by Father Louis Gillet which is today divided into three independent communities with a total of 4,800 members. Teaching, catechetics, nursing and social work are the main occupations. Missions are staffed in Puerto Rico, Chile and Peru. Simple vows are taken.

Sistine Chapel The main chapel of the Vatican Palace. It was begun in 1473 by Pope Sixtus IV, from whom it takes its name (Sistus). It is particularly noted for its paintings by Michelangelo which cover its walls and ceiling. The chapel is used for papal ceremonies not of a public nature. It is the site for the election of a new pope.

Sistine Choir The choir that sings in the Vatican's Sistine Chapel. Formerly it was a standing choir made up of men and boys but today it is not permanently organized and is recruited from other Roman choirs when needed. It is particularly noted for its *a cappella* singing.

skepticism The system of teaching that the real truth of things cannot be known with certainty. Absolute skepticism is self-contradictory since it affirms that even its own principles cannot be known for certain. Relative skepticism doubts only in certain areas while hypothetical skepticism doubts truths until they are examined and proved. Skepticism extends back to the early Greek philosophers. However, Aristotle and St. Thomas teach that the senses and intellect are normally infallible in regard to their proper object, that the ultimate criterion of truth is objective evidence, that skepticism is self-contradictory, and that every man is certain of particular truths such as his own existence.

skull cap The zucchetto. The little round cap worn on the crown of the head by prelates and others, such as Capuchins. The pope wears a white one, cardinals have caps of scarlet, and bishops wear purple ones. At ceremonies these prelates wear the skull cap under the biretta. It is worn at Mass up to the Preface and after the Communion. It evolved from a cap that covered the ears, used in olden days to keep the head warm.

slander A false report intended to injure the character of another; defamation of character. Unjust defamation is a grave sin contrary to justice and charity.

slavery That condition of existence whereby a human being, against his will, is possessed as property by another to be used as the owner wishes, the oldest form of man's inhumanity to man. The enslavement of the weak by the strong had been practiced by all ancient peoples and was utilized by medieval and modern civilizations. In the Middle Ages there was some abatement of slavery due to the influence of the Church's teachings, but it increased rapidly in the 15th century due to Portuguese discoveries along the west coast of Africa. The misery, suffering and death caused by the African slave trade between the 15th and the 19th centuries cannot be estimated. For the African slave, however, the 19th century was the era of freedom. In 1807 the British government abolished the slave trade; in 1809 the United States government followed suit. Although the British government decreed the end of slavery in 1807, it was not until 1833 that Parliament abolished slavery in the colonies. In the United States, President Lincoln issued the Emancipation Proclamation on Jan. 1, 1863; the Thirteenth Amendment to the Constitution, eradicating slavery, was ratified on Dec. 18, 1864. The slaves in Spanish-American colonies won their freedom when the various colonies gained their independence during the first decades of the 19th century. The slaves of Brazil were freed during the 1870's and 1880's, when the government could not cope with a strong, popular anti-slavery movement. It was during the 1880's that the foremost European abolitionist, Cardinal Lavigerie, founder of the White Fathers and Archbishop of Algiers, successfully agitated for the suppression of the slave trade in East Africa and for the destruction of slavery everywhere. He had the full support of Pope Leo XIII in his zealous endeavors to put an end to slavery. The pope provided Lavigerie with traveling expenses as he toured Europe to arouse the people against slavery. His work was so successful that public opinion forced the heads of governments to call a conference, which assembled at Brussels in 1890. At this conference the slave trade in the African colonies of the countries that participated was outlawed forever. Tragically, in our own century slavery has been revived in its most pernicious form under a cloak of secrecy. In the totalitarian countries millions of non-Africans have been reduced to slavery for "reasons of state." Also by some Arab countries, black Africans are kidnaped, smuggled out of Africa and sold into bondage. The United Nations has studied the matter but has taken no effective action.

Slavonic Rite 1. A name given inaccurately to the Byzantine Rite because of its use of Old Slavonic. This language holds second place among languages in which the Liturgy is celebrated. About 865, SS. Cyril and Methodius translated the liturgy of the Byzantine Church into Slavonic to be used by their converts. 2. Toward the end of the 9th century, the Roman Rite was translated into Old Slavonic. It is used in some churches of the Western Rite in Yugoslavia and Czechoslovakia.

sloth The disinclination to spiritual action. St. Thomas defines it as "sorrow in the face of spiritual good inasmuch as it is God's good." It is one of the seven deadly sins because it leads to tepidity in keeping God's law, the desire for that which is forbidden, faint-heartedness and despair of salvation. It is a sin against the first commandment since it is opposed to the love of God, and it becomes grave when it results in the breaking of a grave law.

smoke There are a number of uses of smoke in the Catholic Church. 1. the smoke of incense which is used in various liturgical and paraliturgical functions, such as at Solemn Mass and Benediction. 2. In papal elections ballots are burned in a stove and the smoke which rises outside the Sistine Chapel tells the waiting world if a pope has been elected. When the ballots are burned alone the smoke is black or gray signifying that no conclusion has been reached. When a pope is elected, straw is burned with the ballots making a heavy white smoke.

Snows, Our Lady of the Title of the church first established in Rome on Mount Esquiline in the 4th century. A pious legend claims its foundation was due to a noble patrician's witnessing there a vision of Our Lady during a miraculous fall of snow. The church today is also called St. Mary of the Crib, but it is best known as the Basilica of St. Mary Major. The dedication is celebrated on Aug. 5.

sobriety A moral virtue which regulates a person's desire for and use of intoxicating liquors. It does not require total abstinence except in the case of an alcoholic.

social action (L. *socius,* taking part or sharing in; *actio,* a motion) Efforts undertaken by a group of people (on a local, national or international level) to promote the common good by achieving some useful purpose.

social being The human being considered not in his role as an animal but in his basic and needful relationships to society.

social justice That virtue which directs the external action of all the other virtues to the common good by organizing men into associations, and likewise directing the activities of all social institutions to the attainment of the common good which means for the welfare of all members of society, with no distinction of class or rank. The view of social justice is not merely for individuals to render to others their due, but for all the virtues to be so externally effective as to change the living sociological institutions of society rendering them equitable in every root or concept, likewise in practice. The aim of social justice is to change society and thus promote the common good.

socialism A politico-economic system advocating or aiming at collective or governmental ownership and administration of the means of production and control of the distribution of goods. Official condemnations of socialism by Leo XIII, Pius XI and Pius XII referred to particular forms of socialism prevalent in certain areas of Europe (usually Marxist socialism), which flourished throughout the 19th century and into the 20th. It was clear even at the time of the pronouncements that the popes did not wish to condemn all possible forms of socialism. Pope John XXIII indicated in *Mater et Magistra* and *Pacem in Terris* that certain socialistic (centralistic, collectivistic) directions may be necessary for modern governments in order to ensure justice for all citizens. It has been remarked that the Church, while condemning certain types of socialism, has certainly not canonized capitalism. Some form of socialism, unburdened by European and Marxist dogmas, may well prove the most Christian system for the emerging nations of Africa and Asia.

society A moral organism in which persons are united for a common end. Society has been defined as "the system of social relationships in and through which we live." It is the most inclusive of the many human groups. Man has a need of society and suffers when deprived of human society. Certain elements are necessary for society such as the plurality of persons, a community of aim, a stability of bond, a cooperation of effort, authority. Pope John XXIII in *Mater et Magistra* writes: "Any human society if it is well ordered and productive, must lay down as a foundation this principle: that every human being is a person; his nature is endowed with intelligence and free will. By virtue of this, he has rights and duties of his own, flowing directly and simultaneously from his very nature which are therefore universal, inviolable and inalienable." Society should be differentiated from community which is a group of people occupying a particular area of society, in which they share a "whole set of interests, and activities broad enough to include almost all of their social relationships." It must also be differentiated from an association where the various interests shared by members of a group are very limited.

Society of Jesus Commonly known as the Jesuits (*q.v.*). A religious order of men founded by St. Ignatius of Loyola in 1534. Their primary purpose is to be at the special call of the pope to do whatever he requires. Today their chief labors are in teaching, literary work and foreign missionary work. They are known for their intensive scholarship. They receive a long training before they pronounce their final vows of poverty, chastity and obedience. They are governed by a lifetime Superior General in Rome and provincials throughout the world. In the United States they have over 25 colleges and universities including Fordham, Marquette, Georgetown and Santa Clara. They are the largest religious order in the world having over 28,000 members, the majority of whom are priests.

Society of the Sacred Heart of Jesus Sometimes called the Religious of the Sacred Heart, this community of women was founded in France in 1800 by St. Madeleine Sophie Barat. Blessed Rose Philippine

Duschesne brought the society to Missouri in 1818. The community is both active and contemplative. There are missions in Africa, Brazil, Chile, Colombia, India, Japan, Korea, Puerto Rico and Taiwan. The 1,000 Sisters in the United States are primarily known as teachers.

society, perfect That society which includes within itself the necessary means to accomplish its ends. It pursues a perfect end with full rights in its own order. Thus the Church and the State are said to be perfect societies because the natural and divine law endows them with the necessary authority to accomplish their ends. An imperfect society depends on an outside agency to accomplish its ends, such as a religious order depending on the Church. An imperfect society is incomplete and limited in its rights.

society, religious A religious order or congregation. A body of persons organized under a common rule for the performance of apostolic works and works of religion.

Socinianism A heretical doctrine of the 16th and 17th centuries deriving from the Italian theologian, Faustus Socinus. It held rationalistic views on sin and salvation and denied the divinity of Christ.

sociology A science difficult to define since it embraces so many facets and is still in the process of development, but generally it may be said to be the study of society and social relations.

sodality (L. *sodalis,* companion) An association of lay people organized for some purpose of piety; the term is similar to confraternity. There are said to be some 80,000 Sodalities of Our Lady organized throughout the world.

Sodom, sin of Sodom was a city located in the Jordan Valley near the Dead Sea. Its inhabitants indulged in unnatural sex practices. Sodomy, or unnatural copulation between males, is named for this city. The sin is one that cries to heaven for vengeance. The city was destroyed by God through an earthquake because of its wickedness.

sodomy The unnatural sex act between two males. It is a grave sin and incurs heavy civil penalties.

Solemn Mass *See* Mass, Solemn.

Solemn Vespers *See* Vespers, Solemn.

solemn vows *See* vows, public.

solemnity 1. A rite carried out in full ceremonial observance according to the rubrics. 2. The external solemnity in celebrating certain feasts is sometimes transferred to the following Sunday in order that the faithful may be present and take part. In parishes of the United States, this is particularly true of Corpus Christi where the external solemnity (procession and Benedictions) is held on Sunday.

solemnization of marriage During Advent and Lent the solemn form of matrimony (i.e., Nuptial Mass and blessing) is not permitted except for a grave reason. Later, outside these liturgical seasons, the solemnization of marriage can take place.

solicitation The tempting of another to act against the virtue of purity; in this sense it is synonomous with seduction. In a strict sense it refers to the crime of solicitation which is active when a confessor induces or attempts to induce a penitent to commit with him a sin against the virtue of purity, or passive when a confessor accepts the inducement of a penitent to commit a sin against the virtue of purity. The penalties for solicitation are very severe, ranging from suspension to degradation. A penitent who has been solicited incurs the penalty of excommunication if he or she fails to denounce the confessor to proper ecclesiastical authority within one month. One who makes a false denunciation incurs excommunication specially reserved to the Holy See.

solitary 1. Being alone. In the ancient Church it was the practice for those seeking spiritual perfection to retreat into a desert or other inaccessible place and there live alone, practicing spiritual exercises. This type of spiritual life has disappeared but it still exists in a modified form in such religious orders as the Carthusians. 2. A hermit.

solitude The state of being alone, secluded. Solitude can be exterior or interior. The former is living apart from the world, i.e., such as a hermit; the latter, interior silence or recollection. Solitude, at least interior, is necessary for development in the spiritual life for without it God does not have the opportunity to be heard.

solo (L. *solus,* alone) A solo is permitted as part of liturgical music but according to the *motu proprio* (*q.v.*) "these must never take the chief place in a service or absorb the greater part of the liturgical text; they must rather be points of musical emphasis and accent bound up closely with the rest of the composition which must remain strictly choral."

Solomon's seal A hexagram formed from two triangles similar to the Star of David (*q.v.*) with the upright triangle outlined and the lower triangle made of a heavy line.

son of God One who does the will of God; a name given by St. John (1 Jn. 3). St. Paul uses the same description, referring to the baptized (Rom. 8:16-17.)

Son of God Jesus Christ, Second Person of the Blessed Trinity, begotten by the Father from eternity,

true God, the Word. St. Thomas Aquinas says that the manner of begetting is by the intellect. It is for this reason that Christ is spoken of as the Word. He is the only-begotten of the Father, equal to Him, whom He loves and is loved infinitely in return.

Son of Man A title of Jesus Christ who was born of a human mother but of no human father. It identifies Jesus with all humanity, as the Mediator sent from God, the expected Messias. Jesus uses the term for Himself 81 times.

Sophonia, Book of A book of the Old Testament written by Sophonia, a minor prophet, toward the beginning of the 7th century B.C. The book is made up of predictions of woe, oracles against foreign nations and promises of salvation.

sorcery *See* magic; witchcraft.

sorrow for sin A decisive movement of the will stemming from the sinner's awareness of the evil of sin. It involves a detestation of sin as well as a firm resolve to sin no more. 1. Perfect contrition is based on a motive of love, a desire to respond to love with love. 2. Imperfect contrition is based on fear, whether of the loss of God as source of all good or of the suffering which the betrayal of God entails.

Sorrowful Mysteries The five topics for meditation while saying the Rosary that treat of the Passion and Death of Our Lord. They are: the Agony in the Garden, Scourging at the Pillar, Crowning with Thorns, Carrying of the Cross, and Crucifixion and Death of Our Lord.

soteriology (Gr. *soter,* savior) The theology of salvation and the things related to it.

soul (O.G. *seula,* soul) The principle of life. Although in Scholastic philosophy the soul is understood as the animating principle for any body (plant, animal or human), less technically it is taken as the principle of such spiritual activities as thinking and willing. In this more restricted sense, the soul is substantial and immortal. The analysis of man into soul and body stems directly from Greek philosophy; the Hebrew mind emphasized more the resurrection of the body, by which immortality was given to man as a person.

soul, dark night of the To purify oneself for spiritual perfection, spiritual writers say that the soul must go through two periods of great suffering. The first is the dark night of the senses; there are no sensible gratifications arising from the spiritual life and at the same time there are persistent temptations against chastity, faith and a spirit of prayer. The soul is being made to dispense with the comfort of the interior senses. The second is the dark night of the soul; the soul experiences desolation and abandonment by God while at the same time desiring Him ardently. The brilliance of contemplation gives a realization of the darkness and imperfection of the spiritual life.

souls in purgatory The souls of those dying in the state of grace, but for whom some vestige of sin remains. The Church teaches that some souls must undergo purification for unremitted venial sins or for the temporal punishment due to sins already forgiven. Nothing is defined concerning the nature of this purification, or the number of souls undergoing it. The faithful on earth are encouraged to pray for these souls.

sound bow That heavy part of a bell against which the clapper strikes to make the sound.

soutane (Fr.) The cassock (*q.v.*).

South Africa, Republic of One million Catholics in a population of 16 million. Although the first church was constructed in 1501, it was not until near the middle of the 19th century that serious mission work was begun. Today there are 4 archdioceses, 15 dioceses and 4 prefectures. Factors militating against the Church are the policy of apartheid (racial discrimination), the underdeveloped economy of the Negro and the opposition of the Dutch Reformed Church. Positive factors are the dynamic spirit of the Catholic community, the Church's position on apartheid and the prestige of the Church because of its educational and social work. One priest for every 947 Catholics.

South America The southernmost of the two American continents. It has an area of 6,870,000 square miles and a population estimated at 148,-600,000 in the year 1962. The estimated population in 1964 was 153,000,000; the total Christian population 135,144,000 of whom 132,448,000 were Catholics and 2,-654,000 Protestants. The Catholic Faith came to South America with the Spanish and Portuguese colonists and missioners. The civilization and Christianization of the Indians (though hampered by repacious colonials and adventurers) gave a bright example to the world of the right exercise of responsibility by those who have the riches of Faith towards their brother man who lacks these riches. Later anticlericalism and revolutionary action in some places destroyed much of the work of the Church, but the great body of people are essentially Catholic even where priests are lacking and the laity untaught.

South Carolina The 8th of the 13 original states, it is 40th in area and 26th in population. It was named for

Charles I of England. Many Indian tribes inhabited the area in early days, notably the Catawbas, who aided the American colonists in the Revolution. Spanish explorer Ayllon explored and claimed the land for Spain in 1521. Charles V granted the territory to him and in 1526 he founded a colony—location not known for certain—but Ayllon and many colonists died and the colony was abandoned. Two Dominican priests who came with the settlers no doubt offered Mass there. Later (1569) in a settlement at St. Elena, Jesuit Father Juan Rogel was the first resident priest. Franciscans who arrived in 1573 made St. Elena one of a long line of Indian missions stretching from Florida up the coast. Missions multiplied and many Indians were converted until Governor Moore of the English colony of South Carolina destroyed the missions in 1703. The Anglican Church was established as the state church. Religious liberty was declared in 1789, and the number of Catholics increased with immigration from Ireland and Santo Domingo. The first church was built in 1791, in Charleston, and in 1820 Rev. John England was made bishop of the diocese of the Carolinas and Georgia. He built a cathedral, opened new parishes, brought in Ursuline nuns to teach and founded a new order—Our Lady of Mercy—to nurse the sick. During the Civil War many churches were left in ruins, but rebuilding and growth took place soon after. The Oblate Sisters had been conducting Negro schools in Charleston, and their pupils kept the Faith after the war, built themselves a church, and handed on Catholic doctrine and practice to their children even without priests to care for them. Catholics in South Carolina have always been a small minority. The Diocese of Charleston, established in 1820, comprises the whole state. Catholics number less than 50 thousand in a total population of 2½ million.

South Dakota The 39th or 40th (with North Dakota) state to enter the Union, it is 16th in area and 40th in population. Dakota is a Sioux term meaning friend or ally. In the early days it was inhabited by warlike, buffalo-hunting tribes, mostly Sioux, of whom Chief Sitting Bull is best known. French fur traders arrived in 1659; trader Jacques d'Eglise built the first house in the region in 1794 (the Indians lived in skin tipis). Spain, France and England claimed the area by turns but the United States acquired it in the Louisiana Purchase in 1803. Lewis and Clark traversed the state; John Jacob Astor and his associates built fur-trading posts along the waterways, and Choteau, one of his partners, had a steamboat built which chugged up the Missouri River to Fort Pierre in 1831 and returned with a rich cargo of furs and buffalo tongues. South Dakota was provided with territorial government by Congress in 1861, and became a state in 1889. In the meantime Swedes, Bohemians, Russians, Germans and Irish were swarming into the area, particularly after the railroad was built in 1873 and gold was found in the Black Hills. There were military posts and trading posts where Catholic whites and Indian tribesmen were served by Father De Smet and other priests. The Benedictines came in 1854 from Einsiedeln, Switzerland, and after laying the foundations of St. Meinrad's Abbey in Indiana came on to work among the Dakota Sioux, Abbot Marty in charge. When the Diocese of Sioux

Falls was created in 1889, Abbot Marty was made bishop. He brought in many religious congregations to staff schools, hospitals, orphanages and Indian missions. In 1902 the Diocese of Rapid City was established. Mount Marty College for women was founded in 1950, and Blue Cloud Abbey (Benedictine) was dedicated in 1952. Catholics today number 20 per cent of the population of close to 700 thousand.

sovereignty, national The unconditional affirmation of national sovereignty negates the establishment of any formalized code for international justice through international law. Yet international law is necessary if there is to be objective norms to the settlement of international disputes. Since an international common good exists, it follows that there must be an international order to protect it. Such an order would put certain limitations on national sovereignty.

Spain Probably no nation has contributed as much to the spread and development of the Catholic Church as has Spain. From this nation came the Jesuits, the Dominicans, the Fathers of Mercy, the Reformed Carmelites. Here were born great names in the Church: St. Dominic, St. Ignatius Loyola, St. Francis Xavier, St. Raymond of Penafort, St. Vincent Ferrer, St. Teresa, St. John of the Cross, St. Francis Borgia, St. Alphonsus. From Spain went the explorers and colonizers who planted the Faith in the New World, southeast Asia and the Orient. From Spain has come movements like Opus Dei. In the Spanish Civil War which ended in 1936, 13 bishops, 4,254 priests, 2,489 Sisters, 283 Brothers and 249 seminarians were assassinated for their religion. Despite that terrible bloodletting, today 11,000

Spanish priests and 17,000 Spanish Sisters are serving the Church outside their home country; in Latin America alone, there are over 16,000 Spanish priests and Sisters, evenly divided. Catholicism is the state religion of Spain but in 1964 other religions received moral status before the law. Spain today has 11 archdioceses, 49 dioceses and over 19,000 parishes. The Catholic population is in excess of 31 million, about 99.7 per cent of the total population. The Spanish Church has been accused of being conservative but in recent years many pockets of liberalism have appeared.

speciali modo (L. in a special manner) A Latin term applied to the second type of cases reserved to the Holy See (*q.v.*).

specialissimo modo (L. in a most special manner) A Latin term applied to the first and most important type of cases reserved to the Holy See (*q.v.*).

species (L. a kind) 1. Theology: the Sacred Species, the Eucharistic Species (*qq.v.*). 2. Logic: a division of genus, having common attributes and designated by a common name. 3. Biology: a collection of similar individuals bearing a common name. 4. Metaphysics: an ontological name for essence, that in which a thing is constituted in a determined species.

Species, Eucharistic (L. appearance, form) The accidents or appearances of bread and wine which remain even after the substance has been changed into Christ's Body and Blood in the sacrament of the Eucharist.

spiration (L. *spirare,* to breathe) The manner in which the Holy Spirit proceeds from the Father and the Son; it is the act of love between Father and Son. The Father knows Himself in the Word, and contemplates and loves Himself; while the Son in turn shows Himself in the Father and contemplates and loves. The Holy Spirit is this love-procession, proceeding from the Father and Son as the one sole principle.

spirit That being which can exist apart from the material; thc life principle. The word is sometimes used in contrast to soul and in that case refers to the intellectual faculties as contrasted with the animating principle.

Spirit, Holy *See* Holy Spirit.

spiritism The attempt to communicate with spirits of another world, usually the known dead. The person who makes this attempt is called a medium who is supposed to have special powers. While most of the effects, such as materialization, etc., are the result of trickery it is possible for diabolical intervention to occur. The Church forbids unnatural and useless communication with the spirits of another world. Therefore it is forbidden to be present at a séance, even out of curiosity, and of course, even more strongly forbidden to act as a medium. Also called spiritualism.

spiritual bouquet A spiritual presentation made to someone of good works performed for that person's intention. Among such works are the hearing of Mass, the reception of Holy Communion, Stations of the Cross, ejaculations, Rosaries, sacrifices, etc. The number is given of each.

spiritual dryness Spiritual dryness is a deprivation of sensible and spiritual consolation which makes prayer and the practice of virtue more easy. God allows spiritual dryness in order to humble us and detach us from created things. Spiritual dryness also strengthens us by developing the will

to seek virtue more strongly.

spiritual exercises 1. A series of meditations, reflections, reading and other practices aimed at an understanding and fervent practice of fundamental religious truths in order to advance in the spiritual life. 2. *The Spiritual Exercises.* A book written by St. Ignatius Loyola containing a series of meditations on the most important truths of Christianity and on the life, death and Resurrection of Our Lord, along with many rules and instructions to guide a person on retreat and to train that person in essential practices of the spiritual life such as prayer and examination of conscience. They were completed by St. Ignatius about 1541, and are widely in use today for retreats.

spiritual life The supernatural life. *See* perfection, state of.

spiritual marriage *See* marriage, spiritual.

spiritual reading The reading of spiritual works in order to sustain oneself in the spirit of prayer. Spiritual reading is necessary for the development of supernatural life. A spiritual book is similar to receiving written direction from a spiritual director. The basic reading should be the Scriptures, particularly the New Testament, for therein one finds the teaching and example of Christ. Reading should also include the best of the spiritual writers, particularly among the saints. Finally, modern spiritual writers should be read to know the best in current thought. The world crowds every Christian and a few moments a day given to spiritual reading will do much to aid one's spiritual development.

Spiritual Vessel A title given to Our Lady in the Litany of Loreto. The use of the word "vessel" is found in Acts 9:15 where God refers to St.

Paul as "a chosen vessel to carry my name among nations. . . ."

spiritual works of mercy Seven works of mercy that touch the spiritual side of another. These are: to counsel the doubtful, to instruct the ignorant, to admonish sinners, to forgive offenses, to bear wrongs patiently, to pray for the living and to pray for the dead.

spiritualities All those things belonging to the Church, an ecclesiastic or religion.

spirituality 1. In philosophy: the property of a complete substance by which it exists and performs specific operations, independently of matter; i.e., the spirituality of God, of angels, of the human soul. 2. *In theology*: the quality of a person who, opposed to materialism and secularism, seeks to live within the circumstances of God's providence according to His Will.

sponge, liturgical A small triangular sponge used in the Byzantine Rite in place of the Western purificator. It is used to purify the fingers of celebrant and deacon.

sponsor (L. *spondere,* to promise) The person who offers a person to be baptized or confirmed and who undertakes a spiritual responsibility and contracts a spiritual relation. In Baptism, two sponsors are permitted, a man and a woman, known as the godfather and godmother. Only one sponsor is permitted in Confirmation, of the same sex as the one to be confirmed. Sponsors must be Catholics. In Baptism, the sponsor should have completed the thirteenth year and cannot be mother, father or spouse of the one baptized. The sponsor in Baptism assumes the responsibility for the religious education of the child. The sponsor for Confirmation must be already con-

firmed, and cannot be the parent or spouse of the person to be confirmed

spontaneous generation Abiogenesis. Theory that living things, especially lower forms, may arise *de novo* from the nonliving. Held by the ancients, disputed by moderns, now gaining favor in modified form to explain the origin of life. Although the ancient belief that small forms of life such as worms arose spontaneously in mud through the agency of the sun's heat or even that bacteria do so, has been disproved, the possibility is not excluded that some borderline form similar to viruses arose under favorable conditions. The modern view has been stimulated by the discovery that the chemical DNA (deoxyribosenucleic acid) contains the genetic code and can be synthesized in the laboratory. Many Catholic philosophers have denied the possibility of spontaneous generation on the ground that the effect would exceed the cause. It might be prudent not to assume that we know all the causes in nature at this time. At any rate, the theory is not contrary to Catholic doctrine, provided God is not excluded as the ultimate cause.

spoon, liturgical 1. The small gold or silver spoon used in the Byzantine Rite to give Holy Communion under both species. 2. A small spoon used by some celebrants in the Latin Rite Mass to measure the drops of water to be mixed with the wine in the chalice.

sports, dangerous While sports are generally healthful for participants and entertaining for onlookers, certain sports are coupled with the element of danger both to health and life. According to statistics those sports with the greatest numbers of injuries and death are boxing, football, motor racing and wrestling. In considering the morality of these sports, two basic principles must be kept in mind: 1. no one may expose himself to proximate danger of death except for a proportionately grave reason; 2. one may not engage in activities involving proximate danger to life or health without a grave reason. However, it should be distinguished that proximate danger is not the same for all people. Thus a boxer is trained to avoid and absorb blows, a football player wears protective clothing and a racing driver is skilled by experience. Therefore, to engage in one of the dangerous sports, the participant must properly judge his abilities, training and qualifications. The principle of double effect must also be kept in mind, namely, the participant seeks a good effect, victory over an opponent; he cannot intend the bad effect, possible injury to an opponent. It is never permitted to participate in any sport where injury to an opponent is intended.

spouse   Ordinarily, a husband or wife. The word has been used to indicate a betrothed man or woman but this use today is rare.

Spy Wednesday   Wednesday in Holy Week. The name possibly comes from the tradition that at this time Judas Iscariot was "spying" or watching the movements of Christ in preparation for his betrayal of Him, but more likely it is taken from the Passion of the Mass which refers to Judas as the "betrayer."

Stabat Mater   The first words of the hymn *Stabat Mater dolorosa* (The sad Mother is standing). It is the sequence for the Feast of the Seven Sorrows of the Blessed Virgin Mary, and is often sung at Stations of the Cross. It is believed to have been written by Jacopone da Todi (1220–

1306), a Franciscan.

stability, oath of   1. In general, an oath or vow by which a person expresses his or her intention of persevering in the religious life. 2. In particular, the oath taken by a Benedictine at profession by which the taker expresses the intention of remaining in the religious life and in the particular monastery of profession.

staff   *See* crosier.

stalls   The seats in a choir. They are in long rows, each divided by an arm rest, and with a book holder in front. The seats are usually hinged and can be raised. Many of them have elaborately carved ornamentation.

standing   The normal position for the Christian at prayer; kneeling is the penitential position. In the West the custom of kneeling has become more common but it is seldom seen in the Eastern Rite. In the West, the custom is growing of receiving Holy Communion in a standing position.

star of Bethlehem   The star seen by the Magi. It is not clear from Scripture whether the Magi followed the star to Jerusalem but it did lead them from Jerusalem to Bethlehem. Scriptural scholars are not agreed on the nature of the star, calling it a comet, a single star, a conjunction of planets, a constellation.

Star of David   The Magen David. A hexagram made from two triangles forming a six pointed star and used as a symbol of Israel.

state   1. The body politic. A group of people of a territory gathered under a single government. The state is a natural and perfect society. It is limited, however, by the natural and supernatural law. It can not invade a person's natural rights and, even more importantly, his supernatural rights. 2. The moral condition of a person, such as being in the state of grace or in the state of sin.

state of grace The term which describes the condition of the soul that enjoys habitual grace. It signifies union with God, the absence of mortal sin and the presence of sanctifying grace. A soul in the state of grace is a temple of the Holy Spirit.

statio (stah′tse-oh, L. a standing place) 1. A station of the cross. 2. A Roman station (*q.v.*). 3. The place where the clergy or faithful gather to form a procession. 4. A place where a pilgrim or procession pauses for prayer, such as one of the altars set up for Corpus Christi.

station days Days on which the early Christians fasted until 3 o'clock. On these days the faithful gathered at stated churches for Mass and processions.

Stations of the Cross The name  given to a devotion commonly held in churches on the Fridays in Lent. The priest moves from one to another of 14 crosses attached to the walls of the church, reads meditations on the Passion together with prayers to which the congregation responds. The devotion may also be made privately at any time. The Church grants a plenary indulgence each time the Stations are made under these conditions: perfect sorrow

for sin, intention of gaining the indulgence, movement from station to station, reflection on the Passion and death of Our Lord and prayers for the pope's intentions. Although the wooden crosses affixed to the wall are the essential signs of the Stations, images or pictures are usually attached to them. Although the Stations are a substitute for an actual pilgrimage to the Holy Land, they do not follow the exact arrangement in Jerusalem. Pope Clement XII fixed the number at 14. The Franciscans are given the credit for popularizing the devotion. *See* Way of Cross.

Stations, Roman The churches of Rome where in ancient days the faithful went in procession to assist at a Mass offered by the pope or his delegate. These processions took place on all days of Lent, Ember Days, Sundays in Advent and certain other feasts; there were 84 in all. The place of the station is still noted in the Roman Missal.

statism A philosophical system developed by Hobbes and others that could make the state the determiner of morality. In its most virulent form it becomes totalitarianism in which the state is the source of all rights and which holds that man exists for the state. Statism, like Communism, exaggerates man's social needs.

sterility The inability to reproduce; it must be differentiated from impotency which is the incapacity for the marriage act. Sterility neither impedes nor annuls marriage, while impotency is an impediment. A sterile person can perform the marriage act but it is without fruit.

stigmata (Gr. marks) The reproduction in a person of the wounds of Christ corresponding to the wounds of His hands, feet, side and head.

These wounds appear spontaneously, sometimes disappear to reappear on another occasion. They are accompanied by bleeding and pain. There is also a type of invisible stigmata which causes considerable pain in the wound area but no visible wound. Usually the stigmatist is also an ecstatic, and according to some recorded cases the stigmatist spoke in unknown languages during ecstasy. There are approximately 325 recorded cases, the best known being St. Francis of Assisi. In modern times Theresa Neuman and Padre Pio are among the stigmatists. These cases have undergone medical study and no natural explanation has been forthcoming. However, care must be taken that the stigmata are real and due to genuine holiness and not to self-deception or the result of mental suggestion. St. Catherine of Siena is reputed to have suffered from invisible stigmata.

stigmatist One who bears the stigmata (*q.v.*).

stipend, Mass (L. *stipendium,* recompense, wage) An offering given to a priest with the understanding that the fruits of a Mass the priest offers will be applied for a particular person or purpose. Foundation for such an offering is the real right to support from the faithful of the ministerial priesthood (1. Cor. 9:7-13). Needless to say this is not simony or the buying of the Mass. Likewise the priest is bound to celebrate as many Masses as he receives stipends for. Stipends may be in the form of any material worthwhile object; in the ancient Church the custom was to offer the bread and wine to be used in the Sacrifice.

stipes (L. a stock) That which supports the mensa (*q.v.*) of an altar. It may be a solid block, posts or a central pillar. The stipes should be of stone and cemented to the mensa.

stock A cylindrical metal container in which one of the holy oils is kept. Sometimes it has an interior division and a cap on either end, and thus contains two of the holy oils.

stole (L. *stola,* a garment) A liturgical vestment that is  of the same color as other vestments. According to the manner in which it is worn, it is a mark of the office of priest or deacon. The stole is a long narrow band, several inches wide and approximately 80 inches long; it sometimes flares out at the extremes. A priest wears it about his neck, and it is worn over the left shoulder like a sash by deacons. There is a smaller stole, usually carried in a sick-call case, that is white on one side and purple on the other; this latter type of stole is often used by the priest when hearing confessions, in place of a large purple stole.

stole fees Customary offerings given by the faithful on the occasion of the performance or administration of certain sacraments or even sacramentals. These fees are connected with the ministerial actions of the priesthood and are thus called stole fees (sign of the office). The foundation for such fees is based on the right to the support of the laity by the ministerial clergy (1 Cor. 9:7-13). This is not simony because the ministerial actions are not the basis of sale but the occasion of gifts. *See* simony; stole.

stoup (O.E., a vessel for water) The basin at the entrance of a Catholic church which holds holy water. It is also called a font (*q.v.*).

strike An organized stoppage of

work in order to force the employer to grant some benefit. A strike is defensive when it is undertaken to remove an unjust oppression; it is offensive when it is undertaken to achieve some additional benefit even though the salary or wages are not inadequate, nor the work hours excessive or working conditions unjust. A defensive strike is lawful provided there are no other means to be used against the injustice. An offensive strike is lawful provided it does not take place before the expiration of a contract with the employer, that there is a proportionately grave reason and that the means used to strike are just.

striking the breast A historical sign of humility, penitence and sorrow. In the Latin Rite and in some Oriental churches the gesture has liturgical use. In the Mass the celebrant and servers strike their breasts three times with the right hand during the Confiteor. In addition, the celebrant strikes his breast at the *Nobis quoque peccatoribus,* and each *Agnus Dei,* and at each *Domine non sum dignus* before his Communion. In a Requiem Mass the action is omitted at the *Agnus Dei* because the different form of the prayer no longer refers to the celebrant but to the deceased.

stripping the altar An action that takes place after Mass on Holy Thursday when the linens and other articles are solemnly removed from the altar leaving it bare except for candlesticks and crucifix; also the tabernacle door is left open. It is part of the mourning of the Church.

stylite (Gr. *stylos,* pillar) A solitary ascetic who lived atop a pillar. Stylites preached and helped in a spiritual work. St. Simeon the Elder was said to be the first to adopt this life in 432. Stylites became numerous in

Syria, Palestine and Mesopotamia.

subapostolic The period of time between the death of the Apostles and the deaths of those who were contemporary with them; from approximately A.D. 75 to A.D. 150.

subcincture (L. *subcinctorium*) A liturgical vestment worn only by the pope at a Solemn Mass. It is a square piece of silk with a lamb embroidered on one side and a cross on the other. It is worn hanging from the cincture on the right side. It is a survival of the Oriental epigonation (*q.v.*).

subdeacon (Gr. *diakonos,* a servant) The first of the major orders in the Latin Rite and a minor order in the Oriental. The subdeacon is bound to celibacy and the recitation of the Divine Office. The main duties of the subdeacon are at a Solemn Mass when he sings the Epistle, carries the chalice to the altar and gives the Kiss of Peace to the choir.

subdelegate A person who has been delegated authority or jurisdiction may subdelegate, either for a single act or over an undetermined time, provided there is no restriction in law. A person who has been subdelegated may not in turn subdelegate except when this subdelegation is expressly stated by law.

Subiaco Congregation Benedictines of the Primitive Observance who have their headquarters in the monastery at Subiaco, Italy.

subject 1. *In canon law.* A person subject to the Church and the law of the Church through Baptism. A person subject to a particular jurisdiction by having a domicile or quasi-domicile within that jurisdiction, or by joining a religious institute. 2. *Of a sacrament.* All those who may legitimately receive the sacrament.

subjective Within the subject. It is the opposite of objective. Subjective applies to reality as it is perceived or known, while objective relates to reality as it exists.

subjectivism　A philosophical system based on the principle, "What I think is right." It makes each man a law unto himself and ultimately, if followed to its conclusions, rejects all objective norms of morality.

subprior　The person appointed to assist the prior of a monastery. The feminine form is subprioress.

subreption (L. *subrepere*, to steal into) A canonical term for the act of withholding or misrepresenting the truth in a petition for some favor. It does not invalidate a favorable answer as long as those things needed for validity have been expressed.

subsidiarity, principle of　As defined by Pope Pius XI in his encyclical *Quadragesimo Anno*, it is "a fundamental principle of social philosophy, fixed and unchangeable, that one should not withdraw from individuals and commit to the community what they can accomplish by their own enterprise and industry." By this principle the state and greater collectivities should favor and help private enterprise in order to allow private citizens to accomplish as much as is feasible.

substance (L. *substare*, to be under) That which exists per se and which is not in another as in the subject. In this sense the term can be predicated of God. In a less restricted sense, it is that which exists per se and which serves as a subject in which accidents inhere. In this sense it is predicated of all created things, since God being simple and immutable cannot have accidents. God, therefore, is absolute substance and created things are relative substance. Aristotle distinguishes substance as prime substance and secondary substance.

Prime substance is individuality; it is what makes Peter, Peter and Charles, Charles. Secondary substance is universal nature; it is not in the substance but can be predicated of the subject. Substance is also complete, e.g., man; or incomplete, e.g., the human soul.

subtlety　One of the four qualities of the glorified body. By it the body takes on a spiritual character without ceasing to be a true body.

suburbicarian dioceses　The seven dioceses adjoining Rome; the cardinal sees. They are Ostia, Albano, Frascati, Palestrina, Porto and Santa Rufina, Subina and Poggio Mirteto, and Velletri.

succentor (L. *sub*, under; *canere,* to sing)　1. The assistant to a precentor (*q.v.*). The title is now honorary. 2. Another name for the Synagoga (*q.v.*).

succession　The act of taking over an office from another. Many coadjutor bishops are appointed with the right of succession.

sudarium (L. a towel)　1. A napkin or handkerchief for drying perspiration. 2. The term is also used for the Holy Shroud and Veronica's Veil.

suffragan　A bishop of a see of a province other than the metropolitan; the see or diocese itself in relation to the archdiocese or metropolitan see. A suffragan yields precedence to his archbishop even in his own diocese but does not yield ordinary jurisdiction.

suffrage (L. *suffragium,* a recommendation)　An intercessory prayer to God which depends entirely on God's response to it. The term ordinarily refers to prayers said for souls in purgatory since indulgenced prayers offered for these souls are beyond the Church's jurisdiction. The word also includes acts done by way of suffrage (*per modum suffragii*), such as gaining the Portiuncula Indulgence (*q.v.*).

suicide (L. *sui,* self; *cidere,* to kill) Deliberate self-destruction. Suicide is direct when it is intended as an end or planned as a means to an end. Direct suicide is mortally sinful because it is an infringement of God's power over life. A suicide is not permitted burial from a church. Indirect suicide is placing an act that causes death without that end being intended, e.g., tending plague victims and becoming victim to the disease. *See* felo-de-se.

Sulpician Method *See* meditation.

Sulpicians A society of secular priests, founded in 1642 by Abbe Olier, dedicated to the training of men for the priesthood. The society received its name from its headquarters, the Seminary of St. Sulpice in Paris. (The society now works in France, the United States and Canada.) The society came to the United States in 1791 when four priests arrived in Baltimore and began St. Mary's Seminary, which in 1822 was endowed by Pius VII with all the privileges of a Catholic university. The establishment of the Society of the Propagation of Faith in the United States was largely due to their efforts. They played an important role in the foundation and early spirit of the Catholic Foreign Mission Society of America (Maryknoll). The Sisters of Charity at Emmitsburg, Md., were established at their direction. The Church in the United States owes a great debt to these dedicated men.

Summa (L. the aggregate) The popular name for the *Summa Theologica q.v.* of St. Thomas Aquinas, a compendium of Catholic theology.

Summa Contra Gentiles (L. Summary against the Gentiles) A theological treatise of St. Thomas Aquinas that considers God and His creatures.

Summa Theologica (L. Theological Compendium) The name of the main theological work of St. Thomas Aquinas, the most magnificent and complete theological treatise ever written. It is very logically and orderly in construction, being divided into questions which in turn are divided into articles and they in turn are divided into objections; they are followed by the solution to the article and the reply to the objections.

Sunday The first day of the week, the Lord's Day, the day set aside for the worship of God, the day which weekly commemorates the Resurrection of Christ. It was a day set aside by the Apostles in place of the Jewish Sabbath. Catholics are obliged under pain of sin to attend Mass on this day and to refrain from unnecessary servile work.

Sunday Laws Various laws enacted by civic communities prohibiting the opening of stores and other services on Sunday to sell other than necessary goods. These are under attack in many areas, particularly by those who observe Saturday as the Sabbath.

Sunday school Classes in catechism for children given after Mass on Sunday in many parishes. Formerly very common for children not attending parochial school, Sunday school in many areas has been almost completely replaced by released time (*q.v.*) or shared-time (*q.v.*) classes.

Sung Mass A Missa Cantata or Solemn High Mass (*qq.v.*).

Sunni The orthodox branch of Islam which acknowledges the first four caliphs as the true successors of Muhammad.

supererogation, work of (L. *supererogare,* to spend over and above)

A good act which is not of obligation. A good deed of a person over and above those deeds necessary for salvation. Examples are the counsels and the vows of chastity, poverty and obedience. There are indications of this teaching in Scripture (Mt. 19:16-21; 1 Cor. 7).

superior One who governs or has authority over a religious institute or any division of a religious institute. Canon law distinguishes between major and minor superiors. Major superiors are higher superiors such as a superior general, provincial, an abbot. Minor superiors are local superiors, i.e., superiors of the house in which they live. Local superiors canonically appointed may not remain in office for more than two consecutive terms of three years each in the same community; they may then be appointed to a similar position elsewhere.

superior general The head of a religious order, congregation or society of men or women.

supernatural That which is added over and above to nature. Distinction is made between the absolutely supernatural and the relatively supernatural. An absolutely supernatural gift is one which in its very essence transcends nature. It cannot be demanded by any creature as his due or even be merited. The only absolute supernaturals are the Incarnation and sanctifying grace. That is relatively supernatural which is in itself something that would not be beyond the capacity of creatures but beyond the powers and needs of a certain particular creature. An example is infused knowledge which is beyond the capacity of man but not of angels.

supernatural gift A gift which is above and beyond the nature of the one who receives it. God gave man two supernatural gifts, one absolutely supernatural which was sanctifying grace; one relatively supernatural which was the gift of preternatural integrity, consisting of infused knowledge, freedom from concupiscence and immortality of the body. Adam's sin lost these gifts; but by the Redemption, sanctifying grace was restored to man by Baptism.

supernatural order The state in which man elevated by sanctifying grace directs his activities to his last end which is life with God.

supernatural theology That science which treats of God and creatures in relationship to God through both reason and revelation. Because it is supernatural it involves revelation on the part of God and faith on the part of man. Its formal object is God. It differs from theodicy which is the science of God through the natural light of reason alone.

superstition (L. *superstare,* to stand above) Any act or practice which gives false worship to God or divine worship to a creature. Superstition is an excess and is a sin against the virtue of religion. Worshiping God in an improper manner would include such practices as chain prayers, believing that certain prayers will infallibly give what they promise, worshiping at the site of some reputed miracle against the prohibition of the Church, etc. The second form of superstition in worshiping creatures would include idolatry, divination, vain observance (*qq.v.*), etc.

suppedaneum (L.) The platform of an altar, the footpace (*q.v.*). Also, the platform on a crucifix holding the feet of Christ.

Supplices The first word of the third prayer after the consecration of the Mass. It is believed that at one time it was an *epiklesis* (q.v.). It is the offering of the Body and Blood of the Son to the Father.

supplied ceremonies In cases of emergency or danger of death certain rites are given by a short form. Later when the emergency has disappeared the full ceremonies are supplied. Thus if a person is baptized by the short form and later is freed from the urgency, the omitted ceremonies are supplied but the actual baptismal formula is not repeated.

support of the Church It is one of the commandments of the Church that Catholics should contribute to the support of their parish and the works of the Church, particularly to the evangelization of the world.

surplice (sur′pliss, L. *super,* over;  *pelliceum,* a robe of fur) A liturgical vestment of white linen, cotton or synthetic fiber that is worn by the clergy in choir, in processions, at Benediction, etc. It is worn by a priest performing any blessing or administering the sacraments when the alb is not prescribed. The garment has wide sleeves and reaches slightly below the hips. Its use is permitted to acolytes and choir members who are not clerics. A surplice may be blessed but the blessing is not mandatory.

survival of the fittest Darwin's theory that the evolution of living beings is determined by natural selection and the struggle for existence. *See* evolution.

Suscipe (sus′she-pay; L. receive) 1. The Offertory Hymn. It corresponds to the Entrance and Communion anthems. It was formerly an antiphonal psalm chanted while the faithful in procession presented their offerings to the celebrant at the altar.

2. Another prayer of the Mass said immediately after the first ablution (lavabo). The celebrant bows before the middle of the altar and asks the Blessed Trinity to receive the offering that is about to be made in honor of Jesus Christ and all the saints.

suspension (L. *suspendere,* to hang up) A censure whereby a cleric is denied the use of his office or benefice in whole or in part. A suspension is inflicted only on clerics, while excommunication and interdict can also be applied to the laity.

swearing *See* cursing; oath; profanity.

Swiss Guards, the The Vatican's military guards, first employed by Pope Julius II in 1510. At that time the Swiss cantons of Lucerne and Zurich agreed to supply the pope with a perpetual bodyguard, an agreement which has been kept ever since. The Swiss Guards are carefully chosen and have to meet certain strict conditions for admission. Their duties are to guard the pope during functions, to man all the doors to the pope's palace and living quarters, and to march in processions just after the Noble Guard. They still wear the varicolored uniform of black, red and yellow, as designed by Michelangelo, although they have an informal uniform less spectacular in color and style.

Switzerland Christianity was brought to Helvetia (the ancient name for Switzerland) from Gaul and Italy about 300. Great numbers of Catholics were lost in the Reformation which in Switzerland was accompanied by violence and a civil war. Today one-third of the country (population 5.5 million) is Catholic. There are 6 dioceses and 2 abbeys nullius. Switzerland has contributed generously to the mission of the Church and today Swiss missioners (1,700) are working in India, Japan, Brazil, South Africa, Rhodesia and Bolivia.

Syllabus, the 1. A collection of propositions. 2. When used without qualification the term refers to the *Syllabus* of Pius IX (1864) which listed a series of 80 condemned propositions and which was published along with the encyclical *Quanta Cura*. The sense in which these propositions were condemned must be interpreted from the encyclical. 3. The *Syllabus* of St. Pius X issued in 1907 against Modernism. The decree is named *Lamentabili sane exitu.*

syllogism A form of logical argument. An act of the intellect in which a comparison is made between two extremes which coalesce or do not coalesce on account of the respective agreement or disagreement with a third universally accepted proposition. The two propositions are then compared and a third proposition necessarily follows. Thus: Every animal is a substance. But every man is an animal. Therefore every man is a substance.

symbol (Gr. *symbolon,* a sign by which something is known) 1. A religious creed, such as the Apostles' Creed, Nicene Creed. 2. An emblematic representation of a religious truth, of the Persons of God, the saints and the virtues. They were used widely in the early Church as a way of hiding a truth from persecutors of Christianity. Since the 4th century symbols have been used as religious ornamentation and decoration. Common symbols are a dove for the Holy Spirit, a lamb or a fish for Christ, grapes and wheat for the Eucharist, etc.

symbolism Giving outward things or actions inner meaning to express a religious idea. The Old Testament is full of symbolism, and the use of symbols was adopted by the New Law. Symbolism is found in religious art and in liturgical acts. Thus the use of water in Baptism is symbolic of purification or cleansing.

Synagoga That section of the solemn singing of the Passion in Holy Week that contains the spoken words of those in the Passion narrative other than Christ. It is abbreviated "S."

synagogue (Gr. *synagoge,* gathering place) The place where the Jewish people have traditionally assembled for religious gatherings. It had its origin in the time that the Jews were in exile in Babylon. Deprived of their Temple in which to pray, they felt the need to have a special place to worship. When they returned to Palestine, they kept the institution of the synagogue. In construction the synagogues were rectangular, many having two rows of columns inside, dividing the room into a large central nave and two smaller side aisles. Since the Jews prayed facing Jerusalem, the synagogues were constructed to enable them to do this. At the beginning, the synagogues were used only on the Sabbath and feast days, but later this was extended to other days, especially fast days. Where there was a purely Jewish population, the synagogue was under the civil authority. In other places each synagogue would have its own governing body, usually three men.

synapte (Gr. union) A Byzantine type of litany.

synaxis (Gr. assembly) 1. A coming together of the people for religious worship in the Oriental Church, particularly the Eucharistic Liturgy. 2. A title given certain feasts on which the people of the Oriental Church meet in a particular church, corresponding to the Latin station (*q.v.*).

syncretism The fusion of Christian and pagan beliefs resulting in a theologically untenable amalgam called Christo-paganism. Haiti is an example where Catholic saints and African gods have become identified in the Negro mind and worship. The Christian answer to syncretism is in a practical program of catechetics and leadership training.

syndic apostolic A layman appointed to administer property for the Friars Minor and Capuchins. Since both private and corporate ownership was forbidden the followers of St. Francis of Assisi, the Holy See constitutes itself owner in trust of all legacies, gifts, etc. The syndic is appointed by the minister general or provincial. In recent years, modern conditions have caused the Holy See to dispense from having a syndic in many places and permits corporate possession in civil law only.

synkellos (Gr., *syn*, with; *kellion,* cell) 1. The secretary of a Byzantine bishop. 2. A titular bishop in the Melkite and Syrian Rites. 3. Obsolete, a companion to a bishop who accompanied him at all times.

synod (sin'ud, Gr. *synodos,* an assembly) The meeting of the clergy of a diocese under hierarchical authority to discuss matters pertaining to discipline and liturgy within the diocese. The synod does not diminish the jurisdiction and authority of the ordinary but is merely consultative. Strictly speaking, a national or international meeting can be called a synod but the term generally used is "council."

synod, holy The governing council of each independent Orthodox Church, composed usually of bishops under the patriarch of the Church.

synod, national An ecclesiastical conference of the bishops of a nation. The synod discusses religious and other matters touching the Church. The laws adopted must be submitted to the Holy See for approval before they become binding on the entire nation. The national synods held in the United States are known as the three Baltimore Councils.

synodal examiners Clerics appointed in a diocesan synod by the ordinary to examine the worthiness of candidates for parochial benefits and to judge the fitness of individual priests for pastoral duties.

synodal judges Competent canon lawyers appointed in a synod by the bishop to judge ecclesiastical cases.

Synoptic Gospels (Gr. *synopsis,* a view) A name given to the first three Gospels (Matthew, Mark and Luke) by J. Griesbach in 1776, since they can be arranged in three parallel columns and thus can be seen at one view.

Synoptic Problem The problem of interdependence of the Synoptic authors, with consideration of the points of coincidence and disagreement. The Synoptic Problem (sometimes called the Synoptic Question) is to find the answer to the points of agreement and disagreement by trying to determine how each Gospel was composed. There is no definitive solution to the Synoptic Problem but many theories have been put forward, such as the two-source theory, the theory of oral tradition, and the theory of mutual dependence.

Synoptics, the Also Synoptists. The authors of the Synoptic Gospels, namely SS. Matthew, Mark and Luke.

Syriac A major dialect of the Aramaic language, now no longer spoken, but used as a liturgical language of the Syrian, Maronite, Chaldean and Malabar Rites.

Syrian Church, East 1. The Chaldean Catholics. 2. The Nestorian Church.

Syrian Jacobite Church This is the common name for the native Monophysite Christians of Syria and Iraq. Jacob Baradai organized them in the 6th century. They now number only about 130,000 and are governed by the Patriarch (of Antioch) at Damascus. They use the (West) Syrian Rite; the Arabic language, their orders and sacraments are valid. They admit only the first three ecumenical councils; much of their theological teaching is rather obscure.

Syrian Rite, Catholics of the Catholics of Syria and Iraq who worship according to the (West) Syrian Rite. In existence since 1783, there are more than 60,000 members under their Patriarch of Antioch at Beirut. A seminary at Sharfeh in Lebanon trains their secular clergy. The clergy have been bound to celibacy since 1888 (though a dispensation can be acquired and some priests do marry). Syrians and Maronites represent the native Catholics of Syria and Palestine, others of whom, adopted the Byzantine Rite, are called Melkites.

Syrian Rite (East) This is also known as the Chaldean Rite. It is used among the Chaldean Catholics, the Nestorians, and, in a modified form, the Catholics of Malabar. The liturgical language is Syriac. Holy Communion is under both species separately, but in practice Catholics of this rite receive one species only. About 70 per cent of the users of this rite are Catholics, but if the allied Malabarese are included, 96 per cent. Anglicans call them Assyrians.

Syrian Rite (West) The worship of Syrian and Malankarese (India) Catholics, and also of the Jacobites of Syria and Malabar. The liturgy comes from 4th century Antioch, is called the "worship of St. James," and there are several variations of the canon or *anaphora*. The language of the liturgy is Syriac, but both Catholics and Jacobites have Arabic parts. The words of Consecration are sung aloud and the Eucharist is received under both species. The Office contains seven Hours; part is sung in the evening and the rest before the liturgy. It is made up of many prayers and hymns with few psalms. Baptism is by immersion followed immediately by Confirmation (and among the dissidents, by Communion under the species of wine). There are many strict fasts. The altar is in full view, though there is often an open screen. In the churches there are pictures, but no statues. Benediction, the Rosary and the feast of Corpus Christi have been borrowed from the West by the Catholics, who are one third of the users of the rite in Syria and a small minority in India.

Syro-Antiochene Rite The (West) Syrian Rite (*q.v.*).

Syro-Chaldean Rite The Chaldean Rite (*q.v.*).

Syro-Malabar Rite The version (in the Malayalam language of the East Syrian or Chaldean Rite, used by most of the Catholics of Malabar (Kerala, India).

Syro-Malankara Rite The Indian adaptation of the Syrian Rite of Antioch as used in Kerala, India. The majority of those who use this rite are members of the Jacobite Church. A small group led by Archbishop Mar Ivanios were received into the Catholic Church in 1930. Since then many other Jacobites have followed, so that today there are an archdiocese and diocese to care for the members of the new Syro-Malankara Rite. The same liturgy is used as is used by the Jacobites. It is mainly in the vernacular. Every year approximately 6,000 Jacobites join the Catholics.

Syro-Maronite Rite The version of the West Syrian or Antiochene Rite used by the Maronites (*q.v.*).

T

tabernacle (L. *tabernaculum,* a tent)

1. A boxlike enclosure in the center of an altar for the safekeeping of the Blessed Sacrament. It is of solid construction, lined inside with white silk and capable of being locked. It developed over the centuries and by the 16th century its present form was in common use. 2. In the Old Testament, the tent which sheltered the Ark. It was a wooden frame covered with cloth and ram skins. It was portable.

tabernacle veil A covering of fine cloth which covers the whole tabernacle or at least hangs over the tabernacle doors.

The tabernacle veil is a sign that the Blessed Sacrament is present in the tabernacle. It is usually of a liturgical color.

Tabernacles, Feast of Sukkoth. One of the three principal feasts of the Old Testament, commemorating the sojourn of the Jews in the wilderness. A feast of great joy and merriment, it was held from the 15th to the 23rd of the seventh month and was preceded by ten days of penance, ending in the Day of Atonement (Yom Kippur *q.v.*). It was the Jewish harvest festival.

Tabitha A Christian woman from Joppa mentioned in the New Testament. She made clothing for the poor and was noted for her many charities. St. Peter raised her from the dead.

table of the altar *See* altar table.

talisman A charm worn to avoid evil or obtain good fortune. The use of a talisman is a sin of superstition.

Talmud (Heb. to study) The second greatest literary achievement of the Jewish people. It comprises the Jewish oral interpretations of the law in written form. The first codification of the law is called the Mishnah. This was compiled in written form in the 3rd century A.D. Rabbinical discussion of the Mishnah gave rise to the Jerusalem and Babylonian Talmud.

Tametsi A historic decree of the Council of Trent which takes its name from the first word. It dealt with the Sacrament of Matrimony and ruled invalid any marriage that took place without the parish priest or his representative and two witnesses, except for places where priests are not available. It was modified by the *Ne Temere* of Pope St. Pius X in 1907.

Tantum Ergo　Hymn taken from the last two verses of the *Pange Lingua* which was written by St. Thomas Aquinas for Vespers of Corpus Christi. This hymn is an essential part of the Benediction service.

Tanzania　In 1868 the evangelization of Tanzania (formerly Tanganyika) was begun by the Holy Ghost Fathers and 10 years later the White Fathers arrived. Today in a population of close to 11 million, 16 per cent are Catholic. There are 2 archdioceses, 15 dioceses and 2 abbeys nullius. The first African cardinal was chosen from Tanzania. Cardinal Laurean Rugambwa. The largest American group in Tanzania is the Maryknoll Fathers who staff 2 dioceses, followed by the Holy Ghost Fathers and the Maryknoll Sisters. American Salvatorians and Benedictines are also represented there. The Tanzanian hierarchy is progressive and maintains good relations with the recently independent government.

Targum　(Ar. translation)　A word used to denote an Aramaic translation of the Old Testament for those post-exilic Jews who no longer understood Hebrew. Targums must be used with great caution since they were passed down orally and in many instances became paraphrases of the Old Testament rather than strict translations.

taxation　Theologians are all agreed that the state has the right to tax citizens in order to meet the public expenses of the state and there is further agreement that the payment of taxes is binding in conscience. However, in order to bind in conscience certain provisions must be met: the taxes must be imposed by lawful authority; the taxes must be for a just cause; the taxes should be levied in proportion with the means of the individual citizens.

Te Deum　Psalmlike hymn of praise and thanksgiving usually sung at the end of Matins. It is often sung as a hymn of thanksgiving at great public or religious events. Legend claims that St. Ambrose and St. Augustine, inspired by the Holy Spirit, first sang it at the Baptism of St. Augustine. Today it is attributed to St. Nicetas of Remesiana.

Te igitur　(L.)　The opening words of the Canon of the Mass. This term is used to refer to the first prayer of the Canon: "Wherefore, most merciful Father, we humbly beg and entreat you through Jesus Christ, your Son, our Lord, to accept and bless these gifts, these offerings, these holy and spotless sacrifices which we offer you first for your holy Catholic Church, that you may grant her peace and protection, unity and direction throughout the world, together with your servant (*name*), our Holy Father, and (*name*), our Bishop, and all faithful guardians of the Catholic and Apostolic faith."

teaching office　*See* magisterium.

teaching order　A religious institute founded primarily for the education of youth. For males this would include such groups as Irish Christian Brothers, Xaverian Brothers and Brothers of the Christian Schools; for females the Religious of the Sacred Heart, School Sisters of Notre Dame, Ursulines, Sisters of St. Joseph, etc.

teetotalism　Total abstinence from alcoholic drink. Of itself, teetotalism is morally indifferent; it is praiseworthy when practiced for ascetic motives. For those who are unable to drink in moderation, it becomes necessary and a grave obligation.

teleology　(Gr. *telos,* end; *logos,* word) The science teaching that no complete account of the universe can be given without reference to its final cause. This science imparts the conviction that each creature exists to accomplish something great, that a creature exists because its creator delights in what the creature is capable of accomplishing. Christians believe that God has spoken one living Word to men indicating his desire for all creation: Jesus. By divine decree Christ's mission to the world ought to become each man's personal mission in life if he is to find fulfillment and happiness with his fellow men in the eternal delight of his Creator. This great accomplishment in, through and with Jesus is to love. God Himself does one thing: He loves. Only love delights Him. Thus man's great mission, demanding his attention and energies, is to share God's very life by loving God, his neighbor and himself.

temperament A characteristic or habitual response to situations; a person's disposition. It is a natural disposition by which a person reacts. It has an effect on the will and can lessen the imputability of an act, but never completely.

temperance A cardinal virtue which inclines a man to govern his sensual appetites. It imposes self-control and has for dependent virtues chastity, abstinence and modesty.

Templars, the The Knights of the Temple, or Templars, were founded in 1118 at Jerusalem by nine French knights. They were called Templars because their first quarters were in the Palace of King Baldwin of Jerusalem, which was built on the site of the ancient Temple of Solomon. They received the approval of the Pope at the Council of Troyes (1128). St. Bernard, who was present at the Council, wrote a rule for them based on the Cistercian Rule and did much to spread their order. It is called "In Praise of the New Knighthood." "In this order" the Saint writes, "knighthood has blossomed forth into new life; warriors whose sole aim in life it was once to rob, to plunder, and to kill, have now bound themselves by solemn vow to defend the poor and the Church." During the Crusades the Templars rendered valuable service to the Christian cause. On the fall of Acre they withdrew to the estates which they held in the different countries of Europe. Their wealth excited the cupidity of Philip the Fair, of France. He trumped up charges of heresy and immorality against them and persuaded Pope Clement V to suppress them, burned the last Grand Master at the stake (1312) and appropriated a large share of their property. Masons use symbols in their rituals that are a reminder of this order.

temple (L. *templum*) 1. An enclosed place of worship. 2. The Temple. The place of worship of the Jews. Over time there were a number of temples, the first of which was built by Solomon (*c.* 1000 B.C.) to shelter the Ark in its Holy of Holies. When Nabuchodonosor captured Jerusalem (586 B.C.), he stripped Solomon's Temple of its rich ornamentation and burned it to the ground. It was rebuilt by Zorobabel (*c.* 515) but the new Temple was far less grand. Herod undertook the reconstrunction of the Temple (17 B.C.–A.D. 63) and it was this magnificent structure that Christ knew. However, in accordance with the prophecy of Christ, in A.D. 70 the Temple was burned to the ground by the Romans.

temporal power The civil power of the pope as sovereign of Vatican State which is necessary in order that he may be free from domination in spiritual matters.

temporal punishment An expression commonly used to designate temporary, as opposed to eternal, punishment for sin. Remaining even after the removal of guilt, temporal punishment is one of the means through which the sinner makes his adjustment to God, to the life of grace and ultimately to life eternal. In purgatory it accomplishes the immediate preparation for heaven.

temporalities The material goods attached to an ecclesiastical office, such as a benefice. The word includes the income and revenues of the office.

temporals The transient things of the world as opposed to spiritual matters and eternity.

temporary vows Those vows taken annually or for a number of years before taking perpetual vows. The period is considered one of trial and testing.

temptation Solicitation to evil arising from the world, the flesh or the Devil. God does not tempt His children but He allows them to be tempted in order that they will merit heaven. Temptation is a means of purification. St. Augustine specifies three phases of temptation: suggestion, pleasure and consent. Christ told us to watch and pray lest we fall into temptation. Temptations must be fought promptly, vigorously, continuously and humbly.

tempting God An inaccurate expression since God is incapable of temptation. It refers to an action by which a person challenges God to exercise one of His attributes, e.g., a challenge for Him to work a miracle.

ten tribes, the Sometimes called the "Lost Tribes." The legendary ten tribes of the Jews who were moved to Assyria after the conquest of Israel by Tiglathpileser, or Shalmaneser. According to various legends they became the people of India, Ethiopia, Arabia or Japan; the American Indians, the Hindus; and according to one theory, the English.

Tennessee The 16th state admitted to the Union, it is 34th in size and 17th in population. It was named for Cherokee villages—*"tanasi"*—on the Little Tennessee River. Numerous Indian tribes formerly inhabited the region, notably the Cherokees and Choctaws. De Soto was in the area in 1541, two priests being in his company. In 1673 Father Marquette explored and mapped parts of the Tennessee country. La Salle, with two Franciscans in his party, came in 1682 and erected Fort Prud'homme. It was at this time that Mass was probably offered for the first time. English colonists soon became so numerous that the Spanish and French claims were disregarded. Some settlers organized themselves as the state of Watauga, later called the state of Franklin. It became part of Southwest Territory in 1790. The Indians were induced to give up more land, settlers from the East and from Europe swarmed in, and Tennessee was admitted to the Union in 1796. In 1808 the state was placed in care of the bishop of Bardstown, Ky., and in 1838 Nashville was made a diocese with Rt. Rev. Richard Miles as first bishop. Up to that time, Father Stephen Badin has been taking care of all the Catholics in Kentucky and Tennessee. Bishop Miles built the Cathedral of St. Mary's at Nashville, established a number of parishes with resident priests and brought in some congregations of Sisters to teach in schools. Tennessee, a Confederate state, suffered greatly during and after the Civil War. The Ku Klux Klan originated in 1865 and added to the evils of the times. Yellow fever sprang up in Memphis and hundreds died every day, among them 21 priests and 50 Sisters who perished while tending the plague-stricken. Tennessee however has prospered, with a good educational system and excellent agriculture, prompted greatly by the Tennessee Valley Authority in modern times. Its bishops have built up the Faith among the people and have dotted the state with churches, schools and institutions for charitable work. However, Catholics have always been a small minority. They number less than 100 thousand in a population of over 3½ million.

Terce (L. *tertia,* third)   That part of the Divine Office for the third hour (about 9 A.M.).

terna (L. threefold)   A consultative vote to fill a vacant office in which three names are listed in descending order of worthiness. It is used by the Congregation for the Propagation of the Faith and the Consistorial Congregation in appointing bishops, vicars and prefects.

tertian   1. A Jesuit who is undergoing his third probation. The first probation is upon entering and ends with the reception of the cassock. The second probation is the novitiate. After ordination Jesuits in the United States return to the seminary for an additional year of theology. Upon the completion of this year they enter the tertianship which is equivalent to another novitiate including a thirty-day retreat. 2. A member of a Third Order.

tertiary   A member of a Third Order. It usually refers to a person living in the world although the term does include those Third Order religious who live under vows in community.

testament (L. *testamentum,* a will)   A word extended to mean a covenant and hence used to refer to the covenant between God and man. The covenant made between God and Israel is contained in the Old Testament, while the covenant made in the name of His Father by Christ with all mankind is found in the New Testament.

Testem benevolentiae   A letter written by Pope Leo XIII to Cardinal Gibbons of Baltimore in 1899 which condemned Americanism (*q.v.*).

Tetragrammaton (Gr. of four letters.)   A word indicating the name for God, appearing almost 7,000 times in the Hebrew Bible, which consists of four letters (JHVH) and which is read as "Yahweh." The word was so sacred that at the time of Christ only the High Priest could pronounce it. The name probably derives from the Hebrew for "he who is" from the revelation made to Moses by God who declared: "I am who am."

Texas   The 28th state admitted to the Union, second in area, sixth in population. Its name comes from an Indian term for "friends" or "allies." Early Indians raised crops along the Rio Grande, and the warlike Comanches, Apaches and others fought the white man's advance until as late as 1875. The Spanish Pineda (1519), de Vaca (1528) and Coronado (1541) explored the area, and Father Juan Padilla, who came with Coronado, began missionary work among the Indians. The first permanent Spanish settlement was at Isleta, near El Paso, in 1682. La Salle built Fort St. Louis in 1685, but the Indians drove out the French and martyred Fathers Membre, Le Clercq and Chefdeville. The Spanish settled in the region and built military posts while the Padres began vigorous missionary work, establishing 62 missions from 1690 until Mexico became a republic and the missions were "secularized." Mission San Antonio de Valero, built in 1718, later became famous as the Alamo. The Friars taught arts and crafts as well as religion. More martyrs were made during these years—five by the Indians, one by frontiersmen. In 1821 Texas was part of the new Republic of Mexico, and by 1830 the last mission was taken by the government. Many citizens of the United States had settled in Texas, causing warfare between opposing groups and finally war between Mexico and the United States. Texas was at first an independent republic and then was admitted to the Union in 1845. The Vincentians (Congregation of the Mission) were given the care of the Catholics of Texas, with Father Timon, C.M., as Prefect Apostolic in 1839. In 1842 Texas became a Vicariate Apostolic with Father Odin, C.M., as Vicar Apostolic, and he was made Bishop of the new see of Galveston in 1847. He brought in teaching Sisters and Brothers to staff schools, established new parishes and built churches. Succeeding bishops continued to develop the Church in Texas along the same lines. Catholics today number 2 million, in a total population of 10 million.

text of Scripture   The Church has an infallible text of Scripture that is substantially identical with the original and free from doctrinal error. This text is to be found in Vulgate, which the Council of Trent decreed was certain and authentic.

Thaddeus, St.   *See* Jude, St.

thanksgiving   1. The expression of gratitude to God and the saints for something that has been received. 2.

One of the four ends of the Mass which finds its expression in the Preface.

thaumaturgus (Gr. wonder-worker) A name applied to certain saints because of miraculous powers. The best known is St. Gregory Thaumaturgus, Bishop of Neocaesarea, who lived in the 3rd century. The title is often used in English for St. Anthony of Padua.

theft   The secret taking of another's goods against the owner's reasonable will. The gravity of theft is determined by the value of the thing stolen and the economic condition of the person robbed. Thus, stealing five dollars from a rich man would not have the same gravity as stealing five dollars from a poor widow. A series of small thefts coalesce into grave matter if it is the intention of the thief to steal repeatedly or if committed at frequent intervals. In case of extreme need a person may take as much of the goods of another as will free him from his immediate necessity. Occult compensation (*q.v.*) is permissible in certain circumstances but recourse to it should be rare.

Theism (Gr. *theos,* God) A philosophical system that admits the existence of God and the possibility of revelation but does not necessarily hold belief in the Trinity, the Incarnation, etc. It is opposed to Deism (*q.v.*) which equates with atheism.

theo- (Gr. *theos,* God) A combining form prefixed to words to indicate God.

theocracy (Gr. *theos,* God; *kratein,* to rule) A state governed directly by God through His representatives who control both the civil and religious elements of the country, the classic example being the Jewish nation until its dissolution before Christ's birth. The Catholic Church has never been a theocracy since it has always separated the spiritual from the civil power while teaching that the state must govern in accordance with Christian principles.

theodicy (Gr. *theos,* God; *dike,* justice) Term used from the time of Leibnitz in 1710, when he wrote an essay on the divine attribute of justice. Later it referred to the truly classical term, natural theology. In the later sense, theodicy is the science of God and divine things, acquired through the natural light of reason, and thus may be regarded as the culmination of philosophy.

theologian 1. One skilled in the science of theology. 2. A student of theology or an aspirant for the priesthood who has completed his philosophical course and is studying theology.

theological virtues The three essential virtues in the spiritual life that have as their aim to unite us to God through Jesus Christ. St. Paul names these virtues as faith, hope and charity. He gives them a higher rank than the moral virtues (1 Thess. 1:3; 5:8; 1 Cor. 13:13). St. Paul further states that of the three virtues, charity is the most important (1 Cor. 13:1-13). In the soul that is devoid of charity, faith and hope are imperfect and without life.

theology (Gr. *theos,* god; *logos,* word) The sacred science which treats of God and the things pertaining to God. It is broken down into a number of branches.

theology, ascetical That part of spiritual science which treats of the first degrees of perfection up to contemplation. It deals with the efforts necessary to acquire Christian perfection.

theology, dogmatic The sacred science which deals with the truths

of what we must believe about God. It is concerned with God's divine life; the share of that life which He wills for intelligent creatures, particularly man; the manner in which man lost his share in that divine life by sin, its restoration through the Redemption, its diffusion through the mission of the Church and all Christians, its completion in heaven.

theology, moral The sacred science which shows how man must respond to God's love by cultivating the divine life He has given us to share. It teaches how man must avoid sin, practice virtue, and fulfill the duties of his state in life.

theology, mystical The sacred science that deals with infused or passive contemplation with God. It lays open the secrets to perfection.

theology, natural A theology that has God for its object but which is reached through the use of human reason apart from revelation.

theology, pastoral The sacred science which deals with the care of souls. It takes the principles of moral and dogmatic theology and applies them to situations of everyday life as it is met by priests who work actively with people.

theology, positive A branch of theology restricting itself to the study of the doctrines contained in the sources of revelation, Scripture and Tradition.

theophany (Gr. *theos,* God; *phainesthai,* to appear) The name given to the various manifestations of God to man. It is generally held that these appearances were through angels representing God and speaking for Him. Such manifestations are recorded in the Old Testament; e.g., to Adam (Gen. 3:8), to Abraham (Gen. 12:7), to Isaac (Gen. 24:2), to Moses (Exod. 3:2, 19:20), to

Gedeon (Jgs. 6:2).

theosophy (Gr. *theus* God; *sophia*, wisdom) 1. Teaching that by mystical insight man can arrive at the knowledge of God intuitively because of a natural union of the soul with the Godhead. 2. The beliefs of a modern sect following for the most part Brahmanic or Buddhistic theories. Rejected by the Church.

Thessalonians, Epistles to the About A.D. 51-52 Paul wrote in close proximity two letters to the Thessalonian Christians. The faithful at Thessalonica were put to great suffering by the Jews with the result that they longed for the Second Coming of the Lord. Paul wrote his Epistles to explain the resurrection of the dead and the Parousia (*q.v.*).

third heaven A term used by St. Paul (2 Cor. 12:2-4) to indicate union with God.

Third Mass of Christmas This, the final Mass of Christmas Day, emphasizes the divinity of the Child who has been born. The Epistle, taken from Heb. 1:1-12, tells us that Christ is even above the angels, for He is the Son of God. The Gospel of this Mass is the wonderful prologue to the Gospel of St. John, the classic exposition of the divinity of Jesus. The first Mass having been said at midnight and the second at dawn, this Mass is traditionally said later on Christmas morning, and is the Mass of Christmas Day proper.

Third Order Regular Members of a Third Order who leave the world and lead a religious life in community under simple vows. They developed from members of a Third Order who left the world to devote themselves to good works. Eventually they were allowed to take vows and thus became religious. The majority of them are women.

Third Order Secular A group of faithful living in the world who seek Christian perfection according to the spirit of a particular religious order. They are usually received into the religious order in a particular ceremony and pledge themselves to certain prayers and religious practices. Members are ordinarily given the privilege of being buried in the habit of the religious order. Among the largest in the United States are the Third Order of St. Francis (Franciscan and Capuchin), Third Order of St. Dominic (Dominican), Third Order of Our Lady of Mt. Carmel (Carmelite) and Third Order of St. Augustine (Augustinian).

Thomas More Association An organization founded in Chicago for the promotion and encouragement of Catholic literature and Catholic publishing. The Association operates the largest Catholic bookstore in the United States; publishes the magazine, *The Critic,* which is concerned with articles and reports on Christian culture; makes an annual award for an outstanding contribution to Catholic publishing; and holds various seminars and symposia which are concerned with facts of Christian culture.

Thomas, St. The Apostle, also called Didymus, the Twin. He was the one who doubted the Resurrection of Christ. Ancient tradition has him carrying the Faith to India and being martyred near Mylapore. His feast is Dec. 21.

Thomism The teachings in philosophy and theology as developed by St. Thomas Aquinas and his followers; the philosophy of St. Thomas is also known as Scholastic Philosophy. St. Thomas had a tremendous capacity for synthesizing human knowledge and he drew the best from all who had gone before him. He based his teachings on the fundamental distinction between act and potency which he applied to every section of philosophy and theology. From this principle he developed his doctrine of the real distinction between essence and existence, and outlined a unified position on substance and accidents, the principle of causality, etc. Arguments (proofs) advanced by St. Thomas have never been improved upon. The excellence of his system and teachings has been emphasized by the approving statements of many popes, and canon law commands that the method, doctrine and principles of St. Thomas should be used in the instruction of students.

three children, the The children of Juda named in the book of Daniel. Their names of Anania, Misael and Azaria were changed by the Babylonians to Sidrach, Misach and Abdenago (Dan. 1:17). These three men refused to adore a golden statue and were thrown into a furnace but were miraculously saved (Dan. 3:12 ff.).

Three Hours, the A name given to the period from 12 noon to 3 P.M. on Good Friday in memory of the three hours Jesus hung on the cross. Formerly special services were held during this time but these have been replaced by the present Good Friday Liturgy.

three Marys, the Three women who were closely associated with Christ: Mary Magdalen, Mary Salome and Mary Cleophas.

throne 1. The permanent chair set in a cathedral and used by the bishop when he is pontificating. It is located on the Gospel side of the sanctuary and is usually on a raised platform. The chair has a high back. It is roofed by a square canopy. 2. A temporary throne used by a bishop when in his diocese but outside of his cathedral. A bishop may not use a throne in another diocese, unless he is the metropolitan, without permission of the local ordinary. 3. In the Byzantine Rite the throne is in the apse behind the altar, and this practice is followed in Western churches where the altar extends considerably into the church. 4. A small removable platform on which the monstrance is set when the Blessed Sacrament is exposed.

Thrones The third choir of the highest order of angels. With the Cherubim and Seraphim they form the court of God (Col. 1:16).

thurible (L. *thus,* incense) The metal container extended from chains in which charcoal and incense are burned for use in liturgical services. It has a lid which can be raised. It is also called a censer.

thurifer The person who has charge of the thurible and carries it during liturgical services.

tiara (Gk. royal headdress) The crown worn by the pope. It is shaped like a beehive, made usually wlith three diadems or head bands, elegantly decorated with a cross on the top. It is worn by the pope at his consecration and other nonliturgical ceremonies. It symbolizes the pope's threefold rule over the Church militant, suffering and triumphant.

Timothy, Epistle to *See* Epistles, Pastoral.

Timothy, St. (Gr. *Timotheos,* honoring God) Timothy was the companion and co-worker of St. Paul. He was a native of Lycaonia, born to a pagan father and a Jewish mother. On Paul's first visit to Lyc aonia, Timothy, probably a young man, was converted along with his mother and grandmother. He accompanied Paul on his missionary journeys, was with him during the writing of the Captivity Epistles and performed several missions for Paul.

tithes A tenth part of the fruits of one's revenue or income given for the support of the Church. Much importance was attached to tithes in the Old Testament and they became the acceptable form of Church support under the New Law. Charlemagne in 785 prescribed payment of tithes to the Church. At the time of the French Revolution, tithes were abolished by the government, an action shortly followed in other nations. Gradually other forms of Church support arose. However, the *Code of Canon Law* prescribes that tithes be paid according to local laws and customs. In recent years in the United States, more and more parishes are adopting the system of tithing, usually 5 per cent. Tithing provides a fair and equitable way of supporting the Church, dividing the burden according to one's ability to meet it. The system allows the pastor to make better plans for income and expenses, does away with seat and special collections, and avoids the necessity for frequent sermons on the need of money.

title (L. *titulus*) 1. *Ordination*. That provision made by the Church for the temporal welfare of its clergy. When a cleric is raised to subdiaconate a title stating the source of his material support is announced. There are a number of canons concerned with clerical title. Religious of solemn vows take the title of poverty, or of a common table. 2. *Of a church or altar*. Every church and every altar

has a title given when blessed or consecrated. The main altar of a church usually takes the name of the church. 3. *Of a cardinal*. The title taken by a cardinal priest or deacon from one of Rome's titular churches. 4. One of the conditions necessary for prescription; the reason why a person assumes possession of a thing or proves that what he possesses is his own.

titular 1. *Of a church*. The title of the church, the mystery or saint in whose name the church is blessed or consecrated. 2. *Of an altar*. Every fixed altar must have a title in whose name it is consecrated. The main altar should bear the same title as the church. No two altars in the church should have the same name.

titular church One of the ancient churches in Rome from which the cardinal priests and deacons take their title.

titular see The see assigned to a bishop who has no diocese. These are sees that were formerly Christian but where Islam or paganism now rule.

Titus, Epistle to St. *See* Epistles, Pastoral.

Titus, St. Friend and traveling companion of St. Paul. He was a Gentile Christian.

Tobia (Heb. Yahweh is good) The central character of the Book of Tobia, son of Tobit (the Vulgate refers to both father and son as Tobia). Tobit sends Tobia to collect a sum of money. The angel Raphael offers his service as a guide. On the first day a large fish endangers Tobia but Raphael protects him, knowing also that the fish contains medicinal substance for the cure of Tobia's future wife and of his father's blindness. The book tells of the cure of Sara and her happy marriage to Tobia. Raphael collects the money, and they return to Nineve where Tobit is cured of his blindness. The purpose of the book is to show man's need of God's aid and the importance of trust in God.

Tobias Night A medieval custom whereby, following the example of Tobia and Sara (Tob. 8:4), a newly wed couple would preserve their virginity for one or even three nights.

Toledo Rite Known as the Mozarabic Rite. With the inappropriate improper name Mozarabe (from Mesta and Rab, which means a Christian dominated by the Muslims), this liturgy was followed at one time throughout Spain, and existed long before the Arabs invaded Spain. It was practiced officially from the 11th century. There is no doubt but that the primitive liturgy of Spain was fundamentally Roman on account of the close relations which, from the time of St. Paul's visit to Spain, the Church in Spain maintained with Rome. In the 5th century the sad period of the invasions began. First the Vandals, afterward the Swabians, and finally the Visigoths, semibarbarians who had been converted in the East but were Arians hostile to the Catholic Faith. It was only in 587 when King Recaredo was converted to the Catholic Faith that Spain began to breathe and form itself into a solid national entity. The original liturgy influenced by ancient customs from North Africa also received the influences of the Oriental Liturgy of the invaders—who had their own clergy, churches and their own special rites—as well as from the contact with the customs which existed in France. It is a recognized fact that many elements in the Spanish liturgy, either in the Mass or the Office are influenced by the Oriental Byzantine Liturgy. It is from the end of the 6th century when the nation began to arise that the most important part (formulas, melodies) of the Mozarabic Liturgy was composed by Spanish bishops and Doctors of the Church, the chief among them being the great Bishops St. Leander (+657), St. Ildephonsus (+669) and St. Julian (+690) who composed Masses and liturgical functions. It is a calumny to say that the Mozarabic Liturgy is heretical. This opinion was promulgated by the heterodox Bishop Elipando of Toledo. In spite of the partial invasion of Spain by the Arabs in 711 and 712, and in spite of the persecution of the Faith of the Christians who fell under their power, the traditional religion was practiced and observed as much by those as it was in the part of Spain free from the Arabs. About the middle of the 11th century we hear of the first clashes with the Roman Liturgy which was then followed in all the West. In 1068, Cardinal De Blant, legate of Pope Alexander II to the Council of Barcelona, imposed the Roman Rite in place of the Mozarabic Rite throughout Catalonia. A few years later Gregory VII, addressing the Kings of Castille, Leon and Aragon, invited them "to follow the Rites of the Church of Rome excluding those of Toledo or any other Church." The Pope's invitation was favorably received. A council, celebrated in Burgos in 1085, decreed the abolition of the Mozarabic Liturgy and the adoption of the Roman Liturgy. At the same time King Alphonsus VI in Toledo forbade its use in new churches. The Mozarabic Rite was still in use in some places and in churches under the Moorish regime, but it was on the wane. In 1495 the great Franciscan Cardinal Jimenez de Cisneros as Archbishop of Toledo ordered that the old liturgical books be revised and reprinted. He made a foundation in the same Cathedral of Toledo to re-establish the Mozarabic Rite. Pope Julius II in 1508 approved of his work, which exists until the present day. In the Cathedral of Toledo there is a chapel which is the parish church of those who still follow the Mozarabic Rite. They are baptized according to the rite, and any male from the parish who is ordained follows the rite.

tone One of the eight modes of Gregorian chant.

tongues, the gift of A gift present in the early Church. It was first given to the Apostles on Pentecost when the Holy Spirit descended upon them (Acts 2). St. Paul (1. Cor. 12:10) seems to imply that the gift of tongues was given to both laity and clergy.

tonsure The bare circle worn on the crown of the head.

Tonsure (L. *tondere,* to shear) The ceremony preparatory to minor orders by which a layman becomes a cleric. The bishop or his delegate cuts a small lock of hair in the front, in the back, on each side and on the crown. He then invests the tonsured one in a surplice. In some countries a shaven pot is worn on the head to indicate the clerical state. Some religious orders shave the whole head except for a corona of hair around the crown.

tonus peregrinus (L. wandering tone) A tone used to sing psalms. It varies from the ordinary tone used in recitation and thus seems to wander.

Torah (Heb. instruction) 1. The teaching of the Mosaic and Jewish Law written down in the first five books of the Law, the Pentateuch. 2. The oral Torah which traditional Judaism holds was given to Moses and which has been preserved by tradition.

toties quoties (toe'tee-es quo'tee-es, L. as often as) Referring to a plenary indulgence which may be gained as often as the conditions are met. Thus on the Feast of Portiuncula (Aug. 2) or on All Souls' Day, a plenary indulgence can be gained more than once. The purpose of this privilege is to apply such indulgences to the souls in purgatory. There is no purpose in applying successive plenary indulgences to oneself.

Tower of David A name given the Blessed Virgin in the Litany of Loreto. It refers to her descent from David. Symbolically, as David used a tower for defense against enemies, so Mary is the defense of the Church against heresy and persecution.

Tower of Ivory A name applied to the Blessed Virgin in the Litany of Loreto. It suggests Mary's strength, her beauty and her purity.

tract A short religious treatise or leaflet, very popular with some Protestant sects.

Tract A short penitential prayer that precedes the Gospel. It replaces the Alleluia in Masses from Septuagesima to Easter, in Masses of the Dead and in other penitential Masses. It takes its name because it is sung in one movement (*in uno tractu*).

traditio symboli (L. the handing-on of the Creed) In the early Church the first recitation and explanation of the Apostles' Creed to a catechumen on Wednesday of the 4th week of Lent is referred to in that day's Mass. The *redditio,* or giving back of the *symboli* by the catechumen, took place on the eve of Easter before Baptism.

tradition (L. *tradere,* to transmit) 1. The body of teachings of Christ and His Apostles which are not explicitly contained in the Bible but passed on through the centuries by the teaching Church. 2. The actual transmission of Catholic teaching through the ages by the Church. 3. Something or some action that has been customary in the Church for a long time.

tradition of the instruments and symbols The giving, to one being ordained, of the instrument or symbol of the office to which he is being ordained. They form the matter of minor orders and the subdiaconate.

Traditionalism A philosophical system which affirmed that man's reason alone could not arrive at knowledge of natural religion. The sole source and criterion of truth is a primitive revelation which is handed down to mankind through tradition. It was condemned by the Church. Vatican Council I affirmed that God can be known by the light of reason through the things He made.

traditor (L. traitor) A Christian, often a cleric, who during the persecution of Diocletian delivered up to the persecutors sacred books, the vessels for Mass or the names of other Christians. A canon adopted at the Council of Arles (A.D. 314) ordered that clerical *traditores* should be divested of their clerical office, but allowed those ordained by them to retain jurisdiction.

transcendental (L. *trans,* across; *scandere,* to climb) A term of Scholastic philosophy to describe those notions which transcend all categories, e.g., being.

Transfiguration, the The event which occurred when Christ took Peter, James and John up into the mountain (tradition says Mount Tabor) and for a moment allowed them to see Him in His Glory. The Fathers saw a twofold reason for this event: 1. Jesus in speaking with Moses and Elia confirmed His teachings that He

had not come to destroy the law but fulfill it. 2. As St. Leo says, "Christ meant above all to take away the scandal of the Cross from the hearts of His disciples." Jesus knew that predictions of His death disheartened His disciples. Therefore He wanted to show them that His suffering and death were merely transitional to His glory. The feast is celebrated on Aug. 6; it has greater liturgical importance in the Eastern Churches.

translation 1. The moving of a saint's body from one place to another. 2. The transference of a bishop from one see to another. 3. The transference of a feast to another date.

transmigration of souls Metempsychosis. The transference of a soul from one body to another. It is held by many Asian Indians, theosophists and others. The teaching is incompatible with Catholic teaching.

transubstantiation A term employed by the Catholic Church in explaining its teaching on the Eucharist. In the term "transubstantiation" we find the notion of conversion in which the following condition must be fulfilled: "What was formerly A, is now B." Transubstantiation involves a *substantial* conversion in which the substance is changed into another state of being. The substances bread and wine, at the time of Consecration in the Mass, are converted into an entirely new substance, the true presence of Christ. The accidents of bread and wine—touch, taste and appearance—remain the same, but the repetition of the words of Christ by a validly ordained minister, "This is my Body, . . . this is my Blood" effect the transubstantiation, or conversion, of the total substance of bread and wine into the Body and Blood of Christ.

Trappists Another name for Cistercians of the Strict Observance. They were founded in 1098 in France by St. Robert of Citeaux. The Trappists came to the United States in 1848 and today have foundations in many parts of the country. They take their name from the Abbey of La Trappe. They are a contemplative and penitential order, observe silence, abstain from meat, etc.

Treasury of Merits *See* Treasury of the Church.

Treasury of the Church The infinite store of merits won by Christ as God which were infinitely over and above the satisfaction needed for mankind's salvation. To these are added the merits of the Blessed Virgin and the saints which were beyond their own needs. From this treasury of spiritual riches, the Church can draw and apply graces to any fitting action that is deemed worthy. Indulgences are made possible because of this treasury of merit.

tree of Jesse The genealogical tree of Christ beginning with Jesse, the father of David.

Tree of Life; of Knowledge Within the Garden of Eden there were two trees, the tree of life and the tree of knowledge. The purpose of the tree of life was to keep man from dying. The author of Genesis is saying that death is the result of sin, and after man's Fall the tree of life is not available to him. The fruit of the tree of knowledge enabled man to distinguish clearly between good and evil. After man's Fall he was cut off from grace and supernatural life in God.

Tribunals, Roman The judicial courts of the Holy See; namely the Sacred Apostolic Penitentiary, the Apostolic Signature and the Sacred Roman Rota.

triduum (L. *tres dies,* three days) A religious observance or period of prayer held over three consecutive days. Triduums are usually a preparation for some feast which immediately follows. The name *Triduum Sacrum* is applied to the last three days of Holy Week.

triennial vows The vows made by a religious for a period of three years as a preparation for taking perpetual vows. In some cases, they are renewed yearly during this period and in others are taken but once for the entire period. They are usually made at the conclusion of the novitiate.

trination Unusual faculty granted by an ordinary to a priest permitting him to say three Masses on the same day when this is necessary for the good of the faithful. The general law allows trination on the Feast of All Souls and on Christmas Day.

Trinity, Blessed *See* Blessed Trinity.

Trinity Sunday The first Sunday after Pentecost. The feast is celebrated in the Western Church but is not known in most of the Eastern Rites. It originated in England in the 14th century.

triptych (Gr. *triptychps,* three tablets) A three-leaved, wooden (or metal), hinged surface upon which is painted some spiritual motif or motifs. In the ancient Church they contained the list of the dead. Today they are usually representations of Christ and the saints. *See* diptych.

trope (Gr. *tropos,* a style)   An interpolated versicle or antiphon in a liturgical text. *See* farcing.

tropology (Gr. *tropos,* a style)   The manner of biblical interpretation which concerns the figurative sense of Sacred Scripture.

True Cross, the   The name given to the cross on which Christ died and which was reputedly discovered in a cistern near Calvary by St. Helena, mother of the Emperor Constantine in the year 326. SS. Augustine, Cyril of Jerusalem and Ambrose all testify to the finding. The Church celebrates the Feast of the Exaltation of the Holy Cross on Sept. 14. The Feast of the Finding of the Holy Cross formerly celebrated on May 3 has been suppressed. Many relics of the True Cross are claimed to exist in various parts of the world.

Trusteeism   For many years the peace of the young American Church was disturbed by what was known as the Trustee System, or "Trusteeism." This system originated in New York City. In 1785, shortly after the appointment of Father Daniel Carroll as Prefect Apostolic, the board of "Trustees of the Roman Catholic Church in the City of New York" was incorporated and purchased a site for a church. The trustees, all of them laymen, were not content with holding the property, but maintained that the congregation represented by them had the right not only to choose its pastor, but to dismiss him at pleasure, and that no ecclesiastical superior, bishop or prefect, had any right to interfere. Such a situation, as Father Carroll wrote to the New York Trustees, was bound to result in the formation of distinct churches and independent societies in nearly the same manner as the congregational Presbyterians. As a matter of fact, several churches for a time firmly resisted the authority of the bishops and were put under an interdict. In 1822 Pope Pius VII condemned the Trustee System, but nearly a half century elapsed before Trusteeism was finally abolished and the present system of holding Church property was adopted. The disappearance of the pernicious and thoroughly un-Catholic system was mainly due to the uncompromising stand taken by Bishop Francis Patrick Kenrick of Philadelphia and Bishop John Hughes of New York. It was not a localized movement but infiltrated into nearly all the dioceses.

truth   There are a number of meanings for the word, all of which imply a relationship between a mental reality and objective reality. 1. *Logical.* The conformity between the mind and objective reality. 2. *Ontological.* The conformity of an object to its mental representation. 3. *Moral or ethical.* The conformity of words or thoughts with conscience.

truth, revealed   A truth given by God to man through revelation. This truth may be revealed by the Church through its infallibility, such as when a doctrine is declared dogma, e.g., the Immaculate Conception.

truthfulness   That quality which is in a person by reason of telling the truth. While truth is the conformity of the mind to reality, it is both subjective and objective. Subjective truth is what a person thinks to be true even thought it may not conform to reality. Thus if a person thought it was Thursday when it was really Friday, he would be truthful by stating it was Thursday for to speak otherwise would be a lie.

tumulation (L. *tumulus,* a mound)   Burial above ground in a vault, niche, mausoleum, etc. Except for the state's right of eminent domain, a tomb remains permanently undisturbed. The term derives from the type of burial in areas where it was not possible to dig. The corpse was placed on the ground and then covered with earth and stones. *See* cemetery.

tunic (L. *tunica,* a coat)   1. The outer vestment worn by the subdeacon. He is vested with this vestment during the ordination rite. 2. A vestment worn by cardinals, bishops and abbots at pontifical functions. It is worn under the dalmatic. 3. The loose gown worn as part of the religious habit. Over it is placed the scapular, mantle, etc.

Twelve Apostles   *See* apostle.

typological sense of Scripture   The spiritual or mystical sense of Scripture: persons, things and events which are interpreted as prefigures for persons, things and events which came later. Thus the priesthood of Melchisedech prefigured the priesthood of Christ. The typological sense

is known from later revelation in the New Testament.

tyrannicide (L. *tyrannus,* tyrant)   The killing of a tyrant by a private person or persons for the common good. Tyrants are of two kinds: tyrant by usurpation, one who attacks the community and overthrows the legal authority; tyrant by oppression, one legitimately in office who becomes tyrannical. A tyrant by usurpation may not be killed by a private person or group without a mandate of the legitimate ruler. A tyrant by usurpation is a criminal and may be put to death by legitimate authority. However, if the tyrant by usurpation becomes an unjust aggressor an individual may protect himself. Once the tyrant by usurpation rules peacefully his just laws must be obeyed, but one can assist the legitimate ruler to regain his power. A tyrant by oppression can be punished by the state but no private person has the right to kill him.

U

ubiquity of God (L. *ubique,* everywhere)   Often called the omnipresence of God; indicates that God is present in every thing and in every place. This is so, since God is simple and is not limited by time and space. God is not present in all things as part of their essence (pantheism) but rather as the continuing cause of their existence.

Uganda   Opened to the Church by the White Fathers in 1879, Uganda today has 2 million Catholics in a total population of 7 million. The Church was built on the sacrifice of martyrs. In 1920, 22 Uganda martyrs (*q.v.*) who died in the persecution of 1886 were beatified; they were canonized in 1964, the first Bantu saints. There are 1 archdiocese and 7 dioceses; over one-third of the clergy are Africans.

Uganda Martyrs   The 22 lay Africans who were put to death by King Mwanga of Buganda during the per-secution of 1885–1887, and canonized by Pope Paul VI in 1964. They were representative of more than 300 Christians, both Catholic and Protestant, who were killed during this period in defense of their Faith. The arrival of the White Fathers in Uganda in 1879 was met with friendliness on the part of King Mutesa

who granted them permission to preach freely. However, his successor, Mwanga, feared that the new religion was a threat to his power, particularly since its moral code was in direct opposition to the homosexual vices taught him by Arab traders. The first victim of the persecution was Joseph Musaka, majordomo of the royal court and foremost member of the Christian community. When Joseph protected the royal pages against the king's unnatural advances, the king had him arrested and burned alive on Sunday, Nov. 15, 1885. The Christian pages then looked to Charles Lwanga, chief of pages, as their leader. The king's wrath exploded on May 25, 1886, when he savagely attacked and executed his personal attendant, Denis Ssebuggwawo, for daring to teach catechism to a favorite page. The next morning the king summoned all the pages before him and commanded the Christians among them to step forward. Led by Charles Lwanga the Christians stepped forward and were sentenced to be burned alive. Thirteen martyrs died in the pyre on Namugongo Hill on Ascension Thursday, June 3, 1886. In addition to these Catholic martyrs were nine Protestants who also sacrificed their lives for their beliefs. Before the persecution ended, many more victims perished.

Ukrainians A people originating in what is now the southwestern part of the Soviet Union. When speaking of the "Ukrainians" or "Ruthenians," the Church refers to those who are Catholics of the Byzantine Rite, who are in communion with Rome as a result of the Union of Brest of 1595. They are the largest Eastern Rite body united to Rome, numbering 5.5 million people. In 1945 the Catholic Church in the Ukraine was put in chains by the Russians; priests and Catholics were deported to Siberia; Archbishop Joseph Slipy, Metropolitan of Ukrainian Catholics was imprisoned; all five dioceses of the Ukrainians were liquidated, and 4,400 churches and chapels were desecrated. The Ukrainians have never admitted their enslavement by the Russians, and there is a Ukrainian government-in-exile. Before World War I, a large number of Ukrainians emigrated to the United States and Canada. Since World War II, about 70,000 more have come to America to escape Soviet persecution. Today there are over a half million Ukrainians in the United States and Canada, organized into two archdioceses (Philadelphia and Winnipeg) and five dioceses (Stamford, St. Nicholas of Chicago, Edmonton, Saskatoon and Toronto). Brazil, Argentina, Australia, England, France, Italy and Austria each have a diocese. *See* Ruthenian Catholics.

ultreya A weekly reunion or cell meeting of small groups of those who have made a cursillo. An ultreya usually is attended by four to six cursillistas, and lasts only about 15 minutes. Led by a priest and/or a layman, the cursillistas discuss their successes and failures in their apostolic work of the week just past, and their plans for the coming week.

unam sanctam (L. one, holy) Words found in the Nicene Creed said at Mass, referring to the one holy Catholic and Apostolic Church in which Catholics believe.

unanswered prayer A prayer in which a favor was asked of God but was not received. No prayer, however, is really unanswered because some grace is always bestowed by God upon a person who turns to Him in prayer.

unbaptized infants The common teaching of the Church is that infants who die without Baptism are excluded from heaven. Theologians generally teach that these infants spend eternity in a state of perfect natural happiness. In this state, commonly called Limbo, these souls know and love God with their natural powers. They find perfect contentment in this and experience no grief at lack of the Beatific Vision.

unbaptized, fate of the Every human being who has reached the use of reason, but has not received the Sacrament of Baptism can be saved in one of two ways. 1. By "Baptism of Blood," or martyrdom, whereby a person freely and patiently suffers death for the Christian Faith; e.g., one taking instructions to become a Christian but has not yet been baptized is ordered to give up the instructions or face death—if he refuses to discontinue instructions and is killed, he earns "baptism of blood." 2. By an act of love of God; e.g., someone who through no fault of his own has never become aware of the fact that Christ and His teachings are worthy of belief, nevertheless sees that Someone has been very good to him and he in turn offers gratitude and expresses love for that Someone because He is so good. This person, in his act of love, implicitly says, "I want to do all that you want me to do." But what God wants him to do is to become baptized. Therefore he is saying indirectly, "I want to be baptized." Hence he receives forgiveness of sin and his soul receives sanctifying grace. This act of love is called "baptism of desire." The alternative to these two possibilities for a person who has reached the use of reason and dies without Baptism is eternal damnation.

unclean, ritually A person or thing, e.g., certain foods, that has become ceremonially or legally tainted and is now in need of certain external purifications. This taint or stain is a purely juridical thing. It has no reference to the moral goodness or evil of the person or thing so designated.

unction (L. *ungere,* to anoint) The act of anointing with an especially prepared and blessed oil used for the conferring of spiritual strength. *See* Anointing of the Sick; consecration of a bishop; Holy Orders; etc.

understanding   1. That faculty of the soul (also called intellect, intelligence, reason) as it is exercised in the simple act of judgment. It is that faculty or power of the intellect which renders our experiences intelligible. It enables one to analyze the particulars of our experience and to form reasoned judgments. 2. A gift of the Holy Spirit bestowed upon man in order that he may gain a fuller knowledge and a cogent awareness of the mysteries of faith and of religion. As a consequence, it implies a greater feeling and attachment toward these mysteries.

unfit, killing of the The putting to death of the "socially unfit," e.g., the

deformed, the mentally defective and those suffering from hereditary diseases, based of the claim that they are a burden to themselves and to society. This act, sometimes called euthanasia (mercy killing), is against both the natural and the divine law, as Pope Pius XI pointed out in his encyclical *Mystici Corporis (On the Mystical Body).* It is murder.

Uniate (Russ. *uniya,* union)   A term which designates Eastern Catholic Churches which are in union with Rome; may also be used in referring to members of these Churches. Many Eastern Catholics resent this term because it originated in a hostile nickname given by non-Catholic opponents. Preferable terms would be: Eastern Catholic or Oriental Catholic.

uniformity   Uniformity in the sense of external conformity stifling national genius and qualities is not found in the Catholic Church, although sometimes it is attributed to her. There is unity in the Church, in its teachings, government and sacramental life; but other than this necessary unity of defined faith and morals, there is no principle of uniformity in the Church. This can be seen in the variety of rites and languages used in the official worship of the Church from its earliest times, and confirmed in the Constitution on the Sacred Liturgy promulgated by Vatican Council II, December, 1963.

uniformity of nature, the principle of   A metaphysical principle that natural causes—i.e., those causes operative in the physical universe apart from the free will of man— acting in similar circumstances always and everywhere produce similar results.

Unigenitus (L. *unigenitus,* first born) 1. The Latin term applied to the only-begotten Son of God, Jesus Christ. He alone is generated from all eternity by the Father. 2. The first word of the Apostolic Constitution of Pope Clement XI, given on Sept. 8, 1713, which condemned the Jansenistic doctrines of Quesnel, a Frenchman and member of the Congregation of the Oratory. The Bull was also a factor in the French Gallican struggle, whereby the French Hierarchy under Cardinal Noailles and the French Monarchy of Louis XIV challenged papal jurisdiction over the Church in France. 3. The Jubilee Bull of Clement VI, given in 1343, which dealt with the doctrine of the treasury of merits.

union, mystical An intimate, supernatural union of a soul with God through contemplation. In this union, God operates directly on the soul which responds completely in accord with these actions of God. This union is a gratuitous and extraordinary gift from God. The Mystical union develops by passing through various well-defined stages which are generally four in number: prayer of quiet, full union (in which the soul is more conscious and more certain of God's presence within it), ecstatic union or ecstasy, and the spiritual marriage.

unions Organizations of the faithful who have banded together to pray and perform good works for some specific purpose; e.g., reparation for sin, reparation for outrages against the Church, salvation of the world, etc. Usually these groups are called Unions of Prayer.

Unitarianism A doctrine which denies the Trinity and proposes a single Person in God. The term is most frequently associated with a group of liberal Christians organized in Boston in 1785. Besides the above doctrine, they insist upon absolute freedom in belief, the supreme guidance of reason, devotion to education and philanthropy, and emphasis upon character as the principle of fundamental importance in religion. Although Unitarians claim to be Christians, the assertion is debatable. Many Unitarians today are more proximate to secular humanism than to Christianity.

United States The foundations of the Church in the United States were set in place by the great missioners from Spain and France but it was the successive waves of immigration that gave the Church strength and numbers. Establishing the Church in a hostile Anglo-Saxon culture was not without difficulties; there were discrimination, riots, and movements like the Know Nothings (*q.v.*). Today Catholics make up a substantial part of American life. The 45 million Catholics of 1964 are represented by 28 archdioceses and 120 dioceses. There are 17,000 parishes, staffed by almost 60,000 priests and over 180,000 Sisters. Almost 15,000 educational institutions from elementary school to university have been established. The coordination of the Church in the United States is through the National Catholic Welfare Conference (*q.v.*). Through this organization operate such groups as Catholic Relief Services, National Council of Catholic Men, the Confraternity of Christian Doctrine, Latin America Bureau, National Federation of Catholic College Students, etc. (*qq.v.*). Various societies exist for home mission work: Glenmary Missioners, Josephites, Trinitarians. Well over 7,000 Americans are serving overseas in the foreign missions of the Church. The Catholic press in the United States is not equaled by that of any other country. There are 131 newspapers and some 375 magazines. There are many apostolic movements at work in the United States. Catholic life is far removed from the ghetto of several generations ago.

United States-Vatican relations The United States first began relations with the Papal States on Dec. 15, 1784, and the first consul was appointed in 1797. In 1847 the post was upgraded to a full diplomatic rank and continued as such until the resignation of Rufus King in 1868, following the failure of Congress to appropriate funds. The Papal States, meanwhile, continued to appoint consular officials to the United States until 1895. There was no further diplomatic activity until 1939 when President Franklin Roosevelt appointed Myron C. Taylor as his personal representative to the Vatican. Taylor resigned in 1950, and the following year President Truman named General Mark Clark as Ambassador. Anti-Catholic and secularistic pressures caused General Clark to withdraw his name, and no diplomatic activity has been initiated since.

unitive way The third and last stage of the spiritual life in which the goal is habitual and intimate union with God through Jesus Christ. It is scripturally expressed by St. Paul: "I live, now not I; but Christ liveth in me" (Gal. 2:20).

unity A wholeness or totality that is a union of related parts. This concept is used in many contexts by the Church; e.g., unity of natures in Christ, Church Unity, etc.

unity of God The term "unity" indicates that a thing is undivided in itself and divided from all else. When applied to God, the term indicates the perfection in Him by which we know that He has no composition of any kind and that He is not dependent on any other being for His existence. He is completely simple.

unity of the Church The Church is an external society of men. As an external society, the Church is remarkable for her unity. She is an organic whole, whose members are united in professing the same faith, following the same manner of worship (the Mass and the sacraments), and accepting the same authority of the pope, the visible head of the Church. This external oneness of the Church does not extend to uniformity in nonessential details.

unity of the human race All human beings belong to the same family or species because all have descended from one and the same pair of first parents.

Universalis Ecclesiae (L. the universality of the Church) An apostolic letter of Pope Pius IX dated Sept. 29, 1850. In this document, the pope restored to England and Wales a regular hierarchy of bishops, which had become extinct with the death of the last bishop in the reign of Queen Elizabeth I.

universalism 1. The religious teaching (condemned by the Catholic Church as false) that all men are eventually saved. It has given its name to a sect of American Unitarians who call themselves Universalists. 2. (Catholic). The spirit in the modern world toward a growing unification of mankind. It is the Catholic position that the Mystical Body of Christ is the true and perfect universalism to which all men are called. The universalism of the Church is an incarnational universalism because the Church identifies with Christ in the Mystical Body.

universities, pontifical Those universities which have been canonically erected and given authority by the Sacred Congregation of Seminaries and Universities and therefore have pontifical status. These universities are authorized to award degrees in recognized fields of study. In the United States there are four pontifical universities: Catholic University in Washington, D.C., (1889); Niagara University, Niagara Falls, N.Y. (1956); De Paul University, Chicago, Ill. (1957); Georgetown University, Washington, D.C. (1833). In addition a number of seminaries have pontifical status.

university An educational institution for the teaching of universal knowledge. It is empowered to teach, do research and confer degrees upon students in special departments of knowledge; e.g., theology, law, medicine, the arts, etc. John Henry Cardinal Newman defined the university's primary function as ". . . the diffusion and extension of knowledge."

Unjust Steward A character in a parable told by Christ as found in Lk. 16.

Unknown God When St. Paul was in Athens he found an altar dedicated to the "Unknown God." He later used the expression in a sermon to the Athenians.

Unmerciful Servant A character in a parable told by Christ and recounted in Matt. 18.

unworthy life A term used in reference to a prohibiting impediment by which a marriage between a Catholic and one who is a notorious public sinner, an apostate or under censure, etc., is rendered unlawful (but not invalid).

urbi et orbi (L. to the city and the world) The name given to the solemn blessing of the Holy Father given on special occasions to the people of Rome and the world. The blessing is usually given from the balcony of St. Peter's Basilica. The phrase is also used at times in the address of certain papal pronouncements.

Uriel (Heb. my light is God) The name of an archangel who stands before the throne of God.

Uruguay Modern Uruguay has a history of secularism, laicism and anticlericalism despite the fact that Catholics are 82 per cent of the 3 million population. In 1916 Church and State were separated, the Church was persecuted and laws were enacted against the Church. The University of the Republic was a center of agnosticism. Today the Christian elite is apostolic and the number of Catholics and institutions engaged in the social apostolate is increasing. There are 1 archdiocese and 8 dioceses.

Ursuline Nuns of the Canadian Union Founded in Canada by Venerable Mère Marie of the Incarnation (Marie Guyart) in 1639, the first community of women in Canada or the United States. There are missions in Japan and Latin America. The members take solemn vows and there are both active and contemplative nuns. There are three provinces in Canada with over 1,000 members.

Ursuline Nuns of the Congregation of Paris A community of women founded in France in 1572. There are 8 independent motherhouses in the United States in Kansas, Kentucky (2), Ohio (5). There are approximately 2,200 members engaged primarily in teaching. The Sisters take simple vows.

Ursuline Nuns of the Roman Union Established in New Orleans in 1727 by French Ursulines, the Union now has 4 provinces in the United States with 1,350 members. There are home missions and foreign missions in Latin America, Africa, Asia and Greece. The Union is semi-cloistered with solemn vows. The Divine Office is sung in choir. Work of the community is teaching and catechetics.

Ursulines Formally, Order of St. Ursula, the first community of women dedicated to the education of girls. The Order was founded in Italy in 1535 by St. Angela Merici. The first Ursulines arrived in the New World in 1639 when Venerable Mère Marie of the Incarnation (Marie Guyart) came to Canada. French Ursulines arrived in New Orleans in 1727 and began the first school for girls in what was to become the United States.

use of reason The ability to employ the intellect in judging the moral rightness or wrongness of an act. In canon law, children are presumed to come to the "use of reason" after their seventh year. Unless the contrary is proved, they are assumed not to have the "use of reason" before this age. Adults lacking the "use of reason" (e.g., the insane) are considered in law as infants.

use, special The peculiar modifications in liturgical texts and customs used by a diocese, province or religious order, which are not distinct rites but rather modifications of an existing parent rite. In the Middle Ages many existed, but few of these remained after the reforms initiated by Pope Pius V in the 16th century and the resulting movement toward uniform ritual in the Western Church. The liturgical ceremonies of the Carthusians, the Carmelites and the Dominicans are examples of *"use"* in the Roman Rite. When the term "liturgical uses" is employed, those

laws are meant which regulate the performance of liturgical ceremonies in general, and which allow for the particular modifications mentioned above.

U.S.S.R., the Church in the Long before the revolution of 1917 the official religion of the Czarist empire was the Russian Orthodox Church. The Czar was head of the Church. In 1918, when the Communists came into power, they seized all Church properties, subjugating the Church to the state. In 1925 the program against religion moved into full organization. Antireligious propaganda was openly approved, religious services were allowed to take place as mere targets for the policy of the government. The actual number of Russian-born Catholics in 1917 was very small. The majority of the 2 million members of the Roman Catholic Church were foreigners. These were found chiefly in the west and southwest. There were 4 sees under the Metropolitan See of Mogilev. The gradual disappearance of the clergy, due to persecution, caused the diocesan organization to become defunct, thus placing the Russian Catholics under the responsibility of a special commission at Rome. By 1935 the clergy of the Mogilev Archdiocese was reduced from 435 to 16. Execution, exile, imprisonment and natural death were the main causes. Among those who gave witness to the Faith as martyrs or confessors were Msgr. Budkiewicz, Bishops Sloskan and Malecky, and the Exarch Leonid Feodorov. By 1939 there was said to be only one Catholic priest at liberty in all of Russia. World War II lessened, in some way, the harsh attitude of persecution against religion. The government needed the support of religious people. Due to the annexation of Estonia, Latvia, Lithuania, and parts of Poland and Czechoslovakia, the number of Catholics in the U.S.S.R. increased to 10 million. It is this part of the Catholic Church which is referred to as the "Church in Chains" or the "Church of Silence" or the "Church behind the Iron Curtain." The ironclad policy of the Communist government against religion hardly leaves any doubt that the external practice of Catholicism is greatly hindered. In 1963, in Moscow, there was but one Catholic church which people actually attended. The parish had only one elderly priest, who was allowed to celebrate Mass publicly on Sunday. The Russian Orthodox Church is allowed to hold religious services, and does so with good results. The report is that nearly half of the adult population believes in God and occasionally attends church. Although the official report from the Communist government is that "religion is dying out," the facts confirm the growth in church attendance and liturgical participation. The policy of the state is still against religion —its policy for almost four decades.

usual conditions A phrase used to describe the conditions necessary for gaining a plenary indulgence. In addition to any special conditions which may be attached for the valid gaining of the indulgence, the usual conditions are reception of the Sacraments of Penance and the Eucharist and prayer for the intentions of the pope. This latter condition is usually interpreted as six Our Fathers, Hail Marys and Glorias.

usury (L. *usura,* a use) The loaning of money at an unjustly high rate of interest; a sin against justice and charity. The maximum rate of interest should be set by those in charge of the common good, such a rate covering ordinary risks and justified return. The Church advocates the formation of credit unions in areas where usury is widespread.

Utah The 45th state admitted to the Union, it is 11th in area and 38th in population. It was named for the Ute Indians, a Shoshone tribe. In 1540 Spanish explorers from Mexico came into the area with no lasting results. In 1776 two Franciscans, Fathers Dominquez and Escalante, came with an expedition looking for a route from Santa Fe to the California missions. Other Spanish explorers were acquainted with the region, their maps showing the Great Salt Lake. The Ashley-Smith fur-trading expedition explored northern Utah in 1825, and in 1841 the first permanent settlement was made near Ogden by Miles Goodyear. In the 1840's the Old Spanish Trail was opened, roughly approximating Father Escalante's route. Father De Smet, S.J., who had traversed the region, met the Mormon leaders near Omaha, Neb., in 1846 and in answer to their questions told them of the Salt Lake Valley. They were seeking a place to live, and after their arduous trek westward they settled there, making a lush farming region out of the desert. At that time Utah was part of Mexico but it came to the United States by treaty in 1848. The first Mass celebrated in the territory was most likely said by a chaplain to the troops of Johnston's army, near Salt Lake City, in 1859. Utah was admitted to the Union in 1896. Many non-Mormon settlers, including some Catholics, were employed in mines and railroad work. In 1871 the Archbishop of San Francisco sent a priest, Father Patrick Walsh, to be pastor of Utah. Father Lawrence Scanlon arrived two years later and labored with great zeal among the scattered Catholics. He was made bishop of the new Diocese of Salt Lake in 1891. He brought in teaching Sisters and Brothers, built new churches, and opened schools and hospitals. Succeeding bishops continued to build up the diocese, and though the Church is growing and thriving, Catholics are still a minority. They number about fifty thousand, in a population of less than one million.

utilitarianism A philosophical system devolved from materialism which holds that what is useful is good.

V

vacancy In canon law the official state of an ecclesiastical office when its most recent incumbent has lost his title to that office through death, resignation or official removal from office.

vagus (vah'gus, L. wanderer) A canonical term for a person who has no domicile or quasi-domicile *(q.v.)*. Canon Law makes special provisions for such persons.

vain observance A form of superstition which uses means out of proportion to the determined effect. This would include such practices as mumbling words with supposed magical power, determining the course of the day because a black cat crossed one's path, attempting to heal illness by some "magical" medicine, etc.

vainglory An excessive pride in one's achievements as the result of which the praise of others is desired.

Valentine's Day St. The feast of St. Valentine on Feb. 14. He was a priest and martyr who died in Rome at the end of the 3rd century. Little is known of him. He has nothing to do with the fact that the day has a special meaning for lovers. It was a medieval notion that birds began to mate at this time and thus the day was auspicious for those in love.

valid but illicit Refers to something that has been accomplished, but in an unlawful manner. For example, a marriage which takes place during the closed season when the Church forbids weddings unless proper dispensation has been received, is a true (valid) marriage, but is contracted in an unlawful (*illicit*) manner.

validity of marriage May be effected by a simple renewal of consent when its nullity arises only from a defective consent in one or both parties. When, however, matrimony is invalid on account of the existence of some ecclesiastical impediment, it may be revalidated by simple dispensation or by that known as *sanatio in radice (q.v.)*.

Vatican (L. *Vaticanus*, a hill in Rome) The residence of the pope built upon the Vatican Hill in Rome. Also, in recent use, the papal authorities or the system which they represent; the papacy. *See* Vatican City.

Vatican Basilica More familiarly known as St. Peter's, this magnificent edifice, the largest church in Christendom, marks the spot where, according to tradition, the Prince of the Apostles lies buried. Though commonly regarded as the head church of the world, it ranks second, strictly speaking, to the Basilica of St. John

584

Lateran, the latter being the Cathedral Church of the popes. The present edifice dates from the 16th century. It replaced the original basilica built by Emperor Constantine and consecrated by Pope St. Sylvester in 326. It is a repository of priceless art treasures and of the mortal remains of many popes, emperors and other historical personages. The vast interior of St. Peter's can accommodate as many as 50,000 persons. Functions of world-wide importance, such as canonizations, are held here. A recent example of note: the assemblies of Vatican Council II.

Vatican chant The revision of Gregorian chant melodies along the lines indicated by Pope St. Pius X, who directed that they "be restored in their integrity and identity after the earliest manuscripts." He entrusted the undertaking to the Benedictine monastery at Solesmes, France. The resulting version is the only authentic one for use in churches of the Latin Rite.

Vatican City, the State of (It. *Stato della Citta del Vaticano*) The world's smallest sovereign state, less than 109 acres in area, lies within the city of Rome. The pope is the ruler of this independent territory, belonging to no nation, the pope himself free from national interference (similar to the District of Columbia which belongs to no state, the President and Congress being outside the jurisdiction of any one state). The idea of a territory where the pope ruled as a temporal king began in the time of the Emperor Constantine, shortly after the Edict of Milan (A.D. 313) ended centuries of persecution and gave a period of peace to the Church. Gifts from emperors and noble families converted to Christianity provided the Church with a number of large estates which grew in size and num-

ber, until by the time of Pope Gregory the Great (590–604), the papacy was perhaps the largest landholder in the world. In the time of Charlemagne the Papal States were reorganized, so in 781 they comprised a considerable district around Rome. The popes did not themselves actively govern these states until the fifteenth century. By the beginning of the 16th century the Papal States covered over 15 thousand square miles. From 1860 on, the Kingdom of Italy gradually annexed one after another of the Papal States, and in 1870 the city of Rome itself was seized and the states of the Church no longer existed. In 1929 the pope signed an agreement with the Italian government which determined the independence of Vatican City. This small state is governed by the pope, who delegates his powers to the Pontifical Commission for the Administration of Vatican City. There are about 1,000 citizens of the state, most of them priests and religious engaged in secretarial work and domestic occupations. There are a few hundred lay persons employed in trade and various branches of service. Professional people include the different classes of guards who look after the pope's safety, police Vatican City and serve on ceremonial occasions. Notable buildings in Vatican City are St. Peter's Basilica, built over the tomb of St. Peter, the first pope; the Vatican Palace including the pope's living quarters and the Vatican Library and Museum with some of the world's great treasures of manuscripts and art. Vatican City has its own radio station designed by Marconi (the inventor of radio) and set up under Pope Pius XI in 1931. Extraterritorial possessions of Vatican City are: Castel Gandolfo, the summer home of the pope, which is a few miles outside Rome, the pope's own patriarchal Basilica of St. John Lateran; and a number of other basilicas, besides office buildings belonging to the Roman Curia.

Vatican Council I The twentieth ecumenical council which began Dec. 1, 1869, and adjourned Oct. 20, 1870. While the Council dealt with the nature of the Church, it is best known for its definition of papal infallibility. Some 40 American bishops attended the Council, the majority of whom were opposed to the definition of papal infallibility. The opposition was led by Archbishop Peter Kenrick of St. Louis, Archbishop John Purcell of Cincinnati, and Bishop Michael Domenec of Pittsburgh. Bishop Domenec called the proposed definition an "insurmountable obstacle to the conversion of Protestants in the United States." However, when the final vote was taken only two votes were cast against the new dogma, that of Bishop Edward Fitzgerald of Little Rock and that of an Italian bishop.

Vatican Council II On Christmas Day, 1961, Pope John XXIII published an apostolic constitution which set forth the holding of the Second Vatican Ecumenical Council. The pope charged the Council with updating the Church and working for Christian unity. The Council opened on Oct. 11, 1962. A second session was held at the direction of Pope Paul VI in the fall of 1963, and a third in the fall of 1964. The Council Fathers studied the nature of the Church, Christian unity, the liturgy, mass communications, the role of Mary in the life of the Church, ecumenism, etc. As a result of the work of the Council there has been a liturgical revision of the Mass and Sacraments in which the vernacular and a redirection make them more meaningful to the Christian. See Liturgy, Constitution on the Sacred.

veil (L. vellum, a covering) 1. *Liturgical.* Coverings of cloth of different sizes according to the liturgical use: the chalice veil which covers the chalice and is of the same cloth and color as the vestments used; the tabernacle veil which varies in color according to the liturgical season and the color of the Mass vestments; the humeral veil which covers the shoulders of the priest with which the Blessed Sacrament is covered when being carried in procession or used to cover the base of the monstrance when giving Benediction; the ciborium veil, always white. 2. *Religious.* The head and shoulder covering worn by nuns and Sisters. It is usually black for professed Sisters and white for novices. Some communities of women dispense with the veil entirely, others wear it only outdoors. It was formerly the sign of a married woman and was adopted by Sisters to represent that they are the brides of Christ. 3. *Wedding veil.* Originating in the veil worn by all married women, today it is a symbol of marriage fidelity.

Venerable A title given to a Servant of God whose cause of beatification has been introduced and whose heroic virtue or martyrdom has been declared by official decree. Public veneration cannot yet be given.

Venerable Brother The title used by the pope when addressing a bishop. It is the form of address used in encyclicals, papal bulls and other documents.

veneration The respect shown to saints. It may take the form of prayers, hymns and services; or it may consist in honoring their relics or statues. Above all, we show veneration by asking their prayers for us, and by imitating their virtuous lives. Veneration is distinct from the homage we give to God, usually called adoration.

Venezuela Discovered by Christopher Columbus. Venezuela received its first bishop in 1532. Following independence in 1811, Bolívar assured the Church of his support, but he had other battles to fight in Latin America and the new government did not recognize his promises. The government of Guzman Blanco was very anticlerical. In 1872, convents were dissolved and their goods confiscated. In 1874, religious were expelled. Today the relationship between Church and State is good but the years of turmoil have left a shortage of clergy and a consequent religious ignorance. Illegitimacy has a national average of between 55-60 per cent and about the same percentage of illiteracy. Communism has considerable strength in communications and education, particularly among university students. There are 3 archdioceses and 17 other ecclesiastical territories—dioceses, vicariates and 1 prelature. There is 1 priest for every 5,500 people. The population is approximately 8 million, of which about 95 per cent are claimed to be Catholics. The Christian Democratic Movement in Venezuela, COPEI, is exceptionally strong. Charitable movements such as *Fey y Alegria* give the laity the opportunity for Christian action. There are 4 daily newspapers, 1 of which, *La Religion,* is the dean of the country's newspapers. There is a Catholic university in Carácas conducted by the Jesuits.

Veni Creator Spiritus (L. Come Creator Spirit) Hymn to the Holy Spirit entoned at the ordination of priests, or whenever the Paraclete is solemnly evoked; e.g., at Confirmation, opening of a Council or synod, etc.

Veni Sancte Spiritus (L. Come, Holy Spirit) Opening words of the Golden Sequence of Pentecost and its Octave composed by the medieval Pope Innocent III. It is also used as a hymn.

venia (L. permission) The genuflection or prostration made by a religious as reparation for committing some fault or breach of the rule; the genuflection made to a superior after the granting of a permission.

venial sin *See* sin, venial.

Venice, Patriarch of The bishop of the highest rank in the city of Venice, ruling the diocese of Venice.

Venite (L. come) A liturgical chant which takes its name from the first word of Ps. 94 (95) and which is made up from parts of Ps. 94 (95) and Ps. 95 (96).

Vermont The 14th state admitted to the Union, it is 43rd in area and 47th in population. Its name comes from the French, meaning "green mountain." Abenakis, Algonquins, Iroquois, Mohawks and Mohicans once lived in the area, which was first explored by Champlain in 1609. St. Isaac Jogues, having been captured by the Iroquois, was brought through in 1642. The first white settlement was the fort and shrine of St. Anne on Isle La Motte, in 1666. Father Dollier de Casson, S.S., was the chaplain and offered the first Mass there. Bishop Laval came in from Quebec in 1668, made a visitation and administered Confirmation. English colonials founded Fort Dummer (Brattleboro) in 1724. After 1760, when the English captured Canada, immigrants began to come into Vermont in greater numbers.

The "Green Mountain Boys" led by
Ethan Allen aided in the Revolu
tion. Allen's daughter Frances was
the first New England woman to become a nun. Vermont became a state
in 1791. Irish and French Canadian
settlers and industrial workers later
built up the population. However,
the old English laws discriminated
against Catholics until 1793 when religious freedom was granted. Father
Matignon of Boston visited Vermont
in 1815 and reported that there were
about 100 Catholics in Burlington.
Bishop Fenwick of Boston sent them
a French priest from Canada, and he
himself visited them in 1830. Father
Jeremiah O'Callaghan, from Cork,
was the first resident priest, working
alone in Vermont until 1833. Gradually a few more priests came in to
care for scattered Catholics. Louis
de Goesbriand was the first bishop
of the new Diocese of Burlington,
1853. He built churches, also schools,
hospitals and charitable institutions
staffed by Sisters of various congregations whom he brought in. Succeeding bishops continued to build
up the Church until now the state
numbers a rather high percentage of
Catholics. The first Carthusian monastery in America was founded at
Whitingham in 1951. Catholics today
number one-third of the total population of less than one-half million.

vernacular The mother tongue, or
spoken language of the people. Permission for its wider use in the liturgy is granted by the Constitution
on the Sacred Liturgy prepared by
Vatican Council II: "But since the
use of the mother tongue, whether in
the Mass, the administration of the
sacraments, or other parts of the liturgy, frequently may be of great advantage to the people, the limits of
its employment may be extended."

Greek was the principal vernacular
language of Christian worship in the
first two centuries. Latin liturgy
began in North Africa near the close
of the 2nd century. The transition
from Greek to Latin in Roman Rites
took place between the 3rd and 9th
centuries. Latin too was a vernacular
language at that time.

Veronica's Veil The towel which
tradition says was used to wipe the
face of Christ on the way to Calvary
and His death. Upon it the face of
Christ was miraculously imprinted.
It is one of the major relics preserved
at St. Peter's Basilica in Rome. Very
little is known about the woman
called Veronica. She is sometimes
identified as the woman with the
issue of blood. In legend she cured
the Emperor Tiberius with the veil,
after which she presented it to Pope
St. Clement. There are several other
veils which are said to have miraculous images. One is in St. John
Lateran in Rome and another in
Alicante, Spain.

verse The smallest scriptural division of a chapter. The first such
division was made in 1551 in a
Greek New Testament. In 1555 the
method was applied to the Vulgate.
The system has great practicality for
references.

versicle (L. *versiculum,* a short verse)
Used as part of the responses in the
Divine Office. It is preceded by the
letter *V,* and usually taken from a
psalm.

versions of the Bible Various translations of the original text or other
texts of the Scriptures into the language of certain ethnic groups. The
purpose of translating the Scriptures
was to enable them to be understood
and read by all peoples. In the early
Church there were Greek, Aramaic,
Syriac, Coptic and other ancient ver-

588

sions. St. Jerome (who died in 420) was responsible for the Vulgate, a Latin version that became the standard one in the Church. Since then the Bible, or at least parts of it, has been translated into most of the large language families.

Very Reverend A title applied to certain grades of monsignors, rectors of seminaries, heads of colleges, the provincials of religious orders, etc. It is a title of honor for those lower than the rank of a bishop who hold a special position.

vesperale 1. A vesperal, a book containing the office and chant for Vespers. 2. *See* vespers cloth.

Vespers (L. vesper, evening) The sixth of the canonical hours of the Divine Office, the great evening assembly which with Lauds is the most solemn of the Liturgical hours. In choir Vespers is sung between 3 and 6 P.M. The hour usually consists of five psalms, their antiphons, a short lesson, a versicle and response, a hymn, the Magnificat and its antiphon, and the prayer of the day. Vespers is divided into First Vespers and Second Vespers. First Vespers of a major feast is said on the day before the feast. Second Vespers is the Vespers said on the day of the feast itself.

vespers cloth The cloth used to cover the altar cloth between ceremonies. A vesperale.

Vespers, Solemn Vespers sung with full ecclesiastical ritual. A priest, deacon and subdeacon preside in the sanctuary; cantors wear copes; incense is used; etc.

vessels, sacred *See* sacred vessels.

vestments (L. *vestimentum,* covering) Garments worn by clerics when performing sacred ceremonies. In the early Church no special garments were used but ceremonies were car-

ried out in the regular dress of the times. As the centuries passed they were retained because of their link with apostolic times and thus gradually became distinctive. After the number of vestments was fixed, embellishments and decorations were added and minor styling took place, such as the Gothic-style vestments. 1. *Latin Rite.* Vestments used at Mass include amice, alb, cincture, maniple, stole and chasuble; the deacon wears a dalmatic in place of the chasuble and the subdeacon, a tunicle. A bishop wears all of these plus sandals, buskins, gloves and a mitre. Other vestments are the cope, surplice and pallium. The humeral veil and the bishop's apron are not properly vestments. 2. *Eastern Rite.* Vestments of the Byzantine Rite correspond with those of the Latin Rite but have had their own development. Those worn by priest and deacon are the sticharion (alb). To this the deacon adds the orarion (stole). The priest wears in addition the epitrachelion (stole), embroidered cuffs called epimanika, the zone (cincture) and phelonion (chasuble). Both priest and deacon wear a head covering called an epimanikia. In place of the phelonion a bishop wears a sakkos; he adds the epigonation, the omophorion (pallium), and crown (mitre). Minor clerics wear a kamision (surplice).

viaticum (L. provision for a journey) Holy Eucharist when given in danger of death. Unlike Anointing of the Sick, viaticum may be received even when the person is in good health but is entering a dangerous circumstance (serious operation, a battle, etc.). No period of fasting is required. It is the last preparation for a happy death, and should not be neglected through fear of inconveniencing a priest or

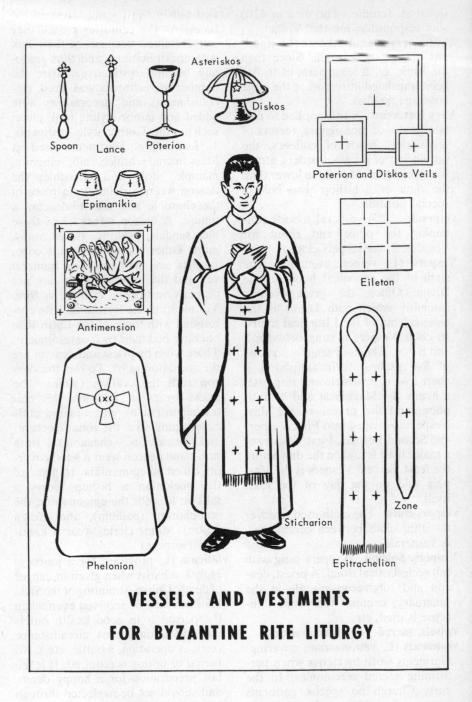

Asteriskos

Diskos

Spoon   Lance   Poterion

Epimanikia

Poterion and Diskos Veils

Eileton

Antimension

Phelonion

Sticharion

Epitrachelion

Zone

VESSELS AND VESTMENTS
FOR BYZANTINE RITE LITURGY

Pall

Paten

Purificator

Corporal

Chalice

Dalmatic

Amice

Stole

Ciborium

Burse

Cincture

Maniple

Veil

Amice

Chasuble

Alb

VESSELS AND VESTMENTS
FOR LATIN RITE LITURGY

alarming a sick person. The priest administers the sacrament with the words: "Receive, my brother (sister), this food for your journey, the body of our Lord Jesus Christ, that he may guard you from the wicked enemy and lead you into everlasting life. Amen."

vicar (L. *vicarius,* a deputy) A cleric who takes the place or acts as representative of another, who acts in the other's name and with his authority, according to the limitations of canon law. Thus the cardinal vicar of Rome represents the pope, as does a vicar apostolic. A vicar general is the first assistant to a superior general or bishop and acts when he is absent. A vicar capitular is elected by a chapter to administer a vacant diocese. A vicar forane represents the bishop in a deanery. A vicar parochial takes the place of a pastor. Among certain religious orders the vicar is the same as a subprior.

vicar apostolic A titular bishop who governs a territory called a vicariate apostolic as the representative of the Holy See. The territory is equivalent to a diocese but it is in a country or region where the ordinary hierarchy has not yet been established. Vicar apostolics come under the jurisdiction of the Congregation for the Propagation of the Faith.

vicar capitular A cleric elected by a cathedral chapter to govern a diocese during a vacancy. If there is no chapter, the Board of Consultors elects an administrator. The one elected is not to make innovations or to act prejudicially to the diocese but merely to provide administration until the new bishop is appointed.

vicar choral A title, seldom used, for an assistant choir director in a cathedral or collegiate church.

vicar forane A rural dean. A priest who has limited jurisdiction over a district in a diocese. He is usually an older and experienced priest who presides at clerical conferences, cares for sick priests, guards ecclesiastical property and protects the discipline of the clergy.

vicar general 1. The first assistant to a superior general. He fulfills the duties assigned by the superior general, takes his place in his absence, and in case of death governs until a new superior general is elected. 2. A priest deputed to assist the bishop in the administration of his diocese. His duties are specified in canon law. He takes precedence over all other clergy of the diocese. His office ends with that of the bishop.

Vicar of Christ The Holy Father, the representative of Christ on earth as spiritual head of the Church Christ founded and the visible head of the Mystical Body.

vicar patriarchal An office in the Eastern Catholic Church somewhat similar to a vicar apostolic. The cleric appointed represents the patriarch in a given area.

vicariate 1. The territory administered by a vicar apostolic, which is under the jurisdiction of the Congregation for the Propagation of the Faith and is divided into various missions. The trend in recent years is to erect fewer vicariates but to give a country an ordinary hierarchy. 2. The office and duties of a vicar.

Vicariate of Rome The diocese of Rome. The bishop is the pope, who delegates administration to a cardinal vicar general. The diocese is made up of the city of Rome and the adjoining suburban area.

vice (L. *vitium,* a defect) An evil habit that is the opposite of virtue and which leads to sin. It is the result of repeated sinful acts.

vice-chancellor The assistant to a chancellor of a diocese or university. In the former case appointment is made by the bishop.

Vicegerent of God The Vicar of Rome, the Holy Father, the pope.

victim (L. *victima,* an animal for sacrifice) That which is offered for sacrifice and immolation. In the Sacrifice of Calvary, Christ was the divine victim, immolating Himself for the sins of the whole human race.

Victimae Paschali (L. Paschal Victim) The Sequence of the Mass of Easter Sunday. It takes its name from the first two words.

Vidi Aquam (L. I saw water) The name given to the antiphon to Ps. 117 which replaces the Asperges during paschal time. It is sung before High Mass while the celebrant sprinkles the people with Holy water. It takes its name from the first two words.

Vietnam The Catholic Church in Vietnam has gone through many trials. Mission work began there in 1615 and by 1629 the first persecution began. In 1658 a new persecution started and missioners were expelled. In 1665, 45 Vietnamese Christians were put to death. That persecution subsided, only for another one to begin in 1698. In 1719 there were 700 churches destroyed and 9 Vietnamese and 2 foreign Jesuits were martyred. In 1737, four Jesuits were beheaded; in 1745, two Dominicans. In 1798, two Vietnamese priests were put to death, Peace came to the Church in 1802 but lasted only until 1833. In the next 30 years, at least 115 priests and 90,000 Christians were put to death; among the victims was the young French priest, Blessed Theophane Venard who died in 1861 by beheading. French occupation of the peninsula brought peace. Then at the end of World War II the Communists began their attacks. In 1947, the Communists (Viet-Minh) put 29 Catholics to death. In 1954, more than 650,000 Catholic refugees fled North Vietnam, completely reversing the proportion of Catholics in the two areas. The apostolic delegation in the north was forcibly closed in 1959 and the following year the remaining foreign missioners were expelled. Since that time the Church in the north has been in chains. In the south, Catholics are subjected to raids by the Communists and there is persecution by Buddhists. There are estimated to be 700,000 Catholics left in the north while South Vietnam has 1.3 million Catholics or 9 per cent of the population.

vigil (L. *vigilia,* a watching) A day preceding certain feasts or solemnities, e.g., Christmas Vigil, Easter Vigil. It is a day of preparation for the feast that follows and sometimes has a penitential character.

vigil light A popular name for the small votive candles burned before a shrine or statue by the faithful. They symbolize the light of prayer.

vimpa The veil worn over the shoulders by the mitre bearer (by which he holds the mitre) at pontifical ceremonies.

Vincentians, the (Congregation of the Mission) A congregation of secular priests with religious vows, founded in Paris in 1625 by St. Vincent de Paul. Born of a poor peasant family, Vincent was ordained in 1600 and devoted himself to the work of a parish priest. He was appointed tutor to the children of the noble family of

Gondi, where he also gave missions to the peasants on the family estates At the urging of Madame Gondi, and with a gift from the Gondis, he founded a society of priests to carry on this mission work. He also founded a seminary at St. Lazare to train them, and established retreats for laymen as a further work for his society to perpetuate. At the outbreak of the Revolution Vincent and his congregation directed 53 major seminaries and 9 minor seminaries. Many of the priests were killed or imprisoned, but after the Revolution growth began again; at his death the congregation numbered 500 priests in France, Italy, Poland and on the foreign missions. Today they are widely spread throughout the world as missioners, conducting seminaries, schools, colleges and universities, and engaged in every kind of parish work. They came to the United States in 1867 and now have almost 900 priests working in all parts of the country.

vine A symbol used by Christ to describe the intimate relation between Himself and Christians (Jn. 15).

violation 1. *Of a church or sacred place*. This type of violation is called local sacrilege. It can be committed in three ways: by defilement of a sacred place, by a grave theft in a sacred place, by violating the immunity of a place. 2. *Personal sacrilege*. This violation is fourfold: violating the *privilegium canonis* (laying violent hands on a cleric or religious), violating the *privilegium fori* (unlawful citation of clerics before a civil court), violating the privilege of personal immunity (exemption from military service), violating the public vow of chastity. 3. *Of an enclosure*. The violation of a papal enclosure, i.e., the cloister in the houses of religious with solemn vows, incurs excommunication simply reserved to the Holy See. This violation is committed by men entering the enclosure of nuns, women entering the enclosure of men, anyone admitting such a person into the enclosure or a nun who leaves her enclosure without permission. 4. *Of the seal of confession*. The obligation of the seal of confession is so strict that no one can dispense from it. Direct violation of the seal is a most grave sin and it incurs excommunication most specially reserved to the Holy See. 5. *Of secrets*. Natural and entrusted secrets bind under grave sin; promised secrets ordinarily bind under venial sin. Violation of a secret, therefore, causes guilt.

violence An extrinsic force or motion brought to bear upon an individual against his will by an external agent. It is one of the strongest obstacles against freedom of the will. In the use of force or violence, the object is guilty in respect to the resulting action in proportion to his failure to resist.

violet (L. *violaceus*) The liturgical color that signifies penance; the color more often is called purple.

Virgin Birth The dogma that Jesus Christ, the Son of God, was born of the Virgin Mary and of no natural father; that she did not lose her virginity, either spiritual or physical. It is also Catholic teaching that Mary remained a virgin all her life. This dogma of the Virgin Birth should not be confused with the dogma of the Immaculate Conception (*q.v.*).

virgin, consecration of a A rite found in the *Pontificale Romanum,* now used only by Carthusian nuns.

Virgin Mary *See* Blessed Virgin.

Virginia The 10th of the original 13 states, it is 36th in area and 14th in

population. It was named by Sir
Walter Raleigh for Elizabeth I, the
Virgin Queen. A confederacy of
Algonquin tribes inhabited the area
when the Spanish arrived in 1526 and
founded a colony in the place where
Jamestown would be founded years
later. Two Dominican Friars were in
the group and no doubt offered Mass
there—the first in Virginia. Eight
Jesuits were martyred by Indians in
the vicinity in 1571. The English settlers in Raleigh's company came to
Roanoke Island in 1585, abandoning
it soon afterward. The first permanent English settlement was at Jamestown in 1607 with Captain John
Smith. The English colonial laws prohibited Catholics; however, a small
group settled in Virginia in 1647 and
were visited by priests from Maryland. The Church of England was established by the state and supported
by taxes. James II granted freedom
of worship in 1687, but Catholics
were not finally emancipated until
1776. The Revolution was largely
brewed in Virginia; the Declaration
of Independence was composed there
by Thomas Jefferson; Virginian
George Washington led the armies
and was made the first President of
the new Union. Father John Dubois
came to Virginia in 1791 and offered
the first Mass in the State Capitol.
Jesuits built the first parish, named
St. Mary's, at Alexandria in 1795.
The first pastor of Richmond was
Father Timothy O'Brien, who arrived in 1834 and built St. Peter's
Church which was to become the
cathedral in later years. The first
bishop was Most Rev. Patrick Kelly.
In the mid-19th century Jesuits
opened the first Catholic school, and
Mother Seton's Sisters of Charity
established an academy and orphanage in Richmond. Numerous other religious congregations staffed schools
and institutions. Churches were left
in ruins and thousands of Catholics
died in the Civil War; Sisters of Charity and of Mercy nursed the wounded.
However the Church and the state
together made a recovery from the
ravages of war. Catholics are however a small minority in Virginia—6
per cent in a population of 4 million.

virginity The state of a person who
has a firm resolution of abstaining
from all venereal pleasure and who
has never been a partner to the sexual
act. Most definitions of virginity refer
to bodily integrity but this is inaccurate because bodily integrity is only
accidental to virginity. A person can
lose bodily integrity through attack
or surgery. The excellence of virginity is praised in Scripture and by the
Fathers. Objections that virginity is
harmful to health have no foundation.

virtue (L. *virtus,* manliness) That
which confers goodness on its owner
and makes his acts good. It is a habit
that operates toward goodness. The
virtuous man is moved to good acts
by right reason aided by grace. Virtues are distinguished by their origin,
which is either acquired (natural) or
infused (supernatural); and by their
object, which is intellectual, moral or
theological.

virtue, heroic Virtue practiced to an
extraordinary degree in motive and
perseverance. Benedict XIV in his
treatise on beatification and canonization defined heroic virtue as the
performance of "virtuous actions
with uncommon promptitude, ease
and pleasure, from supernatural motives and without human reasoning,
with self-abnegation and full control
over natural inclinations." Heroic
virtue must be proved for beatification and canonization.

virtue, infused Those virtues which God infuses into the soul together with sanctifying grace. The Council of Vienne has affirmed that even baptized infants possess the infused virtues. Infused virtues have three special properties: 1. they increase within themselves as often as sanctifying grace increases; 2. all of them except faith and hope are lost by mortal sin; 3. they can be diminished only indirectly.

virtue, moral A habit that perfects the powers of a person in order to enable him to use correctly and well the means to his supernatural end. The chief moral virtues are prudence, justice, religion, obedience, fortitude, temperance, chastity, humility and meekness.

virtue, natural That good habit acquired through the frequent repetition of a good act that renders easy the performance of morally good actions. Thus nonbaptized persons can acquire and gradually perfect the moral virtues of prudence, justice, fortitude and temperance. The help given in acquiring these virtues comes from God's natural concurrence.

Virtues Those angels who compose the second choir of the second or intermediate order of angels. They are mentioned in Eph. 1:21 and 1 Pt. 3:22.

virtues, intellectual Those good habits that perfect man in his understanding of truth; they dispose the intellect for its rightful operations in reference to its object. They are five in number: understanding, wisdom, knowledge, prudence and art (the virtue of the practical intelligence).

virtues, supernatural Those virtues infused in the soul by God. They are principles of action which God in-grafts in every baptized person that they may perform in the soul the function of supernatural faculties and thus enable their possessor to perform supernatural acts. They are made up of the theological virtues and the infused moral virtues.

virtues, theological Those virtues which have God as their immediate object and which are bestowed by God alone. They are three: faith, hope and charity.

vis et metus (L. force and fear) A canonical term referring to the grave fear caused by extrinsic force or violence used by one person to force another into matrimony. It is a diriment impediment to marriage and one of the most frequently used as grounds for seeking an annulment.

visibility of the Church The teaching of the Church that by her essence she is visible both formally and materially. Thus men can see those things that make up the Church such as ministers, liturgy, the pope, etc., but they can also see and know that these ministers and this liturgy are the very Church of Christ. This does not mean that there is not an invisible element also present in the Church which is manifested through the visible element. It is false to affirm that there are two Churches, one visible and one invisible, or that there is only one invisible Church.

vision A supernatural manifestation that is perceived by the eyes or in the imagination or in the intellect. The three kinds are not mutually exclusive but often coalesce. Ascetical writers counsel that visions should not be sought after because of the possibility of deception. They may be counterfeited by the Devil or be the result of a psychosis or hysteria.

visit ad limina *See* ad limina visit.

visitation 1. *Canonical.* The visit of

a religious superior who visits persons and places under his jurisdiction in order to inquire into matters of faith and morals, ensure Church discipline or for some other special purpose. Canon law lays down norms for such visits. 2. *Episcopal.* A bishop is required to visit a part of his diocese each year so that he will complete the whole diocese within five years. If legitimately impeded, he may send his vicar general or another delegate.

Visitation of the Blessed Virgin The journey Mary made to visit her cousin Elizabeth after the Angel Gabriel had told Mary she was to be the mother of God. The liturgy commemorates this feast on July 2. The office for the feast was composed by Cardinal Adam Easton, an Englishman, and its liturgy was celebrated for the first time in the Roman Calendar of Feasts in 1389, during the pontificate of Boniface IX. Elizabeth and her husband Zachary lived in Ain-Karim. According to tradition, to this village, four miles west of Jerusalem, Mary came from Nazareth to tell Elizabeth the good news. When Mary greeted Elizabeth, the Scriptures tell us that Elizabeth's unborn son, John the Baptist, leaped for joy in his mother's womb. Mary responded to Elizabeth's greeting with her own praise for God. This is enshrined in the inspiring prayer, the Magnificat.

Visitation Nuns A contemplative order founded in France in 1610 by St. Jane de Chantal under the inspiration of St. Francis de Sales. It was established in the United States in Washington, D.C., in 1799. Members practice perpetual adoration. Solemn vows are taken. There are 21 monasteries in the United States and 2 in Canada, divided between two federations. Each monastery is inde-

pendent and under the jurisdiction of the local ordinary.

Visitor Apostolic An ecclesiastic appointed by the pope to make a visitation of a diocese or religious order; also the bishop appointed to make the episcopal visitation of the diocese of Rome.

vitandus (vee-tahn'dus, L. *vitare,* to avoid) The name given to an excommunicated person who is to be specially shunned by the faithful. To be a *vitandus* one must be excommunicated expressly as such by name by the Holy See. A *vitandus* cannot be buried in consecrated ground.

vivisection The dissection of a living animal for the scientific purpose of advancing knowledge. Since God has given man animals for his use, vivisection is not immoral in itself as long as the animal is not tortured for the sake of torture and all unnecessary cruelty is avoided. Such experiments greatly advance medical knowledge and have been the means of saving many lives. Scientific research would be gravely handicapped if such experiments were halted.

vocation (L. *vocare,* to call) 1. *In a general sense,* the calling of every man to a particular state and task in life. Everything that happens to a person, sin excepted, is in accordance with the will of God. Therefore, every man has a vocation to both a particular state and task in life, and each person should order his life to carrying out that design. This vocation may be manifested in a particular way but it is ordinarily expressed in the inclinations of an individual which come from temperament, education, particular circumstances, etc. 2. *In a specific sense,* the word is used to mean a particular calling to a priestly or religious life. It is an obvious rule that God knows the needs of His

Church and that He inspires a sufficient number of young people to fill those needs. The problem is for each person to recognize the signs of a vocation. These signs are not spectacular showers of graces, lights, whispers, but usually arise from natural causes. If a person has good morals, sufficient intelligence, generosity and a desire to do God's will, the usual prerequisites for a vocation are present. God's call to a soul is ordinarily through a person's inclinations. A vocation to the priesthood is not clearly revealed until the call by the bishop at the time of ordination. St. Thomas Aquinas says, "It is better to go into religion with a view of testing oneself than not to go in at all." It is the purpose of seminaries, postulancies and novitiates to provide this period for testing one's vocation.

voluntary act That which proceeds from an internal source of action accompanied by knowledge of the end sought (St. Thomas). It is not to be confused with an act which is forced, since that act proceeds from an external source of action. Natural acts (sleeping, breathing) and spontaneous acts are not voluntary acts because knowledge is not required for them; in a voluntary act the will acts freely with knowledge of its end.

voodoo (Creole, Fr. *vaudoux,* a Negro sorcerer) A term applied to superstitious practices found in Haiti, Brazil and other areas. It is related to African fetishism. Voodoo is often connected with devil worship, and practitioners frequently go into self-imposed trances. Those who practice voodoo are not allowed to receive the sacraments. In Haiti, special efforts are made to prevent voodoo worshipers from demeaning Catholic practices.

votive Mass 1. A Mass offered for a special intention, not according to the feast prescribed in the ordo (*q.v.*). 2. Those Masses ordered by the ordo which are strictly called votive Masses, e.g., of the Blessed Virgin on Saturday. 3. Masses ordered by the bishop for a special reason, e.g., the Mass for Peace, For the Election of a Bishop, etc. 4. Those said at the discretion of a celebrant, e.g., daily Mass for the Dead.

votive offerings Something offered to God or a saint because of a vow, promise or act of gratitude.

votive office An office that differs from the assigned office of the day. They were formerly granted as a personal privilege but were abolished in 1911. The only votive office that exists today is that of the Blessed Virgin on Saturday.

vow A voluntary promise made to God. Its primary purpose is God's honor and glory. The spiritual perfection of the individual is its secondary goal.

vows, private A promise made to God by a person to perform an action pleasing to Him. This promise is made without an intermediary official of the Church.

vows, public Those vows made with the authority and intervention of the Church. They are divided into solemn and simple vows. Solemn vows are taken in religious orders after a period of simple vows, and by subdeacons of the Latin Rite as regards the vow of chastity. St. Thomas Aquinas says the essence of solemn vows consists in a certain spiritual consecration and surrender by the person taking the vows, and which the Church officially accepts as the representative of God. Simple vows are solely the spiritual surrender of the individual.

vows of religion Public promises

598

made to God to live a life according to the evangelical counsels of poverty, chastity and obedience. These promises are accepted in the name of the Church by a lawful superior. These vows are made at a public or private ceremony according to the rules of the order.

Vulgate, the   The official Latin translation of the Bible which was prepared almost entirely by St. Jerome from 382 to about A.D. 405. In translating the Psalter, Jerome borrowed heavily from Origen. Wisdom, Ec-clesiasticus, Baruch and the two books of the Machabees were taken directly by Jerome from old Latin texts. The rest of the Bible is his translation from the existing Hebrew, Aramaic or Greek manuscripts. The Council of Trent declared the Vulgate to be "authentic in public readings, disputations, preachings and the original texts and contains no exposition" because it conforms to the original text and contains no errors in faith or morals.

W

wafer bread A term used in England for altar bread. This is the thin, flat bread used in the Eucharistic Liturgy of the Latin, Armenian, Maronite and Malabarese Rites of the Catholic Church.

wake (AS. *wacan,* to awake) To remain awake and on watch with a deceased person. Christian practice would call for simpler funeral customs than are now in use. The practices of dressing the body and restoring it to look alive are not in Christian tradition. Viewing the body is a throwback to a medieval custom of proving that "the king is dead." A Christian funeral should be a symbol of the soul's conquest of death and its departure for the New Jerusalem and the Father. A suggested Christian funeral service begins on the night before burial. The body in a closed casket is taken in procession to the Church where it is met at the door by a priest. It is placed before the altar in the usual manner. A Bible Vigil based on 1 Cor. 15:51-57, Ps. 90, Jn. 6:37-40, Ps. 121 and Ps. 129 follows, interspersed with two homilies and a prayer. The service closes with the recitation of the Apostles' Creed. Afterward, friends visit with the family of the deceased in the Christian atmosphere of the church.

The next morning Requiem Mass is celebrated, followed by the absolutions, a procession to the cemetery (where possible) and the burial. At no time is the coffin opened, and the body is wrapped simply in a burial sheet.

war, the Church's attitude toward A just war must be waged according to international and natural law. The reason must be a grave one: i.e., to repel an invasion or to protect a serious right violated or in defense of the just rights of others. It must be waged only as a last resort after all peaceful means have failed. Wars of aggression, to gain the territory of others, are unjust. The Church lays down repeated blueprints for peace and warns of the horrors of war. ". . . the arms race should cease; the stockpiles . . . reduced equally and simultaneously . . . nuclear weapons banned . . . a general agreement about progressive disarmament and an effective method of control . . . peace will be but an empty-sounding word unless it is founded on truth, built according to justice, vivified and integrated by charity, and put into practice in freedom" (Pope John XXIII, *Pacem in Terris*). The problem of war can only be finally solved by the true conversion of the world to Christ. It is historically evident that so-called Christian nations have waged unjust wars, but those who did so were not truly converted. It is not only the pagan lands who have yet to receive the Gospel and come into the Church. Thousands, millions, who live surrounded by a traditional Christianity have never really heard the Good News in its entirety and dynamic immediacy. The end of war will be either universal slavery and death or a universal turning to God in sincerity.

washing of feet In eastern countries in ancient days it was customary to wash the dust of the road from the feet of a guest. Christ washed His Apostles' feet after the Last Supper. In imitation of this, the custom exists in many dioceses and religious houses for the bishop or superior to wash the feet of a subject on Holy Thursday in order to show humility and charity.

washing of hands A priest washes his fingers before vesting for Mass. He washes his fingers after the Offertory in preparation for the Consecration. He purifies his fingers after the Communion to remove any particles of the Sacred Host which might be clinging to them. Finally, he washes his fingers again after unvesting.

Washington The 42nd state admitted to the Union, it is 20th in area and 23rd in population. It was named for the first President of the United States. Yakimas, Spokanes, Flatheads, Coeur d'Alenes and other tribes of Indians hunted and fished over the area in early days. The Spaniards, Perez and Heceta, made explorations in 1774 and 1775. Captain Cook and Vancouver (1778–1792) made observations along the coast. About the same time Captain Gray from Boston sailed a few miles up the Columbia River and was impressed by the beauty and fertility of the land. Lewis and Clark led the way for other overland expeditions (1805–1806), and fur traders David Thompson for Britain and John Jacob Astor for the United States built up their trading posts and carried on a brisk business. In the War of 1812 the Americans were ousted, the forts taken by the British. The boundary dispute was settled in 1846, placing Washington (then part of Oregon Territory) in American hands. Washington became a state in 1889. In the meantime Seattle, Tacoma and Spokane were settled between 1851 and 1874. The discovery of gold and the building of the Northern Pacific Railway brought in a tide of immigration after 1870. Fathers Blanchet and Demers were sent from Quebec in 1838 to care for the pioneers in the Northwest. Fathers De Smet and Nobili, Jesuits, came to work among the Indians in the '40's, and were later joined by more Jesuits in a fruitful apostolate. Sisters of Notre Dame de Namur came to serve the pioneers as did Sisters of Charity from Halifax. In 1846 Most Rev. Augustin Blanchet was made Bishop of Walla Walla, a see transferred to Nesqually in 1850, and to Seattle in 1907. In the late 19th century the Jesuits consolidated their work among the Indians and founded Gonzaga University. The Benedictines began St. Martin's College, later to be part of St. Martin's Abbey. Many other religious orders of men and women labored in the area. In 1913 the Diocese of Spokane was established. In 1951 Seattle was raised to the rank of Archdiocese and the Diocese of Yakima was created. Catholics today are approaching 400 thousand in a population of almost 3 million.

water A symbol of purity and cleansing. Water has many uses in the Church. 1. In the Eucharistic Liturgy, a few drops of water are mixed with wine in the chalice and consecrated into the Blood of Christ. The water symbolizes the union of Christ with His Church and the water that came from the side of Christ at the Crucifixion. Water is also used during Mass to purify the fingers of the celebrant and to purify the chalice. 2. Natural water is necessary for Baptism. 3. Holy water (*q.v.*) is used in fonts at church doors, for blessings and in homes. 4. Special lustral water is used in the consecration of a church. 5. In the ceremony of blessing of bells, a specially blessed water is used for washing them.

water of consecration *See* Gregorian water.

water, the blessing of Ordinary water sanctified by the blessing of the Church. The blessing consists of exorcisms of water and salt. The salt is added to the water three times in the form of a cross to signify that this water is now preserved from corruption.

wax The candles used in the Church's liturgical worship must be made partly of beeswax. This is just one more instance where the Church demonstrates its respect for the natural and gives it new meaning.

Way of the Cross A devotion that originated in the 14th century and was made popular by the Franciscan Fathers. It consists of meditating successively before 14 Stations of the Cross on the Passion of Christ. The Stations are crosses usually affixed to the walls of a church, although they may be erected outdoors, each representing a particular stage in the Passion of Christ. The common custom is to include with each Station a picture, statuary or some device as an aid to devotion. The Stations must be lawfully erected and blessed by one having authority to do so if the indulgences are to be gained. To gain the indulgences one need not say any prayers but merely go from Station to Station meditating briefly at each on the Passion. If one is unable to move about because of crowds or because the Stations are being performed publicly, it suffices merely to face each Station.

wealth Material possessions, resources, property; that which has money value or economic usefulness. The Christian teaching on wealth approves of private ownership, but with the reservation that man is a steward in charge of his property under God. The right of property is not an end in itself but a means. God created the wealth of the world for the use of all men. This is the end, and the right of property merely guarantees that use. No people have the right to refuse to use natural wealth for the good of all. Pope Pius XII had this in mind when he declared: "Within the limits of a new order founded on moral principles there is no place for that cold and calculating egoism which tends to hoard economic resources and materials destined for the use of all, to such an extent that the nations less favored by nature are not permitted access to them." What applies to nations applies also to individuals. Wealth is to be shared with the poor by alms, by supporting welfare movements, by conducting enterprises that provide jobs with good conditions and ample pay, and in many other ways, bearing in mind that each one is his brother's keeper.

Week, Holy The week immediately preceding Easter. It is the most sublime and solemn week in the Church's liturgy, during which the theme of the cross and the theme of the Resurrection are inseparable. It begins with Palm Sunday when Christ is honored as King. On Holy Thursday the Church commemorates the institution of the Eucharist. Good Friday is devoted to the solemn exaltation of the cross. On Holy Saturday begin the Easter solemnities.

West Indies The island group sometimes called the Antilles, extending between the coasts of Florida and Venezuela, and enclosed by the Caribbean Sea. There are several natural divisions: 1. the Bahamas; 2. the Greater Antilles comprising Cuba, Jamaica, Haiti, the Dominican Republic and Puerto Rico; 3. the Lesser Antilles, made up of the Leeward Islands, the Windward Islands, Trinidad, Tobago, the Barbados, the Dutch Islands and the Venezuelan Islands. Among these are various colonial possessions: the British West Indies, the Dutch West Indies, the French West Indies and the American Virgin Islands. Puerto Rico, an American commonwealth, is self-governing. Margarita and several smaller islands are part of Venezuela. Haiti and the Dominican Republic (both on the island of Hispaniola) are independent, as are Jamaica, Trinidad and Tobago. Cuba after revolting against Spanish rule spent a period of independence and relative prosperity until 1959, when with the encouragement of the United States, Fidel Castro carried out a revolution against a previous dictator, Fulgencio Batista. Once safely in power, Castro showed himself to be a virulent Communist dictator in league with the Soviet Union and Red China. He set up a Marxist economy, resulting in stagnation of industry and agriculture and widespread privation among the people. The West Indies were the first part of the New World discovered by Columbus. Though he died in Spain, his remains, at his own request, rest in a tomb in the cathedral in Santo Domingo on the island of Hispaniola, which he first sighted in 1492. The Spanish missioners left the Church established on the islands. The Dutch West Indies (Netherlands Antilles) number Catholics at almost 151,000, more than 75 per cent of the population. There are two dioceses with numerous schools and Catholic institutions. The French West Indies (Martinique, Guadeloupe and dependencies) have 568,000 Catholics, about 97 per cent of the total. The British West Indies including Trinidad and Tobago, former colonies now independent, and the colonies in the Windward and Leeward Islands, taken all together contain 1 archdiocese and 3 dioceses, with more than 500,000 Catholics, about one-third of the population. Cuba with 2 archdioceses and 4 dioceses, has 6 million Catholics, 84 per cent of the population. The Dominican Republic has 1 archdiocese and 3 dioceses, and over 3 million Catholics, 95 per cent of the population. Haiti has 1 archdiocese and 4 dioceses, but the Church is under government restriction despite the fact that Catholics number nearly 3 million, 79 per cent of the population. In the Virgin Islands there are about 13,000 Catholics, one-third of the population. In Puerto Rico there are 1 archdiocese and 2 dioceses with over 2 million Catholics, 82 per cent of the population.

West Virginia The 35th state admitted to the Union, it is 41st in size and 30th in population. Its name derives from Virginia (*q.v.*). It was a hunting ground for some Indian tribes but was too rugged for homes, even for the Red Man. Lieut. Gov. Spotswood of Virginia first explored the area in 1716, and Morgan made the first settlement in 1726 at Bunker Hill. Germans colonized Sheperdstown about 1750; George Washington surveyed parts of the future state. The Indians sold the area to England for 400 pounds. After the French and Indian War the region began to fill with pioneers, and they led in the fight for independence during the Revolution. In 1863 West Virginia was admitted to the Union. The few Catholics in the area had not been allowed religious freedom until after the Revolution, and priests from Maryland had visited them at intervals, offering Mass in private homes. The first church was built in 1821 at Wheeling, and Father Francis Rolf was made pastor by the Archbishop of Baltimore. The Bishop of Richmond sent in priests and Sisters to do missionary work and staff schools and hospitals after 1846. Wheeling was made a diocese in 1850, Bishop Whelan being transferred there from Richmond. He and succeeding bishops brought in religious congregations of men and women for parish work and for educational and charitable institutions. Priests were always too few, particularly to care for the foreign-language groups who came to work in the mining districts. Catholics today number less than 10 per cent in a population of almost 2 million.

Western Church, the All those parts of the Church which are not only under the jurisdiction of the pope as pope, but also under his jurisdiction as patriarch of the West; that is, today, all Catholics whatever, except those of any Eastern rite.

white A liturgical color that symbolizes purity, innocence and victory. It is the color of the vestments worn on all feasts of the Holy Trinity, of the joyful and glorious mysteries of Our Lord, of Our Lady, of angels, and of saints who were not martyrs.

white friar A name sometimes applied to a Carmelite because of the white habit he wears.

White Fathers Popular title given to members of the Society of Missionaries of Africa because of their white habit. The society was founded in 1868 by Cardinal Lavigerie for the conversion of the Muslims and animists of Africa. The first foundation was made in the United States in 1942. The society has earned an enviable reputation for the sacrifices of its members and the great variety of their mission activities in Africa.

White Sisters Popular title given to the Missionary Sisters of Our Lady of Africa. The society was founded in 1869 to assist the White Fathers in the conversion of Africa. The first American foundation was made in 1929.

Whitsunday (White Sunday) British name for the Feast of Pentecost. It is so called because of the baptismal garments worn in former times on this day.

widow (L. *viduus,* bereft) A woman whose husband is dead and who has not remarried. Widows have always been the solicitous concern of the Church since its foundation (Acts 6:1). The Council of Trent declared that widowhood is more commendable than remarriage; however, this must be determined in each individual case.

wife The wife is the companion to

her husband, subject to him, but both freely exchange with each other the love and respect of the marriage state. As an individual she is equal to her husband in the rights and duties of marital intercourse. A wife has the right of support from her husband for herself and for their children. Love and care for husband and children are her responsibilities.

will (AS. *willa,* will)   The faculty or power which enables a person to make a free choice. Its object is the good apprehended by the intellect. The choice of the will cannot be constrained from without or regulated from within.

will and testament   Every Catholic adult should early draw up a will because to die without one is always troublesome, and may even be tragic for those who survive. If there is no will, property comes under the jurisdiction of the courts, and must be divided according to the law. The first obligation in making a will is to care for family and dependents; after that one has an obligation to remember parish, diocese and world needs of the Church. Just as every Catholic has an obligation to make a will, so he has the duty to include bequests for charity.

will, divine   In the Old Testament, it is thought of as God's counsel, good pleasure, favor or desire. In the New Testament, it is God's eternal plan and purpose based on His deliberation. God's will is absolute, i.e., unconditioned by anything outside Himself; it is not distinct from His divine nature but is in complete harmony with His holiness, righteousness, goodness and truth.

wimple (AS. *wimpel*)   A cloth covering, formerly worn by women over the head and around the neck, which exists today as part of the habit of many nuns.

Winding Sheet   *See* Shroud, Holy.

wine, altar (L. *vinum*)   The fermented juice of the grape that is used in the celebration of Mass and which is changed by the words of consecration into the Blood of Christ. The wine must be pure grape wine and it cannot be sour or otherwise unfit. It is also used at the end of Mass in the purifications.

Wisconsin (Chippewa, grassy place)   The 30th state admitted to the Union, it is 26th in size and 15th in population. The numerous tribes of Indians who inhabited the area were nearly exterminated in the Black Hawk War (1832). Jean Nicolet, French explorer who came to Canada with Champlain, landed at Green Bay in 1634. Explorers Radisson and Groseiliers built a log cabin—the first house of white men—in the state. Father Menard, S.J., started missionary work among the Hurons and was killed by Sioux Indians near Crystal Falls in 1661. Jesuit Father Alouez built the first permanent mission in 1665, and by 1671 the Jesuits were carrying on mission work among twenty tribes. Two Jesuit Brothers were martyred, Brother Jean Guerin by the Foxes in 1672 and Brother Louis Le Boeme in 1687 by Winnebagos. Father Marquette and Louis Joliet, besides other explorers, traversed the region, and a fort was built on Lake Pepin to protect the Canadian fur traders in 1680. After the Seven Years' War Wisconsin became English territory. It was turned over to the United States at the Treaty of Paris in 1783; however, the French Jesuits continued their work among both French settlers and Indians. After 1836 immigrants from Europe and from the eastern United States began to arrive. Priests who came with the European immigrants, refugees from religious and political harassment, cared for the settlers. One famous pioneer priest was Father Mazzuchelli, an architect, who built numerous churches during his 33 years in Wisconsin and established over 30 parishes with schools. The first Catholic Church in Milwaukee was put up by Father Kelly, who came in from Detroit to do mission work. In 1842 the Territory of Wisconsin had 6 priests. Milwaukee Diocese was erected in 1843 with John Henni as first bishop. He built the Cathedral of St. John and established St. Francis Seminary, besides bringing in numerous orders of men and women to staff schools and institutions and to serve the growing population. After the railroads were begun in 1851, immigrants swarmed in; and after the Civil War Catholics became much more numerous. The Jesuits established Marquette University in 1864; schools, hospitals, institutions were multiplied. The Dioceses of Green Bay and La Crosse were erected in 1868; Milwaukee was raised to the rank of archdiocese in 1875; Superior was made a diocese in 1905, followed by Madison in 1946. Catholics today number about 1½ million in a population of 4 million.

wisdom 1. One of the gifts of the Holy Spirit which enables a person to judge rightly in all that pertains to life and conduct. Wisdom also leads to an appreciation of spiritual truths and a preference for divine rather than earthly things. 2. An attribute of God. 3. A name applied to God and to Christ.

Wisdom, Book of This Old Testament book was written in Greek about 100 B.C. by a member of the Jewish community in Alexandria, Egypt. The purpose of the author was to encourage his fellow Jews in time of severe persecution. He points out, speaking in the name of Solomon, how the wisdom of God has guided His people through their history.

witchcraft (AS. *wicce,* witch; *croeft,* craft) A form of black magic practiced through the help of the Devil and evil spirits. It includes the casting of spells, sorcery, enchantment, etc. Great care must be taken before labeling anyone a witch because serious abuses have taken place in this regard both in the United States and in England. However witchcraft does exist in primitive cultures, examples in the Western hemisphere being voodoo (*q.v.*) in Haiti and *macumbo* in Brazil. Witchcraft is gravely sinful both for the practitioners and the users because of cooperation with evil spirits and because its basic purpose is the harm of one's neighbor.

witness In canon law, a person legally competent to give evidence. The canons require a witness for the valid and licit performance of certain acts. Two are requisite for a valid marriage; two are needed for the abjuration of heresy; two or three are usually necessary to establish a fact before an ecclesiastical court, although an official of the Church is sufficient to prove an official act performed by him. Witnesses are also examined in the process of canonization.

woman As individuals, women are morally equal to men. A woman requires man for her social complement and vice versa; each has qualities lacking in the other. In the Christian community she is responsible for the feminine influence; in the family she is the companion of man and mother of children.

wonder-working Another name for the action of performing of a miracle.

Word A term used only by St. John to refer to Christ. It also frequently appears in its Greek form, *Logos*. John uses the term to signify Christ is of one nature with the Father and yet a separate Person. Besides the Gospel (1:1, 14), it also appears in 1 John 1:1, and Apoc. 19:13. St. Thomas describes the Word as a kind of intellectual emanation from the Father. The Word has a divine nature, yet is distinct from the Father. The Greek term means not only "the word" but also the thought expressed by the word. Christ is the thought of the Eternal Father.

Word of God That part of the Mass beginning with the Reading (Epistle) and extending through the Profession of Faith (Creed). The vernacular is permitted in public Masses in all parts except those prayers said secretly by the celebrant before the Gospel. *See* Liturgy of the Word.

work God gave man hands with which to work. It is natural for man to work, and only through work does man find the fulfillment of his person. Because of original sin and the lack of harmony between man and the world around him, work has become a burden. In Christ, work, with its necessary pain, takes on a redemptive value of re-establishing order in the temporal sphere.

workers, rights and duties Man has a natural right and duty to work. *Creative:* because of his dignity as a creature and of his being a child of God. *Redemptive:* because of his dignity through having been redeemed by Christ, as a member of the Mystical Body of Christ, and because of his mission of saving the world. 1. *Rights:* to a choice of work

according to his capabilities; to a living family wage; to form a union for his own protection and collective bargaining with management for job security, good working conditions, wage increases, income stability and to promote better labor-management relations; to expect the state through legislation to protect these basic rights. 2. *Duties:* to use work as a means of accomplishing his salvation; to provide necessities for himself and his family, and for the larger family of the Mystical Body, whenever possible; to perform an honest day's work for his pay; to respect the rights of his employer; to cooperate with fellow workers in forming unions for mutual benefits.

world 1. The universe. 2. A word used by spiritual writers as being in opposition to God and spiritual matters. The forces which draw man away from God are described as "the world, the flesh, and the devil" and in this sense the word refers to all those material allurements which tend to draw the soul away from God. Thus a person entering religion is said "to leave the world."

world Christianity The will of the Father is that all men be saved through and in Christ. Christ's mission is to gather together all men of all times and from all places through His Love. The Church, continuing the mission of Christ to unite all men, must become Christ incarnate, in every age and in all cultures and civilizations. World Christianity will be one of "unity and diversity," unity in essentials but respecting the external manifestations in the life of the Church in a specific culture and time.

worldliness The state of one whose main motivation comes from the world and not from God. It results from being guided by worldly maxims and fashions, accompanied by neglect of religious duties and spiritual needs. A worldly person shows more interest in the pursuits of this life than of the life to come.

worship (AS. *weorthscipe,* being of worth) 1. The state of being worthy of honor. 2. That act of divine worship offered to God alone and based on the recognition of His infinite perfections. We express this worship through posture and prayer. The supreme adoration given only to God is called *latria.* 3. The liturgy.

wreath, Advent It is a growing custom among Catholic families that on the Saturday evening before the first Sunday of Advent an evergreen wreath with a violet bow, and in which are set four candles, is blessed by the head of the house; one of the candles is lighted and appropriate Advent prayers are recited. Each week during Advent an additional candle is lighted until at the end all four are burning. The candles are lighted by the various members of the family. The Advent wreath is a symbol of preparation for Christmas. The evergreen circle symbolizes eternity, the four candles are a reminder of the weeks to prepare for Christmas and the violet ribbon keeps before the mind the spirit of penance that should exist during Advent.

Wyoming The 44th state admitted to the Union, it is ninth in area and 48th in population. It was named for Wyoming Valley, Pa., Algonquin for "Large Prairie Place." Twelve great tribes of Indians lived in the region, hunting and fishing, until the advent of the white man. Now only remnants of two tribes, the Shoshone and the Arapaho remain, living on a reservation in the Wind River country. John Colter, who went out with Lewis and Clark, left the expedition on the way home and went to live as a trapper in the wilderness. He discovered Yellowstone Park in 1807, and was considered a liar afterward when he described its wonders. In the 1840's and 1850's the California gold rush and the trek of settlers over the Oregon Trail brought many travelers through Wyoming territory, and the government built forts to discourage hostile Indians. After the telegraph came in 1861 and the Union Pacific Railroad in 1867, the settlers began drifting into Wyoming. Cheyenne and Laramie sprang up on the plains. Cattlemen found vast and rich grazing lands for their livestock. In 1890 Wyoming was admitted into the Union. Oil wells, mining and other industries combine to make Wyoming a thriving state. The Catholic history begins with Father De Smet, S.J., who offered the first Mass in the state in 1840. The first resident priest was Father William Kelly, who built the first church in Cheyenne in 1867. Sisters of Charity, of the Holy Child Jesus and of St. Dominic contributed to education and hospital work in early days, as did the Jesuits who worked on the Arapaho Indian Reservation. Cheyenne was made a diocese in 1887, with Bishop Maurice Burke in charge. He brought in several religious congregations to care for the children of white citizens and also for the Indian children. Catholics today are 15 per cent in a total population of less than one-half million.

X

Xaverian Brothers Popular name of the Congregation of the Brothers of St. Francis Xavier, an institute of laymen founded in Belgium in 1839. The congregation came to the United States in 1854 and today staffs many Catholic schools. The American Province has missions in Kenya and Uganda. Initials: C.F.X.

XP *See* chi rho.

Y

Yahweh (Heb.) The personal name by which the God of Israel identified Himself to His people, according to Ex. 3:14. Sometimes referred to as the *tetragrammaton* (a Greek expression meaning "four letters"), it is composed of four Hebrew consonants (*YHWH*). A form of the Hebrew verb "to be," the exact meaning of Yahweh is much disputed. Given the circumstances in which it was uttered, however, together with the causal implications of the verb form, there is very likely reference to the divine creative force, in which case the meaning would be "He causes to be" or "He brings into existence."

year, liturgical *See* liturgical cycle.

year of grace Another term to be used for a year of the Christian era, thus the year of grace 1965. It is used in place of Anno Domini (A.D.).

yellow Formerly a liturgical color, sometimes a substitute for white or cloth of gold. Occasionally still seen in France.

Yom Kippur *See* Day of Atonement.

Young Christian Students (YCS) An organization which parallels the Young Christian Workers. It aims to Christianize the school environment and to enlist Catholic students in apostolic movements. It is organized in colleges, universities and high schools. Headquarters: Chicago, Ill.

Young Christian Workers (YCW) Monsignor Joseph Cardijn established the Young Christian Workers (Jocists) in Belgium in 1925 as a specialized Catholic action movement. Its purpose is to train, serve and represent young workers, and to enable them to re-Christianize their own lives, their working and social environments, and their fellow workers. The basic units are parish groups of about 12 people between the ages of 18 and 30. Headquarters: 1655 West Jackson Boulevard, Chicago 12, Ill.

youth, impediment of A matrimonial impediment referring to the age required by Church law for a person to be able to contract marriage. The law was promulgated mainly for those countries where marriages are performed at an early age. Under the new code, boys cannot validly marry before their 16th year and girls before their 14th year. The law attempts to guarantee that the party entering into marriage is old enough to understand and to fulfill the obligations attached to this state.

Yugoslavia The modern history of the Church in Yugoslavia has been one of tension. Following the Communist take-over after World War II, there were arrests and imprisonment of Church officials. In 1959 the direct pressures of the government began to lessen and all the Yugoslavian bishops were allowed to attend Vatican Council II. The Yugo-slavian population is about 20 million. Catholics form 30 per cent of the population and Orthodox about 38 per cent. There are also 2 million followers of Islam.

yule (AS. *geol*)   Christmas or Christmastide.

Z

Zacharia, Book of (Heb. God has remembered) A prophetic book of the Old Testament, part of which was written by the prophet Zacharia whose call dates to about 520 B.C. Because the book, especially the last chapters, speaks of the Messianic age, it is frequently used in the Passion accounts.

Zachary, Canticle of Another name for the Benedictus, the canticle sung by Zachary, at the circumcision of his son, John the Baptist.

zeal (Gr. *zeo,* to boil) Love of God in action.

Zebedee (Heb. *zebed,* gift) The husband of Salome and father of the Apostles James the Greater and John. He was a fisherman on Lake Genesareth, probably well-to-do.

Zecharias Zacharia (*q.v.*).

Zephania Hebrew name for the prophet Sophonia (*q.v.*).

zimarra (It.) The black house cassock worn by prelates. It has purple buttons and piping.

Zion Another name for Israel, the Jewish people. Sion (*q.v.*).

zone A narrow cloth belt worn by the celebrant of the Mass in the Byzantine Rite. It is made from the same cloth as the *epitrachelion* (stole). It corresponds to the cincture of the Roman Rite.

Zoroaster (*also* **Zarathustra**) Founder of an ancient Persian religion about 600 B.C., which spread under the conquests and influence of Cyrus and Darius, but during succeeding centuries died out, only to be revived in early Christian times by the inhabitants of the Mesopotamian regions and India. Shrouded in many superstitions and astrology, it pays homage to Mazda as supreme being. Its adherents today are known as Parsees, and are residents of India. The other followers were converted to Islam.

Zouaves, Pontifical A volunteer military group organized in Rome in 1860 to protect the Papal States. The corps, largely made up of French and Belgians, was disbanded in 1870.

zucchetto (zook-ket′toe, It. *zucca,* head) The small, round skullcap worn by ecclesiastics. The color varies according to rank: white for the pope, red for cardinals, purple for bishops, black for abbots. A small brown skullcap is worn by Capuchins.

612

APPENDICES

Appendix I
Catholic Abbreviations

A DICTIONARY OF ABBREVIATIONS
OF CATHOLIC AND RELIGIOUS TERMS

A

a	albus (white)
A	archpriest
AA	*Congregatio Presbyterorum ab Assumptione,* Assumptionist Fathers, Augustinians of the Assumption; *Congregatio Auxiliorum Apostolatus,* Sisters Auxiliaries of the Apostolate
AAS	*Acta Apostolicae Sedis,* Acts of the Apostolic See
Ab	*Abbas,* abbot
Abd	Abdias
abp	archbishop
abst	abstinence day
AC	*Ante Christum* (*natum*), before (the birth of) Christ
ACJ	*Ancillae Sacri Cordis Jesu,* Handmaids of the Sacred Heart of Jesus
ACTU	Association of Christian Trade Unionists
AD	*Anno Domini,* Year of Our Lord; *Servantes de l'Agneu Divin,* Handmaids of the Lamb of God, Sisters of the Lamb of God
ad lib	*ad libitum,* of your own choice
Ad PPS	*Congregatio Adoratricium u Pretiosissimo Sanguine,* Sisters Adorers of the Most Precious Blood
Ag	Aggeus
alb	albus, white (vestments)
Am	Amos
AM	*Anno Mundi,* in the year of the world
AMDG	*Ad Majorem Dei Gloriam,* For the greater glory of God
ana, ant	*antiphona,* antiphon
Ap, App	Apostle, Apostles
AP	*Adoratrici Perpetuae del Santissimo Sacramento,* Nuns of the Perpetual Adoration of the Blessed Sacrament
APB	*Religiosae Adoratrices Pretiosissimo Sanguinis,* Sisters Adorers of the Precious Blood, (Rel.Ad.PS)
Aram	Aramaic
archieps	*archiepiscopus,* archbishop
ARSSCI	*Ancelle Riparatrici del Sacro Cuore di Gesu,* Congregation of the Handmaids of the Sacred Heart of Jesus of Reparation

617

art	article
AS	Anglo-Saxon
ASV	*Soeurs de l'Assomption de la Sainte-Vierge,* Sisters of the Assumption of the Blessed Virgin Mary
AV	Authorized Version (Anglican) of the Bible

B

b	born
B	*Beatus, Beata,* Blessed (title)
BB	*Beati, Beatae,* Blessed (pl. title)
Bar	Baruch
BC	Before Christ
Bd	*Benedictio* (Blessing)
BGS	Brothers of the Good Shepherd
BHE	Brothers of the Holy Eucharist
bibl	bibliography
Bk	Book
Bl	Blessed
BMVA	*Sorores Franciscanae Beatae Mariae Virginis Angelorum,* Franciscan Sisters of Our Lady of the Holy Angels
bp	bishop
Bro	Brother
BS	Basilian Salvatorian Fathers
BVM	Blessed Virgin Mary; Sisters of Charity of the Blessed Virgin Mary

C

c	*circa,* about; canon
C	celebrant
CA	Catholic Action
CACh	*Sorores Carmelitae a Caritate,* Carmelite Sisters of Charity
CAIP	Catholic Association for International Peace
Cant	Canticle of Canticles
cantat	cantata (sung—opposite to read)
cap	*Caput,* chapter
Card	Cardinal
CCD	Confraternity of Christian Doctrine
CCR	Catholic Committee for Refugees
CCU	Catholic Central Union
CCVI	*Congregatio Caritatis Verbi Incarnati,* Sisters of Charity of the Incarnate Word
CCWL	Catholic Council on Working Life
CDA	Catholic Daughters of America
CDP	Sisters of Divine Providence of San Antonio, Texas
CDS	Congregation of the Divine Spirit
CE	Catholic Encyclopedia
CELAM	Episcopal Committee for Latin America
cf	consult
CFA	*Congregatio Fratrum Cellitarum seu Alexianorum,* Alexian Brothers

618

CFC	Congregation Fathers of Charity "Bigi," Third Order Regular of St. Francis of Assisi
CFM	*Congregatio Filiarum Mariae ab Immaculata Conceptione,* Congregation of the Daughters of Mary of the Immaculate Conception; Christian Family Movement
CFMM	*Congregatio Filiarum Minimarum Mariae,* Minim Daughters of Mary Immaculate
CFMS of A	Catholic Foreign Mission Society of America
CFP	*Congregatio Fratrum Pauperum,* Congregation of Poor Brothers, Poor Brothers of St. Francis
CFX	*Congregatio Fratrum St. Francisci Xaverii,* Brothers of St. Francis Xavier
CHG	Congregation of the Holy Ghost
CIC	Congregation of the Immaculate Conception, Sisters of the Immaculate Conception
CICM	*Congregatio Immaculati Cordis Mariae,* Congregation of the Immaculate Heart of Mary, Immaculate Heart of Mary Mission Society, Scheut Fathers
CIJ	Congregation of the Infant Jesus, Nursing Sisters of the Sick Poor
CIP	Catholic Institute of Press
CJC	Congregation of Jesus Crucified; Code of Canon Law; Poor Sisters of Jesus Crucified and the Sorrowful Mother
CJM	*Congregatio Jesus et Mariae,* Congregation of Jesus and Mary, Eudist Fathers
Cl	Class
CLA	Catholic Library Association
CM	*Congregatio Missionis Sti. Vicentii a Paulo,* Congregation of the Mission, Vincentians
CMF	*Congregatio Missionariorum Filiorum Immaculati Cordis B. Mariae Virginis,* Congregation of the Missionary Sons of the Immaculate Heart of Mary, Claretian Fathers
CMM	*Congregatio Missionariorum de Mariannhill,* Congregation of Mariannhill Missionaries, Mariannhill Fathers
CMP	Congregation of Missionary Sisters, Pallotine
CND	Sisters of the Congregation de Notre Dame
CNT	Confraternity New Testament
CO	*Institutum Oratorii S. Philippi Nerii,* Congregation of the Oratory, Institute of the Oratory of St. Philip Neri, Oratorian Fathers
Col	Colossians
Comp	Compline
Conc Trid	Council of Trent
Conc Vat I (II)	Vatican Council One (Two)
Conf	Confessor
Cor	Corinthians
COT	Confraternity Old Testament
CP	*Congregatio SS. Crucis et Passionis Domini Nostri Jesu Christi,* Congregation of the Most Holy Cross and Passion of Our Lord Jesus Christ, Congregation of the Passion, Passionists; The Nuns of the Most Holy Cross and Passion of Our Lord Jesus Christ, Passionist Nuns
CPA	Catholic Press Association
Cpl	Compline
CPPS	*Congregatio Missionis a Pretioso Sanguine,* Society of the Precious

Blood *Congregatio Pretiosissimi Sanguinis,* Congregation of the Sisters of the Precious Blood, Maria Stein Sisters

CPS   *Congregatio Presbyterorum a SS. Stigmatibus D.N.J.C.,* Congregation of Priests of the Most Holy Wounds of Our Lord Jesus Christ, Stigmatine Fathers; *Congregatio Missionales a Pretiosissimo Sanguine,* Missionary Sisters of the Precious Blood

Cr   Credo

CR   *Congregatio Clericorum Regularium,* Congregation of Clerks Regular, Theatine Fathers; *Congregatio a Resurrectione Domini Nostri Jesu Christi,* Congregation of the Resurrection, Resurrectionist Fathers; Sisters of the Resurrection

CRM   *Clerici Regolari Minori,* Clerics Regular Minor

CRS   Catholic Relief Services

CRSP   *Clericorum Regularium Sancti Pauli,* Clerks Regular of St. Paul, Barnabite Fathers

CSA, CRSA   Canons Regular of St. Augustine; Sisters of Charity of St. Augustine; Sisters of the Congregation of St. Agnes

CSAC   *Congregatio Sororum Apostolatus Catholici,* Congregation of the Sisters of the Catholic Apostolate, Pallotine Sisters

CSB   *Congregatio Presbyterorum a S. Basilio de Toronto,* Congregation of Priests of St. Basil of Toronto, Basilian Fathers; Congregation of St. Bernardine, Bernardine Sisters of the Third Order of St. Francis

CSC   *Congregatio a Sancta Cruce,* Congregation of the Holy Cross, Holy Cross Fathers, Holy Cross Brothers, Holy Cross Sisters; *Sorores Sanctae Crucis et Septem Dolorum,* Congregation of the Sisters of the Holy Cross and of the Seven Dolors

CSFN   *Congregatio Sororum Sacrae Familiae de Nazareth,* Congregation of the Sisters of the Holy Family of Nazareth

CSJ   *Congregatio Sancti Joseph,* Pious Congregation of St. Joseph, Sisters of St. Joseph

CSJB   Sisters of St. John the Baptist

CSL   Sisters of Charity of St. Louis

CSMC   Catholic Student's Mission Crusade

CSSF   Congregation of Sisters of St. Felix of Cantalicio of the Third Order of St. Francis, Felician Sisters

CSSp   *Congregatio Sancti Spiritus sub tutela Immaculati Cordis Beatissimae Virginis Mariae,* Congregation of the Holy Spirit and of the Immaculate Heart of Mary, Holy Ghost Fathers; *Congregatio Sancti Spiritus,* Congregation of the Holy Ghost, Holy Ghost Sisters

CSSR   *Congregatio Sanctissimi Redemptoris,* Congregation of the Most Holy Redeemer, Redemptorist Fathers

CST   *Sorores Carmelitae a Sancta Teresia ab Infante Jesu,* Carmelite Sisters of St. Therese of the Child Jesus

CSV   *Congregatis Clericorum Sancti Viatoris,* Clerics of St. Viator, Viatorians

CSVP   Sisters of Charity of St. Vincent de Paul

Ct   Canticle of Canticles

CU   Catholic University

CYC   Catholic Youth Council

CYO   Catholic Youth Organization

D

D	deacon; *Dominus,* Lord; Dame; Doctor of the Church; Diocese
d	died; double
da	dies assignata (assigned day)
Dan	Daniel
DC	Daughters of Charity of St. Vincent de Paul; Daughters of the Cross; Discalced Carmelite Nuns
DCJ	*Carmelitae Divini Cordis Jesu,* Carmelite Sisters of the Divine Heart of Jesus
DCL	*Doctor Canonicae Legis,* Doctor of Canon Law
DD	Doctor of Divinity
dd	*dono dedit,* gave as a gift
ddd	*dat, dicat, dedicat,* gives, devotes and dedicates
DDR	Daughters of the Divine Redeemer
de Comm	of the Common
de ea	of the feria; of the (weekday)
de oct	of the octave
de seq	*de sequenti,* of the following (day's feast)
decr	decree
Deut	Deuteronomy
dieb	*diebus* (of the day)
DLS	Daughters of Our Lady of the Snows
DM	Daughters of Our Lady of Mercy
DMHR	Daughters of the Most Holy Redeemer
DMJ	*Dames de Marie,* Daughters of Mary and Joseph
Dn	Daniel
DNJC	*Dominus Noster Jesus Christus,* Our Lord Jesus Christ
Dnus	Dominus (Lord)
Doct	Doctor of the Church
Dom	*Dominica,* Sunday
DOM	*Deo Optimo Maximo.* To God, the Best and Greatest.
Dom Prel	Domestic Prelate
dp	*duplex,* double (feast), a term relating to the liturgy
DSF	Daughters of St. Francis of Assisi
DSMP	Daughters of St. Mary of Providence
DSP	Pious Society, Daughters of St. Paul
DSR	Daughters of St. Rita of the Immaculate Heart
DSS	*Doctor Sacrae Scripturae,* Doctor of Holy Scripture
Dt	Deuteronomy
dupl	*duplex,* double
DV	Douay Version; *Deo volente,* God willing
DW	Daughters of Wisdom

E

Ec, Eccles	Ecclesiastes
eccl	ecclesiastical
Eccl	*Ecclesia* (the Church)
Ecclus	Ecclesiasticus

eg	*exempli gratia,* for example
EM	*Episcopus et Martyr,* bishop and martyr
Emus	*Eminentissimus,* Most Eminent
Ep, Epus	*Episcopus,* bishop
Eph	Ephesians
Er Cam	*Congregatio Monachorum Eremitarum Camaldulensium, O.S.B.,* Monk Hermits of Camaldoli
Esd	Esdras
Esth	Esther
Evang, Evgl	*Evangelium,* Gospel; Evangelist
Ex	Exodus
Ezech, Ez	Ezechial

F

F, Fr	Father; Friar; *Frater,* brother
FC	*Congregatio Fratrum Caritate,* Congregation of the Brothers of Charity
FCJ	Society of the Sisters, Faithful Companions of Jesus
FCPS	*Figlie della Carità del Preziosissimo Sangue,* Daughters of Charity of the Most Precious Blood
FCSCJ	*Filiae a Caritate Sacri Corde Jesus,* Daughters of the Charity of the Sacred Heart of Jesus
FCSP	*Filiae Caritatis Servae Pauperum,* Daughters of Charity, Servants of the Poor, Sisters of Charity of Providence
FD, Fest Dev	*Festum devotionis,* Feast of Devotion
FDC	*Filiae Divinae Caritatis,* Daughters of Divine Charity
FDJ	*Filles de Jésus,* Order of the Daughters of Jesus
FDP	*Filii Divinae Providentiae,* Sons of Divine Providence
fer 2,3,4,5,6	*feria secunda,* etc., Monday, Tuesday, Wednesday, Thursday, Friday
FHM	Franciscan Handmaids of the Most Pure Heart of Mary, Franciscan Handmaids of Mary
FIC	*Institutum Fratrum Instructionis Christianae,* Institute of Brothers of Christian Instruction, Brothers of Christian Instruction, La Mennais Brothers
fl	*floruit,* he flourished, i.e., lived
FMA	*Filiae Mariae Auxiliatricis,* Daughters of Mary, Help of Christians, Salesian Sisters of St. John Bosco
FMM	Franciscan Missionaries of Mary; *Fratres de Misericordia,* Brothers of Mercy
FMS	*Institutum Fratrum Maristarum Scholarum,* Institute of the Marist Brothers of the Schools, Marist School Brothers
FMSDC	*Sorores Franciscales Missionariae a Jesu Infante,* Franciscan Missionary Sisters of the Divine Child
FMSI	*Filii Mariae Salutis Infirmorum,* Sons of Mary, Health of the Sick, Daughters of Mary Health of the Sick
FMSJ	Franciscan Missionaries of St. Joseph, Mill Hill Sisters
FSC	*Fratres Scholarum Christianarum,* Brothers of the Christian Schools, Christian Brothers
FSCH	*Fratrum Scholarum Christianarum de Hibernia,* Brothers of the Christian Schools of Ireland, Christian Brothers of Ireland

FSCJ	*Congregatio Filiorum S. Cordis Jesu,* Congregation of the Sons of the Sacred Heart of Jesus, Verona Fathers
FSE	*Filles du Saint-Esprit,* Daughters of the Holy Ghost, White Sisters
FSJ	*Filles de Saint-Joseph,* Religious Daughters of St. Joseph
FSM	*Filles de Sainte-Marie de la Présentation,* Daughters of Saint Mary of the Presentation, Sisters of St. Mary of the Presentation
FSPA	Congregation of the Sisters of the Third Order of St. Francis of Perpetual Adoration
FSSE	Franciscan Sisters of St. Elizabeth
FSSJ	Franciscan Sisters of St. Joseph
FSSS	*Franciscales a Sanctissimo Sacramento,* Franciscan Nuns of the Most Blessed Sacrament

G

Gal	Galatians
Gen	Genesis
Gl	*Gloria in excelsis, Gloria Patri*
Gn	Genesis
GNSH	Grey Nuns of the Sacred Heart
Gr	Greek

H

Hab, Hb	Habacuc
HB	His Beatitude or Blessedness
HCG	*Hermanas Catequistas Guadalupanas,* Sister Catechists of Guadalupe
HE	His Eminence
Heb	Hebrew, Hebrews
HH	His Holiness
HHM	Sisters of the Holy Humility of Mary
HHS	Helpers of the Holy Souls
IIO	Holiday of Obligation
hom	homiletics, homily
Hor	Horae (Little Hours)
HPB	Congregation of the Handmaids of the Precious Blood
HRS	Missionary Sisters of Our Lady of the Holy Rosary, Holy Rosary Sisters
HVM	Sisters, Home Visitors of Mary

I

I	Imperata (Ordered Oration)
IBVM	Institute of the Blessed Virgin Mary, Ladies of Loretto
IC	*Institutum Caritatis,* Institute of Charity, Rosminians
ICA	International Catholic Auxiliaries
ICCC	International Conference of Catholic Charities

ICXC NIKA   Monogram from Greek letters, "Jesus Christ conquers"
ie   *id est,* that is
IFCA   International Federation of Catholic Alumnae
IHM   Sisters, Servants of the Immaculate Heart of Mary, Daughters of the Immaculate Heart of Mary, Sisters of the Most Holy and Immaculate Heart of the Blessed Virgin Mary
IHS   Monogram of the Holy Name in Greek letters
IMC (also MIC)   *Institutum Missionum a Consolata,* Mission Institute of Consolata, Consolata Missionary Fathers, Missionaries of the Consolata of Turin
INRI   *Iesus Nazarenus Rex Iudaeorum,* Jesus of Nazareth, King of the Jews
ipi   *in partibus infidelium,* an episcopal see in non-Christian lands
Is   Isaia
ishs   immediately subject to the Holy See
IWBS, SIWVI   Congregation of the Incarnate Word and Blessed Sacrament of the Archdiocese of San Antonio, Texas; *Congregatio Verbi Incarnati et Sanctissimi Sacramenti,* Sisters of the Incarnate Word and the Blessed Sacrament, Sisters of the Incarnate Word

J

Jas   James
Jb   Job
JC   Jesus Christ
JCD   *Juris Canonici (sive Civilis) Doctor,* Doctor of Canon (or Civil) Law
JCL   Licentiate in Canon Law
jejun   jejunium (fast)
Jer   Jeremia
Jgs   Judges
Jl   Joel
JMJ   Jesus, Mary, Joseph
JMMJ   Missionaries of Jesus, Mary and Joseph
Jn   John
Jon   Jona
Jos   Josue
Jud   Judith

K

K of C   Knights of Columbus
KC   Knight Commander
Kgs   Kings
KHS   Knight of the Holy Sepulcher
KJV   King James Version
KP   Knight of Pius IX; Knight of St. Patrick
KSG   Knight of St. Gregory
KSS   Knight of St. Silvester

L

L	Latin
LAB	Latin America Bureau
Lam	Lamentations
LCM	The Little Company of Mary (Blue Nuns)
Ld	Lauds
LDSJ	The Little Daughters of St. Joseph
lect	Lectio, lecta (Read-opposite to sung).
Lev	Leviticus
Lk	Luke
LL	Late Latin
loc	locus (place)
LSA	Little Sisters of the Assumption
LSIC	Little Servant Sisters of the Immaculate Conception
Lv	Leviticus
LXX	Septuagint

M

M, MM	Martyr, Martyrs
Mac, Mc	Machabees
Mal	Malachia
Mart	Martyr
Mat	Matins
Matt	Matthew
MC	Master of Ceremonies, Consolata Missionary Sisters
MCM	Cordian-Marian Missionary Sisters, Cordi-Marian; *Misioneras del Imaculado Corazón de Mariá,* Missionaries of the Immaculate Heart of Mary
MD	*Madres de los Desamparados,* Mothers of the Helpless
MEP	*Missions Etrangeres de Paris,* Paris Foreign Missions; *Societas Parisiensis Missionum ad Exteros,* Paris Foreign Mission Society
MHM	*Mill Hill Missionaries,* St. Joseph's Society for Foreign Missions
MHS	Sisters of the Most Holy Sacrament
MHSH	Mission Helpers of the Sacred Heart
Mi	Michea
MIC (also SM)	*Congregatio Clericorum Regularium Marianorum sub titulo Immaculatae Conceptionis Beatae Mariae Virginis,* Marian Fathers, Missionaries of the Immaculate Conception, Missionary Sisters of the Immaculate Conception
MISC	Maryknoll International Student Committee
Miss	*Missa,* Mass
Miss Ap	*Missionarius Apostolicus,* Missionary Apostolic
Mk	Mark
MM	Martyrs; Maryknoll Missioner, *Societas de Maryknoll pro Missionibus Exteris,* Catholic Foreign Mission Society of America, Inc., Maryknoll Fathers, Maryknoll Brothers; Missionary Sisters of Mary

MMB	*Mercedarias Misioneras de Bérriz*, Missionaries of Our Lady of Mercy of Berriz
MMM	Medical Missionaries of Mary
MMOM	Missionary Sisters of Our Lady of Mercy
MPF	*Congregatio Sororum Magistrarum Piarum Filippini*, Congregation of the Religious Teachers Filippini, Filippini Sisters, Sisters of St. Lucy Filippini
Mprop	*Missa pro populo*, Mass (said) for the people
MPV	*Magistrae Piae Venerini*, Religious Venerini Teaching Sisters, Venerini Sisters
MRE	Master of Religious Education
ms	manuscript
MS	Mission Sisters of the Holy Ghost; *Missionaires de La Salette*, The Missionaries of Our Lady of La Salette
MSA	Missionary Sisters of the Assumption
MSBT	Missionary Servants of the Most Blessed Trinity
MSC	Marian Society of Catechists; Missionaries of St. Charles, Scalabrini Fathers; *Societas Missionariorum Sacratissi Cordis Jesu*, Missionaries of the Sacred Heart; *Marianistes de la Sainte-Croix*, Sisters, Marianites of the Holy Cross; *Missionarie del Sacro Cuore di Gesu*, Missionary Sisters of the Sacred Heart
MSF	*Congregatio Missionariorum a Sancta Familia*, Congregation of the Missionaries of the Holy Family
Msgr	Monsignor
MSMG	Missionary Sisters of the Mother of God
MSpS	Missionaries of the Holy Ghost, Holy Ghost Missionaries
MSSA	Missionary Servants of St. Anthony, Missionary Sisters of St. Anthony; Missionary Sisters of St. Augustine
MSSCB	Missionary Sisters of St. Charles Borromeo
MSSst	*Missionarii Servi Sanctissimae Trinitas*, Missionary Servants of the Most Holy Trinity, Trinitarians
MSV	Missionary Sisters of Verona
Mt	Matthew
MZSH	Missionary Zelatrices of the Sacred Heart

N

n	name; *niger* (black); number; *natus*, born
Na, Nah	Nahum
nan	*nisi aliter notetur*, unless otherwise noted
NC	National Catholic News Service
NCCM	National Council of Catholic Men
NCCN	National Council of Catholic Nurses
NCCS	National Catholic Community Service
NCCW	National Council of Catholic Women
NCCY	National Council of Catholic Youth
NCEA	National Catholic Education Association
NCWC	National Catholic Welfare Conference (U.S.A.)
ND	*Notre Dame*, Our Lady, Notre Dame University
NDS	Congregation of Notre Dame de Sion
Neh	Nehemia

NFCCS	National Federation of Catholic College Students
nigr	*niger,* black (vestments)
NLD	National Legion of Decency
Nm	Numbers
NNCF	National Newman Club Federation
Noct	Nocturn
NODL	National Office for Decent Literature
NS	new style (in dates)
NT	New Testament
Num	Numbers

O

O	omit
O Cap	Order of Capuchins, Franciscan Capuchin Sisters of the Infant Jesus
O Carm	*Ordo Fratrum Beatissimae Virginis Mariae de Monte Carmelo,* Order of Carmel, Carmelite Fathers, Order of Carmel, Calced Carmelites, Carmelite Nuns of the Ancient Observance
O Cart	*Ordo Cartusianorum,* Order of Carthusians
O Praem	*Ordo Canonicorum Regularium Praemonstratensium,* Canons Regular of Premontre, Norbertine Fathers, Premonstratensians
OA	Oblate Sisters of the Assumption
ob	obit (died)
OCD	Carmelite Nuns, Discalced; *Ordo Carmelitarum Discalceatorum,* Discalced Carmelite Fathers
OCIC	International Catholic Film Office
OCSO	Order of Cistercians of the Strict Observance, Cistercian Nuns of the Strict Observance, Trappistines; *Ordo Cisterciensium Strictioris Observantiae;* The Order Cistercians of the Strict Observance; Trappists
oct	*octava,* octave
ODM	Order of Our Lady of Mercy, Mercedarians
ODN, SMDN	*Ordo Dominae Nostrae, Societas Mariae Dominae Nostrae,* Order of Our Lady, Society of Mary, Our Lady, Company of Mary, Daughters of Mary Our Lady
OE	Old English
OESP	*Ordo Fratrum St. Pauli Primi Eremitae,* Order of St. Paul the First Hermit, Hermits of St. Paul, Paulini Fathers
Off	*Officium* (Office)
OFM	*Ordo Fratrum Minorum,* Order of Friars Minor, Franciscan Fathers
OFM Cap	*Ordinis Fratrum Minorum Capuccinorum,* Order of Friars Minor Capuchin, The Capuchin Fathers
OFM Conv	*Ordo Fratrum Minorum S. Francisci Conventualium,* Conventual Franciscan Fathers, Friars Minor Conventual
OH	Order of Hospitallers, Hospitaller Order of St. John of God
OI	Imperata Omitted
OLCR	Sisters of Our Lady of Charity of Refuge
OLG	Sisters of Our Lady of Guadalupe, Sisters of Guadalupe
OLM	Sisters of Charity of Our Lady of Mercy
OLS	Sisters of Our Lady of Sorrows

OLVM	Our Lady of Victory Missionary Sisters, Missionary Catechists of Our Blessed Lady of Victory
OMI	*Missionarii Oblati Sanctissimae et Immaculatae Virginis Mariae,* Missionary Oblates of the Most Holy and Immaculate Virgin Mary, Oblates of Mary Immaculate
OP	*Patres Sacri Ordinis Fratrum Praedicatorum,* Order of Preachers, Dominican Fathers, Dominican Sisters, Dominican Brothers
op cit	work cited
or	*oratio,* collect, prayer
ORSA	*Ordo Recollectorum Sancti Augustini,* Recollects of St. Augustine, Augustinian Recollects
Os	Osee
OS	old style (in dates)
OSA	*Ordo Eremitarum Sancti Augustini,* Order of Hermits of St. Augustine, Augustinian Fathers
OSB	*Monachorum Silvestrinorum, O.S.B.,* Monks of St. Sylvester, Order of St. Benedict, Sylvestrine Benedictines, Benedictines, Benedictine Fathers; Benedictine Sisters
OSBrig	Brigittine Sisters
OSBM	*Ordo Sancti Basilii Magni,* Order of St. Basil the Great, Basilian Monks; *Moniales Ordinis Sancti Basilii Magni,* Sisters of the Order of St. Basil the Great, Basilian Sisters
OSBS	Oblate Sisters of the Blessed Sacrament.
OSC	*Canonici Regulares Ordinis Sanctae Crucis, Cruciferi,* Canons Regular of the Order of the Holy Cross, Crosier Fathers; Order of Saint Clare, Poor Clares
OS Cam	Order of St. Camillus, Order of Clerks Regular for Ministering to the Sick, Camillian Fathers
OSF	Order of St. Francis, Franciscan Tertiaries of the Holy Cross; *Fratres Missionarii sti Francisci de Sso., Corde Jesu,* Franciscan Missionary Brothers of the Sacred Heart of Jesus; *Fratres Franciscani Brooklyniensis Congregationis Regularis Tertii Ordinis,* The Franciscan Brothers of Brooklyn of the Congregation of the Third Order Regular, Franciscan Brothers of Brooklyn; Franciscan Sisters
OSFK	Franciscan Sisters of Blessed Kunegunda
OSFS	*Congregatio Oblatorum Sancti Francisci Salesii,* Oblates of St. Francis de Sales
OSHJ	Oblate Sisters of the Sacred Heart of Jesus
OSJ	*Congregatio Oblatorum St. Joseph,* Oblates of St. Joseph
OSM	*Ordo Servorum Mariae,* Servants of Mary, Servite Fathers; Order of the Servants of Mary, Mantellate Sisters
OSP	Oblate Sisters of Providence
OSSR	*Oblatas del Santisimo Redentor,* Oblate Sisters of the Most Holy Redeemer
OSSS, OSBrig	*Ordo Sancti Salvatoris,* Order of Holy Savior, Brigittine Sisters
OSST	*Ordo Sanctissimae Trinitatis Redemptionis Captivorum,* The Order of the Most Holy Trinity, Sisters of the Most Holy Trinity
OSU	Order of St. Ursula, Ursuline Nuns
OSV	Our Sunday Visitor
OT	Old Testament
OVSM	*Ordre de la Visitation Sainte-Marie,* Order of the Visitation of St. Mary, Visitation Nuns, Visitandines

P

p	*pater,* father; *papa,* pope
PA, Pref Ap	Prefect Apostolic
Par	Paralipomenon
PBVM	Sisters of the Presentation of the Blessed Virgin Mary
PCJ	Sisters of the Poor Child Jesus
PDM	Pious Disciples of the Divine Master
Pent	Pentecost
PFM	*Petites Franciscaines de Marie,* Little Franciscan Sisters of Mary
PhD	*Philosophiae Doctor,* Doctor of Philosophy
Phil	Philip; Phillipians
PHJC	Poor Handmaids of Jesus Christ, Ancilla Domini Sisters
Phlm	Philemon
PIME	*Pontificium Institutum Missionum Exterarum,* Pontifical Institute for Foreign Missions, Missionaries of SS. Peter and Paul
plen ind	plenary indulgence
PM	Sisters of the Presentation of Mary
Pont	*Pontifex,* bishop
Pont Max	*Pontifex Maximus,* Supreme Pontiff
POSSCC	*Piccole Operaie dei Sacri Cuori di Gesu e Maria,* Little Workers of the Sacret Hearts of Jesus and Mary
PP, Pp	*Papa,* pope
pr	*proprium,* proper
Pr	Prime
Praef	Preface
Prot Ap	Protonotary Apostolic
Prov, Prv	Proverbs
Ps	Psalms
PSdP	*Petites-Soeurs des Pauvres,* Little Sisters of the Poor
PSSF	*Petites-Souers de la Sainte-Famille,* Little Sisters of the Holy Family
Pt	Peter
PVMI	Parish Visitors of Mary Immaculate

Q

Q	question
Quadrag	Quadragesima, Lent
qv, qqv	*quod vide,* which see

R

R	Response
RA	Religious of the Assumption
RC	Religious of the Cenacle, Congregation of Our Lady of the Retreat in the Cenacle

RCD	Religious of Christian Doctrine, Sisters of Our Lady of Christian Doctrine
RCE	Religious of Christian Education
RD	Rural Dean; Reverend Dom; Rheims-Douay
RDC	Religious of Divine Compassion, Sisters of the Divine Compassion
Rev	Reverend
RF	*Religiosas Filipenses,* Sisters of St. Philip Neri
RGS	Religious of the Good Shepherd; Sisters of Our Lady of Charity of the Good Shepherd
RHSJ	Religious Hospitallers of Saint Joseph
RIP	*Requiescat in pace,* may he (she) rest in peace; *requiescant in pace,* may they rest in peace
RJM	Religious of Jesus and Mary
RMJM	Recluse Missionaries of Jesus and Mary
RN	Congregation of the Religious of Nazareth, Ladies of Nazareth
Rom	Romans
rosac	*rosaceus,* rose-colored (vestments)
RP	*Reverendus pater,* Reverend Father
RR	Roman Ritual; *Reverendissimus,* Most Reverend, Right Reverend
RS	Religious of the Order of the Blessed Sacrament and of Our Lady, Sacramentine Nuns
RSCJ	*Religieuses du Sacré-Coeur,* Religious of the Sacred Heart, Society of the Sacred Heart of Jesus
RSD	Religious of St. Dorothy, Institute of the Sisters of St. Dorothy
RSHM	Religious of the Sacred Heart of Mary
RSM	Religious Sisters of Mercy, Sisters of Mercy
RSR	*Soeurs de Notre Dame du Saint Rosaire,* Congregation of Our Lady of the Holy Rosary
RSV	Revised Standard Version
Rt Rev	Right Reverend
Ru	Ruth
RU	Ursuline Nuns of the Congregation of Tildonk, Belgium
rub, r	*ruber,* red (vestments)
RV	Revised Version (Anglican) of the Bible

S

SA	*Societas Adunationis,* Franciscan Friars of the Atonement; Franciscan Sisters of Atonement
Sabb	*Sabbatum,* Saturday
SAC	Society of the Catholic Apostolate, Pallottine Fathers; *Societas Apostolatus Catholici (Sorores),* Sisters of the Catholic Apostolate, Sisters of Mary of the Catholic Apostolate
SBS	Sisters of Bon Secours; Sisters of the Blessed Sacrament, The Sisters of the Blessed Sacrament for Indians and Colored People
SC	*Sacra Congregatio, Sacred Congregation;* Sisters of Charity; *Societas Fratrum Sacris Cordis,* Society of the Brothers of the Sacred Heart, Sacred Heart Brothers
SCC	Sisters of Christian Charity
SCG	*Soeurs de la Charite Grises,* Gray Sisters of Charity, Gray nuns; *Soeurs de la Charite de Quebec,* Sisters of Charity of Quebec
SCIF	Bethlehemite Sisters of the Sacred Heart of Jesus

SCIM	*Congregation des Soeurs Servantes du Coeur Immaculee de Marie,* Sisters, Servants of the Immaculate Heart of Mary; Sisters of the Good Shepherd of Quebec
SCJ	*Congregatio Sacerdotum a SS. Corde Jesu,* Congregation of the Priests of the Sacred Heart
SCK	Society of Christ the King, Sisters of Christ the King
SCL	Sisters of Charity of Leavenworth, Kansas
SCMM	Society of Catholic Medical Missionaries, Medical Mission Sisters
SCMS	Society of Catholic Mission Sisters of St. Francis Xavier
SCN	Sisters of Charity of Nazareth (Kentucky)
SCOLM	Sisters of Charity of Our Lady, Mother of Mercy
Scr	Scripture
SCSC	*Sorores a Caritate Sanctae Crucis,* Sisters of Mercy of the Holy Cross
SD	subdeacon
SDB	*Societas Sancti Francisci Salesii,* Society of St. Francis de Sales, Salesians of St. John Bosco
SdC	*Soeurs de la Divine Charité,* Sisters of Divine Charity, Sisters of Charity of Besancon, Sisters of Charity of St. Joan Antida
SDE	The Society of the Daughters of the Eucharist, Inc.
SdeM	*Siervas de Maria Ministras,* Servants of Mary Ministras, Sisters, Servants of Mary
SDS	*Societas Divini Salvatoris,* Society of the Divine Savior, Salvatorians, Sisters of the Divine Savior
SF	*Congregatio Filiorum Sacrae Familiae,* Sons of the Holy Family
SFP	Franciscan Sisters of the Poor
SFSCM	*Societas Filiarum Sanctissimi Cordis Mariae,* Society of the Daughters of the Heart of Mary, Nardine Sisters, Nardines
SGC	*Soeurs Grises de la Croix,* Gray Nuns of the Cross
SGM	*Soeurs Grises de Montreal,* Gray Nuns, Sisters of Charity of Montreal
SGSH	*Soeurs Grises de Saint-Hyacinthe,* Gray Sisters of St. Hyacinth, Sisters of Charity of St. Hyacinth
SHCJ	Society of the Holy Child Jesus
SHF	Sisters of the Holy Faith, Sisters of the Holy Family
SHG	Sisters of the Holy Ghost, Sister-Servants of the Holy Ghost and Mary Immaculate
SICBMV	*Sorores ab Immaculata Conceptione Beatae Mariae Virginis,* Sisters of the Immaculate Conception of the Blessed Virgin Mary
Sir	Sirach
SJ	*Societas Jesu,* Society of Jesus, Jesuit Fathers
SJA	Sisters of St. Jeanne D'Arc, Institute of St. Joan of Arc, Ottawa
SJC	Sisters of St. Joseph of Cluny
SL	Sisters of Loretto at the Foot of the Cross
Sm	Samuel
SM	Sisters of Misericordia; *Societas Mariae-Marianistae,* Society of Mary, Marianists, Brothers of Mary; *Societas Mariae,* Society of Mary, Marist Fathers
SMA	*Societas Missionum ad Afros,* Society of the African Missions
SMB	*Societas Missionaria de Bethlehem,* Society of Bethlehem Missionaries
SMG	Sisters Poor Servants of the Mother of God

SMIC   Missionary Sisters of the Immaculate Conception, Missionary Poor Clares of the Immaculate Conception, Missionary Sisters of the Immaculate Conception of the Mother of God

SMM   *Societas Mariae Montfortana*, Society of Mary of Montfort, Missionaries of the Company of Mary, Montfort Fathers

SMMG   Sisters of Mary Mother of God

SMR   Society of Mary Reparatrix

SMS   Missionary Sisters of Our Lady of La Salette

SMSH   Sisters of Saint Marthe of St. Hyacinthe

SMSM   Missionary Sisters of the Society of Mary, Inc., Marist Missionary Sisters

SN   Poor Sisters of Nazareth

SND   Sisters of Notre Dame

SNJM   Sisters of the Holy Names of Jesus and Mary

So   Sophonia

SO Cist   Sisters of the Order of Cistercians, Cistercians of the Original Observance; *Sacer Ordo Cisterciensis*, The Holy Order of Cistercians

Soc   *Socius* (pl. *socii*) companion

Solemn   *Solemnis* (solemn)

SOS   Sisters of Service

SP   Sisters of Providence of Saint Mary-of-the-Woods, Indiana; Sisters of Providence; Servants of the Holy Paraclete; Piarist Fathers

SPAp   Sacred Apostolic Penitentiary

SPF   The Society for the Propagation of the Faith

SPM   *Societas Presbyterorum a Misericordia*, Society of the Priests of Mercy, Fathers of Mercy

SPS   St. Patrick's Missionary Society

SPVM   Institute of the Sisters of the Purity of Mary

sq   *sequentes*, and following

Sr   Soror, Sister

SRC   *Sacororum Rituum Congregatio*, Congregation of Sacred Rites; *Soeurs Servantes de Notre-Dame, Reine du Clergé*, Sisters, Servants of Our Lady, Queen of the Clergy

SRCM   Sisters of Reparation of the Congregation of Mary

SRE   *Sancta Roman Ecclesia*, Holy Roman Church

SS   Saints; Servants of the Blessed Sacrament; *Societas Presbyterorum a S. Sulpitio*, Society of the Priests of Saint Sulpice, Sulpicians

SSA   Sisters of St. Anne

SSC   *Societas Sancti Columbani pro missionibus apud Sinenses*, Society of Saint Columban for Missions among the Chinese, St. Columban's Foreign Mission Society, Columban Fathers, Columban Sisters; Sisters of the Most Holy Crucified; Sisters of St. Casimir

SSCC   *Congregatio Sororum a Sanctis Cordibus*, Congregation of the Sacred Hearts, Sisters of the Sacred Heart of Jesus and Mary and of the Perpetual Adoration of the Most Holy Sacrament of the Altar; Picpus Sisters; *Congregatio Sacrorum Cordium*, Fathers of the Sacred Hearts

SSCh   Sisters of Ste. Chretienne

SSCJ   *Sorores a Sacro Corde Jesu*, Sisters of the Sacred Heart of Jesus

SSCK   Sister Servants of Christ the King

SSCM	Sisters of Saints Cyril and Methodius; *Servantes de Saint-Coeur de Marie,* Servants of the Holy Heart of Mary
SSDN	*Sanctissimus Dominus noster,* Our most holy Lord (the pope)
SSE	Sisters of St. Elizabeth; *Societas Sancti Edmundi,* Society of Saint Edmund
SSF	*Congregatio Sororum Sanctae Familiae,* Congregation of the Sisters of the Holy Family
SSHJM	Sisters of the Sacred Hearts of Jesus and Mary
SSHJP	Servants of the Sacred Heart of Jesus and of the Poor
SSJ	*Societas Sancti Joseph SSmi Cordis,* St. Joseph's Society of the Sacred Heart, Josephites; Sisters of St. Joseph of the Third Order of St. Francis; Sisters of St. Joseph
SSJSM	Sisters of St. Joseph of St. Mark
SSM	Sisters of the Sorrowful Mother, Third Order of St. Francis, Sisters of Saint Mary of Namur
SSMI	Sister Servants of Mary Immaculate
SSMIC	Sister Servants of Mary Immaculate of Mariowka
SSMO	Sisters of St. Mary of Oregon
SSND	School Sisters of Notre Dame
SSP	Society of St. Paul for the Apostolate of Communications; Pauline Fathers
SSPC	Sodality of St. Peter Claver, Missionary Sisters of St. Peter Claver
SSpS	*Congregatio Missionalis Servarum Spiritus Sancti,* Missionary Sisters, Servants of the Holy Ghost, Holy Ghost Sisters
SSS	*Congregatio Presbyterorum Sanctissimi Sacramenti,* Congregation of the Blessed Sacrament; Sisters of Social Service
St	Saint
STB	*Sacrae Theologiae Baccalaureus,* Bachelor of Sacred Theology
STD	*Sacrae Theologiae Doctor,* Doctor of Sacred Theology
STdeV	Congregation of Sisters of St. Thomas of Villanova
SThom	St. Thomas Aquinas
STL	*Sacrae Theologiae Licentiatus (sive Lector),* Licentiate (or Lector) of Sacred Theology
STM	*Sacrae Theologiae Magister,* Master of Sacred Theology
STP	*Sacrae Theologiae Professor,* Professor of Sacred Theology
STS	Society of St. Teresa of Jesus, Teresian Sisters
Sts	Saints
suffr	*suffrugium,* the suffrage of the saints
Sum Theol	*The Summa Theologica* of St. Thomas Aquinas
SUSC	*Religieuses de la Sainte-Union des Sacres-Coeurs de Jésus et Marie,* Religious of the Holy Union of the Sacred Hearts of Jesus and Mary, Congregation of the Holy Union of the Sacred Hearts
SVD	*Societas Verbi Divini,* Society of the Divine Word
SVM	Sisters of the Visitation of the Congregation of the Immaculate Heart of Mary
SX	*Pia Societas Sancti Francisci Xaverii pro Exteris Missionibus,* Pius Society of Saint Francis Xavier for Foreign Missions, Saint Francis Xavier Foreign Mission Society, Xaverian Missionary Fathers

T

tant	*tantum* (only)
Thes, Thess	Thessalonians
Ti, Tit	Titus
tit	titular
Tm, Tim	Timothy
Tob, Tb	Tobias
TOR	*Tertius Ordo Regularis de Poenitentia,* Third Order Regular of Penance, Third Order Regular of Saint Francis
TOSD	Tertiary of the Order of St. Dominic
TOSF	Tertiary of the Order of St. Francis
tp	*tempore paschali,* in paschal time

U

ULPAC	Latin American Union of the Catholic Press
UNDA	International Catholic Association for Radio and Television
UTSV	*Soeurs de Sainte-Ursule de la Sainte-Vierge,* Sisters of St. Ursula of the Blessed Virgin

V

V	Versicle; *Venerabilis,* Venerable; Virgin
va, vic ap	*vicarius apostolicus,* vicar apostolic
Ven	Venerable
Vesp	Vespers
vf	*vicarius foraneus,* vicar forane
vg	*vicarius generalis,* vicar general
Vg	vulgate
vic cap	*vicarius capitularis,* vicar capitular
vid	*vidua,* widow
vig	vigil
viol, v	*Violaceus,* purple, violet (vestments)
vir, virid, v	*viridis,* green (vestments)
virg	*virgo,* virgin
viz	*videlicet,* namely
vol	volume
VSC	Vincentian Sisters of Charity

W

w	widow
WF	*Societas Missionariorum Africae,* White Fathers, Missionaries of Africa
Wis	Wisdom
WS	White Sisters, Missionary Sisters of Our Lady of Africa
WSC	White Sisters of Charity of St. Vincent de Paul

634

X

XP   *chi rho*, Christ

Y

YCF   Young Christian Farmers, a form of Catholic Action
YCS   Young Christian Students, a form of Catholic Action
YCW   Young Christian Workers, a form of Catholic Action

Z

Za, Zach   Zacharia

Appendix II
Catholic Forms of Address

ECCLESIASTICAL FORMS OF ADDRESS FOR CATHOLICS RECOGNIZED IN THE UNITED STATES

The following are forms of address used by Catholics in letters and in speech. It is perfectly correct for those who are not Catholics to change the conclusion to something such as: "With every good wish to Your Excellency (Eminence, etc.), I am, Sincerely yours, NN.," or even more simply, "With every best wish. Sincerely yours, NN."

THE POPE:

Addressing a letter: His Holiness Pope N_____.
Salutation: Most Holy Father; Your Holiness.
Concluding a letter: I have the honor to profess myself with the most profound respect, your Holiness' most obedient and humble servant.
In personal speech: Your Holiness

CARDINALS:

Addressing a letter: His Eminence (Christian name) Cardinal (Surname) (If an archbishop or bishop give title and see)
Salutation: Your Eminence:
Concluding a letter: Asking the blessing of Your Eminence, I am, Yours respectfully in Christ, N.
In personal speech: Your Eminence

ARCHBISHOPS:

Addressing a letter: Most Reverend N_____ N_____, Archbishop of _____.
Salutation: Your Excellency:
Concluding a letter: Asking Your Excellency's blessing, I am, Yours respectfully in Christ, N.
In personal speech: Your Excellency

PATRIARCHS, EASTERN:

Addressing a letter: His Beatitude the Patriarch of_____ or, His Beatitude the Lord (Christian name) Patriarch of_____.
Salutation: Your Beatitude:
Concluding a letter: Asking Your Beatitude's blessing, I am, Yours respectfully in Christ, NN.
In personal speech: Your Beatitude

639

Catholic Forms of Address

PATRIARCHS, LATIN TITULAR, AND NUNCIOS:

Addressing a letter: His Excellency the Patriarch (Archbishop) of____
or His Excellency Monsignor N, Patriarch (Archbishop) of____
Salutation: Most Reverend Excellency; Your Excellency:
Concluding a letter: Asking Your Excellency's blessing, I am, Yours respectfully, NN.
In personal speech: Your Excellency.

BISHOPS:

Addressing a letter: Most Reverend N_____ N_____
Bishop of_____
Salutation: Your Excellency:
Concluding a letter: Asking Your Excellency's blessing, I am, Yours respectfully, NN
In personal speech: Bishop

ABBOTS:

Addressing a letter: Right Reverend N_____ N_____ (adding letters designating his Order) Abbott of _____.
Salutation: Right Reverend Abbot:
Concluding a letter: Yours respectfully in Christ, NN.
In personal speech: Father Abbot

PROTONOTARIES APOSTOLIC, DOMESTIC PRELATES AND VICARS GENERAL:

Addressing a letter: Rt. Rev. Msgr. N_____ N_____
Salutation: Right Reverend Monsignor:
Concluding a letter: Yours respectfully in Christ, NN.
In personal speech: Monsignor

PAPAL CHAMBERLAINS:

Address on envelope: Very. Rev. Msgr. N_____N_____
Salutation: Very Reverend Monsignor:
Concluding a letter: Yours respectfully in Christ, NN.
In personal speech: Monsignor

SECULAR PRIESTS:

Address on envelope: Rev. N_____N_____ or Father N_____
Salutation: Dear Father:
Concluding a letter: Respectfully yours in Christ, NN.
In personal speech: Father
(Note. Priests as a group object to being addressed either in a salutation or in personal speech as "Reverend N_____." If "Reverend" is used in the address or in speech so, too, should the first name. "Father" is the preferred form and it should mean nothing more to the person than addressing the Jewish minister as "Rabbi" [Master].)

RELIGIOUS ORDER PRIESTS:

Address on envelope: Rev. N_____N_____ (adding letters designating his Order.)
Salutation: Dear Father:
Concluding a letter: Respectfully yours in Christ, NN
In personal speech: Father

BROTHERS:

> *Address on envelope:* Brother N_____ (adding initials designating his
> Order.)
> *Salutation:* Dear Brother N_____
> *Concluding a letter:* Respectfully yours in Christ, NN
> *In personal speech:* Brother

SISTERS:

> *Address on envelope:* Sister N_____
> *Salutation:* Dear Sister N_____
> *Concluding a letter:* Respectfully yours in Christ, NN
> *In personal speech:* Sister

MOTHER SUPERIOR (or MOTHER GENERAL):

> *Addressing a letter:* The Reverend Mother Superior (General), Convent of_____
> or, The Reverend Mother N_____ (adding initials of her Order.)
> *Salutation:* Dear Reverend Mother:
> *Concluding a letter:* Respectfully yours,
> *In personal speech:* Mother

PROTESTANT MINISTER:

> *Addressing a letter: The Reverend* N_____N_____ or The Reverend
> Doctor N_____N_____.
> *Salutation:* Reverend Sir: or Dear Doctor N_____:
> *Concluding a letter:* Very truly yours,
> *In personal speech:* Mr. N_____ or Doctor

RABBI:

> *Addressing a letter: Rabbi* N_____N_____, *or* The Reverend N_____
> _____N_____.
> *Salutation:* Reverend Sir: *or* Dear Rabbi_____.
> *Concluding a letter:* Very truly yours,
> *In personal speech:* Rabbi

Appendix III
Patron Saints of Occupations and Professions and Their Feast Days

Actors—St. Genesius, Aug. 25.

Alpinists—St. Bernard of Menthon, May 28.

Altar Boys—St. John Berchmans, Aug. 13.

Archers—St. Sebastian, Jan. 20.

Architects—St. Thomas, Apostle, Dec. 21; St. Barbara, Dec. 4.

Armorers—St. Dunstan, May 19.

Artillerymen—St. Barbara, Dec. 4.

Art—St. Catherine (Bologna), Mar. 9.

Artists—St. Luke, Oct. 18.

Astronomers—St. Dominic, Aug. 4.

Athletes—St. Sebastian, Jan. 20.

Authors—St. Francis de Sales, Jan. 29.

Automobilists—St. Frances of Rome, Mar, 9; St. Christopher, July 25.

Aviators—Our Lady of Loreto, Dec. 10; St. Therese of Lisieux, Oct. 3; St. Joseph of Cupertino, Sept. 18.

Bakers—St. Elizabeth of Hungary, Nov. 19; St. Nicholas, Dec. 6.

Bankers—St. Matthew, Sept. 21.

Barbers—SS. Cosmos and Damian, Sept. 27; St. Louis, Aug. 25.

Barren Women—St. Anthony of Padua, June 13; St. Felicitas, Nov. 23.

Basket-makers—St. Anthony, Abbot, Jan. 17.

Beggars—St. Alexius, July 17.

Belt-makers—St. Alexius, July 17.

Blacksmiths—St. Dunstan, May 19.

Blind—St. Odilia, Dec. 13; St. Raphael, Oct. 24.

Bodily Ills—Our Lady of Lourdes, Feb. 11.

Bookbinders—St. Peter Celestine, May 19.

Booksellers—St. John of God, March 8.

Boy Scouts—St. George, April 23.

Brewers—St. Augustine of Hippo, Aug. 28; St. Luke, Oct. 18; St. Nicholas of Myra, Dec. 6.

Bricklayers—St. Stephen, Dec. 26.

Brides—St. Nicholas of Myra, Dec. 6.

Brush-makers—St. Anthony, Abbot, Jan. 17.

Builders—St. Vincent Ferrer, April 5.

Butchers—St. Anthony, Abbot, Jan. 17; St. Hadrian, Sept. 8; St. Luke, Oct. 18.

Cab-drivers—St. Fiacre, Aug. 30.

Cabinet-makers—St. Anne, July 26.

Cancer Patients—St. Peregrine, May 2.

Canonists—St. Raymond of Penafort, Jan. 23.

Carpenters—St. Joseph, March 19.

Catechists—St. Viator, Oct. 21; St. Charles Borromeo, Nov. 4; St. Robert Bellarmine, May 13.

Catholic Action—St. Francis of Assisi, Oct. 4.

Chandlers—St. Ambrose, Dec. 7; St. Bernard of Clairvaux, Aug. 20.

Charitable Societies—St. Vincent de Paul, July 19.

Children—St. Nicholas of Myra, Dec. 6.

Children of Mary—St. Agnes, Jan 21; St. Maria Goretti, July 9.

Choir Boys—H. Innocents, Dec. 28.

Clerics—St. Gabriel of the Sorrowful Mother, Feb. 27.

Comedians—St. Vitus, June 15.

Confessor—St. Alphonsus Ligouri, Aug. 2; St. John Nepomucene, May 16.

Convulsion in Children—St. Scholastica, Feb. 10.

Cooks—St. Lawrence, Aug. 10; St. Martha, July 29.

Coopers—St. Nicholas of Myra, Dec. 6.

Coppersmiths—St. Maurus, Jan. 15.

Dairy Workers—St. Brigid, Feb. 1.

Deaf—St. Francis de Sales, Jan. 29.

Dentists—St. Apollonia, Feb. 9.

Desperate Situations—St. Gregory of Neocaesarea, Nov. 17; St. Jude Thaddeus, Oct. 28.

Domestic Animals—St. Anthony, Abbot, Jan. 17.

Druggists—SS. Cosmas and Damian, Sept. 27; St. James the Less, May 1.

Dyers—SS. Maurice and Lydia, Aug. 3.

Dying—St. Joseph, March 19; St. Barbara, Dec. 4.

Emigrants—St. Francis Xavier Cabrini, Nov. 13.

Engineers—St. Ferdinand III, May 30.

Eucharistic Congresses and Societies—St. Paschal Baylon, May 17.

Expectant Mothers—St. Margaret, July 20; St. Raymond Nonnatus, Aug. 31; St. Gerard Majella, Oct. 16.

Eye Trouble—St. Lucy, Dec. 13.

Falsely Accused—St. Raymond Nonnatus, Aug. 31.

Farmers—St. George, April 23; St. Isidore, Mar. 22.

Farriers—St. John Baptist, Aug. 29.

Firemen—St. Florian, May 4.

Fire Prevention—St. Catherine of Siena, April 30; St. Barbara, Dec. 4.

First Communicants—Bl. Imelda, May 12; St. Tarcisius, Aug. 15.

Fishermen—St. Andrew, Nov. 30.

Florists—St. Dorothy, Feb. 6; St. Therese, Oct. 3.

Forest-workers—St. John Gualbert, July 12.

Founders—St. Barbara, Dec. 4.

Foundlings—Holy Innocents, Dec. 28.

Fullers—St. Anastasius the Fuller, Sept. 7; St. James the Less, May 1.

Funeral Directors—St. Joseph of Arimathea, March 17.

Gardeners—St. Dorothy, Feb. 6; St. Adalard, Jan. 2; St. Tryphon, Nov. 10; St. Fiacre, Aug. 30.

Glass-workers—St. Luke, Oct. 18.

Goldsmiths—St. Dunstan, May 19; St. Anastasius, Sept. 7.

Grave-diggers and Graveyards—St. Anthony, Abbot, Jan. 17.

Greetings—St. Valentine, Feb. 14.

Grocers—St. Michael, Sept. 29.

Gunners—St. Barbara, Dec. 4.

Hatters—St. Severus of Ravenna, Feb. 1; St. James the Less, May 1.

Haymakers—SS. Gervase and Protase, June 19.

Headaches—St. Teresa of Avila, Oct. 15.

Heart Ailments—St. John of God, Mar. 8.

Hospitals—St. Camillus de Lellis, July 18; St. John of God, March 8; St. Jude Thaddeus, Oct. 28.

Housewives—St. Anne, July 26.

Hunters—St. Hubert, Nov. 3.

Huntsmen—St. Eustachius, Sept. 20.

Inn-keepers—St. Amand, Feb. 6.

Invalids—St. Roch, Aug. 16.

Jewellers—St. Eligius, Dec. 1.

Journalists—St. Francis de Sales, Jan. 29.

Jurists—St. Catherine of Alexandria, Nov. 25; St. John Capistran, March 28.

Knights—St. Michael, Sept. 29.

Laborers—St. Isidore, May 10; St. James, July 25.

Lawyers—St. Ivo, May 19; St. Genesius, Aug. 25.

Learning—St. Ambrose, Dec. 7; St. Acca, Nov. 27.

Librarians—St. Jerome, Sept 30.

Locksmiths—St. Dunstan, May 19.

Lost Articles—St. Anthony of Padua, June 13.

Lovers—St. Raphael, Oct. 24.

Marble-workers—St. Clement I, Nov. 23.

Mariners—St. Michael, Sept. 29; St. Nicholas of Tolentino, Sept. 10.

Mentally Ill—St. Dympna, May 15.

Merchants—St. Francis of Assisi, Oct. 4; St. Nicholas of Myra, Dec. 6.

Messengers—St. Gabriel, March 24.

Metalworkers—St. Eligius, Dec. 1.

Millers—St. Arnulph, Aug. 15; St. Victor, July 21.

Miners—St. Barbara, Dec. 4.

Missions—St. Francis Xavier, Dec. 3; St. Therese of Lisieux, Oct. 3; (Home),

St. Leonard of Port Maurice, Nov. 26; (Negro), St. Peter Claver, Sept. 9, St. Benedict the Moor, April 4.

Mothers—St. Monica, May 4.

Motorists—St. Christopher, July 25.

Motorcyclists—Our Lady of Grace, May 31.

Mountaineers—St. Bernard of Menthon, May 28.

Musicians—St. Cecilia, Nov. 22; St. Dunstan, May 19.

Nail-makers—St. Cloud, Sept. 7.

Notaries—St. Luke, Oct. 18; St. Mark, April 25.

Nurses—St. Agatha, Feb. 5; St. Camillus de Lellis, July 18; St. Alexius, July 17; St. John of God, March 8; St. Raphael, Oct. 24.

Old Maids—St. Andrew, Nov. 30.

Orators—St. John Chrysostom, Jan. 27.

Organ Builders—St. Cecilia, Nov. 22.

Orphans—St. Jerome Aemilian, July 20.

Painters—St. Luke, Oct. 18.

Pawnbrokers—St. Nicholas of Myra, Dec. 6.

Philosophers—St. Justin, Apr. 14; St. Catherine of Alex., Nov. 25.

Physicians—St. Pantaleon, July 27; SS. Cosmas and Damian, Sept. 27; St. Luke, Oct. 18; St. Raphael, Oct. 24.

Pilgrims—St. Alexius, July 17; St. James, July 25.

Plasterers—St. Bartholomew, Aug. 24.

Poets—St. David, Dec. 29; St. Cecilia, Nov. 22.

Poisoning—St. Benedict, Mar. 21.

Policemen—St. Michael, Sept. 29.

Poor—St. Lawrence, Aug. 10; St. Anthony of Padua, June 13.

Porters—St. Christopher, July 25.

Possessed—St. Bruno, Oct. 6; St. Denis, Oct. 9.

Postal Employees—St. Gabriel, March 24.

Pregnant Women—St. Margaret, July 20; St. Raymund Nonnatus, Aug. 31; St. Gerard Majella, Oct. 16.

Priests—St. Jean-Baptiste Vianney, Aug. 9.

Printers—St. John of God, March 8; St. Augustine of Hippo, Aug. 28; St. Genesius, Aug. 25.

Prisoners—St. Dismas, Mar. 25; St.

Barbara, Dec. 4.

Prisons—St. Joseph Cafasso, June 23.

Protector of Crops—St. Ansovinus, Mar. 13.

Radiologists—St. Michael, Sept. 29.

Radio-workers—St. Gabriel, March 24.

Retreats—St. Ignatius Loyola, July 31.

Rheumatism—St. James the Greater, July 25.

Saddlers—SS. Crispin and Crispinian, Oct. 25.

Sailors—St. Cuthbert, March 20; St. Brendan, May 16; St. Eulalia, Feb. 12; St. Christopher, July 25; St. Peter Gonzales, April 15; St. Erasmus, June 2.

Scholars—St. Brigid, Feb. 1.

Schools—St. Thomas Aquinas, March 7; St. Joseph Calasanctius, Aug. 27.

Scientists—St. Albert, Nov. 15.

Sculptors—St. Claude, Nov. 8.

Seminarians—St. Charles Borromeo, Nov. 4.

Servants—St. Martha, July 29; St. Zita, April 27.

Shoemakers—SS. Crispin and Crispinian, Oct. 25.

Sick—St. Michael, Sept. 29; St. John of God, March 8; St. Camillus de Lellis, July 18; St. Philomena, Aug. 11.

Silversmiths—St. Andronicus, Oct. 11.

Singers—St. Gregory, March 12; St. Cecilia, Nov. 22.

Skaters—St. Lidwina, Apr. 14.

Skiers—St. Bernard of Menthon, May 28.

Soldiers—St. Hadrian, Sept. 8; St. George, April 23; St. Ignatius, July 31; St. Sebastian, Jan. 20; St. Martin of Tours, Nov. 11; St. Joan of Arc, May 30.

Sore Throat—St. Blaise, Feb. 3.

Stenographers—St. Genesius, Aug. 25; St. Cassian, Dec. 3.

Stone-cutters—St. Clement, Nov. 23.

Stone-masons—St. Stephen, Dec. 26; St. Barbara, Dec. 4.

Students—St. Thomas Aquinas, Mar. 7; St. Catherine of Alexandria, Nov. 25

Surgeons—SS. Cosmas and Damian, Sept. 27.

Swordsmiths—St. Maurice, Sept. 22.

Tailors — St. Homobonus, Nov. 13.

Tanners — SS. Crispin and Crispinian, Oct. 25; St. Simon, May 10.

Tax-gatherers — St. Matthew, Sept. 21.

Teachers — St. Gregory the Great, March 12; St. Catherine of Alexandria, Nov. 25; (principal patron), St. John the Baptist de la Salle, May 15.

Telegraph/Telephone workers — St. Gabriel, March 24.

Television-workers — St. Gabriel, March 24.

Tertiaries — St. Louis of France, Aug. 25; St. Elizabeth of Hungary, Nov. 19.

Theologians — St. Augustine, Aug. 28; (Moral), St. Alphonsus Liguori, Aug. 2.

Travelers — St. Anthony of Padua, June 13; St. Nicholas of Myra, Dec. 6; St. Christopher, July 25; St. Raphael, Oct. 24.

Undertakers — St. Dismas, Mar. 25.

Universal Church — St. Joseph, March 19.

Universities — Blessed Contardo Ferrini, Oct. 5.

Vocations — St. Alphonsus, Aug. 2.

Watchmen — St. Peter of Alcantara, Oct. 19.

Weavers — St. Paul the Hermit, Jan. 15; St. Anastasius the Fuller, Sept. 7; St. Anastasia, Dec. 25.

Wine-growers — St. Vincent, Jan. 22.

Wine-merchants — St. Amand, Feb. 6.

Wheelwrights — St. Catherine of Alexandria, Nov. 25.

Women in labor — St. Anne, July 26.

Women's Army Corps — St. Genevieve, Jan. 3.

Workingmen — St. Joseph, May 1.

Writers — St. Francis de Sales, Jan. 29; St. Lucy, Dec. 13.

Yachtsmen — St. Adjutor, Sept. 1.

Young Girls — St. Agnes, Jan. 21.

Youth — St. Aloysius Gonzaga, June 21; St. John Berchmans, Aug. 13; St. Gabriel Possenti, Feb. 27.

Appendix IV
Patron Saints of Countries and Places

Alsace: St. Odile
Americas: Our Lady of Guadalupe
Argentina: Our Lady of Lujan
Armenia: St. Gregory
Asia Minor: St. John, Apostle
Australia: Our Lady Help of Christians
Basutoland; Immaculate Heart of Mary
Belgium: St. Joseph
Borneo: St. Francis Xavier
Brazil: Immaculate Conception
Canada: St. Anne
Ceylon: St. Lawrence
Chile: St. James, Apostle
China: St. Francis Xavier
Colombia: St. Peter Claver
Cuba: Our Lady of Cobre
Czechoslovakia: St. Wenceslaus
Denmark: St. Anscar
Dominican Republic: Our Lady of Grace
Ecuador: Sacred Heart
Finland: St. Henry
France: Our Lady of the Assumption
Germany: St. Boniface
Greece: St. Nicholas of Myra
Guatemala: Our Lady of Chiantla
Honduras: Our Lady of Suyapa
Hungary: St. Stephen
India: Our Lady of the Assumption
Ireland: St. Patrick

Italy: St. Francis of Assisi
Japan: St. Peter Baptist
Lithuania: St. Casmir
Mexico: Our Lady of Guadalupe
Monaco: St. Devote
Netherlands: St. Willibrord
New Zealand: Our Lady Help of Christians
Norway: St. Olaf
Paraguay: Our Lady of the Assumption
Peru: St. Joseph
Philippines: Sacred Heart of Mary
Poland: St. Stanislaus
Portugal: St. Vincent
Russia: St. Andrew
Scandinavia: St. Anscar
Scotland: St. Andrew
Slovakia: Our Lady of Sorrows
South America: St. Rose of Lima
Spain: St. James, Apostle
Sweden: St. Bridget
Switzerland: St. Nicholas of Myra
South Africa: Our Lady of the Assumption
United States: Immaculate Conception
Uruguay: Our Lady of Lujan
Wales: St. David
West Indies: St. Gertrude

Appendix V
International Catholic Organizations

Pope John XXIII in his Encyclical, PRINCEPS PASTORUM, commented on the value and importance of the help that international Catholic organizations will be able to give to the lay apostolate in mission countries on the scientific level with the study of Christian solutions, especially in the social problems of new nations, and on the apostolic level for the organization of an active Christian laity.

Alcoholism	International Catholic League Against Alcoholism 3, Lowenstrasse Lucerne, Switzerland
Art, Liturgical	International Institute of Liturgical Art Rome, Italy
Charity	International Association of Ladies of Charity of St. Vincent de Paul 10, Avenue Constant Coquelin Paris 7, France Society of St. Vincent de Paul 5, rue de Pre-aux-Clercs Paris VII, France Society of Women of St. Vincent de Paul 8, Via Castiglione Bologna, Italy
Charities	International Conference of Catholic Charities 15 Via della Conciliazione Rome, Italy
Catholic Organizations	Conference of International Catholic Organizations 1, route du Jura Fribourg, Switzerland
Children	International Catholic Child Bureau 42, rue de Chabrol Paris X, France
Education	International Catholic Education Office 9, rue Guimard Brussels, Belgium
Education, Religious	International Study Centre for Religious Education 184, rue Washington Brussels, Belgium
Employers	International Union of Catholic Employers' Ass'n 71, avenue de Cartenberg Brussels, Belgium

Esperanto	International Union of Catholic Esperantists 81, Utrechtsweg Vleuten (Utrecht), Netherlands
Films	International Catholic Film Office 8 rue de l'Orme Brussels, Belgium
Girls	International Catholic Girls' Society 1, route du Jura Fribourg, Switzerland
Hospitals	Catholic International Hospital Federation 72, Badhuisweg The Hague, Netherlands
Intellectual and Cultural Affairs	Pax Romana International Movement for Intellectual and Cultural Affairs 1, route du Jura Fribourg, Switzerland
Lay Apostolate	Permanent Committee for International Congresses of the Apostolate of the Laity Palazzo delle Congregazioni 46, Piazza San Calisto Rome, Italy
Legion of Mary	Legion of Mary International Council De Montfort House North Brunswick Street Dublin, Ireland
Marian Academy	International Marian Academy Piazza Monte Savello, 9 Rome, Italy
Men	International Federation of Catholic Men 4, Via della Conciliazione Rome, Italy
Migration	International Catholic Migration Commission 65 rue de Lausanne Geneva, Switzerland
Nurses	International Committee of Catholic Nurses 16, rue Tiphaine Paris 15, France
Peace	Pax Christi 26, rue Barbet-de-Jouy Paris VII, France
Philosophy	World Union of Catholic Philosophical Societies Abbaye Einsiediln U.W., Switzerland
Physical Education	Catholic International Federation for Physical Education 5, Place St.-Thomas d'Aquin Paris 7, France
Press	International Catholic Press Union 43, rue St.-Augustin Paris II, France

Three Federations belong to the Union:

International Federation of Catholic Journalists
1, Via della Conciliazione
Rome, Italy

International Federation of Catholic Newspaper Publishers
22, Cours Albert 1
Paris VII, France

International Federation of Catholic Press Agencies
c/o KNP
48, Anna Paulownastraat
The Hague, Netherlands

Public Opinion	International Union "Pro Deo" 89, Via Nazionale Rome, Italy
Radio and Television	International Catholic Ass'n for Radio and Television 6, avenue de la Gare Fribourg, Switzerland
Seamen	Apostolatus Maris International Council International General Secretariat 10, Piazza Pio XII Rome, Italy
Singers	International Federation of Little Singers 1420 Avenue of the Americas New York, New York
Social Action	Inter American Catholic Social Action Confederation 1312 Massachusetts Avenue, N.W. Washington, D.C.
Social Research	International Federation of Catholic Institutes for Social Research 1, route du Jura Fribourg, Switzerland
Social Service	Catholic International Union for Social Service 111, rue de la Poste Brussels, Belgium
Social Studies	International Union for Social Studies 19, avenue d'Yser Brussels, Belgium
Social Union	International Christian Social Union 127, rue de la Loi Brussels, Belgium
Sodalities	World Federation of Sodalities of Our Lady 5, Borgo Santo Spirito Rome, Italy
Students	International Young Christian Students 27 rue Linne Paris V, France Pax Romana International Movement of Catholic Students 1, route du Jura Fribourg, Switzerland

Teachers	World Union of Catholic Teachers 3, Via della Conciliazione Rome, Italy
Technologists Agriculturalists Economists	International Secretariat of Catholic Technologists Agriculturalists and Economists 18, rue de Varenne Paris 7, France
Trade Unions	International Federation of Christian Trade Unions 148, rue de la Loi Brussels, Belgium
UNESCO	Centre Catholique International de Coordination aupres de l'UNESCO 98, rue de l'Universite Paris 7, France
Universities	International Federation of Catholic Universities 108, Via della Pineta Sacchetti Rome, Italy
Women	World Union of Catholic Women's Organizations 91, rue de Sevres Paris 6, France
Workers	International Federation of Christian Workers' Movements 127, rue de la Loi Brussels, Belgium
	International Federation of Middle Class Catholics 12 rue de Spa Brussels 4, Belgium
	Young Christian Workers 78, Boulevard Poincare Brussels, Belgium
Youth	International Federation of Catholic Youth 94, Via Torre Rossa Rome, Italy
	World Federation of Catholic Young Women and Girls 8, Springweg Utrecht, Netherlands
Youth, Rural	International Movement of Rural Youth 60 Parijsstraat Leuven, Belgium

Appendix VI
The Popes of the Catholic Church

Although the *Annuario* records the anti-popes in the general listing of popes, they have been separated in the following list to avoid confusion. They will be found in a separate table following. The list below includes the name of the pope, original name when available, birthplace, and dates of rule. When two dates are given, the first refers to election, the second to coronation.

St. Linus: Tuscia; 67–76.
St. Anacletus (Cletus): Rome, 76–88.
St. Clement: Rome, 88–97.
St. Evaristus: Greece; 97–105.
St. Alexander I: Rome; 105–115.
St. Sixtus I: Rome; 115–125.
St. Telesphorus: Greece; 125–136.
St. Hyginus: Greece; 136–140.
St. Pius I: Aquileia; 140–155.
St. Anicetus: Syria; 155–166.
St. Soter: Campania; 166–175.
St. Eleutherius: Nicopoli in Epirus; 175–189.
St. Victor I: Africa; 189–199.
St. Zephyrinus: Rome; 199–217.
St. Callistus I: Rome; 217–222.
St. Urban I: Rome; 222–230.
St. Pontian: Rome; July 21, 230, to Sept. 28, 235.
St. Anterus: Greece; Nov. 21, 235, to Jan. 3, 236.
St. Fabian: Rome; Jan. 10, 236, to Jan. 20, 250.
St. Cornelius: Rome; Mar., 251, to June, 253.
St. Lucius I: Rome; June 25, 253, to Mar. 5, 254.
St. Stephen I: Rome; May 12, 254, to Aug. 2, 257.
St. Sixtus II: Greece; Aug. 30, 257, to Aug. 6, 258.
St. Dionysius: July 22, 259, to Dec. 26, 268.

St. Felix I: Rome; Jan. 5, 269, to Dec. 30, 274.
St. Eutychian: Luni; Jan. 4, 275, to Dec. 7, 283.
St. Caius: Dalmatia; Dec. 17, 283, to Apr. 22, 296.
St. Marcellinus: Rome; June 30, 296, to Oct. 25, 304.
St. Marcellus I: Rome; May 27, 308, or June 26, 308, to Jan. 16, 309.
St. Eusebius: Greece; Apr. 18, 309 or 310, to Aug. 17, 309 or 310.
St. Milziades or Melchiades: Africa; July 2, 311, to Jan. 11, 314.
St. Sylvester I: Rome; Jan. 31, 314, to Dec. 31, 335.
St. Marcus: Rome; Jan. 18, 336, to Oct. 7, 336.
St. Julius I: Rome; Feb. 6, 337, to Apr. 12, 352.
Liberius: Rome; May 17, 352, to Sept. 24, 366.
St. Damasus I: Spain; Oct. 1, 366, to Dec. 11, 384.
St. Siricius: Rome; Dec. 15 or 22 or 29, 384, to Nov. 26, 399.
St. Anastasius I: Rome; Nov. 27, 399, to Dec. 19, 401.
St. Innocent I: Albano; Dec. 22, 401, to Mar. 12, 417.
St. Zozimus: Greece; Mar. 18, 417, to Dec. 26, 418.
St. Boniface I: Rome; Dec. 28 or 29, 418, to Sept. 4, 422.
St. Celestine I: Campania; Sept. 10, 422 to July 27, 432.

* Source for this entry is the *Annuario Pontifico*.

St. Sixtus III: Rome, July 31, 432, to
Aug. 19, 440,

St. Leo I (the Great): Tuscany; Sept. 29,
440, to Nov. 10, 461.

St. Hilary: Sardinia; Nov. 19, 461, to
Feb. 29, 468.

St. Simplicius: Tivoli; Mar. 3, 468, to
Mar. 10, 483.

St. Felix III (II): Rome; Mar. 13, 483,
to Mar. 1, 492.

St. Gelasius I: Africa; Mar. 1, 492, to
Nov. 21, 496.

Anastasius II: Rome; Nov. 24, 496, to
Nov. 19, 498.

St. Symmachus: Sardina; Nov. 22, 498,
to July 19, 514.

St. Hormisdas: Frosinone; July 20, 514,
to Aug. 6, 523.

St. John I, Marytr: Tuscany; Aug. 13,
523, to May 18, 526.

St. Felix IV (III): Samnium; July 12,
526, to Sept. 22, 530.

Boniface II: Rome; Sept. 22, 530, to Oct.
17, 532.

John II: Rome; Jan, 2, 533, to May 8,
535.

St. Agapitus I: Rome; May 13, 535, to
Apr. 22, 536.

St. Silverius, Martyr: Compania; June 1
or 8, 536 to Nov. 11, 537.

Vigilius: Rome; Mar. 29, 537, to June
7, 555.

Pelagius I: Rome; Apr. 16, 556, to Mar.
4, 561.

John III: Rome; July 17, 561, to July 13,
574.

Benedict I: Rome; June 2, 575, to July
30, 579.

Pelagius II: Rome; Nov. 26, 579, to
Feb. 7, 590.

St. Gregory I (the Great): Rome; Sept.
3, 590, to Mar. 12, 604.

Sabinianus: Blera in Tuscany; Sept. 13,
604, to Feb. 22, 606.

Boniface III: Rome; Feb. 19, 607, to
Nov. 12, 607.

St. Boniface IV: Marsi; Aug. 25, 608, to
May 8, 615.

St. Deusdedit (Adeodatus I): Rome;
Oct. 19, 615, to Nov. 8, 618

Boniface V: Naples; Dec. 23, 619, to
Oct. 25, 625.

Honorius I: Campania; Oct. 27, 625, to
Oct. 12, 638.

Severinus: Rome; May 28, 640, to Aug.
2, 640.

John IV: Dalmatia; Dec. 24, 640, to Oct.
12, 642.

Theodore I: Greece; Nov. 24, 642, to
May 14, 649.

St. Martin I, Martyr: Todi; July, 649, to
Sept. 16, 655.

St. Eugene I: Rome; Aug. 10, 654, to
June 2, 657.

St. Vitalian: Segni; July 30, 657, to Jan.
27, 672.

Adeodatus II: Rome; Apr. 11, 672, to
June 17, 676.

Donus: Rome; Nov. 2, 676, to Apr.
11, 678.

St. Agatho: Sicily; June 27, 678, to Jan.
10, 681.

St. Leo II: Sicily; Aug. 17, 682, to July
3, 683.

St. Benedict II: Rome; June 26, 684, to
May 8, 685.

John V: Syria; July 23, 685, to Aug. 2,
686.

Conon: Oct. 21, 686, to Sept. 21, 687.

St. Sergius I: Syria; Dec. 15, 687, to
Sept. 8, 701.

John VI: Greece; Oct. 30, 701, to Jan.
11, 705.

John VII: Greece; Mar. 1, 705, to Oct.
18, 707.

Sisinnius: Syria; Jan. 15, 708, to Feb.
4, 708.

Constantine: Syria; Mar. 25, 708, to
Apr. 9, 715.

St. Gregory II: Rome; May 19, 715, to
Feb. 11, 731.

St. Gregory III: Syria; Mar. 18, 731, to
Nov., 741.

St. Zachary: Greece; Dec. 10, 741, to
Mar. 22, 752.

Stephen II (III): Rome; Mar. 26, 752,
to Apr. 26, 757.

St. Paul I: Rome; Apr. (May 29), 757,
to June 28, 767.

Stephen III (IV); Sicily; Aug. 1 (7), 768,
to Jan. 24, 772.

Adrian I: Rome; Feb. 1 (9), 772, to
Dec. 25, 795.

St. Leo III: Rome; Dec. 26 (27), 795, to
June 12, 816.

Stephen IV (V): Rome; June 22, 816, to Jan. 24, 817.

St. Paschal I: Rome; Jan. 25, 817, to Feb. 11, 824.

Eugene II: Rome; Feb. (May), 824 to Aug., 827.

Valentine: Rome; Aug., 827, to Sept. 827.

Gregory IV: Rome; 827 to Jan., 844.

Sergius II: Rome; Jan., 844, to Jan. 27, 847.

St. Leo IV: Rome; Jan. (Apr. 10), 847, to July 17, 855.

Benedict III: Rome; July (Sept. 29), 855, to Apr. 17, 858.

St. Nicholas I (the Great): Rome; Apr. 24, 858, to Nov. 13, 867.

Adrian II: Rome; Dec. 14, 867, to Dec. 14, 872.

John VIII: Rome; Dec. 14, 872, to Dec. 16, 882.

Marinus I: Gallese; Dec. 16, 882, to May 15, 884.

St. Adrian III: Rome; May 17, 884, to Sept., 885. Cult confirmed June 2, 1891.

Stephen V (VI): Rome; Sept. 885, to Sept. 14, 891.

Formosus: Portus; Oct. 6, 891, to Apr. 4, 896.

Boniface VI: Rome; Apr., 896, to Apr., 896.

Stephen VI (VII): Rome; May, 896, to Aug., 897.

Romanus: Gallese; Aug., 897, to Nov. 897.

Theodore II: Rome; Dec., 897, to Dec., 897.

John IX: Tivoli; Jan., 898, to Jan., 900.

Benedict IV: Rome; Jan. (Feb.), 900, to July, 903.

Leo V: Ardea; July, 903, to Sept., 903.

Sergius III: Rome; Jan., 29, 904, to Apr. 14, 911.

Anastasius III: Rome; Apr., 911, to June, 913.

Landus: Sabina; July, 913, to Feb., 914.

John X: Tossignano (Imola); Mar., 914, to May, 928.

Leo VI: Rome; May, 928, to Dec., 928.

Stephen VII (VIII): Rome; Dec., 928, to Feb., 931.

John XI: Rome; Feb. (Mar.), 931, to Dec., 935.

Leo VII: Rome; Jan. 3, 936, to July 13, 939.

Stephen VIII (IX): Rome; July 14, 939, to Oct. 942.

Marinus II: Rome; Oct. 30, 942, to May, 946.

Agapitus II: Rome; May 10, 946, to Dec., 955.

John XII (Octavius): Tusculum; Dec. 16, 955, to May 14, 964.

Leo VIII: Rome; Dec. 4 (6), 963, to Mar. 1, 965.

Benedict V: Rome; May 22, 964, to July 4, 966.

John XIII: Rome; Oct. 1, 965, to Sept. 6, 972.

Benedict VI: Rome; Jan. 19, 973, to June, 974.

Benedict VII: Rome; Oct. 974, to July 10, 983.

John XIV (Peter Campenora): Pavia; Dec., 983, to Aug. 20, 984.

John XV: Rome; Aug., 985, to Mar., 996.

Gregory V (Bruno of Carinthia): Saxony; May 3, 996, to Feb. 18, 999.

Sylvester II (Gerbert): Auvergne; Apr. 2, 999, to May 12, 1003.

John XVII (Siccone): Rome; June, 1003, to Dec., 1003.

John XVIII (Phasianus): Rome; Jan., 1004, to July, 1009.

Sergius IV (Peter): Rome; July 31, 1009, to May 12, 1012.

Benedict VIII (Theophylactus): Tusculum; May 18, 1012 to Apr. 9, 1024.

John XIX (Romanus): Tusculum; Apr. (May), 1024, to 1032.

Benedict IX (Theophylactus): Tusculum; 1032 to 1044.

Sylvester III (John): Rome; Jan. 20, 1045, to Feb. 10, 1045.

Benedict IX (second time): Apr. 10, 1045, to May 1, 1045.

Gregory VI (John Gratian): Rome; May 5, 1045, to Dec. 20, 1046.

Clement II (Suidger, Lord of Morsleben and Hornburg): Saxony; Dec. 24 (25), 1046, to Oct. 9, 1047.

Benedict IX (third time): Nov. 8, 1047, to July 17, 1048.

Damasus II (Poppo): Bavaria; July 17, 1048, to Aug. 9, 1048.

St. Leo IX (Bruno, of the Counts Egisheim-Dagsburg): Alsace; Feb. 12, 1049, to Apr. 19, 1054.

Victor II (Gebhard, Count of Dollnstein-Hirschberg): Germany; Apr. 16, 1055, to July 28, 1057.

Stephen IX (X) (Frederick): Lorraine; Aug. 3, 1057, to Mar. 29, 1058.

Nicholas II (Gerard): Burgundy; Jan. 24, 1059, to July 27, 1061.

Alexander II (Anselmo da Baggio): Milan; Oct. 1, 1061, to Apr. 21, 1073.

St. Gregory VII (Hildebrand): Tuscany; Apr. 22 (June 30), 1073, to May 25, 1085.

Bl. Victor III (Dauferius; Desiderius): Benevento; May 24, 1086, to Sept. 16, 1087. Cult confirmed July 23, 1887.

Bl. Urban II (Oddone di Largery): France; Mar. 12, 1088, to July 29, 1099. Cult confirmed July 14, 1881.

Paschal II (Ranieri): Ravenna; Aug. 13 (14), 1099 to Jan. 21, 1118.

Gelasius (Giovanni Caetani): Gaeta; Jan. 24 (Mar. 10), 1118 to Jan. 28, 1119.

Callistus II (Guido of Burgundy): Burgundy; Feb. 2, (9), 1119, to Dec. 13, 1124.

Honorius II (Lamberto): Fiagnano (Imola); Dec. 15, (21), 1124, to Feb. 13, 1130.

Innocent II (Gregorio Papareschi): Rome; Feb. 14 (23), 1130, to Sept. 24, 1143.

Celestine II (Guido): Citta di Castello; Sept. 26 (Oct. 3), 1143, to Mar. 8, 1144.

Lucius II (Gerardo Caccianemici): Bologna; Mar. 12, 1144, to Feb. 15, 1145.

Bl. Eugene III (Bernardo Paganelli di Montemagno): Pisa; Feb. 15 (18), 1145, to July 8, 1153. Cult confirmed Oct. 3, 1872.

Anastasius IV (Corrado): Rome; July 12, 1153, to Dec. 3, 1154.

Adrian IV (Nicholas Breakspear): England; Dec. 4 (5), 1154, to Sept. 1, 1159.

Alexander III (Rolando Bandinelli): Siena; Sept. 7 (20), 1159, to Aug. 30, 1181.

Lucius III (Ubaldo Allucingoli): Lucca; Sept. 1 (6), 1181, to Sept. 25, 1185.

Urban III (Uberto Crivelli): Milan; Nov. 25 (Dec. 1), 1185, to Oct. 20, 1187.

Gregory VIII (Alberto de Morra): Benevento; Oct. 21 (25), 1187, to Dec. 17, 1187.

Clement III (Paolo Scolari): Rome; Dec. 19 (20), 1187, to Mar., 1191.

Celestine III (Giacinto Bobone): Rome; Mar. 30 (Apr. 14), 1191, to Jan. 8, 1198.

Innocent III (Lotario dei Conti di Segni): Anagni; Jan. 8 (Feb. 22), 1198, to July 16, 1216.

Honorius III (Cencio Savelli): Rome; July 18 (24), 1216, to Mar. 18, 1227.

Gregory IX (Ugolino, Count of Segni): Anagni; Mar. 19 (21), 1227, to Aug. 22, 1241.

Celestine IV (Goffredo Castiglioni): Milan; Oct. 25 (28), 1241, to Nov. 10, 1241.

Innocent IV (Sinibaldo Fieschi): Genoa; June 25 (28), 1243, to Dec. 7, 1254.

Alexander IV (Rinaldo, Count of Segni): Anagni; Dec. 12 (20), 1254, to May 25, 1261.

Urban IV (Jacques Pantaleon): Troyes; Aug. 29 (Sept. 4), 1261, to Oct. 2, 1264.

Clement IV (Guy Foulques or Guido le Gros): France; Feb. 5 (15), 1265, to Nov. 29, 1268.

Bl. Gregory X (Teobaldo Visconti): Piacenza; Sept. 1, 1271 (Mar. 27, 1272), to Jan. 10, 1276. Cult confirmed Sept. 12, 1713.

Bl. Innocent V (Peter of Tarentaise): Savoy; Jan. 21 (Feb. 22), 1276, to June 22, 1276. Cult confirmed Mar. 13, 1898.

Adrian V (Ottobono Fieschi): Genoa; July 11, 1276, to Aug. 18, 1276.

John XXI (Petrus Juliani or Petrus Hispanus): Portugal; Sept. 8 (20), 1276, to May 20, 1277.

Nicholas III (Giovanni Gaetano Orsini): Rome: Nov. 25 (Dec. 26), 1277, to Aug. 22, 1280.

Martin IV (Simon de Brie): France; Feb. 22 (Mar. 23), 1281, to Mar. 28, 1285.

Honorius IV (Giacomo Savelli): Rome; Apr. 2 (May 20), 1285, to Apr. 3, 1287.

Nicholas IV (Girolamo Masci): Ascoli; Feb. 22, 1288, to Apr. 4, 1292.

St. Celestine V (Pietro del Murrone): Isernia; July 5 (Aug. 29), 1294, to Dec. 13, 1294; d. 1296. Canonized May 5, 1313.

Boniface VIII (Benedetto Caetani): Anagni; Dec. 24, 1294 (Jan. 23, 1295), to Oct. 11, 1303.

Bl. Benedict XI (Niccolo Boccasini): Treviso; Oct. 22 (27), 1303, to July 7, 1304. Cult confirmed Apr. 24, 1736.

Clement V (Bertrand de Got): France; June 5 (Nov. 14), 1305, to Apr. 20, 1314.

John XXII (Jacques d'Euse): Cahors; Aug. 7 (Sept. 5), 1316, to Dec. 4, 1334.

Benedict XII (Jacques Fournier): France; Dec. 20, 1334 (Jan. 8, 1335), to Apr. 25, 1342.

Clement VI (Pierre Roger): France; May 7 (19), 1342 to Dec. 6, 1352.

Innocent VI (Etienne Aubert): France; Dec. 18 (30), 1352 to Sept. 12, 1362.

Bl. Urban V (Guillaume de Grimoard): France; Sept. 28 (Nov. 6), 1362, to Dec. 19, 1370. Cult confirmed Mar. 10, 1870.

Gregory XI (Pierre Roger de Beaufort): France; Dec. 30, 1370 (Jan. 5, 1371), to Mar. 26, 1378.

Urban VI (Bartolomeo Prignano)· Naples; Apr. 8 (18), 1378, to Oct. 15, 1389.

Boniface IX (Pietro Tomacelli): Naples; Nov. 2 (9), 1389, to Oct. 1, 1404.

Innocent VII (Cosma Migliorati): Sulmona; Oct. 17 (Nov. 11), 1404, to Nov. 6, 1406.

Gregory XII (Angelo Correr): Venice; Nov. 30 (Dec. 19), 1406, to July 4, 1415, when he voluntarily resigned from the papacy to permit the election of his successor. (See The Western Schism.)

Martin V (Oddone Colonna): Rome; Nov. 11 (21), 1417, to Feb. 20, 1431.

Eugene IV (Gabriele Condulmer): Venice; Mar. 3 (11), 1431, to Feb. 23, 1447.

Nicholas V (Tommaso Parentucelli): Sarzana; Mar. 6 (19), 1447, to Mar. 24, 1455.

Callistus III (Alfonso Borgia): Jativa; (Valencia); Apr. 8 (20), 1455, to Aug. 6, 1458.

Pius II (Enea Silvio Piccolomini): Siena; Aug. 19 (Sept. 3), 1458, to Aug. 15, 1464.

Paul II (Pietro Barbo): Venice; Aug. 30 (Sept. 16), 1464, to July 26, 1471.

Sixtus IV (Francesco della Rovere): Savona; Aug. 9 (25), 1471, to Aug. 12, 1484.

Innocent VIII (Giovanni Battista Cibo): Genoa; Aug. 29 (Sept. 12), 1484, to July 25, 1492.

Alexander VI (Rodrigo Borgia): Jativa (Valencia); Aug. 11 (26), 1492, to Aug. 18, 1503.

Pius III (Francesco Todeschini-Piccolomini): Siena; Sept. 22 (Oct. 1, 8), 1503, to Oct. 18, 1503.

Julius II (Giuliano della Rovere): Savona; Oct. 31 (Nov. 26), 1503, to Feb. 21, 1513.

Leo X (Giovanni de' Medici): Florence; Mar. 9 (19), 1513, to Dec. 1, 1521.

Adrian VI (Adrian Florensz): Utrecht; Jan. 9 (Aug. 31), 1522, to Sept. 14, 1523.

Clement VII (Giulio de' Medici): Florence; Nov. 19 (26), 1523, to Sept. 25, 1534.

Paul III (Alessandro Farnese): Rome; Oct. 13 (Nov. 3), 1534, to Nov. 10, 1549.

Julius III (Giovanni Maria Ciocchi del Monte): Rome; Feb. 7 (22), 1550, to Mar. 23, 1555.

Marcellus II (Marcello Cervini): Montepulciano; Apr. 9 (10), 1555, to May 1, 1555.

Paul IV (Gian Pietro Carafa): Naples; May 23 (26), 1555, to Aug. 18, 1559.

Pius IV (Giovan Angelo de' Medici): Milan; Dec. 25, 1559 (Jan. 6, 1560), to Dec. 9, 1565.

St. Pius V (Antonio-Michele Ghislieri). Bosco (Alexandria); Jan. 7 (17), 1566, to May 1, 1572. Canonized May 22, 1712.

Gregory XIII (Ugo Boncompagni): Bologna; May 13 (25), 1572, to Apr. 10, 1585.

Sixtus V (Felice Peretti): Grottammere (Ripatransone); Apr. 24 (May 1), 1585, to Aug. 27, 1590.

Urban VII (Giovanni Battista Castagna): Rome; Sept. 15, 1590, to Sept. 27, 1590.

Gregory XIV (Niccolo Sfondrati): Cremona; Dec. 5 (8), 1590, to Oct. 16, 1591.

Innocent IX (Giovanni Antonio Facchinetti): Bologna; Oct. 29 (Nov. 3), 1591, to Dec. 30, 1591.

Clement VIII (Ippolito Aldobrandini): Florence; Jan. 30 (Feb. 9), 1592, to Mar. 3, 1605.

Leo XI (Alessandro de' Medici): Florence; Apr. 1 (10), 1605, to Apr. 27, 1605.

Paul V (Camillo Borghese): Rome; May 16 (29), 1605, to Jan. 28, 1621.

Gregory XV (Alessandro Ludovisi): Bologna; Feb. 9 (14), 1621, to July 8, 1623.

Urban VIII (Maffeo Barberini): Florence; Aug. 6 (Sept. 29), 1623, to July 29, 1644.

Innocent X (Giovanni Battista Pamfili): Rome; Sept. 15 (Oct. 4), 1644, to Jan. 7, 1655.

Alexander VII (Fabio Chigi): Siena; Apr. 7 (18), 1655 to May 22, 1667.

Clement IX (Giulio Rospigliosi): Pistoia; June 20 (26), 1667, to Dec. 9, 1669.

Clement X (Emilio Altieri): Rome; Apr. 29 (May 11), 1670, to July 22, 1676. Elected by acclamation.

Bl. Innocent XI (Benedetto Odescalchi): Como; Sept. 21 (Oct. 4), 1676, to Aug. 12, 1689. Elected by acclamation.

Alexander VIII (Pietro Ottoboni), Venice; Oct. 6 (16), 1689, to Feb. 1, 1691.

Innocent XII (Antonio Pignatelli): Spinazzola; July 12 (15), 1691, to Sept. 27, 1700.

Clement XI (Giovanni Francesco Al-baul). Urbino, Nov. 23, 30 to (Dec 8), 1700, to Mar. 19, 1721.

Innocent XIII (Michelangelo dei Conti): Rome; May 8 (18), 1721, to Mar. 7, 1724.

Benedict XIII (Pietro Francesco—Vincenzo Maria—Orsini): Gravina (Bari); May 29 (June 4), 1724, to Feb. 21, 1730.

Clement XII (Lorenzo Corsini): Florence; July 12 (16), 1730, to Feb. 6, 1740.

Benedict XIV (Prospero Lambertini): Bologna; Aug. 17 (22), 1740, to May 3, 1758.

Clement XIII (Carlo Rezzonico): Venice; July 6 (16), 1758, to Feb. 2, 1769.

Clement XIV (Giovanni Vicenzo Antonio—Lorenzo—Ganganelli): Rimini; May 19, 28 (June 4), 1769, to Sept. 22, 1774.

Pius VI (Giovanni Angelo Braschi): Cesena; Feb. 15 (22), 1775, to Aug. 29, 1799.

Pius VII (Barnaba—Gregorio—Chiaramonti): Cesena; Mar. 14 (21), 1800, to Aug. 20, 1823.

Leo XII (Annibale della Genga): Genga (Fabriano); Sept. 28 (Oct. 5), 1823, to Feb. 10, 1829.

Pius VIII (Francesco Saverio Castiglioni): Cingoli; Mar. 31 (Apr. 5), 1829, to Nov. 30, 1830.

Gregory XVI (Bartolomeo Alberto—Mauro—Cappellari): Belluno; Feb. 2 (6), 1831, to June 1, 1846.

Pius IX (Giovanni M. Mastai Ferretti): Senegallia; June 16 (21), 1846, to Feb. 7, 1878.

Leo XIII (Gioacchino Pecci): Carpineto (Anagni); Feb. 20 (Mar. 3), 1878, to July 20, 1903.

St. Pius X (Giuseppe Sarto): Riese (Treviso); Aug. 4 (9), 1903, to Aug. 20, 1914. Canonized May 29, 1954.

Benedict XV (Giacomo della Chiesa): Genoa; Sept. 3 (6), 1914, to Jan. 22, 1922.

Pius XI (Achille Ratti): Fesio (Milan); Feb. 6 (12), 1922, to Feb. 10, 1939.

Pius XII (Eugenio Pacelli): Rome; Mar 2 (12), 1939, to Oct. 9, 1958.

John XXIII (Angelo Giuseppe Roncalli): Sotto il Monte (Bergamo); Oct. 28 (Nov. 4), 1958, to June 3, 1963.

Paul VI (Giovanni Battista Montini): Concessio; June 21 (June 30), 1963. Gloriously reigning.

The following list contains the names of those men who falsely claimed papal rule, birthplace, and dates of reign.

St. Hippolytus—Rome; 217–235; was reconciled before his death.

Novation—Rome; 251.

Felix II—Rome; 355 to Nov. 22, 365.

Ursinus—366–367.

Eulalius—Dec. 27 or 29, 418, to 419.

Lawrence—498; 501–505

Dioscorus—Alexandria; Sept. 22, 530, to Oct. 14, 530.

Theodore—ended alleged reign, 687.

Paschal—ended alleged reign, 687.

Constantine—Nepi; June 28 (July 5), 767, to 769.

Philip—July 31, 768; retired to his monastery on the same day.

John—ended alleged reign, Jan. 844.

Anastasius—Aug., 855 to Sept., 855.

Christopher—Rome; July or Sept., 903, to Jan. 904.

Boniface VII—Rome; June, 974 to July, 974; Aug., 984, to July, 985.

John XVI—Rossano; Apr., 997, to Feb., 998.

Gregory—ended alleged reign, 1012.

Benedict X—Rome; Apr. 5, 1058, to Jan. 24, 1059.

Honorius II—Verona; Oct. 28, 1061, to 1072.

Clement III—Parma; June 25, 1080 (Mar. 24, 1084), to Sept. 8, 1100.

Theodoric—ended alleged reign, 1100.

Albert—ended alleged reign, 1102.

Sylvester IV—Rome; Nov. 18, 1105, to 1111.

Gregory VIII—France; Mar. 8, 1118, to 1121.

Celestine II—Rome; ended alleged reign, Dec., 1124.

Anacletus II—Rome; Feb. 14 (23), 1130, to Jan. 25, 1138.

Victor IV—Mar. 1138, to May 29, 1138; submitted to Pope Innocent II.

Victor IV—Montecelio; Sept. 7 (Oct. 4), 1159, to Apr. 20, 1164; he did not recognize his predecessor (Victor IV, above).

Paschal III—Apr. 22 (26), 1164, to Sept. 20, 1168.

Callistus III—Arezzo; Sept., 1168, to Aug. 29, 1178; submitted to Pope Alexander III.

Innocent III—Sezze; Sept. 29, 1179, to 1180.

Nicholas V—Corvaro (Rieti); May 12 (22), 1328, to Aug. 25, 1330.

Clement VII—Sept. 20 (Oct. 31), 1378, to Sept. 16, 1394; first antipope of the Western Schism. (See separate article.)

Benedict XIII—Aragon; Sept. 28 (Oct. 11), 1394, to May 23, 1423.

Alexander V—Crete; June 26 (July 7), 1409, to May 3, 1410.

John XXIII—Naples; May 17 (25), 1410, to May 29, 1415; last antipope of the Western Schism.

Felix V—Savoy; Nov. 5, 1439 (July 24, 1440), to April 7, 1449.

* Source: *Annuario Pontifico.*

Appendix VII
Selective Biographies of Deceased Catholics
of the United States and Canada

Albanel, Charles, 1616–1696 Jesuit missioner to Canada's Montagnais Indians.

Albani, Emma, 1847–1930 Stage name for Marie Louise Emma Gye, an internationally celebrated Canadian operatic soprano.

Alemany, Joseph S., 1814–1888 First Archbishop of San Francisco; Dominican missioner in Ohio, Kentucky and Tennessee.

Allen, Frances, 1748–1819 Daughter of Ethan Allen, convert, first nun of New England birth.

Alloues, Claude, 1622–1689 Jesuit missioner; founded De Pere, Wis.

Altham, John, d. 1641 Jesuit missioner, founded first chapel in Maryland.

Ammen, Daniel, 1820–1898 Rear admiral, naval designer.

Anderson, Henry James, 1799–1875 Scientist, educator, author, convert.

Andre, Brother, 1845–1937 Religious name for Alfred Bessette, a Holy Cross Brother, founder of St. Joseph Oratory, Montreal.

Andreis, Venerable Felix de, 1778–1870 Vincentian, pioneer missioner and educator in Middle West.

Anglin, Margaret Mary, 1876–1958 Canadian actress.

Anglin, Timothy W., 1822–1896 Canadian journalist and politician.

Artiquette, Pierre d', 1700–1736 Burned at stake by Chickasaw Indians, near Fulton, Miss.

Auberg, Joseph, 1673–1755 Jesuit missioner to Abenaki Indians.

Audet, Francois Joseph, 1867–1943 Canadian archivist and historian.

Avery, Martha Moore, 1851–1929 Convert, political economist.

Bachelot, Alexis, d. 1837 One of first three priests to Hawaii. Prefect Apostolic of Sandwich Islands.

Bacon, David William, 1813–1874 First Bishop of Portland, Maine.

Baillargeon, Charles F., 1798–1870 Archbishop of Quebec, author.

Baker, Francis Asbury, 1820–1865 Convert, one of founders of Paulists.

Baker, Nelson H., 1841–1936 Priest, philanthropist.

Bapst, John, 1815–1887 Swiss Jesuit who served the Indians of Maine.

Baraga, Frederick, 1797–1868 Indian missioner and chronologist, first Bishop of Marquette.

Barbelin, Felix J., 1808–1869 Priest, educator, philanthropist.

Barre, Antoine Hefeboredela, 1622–1690 Governor-general of New France.

Barrett, Frank A., 1893–1962 Only man to serve Wyoming as U.S. representative, senator and governor.

Barron, Edward, 1801–1854 Bishop, pioneer missioner in Liberia.

Barry, John, 1745–1803 Senior officer in Revolutionary navy, Father U.S. Navy.

Barry, Philip, 1896–1949 Dramatist.

Barrymore, Ethel, 1879–1959 Actress.

Barrymore, Lionel, 1878–1954 Actor.

Barton, George, 1866–1940 Author.

Bayley, James Roosevelt, 1814–1877

Convert, 8th Archbishop of Baltimore, first Bishop of Newark, nephew of Mother Seton.

Bazin, John Stephen, 1796–1848 Missioner in south, bishop.

Beauregard, Pierre Gustave, 1818–1893 Confederate General, commanded Army of the West.

Becker, Thomas Andrew, 1832–1899 Bishop, author.

Begin, Louis Nazaire, 1840–1925 Cardinal, archbishop of Quebec.

Behn, Hernand, 1880–1933 Business executive.

Belmont, Francois Vachon de, 1645–1732 Sulpician missioner to Iroquois, Canadian historian.

Benson, William S., 1855–1932 Admiral, Chief of Naval Operations World War I.

Bentivoglio, Mother Magdalen, d. 1905 Foundress of Poor Clares in U.S.

Benziger, Bruno, 1873–1955 Publisher.

Berenson, Bernard, 1865—1959 Convert, art critic.

Bernal, Juan, d. 1680 Franciscan superior, missions in New Mexico and Arizona, massacred in Pueblo Revolt.

Bertrand, St. Louis, 1526–1581 Missioner in West Indies.

Bessette, Alfred (Brother Andre), 1845–1937 Founder of St. Joseph's Oratory, Montreal.

Blanc, Anthony, 1792–1860 Missioner in Mississippi Valley, first Archbishop of New Orleans.

Blanchet, Francois Norbert, 1795–1883 Pioneer missioner to Oregon country, first bishop in Oregon.

Bohachevsky, Constantine, 1884–1961 Archbishop, Exarch of Ukranian Catholics.

Bolton, Margaret (Mother), 1873–1943 Religious of Cenacle, educator.

Bonaparte, Charles J., 1851–1921 Secretary of Navy, U.S. Attorney General.

Bonaparte, Charles Lucien, 1803–1857 Ornithologist.

Booth, Edwin, 1833–1893 Shakespearian actor.

Boucher, Pierre, 1622–1717 Canadian pioneer, historian.

Bourdon, Jean, 1612–1668 Canadian pioneer, surveyor.

Bourgade, Peter, 1845–1908 Archbishop of Santa Fe, first Bishop of Tucson.

Bourgeoys, Bl. Marguerite, 1620–1700 Teacher, foundress of Congregation of Notre Dame of Montreal.

Bourget, Ignace, 1799–1885 Bishop of Montreal.

Brady, John J., 1884–1950 First Catholic chaplain to attain rank of Rear Admiral.

Brand, Joseph Oliver, 1715–1794 Bishop of Quebec, author of first book printed in Canada.

Braniff, Thomas E., 1883–1954 Airline executive.

Briggs, Walter, 1877–1952 Manufacturer.

Brennan, Patrick Thomas, 1901–1950 Columban missioner in Korea, killed by Reds in Taejon massacre, Sept. 24.

Broderick, Helen, 1891–1959 Actress.

Brophy, John, 1883–1963 Labor leader.

Broun, Heyward, 1888–1939 Convert, columnist, founder of American Newspaper Guild.

Brown, William, 1777–1857 Admiral.

Brownson, Orestes Augustus, 1803–1876 Universalist minister, convert, author and apologist.

Bruce, Frank, 1886–1953 Publisher.

Bruce, William C., 1860–1946 Publisher, civic leader.

Brute, Simon Gabriel, 1779–1839 First Bishop of Vincennes, Sulpician.

Bryant, John D., 1811–1877 Convert, author

Buck, Gene (Edward Eugene), 1885–1957 Lyricist, theatrical producer.

Burke, John J., 1875–1936 Paulist editor, founder NCWC.

Burnett, Peter H., 1807–1895 Convert, governor.

Butler, Mary Joseph (Mother Alphonsus), 1860–1940 Foundress and president of Marymount College, Tarrytown, N.Y.

Butler, Paul, 1905–1961 Politician.

Butler, Pierce, 1866–1939 Supreme Court Justice.

Byrne, Edward, 1802–1862 Missioner, first Bishop of Little Rock.

Byrne, Patrick J., 1888–1950 Pioneer Maryknoll Missioner in Korea, bishop, apostolic delegate; taken prisoner by Communists, he died from effects of infamous Yalu Death March.

Byrne, Richard, 1832–1864 Union general.

Byrne, William, 1780–1833 Missioner in Kentucky.

Caballero y Ocio, Juan, 1644–1707 Mexican priest, refused governorship of California.

Cabeza de Vaca, Alvar Nuñez, c.1490–c.1557 First white man to cross U.S.

Cabot, John, 1450–1498 Italian explorer of New World for England.

Cabral, Pedro Alvares, c.1460–c.1526 Discoverer of Brazil.

Cabrillo, Estevan, d. 1543 Explored California coast.

Cabrini, St. Francis Xavier, 1850–1917 First United States citizen to be canonized, foundress of Missionary Sisters of the Sacred Heart.

Cadillac, Antoine de la Moth, 1657–1730 Founder of Detroit.

Cairns, Robert J., 1884–1941 Maryknoll Missioner, pastor of Sancian Island, deathplace of Francis Xavier. Thrown into China Sea and drowned by Japanese troops.

Callaghan, Daniel H., 1890–1942 Admiral, Chief of Staff South Pacific.

Callahan, Patrick Henry, 1865–1940 Executive, pioneer in profit sharing, co-founder CAIP.

Callierès, Louis de, 1646–1705 Successor to Frontenac as Governor of New France, drew up treaty with Iroquois.

Calvert, Cecil, 1605–1675 Proprietor of Maryland, Second Lord Baltimore.

Calvert, Charles, 1637–1715 Third Lord Baltimore, governor of Maryland.

Calvert, Leonard, 1607–1647 Founder of Maryland, brother of Cecil.

Campbell, James, 1812–1893 Postmaster General, jurist.

Cantwell, John J., 1874–1947 First Archbishop of St. Louis.

Carey, Matthew, 1760–1839 Editor and publisher.

Caron, Rene E., 1800–1876 Jurist, lt. governor of Canada.

Carrel, Alexis, 1873–1944 Physiological surgeon.

Carrell, George A., 1803–1868 First bishop of Covington.

Carroll, Charles, 1737–1832 Statesman, member of Continental Congress, signer of Declaration of Independence, senator from Maryland.

Carroll, Daniel, 1733–1829 Brother John Carroll, framer of Constitution, selected site for National Capital.

Carroll, John, 1735–1815 First bishop of American hierarchy, first Bishop and Archbishop of Baltimore.

Carson, Kit (Christopher), 1809–1868 Convert, mountain man, guide, brigadier general.

Cartier, Georges E., 1814–1873 Premier of Canada.

Cartier, Jacques, 1491–1557 Explorer, discovered St. Lawrence River.

Carver, John, 1576–1640 First governor of Plymouth colony.

Caruso, Enrico, 1873–1921 Operatic singer.

Casgrain, Henri Raymond, 1831–1904 Author, critic, professor of history at Laval University.

Casserly, Eugene, 1822–1883 Senator.

Catala, Magin, 1761–1830 Missioner to Santa Clara Indians, Franciscan.

Champlain, Samuel de, 1570–1635 Explorer, founder of Quebec, father of New France.

Charlevoix, Francis Xavier, 1682–1761 Explorer, Jesuit historian.

Chauveau, Pierre, 1820–1890 Premier of Quebec.

Chavez, Dennis, 1888–1962 Senator.

Cheverus, Jean Louis, 1768–1836 First bishop of Boston.

Chouteau, Auguste, 1786–1838 Fur trader, Indian treaty commissioner, soldier, eldest son of Pierre, Sr. (q.v.)

Chouteau, Pierre, Jr., 1789–1865 Fur trader, founder of Pierre, S.D.

Chouteau, Pierre, Sr., 1758–1849 Fur trader, Indian agent.

Chouteau, Rene Auguste, 1749–1829

Fur trader, co-founder of St. Louis, Mo., brother of Pierre, Sr.

Clark, David W., 1902–1955 Senator from Idaho.

Cleary, William D., 1882–1949 Chaplain, brigadier general.

Cody, William F., 1846–1917 "Buffalo Bill," army scout, Pony Express rider.

Cohan, George M., 1878–1942 Author, theatrical producer, dramatist.

Columbus, Christopher, 1451–1506 Discoverer of America.

Connelly, Cornelia, 1809–1879 Convert, foundress of the Society of the Holy Child Jesus.

Connolly, John, 1750–1825 Second Bishop of New York.

Connolly, Terence, 1888–1961 Author, educator.

Connor, Joseph P., 1896–1952 Composer.

Connors, Francis J., 1900–1939 Maryknoll Missioner, apostle to Chinese lepers.

Conway, Bertrand, 1872–1959 Author, convert-maker, Paulist.

Conway, Katherine E., 1852–1927 Author, educator, winner of Laetare Medal.

Cooper, John M., 1881–1949 Priest, anthropologist.

Corcoran, James A., 1820–1889 Theologian, editor, Orientalist.

Coronado, Francisco Vasques de, 1510–1554 Explored southwest U.S., discovered Grand Canyon.

Coulonge, Louis Dailebout de, 1699–1736 Canadian captain, b. Montreal, burned at stake by Chickasaw Indians, near Fulton, Miss.

Crawford, F. Marion, 1854–1909 Author, convert.

Creighton, Edward, 1820–1874 Builder of roads and telegraph lines, cofounder of Creighton University.

Creighton, John, 1831–1907 Cofounder Creighton U., laid first telegraph line to California.

Crowley, Patrick E., 1864–1953 Railroad president.

Cudahy, Michael, 1841–1910 Merchant, philanthropist.

Cuddihy, Robert J., 1862–1952 Publisher.

Cummings, William J., 1903–1942 Maryknoll Missioner in Philippines, Army chaplain, coined phrase "No atheists in foxholes." Survived Siege of Bataan to die in hold of Japanese prison ship.

Dablon, Claude, 1618–1697 Jesuit missioner in Canada.

Daly, John, 1905–1964 Editor.

Daly, Thomas Augustine, 1871–1948 Poet, journalist.

Damien, Father (Joseph de Veuster), 1840–1888 Missioner to lepers on Molokai, Hawaii.

Danehy, Thomas J., 1914–1959 Mission bishop in Bolivia.

Delany, Selden Peabody, 1874–1935 Convert, priest, author.

Demers, Modeste, 1809–1871 Missioner, Bishop of Vancouver Island.

Dempsey, John J., 1879–1958 Governor.

Denning, Joseph M., 1866–1927 First priest in consular service.

DeRoaldes, Arthur W., 1849–1918 Surgeon.

De Smet, Peter John, 1801–1873 Belgian Jesuit, founder of Missouri Providence of Jesuits, missioner to and peacemaker among Indian tribes of Great Plains.

de Soto, Hernando (or Fernando), c.1500–1542 Explorer, buried in Mississippi River.

Dever, Paul A., 1903–1958 Governor.

DeWohl, Louis, 1903–1961 Author.

Dietz, Peter E., 1878–1947 Priest, pioneer labor organizer.

Donahoe, Patrick, 1811–1901 Publisher, editor.

Donovan, Gerard A., 1904–1938 First Maryknoll Missioner to die violently, murdered by bandits in Manchuria.

Donovan, William (Wild Bill), 1883–1959 World War I colonel, head of O.S.S. World War II.

Dongan, Thomas, 1634–1715 Colonial governor of New York.

Dooley, Thomas A., 1927–1961 Physician, author, co-founder of Medico.

Dorsey, Anna Hanson, 1815–1896 Novelist.

Dougherty, Dennis, 1865–1951 Cardinal, Archbishop of Philadelphia.

Douglas, Stephen A., 1813–1861 Statesman, noted for debate with Lincoln.

Dowling, Austin, 1868–1930 Archbishop, first Bishop of Des Moines.

Doyle, Michael Francis, 1877–1960 Jurist.

Drew, Georgiana, 1856–1893 Actress.

Drexel, Francis A., 1824–1885 Banker, philanthropist.

Drexel, Mother Mary Katharine, 1858–1955 Founded Sisters of the Blessed Sacrament.

Drum, Hugh A., 1879–1951 General.

Drumgoole, John, 1816–1888 Priest and philanthropist.

Duchesne, Philippine Rose, Blessed, 1769–1852, foundress of Religious of Sacred Heart in America.

Duff, Edward A., 1883–1953 First priest to be naval chief of chaplains.

Duffy, Francis P., 1871–1932 Chaplain "Fighting 69th."

Duhamel, Arthur, 1908–1942 Marist missioner from Lawrence, Mass.; bayonetted to death by Japanese on Guadalcanal.

Dunne, Peter Finley, 1867–1936 Journalist.

Duplessis, Maurice, 1890–1959 Premier of Quebec.

Durbin, Elisha J., 1800–1887 Pastor of one-third of Kentucky.

Durkin, Martin P., 1894–1955 Union president, secretary of labor.

Du Tisne, Louis Charles, 1708–1736 Captain, b. Quebec, burned at stake by Chickasaw Indians, near Fulton, Miss.

Dutton, Ira, 1843–1931 Assistant to Father Damien.

Duvernay, Ludger, 1799–1852 Journalist, selected maple leaf as emblem of Canada.

Dwight, Thomas, 1843–1911 Anatomist, convert.

Egan, Michael, 1761–1814 First Bishop of Philadelphia.

Elder, Benedict, 1882–1961 Editor, journalist.

Ellard, Gerald, 1895–1963 Jesuit, theologian, lecturer.

Emmett, Daniel D., 1815–1904 Composer of *Dixie*.

England, John, 1786–1842 First Bishop of Charleston, author.

Ericson, Leif, c. 1000 Possible Norse discoverer of America.

Estaing, Charles Hector d', 1729–1794 French admiral, aided American colonies.

Ewing, Charles, 1835–1883 General in Civil War.

Ewing, Hugh Boyle, 1826–1905 General in Civil War.

Ewing, Thomas, 1789–1871 Lawyer, cabinet secretary.

Fairbault, George B., 1789–1866 Canadian archaeologist.

Farley, John M., 1842–1918 Cardinal, archbishop of New York.

Farrell, Walter, 1902–1951 Dominican, theologian.

Farrow, John, 1906–1963 Author, motion picture director.

Fay, Frank, 1897–1961 Actor

Fenwick, Edward D., 1768–1832 Dominican, first Bishop of Cincinnati.

Finn, Francis, 1859–1928 Jesuit author of juveniles.

Finn, William J., 1881–1961 Paulist, musician.

Fisher, Max, 1893–1954 Journalist, author, convert.

Fiske, Stephen, 1840–1916 Dramatist, author.

Fitton, James, 1805–1881 New England missioner.

Fitzgerald, John F., 1863–1950 Mayor of Boston, grandfather of John F. Kennedy.

Fitzpatrick, Charles, 1853–1942 Canadian jurist.

Fitzpatrick, Thomas, c.1799–1854 Mountain man, guided first wagon train through Rockies.

FitzSimmons, Thomas, 1741–1811 Statesman, member of Continental Congress.

Flaget, Benedict Joseph, 1763–1850 Sulpician, first bishop of Bardstown, Ky.

Flanagan, Edward J., 1886–1948 Sociologist, youth worker, founded Boys Town, priest.

Fleck, Lawrence F., 1856–1938 Physician.

Floyd, John B., 1807–1863 Secretary of war, governor.

Flynn, Edmund J., 1847–1927 Canadian premier.

Ford, Francis X., 1892–1952 Pioneer Maryknoll Missioner, Bishop of Kaying, China; died in Communist prison in Canton, Feb. 21.

Ford, Jeremiah, 1873–1958 Scholar.

Fordney, Joseph W., 1853–1932 Executive.

Foster, John Gray, 1823–1874 U.S. general in Mexican and Civil Wars, convert.

Foucault, Nicholas, d. 1702 Canadian priest, martyred by Arkansas Indians.

Fréchette, Louis Honoré, 1839–1908 Canadian author.

Frontenac, Louis de Baude, Count of, 1622–1698 Governor of New France.

Galitzin, Elizabeth, 1797–1843 Princess, convert, religious.

Gallitzin, Demetrius, 1770–1840 Prince, convert, ordained in United States, missioner in Western Pennsylvania.

Garangouas, Margaret, d. 1692 Daughter of Iroquois chief, tortured and burned to death by her clansmen because she became a Catholic.

Garesche, Edward, 1876–1960 Jesuit, medical missioner.

Garneau, Francis Xavier, 1809–1866 Canadian historian.

Garnier, Julien, 1643–1730 Jesuit missioner, Apostle of Senecas.

Garraghan, Gilbert J., 1871–1942 Historian.

Gaston, William, 1778–1844 Jurist, federalist, congressman.

Gaxton, William, 1894–1963 Actor.

Gayarré, Charles E., 1805–1895 Historian, senator.

Giannini, Amadeo P., 1870–1949 Financier, philanthropist.

Gibbons, Floyd, 1887–1939 Journalist, radio commentator.

Gibbons, James, 1834–1921 Cardinal, Archbishop of Baltimore.

Gibson, Hugh S., 1883–1954 Diplomat.

Gillespie, Eliza Maria, 1824–1887 Religious, Civil War nurse, first superior Sisters of the Holy Cross.

Gillis, James M., 1876–1957 Paulist, orator, author.

Gleason, James, 1884–1959 Actor.

Glennon, John, 1862–1946 Cardinal, Archbishop of St. Louis.

Goldstein, David, 1870–1958 Convert, author.

Grace, Joseph Peter, 1872–1950 Business executive.

Grace, William R., 1832–1904 Ship owner, industrialist.

Grasse, Francois Joseph Paul de, 1722–1788 French Count, admiral, kept British from reinforcing Cornwallis.

Griffin, Martin, 1842–1911 Journalist, author.

Guerin, Mother Theodore, d. 1856 Foundress, Sisters of Providence.

Guiney, Louise Imogen, 1861–1920 Poet and essayist.

Gurian, Waldemar, 1902–1954 Author, educator.

Haldeman, Samuel S., 1812–1880 Convert, educator, first president of National Academy of Sciences.

Hampden, Walter, 1879–1955 Actor.

Hannegan, Robert E., 1901–1949 Postmaster General.

Hanrahan, William J., 1867–1937 Transportation executive.

Hardee, William J., 1817–1873 General in Confederacy.

Harris, Basil, 1889–1948 Executive.

Harris, Joel Chandler, 1848–1908 Journalist, author, convert.

Hartley, James J., 1858–1944 Bishop, founder of Catholic Press Association.

Haughery, Margaret, 1814–1882 New Orleans philanthropist.

Hawks, Edward F., 1879–1955 Convert, priest, scholar.

Hawthorne, Julian, 1846–1934 Author, son of Nathaniel Hawthorne.

Hayes, Carlton J., 1882–1964 Author, diplomat, historian.

Hayes, Patrick J., 1867–1938 Cardinal, Archbishop of New York.

Healy, George, 1808–1894 Portrait painter.

Healy, James A., 1830–1900 First Negro bishop in U.S.

Hebert, Louis Philippe, 1850–1917 Canadian sculptor.

Hecker, Isaac Thomas, 1819–1888 Founder of Paulists, convert.

Henderson, Isaac Austin, 1850–1909 Journalist, philanthropist.

Hennepin, Louis, 1640–1701 Franciscan explorer of the upper Mississippi.

Hingston, William Hales, 1829–1907 Canadian physician, surgeon.

Hogan, John Baptist, 1829–1901 Sulpician educator.

Holland, John P., 1840–1914 Submarine inventor.

Hubbard, Bernard R., 1888–1962 Jesuit, geologist.

Hughes, John, 1797–1864 First Archbishop of New York.

Iberville, Pierre le Moyne D', 1661–1706 Canadian explorer, discovered mouth of Mississippi River.

Ireland, John, 1838–1918 Archbishop of St. Paul.

Ives, Levi Silliman, 1796–1867 Protestant Episcopal bishop, convert, philanthropist.

Jackson, Arthur, 1900–1953 Journalist.

Jeffers, William M., 1876–1953 Railroad transportation.

Jette, Sir Louis A., 1836–1920 Canadian lawyer and statesman.

Joliet, Louis, 1645–1700 Explored Mississippi River with Marquette.

Jones, Arthur E., 1838–1918 Canadian ethnologist.

Kapaun, Emil J., d. 1951 Chaplain, died in Communist prison in North Korea.

Kavanagh, Edward, 1795–1844 Lawyer, legislator, governor.

Kelly, Dennis F., 1868–1938 Merchant.

Kelly, Hugh, 1858–1908 Merchant, civic leader.

Kelly, Thomas H., 1865–1933 Executive, philanthropist.

Kelly, William, 1811–1888 Inventor, discoverer Bessemer process.

Kenkel, Frederick P., d. 1952 Founder of Catholic Verein.

Kenna, John E., 1848–1893 Statesman, lawyer, senator.

Kennedy, John F., 1917–1963 First Catholic president.

Kennedy, Thomas, 1888–1963 Union leader.

Kenrick, Francis P., 1797–1863 Missioner, Bishop of Philadelphia, Archbishop of Baltimore.

Kernan, Francis, 1816–1892 Politician.

Kerwin, Patrick, 1890–1963 Chief Justice of Canada.

Kilmer, Joyce, 1886–1918 Convert, poet.

Kino, Eusebio F., c. 1645–1711 Jesuit pioneer builder of missions in southwest.

Koscuiszko, Tadeusz, 1752–1817 Brigadier general in Revolutionary Army.

Kreisler, Fritz, 1875–1961 Violinist, composer.

Kruegler, William C., 1930–1962 Maryknoll Missioner shot to death in Santa Cruz, Bolivia, while protecting morals of young.

L'Enfant, Pierre Charles, 1754–1825 Engineer, planned Washington, D.C.

Labelle, Francois Xavier, 1833–1891 Priest, Canadian colonizer.

Lacombe, Albert, 1827–1916 Missioner to Indians, peacemaker for Canadian government.

La Farge, Christopher G., 1862–1938 Architect.

LaFarge, John, 1835–1910 Painter and designer of stained glass.

LaFarge, John, 1880–1963 Jesuit, author, interracial leader.

La Gorce, John Oliver, 1879–1959 Geographer.

Lalemont, Charles, 1587–1674 First Jesuit superior in Canada.

Lambert, Louis A., 1835–1910 Editor.

Lamy, John B., 1814–1888 Missioner, Archbishop of Santa Fe.

Lanza, Mario, 1929–1959 Operatic tenor.

LaSalle, Rene Robert, Sieur de, 1643–1687 Canadian explorer.

Lathrop, George Parsons, 1851–1898 Convert, author, husband of Rose Hawthorne Lathrop.

Lathrop, Rose Hawthorne (Mother Alphonsa), 1851–1926 Daughter of Nathaniel Hawthorne, convert, founded Sisterhood Servants of Relief for Incurable Cancer.

Laurier, Sir Wilfred, 1841–1919 Statesman, first French Canadian premier of Canada.

Laval, Francis de Montmorency, 1623–1708 First bishop of Canada.

La Verendrye, Sieur de (Pierre Gualtier de Varinnes), 1685–1749 French Canadian explorer in U.S. and Canada, fur trader.

Leahy, William D., 1875–1959 Admiral, advisor to President F. D. Roosevelt.

Le Caron, Joseph, 1586–1632 Missioner, Recollect, author first Huron dictionary.

Leclerq, Chretien (17th century) Missioner to Canadian Micmac Indians.

Legal, Emile Joseph, 1849–1920 First bishop of Edmonton, Canada.

Le Moyne, Charles, 1626–1683 Canadian pioneer.

Le Moyne, Jean-Baptiste, 1680–1729 Governor of Louisiana, founder of New Orleans.

Le Moyne, Pierre, 1661–1706 Founder of Louisiana.

LeMoyne, Simon, 1604–1665 Jesuit missioner to Onondagas.

Leray, Francis X., 1825–1887 Confederate chaplain, Archbishop of New Orleans.

Lisa, Manuel, 1772–1820 Fur trader, introduced keelboat in West, explorer of upper Missouri River region.

Lloyd, Thomas, 1756–1827 Father of American stenography, soldier, patriot.

Locke, Jesse A., 1859–1952 Convert, educator.

Lockhart, Eugene, 1891–1957 Actor.

Longstreet, James, 1821–1904 Confederate general, Minister to Turkey

Lord, Daniel A., 1889–1955 Jesuit, author, youth worker.

Loughlin, John, 1817–1891 First bishop of Brooklyn.

Lovejoy, Frank, 1914–1962 Actor.

Lynch, Jean Joseph, 1816–1888 First Archbishop of Toronto.

Madeleva, Sister M., 1890–1964 Educator, poet. Family name: Eva Wolff.

Maginnis, Charles, 1867–1955 Architect.

MacDonald, Alexander, 1760–1840 First Bishop of Kingston, Ontario.

Macdonnell, Alexander, 1742–1803 Priest, Canadian pioneer.

Macelwane, James B., 1883–1956 Geophysicist.

Machebeuf, Joseph P., 1812–1889 First Bishop of Colorado.

Maillard, Pierre, 1710–1762 Apostle to Micmacs.

Maisonneuve, Paul, d. 1676 Founder of Montreal.

Mallory, Stephen Russell, 1813–1873 Lawyer, statesman, senator from Florida, Secretary of Confederate Navy.

Maloney, Francis T., 1894–1945 Senator from Connecticut.

Mance, Jeanne, 1606–1673 Founder Hotel Dieu, Montreal.

Mara, Timothy J., 1888–1959 Sportsman.

Marchand, Almanda, 1868–1949 Leader of Canadian Catholic women.

Marcoux, Joseph, 1791–1855 Canadian missionary to Iroquois and linguist extraordinary.

Margil, Antonio (Ven.), 1657–1726 Apostle of Texas, Franciscan.

Marie de l'Incarnation, Mother (Ven.), 1599–1672 Foundress of Ursuline Nuns in Canada.

Marie Victorin, Brother, 1885–1944 Brother of Christian Schools, Canadian botanist. Family name, Kirouac.

Marquette, Jacques, 1636–1675 Jesuit, explorer of Mississippi.

Martin, Abraham, 1587?–1664 Pioneer Canadian settler, owner of Plains of Abraham.

Masson, Louis F., 1833–1903 Governor of Quebec.

Maurin, Peter, 1877–1949 Writer, co-founder of *Catholic Worker*.

Maynard, Theodore, 1890–1956 Author, poet.

Mazzuchelli, Samuel C., 1806–1864 Dominican, missioner.

McAndrew, James, 1862–1922 General, Chief of Staff, World War I.

McCarran, Patrick A., 1876–1954 Senator from Nevada.

McCarthy, Joseph R., 1909–1957 Senator from Wisconsin.

McCloskey, John, 1810–1885 Archbishop of New York (1864), first American cardinal (1875).

McCormick, Anne O'Hare, 1882–1954 Journalist.

McCormack, John, 1884–1945 Concert singer.

McDermott, Arthur V., 1888–1949 General.

McGee, Thomas D'Arcy, 1825–1868 Canadian journalist, poet, politician.

McGillicuddy, Cornelius (Connie Mack), 1862–1956 Sportsman.

Maginn, James, 1911–1950 Columban missioner from Montana, murdered by Reds in Korea on July 4.

McGowan, Raymond A., 1892–1862 Priest, sociologist.

McGraw, John J., 1875–1934 Baseball manager.

McKay, Claude, 1890–1948 Author, poet.

Mackay, John W., 1831–1902 Discoverer of Bonanza Mine, banker.

McKenna, Joseph, 1843–1926 Supreme Court Justice.

McLoughlin, John, 1784–1857 Canadian-born physician, pioneer, "Father of Oregon."

McMahon, Brien, 1903–1952 Senator.

McNicholas, John T., 1877–1950 Archbishop of Cincinnati.

McShane, Daniel L., 1888–1927 Maryknoll missioner.

MacSherry, Richard, 1817–1885 Physician, army surgeon in Seminole War.

Meagher, Thomas F., 1823–1867 Irish patriot, general in Union Army.

Menard, Rene, 1604–1661 Jesuit missioner, martyred by Sioux.

Menendez de Aviles, Pedro, 1519–1574 Spanish admiral, founder of St. Augustine.

Mercier, Louis Honoré, 1840–1894 Canadian statesman.

Mestrovic, Ivan, 1883–1962 Sculptor.

Michel, George Francis (Virgil), 1890–1938 Liturgist.

Miller, Frederick C., 1906–1954 Executive.

Mitchell, John, 1870–1919 Labor leader, president United Mine Workers.

Molyneux, Robert, 1738–1808 Jesuit missioner, opened first parish school and edited first catechism in America.

Monaghan, Msgr. John P., 1890–1961 A founder of ACTU.

Montani, Nicola A., 1880–1948 Composer, conductor.

Montcalm, Louis Joseph, Marquis de, 1712–1759 Commander French Army in Canada, killed in defense of Quebec.

Montmagny, Charles Huault de, d. 1651 Second French governor of Canada.

Moody, John, 1868–1958 Investment executive.

Moon, Parker Thomas, 1892–1936 Educator, author.

Mooney, Edward, 1882–1958 Cardinal, Archbishop of Detroit.

Morrissey, Helen (Sister), 1861–1953 Foundress, hospital administrator.

Muench, Aloysius, 1888–1961 First American cardinal in Curia.

Mullanphy, John, 1758–1833 Philanthropist, fought in war of 1812, brought Sisters of Charity to St. Louis, Mo.

Mundelein, George, 1872–1939 Cardinal, Archbishop of Chicago.

Murphy, John B., 1857–1916 Surgeon.

Murphy, Frank, 1890–1940 Supreme Court Justice, Attorney General U.S.

Murray, Laurence O., 1864–1926 Banker, cabinet minister.

Murray, Philip, 1886–1952 Labor leader, CIO union president.

Murray, Thomas E., 1891–1961 Industrialist, member Atomic Energy Commission.

Murray, Thomas Edward, 1860–1929 Inventor, holder of 1100 patents, formed New York Edison Company.

Nast, Conde, 1874–1942 Publisher.

Nathan, George Jean, 1882–1958 Drama critic.

Narvaez, Panfilo de, c.1480–1528 Explorer of Florida.

Neale, Leonard, 1746–1817 Second archbishop of Baltimore.

Negabomat, Noel, 1600–66 Catholic Montagnais Indian chief of Canada.

Nerinckx, Charles, 1761–1824 Missioner to Kentucky.

Neumann, John N. Blessed, 1811–1860 Redemptorist, Bishop of Philadelphia.

Nevils, William Coleman, 1878–1955 Jesuit educator.

Nieuwland, Julius A., 1878–1936 Holy Cross Father, chemist.

Noll, John F., 1875–1956 Bishop of Fort Wayne, journalist, author, founder of chain of newspapers.

Nourse, Elizabeth, c.1860–1938 Artist.

O'Brien, Edward J., 1890–1941 Critic.

O'Brien, William D., 1878–1962 Archbishop, president Extension Society.

O'Connell, William H., 1859–1944 Cardinal, Archbishop of Boston.

O'Connor, Una, 1881–1959 Actress.

O'Conor, Charles, 1804–1884 Lawyer, nominee for president.

O'Conor, Herbert R., 1897–1960 Governor of Maryland, senator.

O'Dwyer, Joseph, 1841–1898 Physician.

O'Hagan, Thomas, 1855–1939 Canadian author.

O'Hara, Gerald F., 1895–1963 Papal diplomat.

O'Hara, John F., 1888–1960 Cardinal, Archbishop of Philadelphia.

Olcott, Chauncey, 1860–1932 Actor.

Oldenback, Frederick Louis, 1857–1933 Meteorologist.

O'Mahoney, Joseph C., 1885–1963 Senator.

Onate, Juan, de, c.1549–c.1624 Explorer, founder of Santa Fe.

O'Reilly, John Boyle, 1844–1890 Editor, publisher.

O'Ryan, John, 1874–1961 General.

Oursler, Fulton, 1893–1952 Convert, author.

Paderewski, Ignace Jan, 1860–1941 President-in-exile, concert pianist.

Padilla, Juan de, d. 1542 Franciscan, protomartyr of U.S., murdered by Indians near Concordia, Kansas.

Pallen, Condé Benoist, 1858–1929 Poet, writer.

Palmer, Gretta, 1905–1953 Journalist, author, convert.

Palou, Francesco, c.1727–c.1789 Franciscan missioner, biographer of Serra.

Parsons, Wilfred, 1887–1958 Jesuit author, editor.

Payeras, Mariano, 1739–1823 Franciscan missioner.

Phelan, James D., 1861–1930 Senator from California.

Plassman, Thomas B., 1879–1959 Franciscan educator.

Plunkett, Christopher, d. 1697 Capuchin missioner to Virginia, died in English captivity refusing to become a Calvinist.

Pleiss, Joseph Octave, 1763–1825 First Archbishop of Quebec. Won legal rights for Catholic Church in Canada. Held French Canadian loyalty to England in War of 1812.

Ponce de Leon, Juan, c.1460–1521 Discoverer of Florida.

Pope, Generoso, 1891–1950 Publisher, journalist.

Powderly, Terence V., 1849–1924 Labor leader and organizer.

Power, Michael, 1804–1847 First Bishop of Toronto.

Price, Thomas F., 1860–1919 Cofounder Maryknoll, Catholic Foreign Mission Society of America.

Prince, John Charles, 1804–1860 First Bishop of St. Hyacinthe, Quebec.

Provancher, Leon Abel, 1820–1892 "Father of Natural History in Canada."

Pugh, George Ellis, 1822–1876 Jurist, statesman, first native Senator from Ohio.

Pulaski, Casimir, c.1748–1779 Polish

Count, brigadier general in Revolutionary War.

Purcell, John B., 1800–1883 Second Bishop of Cincinnati.

Quigley, Martin, 1890–1964 Publisher.

Randall, James R., 1839–1908 Journalist, song writer, composer of "Maryland, My Maryland."

Raskob, John J., 1879–1950 Banker, financier.

Rauschenbach, Otto A., 1898–1945 Maryknoll Missioner in China, shot to death by bandits while answering sick call.

Raymbault, Charles, 1602–1643 First Jesuit to die in Canada.

Reeve, Arthur B., 1881–1936 Author, convert.

Reid, Richard, 1896–1961 Editor, journalist.

Repplier, Agnes, 1885–1950 Essayist, author.

Rese, Frederick, 1791–1871 First Bishop of Detroit.

Richard, Gabriel, 1767–1832 Pioneer missioner, co-founder University of Michigan, first priest elected to Congress.

Ridder, Charles, 1888–1964 Publisher.

Ridder, Victor F., 1886–1963 Publisher.

Riggs, Thomas L., 1888–1943 Author, chaplain at Yale.

Rochambeau, Jean de, 1725–1807 French Count, fought with Washington in Revolution.

Rockne, Knute, 1883–1931 Educator, football coach.

Rodzinski, Artur, 1894–1958 Symphony conductor.

Rogers, Mary Joseph (Mother), 1883–1955 Foundress, Maryknoll Sisters.

Rosati, Joseph, 1789–1843 First Bishop of St. Louis.

Rose of Lima, St., 1586–1617 First American to be canonized, Patroness of South America.

Rosecrans, William S., 1819–1898 General in Union Army, diplomat, member of Congress.

Rouleau, Felix Raymond Marie, 1866–1931 Cardinal, Archbishop of Quebec.

Routhier, Adolphe, 1839–1920 Canadian jurist.

Roy, Camille Joseph, 1870–1943 Author.

Ruth, George Herman, 1895–1948 Athlete.

Ryan, Abram J., 1838–1886 Priest, poet, Confederate chaplain.

Ryan, John Denis, 1864–1933 Executive.

Ryan, Patrick John, 1831–1911 Lecturer, pioneer in Catholic social thought, Archbishop of Philadelphia.

Ryan, Thomas Fortune, 1851–1928 Financier.

Sales, Raoul de, 1896–1942 Journalist, correspondent.

Sands, Benjamin F., 1812–1883 Rear admiral, superintendent of Naval Observatory.

Sands, James Horan, 1845–1911 Rear admiral, son of Benjamin, commander of Naval Academy.

Savage, Courtenay, 1890–1946 Playwright, author.

Schervier, Mother Frances, 1819–1876 Foundress of Sisters of the Poor of St. Francis, Civil War nurse.

Schlarman, Joseph H., 1879–1951 Archbishop, author.

Schwab, Charles M., 1862–1939 Industrialist.

Scott, Joseph, 1867–1958 Lawyer, civic leader.

Sedella, Antonio de, 1730–1829 Rector St. Louis Cathedral, New Orleans; Capuchin

Seelos, Venerable Francis Xavier, 1819–1867 Redemptorist missioner, d. New Orleans.

Segale, Blandina, 1850–1941 Sister of Charity, pioneer in southwest.

Seghers, Charles J., 1839–1886 Archbishop, Apostle of Alaska, murdered by guide.

Semmes, Raphael, 1809–1877 Rear admiral, Commander Confederate Navy.

Sequin, Juan, d.1836 Mexican captain, defender of Alamo.

Serra, Junipero, 1713–1784 Franciscan Missioner, Father of California.

Delon, Elizabeth Ann, 1800⦙⦙, 1774 1821 Foundress Sisters of Charity.

Shea, Sir Ambrose, 1815–1905 Canadian statesman, diplomat, governor of Bahamas.

Shea, John Gilmary, 1824–1892 Historian of Catholic Church in U.S.

Sheridan, Philip H., 1831–1888 General of the Army.

Shields, James, c.1806–1879 General in Mexican and Civil Wars, senator, governor of Oregon Territory.

Shipman, Andrew J., 1857–1915 Civic leader.

Skinner, Richard Dana, 1893–1941 Drama critic.

Sloane, Thomas O'Conor, 1851–1941 Editor.

Smith, Alfred E., 1873–1944 Governor, presidential candidate.

Smith, Matthew J. W., 1891–1960 Priest, journalist, founder of chain of Catholic newspapers.

Smith, Walter Bedell, 1895–1961 General, director CIA.

Sorin, Edward, 1814–1893 Missioner, Holy Cross Father, founder of Notre Dame University.

Sousa, John Philip, 1854–1932 "March King," composer.

Spalding, John Lancaster, 1840–1916 Archbishop, Bishop of Peoria.

Spalding, Martin John, 1810–1872 Archbishop of Baltimore.

Spearman, Frank H., 1859–1937 Convert, author.

St. Ange, Louis Groston de, 1702–1736 Captain, b. Montreal, burned at stake by Chickasaw Indians, near Fulton, Miss.

Stang, William, 1854–1907 First Bishop of Fall River.

Starr, Eliza Allen, 1824–1901 Artist, writer, first woman to win Laetare Medal.

Stearns, Frank W., 1856–1939 Merchant.

Stephens, Harold M., 1886–1955 Jurist.

Stoddard, Charles Warren, 1843–1909 Author.

Stritch, Samuel A., 1887–1958 Cardinal, Archbishop of Chicago, pro-prefect Congregation of Propaganda

Sugrue, Thomas J., 1907–1953 Author.

Sullivan, John L., 1858–1918 Boxer.

Tabb, John Bannister, 1845–1909 Poet, educator, convert, priest

Taché, Alexander A., 1823–1894 Oblate, Archbishop of St. Boniface, Canada, missioner to Indians.

Taché, Etienne Pascal, 1795–1865 Canadian statesmen, cabinet minister.

Talley, Alfred J., 1878–1952 Jurist.

Taney, Roger Brooke, 1777–1864 Fifth Chief Justice of Supreme Court.

Tascherou, Elzear Alexandre (1820–1898) Cardinal, archbishop of Quebec.

Taschereau, Henri E., 1836–1909 Canadian jurist.

Tegananokoa, Stephen, d. 1690 Christian Indian put to death by Cayuga Indians at Onondaga, N.Y., for his faith.

Tekakwitha, Kateri, 1656–1680 Saintly "Lily of the Mohawks."

Tenney, William Jewett, 1814–1883 Lawyer, author, editor, convert.

Thayer, John, 1775–1815 First native priest of New England.

Thompson, John Sparrow David, 1844–1894 Canada's first Catholic premier.

Tobin, Maurice J., 1901–1953 Secretary of Labor, governor.

Tobin, Richard M., 1867–1952 Diplomat.

Tocqueville, Charles Alexis, 1805–1859 Statesman, French writer of American scene.

Tompkins, J. J., 1871–1953 Educator, pioneer in cooperatives.

Tonty, Pierre Antoine de, 1710–1736 Captain, b. Montreal, burned at stake by Chickasaw Indians, near Fulton, Miss.

Toscanini, Arturo, 1867–1957 Italian operatic and symphonic conductor.

Tracy, Alexandre de Trouville, Marquis de, 1603–1670 Viceroy New France.

Tully, John C., 1884–1919 Executive, founder of Thomas More Assn.

Upsi, Eric, c.1100 Norse bishop, possible first missioner to America.

Vachon, Alexandre, 1885–1953 Archbishop of Ottawa.

VanBuren, William H., 1819–1883 Surgeon.

Vandreuil, Philippe de Rigaud, Marquis de, d. 1725 Governor of Canada.

Vercheres, Marie Madeleine Jarret de, 1678–1747 Heroine of New France who held off Iroquois attack.

Verrazano, Giovanni, 1485–1527 Explorer, gave first description of New York harbor.

Veuster, Joseph de (Father Damien), 1840–1888 Apostle to lepers on Molokai.

Viger, Denis Benjamin, 1774–1861 Journalist, Canadian statesman.

Viger, Jacques, 1787–1858 Archaeologist, historian.

Villeneuve, Jean Marie Rodrigue, 1883–1947 Cardinal, Archbishop of Quebec.

Vincennes, Francois Marie Bissot de, 1700–1736 Canadian captain, burned at stake by Chickasaw Indians, near Fulton, Miss.

Wagner, Robert F., 1877–1953 Senator, labor legislator.

Walker, Frank Comerford, 1886–1959 Postmaster General.

Walsh, Francis P., 1864–1939 Jurist.

Walsh, James A., 1867–1936 Bishop, co-founder Maryknoll, Catholic Foreign Mission Society of America.

Walsh, James J., 1865–1942 Author.

Walsh, Patrick, 1840–1900 Journalist, senator from Georgia.

Walsh, Thomas, 1875–1928 Author.

Walsh, Timothy, 1868–1934 Architect.

Walsh, William Thomas, 1891–1949 Author, biographer.

Ward, James Harman, 1806–1861 Commander, U.S. Navy. One of founders of Naval Academy. First Union naval officer killed in Civil War.

Wattson, Lewis Thomas, 1863–1940 Convert, founder of Society of the Atonement.

Webb, Benjamin J., 1814–1897 Journalist.

Wehrle, August T., 1877–1955 Manufacturer, philanthropist.

Whipple, Amiel Weeks, 1816–1863 Convert, general in Union Army.

White, Andrew, 1579–1656. Mission apostle of Maryland, accompanied first colonists.

White, Edward Douglas, 1825–1921 Chief justice U.S. Supreme Court.

White, Stephen Mallory, 1853–1901 Statesman, U.S. Senator from California.

Williams, John J., 1822–1907 First Archbishop of Boston.

Williams, Joseph J., 1875–1940 Anthropologist.

Williams, Michael, 1877–1950 Editor, author, founder of *Commonweal.*

Willock, Edward F. (Ed), 1916–1960 Editor.

Wood, James F., 1813–1883 First Archbishop of Philadelphia.

Woodlock, Thomas F., 1866–1945 Author.

Wootton, Dick (Richens Lacy), 1816–1893 Fur trader, mountain man, built toll road over Raton Pass.

Wynhoven, Peter M., 1884–1944 Editor.

Wynne, John J., 1859–1948 Jesuit editor, founder of *America.*

Wynne, Robert J., 1851–1922 Postmaster General, journalist.

Yon, Pietro, 1886–1943 Composer, choir master.

Young, John B., 1854–1927 Authority on Church music.

Youville, Bl. Marguérite d', 1701–1771 Foundress of Grey Nuns.

Zahm, John A., 1851–1921 Holy Cross Father, scientist.

Zalvidea, José Maria de, 1780–1846 Franciscan missioner to California Indians.

Appendix VIII
An American Martyrology

(Those who died from violence as the result of their mission work
or because of their Faith)

Name and Community	Mode of death	Place of death	Date
Fr. John de Padilla, O.F.M.	Murdered by Quivira Indians	Kansas	1542
Fr. (or Bro.) John de la Cruz, O,F.M.	Murdered by Indians	New Mexico	1542
Bro. Louis Descalona de Ubeda, O.F.M.	Murdered by Indians	New Mexico	1542
Fr. Diego de Penalosa, O.P.	Murdered by Calusas Indians	Florida	1549
Bro. Fuentes, O.P.	Murdered by Calusas Indians	Florida	1549
Fr. Louis Cancer de Barbastro, O.P.	Murdered by Calusas Indians	Florida	1549
Fr. Hernando Mendez, O.P.	Unattended wounds	Texas	1553
Fr. Diego de la Cruz, O.P.	Unattended wounds	Texas	1553
Bro. John de Mena, O.P.	Shot by Indians	Texas	1553
Fr. John Ferrer, O.P.	Exhaustion after Indian attack	Texas	1553
Fr. Peter de Martinez, S.J.	Clubbed to death by Indians	Florida	1566
Fr. Louis de Quiros, S.J.	Slain by Algonquin Indians	Virginia	1571
Gabriel de Solis, S.J.	Slain by Algonquin Indians	Virginia	1571
Baptista Mendez, S.J.	Slain by Algonquin Indians	Virginia	1571
Fr. John Baptist de Segura, S.J.	Slain by Algonquin Indians	Virginia	1571
Christopher Redondo, S.J.	Slain by Algonquin Indians	Virginia	1571
Bro. Peter Linares, S.J.	Slain by Algonquin Indians	Virginia	1571
Bro. Gabriel Gomez, S.J.	Slain by Algonquin Indians	Virginia	1571
Bro. Sancho Zeballos, S.J.	Slain by Algonquin Indians	Virginia	1571
Fr. John de Santa Maria, O.F.M.	Stoned by Tigua Indians	New Mexico	1581

687

Name and Community	Mode of death	Place of death	Date
Fr. Francis Lopez, O.F.M.	Clubbed to death by Tigua Indians	New Mexico	1582
Bro. Augustine Rodriguez, O.F.M.	Clubbed to death by Tigua Indians	Mexico	1582
Fr. Peter de Corpa, O.F.M.	Tomahawked by Indians	Georgia	1597
Fr. Blas de Rodriguez, O.F.M.	Tomahawked by Indians	Georgia	1597
Fr. Michael de Aunon, O.F.M.	Tomahawked by Indians	Georgia	1597
Bro. Anthony de Badajoz, O.F.M.	Tomahawked by Indians	Georgia	1597
Fr. Francis Verascola, O.F.M.	Tomahawked by Indians	Georgia	1597
Fr. Peter de Ortega, O.F.M.	Poisoned by Jumanos Indians	New Mexico	1631
Fr. Peter Miranda, O.F.M.	Murdered by Taos Indians	New Mexico	1631
Fr. Dominic de Saraoz, O.F.M.	Poisoned by Pueblo Indians	New Mexico	1631
Fr. Francis Letrado, O.F.M.	Murdered by Indians	New Mexico	1632
Fr. Martin de Arvide, O.F.M.	Clubbed & tortured	New Mexico	1632
Fr. Francis Porras, O.F.M.	Poisoned by Moqui Indians	New Mexico	1633
Fr. Diego de San Lucas, O.F.M.	Murdered by Indians	New Mexico	1639
An unnamed Franciscan	Murdered by Apalache Indians	Florida	1647
An unnamed Franciscan	Murdered by Apalache Indians	Florida	1647
An unnamed Franciscan	Murdered by Apalache Indians	Florida	1647
Fr. Rene Menard, S.J.	Murdered by Sioux Indians	Wisconsin	1661
Fr. Peter Avila y Ayala, O.F.M.	Stoned to death by Navajos	New Mexico	1672
Fr. Alonso Gil de Avila, O.F.M.	Killed by Apaches	New Mexico	1675
Fr. Gabriel de la Ribourde, O.F.M.	Murdered by Kickapoo Indians	Illinois	1680
Fr. Anthony de Mora, O.F.M.	Murdered by Pueblo Indians	New Mexico	1680
Bro. John de la Pedrosa, O.F.M.	Murdered by Pueblo Indians	New Mexico	1680
Bartholomew Naranjo, Indian	Murdered by Pueblo Indians	New Mexico	1680
Fr. John Bernal, O.F.M.	Murdered by Pueblo Indians	New Mexico	1680
Fr. Dominic de Vera, O.F.M.	Murdered by Pueblo Indians	New Mexico	1680
Fr. Ferdinand de Velasco, O.F.M.	Murdered by Pueblo Indians	New Mexico	1680
Fr. Emmanuel Tinoco, O.F.M.	Murdered by Pueblo Indians	New Mexico	1680

Name and Community	Mode of death	Place of death	Date
Fr. John Baptist Pio, O.F.M.	Murdered by Pueblo Indians	New Mexico	1680
Fr. Thomas de Torres, O.F.M.	Murdered by Pueblo Indians	New Mexico	1680
Fr. Louis de Morales, O.F.M.	Murdered by Pueblo Indians	New Mexico	1680
Bro. Anthony Sanchez de Pro, O.F.M.	Murdered by Pueblo Indians	New Mexico	1680
Fr. Mathias Rendon, O.F.M.	Murdered by Pueblo Indians	New Mexico	1680
Fr. Francis Anthony de Loren- zana, O.F.M.	Murdered by Pueblo Indians	New Mexico	1680
Fr. John de Talaban, O.F.M.	Murdered by Pueblo Indians	New Mexico	1680
Fr. Joseph de Montesdoca, O.F.M.	Murdered by Pueblo Indians	New Mexico	1680
Fr. John de Jesus, O.F.M.	Murdered by Pueblo Indians	New Mexico	1680
Fr. John del Val, O.F.M.	Murdered by Pueblo Indians	New Mexico	1680
Fr. Luke Maldonado, O.F.M.	Murdered by Pueblo Indians	New Mexico	1680
Fr. Joseph de Figueroa, O.F.M.	Murdered by Pueblo Indians	New Mexico	1680
Fr. Joseph de Trujillo, O.F.M.	Murdered by Pueblo Indians	New Mexico	1680
Fr. Joseph de Espeleta, O.F.M.	Murdered by Pueblo Indians	New Mexico	1680
Fr. Augustine de Santa Maria, O.F.M.	Murdered by Pueblo Indians	New Mexico	1680
Fr. Zenobe Membre, O.F.M.	Murdered by Karan- kawa Indians	Texas	1689
Fr. Maxim LeClercq, O.F.M.	Murdered by Karan- kawa Indians	Texas	1689
Rev. Fr. Chefdeville, S.S.	Murdered by Karan- kawa Indians	Texas	1689
Stephen Tegananokoa, Indian	Tortured by Cayuga Indians	New York	1690
Frances Gonannhatenha, Indian	Stoned to death by Iroquois Indians	New York	1692
Margaret Garangouas, Indian	Burned to death by Iroquois Indians	New York	1692
Fr. Francis Corvera, O.F.M.	Burned to death by Tewa Indians	New Mexico	1696
Fr. Anthony Moreno, O.F.M.	Burned to death by Tewa Indians	New Mexico	1696
Fr. Francis de Jesus Maria Ca- sanas, O.F.M.	Clubbed to death by Jemez Indians	New Mexico	1696
Fr. Joseph de Arbizu, O.F.M.	Murdered by Tanos Indians	New Mexico	1696
Fr. Anthony Carbonel, O.F.M.	Murdered by Tanos Indians	New Mexico	1696

Name and Community	Mode of death	Place of death	Date
Fr. Louis Sanchez, O.F.M.	Murdered by Jororo Indians	Florida	1696
Fr. Christopher Plunkett, O.F.M., Cap.	Harsh treatment in captivity by English	Virginia	1697
Rev. Nicholas Foucault	Slain while asleep by Arkansas Indians	Mississippi	1702
Fr. John Parga Arraiyo, O.F.M.	Beheaded by English and Indians	Florida	1704
Bro. Mark Delgado, O.F.M.	Murdered by Apalache Indians	Florida	1704
Anthony Enixa, Indian	Murdered by English and Indians	Florida	1704
Amador Cuipa Feliciano, Indian	Murdered by English and Indians	Florida	1704
Fr. Manuel de Mendoza, O.F.M.	Shot by English and Indians	Florida	1704
Fr. Dominic Criado, O.F.M.	Murdered by English and Indians	Florida	1704
Fr. Tiburcio de Osorio, O.F.M.	Murdered by English and Indians	Florida	1704
Fr. Augustine Ponze de Leon, O.F.M.	Murdered by English and Indians	Florida	1704
Rev. John Francis Buisson de St. Cosme	Hacked to death by Indians	Louisiana	1706
Fr. Constantine Delhalle, O.F.M.	Shot by Ottawa Indians	Michigan	1706
Fr. James Gravier, S.J.	Wounds by Indians	Alabama	1708
Fr. Leonard Vatier, O.F.M.	Murdered by Fox Indians	Wisconsin	1715
Bro. Louis de Montesdoca, O.F.M.	Burned to death	Texas	1718
Fr. John Minguez, O.F.M.	Murdered by Pawnee Indians	Nebraska	1720
Bro. Joseph Pita, O.F.M.	Murdered by Apache Indians	Texas	1721
Fr. Sebastian Rale, S.J.	Shot by English and Indians	Maine	1724
Fr. Paul Du Poisson, S.J.	Beheaded by Natchez Indians	Mississippi	1729
Fr. John Souel, S.J.	Shot by Yazoo Indians	Mississippi	1729
Rev. Father Gaston	Murdered by Tamarois Indians	Illinois	1730
Father Anthony Senat, S.J.	Burned at stake by Chickasaws	Mississippi	1736
Commander Peter D'Artiquette	Burned at stake by Chickasaws	Mississippi	1736
Captain Francis Marie Bissot de Vincennes	Burned at stake by Chickasaws	Mississippi	1736
Captain Louis Dailebout de Coulonge	Burned at stake by Chickasaws	Mississippi	1736

Name and Community	Mode of death	Place of death	Date
Captain Louis Charles du Tisne	Burned at stake by Chickasaws	Mississippi	1736
Captain Francis Mariauchau d'Esgly	Burned at stake by Chickasaws	Mississippi	1736
Captain Peter Anthony de Tonty	Burned at stake by Chickasaws	Mississippi	1736
Captain Louis Groston de St. Ange, Jr.	Burned at stake by Chickasaws	Mississippi	1736
Fr. John Peter Aulneau, S.J.	Murdered by Indians	Michigan	1736
Fr. Francis X. Silva, O.F.M.	Murdered by Apache Indians	Texas	1749
Fr. Joseph Francis Ganzabal, O.F.M.	Murdered by Indians	Texas	1752
Fr. Alonso Giraldo de Terreros, O.F.M.	Shot by Indians	Texas	1758
Fr. Joseph Santiesteban, O.F.M.	Decapitated by Indians	Texas	1758
Fr. Louis Jalme, O.F.M.	Beaten to death by Indians	California	1775
Fr. John M. Diaz, O.F.M.	Murdered by Indians	California	1781
Fr. Joseph M. Moreno, O.F.M.	Murdered by Indians	California	1781
Fr. Francis H. Garces, O.F.M.	Murdered by Indians	California	1781
Fr. John A. Barreneche, O.F.M.	Murdered by Indians	California	1781
Fr. Andrew Quintana, O.F.M.	Hanged by Indians	California	1812
Fr. Anthony Diaz de Leon, O.F.M.	Murdered by frontiersmen	Texas	1834
Fr. Francis Bassost, O.F.M.	Harsh treatment during expulsion	California	1872
Archbishop Charles J. Seghers	Murdered by his guide	Alaska	1886
Fr. Godfrey Holbein, C.P.	Shot by Red bandits	China	1929
Fr. Clement Seybold, C.P.	Shot by Red bandits	China	1929
Fr. Walter Coveyou, C.P.	Shot by Red bandits	China	1929
Fr. Gerard A. Donovan, M.M.	Garrotted by bandits	Manchuria	1938
Fr. Robert J. Cairns, M.M.	Murdered by drowning	China	1941
Fr. William J. Cummings, M.M.	In Japanese prison	Japan	1942
Fr. Arthur Duhamel, S.M.	Bayonetted by Japanese	Guadalcanal	1942
Fr. James G. Hennessy	In Japanese prison	Japan	1942
Fr. Otto A. Rauschenbach, M.M.	Shot by bandits	China	1945
Most Rev. Patrick J. Byrne, M.M.	In Communist prison	Korea	1950
Fr. James Maginn, S.S.C.	Shot by Communists	Korea	1950
Msgr. Patrick T. Brennan, S.S.C.	Shot by Communists	Korea	1950
Fr. Emil J. Kapaun	In Communist prison	Korea	1951
Most Rev. Francis X. Ford, M.M.	In Communist prison	China	1952
Fr. William C. Kruegler, M.M.	Shot	Bolivia	1962

Appendix IX

Saints' Names
A Partial List

Catholic parents are urged to name their children after saints who are to be patrons of their children. There is no complete list of saints' names, and one name can have many variants. The following list contains the most popular names and gives the origin and feast day for each name.

MALE NAMES

Aaron (Heb., lofty mountain) July 1
Abel (Heb., breath) Jan. 2
Abraham (Heb., father of many) Oct. 9
Abram. Variant of *Abraham.*
Achilles (Gr., lipless) May 15
Adalbert (Teut., nobly bright) Apr. 23
Adam (Heb., first of earth) Dec. 24
Adelbert. Variant of *Adalbert.*
Adolf, Adolph (Teut., noble wolf) June 17
Adrian (Gr., brave) Sept. 8
Aidan (Celt., fire) Aug. 31
Alain. French form of *Alan.*
Alan (Celt., harmony) Sept. 8
Alaric (Teut., all-ruler) Sept. 29
Alastair. Scottish variant of *Alexander.*
Alban (L., white) June 22
Alberic (Teut., skillful ruler) Jan. 26
Albert (Teut., illustrious) Nov. 15
Albin. Variant of *Alban.*
Albrecht, German form of *Albert.*
Alcuin (Teut., noble friend) May 19
Alec. Variant of *Alexander.*
Alexander (Gr., helper of men) Feb. 26
Alexis (Gr., helper) July 17
Alger (Teut., noble spear) Apr. 11
Alfred (Teut., good counsellor) Aug. 15
Allain, Allan, Allen. Variants of *Alan.*
Alois. Variant of *Aloysius.*
Alonso, Alonzo. Variants of *Alphonse.*

Aloysius. Latin form of Luigi (Louis) June 21
Alphonse (Teut., eager for battle) Aug. 2
Alvan, Alvin (Teut., beloved by all) Sept. 5
Amadeus (L., beloved by God) Apr. 18
Ambrose (Gr., immortal) Dec. 7
Americus. Latin form of *Emeric.*
Amory. Variant of *Emeric.*
Amos (Heb., brave) Mar. 31
Anastasius (Gr., who will rise again) Dec. 19
Anatole, (Gr., of the sun) July 3
Andre, Andres. Forms of *Andrew.*
Andrew (Gr., *Andreas,* manly) Nov. 30
Angelo (It., form of Lat. *angelus,* Angel) May 5
Angus (L., narrow) Mar. 11
Ansel, Anselm (Teut., divine helmet) Apr. 21
Ansgar (Teut., divine spear) Feb. 3
Anthony (Gr., priceless) Jan. 17
Anton, Antony. Variants of *Anthony.*
Aquinas, St. Thomas Aquinas Mar. 7
Archibald (Teut., bold prince) Mar. 27
Aristides (Gr., son of the best)
Armand. French form of *Herman.*
Armon. Variant of *Germain.*
Arnaldo, Arnold (Teut., eagle-strong) Mar. 14
Artemas (Gr., gift of Artemis) Jan. 25
Artemus. Variant of *Artemas.*

695

Arthur, Arturo, (Celt., supreme
  ruler) Dec. 11
Athanasius (Gr., immortal May 2
Aubrey (L., fair chief)
Augustine. Diminutive of
  Augustus Aug. 28
Augustus (L., majestic) Oct. 7
Aurelian (L., golden) June 16
Austin. Variant of *Augustine.*
Azarias (Heb., God helps) Dec. 16

Baldwin (Teut., noble friend) July 15
Bathasar (Per., war counsel) July 20
Baptist. From John the
  Baptist June 24
Barnabas (Heb., son of
  consolation) June 11
Barnaby. Variant of *Barnabas.*
Barnard. Variant of *Bernard.*
Barr, Barry. Variants of *Finbar.*
Bart, Bartel. Diminutive of
  Bartholomew.
Bartholomew (Heb., son of
  Talmai) Aug. 24
Basil (Gr., royal) June 14
Bastien. Variant of *Sebastian.*
Becket. From *St. Thomas à*
  Becket. Dec. 29
Bede (Celt., life) May 27
Benedict (Lat., blessed) Mar. 21
Benjamin (Heb., son of the
  right hand) Mar. 31
Bennett. Variant of *Benedict.*
Berchmans. From *St. John*
  Berchmans Aug. 13
Bernard (Ger., bold as a bear) Aug. 20
Bernhard, see *Bernard.*
Berthold (Teut., shining one) Mar. 29
Bert. See *Albert.*
Bertin (Teut., bright friend) Sept. 5
Bertram (Teut., shining haven) June 30
Bertrand. Variant of Bertram Oct. 16
Blaine, Blane (Celt., lean) Aug. 10
Blaise, Blase (Lat., babbler) Feb. 3
Boleslaus, Boleslav (Slav.,
  sorrowful). For *Our Lady of*
  Sorrows, a title of the B.V.M.
Bonaventure (L., good luck) July 14
Boniface (L., well-doer) June 5
Boris (Slav., fighter) July 24
Borromeo. *St. Charles*
  Borromeo Nov. 4
Brandan. Variant of *Brendan.*

Drannock Jan. 7
Brendan (Celt., sword) May 16
Brennan. Variant of *Brendan.* May 6
Brian (Celt., strong) Apr. 23
Briant (Gael., dignified) Dec. 1
Brice (A.S., a breach) Nov. 13
Bruce. Variant of *Brice.*
Bruno (Ger., brown) Oct. 6
Bryan, see *Briant.*
Burton. Substitute for *Bertin.*
Byron (Old Eng., bear) Dec. 3

Caesar, Cesar (etymology un-
  certain) Aug. 27
Cajetan (L., rejoiced in) Aug. 7
Caleb (Heb., fidelity) Oct. 27
Callixtus (L., of the chalice) Oct. 14
Camillus (L., temple servant) July 18
Campion. *Bl. Edmund*
  Campion Dec. 1
Cantius May 31
Canute (Teut., hill) Jan. 19
Caradoc (Celt., beloved) Apr. 13
Carl, Carlo, Carlos. Variant of
  Charles.
Carroll. Irish variant of *Charles.*
Casimir (Slav., peaceful) Mar. 4
Caspar, Casper (Per., treasurer)
  Dec. 29
Cecil (L., dim-sighted) June 3
Celestine (L., heavenly) July 27
Chad (Celt., martial) Mar. 2
Charles (Teut., strong) Nov. 4
Chester (L., camp) Feb. 11
Chet, see *Chester.*
Chretien, see *Christian.*
Christian Mar. 18
Christopher (Gr., Christ-
  bearer) July 25
Chrysostom (Gr., golden-
  mouthed) Jan. 27
Ciril, see *Syril.*
Clarence (L., illustrious) Apr. 26
Claret. *Bl. Anthony Claret.* Oct. 24
Claud, Claude (Lat., lame) Feb. 15
Claus. Variant of *Nicholas.*
Clement (L., merciful) Nov. 23
Clovis. Variant of *Louis.*
Coleman. *Bl. Edward Coleman* Dec. 1
Colin. Scottish variant of *Colum.*
Colman. Contracted form of
  Columbanus Oct. 13
Colum (Gael., dove) June 9

Columbanus (Gael., dove)   Nov. 21

Conan, Conant (Celt.,
  wisdom)   Jan. 26

Conor, Connor. Irish substitutes
  for Cornelius.

Conrad (Teut., bold speech)   Feb. 19

Constantine (L., constant,
  firm)   July 21

Cormac (Celt., charioteer)   Dec. 12

Cornelius (L., *cornu,* horn)   Sept. 16

Cosmas, Cosmo (Gr., order)   Sept. 27

Cronan (Gael., dark tune)   Apr. 28

Curt. Variant of Kurt.

Cuthbert (Old Eng., noted
  splendor)   Mar. 20

Cyprian (Gr., of Cyprus)   Sept. 16

Cyr (Gr., of the Lord)   June 16

Cyril (Gr., lordly)   Feb. 9

Cyrus (Per., sun)   Jan. 31

Damian (Gr., tamer)   Feb. 23

Dan, Daniel (Heb., the Lord
  is judge)   July 21

Darby. Variant of *Dermot.*

Darius (Per., preserver)   Dec. 19

David (Heb., beloved)   Dec. 29

Declan   July 24

Demetrius (Gr., of *Demeter*)   Oct. 8

Denis. From Dionysius.   Oct. 9

Dennis. Variant of *Denis.*

Denys. Variant of *Denis.*

Deret, Derrick. Contracted forms
  of *Theodoric.*

Dermot (Celt., *Diarmuid,* free-
  man)   Jan. 18

Désiré (Fr., desired)   Feb. 10

Dewey, Dewi. Welsh form of
  David   Mar. 1

Dexter (L., right)   May 7

Diederich, Dietrich. German
  forms of *Theodoric.*

Diego. Spanish variant of *James.*

Dion. From *Dionysius.*   July 6

Dionysius (Gr., god of Nyssa)   Apr. 8

Dirck. Dutch contraction of
  Theodoric.

Dismas   Mar. 25

Dixon. See *Benedict.*

Dmitri. Russian form of
  Demetrius.

Dominic (L., the Lord's)   Aug. 4

Don, Donald (Celt., dark
  stranger)   July 15

Dunstan (Old Eng., hill stone)   May 19

Eamon. Irish for *Edmund.*

Edgar (Old Eng., rich spear)   July 8

Edmond, Edmund (Old Eng.,
  happy protection)   Nov. 16

Edward (Old Eng., rich
  guardian)   Oct. 13

Edwin (Old Eng., rich friend)   Oct. 12

Egan. Same as *Aidan.*

Egbert (Old. Eng., strong-
  bright)   Apr. 24

Elgar (Teut., bright spear)   June 14

Elia, Elias (Heb., Yahweh is
  God)   July 20

Eligius (L., worthy of choice)   Dec. 1

Ellis, Eliot, Ely, Variants of
  Elias.

Elmer (A.S., noble)   Aug. 25

Elmo, Italian variant of
  Erasmus.

Emanuel. See *Emmanuel.*

Emeric (Teut., work-ruler)   Nov. 4

Emilian. From *Emil.*   Nov. 12

Emery. English form of *Emeric.*

Emil, Emile (L., excelling)   May 28

Emmanuel (Heb., God with us)
    July 15

Enoch (Heb., consecrated)   Jan. 22

Ephrem (Heb., fruitful)   June 18

Erasmus (Gr., worthy of love)   June 2

Eric, Erik (Norse, ever-ruler)   May 18

Ernest, Ernst (Ger., serious)   Nov. 7

Esdras (Heb., help)   July 13

Ethelbert (Old Eng., noble
  splendor)   Feb. 24

Etienne. French form of
  Stephen.

Eugene (Gr., well-born)   July 8

Eustace (Gr., fruitful)   Sept. 20

Evan. Welsh form of *John.*

Evelyn. Masculine form of
  Eileen.

Everard (Teut., strong boar)   July 30

Ewald (Teut., rich prince)   Oct. 3

Ezechiel (Heb., strength of God)
    Apr. 10

Ezra. Form of *Esdras.*

Fabian (L., bean-grower)   Jan. 20

Fedor. See *Theodore.*

Felician (L., happy)   June 9

Felix (L., happy)   Mar. 8

Ferdinand (Teut., adventurous) May 30
Fergus (Celt., manly strength) Nov. 18
Fiacre (Celt., eagle) Aug. 30
Finbar (Celt., fair headed) Sept. 25
Finian (fair offspring) Sept. 10
Flavian (L., yellow) Feb. 18
Flavio (It., from L. *flavus*, yellow) June 22
Florian (L., flowering) May 4
Foster. English form of *Vedast* Feb. 6
Francis, Frank (Teut., free) Oct. 4
Frederic, Frederick (Teut., peace-ruler) July 18

Gabriel (Heb., God's strength) Mar. 24
Gall (Celt., stranger) Oct. 16
Garcia. Spanish form of *Gerald*.
Gaspar, Gaspard. Spanish and French forms of *Caspar*.
Gaston. French form of *Vedast*. Feb. 6
Gauthier, Gautier. French forms of *Walter*.
Gavin (Teut., battle hawk) Oct. 25
Gedeon (Heb., destroyer) Sept. 1
Gelasius (Gr., laughter) Nov. 21
Geoffrey. Variant of *Godfrey*.
George (Gr., farmer) Apr. 23
Gerald (Teut., spear rule) Mar. 13
Gerard (Teut., strong spear) Oct. 16
Gerhard. Germanic form of *Gerard*.
Germain (Teut., a kin) May 28
Geronimo. Italian form of *Jerome*.
Gervais (Teut., spear-servant) June 19
Gervas, Gervase. English form of *Gervais*.
Gideon. King James Bible spelling of *Gedeon*.
Gilbert (Teut., bright pledge) Feb. 4
Gildas (Celt., servant of God) Jan. 29
Giles (Gr., shield bearer) Sept. 1
Giovanni. Italian form of John. Mar. 28
Girard. Variant of *Gerard*.
Giuseppe. Italian form of *Joseph*. Feb. 4
Godfrey (Teut., God's peace) July 9
Godwin (Old Eng., God's friend) June 30

Gonzaga. St. *Aloysius Gonzaga*. June 21
Gratian (L., favored) June 1
Gregory (Gr., watchman) Mar. 12
Griffith. Welsh form of *Rufus*.
Guido. Italian form of *Guy*.
Gunther Oct. 9
Gustave. Variant of *Augustus*.
Guy (Old Fr., guide) Sept. 12

Hadrian. Variant of *Adrian*.
Hans. From German *Johannes* (*John*).
Harding. *Bl. Stephen Harding* Apr. 17
Harold (Dan., strong warrior) Mar. 25
Harry. Variant of *Henry*.
Hart. *Bl. William Hart* Mar. 13
Harvey (Teut., warrior) June 17
Henry (Teut., home-ruler) July 15
Herbert (Teut., shining warrior) Mar. 20
Herman (Teut., army-man, soldier) Apr. 7
Hermes (Gr., of the gods) Jan. 4
Hilaire. French form of *Hilary*.
Hilary (L., gay, merry) Jan. 14
Hildebrand (Teut., battle sword) May 25
Hobart. Variant of *Hubert*.
Hortensius (L., gardener) Jan. 11
Howard (Old Eng., sword-watcher) Oct. 19
Howell Jan. 6
Hubert (Teut., bright mind) Nov. 3
Hudson. *Bl. James Hudson* Nov. 28
Hugh, Hugo (Teut., thought) Apr. 29
Humbert (Teut., bright mind) Mar. 4
Humphrey (Teut., supporter of peace) Mar. 8

Iago. Spanish form of *James*.
Ian. Scottish for *John*.
Ignace. French form of *Ignatius*.
Ignatius (Gr., fiery) July 31
Igor June 5
Immanuel. Variant of *Emmanuel*.
Inigo. Variant of *Ignatius*.
Innocent July 28
Irvin, Irving. From *Urban*.
Isaac (Heb., he laughs) Mar. 16
Isaias (Heb., God is helper) July 6
Isidore (Gr., strong gift) Apr. 4

Israel (Heb., ruling with the Lord)   Dec. 31

Ivan. Russian form of *John*.

Ives (Teut., archer)   May 19

Ivor, Iver, Ivar. Equivalent of *Ives*.

Jacob (Heb., supplanter) Origin of *James*.

James. English form of *Jacob*   July 25

Jacques. French form of *Jacob*.

Jaime. Spanish form of *Jacob*.

Jared (Heb., descending)   Mar. 1

Jan. Variant of *John*.

Jarvis. Variant of *Gervase*.

Jason or Iason (the healer)   Dec. 3

Jasper. English form of *Caspar*.

Jean. French form of John   Aug. 19

Jeffrey. Variant of *Geoffrey*.

Jeremias (Heb., exalted of the Lord)   May 1

Jeremy. Variant of *Jeremias*.

Jerome (Gr., holy name)   Sept. 30

Jesse, or Isai (Heb., wealthy)   Dec. 2

Jesus. The Holy Name is a common baptismal name in Spain and Latin America.

Joachim (Heb., God prepares)   Aug.16

Joaquin. Spanish form of Joachim   Oct. 28

Job (Heb., persecuted)   May 10

Joel (Heb., strong-willed)   July 13

Johan, Johannes. German forms of *John*.

John (Heb., God has mercy)   Dec. 27

Jonas (Heb., dove)   Sept. 21

Jordan (Heb., flowing down)   Feb. 15

Joris. Dutch for *George*.

Jose. Spanish for *Joseph*.

Josef. German for *Joseph*.

Joseph (Heb., increase)   Mar. 19

Josias. Variant of *Josue*   June 23

Joshua, Josue (Heb., God is salvation)   Sept. 1

Jude (Heb., praised)   Oct. 28

Julian. From *Julius*   Mar. 16

Julius (L., downy beard)   Apr. 12

Jurgen. German variant of *George*.

Justin. Diminutive of *Justus*   Apr. 14

Justus (L., just)   Nov. 10

Karl, German form of *Charles*.

Karol. Slavonic form of *Charles*.

Kenneth (Celt., handsome)   Oct. 11

Kent, (Celt., head chief)   Jan. 14

Kerstan. Variant of *Christian*.

Kevin (Gael., comely)   June 3

Kieran (Gael., black)   Sept. 9

Killian (Celt., church)   July 8

Knute. Variant of *Canute*.

Konrad. German form of *Conrad*.

Kurt. From *Constantine*.

Ladislas (Slav., ruling well)   June 27

Lambert (Teut., land light)   Sept. 17

Lambrecht. German form of *Lambert*.

Lance, Lancelot (Fr., *Lancelot, servant*). Equivalent of *Ladislas;* also given name of *Saint Andrew Avellino*   June 27 or Nov. 10

Larry, Lars. Diminutives of *Laurence*.

Lauren, Laurence, Lawrence (L., laurel)   Aug. 10

Lauritz. Danish form of *Laurence*.

Lazarus (Heb., God will help)   Dec. 17

Leander (Gr., lion-like)   Feb. 27

Leo, Leon (L., lion)   Apr. 11

Leonard (Teut., lion-hearted)   Nov. 26

Leopold (Ger., people's prince)   Nov. 15

Leslie (Teut., leasor)

Lewis. Variant of *Louis*.

Liguori. *St. Alphonsus Liguori*   Aug. 2

Linus (Gr., flaxen-haired)   Sept. 23

Lionel (L., little lion). From Leo.

Llewelyn (Welsh, lion-like)   Apr. 7

Longinus   Mar. 15

Loren, Lorenz, Lorenzo. Forms of *Laurence*.

Lothaire. French form of *Lothar*.

Lothar (Teut., noted warrior)   June 14

Loughlan. Used for *Malachy*.

Louis (Teut., famous warrior)   Aug. 25

Loyola. *St. Ignatius Loyola*   July 31

Lucas. Variant of *Luke*.

Lucian. From *Lucius*. Jan. 7
Lucius (L., light) Mar. 4
Ludwig. German form of *Louis*.
Luis, Spanish form of Louis.
Luke (Gr., *Loukas, Lucius*) Oct. 18

Macaire (Gr., blessed) Jan. 15
Magnus (L., great) Apr. 16
Mainard. Variant of *Maynard*.
Malachi, Malachy (Heb.,
  messenger of the Lord) Nov. 3
Malcolm (Gael., Column's
  servant) June 9
Manasses (Heb., causing to
  forget) June 11
Manfred (Teut., mighty peace)
  Feb. 28
Manuel. Variant of Emmanuel June 17
Marcel, Marcellus. Diminutives
  of *Marcus*. Oct. 30
Marcian. From *Mark* (*Marcius*)
  June 14
Marco, Marcus. Variant of
  Mark.
Mario. Italian form of *Marius*.
Marion. Masculine equivalent of
  Marian.
Marius (L., Mars) Jan. 19
Mark (L., of Mars) Apr. 25
Marshall. Used for *Martial*.
Martial (L., war-like) June 30
Martin (L., of Mars, warlike) Nov. 11
Matthew (Heb., the Lord's gift)
  Sept. 21
Matthias. Variant of *Matthew* Feb. 24
Maur, Maurice (Gr., dark) Sept. 22
Max. Short for *Maximilian*.
Maximilian (L., greatest) Oct. 12
Maynard. Variant of *Meinrad*.
Meinrad (Teut., strong firmness)
  Jan. 21
Melchior (Per. king) Jan. 6
Meredith. Welsh form of
  Murtagh.
Michael (Heb., who is like
  God? Sept. 29
Michel. French form of
  Michael.
Miles (Gr., crusher; or L.,
  soldier) Apr. 30
Modeste, Modestus (L., modest)
  June 15
More. *St. Thomas More* July 9

Morgan (Celt., sea dweller) Mar. 3
Moses (Heb., saved from
  water) Sept. 4
Mungo (Celt., lovable) Cogno-
  men of *St. Kentigern*.
Murdoch. Scottish form of
  Murtagh.
Murphy, Murtagh (Celt., sea
  protector) Aug. 12
Myles. Variant of *Miles*.
Myron (Gr., myrrh) Aug. 8

Napoleon (Gr., of the new
  city) Aug. 15
Nathan (Heb., gift) Dec. 29
Nathanael, Nathaniel (Heb.,
  gift of God) Aug. 24
Neal, Neil (Celt., chief) June 5
Nicholas, Nicol (Gr., people's
  victory) Dec. 6
Niles, Nils. Derivatives of
  Nicholas.
Noah, Noe (Heb., comfort) May 2
Noel (Fr., Christmas) Sept. 26
Norbert (Niord's brightness) June 6

Octave. French form of
  Octavius.
Octavian. Variant of
  Octavius Mar. 22
Octavius (L., eighth-born) Nov. 20
Odilo. Variant of *Odo*.
Odo (Teut., rich) Nov. 18
Olaf (Teut., ancestor's relic) July 30
Oliver, Olivier (Lat., peace) July 11
Orestes (Gr., mountaineer) Nov. 9
Orlando. Italian for *Roland* May 20
Orson (L., bear) Apr. 13
Oscar. Variant of *Ansgar* Feb. 3
Osmond, Osmund (Teut.,
  God's protection) Dec. 4
Oswald (Ger., power of God) Aug. 5
Otto. Variant of *Odo* July 2
Owen. For *St. Audoenus* Aug. 24

Padriac. Irish form of *Patrick*.
Pancratius (Gr., all-ruler) May 12
Pascal, Paschal (Heb., pass-
  over) May 17
Pasquale. Italian form of
  Pascal.
Patrice, Patrick (Lat., nobly
  born) Mar. 17

700

Paul, Pavol (Lat., little)   June 29
Pedro, Sp. for *Peter*.
Percy (Fr., pierce)   Aug. 26
Peter (Gr., rock)   June 29
Philemon (Gr., loving thought)
   Nov. 22
Philibert (Teut., keen will)   Aug. 20
Philip (Gr., horse-lover)   May 1
Philo, Philon, (Gr., friend,
   lover)   Apr. 25
Piers, Pierce, Pierre. Variants
   of *Peter*.
Pius (L., pious)   May 5
Placid   Oct. 5
Plato (Gr. broad)   Apr. 4
Plunkett. *B. Oliver Plunkett*   July 11
Polycarp (Gr., much fruit)   Jan. 26
Porres. *St. Martin de Porres*   Nov. 5
Prosper (L., fortunate)   June 25

Quartus (L., fourth)   Nov. 3
Quentin. From *Quintus*   Oct. 31
Quin, Quinn. Variant of
   Quintus.
Quintus (L., fifth)   Dec. 18

Rafe. Old variant of *Ralph*.
Ralph. (Teut., good omen)   Dec. 1
Ramon. Spanish form of
   Raymond.
Randall. Variant of *Randolph*.
Randolph, (Old. Eng., shied-
   wolf)   May 27
Raoul. French form of *Ralph*.
Raphael (Heb., God's healer)
   Oct. 24
Raymond (Teut., wise
   protection)   Jan. 23
Redmond. Equivalent of
   Raymond.
Reginald (Teut., strong judg-
   ment)   Feb. 17
Regis. *St. Francis Regis*.
Remy (Fr., from Lat. *remex,*
   rower)   Oct. 1
Rene (Fr., reborn)   Sept. 29
Rex. Short for *Reginald* or
   Richard.
Reynold. Variant of *Reginald*   May 4
Ricardo. Italian form of
   Richard.
Richard (Old Eng., firm ruler)   Apr. 3
Robert (Teut., bright fame)   May 13

Roberto. Italian form of *Robert*.
Robin. Short for *Robert*.
Roch, Rock (Fr., *roche,* rock)   Aug. 16
Roderic, Roderick (Teut.,
   noted ruler)   Mar. 13
Roderigo. Spanish form of
   Roderick.
Roger (Teut., famous spear)   July 7
Roland (Teut., wide-famed)   Sept. 13
Rollo. From *Rudolph*.
Romain, Roman, Romeo (L.,
   Romanus)   May 22
Ronald, Scottish for
   Reginald, Reynold   Aug. 20
Ronan (Celt., seal, pledge)   June 1
Rory (Gael, ruddy).
   Equivalent of *Roger*.
Roy (Gael., red)   Dec. 18
Ruben (Heb., behold, a son)   Aug. 4
Rudolf, Rudolph (Teut.,
   famous wolf)   Oct. 17
Rufus (L., ruddy)   Dec. 18
Rupert (Ger., *Ruprecht,*
   Robert)   Mar. 27
Rurik. Russian form of
   Roderick.
Russell (Fr., reddish). Used
   for *Rufus*.

Sacha. Russian diminutive for
   Alexander.
Salvador, Salvatore (L., savior)
   Mar. 18
Samson (Heb., bright sun)   July 28
Samuel (Heb., asked of God)   Aug. 20
Sancho (Sp., from Lat.
   sanctus, saint)   June 5
Sandor. Hungarian for
   Alexander.
Santiago (Sp. for *James*).
Sean, Shane. Irish for *John*.
Sebastian (Gr., venerable)   Jan. 20
Septimus (Lat., seventh)   Aug. 17
Serge. Russian form of *Sergius*.
Sergius. Latin surname   Sept. 8
Seth (Heb., appointed)   July 27
Shamus, Seamus. Irish for *James*.
Shawn. Variant of Sean (*John*).
Sherwin. *Bl. Ralph Sherwin*   Dec. 1
Sherwood. *Bl. Thomas*
   Sherwood   Mar. 7
Sidney, Sydney (*St. Denis*)   Dec. 10

Siegfried (Teut., victorious
peace) Feb. 15
Sigismund. Variant of *Sigmund.*
Sigmund (Teut., victorious
protection) May 1
Silas (L., of the forest) July 13
Silvain, Silvester, Sylvester
L., forester) Dec. 31
Silvio. Italian form of *Silvius.*
Silvius (L., sylvan) Apr. 21
Simeon (Heb., obedient) Feb. 18
Simon. Greek form of *Simeon* Oct. 28
Sinclair. For *St. Clair* Nov. 4
Sixtus (L., sixth) Apr. 6
Solomon (Heb., peaceful) Mar. 13
Stanislaus (Slav., military glory)
glory) Aug. 15
Stanley. English surname; used
for *Stanislaus.*
Stefan, Stephen (Gr., crowned) Dec. 26
Sylvester. Variant of *Silvester.*

Tarsicius Aug. 15
Terrence, Terry (L., smooth) Apr. 10
Thaddeus (Aram., wise) Oct. 28
Theobald (Teut., people's
prince) June 30
Theodore (Gr., God's gift) Sept. 19
Theodoric (Teut., folk-rule) July 1
Thierry. French form of
Theodoric.
Thibaud, Tibault. French
forms of *Theobald.*
Thomas (Aram, twin) Dec. 21
Thurstan (Dan., Thor's stone) Mar. 31
Tiernan, Tierney (Celt., kingly) Apr. 4
Timothy (Gr., god-fearing) Jan. 24
Tito. From *Titus.*
Titus (L., safe) Feb. 6
Tobias (Heb., goodness of God) Nov. 2
Toby. Variant of *Tobias.*
Tomas, Sp. for *Thomas.*
Toussaint (Fr., *All Saints*) Nov. 1
Tudor. From *Theodore.*

Ugo. Italian form of *Hugo.*
Ulric (Teut., noble ruler) July 4
Urban (L., of the city) May 25

Valens, Valente (L., valiant) June 1
Valentine. Diminutive from
Valerius.
Feb. 14
Valerian. From *Valerius* Apr. 14

Valerius (L., valiant, strong) Jan. 29
Vasily, Vassily. Slav. form of
Basil
Vedast Feb. 6
Venard. *Bl. Theophane Venard* Feb. 2
Vergil. Variant of *Virgil.*
Viator (L., traveler) Oct. 21
Victor (L., victor) July 21
Vincent (L., conquering) July 19
Virgil (L., flourishing) Nov. 27
Vito. From *Vitus.*
Vitus (L., life) June 15
Vladimir (Slav., world ruler) July 15
Vladislas. Russian for *Ladislas.*

Walter (Teut., strong warrior) Apr. 8
Ward. *Bl. William Ward* July 26
Warren (Teut., protecting
friend) Feb. 6
Webster. *Bl. Augustine Webster* May 4
Wenceslaus (Slav., great glory) Sept. 28
Wendel, Wendell (Teut.,
wanderer) Oct. 21
Werner (Teut., protecting
army) Apr. 19
Wilbert (Old. Eng., firm bright-
ness) Sept. 11
Wilbur. From *Wilbert.*
Wilfred (Old Eng., firm peace) Oct. 12
Wilhelm. German form of
William.
William (Teut., strong helmet) June 25
Wolfgang (Teut., wolf's way) Feb. 1
Wright. *Bl. Peter Wright* May 19

Xavier, Birthplace of *St.
Francis Xavier.* Dec. 3

Yon. Variant of *Jonas.*
Yves. French form of *Ives.*

Zacharias (Heb., remembered
by God) Sept. 6
Zachary. Variant of *Zacharias* Nov. 5
Zeno (Gr., Zeus) Apr. 12

FEMALE NAMES
Ada (Teut., happy) Dec. 4
Adamina. Feminine of *Adam.*
Adela, Adel (Teut., noble) Dec. 24
Adelaide (Gr., noblewoman) Dec. 16
Adele. French worm of *Adela.*
Adelina (Teut., noble maid) Oct. 20

Adeline, Adile. Variant of
   Adelina.
Adolphina, Adolphine. Feminine
   of *Adolph.*
Adria (L., dark)   Dec. 2
Adriana. Feminine variant of
   Adrian.
Adrienne. Feminine variant of
   Adrian.
Aemilia   Sept. 11
Agatha (Gr., good)   Feb. 5
Agnes (Gr., *agnos,* pure)   Jan. 21
Aileen. Irish variant of *Helen.*
Aimee. French form of *Amata.*
Alacoque. *St. Margaret Mary*
   Alacoque   Oct. 17
Alba. Feminine of *Alban.*
Alberta. Feminine form of
   Albert   Mar. 11
Albertine. French variant of
   Alberta.
Albina (L., white)   Dec. 16
Alena. Lithuanian form of
   Helen.
Alessandra. Italian variant of
   Alexandra.
Alex, Alexa, Alexandra.
   Feminine form of *Alexander*
                                    Mar. 20
Alexandrina. Diminutive of
   Alexandra.
Alexia (Gr., helper)   June 29
Alexis. From *Alexia.*
Alfonsa. Feminine of
   Alphonse.
Alfreda. Feminine of *Alfred*   Aug. 2
Alice (Teut. *Adelicia,* noble
   cheer)   Aug. 24
Alicia. Variant of *Alice.*
Aline (Teut., noble)   June 18
Alison. Scottish variant of
   Louise.
Alix. Variant of *Alice.*
Aliza. See *Elizabeth.*
Allegra. Equivalent of *Hilary.*
Alma (L., loving, sweet). A
   title of Mary.
Aloysia. Variant of *Louise*   Sept. 12
Alphonsa. Feminine of
   Alphonsus (*Alphonse*).
Alphonsine. Feminine diminu-
   tive of *Alphonse.*
Alvernia. For St. Francis' re-

ception of the stigmata on
   Mount Alvernia   Sept. 17
Alvina. From *Albina.*
Alvira   Mar. 6
Alys. Variant of *Alice.*
Amabel (L., amabilis, lovable)   July 11
Amabella. Variant of *Amabel.*
Amanda (L., worthy of love)   Feb. 6
Amarna   July 8
Amata (L., loved)   Feb. 20
Ambrosine. Feminine of
   Ambrose.
Amelia (Teut., *Amelberga,*
   protectress)   July 10
Amy. English form of *Aimee.*
Anastasia (Gr., who will rise
   again)   Dec. 25
Andrea. Feminine of *Andrew.*
Andree. French form of
   Andrea.
Angela (L., angel)   May 31
Angelica. Variant of *Angela.*
Angelina. Diminutive of
   Angela   July 15
Angelique. French form of
   Angelica.
Anita. Spanish diminutive of
   Ann.
Ann, Anne. Variants of *Anna*   July 26
Anna (Heb., grace)   Sept. 1
Annette. Diminutive of *Anne.*
Annunciata. *Feast of the An-*
   nunciation   Mar. 25
Anstice. Contraction of
   Anastasia.
Antoinette. Diminutive of
   Antonia.
Antonia. Feminine of *Anthony.*
Anysia (Gr., complete)   Dec. 30
Apollina, Apollonia (Gr., of
   Apollo)   Feb. 9
Apollinaris (Gr., of *Apollo*)   Jan. 5
Apolline. French form of
   Apollina.
Aquilina (L., like an eagle)   June 13
Ariadne (Gr., very holy)   Sept. 17
Artemia (Gr., gift of Artemis)   Feb. 25
Asteria. Variant of *Esther.*   Aug. 10
Asta. Diminutive of *Augusta.*
Astrid. Norse equivalent of
   Esther.
Athanasia (Gr., immortal)   Aug. 14
Attracta (L., drawn to)   Aug. 11

Audrey. Contracted form of
Ethelreda.
Augusta. Feminine of
Augustus   Mar. 27
Aulaire. From *Eulalia.*
Aurelia (L., golden)   Oct. 15
Ava   Apr. 29
Averil. Feminine variant of
Everard.

Babette. Diminitive of
Barbara.
Baptista. From *John the
Baptist*   June 24
Barbara (Gr., stranger)   Dec. 4
Beata (L., happy)   Mar. 8
Beatrice, Beatrix (L., happi-
ness)   Feb. 13
Bella, Belle. From *Isabel.*
Benedicta (L., blessed)   May 6
Benita. Variant of
Benedicta.
Berenice (Gr., bringer of
victory)   Oct. 4
Bernadette. From *Bernard*   Apr. 16
Bernardine. From *Bernard*   May 20
Bernice. Variant of *Berenice.*
Bertha (Teut., shining one)   July 4
Bertild. From *Bertha.*
Bertilla (Teut., shining warrior) Nov. 5
Beryl. From Saint Beryllus
(Gr., crystal)   Mar. 21
Bessie, Betsy, Beth, Betty. Short
forms of *Elizabeth.*
Beverley, *St. John of Beverley* May 7
Bianca. Italian form of *Blanche.*
Bibiana. Same as *Vivian.*
Blanche (Fr., white)   Nov. 30
Blandina (L., mild)   June 2
Brenda (Teut., sword)   May 16
Bride, Brigid, Brigit. Forms of
Bridget.
Bridget (Celt., strength)   Feb. 1

Callista (L., of the chalice) Sept. 2
Camellia, Camilla, Camille
(L., temple servant)   May 31
Candida (L., white)   Aug. 29
Carina (L., keel)   Nov. 7
Carissima (L., dearest)   Sept. 7
Carita, Caritas (L., charity) Aug. 1
Carleen. From *Carol.*

Carlotta. Feminine variant of
Charles.
Carmel, Carmela, Carmen. *Our
Lady of Mount Carmel,* a title
of the B.V.M.   July 16
Carmelita. Diminutive of
Carmela.
Carol, Carola, Caroline. Femi-
nine variants of *Charles.*
Cassandra. Used for
Alexandra.
Catalina. Spanish variant of
Catherine.
Catherine (Gr., pure)   Nov. 25
Cecilia, Cecile, Cecily (L., dim
sighted   Nov. 22
Celesta, Celeste (L., heavenly) Apr. 16
Celestina. Diminutive of
Celesta.
Celia, Celine (L., heavenly) Oct. 21
Charity. English form of *Caritas*
Charlotte. French feminine
variant of *Charles.*   July 24
Charmaine. From Charlemagne Jan. 28
Christabel (L., *Christus* and
bella, fair).
Christina, Christine. From
Christ   July 24
Claire. French form of *Clara.*
Clara, Clare (L., illustrious) Aug. 12
Clareta, Clarice. Variants of
Clara.
Clarissa. From *Clara*   Jan. 20
Claudette. Feminine variant of
Claud.
Claudia. Feminine of *Claud* Mar. 20
Claudine. French feminine
variant of *Claud.*
Clementine. Feminine diminu-
tive of *Clement*   Nov. 17
Cleo. Short for Cleopatra.
Cleopatra (Gr., of a famous
father)   Oct. 19
Colette. Contracted form of
Nicolette   Mar. 6
Columba (L., dove)   Sept. 17
Conception. *The Immaculate
Conception*   Dec. 8
Constance. Feminine of *Con-
stantine*   Feb. 25
Consuelo (Sp., consolation).
From *Our Lady of Consola-
tion,* a title of the B.V.M.

Cordelia (Celt., daughter of the sea)   Oct. 22

Cornelia. Feminine of *Cornelius*   Mar. 31

Crescentia (L., growing)   June 15

Cynthia. Used for *Diana.*

Cyra (Per., the sun)   Aug. 3

Cyria (Gr., lady)   June 5

Cyrilla (Gr., lordly)   July 5

Damiana. Feminine of *Damian.*

Danette, Daniela. Feminine of *Daniel.*

Daphine (Gr., laurel tree)   May 21

Daria (Per., preserver)   Oct. 25

Davida. Feminine of *David.*

Debora, Deborah (Heb., bee)   Sept. 1

Deidre, Deirdre (Gael., raging)   Jan. 15

Delia, Della. From *Cordelia.*

Delphine (Gr., of *Delphi*)   Dec. 9

Denise. From *Dionysia.*

Desirata (L., Desired, beloved)   May 23

Desiree. French form of *Desirata.*

Devota (L., devoted)   Jan. 27

Diana (L., divine)   June 9

Diane. French form of *Diana.*

Dina. Contracted form of *Geraldine.*

Dionysia. Feminine of *Dionysius*   Dec. 6

Dolores (Sp., sorrows). From *Our Lady of Sorrows,* a title of the B.V.M.   Sept. 15

Dominica, Dominique. Feminine of *Dominic*   July 6

Dona, Donna. From *Donata.*

Donata (L., given)   Dec. 31

Dora. Diminutive of *Theodora.*

Dorcas (Gr., gazelle)   Oct. 25

Doris. Variant of *Dora.*

Dorothy, Dorothea. Inverted forms of *Theodora.*   Feb. 6

Drucilla, Drusilla (L., strong)   Sept. 22

Dymphna (Celt., white wave)   May 15

Eberta. Feminine of *Egbert.*

Edburga (Teut., rich protectress)   June 15

Edith (Old Eng., happiness)   Sept. 16

Edmunda. Feminine of *Edmund.*

Edna (Celt., fire)   July 5

Edwarda, Edwardine. Feminine of *Edward.*

Edwina. Feminine of *Edwin.*

Eileen. Variant of *Aileen* (*Helen*).

Elaine. Variant of *Helen.*

Eleanor, Eleanora. From Provencal *Alienor* (*Helen*)

Elane, Elena, Elene. From *Helen.*

Electa (L., chosen)   Aug. 1

Elfreda (Teut., elf-threatener)   Dec. 8

Elisa, Slise, Eliza. From *Elizabeth.*

Elizabeth (Heb., God has sworn)   Nov. 5

Ella, Ellen. Variants of *Helen.*

Eloisa, Eloise. From French *Heloise* (*Louise*).

Elsa (Teut., noble maiden). Form of *Elizabeth.*

Elsie. From *Elizabeth.*

Elspeth. Variant of *Elizabeth.*

Elvira. Spanish equivalent of *Alfreda*   Jan. 25

Emilia. Same as *Aemilia.*

Emily. Feminine of *Emil*   Aug. 19

Emeline, Emma (Teut., nurse)   June 29

Emmeline. Diminutive of *Emily.*

Enrica. Feminine of *Enrico* (*Henry*).

Erica, Erika. Feminine of *Eric.*

Erma. From *Ermelinda.*

Ermelinda (Teut., world serpent)   Oct. 29

Ernestina, Ernestine. Feminine of *Ernest.*

Estelle. From *Eustella.*

Esther (Per., star)   Dec. 21

Ethel. From *Ethelberta, Ethelreda,* etc.

Ethelreda (Old Eng., noble maiden)   June 23

Etta. From *Henrietta.*

Eudosis, Eudoxia (Gr., approval   Mar. 1

Eugenia, Eugenie. Feminine of *Eugene*   Dec. 25

Eulalia, Eulalie (Gr., fairspoken)   Feb. 12

Eunice (Gr., happy victory)   Oct. 28

Euphemia (Gr., fair speech)   Sept. 16

Eustella (etymology uncertain) May 11
Eva, Eve (Heb., life) May 26
Evelyn. English variant of Irish
   Eibhlhin (*Helen*).

Fabiola (L., bean) Dec. 27
Faith (L., fides) Aug 1
Fanny. For *Frances*.
Faustina, Faustine (L., lucky) Jan. 18
Fay. Variant of *Faith*.
Felicia, Felice (L., happy) June 6
Felicienne. French form of
   Felicia.
Felicity (L., happiness) Mar. 7
Felipa. From *Philip*.
Fernande. From *Ferdinand*.
Fidelity Apr. 24
Flavia (L., yellow) Oct. 5
Flora (L., flowers) July 29
Florence (L., flowering) Nov. 10
Florentina, Florentine (L.,
   flowering) June 20
Fortunata (L., lucky) Oct. 14
Frances. Feminine of *Francis* Mar. 9
Francesca. Italian form of
   Frances.
Freda. Diminutive of *Frederica*
   or *Alfreda*.
Frederica, Fredrika. Feminine
   of *Frederic*.

Gabriela, Gabrielle. Feminine
   of *Gabriel* July 24
Gemma (It., gem) Apr. 11
Genevieve (Celt., white wave) Jan. 3
Georgia. Feminine of *George* Feb. 15
Georgiana, Georgette. Fem-
   inine variants of *George*.
Geralda, Geraldine. Feminine
   of *Gerald*.
Germaine. Feminine of
   Germain June 15
Gertrude (Teut., spear
   strength) Nov. 16
Gilberta. Feminine of *Gilbert*.
Gilda. Feminine of *Gildas*.
Gladys (Cymric, lame) Mar. 29
Gloria, Gloriosa (L., glorious) July 26
Grace, Gratia, (L., favor, grace) July 5
Greta. From *Margaret*.
Gretchen. Diminutive of *Greta*.
Guida. Feminine of *Guido*.
Guadalupe. From Our Lady

Guadalupe Dec. 12
Gwen (Welsh, white) Oct. 18
Gwendoline (Welsh, white
   brow) Mar. 28

Hally. Form of *Henry*.
Hannah. Form of *Anna*.
Harriet. Feminine form of
   Harry (*Henry*).
Harrietta. Variant of *Harriet*.
Hedda. From *Hedwig*.
Hedwig (Teut., war refuge) Oct. 16
Hedy. From *Hedwig*
Helen, Helena (Gr., light) Aug. 18
Helga (Norse, holy). Scan-
   dinavian equivalent of *Olga*.
Heloise. French variant of
   Louise.
Henrietta. Feminine diminu-
   tive of *Henry*.
Henriette. French form of
   Henrietta July 24
Hermione (Gr., high-born) Sept. 4
Hester. Variant of *Esther*.
Hilary (L., merry) Jan. 14
Hilda (Old Eng., battle-maid) Nov. 17
Hildegard (Teut., protecting
   battle-maid) Sept. 17
Honorata (L., honored) Jan. 11
Honore. French form of
   Honorata.
Honoria (L., honor) Feb. 27
Hope (L., *spes*) Aug. 1
Hortense. Feminine of
   Hortensius.
Huette, Huguetta. From *Hugh*.
Hulda, Holda (Heb., weasel) Apr. 10
Humility (L., *humilitas*) May 22
Hyacinth, Hyacinthe (Gr.,
   purple) Jan. 30

Ida (Gr., happy) Sept. 4
Ignacia, Ignatia. Feminine of
   Ignatius.
Ilona. Hungarian for *Helen*.
Ilsa, Ilse. Equivalents of *Alice*.
Imelda May 12
Immaculata. *The Immaculate
   Conception* Dec 8
Imogene. From the shrine of
   the Virgin at Imoge, France.
Imperia (L., commands) Sept. 6

Ina. Short for *Rosina, Justina,* etc.

Ines, Inez. Spanish for *Agnes.*

Ingrid (Norse, Ingvi's ride)   July 1

Irena, Irene (Gr., peace)   Apr. 5

Iris (Gr., rainbow)   Sept. 22

Irma, Irmina   Dec. 24

Isabel. Variant of *Elizabeth.*

Isabella. Spanish form of *Isabel*   July 8

Isadora, Isidora. Feminine of *Isidore*   May 1

Ita (Gael., thirst)   Jan. 15

Jacinta, Jacintha. Variants of *Hyacinth.*

Jacqueline. Feminine diminutive of *Jacques.*

Jane. English form of *Joanna.*

Janet, Janice. Diminutives of *Jane.*

Jean, Jeanne. Feminine of *John.*

Jeanette. Diminutive of *Jeanne.*

Jessica, Jessie. From *Joanna.*

Jennifer. From *Winifred.*

Jill. From *Julia.*

Joan, Joanna. Feminine of *John.* May 30

Johanna. Variant of *Joanna.*

Jocelin, Jocelyn. Feminine diminutive of *Justus.*

Josefa, Josepha. Feminine of *Joseph*   Feb. 14

Josephine. Diminutive of *Josepha*   Oct. 23

Joyce, Joy (L., *jocosa* merry)   July 27

Juana. Spanish form of *Joan, Joanna*   Dec. 8

Juanita. Diminutive of *Juana.*

Judith (Heb., praised)   May 5

Judy. From *Judith.*

Julia (L., downy)   Apr. 8

Juliana. Variant of *Julia*   June 19

Julie. French form of *Julia.*

Juliette, Juliet. Diminutives of *Julia.*

June (L., youthful)   Nov. 14

Justa (L., just)   July 19

Justina. Diminutive of *Justa.*   Oct. 7

Karen. Scandinavian form of *Catherine.*

Kate. Diminutive of *Catherine.*

Kater, *Catherine.*

Katherine, Katheryn. Variants of *Catherine.*

Kathleen. Irish variant of *Catherine.*

Katrina. Slavonic from of *Catherine.*

Kerstin. Swedish form of *Christina.*

Kirsten. Norweigan form of *Christina.*

Kit, Kitty. Diminutives of *Catherine.*

Lamberta. Feminine of *Lambert.*

Laura, Laureen, Laurette. From *Laurence.*

Laurentia. Feminine of *Laurence.*   Oct. 8

Lea, Leah (Heb., weary)   Mar. 22

Lee. Short for *Elizabeth.*

Lelia (Teut., loyal)   Aug. 11

Lena. Short for *Helen* or *Magdalen.*

Lenore, Leonora, Leora. Variants of *Eleanor.*

Leona, Leonie. Feminine of *Leo.*

Leonarda. Feminine of *Leonard.*

Leonce (L., lion-like)   Dec. 6

Leonita. Diminutive of *Leona.*

Leopolda, Leopoldina. From *Leopold.*

Letitia (L., gladness)   Apr. 27

Letty. Short for *Letitia.*

Libby. Short for *Elizabeth.*

Lidwina (Slav., people of Vina)   Apr. 14

Lila, Lilian, Lily (L., lily)   July 27

Lisa, Lise, Lisette. Variants from *Elizabeth.*

Lois, Loisa. Variants of *Louise.*

Lola, Lolita. From *Dolores.*

Lora, Loretta. Same as *Laura, Laurette.*

Loraine. From *Laurentia.*

Lorenza. Feminine of *Lorenzo.*

Lottie. Short for *Charlotte.*

Louella. *Louise-Ella.*

Louisa, Louise. Feminine of *Louis*   Mar. 15

Lucasta, Variant of *Lucia.*

Lucia, Lucy. Feminine of
  Lucius   Dec. 13

Luciana. Feminine of *Lucian.*

Lucile. French form of *Lucilla.*

Lucilla (L., light)   July 29

Lucinda. Variant of *Lucia.*

Lucina (L., lighting)   June 30

Lucrece, Lucretia (L., profit)   Nov. 23

Lucrezia. Italian form of
  Lucretia.

Ludmilla (Slav., people's love) Sept. 16

Ludovica. Feminine of
  Ludovicus (*Louis*)

Luella. Variant of *Louella.*

Luisa, Luise. Forms of *Louisa,*
  Louise.

Lupe. For *Our Lady of*
  Guadalupe   Dec. 12

Lydia (Gr., from *Lydia*)   Aug. 3

Mabel (L., *amabilis*, lovable)   Nov. 1

Macrina   Jan. 14

Madalena. Spanish form of
  Magdalen.

Madeleine. French form of
  Magdalen   May 25

Madge. Contraction from
  Margaret.

Mae. Variant of *May* (*Mary*).

Magda. Short form of *Magdalen.*

Magdalen, Magdalene (Heb.,
  of Magdala)   July 22

Maggie. Diminutive of *Margaret.*

Maisie. Scottish diminutive of
  Margaret.

Manon. French derivative from
  Mary.

Manuela. Feminine of *Manuel.*

Marcella, Marcelle. Feminine
  of *Marcel.*   Jan. 31

Marcia. From *Marcus*   June 5

Marga   Apr. 6

Margaret (Gr., pearl)   June 10

Margery. Variant of *Margaret.*

Margo, Margot. Short forms
  of *Margaret.*

Marguerite. French form of
  Margaret   Oct. 17

Marian, Marianne. Derivatives
  of *Mary.*

Marie. French form of *Mary.*

Marilyn. Diminutive of *Mary.*

Marina (Lat., of the sea)   June 18

Martha, Marthe (Aram., lady)   July 29

Martina, Martine. Feminine of
  Martin   Jan. 30

Mary (Heb., rebellion)   Aug. 15

Marya. Polish form of *Mary.*

Mathilde. French form of
  Matilda.

Matilda (Teut., battle maid)   Mar. 14

Maud, Maude. Variants of
  Matilda.

Maura. Feminine of *Maurice*   Sept. 21

Maureen. Irish variant of *Mary.*

Maxine. Feminine variant of
  Maximilian.

Maybelle. Variant of *Mabel.*

Mayme, Mamie. From *Mary.*

Melania, Melanie (Gr., dark)   Dec. 31

Mercedes (Sp. mercy). *Our*
  Lady of Mercy   Sept. 24

Michaela. Feminine of *Mi-*
  chael.   Aug. 26

Michelle. Feminine of *Michel.*

Mildred (Old Eng., mild
  strength   July 13

Milissa   Mar. 16

Milly, Millie. Short for *Mil-*
  dred, Camille, Emily.

Mimi, Minna, Minnie, Minette.
  For *Wilhelmina.*

Miriam. Hebrew form of *Mary.*

Modesta (L., modest)   Nov. 4

Moira. Anglo-Irish for *Mary.*

Molly. Variant of *Mary.*

Mona. Variant of *Monica.*

Monica (Gr., counsellor)   May 4

Monique. French form of
  Monica.

Myra. Feminine of *Myron.*

Nadine (Russ., hope). Equivalent of *Hope.*

Nan, Nana, Nancy, Nanette.
  From *Anne.*

Narcissa, Narcisse. Feminine of
  Narcissus.

Natalie, Nathalie (L., birth)   Dec. 1

Nell, Nelly. Diminutives of
  Helen or *Eleanor.*

Netta, Nettie. Diminutives of
  Janet.

Neysa. Diminutive of *Agnes.*

Nicolette. Feminine diminutive of *Nicholas.*

Nina, Ninette, Ninon. Diminutives of *Anne.*

Nita. From *Juanita.*

Nona (L., ninth). Used for *Nonna.*

Nonna (L., old woman, nun)　　Aug. 5

Nora, Norah, Norine, Noreen. From *Honoria* or *Honora.*

Nunciata. From *Annunciata.*

Nympha (Gr., bride)　　Nov. 10

Octavia. Feminine of *Octavius.* Apr. 15

Odette. Feminine diminutive of *Odo.*

Odile. Feminine diminutive of *Odo.*　　Dec. 13

Olga. Russian equivalent of *Helga.*　　July 11

Olive, Olivia (L., olive　　June 3

Olympia (Gr., of Olympus, heavenly)　　Dec. 17

Olympe. French form of *Olympia.*

Orlanda. Feminine of *Orlando.*

Ottilia, Ottilie. Variants of *Odile.*

Patience, (L., *Patientia*)　　May 1

Patrice, Patricia. Feminine of *Patrick*　　Aug. 25

Paula. Feminine of *Paul*　　Jan. 26

Pauline, Paulette. Diminutives of *Paula.*　　June 6

Pearl. Equivalent of *Margaret.*

Peg, Peggy. Pet names for *Margaret.*

Perpetua (L., constant)　　Mar. 6

Petronilla. Feminine diminutive of *Peter*　　May 31

Philippa. Feminine of *Philip.*

Philomena (Gr., beloved)　　Aug. 11

Phoebe (Gr., shining)　　Sept. 3

Polly. Variant of *Molly.*

Priscilla (L., ancient)　　Jan. 16

Prosperia. Feminine of *Prosper.*

Prudence (L., *Prudentia*)　　May 6

Rachel (Heb., ewe). Equivalent of *Agnes.*

Raissa　　Sept. 5

Ramona. Feminine of *Ramon* (*Raymond*).

Raphaeal, Rafaela. Feminine of *Raphael.*

Rebecca (Heb., noose)　　No name day

Regina (L., queen).　　Sept. 7

Reine. French form of *Regina.*

Renée. Feminine of *René.*

Richarda. Feminine of *Richard.*

Rita. For *Margarita* (*Margaret*) May 22

Roberta. Feminine of *Robert.*

Roderica. Feminine of *Roderick.*

Romaine. French form of *Romana.*

Romana (L., Roman)　　Feb. 23

Ronalda. Feminine of *Ronald.*

Rosa, Rose (L.)　　Aug. 30

Rosalie, Rosalia, Rosalba. From *Rosa.*　　Sept. 4

Rosalind, Roslyn. Diminutives of *Rosa.*　　Jan. 17

Rosamond (Teut., famous protection)　　Apr. 30

Rosanne, Diminutive of *Rose;* or from *Rose* plus *Anne.*

Rosemarie, Rosemary (Lat., sea-dew). For *Rose* or *Mary.*

Roseria. *Feast of the Rosary*　　Oct. 7

Rosetta. Diminutive of *Rose.*

Roxana (Per., brightness). Equivalent of *Rosanne.*

Roxane. French form of *Roxana.*

Sabina (L., a Sabine)　　Aug. 29

Sacha. Russian for *Alexandra.*

Sadie. Used for Sara.

Sally. From Sara.

Salome, Salomea (Heb., peaceful)　　Oct. 22

Samuela. Feminine of *Samuel.*

Sancta (L., saint, holy)　　Dec. 5

Sandra. Short for *Alexandra.*

Sara, Sarah. (Heb., princess)　　Aug. 19

Savina. Variant of *Sabina.*

Scholastica (L., learner)　　Feb. 10

Selena, Selina. Equivalents of *Helen.*

Selma. Feminine variant of *Anselm.*

Serafina Seraphina (Heb., burning)　　July 29

Sharon. From *Rose of Sharon,* title of the B.V.M.

Sheila. Irish form of *Cecilia.*

Sibyl (Gr., prophetess)   Mar. 18

Silvia, Sylvia (L., of the forest)   Nov. 3

Simona, Simone. Feminine of *Simon.*

Sonia, Sonya. Russian variant of *Sophia.*

Sophia, Sophie, Sofia (Gr., wisdom)   May 25

Stasia, Stacie. From *Anastasia.*

Stella. From *Estelle.*

Stephanie, Stefanie. Feminine of *Stephen.*

Susan, Susanna (Heb., lily)   Aug. 11

Suzanne. French form of *Susan.*

Tabitha (Aram., gazelle)   Oct. 25

Talullah   Jan. 6

Teresa (Gr., reaper)   Oct. 15

Tess, Tessie. Diminutives of *Teresa.*

Thais   Oct. 8

Thecla (Gr., divine fame)   Sept. 23

Theodora. Feminine of *Theodore.*   Apr. 1

Theodosia (Gr., God-given)   Apr. 2

Theresa, Therese. Forms of *Teresa.*

Thomasina, Thomasine. From *Thomas.*

Tilda, Tillie. Diminutives of *Matilda.*

Timothea. Feminine of *Timothy.*

Tina. Short for *Christina, Albertina,* etc.

Tosca. Toscana (L., Tuscan)   Dec. 18

Trina. Short for *Katrina.*

Ulrica. Feminine of *Ulric.*

Una (L., one). Used for *Winifred.*

Ursula (L., little bear)   Oct. 21

Valentina. Feminine of *Valentine.*   July 25

Valeria, Valery. Feminine of *Valerius.*   Apr. 28

Valérie. French form of *Valery.*

Vanessa. Used for *Esther.*

Venetia (Celt. blessed). Used for *Beatrice.*

Vera (L., true)   Jan. 24

Verona   Aug. 29

Veronica (Gr., victory-bringer)   July 9

Veronique. French form of *Veronica.*

Victoria (L., victory)   Dec. 23

Victorine. From *Victor.*

Vicentia. From *Vincent.*

Viola (L., violet)   May 3

Violet, Violette. Diminutive of *Viola.*

Virginia (L., flowering). Used for *Virgana.*   Jan. 7

Vivian (L., lively)   Dec. 2

Vivienne. French form of *Vivian.*

Walburga (Teut., strong protection)   Feb. 25

Wanda (Ger., stem). Used for *Saint Wando.*   Apr. 17

Wendy. From *Wendel.*

Wilfreda. Feminine of *Wilfred.*

Wilhelmina. Feminine diminutive of *Wilhelm.*

Winifred. Same source as *Genevieve.*

Yolanda   Dec. 28

Yolette. From *Violette.*

Yvette. French derivative from *Judith.*

Yvonne. From *Ivor.*

Zita (Sp., *Speransita,* little hope)   Apr. 27

Zoe (Heb. life)   May 2

THE AUTHOR

THE MARYKNOLL CATHOLIC DICTIONARY *was compiled and edited by Father Albert J. Nevins of Maryknoll. Father Nevins' writing and photographic talents are well known to the subscribers to* MARYKNOLL MAGAZINE, *of which he is editor.*

He is the author of over ten books; has turned out a score of documentary films; has lectured widely; and has written for leading religious and secular publications, as well as for national television.

Father Nevins is the recipient of many honors, notably the Maria Moors Cabot Prize from Columbia University "for outstanding journalistic achievement," the Brotherhood Award from the National Conference of Christians and Jews, and the St. Augustine Award of Villanova University.

Father Nevins is a past president of the Catholic Press Association, and has won the same organization's award for the most distinguished contribution to Catholic journalism.